New

American Standard

Bible

New Testament

Reference Edition

THE FOUNDATION PRESS PUBLICATIONS

Box 277, La Habra, Calif.

PUBLISHER

for

THE LOCKMAN FOUNDATION

FOREWORD

The New American Standard Bible has been produced with the conviction that the words of Scripture as originally penned in the Hebrew and Greek were inspired by God. Being the eternal Word of God, the Holy Scriptures speak with fresh power to each generation, to give us wisdom that leads to salvation, that we may serve to the glory of Christ.

It has been the purpose of the Editorial Board to present to the modern reader a revision of the American Standard Version in clear and contemporary language. The attempt has been made to adhere to the original languages of the Holy Scriptures as closely as possible and at the same time to obtain a fluent and readable style according to current English usage.

SCRIPTURAL PROMISE

"The grass withers, the flower fades, but the Word of our God shall stand forever." Isaiah 40:8

FOUR-FOLD AIM

OF

THE LOCKMAN FOUNDATION PUBLICATIONS

1. These publications shall be true to the original Greek.

2. They shall be grammatically correct.

3. They shall be understandable to the masses.

4. They shall give the Lord Jesus Christ His proper place, the place which the Word gives Him, and no work will ever be personalized.

PREFACE TO THE NEW AMERICAN STANDARD BIBLE
A. D. 1963

The producers of this translation were imbued with the conviction that interest in the American Standard Version should be renewed and increased. They have labored with prayerful seriousness to this end. This great responsibility was assumed only after the need was thoroughly established in the minds of many. That which is forever settled in heaven (Psa. 119:89) must ever be available on earth. Such availability is contingent upon (1) clarity of language in its current understanding and (2) the most appealing form of presentation contemporary facilities afford.

All that exists has a cause from which it springs, and this important undertaking was born of no light impulses. It was inspired and encouraged by wholesome and meaningful reasons. The chief inducement, of course, was the recognized value of the version of 1901 which deserves and demands perpetuation. The following observations are advanced as justifiable encouragement:

1. The American Standard Version of 1901 has been in a very real sense the standard for many translations.

2. It is a monumental product of applied scholarship, assiduous labor and thorough procedure.

3. It has enjoyed universal endorsement as a trustworthy translation of the original text.

4. The British and American organizations were governed by rules of procedure which assured accuracy in the completed work.

5. The American Standard Version, itself a revision of the 1881-1885 edition, is the product of international collaboration, invaluable for perspective, accuracy and finesse.

6. Unlike many modern translations of the Scriptures, the American Standard Version retains its acceptability for pulpit reading and for personal memorization.

Perhaps the most weighty impetus for this undertaking can be attributed to a disturbing awareness that the American Standard Version of 1901 was fast disappearing from the scene. As a generation "which knew not Joseph" was born, even so a generation unacquainted with this great and important work has come into being. Recognizing a responsibility to posterity, THE LOCKMAN FOUNDATION felt an urgency to rescue this noble achievement from an inevitable demise, to preserve it as a heritage for coming generations, and to do so in such a form as the demands of passing time dictate.

THE FOUNDATION, a corporation not for profit in the State of California, took the initiative in the work of revision, engaging consultants to lay the groundwork for text arrangement, textual revision, linguistic accuracy and editorial finalizing.

1. TEXT ARRANGEMENT: This initial step was taken with caution and concern. Page construction registers the first impression when attention is given to a volume. But appearance is not the only consideration in designing a format of the printed page; utility is a major factor! Whatever tends to make the reading easier and more enjoyable is the desirable design. To develop this format it was found best to place cross references and marginal notes in a column alongside the text. References are noted by letters and marginal notes by numerals. (See explanation of format.)

2. TEXTUAL REVISION: Words are the vehicle of thought, and most languages, especially the English, have a flexibility which economic and cultural progress utilizes. Passing time with myriads of inventions and innovations automatically renders obsolete and inexpressive words that once were in acceptable usage. The ever-present danger of stripping divine Truth of its dignity and original intent was prominently before the minds of the producers at all times. An editorial board composed of linguists, Greek scholars and pastors undertook the responsibilities of translation and revision.

PRINCIPLES OF REVISION

Greek Text: In revising the ASV, consideration was given to the latest available manuscripts with a view to determining the best Greek text. In most instances the 23rd edition of the Nestle Greek New Testament was followed.

Modern English Usage: The attempt has been made to render the grammar and terminology of the ASV in contemporary English. When it was felt that the word-for-word literalness of the ASV was unacceptable to the modern reader, a change was made in the direction of a more current English idiom. In the instances where this has been done, the more literal rendering has been indicated in the margin.

Marginal Readings: In addition to the more literal renderings, the marginal notations have been made to include alternate translations, readings of variant manuscripts and explanatory equivalents of the text. Only such notations have been used as have been felt justified in assisting the reader's comprehension of the terms used by the original author.

The Appendix to the Old Testament of the 1901 edition listed the particulars in which the 1885 revision differed. The Appendix to the New Testament of the 1901 edition revealed the readings and renderings which appeared in the Revised New Testament of 1881 in place of those preferred by the American New Testament Revision Company.

There has been no attempt in this preface to present illustrations of changes made in the text. This would not only become a rather cumbersome undertaking, but its value would be obviated in that most discerning people have their own favorite proof texts by which they measure the merits and accuracy of new translations.

It is enthusiastically anticipated that the general public will be grateful to learn of the availability, value and need of the New American Standard Bible. It is released with the strong confidence that those who seek a knowledge of the Scriptures will find herein a source of genuine satisfaction for a clear and accurate rendering of divinely-revealed truth.

Editorial Board

The Lockman Foundation

NOTES ON THE TRANSLATION OF GREEK TENSES

1. A careful distinction has been made in the treatment of the Greek aorist tense (usually translated as the English past, "He did") and the Greek imperfect tense (rendered either as English past progressive, "He was doing"; or, if inceptive, as "He *began* to do" or "He started to do"); or else if customary past, as "He used to do." "Began" is italicized if it renders an imperfect tense, in order to distinguish it from the Greek verb for "begin."

2. On the other hand, not all aorists have been rendered as English pasts ("He did"), for some of them are clearly to be rendered as English perfects ("He has done"), or even as past perfects ("He had done"), judging from the context in which they occur. Such aorists have been rendered as perfects or past perfects in this version.

3. As for the distinction between aorists and present imperatives, the Board has usually rendered these imperatives in the customary manner, rather than attempting any such fine distinction as, "Begin to do!" (for the aorist imperative) or, "Continually do!" (for the present imperative).

4. As for sequence of tenses, the Board took care to follow English rules rather than Greek in translating Greek presents, imperfects and aorists. Thus, where English says, "We knew that he was doing," Greek puts it, "We knew that he does"; similarly, "We knew that he had done," is the Greek, "We knew that he did." Likewise, the English, "When he had come, they met him," is represented in Greek by: "When he came, they met him." In all cases a consistent transfer has been made from the Greek tense in the subordinate clause to the appropriate tense in English.

5. In the rendering of negative questions introduced by the particle **mē** (which always expects the answer, "No") the wording has been altered from a mere, "Will he not do this?" to a more accurate, "He will not do this, will he?"

EXPLANATION OF GENERAL FORMAT

MARGINAL NOTES AND CROSS REFERENCES are placed in a column on the outer edge of the page and listed under verse numbers to which they refer. Superior numbers refer to literal renderings, alternate translations, or explanations. Superior letters refer to cross references. Cross references in italics are parallel passages.

PARAGRAPHS are designated by bold face numbers or letters.

QUOTATION MARKS are used in the text in accordance with modern English usage.

PUNCTUATION CHANGES have been made in order to conform with modern practice.

"THOU, THY AND THEE" are changed to "you" except in the language of prayer when addressing Deity.

PERSONAL PRONOUNS are capitalized when pertaining to Deity.

ITALICS are used in the text to indicate words which are not found in the original Greek but implied by it. Italics are used in the marginal notes to signify alternate readings for the text.

SMALL CAPS are used in the text to indicate Old Testament quotes.

ASTERISK—In regard to the use of historical present, the Board recognized that in some contexts the present tense seems more unexpected and unjustified to the English reader than a past tense would have been. But Greek authors frequently used the present tense for the sake of heightened vividness, thereby transporting their readers in imagination to the actual scene at the time of occurrence. However, the Board felt that it would be wise to change these historical presents into English past tenses. Therefore verbs marked with an asterisk (*) represent historical presents in the Greek which have been translated with an English past tense in order to conform to modern usage.

BOOKS OF THE NEW TESTAMENT

THE GOSPEL
ACCORDING TO
MATTHEW
Genealogy of Jesus.

THE book of the genealogy of Jesus Christ, [a]the son of David, [b]the son of Abraham.

2 To Abraham was born Isaac; and to Isaac, Jacob; and to Jacob, [1]Judah and his brothers;

3 and to Judah were born Perez and Zerah by Tamar; and to [a]Perez was born Hezron; and to Hezron, [1]Ram;

4 and to Ram was born Amminadab; and to Amminadab, Nahshon; and to Nahshon, Salmon;

5 and to Salmon was born Boaz by Rahab; and to Boaz was born Obed by Ruth; and to Obed, Jesse;

6 and to Jesse was born David the king.

And to David [a]was born Solomon by her *who had been the wife* of Uriah;

7 and to Solomon [a]was born Rehoboam; and to Rehoboam, Abijah; and to Abijah, [1]Asa;

8 and to Asa was born Jehoshaphat; and to Jehoshaphat, [1]Joram; and to Joram, Uzziah;

9 and to Uzziah was born [1]Jotham; and to Jotham, Ahaz; and to Ahaz, Hezekiah;

10 and to Hezekiah was born Manasseh; and to Manasseh, [1]Amon; and to Amon, Josiah;

11 and to Josiah were born [1]Jeconiah and his brothers, at the time of the [a]deportation to Babylon.

12 And after the [a]deportation to Babylon, to Jeconiah was born [1]Shealtiel; and to Shealtiel, Zerubbabel;

13 and to Zerubbabel was born [1]Abiud; and to Abiud, Eliakim; and to Eliakim, Azor;

14 and to Azor was born Zadok; and to Zadok, Achim; and to Achim, Eliud;

15 and to Eliud was born Eleazar; and to Eleazar, Matthan; and to Matthan, Jacob;

16 and to Jacob was born Joseph the husband of Mary, by whom was born Jesus, [a]who is called [1]Christ.

17 Therefore all the generations from Abraham to David are fourteen generations; and from

---

1 [a]2 Sam. 7:12-16; Ps. 89:3f.; 132:11; Is. 9:6f.; 11:1; Luke 1:32, 69; John 7:42; Acts 13:23; Rom. 1:3; Rev. 22:16; Matt. 9:27 [b]Gen. 22:18; Gal. 3:16; Matt. 1:1-6: *Luke 3:32-34*

2 [1]Gr., *Judas.* Names of Old Testament characters will be given in their Old Testament form throughout this version.

3 [1]Gr., *Aram* [a]Matt. 1:3-6; Ruth 4:18-22; 1 Chr. 2:1-15

6 [a]2 Sam. 11:27; 12:24

7 [1]Gr., *Asaph* [a]1 Chr. 3:10ff.

8 [1]Gr., *Jehoram*

9 [1]Gr., *Joatham*

10 [1]Gr., *Amos*

11 [1]Or, *Jehoiachin* [a]2 Kin. 24:14f.; Jer. 27:20; Matt. 1:17

12 [1]Gr., *Salathiel* [a]2 Kin. 24:14f.; Jer. 27:20; Matt. 1:17

13 [1]Gr., *Abihud*

16 [1]I.e., the Messiah [a]Matt. 27:17, 22; Luke 2:11; John 4:25

1

17 [1]I.e., the Messiah
[a]2 Kin. 24:14f.; Jer. 27:20;
Matt. 1:11, 12

18 [a]Luke 1:27; Matt. 12:46
[b]Luke 1:35

19 [1]Or, *to divorce her*

20 [1]Gr., *begotten*

21 [a]Luke 1:31; 2:21 [b]Luke
2:11; Acts 13:23; John 1:29

22 [1]Or, *has taken place*

23 [1]Or, *Emmanuel*
[a]Is. 7:14

24 [1]Or, *took his wife to
himself*

25 [1]Lit., *was not knowing
her*
[a]Matt. 1:21

1 [1]Pronounced may-ji, a
caste of wise-men
specializing in astrology,
medicine and natural
science
[a]Luke 2:4-7 [b]Luke 1:5

2 [a]Jer. 23:5; 30:9; Zech.
9:9; Matt. 27:11; Luke 19:38;
23:38; John 1:49 [b]Num.
24:17; Rev. 22:16

4 [1]I.e., the Messiah

5 [1]Lit., *through*
[a]John 7:42

6 [a]Mic. 5:2

2

David to the [a]deportation to Babylon fourteen generations; and from the [a]deportation to Babylon to *the time of* [1]Christ fourteen generations.

18　Now the birth of Jesus Christ was as follows. When His [a]mother Mary had been betrothed to Joseph, before they came together she was [b]found to be with child by the Holy Spirit.

19　And Joseph her husband, being a righteous man, and not wanting to disgrace her, desired [1]to put her away secretly.

20　But when he had considered this, behold, an angel of the Lord appeared to him in a dream, saying, "Joseph, son of David, do not be afraid to take Mary as your wife; for that which has been [1]conceived in her is of the Holy Spirit.

21　"And she will bear a Son; and [a]you shall call His name Jesus, for it is He who [b]will save His people from their sins."

22　Now all this [1]took place that what was spoken by the Lord through the prophet might be fulfilled, saying,

23　"[a]BEHOLD, THE VIRGIN SHALL BE WITH CHILD, AND SHALL BEAR A SON, AND THEY SHALL CALL HIS NAME [1]IMMANUEL;" which translated means, "GOD WITH US."

24　And Joseph arose from his sleep, and did as the angel of the Lord commanded him, and [1]took *her* as his wife;

25　and [1]kept her a virgin until she gave birth to a Son; and [a]he called His name Jesus.

CHAPTER 2

NOW after Jesus was [a]born in Bethlehem of Judea in the days of [b]Herod the king, behold, [1]magi from the East arrived in Jerusalem, saying,

2　"Where is He who has been born [a]King of the Jews? For we saw [b]His star in the East, and have come to worship Him."

3　And when Herod the king heard it, he was troubled, and all Jerusalem with him.

4　And gathering together all the chief priests and scribes of the people, he *began* to inquire of them where [1]the Christ was to be born.

5　And they said to him, "[a]In Bethlehem of Judea; for so it has been written [1]by the prophet,

6　'[a]AND YOU, BETHLEHEM, LAND OF JUDAH;

ARE BY NO MEANS LEAST AMONG THE LEADERS
OF JUDAH;
FOR OUT OF YOU SHALL COME FORTH A
RULER,
WHO WILL bSHEPHERD MY PEOPLE ISRAEL.' "

7 Then Herod secretly called the magi, and ascertained from them ¹the time the star appeared.

8 And he sent them to Bethlehem, and said, "Go and make careful search for the Child; and when you have found *Him*, report to me, that I too may come and worship Him."

9 And having heard the king, they went their way; and lo, the star, which they had seen in the East, went on before them, until it came and stood over where the Child was.

10 And when they saw the star, they rejoiced exceedingly, with great joy.

11 And they came into the house and saw the Child with ªMary His mother; and they fell down and worshiped Him; and opening their treasures they presented to Him gifts of gold and frankincense and myrrh.

12 And having been ªwarned *by God* in a dream not to return to Herod, they departed for their own country by another way.

13 Now when they had departed, behold, an angel of the Lord *ªappeared to Joseph in a dream, saying, "Arise and take the Child and His mother, and flee to Egypt, and remain there until I tell you; for Herod is going to search for the Child to destroy Him."

14 And he arose and took the Child and His mother by night, and departed for Egypt;

15 and was there until the death of Herod; that what was spoken by the Lord through the prophet might be fulfilled, saying, "ªOUT OF EGYPT DID I CALL bMY SON."

16 Then when Herod saw that he had been tricked by the magi, he became very enraged, and sent and slew all the male children who were in Bethlehem and in all its environs, from two years old and under, according to the time which he had ascertained from the magi.

17 Then that which was spoken through Jeremiah the prophet was fulfilled, saying,

18 "ªA VOICE WAS HEARD IN RAMAH,
WEEPING AND GREAT MOURNING,
RACHEL WEEPING FOR HER CHILDREN;

6 bJohn 21:16

7 ¹Lit., *the time of the appearing star*

11 ªMatt. 1:18; 12:46

12 ªMatt. 2:22; Acts 10:22; Heb. 8:5; 11:7; Matt. 2:13, 19; Luke 2:26

13 ªMatt. 2:19; 2:12

15 ªHos. 11:1 bEx. 4:22f.

18 ªJer. 31:15

3

19 ᵃMatt. 2:13; 2:12, 22

22 ᵃMatt. 2:12

23 ᵃLuke 1:26 ᵇIs. 11:1
ᶜMark 1:24

1 ¹Or, arrived ²Or,
proclaiming as a herald
ᵃMatt. 3:1-12: Mark 1:3-8;
Luke 3:2-17; John 1:6-8, 19-
28 ᵇJudg. 1:16; Josh. 15:61

2 ¹Lit., of the heavens
²Lit., has come near
ᵃMatt. 4:17 ᵇDan. 2:44;
Matt. 4:17; 6:10; 10:7; Mark
1:15; Luke 10:9f.; 11:20;
21:31; Matt. 4:23

3 ¹Lit., through
ᵃIs. 40:3 ᵇJohn 1:23

4 ¹Lit., his garment
ᵃ2 Kin. 1:8; Zech. 13:4 ᵇLev.
11:2?

5 ᵃLuke 3:3

7 ᵃMatt. 23:13, 15; 16:1ff.
ᵇMatt. 22:23; 16:1ff; Acts
4:1; 5:17; 23:6ff. ᶜMatt.
12:34; 23:33 ᵈ1 Thess. 1:10

8 ᵃActs 26:20

9 ᵃJohn 8:33, 39

4

AND SHE REFUSED TO BE COMFORTED,
BECAUSE THEY WERE NO MORE."

19 But when Herod was dead, behold, an angel of the Lord *ᵃappeared in a dream to Joseph in Egypt, saying,

20 "Arise and take the Child and His mother, and go into the land of Israel; for those who sought the Child's life are dead."

21 And he arose and took the Child and His mother, and came into the land of Israel.

22 But when he heard that Archelaus was reigning over Judea in place of his father Herod, he was afraid to go there; and being ᵃwarned by God in a dream, he departed for the regions of Galilee,

23 and came and resided in a city called ᵃNazareth; that what was spoken through the prophets might be fulfilled, "ᵇHe shall be called a ᶜNazarene."

CHAPTER 3

NOW ᵃin those days John the Baptist *¹came, ²preaching in the ᵇwilderness of Judea, saying,

2 "ᵃRepent, for ᵇthe kingdom of ¹heaven ²is at hand."

3 For this is the one referred to ¹by Isaiah the prophet, saying,
"ᵃTHE VOICE OF ONE CRYING IN THE
WILDERNESS,
'ᵇMAKE READY THE WAY OF THE LORD,
MAKE HIS PATHS STRAIGHT!' "

4 Now John himself had ¹ᵃa garment of camel's hair, and a leather belt about his waist; and his food was ᵇlocusts and wild honey.

5 Then Jerusalem was going out to him, and all Judea, and all ᵃthe district around the Jordan;

6 and they were being baptized by him in the Jordan River, as they confessed their sins.

7 But when he saw many of the ᵃPharisees and ᵇSadducees coming for baptism, he said to them, "You ᶜbrood of vipers, who warned you to flee from ᵈthe wrath to come?

8 "Therefore bring forth fruit ᵃin keeping with your repentance;

9 and do not suppose that you can say to yourselves, 'ᵃWe have Abraham for our father;' for I say to you, that God is able from these stones to raise up children to Abraham.

10 "And the axe is already laid at the root of the trees; ᵃevery tree therefore that does not bear good fruit is cut down, and thrown into the fire.

11 "As for me, ᵃI baptize you ¹in water for repentance; but He who is coming after me is mightier than I, and I am not *even* fit to remove His sandals; ᵇHe Himself will baptize you ¹with the Holy Spirit and fire.

12 "And His ᵃwinnowing fork is in His hand, and He will thoroughly clean His threshing-floor; and He will ᵇgather His wheat into the barn, but He will burn up the chaff with ᶜunquenchable fire."

13 ᵃThen Jesus *arrived ᵇfrom Galilee at the Jordan *coming* to John, to be baptized by him.

14 But John tried to prevent Him, saying, "I have need to be baptized by You, and do You come to me?"

15 But Jesus answering said to him, "Permit *it* at this time; for in this way it is fitting for us to fulfill all righteousness." Then he *permitted Him.

16 And after being baptized, Jesus went up immediately from the water; and behold, the heavens were opened, and ¹ᵃhe saw the Spirit of God descending as a dove, *and* coming upon Him;

17 and behold, a voice out of the heavens, saying, "ᵃThis is ¹My beloved Son, in whom I am well pleased."

ᵃ   Cʜᴀᴘᴛᴇʀ 4

Tʜᴇɴ Jesus was led up by the Spirit into the wilderness to be tempted by the devil.

2 And after He had ᵃfasted forty days and forty nights, He ¹then became hungry.

3 And ᵃthe tempter came and said to Him, "If You are the Son of God, command that these stones become ¹bread."

4 But He answered and said, "It is written, 'ᵃMᴀɴ sʜᴀʟʟ ɴᴏᴛ ʟɪᴠᴇ ᴏɴ ʙʀᴇᴀᴅ ᴀʟᴏɴᴇ, ʙᴜᴛ ᴏɴ ᴇᴠᴇʀʏ ᴡᴏʀᴅ ᴛʜᴀᴛ ᴘʀᴏᴄᴇᴇᴅs ᴏᴜᴛ ᴏғ ᴛʜᴇ ᴍᴏᴜᴛʜ ᴏғ Gᴏᴅ.' "

5 Then the devil *took Him into ᵃthe holy city; and he stood Him on the pinnacle of the temple,

6 and *said to Him, "If You are the Son of God throw Yourself down; for it is written,

---

10 ᵃMatt. 7:19

11 ¹The Greek here can be translated *in, with* or *by* ᵃJohn 1:26 ᵇJohn 1:33

12 ᵃLuke 3:17; Is. 30:24 ᵇMatt. 13:30 ᶜMark 9:43, 48

13 ᵃMatt. 3:13-17: *Mark 1:9-11; Luke 3:21, 22;* John 1:31-34 ᵇMatt. 2:22

16 ¹Or, *He* ᵃJohn 1:32

17 ¹Lit., *My son, the Beloved* ᵃMatt. 12:18; 17:5; Mark 9:7; Luke 9:35; Is. 42:1

1 ᵃMatt. 4:1-11: *Mark 1:12, 13; Luke 4:1-13*

2 ¹Lit., *later, afterward* ᵃEx. 34:28; 1 Kin. 19:8

3 ¹Lit., *loaves* ᵃ1 Thess. 3:5

4 ᵃDeut. 8:3

5 ᵃMatt. 27:53; Neh. 11:1, 18; Dan. 9:24

6 ªPs. 91:11-12

7 ¹Lit., *again* ²Or, *put to the test*
ªDeut. 6:16

10 ¹Or, *fulfill religious duty to Him*
ªDeut. 6:13

11 ªMatt. 26:53; Luke 22:43

12 ¹Lit., *been delivered up*
ªMatt. 14:3; Mark 1:14; Luke 3:20; John 3:24 ᵇMark 1:14; Luke 4:14; John 1:43; 2:11

13 ªMark 1:21; 2:1; Luke 4:23, 31; John 2:12; 4:46f.; Matt. 11:23

15 ¹Or, *toward the sea* ²Or, *nations*
ªIs. 9:1

16 ªIs. 9:2

17 ¹Or, *proclaim*
ªMark 1:14, 15 ᵇMatt. 3:2

18 ªMatt. 4:18-22: *Mark 1:16-20; Luke 5:2-11; John 1:40-42* ᵇMatt. 15:29; Mark 7:31; John 6:1; Luke 5:1 ᶜMatt. 10:2; 16:18; John 1:40, 42

19 ¹Lit., *come here after Me*

21 ¹Or, *Jacob* ²Gr., *Joannes*, Heb., *Johanan*
ªMatt. 10:2; 20:20

6

'ªHE WILL GIVE HIS ANGELS CHARGE CONCERN-
ING YOU;
AND ON THEIR HANDS THEY WILL BEAR YOU
UP,
LEST ·YOU STRIKE YOUR FOOT AGAINST A
STONE.' "

7   Jesus said to him, "¹On the other hand, it is written, 'ªYOU SHALL NOT ²TEMPT THE LORD YOUR GOD.' "

8   Again, the devil *took Him to a very high mountain, and *showed Him all the kingdoms of the world, and their glory;

9   and he said to Him, "All these things will I give You, if You fall down and worship me."

10   Then Jesus *said to him, "Begone, Satan! For it is written, 'ªYOU SHALL WORSHIP THE LORD YOUR GOD, AND ¹SERVE HIM ONLY.' "

11   Then the devil *left Him; and behold, ªangels came and *began to minister to Him.

12   Now when He heard that ªJohn had ¹been taken into custody, ᵇHe withdrew into Galilee;

13   and leaving Nazareth, He came and ªsettled in Capernaum, which is by the sea, in the region of Zebulun and Naphtali.

14   *This was* to fulfill what was spoken through Isaiah the prophet, saying,

15   "ªTHE LAND OF ZEBULUN AND THE LAND OF NAPHTALI,
¹BY THE WAY OF THE SEA, BEYOND THE JOR-
DAN, GALILEE OF THE ²GENTILES.

16   "ªTHE PEOPLE WHO WERE SITTING IN DARKNESS
SAW A GREAT LIGHT,
AND TO THOSE WHO WERE SITTING IN THE
LAND AND SHADOW OF DEATH,
UPON THEM A LIGHT DAWNED."

17   ªFrom that time Jesus began to ¹preach and say, "ᵇRepent; for the kingdom of heaven is at hand."

18   ªAnd walking by ᵇthe sea of Galilee, He saw two brothers, ᶜSimon who was called Peter, and Andrew his brother, casting a net into the sea; for they were fishermen.

19   And He *said to them, "¹Follow Me, and I will make you fishers of men."

20   And they immediately left the nets, and followed Him.

21   And going on from there He saw two other brothers, ¹ªJames the *son* of Zebedee, and ²John

Sermon on the Mount. Beatitudes.
The Disciples and the World.

Matthew 4, 5

his brother, in the boat with Zebedee their father, mending their nets; and He called them.

22 And they immediately left the boat and their father, and followed Him.

23 And *Jesus* was going about ªin all Galilee, ᵇteaching in their synagogues, and ᶜproclaiming the ¹gospel of the kingdom, and ᵈhealing every kind of disease and every kind of sickness among the people.

24 And the news about Him went out ªinto all Syria; and they brought to Him all who were ill, taken with various diseases and pains, ᵇdemoniacs, ¹ᶜepileptics, ᵈparalytics; and He healed them.

25 And great multitudes ªfollowed Him from Galilee and ᵇDecapolis and Jerusalem and Judea and *from* ᶜbeyond the Jordan.

a   CHAPTER 5

AND when He saw the multitudes, He went up on ᵇthe ¹mountain; and after He sat down, His disciples came to Him.

2 And ªopening His mouth He *began* to teach them, saying,

3 "ªBlessed are the poor in spirit, for ᵇtheirs is the kingdom of heaven.

4 "Blessed are ªthose who mourn, for they shall be comforted.

5 "Blessed are ªthe ¹gentle, for they shall inherit the earth.

6 "Blessed are ªthose who hunger and thirst for righteousness, for they shall be satisfied.

7 "Blessed are the merciful, for they shall receive mercy.

8 "Blessed are ªthe pure in heart, for ᵇthey shall see God.

9 "Blessed are the peacemakers, for ªthey shall be called sons of God.

10 "Blessed are those who have been ªpersecuted for the sake of righteousness, for ᵇtheirs is the kingdom of heaven.

11 "Blessed are you when *men* ªrevile you, and persecute you, and say all kinds of evil against you falsely, on account of Me.

12 "Rejoice, and be glad, for your reward in heaven is great, for ªso they persecuted the prophets who were before you.

13 "You are the salt of the earth; but ªif the salt

23 ¹Or, *good news*
ªMark 1:39; Luke 4:15, 44
ᵇMatt. 9:35; 13:54; Mark
1:21; 6:2; Luke 4:15; 6:6;
13:10; John 6:59; 18:20;
Mark 10:1 ᶜMatt. 9:35; Mark
1:14; Matt. 24;14; Luke 4:43;
8:1; 16:16; Acts 20:25; 28:31;
Matt. 3:2 ᵈMatt. 8:16; 9:35;
14:14; 15:30; 19:2; 21:14;
Mark 1:34; 3:10; Luke 4:40;
7:21; Acts 10:38

24 ¹Lit., *moon-smitten*
ªLuke 2:2; Acts 15:23; 18:18;
20:3; 21:3; Gal. 1:21; Mark
7:26 ᵇMatt. 8:16, 28, 33; 9:32;
12:22; 15:22; Mark 1:32;
5:15, 16, 18; Luke 8:36; John
10:21 ᶜMatt. 17:15 ᵈMatt.
8:6; 9:2, 6; Mark 2:3, 4, 5, 9;
Luke 5:24

25 ªMark 3:7, 8; Luke 6:17
ᵇMark 5:20; 7:31 ᶜMatt. 4:15

1 ¹Or, *hill*
ªMatt. 5-7: Luke 6:20-49
ᵇMark 3:13; Luke 9:28; John
6:3, 15; Luke 6:17

2 ªActs 8:35; 10:34; 18:14;
Matt. 13:35

3 ªMatt. 5:3-12; Luke 6:20-
23 ᵇMatt. 5:10; 19:14; 25:34;
Mark 10:14; Luke 6:20;
22:29f.

4 ªIs. 61:2; John 16:20;
Rev. 7:17

5 ¹Or, *humble, meek*
ªPs. 37:11

6 ªIs. 55:1, 2; John 4:14;
6:48ff.; 7:37

8 ªPs. 24:4 ᵇHeb. 12:14;
1 John 3:2; Rev. 22:4

9 ªRom. 8:14; Matt. 5:45;
Luke 6:35

10 ª1 Pet. 3:14 ᵇMatt. 5:3;
19:14; 25:34; Mark 10:14;
Luke 6:20; 22:29f.

11 ª1 Pet. 4:14

12 ª2 Chr. 36:16; Matt.
23:37; Acts 7:52; 1 Thess.
2:15; James 5:10; Heb.
11:33ff.

13 ªMark 9:50; Luke 14:34f.

7

Matthew 5

**Jesus Comes to Fulfill the Law and the Prophets.
Concerning Enmity.**

14 [1]Or, *mountain*
[a]John 8:12

15 [a]Mark 4:21; Luke 8:16;
11:33

16 [a]1 Pet. 2:12 [b]Matt. 9:8

18 [1]Lit., *one iota* or (yodh)
or *one projection of a letter*
(serif)
[a]Luke 16:17; Matt. 24:35

19 [1]Lit., *the men* [2]Lit., *does*

21 [1]Lit., *it was said to the
ancients* [2]Or, *guilty before*
[a]Matt. 5:27, 33, 38, 43 [b]Ex.
20:13; Deut. 5:17 [c]Deut.
16:18; 2 Chr. 19:5f.

22 [1]Some mss. insert here:
without cause [2]Or, *liable to*
[3]Aramaic for *empty-head* or,
good for nothing [4]Lit., *the
Sanhedrin* [5]Gr. *Gehenna*
[a]Deut. 16:18; 2 Chr. 19:5f.
[b]Matt. 10:17; 26:59; Mark
13:9; 14:55; 15:1; Luke 22:66;
John 11:47; Acts 4:15; 5:21;
6:12; 22:30, 23:1; 24:20
[c]Matt. 5:29f.; 10:28; 18:9;
23:15, 33; Mark 9:43ff.; Luke
12:5; James 3:6

23 [1]Or, *gift*

24 [1]Or, *gift*

25 [a]Luke 12:58

26 [1]Lit., *quadrans*
(equaling two lepta or
mites), i.e., 1/64 of a
denarius

8

has become tasteless, how will it be made salty
again? It is good for nothing any more, except to
be thrown out and trampled under foot by men.

14 "You are [a]the light of the world. A city set on
a [1]hill cannot be hidden.

15 "[a]Nor do *men* light a lamp, and put it under
the peck-measure, but on the lampstand; and it
gives light to all who are in the house.

16 "Let your light shine before men in such a
way that they may [a]see your good works, and [b]glo-
rify your Father who is in heaven.

17 "Do not think that I came to abolish the
Law or the Prophets; I did not come to abolish, but
to fulfill.

18 "For truly I say to you, [a]until heaven and
earth pass away, not the [1]smallest letter or stroke
shall pass away from the Law, until all is
accomplished.

19 "Whoever then annuls one of the least of
these commandments, and so teaches [1]others, shall
be called least in the kingdom of heaven; but whoever [2]keeps and teaches *them*, he shall be called
great in the kingdom of heaven.

20 "For I say to you, that unless your righteousness surpasses *that* of the scribes and Pharisees, you
shall not enter the kingdom of heaven.

21 "[a]You have heard that [1]the ancients were
told, '[b]You shall not commit murder;' and 'Whoever
commits murder shall be [2]liable to [c]the court,'

22 but I say to you that every one who is angry
with his brother[1] shall be [2]guilty before [a]the court;
and whoever shall say to his brother, '[3]Raca,' shall
be [2]guilty before [4b]the supreme court; and whoever
shall say, 'You fool,' shall be [2]guilty *enough to go*
into the [5]hell of fire.

23 "If therefore you are presenting your [1]offer-
ing at the altar, and there remember that your
brother has something against you,

24 leave your [1]offering there before the altar,
and go your way, first be reconciled to your brother, and then come and present your [1]offering.

25 "[a]Make friends quickly with your opponent
at law while you are with him on the way; in order
that your opponent may not deliver you to the
judge, and the judge to the officer, and you be
thrown into prison.

26 "Truly I say to you, you shall not come out
of there, until you have paid up the last [1]cent.

27 "ᵃYou have heard that it was said, 'ᵇYOU SHALL NOT COMMIT ADULTERY;'

28 but I say to you, that every one who looks on a woman to lust for her has committed adultery with her already in his heart.

29 "And ᵃif your right eye makes you ¹stumble, tear it out, and throw it from you; for it is better for you that one of the parts of your body perish, ²than for your whole body to be thrown into ³ᵇhell.

30 "And ᵃif your right hand makes you ¹stumble, cut it off, and throw it from you; for it is better for you that one of the parts of your body perish, ²than for your whole body to go into ³ᵇhell.

31 "And it was said, 'ᵃWHOEVER ¹DIVORCES HIS WIFE, LET HIM GIVE HER A CERTIFICATE OF DISMISSAL;'

32 ᵃbut I say to you that every one who divorces his wife, except for *the* cause of unchastity, makes her commit adultery; and whoever marries a divorced woman commits adultery.

33 "Again, ᵃyou have heard that ¹the ancients were told, '²ᵇYOU SHALL NOT ³MAKE FALSE VOWS, BUT SHALL FULFILL YOUR ⁴VOWS TO THE LORD.'

34 "But I say to you, ᵃmake no oath at all; either by heaven, for it is ᵇTHE THRONE OF GOD;

35 or by the earth, for it is the ᵃfootstool of His feet; or ¹by Jerusalem, for it is ᵇTHE CITY OF THE GREAT KING.

36 "Nor shall you make an oath by your head, for you cannot make one hair white or black.

37 "But let your statement be, 'Yes, yes' *or* 'No, no;' and anything beyond these is of ¹ᵃevil.

38 "ᵃYou have heard that it was said, 'ᵇAN EYE FOR AN EYE, AND A TOOTH FOR A TOOTH.'

39 "But I say to you, do not resist him who is evil; but ᵃwhoever slaps you on your right cheek, turn to him the other also.

40 "And if any one wants to sue you, and take your ¹shirt, let him have your ²coat also.

41 "And whoever shall force you to go one mile, go with him two.

42 "ᵃGive to him who asks of you, and do not turn away from him who wants to borrow from you.

43 "ᵃYou have heard that it was said, 'ᵇYou SHALL LOVE YOUR NEIGHBOR, AND HATE YOUR ENEMY.'

44 "But I say to you, ᵃlove your enemies, and pray for those who persecute you;

27 ᵃMatt. 5:21, 33, 38, 43
ᵇEx. 20:14; Deut. 5:18

29 ¹I.e., cause to sin ²Lit., *not your whole body* ³Gr., Gehenna
ᵃMatt. 18:9; Mark 9:47; Matt. 17:27 ᵇMatt. 5:22

30 ¹I.e., cause to sin ²Lit., *not your whole body* ³Gr., Gehenna
ᵃMatt. 18:8; Mark 9:43; Matt. 17:27 ᵇMatt. 5:22

31 ¹Lit., *puts away*
ᵃDeut. 24:1, 3

32 ᵃMatt. 19:9; Mark 10:11f.; Luke 16:18; 1 Cor. 7:11f.

33 ¹Lit., *it was said to the ancients* ²*you* and *your* are singular here ³Or, *break your vows* ⁴Lit., *your oaths*
ᵃMatt. 5:21, 27, 38, 43; 23:16ff. ᵇLev. 19:12; Num. 30:2; Deut. 23:21

34 ᵃJames 5:12 ᵇMatt. 23:22; Is. 66:1

35 ¹Or, *toward*
ᵃIs. 66:1; Acts 7:49 ᵇPs. 48:2

37 ¹Or, *from the evil one*
ᵃMatt. 6:13; 13:19, 38; John 17:15; 2 Thess. 3:3; 1 John 2:13f.; 3:12; 5:18f.

38 ᵃMatt. 5:21, 27, 33, 43
ᵇEx. 21:24; Lev. 24:20; Deut. 19:21

39 ᵃMatt. 5:39-42: *Luke 6:29, 30;* 1 Cor. 6:7

40 ¹*Tunic* or garment worn next to the body ²*Cloak* or outer garment

42 ᵃLuke 6:34f.

43 ᵃMatt. 5:21, 27, 33, 38
ᵇLev. 19:18

44 ᵃLuke 6:27f.; Luke 23:34; Acts 7:60

45 [1]Or, *show yourselves to be*
[a]Matt. 5:9

46 [1]Publicans who collected Roman taxes on commission
[a]Luke 6:32

48 [a]Lev. 19:2

1 [a]Matt. 6:5, 16; 23:5

2 [1]Or, *do an act of charity*
[a]Matt. 6:5, 16; 23:5 [b]Matt. 6:5, 16; Luke 6:24

4 [1]Or, *deeds of charity*
[a]Matt. 6:6, 18

5 [1]Lit., *to be apparent to men*
[a]Mark 11:25; Luke 18:11, 13 [b]Matt. 6:1, 16 [c]Matt. 6:2, 16; Luke 6:24

6 [a]Is. 26:20 [b]Matt. 6:4, 18

7 [a]1 Kin. 18:26f.

8 [a]Matt. 6:32

9 [1]Lit., *the heavens*
[a]Matt. 6:9-13; *Luke 11:2-4*

10 [a]Matt. 3:2

11 [1]Or, *our bread for the coming day* or, *our needful bread*
[a]Prov. 30:8

10

45 in order that you may [1]be [a]sons of your Father who is in heaven; for He causes His sun to rise on *the* evil and *the* good, and sends rain on *the* righteous and *the* unrighteous.

46 "For [a]if you love those who love you, what reward have you? Do not even the [1]tax gatherers do the same?

47 "And if you greet your brothers only, what do you do more *than others?* Do not even the Gentiles do the same?

48 "Therefore [a]you are to be perfect, as your heavenly Father is perfect.

CHAPTER 6

"BEWARE of practicing your righteousness before men [a]to be noticed by them; otherwise you have no reward with your Father who is in heaven.

2 "When therefore you [1]give alms, do not sound a trumpet before you, as the hypocrites do in the synagogues and in the streets, that they [a]may be honored by men. [b]Truly I say to you, they have their reward in full.

3 "But when you give alms, do not let your left hand know what your right hand is doing;

4 that your [1]alms may be in secret; and [a]your Father who sees in secret will repay you.

5 "And when you pray, you are not to be as the hypocrites; for they love to [a]stand and pray in the synagogues and on the street corners, [1b]in order to be seen by men. [c]Truly I say to you, they have their reward in full.

6 "But you, when you pray, [a]GO INTO YOUR INNER ROOM, AND WHEN YOU HAVE SHUT YOUR DOOR, pray to your Father who is in secret, and [b]your Father who sees in secret will repay you.

7 "And when you are praying, do not use meaningless repetition, as the Gentiles do, for they suppose that they will be heard for their [a]many words.

8 "Therefore do not be like them; for [a]your Father knows what you need, before you ask Him.

9 "[a]Pray, then, in this way:
'Our Father who art in [1]heaven,
Hallowed be Thy name.

10 '[a]Thy kingdom come.
Thy will be done,
On earth as it is in heaven.

11 '[a]Give us this day [1]our daily bread.

12 'And forgive us our [1]debts, as we also have forgiven our debtors.

13 'And do not lead us into temptation, but deliver us from [1a]evil. [2][For Thine is the kingdom, and the power, and the glory, forever. Amen].'

14 "[a]For if you forgive men for their transgressions, your heavenly Father will also forgive you.

15 "But if you do not forgive men, then your Father will not forgive your transgressions.

16 "And [a]whenever you fast, do not put on a gloomy face as the hypocrites *do*; for they [1]neglect their appearance in order to be seen fasting by men. [b]Truly I say to you, they have their reward in full.

17 "But you, when you fast, anoint your head, and wash your face;

18 so that you may not be seen fasting by men, but by your Father who is in secret; and your [a]Father who sees in secret will repay you.

19 "Do not lay up for yourselves treasures upon earth, where moth and rust destroy, and where thieves break in and steal;

20 but lay up for yourselves [a]treasures in heaven, where neither moth nor rust destroys, and where thieves do not break in or steal;

21 for [a]where your treasure is, there will your heart be also.

22 "[a]The lamp of the body is the eye; if therefore your eye is [1]clear, your whole body will be full of light.

23 "But if [a]your eye is bad, your whole body will be full of darkness. If therefore the light that is in you is darkness, how great is the darkness!

24 "[a]No one can serve two masters; for either he will hate the one and love the other, or he will hold to one and despise the other. You cannot serve God and [1b]Mammon.

25 "[a]For this reason I say to you, [1]do not be [b]anxious for your life, *as to* what you shall eat, or what you shall drink; nor for your body, *as to* what you shall put on. Is not life more than food, and the body than clothing?

26 "[a]Look at the birds of the [1]air, that they do not sow, neither do they reap, nor gather into barns; and *yet* your heavenly Father feeds them. Are you not worth much more than they?

27 ¹I.e., approximately 18 inches ²Or, *height*
ᵃMatt. 6:25, 28, 31, 34; Luke 10:41; 12:11, 22; Phil. 4:6; 1 Pet. 5:7 ᵇPs. 39:5

28 ᵃMatt. 6:25, 27, 31, 34; Luke 10:41; 12:11, 22; Phil. 4:6; 1 Pet. 5:7

29 ᵃ1 Kin. 10:4-7

30 ᵃMatt. 8:26; 14:31; 16:8

31 ᵃMatt. 6:25, 27, 28, 34; Luke 10:41; 12:11, 22; Phil. 4:6; 1 Pet. 5:7

32 ᵃMatt. 6:8

33 ¹Or, *continually seek* ²Or, *the kingdom* ³Or, *provided*
ᵃMatt. 19:28; Mark 10:29f.; Luke 18:29f.; 1 Tim. 4:8

34 ¹Or, *will worry about itself*
ᵃMatt. 6:25, 27, 28, 31; Luke 10:41; 12:11, 22; Phil. 4:6; 1 Pet. 5:7

1 ¹Or, *do not pass judgments*
ᵃMatt. 7:1-5: Luke 6:37f., 41f.

2 ¹Lit., *by what measure you measure*
ᵃMark 4:24; Luke 6:38

4 ¹Lit., *will*

7 ¹Or, *Keep asking* ²Or, *keep seeking* ³Or, *keep knocking*
ᵃMatt. 7:7-11: Luke 11:9-13 ᵇMatt. 18:19; 21:22; John 14:13; 15:7, 16; 16:23f.; James 1:5f.; 1 John 3:22; 5:14f.; Mark 11:24

12

27 "And which of you by being ᵃanxious can ᵇadd a *single* ¹cubit to his ²life's span?
28 "And why are you ᵃanxious about clothing? Observe how the lilies of the field grow; they do not toil nor do they spin,
29 yet I say to you that even ᵃSolomon in all his glory did not clothe himself like one of these.
30 "But if God so arrays the grass of the field, which is *alive* today and tomorrow is thrown into the furnace, *will He* not much more *do so for* you, ᵃO men of little faith?
31 "Do not be ᵃanxious then, saying, 'What shall we eat?' or, 'What shall we drink?' or, 'With what shall we clothe ourselves?'
32 "For all these things the Gentiles eagerly seek; for ᵃyour heavenly Father knows that you need all these things.
33 "But ¹seek first ²His kingdom, and His righteousness; and ᵃall these things shall be ³added to you.
34 "Therefore do not be ᵃanxious for tomorrow; for tomorrow will ¹care for itself. *Each* day has enough trouble of its own.

CHAPTER 7

"¹ᵃDo not judge lest you be judged *yourselves*.
2 "For in the way you judge, you will be judged; and ¹ᵃby your standard of measure, it shall be measured to you.
3 "And why do you look at the speck in your brother's eye, but do not notice the log that is in your own eye?
4 "Or how ¹can you say to your brother, 'Let me take the speck out of your eye,' and behold, the log is in your own eye?
5 "You hypocrite, first take the log out of your own eye; and then you will see clearly *enough* to take the speck out of your brother's eye.
6 "Do not give what is holy to dogs, and do not throw your pearls before swine, lest they trample them under their feet, and turn and tear you to pieces.
7 "¹ᵃAsk, and ᵇit shall be given to you; ²seek, and you shall find; ³knock, and it shall be opened to you.
8 "For every one who asks receives; and he

who seeks finds; and to him who knocks it shall be opened.

9 "Or what man is there among you, [1]when his son shall ask him for a loaf, [2]will give him a stone?

10 "Or [1]if he shall ask for a fish, he will not give him a snake, will he?

11 "If you then, being evil, know how to give good gifts to your children, how much more shall your Father who is in heaven give what is good to those who ask Him!

12 "[a]Therefore whatever you want others to do for you, [1]do so for them; for [b]this is the Law and the Prophets.

13 "[a]Enter by the narrow gate; for the gate is wide, and the way is broad that leads to destruction, and many are those who enter by it.

14 "For the gate is small, and the way is narrow that leads to life, and few are those who find it.

15 "Beware of the [a]false prophets, who come to you in sheep's clothing, but inwardly are [b]ravenous wolves.

16 "You will [1]know them [a]by their fruits. [2]Grapes are not gathered from thornbushes, nor figs from thistles, are they?

17 "Even so every good tree bears good fruit; but the rotten tree bears bad fruit.

18 "A good tree cannot produce bad fruit, nor can a rotten tree produce good fruit.

19 "[a]Every tree that does not bear good fruit is cut down, and thrown into the fire.

20 "So then, you will [1]know them [a]by their fruits.

21 "[a]Not every one who says to Me, 'Lord, Lord,' will enter the kingdom of heaven; but he who does the will of My Father, who is in heaven.

22 "[a]Many will say to Me on [b]that day, 'Lord, Lord, did we not prophesy in Your name, and in Your name cast out demons, and in Your name perform many [1]miracles?'

23 "And then I will declare to them, 'I never knew you; [a]DEPART FROM ME, YOU WHO PRACTICE LAWLESSNESS.'

24 "Therefore [a]every one who hears these words of Mine, and [1]acts upon them, [2]may be compared to a wise man, who built his house upon the rock;

25 and the rain descended, and the [1]floods came, and the winds blew, and burst against that

9 [1]Lit., *whom* [2]Lit., *he will not give him a stone, will he?*

10 [1]Lit., *also*

12 [1]Or, *you too do so*
[a]Luke 6:31 [b]Matt. 22:40; Gal. 5:14; Rom. 13:8ff.

13 [a]Luke 13:24

15 [a]Matt. 24:11, 24; Mark 13:22; Luke 6:26; Acts 13:6; 2 Pet. 2:1; 1 John 4:1; Rev. 16:13; 19:20; 20:10 [b]Ezek. 22:27; Acts 20:29; John 10:12

16 [1]Or, *recognize* [2]Lit., *they do not gather* [a]Matt. 7:20; 12:33; Luke 6:44; James 3:12

19 [a]Matt. 3:10; Luke 13:7

20 [1]Or, *recognize* [a]Matt. 7:16; 12:33; Luke 6:44; James 3:12

21 [a]Luke 6:46

22 [1]Or, *works of power* [a]Matt. 25:11f.; Luke 13:25ff. [b]Matt. 10:15

23 [a]Matt. 25:41; Luke 13:27; Ps. 6:8

24 [1]Lit., *does* [2]Lit., *will be compared to* [a]Matt. 7:24-27; Luke 6:47-49; James 1:22-25

25 [1]Lit., *rivers*

house; and *yet* it did not fall; for it had been founded upon the rock.

26 "And every one who hears these words of Mine, and does not ¹act upon them, will be like a foolish man, who built his house upon the sand.

27 "And the rain descended, and the ¹floods came, and the winds blew, and burst against that house; and it fell, and great was its fall."

28 ¹ᵃThe result was that when Jesus had finished these words, ᵇthe multitudes were amazed at His teaching;

29 for He was teaching them as *one* having authority, and not as their scribes.

CHAPTER 8

AND when He had come down from the mountain, great multitudes followed Him.

2 And behold, a leper ᵃcame to Him, and ¹ᵇbowed down to Him, saying, "Lord, if You are willing, You can make me clean."

3 And stretching out His hand, He touched him, saying, "I am willing; be cleansed." And immediately his leprosy was cleansed.

4 And Jesus *said to him, "ᵃSee that you tell no one; but ᵇgo, ᶜSHOW YOURSELF TO THE PRIEST, and present the ¹offering that Moses prescribed, for a testimony to them."

5 And ᵃwhen He had entered Capernaum, a centurion came to Him, entreating Him,

6 and saying, "¹Sir, my ²servant is ³lying ᵃparalyzed at home, ⁴suffering great pain."

7 And He *said to him, "I will come and heal him."

8 But the centurion answered and said, "¹Lord, I am not qualified for You to come under my roof, but ²just say the word, and my ³servant will be healed.

9 "For I too am a man under authority, with soldiers under me; and I say to this one, 'Go!' and he goes, and to another, 'Come!' and he comes, and to my slave, 'Do this!' and he does *it*."

10 Now when Jesus heard *this*, He marveled, and said to those who were following, "Truly I say to you, I have not found such great faith ¹with anyone in Israel.

11 "And I say to you, that many ᵃshall come from east and west, and ¹recline *at table* with Abra-

Peter's Mother-in-law Cured, and Others.
Discipleship Exacting. The Tempest Stilled.

Matthew 8

ham, and Isaac, and Jacob, in the kingdom of heaven;

12 but ªthe sons of the kingdom shall be cast out into ᵇthe outer darkness; in that place ᶜthere shall be weeping and gnashing of teeth."

13 And Jesus said to the centurion, "Go your way; let it be done to you ªas you have believed." And the ¹servant was healed that *very* hour.

14 ªAnd when Jesus had come to Peter's ¹home, He saw his mother-in-law lying ²sick in bed with a fever.

15 And He touched her hand, and the fever left her; and she arose, and began to ¹wait on Him.

16 And when evening had come, they brought to Him many ªwho were demon-possessed; and He cast out the spirits with a word, and ᵇhealed all who were ill;

17 in order that what was spoken through Isaiah the prophet might be fulfilled, saying, "ªHE HIMSELF TOOK OUR INFIRMITIES, AND ¹CARRIED AWAY OUR DISEASES."

18 Now when Jesus saw a crowd around Him, ªHe gave orders to depart to the other side.

19 ªAnd a certain scribe came and said to Him, "Teacher, I will follow You wherever You go."

20 And Jesus *said to him, "The foxes have holes, and the birds of the ¹air *have* ²nests; but ªthe Son of Man has nowhere to lay His head."

21 And another of the disciples said to Him, "Lord, permit me first to go and bury my father."

22 But Jesus *said to him, "ªFollow Me; and allow the dead to bury their own dead."

23 ªAnd when He got into the boat, His disciples followed Him.

24 And behold, there arose ¹a great storm in the sea, so that the boat was covered with the waves; but He Himself was asleep.

25 And they came to *Him*, and awoke Him, saying, "Save *us*, Lord; we are perishing!"

26 And He *said to them, "Why are you timid, ªyou men of little faith?" Then He arose, and rebuked the winds and the sea; and ¹it became perfectly calm.

27 And the men marveled, saying, "What kind of a man is this, that even the winds and the sea obey Him?"

28 ªAnd when He had come to the other side into the country of the Gadarenes, two men who

12 ªMatt. 13:38 ᵇMatt. 22:13; 25:30 ᶜMatt. 13:42, 50; 22:13; 24:51; 25:30; Luke 13:28

13 ¹Lit., *boy* ªMatt. 9:29; 9:22

14 ¹Or, *house* ²Lit., *thrown* ªMatt. 8:14-16: *Mark* 1:29-34; *Luke* 4:38-41

15 ¹Or, *serve*

16 ªMatt. 4:24 ᵇMatt. 4:23; 8:33

17 ¹Or, *removed* ªIs. 53:4

18 ªMark 4:35; Luke 8:22

19 ªMatt. 8:19-22: *Luke* 9:57-60

20 ¹Or, *sky* ²Gr., *roosting-places* ªOften; for example, Matt. 9:6; 12:8, 32, 40; 13:41; 16:13, 27f.; 17:9; 19:28; 26:64; Mark 8:38; Luke 12:8; 18:8; 21:36; John 1:51; 3:13f.; 6:27; 12:34; Acts 7:56; Dan. 7:13

22 ªMatt. 9:9; Mark 2:14; Luke 9:59; John 1:43; 21:19

23 ªMatt. 8:23-27: *Mark* 4:36-41; Luke 8:22-25

24 ¹Lit., *a shaking*

26 ¹Lit., *a great calm occurred* ªMatt. 6:30; 14:31; 16:8

28 ªMatt. 8:28-34: *Mark* 5:1-17; Luke 8:26-37

28 ᵇMatt. 4:24

29 ¹I.e., the appointed time
of judgment
ᵃJudg. 11:12; 2 Sam. 16:10;
19:22; 1 Kin. 17:18; 2 Kin.
3:13; 2 Chr. 35:21; Mark
1:24; 5:7; Luke 4:34; 8:28;
John 2:4

33 ¹Lit., *and*
ᵃMatt. 4:24

1 ᵃMatt. 4:13; Mark 5:21

2 ¹Lit., *thrown* ²Gr., *child*
³Lit., *are being forgiven*
ᵃMatt. 9:2-8: *Mark 2:3-12;
Luke 5:18-26* ᵇMatt. 4:24; 9:6
ᶜMatt. 9:22; 14:27; Mark
6:50; 10:49; John 16:33; Acts
23:11 ᵈMark 2:5, 9; Luke
5:20, 23; 7:48

3 ¹Lit., *within*

4 ᵃMatt. 12:25, Luke 6:8;
9:47

5 ¹Lit., *are being forgiven*
ᵃMark 2:5, 9; Luke 5:20, 23;
7:48

6 ᵃMatt. 8:20 ᵇMatt. 4:24;
9:2

7 ¹Or, *departed*

8 ¹Lit., *were afraid*
ᵃMatt. 5:16; 15:31; Mark
2:12; Luke 2:20; 5:25, 26;
7:16; 13:13; 17:15; 23:47;
John 15:8; Acts 4:21; 11:18;
21:20; 2 Cor. 9:13; Gal. 1:24

9 ¹Lit., *at the tax booth*
ᵃMatt. 9:9-17: *Mark 2:14-22;
Luke 5:27-38* ᵇMatt. 10:3;
Mark 3:18; Luke 6:15; Acts
1:13; Mark 2:14 ᶜMatt. 8:22

16

were ᵇdemon-possessed met Him as they were coming out of the tombs; *they were* so exceedingly violent that no one could pass by that road.

29 And behold, they cried out, saying, "ᵃWhat do we have to do with You, Son of God? Have you come here to torment us before ¹the time?"

30 Now there was at a distance from them a herd of many swine feeding.

31 And the demons *began* to entreat Him, saying, "If You are *going to* cast us out, send us into the herd of swine."

32 And He said to them, "Begone!" And they came out, and went into the swine, and behold, the whole herd rushed down the steep bank into the sea, and perished in the waters.

33 And the herdsmen fled, and went away to the city, and reported everything, ¹including the *incident* of the ᵃdemoniacs.

34 And behold, the whole city came out to meet Jesus; and when they saw Him, they entreated *Him* to depart from their region.

CHAPTER 9

And getting into a boat, He crossed over, and came to ᵃHis own city.

2 ᵃAnd behold, they were bringing to Him a ᵇparalytic, ¹lying on a bed; and Jesus seeing their faith said to the paralytic, "ᶜTake courage, My ²son, ᵈyour sins ³are forgiven."

3 And behold, some of the scribes said ¹to themselves, "This *fellow blasphemes.*"

4 And Jesus ᵃknowing their thoughts said, "Why are you thinking evil in your hearts?

5 "For which is easier, to say, 'ᵃYour sins are ¹forgiven,' or to say, 'Rise, and walk'?

6 "But in order that you may know that ᵃthe Son of Man has authority on earth to forgive sins"—then He *said to the ᵇparalytic, "Rise, take up your bed, and go home."

7 And he rose, and ¹went to his home.

8 But when the multitudes saw *this,* they ¹were filled with awe, and ᵃglorified God, who had given such authority to men.

9 ᵃAnd as Jesus passed on from there, He saw a man, called ᵇMatthew, sitting ¹in the tax office; and He *said to him, "ᶜFollow Me!" And he rose, and followed Him.

10 And it happened that as He was reclining *at table* in the house, behold many ¹tax-gatherers and ²sinners came and ³joined Jesus and His disciples *at the table.*

11 And when the Pharisees saw *this*, they said to His disciples, "ªWhy does your Teacher eat with the tax-gatherers and sinners?"

12 But when He heard this, He said, "*It is* not ªthose who are healthy who need a physician, but those who are ill.

13 "But go and learn ªwhat *this* means, 'ᵇI DE-SIRE ¹COMPASSION, ²AND NOT SACRIFICE;' for ᶜI did not come to call *the* righteous, but sinners."

14 Then the disciples of John *came to Him, saying, "Why do we and ªthe Pharisees fast, but Your disciples do not fast?"

15 And Jesus said to them, "The ¹attendants of the bridegroom cannot mourn, as long as the bridegroom is with them, can they? But the days will come when the bridegroom is taken away from them, and then they will fast.

16 "But no one puts a ¹patch of unshrunk cloth on an old garment; for the ²patch pulls away from the garment, and a worse tear results.

17 "Nor do *men* put new wine into old ¹wine-skins; otherwise the wineskins burst, and the wine pours out, and the wineskins are ruined; but they put new wine into fresh wineskins, and both are preserved."

18 ªWhile He was saying these things to them, behold, there came ¹ª ²synagogue official, and ³ᵇbowed down before Him, saying, "My daughter has just died; but come and lay Your hand on her, and she will live."

19 And Jesus rose and *began* to follow him, and *so did* His disciples.

20 And behold, a woman who had been suffering from a hemorrhage for twelve years, came up behind Him and touched ªthe fringe of His ¹cloak;

21 for she was saying ¹to herself, "If I only ªtouch His garment, I shall ²get well."

22 But Jesus turning and seeing her said, "Daughter, ªtake courage; ᵇyour faith has ¹made you well." And ²at once the woman was ¹made well.

23 And when Jesus came into the ¹official's house, and saw ªthe flute-players, and the crowd in noisy disorder,

10 ¹Publicans who collected Roman taxes for profit ²I.e., irreligious or non-practicing Jews ³Lit., reclined with

11 ªMatt. 11:19; Mark 2:16; Luke 5:30; 15:2

12 ªMark 2:17; Luke 5:31

13 ¹Or, *mercy* ²I.e., more than ªMatt. 12:7 ᵇHos. 6:6 ᶜMark 2:17; Luke 5:32; 1 Tim. 1:15

14 ªLuke 18:12

15 ¹Lit., *sons of the bridalchamber*

16 ¹Lit., *that which is put on* ²Lit., *that which fills up*

17 ¹I.e., skins used as bottles

18 ¹Or, *one* ²Lit., *ruler* ³Or, *worshiped* ªMatt. 9:18-26; Mark 5:22-43; Luke 8:41-56 ᵇMatt. 8:2

20 ¹Or, *outer garment* ªNum. 15:38; Deut. 22:12; Matt. 14:36; 23:5

21 ¹Lit., *in herself* ²Lit., *be saved* ªMatt. 14:36; Mark 3:10; Luke 6:19

22 ¹Lit., *saved* ²Lit., *from that hour* ªMatt. 9:2 ᵇMark 5:34; 10:52; Luke 7:50; 8:48; 17:19; 18:42; Matt. 9:29; 15:28

23 ¹Lit., *ruler's* ª2 Chr. 35:25; Jer. 9:17; 16:6; Ezek. 24:17

17

24 ªJohn 11:13; Acts 20:10

25 ¹Or, *was raised up*

26 ªMatt. 9:31; 4:24; 14:1; Mark 1:28, 45; Luke 4:14, 37; 5:15; 7:17

27 ªMatt. 12:23; 15:22; 20:30, 31; 21:9, 15; 22:42; Mark 10:47, 48; 12:35; Luke 18:38, 39; 20:41f.; Matt. 1:1

29 ªMatt 9:22; 8:13

30 ªMatt. 8:4

31 ªMatt. 9:26; 4:24; 14:1; Mark 1:28, 45; Luke 4:14, 37; 5:15; 7:17

32 ¹Lit., *they brought* ªMatt. 12:22, 24 ᵇMatt. 4:24

33 ¹Lit., *ever appeared* ªMark 2:12

34 ªMatt. 12:24; Mark 3:22; Luke 11:15; John 7:20f.

35 ªMatt. 4:23 ᵇMatt. 1.23; Mark 1:14

36 ¹Or, *harassed* ²Lit., *thrown down* ³Lit., *not having* ªMatt. 14:14; 15:32; Mark 6:34; 8:2 ᵇMark 6:34; Num. 27:17; Ezek. 34:5; Zech. 10:2

37 ªLuke 10:2

38 ªLuke 10:2

1 ªMark 3:13-15; 6:7 ᵇMatt. 9:35; Luke 9:1

18

24 He *began* to say, "Depart; for the girl ªis not dead, but is asleep." And they were laughing at Him.

25 But when the crowd had been put out, He entered and took her by the hand; and the girl ¹arose.

26 And ªthis news went out into all that land.

27 And as Jesus passed on from there, two blind men followed Him, crying out, and saying, "Have mercy on us, ªSon of David!"

28 And after He had come into the house, the blind men came up to Him, and Jesus *said to them, "Do you believe that I am able to do this?" They *said to Him, "Yes, Lord."

29 Then He touched their eyes, saying, "Be it done to you ªaccording to your faith."

30 And their eyes were opened. And Jesus ªsternly warned them, saying, "See *here*, let no one know *about this!*"

31 But they went out, and ªspread the news about Him in all that land.

32 And as they were going out, behold, ªa dumb man ᵇdemon-possessed ¹was brought to Him.

33 And after the demon was cast out, the dumb man spoke; and the multitudes marveled, saying, "ªNothing like this was ¹ever seen in Israel."

34 But the Pharisees were saying, "He casts out the demons ªby the ruler of the demons."

35 And Jesus was going about all the cities and the villages, ªteaching in their synagogues, and proclaiming the gospel of the kingdom, and ᵇhealing every kind of disease and every kind of sickness.

36 And ªseeing the multitudes, He felt compassion for them, ᵇbecause they were ¹distressed and ²downcast like sheep ³without a shepherd.

37 Then He *said to His disciples, "ªThe harvest is plentiful, but the workers are few.

38 "ªTherefore beseech the Lord of the harvest to send out workers into His harvest."

CHAPTER 10

AND ªhaving summoned His twelve disciples, He gave them authority over unclean spirits, to cast them out, and to ᵇheal every kind of disease and every kind of sickness.

2 ᵃNow the names of the twelve apostles are these: The first, ᵇSimon, who is called Peter, and ᶜAndrew his brother; and ¹ᵈJames the *son* of Zebedee, and ²John his brother;

3 ᵃPhilip and ¹Bartholomew; ᵇThomas and ᶜMatthew the tax-gatherer; ²ᵈJames the *son* of Alphaeus, and ᵉThaddaeus;

4 Simon the ¹Cananaean, and ᵃJudas Iscariot, the one who betrayed Him.

5 ᵃThese twelve Jesus sent out after instructing them, saying, "Do not ¹go in *the* way of *the* Gentiles, and do not enter *any* city of the ᵇSamaritans;

6 but rather ¹go to ᵃthe lost sheep of the house of Israel.

7 "And as you ¹go, ²preach, saying, 'ᵃThe kingdom of heaven is ³at hand.'

8 "Heal *the* sick, raise *the* dead, cleanse *the* lepers, cast out demons; freely you received, freely give.

9 "ᵃDo not acquire gold, or silver, or copper ¹for your money belts;

10 or a ¹bag for *your* journey, or even two ²tunics, or sandals, or a staff; for ᵃthe worker is worthy of his ³support.

11 "And into whatever city or village you enter, inquire who is worthy in it; and abide there until you go away.

12 "And as you enter the ¹house, ᵃgive it your greeting.

13 "And if the house is worthy, let your *greeting of* peace come upon it; but if it is not worthy, let your *greeting of* peace return to you.

14 "And whoever does not receive you, nor heed your words, as you go out of that house or that city, ᵃshake off the dust of your feet.

15 "Truly I say to you, ᵃit will be more tolerable for *the* land of ᵇSodom and Gomorrah in ᶜthe day of judgment, than for that city.

16 "ᵃBehold, I send you out as sheep in the midst of wolves; therefore ¹be ᵇshrewd as serpents, and ᶜinnocent as doves.

17 "But beware of men; for they will deliver you up to *the* ¹ᵃcourts, and scourge you ᵇin their synagogues;

18 and you shall even be brought before governors and kings for My sake, as a testimony to them and to the Gentiles.

2 ¹Or, *Jacob* ²Gr., *Joannes* from Heb., *Johanan*
ᵃMatt. 10:2-4; Mark 3:16-19; Luke 6:14-16; Acts 1:13
ᵇMatt. 4:18 ᶜMatt. 4:18
ᵈMatt. 4:21

3 ¹I.e., son of Talmai (Aram) ²Or, *Jacob*
ᵃJohn 1:45ff. ᵇJohn 11:16; 14:5; 20:24ff.; 21:2 ᶜMatt 9:9
ᵈMark 15:40 ᵉMark 3:18; Luke 6:16; Acts 1:13

4 ¹Or, *the Zealot*
ᵃLuke 22:3; John 6:71; 13:2, 26; Matt. 26:14

5 ¹Or, *go off to*
ᵃMark 6:7; Luke 9:2 ᵇ2 Kin. 17:24ff.; Luke 9:52; 10:33; 17:16; John 4:9, 39f.; 8:48; Acts 8:25

6 ¹Or, *proceed*
ᵃMatt. 15:24

7 ¹Or, *proceed* ²Or, *proclaim* ³Lit., *has come near*
ᵃMatt. 3:2

9 ¹Lit., *into*
ᵃMatt. 10:9-15; Mark 6:8-11; Luke 9:3-5; 10:4-12; Luke 22:35

10 ¹Or, *knapsack or, beggars' bag* ²Or, *inner garments* ³Lit., *nourishment*
ᵃ1 Cor. 9:14; 1 Tim. 5:18

12 ¹Or, *household*
ᵃ1 Sam. 25:6; Ps. 122:7, 8

14 ᵃActs 13:51

15 ᵃMatt. 11:22, 24 ᵇMatt. 11:24; 2 Pet. 2:6; Jude 7 ᶜMatt. 11:22, 24; 12:36; Acts 17:31; 2 Pet. 2:9; 3:7; 1 John 4:17, Jude 6; Matt. 7:22; 1 Thess. 5:4; Heb. 10:25

16 ¹Or, *show yourselves to be*
ᵃLuke 10:3 ᵇGen. 3:1; Rom. 16:19; Matt. 24:45 ᶜHos. 7:11

17 ¹Or, *Sanhedrins,* or *Councils*
ᵃMatt. 5:22 ᵇMatt. 23:34; Mark 13:9; Acts 5:40; 22:19; 26:11; Luke 12:11

The Twelve Encouraged. The Cost of Service.

19 ªMatt. 10:19-22: *Mark 13:11-13; Luke 21:12-17* ᵇMatt. 6:25

20 ªLuke 12:12; Acts 4:8; 13:9; 2 Cor. 13:3

21 ¹Or, *put them to death* ªMatt. 10:35, 36 ᵇMic. 7:6

22 ªMatt. 24:9; John 15:18ff. ᵇMatt. 24:13

23 ¹Lit., *the other* ªMatt. 23:34 ᵇMatt. 16:27f.

24 ¹Or, *pupil* ªLuke 6:40; John 13:16; 15:20

25 ¹Or, *Beezebul, others read Beelzebub* ªMatt. 9:34 ᵇ2 Kin. 1:2; Matt. 12:24, 27; Mark 3:22; Luke 11:15, 18, 19

26 ªMatt. 10:26-33: *Luke 12:2-9* ᵇMark 4:22; Luke 8:17; 12:2

27 ªLuke 12:3 ᵇMatt. 24:17

28 ¹Gr., *Gehenna* ªHeb. 10:31 ᵇMatt. 5:22

29 ¹Gr., *assarion*, the smallest copper coin ªLuke 12:6

30 ªLuke 21:18; 1 Sam. 14:45; 2 Sam. 14:11; 1 Kin. 1:52; Acts 27:34

31 ªMatt. 12:12

32 ¹Gr., *in Me* ²Gr., *in him* ªRev. 3:5; Luke 12:8

33 ª2 Tim. 2:12; Mark 8:38; Luke 9:26

34 ¹Lit., *cast* ªMatt. 10:34, 35: *Luke 12:51-53*

19 "ªBut when they deliver you up, ᵇdo not become anxious about how or what you will speak; for it shall be given you in that hour what you are to speak.

20 "For ªit is not you who speak, but *it is* the Spirit of your Father who speaks in you.

21 "ªAnd brother will deliver up brother to death, and a father *his* child; and ᵇCHILDREN WILL RISE UP AGAINST PARENTS, and ¹cause them to be put to death.

22 "And ªyou will be hated by all on account of My name, but ᵇit is the one who has endured to the end who will be saved.

23 "But whenever they ªpersecute you in this city, flee to ¹the next; for truly I say to you, you shall not finish *going through* the cities of Israel, ᵇuntil the Son of Man comes.

24 "ªA ¹disciple is not above his teacher, nor a slave above his master.

25 "It is enough for the disciple that he become as his teacher, and the slave as his master. ªIf they have called the head of the house ¹ᵇBeelzebul, how much more the members of his household!

26 "Therefore do not ªfear them, ᵇfor there is nothing covered that will not be revealed, and hidden that will not be known.

27 "ªWhat I tell you in the darkness, speak in the light; and what you hear *whispered* in *your* ear, proclaim ᵇupon the housetops.

28 "And do not fear those who kill the body, but are unable to kill the soul; but rather ªfear Him who is able to destroy both soul and body in ¹ᵇhell.

29 "ªAre not two sparrows sold for a ¹cent? And *yet* not one of them will fall to the ground apart from your Father.

30 "But ªthe very hairs of your head are all numbered.

31 "Therefore do not fear; ªyou are of more value than many sparrows.

32 "Every one therefore who shall confess ¹Me before men, I will also confess ²ªhim before My Father who is in heaven.

33 "But ªwhoever shall deny Me before men, I will also deny him before My Father who is in heaven.

34 "ªDo not think that I came to ¹bring peace on the earth; I did not come to bring peace, but a sword.

35 "For I came to ᵃSET A MAN AGAINST HIS FATHER, AND A DAUGHTER AGAINST HER MOTHER, AND A DAUGHTER-IN-LAW AGAINST HER MOTHER-IN-LAW;

36 and ᵃA MAN'S ENEMIES WILL BE THE MEMBERS OF HIS HOUSEHOLD.

37 "ᵃHe who loves father or mother more than Me is not worthy of Me; and he who loves son or daughter more than Me is not worthy of Me.

38 "And ᵃhe who does not take his cross and follow after Me is not worthy of Me.

39 "ᵃHe who has found his ¹life shall lose it, and he who has lost his ¹life for My sake shall find it.

40 "ᵃHe who receives you receives Me, and ᵇhe who receives Me receives Him who sent Me.

41 "He who receives a prophet in *the* name of a prophet shall receive a prophet's reward; and he who receives a righteous man in the name of a righteous man shall receive a righteous man's reward.

42 "And ᵃwhoever in the name of a disciple gives to one of these ¹little ones even a cup of cold water to drink, truly I say to you he shall not lose his reward."

ᵃ   CHAPTER 11

AND it came about that when Jesus had finished ¹giving instructions to His twelve disciples, He departed from there ᵇto teach and ²preach in their cities.

2   ᵃNow when ᵇJohn in prison heard of the works of Christ, he sent *word* by his disciples,

3   and said to Him, "Are You ᵃthe Coming One, or shall we look for someone else?"

4   And Jesus answered and said to them, "Go and report to John the things which you hear and see:

5   ᵃ*the* BLIND RECEIVE SIGHT and *the* lame walk, *the* lepers are cleansed and *the* deaf hear, and *the* dead are raised up, and *the* POOR HAVE THE ¹GOSPEL PREACHED to them.

6   "And blessed is he ¹who ᵃkeeps from ²stumbling over Me."

7   And as these were going *away*, Jesus began to say to the multitudes concerning John, "What did you go out into ᵃthe wilderness to look at? A reed shaken by the wind?

8   "¹But what did you go out to see? A man

---

35 ᵃMatt. 10:21; Mic. 7:6

36 ᵃMatt. 10:21 Mic. 7:6

37 ᵃLuke 14:26

38 ᵃMatt. 16:24; Mark 8:34; Luke 9:23; 14:27

39 ¹Or, *soul-life* ᵃMatt. 16:25; Mark 8:35; Luke 9:24; 17:33; John 12:25

40 ᵃLuke 10:16; John 13:20; Matt. 18:5; Gal. 4:14 ᵇMark 9:37; Luke 9:48; John 12:44

42 ¹Or, *humble folk* ᵃMark 9:41; Matt. 25:40

1 ¹Or, *commanding* ²Or, *proclaim* ᵃMatt. 7:28 ᵇMatt. 9:35

2 ᵃMatt. 11:2-19: *Luke 7:18-35* ᵇMatt. 14:3; Mark 6:17; Luke 9:7ff.

3 ᵃJohn 6:14; 11:27; Heb. 10:37; Matt. 11:10; Ps. 118:26

5 ¹Or, *good news* ᵃIs. 35:5f.; 61:1

6 ¹Lit., *whoever* ²Or, *taking offense at* ᵃMatt. 13:21, 57; 24:10; 26:31; Mark 6:3; John 6:61; 16:1; Matt. 5:29

7 ᵃMatt. 3:1

8 ¹Or, *Well then,*

21

Matthew 11

John the Baptist's Greatness.
The Unrepenting Cities.

8 [2]Lit., *houses*

9 [1]Or, *Well then,*
[a]Matt. 14:5; 21:26; Luke
1:76; 20:6

10 [1]Lit., *has been written*
[a]Mark 1:2; Mal. 3:1

11 [1]Lit., *less*

12 [1]Or, *is forcibly entered*
[2]Or, *seize it for themselves*
[a]Luke 16:16

13 [a]Luke 16:16

14 [1]Or, *is to come*
[a]Mal. 4:5; Matt. 17:10-13;
Mark 9:11-13; Luke 1:17;
John 1:21

15 [a]Matt. 13:9, 43; Mark
4:9, 23; Luke 8:8; 14:35; Rev.
13:9; 2:7, 11, 17, 29; 3:6, 13,
22

17 [1]Lit., *beat the breast*

18 [a]Matt. 3:4 [b]Luke 1:15
[c]John 7:20; 8:48f., 52; 10:20;
Matt. 9:34

19 [1]Or, *wine-drinker* [2]Or,
publicans who collected
Roman taxes for profit [3]Lit.,
and
[a]Matt. 9:11; Luke 15:2

20 [1]Or, *works of power*

21 [1]Or, *works of power*
[a]Matt. 11:21-23; Luke 10:13-
15 [b]Mark 6:45; 8:22; Luke
9:10; John 1:44; 12:21 [c]Matt.
11:22; 15:21; Mark 3:8; 7:24,
31; Luke 6:17; Acts 12:20;
Luke 4:26; Acts 27:3 [d]Rev.
11:3

22 [a]Matt. 10:15; 11:24
[b]Matt. 10:15

23 [1]Some mss. read, *shall
be brought down* [2]Or, *works
of power*
[a]Matt. 4:13 [b]Is. 14:13, 15;
Ezek. 26:20; 31:14; 32:18, 24
[c]Matt. 16:18; Luke 10:15;
16:23; Acts 2:27, 31; Rev.
1:18; 6:8; 20:13f. [d]Matt.
10:15

dressed in soft *clothing?* Behold, those who wear soft *clothing* are in kings' [2]palaces.
9 "[1]But why did you go out? To see [a]a prophet? Yes, I tell you, and one who is more than a prophet.
10 "This is the one about whom it [1]was written, '[a]BEHOLD, I SEND MY MESSENGER BEFORE YOUR FACE,
WHO WILL PREPARE YOUR WAY BEFORE YOU.'
11 "Truly, I say to you, among those born of women there has not arisen *anyone* greater than John the Baptist; yet he who is [1]least in the kingdom of heaven is greater than he.
12 "And [a]from the days of John the Baptist until now the kingdom of heaven [1]suffers violence, and violent men [2]take it by force.
13 "For [a]all the prophets and the Law prophesied until John.
14 "And if you care to accept *it*, he himself is [a]Elijah, who [1]was to come.
15 "[a]He who has ears to hear, let him hear.
16 "But to what shall I compare this generation? It is like children sitting in the market places, who call out to the other *children,*
17 and say, 'We played the flute for you, and you did not dance; we sang a dirge, and you did not [1]mourn.'
18 "For John came neither [a]eating nor [b]drinking, and they say, '[c]He has a demon!'
19 "The Son of Man came eating and drinking, and they say, 'Behold, a gluttonous man and a [1]drunkard, [a]a friend of [2]tax-gatherers and sinners!' [3]Yet wisdom is vindicated by her deeds."
20 Then He began to reproach the cities in which most of His [1]miracles were done, because they did not repent.
21 "[a]Woe to you, Chorazin! Woe to you, [b]Bethsaida! For if the [1]miracles had occurred in [c]Tyre and [c]Sidon which occurred in you, they would have repented long ago in [d]sackcloth and ashes.
22 "Nevertheless I say to you, [a]it shall be more tolerable for Tyre and Sidon in [b]*the* day of judgment, than for you.
23 "And you, [a]Capernaum, will not be EXALTED TO HEAVEN, will you? You shall [1][b]DESCEND TO [c]HADES; for if the [2]miracles had occurred in [d]Sodom which occurred in you, it would have remained to this day.

24 "Nevertheless I say to you that ᵃit shall be more tolerable for the land of ᵇSodom in ᵇ*the* day of judgment, than for you."

25 ᵃAt that ¹time Jesus ᵇanswered and said, "I ²praise Thee, O ᶜFather, Lord of heaven and earth, that ᵈThou didst hide these things from *the* wise and intelligent and didst reveal them to babes.

26 "Yes, ᵃFather, for thus it was well-pleasing in Thy sight.

27 "ᵃAll things ¹have been handed over to Me by My Father; and no one ²knows the Son, except the Father; nor does anyone ²know the Father, ᵇexcept the Son, and anyone to whom the Son wills to reveal *Him*.

28 "ᵃCome to Me, all who are ¹weary and heavy laden, and I will give you rest.

29 "Take My yoke upon you, and ᵃlearn from Me, for I am gentle and humble in heart; and ᵇYOU SHALL FIND REST FOR YOUR SOULS.

30 "For My yoke is ¹easy, and My load is light."

ᵃ CHAPTER 12

AT that ¹time Jesus went on the Sabbath through the grainfields, and His disciples became hungry and began to ᵇpick the heads of *grain* and eat.

2 But when the Pharisees saw it, they said to Him, "Behold, Your disciples do what ᵃis not lawful to do on a Sabbath."

3 But He said to them, "Have you not read what David did, when he became hungry, he and his companions;

4 how he entered the house of God, and ᵃthey ate the ¹consecrated bread, which was not lawful for him to eat, nor for those with him, but for the priests alone?

5 "Or have you not read in the Law, that on the Sabbath the priests in the temple ¹break the Sabbath, and are innocent?

6 "But I say to you, that something ᵃgreater than the temple is here.

7 "But if you had known what this ¹means, 'ᵃI DESIRE ²COMPASSION, AND NOT A SACRIFICE,' you would not have condemned the innocent.

8 "For ᵃthe Son of Man is Lord of the Sabbath."

9 ᵃAnd departing from there, He went into their synagogue.

24 ᵃMatt. 10:15; 11:22
ᵇMatt. 10:15

25 ¹Or, *occasion* ²Or, *acknowledge to Thy praise*
ᵃMatt. 11:25-27: *Luke 10:21,* 22 ᵇActs 3:12 ᶜLuke 22:42; 23:34; John 11:41; 12:27, 28
ᵈ1 Cor. 1:26ff.

26 ᵃLuke 22:42; 23:34; John 11:41; 12:27, 28

27 ¹Lit., *were given over* ²Or, *perfectly know(s)*
ᵃMatt. 28:18; John 3:35; 13:3; 17:2 ᵇJohn 7:29; 10:15; 17:25

28 ¹Or, *who work to exhaustion*
ᵃJohn 7:37; Jer. 31:25

29 ᵃJohn 13:15; Eph. 4:20; Phil. 2:5; 1 Pet. 2:21; 1 John 2:6 ᵇJer. 6:16

30 ¹Or, *kindly,* or, *pleasant*

1 ¹Or, *occasion*
ᵃMatt. 12:1-8: *Mark 2:23-28; Luke 6:1-5* ᵇDeut. 23:25

2 ᵃMatt. 12:10; Luke 13:14; 14:3; John 5:10; 7:23; 9:16

4 ¹Or, *showbread;* lit., *loaves of presentation*
ᵃ1 Sam. 21:6

5 ¹Or, *profane*

6 ᵃMatt. 12:41, 42

7 ¹Lit., *is* ²Or, *mercy*
ᵃHos. 6:6

8 ᵃMatt. 8:20; 12:32, 40

9 ᵃMatt. 12:9-14: *Mark 3:1-6; Luke 6:6-11*

23

Matthew 12

**Good Deeds on the Sabbath.
A Demon-possessed Man.**

10 ªMatt. 12:2; Luke 13:14;
14:3; John 5:10; 7:23; 9:16

11 ¹Lit., *of*

12 ¹Lit., *well*
ªMatt. 10:31

13 ¹Lit., *healthy, well*

14 ªMatt. 26:4; Mark 14:1;
Luke 22:2; John 7:30, 44;
8:59; 10:31, 39; 11:53

15 ¹Lit., *knowing*
ªMatt. 4:23

16 ¹Lit., *evident*
ªMatt. 8:4

18 ¹Lit., *child* ²Lit., *chose*
³Or, *took pleasure* ⁴Or,
judgment ⁵Or, *nations*
ªIs. 42:1 ᵇMatt. 3:17; 17:5
ᶜLuke 4:18; John 3:34

19 ªIs. 42:2

20 ¹Or, *puts forth* ²Or,
judgment
ªIs. 42:3

21 ¹Or, *nations*
ªIs. 42:4; Rom. 15:12

22 ªMatt. 12:22, 24: *Luke
11:14, 15*; Matt. 9:32, 34
ᵇMatt. 4:24

23 ªMatt. 9:27

24

10　And behold, *there was* a man with a withered hand. And they questioned Him, saying, "ªIs it lawful to heal on the Sabbath?"—in order that they might accuse Him.

11　And He said to them, "What man shall there be ¹among you, who shall have one sheep, and if it falls into a pit on the Sabbath, will he not take hold of it, and lift it out?

12　"Of ªhow much more value then is a man than a sheep! So then, it is lawful to do ¹good on the Sabbath."

13　Then He *said to the man, "Stretch out your hand!" And he stretched it out, and it was restored to ¹normal, like the other.

14　But the Pharisees went out, and ªcounseled together against Him, *as to* how they might destroy Him.

15　But Jesus, ¹aware of *this*, withdrew from there. And many followed Him, and ªHe healed them all,

16　and ªwarned them not to make Him ¹known;

17　in order that what was spoken through Isaiah the prophet, might be fulfilled, saying,

18　"ªBEHOLD, MY ¹SERVANT WHOM I ²HAVE CHOSEN;
ᵇMY BELOVED IN WHOM MY SOUL IS ³WELL PLEASED;
ᶜI WILL PUT MY SPIRIT UPON HIM,
ªAND HE SHALL PROCLAIM ⁴JUSTICE TO THE ⁵GENTILES.

19　"ªHE WILL NOT QUARREL, NOR CRY OUT;
NOR WILL ANY ONE HEAR HIS VOICE IN THE STREETS.

20　"ªA BATTERED REED HE WILL NOT BREAK OFF,
AND A SMOLDERING WICK HE WILL NOT PUT OUT,
UNTIL HE ¹LEADS ²JUSTICE TO VICTORY.

21　"ªAND IN HIS NAME THE ¹GENTILES WILL HOPE."

22　ªThen there was brought to Him a ᵇdemon-possessed man *who was* blind and dumb, and He healed him, so that the dumb man spoke and saw.

23　And all the multitudes were amazed, and *began* to say, "This *man* cannot be the ªSon of David, can he?"

24　But when the Pharisees heard it, they said,

"This man casts out demons only ᵃby ¹Beelzebul the ruler of the demons."

25 ᵃAnd ᵇknowing their thoughts He said to them, "¹Any kingdom divided against itself is laid waste; and ¹any city or house divided against itself shall not stand.

26 "And if ᵃSatan casts out ᵃSatan, he ¹is divided against himself; how then shall his kingdom stand?

27 "And if I ᵃby ¹Beelzebul cast out demons, ᵇby whom do your sons cast them out? Consequently they shall be your judges.

28 "But if I cast out demons by the Spirit of God, then the kingdom of God has come upon you.

29 "Or how can anyone enter the strong man's house and carry off his property, unless he first binds the strong *man*? And then he will plunder his house.

30 "ᵃHe who is not with Me is against Me; and he who does not gather with Me scatters.

31 "ᵃTherefore I say to you, any sin and blasphemy shall be forgiven men; but blasphemy against the Spirit shall not be forgiven.

32 "And whoever shall speak a word against the Son of Man, it shall be forgiven him; but whoever shall speak against the Holy Spirit, it shall not be forgiven him, either in ᵃthis age, or in the *age* to come.

33 "Either make the tree good, and its fruit good; or make the tree rotten, and its fruit rotten; for ᵃthe tree is known by its fruit.

34 "ᵃYou brood of vipers, how can you, being evil, speak ¹what is good? ᵇFor the mouth speaks out of that which fills the heart.

35 "The good man out of *his* good treasure brings forth ¹what is good; and the evil man out of *his* evil treasure brings forth ²what is evil.

36 "And I say to you, that every ¹careless word that men shall speak, they shall render account for it in ᵃthe day of judgment.

37 "For ¹by your words you shall be justified, and ¹by your words you shall be condemned."

38 Then some of the scribes and Pharisees answered Him, saying, "Teacher, ᵃwe want to see a ¹sign from You."

39 But He answered and said to them, "ᵃAn evil and adulterous generation craves for a ¹sign;

24 ¹Or, *Beezebul*; others read *Beelzebub*
ᵃMatt. 9:34

25 ¹Lit., *every*
ᵃMatt. 12:25-29; Mark 3:23-27; Luke 11:17-22 ᵇMatt. 9:4

26 ¹Lit., *was*
ᵃMatt. 4:10

27 ¹vs. 24
ᵃMatt. 9:34 ᵇActs 19:13

30 ᵃLuke 11:23; Mark 9:40; Luke 9:50

31 ᵃMatt. 12:31, 32; Mark 3:28-30; Luke 12:10

32 ᵃMark 10:30; Luke 16:8; 18:30; 20:34, 35; Eph. 1:21; 1 Tim. 6:17; 2 Tim. 4:10; Titus 2:12; Heb. 6:5; Matt. 13:22 and 13:39

33 ᵃMatt. 7:16

34 ¹Lit., *good things*
ᵃMatt. 3:7; 23:33 ᵇMatt. 12:34, 35; Luke 6:45; Matt. 15:18; Eph. 4:29; James 3:2-12; 1 Sam. 24:13

35 ¹Lit., *good things* ²Lit., *evil things*

36 ¹Or, *useless*
ᵃMatt. 10:15

37 ¹Or, *in accordance with*

38 ¹Or, *attesting miracle*
ᵃMatt. 16:1; Mark 8:11, 12; Luke 11:16; John 2:18; 6:30; 1 Cor. 1:22

39 ¹Or, *attesting miracle*
ᵃMatt. 12:39-42; Luke 11:29-32; Matt. 16:4

25

39 ¹Or, *attesting miracle*

40 ªJonah 1:17 ᵇMatt. 8:20
ᶜMatt. 16:21

41 ªJonah 1:2 ᵇJonah 3:5
ᶜMatt. 12:6, 42

42 ª1 Kin. 10:1; 2 Chr. 9:1
ᵇMatt. 12:6, 41

43 ªMatt. 12:43-45: *Luke*
11:24-26

45 ª2 Pet. 2:20

46 ªMatt. 12:46-50: *Mark*
3:31-35; Luke 8:19-21 ᵇMatt.
1:18; 2:11ff.; 3:55; Luke
1:43; 2:33f., 48, 51; John 2:1,
5, 12; 19:25f.; Acts 1:14
ᶜMatt. 13:55; Mark 6:3; John
2:12; 7:3, 5, 10; Acts 1:14;
1 Cor. 9:5; Gal. 1:19

1 ªMatt. 13:36; 9:28; Mark
3:19 ᵇMatt. 13:1-15: *Mark*
4:1-12; Luke 8:4-10

26

and *yet* no ¹sign shall be given to it but the ¹sign of Jonah the prophet;

40 for just as ªJONAH WAS THREE DAYS AND THREE NIGHTS IN THE BELLY OF THE SEA-MONSTER; SO shall ᵇthe Son of Man be ᶜthree days and three nights in the heart of the earth.

41 "ªThe men of Nineveh shall stand up with this generation at the judgment, and shall condemn it because ᵇthey repented at the preaching of Jonah; and behold, ᶜsomething greater than Jonah is here.

42 "ªThe Queen of *the* South shall rise up with this generation at the judgment and shall condemn it; because she came from the ends of the earth to hear the wisdom of Solomon; and behold, ᵇsomething greater than Solomon is here.

43 "ªNow when the unclean spirit goes out of a man, it passes through waterless places, seeking rest, and does not find *it.*

44 "Then it says, 'I will return to my house from which I came;' and when it comes, it finds it unoccupied, swept, and put in order.

45 "Then it goes, and takes along with it seven other spirits more wicked than itself, and they go in and live there; and ªthe last state of that man becomes worse than the first. That is the way it will also be with this evil generation."

40 ªWhile He was still speaking to the multitudes, behold, His ᵇmother and His ᶜbrothers were standing outside, seeking to speak to Him.

47 And someone said to Him, "Behold, Your mother and Your brothers are standing outside seeking to speak to You."

48 But He answered the one who was telling Him and said, "Who is My mother and who are My brothers?"

49 And stretching out His hand toward His disciples, He said, "Behold, My mother and My brothers!

50 "For whoever shall do the will of My Father who is in heaven, he is My brother and sister and mother."

CHAPTER 13

ON that day Jesus went out of ªthe house, and was sitting ᵇby the sea.

2 And great multitudes gathered about Him,

so that ªHe got into a boat and sat down, and the whole multitude was standing on the beach.

3   And He spoke many things to them in ªparables, saying, "Behold, the sower went out to sow;

4   and as he sowed, some *seeds* fell beside the road, and the birds came and devoured them.

5   "And others fell upon the rocky places, where they ¹did not have much soil; and immediately they sprang up, because they had no depth of soil.

6   "But when the sun had risen, they were scorched; and because they had no root, they withered away.

7   "And others fell ¹among the thorns, and the thorns came up and choked them out.

8   "And others fell on the good soil, and *yielded a crop, some a ªhundredfold, some sixty, and some thirty.

9   "ªHe who has ears, let him hear."

10   And the disciples came and said to Him, "Why do You speak to them in parables?"

11   And He answered and said to them, "ªTo you it has been granted to know the mysteries of the kingdom of heaven, but to them it has not been granted.

12   "ªFor whoever has, to him shall *more* be given, and he shall have an abundance; but whoever does not have, even what he has shall be taken away from him.

13   "Therefore I speak to them in parables; because while ªseeing they do not see, and while hearing they do not hear, nor do they understand.

14   "And ¹in their case the prophecy of Isaiah is being fulfilled, which says,

²ªYOU WILL KEEP ON HEARING, ³BUT WILL
NOT UNDERSTAND;
AND ⁴YOU WILL KEEP ON SEEING, BUT WILL
NOT PERCEIVE;

15   ªFOR THE HEART OF THIS PEOPLE HAS BECOME
DULL,
AND WITH THEIR EARS THEY SCARCELY HEAR,
AND THEY HAVE CLOSED THEIR EYES;
LEST THEY SHOULD SEE WITH THEIR EYES,
AND HEAR WITH THEIR EARS,
AND UNDERSTAND WITH THEIR HEART AND
TURN AGAIN,
AND I SHOULD HEAL THEM.'

2 ªLuke 5:3

3 ªMatt. 13:10ff.; Mark 4:2ff.

5 ¹Lit., *were not having*

7 ¹Lit., *upon*

8 ªMatt. 13:23; Gen. 26:12

9 ªMatt. 11:15

11 ªMatt. 19:11; 20:23; John 6:65; 1 Cor. 2:10; Col. 1:27; 1 John 2:20, 27

12 ªMatt. 25:29; Mark 4:25; Luke 8:18; 19:26

13 ªJer. 5:21; Ezek. 12:2; Is. 42:19, 20; Deut. 29:4

14 ¹Lit., *for them* ²Lit., *with a hearing* ³Lit., *and* ⁴Lit., *seeing you will see* ªIs. 6:9; Mark 4:12; Luke 8:10; John 12:40; Acts 28:26, 27; Rom. 10:16; 11:8

15 ªIs. 6:10

27

16 ªMatt. 13:16, 17: *Luke 10:23, 24*

16 "ªBut blessed are your eyes, because they see; and your ears, because they hear.

17 "For truly I say to you, that ªmany prophets and righteous men desired to see what you see, and did not see *it*; and to hear what you hear, and did not hear *it*.

17 ªJohn 8:56; Heb. 11:13; 1 Pet. 1:10-12

18 "ªHear then the parable of the sower.

18 ªMatt. 13:18-23: *Mark 4:13-20; Luke 8:11-15*

19 "When any one hears ªthe word of the kingdom, and does not understand it, ᵇthe evil *one* comes and snatches away what has been sown in his heart. This is the one on whom seed was sown beside the road.

19 ªMatt. 4:23 ᵇMatt. 5:37

20 "And the one on whom seed was sown on the rocky places, this is the man who hears the word, and immediately receives it with joy;

21 yet he has no *firm* root in himself, but is *only* temporary, and when affliction or persecution arises because of the word, immediately he ¹ªfalls away.

21 ¹Lit., *is caused to stumble*
ªMatt. 11:6

22 "And the one on whom seed was sown among the thorns, this is the man who hears the word, and the worry of ªthe ¹world, and the ᵇdeceitfulness of riches choke the word, and it becomes unfruitful.

22 ¹Or, *age*
ªMark 4:19; Rom. 12:2; 1 Cor. 1:20; 2:6, 8; 3:18; 2 Cor. 4:4; Cal. 1:4; Eph. 2:2; Matt. 12:32 and 13:39
ᵇMatt. 19:23; 1 Tim. 6:9, 10, 17

23 "And the one on whom seed was sown on the good ground, this is the man who hears the word and understands it; who indeed bears fruit, and brings forth, some ªa hundredfold, some sixty, and some thirty."

23 ªMatt 13:8

24 He presented another parable to them, saying, "ªThe kingdom of heaven ¹may be compared to ᵇa man who sowed good seed in his field.

24 ¹Lit., *was compared to*
ªMatt. 13:31, 33, 45, 47; 18:23; 20:1; 22 2; 25:1; Mark 4:30; Luke 13:18, 20 ᵇMark 4:26-29

25 "But while men were sleeping, his enemy came and sowed ¹tares also among the wheat, and went away.

25 ¹Or, *darnel*, a weed resembling wheat.

26 "But when the ¹wheat sprang up and bore grain, then the tares became evident also.

26 ¹Lit., *grass*

27 "And the slaves of the landowner came and said to him, 'Sir, did you not sow good seed in your field? ¹How then does it have tares?'

27 ¹Lit., *from where*

28 "And he said to them, 'An ¹enemy has done this!' And the slaves *said to him, 'Do you want us, then, to go and gather them up?'

29 "But he *said, 'No; lest while you are gathering up the tares, you may root up the wheat with them.

28 ¹Lit., *an enemy man*

30 'Allow both to grow together until the harvest; and in the time of the harvest I will say to the

reapers, "First gather up the tares; and bind them in bundles to burn them up; but ᵃgather the wheat into my barn." ' "

31 He presented another parable to them, saying, "ᵃThe kingdom of heaven is like ᵇa mustard seed, which a man took and sowed in his field;

32 and this is smaller than all *other* seeds; but when it is full grown, it is larger than the garden plants, and becomes a tree, so that ᵃTHE BIRDS OF THE ¹AIR come and NEST IN ITS BRANCHES."

33 He spoke another parable to them; "ᵃThe kingdom of heaven is like leaven, which a woman took, and hid in ᵇthree ¹pecks of meal, until it was all leavened."

34 All these things Jesus spoke to the multitudes in parables, and He was not talking to them ᵃwithout a parable,

35 so that what was spoken through the prophet might be fulfilled, saying,

"ᵃI WILL OPEN MY MOUTH IN PARABLES;
I WILL UTTER THINGS HIDDEN SINCE THE
FOUNDATION OF THE WORLD."

36 Then He left the multitudes, and went into ᵃthe house. And His disciples came to Him, saying, "ᵇExplain to us the parable of the ¹tares of the field."

37 And He answered and said, "The one who sows the good seed is ᵃthe Son of Man,

38 and the field is the world; and *as for* the good seed, these are ᵃthe sons of the kingdom; and the tares are ᵇthe sons of ᶜthe evil *one;*

39 and the enemy who sowed them is the devil, and the harvest is ᵃthe ¹end of the age; and the reapers are angels.

40 "Therefore just as the tares are gathered up and burned with fire, so shall it be at ᵃthe ¹end of the age.

41 "ᵃThe Son of Man ᵇwill send forth His angels, and they will gather out of His kingdom all ¹ᶜSTUMBLING-BLOCKS, AND THOSE WHO COMMIT LAWLESSNESS,

42 and ᵃwill cast them into the furnace of fire; in that place ᵇthere shall be weeping and gnashing of teeth.

43 "ᵃThen THE RIGHTEOUS WILL SHINE FORTH AS THE SUN in the kingdom of their Father. ᵇHe who has ears, let him hear.

44 "ᵃThe kingdom of heaven is like a treasure

---

30 ᵃMatt. 3:12

31 ᵃMatt. 13:31, 32: *Mark 4:30-32; Luke 13:18, 19;* Matt. 13:24 ᵇMatt. 17:20; Luke 17:6

32 ¹Or, *sky* ᵃPs. 104:12; Ezek. 17:23; 31:6; Dan. 4:12

33 ¹Gr., *sata* ᵃMatt. 13:33: *Luke 13:21;* Matt. 13:24 ᵇGen. 18:6; Judg. 6:19; 1 Sam. 1:24

34 ᵃMark 4:34; John 10:6; 16:25

35 ᵃPs. 78:2

36 ¹Or, *darnel* cf. vs. 25 ᵃMatt. 13:1 ᵇMatt. 15:15

37 ᵃMatt. 8:20

38 ᵃMatt. 8:12; ᵇJohn 8:44; Acts 13:10; 1 John 3:10 ᶜMatt. 5:37

39 ¹Or, *consummation* ᵃMatt. 13:40, 49; 24:3; 28:20; 1 Cor. 10:11; Heb. 9:26; Matt. 12:32 and 13:22

40 ¹Or, *consummation* ᵃMatt. 13:39, 49; 24:3; 28:20; 1 Cor. 10:11; Heb. 9:26; Matt. 12:32 and 13:22

41 ¹Or, *everything that is offensive* ᵃMatt. 8:20 ᵇMatt. 24:31 ᶜZeph. 1:3

42 ᵃMatt. 13:50 ᵇMatt. 8:12

43 ᵃDan. 12:3 ᵇMatt. 11:15

44 ᵃMatt. 13:24

29

44 bMatt. 13:46

45 aMatt. 13:24

47 aMatt. 13:44

49 1Or, consummation
2Or, separate
aMatt. 13:39, 40

50 aMatt. 13:42 bMatt. 8:12

53 aMatt. 7:28

54 1Or, His own part of the
country 2Or, was teaching
3Or, miracles
aMatt. 13:54-58: Mark 6:1-6
bMatt. 4:23 cMatt. 7:28

55 aMatt. 12:46

56 aMark 6:3

57 1Lit., were being made
to stumble 2Or, his own part
of the country
aMatt. 11:6 bMark 6:4; Luke
4:24; John 4:44

58 1Or, works of power

1 1Or, occasion
aMatt. 14:1-12: Mark 6:14-
29; Matt. 14:1, 2: Luke 9:7-9
bMatt. 14:1-12: Mark 6:14-
29; Matt. 14:1, 2: Luke 9:7-9,
also Mark 8:15; Luke 3:1, 19;
8:3; 13:31; 23:7f., 11f., 15;
Acts 4:27; 12:1

2 aMatt. 16:14; Mark 6:14;
Luke 9:7

hidden in the field; which a man found and hid; and from joy over it he goes and bsells all that he has, and buys that field.

45 "Again, athe kingdom of heaven is like a merchant seeking fine pearls,

46 and upon finding one pearl of great value, he went and sold all that he had, and bought it.

47 "Again, athe kingdom of heaven is like a drag-net cast into the sea, and gathering *fish* of every kind;

48 and when it was filled, they drew it up on the beach; and they sat down, and gathered the good *fish* into containers, but the bad they threw away.

49 "So it will be at athe 1end of the age; the angels shall come forth, and 2take out the wicked from among the righteous,

50 and awill cast them into the furnace of fire; bthere shall be weeping and gnashing of teeth.

51 "Have you understood all these things?" They *said to Him, "Yes."

52 And He said to them, "Therefore every scribe who has become a disciple of the kingdom of heaven is like a head of a household, who brings forth out of his treasure things new and old."

53 aAnd it came about that when Jesus had finished these parables, He departed from there.

54 aAnd coming to 1His home town He 2bbegan teaching them in their synagogue, so that cthey became astonished, and said, "Where *did* this man *get* this wisdom, and *these* 3miraculous powers?

55 "Is not this the carpenter's son? Is not aHis mother called Mary, and His abrothers, James and Joseph and Simon and Judas?

56 "And aHis sisters, are they not all with us? Where then *did* this man *get* all these things?"

57 And they 1took aoffense at Him. But Jesus said to them, "bA prophet is not without honor except in his 2home town, and in his *own* household."

58 And He did not do many 1miracles there because of their unbelief.

a   CHAPTER 14

AT that 1time bHerod the tetrarch heard the news about Jesus,

2 and said to his servants, "aThis is John the

Baptist; ¹he has risen from the dead; and that is why miraculous powers are at work in him."

3 For ªHerod had seized John, and bound him, and put him ᵇin prison on account of ᶜHerodias, the wife of his brother Philip.

4 For John had been saying to him, "ªIt is not lawful for you to have her."

5 And although he wanted to put him to death, he feared the multitude, because ¹they regarded him as ªa prophet.

6 But when Herod's birthday ¹came, the daughter of ªHerodias danced ²before *them* and pleased ᵇHerod.

7 Thereupon he promised with an oath to give her whatever she asked.

8 And having been prompted by her mother, she *said, "Give me here on a platter the head of John the Baptist."

9 And although he was grieved, the king commanded *it* to be given because of his oaths, and because of ¹his dinner-guests.

10 And he sent and had John beheaded in the prison.

11 And his head was brought on a platter and given to the girl; and she brought *it* to her mother.

12 And his disciples came and took away the body and buried ¹it; and they went and reported to Jesus.

13 ªNow when Jesus heard *it*, He withdrew from there in a boat, to a lonely place by Himself; and when the multitudes heard *of this*, they followed Him on foot from the cities.

14 And when He came out, He ªsaw a great multitude, and felt compassion for them, and ᵇhealed their sick.

15 And when it was evening, the disciples came to Him, saying, "The place is desolate, and the time is already past; so send the multitudes away, that they may go into the villages, and buy food for themselves."

16 But Jesus said to them, "They do not need to go away; you give them *something* to eat!"

17 And they *said to Him, "We have here only ªfive loaves, and two fish."

18 And He said, "Bring them here to Me."

19 And ordering the multitudes to recline on the grass, He took the five loaves and the two fish, and looking up toward heaven, He ªblessed *the*

2 ¹Or, *he, himself*

3 ªMatt. 14:1-12: *Mark 6:14-29; Matt. 14:1, 2; Luke 9:7-9*; also Mark 8:15; Luke 3:1, 19; 8:3; 13:31; 23:7f., 11f., 15; Acts 4:27; 12:1 ᵇMatt. 4:12; 11:2 ᶜMatt. 14:6; Mark 6:17, 19, 22; Luke 3:19

4 ªLev. 18:16; 20:21

5 ¹Lit., *they were holding* ªMatt. 11:9

6 ¹Lit., *occurred* ²Lit., *in the midst* ªMatt. 14:3; Mark 6:17, 19, 22; Luke 3:19 ᵇMatt. 14:1-12: *Mark 6:14-29; Matt. 14:1, 2; Luke 9:7-9*; also Mark 8:15; Luke 3:1, 19; 8:3; 13:31; 23:7f. 11f. 15; Acts 4:27; 12:1

9 ¹Lit., *those who reclined at table with him*

12 ¹Lit., *him*

13 ªMatt. 14:13-21: *Mark 6:32-44; Luke 9:10-17; John 6:1-13; Matt. 15:32-38*

14 ªMatt. 9:36 ᵇMatt. 4:23

17 ªMatt. 16:9

19 ª1 Sam. 9:13; Matt. 15:36; 26:26; Mark 6:41; 8:7; 14:22; Luke 24:30; Acts 27:35; Rom. 14:6

31

20 ¹I.e., large-sized baskets
ªMatt. 16:9; Mark 6:43; 8:19;
Luke 9:17; John 6:13

22 ¹Lit., compelled
ªMatt. 14:22-33; Mark 6:45-
51; John 6:15-21

23 ªMark 6:46; Luke 6:12;
9:28; John 6:15

24 ¹A stadion was about
600 feet ²Lit., tormented

25 ¹I.e., 3-6 a.m.
ªMark 13:35; Matt. 21:13

26 ¹Or, troubled
ªLuke 24:37

27 ªMatt. 9:2 ᵇMatt. 17:7;
28:10; Mark 6:50; Luke 5:10;
12:32; John 6:20; Rev. 1:17;
Matt. 28:5; Luke 1:13, 30;
2:10

31 ªMatt. 6:30; 8:26; 16:8

33 ªMatt. 4:3

34 ¹Lit., the land
ªMatt. 14:34-36; Mark 6:53-
56; John 6:24, 25 ᵇMark 6:53;
Luke 5:1

35 ¹Or, knew

36 ªMatt. 9:20 ᵇMatt. 9:21;
Mark 3:10; 6:56; 8:22; Luke
6:19

32

food, and breaking the loaves He gave them to the disciples, and the disciples gave to the multitudes,

20 and they all ate, and were satisfied. And they picked up what was left over of the broken pieces, twelve full ¹ªbaskets.

21 And there were about five thousand men who ate, aside from women and children.

22 ªAnd immediately He ¹made the disciples get into the boat, and go ahead of Him to the other side, while He sent the multitudes away.

23 And after He had sent the multitudes away, ªHe went up to the mountain by Himself to pray; and when it was evening, He was there alone.

24 But the boat was already many ¹stadia away from the land, ²battered by the waves; for the wind was contrary.

25 And in ªthe ¹fourth watch of the night He came to them, walking upon the sea.

26 And when the disciples saw Him walking on the sea, they were ¹frightened, saying, "It is ªa ghost!" And they cried out for fear.

27 But immediately Jesus spoke to them, saying, "ªTake courage, it is I; ᵇdo not be afraid."

28 And Peter answered Him and said, "Lord, if it is You, command me to come to You on the water."

29 And He said, "Come!" And Peter got out of the boat, and walked on the water and came toward Jesus.

30 But seeing the wind, he became afraid, and beginning to sink, he cried out, saying, "Lord, save me!"

31 And immediately Jesus stretched out His hand and took hold of him, and *said to him, "ªO you of little faith, why did you doubt?"

32 And when they got into the boat, the wind stopped.

33 And those who were in the boat worshiped Him, saying, "You are certainly ªGod's Son!"

34 ªAnd when they had crossed over, they came to ¹land at ᵇGennesaret.

35 And when the men of that place ¹recognized Him, they sent into all that surrounding district and brought to Him all who were ill;

36 and they began to entreat Him that they might just touch ªthe fringe of His cloak; and as many as ᵇtouched it were cured.

a   CHAPTER 15

THEN some Pharisees and scribes *came to Jesus ᵇfrom Jerusalem, saying,

2 "Why do Your disciples transgress the tradition of the elders? For they ᵃdo not wash their hands when they eat bread."

3 And He answered and said to them, "And why do ¹you yourselves transgress the commandment of God for the sake of your tradition?

4 "For God said, 'ᵃHONOR YOUR FATHER AND MOTHER,' and, 'ᵇHE WHO SPEAKS EVIL OF FATHER OR MOTHER, LET HIM ¹BE PUT TO DEATH.'

5 "But you say, 'Whoever shall say to *his* father or mother, "Anything of mine you might have been helped by has been ¹given *to* God,"

6 he is not to honor his father ¹or his mother².' And *thus* you invalidated the ³word of God for the sake of your tradition.

7 "You hypocrites, rightly did Isaiah prophesy of you, saying,

8 'ᵃTHIS PEOPLE HONORS ME WITH THEIR LIPS,
BUT THEIR HEART IS FAR AWAY FROM ME.

9 ᵃBUT IN VAIN DO THEY WORSHIP ME,
TEACHING AS THEIR ᵇDOCTRINES THE PRECEPTS OF MEN.' "

10 And He called to Himself the multitude, and said to them, "Hear, and understand.

11 "ᵃNot what enters into the mouth defiles the man, but what proceeds out of the mouth, this defiles the man."

12 Then the disciples *came and *said to Him, "Do You know that the Pharisees were ¹offended when they heard this statement?"

13 But He answered and said, "ᵃEvery plant which My heavenly Father did not plant shall be rooted up.

14 "Let them alone; ᵃthey are blind guides ¹of the blind. And ᵇif a blind man guides a blind man, both will fall into a pit."

15 And Peter answered and said to Him, "ᵃExplain the parable to us."

16 And He said, "Are you also still without understanding?

17 "Do you not understand that everything that goes into the mouth passes into the ¹stomach, and is ²eliminated?

18 "But ᵃthe things that proceed out of the

1 ᵃMatt. 15:1-20: *Mark 7:1-23* ᵇMark 3:22; 7:1; John 1:19; Acts 25:7

2 ᵃLuke 11:38

3 ¹Or, *you also*

4 ¹Lit., *die the death* ᵃEx. 20:12; Deut. 5:16 ᵇEx. 21:17; Lev. 20:9

5 ¹Or, *a gift, an offering*

6 ¹Many mss. omit, *or his mother* ²I.e., by supporting them with it ³Some mss. read, *law*

8 ᵃIs. 29:13

9 ᵃIs. 29:13 ᵇCol. 2:22

11 ᵃActs 10:14, 15; Matt. 15:18; 1 Tim. 4:3

12 ¹Lit., *caused to stumble*

13 ᵃIs. 60:21; 61:3; John 15:2; 1 Cor. 3:9

14 ¹Some mss. omit *of the blind* ᵃMatt. 23:16, 24 ᵇLuke 6:39

15 ᵃMatt. 13:36

17 ¹Lit., *belly* ²Lit., *cast out into the latrine*

18 ᵃMark 7:20; Matt. 12:34

19 ¹I.e., sexual immorality
ᵃGal. 5:19ff.

21 ᵃMatt. 15:21-28: Mark
7:24-30 ᵇMatt. 11:21

22 ᵃMatt. 9:27 ᵇMatt. 4:24

⁎

24 ᵃMatt. 10:6

25 ¹Or, to worship
ᵃMatt. 8:2

26 ¹Or, proper

27 ¹Lit., for

28 ¹Lit., from that hour
ᵃMatt. 9:22

29 ᵃMatt. 15:29-31; Mark
7:31-37 ᵇMatt. 4:18

30 ᵃMatt. 4:23

31 ¹Or, healthy
ᵃMatt. 9:8

32 ¹Lit., are remaining
ᵃMatt. 15:32-39: Mark 8:1-
10; Matt. 14:13-21 ᵇMatt.
9:36

mouth come from the heart, and those defile the man.

19 "ᵃFor out of the heart come evil thoughts, murders, adulteries, ¹fornications, thefts, false witness, slanders.

20 "These are the things which defile the man; but to eat with unwashed hands does not defile the man."

21 ᵃAnd Jesus went away from there, and withdrew into the district of ᵇTyre and ᵇSidon.

22 And behold, a Canaanite woman came out from that region, and began to cry out, saying, "Have mercy on me, O Lord, ᵃSon of David; my daughter is cruelly ᵇdemon-possessed."

23 But He did not answer her a word. And His disciples came to Him and kept asking Him, saying, "Send her away, for she is shouting out after us."

24 But He answered and said, "I was sent only to ᵃthe lost sheep of the house of Israel."

25 But she came and ᵃbegan ¹to bow down before Him, saying, "Lord, help me!"

26 And He answered and said, "It is not ¹good to take the children's bread and throw it to the dogs."

27 But she said, "Yes, Lord; ¹but even the dogs feed on the crumbs which fall from their master's table."

28 Then Jesus answered and said to her, "O woman, ᵃyour faith is great; be it done for you as you wish." And her daughter was healed ¹at once.

29 ᵃAnd departing from there, Jesus went along by ᵇthe sea of Galilee, and having gone up to the mountain, He was sitting there.

30 And great multitudes came to Him, bringing with them those who were lame, crippled, blind, dumb, and many others, and they laid them down at His feet; and ᵃHe healed them,

31 so that the multitude marveled as they saw the dumb speaking, the crippled ¹restored, and the lame walking, and the blind seeing; and they ᵃglorified the God of Israel.

32 ᵃAnd Jesus summoned to Himself His disciples, and said, "ᵇI feel compassion for the multitude, because they ¹have remained with Me now for three days and have nothing to eat; and I do not wish to send them away hungry, lest they faint on the way."

33 And the disciples *said to Him, "Where

would we get so many loaves in a desert place to satisfy such a great multitude?"

34 And Jesus *said to them, "How many loaves do you have?" And they said, "Seven, and a few small fish."

35 And He directed the multitude to ¹sit down on the ground;

36 and He took the seven loaves and the fish; and ᵃgiving thanks, He broke *them* and started giving *them* to the disciples, and the disciples *in turn,* to the multitudes.

37 And they all ate, and were satisfied, and they picked up what was left over of the broken pieces, seven ᵃfull baskets.

38 And those who ate were four thousand men, besides women and children.

39 And dismissing the multitudes, He got into ᵃthe boat, and came to the region of ᵇMagadan.

a   CHAPTER 16

AND the ᵇPharisees and Sadducees came up, and testing Him ᶜasked Him to show them a ¹sign from heaven.

2 ¹But He answered and said to them, "ᵃWhen it is evening, you say, '*It will be* fair weather, for the sky is red.'

3 "And in the morning, '*There will be* a storm today, for the sky is red and threatening.' Do you know how to discern the ¹appearance of the sky, but cannot *discern* the signs of the times?

4 "ᵃAn evil and adulterous generation seeks after a ¹sign; and a ¹sign will not be given it, except the sign of Jonah." And He left them, and went away.

5 And the disciples came to the other side and had forgotten to take bread.

6 And Jesus said to them, "Watch out and ᵃbeware of the ¹leaven of the ᵇPharisees and Sadducees."

7 And they began to discuss among themselves, saying, "*It is* because we took no bread."

8 But Jesus, aware of this, said, "ᵃYou men of little faith, why do you discuss among yourselves because you have no bread?

9 "Do you not yet understand or remember ᵃthe five loaves of the five thousand, and how many large ᵇbaskets you took up?

---

35 ¹Lit., *recline*

36 ᵃMatt. 14:19

37 ᵃMatt. 16:10; Mark 8:8, 20; Acts 9:25

39 ᵃMark 3:9 ᵇMark 8:10

1 ¹Or, *attesting miracle*
ᵃMatt. 16:1-12; *Mark 8:11-21*
ᵇMatt. 16:6, 11, 12; Matt. 3:7
ᶜMatt. 12:38

2 ¹The earliest mss. omit verses 2 & 3
ᵃLuke 12:54f.

3 ¹Lit., *face*

4 ¹Or, *attesting miracle*
ᵃMatt. 12:39

6 ¹Or, *yeast*
ᵃMatt. 16:11; Mark 8.15; Luke 12:1 ᵇMatt. 16:1, 11, 12; 3:7

8 ᵃMatt. 6:30; 8:26; 14:31

9 ᵃMatt. 14:17-21 ᵇMatt. 14:20

10 ªMatt. 15:34-38 ᵇMatt.
15:37

11 ¹Or, yeast
ªMatt. 16:6; Mark 8:15; Luke
12:1 ᵇMatt. 16:6, 12; 3:7

12 ªMatt. 16:6, 11; 3:7

13 ªMatt. 16:13-16: Mark
8:27-29; Luke 9:18-20 ᵇMark
8:27 ᶜMatt. 8:20; 16:27, 28

14 ¹Gr., Elias ²Gr. Jeremias
ªMatt. 14:2 ᵇMark 6:15;
Luke 9:8; Matt. 17:10; John
1:21

16 ¹I.e., the Messiah
ªMatt. 16:20; John 11:27;
Matt. 1:16 ᵇMatt. 4:3 ᶜPs.
12:2; Matt. 26:63; Acts 14:15;
Rom. 9:26; 2 Cor. 3:3; 6:16;
1 Thess. 1:9; 1 Tim. 3:15;
4:10; Heb. 3:12; 9:14; 10:31;
12:22; Rev. 7:2

17 ¹I.e., son of Jonas
ªJohn 1:42; 21:15-17 ᵇ1 Cor.
15:50; Gal. 1:16; Eph. 6:12;
Heb. 2:14

18 ¹Gr., Petros, a stone
²Gr., petra, large rock, bed-
rock ³I.e., the powers of
death
ªMatt. 4:18 ᵇMatt. 11:23

19 ªIs. 22:22; Rev. 1:18; 3:7
ᵇMatt. 18:18; John 20:23

20 ¹Or, strictly admonished
²I.e., the Messiah
ªMark 8:30; Luke 9:21; Matt.
8:4 ᵇMatt. 16:16; John 11:27;
Matt. 1:16

21 ªMatt. 16:21-28: Mark
8:31-9:1; Luke 9:22-27
ᵇMatt. 17:9, 12, 22f.; 20:18f.;
27:63; Mark 9:12, 31; Luke
17:25; 18:32; 24:7; Matt.
12:40; John 2:19

22 ¹Lit., (God be) merciful
to You ²Lit., be

23 ¹Lit., the things of God
ªMatt. 4:10

24 ªMatt. 10:38

36

10 "Or ªthe seven loaves of the four thousand, and how many ᵇbaskets you took up?

11 "How is it that you do not understand that I did not speak to you concerning bread? But ªbeware of the ¹leaven of the ᵇPharisees and Sadducees."

12 Then they understood that He did not say to beware of the leaven of bread, but of the teaching of the ªPharisees and Sadducees.

13 ªNow when Jesus came into the district of ᵇCaesarea Philippi, He *began* asking His disciples, saying, "Who do people say that ᶜthe Son of Man is?"

14 And they said, "Some *say* ªJohn the Baptist; some, ¹ᵇElijah; and others, ²Jeremiah, or one of the prophets."

15 He *said to them, "But who do you say that I am?"

16 And Simon Peter answered and said, "Thou art ¹ªthe Christ, ᵇthe Son of ᶜthe living God."

17 And Jesus answered and said to him, "Blessed are you, ¹ªSimon Barjonas, because ᵇflesh and blood did not reveal *this* to you, but My Father who is in heaven.

18 "And I also say to you that you are ¹ªPeter, and upon this ²rock I will build My church; and ³the gates of ᵇHades shall not overpower it.

19 "I will give you ªthe keys of the kingdom of heaven; and ᵇwhatever you shall bind on earth shall have been bound in heaven, and whatever you shall loose on earth shall have been loosed in heaven."

20 ªThen He ¹warned the disciples that they should tell no one that He was ²ᵇthe Christ.

21 ªFrom that time Jesus Christ began to show His disciples that He must go to Jerusalem, and ᵇsuffer many things from the elders and chief priests and scribes, and be killed, and be raised up on the third day.

22 And Peter took Him aside and began to rebuke Him, saying, "¹God forbid *it*, Lord! This shall never ²happen to You."

23 But He turned and said to Peter, "Get behind Me, ªSatan! You are a stumbling-block to Me; for you are not setting your mind on ¹God's interests, but man's."

24 Then Jesus said to His disciples, "If any one wishes to come after Me, let him deny himself, and ªtake up his cross, and follow Me.

25 "For ᵃwhoever wishes to save his ¹life shall lose it; but whoever loses his ¹life for My sake shall find it.

26 "For what will a man be profited, if he gains the whole world, and forfeits his ¹soul? Or what will a man give in exchange for his ¹soul?

27 "For the ᵃSon of Man ᵇis going to come in the glory of His Father with His angels; and ᶜWILL THEN RECOMPENSE EVERY MAN ACCORDING TO HIS ¹DEEDS.

28 "Truly I say to you, there are some of those who are standing here who shall not taste death until they see the ᵃSon of Man ᵇcoming in His kingdom."

a   CHAPTER 17

AND six days later Jesus *took with him ᵇPeter and ¹James and John his brother, and *brought them up to a high mountain by themselves.

2   And He was transfigured before them; and His face shone like the sun, and His garments became as white as light.

3   And behold, Moses and Elijah appeared to them, talking with Him.

4   And Peter ᵃanswered and said to Jesus, "Lord, it is good for us to be here; if You wish, ᵇI will make three ¹tabernacles here, one for You, and one for Moses, and one for Elijah."

5   While he was still speaking, behold, a bright cloud overshadowed them; and behold, ᵃa voice out of the cloud, saying, "ᵇThis is My beloved Son, with whom I am well pleased: hear Him!"

6   And when the disciples heard *this*, they fell on their faces and were much afraid.

7   And Jesus came to *them* and touched them and said, "Arise, and ᵃdo not be afraid."

8   And lifting up their eyes, they saw no one, except Jesus Himself alone.

9   ᵃAnd as they were coming down from the mountain, Jesus commanded them, saying, "ᵇTell the vision to no one until ᶜthe Son of Man has ᵈrisen from the dead."

10   And His disciples asked Him, saying, "Why then do the scribes say that ᵃElijah must come first?"

11   And He answered and said, "Elijah is coming and will restore all things;

---

25 ¹Or, *soul-life*
ᵃMatt. 10:39

26 ¹Or, *soul-life*

27 ¹Lit., *doing*
ᵃMatt. 8:20 ᵇMatt. 10:23; 24:3, 27, 37, 39; 26:64; Mark 8:38f.; 13:26; Luke 21:27; Acts 1:11; 1 Cor. 15:23; 1 Thess. 1:10; 4:16; 2 Thess. 1:7, 10; 2:1, 8; James 5:7f.; 2 Pet. 1:16; 3:4, 12; 1 John 2:28; Rev. 1:7; John 21:22 ᶜPs. 62:12; Prov. 24:12; Rom. 2:6; 14:12; 2 Cor. 5:10; Eph. 6:8; Col. 3:25; Rev. 2:23; 20:12; 22:12; 1 Cor. 3:13

28 ᵃMatt. 8:20 ᵇMatt. 10:23; 24:3, 27, 37, 39; 26:64; Mark 8:38f.; 13:26; Luke 21:27; Acts 1:11; 1 Cor. 15:23; 1 Thess. 1:10; 4:16; 2 Thess. 1:7, 10; 2:1, 8; James 5:7f.; 2 Pet. 1:16; 3:4, 12; 1 John 2:28; Rev. 1:7; John 21:22

1 ¹Or, *Jacob*
ᵃMatt. 17:1-8: Mark 9:2-8; Luke 9:28-36 ᵇMatt. 26:37; Mark 5:37; Mark 13:3

4 ¹Or, *sacred tents*
ᵃActs 3:12 ᵇMark 9:5; Luke 9:33

5 ᵃ2 Pet. 1:17f. ᵇMatt. 3:17

7 ᵃMatt. 14:27

9 ᵃMatt. 17:9-13: Mark 9:9-13 ᵇMatt. 8:4 ᶜMatt. 17:12, 22; 8:20 ᵈMatt. 16:21

10 ᵃMatt. 11:14; 16:14

37

Matthew 17

The Epileptic Boy Healed.
The Power of Faith. The Temple Tax.

12 ¹Lit., *in him* (or: *in his case*) ²Lit., *by them* ªMatt. 17:9, 22; 8:20

14 ªMatt. 17:14-19: *Mark 9:14-28*; Matt. 17:14-18: *Luke 9:37-42*

15 ¹Or, *Sir* ²Lit., *moon-smitten* ªMatt. 4:24

18 ¹Lit., *from that hour*

20 ªMatt. 21:21f.; Mark 11:23f.; Luke 17:6 ᵇMatt. 13:31; Luke 17:6 ᶜMatt. 17:9; 1 Cor. 13:2 ᵈMark 9:23; John 11:40

21 ¹Some late mss. add verse 21, "*But this kind does not go out except by prayer and fasting.*" ªMark 9:29

22 ¹Or, *betrayed* ªMatt. 17:22, 23: *Mark 9:30-32; Luke 9:44, 45*

23 ªMatt. 16:21; and 17:9

24 ¹Equivalent to two denarii or two days wages paid as a temple tax ªEx. 30:13; 38:26

25 ¹Or, *anticipated what he was going to say,* ªRom. 13:7 ᵇMatt. 22:17, 19

26 ¹Or, *free*

27 ¹Lit., *cause them to stumble* ªMatt. 5:29, 30; 18:6, 8, 9; Mark 9:42, 43, 45, 47; Luke 17:2; John 6:61; 1 Cor. 8:13

38

12 but I say to you, that Elijah already came, and they did not recognize him, but did ¹to him whatever they wished. So also ªthe Son of Man is going to suffer ²at their hands."

13 Then the disciples understood that He had spoken to them about John the Baptist.

14 ªAnd when they came to the multitude, a man came up to Him, falling on his knees before Him, and saying,

15 "¹Lord, have mercy on my son; for he is an ²ªepileptic, and is very ill; for he often falls into the fire, and often into the water.

16 "And I brought him to Your disciples, and they could not cure him."

17 And Jesus answered and said, "O unbelieving and perverted generation, how long shall I be with you? How long shall I put up with you? Bring him here to Me."

18 And Jesus rebuked him, and the demon came out of him, and the boy was cured ¹at once.

19 Then the disciples came to Jesus privately and said, "Why could we not cast it out?"

20 And He *said to them, "Because of the littleness of your faith; for truly I say to you, ªif you have faith as ᵇa mustard seed, you shall say to ᶜthis mountain, 'Move from here to there,' and it shall move; and ᵈnothing shall be impossible to you.

21 (¹ªSee marginal note.)

22 ªAnd while they were gathering together in Galilee, Jesus said to them, "The Son of Man is going to be ¹delivered into the hands of men;

23 and ªthey will kill Him, and He will be raised again on the third day." And they were deeply grieved.

24 And when they had come to Capernaum, those who collected ªthe ¹two-drachma *tax* came to Peter, and said, "Does your teacher not pay ªthe ¹two-drachma *tax*?"

25 He *said, "Yes." And when he came into the house, Jesus ¹spoke to him first, saying, "What do you think, Simon? From whom do the kings of the earth collect ªcustoms or ᵇpoll-tax, from their sons or from strangers?"

26 And upon his saying, "From strangers," Jesus said to him, "Consequently the sons are ¹exempt.

27 "But, lest we ¹ªgive them offense, go to the sea, and throw in a hook, and take the first fish that

Of Rank in the Kingdom of Heaven.
Of Stumbling-blocks.   The Lost Sheep.

Matthew 17, 18

comes up; and when you open its mouth, you will find a ²stater; take that and give it to them for you and Me."

27 ²Or, *shekel*, worth four drachmas

a   CHAPTER 18

1 ¹Lit., *hour* ²Lit., *greater*
ªMatt. 18:1-5; Mark 9:33-37;
Luke 9:46-48

AT that ¹time the disciples came to Jesus, saying, "Who then is ²greatest in the kingdom of heaven?"

2   And He called a child to Himself and stood him in their midst,

3   and said, "Truly I say to you, unless you ¹are converted and ªbecome like children, you shall not enter the kingdom of heaven.

3 ¹Lit., *are turned*
ªMatt. 19:14; Mark 10:15;
Luke 18:17; 1 Cor. 14:20;
1 Pet. 2:2

4   "Whoever then humbles himself as this child, he is the greatest in the kingdom of heaven.

5   "And whoever receives one such child in My name receives Me;

6   but ªwhoever ᵇcauses one of these little ones who believe in Me to stumble, it is better for him that a ¹heavy millstone be hung around his neck, and that he be drowned in the depth of the sea.

6 ¹Lit., *millstone turned by a donkey*
ªMark 9:42; Luke 17:2;
1 Cor. 8:12 ᵇMatt. 17:27

7   "Woe to the world because of *its* stumbling-blocks! For ªit is inevitable that stumbling-blocks come; but woe to that man through whom the stumbling-block comes!

7 ªLuke 17:1; 1 Cor. 11:19;
1 Tim. 4:1

8   "And ªif your hand or your foot ᵇcauses you to stumble, cut it off and throw it from you; it is better for you to enter life crippled or lame, than having two hands or two feet, to be cast into the eternal fire.

8 ªMatt. 5:30; Mark 9:43;
Matt. 17:27 ᵇMatt. 17:27

9   "And ªif your eye ᵇcauses you to stumble, pluck it out, and throw it from you. It is better for you to enter life with one eye, than having two eyes, to be cast into the ¹ᶜhell of fire.

9 ¹Gr. *Gehenna of fire*
ªMatt. 5:29; Mark 9:47;
Matt. 17:27 ᵇMatt. 17:27
ᶜMatt. 5:22

10   "See that you do not despise one of these little ones, for I say to you, that ªtheir angels in heaven continually behold the face of My Father who is in heaven.

10 ªActs 12:15; Luke 1:19;
Rev. 8:2; 2 Kin. 25:19; 1 Kin.
10:8

11   ["¹ªFor the Son of Man has come to save that which was lost.]

12   "What do you think? ªIf any man ¹has a hundred sheep, and one of them has gone astray, does he not leave the ninety-nine on the mountains and go and search for the one that is straying?

11 ¹Most ancient mss. omit this verse
ªLuke 19:10

13   "And if it turns out that he finds it, truly I say to you, he rejoices over it more than over the ninety-nine which have not gone astray.

12 ¹Or, *comes to have*
ªMatt. 18:12-14; Luke 15:4-7

39

Ministering to a Sinning Christian. Multiple Forgiveness. The Unmerciful Slave.

14 ¹Lit., *before*

15 ¹Many mss. add here: *against you* ²Lit., *between you and him alone* ᵃLuke 17:3; Gal. 6:1; 2 Thess. 3:15; James 5:19; Lev. 19:17

16 ¹Lit., *word* ᵃDeut. 19:15; John 8:17; 2 Cor. 13:1; 1 Tim. 5:19; Heb. 10:28

17 ¹Lit., *the* ²A publican who collected Roman taxes ᵃ1 Cor. 6:1ff. ᵇ2 Thess. 3:6, 14f.

18 ¹Or, *forbid* ⁷Or, *permit* ᵃMatt. 16:19; John 20:23

19 ¹Lit., *from* ᵃMatt. 7:7

21 ᵃMatt. 18:15 ᵇLuke 17:4

22 ᵃGen. 4:24

23 ᵃMatt. 13:24 ᵇMatt. 25:19

24 ¹About $10,000,000 in silver content but worth much more in buying power

25 ¹Or, *was unable to* ᵃLuke 7:42 ᵇEx. 21:2; Lev. 25:39; 2 Kin. 4:1; Neh. 5:5

26 ᵃMatt. 8:2

27 ¹Or, *loan*

28 ¹The denarius was worth 18 cents in silver, equivalent to a day's wage

40

14 "Thus it is not *the* will ¹of your Father who is in heaven that one of these little ones perish.

15 "And ᵃif your brother sins¹, go and reprove him ²in private; if he listens to you, you have won your brother.

16 "But if he does not listen *to you,* take one or two more with you, so that ᵃBY THE MOUTH OF TWO OR THREE WITNESSES EVERY ¹FACT MAY BE CONFIRMED.

17 "And if he refuses to listen to them, ᵃtell it to the church; and if he refuses to listen even to the church, ᵇlet him be to you as ¹a Gentile and ¹a ²tax-gatherer.

18 "Truly I say to you, ᵃwhatever you shall ¹bind on earth shall have been bound in heaven; and whatever you ²loose on earth shall have been loosed in heaven.

19 "Again I say to you, that if two of you agree on earth about anything that they may ask, ᵃit shall be done for them ¹by My Father who is in heaven.

20 "For where two or three have gathered together in My name, there I am in their midst."

21 Then Peter came and said to Him, "Lord, ᵃhow often shall my brother sin against me and I forgive him? Up to ᵇseven times?"

22 Jesus *said to him, "I do not say to you, up to seven times, but up to ᵃseventy times seven.

23 "For this reason ᵃthe kingdom of heaven may be compared to a certain king who wished to ᵇsettle accounts with his slaves.

24 "And when he had begun to settle *them,* there was brought to him one who owed him ¹ten thousand talents.

25 "But since he ¹ᵃdid not have *the means* to repay, his lord commanded him ᵇto be sold, along with his wife and children and all that he had, and repayment to be made.

26 "The slave therefore falling down, ᵃprostrated himself before him, saying, 'Have patience with me, and I will repay you everything.'

27 "And the lord of that slave felt compassion and released him and forgave him the ¹debt.

28 "But that slave went out and found one of his fellow-slaves who owed him a hundred ¹denarii; and he seized him and *began* to choke *him,* saying, 'Pay back what you owe.'

29 "So his fellow-slave fell down and *began* to

entreat him, saying, 'Have patience with me and I will repay you.'

30 "He was unwilling however, but went and threw him in prison until he should pay back what was owed.

31 "So when his fellow-slaves saw what had happened, they were deeply grieved and came and reported to their lord all that had happened.

32 "Then summoning him, his lord *said to him, 'You wicked slave, I forgave you all that debt because you entreated me.

33 'Should you not also have had mercy on your fellow-slave, even as I had mercy on you?'

34 "And his lord, moved with anger, handed him over to the torturers until he should repay all that was owed him.

35 "ªSo shall My heavenly Father also do to you, if each of you does not forgive his brother from ¹your heart.'"

a   CHAPTER 19

AND it came about that when Jesus had finished these words, He departed from Galilee, and ᵇcame into the region of Judea beyond the Jordan;

2 and great multitudes followed Him, and ªHe healed them there.

3 And *some* Pharisees came to Him, testing Him, and saying, "ªIs it lawful *for a man* to divorce his wife for any cause at all?"

4 And He answered and said, "Have you not read, ªthat He who created *them* from the beginning made them male and female,

5 and said, 'ªFOR THIS CAUSE A MAN SHALL LEAVE HIS FATHER AND MOTHER, AND SHALL CLEAVE TO HIS WIFE; AND ᵇTHE TWO SHALL BECOME ONE FLESH'?

6 "Consequently they are no more two, but one flesh. What therefore God has joined together, let no man separate."

7 They *said to Him, "ªWhy then did Moses command to GIVE HER A CERTIFICATE AND DIVORCE HER"?

8 He *said to them, "¹Because of your hardness of heart, Moses permitted you to divorce your wives; but from the beginning it has not been this way.

9 "And I say to you, ªwhoever divorces his

35 ¹Lit., *your hearts*
ªMatt. 6:14

1 ªMatt. 7:28 ᵇMatt. 19:1-9: *Mark 10:1-12*

2 ªMatt. 4:23

3 ªMatt. 5:31

4 ªGen. 1:27; 5:2

5 ªEph. 5:31; Gen. 2:24
ᵇ1 Cor. 6:16

7 ªDeut. 24:1-4

8 ¹Or, *with reference to*

9 ªMatt. 5:32

41

Matthew 19

**Jesus Receives Little Children.
The Peril of Riches.**

9 ¹I.e., sexual immorality
²Some early mss. read:
makes her commit adultery
³Some early mss. add: *and
he who marries a divorced
woman commits adultery*

11 ª1 Cor. 7:7ff. 17 ᵇMatt.
13:11

13 ªMatt. 19:13-15: *Mark
10:13-16; Luke 18:15-17*

14 ¹Or, *permit the children*
ªMatt. 18:3; Mark 10:15;
Luke 18:17; 1 Cor. 14:20;
1 Pet. 2:2 ᵇMatt. 5:3

16 ªMatt. 19:16-29: *Mark
10:17-30; Luke 18:18-30;*
Luke 10:25-28 ᵇMatt. 25:46

17 ªLev. 18:5; Neh. 9:29;
Ezek. 20:21

18 ªEx. 20:13-16; Deut.
5:17-20

19 ªEx. 20:12; Deut. 5:16
ᵇLev. 19:18

21 ¹Or, *perfect*
ªLuke 12:33; Luke 16:9; Acts
2:45; 4:34f. ᵇMatt 6:20

23 ªMatt. 13:22; Mark
10:23f; Luke 18:24

24 ªMark 10:25; Luke 18:25

wife, except for ¹immorality, and marries another ²commits adultery."³

10 The disciples *said to Him, "If the relationship of the man with his wife is like this, it is better not to marry."

11 But He said to them, "ªNot all men *can* accept this statement, but ᵇ*only* those to whom it has been given.

12 "For there are eunuchs who were born that way from their mother's womb; and there are eunuchs who were made eunuchs by men; and there are *also* eunuchs who made themselves eunuchs for the sake of the kingdom of heaven. He who is able to accept *this* let him accept *it.*"

13 ªThen *some* children were brought to Him so that He might lay His hands on them and pray; and the disciples rebuked them.

14 But Jesus said, "¹ªLet the children alone, and do not hinder them from coming to Me; for ᵇthe kingdom of heaven belongs to such as these."

15 And after laying His hands on them, He departed from there.

16 ªAnd behold, one came to Him and said, "Teacher, what good thing shall I do that I may obtain ᵇeternal life?"

17 And He said to him, "Why are you asking Me about what is good? There is *only* One who is good; but ªif you wish to enter into life, keep the commandments."

18 He *said to Him, "Which ones?" And Jesus said, "ªYOU SHALL NOT COMMIT MURDER; YOU SHALL NOT COMMIT ADULTERY; YOU SHALL NOT STEAL; YOU SHALL NOT BEAR FALSE WITNESS;

19 ªHONOR YOUR FATHER AND MOTHER; and ᵇYOU SHALL LOVE YOUR NEIGHBOR AS YOURSELF."

20 The young man *said to Him, "All these things I have kept; what am I still lacking?"

21 Jesus said to him, "If you wish to be ¹complete, go *and* ªsell your possessions and give to *the* poor, and you shall have ᵇtreasure in heaven; and come, follow Me."

22 But when the young man heard this statement, he went away grieved; for he was one who owned much property.

23 And Jesus said to His disciples, "Truly I say to you, ªit is hard for a rich man to enter the kingdom of heaven.

24 "And again I say to you, ªit is easier for a

camel to go through the eye of a needle, than for a rich man to enter the kingdom of God."

25 And when the disciples heard *this*, they were very astonished and said, "Then who can be saved?"

26 And looking upon *them* Jesus said to them, "ªWith men this is impossible, but with God all things are possible."

27 Then Peter answered and said to Him, "Behold, we have left everything and followed You; what then will there be for us?"

28 And Jesus said to them, "Truly I say to you, that you who have followed Me, in the regeneration when ªthe Son of Man will sit on ¹His glorious throne, ᵇyou also shall sit upon twelve thrones, judging the twelve tribes of Israel.

29 "And ªeveryone who has left houses or brothers or sisters or father or mother¹ or children or farms for My name's sake, shall receive ²many times as much, and shall inherit eternal life.

30 "ªBut many *who are* first will be last; and *the* last, first.

CHAPTER 20

"For ªthe kingdom of heaven is like ¹a landowner who went out early in the morning to hire laborers ²for his ᵇvineyard.

2 "And when he had agreed with the laborers for a ¹denarius for the day, he sent them into his vineyard.

3 "And he went out about the ¹third hour and saw others standing idle in the market place;

4 and to those he said, 'You too go into the vineyard, and whatever is right I will give you.' And *so* they went.

5 "Again he went out about the ¹sixth and the ninth hour, and did ²the same thing.

6 "And about the ¹eleventh *hour* he went out, and found others standing; and he *said to them, 'Why have you been standing here idle all day long?'

7 "They *said to him, 'Because no one hired us.' He *said to them, 'You too go into the vineyard.'

8 "And when ªevening had come, the ¹owner of the vineyard *said to his ᵇforeman, 'Call the

26 ªGen. 18:14; Job 42:2; Jer. 32:17; Zech. 8:6; Mark 10:27; Luke 18:27; 1:37

28 ¹Lit., *the throne of His glory* ªMatt. 25:31 ᵇLuke 22:30; Rev. 3:21; 4:4; 11:16; 20:4

29 ¹Many mss. add here: *or wife* ²Many mss. read: *a hundredfold* ªMark 10:29f.; Luke 18:29f.; Matt. 6:33

30 ªMatt. 20:16; Mark 10:31; Luke 13:30

1 ¹Lit., *a man, a landowner* ²Lit., *into* ªMatt. 13:24 ᵇMatt. 21:28, 33

2 ¹Cf. Matt. 18:28

3 ¹I.e., 9 a.m.

5 ¹I.e., Noon and 3 p.m. ²Lit., *similarly*

6 ¹I.e., 5 p.m.

8 ¹Or, *lord* ªLev. 19:13 ᵇLuke 8:3

laborers and pay them their wages, beginning with the last *group* to the first.'

9 "And when those *hired* about the eleventh hour came, each one received a ¹denarius.

10 "And when those *hired* first came, they thought that they would receive more; and they also received each one a denarius.

11 "And when they received it, they grumbled at the landowner,

12 saying, 'These last men have worked *only* one hour, and you have made them equal to us who have borne the burden and the ªscorching heat of the day.'

13 "But he answered and said to one of them, 'ªFriend, I am doing you no wrong; did you not agree with me for a denarius?

14 'Take what is yours and go your way, but I wish to give to this last man the same as to you.

15 'Is it not lawful for me to do what I wish with what is my own? Or is your ªeye ¹envious because I am ²generous?'

16 "Thus ªthe last shall be first, and the first last."

17 ªAnd as Jesus was about to go up to Jerusalem, He took the twelve *disciples* aside by themselves, and on the way He said to them,

18 "Behold, we are going up to Jerusalem; and the Son of Man ªwill be ¹delivered up to the chief priests and scribes, and they will condemn Him to death,

19 and ªwill deliver Him up to the Gentiles to mock and scourge and crucify *Him,* and on ᵇthe third day He will be raised up."

20 ªThen the mother of ᵇthe sons of Zebedee came to Him with her sons, ᶜbowing down, and making a request of Him.

21 And He said to her, "What do you wish?" She *said to Him, "Command that in Your kingdom these two sons of mine ªmay sit, one on Your right and one on Your left."

22 But Jesus answered and said, "You do not know what you are asking for. Are you able ªto drink the cup that I am about to drink?" They *said to Him, "We are able."

23 He *said to them, "ªMy cup you shall drink; but to sit on My right and on *My* left, this is not Mine to give, ᵇbut *it is* for those for whom it has been ᶜprepared by My Father."

24   And hearing *this*, the ten became indignant at the two brothers.

25   ᵃBut Jesus called them to Himself, and said, "You know that the rulers of the Gentiles lord it over them, and *their* great men exercise authority over them.

26   "It is not so among you, ᵇbut whoever wishes to become great among you shall be your servant,

27   and whoever wishes to be first among you shall be your slave;

28   just as ᵃthe Son of Man ᵇdid not come to be served, but to serve, and to give His ¹life a ransom for many."

29   ᵃAnd as they were going out from Jericho, a great multitude followed Him.

30   And behold, two blind men sitting by the road, hearing that Jesus was passing by, cried out, saying, "Lord, ᵃhave mercy on us, ᵇSon of David!"

31   And the multitude sternly told them to be quiet; but they cried out all the more, saying, "Lord, have mercy on us, ᵃSon of David!"

32   And Jesus stopped and called them, and said, "What do you wish Me to do for you?"

33   They *said to Him, "Lord, we want our eyes to be opened."

34   And moved with compassion, Jesus touched their eyes; and immediately they received their sight, and followed Him.

ᵃ   CHAPTER 21

AND when they had approached Jerusalem and had come to Bethphage, to ᵇthe Mount of Olives, then Jesus sent two disciples,

2   saying to them, "Go into the village opposite you, and immediately you will find a donkey tied *there* and a colt with her; untie *them*, and bring *them* to Me.

3   "And if anyone says something to you, you shall say, 'The Lord has need of them;' and immediately he will send them."

4   ᵃNow this took place that what was spoken through the prophet might be fulfilled, saying,

5   "ᵃSAY TO THE DAUGHTER OF ZION,
  'BEHOLD YOUR KING IS COMING TO YOU,
  GENTLE, AND MOUNTED UPON A DONKEY,
  EVEN UPON A COLT, THE FOAL OF A BEAST OF
  BURDEN.' "

25 ᵃMatt. 20:25-28; Luke 22:25-27

26 ᵃMatt. 23:11; Mark 9:35; 10:43

28 ¹Or, *soul*
ᵃMatt. 8:20 ᵇMatt. 26:28; John 13:13ff.; 2 Cor. 8:9; Phil. 2:7; 1 Tim. 2:6; Titus 2:14; Heb. 9:28; Rev. 1:5

29 ᵃMatt. 20:29-34: *Mark 10:46-52; Luke 18:35-43;* Matt. 9:27-31

30 ᵃMatt. 20:31 ᵇMatt. 9:27

31 ᵃMatt. 9:27

1 ᵃMatt. 21:1-9: *Mark 11:1-10; Luke 19:29-38* ᵇMatt. 24:3; 26:30; Mark 11:1; 13:3; 14:26; Luke 19:37; 22:39; John 8:1; Luke 19:29; 21:37; Acts 1:12

4 ᵃMatt. 21:4-9: *John 12:12-15*

5 ᵃIs. 62:11; Zech. 9:9

Matthew 21

**The Traders Cast Out of the Temple.
The Withered Fig Tree.**

7 [1]Lit., *on them*

8 [a]2 Kin. 9:13

9 [a]Ps. 118:26f. [b]Matt. 9:27
[c]Luke 2:14

11 [a]John 1:21, 25; 6:14;
7:40; Acts 3:22f.; 7:37; Matt.
21:26; Mark 6:15; Luke 7:16,
39; 13:33; 24:19; John 4:19;
9:17 [b]Matt. 2:23

12 [1]Lit. *the doves*
[a]Matt. 21:12-16: *Mark 11:15-
18; Luke 19:45-47;* Matt.
21:12, 13: *John 2:13-16* [b]Ex.
30:13 [c]Lev. 1:14; 5:7; 12:8

13 [1]Lit., *cave*
[a]Is. 56:7; Jer. 7:11

14 [a]Matt. 4:23

15 [a]Matt. 9:27

16 [a]Ps. 8:2

17 [a]Matt. 26:6; Mark 11:1,
11, 12; 14:3; Luke 19:29;
24:50; John 11:1, 18; 12:1

18 [a]Matt. 21:18-22: *Mark
11:12-14, 20-24*

46

6   And the disciples went and did just as Jesus had directed them,

7   and brought the donkey and the colt, and laid on them their garments; [1]on which He sat.

8   And most of the multitude [a]spread their garments in the road, and others were cutting branches from the trees, and spreading them in the road.

9   And the multitudes going before Him, and those who followed after were crying out, saying,
"[a]Hosanna to the [b]Son of David;
[a]Blessed is He who comes in the name of the Lord;
Hosanna [c]in the highest!"

10   And when He had entered Jerusalem, all the city was stirred, saying, "Who is this?"

11   And the multitudes were saying, "This is [a]the prophet Jesus, from [b]Nazareth in Galilee."

12   [a]And Jesus entered the temple and cast out all those who were buying and selling in the temple, and overturned the tables of the [b]money-changers and the seats of those who were selling [1c]doves.

13   And He *said to them, "It is written, '[a]My house shall be called a house of prayer;' but you are making it a robbers' [1]den."

14   And *the* blind and *the* lame came to Him in the temple, and [a]He healed them.

15   But when the chief priests and the scribes saw the wonderful things that He had done, and the children who were crying out in the temple and saying, "Hosanna to the [a]Son of David," they became indignant,

16   and said to Him, "Do You hear what these are saying?" And Jesus *said to them, "Yes; have you never read, '[a]Out of the mouth of infants and nursing babes Thou hast prepared praise for Thyself'?"

17   And He left them and went out of the city to [a]Bethany, and lodged there.

18   [a]Now in the morning, when He returned to the city, He became hungry.

19   And seeing a lone fig tree by the road, He came to it, and found nothing on it except leaves only; and He *said to it, "No longer shall there ever be *any* fruit from you." And at once the fig tree withered.

20 And seeing *this*, the disciples marveled, saying, "How did the fig tree wither at once?"

21 And Jesus answered and said to them, "Truly I say to you, ªif you have faith, and do not doubt, you shall not only do what was done to the fig tree, but even if you say to this mountain, 'Be taken up and cast into the sea,' it shall happen.

22 "And ªeverything you ask in prayer, believing, you shall receive."

23 ªAnd when He had come into the temple, the chief priests and the elders of the people came to Him as He was teaching, and said, "By what authority are You doing these things, and who gave You this authority?"

24 But Jesus answered and said to them, "I will ask you one ¹thing too, which if you tell Me, I will also tell you by what authority I do these things.

25 "The baptism of John was from what *source*, from heaven or from men?" And they *began* reasoning among themselves, saying, "If we say, 'From heaven,' He will say to us, 'Then why did you not believe him?'

26 "But if we say, 'From men,' we fear the multitude; for they all hold John to be ªa prophet."

27 And they answered Jesus and said, "We do not know." He also said to them, "Neither will I tell you by what authority I do these things.

28 "But what do you think? A man had two ¹sons, and he came to the first and said, '²Son, go work today in the ªvineyard.'

29 "And he answered and said, '¹I will, sir'; and he did not go.

30 "And he came to the second and said ¹the same thing. But he answered and said, '²I will not'; *yet* he afterward regretted *it* and went.

31 "Which of the two did the will of his father?" They *said, "The latter." Jesus *said to them, "Truly I say to you that ªthe ¹tax-gatherers and harlots ²will get into the kingdom of God before you.

32 "For John came to you in the way of righteousness and you did not believe him; but ªthe tax-gatherers and harlots did believe him; and you, seeing this, did not even feel remorse afterward so as to believe him.

33 "Listen to another parable. ªThere was a ¹landowner who ᵇPLANTED A ᶜVINEYARD AND PUT A WALL AROUND IT AND DUG A ᵈWINEPRESS IN IT, AND

21 ªMatt. 17:20; Mark 11:23; Luke 17:6; James 1:6

22 ªMatt. 7:7

23 ªMatt. 21:23-27: *Mark 11:27-33; Luke 20:1-8*

24 ¹Lit., *word*

26 ªMatt. 11:9, Mark 6:20

28 ¹Lit., *children* ²Lit., *Child* ªMatt. 21:33; 20:1

29 ¹Some mss. read '*I will not*'; yet *he afterward regretted and went*

30 ¹Lit., *likewise* ²Some mss. read '*I will*'; *and he did not go*

31 ¹A publican who collected Roman taxes ²Or, *are getting into* ªLuke 7:29, 37-50

32 ªLuke 3:12

33 ¹Lit., *a man, a householder* ªMatt. 21:33-46: *Mark 12:1-12; Luke 20:9-19* ᵇPs. 80:8; Is. 5:1ff. ᶜMatt. 21:28; 20:1 ᵈIs. 5:2

33 [2]Or, *tenant farmers*
(Here and in vss. 34, 35, 38,
40)
[d]Is. 5:2 [e]Matt. 25:14

34 [1]Lit., *the season of the
fruits*
[a]Matt. 22:3

36 [1]Lit., *likewise*
[a]Matt. 22:4

40 [1]Lit., *lord*

41 [a]Matt. 8:11f.; Acts 13:46;
18:6; 28:28

42 [a]Ps. 118:22; Acts 4:11;
1 Pet. 2:7; Rom. 9:33

46 [a]Matt. 21:26 [b]Matt.
21:11

1 [a]Acts 3:12

2 [1]Lit., *a man, a king* [2]Lit.,
made
[a]Matt. 22:2-14; Luke 14:16-
24; Matt. 13:24

[d]BUILT A TOWER, and rented it out to [2]vine-growers, and [e]went on a journey.

34 "And when the [1]harvest time approached, he [a]sent his slaves to the vine-growers to receive his produce.

35 "And the vine-growers took his slaves and beat one, and killed another, and stoned a third.

36 "Again he [a]sent another group of slaves larger than the first; and they did [1]the same thing to them.

37 "But afterward he sent his son to them, saying, 'They will respect my son.'

38 "But when the vine-growers saw the son, they said among themselves, 'This is the heir; come, let us kill him, and seize his inheritance.'

39 "And they took him, and cast him out of the vineyard, and killed *him.*

40 "Therefore when the [1]owner of the vineyard comes, what will he do to those vine growers?"

41 They *said to Him, "He will bring those wretches to a wretched end, and [a]will rent out the vineyard to other vine-growers, who will pay him the proceeds at the *proper* seasons."

42 Jesus *said to them, "Did you never read in the Scriptures,

[a]THE STONE WHICH THE BUILDERS REJECTED,
THIS BECAME THE CHIEF CORNER *STONE*;
THIS CAME ABOUT FROM THE LORD,
AND IT IS MARVELOUS IN OUR EYES'?

43 "Therefore I say to you, the kingdom of God will be taken away from you, and be given to a nation producing the fruit of it.

44 "And he who falls on this stone will be broken to pieces; but on whomever it falls, it will scatter him like dust."

45 And when the chief priests and the Pharisees heard His parables, they understood that He was speaking about them.

46 And when they sought to seize Him, they [a]became afraid of the multitudes, because they held Him to be a [b]prophet.

CHAPTER 22

AND Jesus [a]answered and spoke to them again in parables, saying,

2 "[a]The kingdom of heaven may be compared to [1]a king, who [2]gave a wedding feast for his son.

3 "And he ªsent out his slaves to call those who had been invited to the wedding feast, and they were unwilling to come.

4 "Again he ªsent out other slaves saying, 'Tell those who have been invited, "Behold, I have prepared my dinner; my oxen and my fattened livestock are *all* butchered and everything is ready; come to the wedding feast."'

5 "But they paid no attention and went their way, one to his own ¹farm, another to his business,

6 and the rest seized his slaves and mistreated them and killed them.

7 "But the king was enraged and sent his armies, and destroyed those murderers, and set their city on fire.

8 "Then he *said to his slaves, 'The wedding is ready, but those who were invited were not worthy.

9 'Go therefore to ªthe main highways, and as many as you find *there*, invite to the wedding feast.'

10 "And those slaves went out into the streets, and gathered together all they found, both evil and good; and the wedding hall was filled with ¹dinner-guests.

11 "But when the king came in to look over the dinner-guests, he saw there ªa man not dressed in wedding clothes,

12 and he *said to him, 'ªFriend, how did you come in here ¹without wedding clothes?' And he was speechless.

13 "Then the king said to the servants, 'Bind him hand and foot, and cast him into ªthe outer darkness; in that place ªthere shall be weeping and gnashing of teeth.'

14 "For many are ¹ªcalled, but few *are* ªchosen."

15 ªThen the Pharisees went and counseled together how they might trap Him ¹in what He said.

16 And they *sent their disciples to Him, along with the ªHerodians, saying, "Teacher, we know that You are truthful and teach the way of God in truth, and ¹defer to no one; for You are not partial to any.

17 "Tell us therefore, what do You think? Is it ¹lawful to give a ªpoll-tax to ᵇCaesar, or not?"

18 But Jesus perceived their ¹malice, and said, "Why are you testing Me, you hypocrites?

19 "Show Me the ªcoin *used* for the poll-tax." And they brought Him a ¹denarius.

3 ªMatt. 21:34

4 ªMatt. 21:36

5 ¹Or, *field*

9 ªEzek. 21:21; Obad. 14

10 ¹Lit., *those reclining at table*

11 ª2 Kin. 10:22

12 ¹Lit., *not having* ªMatt. 20:13; 26:50

13 ªMatt. 8:12

14 ¹Or, *invited* ªRev. 17:14; 2 Pet. 1:10; Matt. 24:22

15 ¹Lit., *in word* ªMatt. 22:15-22; Mark 12:13-17; Luke 20:20-26

16 ¹I.e., you court no man's favor ªMark 3:6; 12:13; Mark 8:15

17 ¹Or, *permissible* ªMatt. 17:25 ᵇLuke 2:1; 3:1

18 ¹Or, *wickedness*

19 ¹The denarius was worth 18 cents in silver, equivalent to one day's wage ªMatt. 17:25

21 ªMark 12:17; Luke
20:25; Rom. 13:7

22 ªMark 12:12

23 ªMatt. 22:23-33; *Mark
12:18-27; Luke 20:27-40*
ᵇMatt. 3:7 ᶜActs 23:8

24 ªDeut. 25:5

29 ¹Or, *knowing*
ªJohn 20:9

30 ¹Other mss. add: *of God*
ªMatt. 24:38; Luke 17:27

32 ªEx. 3:6

33 ªMatt. 7:28

34 ªMatt. 22:34-40; *Mark
12:28-31; Luke 10:25-37*
ᵇMatt. 3:7

35 ¹I.e., an expert in the
Mosaic Law
ªLuke 7:30; 10:25; 11:45, 46,
52; 14:3; Titus 3:13

37 ªDeut. 6:5

50

20 And He *said to them, "Whose likeness and inscription is this?"

21 They *said to Him, "Caesar's." Then He *said to them, "ªThen render to Caesar the things that are Caesar's; and to God the things that are God's."

22 And hearing *this*, they marveled, and ªleaving Him, they went away.

23 ªOn that day *some* ᵇSadducees (who say ᶜthere is no resurrection) came to Him and questioned Him,

24 saying, "Teacher, Moses said, 'ªIF A MAN DIES, HAVING NO CHILDREN, HIS BROTHER AS NEXT OF KIN SHALL MARRY HIS WIFE, AND RAISE UP AN OFFSPRING TO HIS BROTHER.'

25 "Now there were seven brothers with us; and the first married and died, and having no offspring left his wife to his brother;

26 so also the second, and the third, down to the seventh.

27 "And last of all, the woman died.

28 "In the resurrection therefore whose wife of the seven shall she be? For they all had her."

29 But Jesus answered and said to them, "You are mistaken, ªnot ¹understanding the Scriptures, or the power of God.

30 "For in the resurrection they neither ªmarry, nor are given in marriage, but are like angels¹ in heaven.

31 "But regarding the resurrection of the dead, have you not read that which was spoken to you by God, saying,

32 'ªI AM THE GOD OF ABRAHAM, AND THE GOD OF ISAAC, AND THE GOD OF JACOB'? God is not *the* God of *the* dead but of *the* living."

33 And when the multitudes heard *this*, ªthey were astonished at His teaching.

34 ªBut when the Pharisees heard that He had put ᵇthe Sadducees to silence, they gathered themselves together.

35 And one of them, ¹ªa lawyer, asked Him a question, testing Him,

36 "Teacher, which is the great commandment in the Law?"

37 And He said to him, " 'ªYOU SHALL LOVE THE LORD YOUR GOD WITH ALL YOUR HEART, AND WITH ALL YOUR SOUL, AND WITH ALL YOUR MIND.'

Pharisaism Exposed, Warned Against, Denounced.

38 "This is the great and [1]foremost commandment.

39 "And a second is like it, '[a]YOU SHALL LOVE YOUR NEIGHBOR AS YOURSELF.'

40 "[a]On these two commandments depend the whole Law and the Prophets."

41 [a]Now while the Pharisees were gathered together, Jesus asked them a question,

42 saying, "What do you think about [1]the Christ, whose son is He?" They *said to Him, "[a]The son of David."

43 He *said to them, "Then how does David [1a]in the Spirit call Him 'Lord,' saying,

44 '[a]THE LORD SAID TO MY LORD,
"SIT AT MY RIGHT HAND,
UNTIL I PUT THINE ENEMIES BENEATH THY FEET."'

45 "If David then calls Him 'Lord', how is He his son?"

46 And [a]no one was able to answer Him a word, nor did anyone dare from that day on to ask Him another question.

[a]   CHAPTER 23

THEN Jesus spoke to the multitudes and to His disciples,

2 saying, "[a]The scribes and the Pharisees have seated themselves in the chair of Moses;

3 therefore all that they tell you, do and observe, but do not do according to their deeds; for they say *things*, and do not do *them*.

4 "And [a]they tie up heavy loads, and lay them on men's shoulders; but they themselves are unwilling to move them with *so much as* a finger.

5 "But they do all their deeds [a]to be noticed by men; for they [b]broaden their [1]phylacteries, and lengthen [c]the tassels *of their garments*.

6 "And they [a]love the place of honor at banquets, and the chief seats in the synagogues,

7 and respectful greetings in the market places, and being called by men, [a]Rabbi.

8 "But [a]do not be called [b]Rabbi; for One is your Teacher, and you are all brothers.

9 "And do not call *anyone* on earth your father; for [a]One is your Father, He who is in heaven.

10 "And do not be called [1]leaders; for One is your Leader, *that is*, Christ.

38 [1]Or, *first*

39 [a]Matt. 19:19; Gal. 5:14; Lev. 19:18

40 [a]Matt. 7:12

41 [a]Matt. 22:41-46: *Mark 12:35-37; Luke 20:41-44*

42 [1]I.e., the Messiah
[a]Matt. 9:27

43 [1]Or, *by inspiration*
[a]Rev. 1:10; 4:2; 2 Sam. 23:2

44 [a]Ps. 110:1; Acts 2:34f.; Heb. 1:13; 1 Cor. 15:25; Heb. 10:13; Matt. 26:64; Mark 16:19

46 [a]Mark 12:34; Luke 14:6; 20:40

1 [a]Matt. 23:1-7: *Mark 12:38, 39; Luke 20:45, 46*

2 [a]Ezra 7:6, 25; Neh. 8:4; Deut. 33:3f.

4 [a]Luke 11:46; Acts 15:10

5 [1]I.e., small boxes containing Scripture texts worn for religious purposes
[a]Matt. 6:1, 5, 16 [b]Ex. 13:9; Deut. 6:8; 11:18 [c]Matt. 9:20

6 [a]Luke 11:43; Luke 14:7; 20:46

7 [a]Matt. 23:8; 26:25, 49; Mark 9:5; 11:21; John 1:38, 49; 3:2, 26; 4:31; 6:25; 9:2; 11:8; Mark 10:51; John 20:16

8 [a]James 3:1 [b]Matt. 23:7; 26:25, 49; Mark 9:5; 11:21; 14:45; John 1:38, 49; 3:2, 26; 4:31; 6:25; 9:2; 11:8; Mark 10:51; John 20:16

9 [a]Matt. 6:9; 7:11

10 [1]Or, *teachers* or *guides*

**Temple Destruction Foretold.
Signs of the Second Coming.**

1 ¹Lit., *and*
ªMatt. 24:1-51; *Mark 13;*
Luke 21:5-36 ᵇMatt. 21:23

2 ªLuke 19:44

3 ¹Or, *presence* ²Or,
consummation
ªMatt. 21:1 ᵇMatt. 24:27, 37,
39; Matt. 16:27f.

4 ªJer. 29:8

5 ¹I.e., Messiah
ªMatt. 24:24; 1 John 2:18;
Matt. 24:11; Acts 5:36f.;
1 John 4:3

7 ª2 Chr. 15:6; Is. 19.2
ᵇActs 11:28

9 ªMatt. 10:17; John 16:2
ᵇMatt. 10:22; John 15.18ff.

10 ¹Lit., *be caused to
stumble* ²Or, *deliver up*
ªMatt. 11:6

11 ªMatt. 24:24; Matt. 7:15

12 ¹Lit., *the love of many*

13 ªMatt. 10:22

14 ¹Lit., *inhabited earth*
ªMatt. 4:23 ᵇRom. 10:18;
Col. 1:6, 23 ᶜLuke 2:1; 4:5;
Acts 11:28; 17:6, 31; 19:27;
Rom. 10:18; Heb. 1:6; 2:5;
Rev. 3:10; 16:14

15 ªDan. 9:27; 11:31; 12:11
ᵇActs 6:13f.; 21:28; John
11:48; Luke 21:20; Mark
13:14 ᶜMark 13:14; Rev. 1:3

17 ªMatt. 10:27; Luke 5:19;
12:3; Acts 10:9; 1 Sam. 9:25;
2 Sam. 11:2

54

ª

CHAPTER 24

AND Jesus ᵇcame out from the temple and was going away ¹when His disciples came up to point out the temple buildings to Him.
2 And He answered and said to them, "Do you not see all these things? Truly I say to you, ªnot one stone here shall be left upon another, which will not be torn down."
3 And as He was sitting on ªthe Mount of Olives, the disciples came to Him privately, saying, "Tell us, when will these things be, and what *will be* the sign of ᵇYour ¹coming, and of the ²end of the age?"
4 And Jesus answered and said to them, "ªSee to it that no one misleads you.
5 "For ªmany will come in My name, saying, 'I am the ¹Christ,' and will mislead many.
6 "And you will be hearing of wars and rumors of wars; see that you are not frightened, for *those things* must take place, but *that* is not yet the end.
7 "For ªnation will rise against nation, and kingdom against kingdom, and in various places there will be ᵇfamines and earthquakes.
8 "But all these things are merely the beginning of birth-pangs.
9 "ªThen they will deliver you up to tribulation, and will kill you, and ᵇyou will be hated by all nations on account of My name.
10 "And at that time many will ¹ªfall away and will ²betray one another and hate one another.
11 "And many ªfalse prophets will arise, and will mislead many.
12 "And because lawlessness is increased, ¹most people's love will grow cold.
13 "ªBut the one who endures to the end, it is he who shall be saved.
14 "And this ªgospel of the kingdom ᵇshall be preached in the whole ¹ᶜworld for a witness to all the nations, and then the end shall come.
15 "Therefore when you see the ªABOMINATION OF DESOLATION which was spoken of through Daniel the prophet, standing in ᵇTHE HOLY PLACE (ᶜlet the reader understand),
16 then let those who are in Judea flee to the mountains;
17 let him who is on ªthe housetop not go down to get the things out that are in his house;

18 and let him who is in the field not turn back to get his cloak.

19 "But ᵃwoe to those who are with child and to those who nurse babes in those days!

20 "But pray that your flight may not be in the winter, or on a Sabbath;

21 for then there will be a ᵃgreat tribulation, such as has not occurred since the beginning of the world until now, nor ever shall.

22 "And unless those days had been cut short, no ¹life would have been saved; but for ᵃthe sake of the ²elect those days shall be cut short.

23 "ᵃThen if any one says to you, 'Behold, here is the ¹Christ,' or '²There *He is*,' do not believe *him*.

24 "For false Christs and ᵃfalse prophets will arise and will show great ¹ᵇsigns and wonders, so as to mislead, if possible, even ᶜthe ²elect.

25 "Behold, I have told you in advance.

26 "If therefore they say to you, 'Behold, He is in the wilderness,' do not go forth, *or*, 'Behold, He is in the inner rooms,' do not believe *them*.

27 "ᵃFor just as the lightning comes from the east, and flashes even to the west, so shall the ¹ᵇcoming of the ᶜSon of Man be.

28 "ᵃWherever the corpse is, there the ¹vultures will gather.

29 "But immediately after the ᵃtribulation of those days ᵇTHE SUN WILL BE DARKENED, AND THE MOON WILL NOT GIVE ITS LIGHT, AND ᶜTHE STARS WILL FALL from ¹the sky, and the POWERS OF ¹THE HEAVENS WILL BE shaken,

30 and then ᵃthe sign of the Son of Man will appear in the sky, and then all the tribes of the earth will mourn, and they will see ᵇthe SON OF MAN COMING ON THE CLOUDS OF THE SKY with power and great glory.

31 "And ᵃHe will send forth His angels WITH ᵇA GREAT TRUMPET and THEY WILL GATHER TOGETHER His ¹ᶜelect FROM ᵈTHE FOUR WINDS, ᵉFROM ONE END OF THE SKY TO THE OTHER.

32 "Now learn the parable FROM THE FIG TREE: when its branch has already become tender, and puts forth its leaves, you know that summer is near;

33 even so you too, when you see all these things, ¹recognize that ²He is near, *right* ᵃat the ³door.

19 ᵃLuke 23:29

21 ᵃDan. 12:1; Joel 2:2; Matt. 24:29

22 ¹Lit., *flesh* ²Or, *chosen ones* ᵃMatt. 24:24, 31; Matt. 22:14; Luke 18:7

23 ¹Or, *the Messiah* ²Lit., *here* ᵃLuke 17:23f.

24 ¹Or, *attesting miracles* ²Or, *chosen ones* ᵃMatt. 24:11; */*:15 ᵇJohn 4:48; 2 Thess. 2:9 ᶜMatt. 24:22, 31; Matt. 22:14 [Gr.]; Luke 18:7

27 ¹Or, *presence* ᵃLuke 17:23f. ᵇMatt. 24:3, 37, 39 ᶜMatt. 8:20

28 ¹Or, *eagles* ᵃLuke 17:37; Job 39:30; Hab. 1:8; Ezek. 39:17

29 ¹Or, *heaven* ᵃMatt. 24:21 ᵇIs. 13:10; 24:23; Ezek. 32:7; Joel 2:10, 31; 3:15; Acts 2:20; Amos 5:20; 8:9; Zeph. 1:15; Rev. 6:12; 8:12 ᶜRev. 6:13; Is. 34:4

30 ᵃMatt. 24:3; Dan. 7:13; Rev. 1:7 ᵇMatt. 24:3, 37, 39; Matt. 16:27

31 ¹Or, *chosen ones* ᵃMatt. 13:41 ᵇIs. 27:13; 1 Cor. 15:52; 1 Thess. 4:16; Ex. 19:16; Zech. 9:14; Rev. 8:2; 11:15; Heb. 12:19 ᶜMatt. 24:22 ᵈDan. 7:2; Zech. 2:6; Rev. 7:1 ᵉDeut. 4:32

33 ¹Lit., *know* ²Or, *it* ³Lit., *doors* ᵃJames 5:9; Rev. 3:20

Matthew 24

**Conditions at the Second Advent.
The Faithful and Unfaithful Servants.**

34 [1]Or, *race*
[a]Matt. 16:28; Matt. 10:23; 23:36

35 [a]Mark 13:31; Luke 21:33; Matt. 5:18

36 [a]Mark 13:32; Acts 1:7

37 [1]Lit., *just as . . . were the days* [2]Or, *presence*
[a]Matt. 24:3, 30, 39; 16:27
[b]Luke 17:26f.; Gen. 6:5; 7:6-23

38 [a]Matt. 22:30 [b]Gen. 7:7

39 [1]Lit., *know* [2]Or, *presence*
[a]Matt. 24:3, 30, 37; Matt. 16:27

40 [1]Lit., *is*

41 [1]I.e., handmill [2]Lit., *is*
[a]Luke 17:35 [b]Deut. 24:6; Ex. 11:5; Is. 47:2

42 [a]Matt. 24:43, 44, 25:10, 13; Luke 12:39f.; Luke 21:36

43 [1]Lit., *know this* [2]Lit., *dug through*
[a]Matt. 24:42, 44; 25:10, 13; Luke 12:39f.; 21:36 [b]Luke 12:38; Matt. 14:25; [b]Luke 6:48; Mark 13:35

44 [a]Matt. 24:42, 43; 25:10, 13; Luke 12:39f.; 21:36
[b]Matt. 24:27

45 [1]Or, *lord*
[a]Matt. 24:45-51; Luke 1:42-46 [b]Matt. 25:21, 23; Luke 16:10 [c]Matt. 7:24; 10:16; 25:2ff. [d]Matt. 25:21, 23

46 [1]Or, *lord*

47 [a]Matt. 25:21, 23

48 [1]Or, *lord* [2]Lit., *lingers*

49 [1]Lit., *those who get drunk*

50 [1]Or, *Lord*

51 [1]Or, *severely scourge him* [2]Lit., *appoint his portion*
[a]Matt. 8:12

56

34 "Truly I say to you, [a]this [1]generation will not pass away until all these things take place.

35 "[a]Heaven and earth will pass away, but My words shall not pass away.

36 "But [a]of that day and hour no one knows, not even the angels of heaven, nor the Son, but the Father alone.

37 "For [1]the [2][a]coming of the Son of Man will be [b]just like the days of Noah.

38 "For as in those days which were before the flood they were eating and drinking, they were [a]marrying and giving in marriage, until the day that [b]NOAH ENTERED THE ARK,

39 and they did not [1]understand until the flood came and took them all away, so shall the [2][a]coming of the Son of Man be.

40 "Then there shall be two men in the field; one [1]will be taken, and one [1]will be left.

41 "[a]Two women *will be* grinding at the [1][b]mill, one [2]will be taken, and one [2]will be left.

42 "Therefore [a]be on the alert, for you do not know which day your Lord is coming.

43 "But [1]be sure of this, that [a]if the head of the house had known [b]at what time of the night the thief was coming, he would have been on the alert and would not have allowed his house to be [2]broken into.

44 "For this reason [a]you be ready too; for [b]the Son of Man is coming at an hour when you do not think *He will.*

45 "[a]Who then is the [b]faithful and [c]sensible slave whom his [1]master [d]put in charge of his household to give them their food at the proper time?

46 "Blessed is that slave whom his [1]master finds so doing when he comes.

47 "Truly I say to you, that [a]he will put him in charge of all his possessions.

48 "But if that evil slave says in his heart, 'My [1]master [2]is not coming for a long time,'

49 and shall begin to beat his fellow-slaves and eat and drink with [1]drunkards;

50 the [1]master of that slave will come on a day when he does not expect *him* and at an hour which he does not know,

51 and shall [1]cut him in pieces and [2]assign him a place with the hypocrites; [a]weeping shall be there and the gnashing of teeth.

Chapter 25

"THEN [a]the kingdom of heaven will be comparable to ten virgins, who took their [b]lamps, and went out to meet the bridegroom.

2 "And five of them were foolish, and five were [a]prudent.

3 "For when the foolish took their lamps, they took no oil with them,

4 but the [a]prudent took oil in flasks along with their lamps.

5 "Now while the bridegroom was delaying, they all got drowsy and *began* to sleep.

6 "But at midnight there was a shout, 'Behold, the bridegroom! Come out to meet *him*.'

7 "Then all those virgins arose, and trimmed their lamps.

8 "And the foolish said to the prudent, 'Give us some of your oil, for our lamps are going out.'

9 "But the [a]prudent answered, saying, 'No, there will not be enough for us and you *too*; go instead to the dealers and buy *some* for yourselves.'

10 "And while they were going away to make the purchase, the bridegroom came, and those who were [a]ready went in with him to [b]the wedding feast; and [c]the door was shut.

11 "And later the other virgins also came, saying, '[a]Lord, Lord, open up for us.'

12 "But he answered and said, 'Truly I say to you, I do not know you.'

13 "[a]Be on the alert then, for you do not know the day nor the hour.

14 "[a]For *it is* just like a man [b]*about* to go on a journey, who called his own slaves, and entrusted his possessions to them.

15 "And to one he gave five [1][a]talents, to another, two, and to another, one, each according to his own ability; and he [b]went on his journey.

16 "Immediately the one who had received the five [a]talents went and traded with them, and gained five more talents.

17 "In the same manner the one who had *received* the two *talents* gained two more.

18 "But he who received the one *talent* went away and dug in the ground, and hid his [1]master's money.

19 "Now after a long time the master of those slaves *came and *[a]settled accounts with them.

1 [a]Matt. 13:24 [b]John 18:3; Acts 20:8; Rev. 4:5; 8:10 [Gr.]

2 [a]Matt. 7:24; 10:16; 25:2ff.

4 [a]Matt. 7:24; 10:16; 25:2ff.

9 [a]Matt. 7:24; 10:16; 25:2ff.

10 [a]Matt. 24:42ff. [b]Luke 12:35f. [c]Luke 13:25; Matt. 7:21ff.

11 [a]Luke 13:25; Matt. 7:21ff.

13 [a]Matt. 24:42ff.

14 [a]Matt. 25:14-30; Luke 19:12-27 [b]Matt. 21:33

15 [1]A talent was $1,000 in silver content, much more in buying power. [a]Matt. 18:24; Luke 19:13 [b]Matt. 21:33

16 [a]Matt. 18:24; Luke 19:13

18 [1]Or, *lord's*

19 [a]Matt. 18:23

20 ªMatt. 18:24; Luke 19:13

20 "And the one who had received the five ªtalents came up and brought five more talents, saying, 'Master, you entrusted five talents to me; see, I have gained five more talents.'

21 ¹Or, *lord*
ªMatt. 25:23; Matt. 24:45, 47

21 "His master said to him, 'Well done, good and ªfaithful slave; you were faithful with a few things, I will put you in charge of many things, enter into the joy of your ¹master.'

22 ªMatt. 18:24; Luke 19:13

22 "The one also who had *received* the two ªtalents came up and said, 'Master, you entrusted to me two talents; see, I have gained two more talents.'

23 ªMatt. 25:21; Matt. 24:45, 47

23 "His master said to him, 'Well done, good and ªfaithful slave; you were faithful with a few things, I will put you in charge of many things; enter into the joy of your master.'

24 ªMatt. 18:24; Luke 19:13

24 "And the one also who had received the one ªtalent came up and said, 'Master, I knew you to be a hard man, reaping where you did not sow, and gathering where you scattered no *seed*.

25 'And I was afraid, and went away and hid your talent in the ground; see, you have what is yours.'

27 ¹Lit., *to the bankers*

26 "But his master answered and said to him, 'You wicked, lazy slave, you knew that I reap where I did not sow, and gather where I scattered no *seed*?

27 'Then you ought to have put my money ¹in the bank, and on my arrival I would have received my *money* back with interest.

28 'Therefore take away the talent from him, and give it to the one who has the ten talents.'

29 ªMatt. 13:12

29 "ªFor to everyone who has shall *more* be given, and he shall have an abundance; but from the one who does not have, even what he does have shall be taken away.

30 ªMatt. 8:12

30 "And cast out the worthless slave into ªthe outer darkness; in that place there shall be weeping and gnashing of teeth.

31 ªMatt. 16:27f. ᵇMatt. 19:28

31 "But when ªthe Son of Man comes in His glory, and all the angels with Him, then ᵇHe will sit on His glorious throne.

32 ªEzek. 34:17, 20

32 "And all the nations will be gathered before Him; and He will separate them from one another, ªas the shepherd separates the sheep from the goats;

33 ª1 Kin. 2:19; Ps. 45:9
ᵇEccles. 10:2

33 and He will put the sheep ªon His right, and the goats ᵇon the left.

34 "Then the King will say to those on His right, 'Come, you who are blessed of My Father, [a]inherit the kingdom prepared for you [b]from the foundation of the world.

35 'For [a]I was hungry, and you gave Me *something* to eat; I was thirsty, and you gave Me drink; [b]I was a stranger, and you invited Me in;

36 [a]naked, and you clothed Me; I was sick, and you [b]visited Me; [c]I was in prison, and you came to Me.'

37 "Then the righteous will answer Him, saying, 'Lord, when did we see You hungry, and feed You, or thirsty, and give You drink?

38 'And when did we see You a stranger, and invite You in, or naked, and clothe You?

39 'And when did we see You sick, or in prison, and come to You?'

40 "And [a]the King will answer and say to them, 'Truly I say to you, [b]to the extent that you did it to one of these brothers of Mine, *even* the least *of them*, you did it to Me.'

41 "Then He will also say to those on His left, '[a]Depart from Me, accursed ones, into the [b]eternal fire which has been prepared for [c]the devil and his angels;

42 for I was hungry, and you gave Me *nothing* to eat; I was thirsty, and you gave Me nothing to drink;

43 I was a stranger, and you did not invite Me in; naked, and you did not clothe Me; sick, and in prison, and you did not visit Me.'

44 "Then they themselves also will answer, saying, 'Lord, when did we see You hungry, or thirsty, or a stranger, or naked, or sick, or in prison, and did not [1]take care of You?'

45 "Then He will answer them, saying, 'Truly I say to you, to the extent that you did not do it to one of the least of these, you did not do it to Me.'

46 "And these will go away into [a]eternal punishment, but the righteous into [b]eternal life."

a   CHAPTER 26

Aₙᴅ it came about that when Jesus had finished all these words, He said to His disciples,

2 "[a]You know that after two days [b]the Passover is coming, and the Son of Man is *to be* [c]delivered up for crucifixion."

---

34 [a]Luke 12:32; 1 Cor. 6:9; 15:50; Gal. 5:21; James 2:5; Matt. 5:3; 19:29 [b]Luke 11:50; Heb. 4:3; 9:26; Rev. 13:8; 17:8; John 17:24; Eph. 1:4; 1 Pet. 1:20; Matt. 13:35

35 [a]Is. 58:7; Ezek. 18:7, 16; James 2:15, 16; [b]Job 31:32; Heb. 13:2

36 [a]Is. 58:7; Ezek. 18:7, 16; James 2:15, 16 [b]James 1:27 [c]2 Tim. 1:16f.

40 [a]Matt. 25:34; Luke 19:38; Rev. 17:14; 19:16 [b]Matt. 10:42; Heb. 6:10; Prov. 19:17

41 [a]Matt. 7:23 [b]Mark 9:48; Luke 16:24; Jude 7 [c]Rev. 12:9; Matt. 4:10

44 [1]Or, *serve*

46 [a]Dan. 12:2; John 5:29; Acts 24:15 [b]Matt. 19:29; John 3:15f., 36; 5:24; 6:27, 40, 47, 54; 17:2f.; Acts 13:46, 48; Rom. 2:7; 5:21; 6:23; Gal. 6:8; 1 John 5:11

1 [a]Matt. 7:28

2 [a]Matt. 26:2-5: *Mark 14:1-2; Luke 22:1-2* [b]John 11:55; 13:1 [c]Matt. 10:4

Matthew 26

The Plot to Kill Jesus.
The Precious Ointment.   The Bargain of Judas.

3 ªJohn 11:47 ᵇMatt.
26:58, 69; Mark 14:54, 66;
15:16; Luke 11:21; 22:55;
John 18:15; Matt. 27:27
ᶜMatt. 26:57; Luke 3:2; John
11:49; 18:13, 14, 24, 28; Acts
4:6

4 ªMatt. 12:14

5 ªMatt. 27:24

6 ªMatt. 26:6-13: *Mark
14:3-9; John 12:1-8; Luke
7:37-39* ᵇMatt. 21:17

11 ªMark 14:7; John 12:8;
Deut. 15:11

12 ªJohn 19:40

13 ªMark 14:9

14 ªMatt. 26:14-16: *Mark
14:10, 11; Luke 22:3-6* ᵇMatt.
10:4; 26:25, 47; 27:3; John
6:71; 12:4; 13:26; Acts 1:16

15 ¹Lit., *and I will* ²Or,
betray ³Or, *silver shekels*
ªMatt. 10:4 ᵇZech. 11:12;
Ex. 21:32

16 ¹Or, *deliver Him up*

17 ªMatt. 26:17-19: *Mark
14:12-16; Luke 22:7-13* ᵇEx.
12:18-20

18 ªMark 14:13; Luke 22:10
ᵇJohn 7:6, 8

20 ªMatt. 26:20-24: *Mark
14:17-21*

21 ªLuke 22:21-23; John
13:21f.

3   ªThen the chief priests and the elders of the people were gathered together in ᵇthe court of the high priest, named ᶜCaiaphas;

4   and they ªplotted together to seize Jesus by stealth, and kill *Him*.

5   But they were saying, "Not during the festival, ªlest a riot occur among the people."

6   ªNow when Jesus was in ᵇBethany, at the home of Simon the leper,

7   a woman came to Him with an alabaster vial of very costly perfume, and she poured it upon His head as He reclined *at table*.

8   But the disciples were indignant when they saw *this*, and said, "What is the point of this waste?

9   "For this *perfume* might have been sold for a high price and *the money* given to the poor."

10   But Jesus, aware of this, said to them, "Why do you bother the woman? For she has done a good deed to Me.

11   "For ªthe poor you have with you always; but you do not always have Me.

12   "For when she poured this perfume upon My body, she did it ªto prepare Me for burial.

13   "Truly I say to you, ªwherever this gospel is preached in the whole world, what this woman has done shall also be spoken of in memory of her."

14   ªThen one of the twelve, named ᵇJudas Iscariot, went to the chief priests,

15   and said, "What are you willing to give me ¹to ²ªdeliver Him up to you?" And ᵇthey weighed out to him thirty ³pieces of silver.

16   And from then on he *began* looking for a good opportunity to ¹betray Him.

17   ªNow on the first *day* of ᵇthe *Feast* of Unleavened Bread the disciples came to Jesus, saying, "Where do You want us to prepare for You to eat the Passover?"

18   And He said, "Go into the city to ªa certain man, and say to him, 'The Teacher says, "ᵇMy time is at hand; I *am to* keep the Passover at your house with My disciples."' "

19   And the disciples did as Jesus had directed them; and they prepared the Passover.

20   ªNow when evening had come, He was reclining *at table* with the twelve disciples.

21   And as they were eating, He said, "ªTruly I say to you that one of you will betray Me."

22   And being deeply grieved, they [1]each one began to say to Him, "Surely not I, Lord?"

23   And He answered and said, "[a]He who dipped his hand with Me in the bowl is the one who will betray Me.

24   "The Son of Man *is to* go, [a]just as it is written of Him; but woe to that man through whom the Son of Man is betrayed! [b]It would have been good [1]for that man if he had not been born."

25   And [a]Judas, who was betraying Him, answered and said, "Surely it is not I, [b]Rabbi?" He *said to him, "[c]You have said *it* yourself."

26   [a]And while they were eating, Jesus took *some* bread, and [1b]after a blessing, He broke it and gave *it* to the disciples, and said, "Take, eat; this is My body."

27   And He took a cup and gave thanks, and gave *it* to them, saying, "Drink from it, all of you;

28   for [a]this is My blood of the covenant, which is *to be* shed on behalf of [b]many for forgiveness of sins.

29   "But I say to you, I will not drink of this fruit of the vine from now on until that day when I drink it new with you in My Father's kingdom."

30   [a]And after singing a hymn, they went out to [b]the Mount of Olives.

31   Then Jesus *said to them, "You will all [1a]fall away because of Me this night, for it is written, '[b]I WILL STRIKE DOWN THE SHEPHERD, AND THE SHEEP OF THE FLOCK SHALL BE [c]SCATTERED.'

32   "But after I have been raised, [a]I will go before you to Galilee."

33   But Peter answered and said to Him, "*Even* though all may [1]fall away because of You, I will never fall away."

34   Jesus said to him, "[a]Truly I say to you that [b]this *very* night, before a cock crows, you shall deny Me three times."

35   Peter *said to Him, "[a]Even if I must die with You, I will not deny You." All the disciples said the same thing too.

36   [a]Then Jesus *came with them to a place called [b]Gethsemane, and *said to His disciples, "Sit here while I go over there and pray."

37   And He took with Him [a]Peter and the two sons of Zebedee, and began to be grieved and distressed.

38   Then He *said to them, "[a]My soul is deeply

22 [1]Or, *one after another*

23 [a]John 13:26; John 13:18

24 [1]Lit., *for him if that man had not been born* [a]Matt. 26:31, 54, 56; Mark 9:12; Luke 24:25-27, 46; Acts 17:2f.; 26:22f.; 1 Cor. 15:3; 1 Pet. 1:10f. [b]Mark 14:21; Matt. 18:7

25 [a]Matt. 26:14 [b]Matt. 23:7; 26:49 [c]Matt. 26:64; 27:11; Luke 22:70

26 [1]Lit., *having blessed* [a]Matt. 26:26-29: *Mark 14:22-25; Luke 22:17-20; 1 Cor. 11.23-25; 1 Cor. 10:16* [b]Matt. 14:19

28 [a]Heb. 9:20 [b]Matt. 20:28

30 [a]Matt. 26:30-35: *Mark 14:26-31; Luke 22:31-34* [b]Matt. 21:1

31 [1]Or, *stumble* [a]Matt. 11:6 [b]Zech. 13:7 [c]John 16:32

32 [a]Matt. 28:7, 10, 16; Mark 16:7

33 [1]Or, *stumble*

34 [a]John 13:38; Matt. 26:75 [b]Mark 14:30

35 [a]John 13:37

36 [a]Matt. 26:36-46: *Mark 14:32-42; Luke 22:40-46* [b]Mark 14:32; Luke 22:39; John 18:1

37 [a]Matt. 17:1; Mark 5:37; Matt. 4:21

38 [a]John 12:27

61

38 bMatt. 26:40, 41

39 aMatt. 20:22 bMatt.
26:42; Mark 14:36; Luke
22:42; John 6:38

40 aMatt. 26:38

41 aMatt. 26:38 bMark
14:38

42 aMatt. 20:22 bMatt.
26:39; Mark 14:36; Luke
22:42; John 6:38

45 1Or, *keep on sleeping
therefore*
aMark 14:41; John 12:27;
13:1

47 1Lit., *and with him*
aMatt. 26:47-56; *Mark 14:43-
50; Luke 22:47-53; John 18:3-
11* bMatt. 26:14

49 aMatt. 23:7; 26:25

50 aMatt. 20:13; 22:12

51 1Lit., *extending the
hand* 2Lit., *took off*
aJohn 18:10; Mark 14:47;
Luke 22:50 bLuke 22:38
cJohn 18:10; Mark 14:47;
Luke 22:50

52 aGen. 9:6; Rev. 13:10

53 1A legion equaled 6,000
troops
aMark 5:9, 15; Luke 8:30
bMatt. 4:11

62

grieved, to the point of death; remain here and
bkeep watch with Me."

39 And He went a little beyond *them*, and fell
on His face and prayed, saying, "My Father, if it is
possible, let athis cup pass from Me; byet not as I
will, but as Thou wilt."

40 And He *came to the disciples and *found
them sleeping, and *said to Peter, "So, you *men*
could not akeep watch with Me for one hour?

41 "aKeep watching and praying, that you may
not enter into temptation; bthe spirit is willing, but
the flesh is weak."

42 He went away again a second time and
prayed, saying, "My Father, if this acannot pass
away unless I drink it, bThy will be done."

43 And He came back and found them sleeping, for their eyes were heavy.

44 And He left them again, and went away and
prayed a third time, saying the same thing once
more.

45 Then He *came to the disciples, and *said
to them, "1Are you still sleeping and taking your
rest? Behold, athe hour is at hand and the Son of
Man is being betrayed into the hands of sinners.

46 "Arise, let us be going; behold, the one who
betrays Me is at hand!"

47 aAnd while He was still speaking, behold,
bJudas, one of the twelve, came up, 1accompanied
by a great multitude with swords and clubs, from
the chief priests and elders of the people.

48 Now he who was betraying Him gave them
a sign, saying, "Whomever I shall kiss, He is the
one; seize Him."

49 And immediately he came to Jesus and said,
"Hail, aRabbi;" and kissed Him.

50 And Jesus said to him, "aFriend, *do* what
you have come for." Then they came and laid
hands on Jesus and seized Him.

51 And behold, aone of those who were with
Jesus 1reached and drew out his bsword, and struck
the cslave of the high priest, and 2cut off his ear.

52 Then Jesus *said to him, "Put your sword
back into its place; for aall those who take up the
sword shall perish by the sword.

53 "Or do you think that I cannot appeal to My
Father, and He will at once put at My disposal
more than twelve 1alegions of bangels?

54 "How then shall [a]the Scriptures be fulfilled, that it must happen this way?"

55 At that time Jesus said to the multitudes, "Have you come out with swords and clubs to arrest Me [1]as though *I were* a robber? [a]Every day I used to sit in the temple teaching and you did not seize Me.

56 "But all this has taken place that [a]the Scriptures of the prophets may be fulfilled." Then all the disciples left Him and fled.

57   [a]And those who had seized Jesus led Him away to [b]Caiaphas, the high priest, where the scribes and the elders were gathered together.

58 But [a]Peter also followed Him at a distance as far as the [b]courtyard of the high priest, and entered in, and sat down with the [1c]officers to see the outcome.

59 Now the chief priests and the whole [1a]Council kept trying to obtain false testimony against Jesus, in order that they might put Him to death;

60 and they did not find it, even though many false witnesses came forward. But later on [a]two came forward,

61 and said, "This man stated, '[a]I am able to destroy the [1]temple of God and to rebuild it [2]in three days.' "

62 And the high priest stood up and said to Him, "Do You make no answer? What is it that these men are testifying against You?"

63 But [a]Jesus kept silent. [b]And the high priest said to Him, "I [1c]adjure You by [d]the living God, that You tell us whether You are [2]the Christ, [e]the Son of God."

64 Jesus *said to him, "[a]You have said it *yourself*; nevertheless I tell you, [1]hereafter you shall see [b]THE SON OF MAN SITTING AT THE RIGHT HAND OF POWER, *and* [c]COMING ON THE CLOUDS OF HEAVEN."

65 Then the high priest [a]tore his [1]robes, saying, "He has blasphemed! What further need do we have of witnesses? Behold, you have now heard the blasphemy;

66 what do you think?" They answered and said, "[a]He is deserving of death!"

67   [a]Then they [b]spat in His face and beat Him with their fists, and others [1]slapped Him,

68 and said, "[a]Prophesy to us, You [1]Christ; who is the one who hit You?"

54 [a]Matt. 26:24

55 [1]Lit., *as against a robber*
[a]Mark 12:35; 14:49; Luke 4:20; 19:47; 20:1; 21:37; John 7:14, 28; 8:2, 20; 18:20

56 [a]Matt. 26:24

57 [a]Matt. 26:57-68; *Mark 14:53-65; John 18:12f., 19-24*
[b]Matt. 26:3

58 [1]Or, *servants*
[a]John 18:15 [b]Matt. 26:3
[c]Matt. 5:25; John 7:32, 45f.; 19:6; Acts 5:22, 26

59 [1]Or, *Sanhedrin*
[a]Matt. 5:22

60 [a]Deut. 19:15

61 [1]Or, *sanctuary* [2]Or, *after*
[a]Matt. 27:40; Mark 14:58; 15:29; John 2:19; Acts 6:14

63 [1]Or, *charge You under oath* [2]I.e., the Messiah
[a]Matt. 27:12, 14; John 19:9
[b]Matt. 26:63-66; Luke 22:67-71 [c]Lev. 5:1 [d]Matt. 16:16
[e]Matt. 4:3

64 [1]Or, *from now on*
[a]Matt. 26:25 [b]Ps. 110:1
[c]Dan. 7:13; Matt. 16:27f.

65 [1]Or, *outer garments*
[a]Mark 14:63; Num. 14:6; Acts 14:14

66 [a]Lev. 24:16; John 19:7

67 [1]Or, possibly, *beat Him with rods*
[a]Matt. 26:67, 68; Luke 22:63-65; John 18:22 [b]Matt. 27:30; Mark 10:34

68 [1]I.e., the Messiah
[a]Mark 14:65; Luke 22:64

Matthew 26, 27

Peter's Three Denials.   Jesus Delivered Up to Pilate.   Judas' Last Words and Act.

69 ᵃMatt. 26:69-75: *Mark 14:66-72; Luke 22:55-62; John 18:16-18, 25-27* ᵇMatt. 26:3

69   ᵃNow Peter was sitting outside in the ᵇcourtyard, and a certain servant-girl came to him and said, "You too were with Jesus the Galilean."

70   But he denied *it* before them all, saying, "I do not know what you are talking about."

71   And when he had gone out to the gateway, another *servant-girl* saw him and *said to those who were there, "This man was with Jesus of Nazareth."

73 ¹Lit., *makes you evident* ᵃMark 14:70; Luke 22:59; John 18:26

72   And again he denied *it* with an oath, "I do not know the man."

73   And a little later the bystanders came up and said to Peter, "Surely you too are *one* of them; ᵃfor the way you talk ¹gives you away."

75 ᵃMatt. 26:34

74   Then he began to curse and swear, "I do not know the man!" And immediately a cock crowed.

75   And Peter remembered the word which Jesus had said, "ᵃBefore a cock crows, you will deny Me three times." And he went out and wept bitterly.

1 ᵃMark 15:1; Luke 22:66; John 18:28

ᵃ

CHAPTER 27

NOW when morning had come, all the chief priests and the elders of the people took counsel against Jesus to put Him to death;

2   and they bound Him, and led Him away, and ᵃdelivered Him up to ᵇPilate the governor.

2 ᵃMatt. 20:19 ᵇLuke 3:1; 13:1; 23:12; Acts 3:13; 4:27; 1 Tim. 6:13

3   Then when ᵃJudas, who had betrayed Him, saw that He had been condemned, he felt remorse and returned ᵇthe thirty ¹pieces of silver to the chief priests and elders,

3 ¹Or, *silver shekels* ᵃMatt. 26:14 ᵇMatt. 26:15

4   saying, "I have sinned by betraying innocent blood." But they said, "What is that to us? ᵃSee *to that* yourself!"

4 ᵃMatt. 27:24

5   And he threw the pieces of silver into ᵃthe sanctuary and departed; and ᵇhe went away and hanged himself.

5 ᵃLuke 1:9, 21; Matt. 26:61 marg. ᵇActs 1:18

6   And the chief priests took the pieces of silver and said, "It is not lawful to put them into the temple treasury, since it is the price of blood."

7 ¹Lit., *them*

7   And they counseled together and with ¹the money bought the Potter's Field as a burial place for strangers.

8   ᵃFor this reason that field has been called the Field of Blood to this day.

8 ᵃActs 1:19

9   Then that which was spoken through Jere-

miah the prophet was fulfilled, saying, "ᵃAND ¹THEY TOOK THE THIRTY PIECES OF SILVER, THE PRICE OF THE ONE WHOSE PRICE HAD BEEN SET BY THE SONS OF ISRAEL;

10   AND ¹THEY GAVE THEM FOR THE POTTER'S FIELD, AS THE LORD DIRECTED ME."

11   ᵃNow Jesus stood before the governor, and the governor questioned Him, saying, "Are You the ᵇKing of the Jews?" And Jesus said to him, "ᶜ*It is as* you say."

12   And while He was being accused by the chief priests and elders, ᵃHe made no answer.

13   Then Pilate *said to Him, "Do You not hear how many things they testify against You?"

14   And ᵃHe did not answer him with regard to even a single ¹charge, so that the governor was quite amazed.

15   ᵃNow at *the* feast the governor was accustomed to release for the multitude *any* one prisoner whom they wanted.

16   And they were holding at that time a notorious prisoner, called Barabbas.

17   When therefore they were gathered together, Pilate said to them, "Whom do you want me to release for you? Barabbas, or Jesus ᵃwho is called Christ?"

18   For he knew that because of envy they had delivered Him up.

19   And ᵃwhile he was sitting on the judgment-seat, his wife sent to him, saying, "Have nothing to do with that ᵇrighteous Man; for ¹last night I suffered greatly ᶜin a dream because of Him."

20   But the chief priests and the elders persuaded the multitudes to ᵃask for Barabbas, and to put Jesus to death.

21   But the governor answered and said to them, "Which of the two do you want me to release for you?" And they said, "Barabbas."

22   Pilate *said to them, "What then shall I do with Jesus ᵃwho is called Christ?" They all *said, "Let Him be crucified!"

23   And he said, "Why, what evil has He done?" But they kept shouting all the more, saying, "Let Him be crucified!"

24   And when Pilate saw that he was accomplishing nothing, but rather that ᵃa riot was starting, he took water and ᵇwashed his hands in front of the

---

9 ¹Some mss. read, *I took*
ᵃZech. 11:12, 13; cf., Jer. 18:2; 19:2, 11; 32:6-9

10 ¹Some mss. read, *I gave*

11 ᵃMatt. 27:11-14: *Mark 15:2-5; Luke 23:2-3; John 18:29-38* ᵇMatt. 2:2 ᶜMatt. 26:25

12 ᵃMatt. 26:63; John 19:9

14 ¹Lit., *word*
ᵃMatt. 27:12; Mark 15:5; John 19:9; Luke 23:9

15 ᵃMatt. 27:15-26: *Mark 15:6-15; Luke 23:[17]-25; John 18:39-19:16*

17 ᵃMatt. 1:16; 27:22

19 ¹Lit., *today*
ᵃJohn 19:13; Acts 12:21 marg.; 18:12, 16f.; 25:6, 10, 17 ᵇMatt. 27:24 ᶜMatt. 1:20; 2:12f., 19, 22; Gen. 20:6; 31:11; Num. 12:6; Job 33:15

20 ᵃActs 3:14

22 ᵃMatt. 1:16

24 ᵃMatt. 26:5 ᵇDeut. 21:6-8

65

24 ¹Many mss. read, *the blood of this righteous Man*
ᶜMatt. 27:19 ᵈMatt. 27:4

25 ᵃJosh. 2:19; Acts 5:28

26 ¹Or, *to them*
ᵃMark 15:15; John 19:1; Luke 23:16

27 ¹Or, *battalion*
ᵃMatt. 27:27-31: *Mark 15:16-20* ᵇJohn 18:28, 33; 19:9; Matt. 26:3 ᶜActs 10:1

28 ᵃMark 15:17; John 19:2

29 ¹Or, *staff* (made of a reed)
ᵃMark 15:17; John 19:2 ᵇMark 15:18; John 19:1

30 ᵃMatt. 26:67; Mark 10:34; 14:65; 15:19

31 ᵃMark 15:20

32 ¹Lit., *a man, a Cyrenian*
ᵃMatt. 27:32: *Mark 15:21; Luke 23:26;* John 19:17 ᵇActs 2:10; 6:9; 11:20; 13:1

33 ᵃMatt. 27:34-44: *Mark 15:22-32; Luke 23:33-43; John 19:17-24* ᵇJohn 19:17; Luke 23:33 and marg.

31 ᵃPs. 69:21 ᵇMark 15:23

35 ¹Lit., *a lot*
ᵃPs. 22:18

36 ᵃMatt. 27:54

37 ¹Lit., *written*
ᵃMark 15:26; Luke 23:38; John 19:19

39 ¹Or, *blaspheming*
ᵃMark 15:29; Job 16:4; Ps. 22:7; 109:25; Lam. 2:15

40 ᵃMatt. 26:61 ᵇMatt. 27:42

42 ¹Or, *can He not save Himself*
ᵃMark 15:31; Luke 23:35

multitude, saying, "I am innocent of ¹ᶜthis Man's blood; ᵈsee *to that* yourselves."

25   And all the people answered and said, "ᵃHis blood *be* on us and on our children!"

26   Then he released Barabbas ¹for them; but Jesus he ᵃscourged and delivered over to be crucified.

27   ᵃThen the soldiers of the governor took Jesus into ᵇthe Praetorium and gathered the whole *Roman* ¹ᶜcohort around Him.

28   And they stripped Him, and ᵃput a scarlet robe on Him.

29   ᵃAnd after weaving a crown of thorns, they put it on His head, and a ¹reed in His right hand; and they kneeled down before Him and mocked Him, saying, "ᵇHail, King of the Jews!"

30   And ᵃthey spat on Him, and took the reed and *began* to beat Him on the head.

31   ᵃAnd after they had mocked Him, they took His robe off and put His garments on Him, and led Him away to crucify *Him.*

32   ᵃAnd as they were coming out, they found a ¹certain ᵇCyrenian named Simon; this man they pressed into service to bear His cross.

33   ᵃAnd when they had come to a place called ᵇGolgotha, which means Place of a Skull,

34   ᵃTHEY GAVE HIM ᵇWINE TO DRINK MINGLED WITH GALL; and after tasting *it,* He was unwilling to drink.

35   And when they had crucified Him, ᵃTHEY DIVIDED UP HIS GARMENTS AMONG THEMSELVES, CASTING ¹LOTS;

36   and sitting down, they *began* to ᵃkeep watch over Him there.

37   And they put up above His head the charge against Him ¹which read, "ᵃTHIS IS JESUS THE KING OF THE JEWS."

38   At that time two robbers *were crucified with Him, one on the right and one on the left.

39   And those who were passing by were ¹hurling abuse at Him, ᵃWAGGING THEIR HEADS,

40   and saying, "ᵃYou who destroy the temple and rebuild it in three days, save Yourself! ᵇIf You are the Son of God, come down from the cross."

41   In the same way the chief priests, along with the scribes and elders, were mocking *Him,* and saying,

42   "ᵃHe saved others; ¹He cannot save Himself.

The Death of Jesus. The Temple Curtain Torn.

Matthew 27

[b]He is the King of Israel; let Him now come down from the cross, and we shall believe in Him.

43 "[a]HE TRUSTS IN GOD; LET HIM DELIVER *Him* now, IF HE TAKES PLEASURE IN HIM; for He said, 'I am the Son of God.'"

44 [a]And the robbers also who had been crucified with Him were casting the same insult at Him.

45 [a]Now from the [1]sixth hour darkness [2]fell upon all the land until the [3]ninth hour.

46 And about the ninth hour Jesus cried out with a loud voice, saying, "ELI, ELI LAMA SABACHTHANI?" that is, "[a]MY GOD, MY GOD, WHY HAST THOU FORSAKEN ME?"

47 And some of those who were standing there, when they heard it, *began* saying, "This man is calling for Elijah."

48 And [a]immediately one of them ran, and taking a sponge, he filled it with sour wine, and put it on a reed, and gave Him a drink.

49 But the rest *of them* said, "[1]Let us see whether Elijah will come to save Him."[2]

50 And Jesus [a]cried out again with a loud voice, and yielded up *His* spirit.

51 [a]And behold, [b]the veil of the temple was torn in two from top to bottom, and [c]the earth shook; and the rocks were split,

52 and the tombs were opened; and many bodies of the [1]saints who had [a]fallen asleep were raised;

53 and coming out of the tombs after His resurrection they entered [a]the holy city and appeared to many.

54 [a]Now the centurion, and those who were with him [b]keeping guard over Jesus, when they saw [c]the earthquake and the things that were happening, became very frightened and said, "Truly this was [1][d]the Son of God!"

55 [a]And many women were there looking on from a distance, who had followed Jesus from Galilee, [1][b]ministering to Him;

56 among whom was [a]Mary Magdalene, *along with* Mary the mother of James and Joseph, and [b]the mother of the sons of Zebedee.

57 [a]And when it was evening, there came a rich man from Arimathea, named Joseph, who himself had also become a disciple of Jesus.

58 This man came to Pilate and asked for the

42 [b]John 1:49; 12:13; Matt. 27:37; Luke 23:37

43 [a]Ps. 22:8

44 [a]Luke 23:39-43

45 [1]I.e., noon [2]Or, *occurred* [3]I.e., 3 p.m. [a]Matt. 27:45-56: *Mark 15:33-41; Luke 23:44-49*

46 [a]Ps. 22:1

48 [a]Mark 15:36; Luke 23:36; John 19:29

49 [1]Lit., *Permit that we see* [2]Some early mss. add: *And another took a spear and pierced His side, and there came out water and blood.* (cf. John 19:34)

50 [a]Mark 15:37; Luke 23:46; John 19:30

51 [a]Matt. 27:51-56: *Mark 15:38-41;* Luke 23:47-49 [b]Mark 15:38; Luke 23:45; Ex. 26:31ff.; Heb. 9:3 [c]Matt. 27:54

52 [1]I.e. true believers; lit., *holy ones* [a]Acts 7:60

53 [a]Matt. 4:5

54 [1]Or, possibly, *a son of God,* or, *a son of a god* [b]Mark 15:39; Luke 23:47 [c]Matt. 27:36 [c]Matt. 27:51 [d]Matt. 4:3; Matt. 27:43

55 [1]Or, *waiting on* [a]Mark 15:40f.; Luke 23:49; John 19:25 [b]Luke 8:2, 3; Mark 15:41

56 [a]Matt. 28:1; Mark 15:40, 47; 16:9; Luke 8:2; John 19:25; 20:1, 18 [b]Matt. 20:20

57 [a]Matt. 27:57-61: *Mark 15:42-47; Luke 23:50-56; John 19:38-42*

Matthew 27, 28

The Burial of Jesus.
Guards Posted.   The Resurrection.

60 ªMark 16:4; Matt. 27:66;
28:2

body of Jesus. Then Pilate ordered *it* to be given over *to him.*

59   And Joseph took the body and wrapped it in a clean linen cloth,

60   and laid it in his own new tomb, which he had hewn out in the rock; and he rolled ªa large stone against the entrance of the tomb and went away.

61 ªMatt. 27:56; 28:1

61   And ªMary Magdalene was there, and the other Mary, sitting opposite the grave.

62 ¹Or, *Friday*
ªMark 15:42; Luke 23:54;
John 19:14, 31, 42

62   Now on the next day, which is *the one* after ¹ªthe preparation, the chief priests and the Pharisees gathered together with Pilate,

63   and said, "Sir, we remember that when he was still alive that deceiver said, 'ªAfter three days I *am to* rise again.'

63 ªMatt. 16:21

64   "Therefore, give orders for the grave to be made secure until the third day, lest the disciples come and steal Him away and say to the people, 'He has risen from the dead,' and the last deception will be worse than the first."

65 ªMatt. 27:66; 28:11

65   Pilate said to them, "You have a ªguard; go, make it *as* secure as you know how."

66 ªMatt. 27:65; 28:11
ᵇDan. 6:17 ᶜMark 16:4;
Matt. 27:60; 28:2

66   And they went and made the grave secure, and along with ªthe guard they set a ᵇseal on ᶜthe stone.

1 ªMatt. 28:1-8: *Mark*
16:1-8; Luke 24:1-10; John
20:1-8 ᵇMatt. 27:56, 61

a   CHAPTER 28

NOW late on the Sabbath, as it began to dawn toward the first *day* of the week, ᵇMary Magdalene and the other Mary came to look at the grave.

2 ªLuke 24:4; John 20:12
ᵇMark 16:4; Matt. 27:66;
28:2

2   And behold, a severe earthquake had occurred, for ªan angel of the Lord descended from heaven and came and rolled away ᵇthe stone and sat upon it.

3 ªDan. 7:9; 10:6; Mark
9:3; John 20:12; Acts 1:10

3   And ªhis appearance was like lightning, and his garment as white as snow;

4   and the guards shook for fear of him, and became like dead men.

5 ¹Or, *Stop being afraid*
ªMatt. 28:10; 14:27

5   And the angel answered and said to the women, "¹ªDo not be afraid; for I know that you are looking for Jesus who has been crucified.

6   "He is not here, for He has risen, ªjust as He said. Come, see the place where He was lying.

6 ªMatt. 27:63; Matt.
12:40; 16:21

7   "And go quickly and tell His disciples that He has risen from the dead; and behold, He is

going before you [a]into Galilee, there you will see Him; behold, I have told you."

8 And they departed quickly from the tomb with fear and great joy and ran to report it to His disciples.

9 And behold, Jesus met them [1]and greeted them. And they came up and took hold of His feet and worshiped Him.

10 Then Jesus *said to them, "[1][a]Do not be afraid; go and take word to [b]My brethren to leave [c]for Galilee, and there they shall see Me."

11 Now while they were on their way, behold, some of [a]the guard came into the city and reported to the chief priests all that had happened.

12 And when they had assembled with the elders and counseled together, they gave a large sum of money to the soldiers,

13 and said, "You are to say, 'His disciples came by night and stole Him away while we were asleep.'

14 "And if this should come to [a]the governor's ears, we will win him over and [1]keep you out of trouble."

15 And they took the money and did as they had been instructed; and this story was widely [a]spread among the Jews, *and is* [b]to this day.

16 But the eleven disciples proceeded [a]to Galilee, to the mountain which Jesus had designated.

17 And when they saw Him, they worshiped *Him*; but [a]some were doubtful.

18 And Jesus came up and spoke to them, saying, "[a]All authority has been given to Me in heaven and on earth.

19 "[a]Go therefore and [b]make disciples of [c]all the nations, [d]baptizing them [1]in the name of the Father and the Son and the Holy Spirit,

20 teaching them to observe all that I commanded you; and lo, [a]I am with you [1]always, even to [b]the end of the age."

7 [a]Matt. 26:32; 28:10, 16

9 [1]Lit., *saying hello*

10 [1]Or, *Stop being afraid*
[a]Matt. 28:5; 14:27 [b]John
20:17; Rom. 8:29; Heb.
2:11f., 17 [c]Matt. 26:32; 28:7,
16

11 [a]Matt. 27:65, 66

14 [1]Lit., *make you free
from care*
[a]Matt. 27:2

15 [a]Matt. 9:31; Mark 1:45
[b]Matt. 27:8

16 [a]Matt. 26:32; 28:7, 10

17 [a]Mark 16:11

18 [a]Matt. 26:64; Dan.
7:13f.; Rom. 14:9; Eph. 1:20-
22; Phil. 2:9f.; Col. 2:10;
1 Pet. 3:22; Matt. 11:27

19 [1]Lit., *into*
[a]Mark 16:15f. [b]Matt.
13:52; Acts 14:21 [c]Luke
24:47; Matt. 25:32 [d]Acts
2:38; 8:16; Rom. 6:3; 1 Cor.
1:13, 15ff.; Gal. 3:27

20 [1]Lit., *all the days*
[a]Matt. 18:20; Acts 18:10
[b]Matt. 13:39

THE GOSPEL

ACCORDING TO

MARK

Preaching of the Baptist. Baptism of Jesus. Temptation of Jesus.

1 ¹Many mss. omit, *the Son of God*
ªMatt. 4:3

2 ªMark 1:2-8: *Matt. 3:1-11; Luke 3:2-16* ᵇMal. 3:1; Matt. 11:10; Luke 7:27

3 ªIs. 40:3; Matt. 3:3; Luke 3:4; John 1:23

4 ¹Or, *proclaiming* ªActs 13:24; ᵇLuke 1:77

6 ¹Lit., *he was eating*

7 ¹Or, *proclaiming*

8 ¹The Greek here can be translated *in, with* or *by*

9 ªMark 1:9-11: *Matt. 3:13-17; Luke 3:21, 22* ᵇMatt. 2:23; Luke 2:51

10 ¹Or, *being parted*

11 ªLuke 3:22; Matt. 3:17

12 ªMark 1:12, 13: *Matt. 4:1-11; Luke 4:1-13*

THE beginning of the gospel of Jesus Christ, ¹ªthe Son of God.

2 ªAs it is written in Isaiah the prophet,
"ᵇBEHOLD, I SEND MY MESSENGER BEFORE YOUR FACE,
WHO WILL PREPARE YOUR WAY;

3 "ªTHE VOICE OF ONE CRYING IN THE WILDERNESS,
'MAKE READY THE WAY OF THE LORD,
MAKE HIS PATHS STRAIGHT.' "

4 John the Baptist appeared in the wilderness ¹ªpreaching a baptism of repentance for the ᵇforgiveness of sins.

5 And all the country of Judea was going out to him, and all the people of Jerusalem; and they were being baptized by him in the Jordan River, confessing their sins.

6 And John was clothed with camel's hair and *wore* a leather belt around his waist, and ¹his diet was locusts and wild honey.

7 And he was ¹preaching, and saying, "After me comes One who is mightier than I, and I am not *even* fit to stoop down and untie the thong of His sandals.

8 "I baptized you ¹with water; but He will baptize you ¹with the Holy Spirit."

9 ªAnd it came about in those days that Jesus ᵇcame from Nazareth in Galilee, and was baptized by John in the Jordan.

10 And immediately coming up out of the water, he saw the heavens ¹opening, and the Spirit like a dove descending upon Him;

11 and a voice came out of the heavens: "ªThou art My beloved Son, in Thee I am well pleased."

12 ªAnd immediately the Spirit *impelled Him *to go* out into the wilderness.

13 And He was in the wilderness forty days

being tempted by ªSatan; and He was with the wild beasts, and the angels were ministering to Him.

14   ªAnd after John had been ¹taken into custody, Jesus came into Galilee, ²ᵇpreaching the gospel of God,

15   and saying, "ªThe time is fulfilled, and the kingdom of God is at hand; ᵇrepent and ¹believe in the gospel."

16   ªAnd as He was going along by the sea of Galilee, He saw Simon and Andrew, the brother of Simon, casting a net in the sea; for they were fishermen.

17   And Jesus said to them, "Follow Me, and I will make you become fishers of men."

18   And they immediately left the nets and followed Him.

19   And going on a little farther, He saw ¹James the *son* of Zebedee, and John his brother, who were also in the boat mending the nets.

20   And immediately He called them; and they left their father Zebedee in the boat with the hired servants, ¹and went away to follow Him.

21   ªAnd they *went into Capernaum; and immediately on the Sabbath ᵇHe entered the synagogue and *began* to teach.

22   And ªthey were amazed at His teaching; for He was teaching them as *one* having authority, and not as the scribes.

23   And just then there was in their synagogue a man with an unclean spirit; and he cried out,

24   saying, "ªWhat do we have to do with You, Jesus of ¹ᵇNazareth? Have You come to destroy us? I know who You are—ᶜthe Holy One of God!"

25   And Jesus rebuked him, saying, "Be quiet, and come out of him!"

26   And throwing him into convulsions, the unclean spirit cried out with a loud voice, and came out of him.

27   And they were all ªamazed, so that they debated among themselves, saying, "What is this? A new teaching with authority! He commands even the unclean spirits, and they obey Him."

28   And immediately the news about Him went out everywhere into all the surrounding district of Galilee.

29   ªAnd immediately ¹after they had come ᵇout of the synagogue, they came into the house of Simon and Andrew, with ²James and John.

13 ªMatt. 4:10

14 ¹Lit., *delivered up* ²Or, *proclaiming* ªMatt. 4:12 ᵇMatt. 4:23

15 ¹Or, *put your trust in* ªGal. 4:4; Eph. 1:10; 1 Tim. 2:6; Titus 1:3 ᵇActs 20:21

16 ªMark 1:16-20: *Matt. 4:18-22; Luke 5:2-11; John 1:40-42*

19 ¹Or, *Jacob*

20 ¹Lit., *after Him*

21 ªMark 1:21-28; Luke 4:31-37 ᵇMatt. 4:23; Mark 1:39; 10:1

22 ªMatt. 7:28

24 ¹Lit., *Nazarene* ªMatt. 8:29 ᵇMark 10:47; 14:67; 16:6; Luke 4:34; 24:19; Matt. 2:23; Acts 24:5 ᶜLuke 4:34; John 6:69; Luke 1:35; Acts 3:14

27 ªMark 10:24, 32; Mark 14:33; 16:5, 6

29 ¹Some mss. read: *after He had come out, He came* ²Or, *Jacob* ªMark 1:29-31: *Matt. 8:14, 15; Luke 4:38, 39* ᵇMark 1:21, 23

Mark 1

Heals Simon's Mother-in-law.   Heals Many and
Casts Out Demons.   Cleanses a Leper.

31 [1]Or, *serve*

32 [a]Mark 1:32-34; *Matt.
8:16, 17; Luke 4:40, 41*
[b]Matt. 8:16; Luke 4:40
[c]Matt. 4:24

33 [a]Mark 1:21

34 [1]Some mss. read: *knew
Him to be Christ*
[a]Matt. 4:23

35 [a]Mark 1:35-38; *Luke
4:42, 43* [b]Luke 5:16; Matt.
14:23

38 [1]Or, *proclaim*

39 [1]Or, *proclaiming*
[a]Matt. 4:23; Mark 1:23; 3:1

40 [a]Mark 1:40-44; *Matt.
8:2-4; Luke 5:12-14* [b]Mark
10:17; Matt. 8:2; Luke 5:12

44 [a]Matt. 8:4 [b]Matt. 8:4

45 [1]Lit., *was*
[a]Luke 5:15; Matt. 28:15
[b]Mark 2:2, 13; 3:7; Luke
5:17; John 6:2

30   Now Simon's mother-in-law was lying sick with a fever; and immediately they *spoke to Him about her.

31   And He came to her and raised her up, taking her by the hand, and the fever left her, and she began to [1]wait on them.

32   [a]And [b]when evening had come, [b]after the sun had set, they *began* bringing to Him all who were ill and those who were [c]demon-possessed.

33   And the whole [a]city had gathered at the door.

34   And He [a]healed many who were ill with various diseases, and cast out many demons; and He was not permitting the demons to speak, because they [1]knew who He was.

35   [a]And in the early morning, while it was still dark, He arose and went out and departed to a lonely place, and [b]was praying there.

36   And Simon and his companions hunted for Him;

37   and they found Him, and *said to Him, "Everyone is looking for You."

38   And He *said to them, "Let us go somewhere else to the towns nearby, in order that I may [1]preach there also; for that is what I came out for."

39   [a]And He went into their synagogues throughout all Galilee, [1]preaching and casting out the demons.

40   [a]And a leper *came to Him, beseeching Him and [b]falling on his knees before Him, and saying to Him, "If You are willing, You can make me clean."

41   And moved with compassion, He stretched out His hand and touched him, and *said to him, "I am willing; be cleansed."

42   And immediately the leprosy left him and he was cleansed.

43   And He sternly warned him and immediately sent him away,

44   and He *said to him, "[a]See that you say nothing to anyone; but [b]go, show yourself to the priest and offer for your cleansing what Moses commanded, for a testimony to them."

45   But he went out and began to [a]proclaim it freely and to [a]spread the news about, to such an extent that Jesus could no longer publicly enter a city, but [1]stayed out in unpopulated areas; and [b]they were coming to Him from everywhere.

CHAPTER 2

A<small>ND</small> when He had come back to Capernaum several days afterward, it was heard that He was at home.

2   And [a]many were gathered together, so that there was no longer room, even near the door; and He was speaking the word to them.

3   [a]And they *came, bringing to Him a [b]paralytic, carried by four men.

4   And being unable to [1]get to Him on account of the crowd, they [a]removed the roof [2]above Him; and when they had dug an opening, they let down the pallet on which the [b]paralytic was lying.

5   And Jesus seeing their faith *said to the paralytic, "My [1]son, [a]your sins are forgiven."

6   But there were some of the scribes sitting there and reasoning in their hearts,

7   "Why does this man speak that way? He is blaspheming; [a]who can forgive sins [1]but God alone?"

8   And immediately Jesus, perceiving [1]in His spirit that they were reasoning that way within themselves, *said to them, "Why are you reasoning about these things in your hearts?

9   "Which is easier, to say to the [a]paralytic, 'Your sins are forgiven;' or to say, 'Arise, and take up your pallet and walk'?

10   "But in order that you may know that the Son of Man has authority on earth to forgive sins"—He *said to the paralytic,

11   "I say to you, rise, take up your pallet and go home."

12   And he rose and immediately took up the pallet and went out in the sight of all; so that they were all amazed and [a]were glorifying God, saying, "[b]We have never seen anything like this."

13   And He went out again by the seashore; and [a]all the multitude were coming to Him, and He was teaching them.

14   [a]And as He passed by, He saw [b]Levi the *son* of Alpheus sitting in the tax office, and He *said to him, "[c]Follow Me!" And he rose and followed Him.

15   And it [1]came about that He was reclining *at table* in his house, and many [2]tax-gatherers and sinners [3]were dining with Jesus and His disciples;

2 [a]Mark 2:13; Mark 1:45

3 [a]Mark 2:3-12: *Matt. 9:2-8; Luke 5:18-26* [b]Matt. 4:24

4 [1]Lit., *bring to* [2]Lit., *where He was* [a]Luke 5:19 [b]Matt. 4:24

5 [1]Lit., *child* [a]Matt. 9:2

7 [1]Lit., *if not one, God* [a]Is. 43:25

8 [1]Lit., *by*

9 [a]Matt. 4:24

12 [a]Matt. 9:8 [b]Matt. 9:33

13 [a]Mark 1:45

14 [a]Mark 2:14-17: *Matt. 9:9-13; Luke 5:27-32* [b]Matt. 9:9 [c]Matt. 8:22

15 [1]Lit., *comes* [2]Publicans who collected Roman taxes for profit [3]Lit., *were reclining with*

Mark 2

"Came . . . to Call Sinners."
Of Fasting. "Lord of the Sabbath."

16 [a]Acts 23:9; Luke 5:30
[b]Matt. 9:11

17 [a]Matt. 9:12, 13; Luke 5:31, 32

18 [a]Mark 2:18-22: Matt. 9:14-17; Luke 5:33-38

19 [1]Lit., sons of the bridalchamber

20 [a]Luke 17:22; Matt. 9:15

21 [1]Lit., that which is put on [2]Lit., that which fills up

22 [1]I.e., skins used as bottles

23 [a]Mark 2:23-28: Matt. 12:1-8; Luke 6:1-5 [b]Deut. 23.25

24 [a]Matt. 12:2

26 [1]Or, showbread; lit., loaves of presentation [a]1 Chr. 24:6; 1 Sam. 21:1; 2 Sam. 8:17

27 [1]Or, came into being [2]Lit., for the sake of [a]Ex. 23:12; Deut. 5:14 [b]Col. 2:16

for there were many of them, and they were following Him.

16 And when [a]the scribes of the Pharisees saw that He was eating with the sinners and tax-gatherers, they *began* saying to His disciples, "[b]Why is He eating and drinking with tax-gatherers and sinners?"

17 And hearing this, Jesus *said to them, "[a]*It is not* those who are healthy who need a physician, but those who are sick; I did not come to call *the* righteous, but sinners."

18 [a]And John's disciples and the Pharisees were fasting; and they *came and *said to Him, "Why do John's disciples and the disciples of the Pharisees fast, but Your disciples do not fast?"

19 And Jesus said to them, "While the bridegroom is with them, [1]the attendants of the bridegroom do not fast, do they? So long as they have the bridegroom with them, they cannot fast.

20 But the [a]days will come when the bridegroom is taken away from them, and then they will fast in that day.

21 "No one sews a [1]patch of unshrunk cloth on an old garment; otherwise the [2]patch pulls away from it, the new from the old, and a worse tear results.

22 "And no one puts new wine into old [1]wineskins; otherwise the wine will burst the skins, and the wine is lost, and the skins *as well;* but *one puts* new wine into fresh wineskins."

23 [a]And it came about that He was passing through the grainfields on the Sabbath, and His disciples began to make their way along while [b]picking the heads *of grain.*

24 And the Pharisees were saying to Him, "See here, [a]why are they doing what is not lawful on the Sabbath?"

25 And He *said to them, "Have you never read what David did when he was in need and became hungry, he and his companions:

26 "How he entered into the house of God in the time of [a]Abiathar *the* high priest, and ate the [1]consecrated bread, which is not lawful for *anyone* to eat except the priests, and he gave *it* also to those who were with him?"

27 And He was saying to them, "[a]The Sabbath [1]was made [2]for man, and [b]not man [2]for the Sabbath.

28 "Consequently, the Son of Man is Lord even of the Sabbath."

1 ªMark 3:1-6: *Matt. 12:9-14; Luke 6:6-11* ᵇMark 1:21, 39

ª CHAPTER 3

AND He ᵇentered again into a synagogue; and a man was there with a withered hand.

2   And ªthey were watching Him *to see* if He would heal him on the Sabbath, ᵇin order that they might accuse Him.

2 ªLuke 6:7; 14:1; 20:20 ᵇMatt. 12:10; Luke 6:7; Luke 11:54

3   And He *said to the man with the withered hand, "[1]Rise and *come* forward!"

3 [1]Lit., *arise into the midst*

4   And He *said to them, "Is it lawful on the Sabbath to do good or to do harm, to save a life or to kill?" But they kept silent.

5   And after ªlooking around at them with anger, grieved at their hardness of heart, He *said to the man, "Stretch out your hand." And he stretched it out, and his hand was restored.

5 ªLuke 6:10

6   And the Pharisees went out and immediately *began* [1]taking counsel with the ªHerodians against Him, *as to* how they might destroy Him.

6 [1]Lit., *giving* ªMatt. 22:16; Mark 12.13

7   ªAnd Jesus withdrew to the sea with His disciples; and ᵇa great multitude from Galilee followed; and *also* from Judea,

7 ªMark 3:7-12: *Matt. 12:15, 16; Luke 6:17-19* ᵇMatt. 4:25; Luke 6:17

8   and from Jerusalem, and from ªIdumea, and beyond the Jordan, and the vicinity of ᵇTyre and Sidon, a great multitude heard of all that He was doing and came to Him.

8 ªJosh. 15:1, 21; Ezek. 35:15; 36:5 ᵇMatt. 11:21

9   And He told His disciples that a boat should stand ready for Him because of the multitude, in order that they might not crowd Him;

10   for He had ªhealed many, with the result that all those who had ᵇafflictions pressed about Him in order to ᶜtouch Him.

10 ªMatt. 4:23 ᵇMark 5:29, 34; Luke 7:21 ᶜMark 6:56; 8:22; Matt 9:21; 14:36

11   And whenever the unclean spirits beheld Him, they would fall down before Him and cry out, saying, "You are ªthe Son of God!"

11 ªMatt. 4:3

12   And He ªearnestly warned them not to [1]reveal His identity.

12 [1]Lit., *make Him manifest* ªMatt. 8:4

13   And He *went up to ªthe mountain and *ᵇsummoned those whom He Himself wanted, and they came to Him.

13 ªLuke 6:12; Matt 5:1 ᵇMatt 10:1; Mark 6:7; Luke 9:1-6

14   And He appointed twelve[1], that they might be with Him, and that He might send them out to preach,

15   and to have authority to cast out the demons.

14 [1]Some early mss. add: *whom He named apostles*

16 aMark 3:16-19: Matt.
10:2-4; Luke 6:14-16; Acts
1:13; names in Matthew's
list.

17 1Or, Jacob

18 1Or, Jacob 2Or, the
Zealot

20 1Lit., into a house 2Lit.,
bread
aMark 2:1; 7:17; 9:28 bMark
1:45; Mark 3:7 cMark 6:31

21 1Or, kinsmen
aMark 3:31f. bJohn 10:20;
Acts 26:24

22 1Or, Beezebul; others
read: Beelzebub
aMatt. 15:1 bMatt. 10:25;
Matt. 11:18 cMatt. 9:34

23 aMark 3:23-27: Matt.
12:25-29; Luke 11:17-22
bMark 4:2; Matt. 13:3ff.;
Mark 4:2ff.; cMatt. 4:10

26 1Lit., he has an end
aMatt. 4:10

27 aIs. 49:24, 25

28 aMark 3:28-30; Matt.
12:31, 32; Luke 12:10

31 aMark 3:31-35: Matt.
12:46-50; Luke 8:19-21

32 1Later mss. add: and
Your sisters

16 And He appointed the twelve: aSimon (to whom He gave the name Peter),

17 and 1James, the *son* of Zebedee, and John the brother of 1James (to them He gave the name Boanerges, which means, "Sons of thunder");

18 and Andrew, and Philip, and Bartholomew, and Matthew, and Thomas, and 1James the *son* of Alphaeus, and Thaddaeus, and Simon 2the Cananaean;

19 and Judas Iscariot, who also betrayed Him.

20 And He *came 1ahome, and the bmultitude *gathered again, cto such an extent that they could not even eat 2a meal.

21 And when aHis own 1people heard *of this*, they went out to take custody of Him; for they were saying, "bHe has lost His senses."

22 And the scribes who came down afrom Jerusalem were saying, "He is possessed by 1bBeelzebul," and "cHe casts out the demons by the ruler of the demons."

23 aAnd He called them to Himself and began speaking to them in bparables, "How can cSatan cast out Satan?

24 "And if a kingdom is divided against itself, that kingdom cannot stand.

25 "And if a house is divided against itself, that house will not be able to stand.

26 "And if aSatan has risen up against himself and is divided, he cannot stand, but 1he is finished!

27 "aBut no one can enter the strong man's house and plunder his property unless he first binds the strong man, and then he will plunder his house.

28 "aTruly I say to you, all sins shall be forgiven the sons of men, and whatever blasphemies they utter;

29 but whoever blasphemes against the Holy Spirit never has forgiveness, but is guilty of an eternal sin;" —

30 because they were saying, "He has an unclean spirit."

31 aAnd His mother and His brothers *arrived, and standing outside they sent *word* to Him, and called Him.

32 And a multitude was sitting around Him, and they *said to Him, "Behold, Your mother and Your brothers1 are outside looking for You."

33 And answering them, He *said, "Who are My mother and My brothers?"

34   And looking about on those who were sitting around Him, He *said, "Behold, My mother and My brothers!

35   "For whoever does the will of God, he is My brother and sister and mother."

ᵃ   CHAPTER 4

AND He began to teach again ᵇby the seashore. And such a very great multitude ¹gathered before Him that He got into a boat in the sea and sat down; and all the multitude were by the seashore on the land.

2   And He was teaching them many things in ᵃparables, and was saying to them in His teaching,

3   "Listen *to this*! Behold, the sower went out to sow;

4   and it came about that as he was sowing, some *seed* fell beside the road, and the birds came and ate it up.

5   "And other *seed* fell on the rocky *ground* where it did not have much soil; and immediately it sprang up because it had no depth of soil.

6   "And after the sun had risen, it was scorched; and because it had no root, it withered away.

7   "And other *seed* fell among the thorns, and the thorns grew up and choked it, and it yielded no crop.

8   "And other *seeds* fell into the good soil and as they grew up and increased, they were yielding a crop and were producing thirty, sixty, and a hundredfold."

9   And He was saying, "ᵃHe who has ears to hear, let him hear."

10   And as soon as He was alone, ¹His followers, along with the twelve, *began* asking Him *about* the parables.

11   And He was saying to them, "To you has been given the mystery of the kingdom of God; but ᵃthose who are outside get everything ᵇin parables;

12   ᵃin order that WHILE SEEING, THEY MAY SEE AND NOT PERCEIVE; AND WHILE HEARING, THEY MAY HEAR AND NOT UNDERSTAND; LEST THEY RETURN AGAIN AND BE FORGIVEN."

13   ᵃAnd He *said to them, "Do you not understand this parable? And how will you understand all the parables?

14   "The sower sows the word.

---

1 ¹Lit., *is gathered*
ᵃMark 4:1-12: *Matt. 13:1-15; Luke 8:4-10* ᵇMark 2:13; 3:7

2 ᵃMark 3:23; Matt. 13:3ff.; Mark 4:2ff.

9 ᵃMatt. 11:15; Mark 4:23

10 ¹Lit., *those about Him*

11 ᵃ1 Cor. 5:12f.; Col. 4:5; 1 Thess. 4:12; 1 Tim. 3:7 ᵇMark 4:2; Mark 3:23

12 ᵃIs. 6:9; Matt. 13:14

13 ᵃMark 4:13-20: *Matt. 13:18-23; Luke 8:11-15*

15 ᵃMatt. 4:10

15 "And these are the ones who are beside the road where the word is sown; and when they hear, immediately ᵃSatan comes and takes away the word which has been sown in them.

16 "And in a similar way these are the ones on whom seed was sown on the rocky *places*, who, when they hear the word, immediately receive it with joy;

17 ¹Lit., *are caused to stumble*

17 and they have no *firm* root in themselves, but are *only* temporary; then, when affliction or persecution arises because of the word, immediately they ¹fall away.

18 "And others are the ones on whom seed was sown among the thorns; these are the ones who have heard the word,

19 ¹Or, *age*
ᵃMatt. 13:22

19 and the worries of ᵃthe ¹world, and the deceitfulness of riches, and the desires for other things enter in and choke the word, and it becomes unfruitful.

20 "And those are the ones on whom seed was sown on the good ground; and they hear the word and accept it, and bear fruit, thirty, sixty, and a hundredfold."

21 ᵃMatt. 5:15; Luke 8:16; 11:33

21 And He was saying to them, "ᵃA lamp is not brought to be put under a peck-measure, is it, or under a bed? Is it not *brought* to be put on the lampstand?

22 ᵃMatt. 10:26; Luke 8:17; 12:2

22 "For nothing is hidden, except to be revealed; nor has *anything* been secret, but that it should come to light.

23 ᵃMark 4:9; Matt. 11:15

23 "ᵃIf any man has ears to hear, let him hear."

24 ¹Lit., *by what measure you measure*
ᵃMatt. 7:2; Luke 6:38

24 And He was saying to them, "Take care what you listen to; ¹ᵃby your standard of measure it shall be measured to you; and more shall be given you besides.

25 ᵃMatt. 13:12

25 "ᵃFor whoever has, to him shall *more* be given; and whoever does not have, even what he has shall be taken away from him."

26 And He was saying, "ᵃThe kingdom of God is like a man who cast seed upon the ground;

26 ᵃMark 4:26-29; Matt. 13:24-30

27 and goes to bed at night and gets up by day, and the seed sprouts up and grows — how, he himself does not know.

28 "The earth produces crops by itself; first the blade, then the head, then the mature grain in the head.

29 ¹Lit., *sends forth*

29 "But when the crop permits, he immediately ¹puts in the sickle, because the harvest has come."

30 aAnd He said, "How shall we 1bpicture the kingdom of God, or by what parable shall we present it?

31 "*It is* like a mustard seed, which, when sown upon the ground, though it is smaller than all the seeds that are upon the ground,

32 yet when it is sown, grows up and becomes larger than all the garden plants and forms large branches; so that the birds of the 1air can nest under its shade."

33 And with many such parables He was speaking the word to them as they were able to hear it;

34 and He was not speaking to them awithout 1parables; but He was explaining everything privately to His own disciples.

35 aAnd on that day, when evening had come, He *said to them, "Let us go over to the other side."

36 And 1leaving the multitude, they *took Him along with them, just as He was, ain the boat; and other boats were with Him.

37 And there *arose a fierce gale of wind, and the waves were breaking over the boat so much that the boat was already filling up.

38 And He Himself was in the stern, asleep on the cushion; and they *awoke Him and *said to Him, "Teacher, do You not care that we are perishing?"

39 And being aroused, He rebuked the wind and said to the sea, "Hush, be still." And the wind died down and 1it became perfectly calm.

40 And He said to them, "Why are you so timid? How is it that you have no faith?"

41 And they became very much afraid and said to one another, "Who then is this, that even the wind and the sea obey Him?"

a   CHAPTER 5

AND they came to the other side of the sea, into the country of the Gerasenes.

2 And when He had come out of athe boat, immediately a man from the tombs bwith an unclean spirit met Him,

3 and he had his dwelling among the tombs; and no one was able to bind him any more, even with a chain;

4 because he had often been bound with

---

30 1Lit., *compare*
aMark 4:30-32: *Matt. 13:31, 32; Luke 13:18, 19* bMatt. 13:24

32 1Or, *sky*

34 1Lit., *a parable*
aMatt. 13:34; John 10:6; 16:25

35 aMark 4:35-41: *Matt. 8:18, 23-27; Luke 8:22, 25*

36 1Or, *sending away*
aMark 4:1; 5:2, 21; Mark 3:9

39 1Lit., *a great calm occurred*

1 aMark 5:1-17: *Matt. 8:28-34; Luke 8:26-37*

2 aMark 4:1, 36; 5:21; Mark 3:9 bMark 1:23

79

7 aMatt. 8:29 bMatt. 4:3
cLuke 8:28; Acts 16:17; Heb.
7:1

9 aMark 5:15; Matt. 26:53;
Luke 8:30

13 1Lit., *were drowning*

15 aMark 5:16, 18; Matt.
4:24 bLuke 8:27 cLuke 8:35
dMark 5:9

16 aMark 5:15; Matt. 4:24

18 1Lit., *be with Him*
aMark 5:18-20; *Luke 8:38, 39*
bMark 5:15, 16; Matt. 4:24

shackles and chains, and the chains had been torn apart by him, and the shackles broken in pieces, and no one was strong enough to subdue him.

5   And constantly night and day, among the tombs and in the mountains, he was crying out and gashing himself with stones.

6   And seeing Jesus from a distance, he ran up and bowed down before Him;

7   and crying out with a loud voice, he *said, "aWhat do I have to do with You, Jesus, bSon of cthe Most High God? I implore You by God, do not torment me!"

8   For He had been saying to him, "Come out of the man, you unclean spirit!"

9   And He was asking him, "What is your name?" And he *said to Him, "My name is aLegion; for we are many."

10   And he *began* to entreat Him earnestly not to send them out of the country.

11   Now there was a big herd of swine feeding there on the mountain side.

12   And they entreated Him, saying, "Send us into the swine so that we may enter them."

13   And He gave them permission. And coming out, the unclean spirits entered the swine; and the herd rushed down the steep bank into the sea, about two thousand *of them;* and they 1were drowned in the sea.

14   And those who tended them ran away and reported it in the city and *out* in the country. And *the people* came to see what it was that had happened.

15   And they *came to Jesus and *observed the man who had been ademon-possessed sitting down, bclothed and cin his right mind, the very man who had had the "dlegion;" and they became frightened.

16   And those who had seen it described to them how it had happened to the ademon-possessed man, and *all* about the swine.

17   And they began to entreat Him to depart from their region.

18   aAnd as He was getting into the boat, the man who had been bdemon-possessed was entreating Him that he might 1accompany Him.

19   And He did not let him, but He *said to him, "Go home to your people and report to them

¹what great things the Lord has done for you, and *how* He had mercy on you."

20 And he went off and began to proclaim in ᵃDecapolis ¹what great things Jesus had done for him; and everyone marveled.

21 ᵃAnd when Jesus had crossed over again in ᵇthe boat to the other side, a great multitude gathered about Him; and He ¹stayed ᶜby the seashore.

22 ᵃAnd one of ᵇthe synagogue ¹officials named Jairus *came up, and upon seeing Him, *fell at His feet,

23 and *entreated Him earnestly, saying, "My little daughter is at the point of death; *please* come and ᵃlay Your hands on her, that she may ¹get well and live."

24 And He went off with him; and a great multitude was following Him and pressing in on Him.

25 And a woman who had had a hemorrhage for twelve years,

26 and had endured much at the hands of many physicians, and had spent all that she had and was not helped at all, but rather had grown worse,

27 after hearing about Jesus, came up in the crowd behind *Him,* and touched His ¹cloak.

28 For she ¹thought, "If I just touch His garments, I shall ²get well."

29 And immediately the flow of her blood was dried up; and she felt in her body that she was healed of her ᵃaffliction.

30 And immediately Jesus, perceiving in Himself that ᵃthe power *proceeding* from Him had gone forth, turned around in the crowd and said, "Who touched My garments?"

31 And His disciples said to Him, "You see the multitude pressing in on You, and You say, 'Who touched Me?' "

32 And He looked around to see the woman who had done this.

33 But the woman fearing and trembling, aware of what had happened to her, came and fell down before Him, and told Him the whole truth.

34 And He said to her, "Daughter, ᵃyour faith has ¹made you well; ᵇgo in peace, and be healed of your ᶜaffliction."

35 While He was still speaking, they *came from the *house of* the ᵃsynagogue official, saying,

19 ¹Or, *everything that*

20 ¹Or, *everything that*
ᵃMark 7:31; Matt. 4:25

21 ¹Lit., *was*
ᵃMatt. 9:1; Luke 8:40 ᵇMark 4:36 ᶜMark 4:1

22 ¹Or, *rulers*
ᵃMark 5:22-43: *Matt. 9:18-26; Luke 8:41-56* ᵇMark 5:35, 36, 38; Luke 8:49; 13:14; Acts 13:15; 18:8, 17; Matt. 9:18

23 ¹Lit., *be saved*
ᵃMark 6:5; 7:32; 8:23; 16:18; Luke 4:40; 13:13; Acts 9:17; 28:8; Acts 6:6

27 ¹Or, *outer garment*

28 ¹Lit., *was saying* ²Lit., *be saved*

29 ᵃMark 5:34; Mark 3:10

30 ᵃLuke 5:17

34 ¹Lit., *saved you*
ᵃMatt. 9:22 ᵇLuke 7:50; 8:48; Acts 16:36; James 2:16 ᶜMark 5:29; Mark 3:10

35 ᵃMark 5:22

Mark 5, 6

**The Daughter Raised.
Jesus Teaches at Nazareth and Is Rejected.**

36 [1]Or, *keep on believing*
[a]Mark 5:22 [b]Luke 8:50

37 [1]Or, *Jacob*
[a]Matt. 17:1; 26:37

38 [a]Mark 5:22

41 [a]Luke 7:14; Acts 9:40

43 [a]Matt. 8:4

1 [1]Or, *His own part of the country*
[a]Mark 6:1-6; Matt. 13:54-58
[b]Luke 4:16, 23; Matt. 13:54, 57

2 [1]Or, *works of power*
[a]Matt. 4:23; Mark 10:1
[b]Matt. 7:28

3 [1]Or, *Jacob* [2]Lit., *were being made to stumble*
[a]Matt. 13:55 [b]Matt. 12:46
[c]Matt. 13:56 [d]Matt. 11:6

4 [1]Or, *his own part of the country*
[a]Matt. 13:57 [b]Mark 6:1

5 [1]Or, *work of power*

"Your daughter has died; why trouble the Teacher any more?"

36 But Jesus, overhearing what was being spoken, *said to the [a]synagogue official, "[b]Do not be afraid *any longer*, only [1]believe."

37 And He allowed no one to follow with Him, except [a]Peter and [1]James and John the brother of [1]James.

38 And they *came to the house of the [a]synagogue official; and He *beheld a commotion, and *people* loudly weeping and wailing.

39 And entering in, He *said to them, "Why make a commotion and weep? The child has not died, but is asleep."

40 And they were laughing at Him. But putting them all out, He *took along the child's father and mother and His own companions, and *entered the *room* where the child was.

41 And taking the child by the hand, He *said to her, "Talitha kum!" (which translated means, "Little girl, [a]I say to you, arise!")

42 And immediately the girl got up and *began* to walk; for she was twelve years old. And immediately they were completely astounded.

43 And He [a]gave them strict orders that no one should know about this; and He said that *something* should be given her to eat.

CHAPTER 6
a

AND He went out from there; and He *came into [1b]His home town; and His disciples *followed Him.

2 And when the Sabbath had come, He began [a]to teach in the synagogue; and the [b]many listeners were astonished, saying, "Where did this man *get* these things, and what is *this* wisdom given to Him, and such [1]miracles as these performed by His hands?

3 "Is not this [a]the carpenter, [b]the son of Mary, and brother of [1]James, and Joses, and Judas, and Simon? Are not [c]His sisters here with us?" And they [2]took [d]offense at Him.

4 And Jesus said to them, "[a]A prophet is not without honor except in [1b]his home town and among his *own* relatives and in his *own* household."

5 And He could do no [1]miracle there except

that He [a]laid His hands upon a few sick people and healed them.

6 And He wondered at their unbelief.

[a]And He was going around the villages teaching.

7 [a]And [b]He *[1]summoned the twelve and began to send them out [c]in pairs; and He was giving them authority over the unclean spirits;

8 [a]and He instructed them that they should take nothing for *their* journey, except a mere staff; no bread, no [1]bag, no money in their belt;

9 but [1]*to* wear sandals; and *He added*, "Do not put on two [2]tunics."

10 And He said to them, "Wherever you enter a house, stay there until you [1]leave town.

11 "And any place that does not receive you or listen to you, as you go out from there, [a]shake off the dust [1]from the soles of your feet for a testimony against them."

12 [a]And they went out and [1]preached that *men* should repent.

13 And they were casting out many demons and [a]were anointing with oil many sick people and healing them.

14 [a]And king Herod heard *of it*; for His name had become well known; and *people* were saying, "[b]John the Baptist has risen from the dead, and therefore these miraculous powers are at work in him."

15 But others were saying, "*He is* [a]Elijah." And others were saying, "*He is* [b]a prophet, like one of the prophets *of old*."

16 But when Herod heard *of it*, he kept saying, "John, whom I beheaded, he has risen!"

17 For Herod himself had sent and had John arrested and bound in prison on account of [a]Herodias, the wife of his brother Philip, because he had married her.

18 For John had been saying to Herod, "[a]It is not lawful for you to have your brother's wife."

19 And [a]Herodias had a grudge against him and wanted to kill him; and could not *do so*;

20 for [a]Herod was afraid of John, knowing that he was a righteous and holy man, and kept him safe. And when he heard him, he was very perplexed; [1]but he [2]used to enjoy listening to him.

21 And a strategic day came when Herod on his birthday [a]gave a banquet for his lords and [1]military commanders and the leading men [b]of Galilee;

5 [a]Mark 5:23

6 [a]Matt. 9:35; Luke 13:22; Mark 1:39; 10:1

7 [1]Lit., *summons*
[a]Mark 6:7-11: *Matt. 10:1, 9-14*; *Luke 9:1, 3-5*; Luke 10:4-11 [b]Mark 3:13; Matt. 10:1, 5; Luke 9:1 [c]Luke 10:1

8 [1]Or, *knapsack* or, *beggar's bag*
[a]Matt. 10:10

9 [1]Lit., *being shod with*
[2]Or, *inner garments*

10 [1]Lit., *go out from there*

11 [1]Lit., *under your feet*
[a]Matt. 10:14

12 [1]Or, *proclaimed as a herald*
[a]Matt. 11:1; Luke 9:6

13 [a]James 5:14

14 [a]Mark 6:14-29: *Matt. 14:1-12*; Mark 6:14-16: *Luke 9:7-9* [b]Matt. 14:2

15 [a]Matt. 16:14; Mark 8:28 [b]Matt. 21:11

17 [a]Matt. 14:3

18 [a]Matt. 14:4

19 [a]Matt. 14:3

20 [1]Lit., *and* [2]Lit., *was hearing him gladly*
[a]Matt. 21:26

21 [1]Lit., chiliarchs in command of a thousand troops
[a]Esther 1:3; 2:18 [b]Luke 3:1

Mark 6

John the Baptist Beheaded.
The Five Thousand Fed.

22 [1]Lit., *those who reclined at table with him*
[a]Matt. 14:3

22 and when the daughter of [a]Herodias herself came in and danced, she pleased Herod and his [1]dinner-guests; and the king said to the girl, "Ask me for whatever you want and I will give it to you."

23 And he swore to her, "Whatever you ask of me, I will give it to you; up to [a]half of my kingdom."

23 [a]Esther 5:3, 6; 7:2

24 And she went out and said to her mother, "What shall I ask for?" And she said, "The head of John the Baptist."

25 And immediately she came in haste before the king and asked, saying, "I want you to give me right away the head of John the Baptist on a platter."

26 [1]Lit., *those reclining at table*

26 And although the king was very sorry, *yet* because of his oaths and because of his [1]dinner-guests, he was unwilling to refuse her.

27 And immediately the king sent an executioner and commanded *him* to bring *back* his head. And he went and beheaded him in the prison,

30 [a]Luke 9.10 [b]Matt. 10.2 [Mark 3:14 in Gr.]; Luke 6:13; 9:10; 17:5; 22:14; 24:10; Acts 1:2, 26

28 and brought his head on a platter, and gave it to the girl; and the girl gave it to her mother.

29 And when his disciples heard *about this*, they came and took away his body and laid it in a tomb.

30 [a]And the [b]apostles *gathered together with Jesus; and they reported to Him all that they had done and taught.

31 [a]Mark 3:20

31 And He *said to them, "Come away by yourselves to a lonely place and rest a while." (For there were many *people* coming and going, and [a]they did not even have time to eat.)

32 [a]Mark 6:32-44: Matt. 14:13-21; Luke 9:10-17; John 6:5-13; Mark 8:2-9 [b]Mark 6:45; 3:9; 4:36

32 [a]And they went away in [b]the boat to a lonely place by themselves.

33 And *the people* saw them going, and many recognized *them*, and they ran there together on foot from all the cities, and got there ahead of them.

34 [1]Lit., *having come forth*
[a]Matt. 9:36

34 And [1]disembarking, He [a]saw a great multitude, and He felt compassion for them because [a]they were like sheep without a shepherd; and He began to teach them many things.

35 And when it was already quite late, His disciples came up to Him and *began* saying, "The place is desolate and it is already quite late;

36 [1]Lit., *what they may eat*

36 send them away so that they may go into the surrounding countryside and villages and buy themselves [1]something to eat."

37   But He answered and said to them, "You give them something to eat!" ªAnd they *said to Him, "Shall we go and spend two hundred ¹ᵇdenarii on bread and give them something to eat?"

38   And He *said to them, "How many loaves do you have? Go look!" And when they found out, they *said, "Five and two fish."

39   And He commanded them all to recline by groups on the green grass.

40   And they reclined in companies of hundreds, and of fifties.

41   And He took the five loaves and the two fish, and looking up toward heaven, He ªblessed *the food* and broke the loaves and He kept giving *them* to the disciples to set before them; and He divided up the two fish among them all.

42   And they all ate and were satisfied.

43   And they picked up twelve full ¹ªbaskets of the broken pieces, and also of the fish.

44   And there were ªfive thousand men who ate the loaves.

45   ªAnd immediately He made His disciples get into ᵇthe boat and go ahead of *Him* to the other side to ᶜBethsaida, while He Himself was sending the multitude away.

46   And after ªbidding them farewell, He departed ᵇto the mountain to pray.

47   And when it was evening, the boat was in the midst of the sea, and He *was* alone on the land.

48   And seeing them ¹straining at the oars, for the wind was against them, at about the ²ªfourth watch of the night, He *came to them, walking on the sea; and He intended to pass by them.

49   But when they saw Him walking on the sea, they supposed that it was a ghost, and cried out;

50   for they all saw Him and were ¹frightened. But immediately He spoke with them and *said to them, "ªTake courage; it is I, ᵇdo not be afraid."

51   And He got into ªthe boat with them, and the wind stopped; and they were greatly astonished,

52   for ªthey ¹had not gained any insight from the *incident of* the loaves, but ²their heart ᵇwas hardened.

53   ªAnd when they had crossed over they came to land at Gennesaret, and moored to the shore.

54   And when they had come out of the boat, immediately *the people* recognized Him,

37 ¹A denarius represented a day's wages for a common laborer
ªJohn 6:7 ᵇMatt. 18:28; Luke 7:41

41 ªMatt. 14:19

43 ¹I.e., large-sized baskets
ªMatt. 14:20

44 ªMatt. 14:21

45 ªMark 6:45-51: *Matt. 14:22-32; John 6:15-21* ᵇMark 6:32 ᶜMatt. 11:21; Mark 8:22

46 ªActs 18:18, 21; 2 Cor. 2:13 ᵇMatt. 14:23

48 ¹Lit., *harassed in rowing* ²I.e., 3-6 a.m.
ªMark 13:35; Matt. 24:43

50 ¹Or, *troubled*
ªMatt. 9:2 ᵇMatt. 14:27

51 ªMark 6:32

52 ¹Lit., *had not understood on the basis of* ²Or, *their mind was closed, made dull, or insensible*
ªMark 8:17ff. ᵇRom. 11:7

53 ªMark 6:53-56: *Matt. 14:34-36; John 6:24, 25*

55 [1]Or, *where they were hearing that He was*

56 [a]Mark 3:10 [b]Matt. 9:20

1 [a]Mark 7:1-23: *Matt. 15:1-20* [b]Matt. 15:1

2 [a]Mark 7:5; Acts 10:14, 28; 11:8; Rom. 14:14; Heb. 10:29; Rev. 21:27; Matt. 15:2; Luke 11:38

3 [1]Lit., *with the fist* [a]Mark 7:5, 8, 9, 13; Gal. 1:14

4 [1]Or, *sprinkle* [2]Lit., *baptizing* [a]Matt. 23:25

5 [a]Mark 7:3, 8, 9, 13; Gal. 1:14 [b]Mark 7:2

6 [a]Is. 29:13

7 [a]Is. 29:13

8 [a]Mark 7:3, 5, 9, 13; Gal. 1:14

9 [a]Mark 7:3, 5, 8, 13; Gal. 1:14

10 [1]Lit., *die the death* [a]Ex. 20:12; Deut. 5:16 [b]Ex. 21:17; Lev. 20:9

11 [1]Or, *a gift, an offering* [a]Lev. 1:2 [Heb.]; Matt. 27:6 marg.

55 and ran about that whole country and began to carry about on their pallets those who were sick, to [1]the place they heard He was.

56 And wherever He entered villages, or cities, or countryside, they were laying the sick in the market places, and entreating Him that they might just [a]touch [b]the fringe of His cloak; and as many as touched it were being cured.

^a

CHAPTER 7

AND the Pharisees and some of the scribes gathered together around Him when they had come [b]from Jerusalem,

2 and had seen that some of His disciples were eating their bread with [a]impure hands, that is, unwashed.

3 (For the Pharisees and all the Jews do not eat unless they [1]carefully wash their hands, *thus* observing the [a]traditions of the elders;

4 and *when they come* from the market place, they do not eat unless they [1]cleanse themselves; and there are many other things which they have received in order to observe, such as the [2]washing of [a]cups and pitchers and copper pots.)

5 And the Pharisees and the scribes *asked Him, "Why do Your disciples not walk according to the [a]tradition of the elders, but eat their bread with [b]impure hands?"

6 And He said to them, "Rightly did Isaiah prophesy of you hypocrites, as it is written,

'[a]THIS PEOPLE HONORS ME WITH THEIR LIPS,
BUT THEIR HEART IS FAR AWAY FROM ME.

7 '[a]BUT IN VAIN DO THEY WORSHIP ME,
TEACHING AS DOCTRINES THE PRECEPTS OF MEN.'

8 "Neglecting the commandment of God, you hold to the [a]tradition of men."

9 He was also saying to them, "You nicely set aside the commandment of God in order to keep your [a]tradition.

10 "For Moses said, '[a]HONOR YOUR FATHER AND YOUR MOTHER;' and, '[b]HE WHO SPEAKS EVIL OF FATHER OR MOTHER, LET HIM [1]BE PUT TO DEATH;'

11 but you say, 'If a man says to *his* father or *his* mother, anything of mine you might have been helped by is [a]Corban (that is to say, [1]given *to* God),'

12 you no longer permit him to do anything for *his* father or *his* mother;

13 *thus* invalidating the word of God by your ªtradition which you have handed down; and you do many such things like that."

14 And summoning the multitude again, He *began* saying to them, "Listen to Me, all of you, and understand:

15 there is nothing outside the man which going into him can defile him; but the things which proceed out of the man are what defile the man."

16 (See marginal note.[1])

17 And when leaving the multitude, He had entered ªthe house, ᵇHis disciples questioned Him about the parable.

18 And He *said to them, "Are you too so uncomprehending? Do you not see that whatever goes into the man from outside cannot defile him;

19 because it does not go into his heart, but into his stomach, and [1]is eliminated?" (*Thus He* declared ªall foods ᵇclean.)

20 And He was saying, "ªThat which proceeds out of the man, that is what defiles the man.

21 "For from within, out of the heart of men, proceed the evil thoughts and [1]fornications, thefts, murders, adulteries,

22 deeds of coveting *and* wickedness, *as well as* deceit, sensuality, [1]ªenvy, slander, [2]pride *and* foolishness.

23 "All these evil things proceed from within and defile the man."

24 ªAnd from there He arose and went away to the region of ᵇTyre[1]. And when He had entered a house, He wanted no one to know *of it*; [2]yet He could not escape notice.

25 But after hearing of Him, a woman whose little daughter had an unclean spirit, immediately came and fell at His feet.

26 Now the woman was a [1]Gentile, of the Syrophoenician race. And she kept asking Him to cast the demon out of her daughter.

27 And He was saying to her, "Let the children be satisfied first, for it is not [1]good to take the children's bread and throw it to the dogs."

28 But she answered and *said to Him, "Yes, Lord, *but* even the dogs under the table feed on the children's crumbs."

29 And He said to her, "Because of this [1]an-

13 ªMark 7:3, 5, 8, 9; Gal. 1:14

16 [1]Later mss. add verse 16: *"If any man has ears to hear, let him hear."*

17 ªMark 9:28; Mark 2:1; 3:19 ᵇMatt. 15:15

19 [1]Lit., *goes out into the latrine* ªRom. 14:1-12; Col. 2:16 ᵇLuke 11:41; Acts 10:15; 11:9

20 ªMatt. 15:18; Mark 7:23

21 [1]I.e., acts of sexual immorality

22 [1]Lit., *an evil eye* [2]Or, *arrogance* ªMatt. 6:23; 20:15

24 [1]Some early mss. add: *and Sidon* [2]Lit., *and* ªMark 7:24-30: Matt. 15:21-28 ᵇMatt. 11:21; Mark 7:31

26 [1]Lit., *Greek*

27 [1]Or, *proper*

29 [1]Lit., *word*

Mark 7, 8

**Cure of a Deaf-mute.
The Four Thousand Fed.**

30 ¹Lit., *thrown* ²Lit., *and the*

31 ªMark 7:31-37: *Matt. 15:29-31* ᵇMatt. 11:21; Mark 7:24 ᶜMatt. 4:18 ᵈMark 5:20; Matt. 4:25

32 ªMark 5:23

33 ªMark 8:23

34 ªMark 8:12

35 ¹Or, *bond* ²Lit., *was loosed*

36 ªMatt. 8:4 ᵇMark 1:45

1 ªMark 8:1-9: [6:34-44] Matt. 15:32-39

2 ªMatt. 9:36; Mark 6:34

4 ¹Lit., *loaves*

6 ¹Lit., *to recline*

swer go your way; the demon has gone out of your daughter."

30   And going back to her home, she found the child ¹lying on the bed, ²the demon having departed.

31   ªAnd again He went out from the region of ᵇTyre, and came through Sidon to ᶜthe sea of Galilee, within the region of ᵈDecapolis.

32   And they *brought to Him one who was deaf and spoke with difficulty, and they *entreated Him to ªlay His hand upon him.

33   And ªHe took him aside from the multitude by himself, and put His fingers into his ears, and after ªspitting, He touched his tongue *with the saliva;*

34   and looking up to heaven with a deep ªsigh, He *said to him, "Ephphatha!" that is, "Be opened!"

35   And his ears were opened, and the ¹impediment of his tongue ²was removed, and he *began* speaking plainly.

36   And ªHe gave them orders not to tell anyone; but the more He ordered them, the more widely they ᵇcontinued to proclaim it.

37   And they were utterly astonished, saying, "He has done all things well; He makes even the deaf to hear, and the dumb to speak."

CHAPTER 8

IN those days again, when there was a great multitude and they had nothing to eat, ªHe summoned His disciples and *said to them,

2   "ªI feel compassion for the multitude because they have remained with Me now three days, and have nothing to eat;

3   and if I send them away fasting to their home, they will faint on the way; and some of them have come from a distance."

4   And His disciples answered Him, "Where will anyone be able to *find enough* to satisfy these men with ¹bread here in the wilderness?"

5   And He was asking them, "How many loaves do you have?" And they said, "Seven."

6   And He *directed the multitude to ¹sit down on the ground; and taking the seven loaves, He gave thanks and broke them, and *began* giving

them to His disciples to [2]serve to them, and they [2]served them to the multitude.

7 They also had a few small fish; and [a]after He had blessed them, He ordered these to be [1]served as well.

8 And they ate and were satisfied; and they picked up seven full [a]baskets of what was left over of the broken pieces.

9 And about four thousand were *there*; and He sent them away.

10 And immediately He entered the boat with His disciples, and came to the district of [a]Dalmanutha.

11 [a]And the Pharisees came out and began to argue with Him, [b]seeking from Him a [1]sign from heaven, [2]to test Him.

12 And [a]sighing deeply [1]in His spirit, He *said, "Why does this generation seek for a [2]sign? Truly I say to you, [3]no [2]sign shall be given to this generation."

13 And leaving them, He again embarked and went away to the other side.

14 And they had forgotten to take bread; and [1]did not have more than one loaf in the boat with them.

15 And He was giving orders to them, saying, "[a]Watch out! Beware of the leaven of the Pharisees and the leaven of [b]Herod."

16 And they *began* to discuss with one another *the fact* that they had no bread.

17 And Jesus, aware of this, *said to them, "Why do you discuss *the fact* that you have no bread? [a]Do you not yet see or understand? Do you have a [1]hardened heart?

18 "[a]HAVING EYES, DO YOU NOT SEE? AND HAVING EARS, DO YOU NOT HEAR? And do you not remember,

19 when I broke [a]the five loaves for the five thousand, how many large [b]baskets full of broken pieces you picked up?" They *said to Him, "Twelve."

20 "And when I *broke* [a]the seven for the four thousand, how many [b]basketfuls of broken pieces did you pick up?" And they *said to Him, "Seven."

21 And He was saying to them, "[a]Do you not yet understand?"

22 And they *came to [a]Bethsaida. And they *brought a blind man to Him, and *entreated Him to [b]touch him.

6 [2]Lit., *set before*

7 [1]Lit., *set before*
[a]Matt. 14:19

8 [a]Mark 8:20; Matt. 15:37

10 [a]Matt. 15:39

11 [1]Or, *attesting miracle*
[2]Lit., *testing Him*
[a]Mark 8:11-21; Matt. 16:1-12
[b]Matt. 12:38

12 [1]Or, *to Himself* [2]Or, *attesting miracle* [3]Lit., *if a sign shall be given*
[a]Mark 7:34

14 [1]Lit., *were not having*

15 [a]Matt. 16:6; Luke 12:1
[b]Matt. 14:1; 22:16

17 [1]Or, *dull, insensible*
[a]Mark 6:52

18 [a]Ezek. 12:2

19 [a]Mark 6:41-44 [b]Matt. 14:20

20 [a]Mark 8:6-9 [b]Mark 8:8

21 [a]Mark 6:52

22 [a]Matt. 11:21; Mark 6:45
[b]Mark 3:10

23 a Mark 7:33 b Mark 5:23

24 1 Or, *gained sight* 2 Or, *they look to me*

26 a Matt. 8:4 b Mark 8:23

27 a Mark 8:27-29: *Matt. 16:13-16; Luke 9:18-20* b Matt. 16:13

28 a Mark 6:14

29 1 I.e., the Messiah

30 1 Or, *strictly admonished* a Matt. 16:20; Luke 9:21; Matt. 8:4

31 a Mark 8:31-9:1: *Matt. 16:21-28; Luke 9:22-27* b Matt. 16:21

32 a John 18:20; John 10:24; 11:14; 16:25, 29 [in Gr.]

33 1 Lit., *the things of God* a Matt. 4:10

34 a Matt. 10:38

35 1 Gr., *soul-life* a Matt. 10:39

36 1 Gr., *soul-life*

37 1 Gr., *soul-life*

38 a Luke 9:26; Matt. 10:33; Heb. 11:16 b Matt. 8:20

23   And taking the blind man by the hand, He a brought him out of the village; and after a spitting on his eyes, and b laying His hands upon him, He asked him, "Do you see anything?"

24   And he 1 looked up and said, "I see men, for 2 I am seeing *them* like trees, walking about."

25   Then again He laid His hands upon his eyes; and he looked intently and was restored, and *began* to see everything clearly.

26   And He sent him to his home, saying, "a Do not even enter b the village."

27   a And Jesus went out, along with His disciples, to the villages of b Caesarea Philippi; and on the way He questioned His disciples saying to them, "Who do people say that I am?"

28   a And they told Him, saying, "John the Baptist; and others *say* Elijah; but still others, one of the prophets."

29   And He *continued* by questioning them, "But who do you say that I am?" Peter *answered and *said to Him, "Thou art 1 the Christ."

30   And a He 1 warned them to tell no one about Him.

31   a And He began to teach them that b the Son of Man must suffer many things and be rejected by the elders and the chief priests and the scribes, and be killed, and after three days rise again.

32   And He was stating the matter a plainly. And Peter took Him aside and began to rebuke Him.

33   But turning around and seeing His disciples, He rebuked Peter, and *said, "Get behind Me, a Satan; for you are not setting your mind on 1 God's interests, but man's."

34   And He summoned the multitude with His disciples, and said to them, "If anyone wishes to come after Me, let him deny himself, and a take up his cross, and follow Me.

35   "For a whoever wishes to save his 1 life shall lose it; and whoever loses his 1 life for My sake and the gospel's shall save it.

36   "For what does it profit a man to gain the whole world, and forfeit his 1 soul?

37   "For what shall a man give in exchange for his 1 soul?

38   "For a whoever is ashamed of Me and My words in this adulterous and sinful generation, b the Son of Man will also be ashamed of him when He

ccomes in the glory of His Father with the holy angels."

38 cMatt. 16:27; Mark 13:26; Luke 9:27

CHAPTER 9

1 aMatt. 16:27; Mark 13:26; Luke 9:27

AND He was saying to them, "aTruly I say to you, there are some of those who are standing here who shall not taste of death until they see the kingdom of God after it has come with power."

2 1Or, Jacob
aMark 9:2-8: Matt. 17:1-8; Luke 9:28-36 bMark 5:37

2   aAnd six days later, Jesus *took with Him bPeter and 1James and John, and *brought them up to a high mountain by themselves. And He was transfigured before them;

3 aMatt. 28:3

3   and aHis garments became radiant and exceedingly white, as no launderer on earth can whiten them.

5 1Or, sacred tents
aMatt. 23:7 bMatt. 17:4; Luke 9:33

4   And Elijah appeared to them along with Moses; and they were conversing with Jesus.

5   And Peter *answered and *said to Jesus, "aRabbi, it is good for us to be here; and blet us make three 1tabernacles, one for You, and one for Moses, and one for Elijah."

7 1Or, occurred 2Or, give constant heed
a2 Pet. 1:17f. bMark 1:11; Matt. 3:17

6   For he did not know what to answer; for they became terrified.

7   Then a cloud 1formed, overshadowing them, and aa voice 1came out of the cloud, "bThis is My beloved Son, 2listen to Him!"

9 1Lit., except when
aMark 9:9-13: Matt. 17:9-13 bMark 5:43; 7:36; Mark 8:30; Matt. 8:4

8   And all at once they looked around and saw no one with them any more, except Jesus only.

9   aAnd as they were coming down from the mountain, He bgave them orders not to relate to anyone what they had seen, 1until the Son of Man should rise from the dead.

10 1Or, kept to themselves
2Lit., the statement 3Lit., what was the rising from the dead

10   And they 1seized upon 2that statement, discussing with one another 3what rising from the dead might mean.

11 aMatt. 11:14

11   And they began questioning Him, saying, "Why is it that the scribes say that first aElijah must come?"

12 aMark 9:31 bMatt. 16:21; 26:24

12   And He said to them, "Elijah does first come and restore everything. And yet how is it written of athe Son of Man that bHe should suffer many things and be treated with contempt?

13 1Lit., also

13   "But I say to you, that Elijah has 1indeed come, and they did to him whatever they wished, just as it is written of him."

14 aMark 9:14-28: Matt. 17:14-19; Luke 9:37-42

14   aAnd when they came back to the disciples,

15 ªMark 14:33; 16:5, 6

18 ¹Or, *wherever* ²Or, *tears him* ³Or, *withers away*

20 ¹Lit., *him*

23 ªMatt. 17:20; John 11:40

25 ¹Or, *running together* ⁷Or, *I Myself command* ³Or, *from now on* ªMark 9:15

28 ªMark 7:17; 2:1

they saw a large crowd around them, and *some* scribes arguing with them.

15   And immediately, when the entire crowd saw Him, they were ªamazed, and *began* running up to greet Him.

16   And He asked them, "What are you discussing with them?"

17   And one of the crowd answered Him, "Teacher, I brought You my son, possessed with a spirit which makes him mute;

18   and ¹whenever it seizes him, it ²dashes him *to the ground* and he foams *at the mouth*, and grinds his teeth, and ³stiffens out. And I told Your disciples to cast it out, and they could not *do it.*"

19   And He *answered them and *said, "O unbelieving generation, how long shall I be with you? How long shall I put up with you? Bring him to Me!"

20   And they brought ¹the boy to Him. And when he saw Him, immediately the spirit threw him into a convulsion, and falling to the ground, he *began* rolling about and foaming *at the mouth.*

21   And He asked his father, "How long has this been happening to him?" And he said, "From childhood.

22   "And it has often thrown him both into the fire and into the water to destroy him. But if You can do anything, take pity on us and help us!"

23   And Jesus said to him, " 'If You can!' ªAll things are possible to him who believes."

24   Immediately the boy's father cried out and *began* saying, "I do believe; help *me in* my unbelief."

25   And when Jesus saw that ªa crowd was ¹rapidly gathering, He rebuked the unclean spirit, saying to it, "You deaf and dumb spirit, I ²command you, come out of him and do not enter him ³again."

26   And after crying out and throwing him into terrible convulsions, it came out; and *the boy* became so much like a corpse that most *of them* said, "He is dead!"

27   But Jesus took him by the hand and raised him; and he got up.

28   And when He had come ªinto *the* house, His disciples *began* questioning Him privately, "Why is it that we could not cast it out?"

29 And He said to them, "This kind cannot come out by anything but prayer."[1]

30 [a]And from there they went out and *began* to go through Galilee, and He was unwilling for anyone to know *about it*.

31 For He was teaching His disciples and telling them, "[a]The Son of Man is to be [1]delivered up into the hands of men, and they will kill Him; and when He has been killed, He will rise again three days later."

32 But [a]they [1]did not understand *this* statement, and they were afraid to ask him.

33 [a]And they came to Capernaum; and when He [1]was in [b]the house, He *began* to question them, "What were you discussing on the way?"

34 But they kept silent, for on the way [a]they had discussed with one another which *of them was* the greatest.

35 And sitting down, He called the twelve and *said to them, "[a]If any one wants to be first, [1]he shall be last of all, and servant of all."

36 And taking a child, He stood him in the midst of them; and taking him in His arms, He said to them,

37 "[a]Whoever receives [1]one child like this in My name is receiving Me; and whoever receives Me is not receiving Me, but Him who sent Me."

38 [a]John said to Him, "Teacher, we saw someone casting out demons in Your name, and [b]we tried to hinder him because he was not following us."

39 But Jesus said, "Do not hinder him, for there is no one who shall perform a miracle in My name, and be able soon afterward to speak evil of Me.

40 "[a]For he who is not against us is [1]for us.

41 "For [a]whoever gives you a cup of water to drink [1]because of your name as *followers* of Christ, truly I say to you, he shall not lose his reward.

42 And [a]whoever causes one of these little ones who believe to stumble, it [1]would be better for him if with a heavy millstone hung around his neck, he [2]had been cast into the sea.

43 "And [a]if your hand causes you to stumble, cut it off; it is better for you to enter life crippled, than having your two hands, to go into [1b]hell, into the [c]unquenchable fire.[2]

44 (See marginal note[2], vs. 43.)

29 [1]Many mss. add: *and fasting*

30 [a]Mark 9:30-32: *Matt. 17:22-23; Luke 9:43-45*

31 [1]Or, *betrayed* [a]Mark 9:12; 8:31; Matt. 16:21

32 [1]Lit., *were not knowing* [a]Luke 2:50; 9:45; 18:34; John 12:16

33 [1]Lit., *had become* [a]Mark 9:33-37: *Matt. [17:24] 18:1-5; Luke 9:46-48* [b]Mark 3:19

34 [a]Luke 22:24; Mark 9:50

35 [1]Or, *let him be* [a]Matt. 20:26

37 [1]Lit., *one of such children* [a]Matt. 10:40

38 [a]Mark 9:38-40: *Luke 9:49-50* [b]Num. 11:27-29

40 [1]Or, *on our side* [a]Matt. 12:30

41 [1]Lit., *in a name that you are Christ's* [a]Matt. 10:42

42 [1]Lit., *is better for him if a millstone turned by a donkey is hung* [2]Lit., *has been cast* [a]Matt. 18:6; Luke 17:2; 1 Cor. 8:12

43 [1]Lit., *Gehenna* [2]Verses 44 and 46, which are identical with verse 48, are omitted by the best ancient mss. [a]Matt. 5:30; 18:8; 17:27 [b]Matt. 5:22 [c]Matt. 3:12; 25:41

93

45 [1]Lit., *Gehenna* [2]cf. vs. 43, note 2
[a]Matt. 5:22

47 [1]Lit., *Gehenna*
[a]Matt. 5:29; 18:9; Matt. 17:27 [b]Matt. 5:22

48 [a]Is. 66:24 [b]Matt. 3:12; Matt. 25:41

50 [1]Lit., *season it*
[a]Matt. 5:13; Luke 14:34f. [b]Col. 4:6 [c]Mark 9:34; Rom. 12:18; 2 Cor. 13:11; 1 Thess. 5:13

1 [a]Mark 10:1-12: *Matt. 19:1-9* [b]Mark 1:21; 2:13; 4:2; 6.2, 6, 34; 12:35; 14:49; Matt. 4:23; 26:55

4 [1]Or, *divorce her*
[a]Deut. 24:1, 3

5 [1]Or, *with reference to*
[a]Matt. 19:8

6 [a]Mark 13:19; 2 Pet. 3:4 [b]Gen. 1:27; 5:2

7 [1]Some mss. add: *and shall cleave to his wife*
[a]Gen. 2:24

8 [a]Gen. 2:24

11 [a]Matt. 5:32

12 [a]1 Cor. 7:11, 13

13 [a]Mark 10:13-16: *Matt. 19:13-15; Luke 18:15-17*

45 "And if your foot causes you to stumble, cut it off; it is better for you to enter life lame, than having your two feet, to be cast into [1a]hell[2].

46 (See marginal note [2], vs. 43.)

47 "And [a]if your eye causes you to stumble, cast it out; it is better for you to enter the kingdom of God with one eye, than having two eyes, to be cast into [1b]hell;

48 [a]where THEIR WORM DOES NOT DIE, AND [b]THE FIRE IS NOT QUENCHED.

49 "For everyone will be salted with fire.

50 "Salt is good, but [a]if the salt becomes unsalty, with what will you [1]make it salty *again?* [b]Have salt in yourselves, and [c]be at peace with one another."

a
CHAPTER 10

AND rising up, He *went from there to the region of Judea, and beyond the Jordan; and crowds *gathered around Him again, and, [b]according to His custom, He once more *began* to teach them.

2 And *some* Pharisees came up to Him, testing Him, and *began* to question Him whether it was lawful for a man to divorce a wife.

3 And He answered and said to them, "What did Moses command you?"

4 And they said, "[a]Moses permitted a man to write a certificate of divorce and [1]send *her* away."

5 But Jesus said to them, "[1a]Because of your hardness of heart he wrote you this commandment.

6 "But [a]from the beginning of creation, God [b]MADE THEM MALE AND FEMALE.

7 "[a]FOR THIS CAUSE A MAN SHALL LEAVE HIS FATHER AND MOTHER,[1]

8 [a]AND THE TWO SHALL BECOME ONE FLESH; consequently they are no longer two, but one flesh.

9 "What therefore God has joined together, let no man separate."

10 And in the house the disciples *began* questioning Him about this again.

11 And He *said to them, "[a]Whoever divorces his wife and marries another woman commits adultery against her;

12 and [a]if she herself divorces her husband and marries another man, she is committing adultery."

13 [a]And they *began* bringing children to Him,

so that He might touch them; and the disciples rebuked them.

14   But when Jesus saw this, He was indignant and said to them, "Permit the children to come to Me; do not hinder them; ªfor the kingdom of God belongs to such as these.

15   "Truly I say to you, ªwhoever does not receive the kingdom of God like a child shall not enter it *at all.*"

16   And He ªtook them in His arms and *began* blessing them, laying His hands upon them.

17   ªAnd as He was setting out on a journey, a man ran up to Him and bknelt before Him, and *began* asking Him, "Good Teacher, what shall I do to cinherit eternal life?"

18   And Jesus said to him, "Why do you call Me good? No one is good except God alone.

19   "You know the commandments, 'ªDo NOT MURDER, DO NOT COMMIT ADULTERY, DO NOT STEAL, DO NOT BEAR FALSE WITNESS, Do not defraud, HONOR YOUR FATHER AND MOTHER.'"

20   And he said to Him, "Teacher, I have kept ªall these things from my youth up."

21   And looking at him, Jesus felt a love for him, and said to him, "One thing you lack: go and sell all you possess, and give *it* to the poor, and you shall have ªtreasure in heaven; and come, follow Me."

22   But at these words ¹his face fell, and he went away grieved, for he was one who owned much property.

23   And Jesus, looking around, *said to His disciples, "ªHow hard it will be for those who are wealthy to enter the kingdom of God!"

24   And the disciples ªwere amazed at His words. But Jesus *answered again and *said to them, "Children, how hard it is ¹to enter the kingdom of God!

25   "ªIt is easier for a camel to go through the eye of ¹a needle than for a rich man to enter the kingdom of God."

26   And they were even more astonished and said ¹to Him, "²Then who can be saved?"

27   Looking upon them, Jesus *said, "ªWith men it is impossible, but not with God; for all things are possible with God."

28   ªPeter began to say to Him, "Behold, we have left everything and followed You."

14 ªMatt. 5:3

15 ªMatt. 18:3; 19:14; Luke 18:17; 1 Cor. 14:20; 1 Pet. 2:2

16 ªMark 9:36

17 ªMark 10:17-31: *Matt. 19:16-30; Luke 18:18-30* bMark 1:40 cLuke 10:25; 18:18; Acts 20:32; Eph. 1:18; 1 Pet. 1:4; Matt. 25:34

19 ªEx. 20:12-16; Deut. 5:16-20

20 ªMatt. 19:20

21 ªMatt. 6:20

22 ¹Or, *he became gloomy*

23 ªMatt. 19:23

24 ¹Later mss. insert: *for those who trust in wealth* ªMark 1:27

25 ¹Lit., *the* ªMatt. 19:24

26 ¹Later mss. read: *to one another* ²Lit., *and*

27 ªMatt. 19:26

28 ªMatt. 4:20-22

29 aMatt. 19:29; Luke
18:29f.; Matt. 6:33

30 1Lit., *this time* 2Or, *age*
aMatt. 12:32

31 aMatt. 19:30

32 aMark 10:32-34: *Matt.
20:17-19; Luke 18:31-33*
bMark 1:27

33 1Or, *betrayed* 2Or,
betray
aMark 8:31; 9:12

34 aMatt. 26:67; 27:30;
Mark 14:65; Matt. 16:21;
Mark 9:31

35 1Or, *Jacob*
aMark 10:35-45: *Matt. 20:20-
28*

37 1Lit., *give to us*
aMatt 19:28

38 aMatt. 20:22 bLuke
12:50

39 aActs 12:2; Rev. 1:9

40 aMatt. 13:11

41 1Or, *Jacob*
aMark 10:42-45; Luke 22:25-
27

29 Jesus said, "Truly I say to you, athere is no one who has left house or brothers or sisters or mother or father or children or farms, for My sake and for the gospel's sake,

30 but that he shall receive a hundred times as much now in the 1present age, houses and brothers and sisters and mothers and children and farms, along with persecutions; and in athe 2world to come, eternal life.

31 "But amany *who are* first, will be last; and the last, first."

32 aAnd they were on the road, going up to Jerusalem, and Jesus was walking on ahead of them; and they bwere amazed, and those who followed were fearful. And again He took the twelve aside and began to tell them what was going to happen to Him,

33 *saying,* "Behold, we are going up to Jerusalem, and athe Son of Man will be 1delivered up to the chief priests and the scribes; and they will condemn Him to death, and will 2deliver Him up to the Gentiles.

34 "And they will mock Him and aspit upon Him, and scourge Him, and kill *Him,* and three days later He will rise again."

35 aAnd 1James and John, the two sons of Zebedee, *came up to Him, saying to Him, "Teacher, we want You to do for us whatever we ask of You."

36 And He said to them, "What do you want Me to do for you?"

37 And they said to Him, "1Grant that we amay sit in Your glory, one on Your right, and one on *Your* left."

38 But Jesus said to them, "You do not know what you are asking for. Are you able ato drink the cup that I drink, or bto be baptized with the baptism with which I am baptized?"

39 And they said to Him, "We are able." And Jesus said to them, "The cup that I drink ayou shall drink; and you shall be baptized with the baptism with which I am baptized.

40 "But to sit on My right or on *My* left, this is not Mine to give; abut *it is for those* for whom it has been prepared."

41 aAnd hearing this, the ten began to feel indignant toward 1James and John.

42 And calling them to Himself, Jesus *said to them, "You know that those who are recognized as

rulers of the Gentiles lord it over them; and their great men exercise authority over them.

43 "But it is not so among you, [a]but whoever wishes to become great among you shall be your servant;

44 and whoever wishes to be first among you shall be slave of all.

45 "For even the Son of Man [a]did not come to be served, but to serve, and to give His [1]life a ransom for many."

46 [a]And they *came to Jericho. And [b]as He was going out from Jericho with His disciples and a great multitude, a blind beggar *named* Bartimaeus, the son of Timaeus, was sitting by the road.

47 And when he heard that it was Jesus the [a]Nazarene, he began to cry out and say, "Jesus, [b]Son of David, have mercy on me!"

48 And many were sternly telling him to be quiet, but he *began* crying out all the more, "[a]Son of David, have mercy on me!"

49 And Jesus stopped and said, "Call him *here*." And they *called the blind man, saying to him, "[a]Take courage, arise! He is calling for you."

50 And casting aside his cloak, he jumped up, and came to Jesus.

51 And answering him, Jesus said, "What do you want Me to do for you?" And the blind man said to Him, "[1a]Rabboni, *I want* to regain my sight!"

52 And Jesus said to him, "Go your way; [a]your faith has [1]made you well." And immediately he received his sight and *began* following Him on the road.

a   CHAPTER 11

AND as they *approached Jerusalem, at Bethphage and [b]Bethany, near [c]the Mount of Olives, He *sent two of His disciples,

2 and *said to them, "Go into the village opposite you, and immediately as you enter it, you will find a colt tied *there*, on which no one yet has ever sat; untie it and bring it *here*.

3 "And if anyone says to you, 'Why are you doing this?' you say, 'The Lord has need of it;' and immediately he [1]will send it back here."

4 And they went away and found a colt tied

43 [a]Matt. 20:26; Mark 9:35

45 [1]Or, *soul*
[a]Matt. 20:28

46 [a]Mark 10:46-52: *Matt. 20:29-34; Luke 18:35-43*
[b]Luke 18:35; 19:1

47 [a]Mark 1:24 [b]Matt. 9:27

48 [a]Matt. 9:27

49 [a]Matt. 9:2

51 [1]I.e., My Master
[a]John 20:16; Matt. 23:7

52 [1]Lit., *saved you*
[a]Matt. 9:22

1 [a]Mark 11:1-10: *Matt. 21:1-9; Luke 19:29-38* [b]Matt. 21:17 [c]Matt. 21:1

3 [1]Lit., *sends*

Mark 11

**The Triumphal Entry.   The Fig Tree Cursed.
The Cleansing of the Temple.**

7 aMark 11:7-10: *John 12:12-15*

9 aMatt. 21:9; Ps. 118:25

10 aMatt. 21:9

11 aMatt. 21:12 bMatt. 21:17

12 aMark 11:12-14 [20-24]: *Matt. 21:18-22*

15 1Lit., *the doves*
aMark 11:15-18: *Matt. 21:12-16; Luke 19:45-47; John 2:13-16*

16 1Lit., *a vessel,* I.e., a receptacle or implement of any kind

17 1Lit., *cave*
aIs. 56:7 bJer. 7:11

18 aMark 12:12; Matt. 21:46; Luke 20:19; John 7:1 bMatt. 7:28

at the door outside in the street; and they *untied it.

5   And some of the bystanders were saying to them, "What are you doing, untying the colt?"

6   And they spoke to them just as Jesus had told *them,* and they gave them permission.

7   aAnd they *brought the colt to Jesus and put their garments on it; and He sat upon it.

8   And many spread their garments in the road, and others *spread* leafy branches which they had cut from the fields.

9   And those who went before, and those who followed after, were crying out,

"aHOSANNA!

BLESSED IS HE WHO COMES IN THE NAME OF THE LORD;

10   "Blessed *is* the coming kingdom of our father David;

HOSANNA ain the highest."

11   And aHe entered Jerusalem *and came* into the temple; and after looking all around, bHe departed for Bethany with the twelve, since it was already late.

12   aAnd on the next day, when they had departed from Bethany, He became hungry.

13   And seeing at a distance a fig tree in leaf, He went *to see* if perhaps He would find anything on it; and when He came to it, He found nothing but leaves, for it was not the season for figs.

14   And He answered and said to it, "May no one ever eat fruit from you again!" And His disciples were listening.

15   aAnd they *came to Jerusalem. And He entered the temple and began to cast out those who were buying and selling in the temple, and overturned the tables of the moneychangers and the seats of those who were selling 1doves;

16   and He would not permit anyone to carry 1goods through the temple.

17   And He *began* to teach and say to them, "Is it not written, 'aMY HOUSE SHALL BE CALLED A HOUSE OF PRAYER FOR ALL THE NATIONS'? bBut you have made it a robber's 1den."

18   And the chief priests and the scribes heard *this,* and abegan seeking how to destroy Him; for they were afraid of Him, for ball the multitude was astonished at His teaching.

19 And ªwhenever evening came, ¹they would go out of the city.

20 ªAnd as they were passing by in the morning, they saw the fig tree withered from the roots *up.*

21 And being reminded, Peter *said to Him, "ªRabbi, behold, the fig tree which You cursed has withered."

22 And Jesus *answered saying to them, "ªHave faith in God.

23 "Truly I say to you, whoever says to this mountain, 'Be taken up and cast into the sea,' and does not doubt in his heart, but believes that what he says is going to happen; it shall be *granted* him.

24 "Therefore I say to you, ªall things for which you pray and ask, believe that you have received them, and they shall be *granted* you.

25 "And whenever you ªstand praying, ᵇforgive, if you have anything against anyone; so that your Father also who is in heaven may forgive you your transgressions."

26 (See marginal note.¹)

27 And they *came again to Jerusalem. ªAnd as He was walking in the temple, the chief priests, and scribes, and elders *came to Him,

28 and *began* saying to Him, "By what authority are You doing these things, or who gave You this authority to do these things?"

29 And Jesus said to them, "I will ask you one question, and you answer Me, and *then* I will tell you by what authority I do these things.

30 "Was the baptism of John from heaven, or from men? Answer Me."

31 And they *began* reasoning with one another, saying, "If we say, 'From heaven,' He will say, 'Then why did you not believe him?'

32 "But ¹shall we say, 'From men'?" —they were afraid of the multitude, for all considered John to have been a prophet indeed.

33 And answering Jesus, they *said, "We do not know." And Jesus *said to them, "Neither ¹will I tell you by what authority I do these things."

a   CHAPTER 12

AND He began to speak to them in parables: "ᵇA man ᶜPLANTED A VINEYARD, AND PUT A ¹WALL AROUND IT, AND DUG A VAT UNDER THE WINEPRESS,

---

19 ¹I.e., Jesus and His disciples
ªLuke 21:37; Matt. 21:17; Mark 11:11

20 ªMark 11:20-24 [Mark 11:12-14]: *Matt. 21:19-22*

21 ªMatt. 23:7

22 ªMatt. 17:20; 21:21f.

24 ªMatt. 7:7f.

25 ªMatt. 6:5 ᵇMatt. 6:14

26 ¹Later mss. add vs. 26: *"But if you do not forgive, neither will your Father who is in heaven forgive your transgressions."* Matt. 6:15; 18:35

27 ªMark 11:27-33: *Matt. 21:23-27; Luke 20:1-8*

32 ¹Or, *if we say*

33 ¹Lit., *do I tell*

1 ¹Or, *fence*
ªMark 3:23; 4:2ff. ᵇMark 12:1-12: *Matt. 21:33-46; Luke 20:9-19* ᶜIs. 5:2

Mark 12

**Parable of the Vine-growers.
Pay Tribute to Caesar?**

1 [2]Here and in verses 2, 7, and 9: or, *tenant farmers*

9 [1]Lit., *lord*

10 [a]Ps. 118:22

11 [a]Ps. 118:23

12 [a]Mark 11:18 [b]Matt. 22:22

13 [a]Mark 12:13-17: *Matt. 22:15-22; Luke 20:20-26* [b]Matt. 22:16 [c]Luke 11:54

14 [1]Lit., *it is not a concern to You about anyone*, I.e., You court no man's favor [2]Or, *permissible*

15 [1]The denarius was worth 18 cents in silver, equivalent to a day's wage

AND BUILT A TOWER, and rented it out to [2]vine-growers and went on a journey.

2 "And at the *harvest* time he sent a slave to the vine-growers, in order to receive *some* of the produce of the vineyard from the vine-growers.

3 "And they took him, and beat him, and sent him away empty-handed.

4 "And again he sent them another slave, and they wounded him in the head, and treated him shamefully.

5 "And he sent another, and that one they killed; and *so with* many others, beating some, and killing others.

6 "He had one more *to send*, a beloved son; he sent him last *of all* to them, saying, 'They will respect my son.'

7 "But those vine-growers said to one another, 'This is the heir; come, let us kill him, and the inheritance will be ours!'

8 "And they took him, and killed him, and threw him out of the vineyard.

9 "What will the [1]owner of the vineyard do? He will come and destroy the vine-growers, and will give the vineyard to others.

10 "Have you not even read this scripture:

'[a]THE STONE WHICH THE BUILDERS REJECTED,

THIS BECAME THE CHIEF CORNER *STONE*;

11 '[a]THIS CAME ABOUT FROM THE LORD,

AND IT IS MARVELOUS IN OUR EYES'?"

12 And [a]they were seeking to seize Him; and *yet* they feared the multitude; for they understood that He had spoken the parable against them. And *so* [b]they left Him, and went away.

13 [a]And they *sent some of the Pharisees and [b]Herodians to Him, in order to [c]trap Him in a statement.

14 And they *came and *said to Him, "Teacher, we know that You are truthful, and [1]defer to no one; for You are not partial to any, but teach the way of God in truth. Is it [2]lawful to pay a poll-tax to Caesar, or not?

15 "Shall we pay, or shall we not pay?" But He, knowing their hypocrisy, said to them, "Why are you testing Me? Bring Me a [1]denarius to look at."

16 And they brought *one*. And He *said to them, "Whose likeness and inscription is this?" And they said to Him, "Caesar's."

17 And Jesus said to them, "ᵃRender to Caesar the things that are Caesar's, and to God the things that are God's." And they ¹were amazed at Him.

18 ᵃAnd *some* Sadducees (who say that there is no resurrection) *came to Him, and *began* questioning Him, saying,

19 "Teacher, Moses wrote for us *a law* that ᵃIF A MAN'S BROTHER DIES, and leaves behind a wife, AND LEAVES NO CHILD, HIS BROTHER SHOULD TAKE THE WIFE, AND RAISE UP OFFSPRING TO HIS BROTHER.

20 "There were seven brothers; and the first one took a wife, and died, leaving no offspring.

21 "And the second one took her, and died, leaving behind no offspring; and the third likewise;

22 and *so* ¹all seven left no offspring. Last of all the woman died too.

23 "In the resurrection, ¹when they rise again, which one's wife will she be? For ²all seven had her as wife."

24 Jesus said to them, "Is this not the reason you are mistaken, that you do not ¹understand the Scriptures, or the power of God?

25 "For when they rise from the dead, they neither marry, nor are given in marriage, but are like angels in heaven.

26 "But ¹regarding the fact that the dead rise again, have you not read in the book of Moses, ᵃin the *passage about the burning* bush, how God spoke to him, saying, 'ᵇI AM THE GOD OF ABRAHAM, AND THE GOD OF ISAAC, AND THE GOD OF JACOB'?

27 "ᵃHe is not *the* God ¹of *the* dead, but of *the* living; you are greatly mistaken."

28 ᵃAnd one of the scribes came and heard them arguing, and ᵇrecognizing that He had answered them well, asked Him, "What commandment is the ¹foremost of all?"

29 Jesus answered, "The foremost is, 'ᵃHEAR, O ISRAEL; THE LORD OUR GOD IS ONE LORD;

30 ᵃAND YOU SHALL LOVE THE LORD YOUR GOD WITH ALL YOUR HEART, AND WITH ALL YOUR SOUL, AND WITH ALL YOUR MIND, AND WITH ALL YOUR STRENGTH.'

31 "The second is this, 'ᵃYOU SHALL LOVE YOUR NEIGHBOR AS YOURSELF.' There is no other commandment greater than these."

32 And the scribe said to Him, "Right, Teacher, You have truly stated that ᵃHE IS ONE; AND THERE IS NO ONE ELSE BESIDES HIM;

17 ¹Or, *were greatly marveling*
ᵃMatt. 22:21

18 ᵃMark 12:18-27: *Matt. 22:23-33; Luke 20:27-38*

19 ᵃDeut. 25:5

22 ¹Lit., *the seven*

23 ¹Most ancient mss. omit: *when they rise again* ²Lit., *the seven*

24 ¹Or, *know*

26 ¹Lit., *concerning the dead, that they rise* ᵃLuke 20:37; Rom. 11:2 ᵇEx. 3:6

27 ¹Or, *of corpses* ᵃMatt. 22:32; Luke 20:38

28 ¹Or, *first* ᵃMark 12:28-34: *Matt. 22:34-40; Luke 10:25-28; 20:39f.* ᵇLuke 20:39; Matt. 22:34

29 ᵃDeut. 6:4

30 ᵃDeut. 6:5

31 ᵃLev. 19:18

32 ᵃDeut. 4:35

33 b1 Sam. 15:22; Hos. 6:6;
Mic. 6:6-8; Matt. 9:13; 12:7
33 aDeut. 6:5

34 aMatt. 22:46

35 1I.e., the Messiah
aMark 12:35-37: Matt. 22:41-
46; Luke 20:41-44 bMatt.
26:55; Mark 10:1 cMatt. 9:27

36 1Or, by
aPs. 110:1

37 1Lit., was gladly hearing
Him
aJohn 12:9

38 aMark 12:38-40: Matt.
23:1-7; Luke 20:45-47 bLuke
11:43; Matt. 23:6

40 aLuke 20:47

41 1I.e., copper coins
aMark 12:41-44: Luke 21:1-4
bJohn 8:20 c2 Kin. 12:9

42 1Lit., lepta 2Lit.,
quadrans, i.e., 1/64 of a
denarius

43 1Lit., those who were
putting in

44 1Or, abundance 2Lit.,
her whole livelihood
aLuke 8:43; 15:12, 30; 21:4

1 1Lit., how great
aMark 13:1-37: Matt. 24;
Luke 21:5-36

33 ᵃAND TO LOVE HIM WITH ALL THE HEART AND WITH ALL THE UNDERSTANDING AND WITH ALL THE STRENGTH, AND TO LOVE ONE'S NEIGHBOR AS HIMSELF, ᵇis much more than all burnt offerings and sacrifices."

34 And when Jesus saw that he had answered intelligently, He said to him, "You are not far from the kingdom of God." ᵃAnd after that, no one would venture to ask Him any more questions.

35 ᵃAnd Jesus answering *began* to say, as He ᵇtaught in the temple, "How *is it that* the scribes say that ¹the Christ is the ᶜson of David?

36 "David himself said ¹in the Holy Spirit,

'ᵃTHE LORD SAID TO MY LORD,

"SIT AT MY RIGHT HAND,

UNTIL I PUT THINE ENEMIES BENEATH THY FEET." '

37 "David himself calls Him 'Lord;' and *so* in what sense is He his son?" And ᵃthe great crowd ¹enjoyed listening to Him.

38 ᵃAnd in His teaching He was saying: "Beware of the scribes who like to walk around in long robes, and *like* ᵇrespectful greetings in the market places,

39 and chief seats in the synagogues, and places of honor at banquets.

40 "ᵃThey *are* the ones who devour widows' houses, and for appearance's sake offer long prayers; these will receive greater condemnation."

41 ᵃAnd He sat down opposite ᵇthe treasury, and *began* observing how the multitude were ᶜputting ¹money into the treasury; and many rich people were putting in large sums.

42 And a poor widow came and put in two ¹small copper coins, which amount to a ²cent.

43 And calling His disciples to Him, He said to them, "Truly I say to you, this poor widow put in more than all ¹the contributors to the treasury;

44 for they all put in out of their ¹surplus, but she, out of her poverty, put in all she owned, ²all she had ᵃto live on."

ᵃ   CHAPTER 13

AND as He was going out of the temple, one of His disciples *said to Him, "Teacher, behold ¹what wonderful stones and ¹what wonderful buildings!"

2 And Jesus said to him, "Do you see these

great buildings? ᵃNot one stone shall be left upon another which will not be torn down."

3　And as He was sitting on ᵃthe Mount of Olives opposite the temple, ᵇPeter and ¹James and John and Andrew were questioning Him privately,

4　"Tell us, when will these things be, and what *will be* the ¹sign when all these things are going to be fulfilled?"

5　And Jesus began to say to them, "See to it that no one misleads you.

6　"Many will come in My name, saying, 'ᵃI am *He!*' and will mislead many.

7　"And when you hear of wars and rumors of wars, do not be frightened; *those things* must take place; but *that is* not yet the end.

8　"For nation will arise against nation, and kingdom against kingdom; there will be earthquakes in various places; there will *also* be famines. These things are *merely* the beginning of birth pangs.

9　"But ¹be on your guard; for they will ᵃdeliver you up to *the* ²courts, and you will be flogged ᵇin *the* synagogues, and you will stand before governors and kings for My sake, as a testimony to them.

10　"ᵃAnd the gospel must first be preached to all the nations.

11　"ᵃAnd when they ¹arrest you and deliver you up, do not be anxious beforehand about what you are to say, but say whatever is given you in that hour; for it is not you who speak, but *it is* the Holy Spirit.

12　"And brother will deliver up brother to death, and a father *his* child; and children will rise up against parents and ¹cause them to be put to death.

13　"And ᵃyou will be hated by all on account of My name, but it is the one who has endured to the end who will be saved.

14　"But ᵃwhen you see the ᵇABOMINATION OF DESOLATION standing where it should not be (let the reader understand), then let those who are in Judea flee to the mountains.

15　"And let him who is on the housetop not go down, or enter in, to get anything out of his house;

16　and let him who is in the field not turn back to get his cloak.

17　"But woe to those who are with child and to those who nurse babes in those days!

2 ᵃLuke 19:44

3 ¹Or, *Jacob*
ᵃMatt. 21:1 ᵇMatt. 17:1

4 ¹Or, *attesting miracle*

6 ᵃJohn 8:24

9 ¹Lit., *look to yourselves*
²Or, *Sanhedrins*, or *councils*
ᵃMatt. 10:17 ᵇMatt. 10:17

10 ᵃMatt. 24:14

11 ¹Lit., *lead*
ᵃMark 13:11-13: *Matt. 10:19-22; Luke 21:12-17*

12 ¹Lit., *put them to death*

13 ᵃJohn 15:21

14 ᵃMatt. 24:15 ᵇDan. 9:27; 11:31; 12:11

19 ªMark 10:6

20 ¹Lit., *flesh* ²Or, *chosen ones*

21 ¹I.e., the Messiah

22 ¹Or, *attesting miracles* ªMatt. 7:15 ᵇMatt. 24:24; John 4:48

24 ªIs. 13:10

25 ¹Or, *heaven* ªIs. 34:4

26 ªDan. 7:13 ᵇMatt. 16:27; Mark 8:38

27 ¹Or, *chosen ones* ªDeut. 30:4 ᵇZech. 2:6

29 ¹Lit., *know* ²Or, *it* ³Lit., *doors*

30 ¹Or, *race*

32 ªMatt. 24:36; Acts 1:7

33 ªEph. 6:18; Col. 4:2

104

18 "But pray that it may not happen in the winter.

19 "For those days will be a *time of* tribulation such as has not occurred ªsince the beginning of the creation which God created, until now, and never shall.

20 "And unless the Lord had shortened *those* days, no ¹life would have been saved; but for the sake of the ²elect whom He chose, He shortened the days.

21 "And then if anyone says to you, 'Behold, here is ¹the Christ;' or, 'Behold, *He is* there;' do not believe *him*;

22 for false Christs and ªfalse prophets will arise, and will show ¹ᵇsigns and ᵇwonders, in order, if possible, to lead the elect astray.

23 "But take heed; behold, I have told you everything in advance.

24 "But in those days, after that tribulation, ªTHE SUN WILL BE DARKENED, AND THE MOON WILL NOT GIVE ITS LIGHT,

25 ªAND THE STARS WILL BE FALLING from heaven, and the POWERS THAT ARE IN ¹THE HEAVENS WILL BE shaken.

26 "ªAND THEN THEY SHALL SEE THE SON OF MAN ᵇCOMING IN CLOUDS with great power and glory.

27 "And then He will send forth the angels, and ªWILL GATHER TOGETHER His ¹elect FROM THE FOUR WINDS, ᵇFROM THE FARTHEST END of the earth, TO THE FARTHEST END OF HEAVEN.

28 "Now learn the parable from the fig tree: when its branch has already become tender, and puts forth its leaves, you know that the summer is near.

29 "Even so you too, when you see these things happening, ¹recognize that ²He is near, *right* at the ³door.

30 "Truly I say to you, this ¹generation will not pass away until all these things take place.

31 "Heaven and earth will pass away, but My words will not pass away.

32 "ªBut of that day or hour no one knows, not even the angels in heaven, nor the Son, but the Father *alone*.

33 "Take heed, ªkeep on the alert; for you do not know when the *appointed* time is.

34 "*It is* like a man, away on a journey, *who*

upon leaving his house and [1]putting his slaves in charge, *assigning* to each one his task, also commanded the doorkeeper to stay on the alert.

35 "Therefore, [a]be on the alert — for you do not know when the [1]master of the house is coming, whether in the evening, at midnight, at [b]cockcrowing, or [c]in the morning;—

36   lest he come suddenly and find you [a]asleep.

37 "And what I say to you I say to all, '[a]Be on the alert!' "

CHAPTER 14

[a] NOW *the feast of* [b]the Passover and Unleavened Bread was two days off; and the chief priests and the scribes [c]were seeking how to seize Him by stealth, and kill *Him*;

2   for they were saying, "Not during the festival, lest there be a riot of the people."

3 [a]And while He was in [b]Bethany at the home of Simon the leper, and reclining *at table*, there came a woman with an alabaster vial of [c]costly perfume of pure nard; *and* she broke the vial and poured it over His head.

4   But some were indignantly *remarking* to one another, "For what purpose has this perfume been wasted?

5 "For this perfume might have been sold for over three hundred [1]denarii, and *the money* given to the poor." And they were scolding her.

6   But Jesus said, "Let her alone; why do you bother her? She has done a good deed to Me.

7 "For [a]the poor you always have with you, and whenever you wish, you can do them good; but you do not always have Me.

8 "She has done what she could; [a]she has anointed My body beforehand for the burial.

9 "And truly I say to you, [a]wherever the gospel is preached in the whole world, that also which this woman has done shall be spoken of in memory of her."

10 [a]And Judas Iscariot, [b]who was one of the twelve, went off to the chief priests, in order to [1]betray Him to them.

11   And they were glad when they heard *this*, and promised to give him money. And he *began* seeking how to betray Him at an opportune time.

12 [a]And on the first day of *the Feast of* [b]Un-

---

34 [1]Lit., *giving the authority to*

35 [1]Lit., *lord*
[a]Mark 13:37; Matt. 24:42
[b]Mark 14:30 [c]Mark 6:48; Matt. 14:25

36 [a]Rom. 13:11

37 [a]Mark 13:35; Matt. 24:42

1 [a]Mark 14:1, 2: *Matt. 26:2-5; Luke 22:1, 2* [b]John 11:55; 13:1; Mark 14:12 [c]Matt. 12:14

3 [a]Mark 14:3-9: *Matt. 26:6-13; Luke 7:37-39; John 12:1-8* [b]Matt. 21:17 [c]Matt. 26:6f.; John 12:3

5 [1]The denarius was worth 18 cents in silver, equivalent to a day's wage

7 [a]Matt. 26:11; John 12:8; Deut. 15:11

8 [a]John 19:40

9 [a]Matt. 26:13

10 [1]Or, *deliver Him up* [a]Mark 14:10, 11: *Matt. 26:14-16; Luke 22:3-6* [b]John 6:71

12 [a]Mark 14:12-16: *Matt. 26:17-19; Luke 22:7-13* [b]Matt. 26:17

12 ¹Lit., *they were sacrificing*
^cLuke 22:7; 1 Cor. 5:7; Deut. 16:5; Mark 14:1

leavened Bread, when the Passover *lamb* was being ¹^csacrificed, His disciples *said to Him, "Where do You want us to go and prepare for You to eat the Passover?"

13   And He *sent two of His disciples, and *said to them, "Go into the city, and a man will meet you carrying a pitcher of water; follow him;

14 ^aLuke 22:11; Luke 2:7 Gr.

14   and wherever he enters, say to the owner of the house, 'The Teacher says, "Where is My ^aguest room in which I may eat the Passover with My disciples?" '

15   "And he himself will show you a large upper room furnished *and* ready; and prepare for us there."

16   And the disciples went out, and came to the city, and found *it* just as He had told them; and they prepared the Passover.

17 ^aMark 14:17-21: Matt. 26:20-24; Luke 22:14, 21-23; John 13:18ff.

17   ^aAnd when it was evening He *came with the twelve.

18   And as they were reclining *at table* and eating, Jesus said, "Truly I say to you that one of you will ¹betray Me, —²one who is eating with Me."

18 ¹Or, *deliver Me up* ²Or, *the one*

19   They began to be grieved and to say to Him one by one, "Surely not I?"

20   And He said to them, "It is one of the twelve, ¹one who dips with Me in the bowl.

20 ¹Or, *the one*

21   "For the Son of Man *is to* go, just as it is written of Him; but woe to that man ¹by whom the Son of Man is betrayed! *It would have been* good ²for that man if he had not been born."

21 ¹Or, *through* ²Lit., *for him if that man had not been born*

22   ^aAnd while they were eating, He took *some* bread, and ¹after a ^bblessing He broke *it*; and gave *it* to them, and said, "Take *it*; this is My body."

23   And He took a cup, and when He had given thanks, He gave *it* to them; and they all drank from it.

22 ¹Lit., *having blessed*
^aMark 14:22-25: Matt. 26:26-29; Luke 22:17-20; 1 Cor. 11:23-25; Mark 10:16 ^bMatt. 14:19

24   And He said to them, "This is My blood of the covenant, which is *to be* shed on behalf of many.

25   "Truly I say to you, I shall never again drink of the fruit of the vine until that day when I drink it new in the kingdom of God."

26 ^aMatt. 26:30 ^bMatt 21:1

26   ^aAnd after singing a hymn, they went out to ^bthe Mount of Olives.

27   ^aAnd Jesus *said to them, "You will all ¹fall away, because it is written, '^bI WILL STRIKE DOWN THE SHEPHERD, AND THE SHEEP SHALL BE SCATTERED.'

27 ¹Or, *stumble*
^aMark 14:27-31: Matt. 26:31-35 ^bZech. 13:7

28 "But after I have been raised, I will go before you to Galilee."

29 But Peter said to Him, "*Even* though all may [1]fall away, yet I will not."

30 And Jesus *said to him, "Truly I say to you, that you yourself [1]athis very night, before [b]a cock crows twice, shall three times deny Me."

31 But *Peter* kept saying insistently, "*Even* if I have to die with You, I will not deny You!" And they all were saying the same thing, too.

32 [a]And they *came to a place named Gethsemane; and He *said to His disciples, "Sit here until I have prayed."

33 And He *took with him Peter and [1]James and John, and began to be very [a]distressed and troubled.

34 And He *said to them, "[a]My soul is deeply grieved to the point of death; remain here and keep watch."

35 And He went a little beyond *them*, and [1]fell to the ground, and *began* praying that if it were possible, [a]the hour might [2]pass Him by.

36 And He was saying, "[a]Abba (Father), all things are possible for Thee; remove this cup from Me; [b]yet not what I will, but what Thou wilt."

37 And He *came and *found them sleeping, and *said to Peter, "Simon, are you asleep? Could you not keep watch for one hour?

38 "[a]Keep watching and praying, that you may not come into temptation; the spirit is willing, but the flesh is weak."

39 And again He went away and prayed, saying the same [1]words.

40 And again He came and found them sleeping, for their eyes were very heavy; and they did not know what to answer Him.

41 And He *came the third time, and *said to them, "[1]Are you still sleeping and taking your rest? It is enough; [a]the hour has come; behold, the Son of Man is being [2]betrayed into the hands of sinners.

42 "Arise, let us be going; behold, the one who betrays Me is at hand!"

43 [a]And immediately while He was still speaking, Judas, one of the twelve, *came up, [1]accompanied by a multitude with swords and clubs, from the chief priests and the scribes and the elders.

44 Now he who was betraying Him had given them a signal, saying, "Whomever I shall kiss, He is

29 [1]Or, *stumble*

30 [1]Lit., *today, on this night*
[a]Matt. 26:34 [b]Mark 14:68, 72; John 13:38

32 [a]Mark 14:32-42: *Matt. 26:36-46; Luke 22:40-46*

33 [1]Or, *Jacob*
[a]Mark 9:15; 16:5, 6

34 [a]Matt. 26:38; John 12:27

35 [1]Lit., *was falling* [2]Lit., *pass from Him*
[a]Mark 14:41; Matt. 26:45

36 [a]Rom. 8:15; Gal. 4:6
[b]Matt. 26:39

38 [a]Matt. 26:41

39 [1]Lit., *word*

41 [1]Or, *keep on sleeping therefore* [2]Or, *delivered up*
[a]Mark 14:35

43 [1]Lit., *and with him*
[a]Mark 14:43 50: *Matt. 26:47-56; Luke 22:47-53; John 18:3-11*

107

44 [1]Lit., *safely*

45 [a]Matt. 23:7

47 [1]Lit., *took off*

49 [1]Or possibly: *let the Scriptures be fulfilled* [a]Mark 12:35

53 [a]Mark 14:53-65: *Matt.* 26:57-68; John 18:12f.; 19-24

54 [1]Or, *servants* [2]Lit., *light* [a]Mark 14:68 [b]Matt. 26:3 [c]Mark 14:67; John 18-18

55 [1]Or, *Sanhedrin* [a]Matt. 5:22

58 [1]Or, *sanctuary* [a]Mark 15:29; Matt. 26:61

60 [1]Or, *what do these testify?*

61 [a]Matt. 26:63 [b]Mark 14:61-63: *Matt. 26:63ff.; Luke 22:67-71*

the one; seize Him, and lead Him away [1]under guard."

45 And after coming, he immediately went up to Him, saying, "[a]Rabbi!" and kissed Him.

46 And they laid hands on Him, and seized Him.

47 But a certain one of those who stood by drew his sword, and struck the slave of the high priest, and [1]cut off his ear.

48 And Jesus answered and said to them, "Have you come out with swords and clubs to arrest Me, as though I were a robber?

49 "Every day I was with you [a]in the temple teaching, and you did not seize Me; but [1]*this has happened* that the Scriptures might be fulfilled."

50 And they all left Him and fled.

51 And a certain young man was following Him, wearing *nothing but* a linen sheet over *his* naked *body*; and they *seized him.

52 But he left the linen sheet behind, and escaped naked.

53 [a]And they led Jesus away to the high priest; and all the chief priests and the elders and the scribes *gathered together.

54 And Peter had followed Him at a distance, [a]right into [b]the courtyard of the high priest; and he was sitting with the [1]officers, and [c]warming himself at the [2]fire.

55 Now the chief priests and the whole [1a]Council kept trying to obtain testimony against Jesus to put Him to death; and they were finding none.

56 For many were giving false testimony against Him, and *yet* their testimony was not consistent.

57 And some stood up and *began* to give false testimony against Him, saying,

58 "We heard Him say, '[a]I will destroy this [1]temple made with hands, and in three days I will build another made without hands.' "

59 And not even in this respect was their testimony consistent.

60 And the high priest arose *and came* forward and questioned Jesus, saying, "Do You make no answer [1]to what these men are testifying against You?"

61 [a]But He kept silent, and made no answer. [b]Again the high priest was questioning Him, and

[1]saying to Him, "Are You [2]the Christ, the Son of the Blessed *One?*"

62   And Jesus said, "I am; and you shall see the [a]SON OF MAN SITTING AT THE RIGHT HAND OF POWER, and [b]COMING WITH THE CLOUDS OF HEAVEN."

63   And [a]tearing his clothes, the high priest *said, "What further need do we have of witnesses?

64   "You have heard the blasphemy; how does it seem to you?" And they all condemned Him to be deserving of death.

65   And some began to [a]spit at Him, and [1b]to blindfold Him, and to beat Him with their fists, and to say to Him, "[c]Prophesy!" And the officers [2]received Him with [3]slaps *in the face.*

66   [a]And as Peter was below in [b]the courtyard, one of the servant-girls of the high priest *came,

67   and seeing Peter [a]warming himself, she looked at him, and *said, "You too, were with Jesus the [b]Nazarene."

68   But he denied *it,* saying, "I neither know nor understand what you are talking about." And he [a]went out onto the [1]porch.[2]

69   And the maid saw him, and began once more to say to the bystanders, "This is *one* of them!"

70   But again [a]he was denying it. And after a little while the bystanders were again saying to Peter, "Surely you are *one* of them, [b]for you are a Galilean too."

71   But he began to [1]curse and swear, "I do not know this fellow you are talking about!"

72   And immediately a cock crowed a second time. And Peter remembered how Jesus had made the remark to him, "Before [a]a cock crows twice, you will deny Me three times." [1]And he *began* to weep.

[a]   CHAPTER 15

AND early in the morning the chief priests with the elders and scribes, and the whole [1b]Council, immediately held a consultation, and binding Jesus, they led Him away, and delivered Him up to Pilate.

2   [a]And Pilate questioned Him, "Are You the King of the Jews?" And answering He *said to him, "*It is as* you say."

---

61 [1]Lit., *says* [2]I.e., the Messiah

62 [a]Ps. 110:1; Mark 13:26 [b]Dan. 7:13

63 [a]Matt. 26:65; Acts 14:14; Num. 14:6

65 [1]Or, *cover over His face* [2]Or, *treated* [3]Or possibly: *blows with rods* [a]Mark 10:34; Matt. 26:67 [b]Esther 7:8 [c]Matt. 26:68; Luke 22:64

66 [a]Mark 14:66-72: *Matt. 26:69-75; Luke 22:56-62; John 18:16-18, 25-27* [b]Mark 14:54

67 [a]Mark 14:54 [b]Mark 1:24

68 [1]Or, *forecourt, gateway* [2]Later mss. add: *and a cock crowed* [a]Mark 14:54

70 [a]Mark 14:68 [b]Matt. 26:73; Luke 22:59

71 [1]Or, *put himself under a curse*

72 [1]Or, *thinking of this, he* began *weeping;* or, *rushing out, he* began *weeping* [a]Mark 14:30, 68

1 [1]Or, *Sanhedrin* [a]Matt. 27:1 [b]Matt. 5:22

2 [a]Mark 15:2-5: *Matt. 27:11-14; Luke 23:2, 3; John 18:29-38*

109

3 [1]Or, *of many things*

5 [a]Matt. 27:12

6 [a]Mark 15:6-15: *Matt.*
27:15-26; Luke 23:18-25;
John 18:39-19:16

11 [a]Acts 3:14

13 [1]Or, *again*

15 [a]Matt. 27:26

16 [1]Or, *court* [2]Or,
battalion
[a]Mark 15:16-20: *Matt.* 27:27-
31 [b]Matt. 27:27; Mark 26:3
[c]Acts 10:1

17 [1]A term for shades
varying from rose to purple

19 [1]Or, *staff* (made of a
reed)

21 [a]Mark 15:21: *Matt.*
27:32; Luke 23:26

3 And the chief priests *began* to accuse Him [1]harshly.

4 And Pilate was questioning Him again, saying, "Do You make no answer? See how many charges they bring against You!"

5 But Jesus [a]made no further answer; so that Pilate was astonished.

6 [a]Now at *the* feast he used to release for them *any* one prisoner whom they requested.

7 And the man named Barabbas had been imprisoned with the insurrectionists who had committed murder in the insurrection.

8 And the multitude went up and began asking him *to do* as he had been accustomed to do for them.

9 And Pilate answered them, saying, "Do you want me to release for you the King of the Jews?"

10 For he was aware that the chief priests had delivered Him up because of envy.

11 But the chief priests stirred up the multitude [a]*to ask* him to release Barabbas for them instead.

12 And answering again, Pilate was saying to them, "Then what shall I do to Him whom you call the King of the Jews?"

13 And they shouted [1]back, "Crucify Him!"

14 But Pilate was saying to them, "Why, what evil has He done?" But they shouted all the more, "Crucify Him!"

15 And wishing to satisfy the multitude, Pilate released Barabbas for them, and after having Jesus [a]scourged, he delivered Him over to be crucified.

16 [a]And the soldiers took Him away into [b]the [1]palace (that is, the Praetorium), and they *called together the whole *Roman* [2c]cohort.

17 And they *dressed Him up in [1]purple, and after weaving a crown of thorns, they put it on Him;

18 and they began to acclaim Him, "Hail, King of the Jews!"

19 And they kept beating His head with a [1]reed, and spitting at Him, and kneeling and bowing before Him.

20 And after they had mocked Him, they took the purple off Him, and put His garments on Him. And they *led Him out to crucify Him.

21 [a]And they *pressed into service a passerby coming from the country, Simon of Cyrene (the

father of Alexander and Rufus), that he might bear His cross.

22   ^aAnd they *brought Him to the place ^bGolgotha, which is translated, Place of a Skull.

23   And they tried to give Him ^awine mixed with myrrh; but He did not take it.

24   And they *crucified Him, and *^aDIVIDED UP HIS GARMENTS AMONG THEMSELVES, CASTING ¹LOTS FOR THEM, *to decide* ²what each should take.

25   And it was the ^{1a}third hour ²when they crucified Him.

26   And the inscription of the charge against Him ¹read, "^aTHE KING OF THE JEWS."

27   And they *crucified two robbers with Him; one on the right and one on the left.

28   (See marginal note.¹)

29   And those passing by were ¹hurling abuse at Him, ^aWAGGING THEIR HEADS, and saying, "Ha! You who *were going to* ^bdestroy the temple and rebuild it in three days,

30   save Yourself, and come down from the cross!"

31   In the same way the chief priests along with the scribes were also mocking *Him* among themselves and saying, "^aHe saved others; ¹He cannot save Himself.

32   "Let *this* Christ, ^athe King of Israel, now come down from the cross, so that we may see and believe!" And ^bthose who were crucified with Him were casting the same insult at Him.

33   ^aAnd when the ^{1b}sixth hour had come, darkness ²fell over the whole land until the ^{3b}ninth hour.

34   And at the ^aninth hour Jesus cried out with a loud voice, "^bELOI, ELOI, LAMA SABACHTHANI?" which is translated, "MY GOD, MY GOD, WHY HAST THOU FORSAKEN ME?"

35   And when some of the bystanders heard it, they *began* saying, "Behold, He is calling for Elijah."

36   And someone ran and filled a sponge with sour wine, put it on a reed, and gave Him a drink, saying, "¹Let us see whether Elijah will come to take Him down."

37   ^aAnd Jesus uttered a loud cry, and breathed His last.

38   ^aAnd the veil of the temple was torn in two from top to bottom.

22 ^aMark 15:22-32: *Matt. 27:33-44; Luke 23:33-43; John 19:17-24* ^bJohn 19:17; Luke 23:33 and marg.

23 ^aMatt. 27:34

24 ¹Lit., *a lot upon* ²Lit., *who should take what* ^aPs. 22:18; John 19:24

25 ¹I.e., 9 a.m. ²Lit., *and* ^aJohn 19:14; Mark 15:33

26 ¹Lit., *had been inscribed* ^aMatt. 27:37

28 ¹Later mss. add verse 28: *And the Scripture was fulfilled which says, "And He was reckoned with transgressors."*

29 ¹Or, *blaspheming* ^aPs. 22:8; Matt. 27:39 ^bMark 14:58

31 ¹Or, *can He not save Himself?* ^aMatt. 27:42; Luke 23:35

32 ^aMatt. 27:42; Mark 15:26 ^bMark 15:27; Matt. 27:44; Luke 23:39-43

33 ¹I.e., noon ²Or, *occurred* ³I.e., 3 p.m. ^aMark 15:33-41: *Matt. 27:45-56; Luke 23:44-49* ^bMatt. 27:45f.; Luke 23:44; Mark 15:25

34 ^aMatt. 27:45f.; Luke 23:44; Matt. 15:25 ^bPs. 22:1; Matt. 27:46

36 ¹Lit., *permit that we see;* or: *hold off, let us see*

37 ^aMatt. 27:50; Luke 23:46; John 19:30

38 ^aMatt. 27:51; Luke 23:45

39 [1]Or, *opposite Him* [2]Lit., *that He thus* [3]Or, possibly: *a son of God*, or, *son of a god*
[a]Matt. 27:54; Luke 23:47; Mark 15:45

40 [1]Or, *Jacob* [2]Lit., *little* (either in stature or age)
[a]Mark 15:40, 41: *Matt. 27:55f.*; Luke 23:49; John 19:25 [b]Luke 19:3 [c]Mark 16:1

41 [1]Or, *wait on*
[a]Matt. 27:55f.

42 [a]Mark 15:42-47: *Matt. 27:57-61; Luke 23:50-56; John 19:38-42* [b]Matt. 27:62

43 [a]Luke 23:51; Acts 13:50; 17:12; Matt. 27:57 [b]Luke 23:51; 2:25, 38; Matt. 27:57; John 19:38 [c]John 19:38

45 [a]Mark 15:39

47 [a]Mark 15:40; 16:1; Matt. 27:56

1 [1]Or, *Jacob*
[a]Mark 16:18: *Matt. 28:1-8; Luke 24:1-10;* John 20:1-8 [b]Mark 15:47 [c]Luke 23:56; John 19:39f.

3 [a]Mark 16:3, 4; 15:46; Matt. 27:60

4 [1]Lit., *for*

39 [a]And when the centurion, who was standing [1]right in front of Him, saw [2]the way He breathed His last, he said, "Truly this man was [3]the Son of God!"

40 [a]And there were also *some* women looking on from afar, among whom *were* Mary Magdalene, and Mary the mother of [1]James [b]the [2]Less and Joses, and [c]Salome.

41 And when He was in Galilee, they used to follow Him and [1a]minister to Him; and *there were* many other women who had come up with Him to Jerusalem.

42 [a]And when evening had already come, because it was [b]the Preparation Day, that is, the day before the Sabbath,

43 Joseph of Arimathea came, a [a]prominent member of the Council, a man who was himself [b]waiting for the kingdom of God; and he [c]gathered up courage and went in before Pilate, and asked for the body of Jesus.

44 And Pilate wondered if He was dead by this time, and summoning the centurion, he questioned him as to whether He was already dead.

45 And ascertaining this from [a]the centurion, he granted the body to Joseph.

46 And *Joseph* bought a linen sheet, took Him down, wrapped Him in the linen sheet, and laid Him in a tomb which had been hewn out in the rock; and he rolled a stone against the entrance of the tomb.

47 And [a]Mary Magdalene and Mary the *mother* of Joses were looking on *to see* where He was laid.

[a]   CHAPTER 16

AND when the Sabbath was over, [b]Mary Magdalene, and Mary the *mother* of [1]James, and Salome, [c]bought spices, that they might come and anoint Him.

2 And very early on the first day of the week, they *came to the tomb when the sun had risen.

3 And they were saying to one another, "Who will roll away [a]the stone for us from the entrance of the tomb?"

4 And looking up, they *saw that the stone had been rolled away, [1]although it was extremely large.

10   And the whole multitude of the people were in prayer ᵃoutside at the hour of the incense offering.

11   And ᵃan angel of the Lord appeared to him, standing to the right of the altar of incense.

12   And Zacharias was troubled when he saw *him*, and fear ¹gripped him.

13   But the angel said to him, "ᵃDo not be afraid, Zacharias, for your petition has been heard, and your wife Elizabeth will bear you a son, and ᵇyou will ¹give him the name John.

14   "And you will have joy and gladness, and many will rejoice at his birth.

15   "For he will be great in the sight of the Lord, and he will ᵃdrink no wine or liquor; and he will be filled with the Holy Spirit, ¹while yet in his mother's womb.

16   "And he will turn back many of the sons of Israel to the Lord their God.

17   "And it is he who will ᵃgo *as a forerunner* before Him in the spirit and power of ᵇElijah, ᶜTO TURN THE HEARTS OF THE FATHERS BACK TO THE CHILDREN, and the disobedient to the attitude of the righteous; so as to ᵃmake ready a people prepared for the Lord."

18   And Zacharias said to the angel, "How shall I know this *for certain?* For I am an old man, and my wife is advanced in ¹years."

19   And the angel answered and said to him, "I am ᵃGabriel, who ¹ᵇstands in the presence of God; and I have been sent to speak to you, and to bring you this good news.

20   "And behold, you shall be silent and unable to speak until the day when these things take place, because you did not believe my words, which shall be fulfilled in their proper time."

21   And the people were waiting for Zacharias, and were wondering at his delay in the temple.

22   But when he came out, he was unable to speak to them; and they realized that he had seen a vision in the temple; and he ᵃkept ¹making signs to them, and remained mute.

23   And it came about, when the days of his priestly service were ended, that he went back home.

24   And after these days Elizabeth his wife became pregnant; and she ¹kept herself in seclusion for five months, saying,

10 ᵃLev. 16:17

11 ᵃLuke 2:9; Acts 5:19

12 ¹Or, *fell upon*

13 ¹Lit., *call his name*
ᵃLuke 1:30; Matt. 14:27
ᵇLuke 1:60, 63

15 ¹Lit., *even from*
ᵃNum. 6:3; Judg. 13:4; Matt. 11:18; Luke 7:33

17 ᵃLuke 1:76 ᵇMatt. 11:14
ᶜMal. 4:6

18 ¹Lit., *days*

19 ¹Lit., *stand beside*
ᵃLuke 1:26; Dan. 8:16; 9:21
ᵇMatt. 18:10

22 ¹Or, *beckoning to*, or, *nodding to*
ᵃLuke 1:62

24 ¹Lit., *was hidden*

115

Luke 1

**Birth of Jesus Foretold.   The Annunciation.
Mary Visits Elizabeth.**

25 ªGen. 30:23; Is. 4:1

26 ªLuke 1:19 ᵇMatt. 2:23

27 ¹Lit., *house*
ªMatt. 1:18 ᵇMatt. 1:16, 20;
Luke 2:4

28 ¹Or, *O woman richly
blessed* ²Or, *be* ³Later mss.
add: *you are blessed among
women*

29 ªLuke 1:12

30 ªLuke 1:13; Matt. 14:27

31 ªMatt. 1:21, 25; Luke
2:21

32 ªLuke 1:35, 76; 6:35;
Acts 7:48; Mark 5:7

33 ªMatt. 1:1 ᵇMatt. 28:18;
Dan. 2:44; 7:14, 18, 27

34 ¹Lit., *shall* ²Lit., *know
no man*

35 ¹Lit., *the holy thing
begotten*
ªMatt. 1:18 ᵇLuke 1:32
ᶜMark 1:24 ᵈMatt. 4:3

36 ¹Lit., *this is the sixth
month to her who*

37 ¹Lit., *not any word*
ªMatt. 19:26

38 ¹Gr. *Mariam*, i.e.,
Miriam; so throughout Luke
²I.e., female slave

39 ¹Lit., *in these days*
ªLuke 1:65; Josh. 20:7; 21:11

41 ªLuke 1:67

25 "This is the way the Lord has dealt with me in the days when He looked *with favor* upon me, to ªtake away my disgrace among men."

26 Now in the sixth month the angel ªGabriel was sent from God to a city in Galilee, called ᵇNazareth,

27 to ªa virgin engaged to a man whose name was Joseph, ᵇof the ¹descendants of David; and the virgin's name was Mary.

28 And coming in, he said to her, "Hail, ¹favored one! The Lord ²*is* with you."³

29 But she ªwas greatly troubled at *this* statement, and kept pondering what kind of salutation this might be.

30 And the angel said to her, "ªDo not be afraid, Mary; for you have found favor with God.

31 "And behold, you will conceive in your womb, and bear a son, and you ªshall name Him Jesus.

32 "He will be great, and will be called the Son of ªthe Most High; and the Lord God will give Him the throne of His father David;

33 ªand He will reign over the house of Jacob forever; ᵇand His kingdom will have no end."

34 And Mary said to the angel, "How ¹can this be, since I ²am a virgin?"

35 And the angel answered and said to her, "ªThe Holy Spirit will come upon you, and the power of ᵇthe Most High will overshadow you; and for that reason ᶜthe ¹holy offspring shall be called ᵈthe Son of God.

36 "And behold, even your relative Elizabeth has also conceived a son in her old age; and ¹she who was called barren is now in her sixth month.

37 "For ¹ªnothing will be impossible with God."

38 And ¹Mary said, "Behold, the ²bondslave of the Lord; be it done to me according to your word." And the angel departed from her.

39 Now ¹at this time Mary arose and went with haste to ªthe hill country, to a city of Judah,

40 and entered the house of Zacharias and greeted Elizabeth.

41 And it came about that when Elizabeth heard Mary's greeting, the baby leaped in her womb; and Elizabeth was ªfilled with the Holy Spirit.

42 And she cried out with a loud voice, and

The 'Magnificat.'

said, "Blessed among w... ...t the
is the fruit of your wo... ...your greet-
43 "And how has ...in my womb
mother of my Lord
44 "For behold, ...lieved ¹that there
ing reached my ea...t had been spoken to
for joy.
45 "And ...bles...
would be a fulfil...
her ²by the Lor...xalts the Lord,
46 And M... spirit has rejoiced in ᵇGod my
47 "ªMy ...or.

48   ...He has had ¹egard for the humble
     state of His ¹bondslave;
     For behold, from this time on all genera-
     tions will count me ªblessed.

49   For the Mighty One has done great
     things for me;
     And holy is His name.

50   ªAND HIS MERCY IS ¹UPON GENERATION AF-
     TER GENERATION
     TOWARDS THOSE WHO FEAR HIM.

51   ªHe has done ¹mighty deeds with His
     arm;
     He has scattered those who were proud
     in the ²thoughts of their heart.

52   He has brought down rulers from their
     thrones,
     And has exalted those who were humble.

53   ªHE HAS FILLED THE HUNGRY WITH GOOD
     THINGS;
     And sent away the rich empty-handed.

54   He has given help to Israel His servant,
     ¹In remembrance of His mercy,

55   ªAs He spoke to our fathers,
     To Abraham and his ¹offspring forever."

56 And Mary stayed with her about three
months, and then returned to her home.

57 Now the time ¹had come for Elizabeth to
...ve birth, and she brought forth a son.

...58 And her neighbors and her relatives heard
...the Lord had ¹ªdisplayed His great mercy
...d her; and they were rejoicing with her.

And it came about that on ªthe eighth day
...ne to circumcise the child, and they were
...all him Zacharias, ¹after his father.

43 ¹Lit., *whence this to me*
ªLuke 2:11

45 ¹Or, possibly: *because
there will be* ²Lit., *from*
ªLuke 1:48; Luke 1:20

46 ¹Lit., *makes great*
ªLuke 1:46-53: 1 Sam. 2:1-10
ᵇPs. 34:2f.

47 ªPs. 35:9 ᵇ1 Tim. 1:1;
2:3; Titus 1:3; 2:10; 3:4; Jude
25

48 ¹I.e., female slave
ªLuke 1:45

50 ¹Lit., *unto generations
and generations*
ªPs. 103:17

51 ¹Lit., *might* ²Lit.,
thought, attitude
ªPs. 98:1; 118:15

53 ªPs. 107:9

54 ¹Lit., *so as to remember*

55 ¹Lit., *seed*
ªGen. 17:19; Ps. 132:11; Gal.
3:16

57 ¹Lit., *was fulfilled*

58 ¹Lit., *magnified*
ªGen. 19:19

59 ¹Lit., *after the name of*
ªGen. 17:12; Lev. 12:3; Luke
2:21; Phil. 3:5

60 a Luke 1:13, 63

62 a Luke 1:22

63 a Luke 1:13, 60

64 a Luke 1:20

65 a Luke 1:39

66 a Acts 11:21

67 a Luke 1:41 b Joel 2:28

68 a Luke 2:38; Heb. 9:12; Luke 1:71; Acts 1:6

69 a 1 Sam. 2:1, 10; Ps. 18:2; 89:17; 132:17; Ezek. 29:21; b Matt. 1:1

70 a Rom. 1:2 b Acts 3:21

71 1 Or, Deliverance a Luke 1:68 b Ps. 106:10

72 a Mic. 7:20 b Ps. 105:8f.; 106:45

73 a Gen. 22:16ff.

76 a Matt. 11:9 b Luke 1:32 c Mal. 3:1 d Luke 1:17

77 1 Or, consisting in a Mark 1:4; Jer. 31:34

78 a Mal. 4:2; Eph. 5:14; 2 Pet. 1:19

John the Baptist.
The 'Benedictus.'

60 And he indeed; but a he

61 And they and said, "No among your relativ

62 And they am ere is no one what he wanted him ca y that name."

63 And he asked for father, as to lows, "a His name is Joh wrote as follows, astonished.

64 a And at once his mout tongue *loosed*, and he *began* tend and his God. in praise of

65 And fear came on all those them; and all these matters were about in all a the hill country of Judea.

66 And all who heard them kept them mind, saying, "What then will this child *turn out* be?" For a the hand of the Lord was certainly with him.

67 And his father Zacharias a was filled with the Holy Spirit, and b prophesied, saying;

68 "Blessed *be* the Lord God of Israel,
    For He has visited us and accomplished a redemption for His people,

69 And has raised up a a horn of salvation for us
    In the house of David b His servant—

70 a As He spoke by the mouth of His holy
        prophets b from of old—

71 1a Salvation b FROM OUR ENEMIES,
    And FROM THE HAND OF ALL WHO HATE US;

72 a To show mercy toward our fathers,
    b And to remember His holy covenant,

73 a The oath which He swore to Abraham our
        father,

74 To grant us that we being delivered from
        the hand of our enemies,
    Might serve Him without fear,

75 In holiness and righteousness before Him
        all our days.

76 And you, child, will be called the a prophet
        of b the Most High;
    For you will go on c BEFORE THE LORD T
        d PREPARE HIS WAYS;

77 To give to His people *the* knowledge
        salvation
    1 By a the forgiveness of their sins,

78 Because of the tender mercy of our
    With which a the Sunrise from on h
        visit us,

118

79   aTO SHINE UPON THOSE WHO SIT IN DARKNESS
AND THE SHADOW OF DEATH,
To guide our feet into the way of peace."

80   aAnd the child continued to grow, and to become strong in spirit, and he lived in the deserts until the day of his public appearance to Israel.

CHAPTER 2

NOW it came about in those days that a decree went out from aCaesar Augustus, that a census be taken of ball [1]the inhabited earth.

2   [1]This was the first census taken while [2]Quirinius was governor of aSyria.

3   And all were proceeding to register for the census, everyone to his own city.

4   And Joseph also went up from Galilee, from the city of Nazareth, to Judea, to the city of David, which is called Bethlehem, because ahe was of the house and family of David;

5   in order to register, along with Mary, who was engaged to him, and was with child.

6   And it came about that while they were there, the days were completed for her to give birth.

7   And she gave birth to her first-born son; and she wrapped Him in cloths, and laid Him in a [1]manger, because there was no room for them in the inn.

8   And in the same region there were *some* shepherds staying out in the fields, and keeping watch over their flock by night.

9   And aan angel of the Lord suddenly bstood before them, and the glory of the Lord shone around them; and they were terribly frightened.

10   And the angel said to them, "aDo not be afraid; for behold, I bring you good news of a great joy which shall be for all the people;

11   for today in the city of David there has been born for you a aSavior, who is [1]bChrist cthe Lord.

12   "And athis *will be* a sign for you: you will find a baby wrapped in cloths, and lying in a [1]manger."

13   And suddenly there appeared with the angel a multitude of the heavenly host praising God, and saying,

14   "aGlory to God in the highest,

79 aIs. 9:1, 2; 59:8; Matt. 4:16

80 aLuke 2:40

1 [1]I.e., the Roman empire
aLuke 3:1; Matt. 22:17
bMatt. 24:14

2 [1]Or, *this took place as a first census* [2]Gr., *Kyrenios*
aMatt. 4:24

4 aLuke 1:27

7 [1]Or, *feeding trough*

9 aLuke 1:11; Acts 5:19
bLuke 24:4; Acts 12:7

10 aMatt. 14:27

11 [1]I.e., Messiah
aJohn 4:42; Acts 5:31; Matt. 1:21 bMatt. 16:16, 20; John 11:27; Matt. 1:16 cActs 2:36; 10:36; Luke 1:43

12 [1]Or, *feeding trough*
a1 Sam. 2:34; 2 Kin. 19:29; 20:8f.; Is. 7:11, 14

14 aLuke 19:38; Matt. 21:9

14 ¹Lit., *of His good
pleasure;* or possibly, *of good
will*
ᵇLuke 3:22; Eph. 1:9; Phil.
2:13

16 ¹Or, *feeding trough*

19 ªLuke 2:51

20 ªMatt. 9:8

21 ¹Lit., *so as to circumcise
Him*
ªLuke 1:59 ᵇLuke 1:31

23 ªEx. 13:2, 12

24 ªLev. 12:8; 5:11

25 ªLuke 1:6 ᵇLuke 2:38;
23:51; Mark 15:43

26 ¹Or, *Messiah*
ªMatt. 2:12 ᵇPs. 89:48; Heb.
11:5; John 8:51

27 ¹Lit., *to do for Him
according to*
ªLuke 2:22

120

And on earth peace among men ¹ᵇwith whom He is pleased."

15 And it came about that when the angels had gone away from them into heaven, the shepherds *began* saying to one another, "Let us go straight to Bethlehem, and see this thing that has happened which the Lord has made known to us."

16 And they came in haste and found their way to Mary and Joseph, and the baby as He lay in the ¹manger.

17 And when they had seen this, they made known the statement which had been told them about this Child.

18 And all who heard it wondered at the things which were told them by the shepherds.

19 But Mary ªtreasured up all these things, pondering them in her heart.

20 And the shepherds went back, ªglorifying and praising God for all that they had heard and seen, just as had been told them.

21 And when ªeight days were completed ¹before His circumcision, ᵇHis name was *then* called Jesus, the name given by the angel before He was conceived in the womb.

22 And when the days for their purification according to the law of Moses were completed, they brought Him up to Jerusalem to present Him to the Lord

23 (as it is written in the Law of the Lord, "ªEVERY *first-born* MALE THAT OPENS THE WOMB SHALL BE CALLED HOLY TO THE LORD"),

24 and to offer a sacrifice according to what was said in the Law of the Lord, "ªA PAIR OF TURTLEDOVES, OR TWO YOUNG PIGEONS."

25 And behold, there was a man in Jerusalem whose name was Simeon; and this man was ªrighteous and devout, ᵇlooking for the consolation of Israel; and the Holy Spirit was upon him.

26 And ªit had been revealed to him by the Holy Spirit that he would not ᵇsee death before he had seen the Lord's ¹Christ.

27 And he came in the Spirit into the temple; and when the parents brought in the child Jesus, ¹ªto carry out for Him the custom of the Law,

28 then he took Him into his arms, and blessed God, and said,

29 "Now Lord, Thou dost let Thy bondservant depart,

In peace, [a]according to Thy word;

30 For mine eyes have [a]seen Thy salvation,

31 Which Thou hast prepared in the presence
of all peoples,

32 [a]A LIGHT [1]OF REVELATION TO THE GENTILES,
And the glory of Thy people Israel."

33 And His father and [a]mother were amazed at
the things which were being said about Him.

34 And Simeon blessed them, and said to
Mary [a]His mother, "Behold, this *Child* is appointed for [b]the fall and [1]rise of many in Israel,
and for a sign to be opposed —

35 and a sword will pierce even your own soul
— to the end that thoughts from many hearts may
be revealed."

36 And there was a [a]prophetess, [1]Anna the
daughter of Phanuel, of [b]the tribe of Asher. She
was advanced in [2]years, [c]having lived with a husband seven years after her [3]marriage,

37 and then as a widow to the age of eightyfour. And she *never* left the temple, serving night
and day with [a]fastings and prayers.

38 And at that very [1]moment she came up and
began giving thanks to God, and continued to
speak of Him to all those who were [a]looking for the
redemption of Jerusalem.

39 And when they had performed everything
according to the Law of the Lord, they returned to
Galilee, to [a]their own city of Nazareth.

40 [a]And the Child continued to grow and become strong, [1]increasing in wisdom; and the grace
of God was upon Him.

41 And His parents used to go to Jerusalem
every year at [a]the Feast of the Passover.

42 And when He became twelve, they went up
there according to the custom of the Feast;

43 and as they were returning, after spending
the [a]full number of days, the boy Jesus stayed behind in Jerusalem. And His parents were unaware
of it,

44 but supposed Him to be in the caravan, and
went a day's journey; and they *began* looking for
Him among their relatives and acquaintances.

45 And when they did not find Him, they returned to Jerusalem, looking for Him.

46 And it came about that after three days
they found Him in the temple, sitting in the midst

29 [a]Luke 2:26

30 [a]Is. 52:10; Luke 3:6

32 [1]Or, *for*
[a]Is. 42:6; 49:6; Acts 13:47; 26:23

33 [a]Matt. 12:46

34 [1]Or, *resurrection*
[a]Matt. 12:46 [b]Matt. 21:44; 1 Cor. 1:23; 2 Cor. 2:16; 1 Pet. 2:8

36 [1]Or, *Hannah* [2]Lit., *days* [3]Lit., *virginity*
[a]Acts 21:9; Luke 2:38 [b]Josh. 19:24 [c]1 Tim. 5:9

37 [a]Luke 5:33; Acts 13:3; 14:23; 1 Tim. 5:5

38 [1]Lit., *hour*
[a]Luke 2:25; Luke 1:68

39 [a]Luke 2:51; 4:16; Luke 1:26; Matt. 2:23

40 [1]Lit., *becoming full of*
[a]Luke 1:80; Luke 2:52

41 [a]Ex. 23:15; Deut. 16:1-6

43 [a]Ex. 12:15

48 ¹Lit., *Child* ²Lit., *are looking*
ªMatt. 12:46 ᵇLuke 3:23; 4:22; Luke 2:49

49 ¹Or, *affairs*; lit., *in the things of My Father*

50 ¹Lit., *had spoken*
ªMark 9:32

51 ¹Lit., *was treasuring* ²Lit., *words*
ªLuke 2:39 ᵇMatt. 12:46
ᶜLuke 2:19

52 ¹Or, *age*
ªLuke 2:40

1 ªMatt. 27:2 ᵇMatt. 14:1

2 ªJohn 18:13, 24; Acts 4:6
ᵇMatt. 26:3 ᶜLuke 3:3-10; Matt. 3:1-10; Mark 1:3-5

3 ªMatt. 3:5

4 ªIs. 40:3

5 ¹Or, *leveled*
ªIs. 40:4

6 ¹Or, *mankind*
ªIs. 40:5 ᵇLuke 2:30

of the teachers, both listening to them, and asking them questions.

47 And all who heard Him were amazed at His understanding and His answers.

48 And when they saw Him, they were astonished; and ªHis mother said to Him, "¹Son, why have You treated us this way? Behold, ᵇYour father and I ²have been anxiously looking for You."

49 And He said to them, "Why is it that you were looking for Me? Did you not know that I had to be in My Father's ¹house?"

50 And ªthey did not understand the statement which He ¹had made to them.

51 And He went down with them, and came to ªNazareth; and He continued in subjection to them; and ᵇHis mother ¹ctreasured all *these* ²things in her heart.

52 And Jesus kept increasing in wisdom and ¹stature, and in ªfavor with God and men.

CHAPTER 3

NOW in the fifteenth year of the reign of Tiberius Caesar, when ªPontius Pilate was governor of Judea, and ᵇHerod was tetrarch of Galilee, and his brother Phillip was tetrarch of the region of Ituraea and Trachonitis, and Lysanias was tetrarch of Abilene,

2 in the high priesthood of ªAnnas and ᵇCaiaphas, ᶜthe word of God came to John, the son of Zacharias, in the wilderness.

3 And he came into all ªthe district around the Jordan, preaching a baptism of repentance for forgiveness of sins;

4 as it is written in the book of the words of Isaiah the prophet, "The voice of one crying in the wilderness,

'ªMAKE READY THE WAY OF THE LORD,
MAKE HIS PATHS STRAIGHT.

5 ªEVERY RAVINE SHALL BE FILLED UP,
AND EVERY MOUNTAIN AND HILL SHALL BE ¹BROUGHT LOW;
AND THE CROOKED SHALL BECOME STRAIGHT,
AND THE ROUGH ROADS SMOOTH;

6 ªAND ALL ¹FLESH SHALL ᵇSEE THE SALVATION OF GOD.'"

7 He therefore *began* saying to the multitudes who were going out to be baptized by him, "You brood of vipers, who warned you to flee from the wrath to come?

8 "Therefore bring forth fruits in keeping with your repentance, and [a]do not begin to say [1]to yourselves, 'We have Abraham for our father,' for I say to you that God is able from these stones to raise up children to Abraham.

9 "And also the axe is already laid at the root of the trees; every tree therefore that does not bear good fruit is cut down and thrown into the fire."

10 And the multitudes were questioning him, saying, "Then what shall we do?"

11 And he would answer and say to them, "Let the man who has two tunics share with him who has none; and let him who has food do likewise."

12 And *some* [1]tax-gatherers also came to be baptized, and they said to him, "Teacher, what shall we do?"

13 And he said to them, "[1]Collect no more than what you have been ordered to."

14 And *some* [1]soldiers were questioning him, saying, "And *what about* us, what shall we do?" And he said to them, "Do not take money from anyone by force, or accuse *anyone* falsely, and be content with your wages."

15 Now while the people were in a state of expectation and all were [1]wondering in their hearts about John, [a]as to whether he might be [2]the Christ;

16 [a]John answered and said to them all, "As for me, I baptize you with water; but He who is mightier than I is coming, and I am not fit to untie the thong of His sandals; He Himself will baptize you [1]in the Holy Spirit and fire.

17 "And His [a]winnowing fork is in His hand to clean out His threshing-floor, and to gather the wheat into His barn; but He will burn up the chaff with [b]unquenchable fire."

18 So with many other exhortations also he preached the gospel to the people.

19 But when [a]Herod the tetrarch was reproved by him on account of [a]Herodias, his brother's wife, and on account of all the wicked things which [b]Herod had done,

20 he added this also to them all, that [a]he locked John up in prison.

8 [1]Or, *in*
[a]Luke 5:21; 13:25, 26; 14:9

12 [1]Publicans who collected Roman taxes on commission

13 [1]Or, *Extort*

14 [1]Lit., men in active military service

15 [1]Or, *reasoning,* or *debating* [2]I.e., the Messiah
[a]John 1:19f.

16 [1]Or, *with*
[a]Luke 3:16, 17; *Matt. 3:11, 12; Mark 1:7, 8*

17 [a]Is. 30:24 [b]Mark 9:43, 48

19 [a]Matt. 14:3; Mark 6:17 [b]Luke 3:1; Matt. 14:1

20 [a]John 3:24

21 ªLuke 3:21, 22: Matt. 3:13-17; Mark 1:9-11 ᵇLuke 5:16; 9:18, 28f.; Matt. 14:23

22 ªMatt. 3:17

23 ¹Lit., as it was being thought ²Also spelled Heli ªMatt. 4:17; Acts 1:1 ᵇLuke 3:23-27; Matt. 1:16

25 ¹Also spelled Esli

27 ¹Gr., Salathiel ªMatt. 1:12

29 ¹Gr., Jesus

30 ¹Gr., Judas

32 ¹Gr., Sala ²Gr., Nausson ªLuke 3:32 34: Matt 1 1-6

33 ¹Gr., Arni

34 ªLuke 3:34-36: Gen. 11:26-30; 1 Chr. 1:24-27

35 ¹Gr., Ragau ²Gr., Eber

36 ªLuke 3:36-38: Gen. 5:3-32; 1 Chr. 1:14

21 ªNow it came about that when all the people were baptized, that Jesus also was baptized, and while He was ᵇpraying, heaven was opened,

22 and the Holy Spirit descended upon Him in bodily form like a dove, and a voice came out of heaven, "ªThou art My beloved Son, in Thee I am well pleased."

23 And ªwhen He began His ministry, Jesus Himself was about thirty years of age, being ¹supposedly *the* son of ᵇJoseph, the *son* of ²Eli,

24 the *son* of Matthat, the *son* of Levi, the *son* of Melchi, the *son* of Jannai, the *son* of Joseph,

25 the *son* of Mattathias, the *son* of Amos, the *son* of Nahum, the *son* of ¹Hesli, the *son* of Naggai,

26 the *son* of Maath, the *son* of Mattathias, the *son* of Semein, the *son* of Josech the *son* of Joda,

27 the *son* of Johanan, the *son* of Resa, ªthe *son* of Zerubbabel, the *son* of ¹Shealtiel, the *son* of Neri,

28 the *son* of Melchi, the *son* of Addi, the *son* of Cosam, the *son* of Elmadam, the *son* of Er,

29 the *son* of ¹Joshua, the *son* of Eliezer, the *son* of Jorim, the *son* of Matthat, the *son* of Levi,

30 the *son* of Simeon, the *son* of ¹Judah, the *son* of Joseph, the *son* of Jonam, the *son* of Eliakim,

31 the *son* of Melea, the *son* of Menna, the *son* of Mattatha, the *son* of Nathan, the *son* of David,

32 ªthe *son* of Jesse, the *son* of Obed, the *son* of Boaz, the *son* of ¹Salmon, the *son* of ²Nahshon,

33 the *son* of Amminadab, the *son* of Admin, the *son* of ¹Ram, the *son* of Hezron, the *son* of Perez, the *son* of Judah,

34 the *son* of Jacob, the *son* of Isaac, ªthe *son* of Abraham, the *son* of Terah, the *son* of Nahor,

35 the *son* of Serug, the *son* of ¹Reu, the *son* of Peleg, the *son* of ²Heber, the *son* of Shelah,

36 the *son* of Cainan, the *son* of Arphaxad, the *son* of Shem, ªthe *son* of Noah, the *son* of Lamech,

37 the *son* of Methuselah, the *son* of Enoch, the *son* of Jared, the *son* of Mahalaleel, the *son* of Cainan,

38 the *son* of Enosh, the *son* of Seth, the *son* of Adam, the *son* of God.

CHAPTER 4

AND Jesus, full of the Holy Spirit, [b]returned from the Jordan and was led about [1]by the Spirit in the wilderness

2   for forty days, while tempted by the devil. And He ate nothing during those days; and when they had ended, He became hungry.

3   And the devil said to Him, "If You are the Son of God, tell this stone to become bread."

4   And Jesus answered him, "It is written, '[a]MAN SHALL NOT LIVE ON BREAD ALONE.' "

5   [a]And he led Him up and showed Him all the kingdoms of [1b]the world in a moment of time.

6   And the devil said to Him, "I will give You all this domain and [1]its glory; [a]for it has been handed over to me, and I give it to whomever I wish.

7   "Therefore if You [1]worship before me, it shall all be Yours."

8   And Jesus answered and said to him, "It is written, '[a]YOU SHALL WORSHIP THE LORD YOUR GOD AND SERVE HIM ONLY.' "

9   [a]And he led Him to Jerusalem and set Him on the pinnacle of the temple, and said to Him, "If You are the Son of God, cast Yourself down from here;

10   for it is written, '[a]HE WILL GIVE HIS ANGELS CHARGE CONCERNING YOU TO GUARD YOU.'

11   and,

'[a]ON THEIR HANDS THEY WILL BEAR YOU UP,
LEST YOU STRIKE YOUR FOOT AGAINST A STONE.' "

12   And Jesus answered and said to him, "It is said, '[a]YOU SHALL NOT [1]FORCE A TEST ON THE LORD YOUR GOD.' "

13   And when the devil had finished every temptation, he departed from Him until an opportune time.

14   And [a]Jesus returned to Galilee in the power of the Spirit; and [b]news about Him spread through all the surrounding district.

15   And He *began* [a]teaching in their synagogues and was praised by all.

16   And He came to [a]Nazareth, where He had been brought up; and as was His custom, [b]He entered the synagogue on the Sabbath, and [c]stood up to read.

1 [1]Or, *under the influence of*, lit., *in*
[a]Luke 4:1-13; Matt. 4:1-11; Mark 1:12, 13 [b]Luke 3:3, 21

4 [a]Deut. 8:3

5 [1]Lit., *the inhabited earth*
[a]Matt. 4:8-10 [b]Matt. 24:14

6 [1]Lit., *their* (referring to the kingdom)
[a]1 John 5:19

7 [1]Or, *bow down*

8 [a]Deut. 6:13

9 [a]Matt. 4:5-7

10 [a]Ps. 91:11

11 [a]Ps. 91:12

12 [1]Or, *tempt*
[a]Deut. 6:16

14 [a]Matt. 4:12 [b]Luke 4:37; Matt. 9:26

15 [a]Matt. 4:23

16 [a]Luke 2:39, 51 [b]Matt. 13:54; Mark 6:1f. [c]Acts 13:14-16

125

17 [1]Or, *scroll*

18 [a]Is. 61:1; Matt. 12:18; Matt. 11:5; John 3:34

19 [a]Is. 61:2; Lev. 25:10

20 [1]Or, *scroll* [a]Luke 4:17 [b]Matt. 26:55

21 [1]Lit., *ears*

22 [1]Or, *testifying* [2]Lit., *were proceeding out of His mouth* [a]Matt. 13:55; Mark 6:3; John 6:42

23 [a]Matt. 4:13; Mark 1:21ff.; 2:1ff.; John 4:46ff.; Luke 4:35ff. [b]Luke 4:16; 2:39, 51; Mark 6:1

24 [a]Matt. 13:57; Mark 6:4; John 4:44

25 [a]1 Kin. 17:1; 18:1; James 5:17

26 [1]Gr., *Serepta* [a]1 Kin. 17:9 [b]Matt. 11:21

27 [a]2 Kin. 5:1-14

29 [a]Acts 7:58; Num. 15:35, Heb. 13:12

30 [a]John 10:39

31 [a]Luke 4:31-37; *Mark 1:21-28* [b]Matt. 4:13; Luke 4:23

17 And the [1]book of the prophet Isaiah was handed to Him. And He opened the [1]book, and found the place where it was written,

18 "[a]THE SPIRIT OF THE LORD IS UPON ME,
BECAUSE HE ANOINTED ME TO PREACH THE GOSPEL TO THE POOR.
HE HAS SENT ME TO PROCLAIM RELEASE TO THE CAPTIVES,
AND RECOVERY OF SIGHT TO THE BLIND,
TO SET FREE THOSE WHO ARE DOWNTRODDEN,

19 [a]TO PROCLAIM THE FAVORABLE YEAR OF THE LORD."

20 And He [a]closed the [1]book, and gave it back to the attendant, and [b]sat down; and the eyes of all in the synagogue were fixed upon Him.

21 And He began to say to them, "Today this Scripture has been fulfilled in your [1]hearing."

22 And all [1]were speaking well of Him, and wondering at the gracious words which [2]were falling from His lips; and they were saying, "[a]Is this not Joseph's son?"

23 And He said to them, "No doubt you will quote this proverb to Me, 'Physician, heal yourself; whatever we heard was done [a]at Capernaum, do here in [b]your home town as well.' "

24 And He said, "Truly I say to you, [a]no prophet is welcome in his home town.

25 "But I say to you in truth, there were many widows in Israel [a]in the days of Elijah, when the sky was shut up for three years and six months, when a great famine came over all the land;

26 and yet Elijah was sent to none of them, but [a]only to [1]Zarephath, in the land of [b]Sidon, to a woman who was a widow.

27 "And there were many lepers in Israel in the time of Elisha the prophet; and none of them was cleansed, but [a]only Naaman the Syrian."

28 And all in the synagogue were filled with rage as they heard these things;

29 and they rose up and [a]cast Him out of the city, and led Him to the brow of the hill on which their city had been built, in order to throw Him down the cliff.

30 But [a]passing through their midst, He went His way.

31 And [a]He came down to [b]Capernaum, a city of Galilee. And He was teaching them on Sabbath days;

**Cures a Demoniac and Simon's
Mother-in-law.   Shuns Publicity.**

Luke 4, 5

32   and [a]they were *continually* amazed at His teaching; for [b]His [1]message was with authority.

33   And there was a man in the synagogue [1]possessed by the spirit of an unclean demon, and he cried out with a loud voice,

34   "[1]Ha! [a]What do we have to do with You, Jesus of [2b]Nazareth? Have You come to destroy us? I know who You are — [b]the Holy One of God!"

35   And Jesus [a]rebuked him, saying, "Be quiet and come out of him!" And when the demon had thrown him down in *their* midst, he went out of him without doing him any harm.

36   And amazement came upon them all, and they *began* discussing with one another, and saying, "What is [1]this message? For [a]with authority and power He commands the unclean spirits, and they come out."

37   And [a]the report about Him was getting out into every locality in the surrounding district.

38   [a]And He arose and *left* the synagogue, and entered Simon's home. Now Simon's mother-in-law was [b]suffering from a high fever; and they made request of Him on her behalf.

39   And standing over her, He [a]rebuked the fever, and it left her; and she immediately arose and *began* to [1]wait on them.

40   [a]And while [b]the sun was setting, all who had any sick with various diseases brought them to Him; and [c]laying His hands on every one of them, He was [d]healing them.

41   And demons also were coming out of many, crying out and saying, "You are [a]the Son of God!" And [b]rebuking them, He would [c]not allow them to speak, because they knew Him to be [1]the Christ.

42   [a]And when day came, He departed and went to a lonely place; and the multitudes were searching for Him, and came to Him, and tried to keep Him from going away from them.

43   But He said to them, "I must preach the kingdom of God to the other cities also, [a]for I was sent for this purpose."

44   And He kept on preaching in the synagogues [a]of [1]Judea.

CHAPTER 5

[a]NOW it came about that while the multitude were pressing around Him and listening to the

---

Marginal notes:

32 [1]Lit., *word*
[a]Matt. 7:28 [b]Luke 4:36; John 7:46

33 [1]Lit., *having a spirit*

34 [1]Or possibly, *Let* us *alone* [2]Lit., *Nazarene*
[a]Matt. 8:29 [b]Mark 1:24

35 [a]Luke 4:39, 41; Matt. 8:26; Mark 4:39; Luke 8:24

36 [1]Or, *this word, that with authority . . . come out?*
[a]Luke 4:32

37 [a]Luke 4:14

38 [a]Luke 4:38, 39: *Matt. 8:14-15; Mark 1:29-31* [b]Matt. 4:24

39 [1]Or, *serve*
[a]Luke 4:35, 41

40 [a]Luke 4:40, 41: *Matt. 8:16-17; Mark 1:32-34* [b]Mark 1:32 [c]Mark 5:23 [d]Matt. 4:23

41 [1]I.e., the Messiah
[a]Matt. 4:3 [b]Luke 4:35 [c]Mark 1:34; Matt. 8:4

42 [a]Luke 4:42, 43: *Mark 1:35-38*

43 [a]Mark 1:38

44 [1]I.e., the country of the Jews (including Galilee); some mss. read, *of Galilee*
[a]Matt. 4:23

1 [a]Luke 5:1-11; Matt. 4:18-22; Mark 1:16-20; John 1:40-42

Luke 5

**The Wonderful Catch of Fish.
Jesus Cleanses a Leper.**

1 bNum. 34:11; Deut. 3:17; Josh. 12:3; 13:27; Matt. 4:18

3 aMatt. 13:2; Mark 4:1

4 aJohn 21:6

5 1Or, *word* aGr. as in Luke 8:24; 9:33, 49; 17:13

8 1Lit., *knees*

10 1Or, *Jacob* aMatt. 14:27 b2 Tim. 2:26

11 aMatt. 4:20, 22; Mark 1:18, 20; Luke 5:28; Matt. 19:29

12 aLuke 5:12-14: *Matt. 8:2-4; Mark 1:40-44*

15 aMatt. 9:26

word of God, He was standing by bthe lake of Gennesaret;

2 and He saw two boats lying at the edge of the lake; but the fishermen had gotten out of them, and were washing their nets.

3 And aHe got into one of the boats, which was Simon's, and asked him to put out a little way from the land. And He sat down and *began* teaching the multitudes from the boat.

4 And when He had finished speaking, He said to Simon, "Put out into the deep water and alet down your nets for a catch."

5 And Simon answered and said, "aMaster, we worked hard all night and caught nothing, but at Your 1bidding I will let down the nets."

6 And when they had done this, they enclosed a great quantity of fish; and their nets *began* to break;

7 and they signaled to their partners in the other boat, for them to come and help them. And they came, and filled both of the boats, so that they began to sink.

8 But when Simon Peter saw *that*, he fell down at Jesus' 1feet, saying, "Depart from me, for I am a sinful man, O Lord!"

9 For amazement had seized him and all his companions because of the catch of fish which they had taken;

10 and so also 1James and John, sons of Zebedee, who were partners with Simon. And Jesus said to Simon, "aDo not fear, from now on you will be bcatching men."

11 And when they had brought their boats to land, athey left everything and followed Him.

12 aAnd it came about that while He was in one of the cities, behold, *there was* a man full of leprosy; and when he saw Jesus, he fell on his face and implored Him, saying, "Lord, if You are willing, You can make me clean."

13 And He stretched out His hand, and touched him, saying, "I am willing; be cleansed." And immediately the leprosy left him.

14 And He ordered him to tell no one, "But go and show yourself to the priest, and make an offering for your cleansing, just as Moses commanded, for a testimony to them."

15 But athe news about Him was spreading

even farther, and great multitudes were gathering to hear *Him* and to be healed of their sicknesses.

16 But He Himself would *often* slip away [1]to the [2]wilderness and [a]pray.

17 And it came about [1]one day that He was teaching; and [a]there were *some* Pharisees and [b]teachers of the law sitting *there*, who had [c]come from every village of Galilee and Judea and *from* Jerusalem; and [d]the power of the Lord was *present* for Him to perform healing.

18 [a]And behold, *some* men *were* carrying on a [1]bed a man who was paralyzed; and they were trying to bring him in, and to set him down in front of Him.

19 And not finding any *way* to bring him in because of the crowd, they went up on [a]the roof and let him down [b]through the tiles with his stretcher, right in the center, in front of Jesus.

20 And seeing their faith, He said, "[1]Friend, [a]your sins are forgiven you."

21 And the scribes and the Pharisees [a]began to reason, saying, "Who is this *man* who speaks blasphemies? [b]Who can forgive sins, but God alone?"

22 But Jesus, [1]aware of their reasonings, answered and said to them, "Why are you reasoning in your hearts?

23 "Which is easier, to say, 'Your sins have been forgiven you,' or to say, 'Rise and walk'?

24 "But in order that you may know that the Son of Man has authority on earth to forgive sins"—He said to the [a]paralytic, "I say to you, rise, and take up your stretcher and go home."

25 And at once he rose up before them, and took up what he had been lying on, and went home, [a]glorifying God.

26 And they were all seized with astonishment and *began* [a]glorifying God; and they were filled [b]with fear, saying, "We have seen remarkable things today."

27 [a]And after that He went out, and noticed a [1]tax-gatherer named [b]Levi, sitting in the tax office, and He said to him, "Follow Me."

28 And he [a]left everything behind, and rose up and *began* to follow Him.

29 And [a]Levi gave a big [1]reception for Him in his house; and there was a great crowd of [b]tax-gatherers and other *people* who were reclining *at table* with them.

16 [1]Lit., *in* [2]Or, *lonely places*
[a]Matt. 14:23; Mark 1:35; Luke 6:12

17 [1]Lit., *on one of the days*
[a]Matt. 15:1 [b]Luke 2:46
[c]Mark 1:45 [d]Mark 5:30; Luke 6:19; 8:46

18 [1]Here, *stretcher*
[a]Luke 5:18-26: *Matt. 9:2-8; Mark 2:3-12*

19 [a]Matt. 24:17 [b]Mark 2:4

20 [1]Lit., *man*
[a]Matt. 9:2

21 [a]Luke 3:8 [b]Is. 43:25

22 [1]Or, *perceiving*

24 [a]Matt. 4:24

25 [a]Matt. 9:8

26 [a]Matt. 9:8 [b]Luke 7:16; 1:65

27 [1]Publicans who collected Roman taxes for profit
[a]Luke 5:27-39: *Matt. 9:9-17; Mark 2:14-22* [b]Matt. 9:9

28 [a]Luke 5:11

29 [1]Or, *banquet*
[a]Matt. 9:9 [b]Luke 15:1

Luke 5, 6

**Is Blamed for Associating with Sinners.
Of Fasting.**

30 aMark 2:16; Acts 23:9

31 aMatt. 9:12, 13; Mark 2:17

33 1Or, *likewise*
aMatt. 9:14; Mark 2:18

34 1Lit., *sons of the bridalchamber*

35 aMatt. 9:15; Mark 2:20; Luke 17:22

36 1Or, *cloak*

37 1I.e., skins used as bottles

1 1Many mss. read, *the second-first Sabbath*; i.e., the second Sabbath after the first
aLuke 5:1-5: *Matt. 12:1-8; Mark 2:23-28* bDeut. 23:25

2 aMatt. 12:2

3 a1 Sam. 21:6

4 1Or, *showbread*, lit., *loaves of presentation*

30 And the Pharisees and ªtheir scribes *began* grumbling at His disciples, saying, "Why do you eat and drink with the tax-gatherers and sinners?"

31 And Jesus answered and said to them, "ª*It is* not those who are well who need a physician, but those who are sick.

32 "I have not come to call righteous men but sinners to repentance."

33 And they said to Him, "ªThe disciples of John often fast and offer prayers; the *disciples* of the Pharisees also do 1the same; but Yours eat and drink."

34 And Jesus said to them, "You cannot make the 1attendants of the bridegroom fast while the bridegroom is with them, can you?

35 "ªBut *the* days will come; and when the bridegroom is taken away from them, then they will fast in those days."

36 And He was also telling them a parable: "No one tears a piece from a new 1garment and puts it on an old 1garment; otherwise he will both tear the new, and the piece from the new will not match the old.

37 "And no one puts new wine into old 1wineskins; otherwise the new wine will burst the 1skins, and it will be spilled out, and the 1skins will be ruined.

38 "But new wine must be put into fresh wineskins.

39 "And no one, after drinking old *wine* wishes for new; for he says, 'The old is good *enough*.'"

a   CHAPTER 6

NOW it came about that on a *certain* 1Sabbath He was passing through *some* grainfields; and His disciples bwere picking and eating the heads *of wheat*, rubbing them in their hands.

2 But some of the Pharisees said, "Why do you do what ªis not lawful on the Sabbath?"

3 And Jesus answering them said, "Have you not even read ªwhat David did when he was hungry, he and those who were with him,

4 how he entered the house of God, and took and ate the 1consecrated bread which is not lawful for any to eat except the priests alone, and gave it to his companions?"

"Lord of the Sabbath." Jesus Heals on the Sabbath. Chooses the Twelve.

Luke 6

5   And He was saying to them, "The Son of Man is lord of the Sabbath."

6   ªAnd it came about ᵇon another Sabbath, that He entered ᶜthe synagogue and was teaching; and there was a man there ¹whose right hand was withered.

7   And the scribes and the Pharisees ªwere watching Him closely, *to see* if He healed on the Sabbath; in order that they might find *reason* to accuse Him.

8   But He ªknew ¹what they were thinking, and He said to the man with the withered hand, "Arise and ²come forward!" And he arose and ³came forward.

9   And Jesus said to them, "I ask you, is it lawful on the Sabbath to do good, or ¹to do evil, to save a life, or to destroy it?"

10   And after ªlooking around at them all, He said to him, "Stretch out your hand!" And he did *so*; and his hand was *completely* restored.

11   But they themselves were filled with ¹rage, and discussed together what they might do to Jesus.

12   And it was ¹at this time that He went off to ªthe mountain to ᵇpray, and He spent the whole night in prayer to God.

13   And when day came, ªHe called His disciples to Him; and chose twelve of them, whom He also named as ᵇapostles:

14   Simon, whom He also named Peter, and Andrew his brother; ¹James and John; Philip and Bartholomew;

15   ªMatthew and Thomas; James *the son* of Alphaeus, and Simon who was called the Zealot;

16   Judas *the son* of James, and Judas Iscariot, who became a traitor.

17   And He ªdescended with them, and stood on a level place; and *there was* ᵇa great multitude of His disciples, and a great throng of people from all Judea and Jerusalem and the coastal region of ᶜTyre and Sidon,

18   ¹who had come to hear Him, and to be healed of their diseases; and those who were troubled with unclean spirits were being cured.

19   And all the multitude were trying to ªtouch Him, for ᵇpower was coming from Him and healing *them* all.

20   And turning His gaze on His disciples, He

---

6 ¹Lit., *and his*
ªLuke 5:6-11; *Matt. 12:9-14;
Mark 3:1-6* ᵇLuke 6:1 ᶜMatt.
4:23

7 ªMark 3:2

8 ¹Lit., *their thoughts*
²Lit., *stand* or *stood into the
midst* ³Lit., *stood*
ªMatt. 9:4

9 ¹Or, *to harm*

10 ªMark 3:5

11 ¹Lit., *folly*

12 ¹Lit., *in these days*
ªMatt. 5:1 ᵇMatt. 14:23;
Luke 9:28; 9:18; 5:16

13 ªLuke 6:13-16: *Matt.
10:2-4; Mark 3:16-19; Acts
1:13* ᵇMark 6:30

14 ¹Here and in verses 15
and 16, Gr., *Jacob*

15 ªMatt. 9:9

17 ªLuke 6:12 ᵇMatt 4:25;
Mark 3:7, 8 ᶜMatt. 11:21

18 ¹Most English versions
begin verse 18 with, *and
those who*

19 ªMark 3:10; Matt. 9:21;
14:36 ᵇLuke 5:17

131

Luke 6

**The Beatitudes.   Of Love to Enemies.
The "Golden Rule."**

20 aLuke 6:20-23; Matt. 5:3-12 bMatt. 5:3

22 aJohn 9:22; 16:2

23 ¹Lit., *do to*
aMal. 4

24 aJames 5:1; Luke 16:25 bMatt. 6:2

25 ¹Lit., *having been filled*

26 ¹Lit., *do to*
aMatt. 7:15

27 aMatt. 5:44; Luke 6:35

28 ¹Or, *revile*
aMatt. 5:44; Luke 6:35

29 ¹Or, *cloak*, or, outer garment ²Or, *tunic*, or, garment worn next to body aLuke 6:29, 30; Matt. 5:39-42

31 ¹Or, *do to*
aMatt. 7:12

32 aMatt. 5:46

34 aMatt. 5:42

35 ¹Or, *not despairing at all* aLuke 6:27 bMatt. 5:9 cLuke 1:32

began to say, "ªBlessed *are* you *who are* poor, for ᵇyours is the kingdom of God.

21 "Blessed *are* you who hunger now, for you shall be satisfied. Blessed *are* you who weep now, for you shall laugh.

22 "Blessed are you when men hate you, and ªostracize you, and heap insults upon you, and spurn your name as evil, for the sake of the Son of Man.

23 "Be glad in that day, and ªleap *for joy*, for behold, your reward is great in heaven; for in the same way their fathers used to ¹treat the prophets.

24 "But woe to ªyou who are rich, for ᵇyou are receiving your comfort in full.

25 "Woe to you who are ¹well-fed now, for you shall be hungry. Woe *to you* who laugh now, for you shall mourn and weep.

26 "Woe to you when all men speak well of you, for in the same way their fathers used to ¹treat the ªfalse prophets.

27 "But I say to you who hear, ªlove your enemies, do good to those who hate you,

28   bless those who curse you, ªpray for those who ¹mistreat you.

29 "ªWhoever hits you on the cheek, offer him the other also; and whoever takes away your ¹coat, do not withhold your ²shirt from him either.

30 "Give to everyone who asks of you, and whoever takes away what is yours, do not demand it back.

31 "ªAnd just as you want men to ¹treat you, ¹treat them in the same way.

32 "And ªif you love those who love you, what credit is *that* to you? For even sinners love those who love them.

33 "And if you do good to those who do good to you, what credit is *that* to you? For even sinners do the same thing.

34 "ªAnd if you lend to those from whom you expect to receive, what credit is *that* to you? Even sinners lend to sinners, in order to receive back the same *amount*.

35 "But ªlove your enemies, and do good, and lend, ¹expecting nothing in return; and your reward will be great, and you will be ᵇsons of ᶜthe Most High; for He Himself is kind to ungrateful and evil *men*.

36 "[1]Be merciful, just as your Father is merciful.

37 "[a]And [1]do not pass judgment and you will not be judged; and do not condemn, and you shall not be condemned; [2b]pardon, and you will be pardoned.

38 "Give, and it will be given to you; [a]good measure, pressed down, shaken together, running over, they will pour [b]into your lap. For whatever measure you deal out *to others*, it will be dealt to you in return."

39 And He also spoke a parable to them: "[a]A blind man cannot guide a blind man, can he? Will they not both fall into a pit?

40 "[a]A [1]pupil is not above his teacher; but everyone, after he has been fully trained, will [2]be like his teacher.

41 "And why do you look at the speck that is in your brother's eye, but do not notice the log that is in your own eye?

42 "Or how can you say to your brother, 'Brother, let me take out the speck that is in your eye,' when you yourself do not see the log that is in your own eye? You hypocrite, first take the log out of your own eye, and then you will see clearly to take out the speck that is in your brother's eye.

43 "[a]For there is no good tree which produces bad fruit; nor [1]on the other hand, a bad tree which produces good fruit.

44 "[a]For each tree is known by its own fruit. For men do not gather figs from thorns, nor do they pick grapes from a briar bush.

45 "[a]The good man out of the good [1]treasure of his heart brings forth what is good; and the evil *man* out of the evil [1]*treasure* brings forth what is evil; [b]for his mouth speaks from [2]that which fills his heart.

46 "And [a]why do you call Me, 'Lord, Lord,' and do not do what I say?

47 "[a]Everyone who comes to Me, and hears My words, and [1]acts upon them, I will show you whom he is like:

48 he is like a man building a house, who [1]dug deep and laid a foundation upon the rock; and when a flood arose, the river burst against that house and could not shake it, because it had been well built.

49 "But the one who has heard, and has not acted *accordingly*, is like a man who built a house

---

36 [1]Or, *become*

37 [1]Lit., *do not judge* [2]Lit., *release*
[a]Luke 6:37-42: *Matt. 7:1-5*
[b]Luke 23:16; Acts 3:13; Matt. 6:14

38 [a]Mark 4:24 [b]Ps. 79:12; Is. 65:6, 7; Jer. 32:18

39 [a]Matt. 15:14

40 [1]Or, *disciple* [2]Or, *reach his teacher's level*
[a]Matt. 10:24

43 [1]Lit., *again*
[a]Luke 6:43, 44: *Matt. 7:16, 18, 20*

44 [a]Matt. 7:16

45 [1]Or, *treasury, storehouse* [2]Lit., *the abundance of*
[a]Matt. 12:35 [b]Matt. 12:34

46 [a]Matt. 7:21; Mal. 1:6

47 [1]Lit., *does*
[a]Luke 6:47-49; *Matt. 7:24-27*

48 [1]Lit., *dug and went deep*

133

1 ªMatt. 7:28 ᵇLuke 7:1-
10: *Matt. 8:5-13*

2 ¹Lit., *to whom he was
honorable*

3 ¹Lit., *elders of the Jews*
²Lit., *bring safely through,
rescue*
ªMatt. 8:5

6 ¹Or, *Sir*

7 ¹Lit., *speak with a word*
²Or, *boy*

9 ªMatt. 8:10; Luke 7:50

11 ¹Some mss read, *on the
next day* ²Lit., *and*

12 ¹Lit., *one who had died*
²Or, *only begotten*

13 ¹Or, *stop weeping*
ªLuke 7:19; 10:1; 11:1, 39;
12:42; 13:15; 17:5, 6; 18:6;
19:8; 22:61; 24:34; John 4:1;
6:23; 11:2

134

upon the ground without any foundation; and the river burst against it and immediately it collapsed, and the ruin of that house was great."

ª   CHAPTER 7

WHEN He had completed all His discourse in the hearing of the people, ᵇHe went to Capernaum.

2   And a certain centurion's slave, ¹who was highly regarded by him, was sick and about to die.

3   And when he heard about Jesus, ªhe sent some ¹Jewish elders asking Him to come and ²save the life of his slave.

4   And when they had come to Jesus, they earnestly entreated Him, saying, "He is worthy for You to grant this to him;

5   for he loves our nation, and it was he who built us our synagogue."

6   Now Jesus *started* on His way with them; and when He was already not far from the house, the centurion sent friends, saying to Him, "¹Lord, do not trouble Yourself further, for I am not fit for You to come under my roof;

7   for this reason I did not even consider myself worthy to come to You, but just ¹say the word, and my ²servant will be healed.

8   "For indeed, I am a man under authority, with soldiers under me; and I say to this one, 'Go!' and he goes; and to another, 'Come!' and he comes; and to my slave, 'Do this!' and he does it."

9   And when Jesus heard this, He marveled at him, and turned and said to the multitude that was following Him, "I say to you, ªnot even in Israel have I found such great faith."

10   And when those who had been sent returned to the house, they found the slave in good health.

11   And it came about ¹soon afterwards, that He went to a city called Nain; and His disciples were going along with Him, ²accompanied by a large multitude.

12   Now as He approached the gate of the city, behold, ¹a dead man was being carried out, the ²only son of his mother, and she was a widow; and a sizeable crowd from the city was with her.

13   And when ªthe Lord saw her, He felt compassion for her, and said to her, "¹Do not weep."

14   And He came up and touched the coffin; and the bearers came to a halt. And He said, "Young man, I say to you, arise!"

15   And the ¹dead man sat up, and began to speak. And *Jesus* gave him back to his mother.

16   And ᵃfear gripped them all, and they *began* ᵇglorifying God, saying, "A great ᶜprophet has arisen among us!" and, "God has ¹visited His people!"

17   ᵃAnd this report concerning Him went out all over Judea, and in all the surrounding district.

18   ᵃAnd the disciples of John reported to him about all these things.

19   And summoning ¹two of his disciples, John sent them to ᵃthe Lord, saying, "Are You the One who is coming, or do we look for someone ²else?"

20   And when the men had come to Him, they said, "John the Baptist has sent us to You, saying, 'Are You the One who is coming, or do we look for someone else?'"

21   At that ¹very time He ᵃcured many *people* of diseases and ᵇafflictions and evil spirits; and He granted sight to many *who were* blind.

22   And He answered and said to them, "Go and report to John what you have seen and heard: *the* ᵃBLIND RECEIVE SIGHT, *the* lame walk, *the* lepers are cleansed, and *the* deaf hear, *the* dead are raised up, *the* ᵃPOOR HAVE THE GOSPEL PREACHED TO THEM.

23   "And blessed is he ¹who keeps from stumbling over Me."

24   And when the messengers of John had left, He began to speak to the multitudes about John, "What did you go out into the wilderness to look at? A reed shaken by the wind?

25   "¹But what did you go out to see? A man dressed in soft ²clothing? Behold, those who are splendidly clothed and live in luxury are *found* in royal palaces.

26   "But what did you go out to see? A prophet? Yes, I say to you, and one who is more than a prophet.

27   "This is the one about whom it ¹is written,
'ᵃBEHOLD, I SEND MY MESSENGER BEFORE
    YOUR FACE,
WHO WILL PREPARE YOUR WAY BEFORE YOU.'

28   "I say to you, among those born of women, there is no one greater than John; yet he who is ¹least in the kingdom of God is greater than he."

29   And when all the people and the ¹tax-gath-

15 ¹Or, *corpse*

16 ¹Or, *cared for*
ᵃLuke 5:26 ᵇMatt. 9:8 ᶜMatt. 21:11; Luke 7:39

17 ᵃMatt. 9:26

18 ᵃLuke 7:18-35: *Matt. 11:2-19*

19 ¹Lit., *a certain two* ²Some early mss. read, *one who is different*
ᵃLuke 7:13; 10:1; 11:1, 39; 12:42; 13:15; 17:5, 6; 18:6; 19:8; 22:61; 24:34; John 4:1; 6:23; 11:2

21 ¹Lit., *hour*
ᵃMatt. 4:23 ᵇMark 3:10

22 ᵃIs. 61:1

23 ¹Lit., *whoever*

25 ¹Or, *Well then, what* ²Or, *garments*

27 ¹Lit., *has been written*
ᵃMal. 3:1; Matt. 11:10; Mark 1:2

28 ¹Lit., *less*

29 ¹Publicans who collected Roman taxes on commission

135

29 [2]Or, *justified God*
[a]Luke 7:35 [b]Luke 3:12;
Matt. 21:32 [c]Acts 18:25; 19:3

30 [1]I.e., experts on the
Mosaic Law [2]Lit., *him*
[a]Matt. 22:35

33 [a]Luke 1:15

34 [1]Or, *wine-drinker*
[2]Publicans who collected
Roman taxes on commission

35 [1]Lit., *And*
[a]Luke 7:29

36 [1]Lit., *eat*

37 [1]I.e., an immoral woman
[a]Luke 7:37 39; Matt 26:6-13;
Mark 14:3-9; John 12:1-8

39 [1]Lit., *to himself, saying*
[2]Some mss. read, *the
prophet* [3]I.e., an immoral
woman
[a]Luke 7:16; John 4:19

40 [1]Lit., *says*

41 [1]The denarius was worth
18 cents in silver, equivalent
to a day's wage
[a]Matt. 18:28; Mark 6:37

42 [a]Matt. 18:25

erers heard *this*, they [2]acknowledged [a]God's justice, [b]having been baptized with [c]the baptism of John.

30 But the Pharisees and the [1]lawyers rejected God's purpose for themselves, not having been baptized by [2]John.

31 "To what then shall I compare the men of this generation, and what are they like?

32 "They are like children who sit in the market place and call to one another; and they say, 'We played the flute for you, and you did not dance; we sang a dirge, and you did not weep.'

33 "For John the Baptist has come [a]eating no bread and drinking no wine; and you say, 'He has a demon!'

34 "The Son of Man has come eating and drinking; and you say, 'Behold, a gluttonous man, and a [1]drunkard, a friend of [2]tax-gatherers and sinners!'

35 "[1]Yet wisdom [a]is vindicated by all her children."

36 Now one of the Pharisees was requesting Him to [1]dine with him. And He entered the Pharisee's house, and reclined *at table*.

37 [a]And behold, there was a woman in the city who was a [1]sinner; and when she learned that He was reclining *at table* in the Pharisee's house, she brought an alabaster vial of perfume,

38 and standing behind *Him* at His feet, weeping, she began to wet His feet with her tears, and kept wiping them with the hair of her head, and kissing His feet, and anointing them with the perfume.

39 Now when the Pharisee who had invited Him saw this, he said [1]to himself, "If this man were [2]a prophet He would know who and what sort of person this woman is who is touching Him, that she is a [3]sinner."

40 And Jesus answered and said to him, "Simon, I have something to say to you." And he [1]replied, "Say it, Teacher."

41 "A certain money-lender had two debtors: one owed five hundred [1a]denarii, and the other fifty.

42 "When they [a]were unable to repay, he graciously forgave them both. Which of them therefore will love him more?"

43 Simon answered and said, "I suppose the one whom he forgave more." And He said to him,

"You have judged correctly."

44 And turning toward the woman, He said to Simon, "Do you see this woman? I entered your house; you [a]gave Me no water for My feet, but she has wet My feet with her tears, and wiped them with her hair.

45 "You [a]gave Me no kiss; but she, since the time I came in, [1]has not ceased to kiss My feet.

46 "[a]You did not anoint My head with oil, but she anointed My feet with perfume.

47 "For this reason I say to you, her sins, which are many, have been forgiven, for she loved much, but he who is forgiven little, loves little."

48 And He said to her, "[a]Your sins have been forgiven."

49 And those who were reclining *at table* with Him began to say [1]to themselves, "Who is this *man* who even forgives sins?"

50 And He said to the woman, "[a]Your faith has saved you; [b]go in peace."

CHAPTER 8

AND it came about soon afterwards, that He *began* going about from one city and village to another, [a]proclaiming and preaching the kingdom of God; and the twelve were with Him,

2 and *also* [a]some women who had been healed of evil spirits and sicknesses: [a]Mary who was called Magdalene, from whom seven demons had gone out,

3 and Joanna the wife of Chuza, [a]Herod's [b]steward, and Susanna, and many others who were contributing to their support out of their private means.

4 [a]And when a great multitude were coming together, and those from the various cities were journeying to Him, He spoke by way of a parable:

5 "The sower went out to sow his seed; and as he sowed, some fell beside the road; and it was trampled under foot, and the birds of the [1]air devoured it.

6 "And other *seed* fell on rocky *soil*, and as soon as it grew up, it withered away, because it had no moisture.

7 "And other *seed* fell among the thorns; and the thorns grew up with it, and choked it out.

8 "And other *seed* fell into the good ground, and grew up, and produced a crop a hundred times

44 [a]Gen. 18:4; 19:2; 43:24; Judg. 19:21; 1 Tim. 5:10

45 [1]Lit., *was not ceasing*
[a]2 Sam. 15:5

46 [a]Ps. 23:5; Eccles. 9:8; 2 Sam. 12:20; Dan. 10:3

48 [a]Matt. 9:2

49 [1]Or, *among*

50 [a]Matt. 9:22 [b]Luke 8:48; Mark 5:34

1 [a]Matt. 4:23

2 [a]Matt. 27:55f.; Luke 23:49

3 [a]Matt. 14:1 [b]Matt. 20:8

4 [a]Luke 8:4-8; *Matt. 13:2-9; Mark 4:1-9*

5 [1]Lit., *heaven*

8 ᵃMatt. 11:15

9 ᵃLuke 8:9-15: *Matt. 13:10-23; Mark 4:10-20*

10 ᵃMatt. 13:11 ᵇIs. 6:9; Matt. 13:14

11 ᵃ1 Pet. 1:23

13 ¹Lit., *who believe*

15 ¹Or, *steadfastness*

16 ᵃMatt. 5:15; Mark 4:21; Luke 11:33

17 ᵃLuke 12:2; Matt. 10:26; Mark 4:22

18 ¹Or, *seems to have* ᵃMatt. 13:12; Luke 19:26

19 ᵃLuke 8:19-21: *Matt. 12:46-50; Mark 3:31-35*

21 ᵃLuke 11:28

22 ᵃLuke 8:22-25: *Matt. 8:23-27; Mark 4:36-41*

138

as great." As He said these things, He would call out, "ᵃHe who has ears to hear, let him hear."

9   ᵃAnd His disciples *began* questioning Him as to what this parable might be.

10   And He said, "ᵃTo you it is granted to know the mysteries of the kingdom of God, but to the rest in parables; in order that ᵇSEEING THEY MAY NOT SEE, AND HEARING THEY MAY NOT UNDERSTAND.

11   "Now the parable is this: ᵃthe seed is the word of God.

12   "And those beside the road are those who have heard; then the devil comes and takes away the word from their heart, so that they may not believe and be saved.

13   "And those on the rocky *soil are* those who, when they hear, receive the word with joy; and these have no *firm* root; ¹they believe for a while, and in time of temptation fall away.

14   "And the *seed* which fell among the thorns, these are the ones who have heard, and as they go on their way they are choked with worries and riches and pleasures of *this* life, and bring no fruit to maturity.

15   "And the *seed* in the good ground, these are the ones who have heard the word in an honest and good heart, and hold it fast, and bear fruit with ¹perseverance.

16   "Now ᵃno one after lighting a lamp covers it over with a container, or puts it under a bed; but he puts it on a lampstand, in order that those who come in may see the light.

17   "ᵃFor nothing is hidden that shall not become evident, nor *anything* secret that shall not be known and come to light.

18   "Therefore take care how you listen; ᵃfor whoever has, to him shall *more* be given; and whoever does not have, even what he ¹thinks he has shall be taken away from him."

19   ᵃAnd His mother came to Him and *His* brothers *also*, and they were unable to get to Him because of the crowd.

20   And it was reported to Him, "Your mother and Your brothers are standing outside, wishing to see You."

21   But He answered and said to them, "My mother and My brothers are these ᵃwho hear the word of God and do it."

22   ᵃNow it came about on one of *those* days,

that He and His disciples got into a boat, and He said to them, "Let us go over to the other side of ^bthe lake." And they launched out.

23 But as they were sailing along He fell asleep; and a fierce gale of wind descended upon ^athe lake, and they *began* to be swamped and to be in danger.

24 And they came to Him, and woke Him up, saying, "^aMaster, Master, we are perishing!" And being aroused, He ^brebuked the wind and the surging waves, and they stopped, and ¹it became calm.

25 And He said to them, "Where is your faith?" And they were fearful and amazed, saying to one another, "Who then is this, that He commands even the winds and the water, and they obey Him?"

26 ^aAnd they sailed to the country of the ¹Gerasenes, which is opposite Galilee.

27 And when He had come out onto the land, a certain man from the city met Him who was possessed with demons; and who had not put on any clothing for a long time, and was not living in a house, but in the tombs.

28 And seeing Jesus, he cried out and fell before Him, and said in a loud voice, "^aWhat do I have to do with You, Jesus, Son of ^bthe Most High God? I beg You, do not torment me."

29 For He ¹had been commanding the unclean spirit to come out of the man. For it had seized him many times; and he was bound with chains and shackles and kept under guard; and *yet* he would burst his fetters and be driven by the demon into the deserts.

30 And Jesus asked him, "What is your name?" And he said, "^aLegion"; for many demons had entered him.

31 And they were entreating Him not to command them to depart into ^athe abyss.

32 Now there was a herd of many swine feeding there on the mountain; and *the demons* entreated Him to permit them to enter ¹the swine. And He gave them permission.

33 And the demons came out from the man and entered the swine; and the herd rushed down the steep bank into ^athe lake, and were drowned.

34 And when those who tended them saw what had happened, they ran away and reported it in the city and *out* in the country.

22 ^bLuke 8:23; 5:1f.

23 ^aLuke 8:22; 5:1f.

24 ¹Lit., *a calm occurred*
^aLuke 5:5 ^bLuke 4:39

26 ¹Other mss. read,
Gergesenes, or *Gadarenes*
^aLuke 8:26-37: Matt. 8:28-34; Mark 5:1-17

28 ^aMatt. 8:29 ^bMark 5:7

29 ¹Or, *was commanding*

30 ^aMatt. 26:53

31 ^aRom. 10:7; Rev. 9:1f., 11; 11:7; 17:8; 20:1, 3

32 ¹Lit., *them*

33 ^aLuke 8:22; 5:1f.

139

35 aLuke 10:39

36 1Or, *saved*
aMatt. 4:24

37 1Other mss. read,
Gergesenes or *Gadarenes*

38 1Lit., *be with*
aLuke 8:38, 39: *Mark 5:18-20*

40 aMatt. 9:1; Mark 5:21

41 1Lit., *ruler*
aLuke 8:41-56: *Matt. 9:18-
26; Mark 5:22-43* bLuke 8:49;
Mark 5:22

42 1Or, *only begotten*

43 1Some mss. add, *who
had spent all her living upon
physicians*

44 1Or, *outer garment*

45 1Some early mss. add,
and those with him
aLuke 5:5

46 aLuke 5:17

48 1Lit., *saved you*
aMatt. 9:22 bLuke 7:50;
Mark 5:34

49 aLuke 8:41

35   And *the people* went out to see what had happened; and they came to Jesus, and found the man from whom the demons had gone out, sitting down aat the feet of Jesus, clothed and in his right mind; and they became frightened.

36   And those who had seen it reported to them how the man who was ademon-possessed had been 1made well.

37   And all the people of the country of the 1Gerasenes and the surrounding district asked Him to depart from them; for they were gripped with great fear; and He got into a boat, and returned.

38   aBut the man from whom the demons had gone out was begging Him that he might 1accompany Him; but He sent him away, saying,

39   "Return to your house and describe what great things God has done for you." And he departed, proclaiming throughout the whole city what great things Jesus had done for him.

40   aAnd as Jesus returned, the multitude welcomed Him, for they had all been waiting for Him.

41   aAnd behold, there came a man named Jairus, and he was an 1bofficial of the synagogue; and he fell at Jesus' feet, and *began* to entreat Him to come to his house;

42   for he had an 1only daughter, about twelve years old, and she was dying. But as He went, the multitudes were pressing against Him.

43   And a woman who had a hemorrhage for twelve years, 1and could not be healed by anyone,

44   came up behind Him, and touched the fringe of His 1cloak; and immediately her hemorrhage stopped.

45   And Jesus said, "Who is the one who touched Me?" And while they were all denying it, Peter said,1 "aMaster, the multitudes are crowding and pressing upon You."

46   But Jesus said, "Someone did touch Me, for I was aware that apower had gone out of Me."

47   And when the woman saw that she had not escaped notice, she came trembling and fell down before Him, and declared in the presence of all the people the reason why she had touched Him, and how she had been immediately healed.

48   And He said to her, "Daughter, ayour faith has 1made you well; bgo in peace."

49   While He was still speaking, someone *came from *the house of* athe synagogue official,

saying, "Your daughter has died; do not trouble the Teacher any more."

50 But when Jesus heard *this*, He answered him, "[a]Do not be afraid *any longer*; only believe, and she shall be [1]made well."

51 And when He had come to the house, He did not allow anyone to enter with Him, except Peter, John and James, and the girl's father and mother.

52 Now they were all weeping and [a]lamenting for her; but He said, "Stop weeping, for she has not died, but [b]is asleep."

53 And they *began* laughing at Him, knowing that she had died.

54 He, however, took her by the hand and called, saying, "Child, arise!"

55 And her spirit returned, and she rose up immediately; and He gave orders for *something* to be given her to eat.

56 And her parents were amazed; but He [a]instructed them to tell no one what had happened.

a   CHAPTER 9

AND He called the twelve together, and gave them power and authority over all the demons, and to heal diseases.

2 And He sent them out to [a]proclaim the kingdom of God, and [1]to perform healing.

3 And He said to them, "[a]Take nothing for *your* journey, [b]neither a staff, nor a [1]bag, nor bread, nor money; and do not *even* have [2]two tunics apiece.

4 "And whatever house you enter, stay there, and take your leave from there.

5 "And as for those who do not receive you, when you depart from that city, [a]shake off the dust from your feet as a testimony against them."

6 And departing, they *began* going about [1]among the villages, [a]preaching the gospel, and healing everywhere.

7 [a]Now [b]Herod the tetrarch heard of all that was happening; and he was greatly perplexed, because it was said by some that [c]John had risen from the dead,

8 and by some that [a]Elijah had appeared, and by others, that one of the prophets of old had risen again.

50 [1]Or, *saved*
[a]Mark 5:36

52 [a]Luke 23:27; Matt. 11:17
[b]John 11:13

56 [a]Matt. 8:4

1 [a]Matt. 10:5; Mark 6:7

2 [1]Some mss. read, *to heal the sick*
[a]Matt. 10:7

3 [1]Or, *knapsack,* or *beggar's bag* [2]Or, *inner garment*
[a]Luke 9:3-5; *Matt.* 10:9-15; *Mark* 6:8-11; Luke 10:4-12; 22:35 [b]Matt. 10:10; Mark 6:8; Luke 22:35f.

5 [a]Acts 13:51; Luke 10:11

6 [1]Or, *from village to village*
[a]Luke 8:1; Mark 6:12

7 [a]Luke 9:7-9: *Matt.* 14:1, 2; Mark 6:14f. [b]Matt. 14:1; Luke 3:1; 13:31; 23:7 [c]Matt. 14:2

8 [a]Matt. 16:14

9 aLuke 23:8

9   And Herod said, "I myself had John beheaded; but who is this man about whom I hear such things?" And ahe kept trying to see Him.

10 aMark 6:30 bMark 6:30
cLuke 9:10-17: Matt. 14:13-
21; Mark 6:32-44; John 6:5-
13 dMatt. 11:21

10   aAnd when the bapostles returned, they gave an account to Him of all that they had done. cAnd taking them with Him, He withdrew privately to a city called dBethsaida.

11   But the multitudes were aware of this and followed Him; and welcoming them, He *began* speaking to them about the kingdom of God and curing those who had need of healing.

12 1Lit., provisions

12   And the day began to decline, and the twelve came and said to Him, "Send the multitude away, that they may go into the surrounding villages and countryside and find lodging and get 1something to eat; for here we are in a desolate place."

13   But He said to them, "You give them something to eat!" And they said, "We have no more than five loaves and two fish, unless perhaps we go and buy food for all these people."

14 aMark 6:39

14   (For there were about five thousand men). And He said to His disciples, "Have them recline *to eat* ain groups of about fifty each."

15   And they did so, and had them all recline.

16   And He took the five loaves and the two fish, and looking up to heaven, He blessed them, and broke *them*, and kept giving *them* to the disciples to set before the multitude.

17 1I.e., large-sized baskets
aMatt. 14:20

17   And they all ate and were satisfied; and that which was left over to them of the broken pieces was picked up, twelve 1abaskets *full*.

18 aLuke 9.18-20: Matt
16:13-16; Mark 8:27-29
bMatt. 14:23; Luke 6:12; 9:28

18   aAnd it came about that while He was bpraying alone, the disciples were with Him, and He questioned them, saying, "Who do the multitudes say that I am?"

19   And they answered and said, "John the Baptist; but others *say*, Elijah; and others, that one of the prophets of old has risen again."

20 1I.e., Messiah
aJohn 6:68f.

20   And He said to them, "But who do you say that I am?" And Peter answered and said, "aThe 1Christ of God."

21 1Or, strictly admonished
aMatt. 16:20; Mark 8:30;
Matt. 8:4

21   But He 1awarned them, and instructed *them* not to tell this to anyone,

22 aLuke 9:22-27: Matt.
16:21-28; Mark 8:31-9:1
bMatt. 16:21; Luke 9:44

22   asaying, "bThe Son of Man must suffer many things, and be rejected by the elders and chief priests and scribes, and be killed, and be raised up on the third day."

23   And He was saying to *them* all, "If anyone wishes to come after Me, let him deny himself, and [a]take up his cross daily, and follow Me.

24   "For [a]whoever wishes to save his [1]life shall lose it, but whoever loses his [1]life for My sake, he is the one who will save it.

25   "For what is a man profited if he gains the whole world, and [a]loses or forfeits himself?

26   "[a]For whoever is ashamed of Me and My words, of him will the Son of Man be ashamed when He comes in His glory, and *the glory* of the Father and of the holy angels.

27   "But I tell you truly, [a]there are some of those standing here who shall not taste death until they see the kingdom of God."

28   [a]And some eight days after these sayings, it came about that He took along [b]Peter and John and James, and [c]went up to the mountain [d]to pray.

29   And while He was [a]praying, the appearance of His face [b]became different, and His clothing *became* white *and* [1]gleaming.

30   And behold, two men were talking with Him; and they were Moses and Elijah,

31   who, appearing in [1]glory, were speaking of His [a]departure which He was about to accomplish at Jerusalem.

32   Now Peter and his companions [a]had been overcome with sleep; but when they were fully awake, they saw His glory and the two men standing with Him.

33   And it came about, as [1]these were parting from Him, Peter said to Jesus, "[a]Master, it is good for us to be here; and [b]let us make three [2]tabernacles: one for You, and one for Moses, and one for Elijah"—[c]not realizing what he was saying.

34   And while he was saying this, a cloud [1]formed and *began* to overshadow them; and they were afraid as they entered the cloud.

35   And [a]a voice came out of the cloud, saying, "[b]This is My Son, *My* Chosen One; listen to Him!"

36   And when the voice [1]had spoken, Jesus was found alone. And [a]they kept silent, and reported to no one in those days any of the things which they had seen.

37   [a]And it came about on the next day, that when they had come down from the mountain, a great multitude met Him.

23 [a]Matt. 10:38

24 [1]Gr., *soul-life*
[a]Matt. 10:39

25 [a]Heb. 10:34 marg.

26 [a]Luke 12:9; Matt. 10:33

27 [a]Matt. 16:28

28 [a]Luke 9:28-36: *Matt. 17:1-8; Mark 9:2-8* [b]Matt. 17:1 [c]Matt. 5:1 [d]Luke 3:21; 5:16; 6:12; 9:18

29 [1]Lit., *flashing like lightning* [a]Luke 3:21; 5:16; 6:12; 9:18 [b]Mark 16:12

31 [1]Or, *splendor* [a]2 Pet. 1:15

32 [a]Matt. 26:43; Mark 14:40

33 [1]Lit., *they* [2]Or, *sacred tents* [a]Luke 5:5; 9:49 [b]Matt. 17:4; Mark 9:5 [c]Mark 9:6

34 [1]Or, *occurred*

35 [a]2 Pet. 1:17f. [b]Matt. 3:17; Luke 3:22

36 [1]Lit., *occurred* [a]Matt. 17:9; Mark 9:9f.

37 [a]Luke 9:37-42: *Matt. 17:14-18; Mark 9:14-27*

38 [1]Or, *only begotten*

42 [1]Or, *tore him*

43 [1]Or, *majesty*
[a]2 Pet. 1:16 [b]Luke 9:43-45;
Matt. 17:22f.; Mark 9:30-32

44 [1]Or, *betrayed*
[a]Luke 9:22

45 [1]Lit., *were not knowing*
[a]Mark 9:32

46 [1]Lit., *entered in*
[a]Luke 9:46-48; Matt. 18:1-5;
Mark 9:33-37

47 [1]Lit., *the reasoning or
argument*
[a]Matt. 9:4

48 [1]Or, *lowliest*
[a]Matt. 10:40 [b]Luke 22:26

49 [a]Luke 9:49, 50: Mark
9:38-40 [b]Luke 5:5; 9:33

50 [1]Or, *on your side*
[a]Matt. 12:30; Luke 11:23

51 [1]Lit., *taking up*
[a]Mark 16:19 [b]Luke 13:22;
17:11; 18:31; 19:11, 28

38 And behold, a man from the multitude shouted out, saying, "Teacher, I beg You to look at my son, for he is my [1]only *boy,*

39 and behold, a spirit seizes him, and he suddenly screams, and it throws him into a convulsion with foaming *at the mouth,* and as it mauls him, it scarcely leaves him.

40 "And I begged Your disciples to cast it out, and they could not."

41 And Jesus answered and said, "O unbelieving and perverted generation, how long shall I be with you, and put up with you? Bring your son here."

42 And while he was still approaching, the demon [1]dashed him *to the ground,* and threw him into a violent convulsion. But Jesus rebuked the unclean spirit, and healed the boy, and gave him back to his father.

43 And they were all amazed at the [1a]greatness of God.

[b]But while everyone was marveling at all that He was doing, He said to His disciples,

44 "Let these words sink into your ears; [a]for the Son of Man is going to be [1]delivered into the hands of men."

45 But [a]they [1]did not understand this statement, and it was concealed from them so that they might not perceive it; and they were afraid to ask Him about this statement.

46 [a]And an argument [1]arose among them as to which of them might be the greatest.

47 But Jesus, [a]knowing [1]what they were thinking in their heart, took a child and stood him by His side,

48 and said to them, "[a]Whoever receives this child in My name receives Me; and whoever receives Me receives Him who sent Me; [b]for he who is [1]least among you, this is the one who is great."

49 [a]And John answered and said, "[b]Master, we saw someone casting out demons in Your name; and we tried to hinder him because he does not follow along with us."

50 But Jesus said to him, "Do not hinder *him;* [a]for he who is not against you is [1]for you."

51 And it came about, when the days were approaching for [a]His [1]ascension, that He resolutely set His face [b]to go to Jerusalem;

52   and He sent messengers on ahead of Him. And they went, and entered a village of the ªSamaritans, to ¹make arrangements for Him.

53   And they did not receive Him, ªbecause ¹He was journeying with His face toward Jerusalem.

54   And when His disciples ªJames and John saw *this*, they said, "Lord, do You want us to command fire to come down from heaven and consume them¹?"

55   But He turned and rebuked them.¹

56   And they went on to another village.

57   And ªas they were going along the road, ᵇsomeone said to Him, "I will follow You wherever You go."

58   And Jesus said to him, "The foxes have holes, and the birds of the ¹air *have* ²nests, but ªthe Son of Man has nowhere to lay His head."

59   And He said to another, "ªFollow Me." But he said, "¹Permit me first to go and bury my father."

60   But He said to him, "Allow the dead to bury their own dead; but as for you, go and ªproclaim everywhere the kingdom of God."

61   And another also said, "I will follow You, Lord; but ªfirst permit me to say good-bye to those at home."

62   But Jesus said to him, "ªNo one, after putting his hand to the plow and looking back, is fit for the kingdom of God."

CHAPTER 10

Now after this ªthe Lord appointed ¹seventy ᵇothers, and sent them ᶜtwo and two ahead of Him to every city and place where He Himself was going to come.

2   And He was saying to them, "ªThe harvest is plentiful, but the laborers are few; therefore beseech the Lord of the harvest to send out laborers into His harvest.

3   "Go your ways; ªbehold, I send you out as lambs in the midst of wolves.

4   "ªCarry no purse, no ¹bag, no shoes; and greet no one on the way.

5   "And whatever house you enter, first say, 'Peace *be* to this house.'

6   "And if a ¹man of peace is there, your peace will rest upon him; but if not, it will return to you.

52 ¹Or, *prepare*
ªMatt. 10:5; Luke 10:33; 17:16; John 4:4

53 ¹Lit., *His face was proceeding toward*
ªJohn 4:9

54 ¹Some mss. add, *as Elijah did*
ªMark 3:17

55 ¹Later mss. add, *and said, "You do not know what kind of spirit you are of.*

56 *"For the Son of Man did not come to destroy men's lives, but to save them."*

57 ªLuke 9:51 ᵇLuke 9:57-60: *Matt. 8:19-22*

58 ¹Or, *sky* ²Gr., *roosting-places*
ªMatt. 8:20

59 ¹Some mss. add, *Lord*
ªMatt. 8:22

60 ªMatt. 4:23

61 ª1 Kin. 19:20

62 ªPhil. 3:13

1 ¹Some mss. read, *seventy-two*
ªLuke 7:13 ᵇLuke 9:1f., 52 ᶜMark 6:7

2 ªMatt. 9:37, 38; John 4.35

3 ªMatt. 10:16

4 ¹Gr., *knapsack,* or *beggar's bag*
ªLuke 10:4-12; Matt. 10:9-14; Mark 6:8-11; Luke 9:3-5

6 ¹Lit., *son*

7 [1]Or, *the house itself*
[2]Lit., *the things from them*
[a]Matt. 10:10; 1 Cor. 9:14;
1 Tim. 5:18

8 [a]1 Cor. 10:27

9 [a]Matt. 3:2; 10:7; Luke
10:11

11 [1]Lit., *know*
[a]Matt. 10:14; Mark 6:11;
Luke 9:5 [b]Matt. 3:2; 10:7;
Luke 10:9

12 [a]Matt. 10:15; 11:24
[b]Matt. 10:15

13 [1]Or, *works of power*
[a]Luke 10:13-15; Matt. 11:21-
23 [b]Matt. 11:21 [c]Rev. 11:3

14 [a]Matt. 11:21

15 [a]Matt. 4:13 [b]Matt. 11:23

16 [a]Matt. 10:40; John
13:20; Gal. 4:14 [b]John 12:48;
1 Thess. 4:8

17 [1]Some mss. read,
seventy-two
[a]Mark 16:17

18 [a]Matt. 4:10

19 [a]Mark 16:18

20 [a]Ex. 32:32; Ps. 69:28; Is.
4:3; Ezek. 13:9; Dan. 12:1;
Phil. 4:3; Heb. 12:23; Rev.
3:5; 13:8; 17:8; 20:12, 15;
21:27

21 [1]Lit., *hour* [2]Or,
acknowledge to Thy praise
[a]Luke 10:21, 22: Matt.
11:25-27

7 "And stay in [1]that house, eating and drinking [2]what they give you; for [a]the laborer is worthy of his wages. Do not keep moving from house to house.

8 "And whatever city you enter, and they receive you, [a]eat what is set before you;

9 and heal those in it who are sick, and say to them, '[a]The kingdom of God has come near to you.'

10 "But whatever city you enter and they do not receive you, go out into its streets and say,

11 '[a]Even the dust of your city which clings to our feet, we wipe off *in protest* against you; yet [1]be sure of this, that [b]the kingdom of God has come near.'

12 "I say to you, [a]it will be more tolerable in that day for [b]Sodom, than for that city.

13 "[a]Woe to you, [b]Chorazin! Woe to you, [b]Bethsaida! For if the [1]miracles had been performed in [b]Tyre and Sidon which occurred in you, they would have repented long ago, sitting in [c]sackcloth and ashes.

14 "But it will be more tolerable for [a]Tyre and Sidon in the judgment, than for you.

15 "And you, [a]Capernaum, will not be exalted to heaven, will you? You will be brought down to [b]Hades!

16 "[a]The one who listens to you listens to Me, and [b]the one who rejects you rejects Me; and he who rejects Me rejects the One who sent Me."

17 And the [1]seventy returned with joy, saying, "Lord, even [a]the demons are subject to us in Your name."

18 And He said to them, "I was watching [a]Satan fall from heaven like lightning.

19 "Behold, I have given you authority to [a]tread upon serpents and scorpions, and over all the power of the enemy, and nothing shall injure you.

20 "Nevertheless do not rejoice in this, that the spirits are subject to you, but rejoice that [a]your names are recorded in heaven."

21 [a]At that very [1]time He rejoiced greatly in the Holy Spirit, and said, "I [2]praise Thee, O Father, Lord of heaven and earth, that Thou didst hide these things from *the* wise and intelligent and didst reveal them to babes. Yes, Father, for thus it was well-pleasing in Thy sight.

22 "All things have been handed over to Me by My Father, and no one knows who the Son is ex-

cept the Father, and who the Father is except the Son, and anyone to whom the Son wills to reveal *Him.*"

23 [a]And turning to the disciples, He said privately, "Blessed *are* the eyes which see the things you see,

24 for I say to you, that many prophets and kings wished to see the things which you see, and did not see *them*, and to hear the things which you hear, and did not hear *them.*"

25 [a]And behold, a certain [1b]lawyer stood up and put Him to the test, saying, "Teacher, what shall I do to inherit eternal life?"

26 And He said to him, "What is written in the Law? How [1]does it read to you?"

27 And he answered and said, "[a]YOU SHALL LOVE THE LORD YOUR GOD WITH ALL YOUR HEART, AND WITH ALL YOUR SOUL, AND WITH ALL YOUR STRENGTH, AND WITH ALL YOUR MIND; AND YOUR NEIGHBOR AS YOURSELF."

28 And He said to him, "You have answered correctly; [a]DO THIS, AND YOU WILL LIVE."

29 But wishing [a]to justify himself, he said to Jesus, "And who is my neighbor?"

30 Jesus replied and said, "A certain man was [a]going down from Jerusalem to Jericho; and he fell among robbers, and they stripped him and [1]beat him, and went off leaving him half dead.

31 "And by chance a certain priest was going down on that road, and when he saw him, he passed by on the other side.

32 "And likewise a Levite also, when he came to the place and saw him, passed by on the other side.

33 "But a certain [a]Samaritan, who was on a journey, came upon him; and when he saw him, he felt compassion,

34 and came to him, and bandaged up his wounds, pouring oil and wine on *them*; and he put him on his own beast, and brought him to an inn, and took care of him.

35 "And on the next day he took out two [1]denarii and gave them to the innkeeper and said, 'Take care of him; and whatever more you spend, when I return, I will repay you.'

36 "Which of these three do you think proved to be a neighbor to the man who fell into the robbers' *hands?*"

37 And he said, "The one who showed mercy

23 [a]Luke 10:23, 24: *Matt. 13:16, 17*

25 [1]I.e., an expert in the Mosaic law
[a]Luke 10:25-28: *Matt. 22:34-40; Mark 12:28-31*; Matt. 19:16-19 [b]Matt. 22:35

26 [1]Lit., *do you read*

27 [a]Deut. 6:5; Lev. 19:18

28 [a]Matt. 19:17; Lev. 18:5

29 [a]Luke 16:15

30 [1]Lit., *laid blows upon*
[a]Luke 18:31; 19:28

33 [a]Matt. 10:5; Luke 9:52

35 [1]The denarius was worth 18 cents in silver, equivalent to a day's wage

37 [1]Or, *likewise*

38 [1]Lit., *certain woman*
[a]Luke 10:40f.; John 11:1, 5, 19ff., 30, 39; 12:2

39 [a]Luke 10:42; John 11:1f., 19f., 28, 31f., 45; 12:3 [b]Luke 8:35; Acts 22:3

40 [1]Lit., *much service*
[a]Luke 10:38, 41; John 11:1, 5, 19ff., 30, 39; 12:2

41 [a]Luke 10:38, 40; John 11:1, 5, 19ff., 30, 39; 12:2 [b]Matt. 6:25

42 [1]Some mss. read, *but one thing is necessary* [2]Lit., *or*
[a]John 6:27; Ps. 27:4 [b]Luke 10:39; John 11:1f., 19f., 28, 31f., 45; 12:3

1 [a]Luke 7:13

2 [1]Some mss. insert phrases from Matt. 6:9-13 to make the two passages closely similar
[a]Luke 11:2-4; Matt. 6:9-13

3 [1]Or, *bread for the coming day*, or *needful bread*
[a]Acts 17:11

4 [a]Luke 13:4 marg.

5 [1]Lit., *which one of you*

7 [1]Lit., *with me*

8 [1]Or, *shamelessness*
[a]Luke 18:1-6

toward him." And Jesus said to him, "Go and do [1]the same."

38 Now as they were traveling along, He entered a certain village; and a [1]woman named [a]Martha welcomed Him into her home.

39 And she had a sister called [a]Mary, who moreover was listening to the Lord's word, [b]seated at His feet.

40 But [a]Martha was distracted with [1]all her preparations; and she came up *to Him*, and said, "Lord, do You not care that my sister has left me to do all the serving alone? Then tell her to help me."

41 But the Lord answered and said to her, "[a]Martha, Martha, you are [b]worried and bothered about so many things;

42 [1a]but *only* a few things are necessary, [2]really *only* one: for [b]Mary has chosen the good part, which shall not be taken away from her."

CHAPTER 11

AND it came about that while He was praying in a certain place, after He had finished, one of His disciples said to Him, "[a]Lord, teach us to pray just as John also taught his disciples."

2 And He said to them, "[a]When you pray, say:

'[1]Father, hallowed be Thy name.
Thy kingdom come.

3 Give us [a]each day our [1]daily bread.

4 And forgive us our sins,
For we ourselves also forgive everyone who [a]is indebted to us.
And lead us not into temptation.' "

5 And He said to them, "[1]Suppose one of you shall have a friend, and shall go to him at midnight, and say to him, 'Friend, lend me three loaves;

6 for a friend of mine has come to me from a journey, and I have nothing to set before him';

7 and from inside he shall answer and say, 'Do not bother me; the door has already been shut and my children [1]and I are in bed; I cannot get up and give you *anything*.'

8 "I tell you, even though he will not get up and give him *anything* because he is his friend, yet [a]because of his [1]persistence he will get up and give him as much as he needs.

9 "And I say to you, [1a]ask, and it shall be given to you; [2]seek, and you shall find; [3]knock, and it shall be opened to you.

10 "For everyone who asks receives; and he who seeks finds; and to him who knocks it shall be opened.

11 "Now [1]suppose one of you fathers is asked by his son for a [2]fish; he will not give him a snake instead of a fish, will he?

12 "Or if he is asked for an egg, he will not give him a scorpion, will he?

13 "[a]If you then, being evil, know how to give good gifts to your children, how much more shall your [1]Heavenly Father give the [b]Holy Spirit to those who ask Him?"

14 [a]And He was casting out a demon, *and it was* dumb; and it came about that when the demon had gone out, the dumb man spoke; and the multitudes marveled.

15 But some of them said, "He casts out demons [a]by [1b]Beelzebul, the ruler of the demons."

16 And others, [1]to test *Him*, [a]were demanding of Him a [2]sign from heaven.

17 [a]But He knew their thoughts, and said to them, "[1]Any kingdom divided against itself is laid waste; and [2]a house divided against itself falls.

18 "And if [a]Satan also is divided against himself, how shall his kingdom stand? For you say that I cast out demons by [b]Beelzebul.

19 "And if I by [a]Beelzebul cast out demons, by whom do your sons cast them out? Consequently they shall be your judges.

20 "But if I cast out demons by the [a]finger of God, then [b]the kingdom of God has come upon you.

21 "When [1]a strong *man* fully armed guards his own [a]homestead, his possessions are [2]undisturbed;

22 but when someone stronger than he attacks him and overpowers him, he takes away from him all his armor on which he had relied, and distributes his plunder.

23 "[a]He who is not with Me is against Me; and he who does not gather with Me, scatters.

24 "[a]When the unclean spirit goes out of [1]a man, it passes through waterless places seeking rest, and not finding any, it says, 'I will return to my house from which I came.'

9 [1]Or, *keep asking* [2]Or, *keep seeking* [3]Or, *keep knocking*
[a]Luke 11:9-13: *Matt. 7:7-11*

11 [1]Lit., *which of you shall a son ask the father* [2]Some early mss. insert: *loaf, he will not give him a stone, will he, or for a . . .*

13 [1]Lit., *Father from heaven*
[a]Luke 18:7f. [b]Matt. 7:11

14 [a]Luke 11:14, 15: *Matt. 12:22, 24; Matt. 9:32-34*

15 [1]Here and in verses 18 and 19 some mss. read, *Beezebul*
[a]Matt. 9:34 [b]Matt. 10:25

16 [1]Lit., *were testing* [2]Or, *attesting miracle*
[a]Matt. 12:38

17 [1]Lit., *every* [2]Lit., *a house against a house falls*
[a]Luke 11:17-22: *Matt. 12:25-29; Mark 3:23-27*

18 [a]Matt. 4:10 [b]Matt. 10:25

19 [a]Matt. 10:25

20 [a]Ex. 8:19 [b]Matt. 3:2

21 [1]Lit., *the* [2]Lit., *in peace*
[a]Matt. 26:3

23 [a]Matt. 12:30

24 [1]Lit., *the*
[a]Luke 11:24-26: *Matt. 12:43-45*

Luke 11

The Craving for Signs Rebuked.
Pharisaism Exposed and Denounced.

27 a Luke 23:29

28 a Luke 8:21

29 [1]Or, *attesting miracle*
a Luke 11:29-32: *Matt. 12:39-42* b Luke 11:16; Matt. 12:38

30 [1]Or, *attesting miracle*

33 a Luke 8:16; Matt. 5:15; Mark 4:21

34 [1]Or, *healthy*
a Luke 11:34, 35: *Matt. 6:22, 23*

38 [1]Gr., *baptized* [2]Or, *lunch*
a Matt. 15:2; Mark 7:3f.

150

25 "And when it comes, it finds it swept and put in order.

26 "Then it goes and takes *along* seven other spirits more evil than itself, and they go in and live there; and the last state of that man becomes worse than the first."

27 And it came about while He said these things, one of the women in the crowd raised her voice, and said to Him, "[a]Blessed is the womb that bore You, and the breasts at which You nursed."

28 But He said, "On the contrary, blessed are [a]those who hear the word of God, and observe it."

29 And as the crowds were increasing, He began to say, "[a]This generation is a wicked generation; it [b]seeks for a [1]sign, and *yet* no [1]sign shall be given to it but the [1]sign of Jonah.

30 "For just as Jonah became a [1]sign to the Ninevites, so shall the Son of Man be to this generation.

31 "The Queen of the South shall rise up with the men of this generation at the judgment and condemn them, because she came from the ends of the earth to hear the wisdom of Solomon; and behold, something greater than Solomon is here.

32 "The men of Nineveh shall stand up with this generation at the judgment and condemn it, because they repented at the preaching of Jonah; and behold, something greater than Jonah is here.

33 "No [a]one, after lighting a lamp, puts it away in a cellar, nor under a peck-measure, but on the lampstand, in order that those who enter may see the light.

34 "[a]The lamp of your body is your eye; when your eye is [1]clear, your whole body also is full of light; but when it is bad, your body also is full of darkness.

35 "Then watch out that the light in you may not be darkness.

36 "If therefore your whole body is full of light, with no dark part in it, it shall be wholly illumined, as when the lamp illumines you with its rays."

37 Now when He had spoken, a Pharisee *asked Him to have lunch with him; and He went in , and reclined *at table*.

38 And when the Pharisee saw it, he was surprised that He had not first [1a]ceremonially washed before the [2]meal.

39 But [a]the Lord said to him, "Now [b]you Pharisees clean the outside of the cup and of the platter; but [1]inside of you, you are full of robbery and wickedness.

40 "[a]You foolish ones, did not He who made the outside make the inside also?

41 "But [a]give that which is within as charity, and [1]then all things are [b]clean for you.

42 "[a]But woe to you Pharisees! For you [b]pay tithe of mint and rue and every *kind of* garden herb, and *yet* disregard justice and the love of God; but these are the things you should have done without neglecting the others.

43 "Woe to you Pharisees! For you [a]love the front seats in the synagogues, and the respectful greetings in the market places.

44 "[a]Woe to you! For you are like [1]concealed tombs, and the people who walk over *them* are unaware *of it*."

45 And one of the [1a]lawyers *said to Him in reply, "Teacher, when You say this, You insult us too."

46 But He said, "Woe to you [a]lawyers as well! For [b]you weigh men down with burdens hard to bear, [1]while you yourselves will not even touch the burdens with one of your fingers.

47 "[a]Woe to you! For you build the [1]tombs of the prophets, and *it was* your fathers *who* killed them.

48 "Consequently, you are witnesses and approve the deeds of your fathers; because it was they who killed them, and you build *their tombs*.

49 "For this reason also [a]the Wisdom of God said, '[b]I will send to them prophets and apostles, and *some* of them they will kill and *some* they will [1]persecute,

50 in order that the blood of all the prophets, shed [a]since the foundation of the world, may be [1]charged against this generation,

51 from the blood of Abel to the blood of Zechariah, who perished between the altar and the House *of* God, yes, I tell you, it shall be [1]charged against this generation.'

52 "Woe to you [1a]lawyers! For you have taken away the key of knowledge; [b]you did not enter in yourselves, and those who were entering in you hindered."

39 [1]Lit., *your inside is full*
[a]Luke 7:13 [b]Matt. 23:25f.

40 [a]Luke 12:20; 1 Cor. 15:36

41 [1]Lit., *behold*
[a]Luke 12:33; 16:9 [b]Mark 7:19; Titus 1:15

42 [a]Matt. 23:23 [b]Luke 18:12

43 [a]Matt. 23:6f.; Mark 12:38f., Luke 20:46; 14:7

44 [1]Or, *indistinct, unseen*
[a]Matt. 23:27

45 [1]I.e., experts in the Mosaic law
[a]Luke 11:46, 52; Matt. 22:35

46 [1]Lit., *and*
[a]Luke 11:45, 52; Matt. 22:35
[b]Matt. 23:4

47 [1]Or, *monuments to*
[a]Matt. 23:29ff.

49 [1]Or, *drive out*
[a]1 Cor. 1:24, 30; Col. 2:3
[b]Luke 11:49-51; Matt. 23:34-36

50 [1]Or, *required of*
[a]Matt. 25:34

51 [1]Or, *required of*

52 [1]I.e., experts in the Mosaic law
[a]Luke 11:45, 46; Matt. 22:35
[b]Matt. 23:13

54 [1]Lit., *something out of His mouth*
[a]Acts 23:21; Luke 20:20; Mark 3:2 [b]Mark 12:13

1 [1]Gr., *myriads*
[a]Matt. 16:6, 11ff.; Mark 8:15

2 [a]Luke 12:2-9: *Matt. 10:26-33;* Luke 8:17; Matt. 10:26; Mark 4:22

3 [1]Lit., *spoken in the ear*
[a]Matt. 10:27; Matt. 24:17

4 [a]John 15:13 15

5 [1]Or, *show* [2]Gr. *Gehenna*
[a]Heb. 10:31 [b]Matt. 5:22

6 [1]Gr., *assaria*, the smallest of copper coins
[a]Matt. 10:29

7 [a]Matt. 10:30

8 [a]Matt. 10:32; Luke 15:10; Rom. 10:9

9 [a]Luke 9:26; Matt. 10:33 [b]Matt. 10:32; Luke 15:10; Rom. 10:9

10 [a]Matt. 12:31, 32; Mark 3:28-30

11 [a]Matt. 10:17 [b]Luke 12:22; Matt. 6:25; 10:19; Mark 13:11; Luke 21:14

12 [a]Matt. 10:20; Luke 21:15

53 And when He left there, the scribes and the Pharisees began to be very hostile and to question Him closely on many subjects,

54 [a]plotting against Him, [b]to catch *Him* [1]in something He might say.

CHAPTER 12

UNDER these circumstances, after [1]so many thousands of the multitude had gathered together that they were stepping on one another, He began saying to His disciples first *of all,* "[a]Beware of the leaven of the Pharisees, which is hypocrisy.

2 "[a]But there is nothing covered up that will not be revealed, and hidden that will not be known.

3 "Accordingly whatever you have said in the dark shall be heard in the light, and what you have [1]whispered in the inner rooms shall be proclaimed upon [a]the housetops.

4 "And I say to you [a]my friends, do not be afraid of those who kill the body, and after that have no more that they can do.

5 "But I will [1]warn you whom to fear: [a]Fear the One who after He has killed has authority to cast into [2][b]hell; yes, I tell you, fear Him!

6 "Are not [a]five sparrows sold for two [1]cents? And *yet* not one of them is forgotten before God.

7 "[a]Indeed the very hairs of your head are all numbered. Do not fear; you are of more value than many sparrows.

8 "And I say to you, everyone who confesses Me before men, the Son of Man shall confess him also [a]before the angels of God;

9 but [a]he who denies Me before men shall be denied [b]before the angels of God.

10 "[a]And everyone who will speak a word against the Son of Man, it shall be forgiven him; but he who blasphemes against the Holy Spirit, it shall not be forgiven him.

11 "And when they bring you before [a]the synagogues and the rulers and the authorities, do not become [b]anxious about how or what you should speak in your defense, or what you should say;

12 for [a]the Holy Spirit will teach you in that very hour what you ought to say."

13   And someone ¹in the crowd said to Him, "Teacher, tell my brother to divide the *family* inheritance with me."

14   But He said to him, "ᵃMan, who appointed Me a judge or arbiter over you?"

15   And He said to them, "ᵃBeware, and be on your guard against every form of greed; for not *even* when one has an abundance does his life consist of his possessions."

16   And He told them a parable, saying, "The land of a certain rich man was very productive.

17   "And he began reasoning to himself, saying, 'What shall I do, since I have no place to store my crops?'

18   "And he said, 'This is what I will do: I will tear down my barns and build larger ones, and there I will store all my grain and my goods.

19   'And I will say to my soul, "Soul, ᵃyou have many goods laid up for many years *to come*; take your ease, eat, drink *and* be merry." '

20   "But God said to him, 'ᵃYou fool! This *very* night ¹ᵇyour soul is required of you; and ᶜ*now* who will own what you have prepared?'

21   "So is the man who ᵃlays up treasure for himself, and is not rich toward God."

22   And He said to His disciples, "ᵃFor this reason I say to you, do not be anxious for *your* ¹life, *as to* what you shall eat; nor for your body, *as to* what you shall put on.

23   "For life is more than food, and the body than clothing.

24   "Consider the ᵃravens, for they neither sow nor reap; and they have no storeroom nor ᵇbarn; and *yet* God feeds them; how much more valuable you are than the birds!

25   "And which of you by being anxious can add a *single* ¹ᵃcubit to his ²life's span?

26   "If then you cannot do even a very little thing, why are you anxious about other matters?

27   "Consider the lilies, how ¹they grow; they neither toil nor spin; but I tell you, even ᵃSolomon in all his glory did not clothe himself like one of these.

28   "But if God so *arrays* the grass in the field, which is *alive* today and tomorrow is thrown into the furnace, how much more *will He clothe* you, ᵃO men of little faith!

13 ¹Lit., *out of*

14 ᵃMic. 6:8; Rom. 2:1, 3; 9:20

15 ᵃ1 Tim. 6:6-10

19 ᵃEccles. 11:9

20 ¹Lit., *they are demanding your soul from you*
ᵃJer. 17:11; Luke 11:40 ᵇJob 27:8 ᶜPs. 39:6

21 ᵃLuke 12:33

22 ¹Gr., *soul-life*
ᵃLuke 12:22-31: Matt. 6:25-33

24 ᵃJob 38:41 ᵇLuke 12:18

25 ¹I.e., 18 inches ²Or, *height*
ᵃPs. 39:5

27 ¹Some mss. omit, *they grow*
ᵃ1 Kin. 10:4-7

28 ᵃMatt. 6:30

153

Luke 12

The True Treasure.   Watchfulness Enjoined.
Of Faithful and Unfaithful Servants.

29 ªMatt. 6:31

30 ¹Or, *these things all the nations of the world*

31 ªMatt. 6:33

32 ªMatt. 14:27 ᵇJohn 21:15-17 ᶜEph. 1:5, 9

33 ªMatt. 19:21; Luke 18:22; 11:41 ᵇMatt. 6:20; Luke 12:21

34 ªMatt. 6:21

35 ¹Lit., *Let your loins be girded* ªLuke 12:35, 36; Matt. 25:1ff. ᵇEph. 6:14; 1 Pet. 1:13

37 ªMatt. 24:42 ᵇLuke 17:8; John 13:4

38 ¹I.e., 9 p.m. to midnight ²I.e., Midnight to 3 a.m. ªMatt. 24:43

39 ¹Lit., *know* ²Lit., *dug through* ªLuke 12:39, 40; Matt. 24:43, 44 ᵇMatt. 6:19

40 ¹Lit., *think, suppose* ªLuke 21:36; Mark 13:33

41 ªLuke 12:47, 48

42 ¹Lit., *service* ªLuke 7:13 ᵇLuke 12:42-46; Matt. 24:45-51 ᶜMatt. 24:45; Luke 16:1ff.

43 ¹Or, *lord* ªLuke 12:42

45 ¹Lit., *is delaying to come*

154

29 "And do not seek what you shall eat, and what you shall drink, and do not ªkeep worrying.

30 "For ¹all these things the nations of the world eagerly seek; but your Father knows that you need these things.

31 "But seek for His kingdom, and ªthese things shall be added to you.

32 "ªDo not be afraid, ᵇlittle flock, for ᶜyour Father has chosen gladly to give you the kingdom.

33 "ªSell your possessions and give to charity; make yourselves purses which do not wear out, ᵇan unfailing treasure in heaven, where no thief comes near, nor moth destroys.

34 "For ªwhere your treasure is, there will your heart be also.

35 "¹ªBe dressed in ᵇreadiness, and *keep* your lamps alight.

36 "And be like men who are waiting for their master when he returns from the wedding feast, so that they may immediately open *the door* to him when he comes and knocks.

37 "Blessed are those slaves whom the master shall find ªon the alert when he comes; truly I say to you, that ᵇhe will gird himself *to serve*, and have them recline *at table*, and will come up and wait on them.

38 "Whether he comes in the ¹ªsecond watch, or even in the ²ªthird, and finds *them* so, blessed are those *slaves*.

39 "ªAnd ¹be sure of this, that if the head of the house had known at what hour the thief was coming, he would not have allowed his house to be ²ᵇbroken into.

40 "ªYou too, be ready; for the Son of Man is coming at an hour that you do not ¹expect."

41 And Peter said, "Lord, are You addressing this parable to us, or ªto everyone *else* as well?"

42 And ªthe Lord said, "ᵇWho then is the faithful and sensible ᶜsteward, whom his master will put in charge of his ¹servants, to give them their rations at the proper time?

43 "Blessed is that ªslave whom his ¹master finds so doing when he comes.

44 "Truly I say to you, that he will put him in charge of all his possessions.

45 "But if that slave says in his heart, 'My master ¹will be a long time in coming,' and begins to

beat the slaves, *both* men and women, and to eat and drink and get drunk;

46 the master of that slave will come on a day when he does not expect *him,* and at an hour he does not know, and will cut him in pieces, and assign him a place with the unbelievers.

47 "And that slave who knew his master's will and did not get ready or act in accord with his will, shall ªreceive many *lashes,*

48 but the one who did not ªknow *it,* and committed deeds worthy of ¹a flogging, will receive but few. ᵇAnd from everyone who has been given much shall much be required; and to whom they entrusted much, of him they will ask all the more.

49 "I ¹have come to cast fire upon the earth; and ²how I wish it were already kindled!

50 "But I have a ªbaptism to ¹undergo, and how distressed I am until it is accomplished!

51 "ªDo you suppose that I came to grant peace on earth? I tell you, no, but rather division;

52 for from now on five *members* in one household will be divided, three against two, and two against three.

53 "They will be divided, ªfather against son, and son against father; mother against daughter, and daughter against mother; mother-in-law against daughter-in-law, and daughter-in-law against mother-in-law."

54 And He was also saying to the multitudes, "ªWhen you see a cloud rising in the west, immediately you say, 'A shower is coming,' and so it turns out.

55 "And when *you see* a south wind blowing, you say, 'It will be a ªhot day,' and it turns out *that way.*

56 "You hypocrites! ªYou know how to analyze the appearance of the earth and the sky, but ¹why do you not analyze this present time?

57 "And ªwhy do you not even on your own initiative judge what is right?

58 "For ªwhile you are going with your opponent to appear before the magistrate, on *your* way *there* make an effort to ¹settle with him, in order that he may not drag you before the judge, and the judge turn you over to the constable, and the constable throw you into prison.

59 "I say to you, you shall not get out of there until you have paid the very last ¹ªcent."

47 ªDeut. 25:2

48 ¹Lit., *blows* ªLev. 5:17; Num. 15:29f. ᵇMatt. 13:12

49 ¹Or, *came* ²Lit., *what do I wish if . . . ?*

50 ¹Lit., *be baptized with* ªMark 10:38

51 ªLuke 12:51-53: *Matt. 10:34-36*

53 ªMic. 7:6; Matt. 10:21

54 ªMatt. 16:2f.

55 ªMatt. 20:12

56 ¹Lit., *how* ªMatt. 16:3

57 ªLuke 21:30

58 ¹Lit., *be released from him* ªLuke 12:58, 59: *Matt. 5:25, 26*

59 ¹Lit., *lepton,* i.e., 1/128 of a denarius ªMark 12:42

Luke 13

**The Barren Fig Tree.
A Cure on the Sabbath Defended.**

1 ¹Or, *shed along with*
ªMatt. 27

2 ªJohn 9:2f.

3 ¹Or, *are repentant*

4 ¹Lit., *debtors*
ªIs. 8:6 [Neh. 3:15]; John 9:7,
11 ᵇMatt. 6:12; Luke 11:4

6 ªMatt. 21:19

7 ¹Lit., *and I do not find*
ªMatt. 3:10; 7:19; Luke 3:9

10 ªMatt. 4:23

11 ªLuke 13:16

13 ªMark 5:23 ᵇMatt. 9:8

14 ªMark 5:22 ᵇMatt. 12:2;
Luke 14:3 ᶜEx. 20:9; Deut.
5:13

CHAPTER 13

NOW on the same occasion there were some present who reported to Him about the Galileans, whose blood ªPilate had ¹mingled with their sacrifices.

2 And He answered and said to them, "ªDo you suppose that these Galileans were *greater* sinners than all *other* Galileans, because they suffered this *fate?*

3 "I tell you, no, but, unless you ¹repent, you will all likewise perish.

4 "Or do you suppose that those eighteen on whom the tower in ªSiloam fell and killed them, were *worse* ¹ᵇculprits than all the men who live in Jerusalem?

5 "I tell you, no, but, unless you repent, you will all likewise perish."

6 And He *began* telling this parable: "A certain man had ªa fig tree which had been planted in his vineyard; and he came looking for fruit on it, and did not find any.

7 "And he said to the vineyard-keeper, 'Behold, for three years I have come looking for fruit on this fig tree ¹without finding any. ªCut it down! Why does it even use up the ground?'

8 "And he answered and said to him, 'Let it alone, sir, for this year too, until I dig around it and put in fertilizer;

9 and if it bears fruit next year, *fine*; but if not, cut it down.' "

10 And He was ªteaching in one of the synagogues on the Sabbath.

11 And behold, there was a woman who for eighteen years had had ªa sickness caused by a spirit; and she was bent double, and could not straighten up at all.

12 And when Jesus saw her, He called her over and said to her, "Woman, you are freed from your sickness."

13 And He ªlaid His hands upon her; and immediately she was made erect again, and *began* ᵇglorifying God.

14 And ªthe synagogue official, indignant because Jesus ᵇhad healed on the Sabbath, *began* saying to the multitude in response, "ᶜThere are six days in which work should be done; therefore come

during them and get healed, and not on the Sabbath day."

15 But ªthe Lord answered him and said, "You hypocrites, ᵇdoes not each of you on the Sabbath untie his ox or his donkey from the stall, and lead him away to water *him?*

16 "And this woman, ªa daughter of Abraham as she is, whom ᵇSatan has bound for eighteen long years, should she not have been released from this bond on the Sabbath day?"

17 And as He said this, all his opponents were being humiliated; and ªthe entire multitude was rejoicing over all the glorious things being done by Him.

18 Therefore ªHe was saying, "ᵇWhat is the kingdom of God like, and to what shall I compare it?

19 "It is like a mustard seed, which a man took and threw into his own garden; and it grew and became a tree; and the birds of the ¹air nested in its branches."

20 And again He said, "ªTo what shall I compare the kingdom of God?

21 "ªIt is like leaven, which a woman took and hid in ᵇthree ¹pecks of meal, until it was all leavened."

22 And He was passing through from one city and village to another, teaching, and ªproceeding on His way to Jerusalem.

23 And someone said to Him, "Lord, are there *just* a few who are being saved?" And He said to them,

24 "ªStrive to enter by the narrow door; for many, I tell you, will seek to enter and will not be able.¹

25 "Once the head of the house gets up and ªshuts the door, and you ᵇbegin to stand outside and knock on the door, saying, 'ᶜLord, open up to us!' ¹then He will answer and say to you, 'ᵈI do not know where you are from.'

26 "Then you will ªbegin to say, 'We ate and drank in Your presence, and You taught in our streets';

27 and He will say, 'I tell you, ªI do not know where you are from; ᵇDEPART FROM ME, ALL YOU EVILDOERS.'

28 "ªThere will be weeping and gnashing of teeth there when you see Abraham and Isaac and

15 ªLuke 7:13 ᵇLuke 14:5

16 ªLuke 19:9 ᵇMatt. 4:10; Luke 13:11

17 ªLuke 18:43

18 ªLuke 13:18, 19: *Matt. 13:31, 32; Mark 4:30-32* ᵇMatt. 13:24; Luke 13:20

19 ¹Or, *sky*

20 ªMatt. 13:24; Luke 13:18

21 ¹Gr., *sata* ªLuke 13:20, 21: *Matt. 13:33* ᵇMatt. 13:33

22 ªLuke 9:51

24 ¹Or, *able, once . . .* ªMatt. 7:13

25 ¹Lit., *and* ªMatt. 25:10 ᵇLuke 3:8 ᶜMatt. 25:11; 7:22 ᵈLuke 13:27; Matt. 7:23; 25:12

26 ªLuke 3:8

27 ªLuke 13:25 ᵇPs. 6:8; Matt. 25:41

28 ªMatt. 8:12

Luke 13, 14

His Yearning for Jerusalem.
Jesus Heals on the Sabbath.

29 ªMatt. 8:11

30 ªMatt. 19:30

31 ªMatt. 14:1; Luke 3:1; 9:7; 23:7

32 ¹Or possibly, *am perfected*
ªHeb. 2:10; 5:9; 7:28

33 ªJohn 11:9 ᵇMatt. 21:11

34 ªLuke 13:34, 35; Matt. 23:37-39; Luke 19:41 ᵇMatt. 23:37

35 ¹Later mss. add, *desolate*
ªPs. 118:26; Matt. 21:9; Luke 19:38

1 ¹I.e., members of the Sanhedrin
ªMark 3:2

2 ¹Lit., *behold*

3 ¹I.e., experts in Mosaic Law
ªActs 3:12 ᵇMatt. 22:35
ᶜMatt. 12:2; Luke 13:14

5 ¹Some ancient mss. read, *donkey*
ªLuke 13:15

6 ªMatt. 22:46; Luke 20:40

7 ªMatt. 23:6

Jacob and all the prophets in the kingdom of God, and yourselves being cast out.

29 "And they ªwill come from east and west, and from north and south, and will recline *at table* in the kingdom of God.

30 "And behold, ªsome are last who will be first and *some* are first who will be last."

31 Just at that time some Pharisees came up, saying to Him, "Go away and depart from here, for ªHerod wants to kill You."

32 And He said to them, "Go and tell that fox, 'Behold, I cast out demons and perform cures today and tomorrow, and the third *day* I ¹ªreach My goal.'

33 "Nevertheless ªI must journey on today and tomorrow and the next *day*; for it cannot be that a ᵇprophet should perish outside of Jerusalem.

34 "ªO Jerusalem, Jerusalem, *the city* that kills the prophets and stones those sent to her! How often I wanted to gather your children together, ᵇjust as a hen *gathers* her brood under her wings, and you would not *have it!*

35 "Behold, your house is left to you ¹*desolate*; and I say to you, you shall not see Me until *the time* comes when you say, 'ªBlessed *is* He who comes in the name of the Lord!' "

CHAPTER 14

AND it came about that when He went into the house of one of the ¹leaders of the Pharisees on *the* Sabbath to eat bread, ªthey were watching Him closely.

2 And ¹there, in front of Him was a certain man suffering from dropsy.

3 And Jesus ªanswered and spoke to the ¹ᵇlawyers and Pharisees, saying, "ᶜIs it lawful to heal on the Sabbath, or not?"

4 But they kept silent. And He took hold of him, and healed him, and sent him away.

5 And He said to them, "ªWhich one of you shall have a ¹son or an ox fall into a well, and will not immediately pull him out on a Sabbath day?"

6 ªAnd they could make no reply to this.

7 And He *began* speaking a parable to the invited guests when He noticed how ªthey had been picking out the places of honor *at the table*; saying to them,

8 "When you are invited by someone to a wedding feast, [a]do not [1]take the place of honor, lest someone more distinguished than you may have been invited by him,

9   and he who invited you both shall come and say to you, 'Give place to this man', and then [a]in disgrace you [1]proceed to occupy the last place.

10 "But when you are invited, go and recline at the last place, so that when the one who has invited you comes, he may say to you, 'Friend, [a]move up higher'; then you will have honor in the sight of all who [1]are at the table with you.

11 "[a]For everyone who exalts himself shall be humbled, and he who humbles himself shall be exalted."

12   And He also went on to say to the one who had invited Him, "When you give a luncheon or a dinner, do not invite your friends or your brothers or your relatives or rich neighbors, lest they also invite you in return, and repayment come to you.

13 "But when you give a [1]reception, invite *the* poor, *the* crippled, *the* lame, *the* blind,

14   and you will be [1]blessed, since they [2]do not have *the means* to repay you; for you will be repaid at [a]the resurrection of the righteous."

15   And when one of those who were reclining *at table* with Him heard this, he said to Him, "[a]Blessed is everyone who shall eat bread in the kingdom of God!"

16   But He said to him, "[a]A certain man was giving a big dinner, and he invited many;

17   and at the dinner hour he sent his slave to say to those who had been invited, 'Come; for everything is ready now.'

18 "But they all alike began to make excuses. The first one said to him, 'I have bought a [1]piece of land and I need to go out and look at it; [2]please consider me excused.'

19 "And another one said, 'I have bought five yoke of oxen, and I am going to try them out; [1]please consider me excused.'

20 "And another one said, '[a]I have married a wife, and for that reason I cannot come.'

21 "And the slave came *back* and reported this to his master. Then the head of the household became angry and said to his slave, 'Go out at once into the streets and lanes of the city and bring in here the poor and crippled and blind and lame.'

8 [1]Lit., *recline at*
[a]Prov. 25:6, 7

9 [1]Lit., *begin*
[a]Luke 3:8

10 [1]Lit., *recline at table*
[a]Prov. 25:6, 7

11 [a]Luke 18:14; Matt. 23:12

13 [1]Or, *banquet*

14 [1]Or, *happy* [2]Or, *are unable to*
[a]John 5:29; Acts 24:15; Rev. 20:4, 5[?]

15 [a]Rev. 19:9

16 [a]Luke 14:16-24; Matt. 22:2-14

18 [1]Or, *field* [2]Lit., *I request you*

19 [1]Lit., *I request you*

20 [a]Deut. 24:5; 1 Cor. 7:33

159

Luke 14, 15

Discipleship Exacting.
God's Interest in Sinners:—The Lost Sheep.

26 [1] I.e., by comparison of his love for Me
[a] Matt. 10:37f.

27 [a] Matt. 10:38

32 [1] Or, *embassy*

33 [a] Phil. 3:7; Heb. 11:26

34 [a] Matt. 5:13; Mark 9:50

35 [1] Lit., *they throw it out*
[a] Matt. 11:15

1 [1] Publicans who collected Roman taxes for profit [2] I.e., irreligious or non-practicing Jews
[a] Luke 5:29

2 [1] Lit., *grumble among themselves*
[a] Matt. 9:11

4 [a] Luke 15:4-7; Matt. 18:12-14

160

22 "And the slave said, 'Master, what you commanded has been done, and still there is room.'

23 "And the master said to the slave, 'Go out into the highways along the hedges, and compel *them* to come in, that my house may be filled.

24 'For I tell you, none of those men who were invited shall taste of my dinner.' "

25 Now great multitudes were going along with Him; and He turned and said to them,

26 "[a]If anyone comes to Me, and does not [1]hate his own father and mother and wife and children and brothers and sisters, yes, and even his own life, he cannot be My disciple.

27 "Whoever does not [a]carry his own cross and come after Me cannot be My disciple.

28 "For which one of you, when he wants to build a tower, does not first sit down and calculate the cost, to see if he has enough to complete it?

29 "Otherwise, when he has laid a foundation, and is not able to finish, all who observe it begin to ridicule him,

30 saying, 'This man began to build and was not able to finish.'

31 "Or what king, when he sets out to meet another king in battle, will not first sit down and take counsel whether he is strong enough with ten thousand *men* to encounter the one coming against him with twenty thousand?

32 "Or else, while the other is still far away, he sends a [1]delegation and asks terms of peace.

33 "So therefore, no one of you can be My disciple who [a]does not give up all his own possessions.

34 "Therefore, salt is good; but [a]if even salt has become tasteless, with what will it be seasoned?

35 "It is useless either for the soil or for the manure pile; [1]it is thrown out. [a]He who has ears to hear, let him hear."

CHAPTER 15

NOW all the [1][a]tax-gatherers and the [2]sinners were coming near Him to listen to Him.

2 And both the Pharisees and the scribes [1]*began* to grumble, saying, "This man receives sinners and [a]eats with them."

3 And He told them this parable, saying,

4 "[a]What man among you, if he has a hundred sheep and has lost one of them, does not leave the

ninety-nine in the [1]open pasture, and go after the one which is lost, until he finds it?

5 "And when he has found it, he lays it on his shoulders, rejoicing.

6 "And when he comes home, he calls together his friends and his neighbors, saying to them, 'Rejoice with me, for I have found my sheep which was lost!'

7 "I tell you that in the same way, there will be *more* joy in heaven over one sinner who repents, than over ninety-nine righteous persons who need no repentance.

8 "Or what woman, if she has ten [1]silver coins and loses one coin, does not light a lamp and sweep the house and search carefully until she finds it?

9 "And when she has found it, she calls together her [1]friends and neighbors, saying, 'Rejoice with me, for I have found the coin which I had lost!'

10 "In the same way, I tell you, there is joy [a]in the presence of the angels of God over one sinner who repents."

11 And He said, "A certain man had two sons;

12 and the younger of them said to his father, 'Father, give me [a]the share of the estate that falls to me.' And he divided his [1b]wealth between them.

13 "And not many days later, the younger son gathered everything together and went on a journey into a distant country, and there he squandered his estate with loose living.

14 "Now when he had spent everything, a severe famine occurred in that country, and he began to be in need.

15 "And he went and [1]attached himself to one of the citizens of that country, and he sent him into his fields to feed swine.

16 "And he was longing [1]to fill his [2]stomach with the [3]pods that the swine were eating, and no one was giving *anything* to him.

17 "But when he came to [1]his senses, he said, 'How many of my father's hired men have more than enough bread, but I am dying here with hunger!

18 'I will get up and go to my father, and will say to him, "Father, I have sinned against heaven, and [1]in your sight;

19 "I am no longer worthy to be called your son; make me as one of your hired men."'

---

4 [1]Lit., *wilderness*

8 [1]Gr., *drachmas*, one drachma was equivalent to a day's wages

9 [1]Lit., *women friends and neighbors*

10 [a]Luke 15:7; Matt. 10:32

12 [1]Lit., *living* [a]Deut. 21:17 [b]Mark 12:44; Luke 15:30

15 [1]Lit., *was joined to*

16 [1]Some mss. read *to be satisfied with* [2]Lit., *belly* [3]I.e., of the carob tree

17 [1]Lit., *himself*

18 [1]Lit., *before you*

161

20 [1]Lit., *his own* [2]Lit., *fell on his neck* [3]Lit., *kissed him again and again*
[a]Gen. 45:14; 46:29; Acts 20:37

21 [1]Some ancient mss. add: *make me as one of your hired men*

22 [a]Zech. 3:4; Rev. 6:11
[b]Gen. 41:42

24 [a]Luke 15:32; Matt. 8:22; Luke 9:60; 1 Tim. 5:6; Eph. 2:1, 5; 5:14; Col. 2:13; Rom. 11:15

29 [1]Or, *disobeyed* [2]Or, *young goat*

30 [1]Lit., *living*
[a]Luke 15:12; Prov. 29:3

31 [1]Lit., *are always with me*

32 [1]Lit., *it was necessary*
[a]Luke 15:24

1 [1]Or, *accused*
[a]Luke 15:13

20 "And he got up and came to [1]his father. But while he was still a long way off, his father saw him, and felt compassion *for him*, and ran and [2a]embraced him, and [3]kissed him.

21 "And the son said to him, 'Father, I have sinned against heaven and in your sight; I am no longer worthy to be called your son.'[1]

22 "But the father said to his slaves, 'Quickly bring out [a]the best robe and put it on him, and [b]put a ring on his hand and sandals on his feet;

23 and bring the fattened calf, kill it, and let us eat and be merry;

24 for this son of mine was [a]dead, and has come to life again; he was lost, and has been found.' And they began to be merry.

25 "Now his older son was in the field, and when he came and approached the house, he heard music and dancing.

26 "And he summoned one of the servants and *began* inquiring what these things might be.

27 "And he said to him, 'Your brother has come, and your father has killed the fattened calf, because he has received him back safe and sound.'

28 "But he became angry, and was not willing to go in; and his father came out and *began* entreating him.

29 "But he answered and said to his father, 'Look! For so many years I have been serving you, and I have never [1]neglected a command of yours; and *yet* you have never given me a [2]kid, that I might be merry with my friends;

30 but when this son of yours came, who has devoured your [1a]wealth with harlots, you killed the fattened calf for him.'

31 "And he said to him, 'My child you [1]have always been with me, and all that is mine is yours.

32 'But [1]we had to be merry and rejoice, for this brother of yours was [a]dead and *has begun* to live, and *was* lost and has been found.' "

CHAPTER 16

NOW He was also saying to the disciples, "There was a certain rich man who had a steward, and this *steward* was [1]reported to him as [a]squandering his possessions.

2 "And he called him and said to him, 'What is

this I hear about you? Give an account of your stewardship, for you can no longer be steward.'

3 "And the steward said to himself, 'What shall I do, since my [1]master is taking the stewardship away from me? I am not strong enough to dig; I am ashamed to beg.

4 'I [1]know what I shall do, so that when I am removed from the stewardship, they will receive me into their homes.'

5 "And he summoned each one of his [1]master's debtors, and he *began* saying to the first, 'How much do you owe my master?'

6 "And he said, 'A hundred [1]measures of oil.' And he said to him, 'Take your bill, and sit down quickly and write fifty.'

7 "Then he said to another, 'And how much do you owe?' And he said, 'A hundred [1]measures of wheat.' He *said to him, 'Take your bill, and write eighty.'

8 "And his [1]master praised the unrighteous steward because he had acted shrewdly; for the sons of [a]this age are more shrewd in relation to their own [2]kind than the [b]sons of light.

9 "And I say to you, [a]make friends for yourselves by means of the [1b]Mammon of unrighteousness; that when it fails, [c]they may receive you into the eternal dwellings.

10 "[a]He who is faithful in a very little thing is faithful also in much; and he who is unrighteous in a very little thing is unrighteous also in much.

11 "If therefore you have not been faithful in the *use of* unrighteous [1a]Mammon, who will entrust the true *riches* to you?

12 "And if you have not been faithful in *the use of* that which is another's, who will give you that which is [1]your own?

13 "[a]No [1]servant can serve two masters; for either he will hate the one, and love the other, or else he will hold to one, and despise the other. You cannot serve God and [2b]Mammon."

14 Now the Pharisees, who were [a]lovers of money, were listening to all these things, and they [b]were scoffing at Him.

15 And He said to them, "You are those who [a]justify yourselves [1]in the sight of men, but [b]God knows your hearts; for that which is [2]highly esteemed among men is detestable [3]in the sight of God.

3 [1]Or, *lord*

4 [1]Lit., *have come to the knowledge of*

5 [1]Or, *lord's*

6 [1]Gr., *baths*, one bath equals between 8 and 9 gallons

7 [1]Gr., *cors*, one cor equals between 10 and 12 bushels.

8 [1]Or, *lord* [2]Lit., *generation*
[a]Matt. 12:32; Luke 20:34
[b]John 12:36; Eph. 5:8; 1 Thess. 5:5

9 [1]Or, *riches*
[a]Matt. 19:21; Luke 11:41; 12:33 [b]Luke 16:11, 13; Matt. 6:24 [c]Luke 16:4

10 [a]Matt. 25:21, 23

11 [1]Or, *riches*
[a]Luke 16:9

12 [1]Some mss. read, *our own*

13 [1]Or, *house-servant* [2]Or, *riches*
[a]Matt. 6:24 [b]Luke 16:9

14 [a]2 Tim. 3:2 [b]Luke 23:35

15 [1]Lit., *before men* [2]Lit., *high* [3]Lit., *before God*
[a]Luke 10:29; 18:9, 14
[b]1 Sam. 16:7; Prov. 21:2; Rom. 8:27; Acts 1:24

16 aMatt. 11:12f. bMatt. 4:23

17 1I.e., projection of a letter (serif) aMatt. 5:18

18 aMatt. 5:32

20 aActs 3:2

22 aJohn 13:23; 1:18

23 1Lit., *having lifted up* aMatt. 11:23

24 aLuke 16:30; Luke 3:8; 19:9 bMatt. 25:41

25 aLuke 6:24

26 1Lit., *in all these things*

28 aActs 2:40; 8:25; 10:42; 18:5; 20:21ff.; 23:11; 28:23; Gal. 5:3; Eph. 4:17; 1 Thess. 2:11; 4:6

29 aLuke 4:17; Acts 15:21; John 5:45-47

30 aLuke 16:24; 3:8; 19:9

16 "aThe Law and the Prophets *were* proclaimed until John; since then bthe gospel of the kingdom of God is preached, and every one is forcing his way into it.

17 "aBut it is easier for heaven and earth to pass away than for one 1stroke of a letter of the Law to fail.

18 "aEvery one who divorces his wife and marries another commits adultery; and he who marries one who is divorced from a husband commits adultery.

19 "Now there was a certain rich man, and he habitually dressed in purple and fine linen, gaily living in splendor every day.

20 "And a certain poor man named Lazarus awas laid at his gate, covered with sores,

21 and longing to be fed with the *crumbs* which were falling from the rich man's table; besides, even the dogs were coming and licking his sores.

22 "Now it came about that the poor man died and he was carried away by the angels to aAbraham's bosom; and the rich man also died and was buried.

23 "And in aHades 1he lifted up his eyes, being in torment, and *saw Abraham far away, and Lazarus in his bosom.

24 "And he cried out and said, 'aFather Abraham, have mercy on me, and send Lazarus, that he may dip the tip of his finger in water and cool off my tongue; for I am in agony in bthis flame.'

25 "But Abraham said, 'Child, remember that aduring your life you received your good things, and likewise Lazarus bad things; but now he is being comforted here, and you are in agony.

26 'And 1besides all this, between us and you there is a great chasm fixed, in order that those who wish to come over from here to you may not be able, and *that* none may cross over from there to us.'

27 "And he said, 'Then I beg you, Father, that you send him to my father's house —

28 for I have five brothers — that he may awarn them, lest they also come to this place of torment.'

29 "But Abraham *said, 'They have aMoses and the Prophets; let them hear them.'

30 "But he said, 'No, aFather Abraham, but if

someone goes to them from the dead, they will repent!'

31 "But he said to him, 'If they do not listen to Moses and the Prophets, neither will they be persuaded if someone rises from the dead.' "

CHAPTER 17

AND He said to His disciples, "^aIt is inevitable that ¹stumbling-blocks should come, but woe to him through whom they come!

2 "^aIt would be better for him if a millstone were hung around his neck and he were thrown into the sea, than that he should cause one of these little ones to stumble.

3 "¹Be on your guard! ^aIf your brother sins, rebuke him; and if he repents, forgive him.

4 "And if he sins against you ^aseven times a day, and returns to you seven times, saying, 'I repent,' ¹forgive him.''

5 And ^athe apostles said to ^bthe Lord, "Increase our faith!"

6 And ^athe Lord said, "If you had faith like ^ba mustard seed, you would say to this ^cmulberry tree, 'Be uprooted and be planted in the sea'; and it would ¹obey you.

7 "But which of you, having a slave plowing or tending sheep, will say to him when he has come in from the field, 'Come immediately and ¹sit down to eat'?

8 "But will he not say to him, '^aPrepare something for me to eat, and *properly* ¹clothe yourself and serve me until I have eaten and drunk; and ²afterward you will eat and drink'?

9 "He does not thank the slave because he did the things which were commanded, does he?

10 "So you too, when you do all the things which are commanded you, say, 'We are unworthy slaves; we have done *only* that which we ought to have done.' "

11 And it came about while He was ^aon the way to Jerusalem, that ^bHe was passing ¹between Samaria and Galilee.

12 And as He entered a certain village, there met Him ten leprous men, who ^astood at a distance;

13 and they raised their voices, saying, "Jesus, ^aMaster, have mercy on us!"

---

1 ¹Or, *temptations to sin*
^aMatt. 18:7; 1 Cor. 11:19; 1 Tim. 4:1

2 ^aMatt. 18:6; Mark 9:42; 1 Cor. 8:12

3 ¹Lit., *Take heed to yourselves*
^aMatt. 18:15

4 ¹Lit., *you shall forgive*
^aMatt. 18:21f.

5 ^aMark 6:30 ^bLuke 7:13

6 ¹Gr., *have obeyed*
^aLuke 7:13 ^bMatt. 13:31; 17:20; Mark 4:31; Luke 13:19
^cLuke 19:4

7 ¹Lit., *recline*

8 ¹Lit., *gird* ²Lit., *after these things*
^aLuke 12:37

11 ¹Lit., *through the midst of*, or, *along the borders of*
^aLuke 9:51 ^bLuke 9:52ff.; John 4:3f.

12 ^aLev. 13:45f.

13 ^aLuke 5:5

Luke 17

**The Samaritan Leper.
The Coming of the Kingdom.**

14 aLuke 5:14; Matt. 8:4

15 aMatt. 9:8

16 aMatt. 10:5

18 ¹Lit., *were there not found those who* aMatt. 9:8

19 ¹Lit., *has saved you* aMatt. 9:22; Luke 18:42

20 ¹Or, *observation* aLuke 19:11; Acts 1:6 bLuke 14:1 [Gr.]

21 ¹Or, *within you* aLuke 17:23

22 aMatt. 9:15; Mark 2:20, Luke 5:35

23 aMatt. 24:23; Mark 13:21; Luke 21:8

24 ¹Lit., *under heaven* aMatt. 24:27

25 aMatt. 16:21; Luke 9:22

26 aLuke 17:26, 27: *Matt.* 24:37-39 bGen. 7

28 ¹Lit., *in the same way as* aGen. 19

29 ¹Or, *sulphur*

14 And when He saw them, He said to them, "ªGo and show yourselves to the priests." And it came about that as they were going, they were cleansed.

15 Now one of them, when he saw that he had been healed, turned back, ªglorifying God with a loud voice,

16 and he fell on his face at His feet, giving thanks to Him. And he was a ªSamaritan.

17 And Jesus answered and said, "Were there not ten cleansed? But the nine — where are they?

18 "¹Were none found who turned back to ªgive glory to God, except this foreigner?"

19 And He said to him, "Rise, and go your way; ªyour faith ¹has made you well."

20 Now having been questioned by the Pharisees ªas to when the kingdom of God was coming, He answered them and said, "The kingdom of God is not coming with ¹bsigns to be observed;

21 nor will ªthey say, 'Look, here *it is!*' or, 'There *it is!*' For behold, the kingdom of God is ¹in your midst."

22 And He said to the disciples, "ªThe days shall come when you will long to see one of the days of the Son of Man, and you will not see it.

23 "ªAnd they will say to you, 'Look there! Look here!' Do not go away, and do not run after *them.*

24 "ªFor just as the lightning, when it flashes out of one part ¹of the sky, shines to the other part ¹of the sky, so will the Son of Man be in His day.

25 "ªBut first He must suffer many things and be rejected by this generation.

26 "ªAnd just as it happened ᵇin the days of Noah, so it shall be also in the days of the Son of Man:

27 they were eating, they were drinking, they were marrying, they were being given in marriage, until the day that Noah entered the ark, and the flood came and destroyed them all.

28 "¹It was the same as happened in ªthe days of Lot: they were eating, they were drinking, they were buying, they were selling, they were planting, they were building;

29 but on the day that Lot went out from Sodom it rained fire and ¹brimstone from heaven and destroyed them all.

30 "It will be ¹just the same on the day that the Son of Man ªis revealed.

31 "On that day, let not the one who is ªon the housetop and whose goods are in the house go down to take them away; and likewise let not the one who is in the field turn back.

32 "ªRemember Lot's wife.

33 "ªWhoever seeks to keep his ¹life shall lose it, and whoever loses *his life* shall preserve it alive.

34 "I tell you, on that night there will be two men in one bed; one will be taken, and the other will be left.

35 "ªThere will be two women grinding at the same place; one will be taken, and the other will be left."

36 (See marginal note.¹)

37 And answering they *said to Him, "Where, Lord?" And He said to them, "ªWhere the body *is*, there also will the ¹vultures be gathered."

CHAPTER 18

NOW He was telling them a parable to show that at all times they ªought to pray and not to ᵇlose heart,

2 saying, "There was in a certain city a judge who did not fear God, and did not ªrespect man.

3 "And there was a widow in that city, and she kept coming to him, saying, '¹Give me legal protection from my opponent.'

4 "And for a while he was unwilling; but afterward he said to himself, 'Even though I do not fear God nor ªrespect man,

5 yet ªbecause this widow bothers me, I will ¹give her legal protection, lest by continually coming she ²ᵇwear me out.' "

6 And ªthe Lord said, "Hear what the unrighteous judge *said;

7 now shall not God ªbring about justice for His ᵇelect, who cry to Him day and night, ¹and will He ᶜdelay long over them?

8 "I tell you that He will bring about justice for them speedily. However, when the Son of Man comes, ªwill He find ¹faith on the earth?"

9 And He also told this parable to certain ones who ªtrusted in themselves that they were righteous, and ᵇviewed others with contempt:

30 ¹Lit., *according to the same things*
ª1 Cor. 1:7; 2 Thess. 1:7; 1 Pet. 1:7; Col. 3:4; 1 John 2:28; 1 Pet. 4:13; Matt. 16:27

31 ªMatt. 24:17, 18; Mark 13:15f.; Luke 21:21

32 ªGen. 19:26

33 ¹Or, *soul-life*
ªMatt. 10:39

35 ªMatt. 24:41

36 ¹Some mss. add verse 36, *Two men will be in the field; one will be taken and the other will be left.* cf. Matt. 24:40

37 ¹Or, *eagles*
ªMatt. 24:28

1 ªLuke 11:5-10 ᵇ2 Cor. 4:1

2 ªLuke 18:4; 20:13; Heb. 12:9

3 ¹Lit., *do me justice*

4 ªLuke 18:2; 20:13; Heb. 12:9

5 ¹Lit., *do her justice* ²Lit., *hit me under the eye*
ªLuke 11:8 ᵇ1 Cor. 9:27 [Gr.]

6 ªLuke 7:13

7 ¹Or, *and yet He is long-suffering over them*
ªRev. 6:10 ᵇMatt. 24:22; Rom. 8:33; Col. 3:12; 2 Tim. 2:10; Titus 1:1 ᶜ2 Pet. 3:9

8 ¹Lit., *the faith*
ªLuke 17:26ff.

9 ªLuke 16:15 ᵇRom. 14:3, 10

Luke 18

The Pharisee and the Publican.   Jesus Receives Little Children.   The Peril of Riches.

10 ¹A publican who collected Roman taxes for profit
ᵃActs 3:1; 2 Kin. 20:5, 8; 1 Kin. 10:5

11 ¹Note, verse 10
ᵃMatt. 6:5; Mark 11:25; Luke 22:41

12 ᵃMatt. 9:14 ᵇLuke 11:42

13 ¹Note, verse 10 ²Or, *propitious*
ᵃMatt. 6:5; Mark 11:25; Luke 22:41 ᵇEzra 9:6 ᶜLuke 23:48

14 ᵃLuke 14:11; Matt. 23:12

15 ᵃLuke 18:15-17: *Matt. 19:13-15; Mark 10:13-16*

17 ᵃMatt. 18:3; 19:14; Mark 10:15; 1 Cor. 14:20; 1 Pet. 2:2

18 ᵃLuke 18:18-30. *Matt. 19:16-29; Mark 10:17-30;* Luke 10:25-28

20 ᵃEx. 20:12-16; Deut. 5:16-20

22 ᵃLuke 12:33; Matt. 19:21 ᵇMatt. 6:20

24 ᵃMatt. 19:23; Mark 10:23f.

25 ¹Lit., *enter*
ᵃMatt. 19:24; Mark 10:25

10 "Two men ᵃwent up into the temple to pray, one a Pharisee, and the other a ¹tax-gatherer.

11 "The Pharisee ᵃstood and was praying thus to himself, 'God, I thank Thee that I am not like other people, swindlers, unjust, adulterers, or even like this ¹tax-gatherer.

12 'I ᵃfast twice a week; I ᵇpay tithes of all that I get.'

13 "But the ¹tax-gatherer, ᵃstanding some distance away, ᵇwas even unwilling to lift up his eyes to heaven, but ᶜwas beating his breast, saying, 'God, be ²merciful to me, the sinner!'

14 "I tell you, this man went down to his house justified rather than the other; ᵃfor every one who exalts himself shall be humbled, but he who humbles himself shall be exalted."

15 ᵃAnd they were bringing even their babies to Him, in order that He might touch them, but when the disciples saw it, they *began* rebuking them.

16 But Jesus called for them, saying, "Permit the children to come to Me, and stop hindering them, for the kingdom of God belongs to such as these.

17 "Truly I say to you, ᵃwhoever does not receive the kingdom of God like a child shall not enter it *at all*."

18 ᵃAnd a certain ruler questioned Him, saying, "Good Teacher, what shall I do to obtain eternal life?"

19 And Jesus said to him, "Why do you call Me good? No one is good except God alone.

20 "You know the commandments, 'ᵃDo not commit adultery, Do not murder, Do not steal, Do not bear false witness, Honor your father and mother.' "

21 And he said, "All these things I have kept from *my* youth."

22 And when Jesus heard *this*, He said to him, "One thing you still lack; ᵃsell all that you possess, and distribute it to the poor, and you shall have ᵇtreasure in heaven; and come, follow Me."

23 But when he had heard these things, he became very sad; for he was extremely rich.

24 And Jesus looked at him and said, "ᵃHow hard it is for those who are wealthy to enter the kingdom of God!

25 "For ᵃit is easier for a camel to ¹go through

the eye of a needle, than for a rich man to enter the kingdom of God."

26 And they who heard it said, "[1]Then who can be saved?"

27 But He said, "[a]The things impossible with men are possible with God."

28 And Peter said, "Behold, [a]we have left [1]our own *homes*, and followed You."

29 And He said to them, "Truly I say to you, [a]there is no one who has left house or wife or brothers or parents or children, for the sake of the kingdom of God,

30 who shall not receive many times as much at this time and in [a]the age to come, eternal life."

31 [a]And He took the twelve aside and said to them, "Behold, [b]we are going up to Jerusalem, and [c]all things which are written through the prophets about the Son of Man will be accomplished.

32 "[a]For He will be [1]delivered up to the Gentiles, and will be mocked and mistreated and spit upon,

33 and after they have scourged Him, they will kill Him; and the third day He will rise again."

34 And [a]they understood none of these things, and this saying was hidden from them, and they did not comprehend the things that were said.

35 [a]And it came about that [b]as He was approaching Jericho, a certain blind man was sitting by the road, begging.

36 Now hearing a multitude going by, he *began* to inquire what this might be.

37 And they told him that Jesus of Nazareth was passing by.

38 And he called out, saying, "Jesus, [a]Son of David, have mercy on me!"

39 And those who led the way were sternly telling him to be quiet; but he kept crying out all the more, "[a]Son of David, have mercy on me!"

40 And Jesus [1]stopped and commanded that he be brought to Him; and when he had come near, He questioned him,

41 "What do you want Me to do for you?" And he said, "Lord, *I want* to receive my sight!"

42 And Jesus said to him, "Receive your sight; [a]your faith has [1]made you well."

43 And immediately he received his sight, and *began* following Him, [a]glorifying God; and when [b]all the people saw it, they gave praise to God.

---

26 [1]Lit., *and*

27 [a]Matt. 19:26

28 [1]Lit., *our own things*
[a]Luke 5:11

29 [a]Matt. 19:29; Mark 10:29f.; Matt. 6:33

30 [a]Matt. 12:32

31 [a]Luke 18:31-33: *Matt. 20:17-19; Mark 10:32-34*
[b]Luke 9:51 [c]Ps. 22; Is. 53

32 [1]Or, *betrayed*
[a]Matt. 16:21

34 [a]Mark 9:32; Luke 9:45

35 [a]Luke 18:35-43: *Matt. 20:29-34; Mark 10:46-52*
[b]Matt. 20:29; Mark 10:46; Luke 19:1

38 [a]Luke 18:39; Matt. 9:27

39 [a]Luke 18:38

40 [1]Lit., *stood*

42 [1]Or, *saved you*
[a]Matt. 9:22

43 [a]Matt. 9:8 [b]Luke 13:17; Luke 9:43; 19:37

Luke 19

**Zaccheus the Tax-gatherer.
The Parable of the Money.**

CHAPTER 19

AND He [a]entered and was passing through Jericho.

2 And behold, there was a man called by the name of Zaccheus; and he was a chief [1]tax-gatherer, and he was rich.

3 And he was trying to see who Jesus was, and he was unable because of the crowd, for he was small in stature.

4 And he ran on ahead and climbed up into a [1]sycamore tree in order to see Him, for He was about to pass through that way.

5 And when Jesus came to the place, He looked up and said to him, "Zaccheus, hurry and come down, for today I must stay at your house."

6 And he hurried and came down, and received Him [1]gladly.

7 And when they saw it, they all *began* to [1]grumble, saying, "He has gone [2]to be the guest of a man who is a sinner."

8 And Zaccheus [1]stopped and said to [a]the Lord, "Behold, Lord, half of my possessions I will give to the poor, and if I have [b]defrauded anyone of anything, I will give back [c]four times as much."

9 And Jesus said to him, "Today salvation has come to this house, because he, too, is [a]a son of Abraham.

10 "For [a]the Son of Man has come to seek and to save that which was lost."

11 And while they were listening to these things, He went on to tell a parable, because [a]He was near Jerusalem, and they supposed that [b]the kingdom of God was going to appear immediately.

12 He said therefore, "[a]A certain nobleman went to a distant country to receive a kingdom for himself, and *then* return.

13 "And he called ten of his slaves, and gave them ten [1]minas, and said to them, 'Do business *with this* [2]until I come *back*.'

14 "But his citizens hated him, and sent [1]a delegation after him, saying, 'We do not want this man to reign over us.'

15 "And it came about that when he returned, after receiving the kingdom, he ordered that these slaves, to whom he had given the money, be called to him in order that he might know what business they had done.

---

1 [a]Luke 18:35

2 [1]A publican who collected Roman taxes for profit

4 [1]I.e., a fig-mulberry
[a]1 Kin. 10:27; 1 Chr. 27:28; 2 Chr. 1:15; 9:27; Ps. 78:47; Is. 9:10; Luke 17:6 [?]

6 [1]Lit., *rejoicing*

7 [1]Lit., *grumble among themselves* [2]Or, *to find lodging*

8 [1]Lit., *stood*
[a]Luke 7:13 [b]Luke 3:14 [Gr.] [c]Ex. 22:1; Lev. 6:5; Num. 5:7; 2 Sam. 12:6

9 [a]Luke 3:8; 13:16; Rom. 4:16; Gal. 3:7

10 [a]Matt. 18:11 marg.

11 [a]Luke 9:51 [b]Luke 17:20

12 [a]Luke 19:12-27; Matt. 25:14-30

13 [1]A mina is equal to about 100 days' wages or nearly $20 [2]Lit., *while I am coming*

14 [1]Or, *an embassy*

170

16 "And the first appeared, saying, '¹Master, your ²mina has made ten minas more.'

17 "And he said to him, 'Well done, good slave, because you have been ªfaithful in a very little thing, be in authority over ten cities.'

18 "And the second came, saying, 'Your ¹mina, ²master, has made five minas.'

19 "And he said to him also, 'And you are to be over five cities.'

20 "And another came, saying, 'Master, behold your mina, which I kept put away in a handkerchief;

21 for I was afraid of you, because you are an exacting man; you take up what you did not lay down, and reap what you did not sow.'

22 "He *said to him, '¹By your own words I will judge you, you worthless slave. Did you know that I am an exacting man, taking up what I did not lay down, and reaping what I did not sow?

23 '¹Then why did you not put the money in the bank, and having come, I would have collected it with interest?'

24 "And he said to the bystanders, 'Take the mina away from him, and give it to the one who has the ten minas.'

25 "And they said to him, 'Master, he has ten minas *already*.'

26 "ªI tell you, that to everyone who has shall *more* be given, but from the one who does not have, even what he does have shall be taken away.

27 'But ªthese enemies of mine, who did not want me to reign over them, bring them here, and ᵇslay them in my presence.' "

28 And after He had said these things, He ªwas going on ahead, ᵇascending to Jerusalem.

29 And it came about that ªwhen He approached Bethphage and ᵇBethany, near the ¹mount that is called ²ᶜOlivet, He sent two of the disciples,

30 saying, "Go into the village opposite *you*, in which as you enter you will find a colt tied, on which no one yet has ever sat; untie it, and bring it *here*.

31 "And if anyone asks you, 'Why are you untying it?' thus shall you speak, 'The Lord has need of it.' "

32 And those who were sent went away and found it just as He had told them.

---

16 ¹Lit., *Lord* ²Note, verse 13

17 ªLuke 16:10

18 ¹Note, verse 13 ²Lit., *lord*

22 ¹Lit., *out of your own mouth*

23 ¹Lit., *and*

26 ªMatt. 13:12; Luke 8:18

27 ªLuke 19:14 ᵇMatt. 22:7; Luke 20:16

28 ªMark 10:32 ᵇLuke 9:51

29 ¹Or, *hill* ²Or, *Olive Grove* ªLuke 19:29-38: *Matt. 21:1-9; Mark 11:1-10* ᵇMatt. 21:17 ᶜLuke 21:37; Acts 1:12

171

Luke 19

**Triumphal Entry Into Jerusalem.
He Cleanses the Temple.**

33 [1]Lit., *lords*

35 [a]Luke 19:35-38: *John
12:12-15*

37 [1]Lit., *as they were
rejoicing* [2]Or, *works of
power*
[a]Matt. 21:1; Luke 19:29
[b]Luke 18:43

38 [a]Ps. 118:26 [b]Matt. 2:2;
Matt. 25:34 [c]Luke 2:14;
Matt. 21:9

39 [1]Lit., *from*
[a]Matt. 21:15f.

40 [a]Hab. 2:11

41 [a]Luke 13:34, 35

43 [1]Lit., *and* [2]I.e., a dirt
wall or mound for siege
purposes
[a]Eccles. 9:14; Is. 29:3; 37:33;
Jer. 6:6; Ezek. 4:2; 26:8
[b]Luke 21:20

44 [a]Matt. 24:2; Mark 13:2,
Luke 21:6 [b]1 Pet. 2:12

45 [a]Luke 19:45, 46: *Matt.
21:12-16; Mark 11:15-18;
John 2:13-16*

46 [1]Lit., *cave*
[a]Is. 56:7; Jer. 7:11; Matt.
21:13; Mark 11:17

47 [a]Matt. 26:55 [b]Luke
20:19

48 [1]Lit., *what they might
do* [2]Lit., *Him, listening*

33 And as they were untying the colt, its [1]owners said to them, "Why are you untying the colt?"

34 And they said, "The Lord has need of it."

35 And they brought it to Jesus, [a]and they threw their garments on the colt, and put Jesus *on it.*

36 And as He was going, they were spreading their garments in the road.

37 And as He was now approaching, near the descent of [a]the Mount of Olives, the whole multitude of the disciples began to [b]praise God [1]joyfully with a loud voice for all the [2]miracles which they had seen,

38 saying,

"[a]BLESSED IS THE [b]King WHO COMES IN THE
NAME OF THE LORD;
Peace in heaven and [c]glory in the
highest!"

39 [a]And some of the Pharisees [1]in the multitude said to Him, "Teacher, rebuke Your disciples."

40 And He answered and said, "I tell you, if these become silent, [a]the stones will cry out!"

41 And when He approached, He saw the city and [a]wept over it,

42 saying, "If you had known in this day, even you, the things which make for peace! But now they have been hidden from your eyes.

43 "For the days shall come upon you [1]when your enemies will [a]throw up a [2]bank before you, and [b]surround you, and hem you in on every side,

44 and will level you to the ground and your children within you, and [a]they will not leave in you one stone upon another, because you did not recognize [b]the time of your visitation."

45 [a]And He entered the temple and began to cast out those who were selling,

46 saying to them, "It is written, '[a]AND MY HOUSE SHALL BE A HOUSE OF PRAYER,' but you have made it a robbers' [1]den."

47 And [a]He was teaching daily in the temple; but the chief priests and the scribes and the leading men among the people [b]were trying to destroy Him,

48 and they could not find [1]anything that they might do, for all the people were hanging upon [2]His words.

CHAPTER 20

a

AND it came about on one of the days while [b]He was teaching the people in the temple and [c]preaching the gospel, that the chief priests and the scribes with the elders [d]confronted *Him,*

2 and they spoke, saying to Him, "Tell us by what authority You are doing these things, or who is the one who gave You this authority?"

3 And He answered and said to them, "I shall also ask you a [1]question, and you tell Me:

4 "Was the baptism of John from heaven or from men?"

5 And they reasoned among themselves, saying, "If we say, 'From heaven,' He will say, 'Why did you not believe him?'

6 "But if we say, 'From men,' all the people will stone us to death, for they are convinced that John was a [a]prophet."

7 And they answered that they did not know where *it came* from.

8 And Jesus said to them, "Neither [1]will I tell you by what authority I am doing these things."

9 [a]And He began to tell the people this parable: "A man planted a vineyard and rented it out to [1]vine-growers, and went on a journey for a long time.

10 "And at the *harvest* time he sent a slave to the vine-growers, in order that they might give him *some* of the produce of the vineyard; but the vine-growers beat him and sent him away empty-handed.

11 "And he proceeded to send another slave; and they beat him also and treated him shamefully, and sent him away empty-handed.

12 "And he proceeded to send a third; and this one also they wounded and cast out.

13 "And the [1]owner of the vineyard said, 'What shall I do? I will send my beloved son; perhaps they will [a]respect him.'

14 "But when the vine-growers saw him, they reasoned with one another, saying, 'This is the heir; let us kill him that the inheritance may be ours.'

15 "And they cast him out of the vineyard and killed him. What, therefore, will the [1]owner of the vineyard do to them?

16 "He will come and [a]destroy these vine-grow-

1 [a]Luke 20:1-8: *Matt. 21:23-27; Mark 11:27-33* [b]Matt. 26:55 [c]Luke 8:1 [d]Acts 4:1; 6:12

3 [1]Lit., *word*

6 [a]Matt. 11:9; Luke 7:29, 30

8 [1]Lit., *do I tell*

9 [1]Here and in verses 10, 14 and 16, or, *tenant farmers* [a]Luke 20:9-19: *Matt. 21:33-46; Mark 12:1-12*

13 [1]Lit., *lord* [a]Luke 18:2 [Gr.]

15 [1]Lit., *lord*

16 [a]Luke 19:27; Matt. 21:41; Mark 12:9

173

Luke 20

Captious Questions: Pay Tribute to Caesar? Is There a Resurrection?

16 [b]Rom. 3:4, 6, 31; 6:2, 15; 7:7, 13; 9:14; 11:1, 11; 1 Cor. 6:15; Gal. 2:17; 3:21; 6:14, [Gr.]

17 [a]Ps. 118:22 [b]Eph. 2:20; 1 Pet 2:6

18 [a]Matt. 21:44

19 [a]Luke 19:47

20 [1]Lit., *feigned themselves* [2]Lit., *take hold of His word* [a]Luke 20:20-26: Matt. 22:15-22; *Mark* 12:13-17; Mark 3:2 [b]Luke 11:54; 20:26 [c]Matt. 27:2

21 [1]Lit., *do not receive a face*

22 [1]Or, *permissible* [a]Luke 23:2; Matt. 17:25

24 [1]The denarius was worth 18 cents in silver, equivalent to one day's wages [2]Lit., *image*

25 [a]Matt. 22:21; Mark 12:17

26 [1]Lit., *take hold of His saying* [a]Luke 11:54; 20:26

27 [a]Luke 20:27-40: Matt. 22:23-33; Mark 12:18-27

28 [a]Deut. 25:5

31 [1]Lit., *left no children, and died*

ers and will give the vineyard to others." And when they heard it, they said, "[b]May it never be!"

17 But He looked at them and said, "What then is this that is written,

'[a]The STONE WHICH THE BUILDERS REJECTED, THIS BECAME THE CHIEF CORNER *STONE*'?

18 "[a]Every one who falls on that stone will be broken to pieces; but on whomever it falls, it will scatter him like dust."

19 And the scribes and the chief priests [a]tried to lay hands on Him that very hour, and they feared the people; for they understood that He spoke this parable against them.

20 [a]And they watched Him, and sent spies who [1]pretended to be righteous, in order [b]that they might [2]catch Him in some statement, so as to deliver Him up to the rule and the authority of [c]the governor.

21 And they questioned Him, saying, "Teacher, we know that You speak and teach correctly, and You [1]are not partial to any, but teach the way of God in truth.

22 "Is it [1]lawful for us [a]to pay taxes to Caesar, or not?"

23 But He detected their trickery and said to them,

24 "Show Me a [1]denarius. Whose [2]head and inscription does it have?" And they said, "Caesar's."

25 And He said to them, "Then [a]render to Caesar the things that are Caesar's, and to God the things that are God's."

26 And they were unable to [1a]catch Him in a saying in the presence of the people; and marveling at His answer, they became silent.

27 [a]Now there came to Him some of the Sadducees (who say that there is no resurrection),

28 and they questioned Him, saying, "Teacher, Moses wrote us that [a]IF A MAN'S BROTHER DIES, having a wife, AND HE IS CHILDLESS, HIS BROTHER SHOULD TAKE THE WIFE AND RAISE UP OFFSPRING TO HIS BROTHER.

29 "Now there were seven brothers; and the first took a wife, and died childless;

30 and the second

31 and the third took her; and in the same way the seven also [1]died, leaving no children.

32 "Finally the woman died also.

33 "In the resurrection therefore, which one's

wife will the woman be? For the seven had her as wife."

34 And Jesus said to them, "The sons of ªthis age marry and are given in marriage,

35 but those who are considered worthy to attain to ªthat age and the resurrection from the dead, neither marry, nor are given in marriage;

36 for neither can they die any more, for they are like angels, and are ªsons of God, being sons of the resurrection.

37 "But that the dead are raised, even Moses showed, in ªthe *passage about the burning* bush, where he calls the Lord ᵇTHE GOD OF ABRAHAM, AND THE GOD OF ISAAC, AND THE GOD OF JACOB.

38 "ªNow He is not the God of the dead, but of the living; for ᵇall live to Him."

39 And some of the scribes answered and said, "Teacher, You have spoken well."

40 For ªthey did not have courage to question Him any longer about anything.

41 ªAnd He said to them, "How *is it that* they say ¹the Christ is ᵇDavid's son?

42 "For David himself says in the book of Psalms,

'ªTHE LORD SAID TO MY LORD,
"SIT AT MY RIGHT HAND,

43 ªUNTIL I MAKE THINE ENEMIES A FOOTSTOOL FOR THY FEET." '

44 "David therefore calls Him 'Lord,' and how is He his son?"

45 ªAnd while all the people were listening, He said to the disciples,

46 "Beware of the scribes, ªwho like to walk around in long robes, and love respectful greetings in the market places, and chief seats in the synagogues, and places of honor at banquets,

47 who devour widows' houses, and for appearance's sake offer long prayers; these will receive greater condemnation."

ª   CHAPTER 21

AND He looked up and saw the rich putting their gifts into the treasury.

2 And He saw a certain poor widow putting ¹in ªtwo ²small copper coins.

3 And He said, "Truly I say to you, this poor widow put in more than all *of them*;

---

34 ªMatt. 12:32; Luke 16:8

35 ªMatt. 12:32; Luke 16:8

36 ªRom. 8:16f.; 1 John 3:1, 2

37 ªMark 12:26 ᵇEx. 3:6

38 ªMatt. 22:32; Mark 12:27 ᵇRom. 14:8

40 ªMatt. 22:46; Luke 14:6

41 ¹I.e., the Messiah ªLuke 20:41-44: *Matt. 22:41-46; Mark 12:35-37* ᵇMatt. 9:27

42 ªPs. 110:1

43 ªPs. 110:1

45 ªLuke 20:45-47: *Matt. 23:1-7; Mark 12:38-40*

46 ªLuke 11:43; Luke 14:7

1 ªLuke 21:1-4: *Mark 12:41-44*

2 ¹Or, *therein* ²Lit., *lepta* ªMark 12:42

4 [1]Or, *abundance* [2]Lit.,
gifts [3]Lit., *the living that she
had*
[a]Mark 12:44

5 [a]Luke 21:5-36: *Matt. 24;
Mark 13*

6 [a]Luke 19:44

7 [1]Or, *attesting miracle*

8 [a]John 8:24 [b]Luke 17:23

11 [1]Or, *attesting miracles*

12 [1]Lit., *being brought*
[a]Luke 21:12-17: *Matt. 10:19-
22; Mark 13:11-13*

13 [1]Lit., *a testimony for
you*
[a]Phil. 1:12

14 [a]Luke 12:11

15 [1]Lit., *a mouth*
[a]Luke 12:12

18 [a]Matt. 10:30; Luke 12:7

19 [a]Matt. 10:22; 24:13;
Rom. 2:7; 5:3f.; James 1:3;
Heb. 10:36; 2 Pet. 1:6

4   for they all out of their [1]surplus put into the [2]offering; but she out of her poverty put in all [3]that she had [a]to live on."

5   [a]And while some were talking about the temple, that it was adorned with beautiful stones and votive gifts, He said,

6   "*As for* these things which you are looking at, the days will come in which [a]there will not be left one stone upon another which will not be torn down."

7   And they questioned Him, saying, "Teacher, when therefore will these things be? And what *will be* the [1]sign when these things are about to take place?"

8   And He said, "Take heed that you be not misled; for many will come in My name, saying, '[a]I am *He*,' and, 'The time is at hand'; [b]do not go after them

9   "And when you hear of wars and disturbances, do not be terrified; for these things must take place first, but the end *does* not *follow* immediately."

10   Then He continued by saying to them, "Nation will rise against nation, and kingdom against kingdom,

11   and there will be great earthquakes, and in various places plagues and famines; and there will be terrors and great [1]signs from heaven.

12   "But before all these things, [a]they will lay their hands on you and will persecute you, delivering you to the synagogues and prisons, [1]bringing you before kings and governors for My name's sake.

13   "[a]It will lead to an [1]opportunity for your testimony.

14   "[a]So make up your minds not to prepare beforehand to defend yourselves;

15   for [a]I will give you [1]utterance and wisdom which none of your opponents will be able to resist or refute.

16   "But you will be betrayed even by parents and brothers and relatives and friends, and they will put *some* of you to death,

17   and you will be hated by all on account of My name.

18   "Yet [a]not a hair of your head will perish.

19   "[a]By your perseverance you will win your souls.

20 "But when you see Jerusalem ᵃsurrounded by armies, then ¹recognize that her desolation is at hand.

21 "Then let those who are in Judea flee to the mountains, and let those who are in the midst of ¹the city depart, and ᵃlet not those who are in the country enter ¹the city;

22 because these are ᵃdays of vengeance, in order that all things which are written may be fulfilled.

23 "Woe to those who are with child and to those who nurse babes in those days; for ᵃthere will be great distress upon the ¹land, and wrath to this people,

24 and they will fall by ᵃthe edge of the sword, and will be led captive into all the nations; and ᵇJerusalem will be ᶜtrampled underfoot by the Gentiles until ᵈthe times of the Gentiles be fulfilled.

25 "And there will be ¹signs in sun and moon and stars, and upon the earth dismay among nations, in perplexity at the roaring of the sea and the waves,

26 men fainting from fear and the expectation of the things which are coming upon the ¹world; for the powers of ²the heavens will be shaken.

27 "And ᵃthen will they see ᵇᴛʜᴇ Sᴏɴ ᴏꜰ Mᴀɴ ᴄᴏᴍɪɴɢ ɪɴ ᴀ ᴄʟᴏᴜᴅ with power and great glory.

28 "But when these things begin to take place, straighten up and lift up your heads, because ᵃyour redemption is drawing near."

29 And He told them a parable: "Behold the fig tree, and all the trees;

30 as soon as they put forth *leaves*, you see it and ᵃknow for yourselves that the summer is now near.

31 "Even so you too, when you see these things happening, ¹recognize that ᵃthe kingdom of God is near.

32 "Truly I say to you, this ¹generation will not pass away until all things take place.

33 "ᵃHeaven and earth will pass away, but My words will not pass away.

34 "ᵃBe on guard, that your hearts may not be weighted down with dissipation and drunkenness and the worries of life, and that day come on you suddenly like a trap;

20 ¹Lit., *know*
ᵃLuke 19:43

21 ¹Lit., *her*
ᵃLuke 17:31

22 ᵃIs. 63:4; Hos. 9:7; Dan. 9:24-27

23 ¹Or, *earth*
ᵃDan. 8:19; 1 Cor. 7:26

24 ᵃGen. 34:26; Ex. 17:13; Heb. 11:34 ᵇIs. 63:18; Dan. 8:13; Rev. 11:2 ᶜRev. 11:2 ᵈRom. 11:25

25 ¹Or, *attesting miracles*

26 ¹Lit., *inhabited earth*
²Or, *heaven*

27 ᵃMatt. 24:30; Mark 13:26; Matt. 16:27; 26:64 ᵇDan. 7:13

28 ᵃLuke 18:7

30 ᵃLuke 12:57

31 ¹Lit., *know*
ᵃMatt. 3:2

32 ¹Or, *race*

33 ᵃMatt. 5:18; Luke 16:17

34 ᵃMatt. 24:42-44; Luke 12:40, 45; Mark 4:19; 1 Thess. 5:2ff.

Luke 21, 22

**The Rulers Plot to Kill Jesus.
The Bargain of Judas.**

36 aMark 13:33; Luke 12:40
bLuke 1:19; Rev. 7:9; 8:2;
11:4

37 1Lit., days 2Lit., nights
3Or, the hill 4Or, Olive
Grove
aMatt. 26:55 bMark 11:19
cMatt. 21:1

38 aJohn 8:2

1 aLuke 22:1, 2: Matt.
26:2 5; Mark 14:1, 2 bJohn
11:55; 13:1

2 aMatt. 12:14

3 1Lit., being of
aLuke 22:3-6: Matt. 26:14-
16; Mark 14:10-11 bMatt.
4:10; John 13:2, 27

4 aLuke 22:52; Acts 4:1;
5.24, 26, 1 Chr. 9.11, Neh.
11:11

6 1Or, without a
disturbance

7 aLuke 22:7-13: Matt.
26:17-19; Mark 14:12-16
bMark 14:12

8 aActs 3:1, 11; 4:13, 19;
8:14; Gal. 2:9

35   for it will come upon all those who dwell on the face of all the earth.

36   "But [a]keep on the alert at all times, praying in order that you may have strength to escape all these things that are about to take place, and to [b]stand before the Son of Man."

37   Now [1]during the day He was [a]teaching in the temple, but [2b]at evening He would go out and spend the night on [3c]the mount that is called [4]Olivet.

38   And all the people would get up [a]early in the morning *to come* to Him in the temple to listen to Him.

a

CHAPTER 22

NOW the Feast of Unleavened Bread, which is called the [b]Passover, was approaching.

2   And the chief priests and the scribes [a]were seeking how they might put Him to death; for they were afraid of the people.

3   [a]And [b]Satan entered into Judas who was called Iscariot, [1]belonging to the number of the twelve.

4   And he went away and discussed with the chief priests and [a]officers how he might betray Him to them.

5   And they were delighted, and agreed to give him money.

6   And he consented, and *began* seeking a good opportunity to betray Him to them [1]apart from the multitude.

7   [a]Then came the day of Unleavened Bread on which [b]the Passover *lamb* had to be sacrificed.

8   And He sent [a]Peter and John, saying, "Go and prepare the Passover for us, that we may eat it."

9   And they said to Him, "Where do You want us to prepare it?"

10   And He said to them, "Behold, when you have entered the city, a man will meet you carrying a pitcher of water; follow him into the house that he enters.

11   "And you shall say to the owner of the house, 'The Teacher says to you, "Where is the guest room in which I may eat the Passover with My disciples?" '

12 "And he will show you a large, furnished, upper room; prepare it there."

13   And they departed and found *everything* just as He had told them; and they prepared the Passover.

14   [a]And when the hour had come He reclined *at table*, and [b]the apostles with Him.

15   And He said to them, "I have earnestly desired to eat this Passover with you before I suffer;

16   for I say to you, I shall never again eat it [a]until it is fulfilled in the kingdom of God."

17   [a]And having taken a cup, [b]when He had given thanks, He said, "Take this and share it among yourselves;

18   for [a]I say to you, I will not drink of the fruit of the vine from now on until the kingdom of God comes."

19   And having taken *some* bread, [a]when He had given thanks, He broke *it*, and gave *it* to them, saying, "This is My body [1]which is given for you; do this in remembrance of Me."

20   And in the same way *He took* the cup after they had eaten, saying, "This cup which is [a]poured out for you is the [b]new covenant in My blood.

21   "[a]But behold, the hand of the one betraying Me is with Me on the table.

22   "For indeed, the Son of Man is going [a]as it has been determined; but woe to that man through whom He is betrayed!"

23   And they began to discuss among themselves which one of them it might be who was going to do this thing.

24   And there arose also [a]a dispute among them *as to* which one of them was regarded to be greatest.

25   [a]And He said to them, "The kings of the Gentiles lord it over them; and those who have authority over them are called 'Benefactors.'

26   "But not so with you, [a]but let him who is the greatest among you become as [b]the youngest, and the leader as the servant.

27   "For [a]who is greater, the one who reclines *at table*, or the one who serves? Is it not the one who reclines *at table*? But [b]I am among you as the one who serves.

28   "And you are those who have stood by Me in My [a]trials;

14 [a]Matt. 26:20; Mark 14:17 [b]Mark 6:30

16 [a]Luke 22:18, 30; 14:15; Rev. 19:9

17 [a]Luke 22:17-20: *Matt. 26:26-29; Mark 14:22-25; 1 Cor. 11:23-25; 10:16* [b]Matt. 14:19

18 [a]Matt. 26:29; Mark 14:25

19 [1]Some ancient mss. omit the remainder of verse 19 and all of verse 20 [a]Matt. 14:19

20 [a]Matt. 26:28; Mark 14:24 [b]1 Cor. 11:25; 2 Cor. 3:6; Heb. 9:15; 8:8; Jer. 31:31; Ex. 24:8 [Heb. 8:13]

21 [a]Luke 22:21-23: *Matt. 26:21-24; Mark 14:18-21;* John 13:18, 21, 22, 26

22 [a]Acts 2:23; 4:28; 10:42; 17:31

24 [a]Mark 9:34; Luke 9:46

25 [a]Luke 22:25-27: *Matt. 20:25-28; Mark 10:42-45*

26 [a]Luke 9:48 [b]1 Pet. 5:5

27 [a]Luke 12:37 [b]Matt. 20:28

28 [a]Heb. 2:18; 4:15

Luke 22

**Peter's Denial Foretold.   The Apostles'
Changed Condition.   Gethsemane.**

29 ªMatt. 5:3; 2 Tim. 2:12

30 ªLuke 22:16 ᵇMatt. 5:3;
2 Tim. 2:12 ᶜMatt. 19:28

31 ¹Or, *obtained by asking*
ªMatt. 4:10; Job 1:6-12; 2:1-6
ᵇAmos 9:9

32 ªJohn 17:9, 15 ᵇJohn
21:15-17

33 ªLuke 22:33, 34: *Matt.
26:33-35; Mark 14:29-31;
John 13:37, 38*

35 ªLuke 9:3ff.; 10:4; Matt.
10:9f.; Mark 6:8

36 ¹Or, *outer garment*

37 ¹Or, *reckoned with
transgressors*
ªIs. 53:12 ᵇJohn 17:4; 19:30

38 ªLuke 22:36, 49

39 ªMatt. 26:30; Mark
14:26; John 18:1 ᵇLuke 21:37
ᶜMatt. 21:1

40 ªLuke 22:40-46: *Matt.
26:36-46; Mark 14:32-42*
ᵇLuke 22:46; Matt. 6:13

41 ªMatt. 26:39; Mark
14:35; Luke 18:11

42 ªMatt. 20:22 ᵇMatt.
26:39

43 ¹Some ancient mss. omit
verses 43 and 44
ªMatt. 4:11

44 ªHeb. 5:7

29 and just as My Father has granted Me a
ªkingdom, I grant you

30 that you may ªeat and drink at My table in
My ᵇkingdom, and ᶜyou will sit on thrones judging
the twelve tribes of Israel.

31 "Simon, Simon, behold, ªSatan has ¹de-
manded *permission* to ᵇsift you like wheat;

32 but I ªhave prayed for you, that your faith
may not fail; and you, when once you have turned
again, ᵇstrengthen your brothers."

33 ªAnd he said to Him, "Lord, with You I am
ready to go both to prison and to death!"

34 And He said, "I tell you, Peter, the cock will
not crow today until you have denied three times
that you know Me."

35 And He said to them, "ªWhen I sent you
out without purse and bag and sandals, you did not
lack anything, did you?" And they said, "*No,
nothing.*"

36 And He said to them, "But now, let him
who has a purse take it along, likewise also a bag,
and let him who has no sword sell his ¹robe and buy
one.

37 "For I tell you, that this which is written
must be fulfilled in Me, 'ªAND HE WAS ¹CLASSED
AMONG CRIMINALS'; for ᵇthat which refers to Me has
its fulfillment."

38 And they said, "Lord, look, here are two
ªswords." And He said to them, "It is enough."

39 ªAnd He came out and proceeded ᵇas was
His custom to ᶜthe Mount of Olives; and the disciples also followed Him.

40 ªAnd when He arrived at the place, He said
to them, "ᵇPray that you may not enter into
temptation."

41 And He withdrew from them about a
stone's throw, and He ªknelt down and *began* to
pray,

42 saying, "Father, if Thou art willing, remove
this ªcup from Me; ᵇyet not My will, but Thine be
done."

43 ¹Now an ªangel from heaven appeared to
Him, strengthening Him.

44 And ªbeing in agony He was praying very
fervently; and His sweat became like drops of
blood, falling down upon the ground.

45 And when He rose from prayer, He came to
His disciples and found them sleeping from sorrow,

46 and said to them, "Why are you sleeping? Rise and ªpray that you may not enter into temptation."

47 ªWhile He was still speaking, behold, a multitude *came*, and the one called Judas, one of the twelve, was preceding them; and he approached Jesus to kiss Him.

48 But Jesus said to him, "Judas, are you betraying the Son of Man with a kiss?"

49 And when those who were around Him saw what was going to happen, they said, "Lord, shall we strike with the ªsword?"

50 And a certain one of them struck the slave of the high priest and cut off his right ear.

51 But Jesus answered and said, "¹Stop! No more of this." And He touched his ear and healed him.

52 And Jesus said to the chief priests and ªofficers of the temple and elders who had come against Him, "Have you come out with swords and clubs ᵇas against a robber?

53 "While I was with you daily in the temple, you did not lay hands on Me; but ¹this hour and the power of darkness are yours."

54 ªAnd having arrested Him, they led Him *away*, and brought Him to the house of the high priest; but ᵇPeter was following at a distance.

55 ªAnd after they had kindled a fire in the middle of ᵇthe courtyard and had sat down together, Peter was sitting among them.

56 And a certain servant-girl, seeing him as he sat in the firelight, and looking intently at him, said, "This man was with Him too."

57 But he denied *it*, saying, "Woman, I do not know Him."

58 And a little later, ªanother saw him and said, "You are *one* of them too!" But Peter said, "Man, I am not!"

59 And after about an hour had passed, another man *began* to insist, saying, "Certainly this man also was with Him, ªfor he is a Galilean too."

60 But Peter said, "Man, I do not know what you are talking about." And immediately, while he was still speaking, a cock crowed.

61 And ªthe Lord turned and looked at Peter. And Peter remembered the word of the Lord, how He had told him, "ᵇBefore a cock crows today, you will deny Me three times."

46 ªLuke 22:40

47 ªLuke 22:47-53: *Matt. 26:47-56; Mark 14:43-50; John 18:3-11*

49 ªLuke 22:38

51 ¹Or, "*Let Me at least do this," and He touched . . .*

52 ªLuke 22:4 ᵇLuke 22:37

53 ¹Lit., *this is your hour and power of darkness*

54 ªMatt. 26:57; Mark 14:53 ᵇMatt. 26:58; Mark 14:54; John 18:15

55 ªLuke 22:55-62: *Matt. 26:69-75; Mark 14:66-72; John 18:16-18, 25-27* ᵇMatt. 26:3

58 ªJohn 18:26

59 ªMatt. 26:73; Mark 14:70

61 ªLuke 7:13 ᵇLuke 22:34

F18

Luke 22, 23

The Mockery. Trial Before the Sanhedrin.
Jesus Before Pilate. Jesus Before Herod.

63 ¹Lit., *Him*
ªLuke 22:63-65: Matt. 26:67f.; Mark 14:65; John 18:22f.

64 ªMatt. 26:68; Mark 14:65

65 ªMatt. 27:39 Gr.

66 ¹Or, *Sanhedrin*
ªMatt. 27:1f.; Mark 15:1; John 18:28 ᵇActs 22:5 Gr. ᶜMatt. 5:22

67 ¹I.e., Messiah
ªLuke 22:67-71: Matt. 26:63-66; Mark 14:61-63; John 18:19-21

69 ªMatt. 26:64; Mark 14:62; Mark 16:19 ᵇPs. 110:1

70 ¹Lit., *you say that I am*
ªMatt. 4:3 ᵇMatt. 27:11; Luke 23:3; Matt. 26:64

1 ªMatt. 27:2; Mark 15:1; John 18:28

2 ¹I.e., Messiah
ªLuke 23:2, 3: *Matt. 27:11-14; Mark 15:2-5; John 18:29-37* ᵇLuke 23:14 ᶜLuke 20:22; John 16:3ff., 19:12, Acts 17:7

3 ªLuke 22:70

4 ªLuke 23:14, 22; Matt. 27:23; Mark 15:14; John 18:38; 19:4, 6

5 ªMatt. 4:12

7 ¹Lit., *in these days*
ªMatt. 14:1; Mark 6:14; Luke 3:1; 9:7; 13:31

8 ªLuke 9:9

182

62   And he went outside and wept bitterly.

63   ªAnd the men who were holding ¹Jesus in custody were mocking Him, and beating Him,

64   and they blindfolded Him and were asking Him, saying, "ªProphesy, who is the one who hit You?"

65   And they were saying many other things against Him, ªblaspheming.

66   ªAnd when it was day, ᵇthe ¹Council of Elders of the people assembled, both chief priests and scribes, and they led Him away to their ᶜcouncil *chamber*, saying,

67   "ªIf You are the ¹Christ, tell us." But He said to them, "If I tell you, you will not believe;

68   and if I ask a question, you will not answer.

69   "ªBut from now on ᵇTHE SON OF MAN WILL BE SEATED AT THE RIGHT HAND of the power OF GOD."

70   And they all said, "Are You ªthe Son of God, then?" And He said to them, "¹ᵇYes, I am."

71   And they said, "What further need do we have of testimony? For we have heard it ourselves from His own mouth."

CHAPTER 23

THEN the whole body of them arose and ªbrought Him before Pilate.

2   ªAnd they began to accuse Him, saying, "We found this man ᵇmisleading our nation and ᶜforbidding to pay taxes to Caesar, and saying that He Himself is ¹Christ, a King."

3   And Pilate asked Him, saying, "Are You the King of the Jews?" And He answered him and said, "ªIt is *as* you say."

4   And Pilate said to the chief priests and the multitudes, "ªI find no guilt in this man."

5   But they kept on insisting, saying, "He stirs up the people, teaching all over Judea, ªstarting from Galilee, even as far as this place."

6   But when Pilate heard it, he asked whether the man were a Galilean.

7   And when he learned that He belonged to Herod's jurisdiction, he sent Him to ªHerod, who himself also was in Jerusalem ¹at that time.

8   Now Herod was very glad when he saw Jesus; for ªhe had wanted to see Him for a long

time, because he had been hearing about Him and was hoping to see some [1]sign performed by Him.

9 And he questioned Him [1]at some length; but [a]He answered him nothing.

10 And the chief priests and the scribes were standing there, accusing Him vehemently.

11 And Herod with his soldiers, after treating Him with contempt and mocking Him, [a]dressed Him in a gorgeous robe and sent Him back to Pilate.

12 Now [a]Herod and Pilate became friends with one another that very day; for before they had been at enmity with each other.

13 And Pilate summoned the chief priests and the [a]rulers and the people,

14 and said to them, "You brought this man to me as one who [a]incites the people to rebellion, and behold, having examined Him before you, I [b]have found no guilt in this man regarding the charges which you make against Him.

15 "No, nor has [a]Herod, for he sent Him back to us; and behold, nothing deserving death has been done by Him.

16 "I will therefore [a]punish Him and release Him."

17 (See marginal note.[1])

18 But they cried out all together, saying, "[a]Away with this man, and release for us Barabbas!"

19 (He was one who had been thrown in prison for a certain insurrection made in the city, and for murder.)

20 And Pilate, wanting to release Jesus, addressed them again,

21 but they kept on calling out, saying, "Crucify, crucify Him!"

22 And he said to them the third time, "Why, what evil has this man done? I have found in Him no guilt *demanding* death; I will therefore [a]punish Him and release Him."

23 But they were insistent, with loud voices asking that He be crucified. And their voices *began* to prevail.

24 And Pilate pronounced sentence that their demand should be granted.

25 And he released the man they were asking for who had been thrown into prison for insurrection and murder, but he turned Jesus over to their will.

8 [1]Or, *attesting miracle*

9 [1]Lit., *in many words*
[a]Matt. 27:12, 14; Mark 15:5; John 19:9

11 [a]Matt. 27:28

12 [a]Acts 4:27

13 [a]Luke 23:35; John 7:26, 48; 12:42; Acts 3:17; 4:5, 8; 13:27

14 [a]Luke 23:2 [b]Luke 23:4

15 [a]Luke 9:9

16 [a]Matt. 27:26; Mark 15:15; John 19:1; Acts 16:37; Luke 23:22

17 [1]Some mss. insert verse 17, *Now he was obliged to release to them at the feast one prisoner*

18 [a]Luke 23:18-25: *Matt. 27:15-26; Mark 15:6-15; John 18:39-19:16*

22 [a]Luke 23:16

183

26 aLuke 23:26: *Matt. 27:32; Mark 15:21;* John 19:17 bMatt. 27:32

27 1Lit., *beating the breast* aLuke 8:52

29 aMatt. 24:19; Luke 21:23; 11:27

30 aHos. 10:8; Rev. 6:16; Is. 2:19, 20

32 aMatt. 27:38; Mark 15:27; John 19:18

33 1In Latin, *Calvaria,* or *Calvary* aLuke 23:33-43: Matt. 27:33-44; Mark 15:22-32; John 19:17-24

34 1Some mss. omit, *"But Jesus was saying. . . doing."* aMatt. 11:25; Luke 22:42 bPs. 22:18; John 19:24

35 1I.e., Messiah aLuke 23:13 bMatt. 27:43

36 aMatt. 27:48

37 aMatt. 27:43

38 aMatt. 27:37; Mark 15:26; John 19:19

39 1Or, *blaspheming* 2I.e., Messiah aLuke 23:39-43: Matt. 27:44; Mark 15:32 bLuke 23:35, 37

41 1Lit., *things worthy of what we have done*

42 1Or, *into*

26 aAnd when they led Him away, they laid hold of one Simon, a bCyrenian, coming in from the country, and placed on him the cross to carry behind Jesus.

27 And there were following Him a great multitude of the people, and of women who were 1amourning and lamenting Him.

28 But Jesus turning to them said, "Daughters of Jerusalem, stop weeping for Me, but weep for yourselves and for your children.

29 "For behold, the days are coming when they will say, 'aBlessed are the barren, and the wombs that never bore, and the breasts that never nursed.'

30 "Then they will begin TO aSAY TO THE MOUNTAINS, 'FALL ON US,' AND TO THE HILLS, 'COVER US.'

31 "For if they do these things in the green tree, what will happen in the dry?"

32 aAnd two others also, who were criminals, were being led away to be put to death with Him.

33 aAnd when they came to the place called 1The Skull, there they crucified Him and the criminals, one on the right and the other on the left.

34 1But Jesus was saying, "aFather forgive them; for they do not know what they are doing." bAND THEY CAST LOTS, DIVIDING UP HIS GARMENTS AMONG THEMSELVES.

35 And the people stood by, looking on. And even the arulers were sneering at Him, saying, "He saved others; blet Him save Himself if this is the 1Christ of God, His Chosen One."

36 And the soldiers also mocked Him, coming up to Him, aoffering Him sour wine,

37 and saying, "aIf You are the King of the Jews, save Yourself!"

38 Now there was also an inscription above Him, "aTHIS IS THE KING OF THE JEWS."

39 aAnd one of the criminals who were hanged *there* was 1hurling abuse at Him, saying, "Are You not the 2Christ? bSave Yourself and us!"

40 But the other answered, and rebuking him said, "Do you not even fear God, since you are under the same sentence of condemnation?

41 "And we indeed justly, for we are receiving 1what we deserve for our deeds; but this man has done nothing wrong."

42 And he was saying, "Jesus, remember me when You come 1in Your kingdom!"

43   And He said to him, "Truly I say to you, today you shall be with Me in ªParadise."

44   ªAnd it was now about 1bthe sixth hour, and darkness 2fell over the whole land until 3the ninth hour,

45   the sun 1being obscured; and ªthe veil of the temple was torn 2in two.

46   And Jesus, ªcrying out with a loud voice, said, "Father, bINTO THY HANDS I COMMIT MY SPIRIT." And having said this, He breathed His last.

47   ªNow when the centurion saw what had happened, he *began* bpraising God, saying, "Certainly this man was 1innocent."

48   And all the multitudes who came together for this spectacle, when they observed what had happened, *began* to return, ªbeating their breasts.

49   ªAnd all His acquaintances and ªthe women who accompanied Him from Galilee, were standing at a distance, seeing these things.

50   ªAnd behold, a man named Joseph, who was a bmember of the Council, a good and righteous man,

51   (he had not consented to their plan and action) *a man* from Arimathea, a city of the Jews, who was ªwaiting for the kingdom of God,

52   this man went to Pilate and asked for the body of Jesus.

53   And he took it down and wrapped it in a linen cloth, and laid Him in a tomb cut into the rock, where no one had ever lain.

54   And it was ªthe Preparation Day, and the Sabbath was about to 1begin.

55   Now ªthe women who had come with Him out of Galilee followed after, and saw the tomb and how His body was laid.

56   And they returned and ªprepared spices and perfumes.

And on the Sabbath they rested according to bthe commandment.

a

CHAPTER 24

BUT on the first day of the week, at early dawn, they came to the tomb, bringing the spices which they had prepared.

2   And they found the stone rolled away from the tomb,

---

43 ª2 Cor. 12:4; Rev. 2:7; Gen. 2:8 [Sept.]

44 1I.e., 12 noon 2Or, *occurred* 3I.e., 3 p.m. ªLuke 23:44-49: *Matt. 27:45-56; Mark 15:33-41* bJohn 19:14

45 1Lit., *failing* 2Lit., *in the middle* ªMatt. 27:51

46 ªMatt. 27:50; Mark 15:37; John 19:30 bPs. 31:5

47 1Lit., *righteous* ªMatt. 27:54; Mark 15:39 bMatt. 9:8

48 ªLuke 18:13; Luke 8:52

49 ªMatt. 27: 55f.; Mark 15:40f.; Luke 8:2; John 19:25

50 ªLuke 23:50-56: *Matt. 27:57-61; Mark 15:42-47; John 19:38-42* bMark 15:43

51 ªMark 15:43; Luke 2:25

54 1Lit., *dawn* ªMark 15:42; Matt. 27:62

55 ªLuke 23:49

56 ªMark 16:1; Luke 24:1 bEx. 20:10

1 ªLuke 24:1-10: *Matt. 28:1-8; Mark 16:1-8; John 20:1-8*

Luke 24

**The Empty Tomb.
The Interview on the Way to Emmaus.**

3 ªActs 1:21; Luke 7:13

4 ªJohn 20:12 ᵇLuke 2:9;
Acts 12:7

6 ¹Some ancient mss.
omit: *He is not here, but He
has risen* ²Or, *been raised*
ªMark 16:6 ᵇMatt. 17:22f.;
Mark 9:30f.; Luke 9:44; Luke
24:44

7 ªMatt. 16:21; Luke 24:46

8 ªJohn 2:22

10 ªMatt. 27:56 ᵇMark 6:30

11 ¹Lit., *in their sight*
ªMark 16:11

12 ¹Some ancient mss. omit
verse 12 ²Or, *by themselves*
ªJohn 20:3-6 ᵇJohn 20:10

13 ¹I.e., 60 stadia, one
stadion equals 600 feet
ªMark 16:12

16 ¹Lit., *were being
prevented*
ªJohn 20:14; 21:4; Luke
24:31

18 ¹Or, *Are You visiting
Jerusalem alone . . .*

19 ªMark 1:24 ᵇMatt. 21:11

3 but when they entered, they did not find the body of ªthe Lord Jesus.

4 And it happened that while they were perplexed about this, behold, ªtwo men suddenly ᵇstood near them in dazzling apparel;

5 and as *the women* were terrified and bowed their faces to the ground, *the men* said to them, "Why do you seek the living One among the dead?

6 ¹"He is not here, but He ªhas ²risen. Remember how He spoke to you ᵇwhile He was still in Galilee,

7 saying that ªthe Son of Man must be delivered into the hands of sinful men, and be crucified, and the third day rise again."

8 And ªthey remembered His words,

9 and returned from the tomb and reported all these things to the eleven and to all the rest.

10 Now they were ªMary Magdalene and Joanna and Mary the *mother* of James; also the other women with them were telling these things to ᵇthe apostles.

11 And these words appeared ¹to them as nonsense, and they ªwould not believe them.

12 [¹But Peter arose and ªran to the tomb; ªstooping and looking in, he *saw the linen wrappings ²only; and he went away ᵇto his home marveling at that which had happened.]

13 And behold, ªtwo of them were going that very day to a village named Emmaus, which was ¹about seven miles from Jerusalem.

14 And they were conversing with each other about all these things which had taken place.

15 And it came about that while they were conversing and discussing, Jesus Himself approached, and *began* traveling with them.

16 But ªtheir eyes ¹were prevented from recognizing Him.

17 And He said to them, "What are these words that you are exchanging with one another as you are walking?" And they stood still, looking sad.

18 And one of them, named Cleopas, answered and said to Him, "¹Are You the only one visiting Jerusalem and unaware of the things which have happened here in these days?"

19 And He said to them, "What things?" And they said to Him, "The things about ªJesus the Nazarene, who was a ᵇprophet mighty in deed and word in the sight of God and all the people,

20 and how the chief priests and our [a]rulers delivered Him up to the sentence of death, and crucified Him.

21 "But we were hoping that it was He who was going to [a]redeem Israel. Indeed, besides all this, it is the third day since these things happened.

22 "But also some women among us amazed us. [a]When they were at the tomb early in the morning,

23 and did not find His body, they came, saying that they had also seen a vision of angels, who said that He was alive.

24 "And some of those who were with us went to the tomb and found it just exactly as the women also had said; but Him they did not see."

25 And He said to them, "O foolish men and slow of heart to believe in all that [a]the prophets have spoken!

26 "[a]Was it not necessary for the [1]Christ to suffer these things and to enter into His glory?"

27 And beginning [1]with [a]Moses and [1]with all the [b]prophets, He explained to them the things concerning Himself in all the Scriptures.

28 And they approached the village where they were going, and [a]He acted as though He would go farther.

29 And they urged Him, saying, "Stay with us, for it is *getting* toward evening, and the day [1]is now nearly over." And He went in to stay with them.

30 And it came about that when He had reclined *at table* with them, He took the bread and [a]blessed *it*, and breaking *it*, He *began* giving *it* to them.

31 And their [a]eyes were opened and they recognized Him; and He vanished from [1]their sight.

32 And they said to one another, "[1]Were not our hearts burning within us while He was speaking to us on the road, while He [a]was [2]explaining the Scriptures to us?"

33 And they arose that very hour and returned to Jerusalem, and [a]found gathered together the eleven and [b]those who were with them,

34 saying, "[a]The Lord has really risen, and [b]has appeared to Simon."

35 And they *began* to relate [1]their experiences on the road and how [a]He was recognized by them in the breaking of the bread.

36 And while they were telling these things, [a]He Himself stood in their midst.[1]

20 [a]Luke 23:13

21 [a]Luke 1:68

22 [a]Luke 24:1ff.

25 [a]Matt. 26:24

26 [1]I.e., Messiah
[a]Luke 24:7, 44ff.; Heb. 2:10;
1 Pet. 1:11

27 [1]Lit., *from*
[a]Gen. 3:15; 12:3; Num. 21:9
[John 3:14]; Deut. 18:15
[John 1:45]; John 5:46
[b]2 Sam. 7:12-16: Is. 7:14
[Matt. 1:23]; 9:1f. [Matt.
4:15f.]; 42: [Matt. 12:18ff.];
53: [Matt. 8:17; Luke 22:37];
Dan. 7:13 [Matt. 24:30];
Mic. 5:2 [Matt. 2:6]; Zech.
9:9 [Matt. 21:5]; Acts 13:27

28 [a]Mark 6:48

29 [1]Lit., *has now declined*

30 [a]Matt. 14:19

31 [1]Lit., *them*
[a]Luke 24:16

32 [1]Lit., *was not our heart*
[2]Lit., *opening*
[a]Luke 24:45

33 [a]Mark 16:13 [b]Acts 1:14

34 [a]Luke 24:6 [b]1 Cor. 15:5

35 [1]Lit., *the things*
[a]Luke 24:30f.

36 [1]Some ancient mss.
insert, *And He says to them,
"Peace be to you."*
[a]Mark 16:14

187

37 ᵃMatt. 14:26; Mark 6:49

38 ¹Lit., *heart*

39 ᵃJohn 20:20, 27 ᵇ1 John 1:1; John 20:27

40 ¹Some mss. add verse 40, *And when He had said this, He showed them His hands and His feet.*

41 ¹Lit., *were disbelieving* ᵃLuke 24:11 ᵇJohn 21:5

43 ¹Lit., *before them* ᵃActs 10:41

44 ᵃLuke 9:22, 44f.; 18:31-34; 22:37 ᵇLuke 24:27 ᶜPs. 2 [Acts 13:33]; Ps. 16 [Acts 2:27]; Ps. 22 [Matt. 27:34-46]; Ps. 69 [John 19:28ff.]; Ps. 72; 110 [Matt. 22:43f.]; Ps. 118 [Matt. 21:42]

45 ¹Lit., *mind* ᵃLuke 24:32; Acts 16:14; 1 John 5:20

46 ¹I.e., Messiah ᵃLuke 24:26, 44 ᵇLuke 24:7

47 ¹Some mss. read, *and forgiveness* ²Or, *on the basis of* ᵃActs 5:31; 10:43; 13:38; 26:18 ᵇMatt. 28:19

48 ᵃActs 1:8, 22; 2:32; 3:15; 4:33; 5:32; 10:39, 41; 13:31; 1 Pet. 5:1

49 ᵃJohn 14:26 ᵇActs 1:4

50 ᵃMatt. 21:17; Acts 1:12

51 ¹Some mss. add, *and was carried up into heaven*

52 ¹Some mss. insert, *worshiped Him, and . . .*

53 ¹Lit., *blessing*

37 But they were startled and frightened and thought that they were seeing ᵃa spirit.

38 And He said to them, "Why are you troubled, and why do doubts arise in your ¹hearts?

39 "See My hands and My feet, that it is I Myself; ᵇtouch Me and see, for a spirit does not have flesh and bones as you see that I have."

40 (See marginal note.¹)

41 And while they still ¹ᵃcould not believe *it* for joy and were marveling, He said to them, "ᵇHave you anything here to eat?"

42 And they gave Him a piece of a broiled fish;

43 and He took it and ᵃate *it* ¹in their sight.

44 Now He said to them, "ᵃThese are My words which I spoke to you while I was still with you, that all things which are written about Me in the ᵇLaw of Moses and ᵇthe Prophets and ᶜthe Psalms must be fulfilled."

45 Then He ᵃopened their ¹minds to understand the Scriptures.

46 and He said to them, "ᵃThus it is written, that the ¹Christ should suffer and ᵇrise again from the dead the third day;

47 and that ᵃrepentance ¹for forgiveness of sins should be proclaimed ²in His name to ᵇall the nations—beginning from Jerusalem.

48 "You are ᵃwitnesses of these things.

49 "And behold, ᵃI am sending forth the promise of My Father upon you; but ᵇyou are to stay in the city until you are clothed with power from on high."

50 And He led them out as far as ᵃBethany, and He lifted up His hands and blessed them.

51 And it came about that while He was blessing them, He parted from them.¹

52 And they¹ returned to Jerusalem with great joy,

53 and were continually in the temple, ¹praising God.

THE GOSPEL

ACCORDING TO

JOHN

The Prologue. The Word Made Flesh
Announced by John

^a

IN the beginning was ^bthe Word, and the Word was ^cwith God, and ^dthe Word was God.

2 ¹He was in the beginning with God.

3 ^aAll things came into being through Him; and apart from Him nothing came into being that has come into being.

4 ^aIn Him was life; and the life was ^bthe light of men.

5 And ^athe light shines in the darkness; and the darkness did not ¹comprehend it.

6 There ¹came a man, sent from God, whose name was ^aJohn.

7 ¹He came ^afor a witness, that he might bear witness of the light, ^bthat all might believe through him.

8 ^{1a}He was not the light, but *came* that he might bear witness of the light.

9 There was ^athe true light ¹which, coming into the world, enlightens every man.

10 He was in the world, and ^athe world was made through Him, and the world did not know Him.

11 He came to His ¹own, and those who were His own did not receive Him.

12 But as many as received Him, to them He gave the right to become ^achildren of God, *even* ^bto those who believe in His name:

13 ^awho were ¹born not of ²blood, nor of the will of the flesh, nor of the will of man, but of God.

14 And ^athe Word ^bbecame flesh, and ^{1c}dwelt among us, and ^dwe beheld His glory, glory as of ²the only begotten from the Father, full of ^egrace and ^ftruth.

15 John *^abore witness of Him, and cried out, saying, "This was He of whom I said, '^bHe who comes after me ¹has a higher rank than I, ^cfor He existed before me.' "

16 For of His ^afulness ¹we have all received, and ²grace upon grace.

1 ^aGen. 1:1; Col. 1:17; 1 John 1:1 ^bJohn 1:14; Rev. 19:13 ^c1 John 1:2; John 17:5 ^dPhil. 2:6

2 ¹Lit., *This One*

3 ^aJohn 1:10; 1 Cor. 8:6; Col. 1:16; Heb. 1:2

4 ^aJohn 5:26; John 11:25; 14:6 ^bJohn 8:12; 9:5; 12:46

5 ¹Or, *overpower* ^aJohn 3:19

6 ¹Or, *came into being* ^aMatt. 3:1

7 ¹Lit., *This One* ^aJohn 1:15, 19, 32; 3:26; 5:33 ^bJohn 1:12; Acts 19:4; Gal. 3:26

8 ¹Lit., *That One* ^aJohn 1:20

9 ¹Or, *which enlightens every man coming into the world* ^a1 John 2:8

10 ^a1 Cor. 8:6; Col. 1:16; Heb. 1:2

11 ¹Gr., *His own things, possessions, domain*

12 ^aJohn 11:52; Gal. 3:26 ^bJohn 1:7; 3:18; 1 John 5:13; 1 John 3:23

13 ¹Or, *begotten* ²Or, Gr., *bloods* ^aJohn 3:5f.; 1 Pet. 1:23; James 1:18; 1 John 2:29; 3:9

14 ¹Or, Gr., *tabernacle* ²Lit., *an only or unique one* or, *an only begotten from a father* ^aRev. 19:13 ^bRom. 1:3; Gal. 4:4; Phil. 2:7f., 1 Tim. 3:16; Heb. 2:14; 1 John 1:1f.; 4:2; 2 John 7 ^cRev. 21:3 ^dLuke 9:32; John 2:11; 17:22, 24; 2 Pet. 1:16f.; 1 John 1:1 ^eJohn 1:17; Rom. 5:21; 6:14 ^fJohn 8:32; 14:6; 18:37

15 ¹Lit., *is become before me* ^aJohn 1:7 ^bJohn 1:27, 30; Matt. 3:11 ^cJohn 1:30

16 ¹Lit., *we all received* ²Lit., *grace for grace* ^aEph. 1:23; 3:19; 4:13; Col. 1:19; 2:9

17 ªJohn 7:19 ᵇJohn 1:14; Rom. 5:21; 6:14 ᶜJohn 8:32; 14:6; 18:37

18 ¹Some later mss. read, *Son* ªEx. 33:20; John 6:46; Col. 1:15; 1 Tim. 6:16; 1 John 4:12 ᵇJohn 3:16, 18; 1 John 4:9 ᶜJohn 13:23; Luke 16:22 ᵈJohn 3:11

19 ªJohn 1:7 ᵇJohn 2:18, 20; 5:10, 15f., 18; 6:41, 52; 7:1, 11, 13, 15, 35; 8:22, 48, 52, 57; 9:18, 22; 10:24, 31, 33 ᶜMatt. 15:1

20 ¹I.e., the Messiah ªJohn 3:28; cf. Luke 3:15f.

21 ªMatt. 11:14; 16:14 ᵇDeut. 18:15, 18; John 1:25; Matt. 21:11

23 ªMatt. 3:3; Mark 1:3; Luke 3:4 ᵇIs. 40:3

25 ¹I.e., Messiah ªDeut. 18:15, 18; John 1:21; Matt. 21:11

26 ¹The Gr. here can be translated *in, with,* or *by* ªMatt. 3:11; Mark 1:8; Luke 3:16; Acts 1:5

27 ªJohn 1:30; Matt. 3:11 ᵇMark 1:7; Luke 3:16; Matt. 3:11

28 ªJohn 3:26; 10:40

29 ªIs. 53:7; John 1:36; Acts 8:32; 1 Pet. 1:19; Rev. 5:6, 8, 12f.; 6:1 ᵇ1 John 3:5; Matt. 1:21

30 ¹Lit., *has become before me* ªJohn 1:27; Matt. 3:11 ᵇJohn 1:15

31 ¹I.e., as the Messiah ²The Gr. here can be translated *in, with,* or *by*

32 ªJohn 1:7 ᵇMatt. 3:16; Mark 1:10; Luke 3:22

33 ¹I.e., as the Messiah ²The Gr. here can be translated *in, with,* or *by* ªMatt. 3:11; Mark 1:8; Luke 3:16; Acts 1:5

17 For ªthe law was given through Moses; ᵇgrace and ᶜtruth were realized through Jesus Christ.

18 ªNo man has seen God at any time; ᵇthe only begotten ¹God, who is ᶜin the bosom of the Father, ᵈHe has explained *Him*.

19 And this is ªthe witness of John, when ᵇthe Jews sent to him priests and Levites ᶜfrom Jerusalem to ask him, "Who are you?"

20 And he confessed, and did not deny, and he confessed, "ªI am not ¹the Christ."

21 And they asked him, "What then? Are you ªElijah?" And he *said, "I am not." "Are you ᵇthe Prophet?" And he answered, "No."

22 They said then to him, "Who are you, so that we may give an answer to those who sent us? What do you say about yourself?"

23 He said, "ªI am a voice of one crying in the wilderness, 'ᵇMAKE STRAIGHT THE WAY OF THE LORD,' as Isaiah the prophet said."

24 Now they had been sent from the Pharisees.

25 And they asked him, and said to him, "Why then are you baptizing, if you are not the ¹Christ, nor Elijah, nor ªthe Prophet?"

26 John answered them saying, "ªI baptize ¹in water, *but* among you stands One whom you do not know.

27 "*It is* ªHe who comes after me, the ᵇthong of whose sandal I am not worthy to untie."

28 These things took place in Bethany ªbeyond the Jordan, where John was baptizing.

29 The next day he *saw Jesus coming to him, and *said, "Behold, ªthe Lamb of God who ᵇtakes away the sin of the world!

30 "This is He on behalf of whom I said, 'ªAfter me comes a Man who ¹has a higher rank than I, ᵇfor He existed before me.'

31 "And I did not recognize ¹Him, but in order that He might be manifested to Israel, I came baptizing ²in water."

32 And John ªbore witness saying, "ᵇI have beheld the Spirit descending as a dove out of heaven; and He remained upon Him.

33 "And I did not recognize ¹Him, but He who sent me to baptize ²in water said to me, 'He upon whom you see the Spirit descending and remaining upon Him, ªthis is the one who baptizes ²in the Holy Spirit.'

34 "And I have seen, and have borne witness that this is [a]the Son of God."

35 Again [a]the next day John was standing, and two of his disciples;

36 and he looked upon Jesus as He walked, and *said, "Behold, [a]the Lamb of God!"

37 And the two disciples heard him speak, and they followed Jesus.

38 And Jesus turned, and beheld them following, and *said to them, "What do you seek?" And they said to Him, "[a]Rabbi (which translated means Teacher), where are You staying?"

39 He *said to them, "Come, and you will see." They came therefore and saw where He was staying; and they stayed with Him that day, for it was about the [1]tenth hour.

40 [a]One of the two who heard John *speak*, and followed Him, was Andrew, Simon Peter's brother.

41 He *found first his own brother Simon, and *said to him, "We have found the [a]Messiah" (which translated means [1]Christ).

42 He brought him to Jesus. Jesus looked at him, and said, "You are Simon the son of [1a]John; you shall be called [b]Cephas" (which translated means [2c]Peter).

43 [a]The next day *He* purposed to go forth into [b]Galilee, and He *found [c]Philip, and Jesus *said to him, "[d]Follow Me."

44 Now [a]Philip was from [b]Bethsaida, of the city of Andrew and Peter.

45 [a]Philip *found [b]Nathanael, and *said to him, "We have found Him, of whom [c]Moses in the Law and also [c]the Prophets wrote, Jesus of [d]Nazareth, [e]the son of Joseph."

46 And Nathanael *said to him, "[a]Can any good thing come out of Nazareth?" [b]Philip *said to him, "Come and see."

47 Jesus saw Nathanael coming to Him, and *said of him, "Behold, an [a]Israelite indeed, in whom is no guile!"

48 Nathanael *said to Him, "How do You know me?" Jesus answered and said to him, "Before [a]Philip called you, when you were under the fig tree, I saw you."

49 Nathanael answered Him, "[a]Rabbi, You are [b]the Son of God; You are the [c]King of Israel."

50 Jesus answered and said to him, "Because I

34 [a]John 1:49; Matt. 4:3

35 [a]John 1:29

36 [a]John 1:29

38 [a]Matt. 23:7f.; John 1:49

39 [1]I.e., 4 p.m.

40 [a]John 1:40-42; Matt. 4:18-22; Mark 1:16-20; Luke 5:2-11

41 [1]Greek for *Anointed One* [a]Dan. 9:25 marg.; John 4:25

42 [1]Gr. *Joannes*, called in Matt. 16:17, Jonas [2]I.e., Rock or Stone [a]John 21:15-17 [b]1 Cor. 1:12; 3:22; 9:5; 15:5; Gal. 1:18; 2:9, 11, 14 [c]Matt. 16:18

43 [a]John 1:35; John 1:29 [b]John 1:28; Matt. 4:12; John 2:11 [c]Matt. 10:3; John 1:44-48; John 6:5, 7; 12:21f.; 14:8f. [d]Matt. 8:22

44 [a]Matt. 10:3; John 1:44-48; John 6:5, 7; 12:21f.; 14:8f. [b]Matt. 11:21

45 [a]Matt. 10:3; John 1:44-48; John 6:5, 7; 12:21f.; 14:8f. [b]John 1:46-49; 21:2 [c]Luke 24:27 [d]Matt. 2:23 [e]Luke 3:23; 2:48; 4:22; John 6:42

46 [a]John 7:41, 52 [b]Matt. 10:3; John 1:44-48: John 6:5, 7; 12:21f.; 14:8f.

47 [a]Rom. 9:4

48 [a]Matt. 10:3; John 1:44-48: John 6:5, 7; 12:21f.; 14:8f.

49 [a]John 1:38 [b]John 1:34 [c]Matt. 2:2; 27:42; Mark 15:32; John 12:13

51 ªEzek. 1:1; Matt. 3:16; Luke 3:21; Acts 7:56; 10:11; Rev. 19:11 ᵇGen. 28:12 ᶜMatt. 8:20

1 ªJohn 1:29, 35, 43 ᵇJohn 2:11; 4:46; 21:2 ᶜMatt. 12:46

2 ªJohn 1:40-49; 2:12, 17, 22; 3:22; 4:2, 8, 27ff.; 6:8, 12, 16:22, 24; John 6:60f., 66; 7:3; 8:31

4 ¹Lit., what to Me and to you (a Hebrew idiom) ªJohn 19:26 ᵇMatt. 8:29 ᶜJohn 7:6, 8, 30; 8:20

5 ªMatt 12:46

6 ¹Two or three metretai ªMark 7:3f.; John 3:25

8 ¹Or, steward

9 ªJohn 4:46

10 ¹Lit., have become drunk ªMatt. 24:49; Luke 12:45; Acts 2:15; 1 Cor. 11:21; Eph. 5:18; 1 Thess. 5:7; Rev. 17:2, 6

11 ¹Or, attesting miracles, I.e., one which points to the supernatural power of God in redeeming grace ªJohn 2:23; 3:2; 4:54; 6:2, 14, 26, 30; 7:31; 9:16; 10:41; 11:47; 12:18, 37; 20:30 ᵇJohn 1:43 ᶜJohn 1:14

12 ªMatt. 4:13 ᵇMatt. 12:46 ᶜJohn 2:2

13 ªJohn 6:4; 11:55; John 5:1 marg. ᵇDeut. 16:1-6; Luke 2:41; John 2:23

192

said to you that I saw you under the fig tree, do you believe? You shall see greater things than these."

51   And He *said to him, "Truly, truly, I say to you, you shall see ªthe heavens opened, and ᵇthe angels of God ascending and descending upon ᶜthe Son of Man."

CHAPTER 2

AND on ªthe third day there was a wedding in ᵇCana of Galilee; and the ᶜmother of Jesus was there;

2   and Jesus also was invited, and His ªdisciples, to the wedding.

3   And when the wine gave out, the mother of Jesus *said to Him, "They have no wine."

4   And Jesus *said to her, "ªWoman, ¹ᵇwhat do I have to do with you? ᶜMy hour has not yet come."

5   His ªmother *said to the servants, "Whatever He says to you, do it."

6   Now there were six stone waterpots set there ªfor the Jewish custom of purification, containing ¹twenty or thirty gallons each.

7   Jesus *said to them, "Fill the waterpots with water." And they filled them up to the brim.

8   And He *said to them, "Draw *some* out now, and take it to the ¹headwaiter." And they took it *to him.*

9   And when the headwaiter tasted the water ªwhich had become wine, and did not know where it came from (but the servants who had drawn the water knew), the headwaiter *called the bride-groom,

10   and *said to him, "Every man serves the good wine first, and when *men* ªhave ¹drunk freely, *then* that which is poorer; you have kept the good wine until now."

11   This beginning of *His* ¹ªsigns Jesus did in Cana of ᵇGalilee, and manifested His ᶜglory, and His disciples believed in Him.

12   After this He went down to ªCapernaum, He and His ᵇmother, and *His* ᵇbrothers, and His ᶜdisciples; and there they stayed a few days.

13   And ªthe Passover of the Jews was at hand, and Jesus ᵇwent up to Jerusalem.

14 [a]And He found in the temple those who were selling oxen and sheep and doves, and the money-changers seated.

15 And He made a scourge of cords, and drove *them* all out of the temple, with the sheep and the oxen; and He poured out the coins of the money-changers, and overturned their tables;

16 and to those who were selling [a]the doves He said, "Take these things away; stop making [b]My Father's house a house of merchandise."

17 His [a]disciples remembered that it was written, "[b]Zeal for Thy house will consume me."

18 [a]The Jews therefore answered and said to Him, "[b]What sign do You show to us, seeing that You do these things?"

19 Jesus answered and said to them, "[a]Destroy this [1]temple, and in three days I will raise it up."

20 [a]The Jews therefore said, "It took [b]forty-six years to build this [1]temple, and will You raise it up in three days?"

21 But He was speaking of [1a] the temple of His body.

22 When therefore He was raised from the dead, His [a]disciples [b]remembered that He said this; and they believed [c]the Scripture, and the word which Jesus had spoken.

23 Now when He was in Jerusalem at [a]the Passover, during the feast, many believed in His name, [b]beholding His signs which He was doing.

24 But Jesus, on His part, was not entrusting Himself to them, for He knew all men,

25 and because He did not need any one to bear witness concerning man [a]for He Himself knew what was in man.

CHAPTER 3

NOW there was a man of the Pharisees, named [a]Nicodemus, a [b]ruler of the Jews;

2 this man came to Him by night, and said to Him, "[a]Rabbi, we know that You have come from God *as* a teacher; for no one can do these [1b]signs that You do unless [c]God is with him."

3 Jesus answered and said to him, "Truly, truly, I say to you, unless one [a]is born [1]again, he cannot see [b]the kingdom of God."

14 [a]John 2:14-16; *Matt. 21:12ff.; Mark 11:15, 17; Luke 19:45f.; Mal. 3:1ff.*

16 [a]Matt. 21:12 [b]Luke 2:49

17 [a]John 2:2 [b]Ps. 69:9

18 [a]John 1:19 [b]Matt. 12:38

19 [1]Or, *sanctuary* [a]Matt. 26:61; 27:40; Mark 14:58; 15:29; Acts 6:14

20 [1]Or, *sanctuary* [a]John 1:19 [b]Ezra 5:16

21 [1]Or, *sanctuary* [a]1 Cor. 6:19

22 [a]John 2:2 [b]Luke 24:8; John 12:16; 2:17; 14:26 [c]Ps. 16:10; John 20:9; Luke 24:26f.; Acts 13:33

23 [a]John 2:13 [b]John 2:11

25 [a]John 6:61, 64; 13:11; Matt. 9:4; John 1:42, 47

1 [a]John 7:50; 19:39 [b]Luke 23:13; John 7:26, 48

2 [1]Or, *attesting miracles* [a]Matt. 23:7; John 3:26 [b]John 2:11 [c]Acts 10:38; John 9:33; 10:38; 14:10f.; Acts 2:22

3 [1]Or, *from above* [a]1 Pet. 1:23; 2 Cor. 5:17 [b]John 3:5; Matt. 19:24; 21:31; Mark 9:47; 10:14f.

John 3

**Nicodemus Visits Jesus.
"God So Loved the World."**

5 ªEzek. 36:25-27; Eph.
5:26; Titus 3:5 ᵇJohn 3:3;
Matt. 19:24; 21:31; Mark
9:47; 10:14f.

6 ªJohn 1:13; 1 Cor. 15:50

7 ¹Or, *from above*

8 ªEccles. 11:5; Ezek. 37:9;
Ps. 135:7

10 ªLuke 2:46; 5:17; Acts
5:34

11 ªJohn 7:16f.; 8:26, 28;
12:49; 14:24; John 1:18 ᵇJohn
3:32

13 ¹Later manuscripts add,
who is in heaven
ªProv. 30:4; Deut. 30:12;
Acts 2:34; Rom. 10:6; Eph.
4:9 ᵇJohn 3:31; 6:38, 42
ᶜMatt. 8:20

14 ªNum. 21:9 ᵇMatt. 8:20
ᶜJohn 8:28; 12:34

15 ¹Some mss. read,
*believes in Him may have
eternal life*
ªJohn 20:31; 1 John 5:11-13

16 ¹Or, *unique, only one of
His kind*
ªRom. 5:8; Eph. 2:4; 2 Thess.
2:16; 1 John 4:10; Rev. 1:5
ᵇRom. 8:32; 1 John 4:9 ᶜJohn
1:18; 3:18; 1 John 4:9 ᵈJohn
3:36; 6:40; 11:25f.

17 ªJohn 3:34; 5:36, 38;
6:29, 38, 57; 7:29; 8:42; 10:36;
11:42; 17:3, 8, 18, 21, 23, 25;
20:21 ᵇJohn 8:15; 12:47;
Luke 19:10; 1 John 4:14

18 ¹Or, *unique, only one of
His kind*
ªMark 16:16; John 5:24
ᵇJohn 1:18; 1 John 4:9

19 ªJohn 1:4; 8:12; 9:5;
12:46 ᵇJohn 7:7

20 ªJohn 3:20, 21; Eph.
5:11, 13

4 Nicodemus *said to Him, "How can a man be born when he is old? He cannot enter a second time into his mother's womb and be born, can he?"

5 Jesus answered, "Truly, truly, I say to you, unless one is born of ªwater and the Spirit, he cannot enter into ᵇthe kingdom of God.

6 "ªThat which is born of the flesh is flesh; and that which is born of the Spirit is spirit.

7 "Do not marvel that I said to you, 'You must be born ¹again.'

8 "ªThe wind blows where it wishes and you hear the sound of it, but do not know where it comes from and where it is going; so is every one who is born of the Spirit."

9 Nicodemus answered and said to Him, "How can these things be?"

10 Jesus answered and said to him, "Are you ªthe teacher of Israel, and do not understand these things?

11 "Truly, truly, I say to you, ªwe speak that which we know, and ᵇbear witness of that which we have seen; and ᵇyou do not receive our witness.

12 "If I told you earthly things and you do not believe, how shall you believe if I tell you heavenly things?

13 "And ªno one has ascended into heaven, but ᵇHe who descended from heaven, *even* ᶜthe Son of Man.¹

14 "And as ªMoses lifted up the serpent in the wilderness, even so must ᵇthe Son of Man ᶜbe lifted up;

15 that whoever ¹believes may ªin Him have eternal life.

16 "For God so ªloved the world, that He ᵇgave His ¹ᶜonly begotten Son, that whoever ᵈbelieves in Him should not perish, but have eternal life.

17 "For God ªdid not send the Son into the world ᵇto judge the world; but that the world should be saved through Him.

18 "ªHe who believes in Him is not judged; he who does not believe has been judged already, because he has not believed in the name of ᵇthe ¹only begotten Son of God.

19 "And this is the judgment, that ªthe light is come into the world, and men loved the darkness rather than the light; for ᵇtheir deeds were evil.

20 "ªFor everyone who does evil hates the light,

and does not come to the light, lest his deeds should be exposed.

21 "But he who ªpractices the truth comes to the light, that his deeds may be manifested as having been wrought in God."

22 After these things Jesus and His ªdisciples came into the land of Judea; and there He was spending time with them, and ᵇbaptizing.

23 And John also was baptizing in Aenon near Salim, because there was much ¹water there; and they were coming, and were being baptized.

24 For ªJohn had not yet been thrown into prison.

25 There arose therefore a discussion on the part of John's disciples with a Jew about ªpurification.

26 And they came to John, and said to him, "ªRabbi, He who was with you ᵇbeyond the Jordan, to whom you ᶜhave borne witness, behold, He is baptizing, and all are coming to Him."

27 John answered and said, "ªA man can receive nothing, unless it has been given him from heaven.

28 "You yourselves bear me witness, that I said, 'ªI am not the ¹Christ', but, 'I have been sent before Him.'

29 "He who has the bride is ªthe bridegroom; but the friend of the bridegroom, who stands and hears him, rejoices greatly because of the bridegroom's voice. And so this ᵇjoy of mine has been made full.

30 "He must increase, but I must decrease.

31 "ªHe who comes from above is above all, he who is of the earth is from the earth and speaks ᵇof the earth. ªHe who comes from heaven is above all.

32 "What He has seen and heard, of that He ªbears witness; and ªno man receives His witness.

33 "He who has received His witness ªhas set his seal to *this*, that God is true.

34 "For He whom God has ªsent speaks the words of God; ¹ᵇfor He gives the Spirit without measure.

35 "ªThe Father loves the Son, and has given all things into His hand.

36 "He who ªbelieves in the Son has eternal life; but he who ᵇdoes not ¹obey the Son shall not see life, but the wrath of God abides on him."

21 ª1 John 1:6

22 ªJohn 2:2 ᵇJohn 4:1, 2

23 ¹Lit., *many waters*

24 ªMatt. 4:12

25 ªJohn 2:6

26 ªJohn 3:2; Matt. 23:7 ᵇJohn 1:28 ᶜJohn 1:7

27 ª1 Cor. 4:7; Heb. 5:4

28 ¹I.e., Messiah ªJohn 1:20, 23

29 ªMatt. 25:1; 9:15 ᵇJohn 15:11; 16:24; 17:13; Phil. 2:2; 1 John 1:4; 2 John 12

31 ªJohn 3:13; 8:23 ᵇ1 John 4:5

32 ªJohn 3:11

33 ªJohn 6:27; Rom. 4:11; 15:28; 1 Cor. 9:2; 2 Cor. 1:22; Eph. 1:13; 4:30; 2 Tim. 2:19; Rev. 7:3-8

34 ¹Lit., *for He does not give the Spirit by measure* ªJohn 3:17 ᵇMatt. 12:18; Luke 4:18; Acts 1:2; 10:38

35 ªJohn 5:20; 17:2; Matt. 28:18

36 ¹Or, *believe* ªJohn 3:16 ᵇActs 14:2; Heb. 3:18

1 ªLuke 7:13 ᵇJohn 3:22,
26; 1 Cor. 1:17

2 ªJohn 3:22, 26; 1 Cor.
1:17 ᵇJohn 2:2

3 ªJohn 3:22 ᵇJohn 2:11f.

4 ªLuke 9:52

5 ªLuke 9:52 ᵇGen. 33:19;
48:22; Josh. 24:32; John 4:12

6 ¹I.e., Noon

8 ªJohn 2:2 ᵇJohn 4:5, 39

9 ªLuke 9:52 ᵇMatt. 10:5;
John 8:48; Ezra 4:3-6, 11ff.

10 ªJohn 7:37f.; Rev. 21:6;
22:17

11 ¹Or, *Lord*
ªJohn 7:37f.; Rev. 21:6; 22:17

12 ªJohn 4:6

14 ªJohn 6:35; 7:38 ᵇMatt.
25:46; John 6:27

15 ¹Or, *Lord*
ªJohn 6:34

CHAPTER 4

WHEN therefore ªthe Lord knew that the Pharisees had heard that Jesus was making and ᵇbaptizing more disciples than John

2   (although ªJesus Himself was not baptizing, but His ᵇdisciples were),

3   He left ªJudea, and departed ᵇagain into Galilee.

4   And He had to pass through ªSamaria.

5   So He *came to a city of ªSamaria, called Sychar, near the parcel of ground that ᵇJacob gave to his son Joseph;

6   and Jacob's well was there. Jesus therefore, being wearied from His journey, was sitting thus by the well. It was about the ¹sixth hour.

7   There *came a woman of Samaria to draw water. Jesus *said to her, "Give Me a drink."

8   For His ªdisciples had gone away into ᵇthe city to buy food.

9   The ªSamaritan woman therefore *said to Him, "How is it that You, being a Jew, ask me for a drink since I am a Samaritan woman?" (For ᵇJews have no dealings with Samaritans.)

10   Jesus answered and said to her, "If you knew the gift of God, and who it is who says to you, 'Give Me a drink,' you would have asked Him, and He would have given you ªliving water."

11   She *said to Him, "¹Sir, You have nothing to draw with and the well is deep; where then do You get that ªliving water?

12   "You are not greater than our father Jacob, are You, who ªgave us the well, and drank of it himself, and his sons, and his cattle?"

13   Jesus answered and said to her, "Everyone who drinks of this water shall thirst again;

14   but whoever drinks of the water that I shall give him ªshall never thirst; but the water that I shall give him shall become in him a well of water springing up to ᵇeternal life."

15   The woman *said to Him, "¹Sir, ªgive me this water, so I will not be thirsty, nor come all the way here to draw."

16   He *said to her, "Go, call your husband, and come here."

17   The woman answered and said, "I have no husband." Jesus *said to her, "You have well said, 'I have no husband;'

18 for you have had five husbands; and the one whom you now have is not your husband; this you have said truly."

19 The woman *said to Him, "[1]Sir, I perceive that You are [a]a prophet.

20 "[a]Our fathers worshiped in [b]this mountain; and you *people* say that [c]in Jerusalem is the place where men ought to worship."

21 Jesus *said to her, "Woman, believe Me, [a]an hour is coming when [b]neither in this mountain, nor in Jerusalem, shall you worship the Father.

22 "[a]You worship that which you do not know; we worship that which we know; for [b]salvation is from the Jews.

23 "But [a]an hour is coming, and now is, when the true worshipers shall worship the Father [b]in spirit and truth; for such people the Father seeks to be His worshipers.

24 "God is [1]spirit; and those who worship Him must worship [a]in spirit and truth."

25 The woman *said to Him, "I know that [a]Messiah is coming ([b]He who is called Christ); when that One comes, He will declare all things to us."

26 Jesus *said to her, "[a]I who speak to you am He."

27 And at this point His [a]disciples [b]came, and they marveled that He had been speaking with a woman; yet no one said, "What do You seek?" or, "Why do You speak with her?"

28 So the woman left her waterpot, and went into the city, and *said to the men,

29 "Come, see a man [a]who told me all the things that I *have* done; [b]this is not [1]the Christ, is it?"

30 They went out of the city, and were coming to Him.

31 In the meanwhile the disciples were requesting Him, saying, "[a]Rabbi, eat."

32 But He said to them, "I have food to eat that you do not know about."

33 The [a]disciples therefore were saying to one another, "No one brought Him *anything* to eat, did he?"

34 Jesus *said to them, "My food is to [a]do the will of Him who sent Me, and to [b]accomplish His work.

35 "Do you not say, 'There are yet four months,

19 [1]Or, *Lord*
[a]Matt. 21:11; Luke 7:39

20 [a]Gen. 33:20? [John 4:12] [b]Deut. 11:29; Josh. 8:33 [c]Luke 9:53

21 [a]John 5:28; 16:2; John 4:23; 5:25; 16:32 [b]Mal. 1:11; 1 Tim. 2:8

22 [a]2 Kin. 17:28-41 [b]Is. 2:3; Rom. 3:1f.; 9:4f.

23 [a]John 5:25; 16:32; John 4:21; 5:28; 16:2 [b]Phil. 3:3

24 [1]Or, *God is a Spirit* [a]Phil. 3:3

25 [a]John 1:41 [b]Matt. 1:16

26 [a]John 8:24; John 9:35-37

27 [a]John 4:8 [b]John 2:2

29 [1]I.e., The Messiah [a]John 4:17f. [b]John 7:26, 31; Matt. 12:23

31 [a]Matt. 23:7

33 [a]John 2:2

34 [a]John 5:30; 6:38 [b]John 5:36; 17:4; 19:28, 30

John 4

**Many Samaritans Believe.
Jesus Received in Galilee. Nobleman's Son.**

and *then* comes the harvest'? Behold, I say to you, lift up your eyes, and look on the fields, that they are white [a]for harvest.

36 "Already he who reaps is receiving [a]wages, and is gathering [b]fruit for [c]life eternal; that he who sows and he who reaps may rejoice together.

37 "For in this *case* the saying is true, '[a]One sows, and another reaps.'

38 "I sent you to reap that for which you have not labored; others have labored, and you have entered into their labor."

39 And from [a]that city many of the Samaritans believed in Him because of the word of the woman who testified, "[b]He told me all the things that I *have* done."

40 So when the Samaritans came to Him, they were asking Him to stay with them; and He stayed there two days.

41 And many more believed because of His word;

42 and they were saying to the woman, "It is no longer because of what you said that we believe, for we have heard for ourselves and know that this One is indeed [a]the Savior of the world."

43 And after [a]the two days He went forth from there into Galilee.

44 For Jesus Himself testified that [a]a prophet has no honor in his own country.

45 So when He came to Galilee, the Galileans received Him, [a]having seen all the things that He did in Jerusalem at the feast; for they themselves also went to the feast.

46 He came therefore again to [a]Cana of Galilee [b]where He had made the water wine. And there was a certain royal official, whose son was sick at [c]Capernaum.

47 When he heard that Jesus had come [a]out of Judea into Galilee, he went to Him, and was requesting *Him* to come down and heal his son; for he was at the point of death.

48 Jesus therefore said to him, "Unless you *people* see [1a]signs and [a]wonders, you *simply* will not believe."

49 The royal official *said to Him, "[1]Sir, come down before my child dies."

50 Jesus *said to him, "Go your way; your son lives." The man believed the word that Jesus spoke to him, and he started off.

35 [a]Luke 10:2

36 [a]1 Cor. 9:17f. [b]Rom. 1:13 [c]John 4:14

37 [a]Job 31:8; Mic. 6:15

39 [a]John 4:5, 30 [b]John 4:29

42 [a]1 John 4:14; 1 Tim. 1.10, Luke 7:11; Acts 5:31; 13:23

43 [a]John 4:40

44 [a]Matt. 13:57

45 [a]John 2:23

46 [a]John 2:1 [b]John 2:9 [c]John 2:12; Luke 4:23

47 [a]John 4:3, 54

48 [1]Or, *attesting miracles* [a]Dan. 4:2f.; 6:27; Matt. 24:24; Mark 13:22; Acts 2:19, 22, 43; 4:30; 5:12; 6:8; 7:36; 14:3; 15:12; Rom. 15:19; 2 Cor. 12:12; 2 Thess. 2:9; Heb. 2:4; 1 Cor. 1:22

49 [1]Or, *Lord*

The Healing at Bethesda. Jesus Censured for Breaking Sabbath; Justifies His Actions.

John 4, 5

51 And as he was now going down, *his* slaves met him, saying that his [1]son was living.

52 So he inquired of them the hour when he began to get better. They said therefore to him, "Yesterday at the [1]seventh hour the fever left him."

53 So the father knew that *it was* at that hour in which Jesus said to him, "Your son lives;" and he himself believed, and [a]his whole household.

54 This is again a [a]second [1]sign that Jesus performed, when He had [b]come out of Judea into Galilee.

Chapter 5

AFTER these things there was [1]a feast of the Jews; and Jesus went up to Jerusalem.

2 Now there is in Jerusalem by [a]the sheep *gate* a pool, which is called [b]in [1]Hebrew [2]Bethesda, having five porticoes.

3 In these lay a multitude of those who were sick, blind, lame, withered.

4 (See marginal note.)

5 And a certain man was there, who had been thirty-eight years in his sickness.

6 When Jesus saw him lying there, and knew that he had already been a long time *in that condition*, He *said to him, "Do you wish to get well?"

7 The sick man answered Him, "Sir, I have no man to put me into the pool when [a]the water is stirred up, but while I am coming, another steps down before me."

8 Jesus *said to him, "[a]Arise, take up your pallet, and walk."

9 And immediately the man became well, and took up his pallet and *began* to walk.
[a]Now it was the Sabbath on that day.

10 Therefore [a]the Jews were saying to him who was cured, "It is the Sabbath, and [b]it is not permissible for you to carry your pallet."

11 But he answered them, "He who made me well was the one who said to me, 'Take up your pallet and walk.' "

12 They asked him, "Who is the man who said to you, 'Take up *your* pallet, and walk'?"

13 But he who was healed did not know who it was; for Jesus had slipped away while there was a crowd in *that* place.

---

51 [1]Or, *boy*

52 [1]I.e., 1 p.m.

53 [a]Acts 11:14

54 [1]Or, *attesting miracle* [a]John 2:11 [b]John 4:45f.

1 [1]Many good mss. read, *the feast*, i.e., the Passover

2 [1]I.e., Jewish Aramaic [2]Many good mss. read, *Bethsaida* or *Bethzatha* [a]Neh. 3:1, 32; 12:39 [b]John 19:13, 17, 20; 20:16; Rev. 9:11; 16:16; Acts 21:40

4 Many authorities insert, wholly or in part, *waiting for the moving of the waters*; V. 4 *for an angel of the Lord went down at certain seasons into the pool, and stirred up the water: whoever then first after the stirring up of the water stepped in was made well from whatever disease with which he was afflicted.*

7 [a]John 5:4 in marg.

8 [a]Matt. 9:6; Mark 2:11; Luke 5:24

9 [a]John 9:14

10 [a]John 5:15, 16, 18; 1:19 [b]Neh. 13:19; Jer. 17:21f.; John 7:23; 9:16; Matt. 12:2

199

14 aJohn 8:11; Mark 2:5
bEzra 9:14

15 aJohn 5:16, 18; 1:19

16 aJohn 5:10, 15, 18; 1:19

18 aJohn 5:15, 16; 1:19
bJohn 5:16; 7:1 cJohn 10:33;
19:7

19 aJohn 5:30; 8:28; 12:49;
14:10

20 aJohn 5:35 bJohn 14:12

21 aRom. 4:17; 8:11 bJohn
11:25

22 aJohn 5:27; 9:39; Acts
10:42; 17:31

23 aLuke 10:16; 1 John 2:23

24 aJohn 3:18; 12:44; 20:31;
1 John 5:13 bJohn 3:18
cI John 3:14

25 aJohn 4:23; 5:28; 4:21
bLuke 15:24 cJohn 6:60; 8:43,
47; 9:27

26 aJohn 1:4; 6:57

27 1Or, a son of man
aJohn 9:39; Acts 10:42; 17:31

28 aJohn 4:21 bJohn 11:24;
1 Cor. 15:52

29 aDan. 12:2; Acts 24:15;
Matt. 25:46

14 Afterward Jesus *found him in the temple, and said to him, "Behold, you have become well; do not ªsin any more, ᵇso that nothing worse may befall you."

15 The man went away, and told ªthe Jews that it was Jesus who had made him well.

16 And for this reason ªthe Jews were persecuting Jesus, because He was doing these things on the Sabbath.

17 But He answered them, "My Father is working until now, and I Myself am working."

18 For this cause therefore ªthe Jews ᵇwere seeking all the more to kill Him, because He not only was breaking the Sabbath, but also was calling God His own Father, ᶜmaking Himself equal with God.

19 Jesus therefore answered and was saying to them, "Truly, truly, I say to you, ªthe Son can do nothing of Himself, unless *it is* something He sees the Father doing; for whatever *the Father* does, these things the Son also does in like manner.

20 "ªFor the Father loves the Son, and shows Him all things that He Himself is doing; and ᵇgreater works than these will He show Him, that you may marvel.

21 "For just as the Father raises the dead and ªgives them life, even so ᵇthe Son also gives life to whom He wishes.

22 "For not even the Father judges any one, but ªHe has given all judgment to the Son,

23 in order that all may honor the Son, even as they honor the Father. ªHe who does not honor the Son does not honor the Father who sent Him.

24 "Truly, truly, I say to you, he who hears My word, and ªbelieves Him who sent Me, has eternal life, and ᵇdoes not come into judgment, but has ᶜpassed out of death into life.

25 "Truly, truly, I say to you, ªan hour is coming and now is, when ᵇthe dead shall hear the voice of the Son of God; and those who ᶜhear shall live.

26 "For just as the Father has life in Himself, even so He ªgave to the Son also to have life in Himself;

27 and He gave Him authority to ªexecute judgment, because He is ¹the Son of Man.

28 "Do not marvel at this; for ªan hour is coming, in which ᵇall who are in the tombs shall hear His voice,

29 and shall come forth; ªthose who did the

good *deeds,* to a resurrection of life, those who committed the evil *deeds* to a resurrection of judgment.

30 "[a]I can do nothing on My own initiative, as I hear, I judge; and [b]My judgment is just; because I do not seek My own will but [c]the will of Him who sent Me.

31 "[a]If I *alone* bear witness of Myself, My testimony is not [1]true.

32 "There is [a]another who bears witness of Me; and I know that the testimony which He bears of Me is true.

33 "You have sent to John, and he [a]has borne witness to the truth.

34 "But [a]the witness which I receive is not from man; but I say these things, that you may be saved.

35 "He was [a]the lamp that was burning and was shining and you [b]were willing to rejoice for a while in his light.

36 "But the witness which I have is greater than *that of* John; for [a]the works which the Father has given Me [b]to accomplish, the very works that I do, bear witness of Me, that the Father [c]has sent Me.

37 "And the Father who sent Me, [a]He has borne witness of Me. You have neither heard His voice at any time, nor seen His form.

38 "And you do not have [a]His word abiding in you, for you do not believe Him whom He [b]sent.

39 "[1a]You search the Scriptures, because you think that in them you have eternal life; and it is [b]these that bear witness of Me;

40 and you are unwilling to come to Me, that you may have life.

41 "[a]I do not receive glory from men;

42 but I know you, that you do not have the love of God in yourselves.

43 "I have come in My Father's name, and you do not receive Me; [a]if another shall come in his own name, you will receive him.

44 "How can you believe, when you [a]receive [1]glory from one another, and you do not seek [b]the [1]glory that is from [c]the *one and* only God?

45 "Do not think that I will accuse you before the Father; the one who accuses you is [a]Moses, in whom you have set your hope.

46 "For if you believed Moses, you would believe Me; for [a]he wrote of Me.

30 [a]John 5:19 [b]John 8:16 [c]John 4:34; 6:38

31 [1]I.e., admissible as legal evidence [a]John 8:14

32 [a]John 5:37

33 [a]John 1:7

34 [a]1 John 5:9; John 5:32

35 [a]2 Sam. 21:17; 2 Pet. 1:19 [b]Mark 1:5

36 [a]John 10:25, 38; 14:11; 15:24; 2:23; Matt. 11:4 [b]John 4:34 [c]John 3:17

37 [a]John 8:18; Luke 24:27

38 [a]1 John 2:14 [b]John 3:17

39 [1]Or, (a command) *Search the Scriptures!* [a]John 7:52; Rom. 2:17ff. [b]Luke 24:25, 27; Acts 13:27

41 [a]John 5:44; 7:18

43 [a]Matt. 24:5

44 [1]Or, *honor or fame* [a]John 5:41 [b]Rom. 2:29 [c]John 17:3; 1 Tim. 1:17

45 [a]John 9:28; Rom. 2:17ff.

46 [a]Luke 24:27

47 aLuke 16:29, 31

1 aJohn 6:1-13: *Matt. 14:13-21; Mark 6:32-44; Luke 9:10-17* bMatt. 4:18; Luke 5:1 cJohn 21:1; 6:23

2 ¹Or, *attesting miracles* aJohn 2:11

3 aJohn 6:15; Matt. 5:1

4 aJohn 2:13

5 aJohn 1:43

6 a2 Cor. 13:5 and Rev. 2:2 in Gr.

7 ¹A denarius represented a days wages for a common laborer aJohn 1:43 bMark 6:37

8 aJohn 2:2 bJohn 1:40

9 aJohn 21:9, 10, 13; John 6:11

10 ¹Lit., *recline(d)* aJohn 6:4; Mark 6:39 bMatt. 14:21

11 aJohn 6:23; Matt. 15:36 bJohn 21:9, 10, 13; John 6:9

12 aJohn 2:2

13 aMatt. 14:20

14 ¹Or, *attesting miracle* aJohn 1:21; Matt. 11:3; 21:11

15 ¹Or, *about* aJohn 18:36f.

47 "But aif you do not believe his writings, how will you believe My words?"

CHAPTER 6

AFTER these things aJesus went away to the other side of bthe sea of Galilee (or cTiberias).

2　And a great multitude was following Him, because they were seeing the ¹asigns which He was performing on those who were sick.

3　And Jesus went up on athe mountain, and there He sat with His disciples.

4　Now athe Passover, the feast of the Jews, was at hand.

5　Jesus therefore lifting up His eyes, and seeing that a great multitude was coming to Him, *said to aPhilip, "Where are we to buy bread, that these may eat?"

6　And this He was saying to atest him; for He Himself knew what He was intending to do.

7　aPhilip answered Him, "bTwo hundred ¹denarii worth of bread is not sufficient for them, for every one to receive a little."

8　One of His adisciples, bAndrew, Simon Peter's brother, *said to Him,

9　"There is a lad here, who has five barley loaves, and two afish; but what are these for so many people?"

10　Jesus said, "Have the people ¹sit down." Now there was amuch grass in the place. So the men ¹sat down, in number about bfive thousand.

11　Jesus therefore took the loaves; and ahaving given thanks, He distributed to those who were seated; likewise also of the bfish as much as they wanted.

12　And when they were filled, He *said to His adisciples. "Gather up the left-over fragments that nothing may be lost."

13　And so they gathered them up, and filled twelve abaskets with fragments from the five barley loaves, which were left over by those who had eaten.

14　When therefore the people saw the ¹sign which He had performed, they said, "This is of a truth the aProphet who is to come into the world."

15　Jesus therefore perceiving that they were ¹intending to come and take Him by force, ato

make Him king, [b]withdrew again to [c]the mountain by Himself alone.

16 Now when evening came, His [a]disciples went down to the sea,

17 and after getting into a boat, they *started to* cross the sea [a]to Capernaum. And it had already become dark, and Jesus had not yet come to them.

18 And the sea *began* to be stirred up because a strong wind was blowing.

19 When therefore they had rowed about [1]three or four miles, they *beheld Jesus walking on the sea, and drawing near to the boat; and they were frightened.

20 But He *said to them, "It is I; [1a]do not be afraid."

21 They were willing therefore to receive Him into the boat; and immediately the boat was at the land to which they were going.

22 The next day [a]the multitude that stood on the other side of the sea saw that there was no other small boat there, except one, and that Jesus [b]had not entered with His disciples into the boat, but *that* His disciples had gone away alone.

23 There came other small boats from [a]Tiberias near to the place where they ate the bread after the [b]Lord [c]had given thanks.

24 When the multitude therefore saw that Jesus was not there, nor His disciples, they themselves got into the small boats, and [a]came to Capernaum, seeking Jesus.

25 And when they found Him on the other side of the sea, they said to Him, "[a]Rabbi, when did You get here?"

26 Jesus answered them and said, "Truly, truly, I say to you, you [a]seek Me, not because you saw [b]signs, but because you ate of the loaves, and were filled.

27 "Do not [a]work for the food which perishes, but for the food which endures to [b]eternal life, which [c]the Son of Man shall give to you, for on Him the Father, *even* God, [d]has set His seal."

28 They said therefore to Him, "What shall we do, that we may work the works of God?"

29 Jesus answered and said to them, "This is [a]the work of God, that you believe in Him whom He [b]has sent."

30 They said therefore to Him, "[a]What then

15 [b]John 6:15-21: *Matt. 14:22-33; Mark 6:45-51* [c]John 6:3

16 [a]John 2:2

17 [a]Mark 6:45; John 6:24, 59

19 [1]Lit., 25 or 30 stadia

20 [1]Or, *stop fearing* [a]Matt. 14:27

22 [a]John 6:2 [b]John 6:15ff.

23 [a]John 6:1 [b]Luke 7:13 [c]John 6:11

24 [a]John 6:17, 59; Matt. 14:34; Mark 6:53

25 [a]Matt. 23:7

26 [a]John 6:24 [b]John 6:2, 14, 30

27 [a]Is. 55:2 [b]John 6:40, 47, 54; 3:15f.; 4:14; 10:28; 17:2f. [c]Matt. 8:20; John 6:53, 62 [d]John 3:33

29 [a]1 Thess. 1:3; James 2:22; 1 John 3:23; Rev. 2:26 [b]John 3:17

30 [a]Matt. 12:38

30 bJohn 6:2, 14, 26

31 aEx. 16:21; Num. 11:8;
John 6:49, 58 bNeh. 9:15; Ex.
16:4, 15; Ps. 78:24; 105:40

33 1Or, *He who comes*
aJohn 6:50; 6:41

34 aJohn 4:15

35 aJohn 6:48, 51 bJohn
4:14

36 aJohn 6:26

37 aJohn 6:39; 17:2, 24

38 aJohn 3:13 bMatt. 26:39
cJohn 4:34; 5:30 dJohn 6:29

39 aJohn 6:37; 17:2, 24
bJohn 17:12; 18:9 cJohn 6:40,
44, 54; 11:24; Matt. 10:15

40 aJohn 12:45; 14:17, 19
bJohn 3:16 cJohn 6:39, 44, 54;
11:24; Matt. 10:15

41 aJohn 1:19; 6:52 bJohn
6:51, 58; 6:33

42 aLuke 4:22 bJohn 7:27f.
cJohn 6:38, 62

44 aJer. 31:3; Hos. 11:4;
John 12:32; 6:65 bJohn 6:39

45 aActs 7:42; 13:40; Heb.
8:11 bIs. 54:13; Jer. 31:34
cl Thess. 4:9; Phil. 3:15;
1 John 2:27

46 aJohn 1:18

do You do for a bsign, that we may see, and believe You? What work do You perform?

31 "aOur fathers ate the manna in the wilderness; as it is written, 'bHE GAVE THEM BREAD OUT OF HEAVEN TO EAT.' "

32 Jesus therefore said to them, "Truly, truly, I say to you, it is not Moses who has given you the bread out of heaven, but it is My Father who gives you the true bread out of heaven.

33 "For the bread of God is 1that which acomes down out of heaven, and gives life to the world."

34 They said therefore to Him, "Lord, evermore agive us this bread."

35 Jesus said to them, "aI am the bread of life; he who comes to Me shall not hunger, and he who believes in Me bshall never thirst.

36 "But aI said to you, that you have seen Me, and yet do not believe.

37 "aAll that the Father gives Me shall come to Me; and the one who comes to Me I will certainly not cast out.

38 "For aI have come down from heaven, bnot to do My own will, but cthe will of Him who dsent Me.

39 "And this is the will of Him who sent Me, that of aall that He has given Me I blose nothing, but craise it up on the last day.

40 "For this is the will of My Father, that every one who abeholds the Son, and bbelieves in Him, may have eternal life; and I Myself will craise him up on the last day."

41 aThe Jews therefore were grumbling about Him, because He said, "I am the bread that bcame down out of heaven."

42 And they were saying, "aIs not this Jesus, the son of Joseph, whose father and mother bwe know? How does He now say, 'cI have come down out of heaven'?"

43 Jesus answered and said to them, "Do not grumble among yourselves.

44 "No one can come to Me, unless the Father who sent Me adraws him; and I will braise him up on the last day.

45 "It is written ain the prophets, 'bAND THEY SHALL ALL BE cTAUGHT OF GOD.' Every one who has heard and learned from the Father, comes to Me.

46 "aNot that any man has seen the Father,

except the One who is from God, He has seen the Father.

47 "Truly, truly, I say to you, he who believes [a]has eternal life.

48 "[a]I am the bread of life.

49 "[a]Your fathers ate the manna in the wilderness, and they died.

50 "This is the bread which [a]comes down out of heaven, so that one may eat of it and [b]not die.

51 "[a]I am the living bread that [b]came down out of heaven; if any one eats of this bread, [c]he shall live forever; and the bread also which I shall give [d]for the life of the world is [e]My flesh."

52 [a]The Jews therefore [b]*began* to argue with one another, saying, "How can this man give us *His* flesh to eat?"

53 Jesus therefore said to them, "Truly, truly, I say to you, unless you eat the flesh of [a]the Son of Man and drink His blood, you have no life in yourselves.

54 "He who eats My flesh and drinks My blood has eternal life; and I will [a]raise him up on the last day.

55 "For My flesh is true food, and My blood is true drink.

56 "He who eats My flesh and drinks My blood [a]abides in Me, and I in him.

57 "As the [a]living Father [b]sent Me, and I live because of the Father; so he who eats Me, he also shall live because of Me.

58 "This is the bread which [a]came down out of heaven; not as [b]the fathers ate, and died; he who eats this bread [c]shall live forever."

59 These things He said [a]in the synagogue, as He taught [b]in Capernaum.

60 Many therefore of His [a]disciples, when they heard *this* said, "[b]This is a difficult statement; who can listen to it?"

61 But Jesus, [a]conscious that His disciples grumbled at this, said to them, "Does this [b]cause you to stumble?

62 "*What* then if you should behold [a]the Son of Man [b]ascending where He was before?

63 "[a]It is the Spirit who gives life; the flesh profits nothing; [b]the words that I have spoken to you are spirit and are life.

64 "But there are [a]some of you who do not believe." For Jesus [b]knew from the beginning who

47 [a]John 6:51, 58; 3:36; 5:24; 11:26

48 [a]John 6:35, 51

49 [a]John 6:31, 58

50 [a]John 6:33 [b]John 6:47, 51, 58; 3:36; 5:24; 11:26

51 [a]John 6:35, 48 [b]John 6:41, 58 [c]John 6:47, 58; 3:36; 5:24; 11:26 [d]John 1:29; 3:14f.; Heb. 10:10; 1 John 4:10 [e]John 6:53-56

52 [a]John 1:19; 6:41 [b]John 9:16; 10:19

53 [a]John 6:27, 62; Matt. 8:20

54 [a]John 6:39

56 [a]John 15:4f.; 1 John 2:24; 3:24; 4:15f.; John 17:23

57 [a]Matt. 16:16; John 5:26 [b]John 6:29, 38; 3:17

58 [a]John 6:41, 51; 6:33 [b]John 6:31, 49 [c]John 6:47, 51; 3:36; 5:24; 11:26

59 [a]Matt. 4:23 [b]John 6:24

60 [a]John 2:2; 6:66; 7:3 [b]John 6:52

61 [a]John 6:64 [b]Matt. 11:6

62 [a]John 6:27, 53; Matt. 8:20 [b]Mark 16:19; John 3:13

63 [a]2 Cor. 3:6 [b]John 6:68

64 [a]John 6:60, 66 [b]John 2:25

64 ¹Or, *deliver Him up*
cJohn 6:71; 13:11; Matt. 10:4

65 aJohn 6:37, 44 bMatt.
13:11; John 3:27

66 aJohn 2:2; 7:3 bJohn
6:60, 64

67 aJohn 6:70f.; 20:24;
Matt. 10:2; John 2:2

68 aMatt. 16:16 bJohn 6:63;
12:49f.; 17:8

69 aMark 1:24

70 aJohn 15:16, 19 bJohn
6:71; 20:24; Matt. 10:2; John
2:2 cJohn 13:2, 27; 8:44;
17:12

71 ¹Or, *was intending to*
aJohn 13:26; 12:4; 13:2
bMark 14:10 cJohn 6:70f.;
20:24; Matt. 10:2; John 2:2

1 aJohn 4:3; 6:1; 11:54
bJohn 1:19; 7:11, 13, 15, 35
cJohn 7:19; 5:18; 8:37, 40;
11:53

2 aLev. 23:34; Zech. 14:16-
19; Deut. 16:16

3 aMatt. 12:46; John 7:5,
10; Mark 3:21 bJohn 6:60

4 ¹Lit., *and*

5 aMatt. 12:46; John 7:3,
10; Mark 3:21

6 aMatt. 26:18; John 7:8,
30; 2:4

7 aJohn 15:18f. bJohn
3:19f.

8 ¹Some authorities add
yet
aJohn 7:6

10 aMatt. 12:46; John 7:3, 5;
Mark 3:21

206

they were who did not believe, and cwho it was that would ¹betray Him.

65　And He was saying, "For this reason I have asaid to you, that no one can come to Me, unless bit has been granted him from the Father."

66　As a result of this many of His adisciples bwithdrew, and were not walking with Him any more.

67　Jesus said therefore to athe twelve, "You do not want to go away also, do you?"

68　aSimon Peter answered Him, "Lord, to whom shall we go? You have bwords of eternal life.

69　"And we have believed and have come to know that You are athe Holy One of God."

70　Jesus answered them, "aDid I Myself not choose you, bthe twelve, and *yet* one of you is ca devil?"

71　Now He meant Judas a*the son* of Simon Iscariot, for he, bone of cthe twelve, ¹was going to betray Him.

CHAPTER 7

AND after these things Jesus awas walking in Galilee; for He was unwilling to walk in Judea, because bthe Jews cwere seeking to kill Him.

2　Now the feast of the Jews, athe Feast of Tabernacles, was at hand.

3　His abrothers therefore said to Him, "Depart from here, and go into Judea, that Your bdisciples also may behold Your works which You are doing.

4　"For no one does anything in secret, ¹when he himself seeks to be *known* publicly. If You do these things, show Yourself to the world."

5　For not even His abrothers were believing in Him.

6　Jesus therefore *said to them, "aMy time is not yet at hand; but your time is always opportune.

7　"aThe world cannot hate you; but it hates Me, because I testify of it, that bits deeds are evil.

8　"Go up to the feast yourselves; I do not go up ¹to this feast because aMy time has not yet fully come."

9　And having said these things to them, He stayed in Galilee.

10　But when His abrothers had gone up to the

feast, then He Himself also went up, not publicly, but as it were, in secret.

11 [a]The Jews therefore [b]were seeking Him at the feast, and were saying, "Where is He?"

12 And there was much grumbling among the multitudes concerning Him; [a]some were saying, "He is a good man;" others were saying, "No, on the contrary, He leads the multitude astray."

13 Yet no one was speaking openly of Him for [a]fear of the Jews.

14 But when it was now the midst of the feast Jesus went up into the temple, and *began to* [a]teach.

15 [a]The Jews therefore were marveling, saying, "How has this man [b]become learned, having never been educated?"

16 Jesus therefore answered them, and said, "[a]My teaching is not Mine, but His who sent Me.

17 "[a]If any man is willing to do His will, he shall know of the teaching, whether it is of God, or *whether* I speak from Myself.

18 "He who speaks from himself [a]seeks his own glory; but He who is seeking the glory of the one who sent Him, He is true, and there is no unrighteousness in Him.

19 "[a]Did not Moses give you the law, and *yet* none of you carries out the law? Why do you [b]seek to kill Me?"

20 The multitude answered, "[a]You have a [1]demon! Who seeks to kill You?"

21 Jesus answered and said to them, "I did [a]one [1]deed, and you all marvel.

22 "On this account [a]Moses has given you circumcision (not because it is from Moses, but from [b]the fathers); and on *the* Sabbath you circumcise a man.

23 "[a]If a man receives circumcision on *the* Sabbath that the Law of Moses may not be broken, are you angry with Me because I made an entire man well on *the* Sabbath?

24 "Do not [a]judge according to appearance, but [1]judge with righteous judgment."

25 Therefore some of the people of Jerusalem were saying, "Is this not the man whom they are seeking to kill?

26 "And look, He is speaking publicly, and they are saying nothing to Him. [a]The rulers do not really know that this is [1]the Christ, do they?

27 "However [a]we know where this man is from;

11 [a]John 7:13, 15, 35 [b]John 11:56

12 [a]John 7:40-43

13 [a]John 19:38; 20:19; 9:22; 12:42

14 [a]John 7:28; Matt. 26:55

15 [a]John 1:19; John 7:11, 13, 35 [b]Acts 26:24 [Gr.]

16 [a]John 3:11

17 [a]John 3:21; 8:43f.; Ps. 25:9, 14; Prov. 3:32; Dan. 12:10

18 [a]John 5:41; 8:50, 54; 12:43

19 [a]John 1:17 [b]John 7:1; Mark 11:18

20 [1]Or, *you are demented* [a]John 8:48f., 52; 10:20; Matt. 11:18

21 [1]Or, *work* [a]John 7:23; 5:2-9, 16

22 [a]Lev. 12:3 [b]Gen. 17:10ff.; 21:4; Acts 7:8

23 [a]Matt. 12:2; John 5:10

24 [1]Lit., *judge the righteous judgment* [a]Lev. 19:15; Is. 11:3; Zech. 7:9; John 8:15

26 [1]I.e., the Messiah [a]Luke 23:13; John 3:1

27 [a]John 6:42; 7:41f.; 9:29

28 ^aJohn 7:14 ^bJohn 6:42;
7:14f.; 9:29 ^cJohn 8:42

29 ^aJohn 8:55; 17:25; Matt.
11:27 ^bJohn 6:46 ^cJohn 3:17

30 ^aJohn 7:32, 44; 10:39;
Matt. 21:46 ^bJohn 8:20; John
7:6

31 ¹I.e., the Messiah ²Or,
attesting miracles
^aJohn 8:30; 10:42; 11:45;
12:11, 42; 2:23 ^bJohn 7:26
^cJohn 2:11

32 ^aJohn 7:45f., Matt. 26:58
^bMatt. 12:14

33 ^aJohn 12:35; 13:33;
14:19; 16:16-19 ^bJohn 16:5,
10, 17, 28; John 14:12, 28;
20:17

34 ^aJohn 7:36; 8:21; 13:33

35 ^aJohn 7:1 ^bJohn 8:22
^cJames 1:1; 1 Pet. 1:1; in the
Gr. Ps. 147:2; Is. 11:12; 56:8;
Zeph. 3:10 ^dJohn 12:20; Acts
14:1; 17:4; 18:4; Rom. 1:16

36 ^aJohn 7:34; 8:21; 13:33

37 ¹I.e., let him keep
coming to Me and let him
keep drinking
^aLev. 23:36; Num. 29:35;
Neh. 8:18 ^bJohn 4:10, 14;
6:35

38 ¹Lit., *out of his belly*
^aIs. 44:3; 55:1; 58:11 ^bJohn
4:10

39 ¹Other mss. read, *for the
Holy Spirit was not yet given*
^aJoel 2:28; John 1:33 ^bActs
1:4f.; 2:4, 33; 19:2; John
20:22 ^cJohn 12:16, 23;
13:31f.; 16:14; 17:1

40 ^aMatt. 21:11; John 1:21

41 ¹I.e., The Messiah
^aJohn 7:52; 1:46

but whenever the Christ may come, no one knows where He is from."

28 Jesus therefore cried out in the temple, ^ateaching and saying, "^bYou both know Me, and know where I am from; and ^cI have not come of Myself, but He who sent Me is true, whom you do not know.

29 "^aI know Him; because ^bI am from Him, and ^cHe sent Me."

30 They ^awere seeking therefore to seize Him; and no man laid his hand on Him, because His ^bhour had not yet come.

31 But ^amany of the multitude believed in Him; and they were saying, "^bWhen ¹the Christ shall come, He will not perform more ^{2c}signs than those which this man has, will He?"

32 The Pharisees heard the multitude muttering these things about Him; and the chief priests and the Pharisees sent ^aofficers to ^bseize Him.

33 Jesus therefore said, "^aFor a little while longer I am with you, then ^bI go to Him who sent Me.

34 "^aYou shall seek Me, and shall not find Me; and where I am, you cannot come."

35 ^aThe Jews therefore said to one another, "^bWhere does this man intend to go that we shall not find Him? He is not intending to go to ^cthe Dispersion among ^dthe Greeks, and teach the Greeks, is He?

36 "What is this statement that He said, '^aYou will seek Me, and will not find Me; and where I am, you cannot come'?"

37 Now on ^athe last day, the great *day* of the feast, Jesus stood and cried out, saying, "^bIf any man is thirsty, let him ¹come to Me and drink.

38 "He who believes in Me, ^aas the Scripture said, 'From ¹his innermost being shall flow rivers of ^bliving water.' "

39 But this He spoke ^aof the Spirit, whom those who believed in Him were to receive; ¹for ^bthe Spirit was not yet *given*, because Jesus was not yet ^cglorified.

40 *Some* of the multitude therefore, when they heard these words, were saying, "This certainly is ^athe Prophet."

41 Others were saying, "This is ¹the Christ." Still others were saying, "^aSurely ¹the Christ is not going to come from Galilee, is He?

42 "Has not the Scripture said that THE CHRIST

COMES FROM ᵃTHE OFFSPRING OF DAVID, AND FROM BETHLEHEM, the village where David was?"

43 So ᵃthere arose a division in the multitude because of Him.

44 And ᵃsome of them wanted to seize Him, but no one laid hands on Him.

45 The ᵃofficers therefore came to the chief priests and Pharisees, and they said to them, "Why did you not bring Him?"

46 The ᵃofficers answered, "ᵇNever did a man speak the way this man speaks."

47 The Pharisees therefore answered them, "ᵃYou have not also been led astray, have you?

48 "ᵃNo one of ᵇthe rulers or Pharisees has believed in Him, has he?

49 "But this multitude which does not know the Law is accursed."

50 ᵃNicodemus *said to them (he who came to Him before, being one of them),

51 "ᵃOur Law does not judge a man, unless it first hears from him and knows what he is doing, does it?"

52 They answered and said to him, "ᵃYou are not also from Galilee, are you? Search, and see that no prophet arises out of Galilee."

53 [¹And everyone went to his home;

CHAPTER 8

Bᴜᴛ Jesus went to ᵃthe Mount of Olives.

2 And early in the morning He came again into the temple, and all the people were coming to Him; and ᵃHe sat down and *began* to teach them.

3 And the scribes and the Pharisees *brought a woman caught in adultery, and having set her in the midst,

4 they *said to Him, "Teacher, this woman has been caught in adultery, in the very act.

5 "Now in the Law ᵃMoses commanded us to stone such women; what then do You say?"

6 And they were saying this, ᵃtesting Him, ᵇin order that they might have grounds for accusing Him. But Jesus stooped down, and with His finger wrote on the ground.

7 But when they persisted in asking Him, ᵃHe straightened up, and said to them, "ᵇHe who is without sin among you, let him *be the* ᶜfirst to throw a stone at her."

42 ᵃMatt. 1:1; 2:5f.; Luke 2:4ff.; Ps. 89:4; Micah 5:2

43 ᵃJohn 10:19; 9:16

44 ᵃJohn 7:30

45 ᵃJohn 7:32

46 ᵃJohn 7:32 ᵇMatt. 7:28

47 ᵃJohn 7:12

48 ᵃJohn 12:42 ᵇLuke 23:13; John 7:26

50 ᵃJohn 3:1; 19:39

51 ᵃEx. 23:1; Deut. 17:6; 19:15; Prov. 18:13; Acts 23:3

52 ᵃJohn 7:41; 1:46

53 ¹John 7:53-8:11 is not found in most of the old mss.

1 ᵃMatt. 21:1

2 ᵃMatt. 26:55; John 8:20

5 ᵃLev. 20:10; Deut. 22:22f.

6 ᵃMatt. 16:1; 19:3; 22:18, 35; Mark 8:11; 10:2; 12:15; Luke 10:25; 11:16 ᵇMark 3:2

7 ᵃJohn 8:10 ᵇMatt. 7:1; Rom. 2:1 ᶜDeut. 17:7

10 ªJohn 8:7

11 ¹Or, *Sir*
ªJohn 3:17 ᵇJohn 5:14

12 ªJohn 1:4; 12:35 ᵇMatt.
5:14

13 ¹Or, *valid*
ªJohn 5:31

14 ªJohn 18:37; Rev. 1:5;
3:14 ᵇJohn 13:3; 16:28; 8:42
ᶜJohn 7:28; 9:29

15 ¹I.e., a carnal standard
ª1 Sam. 16:7; John 7:24
ᵇJohn 3:17

16 ¹Many ancient mss.
read, *the Father who sent
Me*
ªJohn 5:30

17 ¹I.e., *valid or admissible*
ªDeut. 19:15; 17:6 ᵇMatt.
18:16

18 ªJohn 5:37; 1 John 5:9

19 ªJohn 14:7; 16:3; 7:28;
14:9; 8:55

20 ªMark 12:41, 43; Luke
21:1 ᵇJohn 7:14; John 8:2
ᶜJohn 7:30

21 ªJohn 7:34 ᵇJohn 8:24

22 ªJohn 1:19; John 8:48,
52, 57 ᵇJohn 7:35

23 ªJohn 3:31

8   And again He stooped down, and wrote on the ground.

9   And when they heard it, they *began* to go out one by one, beginning with the older ones, and He was left alone, and the woman, *where she had been*, in the midst.

10   And ªstraightening up, Jesus said to her, "Woman, where are they? Did no one condemn you?"

11   And she said, "No one, ¹Lord." And Jesus said, "ªNeither do I condemn you; go your way; from now on ᵇsin no more."]

12   Again therefore Jesus spoke to them, saying, "ªI am the light of the world; ᵇhe who follows Me shall not walk in the darkness, but shall have the light of life."

13   The Pharisees therefore said to Him, "ªYou are bearing witness of Yourself; Your witness is not ¹true."

14   Jesus answered and said to them, "ªEven if I bear witness of Myself, My witness is true; for I know ᵇwhere I came from, and where I am going; but ᶜyou do not know where I come from, or where I am going.

15   "ªYou people judge ¹according to the flesh; ᵇI am not judging any one.

16   "But even ªif I do judge, My judgment is true; for I am not alone *in it*, but I and ¹He who sent Me.

17   "Even in ªyour law it has been written, that the testimony of ᵇtwo men is ¹true.

18   "I am He who bears witness of Myself, and ªthe Father who sent Me bears witness of Me."

19   And so they were saying to Him, "Where is Your Father?" Jesus answered, "You know neither Me, nor My Father; ªif you knew Me, you would know My Father also."

20   These words He spoke in ªthe treasury, as ᵇHe taught in the temple; and no one seized Him, because ᶜHis hour had not yet come.

21   He said therefore again to them, "I go away, and ªyou shall seek Me, and ᵇshall die in your sin; where I am going, you cannot come."

22   Therefore ªthe Jews were saying, "Surely He will not kill Himself, will He, since He says, ᵇ'Where I am going, you cannot come'?"

23   And He was saying to them, "ªYou are from

below, I am from above; [b]you are of this world; [c]I am not of this world.

24 "I said therefore to you, that you [a]shall die in your sins; for unless you believe that [1b]I am *He*, [a]you shall die in your sins."

25 And so they were saying to Him, "Who are You?" Jesus said to them, "[1]What have I been saying to you *from* the beginning?

26 "I have many things to speak and to judge concerning you, but [a]He who sent Me is true; and [b]the things which I heard from Him, these I speak to the world."

27 They did not realize that He had been speaking to them about the Father.

28 Jesus therefore said, "When you [a]lift up the Son of Man, then you will know that [1b]I am *He*, and [c]I do nothing on My own initiative, but I speak these things as the Father taught Me.

29 "And He who sent Me is with Me; [a]He [1]has not left Me alone, for [b]I always do the things that are pleasing to Him."

30 As He spoke these things, [a]many came to believe in Him.

31 Jesus therefore was saying to those Jews who had believed Him, "[a]If you abide in My word, *then* you are truly [b]disciples of Mine;

32 and [a]you shall know the truth, and [b]the truth shall make you free."

33 They answered Him, "[a]We are Abraham's offspring, and have never yet been enslaved to any one; how is it that You say, 'You shall become free'?"

34 Jesus answered them, "Truly, truly, I say to you, [a]every one who commits sin is the slave of sin.

35 "And [a]the slave does not remain in the house forever; [b]the son does remain forever.

36 "If therefore the Son [a]shall make you free, you shall be free indeed.

37 "I know that you are [a]Abraham's offspring; yet [b]you seek to kill Me, because My word [1]has no place in you.

38 "I speak the things which I have seen [1]with *My* Father; therefore you also do the things which you heard from [a]*your* father."

39 They answered and said to Him, "Abraham is [a]our father." Jesus *said to them, "[b]If you are Abraham's children, do the deeds of Abraham.

40 "But as it is, [a]you are seeking to kill Me, a

23 [b]1 John 4:5 [c]John 17:14, 16

24 [1]Most auth. connect this with Ex. 3:14 *I AM THAT I AM*
[a]John 8:21 [b]John 8:28; Mark 13:6; Luke 21:8 [Matt. 24:5]; John 4:26; 13:19

25 [1]Or, *that which I have been saying to you from the beginning.*

26 [a]John 7:28; 3:33 [b]John 12:49; 15:15; 8:40

28 [1]Lit., *I am* (vs. 24 note) [a]John 3:14; 12:32 [b]John 8:24; Mark 13:6; Luke 21:8 [Matt. 24:5]; John 4:26; 13:19 [c]John 5:19; 3:11

29 [1]Or, *did not leave* [a]John 8:16; 16:32 [b]John 4:34

30 [a]John 7:31

31 [a]John 15:7; 2 John 9 [b]John 2:2

32 [a]John 1:14, 17 [b]John 8:36; Rom. 8:2; 2 Cor. 3:17; Gal. 5:1, 13; James 2:12; 1 Pet. 2:16

33 [a]John 8:37, 39; Matt. 3:9

34 [a]Rom. 6:16; 2 Pet. 2:19

35 [a]Gen. 21:10; Gal. 4:30 [b]Luke 15:31

36 [a]John 8:32

37 [1]Or, *makes no progress* [a]John 8:39; Matt. 3:9 [b]John 8:40; 7:1

38 [1]Or, *in the presence of* [a]John 8:41, 44

39 [a]John 8:37; Matt. 3:9 [b]Rom. 9:7; Gal. 3:7

40 [a]John 8:37; 7:1

40 [b]John 8:26

41 [a]John 8:38, 44 [b]Deut. 32:6; Is. 63:16; 64:8

42 [1]Lit., *that One* [a]1 John 5:1 [b]John 13:3; 16:28, 30; 17:8 [c]John 7:28 [d]John 3:17

43 [1]Or, *My mode of speaking* [a]John 8:33, 39, 41 [b]John 5:25

44 [1]Lit., *the lie* [2]Lit., *the father of it* [a]1 John 3:8 [b]John 8:38, 41 [c]John 7:17 [d]Gen. 3:4; 1 John 3:8, 15 [e]1 John 2:4 [f]Matt. 12:34

45 [a]John 18:37

46 [a]John 18:37

47 [a]1 John 4:6

48 [a]John 1:19 [b]Matt. 10:5; John 4:9 [c]John 7:20

49 [a]John 7:20

50 [a]John 5:41; 8:54

51 [a]John 14:23; 15:20; 17:6; John 8:55 [b]Luke 2:26; Heb. 11:5; Matt. 16:28; Heb. 2:9; John 8:52

52 [a]John 1:19 [b]John 7:20 [c]John 14:23; 15:20; 17:6; 8:55 [d]John 8:51

53 [a]John 4:12

54 [a]John 8:50 [b]John 7:39

55 [a]John 8:19; 15:21 [b]John 7:29 [c]John 8:44 [d]John 15:10; 8:51

man who has [b]told you the truth, which I heard from God; this Abraham did not do.

41 "You are doing the deeds of [a]your father." They said to Him, "We were not born of fornication; [b]we have one Father, *even* God."

42 Jesus said to them, "If God were your Father, [a]you would love Me; [b]for I proceeded forth and have come from God, for I have [c]not even come on My own initiative, but [1d]He sent Me.

43 "Why do you not understand [1a]what I am saying? *It is* because you cannot [b]hear My word.

44 "[a]You are of [b]your father the devil, and [c]you want to do the desires of your father. [d]He was a murderer from the beginning, and does not stand in the truth, because [e]there is no truth in him. Whenever he speaks a [1]lie, he [f]speaks from his own nature, for he is a liar, and the father of [2]lies.

45 "But because [a]I speak the truth, you do not believe Me.

46 "Which one of you convicts Me of sin? If [a]I speak truth, why do you not believe Me?

47 "[a]He who is of God hears the words of God; for this reason you do not hear *them*, because you are not of God."

48 [a]The Jews answered and said to Him, "Do we not say rightly that You are a [b]Samaritan and [c]have a demon?"

49 Jesus answered, "I do not [a]have a demon; but I honor My Father, and you dishonor Me.

50 "But [a]I do not seek My glory; there is One who seeks and judges.

51 "Truly, truly, I say to you, if anyone [a]keeps My word he shall never [b]see death."

52 [a]The Jews said to Him, "Now we know that You [b]have a demon. Abraham died, and the prophets *also*; and You say, 'If anyone [c]keeps My word, he shall never [d]taste of death.'

53 "Surely You [a]are not greater than our father Abraham, who died? The prophets died too; whom do You make Yourself out *to be*?"

54 Jesus answered, "[a]If I glorify Myself, My glory is nothing; [b]it is My Father who glorifies Me, of whom you say, 'He is our God;'

55 and [a]you have not come to know Him, [b]but I know Him; and if I say that I do not know Him, I shall be [c]a liar like you, [b]but I do know Him, and [d]keep His word.

56 "[a]Your father Abraham [b]rejoiced [1]to see My day; and he saw *it*, and was glad."

57 [a]The Jews therefore said to Him, "You are not yet fifty years old, and have You seen Abraham?"

58 Jesus said to them, "Truly, truly, I say to you, before Abraham [1]was born, [2a]I AM."

59 Therefore they [a]picked up stones to throw at Him; but Jesus [1b]hid Himself, [2]and went out of the temple.

CHAPTER 9

AND as He passed by, He saw a man blind from birth.

2 And His disciples asked Him, saying, "[a]Rabbi, who sinned, [b]this man, or his [c]parents, that he should be born blind?"

3 Jesus answered, "*It was* neither *that* this man sinned, nor his parents; but *it was* in order [a]that the works of God might be displayed in him.

4 "We must work the works of Him who sent Me, [a]as long as it is day; night is coming, when no man can work.

5 "While I am in the world, I am [a]the light of the world."

6 When He had said this, He [a]spat on the ground, and made clay of the spittle, and applied the clay to his eyes,

7 and said to him, "Go, wash in [a]the pool of Siloam" (which is translated, Sent). And so he went away and washed, and [b]came *back* seeing.

8 The neighbors therefore, and those who previously saw him as a beggar, were saying, "Is not this the one who used to [a]sit and beg?"

9 Others were saying, "This is he," *still* others were saying, "No, but he is like him." He kept saying, "I am the one."

10 Therefore they were saying to him, "How then were your eyes opened?"

11 He answered, "The man who is called Jesus made clay, and anointed my eyes, and said to me, 'Go to [a]Siloam, and wash'; so I went away and washed, and I received sight."

12 And they said to him, "Where is He?" He *said, "I do not know."

13 They *brought to the Pharisees him who was formerly blind.

56 [1]Lit., *in order that he might see*
[a]John 8:37, 39 [b]Matt. 13:17; Heb. 11:13

57 [a]John 1:19

58 [1]Lit., *came into being* [2]Or, *I have been* [a]John 17:5, 24; 1:1

59 [1]Lit., *was hidden* [2]Some mss. add, *and going through the midst of them went His way and so passed by* [a]John 10:31; 11:8; Matt. 12:14 [b]John 12:36

2 [a]Matt. 23:7 [b]John 9:34; Luke 13:2; Acts 28:4 [c]Ex. 20:5

3 [a]John 11:4

4 [a]John 11:9; 12:35; 7:33; Gal. 6:10

5 [a]John 1:4; 8:12; 12:46

6 [a]Mark 7:33; 8:23

7 [a]John 9:11; Luke 13:4 [b]John 11:37

8 [a]Acts 3:2, 10

11 [a]John 9:7

213

14 aJohn 5:9

14 aNow it was a Sabbath on the day when Jesus made the clay, and opened his eyes.

15 aAgain therefore the Pharisees also were asking him how he received his sight. And he said to them, "He applied clay to my eyes, and I washed, and I see."

15 aJohn 9:10

16 Therefore some of the Pharisees were saying, "aThis man is not from God, because he does not keep the Sabbath." But others were saying, "How can a man who is a sinner perform such 1bsigns?" And cthere was a division among them.

16 1Or, attesting miracles
aMatt. 12:2 bJohn 2:11 cJohn 6:52; 7:43; 10:19

17 They *said therefore to the blind man aagain, "What do you say about Him, since He opened your eyes?" And he said, "He is a bprophet."

18 aThe Jews therefore did not believe it of him, that he had been blind, and had received sight, until they called the parents of the very one who had received his sight,

17 aJohn 9:15 bMatt. 21:11

19 and questioned them, saying, "Is this your son, who you say was born blind? Then how does he now see?"

20 His parents answered then, and said, "We know that this is our son, and that he was born blind;

21 but how he now sees, we do not know; or who opened his eyes, we do not know. Ask him; he is of age, he shall speak for himself."

18 aJohn 1:19; 9:22

22 His parents said this because they awere afraid of the Jews; for the Jews bhad already agreed, that if any one should confess Him to be 1Christ, che should be put out of the synagogue.

22 1I.e., the Messiah
aJohn 7:13 bJohn 7:45-52
cJohn 12:42; 16:2; Luke 6:22

23 For this reason his parents said, "aHe is of age; ask him."

24 So a second time they called the man who had been blind, and said to him, "aGive glory to God; we know that bthis man is a sinner."

23 aJohn 9:21

25 He therefore answered, "Whether He is a sinner, I do not know; one thing I do know, that, whereas I was blind, now I see."

26 They said therefore to him, "What did He do to you? How did He open your eyes?"

27 He answered them, "aI told you already, and you did not blisten; why do you want to hear it again? You do not want to become His disciples too, do you?"

24 aJosh 7:19; Ezra 10:11;
Rev. 11:13 bJohn 9:16

27 aJohn 9:15 bJohn 5:25

28 And they reviled him, and said, "You are His disciple; but [a]we are disciples of Moses.

29 "We know that God has spoken to Moses; but as for this man, [a]we do not know where He is from."

30 The man answered and said to them, "Well, here is an amazing thing, that you do not know where He is from, and *yet* He opened my eyes.

31 "We know that [a]God does not hear sinners; but if any one is God-fearing, and does His will, He hears him.

32 "[1]Since the beginning of time it has never been heard that any one opened the eyes of a person born blind.

33 "[a]If this man were not from God, He could do nothing."

34 They answered and said to him, "[a]You were born entirely in sins, and are you teaching us?" And they [b]put him out.

35 Jesus heard that they had [a]put him out; and finding him, He said, "Do you believe in the [b]Son of Man?"

36 He answered and said, "And [a]who is He, [1]Lord, that I may believe in Him?"

37 Jesus said to him, "You have both seen Him, and [a]He is the one who is talking with you."

38 And he said, "Lord, I believe." And he [a]worshiped Him.

39 And Jesus said, "[a]For judgment I came into this world, that [b]those who do not see may see; and that [c]those who see may become blind."

40 Those of the Pharisees who were with Him heard these things, and said to Him, "[a]We are not blind too, are we?"

41 Jesus said to them, "[a]If you were blind, you would have no sin; but now you say, '[b]We see;' your sin remains.

CHAPTER 10

"TRULY, truly, I say to you, he who does not enter by the door into the fold of the sheep, but climbs up some other way, he is [a]a thief and a robber.

2 "But he who enters by the door is [a]a shepherd of the sheep.

3 "To him the doorkeeper opens; and the

28 [a]John 5:45; Rom. 2:17

29 [a]John 8:14

31 [a]Job 27:8f.; 35:13; Ps. 34:15f.; 66:18; 145:19; Prov. 15:29; 28:9; Is. 1:15; James 5:16ff.

32 [1]Lit., *from antiquity it was not heard*

33 [a]John 9:16; 3:2

34 [a]John 9:2 [b]John 9:22, 35; 3 John 10

35 [a]John 9:22, 34; 3 John 10 [b]Matt. 4:3

36 [1]Or, *Sir* [a]Rom. 10:14

37 [a]John 4:26

38 [a]Matt. 8:2

39 [a]John 5:22, 27; 3:19 [b]Luke 4:18 [c]Matt. 13:13; 15:14

40 [a]Rom. 2:19

41 [a]John 15:22, 24 [b]Prov. 26:12

1 [a]John 10:8

2 [a]John 10:11f.

3 aJohn 10:4f., 16, 27
bJohn 10:9

4 aJohn 10:5, 16, 27

5 aJohn 10:4f., 16, 27

6 aJohn 16:25, 29; 2 Pet. 2:22

7 aJohn 10:1f., 9

8 aJohn 10:1; Jer. 23:1f.; Ezek. 34:2ff.

9 aJohn 10:1f., 9

10 1Or, *have abundance*
aJohn 5:40

11 aJohn 10:14; Is. 40:11; Ezek. 34:11-16, 23; Heb. 13:20; 1 Pet. 5:4; Rev. 7:17 bJohn 10:15, 17, 18; 1 John 3:16; John 15:13

12 aJohn 10:2

14 aJohn 10:11 bJohn 10:27

15 aMatt. 11:27 bJohn 10:11, 17, 18

16 aIs. 56:8 bJohn 11:52; 17:20f.; Eph. 2:13-18; 1 Pet. 2:25 cEzek. 34:23; 37:24

17 aJohn 10:11, 15, 18

18 1Many Greek mss. read, *takes*
aMatt. 26:53; John 2:19; 5:26 bJohn 10:11, 15, 17 cJohn 14:31; 15:10; Phil. 2:8; Heb. 5:8

19 aJohn 7:43; 9:16

20 aJohn 7:20 bMark 3:21

sheep hear ahis voice; and he calls his own sheep by name, and bleads them out.

4 "When he puts forth all his own, he goes before them, and the sheep follow him because they know ahis voice.

5 "And a stranger they simply will not follow, but will flee from him, because they do not know athe voice of strangers."

6 This afigure of speech Jesus spoke to them, but they did not understand what those things were which He had been saying to them.

7 Jesus therefore said to them again, "Truly, truly, I say to you, I am athe door of the sheep.

8 "All who came before Me are athieves and robbers; but the sheep did not hear them.

9 "aI am the door; if anyone enters through Me, he shall be saved, and shall go in and out, and find pasture.

10 "The thief comes only to steal, and kill, and destroy; I came that they amight have life, and might 1have *it* abundantly.

11 "aI am the good shepherd; the good shepherd blays down His life for the sheep.

12 "He who is a hireling, and not a ashepherd, who is not the owner of the sheep, beholds the wolf coming, and leaves the sheep, and flees, and the wolf snatches them, and scatters *them.*

13 "He flees because he is a hireling, and is not concerned about the sheep.

14 "aI am the good shepherd; and bI know My own, and My own know Me,

15 even as athe Father knows Me and I know the Father; and bI lay down My life for the sheep.

16 "And I have aother sheep, which are not of this fold; I must bring them also, and they shall hear My voice; and they shall become bone flock *with* cone Shepherd.

17 "For this reason the Father loves Me, because I alay down My life that I may take it again.

18 "aNo one 1has taken it away from Me, but I blay it down on My own initiative. I have authority to lay it down, and I have authority to take it up again. cThis commandment I received from My Father."

19 aThere arose a division again among the Jews because of these words.

20 And many of them were saying, "He ahas a demon, and bis insane; why do you listen to Him?"

21 Others were saying, "These are not the sayings of one ᵃdemon-possessed. ᵇA demon cannot open the eyes of the blind, can he?"

22 At that time the Feast of the Dedication took place at Jerusalem;

23 it was winter, and Jesus was walking in the temple in the portico of ᵃSolomon.

24 ᵃThe Jews therefore gathered around Him, and were saying to Him, "How long will You keep us in suspense? If You are ¹the Christ, tell us ᵇplainly."

25 Jesus answered them, "ᵃI told you, and you do not believe; ᵇthe works that I do in My Father's name, these bear witness of Me.

26 "But you do not believe, because ᵃyou are not of My sheep.

27 "My sheep ᵃhear My voice, and ᵇI know them, and they follow Me;

28 and I give ᵃeternal life to them; and they shall never perish, and ᵇno one shall snatch them out of My hand.

29 "¹My Father, who has given *them* to Me, is greater than all; and no one is able to snatch *them* out of the Father's hand.

30 "ᵃI and the Father are ¹one."

31 The Jews ᵃtook up stones again to stone Him.

32 Jesus answered them, "I showed you many good works from the Father; for which of them are you stoning Me?"

33 The Jews answered Him, "For a good work we do not stone You, but for ᵃblasphemy; and because You, being a man, ᵇmake Yourself out *to be* God."

34 Jesus answered them, "Has it not been written in ᵃyour ᵇLaw, 'I said, ᶜyou are gods'?

35 "If he called them gods, to whom the word of God came (and the Scripture cannot be broken),

36 do you say of Him, whom the Father ᵃsanctified and ᵇsent into the world, 'You are blaspheming'; because I said, ᶜI am the Son of God'?

37 "ᵃIf I do not do the works of My Father, do not believe Me;

38 but if I do them, though you do not believe Me, believe ᵃthe works; that you may ¹know and understand that ᵇthe Father is in Me, and I in the Father."

21 ᵃMatt. 4:24 ᵇJohn 9:32f.; Ex. 4:11

23 ᵃActs 3:11; 5:12

24 ¹I.e., the Messiah ᵃJohn 1:19; 10:31, 33 ᵇJohn 16:25; Luke 22:67

25 ᵃJohn 8:56, 58 ᵇJohn 5:36; 10:38

26 ᵃJohn 8:47

27 ᵃJohn 10:16; John 10:4 ᵇJohn 10:14

28 ᵃJohn 17:2f.; 1 John 2:25; 5:11 ᵇJohn 6:37, 39

29 ¹Some early mss. read, *What My Father has given Me is greater than all*

30 ¹(Lit. neuter) *a unity*, or, *one essence.* ᵃJohn 17:21ff.

31 ᵃJohn 8:59

33 ᵃLev. 24:16 ᵇJohn 5:18

34 ᵃJohn 8:17 ᵇJohn 12:34; 15:25; Rom. 3:19; 1 Cor. 14.21 ᶜPs. 82:6

36 ᵃJohn 6:69; Jer. 1:5 ᵇJohn 3:17 ᶜJohn 10:30; 5:17f.

37 ᵃJohn 15:24; 10:25

38 ¹Lit., *know and continue knowing* ᵃJohn 10:25; 14:11 ᵇJohn 14:10f., 20; 17:21, 23

39 ᵃJohn 7:30 ᵇJohn 8:59;
Luke 4:30

40 ᵃJohn 1:28

41 ᵃJohn 2:11 ᵇJohn 1:27,
30, 34; 3:27-30

42 ᵃJohn 7:31

1 ᵃMatt. 21:17; John 11:18
ᵇJohn 11:5, 19ff.; Luke 10:38

2 ᵃJohn 12:3; Luke 7:38
ᵇLuke 7:15; John 11:3, 21,
32; 13:13f.

3 ᵃLuke 7:13; John 11:2,
21, 32; 13:13f. ᵇJohn 11:5, 11,
36

4 ᵃJohn 11:40, 9.3; 10:38

5 ᵃJohn 11:1

7 ᵃJohn 10:40

8 ᵃMatt. 23:7 ᵇJohn 10:31;
8:59

9 ᵃLuke 13:33; John 9:4;
12:35

11 ᵃJohn 11:3 ᵇMatt. 27:52;
Mark 5:39; John 11:13; Acts
7:60

12 ¹Lit., *he will be saved*

13 ¹Lit., *the slumber of
sleep*
ᵃMatt. 9:24; Luke 8:52

218

39 Therefore ᵃthey were seeking again to seize Him; and ᵇHe eluded their grasp.

40 And He went away ᵃagain beyond the Jordan to the place where John was first baptizing; and He was staying there.

41 And many came to Him; and they were saying, "While John performed no ᵃsign, yet ᵇeverything John said about this man was true."

42 And ᵃmany believed in Him there.

CHAPTER 11

NOW a certain man was sick, Lazarus of ᵃBethany, of the village of Mary and her sister ᵇMartha.

2 And it was the Mary who ᵃanointed ᵇthe Lord with ointment, and wiped His feet with her hair, whose brother Lazarus was sick.

3 The sisters therefore sent to Him, saying, "ᵃLord, behold, ᵇhe whom You love is sick."

4 But when Jesus heard it, He said, "This sickness is not unto death, but for ᵃthe glory of God, that the Son of God may be glorified by it."

5 Now Jesus loved ᵃMartha, and her sister, and Lazarus.

6 When therefore He heard that he was sick, He stayed then two days *longer* in the place where He was.

7 Then after this He *said to the disciples, "ᵃLet us go to Judea again."

8 The disciples *said to Him, "ᵃRabbi, the Jews were just now seeking ᵇto stone You; and are You going there again?"

9 Jesus answered, "ᵃAre there not twelve hours in the day? If anyone walks in the day, he does not stumble, because he sees the light of this world.

10 "But if anyone walks in the night, he stumbles, because the light is not in him."

11 This He said, and after that He *said to them, "Our ᵃfriend Lazarus ᵇhas fallen asleep; but I go, that I may awaken him out of sleep."

12 The disciples therefore said to Him, "Lord, if he has fallen asleep, he will ¹recover."

13 Now ᵃJesus had spoken of his death; but they thought that He was speaking of ¹literal sleep.

14 Then Jesus therefore said to them plainly, "Lazarus is dead,

15 and I am glad for your sakes that I was not

there, so that you may believe; but let us go to him."

16 [a]Thomas therefore, who is called [1b]Didymus, said to *his* fellow disciples, "Let us also go, that we may die with Him."

17 So when Jesus came, He found that he had already been in the tomb [a]four days.

18 Now [a]Bethany was near Jerusalem, about [1]two miles off;

19 and many of [a]the Jews had come to [b]Martha and Mary, [c]to console them concerning *their* brother.

20 [a]Martha therefore, when she heard that Jesus was coming, went to meet Him; but [a]Mary still sat in the house.

21 Martha therefore said to Jesus, "[a]Lord, [b]if You had been here, my brother would not have died.

22 "Even now I know that [a]whatever You ask of God, God will give You."

23 Jesus *said to her, "Your brother shall rise again."

24 Martha *said to Him, "[a]I know that he will rise again in the resurrection on the last day."

25 Jesus said to her, "[a]I am the resurrection, and the life; he who believes in Me shall live even if he dies,

26 and everyone who lives and believes in Me [a]shall never die. Do you believe this?"

27 She *said to Him, "Yes, Lord; I have believed that You are [1a]the Christ, the Son of God, *even* [2b]He who comes into the world."

28 And when she had said this, she [a]went away, and called Mary her sister, saying secretly, "[b]The Teacher is here, and is calling for you."

29 And when she heard it, she *arose quickly, and was coming to Him.

30 Now Jesus had not yet come into the village, but [a]was still in the place where Martha met Him.

31 [a]The Jews then who were with her in the house, and [b]consoling her, when they saw that Mary rose up quickly and went out, followed her, supposing that she was going to the tomb to [1]weep there.

32 Therefore, when Mary came where Jesus was, she saw Him, and fell at His feet, saying to

16 [1]I.e., the Twin
[a]Matt. 10:3; Mark 3:18; Luke 6:15; John 14:5; 20:26-28; Acts 1:13 [b]John 20:24; 21:2

17 [a]John 11:39

18 [1]Lit., 15 stadia (9090 ft.)
[a]John 11:1

19 [a]John 1:19; 11:8 [b]John 11:1 [c]John 11:31; Job 2:11; 1 Sam. 31:13; 1 Chr. 10:12

20 [a]Luke 10:38-42

21 [a]John 11:2 [b]John 11:32, 37

22 [a]John 11:41f.; 9:31

24 [a]Dan. 12:2; Acts 24:15; John 5:28f.

25 [a]John 1:4; 5:26; 6:39f.; Rev. 1:18

26 [a]John 6:47, 50, 51; 8:51

27 [1]I.e., the Messiah [2]The Coming One was the Messianic title
[a]Matt. 16:16; Luke 2:11 [b]John 6:14

28 [a]John 11:30 [b]Matt. 26:18; Mark 14:14; Luke 22:11; John 13:13

30 [a]John 11:20

31 [1]Lit., *wail*
[a]John 11:19, 33 [b]John 11:19

32 ªJohn 11:2 ᵇJohn 11:21

33 ¹Lit., *wailing* ²Lit., *troubled Himself* ªJohn 11:19 ᵇJohn 11:38 ᶜJohn 12:27; 13:21

35 ªLuke 19:41 [where Gr. as in John 11:33 marg.]

36 ¹Lit., *was loving* ªJohn 11:19 ᵇJohn 11:3

37 ¹Lit., *have caused that this man also not die* ªJohn 9:7

38 ªMatt. 27:60; Mark 15:46; Luke 24:2; John 20:1

39 ¹Lit., *he stinks* ªJohn 11:17

40 ªJohn 11:4, 23ff.

41 ªMatt. 27:60; Mark 15:46; Luke 24:2; John 20:1 ᵇJohn 17:1; Acts 7:55 ᶜMatt. 11:25

42 ªJohn 12:30; 17:21 ᵇJohn 3:17

44 ªJohn 19:40 ᵇJohn 20:7

45 ªJohn 7:31 ᵇJohn 11:19; John 12:17f. ᶜJohn 2:23

46 ªJohn 11:57; John 7:32, 45

47 ¹Or, *attesting miracles* ªJohn 11:57; John 7:32, 45 ᵇMatt. 26:3 ᶜMatt. 5:22 ᵈJohn 2:11

48 ªMatt. 24:15

Him, "ªLord, ᵇif You had been here, my brother would not have died."

33 When Jesus therefore saw her ¹weeping, and ªthe Jews who came with her, *also* ¹weeping, He ᵇwas deeply moved in spirit, and ²ᶜwas troubled,

34 and said, "Where have you laid him?" They *said to Him, "Lord, come and see."

35 Jesus ªwept.

36 And so ªthe Jews were saying, "Behold how He ¹ᵇloved him!"

37 But some of them said, "Could not this man, who ªopened the eyes of him who was blind, ¹have kept this man also from dying?"

38 Jesus therefore again being deeply moved within, *came to the tomb. Now it was a ªcave, and a stone was lying against it.

39 Jesus *said, "Remove the stone." Martha, the sister of the deceased, *said to Him, "Lord, by this time ¹there will be a stench; for he *has been dead* ªfour days."

40 Jesus *said to her, "ªDid I not say to you, if you believe, you will see the glory of God?"

41 And so they removed the ªstone. And Jesus ᵇraised His eyes, and said, "ᶜFather, I thank Thee that Thou heardest Me.

42 "And I knew that Thou hearest Me always; but ªbecause of the people standing around I said it, that they may believe that ᵇThou didst send Me."

43 And when He had said these things, He cried out with a loud voice, "Lazarus, come forth."

44 He who had died came forth, ªbound hand and foot with wrappings; and ᵇhis face was wrapped around with a cloth. Jesus *said to them, "Unbind him, and let him go."

45 ªMany therefore of the Jews, ᵇwho had come to Mary and ᶜbeheld what He had done, believed in Him.

46 But some of them went away to the ªPharisees, and told them the things which Jesus had done.

47 Therefore ªthe chief priests and the Pharisees ᵇconvened a ᶜcouncil, and were saying, "What are we doing? For this man is performing many ¹ᵈsigns.

48 "If we let Him *go on* like this, all men will believe in Him, and the Romans will come and take away both our ªplace and our nation."

49   But a certain one of them, ªCaiaphas, ᵇwho was high priest that year, said to them, "You know nothing at all,

50   nor do you take into account that ªit is expedient for you that one man should die for the people, and that the whole nation should not perish."

51   Now this he did not say ¹on his own initiative; but ªbeing high priest that year, he ᵇprophesied that Jesus was going to die for the nation;

52   and not for the nation only, but that He might also ªgather together into one the children of God who are scattered abroad.

53   So from that day on they ªplanned together to kill Him.

54   Jesus therefore ªno longer continued to walk publicly among the Jews, but went away from there to the country near the wilderness, into a city called ᵇEphraim; and there He stayed with the disciples.

55   Now ªthe Passover of the Jews was at hand, and many went up to Jerusalem out of the country before the Passover, ᵇto purify themselves.

56   Therefore they ªwere seeking for Jesus, and were saying to one another, as they stood in the temple, "What do you think; that He will not come to the feast at all?"

57   Now ªthe chief priests and the Pharisees had given orders that if any one knew where He was, he should report it, that they might seize Him.

ª   CHAPTER 12

JESUS therefore six days before ᵇthe Passover, came to ᶜBethany where Lazarus was, whom Jesus had raised from the dead.

2   So they made Him a supper there; and ªMartha was serving; but Lazarus was one of those reclining *at the table* with Him.

3   ªMary therefore took a pound of very costly, ᵇgenuine spikenard-ointment, and anointed the feet of Jesus, and wiped His feet with her hair; and the house was filled with the fragrance of the ointment.

4   But ªJudas Iscariot, one of His disciples, who was intending to ¹betray Him, *said,

5   "Why was this ointment not sold for ¹three hundred denarii, and given to poor *people?*"

49 ªMatt. 26:3 ᵇJohn 11:51; 18:13

50 ªJohn 18:14

51 ¹Lit., *from himself*
ªJohn 11:51; 18:13 ᵇEx. 28:30; Num. 27:21; 1 Sam. 23:9; 30:7; Ezra 2:63

52 ªJohn 10:16

53 ªMatt. 26:4

54 ªJohn 7:1 ᵇ2 Chr. 13:19 marg.

55 ªMatt. 26:1f.; Mark 14:1; Luke 22:1; John 12:1; 13:1; John 2:13 ᵇNum. 9:10; 2 Chr. 30:17f.; John 18:28

56 ªJohn 7:11

57 ªJohn 11:47

1 ªJohn 12:1-8: *Matt.* 26:6-13; *Mark* 14:3-9; also *Luke* 7:37-39 ᵇJohn 11:55; John 12:20 ᶜMatt. 21:17; John 11:43f.

2 ªLuke 10:38

3 ªJohn 11:2 ᵇMark 14:3

4 ¹Or, *deliver Him up*
ªJohn 6:71

5 ¹Monetary value $50, but equal to 11 month's wages

6 aJohn 13:29 bLuke 8:3

7 1I.e., The custom of
anointing for burial
aJohn 19:40

8 aMatt. 26:11; Mark 14:7;
Deut. 15:11

9 aMark 12:37; John 12:12
marg. bJohn 11:43f.; 12:1,
17f.

11 aJohn 12:18; 11:45f.
bJohn 7:31; 11:47

12 1Or, the common
people
aJohn 12:12-15: Matt. 21:4-9:
Mark 11:7-10; Luke 19:35-38
bJohn 12:1

13 aPs. 118:25f. bJohn 1:49

15 aZech. 9:9

16 aMark 9:32; John 2:22;
14:26 bJohn 7:39; 12:23

17 aJohn 11:42

18 1Or, attesting miracle
aLuke 19:37; John 12:12
bJohn 12:11

20 aJohn 7:35 bJohn 12:1

21 aJohn 1:44 bMatt. 11:21

6 Now he said this, not because he was concerned about the poor, but because he was a thief, and as he ahad the money box, he used to pilfer bwhat was put into it.

7 Jesus therefore said, "Let her alone, in order that she may keep 1it for athe day of My burial.

8 "aFor the poor you always have with you; but you do not always have Me."

9 The agreat multitude therefore of the Jews learned that He was there; and they came, not for Jesus' sake only, but that they might also see Lazarus, bwhom He raised from the dead.

10 But the chief priests took counsel that they might put Lazarus to death also;

11 because aon account of him bmany of the Jews were going away, and were believing in Jesus.

12 On the next day 1athe great multitude who had come to bthe feast, when they heard that Jesus was coming to Jerusalem,

13 took the branches of the palm trees, and went out to meet Him, and *began* to cry out, "aHosanna: BLESSED *is* HE WHO COMES IN THE NAME OF THE LORD, even the bKing of Israel."

14 And Jesus, finding a young donkey, sat on it; as it is written,

15 "aFEAR NOT, DAUGHTER OF ZION; BEHOLD, YOUR KING COMES SITTING ON A DONKEY'S COLT."

16 aThese things His disciples did not understand at the first; but when Jesus bwas glorified, then they remembered that these things were written of Him, and that they had done these things to Him.

17 And so athe multitude who were with Him when He called Lazarus out of the tomb, and raised him from the dead, were bearing Him witness.

18 aFor this cause also the multitude went and met Him, bbecause they heard that He had performed this 1sign.

19 The Pharisees therefore said to one another, "You see that you are not doing any good; look, the world has gone after Him."

20 Now there were certain aGreeks among those who were going up to worship at bthe feast;

21 these therefore came to aPhilip, who was from bBethsaida of Galilee, and *began to* ask him, saying, "Sir, we wish to see Jesus."

22   Philip *came and *told [a]Andrew; Andrew and Philip *came, and they *told Jesus.

23   And Jesus *answered them, saying, "[a]The hour has come for the Son of Man to [b]be glorified.

24   "Truly, truly, I say to you, [a]unless a grain of wheat falls into the earth and dies, it remains by itself alone; but if it dies, it bears much fruit.

25   "[a]He who loves his [1]life loses it; and he who [b]hates his [1]life in this world shall keep it to life eternal.

26   "If any one serves Me, let him follow Me; and [a]where I am, there shall My servant also be; if any one serves Me, the Father will [b]honor him.

27   "[a]Now My soul has become troubled; and what shall I say, '[b]Father, save Me from [c]this hour?' But for this purpose I came to this hour.

28   "[a]Father, glorify Thy name." There came therefore a [b]voice out of heaven: "I have both glorified it, and will glorify it again."

29   The multitude therefore, who stood by and heard it, were saying that it had thundered; others were saying, "[a]An angel has spoken to Him."

30   Jesus answered and said, "[a]This voice has not come for My sake, but for your sakes.

31   "[a]Now judgment is upon this world; now [b]the ruler of this world shall be cast out.

32   "And I, if I [a]be lifted up from the earth, will [b]draw all men to Myself."

33   But He was saying this [a]to indicate the kind of death by which He was to die.

34   The multitude therefore answered Him, "We have heard out of [a]the Law that [1][b]the Christ is to remain forever; and how can You say, 'The [c]Son of Man must be [d]lifted up'? Who is this [c]Son of Man?"

35   Jesus therefore said to them, "[a]For a little while longer [b]the light is among you. [c]Walk while you have the light, that darkness may not overtake you; he who [d]walks in the darkness does not know where he goes.

36   "While you have the light, [a]believe in the light, in order that you may become [b]sons of light."

These things Jesus spoke, and He departed and [1c]hid Himself from them.

37   But though He had performed so many [1]signs before them, *yet* they were not believing in Him;

38   that the word of Isaiah the prophet might

22 [a]John 1:44

23 [a]John 13:1, 32; 17:1; Matt. 26:45; Mark 14:35, 41 [b]John 7:39; 12:16

24 [a]1 Cor. 15:36; Rom. 14:9

25 [1]Or, *soul* [a]Matt. 10:39 [b]Luke 14:26

26 [a]John 14:3; 17:24; 2 Cor. 5:8; Phil. 1:23; 1 Thess. 4:17 [b]1 Sam. 2:30; Ps. 91:15; Luke 12:37

27 [a]Matt. 26:38; Mark 14:34; John 11:33 [b]Matt. 11:25 [c]John 12:23

28 [a]Matt. 11:25 [b]Matt. 3:17; 17:5; Mark 1:11; 9:7; Luke 3:22; 9:35

29 [a]Acts 23:9

30 [a]John 11:42

31 [a]John 16:11; 3:19; 9:39 [b]John 14:30; 16:11; 2 Cor. 4:4; Eph. 2:2; Eph. 6:12; 1 John 4:4; 5:19

32 [a]John 3:14; 8:28; 12:34 [b]John 6:44

33 [a]John 18:32; 21:19

34 [1]I.e., The Messiah [a]John 10:34 [b]Ps. 110:4; Is. 9:7; Ezek. 37:25; Dan. 7:14 [c]Matt. 8:20 [d]John 3:14; 8:28; 12:32

35 [a]John 7:33; 9:4; 1 John 2:10 [b]John 12:46 [c]Eph. 5:8; Gal. 6:10 [d]1 John 1:6; 2:11

36 [1]Lit., *was hidden* [a]John 12:46 [b]Luke 16:8; John 8:12 [c]John 8:59

37 [1]Or, *attesting miracles*

be fulfilled, which he spoke, "[a]LORD, WHO HAS BELIEVED OUR REPORT? AND TO WHOM HAS THE ARM OF THE LORD BEEN REVEALED?"

39 For this cause they could not believe, for Isaiah said again,

40 "[a]HE HAS BLINDED THEIR EYES, AND HE [b]HARDENED THEIR HEART; LEST THEY SEE WITH THEIR EYES, AND PERCEIVE WITH THEIR HEART, AND [1]BE CONVERTED, AND I HEAL THEM."

41 These things Isaiah said, because [a]he saw His glory, and [b]he spoke of Him.

42 Nevertheless [a]many even of [b]the rulers believed in Him, but [c]because of the Pharisees they were not confessing *Him*, lest they should be [1d]put out of the synagogue;

43 [a]for they loved the approval of men rather than the approval of God.

44 And Jesus cried out and said, "[a]He who believes in Me does not believe in Me, but in Him who sent Me.

45 "And [a]he who beholds Me beholds the One who sent Me.

46 "[a]I have come *as* light into the world, that everyone who believes in Me may not remain in darkness.

47 "And if any one hears My sayings, and does not keep them, I do not judge him; for [a]I did not come to judge the world, but to save the world.

48 "[a]He who rejects Me, and does not receive My sayings, has one who judges him; [b]the word I spoke is what will judge him at [c]the last day.

49 "[a]For I did not speak [1]on My own initiative, but the Father Himself who sent Me [b]has given Me commandment, what to say, and what to speak.

50 "And I know that [a]His commandment is eternal life; therefore the things I speak, I speak [b]just as the Father has told Me."

CHAPTER 13

NOW before the feast of [a]the Passover, Jesus knowing that [b]His hour had come that He should depart out of this world [c]to the Father, having loved His own who were in the world, He loved them [1]to the end.

2 And during supper, [a]the devil having already put into the heart of [b]Judas Iscariot, *the son* of Simon, to betray Him,

38 [a]Is. 53:1; Rom. 10:16

40 [1]Lit., *should be turned,* i.e., *turn about* [a]Is. 6:10; Matt. 13:14f. [b]Mark 6:52

41 [a]Is. 6:1ff. [b]Luke 24:27

42 [1]I.e., excommunicated [a]John 7:48; 12:11 [b]Luke 23:13 [c]John 7:13 [d]John 9:22

43 [a]John 5:41, 44

44 [a]Matt. 10:40; John 5:24

45 [a]John 14:9

46 [a]John 1:4; 3:19; 8:12; 9:5; 12:35f.

47 [a]John 3:17; 8:15f.

48 [a]Luke 10:16 [b]Deut. 18:18f.; John 5:45ff.; 8:47 [c]Matt. 10:15

49 [1]Lit., *of Myself* [a]John 3:11 [b]John 14:31; 17:8

50 [a]John 6:68 [b]John 8:28

1 [1]Lit., *to the uttermost* or, *eternally* [a]John 11:55; 2:13 [b]John 12:23 [c]John 16:28; 13:3

2 [a]John 6:70; 13:27 [b]John 6:71

3 *Jesus*, ªknowing that the Father had given all things into His hands, and that ᵇHe had come forth from God, and was going back to God,

4 *rose from supper, and *laid aside His garments; and taking a towel, ªgirded Himself about.

5 Then He *poured water into the basin, and began to ªwash the disciples' feet, and to wipe them with the towel with which He was girded.

6 And so He *came to Simon Peter. He *said to Him, "Lord, do You wash my feet?"

7 Jesus answered and said to him, "What I do you do not realize now; but you shall understand ªhereafter."

8 Peter *said to Him, "Never shall You wash my feet!" Jesus answered him, "If I do not wash you, ªyou have no part with Me."

9 Simon Peter *said to Him, "Lord, not my feet only, but also my hands and my head."

10 Jesus *said to him, "He who has bathed needs only to wash his feet, but is completely clean; and ªyou are clean, but not all *of you.*"

11 For ªHe knew the one who was betraying Him; for this reason He said, "Not all of you are clean."

12 And so when He had washed their feet, and ªtaken His garments, and reclined *at table* again, He said to them, "Do you know what I have done to you?

13 "You call me ªTeacher, and ᵇLord; and ¹you are right; for *so* I am.

14 "If I then, ªthe Lord and the Teacher, washed your feet, you also ought to wash one another's feet.

15 "For I gave you ªan example that you also should do as I did to you.

16 "Truly, truly, I say to you, ªa slave is not greater than his master; neither ᵇone who is sent greater than the one who sent him.

17 "If you know these things, you are ªblessed if you do them.

18 "ªI do not speak of all of you. I know the ones I have ᵇchosen; but *it is* ᶜthat the Scripture may be fulfilled, 'ᵈHᴇ ᴡʜᴏ ᴇᴀᴛs Mʏ ʙʀᴇᴀᴅ ʜᴀs ʟɪꜰᴛᴇᴅ ᴜᴘ ʜɪs ʜᴇᴇʟ ᴀɢᴀɪɴsᴛ Mᴇ.'

19 "From now on ªI am telling you before *it* comes to pass, so that when it does occur, you may believe that ᵇI am *He.*

20 "Truly, truly, I say to you, ªhe who receives

---

3 ªJohn 3:35 ᵇJohn 8:42

4 ªLuke 12:37

5 ªLuke 7:44

7 ªJohn 13:12ff.

8 ªDeut. 12:12; 2 Sam. 20:1; 1 Kin. 12:16

10 ªJohn 15:3

11 ªJohn 6:64; 13:2

12 ªJohn 13:4

13 ¹Lit., *you say well* ªJohn 11:28 ᵇJohn 11:2; 1 Cor. 12:3; Phil. 2:11

14 ªJohn 11:2; 1 Cor. 12:3; Phil. 2:11

15 ª1 Pet. 5:3

16 ªMatt. 10:24 ᵇ2 Cor. 8:23; Phil. 2:25

17 ªLuke 11:28; James 1:25; Matt. 7:24ff.

18 ªJohn 13:10f. ᵇJohn 6:70; 15:16, 19 ᶜJohn 17:12; 19:24, 36; 15:25; 18:32 ᵈPs. 41:9; John 13:18, 21, 22, 26; Matt. 26:21ff. Mark 14:18f.; Luke 22:21ff.

19 ªJohn 14:29; 16:4 ᵇJohn 8:24

20 ªMatt. 10:40; Luke 10:16; Gal. 4:14

225

21 ¹Or, *deliver Me up*
ªJohn 11:33 ᵇJohn 13:18, 21, 22, 26: Matt. 26:21f.; Mark 14:18ff. Luke 22:21ff.

22 ªJohn 13:18, 21, 22, 26: Matt. 26:21ff.; Mark 14:18ff.; Luke 22:21ff.

23 ªJohn 1:18 ᵇJohn 19:26; 20:2; 21:7, 20

25 ªJohn 21:20

26 ªJohn 6:71

27 ªMatt. 4:10 ᵇLuke 22:3; John 13:2

29 ªJohn 12:6 ᵇJohn 13:1 ᶜJohn 12:5

30 ªLuke 22:53

31 ¹Or, *was*
ªMatt. 8:20 ᵇJohn 7:39 ᶜJohn 14:13; 17:4, 1 Pet. 4:11

32 ¹Some ancient mss. omit this phrase
ªJohn 17:1

33 ª1 John 2:1 ᵇJohn 7:33 ᶜJohn 7:34

34 ª1 John 2:7f.; 3:11, 23; 2 John 5; John 15:12, 17 ᵇLev. 19:18; 1 Thess. 4:9; 1 Pet. 1:22; 1 John 4:7; Heb. 13:1; Gal. 5:14; Matt. 5:44 ᶜEph. 5:2; 1 John 4:10f.

35 ª1 John 3:14; 4:20

whomever I send receives Me; and he who receives Me receives Him who sent Me."

21 When Jesus had said this, He ªbecame troubled in spirit, and testified, and said, "Truly, truly, I say to you, that ᵇone of you will ¹betray Me."

22 The disciples *began* looking at one another, ªat a loss *to know* of which one He was speaking.

23 There was reclining on ªJesus' breast one of His disciples, ᵇwhom Jesus loved.

24 Simon Peter therefore *gestured to him, and *said to him. "Tell *us* who it is of whom He is speaking."

25 He, ªleaning back thus on Jesus' breast, *said to Him, "Lord, who is it?"

26 Jesus therefore *answered, "That is the one for whom I shall dip the morsel, and give it to him." So when He had dipped the morsel, He *took and *gave it to Judas, ªthe son of Simon Iscariot.

27 And after the morsel, ªSatan then ᵇentered into him. Jesus therefore *said to him, "What you do, do quickly."

28 Now no one of those reclining *at table* knew for what purpose He had said this to him.

29 For some were supposing, because Judas ªhad the money box, that Jesus was saying to him, "Buy the things we have need of ᵇfor the feast"; or else, that he should ᶜgive something to the poor.

30 And so after receiving the morsel he went out immediately; and ªit was night.

31 When therefore he had gone out, Jesus *said, "Now ¹is ªthe Son of Man ᵇglorified, and ᶜGod ¹is glorified in Him;

32 ¹if God is glorified in Him, ªGod will also glorify Him in Himself, and will glorify Him immediately.

33 "ªLittle children, I am with you ᵇa little while longer. ᶜYou shall seek Me; and as I said to the Jews, 'Where I am going, you cannot come', now I say to you also.

34 "A ªnew commandment I give to you, ᵇthat you love one another, ᶜeven as I have loved you, that you also love one another.

35 "ªBy this all men will know that you are My disciples, if you have love for one another."

36 Simon Peter *said to Him, "Lord, where

are You going?" Jesus answered, "ªWhere I go, you cannot follow Me now; but ᵇyou shall follow later."

37 Peter *said to Him, "Lord, why can I not follow You right now? ªI will lay down my life for You."

38 Jesus *answered, "Will you lay down your life for Me? Truly, truly, I say to you, ªa cock shall not crow, until you deny Me three times.

CHAPTER 14

"ªLET not your heart be troubled; ¹believe in God, believe also in Me.

2 "In My Father's house are many dwelling places; if it were not so, I would have told you; for ªI go to prepare a place for you.

3 "And if I go and prepare a place for you, ªI will come again, and receive you to Myself; that ᵇwhere I am, *there* you may be also.

4 "¹And you know the way where I am going."

5 ªThomas *said to Him, "Lord, we do not know where You are going; how do we know the way?"

6 Jesus *said to him, "I am ªthe way, and ᵇthe truth, and ᶜthe life; no one comes to the Father, but through Me.

7 "ªIf you had known Me, you would have known My Father also; from now on you ᵇknow Him, and have ᶜseen Him."

8 ªPhilip *said to Him, "Lord, show us the Father, and it is enough for us."

9 Jesus *said to him, "Have I been so long with you, and *yet* you have not come to know Me, Philip? ªHe who has seen Me has seen the Father; how do you say, 'Show us the Father'?

10 "Do you not believe that ªI am in the Father, and the Father is in Me? ᵇThe words that I say to you I do not speak on My own initiative, but the Father abiding in Me does His works.

11 "Believe Me that ªI am in the Father, and the Father in Me; otherwise ᵇbelieve on account of the works themselves.

12 "Truly, truly, I say to you, he who believes in Me, the works that I do shall he do also; and ªgreater *works* than these shall he do; because ᵇI go to the Father.

13 "And ªwhatever you ask in My name, that

36 ªJohn 13:33; John 14:2; 16:5 ᵇJohn 21:18f.; 2 Pet. 1:14

37 ªJohn 13:37, 38: *Matt. 26:33-35; Mark 14:29-31; Luke 22:33-34*

38 ªJohn 18:27; Mark 14:30

1 ¹Or, *you believe in God* ªJohn 14:27; 16:22, 24

2 ªJohn 13:33, 36

3 ªJohn 14:18, 28 ᵇJohn 12:26

4 ¹Many ancient authorities read, *And where I go you know, and the way you know*

5 ªJohn 11:16

6 ªJohn 10:9; Rom. 5:2; Heb. 10:20; Eph. 2:18 ᵇJohn 1:14 ᶜJohn 1:4; 11:25; 1 John 5:20

7 ªJohn 8:19 ᵇ1 John 2:13 ᶜJohn 6:46

8 ªJohn 1:43

9 ªJohn 12:45; 1:14; Col. 1:15; Heb. 1:3

10 ªJohn 10:38; 14:11, 20 ᵇJohn 14:24; 5:19

11 ªJohn 10:38; 14:10, 20 ᵇJohn 5:36

12 ªJohn 5:20; 4:37f. ᵇJohn 7:33; 14:28

13 ªMatt. 7:7

227

13 bJohn 13:31

14 aJohn 15:16; 16:23f.

15 aJohn 14:21, 23; John 15:10; 1 John 5:3; 2 John 6

16 1Gr., *Paracletos*, equals one called alongside to help, or *Intercessor* aJohn 14:26; 15:26; 16:7; 1 John 2:1 marg.; John 7:39; Rom. 8:26

17 aJohn 15:26; 16:13; 1 John 4:6; 5:7 b1 Cor. 2:14

18 aJohn 14:3, 28

19 1Lit., *yet a little and the world* aJohn 7:33 bJohn 16:16, 22 cJohn 6:57

20 aJohn 16:23, 26 bJohn 10:38; 14:11

21 aJohn 14:15, 23; 15:10; 1 John 5:3; 2 John 6 bJohn 16:27; 14:23 cEx. 33:18f.; Prov. 8:17

22 aLuke 6:16; Acts 1:13; Matt. 10:3 bActs 10:40, 41

23 aJohn 14:15, 21; 15:10; 1 John 5:3; 2 John 6 bJohn 8:51; 1 John 2:5 cJohn 14:21 dRev. 3:20; Eph. 5:17; 1 John 2:24; Rev. 21:3; 2 Cor. 6:16 for O.T.

24 aJohn 14:23 bJohn 14:10; 7:16

26 aJohn 14:16 bJohn 1:33; 15:26; 16:7; Luke 24:49; and esp. Acts 2:33 cJohn 16:13f.; 1 John 2:20, 27 dJohn 2:22

27 aJohn 16:33; Col. 3:15; Phil. 4:7; John 20:19 bJohn 14:1

28 aJohn 14:2-4 bJohn 14:3, 18 cJohn 14:12 dJohn 10:29; Phil. 2:6

29 aJohn 13:19

228

will I do, that bthe Father may be glorified in the Son.

14 "If you ask Me anything ain My name, I will do *it*.

15 "aIf you love Me, you will keep My commandments.

16 "And I will ask the Father, and He will give you another 1aHelper, that He may be with you forever;

17 *that is* athe Spirit of truth, bwhom the world cannot receive, because it does not behold Him or know Him, *but* you know Him because He abides with you, and will be in you.

18 "I will not leave you as orphans; aI will come to you.

19 "1aAfter a little while bthe world will behold Me no more; but you *will* behold Me; cbecause I live, you shall live also.

20 "aIn that day you shall know that bI am in My Father, and you in Me, and I in you.

21 "aHe who has My commandments, and keeps them, he it is who loves Me; and bhe who loves Me shall be loved by My Father, and I will love him, and will cdisclose Myself to him."

22 aJudas (not Iscariot) *said to Him, "Lord, what then has happened bthat You are going to disclose Yourself to us, and not to the world?"

23 Jesus answered and said to him, "aIf anyone loves Me, he will bkeep My word; and cMy Father will love him, and We dwill come to him, and make Our abode with him.

24 "He who does not love Me adoes not keep My words; and bthe word which you hear is not Mine, but the Father's who sent Me.

25 "These things I have spoken to you, while abiding with you.

26 "But the aHelper, the Holy Spirit, bwhom the Father will send in My name, cHe will teach you all things, and dbring to your remembrance all that I said to you.

27 "aPeace I leave with you; My peace I give to you; not as the world gives, do I give to you. bLet not your heart be troubled, nor let it be fearful.

28 "aYou heard that I said to you, 'I go away, and bI will come to you.' If you loved Me, you would have rejoiced, because cI go to the Father; for dthe Father is greater than I.

29 "And now aI have told you before it comes

to pass, that when it comes to pass, you may believe.

30 "I will not speak much more with you, for [a]the ruler of the world is coming, and [b]he has nothing in Me;

31 but that the world may know that I love the Father, and as [a]the Father gave Me commandment, even so I do. Arise, [b]let us go from here.

CHAPTER 15

"[a]I AM the true vine, and My Father is the [b]vinedresser.

2 "Every branch in Me that does not bear fruit, He takes away; and every *branch* that bears fruit, He [1]prunes it, that it may bear more fruit.

3 "[a]You are already clean because of the word which I have spoken to you.

4 "[a]Abide in Me, and I in you. As the branch cannot bear fruit of itself, unless it abides in the vine, so neither *can* you, unless you abide in Me.

5 "I am the vine, you are the branches; he who abides in Me, and I in him, he [a]bears much fruit; for apart from Me you can do nothing.

6 "If anyone does not abide in Me, he is [a]thrown away as a branch, and dries up; and they gather them, and cast them into the fire, and they are burned.

7 "If you abide in Me, and My words abide in you, [a]ask whatever you wish, and it shall be done for you.

8 "[a]By this is My Father glorified, [1]that you bear much fruit, and *so* [b]prove to be My disciples.

9 "Just as [a]the Father has loved Me, I have also loved you; abide in My love.

10 "[a]If you keep My commandments, you will abide in My love; just as [b]I have kept My Father's commandments, and abide in His love.

11 "[a]These things I have spoken to you, that My joy may be in you, and *that* your [b]joy may be made full.

12 "This is [a]My commandment, that you love one another, just as I have loved you.

13 "[a]Greater love has no one than this, that one [b]lay down his life for his friends.

14 "You are My [a]friends, if [b]you do what I command you.

15 "No longer do I call you slaves; for the slave

30 [a]John 12:31 [b]Heb. 4:15

31 [a]John 10:18; 12:49 [b]John 13:1; 18:1

1 [a]Is. 5:1ff.; Ezek. 19:10ff.; Ps. 80:8ff.; Matt. 21:33ff. [b]Matt. 15:13; Rom. 11:17; 1 Cor. 3:9

2 [1]Lit., *cleanses*

3 [a]John 13:10; 17:17; Eph. 5:26

4 [a]John 15:4-7; 1 John 2:6; John 6:56

5 [a]John 15:16

6 [a]John 15:2

7 [a]Matt. 7:7; John 15:16

8 [1]Another reading, *that you bear much fruit, and become My disciples* [a]Matt. 5:16 [b]John 8:31

9 [a]John 17:23, 24, 26; 3:35

10 [a]John 14:15 [b]John 8:29

11 [a]John 17:13 [b]John 3:29

12 [a]John 13:34; 15:17

13 [a]Rom. 5:7f. [b]John 10:11

14 [a]Luke 12:4 [b]Matt. 12:50

15 ªJohn 8:26; 16:12

16 ªJohn 15:19; 6:70; 13:18
ᵇJohn 15:5 ᶜJohn 14:13;
16:23; 15:7

17 ªJohn 15:12

18 ¹Or, (imperative) *know that*
ªJohn 7:7; 1 John 3:13

19 ªMatt. 10:22; 24:9 ᵇJohn 15:16 ᶜJohn 17:14

20 ªJohn 13:16 ᵇ1 Cor. 4:12;
2 Cor. 4:9; 2 Tim. 3:12 ᶜJohn 8:51

21 ªMatt. 10:22; 24:9; Mark 13:13; Luke 21:12, 17; Acts 4:17; 5:41; 9:14; 26:9; 1 Pet. 4:14; Rev. 2:3 ᵇJohn 16:3; John 8:19, 55; 17:25; Acts 3:17; 1 John 3:1

22 ¹I.e., guilt
ªJohn 9:41; John 15:24

24 ¹I.e., guilt
ªJohn 9:41; 15:21 ᵇJohn 5:36; 10:37

25 ªJohn 10:34 ᵇPs. 35:19; 69.4

26 ¹Gr. *Paracletos*, equals one called alongside to help, or, *Intercessor*
ªJohn 14:16 ᵇJohn 14:26
ᶜJohn 14:17 ᵈ1 John 5:7

27 ¹Or (imperative), *and bear witness*
ªJohn 19:35; 21:24; 1 John 1:2; 4:14; Luke 24:48 ᵇLuke 1:2

1 ªJohn 15:18-27 ᵇMatt. 11:6

2 ¹Or, *they will make you excommunicated*
ªJohn 9:22 ᵇJohn 4:21; 16:25
ᶜActs 26:9-11; Is. 66:5; Rev. 6:9

does not know what his master is doing; but I have called you friends, for ªall things that I have heard from My Father I have made known to you.

16 "ªYou did not choose Me, but I chose you, and appointed you, that you should go and ᵇbear fruit, and *that* your fruit should remain; that ᶜwhatever you ask of the Father in My name, He may give to you.

17 "This ªI command you, that you love one another.

18 "ªIf the world hates you, ¹you know that it has hated Me before *it hated* you.

19 "ªIf you were of the world, the world would love its own; but because you are not of the world, but ᵇI chose you out of the world, ᶜtherefore the world hates you.

20 "Remember the word that I said to you, 'ªA slave is not greater than his master.' If they persecuted Me, ᵇthey will also persecute you; if they ᶜkept My word, they will keep yours also.

21 "But all these things they will do to you ªfor My name's sake, ᵇbecause they do not know the One who sent Me.

22 "ªIf I had not come and spoken to them, they would not have ¹sin, but now they have no excuse for their sin.

23 "He who hates Me hates My Father also.

24 "ªIf I had not done among them ᵇthe works which no one else did, they would not have ¹sin; but now they have both seen and hated Me and My Father as well.

25 "But *they have done this* in order that the word may be fulfilled that is written in their ªLaw, 'ᵇTHEY HATED ME WITHOUT A CAUSE.'

26 "When the ¹ªHelper comes, ᵇwhom I will send to you from the Father, *that is* ᶜthe Spirit of truth, who proceeds from the Father, ᵈHe will bear witness of Me,

27 ¹and ªyou *will* bear witness also, because you have been with Me ᵇfrom the beginning.

CHAPTER 16

"ªTHESE things I have spoken to you, that you may be kept from ᵇstumbling.

2 "¹They will ªmake you outcasts from the synagogue; but ᵇan hour is coming for everyone ᶜwho kills you to think that he is offering service to God.

3 "And these things they will do, [a]because they have not known the Father, or Me.

4 "But these things I have spoken to you, [a]that when their hour comes, you [1]may remember that I told you of them. And these things I did not say to you [b]at the beginning, because I was with you.

5 "But now [a]I am going to Him who sent Me; and none of you asks Me, '[b]Where are You going?'

6 "But because I have said these things to you, [a]sorrow has filled your heart.

7 "But I tell you the truth, it is to your advantage that I go away; for if I do not go away, the [1a]Helper shall not come to you; but if I go, [b]I will send Him to you.

8 "And He, when He comes, will convict the world concerning sin, and righteousness, and judgment.

9 concerning sin, [a]because they do not believe in Me;

10 and concerning [a]righteousness, because [b]I go to the Father, and you no longer behold Me;

11 [a]and concerning judgment, because the ruler of this world has been judged.

12 "I have many more things to say to you, but you cannot bear *them* now.

13 "But when He, [a]the Spirit of truth, comes, He will [b]guide you into all the truth; for He will not speak on His own initiative, but whatever He hears, He will speak; and He will disclose to you what is to come.

14 "He shall [a]glorify Me; for He shall take of Mine, and shall disclose *it* to you.

15 "[a]All things that the Father has are Mine; therefore I said, that He takes of Mine, and will disclose *it* to you.

16 "[a]A little while, and [b]you *will* no longer behold Me; and again a little while, and [c]you will see Me."

17 *Some* of His disciples therefore said to one another, "What is this thing He is telling us, '[a]A little while, and you *will* not behold Me; and again a little while, and you will see Me'; and, 'Because [b]I go to the Father'?"

18 And so they were saying, "What is this that He says, 'A little while'? We do not know what He is talking about."

19 [a]Jesus knew that they wished to question Him, and He said to them, "Are you deliberating

3 [a]John 15:21; 8:19, 55; 17:25; Acts 3:17; 1 John 3:1

4 [1]Lit., *may remember them, that I told you* [a]John 13:19 [b]Luke 1:2

5 [a]John 7:33; 16:10, 17, 28 [b]John 13:36; 14:5

6 [a]John 16:22; 14:1

7 [1]Gr. *Paracletos*, equals one called alongside to help, or, *Intercessor* [a]John 14:16 [b]John 14:26

9 [a]John 15:22, 24

10 [a]Acts 3:14; 7:52; 17:31; 1 Pet. 3:18 [b]John 16:5

11 [a]John 12:31

13 [a]John 14:17 [b]John 14:26

14 [a]John 7:39

15 [a]John 17:10

16 [a]John 7:33 [b]John 16:16-24; 14:18-24 [c]John 16:22

17 [a]John 16:16 [b]John 16:5

19 [a]John 6:61; Mark 9:32

20 aMark 16:10; Luke 23:27
bJohn 20:20

21 1Lit., a human being
aIs. 13:8; 21:3; 26:17; 66:7;
Hos. 13:13; Mic. 4:9;
1 Thess. 5:3

22 aJohn 16:6 bJohn 16:16

23 1Lit., will question Me
nothing
aJohn 16:26; 14:20 bJohn
16:19, 30 cJohn 15:16

24 aJohn 14:14 bJohn 3:29;
15:11

25 1Lit., in proverbs or, in
figures of speech
aJohn 16:29; 10:6; Matt.
13:34 bJohn 16:2

26 aJohn 16:23; 14:20 bJohn
16:19, 30

27 aJohn 14:21, 23 bJohn
16:30; 2:11 cJohn 8:42; 16:30

28 aJohn 8:42; 16:30 bJohn
16:5, 10, 17; 13:1, 3

29 1Lit., a proverb
aJohn 16:25; 10:6; Matt.
13:34

30 aJohn 16:27; 2:11 bJohn
8:42; 16:28

32 aJohn 4:23; 16:2, 25
bMatt. 26:31; Zech. 13:7
cJohn 19:27 dJohn 8:29

33 aJohn 14:27 bJohn
15:18ff.

together about this, that I said, 'A little while, and you *will* not behold Me, and again a little while, and you *will* see Me'?

20 "Truly, truly, I say to you, that ªyou will weep and lament, but the world will rejoice; you will be sorrowful, but ᵇyour sorrow will be turned to joy.

21 "ªWhenever a woman is in travail she has sorrow, because her hour has come; but when she gives birth to the child, she remembers the anguish no more, for joy that a ¹child has been born into the world.

22 "Therefore ªyou, too, now have sorrow; but ᵇI will see you again, and your heart will rejoice, and no one takes your joy away from you.

23 "And ªin that day ᵇyou will ¹ask Me no question. Truly, truly, I say to you, cif you shall ask the Father for anything, He will give it to you in My name.

24 "ªUntil now you have asked for nothing in My name; ask, and you will receive, that your ᵇjoy may be made full.

25 "These things I have spoken to you in ¹ªfigurative language; ᵇan hour is coming, when I will speak no more to you in ¹figurative language, but will tell you plainly of the Father.

26 "ªIn that day ᵇyou will ask in My name; and I do not say to you that I will request the Father on your behalf;

27 for ªthe Father Himself loves you, because you have loved Me, and ᵇhave believed that cI came forth from the Father.

28 "ªI came forth from the Father, and have come into the world; I am leaving the world again, and ᵇgoing to the Father."

29 His disciples *said, "Lo, now You are speaking plainly, and are not using ªa ¹figure of speech.

30 "Now we know that You know all things, and have no need for anyone to question You; by this we ªbelieve that You ᵇcame from God."

31 Jesus answered them, "Do you now believe?

32 "Behold, ªan hour is coming, and has *already* come, for ᵇyou to be scattered, each to chis own *home*, and to leave Me alone; and *yet* dI am not alone, because the Father is with Me.

33 "These things I have spoken to you, that ªin Me you may have peace. ᵇIn the world you have

tribulation, but ᶜtake courage; ᵈI have overcome the world."

33 ᶜMatt. 9:2 ᵈRom. 8:37;
2 Cor. 2:14; 4:7ff.; 6:4ff.;
Rev. 3:21; 12:11

CHAPTER 17

1 ªJohn 11;41 ᵇJohn 7:39;
13:31f.

THESE things Jesus spoke; and ªlifting up His eyes to heaven, He said, "Father, the hour has come; ᵇglorify Thy Son, that the Son may glorify Thee,

2 ¹Lit., *flesh* ²Lit., *all that
which Thou hast given Him,
to them He*
ªJohn 3:35 ᵇJohn 17:6, 9, 24;
6:37, 39 ᶜJohn 10:28

2   even as ªThou gavest Him authority over all ¹mankind, that ᵇto ²all whom Thou hast given Him, ᶜHe may give eternal life.

3 ªJohn 5:44 ᵇJohn 3:17;
17:8, 21, 23, 25

3   "And this is eternal life, that they may know Thee ªthe only true God, and Jesus Christ whom ᵇThou hast sent.

4 ªJohn 13:31 ᵇJohn 4:34;
Luke 22:37

4   "ªI glorified Thee on the earth, ᵇhaving accomplished the work which Thou hast given Me to do.

5 ªJohn 17:1 ᵇJohn 1:1;
8:58; Phil. 2:6; John 17:24

5   "And now, ªglorify Thou Me together with Thyself, Father, with the glory which I ever had ᵇwith Thee before the world was.

6 ªJohn 17:26 ᵇJohn 17:2,
9, 24; John 6:37, 39 ᶜJohn
17:9 ᵈJohn 8:51

6   "ªI manifested Thy name to the men whom ᵇThou gavest Me out of the world; ᶜThine they were, and Thou gavest them to Me, and they have ᵈkept Thy word.

8 ªJohn 6:68; 12:49 ᵇJohn
17:14, 26; 15:15 ᶜJohn 8:42;
16:27, 30 ᵈJohn 3:17; 17:18,
21, 23, 25

7   "Now they have come to know that everything Thou hast given Me is from Thee;

8   for ªthe words which ªThou gavest Me ᵇI have given to them; and they received *them*, and truly understood that ᶜI came forth from Thee, and they believed that ᵈThou didst send Me.

9 ªLuke 22:32; John 14:16
ᵇJohn 17:20f.; Luke 23:34
ᶜJohn 17:2, 6, 24; 6:37, 39
ᵈJohn 17:6

9   "ªI ask on their behalf; ᵇI do not ask on behalf of the world, but of those whom ᶜThou hast given Me; for ᵈthey are Thine;

10 ªJohn 16:15

10   and ªall things that are Mine are Thine, and Thine are Mine; and I have been glorified in them.

11 ªJohn 13:1 ᵇJohn 17:13;
7:33 ᶜJohn 17:25 ᵈPhil. 2:9;
Rev. 19:12; John 17:6 ᵉJohn
17:21f.; Rom. 12:5; Gal. 3:28

11   "And I am no more in the world; and *yet* ªthey themselves are in the world, and ᵇI come to Thee. ᶜHoly Father, keep them in Thy name, *the name* ᵈwhich Thou hast given Me, that ᵉthey may be one, even as We *are*.

12 ªPhil. 2:9; Rev. 19:12;
John 17:6 ᵇJohn 6:39; 18:9
ᶜJohn 6:70 ᵈPs. 41:9

12   "While I was with them, I was keeping them in Thy name ªwhich Thou hast given Me; and I guarded them, and ᵇnot one of them perished but ᶜthe son of perdition, that the ᵈScripture might be fulfilled.

13 ªJohn 17:11; 7:33 ᵇJohn
15:11

13   "But now ªI come to Thee; and ᵇthese things

13 cJohn 3:29

14 aJohn 15:19 bJohn 17:16; 8:23

15 1Or, *out of* the power of
2Or, *evil*
aMatt. 5:37

16 aJohn 17:14

17 aJohn 15:3

18 aJohn 17:3, 8, 21, 23, 25; 3:17 bJohn 20:21; Matt. 10:5; John 4:38

19 aJohn 15:13 bJohn 15:3 c2 Cor. 7:14; Col. 1:6; 1 John 3:18

21 1Gr. tense indicates *continually believe* aJohn 10:38; 17:23; 17:11 bJohn 17:8 cJohn 17:3, 8, 18, 23, 25; 3:17

22 aJohn 17:24; 1:14

23 1Lit., *into a unit* 2Gr. tense indicates *continually know* aJohn 10:38; 17:21; John 17:11 bJohn 17:3, 8, 18, 21, 25; John 3:17 cJohn 16:27

24 1Gr., *that which Thou hast given Me, I desire that where I am, they also may be with Me, that* aJohn 17:2 bJohn 12:26 cJohn 17:22; 1:14 dMatt. 25:34; John 17:5

25 1Lit., *and* aJohn 17:11; 1 John 1:9 bJohn 7:29; 15:21 cJohn 17:3, 8, 18, 21, 23; 3:17

26 aJohn 17:6 bJohn 15:9

1 1Gr., *winter-torrent* aMatt. 26:30, 36; Mark 14:26, 32; Luke 22:39 b2 Sam. 15:23; 1 Kin. 2:37; 15:13; 2 Kin. 23:4, 6, 12; 2 Chr. 15:16; 29:16; 30:14; Jer. 31:40 cMatt. 26:36; Mark 14:32; John 18:26

2 1Or, *delivering Him up*

I speak in the world, that they may have My cjoy made full in themselves.

14 "I have given them Thy word; and athe world has hated them, because bthey are not of the world, even as I am not of the world.

15 "I do not ask Thee to take them out of the world, but to keep them 1from 2athe evil *one*.

16 "aThey are not of the world, even as I am not of the world.

17 "aSanctify them in the truth; Thy word is truth.

18 "As aThou didst send Me into the world, bI also have sent them into the world.

19 "And for their sakes I asanctify Myself, that they themselves also may be bsanctified cin truth.

20 "I do not ask in behalf of these alone, but for those also who believe in Me through their word;

21 that they may all be one; aeven as Thou, Father, *art* in Me, and I in Thee, that they also may be in Us; bthat the world may 1believe that cThou didst send Me.

22 "And the aglory which Thou hast given Me I have given to them; that they may be one, just as We are one;

23 aI in them, and Thou in Me, that they may be perfected 1in unity, that the world may 2know that bThou didst send Me, and didst clove them, even as Thou didst love Me.

24 "Father, 1I desire that athey also whom Thou hast given Me bbe with Me where I am, in order that they may behold My cglory, which Thou hast given Me; for Thou didst love Me before dthe foundation of the world.

25 "O arighteous Father, 1although bthe world has not known Thee, 1yet I have known Thee; and these have known that cThou didst send Me;

26 and aI have made Thy name known to them, and will make it known; that bthe love wherewith Thou didst love Me may be in them, and I in them."

CHAPTER 18

WHEN Jesus had spoken these words, aHe went forth with His disciples over bthe 1ravine of the Kidron, where there was ca garden, into which He Himself entered, and His disciples.

2 Now Judas also, who was 1betraying Him,

knew the place; for Jesus had [a]often met there with His disciples.

3   [a]Judas then, having received [b]the [1]*Roman* cohort, and [c]officers from the chief priests and the Pharisees, *came there with lanterns and [d]torches and weapons.

4   Jesus therefore, [a]knowing all the things that were coming upon Him, went forth, and *said to them, "[b]Whom do you seek?"

5   They answered Him, "Jesus the Nazarene." He *said to them, "I am *He*." And Judas also who was betraying Him, was standing with them.

6   When therefore He said to them, "I am *He*", they drew back, and fell to the ground.

7   Again therefore He asked them, "[a]Whom do you seek?" And they said, "Jesus the Nazarene."

8   Jesus answered, "I told you that I am *He*; if therefore you seek Me, let these go their way,"

9   that the word might be fulfilled which He spoke, "[a]Of those whom Thou hast given Me I lost not one."

10   Simon Peter therefore [a]having a sword, drew it, and struck the high priest's slave, and cut off his right ear; and the slave's name was Malchus.

11   Jesus therefore said to Peter, "Put the sword into the sheath; [a]the cup which the Father has given Me, shall I not drink it?"

12   [a]So [b]the *Roman* [1]cohort and the [2]commander, and the [b]officers of the Jews, arrested Jesus and bound him,

13   and led Him to [a]Annas first; for he was father-in-law of [b]Caiaphas, who was high priest that year.

14   Now Caiaphas was the one who had advised the Jews that [a]it was expedient for one man to die on behalf of the people.

15   And [a]Simon Peter was following Jesus, and *so was* another disciple. Now that disciple was known to the high priest, and entered with Jesus into [b]the court of the high priest,

16   [a]but Peter was standing at the door outside. So the other disciple, who was known to the high priest, went out and spoke to the doorkeeper, and brought in Peter.

17   [a]The slave-girl therefore who kept the door *said to Peter, "[b]You are not also *one* of this man's disciples, are you?" He *said, "I am not."

18   Now the slaves and the [a]officers were stand-

2 [a]Luke 21:37; 22:39

3 [1]Normally 600 men; *a battalion*
[a]John 18:3-11; *Matt.* 26:47-56; *Mark* 14:43-50; *Luke* 22:47-53 [b]John 18:12; *Acts* 10:1 [c]John 7:32; 18:12, 18
[d]Matt. 25:1 and marg.

4 [a]John 6:64; 13:1, 11
[b]John 18:7

7 [a]John 18:4

9 [a]John 17:12

10 [a]Matt. 26:51; Mark 14:47

11 [a]Matt. 20:22

12 [1]Or, *battalion* [2]Lit., *chiliarch*, in command of a thousand troops
[a]John 18:12f.: *Matt.* 26:57ff.
[b]John 18:3

13 [a]John 18:24; Luke 3:2
[b]Matt. 26:3; John 11:49, 51

14 [a]John 11:50

15 [a]Matt. 26:58; Mark 14:54; Luke 22:54 [b]Matt. 26:3; John 18:24, 28

16 [a]John 18:16-18: *Matt.* 26:69f.; *Mark* 14:66-68; *Luke* 22:55-57

17 [a]Acts 12:13 [b]John 18:25

18 [a]John 18:3

18 bMark 14:54, 67 cJohn 21:9

19 aJohn 18:19-24: Matt. 26:59-68; Mark 14:55-65; Luke 22:63-71

20 1Lit., synagogue aJohn 7:26; 8:26 bMatt. 4:23; John 6:59 cMatt. 26:55

22 aJohn 18:3 bJohn 19:3

23 aMatt. 5:39; Acts 23:2-5

24 aJohn 18:13

25 aJohn 18:25-27; Matt. 26:71-75; Mark 14:69-72; Luke 22:58-62 bJohn 18:18 cJohn 18:17

26 aJohn 18:10 bJohn 18:1

27 aJohn 13:38

28 1Or, governor's official residence aMatt. 27:2; Mark 15:1; Luke 23:1 bJohn 18:13 cJohn 18:33; 19:9; Matt. 27:27 dJohn 11:55; Acts 11:3

29 aJohn 18:29-38; Matt. 27:11-14; Mark 15:2-5; Luke 23:2, 3

32 aJohn 12:32f.; 3:14; 8:28; Matt. 20:19; 26:2; Mark 10:33f.; Luke 18:32f.

33 aJohn 18:28, 29; 19:9

ing *there*, bhaving made ca charcoal fire, for it was cold and they were warming themselves; and Peter also was with them, standing and warming himself.

19 aThe high priest therefore questioned Jesus about His disciples, and about His teaching.

20 Jesus answered him, "I ahave spoken openly to the world; I always btaught in 1synagogues, and cin the temple, where all the Jews come together; and I spoke nothing in secret.

21 "Why do you question Me? Question those who have heard what I spoke to them; behold, these know what I said."

22 And when He had said this, one of the aofficers standing by bgave Jesus a blow, saying, "Is that the way You answer the high priest?"

23 aJesus answered him, "If I have spoken wrongly, bear witness of the wrong; but if rightly, why do you strike Me?"

24 aAnnas therefore sent Him bound to aCaiaphas the high priest.

25 aNow bSimon Peter was standing and warming himself. They said therefore to him, "cYou are not also *one* of His disciples, are you?" He denied *it*, and said, "I am not."

26 One of the slaves of the high priest, being a relative of the one awhose ear Peter cut off, *said, "Did I not see you in bthe garden with Him?"

27 Peter therefore denied *it* again; and immediately aa cock crowed.

28 aThey *led Jesus therefore from bCaiaphas into cthe 1Praetorium; and it was early; and they themselves did not enter into cthe 1Praetorium in order that dthey might not be defiled, but might eat the Passover.

29 aPilate therefore went out to them, and *said, "What accusation do you bring against this Man?"

30 They answered and said to him, "If this Man were not an evildoer, we would not have delivered Him up to you."

31 Pilate therefore said to them, "Take Him yourselves, and judge Him according to your law." The Jews said to him, "We are not permitted to put any one to death,"

32 that athe word of Jesus might be fulfilled, which He spoke, signifying by what kind of death He was about to die.

33 Pilate therefore aentered again into the

Praetorium, and summoned Jesus, and said to Him, "ᵇYou are the King of the Jews?"

34 Jesus answered, "Are you saying this ¹on your own initiative, or did others tell you about Me?"

35 Pilate answered, "I am not a Jew, am I? Your own nation and the chief priests delivered You up to me; what have You done?"

36 Jesus answered, "ᵃMy kingdom ¹is not of this world. If My kingdom were of this world, then My servants would be fighting, that I might not be delivered up to the Jews; but as it is My kingdom is not ²of this realm."

37 Pilate therefore said to Him, "So You are a king?" Jesus answered, "ᵃYou say *correctly* that I am a king. For this I have been born, and for this I have come into the world, ᵇto bear witness to the truth. ᶜEvery one who is of the truth hears My voice."

38 Pilate *said to Him, "What is truth?"

And when he had said this, he ᵃwent out again to the Jews, and *said to them, "ᵇI find no guilt in Him.

39 "ᵃBut you have a custom, that I should release someone ¹for you at the Passover; do you wish then that I release ¹for you the King of the Jews?"

40 Therefore they cried out again, saying, "ᵃNot this Man, but Barabbas." Now Barabbas was a robber.

CHAPTER 19

THEN Pilate therefore took Jesus, and ¹ᵃscourged Him.

2 ᵃAnd the soldiers wove a crown of thorns and put it on His head, and arrayed Him in a purple robe;

3 and they *began* to come up to Him, and say, "ᵃHail, King of the Jews!" and to ᵇgive Him blows in the face.

4 And Pilate ᵃcame out again, and *said to them, "Behold, I am bringing Him out to you, that you may know that ᵇI find no guilt in Him."

5 Jesus therefore came out, ᵃwearing the crown of thorns and the purple robe. And *Pilate* *said to them, "Behold, the Man!"

6 When therefore the chief priests and the

33 ᵇLuke 23:3; John 19:12

34 ¹Lit., *from yourself*

36 ¹Or, *is not derived from* ²Lit., *from here* ᵃJohn 6:15; Matt. 26:53; Luke 17:21

37 ᵃMatt. 27:11; Mark 15:2; Luke 22:70; 23:3 ᵇJohn 3:32; 8:14; 1:14 ᶜJohn 8:47; 1 John 4:6

38 ᵃJohn 19:4; 18:33 ᵇLuke 23:4; John 19:4

39 ¹Or, *to you* ᵃJohn 18:39-19:16: Matt. 27:15-18, 20-23; Mark 15:6-15; Luke 23:18-25

40 ᵃActs 3:14

1 ¹Or, *had Him scourged* ᵃMatt. 27:26

2 ᵃMatt. 27:27-30: Mark 15:16-19

3 ᵃMatt. 27:29; Mark 15:18 ᵇJohn 18:22

4 ᵃJohn 18:38; 18:33 ᵇJohn 18:38; 19:6; Luke 23:4

5 ᵃJohn 19:2

237

John 19

**Pilate Releases Jesus to the Jews.
The Crucifixion.**

6 ªJohn 18:3; Matt. 26:58
ᵇJohn 18:38; 19:4; Luke 23:4

7 ªLev. 24:16; Matt. 26:63-
66 ᵇJohn 5:18; 10:33

9 ¹Or, governor's official
residence
ªJohn 18:33 ᵇMatt. 26:63;
27:12, 14; John 18:34-37

11 ¹Lit., against
ªRom. 13:1 ᵇJohn 18:13f.,
28ff.; Acts 3:13

12 ¹Lit., was seeking to ²Or,
speaks against
ªLuke 23:2; John 18:33ff.

13 ¹Gr., The Lithostrotos
²I.e., Jewish Aramaic
ªMatt. 27:19 ᵇJohn 5:2;
19:17, 20

14 ¹I.e., noon
ªMatt. 27:62; John 19:31, 42
ᵇMark 15:25; Matt. 27:45
ᶜJohn 19:19, 21

15 ªLuke 23:18

16 ªMatt. 27:26; Mark
15:15; Luke 23:25

17 ¹Lit., bearing the cross
for Himself ²I.e., Jewish
Aramaic
ªJohn 19:17-24; Matt. 27:33-
44; Mark 15:22-32; Luke
23:33-43 ᵇLuke 14:27; Matt.
27:32; Mark 15:21; Luke
23:26 ᶜLuke 23:33 and marg.
ᵈJohn 19:13

18 ªLuke 23:32

19 ªMatt. 27:37; Mark
15:26; Luke 23:38

ªofficers saw Him, they cried out, saying, "Crucify, crucify!" Pilate *said to them, "Take Him yourselves, and crucify Him, for ᵇI find no guilt in Him."

7 The Jews answered him, "ªWe have a law, and by that law He ought to die because He ᵇmade Himself *to be* the Son of God."

8 When Pilate therefore heard this statement, he was the more afraid;

9 and he ªentered into the ¹Praetorium again, and *said to Jesus, "Where are You from?" But ᵇJesus gave him no answer.

10 Pilate therefore *said to Him, "You do not speak to me? Do You not know that I have authority to release You, and I have authority to crucify You?"

11 Jesus answered, "ªYou would have no authority ¹over Me, unless it had been given you from above; for this reason ᵇhe who delivered Me up to you has *the* greater sin."

12 As a result of this Pilate ¹made efforts to release Him, but the Jews cried out, saying, "ªIf you release this Man, you are no friend of Caesar; every one who makes himself out *to be* a king ²opposes Caesar."

13 When Pilate therefore heard these words, he brought Jesus out, and ªsat down on the judgment-seat at a place called ¹The Pavement, but ᵇin ²Hebrew, Gabbatha.

14 Now it was ªthe day of preparation for the Passover; it was about the ¹ᵇsixth hour. And he *said to the Jews, "Behold, ᶜyour King!"

15 They therefore cried out, "ªAway with *Him*, away with *Him*, crucify Him!" Pilate *said to them, "Shall I crucify your King?" The chief priests answered, "We have no king but Caesar."

16 And so he then ªdelivered Him up to them to be crucified.

17 ªThey took Jesus therefore; and He went out, ¹ᵇbearing His own cross, to the place called ᶜthe Place of a Skull, which is called ᵈin ²Hebrew Golgotha;

18 where they crucified Him, and with Him ªtwo other men, one on either side, and Jesus in between.

19 And Pilate wrote an inscription also, and put it on the cross. And it was written, "ªJESUS

"Woman, Behold Your Son!" "Behold, Your Mother!" "I Thirst." "It Is Finished."

John 19

THE NAZARENE, [b]THE KING OF THE JEWS."

20   Therefore this inscription many of the Jews read, for the place where Jesus was crucified was near the city; and it was written [a]in [1]Hebrew, Latin, *and* in Greek.

21   And so the chief priests of the Jews were saying to Pilate, "Do not write, '[a]The King of the Jews'; but that He said, 'I am [a]King of the Jews.' "

22   Pilate answered, "[a]What I have written I have written."

23   [a]The soldiers therefore, when they had crucified Jesus, took His outer garments and made [b]four parts, a part to every soldier and *also* the [1]tunic; now the tunic was seamless, woven [2]in one piece.

24   They said therefore to one another, "[a]Let us not tear it, but cast [1]lots for it, *to decide* whose it shall be;" [b]that the Scripture might be fulfilled, "They [c]divided My outer garments among them, and for My clothing they cast [1]lots."

25   Therefore the soldiers did these things. [a]But there were standing by the cross of Jesus [b]His mother, and His mother's sister, Mary the *wife* of [c]Clopas, and [d]Mary Magdalene.

26   When Jesus therefore saw His mother, and [a]the disciple whom He loved standing nearby, He *said to His mother, "[b]Woman, behold, your son!"

27   Then He *said to the disciple, "Behold, your mother!" And from that hour the disciple took her into [a]his own *household*.

28   After this Jesus, [a]knowing that all things had already been accomplished, [b]in order that the Scripture might be fulfilled, *said, "[c]I am thirsty."

29   A jar full of sour wine was standing there; so [a]they put a sponge full of the sour wine upon *a branch of* hyssop, and brought it up to His mouth.

30   When Jesus therefore had received the sour wine, He said, "[a]It is finished!" And He bowed His head, and [b]gave up His spirit.

31   The Jews therefore, because it was [a]the day of preparation, so that [b]the bodies should not remain on the cross on the Sabbath ([1]for that Sabbath was a [c]high *day*), asked Pilate that their legs might be broken, and *that* they might be taken away.

32   The soldiers therefore came, and broke the

19 [b]John 19:14, 21

20 [1]I.e., Jewish Aramaic
[a]John 19:13

21 [a]John 19:14, 19

22 [a]Gen. 43:14; Esther 4:16

23 [1]Gr., *khiton*, the garment worn next to the skin [2]Lit., *woven from the upper part through the whole*
[a]Matt. 27:35; Mark 15:24; Luke 23:34 [b]Acts 12:4

24 [1]Lit., *a lot*
[a]Matt. 27:35; Mark 15:24; Luke 23:34; Ex. 28:32 [b]John 19:28, 36f. [c]Ps. 22:18

25 [a]Matt. 27:55f.; Mark 15:40f.; Luke 23:49 [b]Matt. 12:46 [c]Luke 24:18 [d]John 20:1, 18; Luke 8:2

26 [a]John 13:23 [b]John 2:4

27 [a]Luke 18:28 marg.; John 1:11; 16:32; Acts 21:6 [Gr.]

28 [a]John 13:1; 17:4 [b]John 19:24, 36f. [c]Ps. 69:21

29 [a]John 19:29, 30, Matt. 27:48, 50; Mark 15:36f.; Luke 23:36

30 [a]John 17:4 [b]Matt. 27:50; Mark 15:37; Luke 23:46

31 [1]Lit., *for the day of that Sabbath was great*
[a]John 19:14, 42 [b]Deut. 21:23; Josh. 8:29; 10:26f. [c]Ex. 12:16

239

32 [a]John 19:18

34 [a]1 John 5:6, 8

35 [a]John 15:27; 21:24

36 [1]Or, *crushed* or *shattered* [a]John 19:24, 28 [b]Ex. 12:46; Num. 9:12; Ps. 34:20

37 [a]Zech. 12:10

38 [a]John 19:38-42: *Matt. 27:57-61; Mark 15:42-47; Luke 23:50-56* [b]Mark 15:43 [c]John 7:13

39 [1]Another reading, *package of* [2]Lit., 100 litras (12 oz. each) [a]John 3:1 [b]Mark 16:1 [c]Ps. 45:8; Prov. 7:17; Song 4:14; Matt. 2:11 [d]John 12:3

40 [a]John 11:44; Matt. 26:12; Mark 14:8 [b]John 20:5, 7; Luke 24:12

41 [a]Matt. 27:60 [b]Luke 23:53

42 [a]John 19:14, 31 [b]John 19:20, 41

1 [a]John 20:1-8: Matt. 28:1-8; Mark 16:1-8; Luke 24:1-10 [b]John 19:25; John 20:18 [c]Matt. 27:60, 66; 28:2; Mark 15:46; 16:3f.; Luke 24:2; John 11:38

2 [1]Lit., *was loving* [a]John 13:23 [b]John 20:13

3 [a]John 20:3-10; Luke 24:12

240

legs of the first man, and of the other man who was [a]crucified with Him;

33　but coming to Jesus, when they saw that He was already dead, they did not break His legs;

34　but one of the soldiers pierced His side with a spear, and immediately there came out [a]blood and water.

35　And he who has seen has [a]borne witness, and his witness is true; and he knows that he is telling the truth, so that you also may believe.

36　For these things came to pass, [a]that the Scripture might be fulfilled, "[b]Nᴏᴛ ᴀ ʙᴏɴᴇ ᴏғ Hɪᴍ sʜᴀʟʟ ʙᴇ [1]ʙʀᴏᴋᴇɴ."

37　And again another Scripture says, "[a]Tʜᴇʏ sʜᴀʟʟ ʟᴏᴏᴋ ᴏɴ Hɪᴍ ᴡʜᴏᴍ ᴛʜᴇʏ ᴘɪᴇʀᴄᴇᴅ."

38　[a]And after these things Joseph of Arimathea, being a disciple of Jesus, but a [b]secret *one*, for [c]fear of the Jews, asked Pilate that he might take away the body of Jesus; and Pilate granted permission. He came therefore, and took away His body.

39　And [a]Nicodemus came also, who had first come to Him by night; [b]bringing a [1]mixture of [c]myrrh and aloes, about a [d]hundred [2]pounds *weight*.

40　And so they took the body of Jesus, and [a]bound it in [b]linen wrappings with the spices, as is the burial custom of the Jews.

41　Now in the place where He was crucified there was a garden; and in the garden a [a]new tomb, [b]in which no one had yet been laid.

42　Therefore on account of the Jewish day of [a]preparation, because the tomb was [b]nearby, they laid Jesus there.

^a

Cʜᴀᴘᴛᴇʀ 20

Nᴏᴡ on the first *day* of the week [b]Mary Magdalene *came early to the tomb, while it *was still dark, and *saw [c]the stone *already* taken away from the tomb.

2　And so she *ran and *came to Simon Peter, and to the other [a]disciple whom Jesus [1]loved, and *said to them, "[b]They have taken away the Lord out of the tomb, and we do not know where they have laid Him."

3　[a]Peter therefore went forth, and the other disciple, and they were going to the tomb.

4　And the two were running together; and the

other disciple ran ahead faster than Peter, and came to the tomb first;

5   and [a]stooping and looking in, he *saw the [b]linen wrappings lying *there;* but he did not go in.

6   Simon Peter therefore also *came, following him, and entered the tomb; and he *beheld the linen wrappings lying *there,*

7   and [a]the face-cloth, which had been on His head, not lying with the [b]linen wrappings, but rolled up in a place by itself.

8   Then entered in therefore the other disciple also, who [a]had first come to the tomb, and he saw, and believed.

9   For as yet [a]they did not understand the Scripture, [b]that He must rise again from the dead.

10   So the disciples went away again [a]to their own homes.

11   [a]But Mary was standing outside the tomb weeping; and so, as she wept, she [b]stooped and looked into the tomb;

12   and she *beheld [a]two angels in white sitting, one at the head, and one at the feet, where the body of Jesus had been lying.

13   And they *said to her, "[a]Woman, why are you weeping?" She *said to them, "Because [b]they have taken away my Lord, and I do not know where they have laid Him."

14   When she had said this, she turned around, and *[a]beheld Jesus standing *there,* and [b]did not know that it was Jesus.

15   Jesus *said to her, "[a]Woman, why are you weeping? Whom are you seeking?" Supposing Him to be the gardener, she *said to Him, "Sir, if you have carried Him away, tell me where you have laid Him, and I will take Him away."

16   Jesus *said to her, "Mary!" She *turned and *said to Him [a]in [1]Hebrew, "[b]Rabboni," (which means, Teacher.)

17   Jesus *said to her, "Stop clinging to Me; for I have not yet ascended to the Father; but go to [a]My brethren, and say to them, 'I [b]ascend to My Father and your Father, and My God and your God.' "

18   [a]Mary Magdalene *came, [b]announcing to the disciples, "I have seen the Lord;" and *that* He had said these things to her.

19   When therefore it was evening, on that day, the first *day* of the week, and when the doors were

5 [a]John 20:11 [b]John 19:40

7 [a]John 11:44 [b]John 19:40

8 [a]John 20:4

9 [a]Matt. 22:29; John 2:22 [b]Luke 24:26ff., 46

10 [a]Luke 24:12

11 [a]Mark 16:5 [b]John 20:5

12 [a]Luke 24:4; Matt. 28:2f.; Mark 16:5

13 [a]John 20:15 [b]John 20:2

14 [a]Mark 16:9; Matt. 28:9 [b]John 21:4

15 [a]John 20:13

16 [1]I.e., Jewish Aramaic [a]John 5:2 [b]Mark 10:51; Matt. 23:7

17 [a]Matt. 28:10 [b]John 7:33; Mark 16:19; 12:26

18 [a]John 20:1 [b]Mark 16:10; Luke 24:10, 23

19 ¹Lit., *Peace to you*
ᵃJohn 7:13 ᵇJohn 20:21, 26;
Luke 24:36; John 14:27

20 ᵃLuke 24:39, 40; John
19:34 ᵇJohn 16:20, 22

21 ¹Here as in verse 19 and
26
ᵃJohn 20:19, 26; Luke 24:36;
John 14:27 ᵇJohn 17:18

23 ¹I.e., have previously
been forgiven
ᵃMatt. 18:18; Matt. 16:19

24 ¹I.e., the Twin
ᵃJohn 11:16 ᵇJohn 6:67

25 ᵃJohn 20:20 ᵇMark 16:11

26 ¹Or, *a week later* ²Or,
locked
ᵃJohn 20:19, 21; Luke 24:36;
John 14:27

27 ᵃJohn 20:25; Luke 24:40

29 ᵃ1 Pet. 1:8

30 ¹Or, *attesting miracles*
ᵃJohn 21:25 ᵇJohn 2:11

31 ¹I.e., The Messiah
ᵃJohn 19:35 ᵇMatt. 4:3 ᶜJohn
3:15

1 ¹Or, *made Himself
visible*
ᵃJohn 21:14; Mark 16:12
ᵇJohn 20:19, 26 ᶜJohn 6:1

242

shut where the disciples were, for ᵃfear of the Jews, Jesus came and stood in their midst, and *said to them, "¹ᵇPeace *be* with you."

20 And when He had said this, ᵃHe showed them both His hands and His side. The disciples therefore ᵇrejoiced when they saw the Lord.

21 Jesus therefore said to them again, "¹ᵃPeace *be* with you; ᵇas the Father has sent Me, I also send you."

22 And when He had said this, He breathed on them, and *said to them, "Receive the Holy Spirit.

23 "ᵃIf you forgive the sins of any, *their sins* ¹have been forgiven them; if you retain the *sins* of any, they have been retained."

24 But ᵃThomas, one of ᵇthe twelve, called ¹ᵃDidymus, was not with them when Jesus came.

25 The other disciples therefore were saying to him, "We have seen the Lord!" But he said to them, "Unless I shall see in ᵃHis hands the imprint of the nails, and put my finger into the place of the nails, and put my hand into His side, ᵇI will not believe."

26 And ¹after eight days again His disciples were inside, and Thomas with them. Jesus *came, the doors having been ²shut, and stood in their midst, and said, "ᵃPeace *be* with you."

27 Then He *said to Thomas, "ᵃReach here your finger, and see My hands; and reach here your hand, and put it into My side; and be not unbelieving, but believing."

28 Thomas answered and said to Him, "My Lord and my God!"

29 Jesus *said to him, "Because you have seen Me, have you believed? ᵃBlessed *are* they who did not see, and *yet* believed."

30 ᵃMany other ¹ᵇsigns therefore Jesus also performed in the presence of the disciples, which are not written in this book;

31 but these have been written ᵃthat you may believe that Jesus is ¹the Christ, ᵇthe Son of God; and that ᶜbelieving you may have life in His name.

CHAPTER 21

AFTER these things Jesus ¹ᵃmanifested Himself ᵇagain to the disciples at the ᶜsea of Tiberias; and He manifested *Himself* in this way.

2 There were together Simon Peter, and

ªThomas called ¹Didymus, and ᵇNathanael of ᶜCana in Galilee, and ᵈthe *sons* of Zebedee, and two others of His disciples.

3 Simon Peter *said to them, "I am going fishing." They *said to him, "We will also come with you." They went out, and got into the boat; and ªthat night they caught nothing.

4 But when the day was now breaking, Jesus stood on the beach; yet the disciples did not ªknow that it was Jesus.

5 Jesus therefore *said to them, "Children, ªyou do not have any ¹fish, do you?" They answered Him, "No."

6 And He said to them, "ªCast the net on the right-hand side of the boat, and you will find *a catch.*" They cast therefore, and then they were not able to haul it in because of the great number of fish.

7 ªThat disciple therefore whom Jesus ¹loved *said to Peter, "It is the Lord." And so when Simon Peter heard that it was the Lord, he put his outer garment on (for he was stripped *for work*), and threw himself into the sea.

8 But the other disciples came in the little boat, for they were not far from the land, but about ¹one hundred yards away, dragging the net *full* of fish.

9 And so when they got out upon the land, they *saw a charcoal ªfire *already* laid, and ᵇfish placed on it, and bread.

10 Jesus *said to them, "Bring some of the ªfish which you have now caught."

11 Simon Peter went up, and drew the net to land, full of large fish, a hundred and fifty-three; and although there were so many, the net was not torn.

12 Jesus *said to them, "Come *and* have ªbreakfast." None of the disciples ventured to question Him, "Who are You?" knowing that it was the Lord.

13 Jesus *came and *took ªthe bread, and *gave them, and the ᵇfish likewise.

14 This is now the ªthird time that Jesus ¹was manifested to the disciples, after He was raised from the dead.

15 So when they had ªfinished breakfast, Jesus *said to Simon Peter, "Simon, ¹*son* of John, do you ²ᵇlove Me more than these?" He *said to Him,

2 ¹I.e., the Twin
ªJohn 11:16 ᵇJohn 1:45ff.
ᶜJohn 2:1 ᵈMatt. 4:21; Mark 1:19; Luke 5:10

3 ªLuke 5:5

4 ªJohn 20:14; Luke 24:16

5 ¹Lit., *something eaten with bread*
ªLuke 24:41

6 ªLuke 5:4ff.

7 ¹Lit., *was loving*
ªJohn 13:23; John 21:20

8 ¹Lit., *200 cubits*

9 ªJohn 18:18 ᵇJohn 21, 10, 13; John 6:9, 11

10 ªJohn 21:10, 13; John 6:9, 11

12 ªJohn 21:15

13 ªJohn 21:9 ᵇJohn 21:9, 10; 6:9, 11

14 ¹Or, *made Himself visible*
ªJohn 20:19, 26

15 ¹Here and in verses 16 and 17 some mss. read, *son of Jonas* ²Gr., agapao
ªJohn 21:12 ᵇJohn 13:37; Matt. 26:33; Mark 14:29

243

15 ³Gr., phileo
cLuke 12:32

16 ¹Gr., agapao ²Gr., phileo
aMatt. 2:6; Acts 20:28; 1 Pet.
5:2; Rev. 7:17

17 ¹Gr., phileo
aJohn 13:38 bJohn 16:30
cJohn 21:16

19 aJohn 12:33; 18:32
b2 Pet. 1:14 cMatt. 8:22;
16:24; John 21:22

20 aJohn 21:7 bJohn 13:25

22 a1 Cor. 4:5; 11:26; James
5:7; Rev. 2:25; Matt. 16:27f.
bMatt. 8:22; 16:24; John
21:19

23 aActs 1:15 b1 Cor. 4:5;
11:26; James 5:7; Rev. 2:25;
Matt. 16:27f.

24 aJohn 15:27

25 aJohn 20:30

244

"Yes, Lord; You know that I ³love You." He *said to him, "Tend cMy lambs."

16 He *said to him again a second time, "Simon, *son* of John, do you ¹love Me?" He *said to Him, "Yes, Lord; You know that I ²love You." He *said to him, "aShepherd My sheep."

17 He *said to him the third time, "Simon, *son* of John, do you ¹love Me?" Peter was grieved because He said to him athe third time, "Do you ¹love Me?" And he said to Him, "Lord, bYou know all things; You know that I ¹love You." Jesus *said to him, "cTend My sheep."

18 "Truly, truly, I say to you, when you were younger, you used to gird yourself, and walk wherever you wished; but when you grow old, you will stretch out your hands, and someone else will gird you, and bring you where you do not wish to go."

19 Now this He said, asignifying by bwhat kind of death he would glorify God. And when He had spoken this, He *said to him, "cFollow Me!"

20 Peter, turning around, *saw the adisciple whom Jesus loved following *them*; the one who also had bleaned back on His breast at the supper, and said, "Lord, who is the one who betrays You?"

21 Peter therefore seeing him *said to Jesus, "Lord, and what about this man?"

22 Jesus *said to him, "If I want him to remain auntil I come, what *is that* to you? You bfollow Me!"

23 This saying therefore went out among athe brethren that that disciple would not die; yet Jesus did not say to him that he would not die; but *only*, "If I want him to remain buntil I come, what *is that* to you?"

24 This is the disciple who abbears witness of these things, and wrote these things; and we know that his witness is true.

25 And there are also amany other things which Jesus did, which if they *were written in detail, I suppose that even the world itself *would not contain the books which *were written.

THE ACTS
OF THE APOSTLES

The Introduction. The Ascension.

THE first account I [1]composed, [a]Theophilus, about all that Jesus [b]began to do and teach,

2 until the day when He [a]was taken up, after He [b]had [1]by the Holy Spirit given orders to [c]the apostles whom He had [d]chosen.

3 To [1]these [a]He also presented Himself alive, after His suffering, by many convincing proofs, appearing to them over *a period of* forty days, and speaking of [b]the things concerning the kingdom of God.

4 And [1]gathering them together, He commanded them [a]not to leave Jerusalem, but to wait for [2b]what the Father had promised, "Which," *He said,* "you heard of from Me;

5 for [a]John baptized with water, but you shall be baptized [1]with the Holy Spirit [2b]not many days from now."

6 And so when they had come together, they were asking Him, saying, "Lord, [a]is it at this time You are restoring the kingdom to Israel?"

7 He said to them, "It is not for you to know times or epochs which [a]the Father has fixed by His own authority;

8 but you shall receive power [a]when the Holy Spirit has come upon you; and you shall be [b]My witnesses both in Jerusalem, and in all Judea and [c]Samaria, and even to [d]the remotest part of the earth."

9 And after He had said these things, [a]He was lifted up while they were looking on, and a cloud received Him out of their sight.

10 And as they were gazing intently into [1]the sky while He was departing, [2]behold, [a]two men in white clothing stood beside them;

11 and they also said, "[a]Men of Galilee, why do you stand looking into [1]the sky? This Jesus, who [b]has been taken up from you into heaven, will [c]come in just the same way as you have watched Him go into heaven."

12 Then they [a]returned to Jerusalem from the

1 [1]Lit., *made*
[a]Luke 1:3 [b]Luke 3:23

2 [1]Or, *through*
[a]Mark 16:19; Acts 1:9, 11, 22 [b]Matt. 28:19f.; Mark 16:15; John 20:21f.; Acts 10:42 [c]Mark 6:30 [and so elsewhere] [d]John 13:18; Acts 10:41

3 [1]Lit., *whom*
[a]Matt. 28:17; Mark 16:12, 14; Luke 24:34, 36; John 20:19, 26; 21:1, 14; 1 Cor. 15:5-7 [b]Acts 8:12; 19:8; 28:23, 31

4 [1]Or, *eating with;* or possibly, *lodging with* [2]Lit., *the promise of the Father* [a]Luke 24:49 [b]Acts 2:33; John 14:16, 26; 15:26

5 [1]Or, *in* [2]Lit., *after these many days* [a]Acts 11:16; Matt. 3:11 [b]Acts 2:1-4

6 [a]Matt. 17:11; Mark 9:12; Luke 17:20; 19:11

7 [a]Matt. 24:36; Mark 13:32

8 [a]Acts 2:1-4 [b]Luke 24:48; John 15:27 [c]Acts 8:1, 5, 14 [d]Matt. 28:19; Mark 16:15; Col. 1:23; Rom. 10:18

9 [a]Acts 1:2

10 [1]Or, *heaven* [2]Lit., *and behold* [a]Luke 24:4; John 20:12

11 [1]Or, *heaven* [a]Acts 2:7; 13:31 [b]Mark 16:19; Acts 1:9, 22 [c]Matt. 16:27f., Acts 3:21

12 [a]Luke 24:50, 52

F22

12 ¹Or, *hill* ²Or, *Olive Grove*
ᵇMatt. 21:1

13 ¹Or, *Jacob* ²Or possibly, *brother*
ᵃActs 9:37, 39; 20:8; Mark 14:15; Luke 22:12 ᵇActs 1:13; *Matt. 1:2-4; Mark 3:16-19; Luke 6:14-16* ᶜJohn 14:22

14 ¹Or, *certain women*
ᵃActs 2:42; 6:4; Rom. 12:12; Col. 4:2; Eph. 6:18 ᵇLuke 8:2f. ᶜMatt. 12:46

15 ¹Lit., *in these days* ²Lit., *names*
ᵃJohn 21:23; Acts 6:3; 9:30; 10:23; 11:1, 12, 29; 12:17; 14:2; 15:1, 3, 22, 23, 32f., 40; 16:2, 40; 17:6, 10, 14; 18:18, 27; 21:7, 17; 22:5; 28:14f.; Rom. 1:13; Acts 11:26

16 ᵃActs 1:20; John 13:18; 17:12 ᵇMatt. 26:47; Mark 14:43; Luke 22:47; John 18:3

17 ᵃJohn 6:70f. ᵇActs 1:25; 20:24; 21:19

18 ᵃMatt. 27:3-10 ᵇMatt. 26:14f.

19 ¹Some early mss. read, *Hakoldamach*
ᵃActs 21:40; Matt. 27:8

20 ¹Lit., *position as overseer*
ᵃPs. 69:25 ᵇPs. 109:8

21 ¹Lit., *to us*
ᵃLuke 24:3

22 ¹Lit., *from*
ᵃMark 1:1-4 ᵇActs 1:2 ᶜActs 1:8; 2:32

23 ᵃActs 1:26

24 ᵃActs 6:6; 13:3; 14:23 ᵇActs 15:8; Rom. 8:27; 1 Sam. 16:7; Jer. 17:10

¹ᵇmount called ²Olivet, which is near Jerusalem, a Sabbath day's journey away.

13 And when they had entered, they went up to ᵃthe upper room, where they were staying; ᵇthat is, Peter and John and ¹James and Andrew, Philip and Thomas, Bartholomew and Matthew, ¹James *the son* of Alphaeus, and Simon the Zealot, and ᶜJudas *the* ²*son* of ¹James.

14 These all with one mind ᵃwere continually devoting themselves to prayer, along with ¹ᵇ*the* women, and Mary the ᶜmother of Jesus, and with His ᶜbrothers.

15 And ¹at this time Peter stood up in the midst of ᵃthe brethren (a gathering of about one hundred and twenty ²persons was there together), and said,

16 "Brethren, ᵃthe Scripture had to be fulfilled, which the Holy Spirit foretold by the mouth of David concerning Judas, ᵇwho became a guide to those who arrested Jesus.

17 "For he was ᵃcounted among us, and received his portion in ᵇthis ministry."

18 (Now this man ᵃacquired a field with ᵇthe price of his wickedness; and falling headlong, he burst open in the middle and all his bowels gushed out.

19 And it became known to all who were living in Jerusalem; so that in ᵃtheir own language that field was called ¹Hakeldama, that is, Field of Blood).

20 "For it is written in the book of Psalms,

'ᵃLᴇᴛ ʜɪs ʜᴏᴍᴇsᴛᴇᴀᴅ ʙᴇ ᴍᴀᴅᴇ ᴅᴇsᴏʟᴀᴛᴇ,
Aɴᴅ ʟᴇᴛ ɴᴏ ᴍᴀɴ ᴅᴡᴇʟʟ ɪɴ ɪᴛ;'

and,

'ᵇHɪs ¹ᴏғғɪᴄᴇ ʟᴇᴛ ᴀɴᴏᴛʜᴇʀ ᴍᴀɴ ᴛᴀᴋᴇ.'

21 "It is therefore necessary that of the men who have accompanied us all the time that ᵃthe Lord Jesus went in and out ¹among us—

22 ᵃbeginning ¹with the baptism of John, until the day that He ᵇwas taken up from us—one of these should become a ᶜwitness with us of His resurrection."

23 And they put forward two men, Joseph called Barsabbas (who was also called Justus), and ᵃMatthias.

24 And they ᵃprayed, and said, "Thou, Lord, ᵇwho knowest the hearts of all men, show which one of these two Thou hast chosen

25 to [1]occupy [a]this ministry and [b]apostleship from which Judas turned aside to go to his own place."

26 And they [1a]drew lots for them, and the lot fell [2]to [b]Matthias; and he was [3]numbered with [c]the eleven apostles.

CHAPTER 2

AND when [a]the day of Pentecost [1]had come, they were all together in one place.

2 And suddenly there came from heaven a noise like a violent, rushing wind, and it filled [a]the whole house where they were sitting.

3 And there appeared to them tongues as of fire [1]distributing themselves, and [2]they [3]rested on each one of them.

4 And they were all [a]filled with the Holy Spirit and began to [b]speak with other tongues, as the Spirit was giving them [1]utterance.

5 Now there were Jews living in Jerusalem, [a]devout men, from every nation under heaven.

6 And when [a]this sound occurred, the multitude came together, and were bewildered, because they were each one hearing them speak in his own [1]language.

7 And [a]they were amazed and marveled, saying, "[1]Why, are not all these who are speaking [b]Galileans?

8 "And how is it that we each hear *them* in our own [1]language [2]to which we were born?

9 "Parthians and Medes and Elamites, and residents of Mesopotamia, Judea and [a]Cappadocia, [b]Pontus and [1c]Asia,

10 [a]Phrygia and [b]Pamphylia, Egypt and the districts of Libya around [c]Cyrene, and [1d]visitors from Rome, both Jews and [2e]proselytes,

11 Cretans and Arabs—we hear them in our *own* tongues speaking of the mighty deeds of God."

12 And [a]they continued in amazement and great perplexity, saying to one another, "What does this mean?"

13 But others were mocking and saying, "[a]They are full of [1]sweet wine."

14 But Peter, [1]taking his stand with [a]the eleven, raised his voice and declared to them: "Men of

25 [1]Lit., *take the place of*
[a]Acts 1:17 [b]Rom. 1:5; 1 Cor. 9:2; Gal. 2:8

26 [1]Lit., *gave* [2]Or, *upon* [3]Lit., *chosen*
[a]Lev. 16:8; Josh. 14:2; 1 Sam. 14:41f.; Neh. 10:34; 11:1; Prov. 16:33 [b]Acts 1:23 [c]Acts 2:14

1 [1]Lit., *was being fulfilled*
[a]Acts 20:16; 1 Cor. 16:8; Lev. 23:15f.

2 [a]Acts 4:31

3 [1]Or, *being distributed* [2]Lit., *it* [3]Or, *sat*

4 [1]Or, *ability to speak out*
[a]Acts 4:8, 31; 9:17; 13:9, 52; 1:5, 8; 6:3, 5; 7:55; 8:17; 11:15; Matt. 10:20 [b]Mark 16:17; 1 Cor. 12:10f.; 14:21

5 [a]Acts 8:2; Luke 2:25

6 [1]Or, *dialect*
[a]Acts 2:2

7 [1]Lit., *behold*
[a]Acts 2:12 [b]Acts 1:11; Matt. 26:73

8 [1]Or, *dialect* [2]Lit., *in*

9 [1]I.e., west coast province of Asia Minor
[a]1 Pet. 1:1 [b]1 Pet. 1:1; Acts 18:2 [c]Acts 6:9; 16:6; 19:10, 20:4; 21:27; 24:18; 27:2; Rom. 16:5; 1 Cor. 16:19; 2 Cor. 1:8; 2 Tim. 1:15; Rev. 1:4

10 [1]Lit., *the sojourning Romans* [2]I.e., Gentile converts to Judaism
[a]Acts 16:6; 18:23 [b]Acts 13:13; 14:24; 15:38; 27:5 [c]Matt. 27:32 [d]Acts 17:21 [e]Matt. 23:15

12 [a]Acts 2:7

13 [1]Or, *new wine*
[a]1 Cor. 14:23

14 [1]Or, *being put forward as spokesman*
[a]Acts 1:26

15 [1]I.e., 9 a.m.
[a]1 Thess. 5:7

17 [1]Lit., *flesh*
[a]Joel 2:28-32

21 [a]Rom. 10:13

22 [1]Or, *exhibited;* or
accredited [2]Or, *works of
power* [3]Or, *attesting
miracles*
[a]Acts 10:38; 3.6; 4:10 [b]John
3:2 [c]Acts 2:19, 43; John 4:48

23 [1]Or, *men without the
Law,* i.e., heathen
[a]Acts 3:18; 4:28; Luke 22:22;
1 Pet. 1:20 [b]Acts 3:13; Luke
21:20

24 [1]Lit., *Whom God raised
up* [2]Lit., *birth pangs*
[a]Acts 2:32; 3:15, 26; 4:10;
5:30; 10:40; 13:30, 33, 34, 37;
17:31; Rom. 4:24; 6:4; 8:11;
10:9; 1 Cor. 6:14; 15:15;
2 Cor. 4:14; Gal. 1:1; Eph.
1:20; Col. 2:12; 1 Thess. 1:10;
Heb. 13:20; 1 Pet. 1:21 [b]John
20:9

25 [a]Ps. 16:8-11

Judea, and all you who live in Jerusalem, let this be known to you, and give heed to my words.

15 "For these men are not drunk, as you suppose, [a]for it is *only* the [1]third hour of the day;

16 but this is what was spoken of through the prophet Joel:

17 '[a]AND IT SHALL BE IN THE LAST DAYS, GOD
SAYS,
THAT I WILL POUR FORTH OF MY SPIRIT
UPON ALL [1]MANKIND;
AND YOUR SONS AND YOUR DAUGHTERS SHALL
PROPHESY,
AND YOUR YOUNG MEN SHALL SEE VISIONS,
AND YOUR OLD MEN SHALL DREAM DREAMS;

18 'EVEN UPON MY BONDSLAVES, BOTH MEN AND
WOMEN,
I WILL IN THOSE DAYS POUR FORTH OF MY
SPIRIT
And they shall prophesy.

19 'AND I WILL GRANT WONDERS IN THE SKY
ABOVE,
AND SIGNS ON THE EARTH BENEATH,
BLOOD, AND FIRE, AND VAPOR OF SMOKE.

20 'THE SUN SHALL BE TURNED INTO DARKNESS,
AND THE MOON INTO BLOOD,
BEFORE THE GREAT AND GLORIOUS DAY OF THE
LORD SHALL COME.

21 'AND IT SHALL BE, THAT [a]EVERY ONE WHO
CALLS ON THE NAME OF THE LORD SHALL
BE SAVED.'

22 "Men of Israel, listen to these words: [a]Jesus the Nazarene, [b]a man [1]attested to you by God with [2]miracles and [c]wonders and [3]signs which God performed through Him in your midst, just as you yourselves know—

23 this *Man*, delivered up by the [a]predetermined plan and foreknowledge of God, [b]you nailed to a cross by the hands of [1]godless men and put *Him* to death.

24 "[1]And [a]God raised Him up again, putting an end to the [2]agony of death, since it [b]was impossible for Him to be held in its power.

25 "For David says of Him,
'[a]I WAS ALWAYS BEHOLDING THE LORD IN
MY PRESENCE;
FOR HE IS AT MY RIGHT HAND, THAT I MAY
NOT BE SHAKEN.

26   'THEREFORE MY HEART WAS GLAD AND MY
      TONGUE EXULTED;
    MOREOVER MY FLESH ALSO WILL ABIDE IN
      HOPE;

27   'BECAUSE THOU WILT NOT ABANDON MY
      SOUL TO [a]HADES,
    [b]NOR [1]ALLOW THY [2]HOLY ONE TO [3]UNDER-
      GO DECAY.

28   'THOU HAST MADE KNOWN TO ME THE WAYS
      OF LIFE;
    THOU WILT MAKE ME FULL OF GLADNESS
      WITH THY PRESENCE.'

29 "[1]Brethren, I may confidently say to you regarding the [a]patriarch David that he both [b]died and [c]was buried, and [d]his tomb is [2]with us to this day.

30 "And so, because he was [a]a prophet, and knew that [b]God had sworn to him with an oath to seat [1]one of his descendants upon his throne,

31 he looked ahead and spoke of the resurrection of [1]the Christ, that He was neither abandoned to [a]Hades, nor did His flesh [2]suffer decay.

32 "This Jesus [a]God raised up again, to which we are all [b]witnesses.

33 "Therefore having been exalted [1a]to the right hand of God, and [b]having received from the Father [c]the promise of the Holy Spirit, He has [d]poured forth this which you both see and hear.

34 "For it was not David who ascended into [1]heaven, but he himself says:
    '[a]THE LORD SAID TO MY LORD,
    "SIT AT MY RIGHT HAND,

35   UNTIL I MAKE THINE ENEMIES A FOOTSTOOL
      FOR THY FEET."'

36 "Therefore let all the [a]house of Israel know for certain that God has made Him both [b]Lord and [1]Christ—this Jesus [c]whom you crucified."

37 Now when they heard *this*, they were [1]pierced to the heart, and said to Peter and the rest of the apostles, "[2]Brethren, [a]what shall we do?"

38 And Peter *said* to them, "[a]Repent, and let each of you be [b]baptized in the name of Jesus Christ for the forgiveness of your sins; and you shall receive the gift of the Holy Spirit.

39 "For [a]the promise is for you and your children, and for all who are [b]far off, as many as the Lord our God shall call to Himself."

40 And with many other words he solemnly

27 [1]Lit., *give* [2]Or, *devout* or *pious* [3]Lit., *see corruption* [a]Matt. 11:23; Acts 2:31 [b]Acts 13:35

29 [1]Lit., *men brothers* [2]Lit., *among* [a]Acts 7:8f.; Heb. 7:4 [b]Acts 13:36 [c]1 Kin. 2:10 [d]Neh. 3:16

30 [1]Lit., *of the fruit of his loins* [a]Matt. 22:43 [b]2 Sam. 7:12f.; Ps. 89:3f.; 132:11

31 [1]I.e., the Messiah [2]Lit., *see corruption* [a]Matt. 11:23; Acts 2:27

32 [a]Acts 2:24; 3:15, 26; 4:10; 5:30; 10:40; 13:30, 33, 34, 37; 17:31; Rom. 4:24; 6:4; 8:11; 10:9; 1 Cor. 6:14; 15:15; 2 Cor. 4:14; Gal. 1:1; Eph. 1:20; Col. 2:12; 1 Thess. 1:10; Heb. 13:20; 1 Pet. 1:21 [b]Acts 1:8

33 [1]Or, *by* [a]Acts 5:31; Mark 16:19 [b]Acts 1:4 [c]Gal. 3:14; John 7:39 [d]Acts 2:17; 10:45

34 [1]Lit., *the heavens* [a]Ps. 110:1; Matt. 22:44f.

36 [1]I.e., Messiah [a]Ezek. 36:22, 32, 37; 45:6 [b]Luke 2:11 [c]Acts 2:23

37 [1]Or, *smitten in conscience* [2]Lit., *men brothers* [a]Luke 3:10, 12, 14

38 [a]Acts 3:19; 5:31; 20:21; Luke 24:47; Mark 1:15 [b]Acts 8:12, 16; 22:16; Mark 16:16

39 [a]Rom. 9:4; Is. 44:3; 54:13; 57:19; Joel 2:32; Eph. 2:12 [b]Eph. 2:13, 17

40 [1]Or, *Escape*
[a]Luke 16:28 [b]Deut. 32:5;
Phil. 2:15; Matt. 17:17

41 [1]I.e., persons
[a]Acts 3:23; 7:14; 27:37; Rom.
13:1; 1 Pet. 3:20; Rev. 16:3

42 [1]Lit., *the prayers*
[a]Acts 1:14 [b]Luke 24:30; Acts
20:7; 1 Cor. 10:16; Acts 2:46

43 [1]Lit., *fear was occurring
to every soul* [2]Or, *attesting
miracles* [3]Some ancient mss.
add, *in Jerusalem; and great
fear was upon all*
[a]Acts 2:22

44 [1]Some ancient mss.
omit, *were*
[a]Acts 4:32; Acts 4:37; 5:2

45 [a]Matt. 19:21; Acts 4:34

46 [1]Or, *in the various
private homes* [2]Lit., *food*
[3]Or, *simplicity*
[a]Acts 5:42 [b]Luke 24:30; Acts
20:7; 1 Cor. 10:16; Acts 2:42

47 [1]Lit., *together*
[a]Acts 5:13 [b]Acts 2:11; 5:14;
6:1, 7; 11:24; Acts 4:4; 9:31,
35, 42; 11:21; 14:1, 21; 16:5;
17:12 [c]1 Cor. 1:18

1 [1]I.e., 3 p.m.
[a]Luke 22:8; Acts 3:3, 4, 11
[b]Ps. 55:17; Acts 10:30; Matt.
27:45

2 [1]Or, *a gift of charity*
[a]Acts 14:8 [b]Luke 16:20 [c]Acts
3:10; John 9:8

3 [a]Luke 22:8; Acts 3:1, 4,
11

4 [a]Acts 10:4

6 [a]Acts 4:10; 3:16; 2:22

8 [1]Lit., *leaping up*
[a]Acts 14:10

[a]testified and kept on exhorting them, saying, "[1]Be saved from this [b]perverse generation!"

41 So then, those who had received his word were baptized; and there were added that day about three thousand [1a]souls.

42 And they were [a]continually devoting themselves to the apostles' teaching and to fellowship, to [b]the breaking of bread and [1a]to prayer.

43 And [1]everyone kept feeling a sense of awe; and many [a]wonders and [2]signs were taking place through the apostles[3].

44 And all those who had believed [1]were together, and [a]had all things in common;

45 and they [a]*began* selling their property and possessions, and were sharing them with all, as anyone might have need.

46 [a]And day by day continuing with one mind in the temple, and [b]breaking bread [1]from house to house, they were taking their [2]meals together with gladness and [3]sincerity of heart,

47 praising God, and [a]having favor with all the people. And the Lord [b]was adding [1]to their number day by day [c]those who were being saved.

CHAPTER 3

NOW [a]Peter and John were going up to the temple at the [1]ninth *hour,* [b]the hour of prayer.

2 And [a]a certain man who had been lame from his mother's womb was being carried along, whom they [b]used to set down every day at the gate of the temple which is called Beautiful, [c]in order to beg [1]alms of those who were entering the temple.

3 And when he saw [a]Peter and John about to go into the temple, he *began* asking to receive alms.

4 And Peter, along with John, [a]fixed his gaze upon him and said, "Look at us!"

5 And he *began* to give them his attention, expecting to receive something from them.

6 But Peter said, "I do not possess silver and gold, but what I do have I give to you: [a]In the name of Jesus Christ the Nazarene—walk!"

7 And seizing him by the right hand, he raised him up; and immediately his feet and his ankles were strengthened.

8 [a]And [1]with a leap, he stood upright and

began to walk; and he entered the temple with them, walking and leaping and praising God.

9 And ᵃall the people saw him walking and praising God;

10 and they were taking note of him as being the one who used to ᵃsit at the Beautiful Gate of the temple to *beg* alms, and they were filled with wonder and amazement at what had happened to him.

11 And while he was clinging to ᵃPeter and John, all the people ran together to them at the so-called ¹ᵇportico of Solomon, full of amazement.

12 But when Peter saw *this*, he ᵃreplied to the people, "Men of Israel, why do you marvel at this, or why do you gaze at us, as if by our own power or piety we had made him walk?

13 "ᵃThe God of Abraham, Isaac, and Jacob, ᵇthe God of our fathers, has glorified His ¹ᶜServant Jesus, *the one* whom ᵈyou delivered up, and disowned in the presence of ᵉPilate, when he had ᶠdecided to release Him.

14 "But you disowned ᵃthe Holy and Righteous One, and ᵇasked for a murderer to be granted to you,

15 but put to death the ¹ᵃPrince of life, *the one* whom ᵇGod raised from the dead,—*a fact* to which we are ᶜwitnesses.

16 "And on the basis of faith ᵃin His name, *it is* the name of ¹Jesus which has strengthened this man whom you see and know; and the faith which *comes* through Him has given him this perfect health in the presence of you all.

17 "And now, brethren, I know that you acted ᵃin ignorance, just as your ᵇrulers did also.

18 "But the things which ᵃGod announced beforehand by the mouth of all the prophets, ᵇthat His ¹Christ should suffer, He has thus fulfilled.

19 "ᵃRepent therefore and return, that your sins may be wiped away, in order that ᵇtimes of refreshing may come from the presence of the Lord;

20 and that he may send Jesus, the ¹Christ appointed for you,

21 ᵃwhom heaven must receive until *the* ¹period of ᵇrestoration of all things, about which ᶜGod spoke by the mouth of His holy prophets from ancient time.

22 "Moses said, 'ᵃThe Lord God shall raise up for you a Prophet ¹like me from your brethren;

---

9 ᵃActs 4:16, 21

10 ᵃActs 3:2; John 9:8

11 ¹Or, *colonnade*
ᵃLuke 22:8; Acts 3:3, 4 ᵇActs 5:12; John 10:23

12 ᵃMatt. 11:25; 17:4; 22:1; Luke 14:3; Acts 5:8; 10:46

13 ¹Or, *Child*
ᵃMatt. 22:32 ᵇActs 5:30; 7:32; 22:14; Ex. 3:13, 15 ᶜActs 3:26; 4:27, 30 ᵈActs 2:23; Matt. 20:19; John 19:11 ᵉMatt. 27:2 ᶠLuke 23:4

14 ᵃMark 1:24; Acts 4:27; 7:52; 2 Cor. 5:21 ᵇMatt. 27:20; Mark 15:11; Luke 23:18-25

15 ¹Or, *Author*
ᵃActs 5:31; Heb. 2:10; 12:2 ᵇActs 2:24 ᶜLuke 24:48

16 ¹Lit., *His*
ᵃActs 3:6

17 ᵃLuke 23:34; Acts 13:27; 26:9; John 15:21; Eph. 4:18 ᵇLuke 23:13

18 ¹Or, *Anointed One, Messiah*
ᵃActs 2:23 ᵇLuke 24:27; Acts 17:3; 26:23

19 ᵃActs 2:38; 26:20 ᵇ2 Thess. 1:7; Heb. 4:1ff.

20 ¹I.e., Messiah

21 ¹Lit., *periods, times*
ᵃActs 1:11 ᵇMatt. 17:11; Rom. 8:21 ᶜLuke 1:70

22 ¹Or, *as He raised up me*
ᵃDeut. 18:15; Acts 7:37

251

Acts 3, 4

**Peter and John Arrested.
Brought Before the Council.**

23 ^aDeut. 18:19 ^bActs 2:41

24 ^aLuke 24:27; Acts 17:3;
26:23

25 ¹Lit., *covenanted*
^aActs 2:39 ^bRom. 9:4f. ^cGen.
22:18

26 ¹Or, *Child*
^aActs 13:46; Rom. 1:16; 2:9f.;
Matt. 15:24; John 4:22 ^bActs
2:24

1 ^aLuke 22:4 ^bMatt. 3:7
^cLuke 20:1; Acts 6:12

2 ¹Or, *in the case of*
^aActs 17:18; 3:15

3 ^aActs 5:18

4 ¹Or, *word*
^aActs 2:41

5 ^aLuke 23:13; Acts 4:8

6 ^aLuke 3:2 ^bMatt. 26:3

8 ¹Or, *having just been
filled* ²Or, *rulers of the
people and elders*
^aActs 13:9; 2:4 ^bLuke 23:13;
Acts 4:5

9 ¹Or, *by whom*
^aActs 3:7f.

10 ¹Or, *in*
^aActs 3:6; 2:22 ^bActs 2:24

TO HIM YOU SHALL GIVE HEED IN EVERYTHING HE SAYS TO YOU.

23 '^aAND IT SHALL BE THAT EVERY ^bSOUL THAT DOES NOT HEED THAT PROPHET SHALL BE UTTERLY DESTROYED FROM AMONG THE PEOPLE.'

24 "And likewise, ^aall the prophets who have spoken, from Samuel and *his* successors onward, also announced these days.

25 "It is you who are ^athe sons of the prophets, and of the ^bcovenant which God ¹made with your fathers, saying to Abraham, '^cAND IN YOUR SEED ALL THE FAMILIES OF THE EARTH SHALL BE BLESSED.'

26 "For you ^afirst, God ^braised up His ¹Servant, and sent Him to bless you by turning every one *of you* from your wicked ways."

CHAPTER 4

A<small>ND</small> as they were speaking to the people, the priests and ^athe captain of the temple *guard*, and ^bthe Sadducees, ^ccame upon them,

2 being greatly disturbed because they were teaching the people and proclaiming ^{1a}in Jesus the resurrection from the dead.

3 And they laid hands on them, and ^aput them in jail until the next day, for it was already evening.

4 But many of those who had heard the ¹message believed; and ^athe number of the men came to be about five thousand.

5 And it came about on the next day, that their ^arulers and elders and scribes were gathered together in Jerusalem;

6 and ^aAnnas the high priest *was there*, and ^bCaiaphas and John and Alexander, and all who were of high-priestly descent.

7 And when they had placed them in the center, they *began to* inquire, "By what power, or in what name, have you done this?"

8 Then Peter, ^{1a}filled with the Holy Spirit, said to them, "^{2b}Rulers and elders of the people,

9 if we are on trial today for ^aa benefit done to a sick man, ¹as to how this man has been made well,

10 let it be known to all of you, and to all the people of Israel, that ^{1a}by the name of Jesus Christ the Nazarene, whom you crucified, whom ^bGod

raised from the dead,—¹by ²this *name* this man stands here before you in good health.

11 "¹aHe is the bSTONE WHICH WAS cREJECTED by you, THE BUILDERS, *but* WHICH BECAME THE VERY CORNER *STONE*.

12 "And there is salvation in ano one else; for there is no other name under heaven that has been given among men, by which we must be saved."

13 Now as they observed the aconfidence of bPeter and John, and understood that they were uneducated and untrained men, they were marveling, and cbegan to recognize them ¹as having been with Jesus.

14 And seeing the man who had been healed standing with them, they had nothing to say in reply.

15 But when they had ordered them to go aside out of the ¹aCouncil, they *began* to confer with one another,

16 saying, "aWhat shall we do with these men? For the fact that a bnoteworthy ¹miracle has taken place through them is apparent to all who live in Jerusalem, and we cannot deny it.

17 "But in order that it may not spread any further among the people, let us warn them to speak no more to any man ain this name."

18 And when they had summoned them, they acommanded them not to speak or teach at all ¹in the name of Jesus.

19 But aPeter and John answered and said to them, "bWhether it is right in the sight of God to give heed to you rather than to God, you be the judge;

20 for awe cannot stop speaking what we have seen and heard."

21 And when they had threatened them further, they let them go (finding no basis on which they might punish them) aon account of the people, because they were all bglorifying God for what had happened;

22 for the man was more than forty years old on whom this ¹miracle of healing had been performed.

23 And when they had been released, they went to their own *companions*, and reported all that the chief priests and the elders had said to them.

24 And when they heard *this*, they lifted their

---

10 ¹Or, *in* ²Or, *him*

11 ¹Lit., *This One*
aMatt. 21:42 bPs. 118:22
cMark 9:12

12 a1 Tim. 2:5; Matt. 1:21; Acts 10:43

13 ¹Lit., *that they had been*
aActs 4:31 bLuke 22:8; Acts 4:19 cJohn 7:15

15 ¹Or, *Sanhedrin*
· aMatt. 5:22

16 ¹Or, *sign*
aJohn 11:47 bActs 3:7-10

17 aJohn 15:21

18 ¹Or, *on the basis of*
aActs 5:28f.

19 aActs 4:13 bActs 5:28f.

20 a1 Cor. 9:16

21 aActs 5:26 bMatt. 9:8

22 ¹Or, *sign*

24 [1]Or, *Master*
[a]Ex. 20:11; Ps. 146:6

25 [1]This word is missing in the Greek [2]Or, *Nations*
[a]Acts 1:16 [b]Ps. 2:1

26 [1]Or, *approached* [2]I.e., Messiah, Anointed One
[a]Ps. 2:2 [b]Dan. 9:24f.; Luke 4:18; Acts 10:38; Heb. 1:9

27 [1]Or, *Child* [2]Or, *nations*
[a]Acts 4:30; 3:13 [b]Matt. 14:1 [c]Luke 23:12; Matt. 27:2 [d]Matt. 20:19

28 [a]Acts 2:23

29 [1]Or, *as for the present situation*
[a]Phil. 1:14 [b]Acts 4:13, 31; 14:3

30 [1]Or, *attesting miracles* [2]Or, *Child*
[a]John 4:48 [b]Acts 4:27; 3:13

31 [a]Acts 2:1 [b]Acts 2:4 [c]Phil. 1:14 [d]Acts 4:13; 14:3

32 [1]Or, *multitude* [2]Lit., *was saying*
[a]Acts 2:44

33 [1]Some mss. add, *Christ*
[a]Acts 1:8 [b]Luke 24:48

34 [1]Lit., *the prices of the things being sold*
[a]Matt. 19:21; Acts 2:45

35 [a]Acts 4:37; 5:2 [b]Acts 6:1; 2:45

36 [1]Or, *Exhortation*, or, *Consolation*
[a]Acts 11:19f.; 13:4; 15:39; 21:3, 16; 27:4 [b]Acts 9:27; 11:22, 30; 12:25; 13:15; 1 Cor. 9:6; Gal. 2:1, 9, 13; Col. 4:10 [c]Acts 13:15; 1 Cor. 14:3; 1 Thess. 2:3; Acts 2:40; 11:23

37 [a]Acts 4:35; 5:2

voice to God with one accord and said, "O [1]Lord, it is Thou who [a]DIDST MAKE THE HEAVEN AND THE EARTH AND THE SEA, AND ALL THAT IS IN THEM,

25 who [a]by the Holy Spirit, [1]*through* the mouth of our father David Thy servant, didst say,

'[b]WHY DID THE [2]GENTILES RAGE,
AND THE PEOPLES DEVISE FUTILE THINGS?

26 '[a]THE KINGS OF THE EARTH [1]TOOK THEIR STAND,
AND THE RULERS WERE GATHERED TOGETHER,
AGAINST THE LORD, AND AGAINST HIS [2b]CHRIST.'

27 "For truly in this city there were gathered together against Thy holy [1a]Servant Jesus, whom Thou didst anoint, both [b]Herod and [c]Pontius Pilate, along with [d]the [2]Gentiles and the peoples of Israel,

28 to do whatever Thy hand and [a]Thy purpose predestined to occur.

29 "And [1]now, Lord, take note of their threats, and grant that Thy bond-servants may [a]speak Thy word with all [b]confidence,

30 while Thou dost extend Thy hand to heal, and [1a]signs and wonders take place through the name of Thy holy [2b]Servant Jesus."

31 And when they had prayed, the [a]place where they had gathered together was shaken, and they were all [b]filled with the Holy Spirit, and *began* to [c]speak the word of God with [d]boldness.

32 And the [1]congregation of those who believed were of one heart and soul; and not one of *them* [2]claimed that anything belonging to him was his own; but [a]all things were common property to them.

33 And [a]with great power the apostles were giving [b]witness to the resurrection of the Lord Jesus[1], and abundant grace was upon them all.

34 For there was not a needy person among them, for all who were owners of lands or houses [a]would sell them and bring the [1]proceeds of the sales,

35 and [a]lay them at the apostles' feet; and they would be [b]distributed to each, as any had need.

36 And Joseph, a Levite of [a]Cyprian birth, who was also called [b]Barnabas by the apostles (which translated means, Son of [1c]Encouragement),

37 and who owned a tract of land, sold it and brought the money and [a]laid it at the apostles' feet.

CHAPTER 5

BUT a certain man named Ananias, with his wife Sapphira, sold a piece of property,

2 and [a]kept back *some* of the price for himself, with his wife's [1]full knowledge, and bringing a portion of it, he [b]laid it at the apostles' feet.

3 But Peter said, "Ananias, why has [a]Satan filled your heart to lie [b]to the Holy Spirit, and to [c]keep back *some* of the price of the land?

4 "While it remained *unsold*, did it not remain your own? And after it was sold, was it not [1]under your control? Why is it that you have [2]conceived this deed in your heart? You have not lied to men, but [a]to God."

5 And as he heard these words, Ananias [a]fell down and breathed his last; and [b]great fear came upon all who heard of it.

6 And the [1]young men arose and [a]covered him up, and after carrying him out, they buried him.

7 Now there elapsed an interval of about three hours, and his wife came in, not knowing what had happened.

8 And Peter [a]responded to her, "Tell me whether you sold the land [1b]for such and such a price?" And she said, "Yes, [1]that was the price."

9 Then Peter *said* to her, "Why is it that you have agreed together to [a]put [b]the Spirit of the Lord to the test? Behold, the feet of those who have buried your husband are at the door, and they shall carry you out *as well.*"

10 And she [a]fell immediately at his feet, and breathed her last; and the young men came in and found her dead, and they carried her out and buried her beside her husband.

11 And [a]great fear came upon the whole church, and upon all who heard of these things.

12 And [1]at the hands of the apostles many [a]signs and wonders were taking place among the people; and they were all with one accord in [b]Solomon's portico.

13 But none of the rest dared to associate with them; however, [a]the people [1]held them in high esteem.

14 And all the more [a]believers in the Lord, multitudes of men and women, were constantly [b]added to *their number;*

2 [1]Or, *collusion*
[a]Acts 5:3 [b]Acts 4:35, 37

3 [a]Matt. 4:10; Luke 22:3; John 13:2, 27 [b]Acts 5:4, 9 [c]Acts 5:2

4 [1]Or, *in your authority* [2]Or, *placed* [a]Acts 5:3, 9

5 [a]Acts 5:10; Ezek. 11:13 [b]Acts 5:11; 2:43

6 [1]Lit., *younger* [a]John 19:40

8 [1]Lit., *for so much* [a]Acts 3:12 [b]Acts 5:2

9 [a]Acts 15:10 [b]Acts 5:3, 4

10 [a]Acts 5:5; Ezek. 11:13

11 [a]Acts 5:5; 2:43

12 [1]Lit., *through* [a]John 4:48 [b]Acts 3:11; John 10:23

13 [1]Lit., *were holding* [a]Acts 2:47; 4:21

14 [a]2 Cor. 6:15 [b]Acts 2:47; 11:24

15 ªActs 19:12

16 ¹Lit., *multitude* ²Lit.,
and

17 ªActs 15:5 ᵇMatt. 3:7;
Acts 4:1

18 ªActs 4:3

19 ªMatt. 1:20, 24; 2:13, 19;
28:2; Luke 1:11; 2:9; Acts
8.26, 12:7, 23; 16:9; 27:23

20 ¹Or, *continue to speak*
²Lit., *all the words*
ªJohn 6:63, 68

21 ¹Or, *Sanhedrin*
ªJohn 8:2 ᵇActs 4:6 ᶜMatt.
5:22, Acts 5:27, 34, 41

22 ªMatt. 26:58; Acts 5:26

24 ¹Lit., *this would become*
ªActs 4:1; 5:26

26 ªActs 5:24 ᵇActs 5:22
ᶜActs 4:21; 5:13

27 ¹Lit., *in*
ªMatt. 5:22; Acts 5:21, 34, 41

28 ªActs 4:18

15 to such an extent that they even carried the sick out into the streets, and laid them on cots and pallets, so that when Peter came by, ªat least his shadow might fall on any one of them.

16 And also the ¹people from the cities in the vicinity of Jerusalem were coming together, bringing people who were sick ²or afflicted with unclean spirits; and they were all being healed.

17 But the high priest rose up, along with all his associates (that is ªthe sect of ᵇthe Sadducees), and they were filled with jealousy;

18 and they laid hands on the apostles, and ªput them in a public jail.

19 But ªan angel of the Lord during the night opened the gates of the prison, and taking them out he said,

20 "Go your way, stand and ¹speak to the people in the temple ²ªthe whole message of this Life."

21 And upon hearing *this*, they entered into the temple ªabout daybreak, and *began* to teach. Now when ᵇthe high priest and his associates had come, they called ᶜthe ¹Council together, and all the Senate of the sons of Israel, and sent *orders* to the prison-house for them to be brought.

22 But ªthe officers who came did not find them in the prison; and they returned, and reported back,

23 saying, "We found the prison-house locked quite securely and the guards standing at the doors; but when we had opened up, we found no one inside."

24 Now when ªthe captain of the temple *guard* and the chief priests heard these words, they were greatly perplexed about them as to what ¹would come of this.

25 But someone came and reported to them, "Behold, the men whom you put in prison are standing in the temple and teaching the people!"

26 Then ªthe captain went along with ᵇthe officers and *proceeded* to bring them *back* without violence; (for ᶜthey were afraid of the people, lest they should be stoned).

27 And when they had brought them, they stood them ¹before ªthe Council. And the high priest questioned them,

28 saying, "We gave you ªstrict orders not to continue teaching in this name, and behold, you

have filled Jerusalem with your teaching, and [b]intend to bring this man's blood upon us."

29 But Peter and the apostles answered and said, "[a]We must obey God rather than men.

30 "[a]The God of our fathers [b]raised up Jesus, [1]whom you had [c]put to death by hanging Him on a [2]cross.

31 "[a]He is the one whom God exalted [1]to His right hand as a [2b]Prince and a [c]Savior, to grant [d]repentance to Israel, and forgiveness of sins.

32 "And we are [a]witnesses[1] of these things; and [b]*so is* the Holy Spirit, whom God has given to those who obey Him."

33 But when they heard this, they were [1a]cut to the quick and were intending to slay them.

34 But a certain Pharisee named [a]Gamaliel, a [b]teacher of the Law, respected by all the people, stood up in [c]the Council and gave orders to put the men outside for a short time.

35 And he said to them, "Men of Israel, take care what you propose to do with these men.

36 "For sometime ago Theudas rose up, [a]claiming to be somebody; and a group of about four hundred men joined up with him. [1]And he was slain; and all who [2]followed him were dispersed and came to nothing.

37 "After this man Judas of Galilee rose up in the days of [a]the census, and drew away *some* people after him; he too perished, and all those who [1]followed him were scattered.

38 "And so in the present case, I say to you, stay away from these men and let them alone, for if this plan or [1]action should [a]be of men, it will be overthrown;

39 but if it is of God, you will not be able to overthrow them; or else you may even be found [a]fighting against God."

40 And they [1]took his advice; and after calling the apostles in, they [a]flogged them and ordered them to [2]speak no more in the name of Jesus, and *then* released them.

41 So they went on their way from the presence of the [1a]Council, [b]rejoicing that they had been considered worthy to suffer shame [c]for [2]*His* name.

42 [a]And every day, in the temple and [1]from house to house, they [2]kept right on teaching and [3b]preaching Jesus *as* the [4]Christ.

---

28 [b]Acts 2:23, 36; 3:14f.; 7:52; Matt. 23:35; 27:25

29 [a]Acts 4:19

30 [1]Or, *on whom you had laid violent hands* [2]Lit., *wood* [a]Acts 3:13 [b]Acts 2:24 [c]Acts 10:39; 13:29; Gal. 3:13; 1 Pet. 2:24

31 [1]Or, *by* [2]Or, *Leader* [a]Acts 2:33 [b]Acts 3:15 [c]Luke 2:11 [d]Luke 24:47; Acts 2:38

32 [1]Some mss. add, *in Him* or, *of Him* [a]Luke 24:48 [b]John 15:26; Acts 15:28; Rom. 8:16; Heb. 2:4

33 [1]Lit., *being sawed through* [a]Acts 7:54; 2:37

34 [a]Acts 22:3 [b]Luke 2:46; 5:17 [c]Acts 5:21

36 [1]Lit., *who was slain* [2]Lit., *were obeying* [a]Acts 8:9; Gal. 2:6; 6:3

37 [1]Lit., *were obeying* [a]Luke 2:2

38 [1]Or, *work* [a]Mark 11:30

39 [a]Acts 11:17; Prov. 21:30

40 [1]Lit., *were persuaded by him* [2]Lit., *not be speaking* [a]Matt. 10:17

41 [1]Or, *Sanhedrin* [2]Lit., *the name* (par excellence) [a]Acts 5:21 [b]1 Pet. 4:14, 16 [c]John 15:21

42 [1]Or, *in the various private homes* [2]Lit., *were not ceasing to* [3]Or, *telling the good news of* [4]I.e., Messiah [a]Acts 2:46 [b]Acts 8:35; 11:20; 17:18; Gal. 1:16

1 ¹Lit., *in these days* ²I.e.,
non-Palestinian Jews who
normally spoke Greek
ªActs 11:26 ᵇActs 6:7; 2:47
ᶜActs 9:29; 11:20 marg.
ᵈ2 Cor. 11:22; Phil. 3:5 ᵉActs
9:39, 41; 1 Tim. 5:3 ᶠActs
4:35; 11:29

2 ¹Or, *multitude*

3 ªActs 1:15; John 21:23
ᵇActs 2:4

4 ¹Or, *service*
ªActs 1:14

5 ¹Lit., *multitude* ²Gr,
Nikolaos ³I.e., a former
convert to Judaism
ªActs 6:8ff.; 11:19; 22:20
ᵇActs 6:3; Acts 11:24 ᶜActs
8.5ff.; 21:8 ᵈMatt. 23:15
ᶜActs 11:19

6 ªActs 1:24 ᵇActs 13:3;
1 Tim. 4:14; 2 Tim. 1:6;
Num. 8:10; 27:18; Deut.
34:9; Acts 8:17ff.; 9:17; 19:6;
Heb. 6:2; Mark 5:23

7 ªActs 12:24; 19:20 ᵇActs
6:1 ᶜActs 13:8; 14:22; Gal.
1:23; 6:10; Jude 3, 20

8 ¹Or, *attesting miracles*
ªJohn 4:48

9 ¹I.e., west coast province
of Asia Minor
ªActs 2:10; Matt. 27:32 ᵇActs
18:24 ᶜActs 15:23, 41; 21:39;
22:3; 23:34; 27:5; Gal. 1:21
ᵈActs 16:6; 19:10; 21:27;
24:18

11 ¹Lit., *saying*

12 ¹Lit., *into* ²Or,
Sanhedrin
ªActs 4:1; Luke 20:1 ᵇMatt.
5:22

13 ªMatt. 26:59-61; Acts
7:58 ᵇMatt. 24:15; Acts
21:28; Acts 25:8

14 ªMatt. 26:61

Chapter 6

Now ¹at this time while the ªdisciples were increasing ᵇ*in number*, a complaint arose on the part of the ²ᶜHellenistic *Jews* against the *native* ᵈHebrews, because their ᵉwidows were being overlooked in ᶠthe daily serving *of food*.

2 And the Twelve summoned the ¹congregation of the disciples and said, "It is not desirable for us to neglect the word of God in order to serve tables.

3 "But select from among you, ªbrethren, seven men of good reputation, ᵇfull of the Spirit and of wisdom, whom we may put in charge of this task.

4 "But we will ªdevote ourselves to prayer, and to the ¹ministry of the word."

5 And the statement found approval with the whole ¹congregation; and they chose ªStephen, a man ᵇfull of faith and of the Holy Spirit, and ᶜPhilip, Prochorus, Nicanor, Timon, Parmenas and ²Nicolas, a ³ᵈproselyte from ᶜAntioch.

6 And these they brought before the apostles; and after ªpraying, they ᵇlaid their hands on them.

7 And ªthe word of God kept on spreading; and ᵇthe number of the disciples continued to increase greatly in Jerusalem, and a great many of the priests were becoming obedient to ᶜthe faith.

8 And Stephen, full of grace and power, was performing great ªwonders and ¹signs among the people.

9 But some men from what was called the Synagogue of the Freedmen, *including* both ªCyrenians and ᵇAlexandrians, and some from ᶜCilicia and ¹ᵈAsia, rose up and argued with Stephen.

10 And *yet* they were unable to cope with the wisdom and the Spirit with which he was speaking.

11 Then they secretly induced men ¹to say, "We have heard him speak blasphemous words against Moses and *against* God."

12 And they stirred up the people, the elders and the scribes, and they ªcame upon him and dragged him away, and brought him ¹before ᵇthe ²Council.

13 And they put forward ªfalse witnesses who said, "This man incessantly speaks against this ᵇholy place, and the Law;

14 for we have heard him say that ªthis Naza-

rene, Jesus, will destroy this place and alter ᵇthe customs which Moses handed down to us."

15 And fixing their gaze on him, all who were sitting in the ¹ᵃCouncil saw his face like the face of an angel.

CHAPTER 7

Aᴎᴅ the high priest said, "Are these things so?"

2 And he said, "Hear me, ᵃbrethren and fathers! ᵇThe God of glory ᶜappeared to our father Abraham when he was in Mesopotamia, before he lived in ¹Haran,

3 ᴀɴᴅ sᴀɪᴅ ᴛᴏ ʜɪᴍ, 'ᵃDᴇᴘᴀʀᴛ ꜰʀᴏᴍ ʏᴏᴜʀ ᴄᴏᴜɴᴛʀʏ ᴀɴᴅ ʏᴏᴜʀ ʀᴇʟᴀᴛɪᴠᴇs, ᴀɴᴅ ᴄᴏᴍᴇ ɪɴᴛᴏ ᴛʜᴇ ʟᴀɴᴅ ᴛʜᴀᴛ I ᴡɪʟʟ sʜᴏᴡ ʏᴏᴜ.'

4 "ᵃThen he departed from the land of the Chaldeans, and settled in ¹Haran. And ᵇfrom there, after his father died, God removed him into this country in which you are now living.

5 "And He gave him no inheritance in it, not even a foot of ground; and *yet*, even when he had no child, ᵃHe promised that Hᴇ ᴡᴏᴜʟᴅ ɢɪᴠᴇ ɪᴛ ᴛᴏ ʜɪᴍ ᴀs ᴀ ᴘᴏssᴇssɪᴏɴ, ᴀɴᴅ ᴛᴏ ʜɪs ᴏꜰꜰsᴘʀɪɴɢ ᴀꜰᴛᴇʀ ʜɪᴍ.

6 "But ᵃGod spoke to this effect, that ʜɪs ᴏꜰꜰsᴘʀɪɴɢ ᴡᴏᴜʟᴅ ʙᴇ ᴀʟɪᴇɴs ɪɴ ᴀ ꜰᴏʀᴇɪɢɴ ʟᴀɴᴅ, ᴀɴᴅ ᴛʜᴀᴛ ᴛʜᴇʏ ᴡᴏᴜʟᴅ ¹ʙᴇ ᴇɴsʟᴀᴠᴇᴅ ᴀɴᴅ ᴍɪsᴛʀᴇᴀᴛᴇᴅ ꜰᴏʀ ꜰᴏᴜʀ ʜᴜɴᴅʀᴇᴅ ʏᴇᴀʀs.

7 " 'Aɴᴅ ᴡʜᴀᴛᴇᴠᴇʀ ɴᴀᴛɪᴏɴ ᴛᴏ ᴡʜɪᴄʜ ᴛʜᴇʏ sʜᴀʟʟ ʙᴇ ɪɴ ʙᴏɴᴅᴀɢᴇ I Mʏsᴇʟꜰ ᴡɪʟʟ ᴊᴜᴅɢᴇ,' said God, 'ᴀɴᴅ ᵃᴀꜰᴛᴇʀ ᴛʜᴀᴛ ᴛʜᴇʏ ᴡɪʟʟ ᴄᴏᴍᴇ ᴏᴜᴛ ᴀɴᴅ ¹sᴇʀᴠᴇ Mᴇ ɪɴ ᴛʜɪs ᴘʟᴀᴄᴇ.'

8 "And He ᵃgave him ¹the covenant of circumcision; and so ᵇ*Abraham* became the father of Isaac, and circumcised him on the eighth day; and ᶜIsaac *became the father of* Jacob, and ᵈJacob *of* the twelve ᵉpatriarchs.

9 "And the patriarchs ᵃʙᴇᴄᴀᴍᴇ ᴊᴇᴀʟᴏᴜs ᴏꜰ Jᴏsᴇᴘʜ ᴀɴᴅ sᴏʟᴅ ʜɪᴍ ɪɴᴛᴏ Eɢʏᴘᴛ. And *yet* God ᴡᴀs ᴡɪᴛʜ ʜɪᴍ,

10 and rescued him from all his afflictions, and ᵃɢʀᴀɴᴛᴇᴅ ʜɪᴍ ꜰᴀᴠᴏʀ and wisdom ɪɴ ᴛʜᴇ sɪɢʜᴛ ᴏꜰ Pʜᴀʀᴀᴏʜ, ᴋɪɴɢ ᴏꜰ Eɢʏᴘᴛ; ᴀɴᴅ ʜᴇ ᴍᴀᴅᴇ ʜɪᴍ ɢᴏᴠᴇʀɴᴏʀ ᴏᴠᴇʀ Eɢʏᴘᴛ ᴀɴᴅ ᴀʟʟ ʜɪs ʜᴏᴜsᴇʜᴏʟᴅ.

11 "Now ᵃᴀ ꜰᴀᴍɪɴᴇ ᴄᴀᴍᴇ ᴏᴠᴇʀ ᴀʟʟ Eɢʏᴘᴛ ᴀɴᴅ Cᴀɴᴀᴀɴ, and great affliction *with it*; and our fathers ¹could find no ²food.

14 ᵇActs 15:1; 21:21; 26:3; 28:17

15 ¹Or, *Sanhedrin*
ᵃMatt. 5:22

2 ¹Gr., *Kharran*
ᵃActs 22:1 ᵇPs. 29:3; 1 Cor. 2:8 ᶜGen. 11:31; 15:7

3 ᵃGen. 12:1

4 ¹Gr., *Kharran*
ᵃGen. 11:31; 15:7 ᵇGen. 12:5

5 ᵃGen. 12:7; 17:8

6 ¹Lit., *enslave them and mistreat them*
ᵃGen. 15:13f.

7 ¹Or, *worship*
ᵃEx. 3:12

8 ¹Or, *a*
ᵃGen. 17:10ff. ᵇGen. 21:2-4 ᶜGen. 25:26 ᵈGen. 29:31ff.; 30:5ff.; 35:23ff. ᵉActs 2:29

9 ᵃGen. 37:11, 28; 45:4; 39:2, 21f.

10 ᵃGen. 39:21; 41:40-46; Ps. 105:21

11 ¹Lit., *were not finding* ²Or, *fodder*
ᵃGen. 41:54ff.; 42:5

12 ªGen. 42:2

13 ¹Or, *was made known*
ªGen. 45:1-4

14 ªGen. 45:9f. ᵇGen.
46:26f.; Ex. 1:5; Deut. 10:22
ᶜActs 2:41

15 ªGen. 46:5; 49:33; Ex.
1:6

16 ¹Gr., *Sychem* ²Gr.,
Emmor
ªGen. 23:16; 50:13; 33:19;
Josh. 24:32

17 ªEx. 1:7f.

18 ªEx. 1:8

19 ¹Or, *put out to die*
ªEx. 1:10f., 16ff.

20 ¹Lit., *to God*
ªEx. 2:2

21 ¹Or, *put out to die* ²Or,
adopted him
ªEx. 2:5f., 10

22 ª1 Kin. 4:30; Is. 19:11

23 ¹Lit., *heart*
ªEx. 2:11f.

25 ¹Lit., *was thinking* ²Or,
salvation ³Lit., *through his
hand*

26 ªEx. 2:13f.

27 ªEx. 2:14; Acts 7:35

12 "But ªWHEN JACOB HEARD THAT THERE WAS GRAIN IN EGYPT, he sent our fathers *there* the first time.

13 "And on the second *visit* ªJoseph ¹made himself known to his brothers, and Joseph's family was disclosed to Pharaoh.

14 "And ªJoseph sent *word* and invited Jacob his father and all his relatives to come to him, ᵇseventy-five ᶜpersons *in all.*

15 "And ªJacob WENT DOWN TO EGYPT AND *there* PASSED AWAY, he and our fathers.

16 "And *from there* they were removed to ¹ªShechem, and laid in the tomb which Abraham had purchased for a sum of money from the sons of ²Hamor in ¹Shechem.

17 "But as the time of the promise was approaching which God had assured to Abraham, ªthe people increased and multiplied in Egypt,

18 until ªTHERE AROSE ANOTHER KING OVER EGYPT WHO KNEW NOTHING ABOUT JOSEPH.

19 "It was he who took ªshrewd advantage of our race, and mistreated our fathers so that they would ¹expose their infants and they would not survive.

20 "And it was at this time that ªMoses was born; and he was lovely ¹in the sight of God; and he was nurtured three months in his father's home.

21 "And after he had been ¹exposed, ªPharaoh's daughter ²took him away, and nurtured him as her own son.

22 "And Moses was educated in all ªthe learning of the Egyptians, and he was a man of power in words and deeds.

23 "But when he was approaching the age of forty, ªit entered his ¹mind to visit his brethren, the sons of Israel.

24 "And when he saw one *of them* being treated unjustly, he defended him and took vengeance for the oppressed by striking down the Egyptian.

25 "And he ¹supposed that his brethren understood that God was granting them ²deliverance ³through him; but they did not understand.

26 "ªAnd on the following day he appeared to them as they were fighting together, and he tried to reconcile them in peace, saying, 'Men, you are brethren, why do you injure one another?'

27 "ªBUT THE ONE WHO WAS INJURING HIS NEIGH-

BOR pushed him away, saying, 'WHO MADE YOU A RULER AND JUDGE OVER US?

28 'ªYOU DO NOT MEAN TO KILL ME AS YOU KILLED THE EGYPTIAN YESTERDAY, DO YOU?'

29 "AND AT THIS REMARK ªMOSES FLED, AND BECAME AN ALIEN IN THE LAND OF ¹MIDIAN, where he became the father of two sons.

30 "And after forty years had passed, ªAN ANGEL APPEARED TO HIM IN THE WILDERNESS OF MOUNT SINAI, IN THE FLAME OF A BURNING THORN-BUSH.

31 "And when Moses saw it, he *began* to marvel at the sight; and as he approached to look *more* closely, there came the voice of the Lord:

32 'ªI AM THE GOD OF YOUR FATHERS, THE GOD OF ABRAHAM AND ISAAC AND JACOB.' And Moses shook *with fear* and would not venture to look.

33 "BUT THE LORD SAID TO HIM, 'ªTAKE OFF THE SANDALS FROM YOUR FEET, FOR THE PLACE ON WHICH YOU ARE STANDING IS HOLY GROUND.

34 'ªI HAVE CERTAINLY SEEN THE OPPRESSION OF MY PEOPLE IN EGYPT, AND HAVE HEARD THEIR GROANS, AND I HAVE COME DOWN TO DELIVER THEM; ¹ᵇCOME NOW, AND I WILL SEND YOU TO EGYPT.'

35 "This Moses whom they ªdisowned, saying, 'WHO MADE YOU A RULER AND A JUDGE?' is the one whom God ¹sent *to be* both a ruler and a deliverer with the ²help of the angel who appeared to him in the thorn-bush.

36 "ªThis man led them out, performing ᵇwonders and ¹signs in the land of Egypt and in the Red Sea and in the ᶜwilderness for forty years.

37 "This is the Moses who said to the sons of Israel, 'GOD SHALL RAISE UP FOR YOU ªA PROPHET ¹LIKE ME FROM YOUR BRETHREN.'

38 "This is the one who was in ªthe ¹congregation in the wilderness together with ᵇthe angel who was speaking to him in Mount Sinai, and *who was* with our fathers; and he received ᶜliving ᵈoracles to pass on to you.

39 "And our fathers were unwilling to be obedient to him, but ªrepudiated him and in their hearts turned back to Egypt,

40 SAYING TO AARON, 'ªMAKE FOR US GODS WHO WILL GO BEFORE US; FOR THIS MOSES WHO LED US OUT OF THE LAND OF EGYPT—WE DO NOT KNOW WHAT HAPPENED TO HIM.'

41 "And ¹at that time ªthey made a ²calf and

28 ªEx. 2:14

29 ¹Gr., *Madiam*
ªEx. 2:15, 22

30 ªEx. 3:1f.

32 ªEx. 3:6

33 ªEx. 3:5

34 ¹Lit., *and now hither!*
ªEx. 3:7 ᵇEx. 3:10

35 ¹Lit., *has sent* ²Lit., *hand*
ªActs 7:27

36 ¹Or, *attesting miracles*
ªEx. 12:41; 33:1; Heb. 8:9
ᵇEx. 7:3; John 4:48 ᶜEx. 16:35; Num. 14:33; Ps. 95:8-10; Heb. 3:8f.; Acts 7:42; 13:18

37 ¹Or, *as He raised up me*
ªDeut. 18:15; Acts 3:22

38 ¹Or, *church* (Gr. *ekklesia*)
ªEx. 19:17 ᵇActs 7:53 ᶜDeut. 32:47; Heb. 4:12 ᵈRom. 3:2; Heb. 5:12; 1 Pet. 4:11

39 ªNum. 14:3f.

40 ªEx. 32:1, 23

41 ¹Lit., *in those days* ²Or, *young bull*
ªEx. 32:4, 6

41 [b]Rev. 9:20

42 [1]Or, *worship* [2]I.e.,
heavenly bodies
[a]Josh. 24:20; Is. 63:10; Jer.
19:13; Ezek. 20:39 [b]Amos
5:25 [c]Acts 7:36

43 [1]Other mss. spell it:
Romphan, or *Rempham*, or
Raiphan, or *Rephan*
[a]Amos 5:26, 27

44 [a]Ex. 25:8, 9; 38:21

45 [1]Gr., *Jesus* [2]Or, *Gentiles*
[a]Josh. 3:14ff.; 18:1; 23:9;
24:18; Deut. 32:49; Ps. 44:2f.

46 [1]The earliest mss. read
house instead of *God;* the
Septuagint reads, *God*
[a]2 Sam. 7:8ff.; Ps. 132:1-5;
Acts 13:22

47 [a]1 Kin. 8:20

48 [a]Luke 1:32

49 [a]Is. 66:1; Matt. 5:34f.

50 [a]Is. 66:2

51 [a]Ex. 32:9; 33:3, 5; Lev.
26:41; Num. 27:14; Is. 63:10;
Jer. 6:10; 9:26

52 [a]2 Chr. 36:15f.; Matt.
23:31, 37; 5:12 [b]Acts 22:14;
3:14; 1 John 2:1 [c]Acts 3:14;
5:28

53 [a]Acts 7:38; Gal. 3:19;
Heb. 2:2; Deut. 33:2 [Sept.]

54 [1]Lit., *in their hearts*
[a]Acts 5:33

55 [a]Acts 2:4 [b]John 11:41

brought a sacrifice to the idol, and were rejoicing in [b]the works of their hands.

42 "But God [a]turned away and delivered them up to [1]serve the [2]host of heaven; as it is written in the book of the prophets, '[b]IT WAS NOT TO ME THAT YOU OFFERED VICTIMS AND SACRIFICES [c]FORTY YEARS IN THE WILDERNESS, WAS IT, O HOUSE OF ISRAEL?

43 '[a]YOU ALSO TOOK ALONG THE TABERNACLE OF MOLOCH AND THE STAR OF THE GOD [1]ROMPHA, THE IMAGES WHICH YOU MADE TO WORSHIP THEM. I ALSO WILL REMOVE YOU BEYOND BABYLON.'

44 "Our fathers had [a]the tabernacle of testimony in the wilderness, just as He who spoke to Moses directed *him* to make it according to the pattern which he had seen.

45 "And having received it in their turn, our fathers [a]brought it in with [1]Joshua upon dispossessing the [2]nations whom God drove out before our fathers, until the time of David.

46 "And [a]*David* found favor in God's sight, and asked that he might find a dwelling place for the [1]God of Jacob.

47 "But it was [a]Solomon who built a house for Him.

48 "However, [a]the Most High does not dwell in *houses* made by *human* hands; as the prophet says:

49 '[a]HEAVEN IS MY THRONE,
AND EARTH IS THE FOOTSTOOL OF MY FEET;
WHAT KIND OF HOUSE WILL YOU BUILD FOR ME? says the Lord;
OR WHAT PLACE IS THERE FOR MY REPOSE?

50 '[a]WAS IT NOT MY HAND WHICH MADE ALL THESE THINGS?'

51 "You men who are [a]stiffnecked and uncircumcised in heart and ears are always resisting the Holy Spirit; you are doing just as your fathers did.

52 "[a]Which one of the prophets did your fathers not persecute? And they killed those who had previously announced the coming of [b]the Righteous One, whose betrayers and murderers [c]you have now become;

53 you who received the law as [a]ordained by angels, and *yet* did not keep it."

54 Now when they heard this, they were [a]cut [1]to the quick, and they *began* gnashing their teeth at him.

55 But being [a]full of the Holy Spirit, he [b]gazed

intently into heaven and saw the glory of God, and Jesus standing ᶜat the right hand of God;

56   and he said, "Behold, I see the ᵃheavens opened up and ᵇthe Son of Man standing at the right hand of God."

57   But they cried out with a loud voice, and covered their ears, and they rushed upon him with one impulse.

58   And when they had ᵃdriven him out of the city, they *began* stoning *him*, and ᵇthe witnesses ᶜlaid aside their robes at the feet of ᵈa young man named Saul.

59   And they went on stoning Stephen as he ᵃcalled upon *the Lord* and said, "Lord Jesus, receive my spirit!"

60   And ᵃfalling on his knees, he cried out with a loud voice, "Lord, ᵇdo not hold this sin against them!" And having said this, he ¹ᶜfell asleep.

CHAPTER 8

Aɴᴅ ᵃSaul was in hearty agreement with putting him to death.

And on that day a great persecution arose against ᵇthe church in Jerusalem; and they were all ᶜscattered throughout the regions of Judea and ᵈSamaria, except the apostles.

2   And *some* devout men buried Stephen, and made loud lamentation over him.

3   But ᵃSaul *began* ravaging the church, entering house after house; and ᵇdragging off men and women, he would put them in prison.

4   Therefore, those ᵃwho had been scattered went about ¹ᵇpreaching the word.

5   And ᵃPhilip went down to the city of Samaria and *began* proclaiming ¹Christ to them.

6   And the multitudes with one accord were giving attention to what was said by Philip, as they heard and saw the ¹signs which he was performing.

7   For *in the case of* many who had ᵃunclean spirits, they were coming out *of them* shouting with a loud voice; and many who had been ᵇparalyzed and lame were healed.

8   And there was ᵃmuch rejoicing in that city.

9   Now there was a certain man named

55 ᶜMark 16:19

56 ᵃJohn 1:51 ᵇMatt. 8:20

58 ᵃLev. 24:14, 16; Luke 4:29 ᵇActs 6:13; Deut. 13:9f.; 17:7 ᶜActs 22:20 ᵈActs 8:1; 22:20; 26:10

59 ᵃActs 9:14, 21; 22:16; Rom. 10:12, 13f.; 1 Cor. 1:2; 2 Tim. 2:22

60 ¹Or, *expired* ᵃLuke 22:41 ᵇMatt. 5:44; Luke 23:34 ᶜDan. 12:2; Matt. 27:52; John 11:11f., Acts 13:36; 1 Cor. 15:6, 18, 20; 1 Thess. 4:13ff.; 2 Pet. 3:4

1 ᵃActs 7:58; 22:20; 26:10 ᵇActs 9:31 ᶜActs 8:4; 11:19 ᵈActs 1:8; 8:5, 14; 9:31

3 ᵃActs 9:1, 13, 21; 22:4, 19; 26:10f.; 1 Cor. 15:9; Gal. 1:13; Phil. 3:6; 1 Tim. 1:13 ᵇJames 2:6

4 ¹Or, *bringing the good tidings of* ᵃActs 8:1 ᵇActs 8:12; 15:35

5 ¹I.e., the Messiah ᵃActs 6:5; 8:26, 30

6 ¹Or, *attesting miracles*

7 ᵃMark 16:17 ᵇMatt. 4:24

8 ᵃActs 8:39; John 4:40-42

263

9 ªActs 8:11; 13:6 ᵇActs 5:36

10 ªActs 14:11; 28:6

11 ªActs 8:9; 13:6

12 ªActs 8:4; 1:3 ᵇActs 2:38

13 ªActs 8:6 ᵇActs 19:11

14 ªActs 8:1 ᵇLuke 22:8

15 ªActs 2:38; 19:2

16 ¹Lit., *into*
ªMatt. 28:19

17 ªActs 6:6; Mark 5:23
ᵇActs 2:4

20 ªActs 2:38; Matt. 10:8;
Is. 55:1; 2 Kin. 5:16; Dan.
5:17

21 ¹Or, *teaching*; lit., *word*
ªDeut. 10:9; 12:12; Eph. 5:5
ᵇPs. 78:37

23 ¹Or, *fetter*
ªIs. 58:6

25 ªLuke 16:28

Simon, who formerly was practicing ªmagic in the city, and astonishing the people of Samaria, ᵇclaiming to be someone great;

10 and they all, from smallest to greatest, were giving attention to him, saying, "ªThis man is what is called the Great Power of God."

11 And they were giving him attention because he had for a long time astonished them with his ªmagic arts.

12 But when they believed Philip ªpreaching the good news about the kingdom of God and the name of Jesus Christ, they were being ᵇbaptized, men and women alike.

13 And even Simon himself believed; and after being baptized, he continued on with Philip; and as he observed ªsigns and ᵇgreat miracles taking place, he was constantly amazed.

14 Now when ªthe apostles in Jerusalem heard that Samaria had received the word of God, they sent them ᵇPeter and John,

15 who came down and prayed for them, ªthat they might receive the Holy Spirit.

16 For He had not yet fallen upon any of them; they had simply been ªbaptized ¹in the name of the Lord Jesus.

17 Then they ª*began* laying their hands on them, and they were ᵇreceiving the Holy Spirit.

18 Now when Simon saw that the Spirit was bestowed through the laying on of the apostles' hands, he offered them money,

19 saying, "Give this authority to me as well, so that everyone on whom I lay my hands may receive the Holy Spirit."

20 But Peter said to him, "May your silver perish with you, because you thought you could ªobtain the gift of God with money!

21 "You have ªno part or portion in this ¹matter, for your heart is not ᵇright before God.

22 "Therefore repent of this wickedness of yours, and pray the Lord that if possible, the intention of your heart may be forgiven you.

23 "For I see that you are in the gall of bitterness and in ªthe ¹bondage of iniquity."

24 But Simon answered and said, "Pray to the Lord for me yourselves, so that nothing of what you have said may come upon me."

25 And so, when they had solemnly ªtestified

and spoken [b]the word of the Lord, they started back to Jerusalem, and were [c]preaching the gospel to many villages of the [d]Samaritans.

26 But [a]an angel of the Lord spoke to [b]Philip saying, "Arise and go south to the road that descends from Jerusalem to [c]Gaza." ([1]This is a desert *road*.)

27 And he arose and went; and behold, [a]there was an Ethiopian eunuch, a court official of Candace, queen of the Ethiopians, who was in charge of all her treasure; and he [b]had come to Jerusalem to worship.

28 And he was returning and sitting in his [1]chariot, and was reading the prophet Isaiah.

29 And [a]the Spirit said to Philip, "Go up and join this [1]chariot."

30 And when Philip had run up, he heard him reading Isaiah the prophet, and said, "Do you understand what you are reading?"

31 And he said, "Well, how could I, unless someone guides me?" And he invited Philip to come up and sit with him.

32 Now the passage of Scripture which he was reading was this:

"[a]He was led as a sheep to slaughter;

And as a lamb before its shearer is silent,

So He does not open His mouth.

33 "[a]In humiliation His judgment was taken away;

Who shall [1]relate His [2]generation?

For His life is removed from the earth."

34 And the eunuch answered Philip and said, "Please *tell me*, of whom does the prophet say this? Of himself, or of someone else?"

35 And Philip [a]opened his mouth, and [b]beginning from this Scripture he [c]preached Jesus to him.

36 And as they went along the road they came to some water; and the eunuch *said, "Look! Water! [a]What prevents me from being baptized?"

37 (See marginal note.)

38 And he ordered the [1]chariot to stop; and they both went down into the water, Philip as well as the eunuch; and he baptized him.

39 And when they came up out of the water, [a]the Spirit of the Lord snatched Philip away; and the eunuch saw him no more, but went on his way rejoicing.

25 [b]Acts 13:12 [c]Acts 8:40 [d]Matt. 10:5

26 [1]Or, *this city is deserted* [a]Acts 5:19; 8:29 [b]Acts 8:5 [c]Gen. 10:19

27 [a]Ps. 68:31; 87:4; Is. 56:3ff. [b]1 Kin. 8:41f.; John 12:20

28 [1]Or, *carriage*

29 [1]Or, *carriage* [a]Acts 10:19; 11:12; 13:2; 20:23; 21:11; 16:6, 7; 28:25; Heb. 3:7; Acts 8:39

32 [a]Is. 53:7

33 [1]Or, *describe* [2]Or, *family*, or, *origin* [a]Is. 53:8f.

35 [a]Matt. 5:2 [b]Luke 24:27; Acts 17:2; 18:28; 28:23 [c]Acts 5:42

36 [a]Acts 10:47

37 Late mss. insert verse 37: *And Philip said, "If you believe with all your heart, you may." And he answered and said "I believe that Jesus Christ is the Son of God."*

38 [1]Or, *carriage*

39 [a]1 Kin. 18:12; 2 Kin. 2:16; Ezek. 3:12, 14; 8:3; 11:1, 24; 43:5; 2 Cor. 12:2

40 ¹Or, *was found* ²O.T.: Ashdod
ᵃJosh. 11:22; 1 Sam. 5:1
ᵇActs 8:25 ᶜActs 9:30; 10:1, 24; 11:11; 12:19; 18:22; 21:8, 16; 23:23, 33; 25:1, 4, 6, 13

1 ¹Lit., *threat*
ᵃActs 9:1-22; 22:3-16; 26:9-18
ᵇActs 8:3; Acts 9:13-21

2 ᵃActs 22:5; 26:10; 9:14, 21 ᵇActs 9:2 ᶜGen. 14:15; 2 Cor. 11:32; Gal. 1:17 ᵈActs 19:9, 23; 22:4; 24:14, 22; 18:25f.; John 14:6

3 ᵃ1 Cor. 15:8

4 ᵃActs 22:7; 26:14

6 ᵃActs 9:16

7 ¹Or, *sound*
ᵃActs 26:14 ᵇActs 22:9 [John 12:29f.]

8 ¹Lit., *was seeing*
ᵃActs 22:11, 9:18 ᵇGen. 14:15 2 Cor. 11:32; Gal. 1:17

10 ᵃGen. 14:15; 2 Cor. 11:32; Gal. 1:17 ᵇActs 22:12 ᶜActs 10:3, 17, 19; 11:5; 12:9; 16:9f.; 18:9

11 ᵃActs 9:30; 11:25; 21:39; 22:3

12 ¹Some mss. omit, *in a vision*
ᵃActs 9:17; Mark 5:23; Acts 6:6

13 ¹I.e., true believers; lit., *holy ones*
ᵃActs 8:3 ᵇActs 9:32, 41; 26:10; Rom 1:7; 15:25f., 31; 16:2, 15; 1 Cor. 1:2

14 ᵃActs 9:2, 21 ᵇActs 7:59

15 ᵃActs 13:2; Rom. 1:1; Gal. 1:15; Eph. 3:7; Rom. 9:23

40 But Philip ¹found himself at ²ᵃAzotus; and as he passed through he ᵇkept preaching the gospel to all the cities, until he came to ᶜCaesarea.

a

<h3 style="text-align:center">CHAPTER 9</h3>

NOW Saul, still ᵇbreathing ¹threats and murder against the disciples of the Lord, went to the high priest,

2 and asked for ᵃletters from him to ᵇthe synagogues at ᶜDamascus, so that if he found any belonging to ᵈthe Way, both men and women, he might bring them bound to Jerusalem.

3 And it came about that as he journeyed, he was approaching Damascus, and ᵃsuddenly a light from heaven flashed around him;

4 and ᵃhe fell to the ground, and heard a voice saying to him, "Saul, Saul, why are you persecuting Me?"

5 And he said, "Who art Thou, Lord?" And He *said*, "I am Jesus whom you are persecuting,

6 but rise, and enter the city, and ᵃit shall be told you what you must do."

7 And the men who traveled with him ᵃstood speechless, ᵇhearing the ¹voice, but seeing no one.

8 And Saul got up from the ground, and ᵃthough his eyes were open, he ¹could see nothing; and leading him by the hand, they brought him into ᵇDamascus.

9 And he was three days without sight, and neither ate nor drank.

10 Now there was a certain disciple at ᵃDamascus, named ᵇAnanias; and the Lord said to him in ᶜa vision, "Ananias." And he said, "Behold, *here am* I, Lord."

11 And the Lord *said* to him, "Arise and go to the street called Straight, and inquire at the house of Judas for a man from ᵃTarsus named Saul, for behold, he is praying,

12 and he has seen ¹in a vision a man named Ananias come in and ᵃlay his hands on him, so that he might regain his sight."

13 But Ananias answered, "Lord, I have heard from many about this man, ᵃhow much harm he did to ᵇThy ¹saints at Jerusalem;

14 and here he ᵃhas authority from the chief priests to bind all who ᵇcall upon Thy name."

15 But the Lord said to him, "Go, for ᵃhe is a

chosen ¹instrument of Mine, to bear My name before ᵇthe Gentiles and ᶜkings and the sons of Israel;

16 for ᵃI will show him how much he must suffer for My name's sake."

17 And Ananias departed and entered the house, and after ᵃlaying his hands on him said, "ᵇBrother Saul, the Lord Jesus, who appeared to you on the road by which you were coming, has sent me so that you may regain your sight, and be ᶜfilled with the Holy Spirit."

18 And immediately there fell from his eyes something like scales, and he regained his sight, and he arose and was baptized;

19 and he took food and was strengthened.

Now ᵃfor several days he was with ᵇthe disciples who were at Damascus,

20 and immediately he *began* to proclaim Jesus ᵃin the synagogues, ¹saying, "He is ᵇthe Son of God."

21 And all those hearing him continued to be amazed, and were saying, "Is this not he who in Jerusalem ᵃdestroyed those who ᵇcalled on this name, and *who* had come here for the purpose of bringing them bound before the chief priests?"

22 But Saul kept increasing in strength and confounding the Jews who lived at Damascus by proving that this *Jesus* is the ¹Christ.

23 And when ᵃmany days had elapsed, ᵇthe Jews plotted together to do away with him,

24 but ᵃtheir plot became known to Saul. And ᵇthey were also watching the gates day and night so that they might put him to death;

25 but his disciples took him by night, and let him down through *an opening in* the wall, lowering him in a ᵃbasket.

26 And ᵃwhen he had come to Jerusalem, he was trying to associate with the disciples; and they were all afraid of him, not believing that he was a disciple.

27 But ᵃBarnabas took hold of him and brought him to the apostles and described to them how he had ᵇseen the Lord on the road, and that He had talked to him, and how ᶜat Damascus he had ᵈspoken out boldly in the name of Jesus.

28 And he was with them ¹moving about freely in Jerusalem, ᵃspeaking out boldly in the name of the Lord.

29 And he was talking and arguing with the

15 ¹Or, *vessel* ᵇRom. 1:5 marg.; 11:13; 15:16; Gal. 1:16; 2:7ff.; Eph. 3:2, 8; 1 Tim. 2:7; 2 Tim. 4:17; Acts 22:21; 26:17 ᶜActs 25:22f.; 26:1, 32; 2 Tim. 4:16

16 ᵃActs 20:23; 21:11 [4 and 13]; 1 Thess. 3:3; 2 Cor. 6:4f.; 11:23-27

17 ᵃActs 9:12; Mark 5:23; Acts 6:6 ᵇActs 22:13 ᶜActs 2:4

19 ᵃActs 26:20 ᵇActs 11:26; 9:26, 38

20 ¹Lit., *that* ᵃActs 13:5, 14; 14:1; 17:2, 10; 18:4, 19; 19:8; 16:13; 28:17 ᵇMatt. 4:3; Acts 13:33; 9:22

21 ᵃActs 8:3; 9:13; Gal. 1:13, 23 ᵇActs 9:14

22 ¹I.e., Messiah

23 ᵃGal. 1:17, 18 ᵇ1 Thess. 2:16

24 ᵃActs 20:3, 19; 23:12, 30; 25:3 ᵇ2 Cor. 11:32f.

25 ᵃMatt. 15:37

26 ᵃActs 22:17-20; 26:20

27 ᵃActs 4:36 ᵇActs 9:3-6 ᶜActs 9:20, 22 ᵈActs 9:29; 4:13, 29

28 ¹Lit., *going in and going out* ᵃActs 9:29; 4:13, 29

Acts 9

Saul Escapes Plot of the Jews, Is Sent to Tarsus.   Raising of Dorcas.

29 ^aActs 6:1

30 ^aActs 1:15 ^bActs 8:40
^cGal. 1:21 ^dActs 9:11

31 ¹Lit., *was having*
^aActs 5:11; 8:1; 16:5

32 ¹I.e., true believers; lit.,
holy ones
^aActs 9:13 ^b1 Chr. 8:12; Ezra
2:33; Neh. 7:37; 11:35

35 ^a1 Chr. 8:12; Ezra 2:33;
Neh. 7:37; 11:35 ^b1 Chr.
5:16; 27:29; Is. 33:9; 35:2;
65:10 ^cActs 11:21; 2:47; 9:42

36 ¹Or, *Gazelle*
^aJosh. 19:46; 2 Chr. 2:16;
Ezra 3:7; Jonah 1:3; Acts
9:38, 42f.; 10:5, 8, 23, 32;
11:5, 13

37 ¹Lit., *in those days*
^aActs 9:39; 1:13

38 ^aJosh. 19:46; 2 Chr. 2:16;
Ezra 3:7; Jonah 1:3; Acts
9:36, 42f.; 10:5, 8, 23, 32;
11:5, 13 ^bActs 11:26

39 ¹Or, *inner garments*
^aActs 9:37; 1:13 ^bActs 6:1

40 ^aMatt. 9:25 ^bActs 7:60;
Luke 22:41 ^cMark 5:41

41 ¹Note vs. 32
^aActs 9:13 ^bActs 6:1

42 ^aJosh. 19:46; 2 Chr. 2:16;
Jonah 1:3; Acts 9:38, 42f.;
10:5, 8, 23, 32; 11:5, 13 ^bActs
9:35

43 ^aJosh. 19:46; 2 Chr. 2:16;
Ezra 3:7; Jonah 1:3; Acts
9:38, 42f.; 10:5, 8, 23, 32;
11:15, 13 ^bActs 10:6

^aHellenistic *Jews;* but they were attempting to put him to death.

30   But when ^athe brethren learned *of it,* they brought him down to ^bCaesarea and ^csent him away to ^dTarsus.

31   So ^athe church throughout all Judea and Galilee and Samaria ¹enjoyed peace, being built up; and, going on in the fear of the Lord and in the comfort of the Holy Spirit, it continued to increase.

32   Now it came about that as Peter was traveling through all *those parts,* he came down also to ^athe ¹saints who lived at ^bLydda.

33   And there he found a certain man named Aeneas, who had been bedridden eight years, for he was paralyzed.

34   And Peter said to him, "Aeneas, Jesus Christ heals you; arise, and make your bed." And immediately he arose.

35   And all who lived at ^aLydda and ^bSharon saw him, and they ^cturned to the Lord.

36   Now in ^aJoppa there was a certain disciple named Tabitha (which translated *in Greek* is called ¹Dorcas); this woman was abounding with deeds of kindness and charity, which she continually did.

37   And it came about ¹at that time that she fell sick and died; and when they had washed her body, they laid it in an ^aupper room.

38   And since Lydda was near ^aJoppa, ^bthe disciples, having heard that Peter was there, sent two men to him, entreating him, "Do not delay to come to us."

39   And Peter arose and went with them. And when he had come, they brought him into the ^aupper room; and all the ^bwidows stood beside him weeping, and showing all the ¹tunics and garments that Dorcas used to make while she was with them.

40   But Peter ^asent them all out and ^bknelt down and prayed, and turning to the body, he said, "^cTabitha, arise." And she opened her eyes, and when she saw Peter, she sat up.

41   And he gave her his hand and raised her up; and calling ^athe ¹saints and ^bwidows, he presented her alive.

42   And it became known all over ^aJoppa, and ^bmany believed in the Lord.

43   And it came about that he stayed many days in ^aJoppa with ^b a certain tanner, Simon.

CHAPTER 10

NOW *there was* a certain man at ᵃCaesarea named Cornelius, a centurion of what was ᵇcalled the Italian ¹cohort,

2 a devout man, and ᵃone who feared God with all his household, and ᵇgave many ¹alms to the *Jewish* people, and prayed to God continually.

3 About ᵃthe ¹ninth hour of the day he clearly saw ᵇin a vision ᶜan angel of God who had *just* come in to him, and said to him, "Cornelius!"

4 And ᵃfixing his gaze upon him and being much alarmed, he said, "What is it, Lord?" And he said to him, "Your prayers and ¹alms ᵇhave ascended ᶜas a memorial before God.

5 "And now dispatch *some* men to ᵃJoppa, and send for a man *named* Simon, who is also called Peter;

6 he ¹is staying with a certain tanner *named* ᵃSimon, whose house is by the sea."

7 And when the angel who was speaking to him had departed, he summoned two of his ¹servants and a devout soldier of those who were in constant attendance upon him,

8 and after he had explained everything to them, he sent them to ᵃJoppa.

9 And on the next day, as they were on their way, and approaching the city, ᵃPeter went up on ᵇthe housetop about ᶜthe ¹sixth hour to pray.

10 And he became hungry, and was desiring to eat; but while they were making preparations, he ᵃfell into a trance;

11 and he *beheld ᵃthe ¹sky opened up, and a certain ²object like a great sheet coming down, lowered by four corners to the ground,

12 and there were in it all *kinds of* four-footed animals and ¹crawling creatures of the earth and birds of the ²air.

13 And a voice came to him, "Arise, Peter, ¹kill and eat!"

14 But Peter said, "By no means, ᵃLord, for ᵇI have never eaten anything ¹unholy and unclean."

15 And again a voice *came* to him a second time, "ᵃWhat God has cleansed, no *longer* consider ¹unholy."

16 And this happened three times; and immediately the ¹object was taken up into the ²sky.

17 Now while Peter was greatly perplexed ¹in

1 ¹Or, *battalion*
ᵃActs 8:40; 10:24 ᵇMatt. 27:27; Mark 15:16; John 18:3, 12; Acts 21:31, 27:1

2 ¹Or, *gifts of charity*
ᵃActs 10:22, 35; 13:16, 26 ᵇLuke 7:4f.

3 ¹I.e., 3 p.m.
ᵃActs 3:1 ᵇActs 9:10; 10:17, 19 ᶜActs 5:19

4 ¹Or, *deeds of charity*
ᵃActs 3:4 ᵇRev. 8:4 ᶜMatt. 26:13; Phil. 4:18; Heb. 6:10

5 ᵃActs 9:36

6 ¹Or, *is lodging*
ᵃActs 9:43

7 ¹Or, *household slaves*

8 ᵃActs 9:36

9 ¹I.e., noon
ᵃActs 10:9-32; 11:5-14 ᵇMatt. 24:17; Jer. 19:13; 32:29; Zeph. 1:5 ᶜActs 10:3; Ps. 55:17

10 ᵃActs 22:17; 11:5

11 ¹Or, *heaven* ²Or, *vessel*
ᵃJohn 1:51

12 ¹Or possibly, *reptiles*
²Or, *heaven*

13 ¹Or, *sacrifice*

14 ¹Or, *profane*; lit., *common*
ᵃMatt. 8:2ff.; John 4:11ff.; Acts 9:5; 22:8; ᵇActs 10:28; Ezek. 4:14; Dan. 1:8; Lev. 11: 20-25; Deut. 14:4-20

15 ¹Lit., *make common*
ᵃMark 7:19; Rom. 14:14; 1 Cor. 10:25ff.; 1 Tim. 4:4f.; Titus 1:15; Matt. 15:11

16 ¹Or, *vessel* ²Or, *heaven*

17 ¹Lit., *himself*

17 ªActs 10:3 ᵇActs 10:8

18 ¹Or, *lodging*

19 ¹One early ms. reads,
two
ªActs 10:3 ᵇActs 8:29

20 ¹Lit., *doubting nothing*
ªActs 15:7-9

22 ¹Lit., *words*
ªActs 10:2 ᵇMatt. 2:12 ᶜMark
8:38; Luke 9:26; Rev. 14:10
ᵈActs 11:14

23 ªActs 10:45; 11:12 ᵇActs
1:15 ᶜActs 9:36

24 ªActs 10:1; 8:40

25 ¹Or, *prostrated himself
in reverence*
ªMatt. 8:2

26 ªRev. 19:10; 22:8f.; Acts
14:15

27 ¹Lit., *finds*
ªActs 10:24

28 ¹Or, *profane*; lit.,
common
ªActs 11:3; John 4:9; 18:28
ᵇActs 10:14f.; 10:35; 15:9

30 ¹I.e., 3 to 4 p.m.
ªActs 10:9, 22f. ᵇActs 10:3;
3:1 ᶜActs 10:30-32; 10:3-6

mind as to what ªthe vision which he had seen
might be, behold, ᵇthe men who had been sent by
Cornelius, having asked directions for Simon's
house, appeared at the gate;

18   and calling out, they were asking whether
Simon, who was also called Peter, was ¹staying
there.

19   And while Peter was reflecting on ªthe vision, ᵇthe Spirit said to him, "Behold, ¹three men
are looking for you.

20   "But arise, go downstairs, and ªaccompany
them ¹without misgivings; for I have sent them
Myself."

21   And Peter went down to the men and said,
"Behold, I am the one you are looking for; what is
the reason for which you have come?"

22   And they said, "Cornelius a centurion, a righteous and ªGod-fearing man well spoken of by the
entire nation of the Jews, ᵇwas *divinely* directed by
a ᶜholy angel to send for you *to come* to his house
and hear ᵈa ¹message from you."

23   And so he invited them in and gave them
lodging.

    And on the next day he arose and went away
with them, and ªsome of ᵇthe brethren from ᶜJoppa
accompanied him.

24   And on the following day he entered ªCaesarea. Now Cornelius was waiting for them, and
had called together his relatives and close friends.

25   And when it came about that Peter entered,
Cornelius met him, and fell at his feet and ¹awor-
shiped *him*.

26   But Peter raised him up, saying, "ªStand up;
I too am *just* a man."

27   And as he talked with him, he entered, and
¹found ªmany people assembled.

28   And he said to them, "You yourselves know
how ªunlawful it is for a man who is a Jew to associate with a foreigner or to visit him; and *yet* ᵇGod
has shown me that I should not call any man ¹unholy or unclean.

29   "That is why I came without even raising any
objection when I was sent for. And so I ask for what
reason you have sent for me."

30   And Cornelius said, "ªFour days ago to this
hour, I was praying in my house during ᵇthe ¹ninth
hour; and behold, ᶜa man stood before me in shining garments,

31 and he *said, 'Cornelius, your prayer has been heard and your ¹alms have been remembered before God.

32 'Send therefore to ªJoppa and invite Simon, who is also called Peter, to come to you; he is ¹staying at the house of Simon *the* tanner by the sea.'

33 "And so I sent to you immediately, and you have ¹been kind enough to come. Now then, we are all here present before God to hear all that you have been commanded by the Lord."

34 And ªopening his mouth, Peter said:

"I most certainly understand *now* that ᵇGod is not one to show partiality,

35 but ªin every nation the man who ¹ᵇfears Him and ²does what is right, is welcome to Him.

36 "¹The word which He sent to the sons of Israel, ªpreaching ²ᵇpeace through Jesus Christ (He is ᶜLord of all) —

37 you yourselves know the thing which took place throughout all Judea, starting from Galilee, after the baptism which John proclaimed.

38 "¹*You know of* ªJesus of Nazareth, how God ᵇanointed Him with the Holy Spirit and with power, ²ᶜand *how* He went about doing good, and healing all who were oppressed by the devil; for ᵈGod was with Him.

39 "And we are ªwitnesses of all the things He did both in the ¹land of the Jews and in Jerusalem. And they also ᵇput Him to death by hanging Him on a ²cross.

40 "ªGod raised Him up on the third day, and granted that He should become visible,

41 ªnot to all the people, but to ᵇwitnesses who were chosen beforehand by God, *that is,* to us, ᶜwho ate and drank with Him after He arose from the dead.

42 "And He ªordered us to ¹preach to the people, and solemnly to ᵇtestify that this is the One who has been ᶜappointed by God as ᵈJudge of the living and the dead.

43 "Of Him ªall the prophets bear witness that through ᵇHis name every one who believes in Him has received forgiveness of sins."

44 While Peter was still speaking these words, ªthe Holy Spirit fell upon all those who were listening to the ¹message.

45 And ªall the ¹circumcised believers who had

---

31 ¹Or, *deeds of charity*

32 ¹Or, *lodging*
ªActs 11:3; John 4:9; 18:28

33 ¹Lit., *done well in coming*

34 ªMatt. 5:2 ᵇDeut. 10:17; 2 Chr. 19:7; Rom. 2:11; Gal. 2:6; Eph. 6:9; Col. 3:25; 1 Pet. 1:17

35 ¹Or, *reverences* ²Lit., *works righteousness*
ªActs 10:28 ᵇActs 10:2

36 ¹Some mss. read, *He sent the word to* ²Or, *preaching the gospel of peace*
ªActs 13:32 ᵇLuke 1:79; 2·14; Rom. 5:1; Eph. 2:17 ᶜRom. 10:12; Acts 2:36; Matt. 28:18

38 ¹Or, possibly, *how God anointed Jesus of Nazareth* ²Lit., *who went*
ªActs 2:22 ᵇActs 4:26 ᶜMatt. 4:23 ᵈJohn 3:2

39 ¹Or, *countryside* ²Lit., *wood*
ªLuke 24:48; Acts 10:41 ᵇActs 5:30

40 ªActs 2:24

41 ªJohn 14:19, 22; 15:27 ᵇLuke 24:48; Acts 10:39 ᶜLuke 24:43; Acts 1:4 marg.

42 ¹Or, *proclaim*
ªActs 1:2 ᵇLuke 16:28 ᶜLuke 22:22 ᵈ2 Tim. 4:1; 1 Pet. 4:5; John 5:22, 27; Acts 17:31

43 ªActs 3:18 ᵇLuke 24:47; Acts 2:38; 4:12

44 ¹Lit., *word*
ªActs 11:15; 15:8

45 ¹Lit., *believers from among the circumcision;* i.e., Jewish Christians
ªActs 10:23

45 bActs 2:33, 38

46 aActs 2:4; 19:6; Mark 16:17 bActs 3:12

47 aActs 8:36 bActs 10:44f.; 11:17; 15:8; 2:4

48 a1 Cor. 1:14-17 bActs 2:38; 8:16; 19:5

1 aActs 1:15

2 1Lit., *those of the circumcision; i.e.,* Jewish Christians aActs 10:45

3 1Or, *entered the house of* aMatt. 9:11; Gal 2.12; Acts 10:28

4 aLuke 1:3

5 1Or, *vessel* 2Or, *heaven* aActs 11:5-14; Acts 10.9-32 bActs 9:10

6 1Lit., *and I saw* 2Or possibly, *reptiles* 3Or, *heaven*

7 1Or, *sacrifice*

8 1Or, *profane;* lit., *common*

9 1Lit., *make common* aActs 10:15

10 1Or, *heaven*

11 aActs 8:40

12 1Or, *without making any distinction* aActs 8:29 bActs 15:9; Rom. 3:22 cActs 10:23

13 1Or, *after he had stood in his house and said*

come with Peter were amazed, because the gift of the Holy Spirit had been bpoured out upon the Gentiles also.

46 For they were hearing them aspeaking with tongues and exalting God. Then Peter banswered,

47 "aSurely no one can refuse the water for these to be baptized who bhave received the Holy Spirit just as we *did*, can he?"

48 And he aordered them to be baptized bin the name of Jesus Christ. Then they asked him to stay on for a few days.

Chapter 11

NOW the apostles and athe brethren who were throughout Judea heard that the Gentiles also had received the word of God.

2 And when Peter came up to Jerusalem, 1athose who were circumcised took issue with him,

3 saying, "aYou 1went to uncircumcised men and ate with them."

4 But Peter began *speaking* and *proceeded* to explain to them ain orderly sequence, saying,

5 "aI was in the city of Joppa praying; and in a trance I saw ba vision, a certain 1object coming down like a great sheet lowered by four corners from 2the sky; and it came right down to me,

6 and when I had fixed my gaze upon it and was observing it 1I saw the four-footed animals of the earth and the wild beasts and the 2crawling creatures and the birds of the 3air.

7 "And I also heard a voice saying to me, 'Arise, Peter; 1kill and eat.'

8 "But I said, 'By no means, Lord, for nothing 1unholy or unclean has ever entered my mouth.'

9 "But a voice from heaven answered a second time, 'aWhat God has cleansed, no longer 1consider unholy.'

10 "And this happened three times, and everything was drawn back up into 1the sky.

11 "And behold, at that moment three men appeared before the house in which we were *staying*, having been sent to me from aCaesarea.

12 "And athe Spirit told me to go with them 1bwithout misgivings. And cthese six brethren also went with me, and we entered the man's house.

13 "And he reported to us how he had seen the angel 1standing in his house, and saying, 'Send to

Joppa, and have Simon, who is also called Peter, brought here;

14 and he shall speak [a]words to you by which you will be saved, you and [b]all your household.'

15 "And as I began to speak, [a]the Holy Spirit fell upon them, just [b]as *He did* upon us at the beginning.

16 "And I remembered the word of the Lord, how He used to say, '[a]John baptized with water, but you shall be baptized [1]with the Holy Spirit.'

17 "If [a]God therefore gave to them the same gift as *He gave* to us also after believing in the Lord Jesus Christ, [b]who was I that I could [1]stand in God's way?"

18 And when they heard this, they [1]quieted down, and [a]glorified God, saying, "Well then, God has granted to the Gentiles also the [b]repentance *that leads* to life."

19 [a]So then those who were scattered because of the [1]persecution that arose in connection with Stephen made their way [2]to [b]Phoenicia and [c]Cyprus and [d]Antioch, speaking the word to no one except to Jews alone.

20 But there were some of them, men of [a]Cyprus and [b]Cyrene, who came to [c]Antioch and *began* speaking to the [1d]Greeks also, [2e]preaching the Lord Jesus.

21 And [a]the hand of the Lord was with them, and [b]a large number who believed turned to the Lord.

22 And the [1]news about them [2]reached the ears of the church at Jerusalem, and they sent [a]Barnabas off [3]to [b]Antioch.

23 Then when he had come and [1]witnessed [a]the grace of God, he rejoiced and *began* to encourage them all with [2]resolute heart to remain *true* to the Lord;

24 for he was a good man, and [a]full of the Holy Spirit and of faith. And [b]considerable [1]numbers were [2]brought to the Lord.

25 And he left for [a]Tarsus to look for Saul;

26 and when he had found him, he brought him to [a]Antioch. And it came about that for an entire year they [1]met with the church, and taught considerable [2]numbers; and [b]the disciples were first called [c]Christians in [a]Antioch.

27 Now [1]at this time [a]some prophets [b]came down from Jerusalem to [c]Antioch.

14 [a]Acts 10:22 [b]Acts 10:2; 16:15, 31-34; 18:8; John 4:53; 1 Cor. 1:16

15 [a]Acts 10:44 [b]Acts 2:4

16 [1]Or, *in* [a]Acts 1:5

17 [1]Or, *prevent God* [a]Acts 10:45, 47 [b]Acts 5:39

18 [1]Lit., *became silent* [a]Matt. 9:8 [b]2 Cor. 7:10

19 [1]Or, *tribulation* [2]Lit., *as far as* [a]Acts 8:1, 4 [b]Acts 15:3; 21:2 [c]Acts 4:36 [d]Acts 11:20, 22, 27; 6:5; 13:1; 14:26; 15:22f. 30, 35; 18:22; Gal. 2:11

20 [1]Some mss. read, *Greek-speaking Jews* [2]Or, *bringing the good news of* [a]Acts 4:36 [b]Acts 2:10; 6:9; 13:1; Matt. 27:32 [c]Acts 11:19, 22, 27; 6:5; 13:1; 14:26; 15:22f. 30, 35; 18:22; Gal. 2:11 [d]John 7:35 [e]Acts 5:42

21 [a]Luke 1:66 [b]Acts 2:47

22 [1]Lit., *word* [2]Lit., *was heard in* [3]Lit., *as far as* [a]Acts 4:36 [b]Acts 11:19, 20, 27; 6:5; 13:1; 14:26; 15:22f. 30, 35; 18:22; Gal. 2:11

23 [1]Lit., *seen* [2]Lit., *purpose of heart* [a]Acts 13:43; 14:26; 15:40; 20:24, 32

24 [1]Lit., *multitudes* [2]Lit., *added* [a]Acts 2:4 [b]Acts 5:14; 2:47; 11:21

25 [a]Acts 9:11

26 [1]Or, *were gathered together* [2]Lit., *multitude* [a]Acts 11:20, 22, 27; 6:5; 13:1; 14:26; 15:22f., 30, 35; Gal. 2:11 [b]Acts 6:1f.; 9:19, 26, 38; 11:29; 13:52; 14:20, 22, 28; John 2:2; Acts 9:25; 1:15 [c]Acts 26:28; 1 Pet. 4:16

27 [1]Lit., *in these days* [a]Acts 13:1; 2:17; Luke 11:49; 1 Cor. 12:10, 28f. [b]Acts 18:22 [c]Acts 11:20, 22, 26; 6:5; 13:1; 14:26; 15:22f., 30, 35; 18:22; Gal. 2:11

28 [1]Or, *through* [2]Lit.,
inhabited earth
[a]Acts 21:10 [b]Matt. 24:14
[c]Acts 18:2

29 [1]Lit., *service*
[a]Acts 6:1f.; 9:19, 26, 38; Acts
11:26; 13:52; 14:20, 22, 28;
John 2:2; Acts 9:25; 1:15
[b]Acts 11:1

30 [1]Lit., *through the hand
of*
[a]Acts 12:25 [b]Acts 4:36 [c]Acts
14:23; 15:2, 4, 6, 22f.; 16:4;
20:17; 21:18; 1 Tim. 5:17, 19;
Titus 1:5; James 5:14; 1 Pet.
5:1; 2 John 1; 3 John 1

1 [1]I.e., Herod Agrippa I

2 [a]Matt. 4:21; 20:23 [b]Mark
10:39

3 [1]Lit., *they were the days*
[a]Acts 24:27; 25:9 [b]Ex. 12:15;
23:15; Acts 20:6

4 [1]Lit., *quaternions*, one
quaternion is composed of
four soldiers
[a]John 19:23 [b]Mark 14:1; Acts
12:3

6 [a]Acts 21:33

7 [a]Acts 5:19 [b]Luke 2:9;
24:4 [c]Acts 16:26

8 [1]Lit., *bind*

9 [a]Acts 9:10

28   And one of them named [a]Agabus stood up and *began* to indicate [1]by the Spirit that there would certainly be a great famine [b]all over the [2]world. And this took place in the *reign* of [c]Claudius.

29   And in the proportion that any of [a]the disciples had means, each of them determined to send *a contribution* for the [1]relief of [b]the brethren living in Judea.

30   [a]And this they did, sending it [1]in charge of [b]Barnabas and Saul to the [c]elders.

CHAPTER 12

NOW about that time [1]Herod the king laid hands on some who belonged to the church, in order to mistreat them.

2   And he [a]had James the brother of John [b]put to death with a sword.

3   And when he saw that it [a]pleased the Jews, he proceeded to arrest Peter also. Now [1]it was during [b]the days of *the Feast of* Unleavened Bread.

4   And when he had seized him, he put him in prison, delivering him to four [1a]squads of soldiers to guard him, intending after [b]the Passover to bring him out before the people.

5   So Peter was kept in the prison, but prayer for him was being made fervently by the church to God.

6   And on the very night when Herod was about to bring him forward, Peter was sleeping between two soldiers, [a]bound with two chains; and guards in front of the door were watching over the prison.

7   And behold, [a]an angel of the Lord suddenly [b]appeared, and a light shone in the cell; and he struck Peter's side and roused him, saying, "Get up quickly." And [c]his chains fell off his hands.

8   And the angel said to him, "Gird yourself and [1]put on your sandals." And he did so. And he *said to him, "Wrap your cloak around you and follow me."

9   And he went out and continued to follow, and he did not know that what was being done by the angel was real, but thought he was seeing [a]a vision.

10   And when they had passed the first and second guard, they came to the iron gate that leads

into the city, which [a]opened for them by itself; and they went out and went along one street; and immediately the angel departed from him.

11   And when Peter [a]came to himself, he said, "Now I know for sure that [b]the Lord has sent forth His angel and rescued me from the hand of Herod and from all [1]that the Jewish people were expecting."

12   And when he realized *this*, he went to the house of Mary, the mother of [a]John who was also called Mark, where many were gathered together and [b]were praying.

13   And when he knocked at the door of the gate, [a]a servant-girl named Rhoda came to answer.

14   And when she recognized Peter's voice, [a]because of her joy she did not open the gate, but ran in and announced that Peter was standing in front of the gate.

15   And they said to her, "You are out of your mind!" But she kept insisting that it was so. And they kept saying, "It is [a]his angel."

16   But Peter continued knocking; and when they had opened, they saw him and were amazed.

17   But [a]motioning to them with his hand to be silent, he described to them how the Lord had led him out of the prison. And he said, "Report these things to [1][b]James and [c]the brethren." And he departed and went to another place.

18   Now when day came, there was no small disturbance among the soldiers *as to* [1]what could have become of Peter.

19   And when Herod had searched for him and had not found him, he examined the guards and ordered that they [a]be led away *to execution*. And he went down from Judea to [b]Caesarea and was spending time there.

20   Now he was very angry with the people of [a]Tyre and Sidon; and with one accord they came to him, and having won over Blastus the king's chamberlain, they were asking for peace, because [b]their country was fed by the king's country.

21   And on an appointed day Herod, having put on his royal apparel, took his seat on the [1]rostrum and *began* delivering an address to them.

22   And the people kept crying out, "The voice of a god and not of a man!"

23   And immediately [a]an angel of the Lord

---

10 [a]Acts 5:19; 16:26

11 [1]Lit., *the expectation of the people of the Jews*
[a]Luke 15:17 [b]Dan. 3:28; 6:22

12 [a]Acts 12:25; 13:5, 13; 15:37, 39; Col. 4:10; 2 Tim. 4:11; Philem. 24; 1 Pet. 5:13 [b]Acts 12:5

13 [a]John 18:16f.

14 [a]Luke 24:41

15 [a]Matt. 18:10

17 [1]Or, *Jacob*
[a]Acts 13:16; 19:33; 21:40 [b]Acts 15:13; 21:18; 1 Cor. 15:7; Gal. 1:19; 2:9, 12; Mark 6:3 [c]Acts 1:15

18 [1]Lit., *what therefore had become*

19 [a]Acts 16:27; 27:42 [b]Acts 8:40

20 [a]Matt. 11:21 [b]1 Kin. 5:11; Ezra 3:7; Ezek. 27:17

21 [1]Or, *judgment-seat*

23 [a]Acts 5:19; 2 Sam. 24:16; 2 Kin. 19:35

Acts 12, 13

**The Death of Herod.
Paul and Barnabas Commissioned.**

23 ¹Lit., *breathed his last*

24 ªActs 6:7; 19:20

25 ¹Some ancient mss. read, *to Jerusalem* ²Lit., *ministry*
ªActs 13:1ff.; 4:36 ᵇActs 11:30 ᶜActs 12:12

1 ªActs 11:19 ᵇActs 11:26 ᶜActs 11:27; 15:32; 1 Cor. 14:29, 32, 37; Acts 19:6; 21:9; 1 Cor. 11:4f.; 13:2, 8f. ᵈl Cor. 12:28f.; Eph. 4:11; Rom. 12:6f.; James 3:1 ᵉActs 13:1ff.; 4:36 ᶠMatt. 27:32; Acts 11:20 ᵍMatt. 14:1

2 ªActs 8:29; 13:4 ᵇActs 13:1ff.; 4:36 ᶜActs 9:15

3 ªActs 1:24 ᵇActs 6:6 ᶜActs 14:26; 13:4

4 ªActs 13:2f. ᵇActs 4:36

5 ªActs 9:20; 13:14 ᵇActs 12:12

6 ªActs 8:9 ᵇMatt. 7.15

7 ªActs 13:8, 12; 18:12; 19:38

8 ªActs 8:9 ᵇActs 13:7, 12; Acts 18:12; 19:38 ᶜActs 6:7

9 ¹Or, *having just been filled*
ªActs 4:8; 2:4

10 ªMatt. 13:38; John 8:44 ᵇHos. 14:9; 2 Pet. 2:15

11 ªEx. 9:3; 1 Sam. 5:6f.; Ps. 32:4; Job 19:21; Heb. 10:31

struck him because he did not give God the glory, and he was eaten by worms and ¹died.

24 But ªthe word of the Lord continued to grow and to be multiplied.

25 And ªBarnabas and ªSaul returned ¹from Jerusalem ᵇwhen they had fulfilled their ²mission, taking along with *them* ᶜJohn, who was also called Mark.

CHAPTER 13

Now there were at ªAntioch, in the ᵇchurch that was *there*, ᶜprophets and ᵈteachers: ᵉBarnabas, and Simeon who was called Niger, and Lucius of ᶠCyrene, and Manaen who had been brought up with ᵍHerod the tetrarch, and ᵉSaul.

2 And while they were ministering to the Lord and fasting, ªthe Holy Spirit said, "Set apart for Me ᵇBarnabas and Saul for ᶜthe work to which I have called them."

3 Then, when they had fasted and ªprayed and ᵇlaid their hands on them, ᶜthey sent them away.

4 So, being ªsent out by the Holy Spirit, they went down to Seleucia and from there they sailed to ᵇCyprus.

5 And when they reached Salamis, they *began* to proclaim the word of God in ªthe synagogues of the Jews; and they also had ᵇJohn as their helper.

6 And when they had gone through the whole island as far as Paphos, they found a certain ªmagician, a Jewish ᵇfalse prophet whose name was Bar-Jesus,

7 who was with the ªproconsul, Sergius Paulus, a man of intelligence. This man summoned Barnabas and Saul and sought to hear the word of God.

8 But Elymas the ªmagician (for thus his name is translated) was opposing them, seeking to turn the ᵇproconsul away from ᶜthe faith.

9 But Saul, who was also *known as* Paul, ¹ªfilled with the Holy Spirit, fixed his gaze upon him,

10 and said, "You who are full of all deceit and fraud, you ªson of the devil, you enemy of all righteousness, will you not cease to make crooked ᵇthe straight ways of the Lord?

11 "And now, behold, ªthe hand of the Lord is

**Elymas the Magician Struck Blind.
Paul's Sermon.**

Acts 13

upon you, and you will be blind and not see the sun for a time." And immediately a mist and a darkness fell upon him, and he went about seeking those who would lead him by the hand.

12 Then the ªproconsul believed when he saw what had happened, being amazed at ᵇthe teaching of the Lord.

13 Now Paul and his companions put out to sea from ªPaphos and came to ᵇPerga in ᶜPamphylia; and ᵈJohn left them and returned to Jerusalem.

14 But going on from Perga, they arrived at ªPisidian ᵇAntioch, and on ᶜthe Sabbath day they went into ᵈthe synagogue and sat down.

15 And after ªthe reading of the Law and ᵇthe Prophets ᶜthe synagogue officials sent to them, saying, "Brethren, if you have any word of exhortation for the people, say it."

16 And Paul stood up, and ªmotioning with his hand, he said,

"**M**en of Israel, and ᵇyou who fear God, listen:

17 "The God of this people Israel ªchose our fathers, and ¹made the people great during their stay in the land of Egypt, and with an uplifted arm He led them out from it.

18 "And for about ªa period of forty years ᵇHe ¹put up with them in the wilderness.

19 "And ªwhen He had destroyed ᵇseven nations in the land of Canaan, He ᶜdistributed their land as an inheritance—*all of which took* ᵈabout four hundred and fifty years.

20 "And after these things He ªgave *them* judges until ᵇSamuel the prophet.

21 "And then they ªasked for a king, and God gave them ᵇSaul the son of Kish, a man of the tribe of Benjamin, for forty years.

22 "And after He had ªremoved him, He raised up David to be their king, concerning whom He also testified and said, 'I have found ᵇDavid the son of Jesse, a man after My heart, who will do all My ¹will.'

23 "ªFrom the offspring of this man ᵇaccording to promise God has brought to Israel ᶜa Savior, Jesus,

24 after ªJohn had proclaimed before ¹His coming a baptism of repentance to all the people of Israel.

25 "And while John ªwas completing his course, ᵇhe kept saying, 'What do you suppose that I am? I

12 ªActs 13:7, 8; 18:12; 19:38 ᵇActs 13:49; 8:25; 15:35f.; 19:10, 20

13 ªActs 13:6 ᵇActs 14:25 ᶜActs 2:10; 14:24; 15:38; 27:5 ᵈActs 12:12

14 ªActs 14:24 ᵇActs 14:19, 21; 2 Tim. 3:11 ᶜActs 13:42, 44; 16:13; 18:4; 17:2 ᵈActs 9:20; 13:5

15 ªActs 15:21; 2 Cor. 3:14f. ᵇActs 13:27 ᶜMark 5:22

16 ªActs 12:17 ᵇActs 10:2; 13:26

17 ¹Or, *exalted* ªDeut. 7.6-8, Ex. 6.1, 6; 13:14, 16; Acts 7:17ff.

18 ¹Some ancient mss. read, *bore them up in His arms as a nurse in the wilderness* ªActs 7:36 ᵇDeut. 1:31

19 ªActs 7:45 ᵇDeut. 7:1 ᶜJosh. 19:51; Ps. 78:55 ᵈJudg. 11:26; 1 Kin. 6:1

20 ªJudg. 2:16 ᵇActs 3:24

21 ª1 Sam. 8:5 ᵇ1 Sam. 10:1; 9:1f.

22 ¹Lit., *wills* ª1 Sam. 15:23, 26, 28; 16:1, 13 ᵇ1 Sam. 13:14; Ps. 89:20; Acts 7:46

23 ªMatt. 1:1 ᵇActs 13:32f. ᶜLuke 2:11; John 4:42

24 ¹Lit., *the face of His entering* ªMark 1:1-4; Acts 1:22; 19:4

25 ªActs 20:24 ᵇJohn 1:20, 27; Matt. 3:11; Mark 1:7; Luke 3:16

26 ªActs 28:28; Acts 5:20;
4:12; 13:46; John 6:68

27 ¹Lit., *voices*
ªLuke 23:13 ᵇActs 3:17
ᶜLuke 24:27 ᵈActs 13:15

28 ¹Lit., *destroyed*
ªActs 3:14

29 ¹Lit., *wood*
ªActs 26:22 ᵇLuke 23:53
ᶜActs 5:30

30 ªActs 13:33, 34, 37; 2:24

31 ªActs 1:11 ᵇLuke 24:48

32 ªActs 5:42; 14:15 ᵇActs
26:6; Rom. 1:2; 4:13; 9:4;
Acts 13:23

33 ¹Some mss. read, *to us
their children*
ªActs 13:30, 34, 37; 2:24 ᵇPs.
2:7

34 ªActs 13:30, 33, 37; 2:24
ᵇIs. 55:3

35 ¹Lit., *give* ²Or, *Devout,
or, Pious* ³Lit., *see
corruption*
ªPs. 16:10; Acts 2:27

36 ¹Or, *served his own
generation by the purpose of
God* ²Lit., *saw corruption*
ªActs 2:29 ᵇActs 13:22; 20:27
ᶜActs 8:1; 1 Kin. 2:10

37 ¹Lit., *see corruption*
ªActs 13:30, 33, 34; 2:24

38 ¹Lit., *this One*
ªLuke 24:47; Acts 2:38

39 ¹Lit., *justified* ²In the
Greek text the remainder of
this vs. is part of vs. 38
ªRom. 3:28; 10:4; Acts 10:43

40 ªJohn 6:45; Acts 7:42;
Luke 24:44

41 ¹Lit., *disappear*
ªHab. 1:5

am not *He*. But behold, one is coming after me the sandals of whose feet I am not worthy to untie.'

26 "Brethren, sons of Abraham's family, and those among you who fear God, to us the word of ªthis salvation is sent out.

27 "For those who live in Jerusalem, and their ªrulers, ᵇrecognizing neither Him nor the ¹utterances of ᶜthe prophets which are ᵈread every Sabbath, fulfilled *these* by condemning *Him*.

28 "And though they found no ground for *putting Him to* death, they ªasked Pilate that He be ¹executed.

29 "And when they had ªcarried out all that was written concerning Him, ᵇthey took Him down from ᶜthe ¹cross and laid Him in a tomb.

30 "But God ªraised Him from the dead;

31 and for many days He appeared to those who came up with Him ªfrom Galilee to Jerusalem, the very ones who are now ᵇHis witnesses to the people.

32 "And we ªpreach to you the good news of ᵇthe promise made to the fathers,

33 that God has fulfilled this *promise* ¹to our children in that He ªraised up Jesus, as it is also written in the second Psalm, 'ᵇThou art My Son; today I have begotten Thee.'

34 "*And as for the fact* that He ªraised Him up from the dead, no more to return to decay, He has spoken in this way: 'ᵇI will give you the holy *and* sure *blessings* of David.'

35 "Therefore He also says in another *Psalm*, 'ªThou wilt not ¹allow Thy ²Holy One to ³undergo decay.'

36 "For ªDavid, after he had ¹served ᵇthe purpose of God in his own generation, ᶜfell asleep, and was laid among his fathers, and ²underwent decay;

37 but He whom God ªraised did not ¹undergo decay.

38 "Therefore let it be known to you, brethren, that ªthrough ¹Him forgiveness of sins is proclaimed to you,

39 and through Him ªeveryone who believes is ¹freed² from all things, from which you could not be ¹freed through the Law of Moses.

40 "Take heed therefore, so that the thing spoken of ªin the Prophets may not come upon *you*:

41 'ªBehold, you scoffers, and marvel, and ¹perish;

FOR I AM ACCOMPLISHING A WORK IN YOUR
DAYS,
A WORK WHICH YOU WILL NEVER BELIEVE,
THOUGH SOMEONE SHOULD DESCRIBE IT
TO YOU.' "

42 And as [1]Paul and Barnabas were going out,
[2]the people kept begging that these [3]things might
be spoken to them the next [a]Sabbath.

43 Now when *the meeting of* the synagogue
had broken up, many of the Jews and of the [a]God-
fearing [1b]proselytes followed Paul and Barnabas,
who, speaking to them, were urging them to continue in [c]the grace of God.

44 And the next [a]Sabbath nearly the whole city
assembled to hear the word of [1]God.

45 But when [a]the Jews saw the crowds, they
were filled with jealousy, and *began* contradicting
the things spoken by Paul, and were [1]blaspheming.

46 And Paul and Barnabas spoke out boldly
and said, "It was necessary that the word of God
should be spoken to you [a]first; since you repudiate
it, and judge yourselves unworthy of eternal life,
behold, [b]we are turning to the Gentiles.

47 "For thus the Lord has commanded us,
'[a]I HAVE PLACED YOU AS A [b]LIGHT FOR THE
GENTILES,
THAT YOU SHOULD [b]BRING SALVATION TO
THE END OF THE EARTH.' "

48 And when the Gentiles heard this, they *began* rejoicing and glorifying [a]the word of [1]the Lord;
and as many as [b]had been appointed to eternal life
believed.

49 And [a]the word of the Lord was being spread
through the whole region.

50 But [a]the Jews aroused the [1b]devout women
[c]of prominence and the leading men of the city,
and instigated a persecution against Paul and Barnabas, and drove them out of their [2]district.

51 But [a]they shook off the dust of their feet *in
protest* against them and went to [b]Iconium.

52 And the disciples were continually [a]filled
with joy and with the Holy Spirit.

CHAPTER 14

AND it came about that in [a]Iconium [b]they entered the synagogue of the Jews together, and

42 [1]Lit., *they were* [2]Lit.,
they [3]Lit., *words*
[a]Acts 13:14

43 [1]I.e., Gentile converts to
Judaism
[a]Acts 13:50; 17:4, 17; Acts
16:14; 18:7 [b]Matt. 23:15
[c]Acts 11:23

44 [1]Some ancient mss.
read, *the Lord*
[a]Acts 13:14

45 [1]Or, *reviling*
[a]Acts 13:50; 14:2, 4, 5, 19;
1 Thess. 2:16

46 [a]Acts 3:26; 13:5, 14; 9:20
[b]Acts 18:6; 22:21; 26:20;
28:28; 19:9, 15

47 [1]Lit., *be for salvation*
[a]Is. 49:6 [b]Luke 2:32

48 [1]Some ancient mss.
read, *God*
[a]Acts 13:12 [b]Rom. 8:28ff.;
Eph. 1:4f., 11

49 [a]Acts 13:12

50 [1]Or, *worshipping* [2]Lit.,
boundaries
[a]Acts 13:45; 14:2, 4, 5, 19;
1 Thess. 2:16 [b]Acts 13:43;
17:4, 17; 16:14; 18:7 [c]Mark
15:43

51 [a]Matt. 10:14; Acts 18:6
[b]Acts 14:1, 19, 21; 16:2;
2 Tim. 3:11

52 [a]Acts 2:4

1 [a]Acts 13:51; 14:19, 21;
16:2; 2 Tim. 3:11 [b]Acts 13:5

279

1 cActs 2:47 dJohn 7:35;
Acts 18:4

2 1Or, *disobeyed* 2Lit.,
souls
aActs 13:45, 50; 14:4, 5, 19;
1 Thess. 2:16 bJohn 3:36
cActs 1:15

3 1Or, *attesting miracles*
aActs 4:29f.; 20:32; Heb. 2:4
bJohn 4:48

4 1Lit., *were*
aActs 17:4f.; 19:9; 28:24
bActs 13:45, 50; 14:2, 5, 19;
1 Thess. 2:16 cActs 14:14

5 aActs 13:45, 50; 14:2, 4,
19; 1 Thess. 2:16 bActs 14:19

6 aActs 14:11 bActs 14:8,
21; 16:1f.; 2 Tim. 3:11 cActs
14:20; 16:1; 20:4

7 aActs 14:21; 16:10; 14:15

8 aActs 14:6, 21; Acts
16:1f.; 2 Tim. 3:11 bActs 3:2

9 1Lit., *saved*
aActs 3:4; 10:4 bMatt. 9:28

10 aActs 3:8

11 aActs 14:6 bActs 8:10;
28:6

12 1Lat., Jupiter 2Lat.,
Mercurius 3Lit., *the leader
of the speaking*

13 1Lit., *in front of*
aDan. 2:46

14 1Or, *outer garments*
aActs 14:4 bNum. 14:6;
Matt. 26:65; Mark 14:63

15 1I.e., idols
aJames 5:17; Acts 10:26 bActs
13:32; Acts 14:7, 21 cDeut.
32:21; 1 Sam. 12:21; Jer.
8:19; 14:22; 1 Cor. 8:4 dMatt.
16:16

spoke in such a manner cthat a great multitude believed, both of Jews and of dGreeks.

2   But athe Jews who 1bdisbelieved stirred up the 2minds of the Gentiles, and embittered them against cthe brethren.

3   Therefore they spent a long time *there* aspeaking boldly *with reliance* upon the Lord, who was bearing witness to the word of His grace, granting that 1bsigns and wonders be done by their hands.

4   aBut the multitude of the city was divided; and some 1sided with bthe Jews, and some with cthe apostles.

5   And when an attempt was made by both the Gentiles and athe Jews with their rulers, to mistreat and to bstone them,

6   they became aware of it and fled to the cities of aLycaonia, bLystra and cDerbe, and the surrounding region;

7   and there they continued to apreach the gospel.

8   And at aLystra there was sitting ba certain man, without strength in his feet, lame from his mother's womb, who had never walked.

9   This man was listening to Paul as he spoke, who, awhen he had fixed his gaze upon him, and had seen that he had bfaith to be 1made well,

10   said with a loud voice, "Stand upright on your feet." aAnd he leaped up and *began* to walk.

11   And when the multitudes saw what Paul had done, they raised their voice, saying in the aLycaonian language, "bThe gods have become like men and have come down to us."

12   And they *began* calling Barnabas, 1Zeus, and Paul, 2Hermes, because he was 3the chief speaker.

13   And the priest of Zeus, whose *temple* was 1just outside the city, brought oxen and garlands to the gates, and awanted to offer sacrifice with the crowds.

14   But when athe apostles, Barnabas and Paul, heard of it, they btore their 1robes and rushed out into the crowd, crying out

15   and saying, "Men, why are you doing these things? We are also amen of the same nature as you, and bpreach the gospel to you in order that you should turn from these 1cvain things to a dliving

God, cWHO MADE THE HEAVEN AND THE EARTH AND THE SEA, AND ALL THAT IS IN THEM.

16 "¹And in the generations gone by He ªpermitted all the ²nations to ᵇgo their own ways;

17 and yet ªHe did not leave Himself without witness, in that He did good and ᵇgave you rains from heaven and fruitful seasons, ¹satisfying your hearts with food and gladness."

18 And *even* saying these things, they with difficulty restrained the crowds from offering sacrifice to them.

19 But ªJews came from ᵇAntioch and cIconium, and having won over the multitudes, they ᵈstoned Paul and ¹dragged him out of the city, supposing him to be dead.

20 But while ªthe disciples stood around him, he arose and entered the city. And the next day he went away with Barnabas to ᵇDerbe.

21 And after they had ªpreached the gospel to that city and had ᵇmade many disciples, they returned to cLystra and to ᵈIconium and to ᵉAntioch,

22 strengthening the souls of ªthe disciples, encouraging them to continue in ᵇthe faith, and *saying*, "cThrough many tribulations we must enter the kingdom of God."

23 And when ªthey had appointed ᵇelders for them in every church, having cprayed with fasting, they ᵈcommended them to the Lord in whom they had believed.

24 And they passed through ªPisidia and came into ᵇPamphylia.

25 And when they had spoken the word in ªPerga, they went down to Attalia;

26 and from there they sailed to ªAntioch, from ᵇwhich they had been ccommended to the grace of God for the work that they had ¹accomplished.

27 And when they had arrived and gathered the church together, they *began* to ªreport all things that God had done with them and ¹how He had opened a ᵇdoor of faith to the Gentiles.

28 And they spent ¹a long time with ªthe disciples.

CHAPTER 15

AND ªsome men came down from Judea and *began* teaching ᵇthe brethren, "Unless you are ccircumcised according to ᵈthe custom of Moses, you cannot be saved."

15 cEx. 20:11; Ps. 146:6; Rev. 14:7; Acts 4:24; 17:24

16 ¹Lit., *who in the generations gone by permitted* ²Or, *Gentiles* ªActs 17:30 ᵇMic. 4:5; Ps. 81:12

17 ¹Lit., *filling* ªActs 17:26f.; Rom. 1:19f. ᵇDeut. 11:14; Job 5:10; Ps. 65:10f.; Ezek. 34:26f.; Joel 2:23

19 ¹Lit., *were dragging* ªActs 13:45, 50; 14:2, 4, 5; 1 Thess. 2:16 ᵇActs 13:14; 14:21, 26 cActs 13:51; 14:1, 21 ᵈActs 14:5; 2 Cor. 11:25; 2 Tim. 3:11

20 ªActs 11:26; 14:22, 28 ᵇActs 14:6

21 ªActs 14:7 ᵇActs 2:47 cActs 14:6 ᵈActs 13:51; 14:1, 19 ᵉActs 13:14; Acts 14:19, 26

22 ªActs 11:26; Acts 14:28 ᵇActs 6:7 cJohn 16:33; 1 Thess. 3:3; 2 Tim. 3:12; Mark 10:30; John 15:18, 20; 1 Pet. 2:21; Rev. 1:9; Acts 9:16

23 ªTitus 1:5; 2 Cor. 8:19 ᵇActs 11:30 cActs 13:3; 1:24 ᵈActs 20:32

24 ªActs 13:14 ᵇActs 13:13

25 ªActs 13:13

26 ¹Lit., *fulfilled* ªActs 11:19 ᵇActs 13:3 cActs 15:40; 11:23

27 ¹Lit., *that* ªActs 15:4; 15:3, 12; 21:19 ᵇ1 Cor. 16:9; 2 Cor. 2:12; Col. 4:3; Rev. 3:8

28 ¹Lit., *not a little* ªActs 11:26; 14:22

1 ªActs 15:24 ᵇActs 1:15; 15:3, 22, 32 cActs 15:5; Gal. 5:2f.; 1 Cor. 7:18; Gal. 2:11, 14 ᵈActs 6:14

2 [1]Lit., *not a little* [2]Or, *it was determined*
[a]Acts 15:7 [b]Gal. 2:2 [c]Acts 15:4, 6, 22, 23; 16:4; 11:30

3 [a]Acts 20:38; 21:5; Rom. 15:24; 1 Cor. 16:6, 11; 2 Cor. 1:16; Titus 3:13; 3 John 6 [b]Acts 11:19 [c]Acts 14:27; 15:4, 12 [d]Acts 1:15; 15:22, 32

4 [a]Acts 15:6, 22, 23; 16:4; 11:30 [b]Acts 14:27; Acts 15:12

5 [a]Acts 5:17; 24:5, 14; 26:5; 28:22 [b]Matt. 3:7; Acts 26:5 [c]Gal. 5:2f.; 1 Cor. 7:18; Gal. 2:11, 14

6 [1]Lit., *see about* [2]Lit., *word*
[a]Acts 15:4, 22, 23; 16:4; 11:30

7 [1]Lit., *from days of old* [a]Acts 15:2 [b]Acts 10:19f. [c]Acts 20:24

8 [a]Acts 1:24 [b]Acts 10:47

9 [a]Acts 10:28, 34; 11:12 [b]Acts 10:43

10 [a]Acts 5:9 [b]Matt. 23:4, Gal. 5:1

11 [a]Rom. 5:15, 3.24; 2 Cor. 13:14; Eph. 2:5-8

12 [a]Acts 14:27; 15:3, 4 [b]John 4:48

13 [1]Or, *Jacob* [a]Acts 12:17

14 [a]2 Pet. 1:1 marg.; Acts 15:7

15 [a]Acts 13:40

2   And when Paul and Barnabas had [1]great dissension and [a]debate with them, [2b]*the brethren* determined that Paul and Barnabas and certain others of them, should go up to Jerusalem to the [c]apostles and elders concerning this issue.

3   Therefore, being [a]sent on their way by the church, they were passing through both [b]Phoenicia and Samaria, [c]describing in detail the conversion of the Gentiles, and were bringing great joy to all [d]the brethren.

4   And when they arrived at Jerusalem, they were received by the church and [a]the apostles and the elders, and they [b]reported all that God had done with them.

5   But certain ones of [a]the sect of the [b]Pharisees who had believed, stood up, saying, "It is necessary to [c]circumcise them, and to direct them to observe the Law of Moses."

6   And [a]the apostles and the elders came together to [1]look into this [2]matter.

7   And after there had been much [a]debate, Peter stood up and said to them, "Brethren, you know that [1]in the early days [b]God made a choice among you, that by my mouth the Gentiles should hear the word of [c]the gospel and believe.

8   "And God, [a]who knows the heart, bore witness to them, [b]giving them the Holy Spirit, just as He also did to us;

9   and [a]He made no distinction between us and them, [b]cleansing their hearts by faith.

10   "Now therefore why do you [a]put God to the test by placing upon the neck of the disciples a yoke which [b]neither our fathers nor we have been able to bear?

11   "But we believe that we are saved through [a]the grace of the Lord Jesus, in the same way as they also are."

12   And all the multitude kept silent, and they were listening to Barnabas and Paul as they were [a]relating what [b]signs and wonders God had done through them among the Gentiles.

13   And after they had stopped speaking, [1a]James answered, saying, "Brethren, listen to me.

14   "[a]Simeon has related how God first concerned Himself about taking from among the Gentiles a people for His name.

15   "And with this the words of [a]the Prophets agree, just as it is written,

16 'ᵃAFTER THESE THINGS ᵇI WILL RETURN,
   AND I WILL REBUILD THE ¹TABERNACLE OF
     DAVID WHICH HAS FALLEN,
   AND I WILL REBUILD ITS RUINS,
   AND I WILL RESTORE IT,

17 'ᵃIN ORDER THAT THE REST OF ¹MANKIND MAY
    SEEK THE LORD,
   AND ALL THE GENTILES ²ᵇWHO ARE CALLED
    BY MY NAME,

18 'ᵃSAYS THE LORD, WHO ¹ᵇMAKES THESE THINGS
    KNOWN FROM OF OLD.'

19 "Therefore it is ᵃmy judgment that we do not trouble those who are turning to God from among the Gentiles,

20 but that we write to them that they abstain from ¹ᵃthings contaminated by idols and from fornication and from ᵇwhat is strangled and from blood.

21 "For ᵃMoses from ancient generations has in every city those who preach him, since he is read in the synagogues every Sabbath."

22 Then it seemed good to ᵃthe apostles and the elders, with the whole church, to choose men from among them to send to ᵇAntioch with Paul and Barnabas—Judas called Barsabbas, and ᶜSilas, leading men among ᵈthe brethren,

23 and they ¹sent this letter by them,

"ᵃThe apostles and the brethren who are elders, to ᵇthe brethren in ᶜAntioch and ᵈSyria and ᵉCilicia who are from the Gentiles, ᶠgreetings.

24 "Since we have heard that ᵃsome ¹of our number to whom we gave no instruction have ᵇdisturbed you with *their* words, unsettling your souls,

25 ᵃit seemed good to us, having ¹become of one mind, to select men to send to you with our beloved Barnabas and Paul,

26 men who have ¹ᵃrisked their lives for the name of our Lord Jesus Christ.

27 "Therefore we have sent ᵃJudas and ᵇSilas, who themselves will also report the same things by word *of mouth.*

28 "For ᵃit seemed good to ᵇthe Holy Spirit and to ᶜus to lay upon you no greater burden than these essentials:

29 that you abstain from ᵃthings sacri-

---

16 ¹Or, *tent*
ᵃAmos 9:11 ᵇJer. 12:15

17 ¹Lit., *men* ²Lit., *upon whom My name is called*
ᵃAmos 9:12 ᵇJames 2:7 marg.; Sept. of Deut. 28:10; Is. 63:19; Jer. 14:9; Dan. 9:19.

18 ¹Or, *does these things which were known*
ᵃAmos 9:12 ᵇIs. 45:21

19 ᵃActs 15:28; 21:25

20 ¹Lit., *the pollutions of*
ᵃActs 15:29; Dan. 1:8; 1 Cor. 8:7-13; 10:7f., 14-28; Rev. 2:14, 20 ᵇGen. 9:4; Lev. 3:17; 7:26; 17:10, 14; 19:26; Deut. 12:16, 23; 15:23; 1 Sam. 14:33

21 ᵃActs 13:15; 2 Cor. 3:14f.

22 ᵃActs 15:2 ᵇActs 11:20 [not 13:14] ᶜActs 15:27, 32, 40; 16:19, 25, 29; 17:4, 10, 14f.; 18:5; 2 Cor. 1:19; 1 Thess. 1:1; 2 Thess. 1:1; 1 Pet. 5:12 ᵈActs 15:1

23 ¹Lit., *wrote by their hand*
ᵃActs 15:2 ᵇActs 15:1 ᶜActs 11:20 ᵈMatt. 4:24; Acts 15:41; Gal. 1:21 ᵉActs 6:9 ᶠActs 23:26; James 1:1; 2 John 10f.

24 ¹Lit., *from us*
ᵃActs 15:1 ᵇGal. 1:7; 5:10

25 ¹Or, *met together*
ᵃActs 15:28

26 ¹Lit., *given over*
ᵃActs 9:23ff.; 14:19

27 ᵃActs 15:22, 32 ᵇActs 15:22

28 ᵃActs 15:25 ᵇActs 15:8; 5:32 ᶜActs 15:19, 25

29 ᵃActs 15:20

29 [1]Lit., *from which keeping yourselves free*
[a]Acts 15:20

30 [1]Or, *multitude*
[a]Acts 15:22f.

31 [1]Or, *exhortation*

32 [1]Or, *exhorted*
[a]Acts 15:22, 27 [b]Acts 15:22
[c]Acts 13:1 [d]Acts 15:1

33 [a]Mark 5:34; Acts 16:36;
1 Cor. 16:11; Heb. 11:31
[b]Acts 15:22

34 [1]Some mss. add verse 34,
*But it seemed good to Silas
to remain there*

35 [a]Acts 12:25 [b]Acts 8:4
[c]Acts 13:12

36 [a]Acts 13:4, 13, 14, 51;
14:6, 24f. [b]Acts 13:12

37 [a]Acts 12:12

38 [1]Lit., *from*
[a]Acts 13:13

39 [a]Col. 4:10; Acts 12:12;
15:37 [b]Acts 4:36

40 [a]Acts 15:22 [b]Acts 14:26;
11:23

41 [a]Matt. 4:24; Acts 15:23
[b]Acts 6:9

1 [a]Acts 14:6 [b]Acts 17:14f.;
18:5; 19:22; 20:4; Rom.
16:21; 1 Cor. 4:17; 16:10;
2 Cor. 1:1, 19; Phil. 1:1; 2:19;
Col. 1:1; 1 Thess. 1:1; 3:2, 6;
2 Thess. 1:1; 1 Tim. 1:2, 18;
6:20; 2 Tim. 1:2; Philem. 1;
Heb. 13:23 [c]2 Tim. 1:5; 3:15

2 [a]Acts 16:40 [b]Acts 14:6
[c]Acts 13:51

3 [1]Lit., *go out*
[a]Gal. 2:3

ficed to idols and from [a]blood and from [a]things strangled and from [a]fornication; [1]if you keep yourselves free from such things, you will do well. Farewell."

30 So, when they were sent away, [a]they went down to Antioch; and having gathered the [1]congregation together, they delivered the letter.

31 And when they had read it, they rejoiced because of its [1]encouragement.

32 And [a]Judas and [b]Silas, also being [c]prophets themselves, [1]encouraged and strengthened [d]the brethren with a lengthy message.

33 And after they had spent time *there*, they were sent away from the brethren [a]in peace to those who had [b]sent them out.

34 (See marginal note.[1])

35 But [a]Paul and Barnabas stayed in Antioch, teaching and [b]preaching with many others also [c]the word of the Lord.

36 And after some days Paul said to Barnabas, "Let us return and visit the brethren in [a]every city in which we proclaimed [b]the word of the Lord, *and see* how they are."

37 And Barnabas was desirous of taking [a]John, called Mark, along with them also.

38 But Paul kept insisting that they should not take him along who had [a]deserted them [1]in Pamphylia and had not gone with them to the work.

39 And there arose such a sharp disagreement that they separated from one another, and Barnabas took [a]Mark with him and sailed away to [b]Cyprus.

40 But Paul chose [a]Silas and departed, being [b]committed by the brethren to the grace of the Lord.

41 And he was traveling through [a]Syria and [b]Cilicia, strengthening the churches.

CHAPTER 16

AND he came also to [a]Derbe and to [a]Lystra. And behold, a certain disciple was there, named [b]Timothy, the son of a [c]Jewish woman who was a believer, but his father was a Greek,

2 and he was well spoken of by [a]the brethren who were in [b]Lystra and [c]Iconium.

3 Paul wanted this man to [1]go with him; and he [a]took him and circumcised him because of the

Jews who were in those parts, for they all knew that his father was a Greek.

4   Now while they were passing through the cities, they were delivering ªthe decrees, which had been decided upon by ᵇthe apostles and ᶜelders who were in Jerusalem, for them to observe.

5   So ªthe churches were being strengthened ¹in the faith, and were ᵇincreasing in number daily.

6   And they passed through the ¹ªPhrygian and ᵇGalatian region, having been forbidden by the Holy Spirit to speak the word in ²ᶜAsia;

7   and when they had come to ªMysia, they were trying to go into ᵇBithynia, and the ᶜSpirit of Jesus did not permit them;

8   and passing ¹by ªMysia, they came down to ᵇTroas.

9   And ªa vision appeared to Paul in the night: ¹A certain man of ᵇMacedonia was standing and appealing to him, and saying, "Come over to Macedonia and help us."

10   And when he had seen ªthe vision, immediately ᵇwe sought to ¹go into Macedonia, concluding that God had called us to ᶜpreach the gospel to them.

11   ¹Therefore putting out to sea from ªTroas, we ran ᵇa straight course to Samothrace, and on the day following to Neapolis;

12   and from there to ªPhilippi, which is a leading city of the district of ᵇMacedonia, ᶜa *Roman* colony; and we were staying in this city for some days.

13   And on ªthe Sabbath day we went outside the gate to a river side, where we were supposing that there would be a place of prayer; and we sat down and began speaking to the women who had assembled.

14   And a certain woman named Lydia, from the city of ªThyatira, a seller of purple fabrics, ᵇa worshiper of God, was listening; ¹and the Lord ᶜopened her heart to respond to the things spoken by Paul.

15   And when she and ªher household had been baptized, she urged us, saying, "If you have judged me to be faithful to the Lord, come into my house and stay." And she prevailed upon us.

16   And it happened that as we were going to ªthe place of prayer, a certain slave-girl having ᵇa

4 ªActs 15:28f. ᵇActs 15:2 ᶜActs 11:30

5 ¹Or, *in faith* ªActs 9:31 ᵇActs 2:47

6 ¹Or, *Phrygia and the Galatian region* ²I.e., west coast province of Asia Minor ªActs 2:10; 18:23 ᵇActs 18:23; 1 Cor. 16:1; Gal. 1:2; 3:1; 2 Tim. 4:10; 1 Pet. 1:1 ᶜActs 2:9

7 ªActs 16:8 ᵇ1 Pet. 1:1 ᶜLuke 24:49; Rom. 8:9; Gal. 4:6; Phil. 1:19; 1 Pet. 1:11; Acts 8:29

8 ¹Or, *through* ªActs 16:7 ᵇActs 16:11; 20:5f.; 2 Cor. 2:12; 2 Tim. 4:13

9 ¹Or, *A man* ªActs 9:10 ᵇActs 16:10, 12; 18:5; 19:21f., 29; 20:1, 3; 27:2; Rom. 15:26

10 ¹Lit., *go out* ªActs 9:10 ᵇ[we] Acts 16:10-17; 20:5-15; 21:1-18; 27:1-28:16 ᶜActs 14:7

11 ¹Some ancient mss. read, *and* ªActs 16:8; 20:5f.; 2 Cor. 2:12; 2 Tim. 4:13 ᵇActs 21:1

12 ªActs 20:6; Phil. 1:1; 1 Thess. 2:2 ᵇActs 16:9, 10; 18:5; 19:21f., 29; 20:1, 3; 27:2; Rom. 15:26 ᶜActs 16:21

13 ªActs 13:14

14 ¹Lit., *whose heart the Lord opened* ªRev. 1:11; 2:18, 24 ᵇActs 18:7; 13:43 ᶜLuke 24:45

15 ªActs 11:14

16 ªActs 16:13 ᵇLev. 19:31; 20:6, 27; Deut. 18:11; 1 Sam. 28:3, 7; 2; Kin. 21:6; 1 Chr. 10:13; Is. 8:19

285

17 ¹Lit., *a way*
ᵃMark 5:7

18 ¹Lit., *hour*
ᵃMark 16:17

19 ¹Lit., *gone out*
ᵃActs 16:16; 19:25f. ᵇActs
15:40; 16:25, 29; Acts 15:22
ᶜActs 17:6f.; 21:30; James
2:6; Acts 8:3

21 ᵃEsther 3:8 ᵇActs 16:12

22 ¹Or, *outer garments*
²Lit., *to beat with rods*
ᵃ2 Cor. 11:25; 1 Thess. 2:2

23 ᵃActs 16:27, 36

24 ¹Lit., *who, having
received*
ᵃJob 13:27; 33:11; Jer. 20:2f.;
29:26

25 ᵃActs 16:19 ᵇEph. 5:19

26 ᵃActs 4:31 ᵇActs 12:10
ᶜActs 12:7

27 ᵃActs 16:23, 36 ᵇActs
12:19

29 ᵃActs 16:19

spirit of divination met us, who was bringing her masters much profit by fortune-telling.

17 Following after Paul and us, she kept crying out, saying, "These men are bond-servants of ᵃthe Most High God, who are proclaiming to you ¹the way of salvation."

18 And she continued doing this for many days. But Paul was greatly annoyed, and turned and said to the spirit, "I command you ᵃin the name of Jesus Christ to come out of her!" And it came out at that very ¹moment.

19 But when her masters saw that their hope of ᵃprofit was ¹gone, they seized ᵇPaul and Silas and ᶜdragged them into the market place before the authorities,

20 and when they had brought them to the chief magistrates, they said, "These men are throwing our city into confusion, being Jews,

21 and ᵃare proclaiming customs which it is not lawful for us to accept or to observe, being ᵇRomans."

22 And the crowd rose up together against them, and the chief magistrates tore their ¹robes off them, and proceeded to order ²*them* to be ᵃbeaten with rods.

23 And when they had inflicted many blows upon them, they threw them into prison, commanding ᵃthe jailer to guard them securely;

24 ¹and he, having received such a command, threw them into the inner prison, and fastened their feet in ᵃthe stocks.

25 But about midnight ᵃPaul and Silas were praying and ᵇsinging hymns of praise to God, and the prisoners were listening to them;

26 and suddenly ᵃthere came a great earthquake, so that the foundations of the prison-house were shaken; and immediately ᵇall the doors were opened, and everyone's ᶜchains were unfastened.

27 And when ᵃthe jailer had been roused out of sleep and had seen the prison doors opened, he drew his sword and was about ᵇto kill himself, supposing that the prisoners had escaped.

28 But Paul cried out with a loud voice, saying, "Do yourself no harm, for we are all here!"

29 And he called for lights and rushed in and trembling with fear, he fell down before ᵃPaul and Silas,

30   and after he brought them out, he said, "Sirs, ªwhat must I do to be saved?"

31   And they said, "ªBelieve in the Lord Jesus, and you shall be saved, you and ᵇyour household."

32   And they spoke the word of ¹the Lord to him together with all who were in his house.

33   And he took them ªthat *very* hour of the night and washed their wounds, and immediately he was baptized, he and all his *household.*

34   And he brought them into his house and set ¹food before them, and rejoiced ²greatly, having believed in God with ªhis whole household.

35   Now when day came, the chief magistrates sent their policemen, saying, "Release those men."

36   And ªthe jailer reported these words to Paul, *saying,* "The chief magistrates have sent to release you. Now therefore come out and go ᵇin peace."

37   But Paul said to them, "They have beaten us in public without trial, ªmen who are Romans, and have thrown us into prison; and now are they sending us away secretly? No indeed! But let them come themselves and bring us out."

38   And the policemen reported these words to the chief magistrates. And ªthey were afraid when they heard that they were Romans,

39   and they came and appealed to them, and when they had brought them out, they kept begging them ªto leave the city.

40   And they went out of the prison and entered *the house of* ªLydia, and when they saw ᵇthe brethren, they ¹encouraged them and departed.

CHAPTER 17

NOW when they had traveled through Amphipolis and Apollonia, they came to ªThessalonica, where there was a synagogue of the Jews.

2   And ªaccording to Paul's custom, he went to them, and for three ᵇSabbaths reasoned with them from ᶜthe Scriptures,

3   ¹explaining and ²giving evidence that the ³Christ ªhad to suffer and ᵇrise again from the dead, and *saying,* "ᶜThis Jesus whom I am proclaiming to you is the ³Christ."

4   ªAnd some of them were persuaded and joined ᵇPaul and Silas, ¹along with a great multi-

30 ªActs 2:37; 22:10

31 ªMark 16:16 ᵇActs 11:14; 16:15

32 ¹Some ancient mss. read, *God*

33 ªActs 16:25

34 ¹Lit., *a table* ²Or, *greatly with his whole household, having believed in God* ªActs 11:14; 16:15

36 ªActs 16:27 ᵇActs 15:33

37 ªActs 22:25-29

38 ªActs 22:29

39 ªMatt. 8:34

40 ¹Or, *exhorted* ªActs 16:14 ᵇActs 16:2; 1:15

1 ªActs 17:11, 13; 27:2; Phil. 4:16; 2 Tim. 4:10; Acts 20:4; 1 Thess. 1:1; 2 Thess. 1:1

2 ªActs 9:20; 17:10, 17 ᵇActs 13:14 ᶜActs 8:35

3 ¹Lit., *opening* ²Lit., *placing before* ³I.e., Messiah ªActs 3:18 ᵇJohn 20:9 ᶜActs 9:22; 18:5, 28

4 ¹Lit., *and a great* ªActs 14:4 ᵇActs 17:10; 15:40; 15:22; 17:14f.

4 [2]Lit., *not a few*
[c]Acts 17:17; 13:43 [d]John 7:35
[e]Acts 13:50

5 [a]Acts 17:13; 1 Thess.
2:16 [b]Acts 17:6, 7, 9; Rom.
16:21

6 [1]Lit., *the inhabited
earth*
[a]Acts 16:19f. [b]Acts 17:31;
Matt. 24:14

7 [1]Lit., *whom Jason has
welcomed*
[a]Luke 10:38; James 2:25
[b]Luke 23:2

9 [1]Or, *bond*
[a]Acts 17:5

10 [1]Lit., *who
when . . . arrived went*
[a]Acts 17:6, 14f.; 1:15 [b]Acts
17:4 [c]Acts 17:13; 20:4 [d]Acts
17:2

11 [1]Lit., *who received* [2]Lit.,
all
[a]Acts 17:1

12 [1]Lit., *and not a few*
[a]Acts 2:47 [b]Mark 15:43 [c]Acts
13:50

13 [a]Acts 17:1 [b]Acts 17:10;
20:4

14 [a]Acts 17:6, 10; 1:15 [b]Acts
17:4, 10; 15:22 [c]Acts 16:1

15 [a]Acts 15:3 [b]Acts 17:16,
21f.; 18:1; 1 Thess. 3:1 [c]Acts
17:14 [d]Acts 18:5

16 [a]Acts 17:15, 21f.; 18:1;
1 Thess. 3:1

17 [a]Acts 9:20; 17:2 [b]Acts
17:4

18 [1]Or, *disputing*

288

tude of the [c]God-fearing [d]Greeks and [2]a number of the [e]leading women.

5 But [a]the Jews, becoming jealous and taking along some wicked men from the market place, formed a mob and set the city in an uproar; and coming upon the house of [b]Jason, they were seeking to bring them out to the people.

6 And when they did not find them, they *began* [a]dragging Jason and some brethren before the city authorities, shouting, "These men who have upset [1b]the world have come here also;

7 [1]and Jason [a]has welcomed them, and they all act [b]contrary to the decrees of Caesar, saying that there is another king, Jesus."

8 And they stirred up the crowd and the city authorities who heard these things.

9 And when they had received a [1]pledge from [a]Jason and the others, they released them.

10 And [a]the brethren immediately sent [b]Paul and Silas away by night to [c]Berea; [1]and when they arrived, they went into [d]the synagogue of the Jews.

11 Now these were more noble-minded than those in [a]Thessalonica, [1]for they received the word with [2]great eagerness, examining the Scriptures daily, *to see* whether these things were so.

12 [a]Many of them therefore believed, [1]along with a number of [b]prominent Greek [c]women and men.

13 But when the Jews of [a]Thessalonica found out that the word of God had been proclaimed by Paul in [b]Berea also, they came there likewise, agitating and stirring up the crowds.

14 And then immediately [a]the brethren sent Paul out to go as far as the sea; and [b]Silas and [c]Timothy remained there.

15 Now [a]those who conducted Paul brought him as far as [b]Athens; and receiving a command for [c]Silas and Timothy to [d]come to him as soon as possible, they departed.

16 Now while Paul was waiting for them at [a]Athens, his spirit was being provoked within him as he was beholding the city full of idols.

17 So he was reasoning [a]in the synagogue with the Jews and [b]the God-fearing *Gentiles*, and in the market place every day with those who happened to be present.

18 And also some of the Epicurean and Stoic philosophers were [1]conversing with him. And some

were saying, "What would [a]this [2]idle babbler wish to say?" Others, "He seems to be a proclaimer of strange [3]deities,"—because he was preaching [b]Jesus and the resurrection.

19 And they [a]took him and brought him [1]to the [2b]Areopagus, saying, "May we know what [c]this new teaching is [3]which you are proclaiming?

20 "For you are bringing some strange things to our ears; we want to know therefore what these things mean."

21 (Now all the Athenians and the strangers [a]visiting there used to spend their time in nothing other than telling or hearing something new.)

22 And Paul stood in the midst of the [1]Areopagus and said, "Men of [a]Athens, I observe that you are very [b]religious in all respects.

23 "For while I was passing through and examining the [a]objects of your worship, I also found an altar with this inscription, 'TO AN UNKNOWN GOD.' What therefore [b]you worship in ignorance, this I proclaim to you.

24 "[a]The God who made the world and all things in it, since He is [b]Lord of heaven and earth, does not [c]dwell in temples made with hands;

25 neither is He served by human hands, [a]as though He needed anything, since He Himself gives to all life and breath and all things;

26 and [a]He made from [1]one every nation of mankind to live on all the face of the earth, having [b]determined *their* appointed times, and the boundaries of their habitation,

27 that they should seek God, if perhaps they might grope for Him and find Him, [a]though He is not far from each one of us;

28 for [a]in Him we live and move and [1]exist, as even some of your own poets have said, 'For we also are His offspring.'

29 "Being then the offspring of God, we [a]ought not to think that the Divine Nature is like gold or silver or stone, an image formed by the art and thought of man.

30 "Therefore having [a]overlooked [b]the times of ignorance, God is [c]now declaring to men that all everywhere should repent,

31 because He has fixed [a]a day in which [b]He will judge [1c]the world in righteousness through a Man whom He has [d]appointed, having furnished proof to all men [2]by [e]raising Him from the dead."

18 [2]I.e., one who makes his living by picking up scraps [3]Lit., *demons*
[a]1 Cor. 4:10; 1:20 [b]Acts 4:2; 17:31f.

19 [1]Or, *before* [2]Or, *Hill of Ares*, god of war [3]Lit., *which is being spoken by you*
[a]Acts 23:19 [b]Acts 17:22 [c]Mark 1:27

21 [a]Acts 2:10

22 [1]Or possibly, the Council of the Areopagus
[a]Acts 17:15 [b]Acts 25:19

23 [a]2 Thess. 2:4 marg.
[b]John 4:22

24 [a]Is. 42:5; Acts 14:15 [b]Matt. 11:25; Deut. 10:14; Ps. 115:16 [c]Acts 7:48

25 [a]Ps. 50:10-12; Job 22:2

26 [1]Some later mss. read, *one blood*
[a]Mal. 2:10 [b]Deut. 32:8; Job 12:23

27 [a]Deut. 4:7; Jer. 23:23f.; Acts 14:17

28 [1]Lit., *are*
[a]Job 12:10; Dan. 5:23

29 [a]Is. 40:18ff.; Rom. 1:23

30 [a]Acts 14:16; Rom. 3:25 [b]Acts 17:23 [c]Luke 24:47; Acts 26:20; Titus 2:11f.

31 [1]Lit., *the inhabited earth* [2]Or, *when He raised*
[a]Matt. 10:15 [b]John 5:22, 27; Acts 10:42; Ps. 9:8; 96:13; 98:9 [c]Matt. 24:14; Acts 17:6 [d]Luke 22:22 [e]Acts 2:24

Paul at Corinth Preaches in the Synagogue.

32 ¹Lit., *also again*
ªActs 17:18, 31

34 ªActs 17:19, 22

1 ªActs 17:15 ᵇActs 19:1;
1 Cor. 1:2; 2 Cor. 1:1, 23;
2 Tim. 4:20; Acts 18:8;
2 Cor. 6:11

2 ªActs 18:18, 26; Rom.
16:3; 1 Cor. 16:19; 2 Tim.
4:19 ᵇActs 2:9 ᶜActs 27:1, 6;
Heb. 13:24 ᵈActs 11:28

3 ªActs 20:34; 1 Cor. 4:12;
1 Thess. 2:9; 2 Thess. 3:8;
1 Cor. 9:15; 2 Cor. 11:7;
12:13; 1 Thess. 4:11

4 ªActs 9:20; 18:19 ᵇActs
13:14 ᶜActs 14:1

5 ¹I.e., Messiah
ªActs 17:14; 15:22; 16:1 ᵇActs
17:15 ᶜActs 16:9 ᵈActs 20:21;
Luke 16:28 ᵉActs 17:3; 18:28

6 ªNeh. 5:13; Acts 13:51
ᵇ2 Sam. 1:16; 1 Kin. 2:33;
Ezek. 18:13; 33:4, 6, 8; Matt.
27:25; Acts 20:26 ᶜActs 13:46

7 ¹Some ancient mss.
read, *Titus*, others omit it
altogether
ªActs 16:14; Acts 13:43

8 ª1 Cor. 1:14 ᵇMark 5:22
ᶜActs 11:14 ᵈActs 19:1;
1 Cor. 1:2; 2 Cor. 1:1, 23;
2 Tim. 4:20; Acts 18:1;
2 Cor. 6:11

9 ªActs 9:10

32 Now when they heard of ªthe resurrection of the dead, some *began* to sneer, but others said, "We shall hear you ¹again concerning this."

33 So Paul went out of their midst.

34 But some men joined him and believed, among whom also was Dionysius the ªAreopagite and a woman named Damaris and others with them.

CHAPTER 18

Aͬ͟FTER these things he left ªAthens and went to ᵇCorinth.

2 And he found a certain Jew named ªAquila, a native of ᵇPontus, having recently come from ᶜItaly with his wife ªPriscilla, because ᵈClaudius had commanded all the Jews to leave Rome. He came to them,

3 and because he was of the same trade, he stayed with them and ªthey were working; for by trade they were tent-makers.

4 And he was reasoning ªin the synagogue every ᵇSabbath and trying to persuade ᶜJews and Greeks.

5 But when ªSilas and Timothy ᵇcame down from ᶜMacedonia, Paul *began* devoting himself completely to the word, solemnly ᵈtestifying to the Jews that ᵉJesus was the ¹Christ.

6 And when they resisted and blasphemed, he ªshook out his garments and said to them, "ᵇYour blood *be* upon your own heads, I am clean; from now on I shall go ᶜto the Gentiles."

7 And he departed from there and went to the house of a certain man named ¹Titius Justus, ªa worshiper of God, whose house was next to the synagogue.

8 And ªCrispus, ᵇthe leader of the synagogue, believed in the Lord ᶜwith all his household, and many of the ᵈCorinthians when they heard were believing and being baptized.

9 And the Lord said to Paul in the night by ªa vision, "Do not be afraid *any longer*, but go on speaking and do not be silent;

10 for I am with you, and no man will attack you in order to harm you, for I have many people in this city."

11 And he settled *there* a year and six months, teaching the word of God among them.

12 But while Gallio was ᵃproconsul of ᵇAchaia, ᶜthe Jews with one accord rose up against Paul and brought him before ᵈthe judgment-seat,

13 saying, "This man persuades men to worship God contrary to ᵃthe law."

14 But when Paul was about to ᵃopen his mouth, Gallio said to the Jews, "If it were a matter of wrong or of vicious crime, O Jews, it would be reasonable for me to put up with you;

15 but if there are ᵃquestions about words and names and your own Law, look after it yourselves; I am unwilling to be a judge of these matters."

16 And he drove them away from ᵃthe judgment-seat.

17 And they all took hold of ᵃSosthenes, ᵇthe leader of the synagogue, and *began* beating him in front of ᶜthe judgment-seat. And Gallio was not concerned about any of these things.

18 And Paul, having remained many days longer, ᵃtook leave of ᵇthe brethren and put out to sea for ᶜSyria, and with him were ᵈPriscilla and ᵈAquila. In ᵉCenchrea ¹he ᶠhad his hair cut, for he was keeping a vow.

19 And they came to ᵃEphesus, and he left them there. Now he himself entered ᵇthe synagogue and reasoned with the Jews.

20 And when they asked him to stay for a longer time, he did not consent,

21 but ᵃtaking leave of them and saying, "I will return to you again ᵇif God wills," he set sail from ᶜEphesus.

22 And when he had landed at ᵃCaesarea, he went up and greeted the church, and went down to ᵇAntioch.

23 And having spent some time *there*, he departed and passed successively through the ᵃGalatian region and Phrygia, strengthening all the disciples.

24 Now a certain Jew named ᵃApollos, an ᵇAlexandrian by birth, ¹an eloquent man, came to ᶜEphesus; and he was mighty in the Scriptures.

25 This man had been instructed in ᵃthe way of the Lord; and being fervent in spirit, he was speaking and teaching accurately the things concerning Jesus, being acquainted only with ᵇthe baptism of John;

26 and he began to speak out boldly in the synagogue. But when ᵃPriscilla and Aquila heard

12 ᵃActs 13:7 ᵇActs 18:27; 19:21; Rom. 15:26; 1 Cor. 16:15; 2 Cor. 1:1; 9:2; 11:10; 1 Thess. 1:7f. ᶜ1 Thess. 2:16 ᵈMatt. 27:19

13 ᵃActs 18:15; John 19:7

14 ᵃMatt. 5:2

15 ᵃActs 23:29; 25:19

16 ᵃMatt. 27:19

17 ᵃ1 Cor. 1:1 ᵇActs 18:8 ᶜMatt. 27:19

18 ¹Lit., *having his hair cut* ᵃMark 6:46 ᵇActs 18:27 ᶜMatt. 4:24 ᵈActs 18:2, 26 ᵉRom. 16:1 ᶠNum. 6:2, 5, 9, 18; Acts 21:24

19 ᵃActs 18:21, 24; 19:1, 17, 26 [28, 34f.]; 20:16f.; [21:29]; 1 Cor. 15:32; 16:8; Eph. 1:1; 1 Tim. 1:3; 2 Tim. 1:18; 4:12; Rev. 1:11; 2:1 ᵇActs 18:4

21 ᵃMark 6:46 ᵇ1 Cor. 4:19; 16:7; Heb. 6:3; James 4:15; Rom. 1:10; 15:32; 1 Pet. 3:17 ᶜActs 18:19, 24; 19:1, 17, 26 [28, 34f.]; 20:16f.; [21:29]; 1 Cor. 15:32; 16:8; Eph. 1:1; 1 Tim. 1:3; 2 Tim. 1:18; 4:12; Rev. 1:11; 2:1

22 ᵃActs 8:40 ᵇActs 11:19

23 ᵃActs 16:6

24 ¹Or, *a learned man* ᵃActs 19:1; 1 Cor. 1:12; 3:5, 6, 22; 4:6; 16:12; Titus 3:13 ᵇActs 6:9 ᶜActs 18:19

25 ᵃActs 9:2; 18:26 ᵇLuke 7:29; Acts 19:3

26 ᵃActs 18:2, 18

26 ᵇActs 18:25

27 ¹Or, *helped greatly through grace those who had believed*
ᵃActs 18:12; 19:1 ᵇActs 18:18 ᶜActs 11:26

28 ¹I.e., Messiah
ᵃActs 8:35 ᵇActs 18:5

1 ᵃActs 18:24; 1 Cor. 1:12; 3:5, 6, 22; 4:6; 16:12; Titus 3:13 ᵇActs 18:1 ᶜActs 18:23 ᵈActs 18:21, 24; 19:1, 17, 26 [28, 34f.]; 20:16f.; [21:29]; 1 Cor. 15:32; 16:8; Eph. 1:1; 1 Tim. 1:3; 2 Tim. 1:18; 4:12; Rev. 1:11; 2:1

2 ¹Or, *the Holy Spirit has been given*
ᵃActs 8:15f.; 11:16f. ᵇJohn 7:39

3 ᵃLuke 7:29; Acts 18:25

4 ᵃActs 13:24 ᵇJohn 1:7

5 ¹Lit., *into*
ᵃActs 8:12, 16; 10:48

6 ᵃActs 6:6; 8:17 ᵇActs 2:4; 10:46; Mark 16:17 ᶜActs 13:1

8 ¹Some ancient mss. read, *persuading* as to the things about
ᵃActs 9:20; 18:26 ᵇActs 1:3

9 ᵃActs 14:4 ᵇActs 9:2; 19:23 ᶜActs 11:26; 19:30

10 ¹I.e., west coast province of Asia Minor
ᵃActs 19:8; 20:31 ᵇActs 16:6; 19:22, 26, 27 ᶜActs 13:12; 19:20

11 ¹Or, *works of power*
ᵃActs 8:13

12 ᵃActs 5:15

him, they took him aside and explained to him ᵇthe way of God more accurately.

27 And when he wanted to go across to ᵃAchaia, ᵇthe brethren encouraged him and wrote to ᶜthe disciples to welcome him; and when he had arrived, he ¹helped greatly those who had believed through grace;

28 for he powerfully refuted the Jews in public, demonstrating ᵃby the Scriptures that ᵇJesus was the ¹Christ.

CHAPTER 19

AND it came about that while ᵃApollos was at ᵇCorinth, Paul having passed through the ᶜupper country came to ᵈEphesus, and found some disciples,

2 and he said to them, "ᵃDid you receive the Holy Spirit when you believed?" And they *said* to him, "No, ᵇwe have not even heard whether ¹there is a Holy Spirit."

3 And he said, "Into what then were you baptized?" And they said, "ᵃInto John's baptism."

4 And Paul said, "ᵃJohn baptized with the baptism of repentance, telling the people ᵇto believe in Him who was coming after him, that is, in Jesus."

5 And when they heard this, they were ᵃbaptized ¹in the name of the Lord Jesus.

6 And when Paul had ᵃlaid his hands upon them, the Holy Spirit came on them, and they *began* ᵇspeaking with tongues and ᶜprophesying.

7 And there were in all about twelve men.

8 And he entered ᵃthe synagogue and continued speaking out boldly for three months, reasoning and ¹persuading *them* ᵇabout the kingdom of God.

9 But when ᵃsome were becoming hardened and disobedient, speaking evil of ᵇthe Way before the multitude, he withdrew from them and took away ᶜthe disciples, reasoning daily in the school of Tyrannus.

10 And this took place for ᵃtwo years, so that all who lived in ¹ᵇAsia heard ᶜthe word of the Lord, both Jews and Greeks.

11 And God was performing ᵃextraordinary ¹miracles by the hands of Paul,

12 ᵃso that handkerchiefs or aprons were even

carried from his body to the sick, and the diseases left them and [b]the evil spirits went out.

13 But also some of the Jewish [a]exorcists, who went from place to place, attempted to name over those who had the evil spirits the name of the Lord Jesus, saying, "I adjure you by Jesus whom Paul preaches."

14 And seven sons of one Sceva, a Jewish chief priest, were doing this.

15 And the evil spirit answered and said to them, "I recognize Jesus, and I know about Paul, but who are you?"

16 And the man in whom was the evil spirit leaped on them and subdued both of them and overpowered them, so that they fled out of that house naked and wounded.

17 And this became known to all, both Jews and Greeks, who lived in [a]Ephesus; and fear fell upon them all and the name of the Lord Jesus was being magnified.

18 Many also of those who had believed kept coming, confessing and disclosing their practices.

19 And many of those who practiced magic brought their books together and *began* burning them in the sight of all; and they counted up the price of them and found it [1]fifty thousand [a]pieces of silver.

20 So [1a]the word of the Lord [b]was growing mightily and prevailing.

21 Now after these things were finished, Paul purposed in the [1]spirit to [a]go to Jerusalem [b]after he had passed through [c]Macedonia and [d]Achaia, saying, "After I have been there, [e]I must also see Rome."

22 And having sent into [a]Macedonia two of [b]those who ministered to him, [c]Timothy and [d]Erastus, he himself stayed in [1e]Asia for a while.

23 And about that time there arose no small disturbance concerning [a]the Way.

24 For a certain man named Demetrius, a silversmith, who made silver shrines of [1]Artemis, [a]was bringing no little [2]business to the craftsmen;

25 these he gathered together with the workmen of similar *trades*, and said, "Men, you know that our prosperity [1]depends upon this business.

26 "And you see and hear that not only in [a]Ephesus, but in almost all of [1b]Asia, this Paul has persuaded and turned away a considerable number

12 [b]Mark 16:17

13 [a]Matt. 12:27; Luke 11:19

17 [a]Acts 18:19

19 [1]Or probably, fifty thousand Greek drachmas. A drachma approximated a day's wage.
[a]Luke 15:8 and marg.

20 [1]Or, *according to the power of the Lord the word was growing*
[a]Acts 19:10 [b]Acts 6:7; 12:24

21 [1]Or, *Spirit*
[a]Acts 20:16, 22; 21:15; Rom. 15:25; 2 Cor. 1:16 [b]1 Cor. 16:5; Acts 20:1 [c]Rom. 15:26; 1 Thess. 1:7f.; Acts 16:9; 19:22, 29 [d]Acts 18:12 [e]Rom. 15:24, 28; Acts 23:11

22 [1]I.e., west coast province of Asia Minor
[a]Acts 16:9; 19:21, 29 [b]Acts 19:29; 13:5; 20:34; 2 Cor. 8:19 [c]Acts 16:1 [d]Rom. 16:23; 2 Tim. 4:20 [e]Acts 19:10

23 [a]Acts 19:9

24 [1]Latin, *Diana* [2]Or, *profit*
[a]Acts 16:16, 19f.

25 [1]Lit., *is from*

26 [1]Note vs. 22
[a]Acts 18:19 [b]Acts 19:10

26 cActs 17:29; 1 Cor. 8:4;
10:19; Deut. 4:28; Ps. 115:4;
Is. 44:10-20; Jer. 10:3ff.; Rev.
9:20

27 ¹Latin, *Diana* ²Note vs.
22 ³Lit., *the inhabited earth*
aActs 19:10 bMatt. 24:14

28 ¹Latin, *Diana*
aActs 18:19

29 ¹Lit., *having dragged*
aActs 20:4 bActs 20:4; 27:2;
Col. 4:10; Philem. 24 cActs
19:22; 13:5; 20:34; 2 Cor.
8:19 dActs 16:9; 19:22

30 ¹Lit., *people*
aActs 19:9

31 ¹I.e., political or
religious officials of the
province of Asia ²Lit., *give
himself*

32 ¹Gr., ekklesia ²Or, *on
whose account*
aActs 21:34

33 ¹Or, *instructed
Alexander* ²Lit., *people*
aActs 12:17

34 ¹Latin, *Diana*

35 ¹Latin, *Diana* ²Lit.,
Zeus or, *Jupiter*
aActs 18:19

37 aRom. 2:22

38 ¹Or, *provincial
governors*
aActs 13:7

294

of people, saying that cgods made with hands are no gods *at all*.

27 "And not only is there danger that this trade of ours fall into disrepute, but also that the temple of the great goddess ¹Artemis be regarded as worthless and that she whom all of ²aAsia and bthe ³world worship should even be dethroned from her magnificence."

28 And when they heard *this* and were filled with rage, they *began* crying out, saying, "Great is ¹Artemis of the aEphesians!"

29 And the city was filled with the confusion, and they rushed with one accord into the theater, ¹dragging along aGaius and bAristarchus, Paul's traveling ccompanions from dMacedonia.

30 And when Paul wanted to go in to the ¹assembly, athe disciples would not let him.

31 And also some of the ¹Asiarchs who were friends of his sent to him and repeatedly urged him not to ²venture into the theater.

32 aSo then, some were shouting one thing and some another, for the ¹assembly was in confusion, and the majority did not know ²for what cause they had come together.

33 And some of the crowd ¹concluded *it was* Alexander, since the Jews had put him forward; and having amotioned with his hand, Alexander was intending to make a defense to the ²assembly.

34 But when they recognized that he was a Jew, a single outcry arose from them all as they shouted for about two hours, "Great is ¹Artemis of the Ephesians!"

35 And after quieting the multitude the town-clerk *said, "Men of aEphesus, what man is there after all who does not know that the city of the Ephesians is guardian of the temple of the great ¹Artemis, and of the *image* which fell down from ²heaven?

36 "Since then these are undeniable facts, you ought to keep calm and to do nothing rash.

37 "For you have brought these men *here* who are neither arobbers of temples nor blasphemers of our goddess.

38 "So then, if Demetrius and the craftsmen who are with him have a complaint against any man, the courts are in session and ¹aproconsuls are *available*; let them bring charges against one another.

39 "But if you want anything beyond this, it shall be settled in the ¹lawful ²assembly.

40 "For indeed we are in danger of being accused of a riot in connection with today's affair, since there is no *real* cause *for it;* and in this connection we shall be unable to account for this disorderly gathering."

41 And after saying this he dismissed the ¹assembly.

CHAPTER 20

AND after the uproar had ceased, Paul sent for ᵃthe disciples and when he had exhorted them and taken his leave of them, he departed ᵇto go to ᶜMacedonia.

2 And when he had gone through those districts and had given them much exhortation, he came to Greece.

3 And *there* he spent three months, and when ᵃa plot was formed against him by the Jews as he was about to set sail for ᵇSyria, he determined to return through ᶜMacedonia.

4 And ¹he was accompanied by Sopater of ᵃBerea, *the son* of Pyrrhus; and by ᵇAristarchus and Secundus of the ᶜThessalonians; and ᵈGaius of ᵉDerbe, and ᶠTimothy; and ᵍTychicus and ʰTrophimus of ²ⁱAsia.

5 But these had gone on ahead and were waiting for ᵃus at ᵇTroas.

6 And ᵃwe sailed from ᵇPhilippi after ᶜthe days of Unleavened Bread, and came to them at ᵈTroas within five days; and there we stayed seven days.

7 And on ᵃthe first day of the week, when ᵇwe were gathered together to ᶜbreak bread, Paul *began* talking to them, intending to depart the next day, and he prolonged his ¹message until midnight.

8 And there were many ᵃlamps in the ᵇupper room where we were gathered together.

9 And there was a certain young man named Eutychus sitting ¹on the window-sill, sinking into a deep sleep; and as Paul kept on talking, he was overcome by sleep and fell down from the third floor, and was picked up dead.

10 But Paul went down and ᵃfell upon him and after embracing him, he ᵇsaid, "¹Do not be troubled, for his life is in him."

39 ¹Or, *regular* ²Gr., ekklesia

41 ¹Gr., ekklesia

1 ᵃActs 11:26 ᵇActs 19:21 ᶜActs 16:9; 20:3

3 ᵃActs 9:24; Acts 20:19 ᵇMatt. 4:24 ᶜActs 16:9; 20:1

4 ¹Lit., *there accompanied him* ²I.e., west coast province of Asia Minor ᵃActs 17:10 ᵇActs 19:29 ᶜActs 17:1 ᵈActs 19:29 ᵉActs 14:6 ᶠActs 16:1 ᵍEph. 6:21; Col. 4:7; 2 Tim. 4:12; Titus 3:12 ʰActs 21:29; 2 Tim. 4:20 ⁱActs 16:6; 20:16, 18

5 ᵃActs 20:5-15; 16:10 ᵇActs 16:8

6 ᵃActs 20:5-15; 16:10 ᵇActs 16:12 ᶜActs 12:3 ᵈActs 16:8

7 ¹Lit., *word, speech* ᵃ1 Cor. 16:2; Rev. 1:10 ᵇActs 20:5-15; 16:10 ᶜActs 2:42; 20:11

8 ᵃMatt. 25:1 ᵇActs 1:13

9 ¹Or, *at the window*

10 ¹Or, *Stop being troubled* ᵃ1 Kin. 17:21; 2 Kin. 4:34 ᵇMatt. 9:23f.; Mark 5:39

11 ¹Lit., *tasted*
ᵃActs 2:42; 20:7

12 ¹Lit., *not moderately*

13 ¹Or, *on foot*
ᵃActs 20:5-15; 16:10

15 ¹Later mss. add, *after
staying at Trogyllium, the
day following . . .*
ᵃActs 20:17; 2 Tim. 4:20

16 ¹I.e., west coast province
of Asia Minor
ᵃActs 18:19 ᵇActs 16:6; 20:4,
18 ᶜActs 19:21; 20:22; 20:6;
1 Cor. 16:8 ᵈActs 2:1

17 ᵃActs 18:19 ᵇActs 11:30

18 ¹Note vs. 16
ᵃActs 18:19; 19:1, 10; 20:4, 16

19 ᵃActs 20:3

20 ¹Or, *in the various
private homes*
ᵃActs 20:27

21 ᵃActs 18:5; Luke 16:28;
Acts 20:23, 24 ᵇActs 2:38;
11:18; 26:20 ᶜActs 24:24;
26:18; Eph. 1:15; Col. 2:5;
Philem. 5

22 ¹Or, *the Spirit*
ᵃActs 20:16; 17:16

23 ᵃActs 8:29 ᵇActs 18:5;
Luke 16:28; Acts 20:21, 24
ᶜActs 9:16; 21:33

24 ᵃActs 21:13 ᵇActs 13:25
ᶜActs 1:17 ᵈActs 18:5; Luke
16:28; Acts 20:21 ᵉActs
11:23; 20:32

296

11 And when he had gone *back* up, and had ᵃbroken the bread and ¹eaten, he talked with them a long while, until daybreak, and so departed.

12 And they took away the boy alive, and were ¹greatly comforted.

13 But ᵃwe, going ahead to the ship, set sail for Assos, intending from there to take Paul on board; for thus he had arranged it, intending himself to go ¹by land.

14 And when he met us at Assos, we took him on board and came to Mitylene.

15 And sailing from there, we arrived the following day opposite Chios; and the next day we crossed over to Samos; and ¹the day following we came to ᵃMiletus.

16 For Paul had decided to sail past ᵃEphesus in order that he might not have to spend time in ¹ᵇAsia; for he was hurrying ᶜto be in Jerusalem, if possible, ᵈon the day of Pentecost.

17 And from Miletus he sent to ᵃEphesus and called to him ᵇthe elders of the church.

18 And when they had come to him, he said to them,

"**Y**ou yourselves know, ᵃfrom the first day that I set foot in ¹ᵃAsia, how I was with you the whole time,

19 serving the Lord with all humility and with tears and with trials which came upon me through ᵃthe plots of the Jews;

20 how I ᵃdid not shrink from declaring to you anything that was profitable, and teaching you publicly and ¹from house to house,

21 solemnly ᵃtestifying to both Jews and Greeks of ᵇrepentance toward God and ᶜfaith in our Lord Jesus Christ.

22 "And now, behold, bound in ¹spirit, ᵃI am on my way to Jerusalem, not knowing what will happen to me there,

23 except that ᵃthe Holy Spirit solemnly ᵇtestifies to me in every city, saying that ᶜbonds and afflictions await me.

24 "But ᵃI do not consider my life of any account as dear to myself, in order that I may ᵇfinish my course, and ᶜthe ministry which I received from the Lord Jesus, to ᵈtestify solemnly of the gospel of ᵉthe grace of God.

25 "And now, behold, I know that you all,

among whom I went about [a]preaching the kingdom, will see my face no more.

26 "Therefore I [1]testify to you this day, that [a]I am [2]innocent of the blood of all men.

27 "For I [a]did not shrink from declaring to you the whole [b]purpose of God.

28 "Be on guard for yourselves and for all [a]the flock, among which the Holy Spirit has made you [1]overseers, to shepherd [b]the church of [2]God which [c]He [3]purchased with His own blood.

29 "I know that after my departure [a]savage wolves will come in among you, not sparing [b]the flock;

30 and from among your own selves men will arise, speaking perverse things, to draw away [a]the disciples after them.

31 "Therefore be on the alert, remembering that night and day for a period of [a]three years I did not cease to admonish each one [b]with tears.

32 "And now I [a]commend you to [1]God and to [b]the word of His grace, which is able to [c]build *you* up and to give *you* [d]the inheritance among all those who are sanctified.

33 "[a]I have coveted no one's silver or gold or clothes.

34 "You yourselves know that [a]these hands ministered to my *own* needs and to the [b]men who were with me.

35 "In every thing I showed you that by working hard in this manner you must help the weak and remember the words of the Lord Jesus, that He Himself said, 'It is more blessed to give than to receive.' "

36 And when he had said these things, he [a]knelt down and prayed with them all.

37 And [1]they *began* to weep aloud and [2a]embraced Paul, and repeatedly kissed him,

38 [1]grieving especially over [a]the word which he had spoken, that they should see his face no more. And they were [b]accompanying him to the ship.

CHAPTER 21

A̲N̲D̲ when it came about that [a]we had parted from them and had set sail, we ran [b]a straight course to Cos and the next day to Rhodes and from there to Patara;

25 [a]Acts 28:31; Matt. 4:23

26 [1]Or, *call you to witness*
[2]Lit., *pure from*
[a]Acts 18:6

27 [a]Acts 20:20 [b]Acts 13:36

28 [1]Or, *bishops* [2]Some ancient mss. read, *the Lord*
[3]Lit., *acquired*
[a]Acts 20:29; Luke 12:32; 1 Pet. 5:2f.; John 21:15-17
[b]Matt. 16:18; Rom. 16:16; 1 Cor. 10:32 [c]Eph. 1:7, 14: Titus 2:14; 1 Pet. 1:19; 2:9; Rev. 5:9

29 [a]Ezek. 22:27; Matt. 7:15
[b]Acts 20:28; Luke 12:32, 1 Pet. 5:2f.; John 21:15-17

30 [a]Acts 11:26

31 [a]Acts 19:1, 8, 10; 24:17
[b]Acts 20:19

32 [1]One ancient mss. reads, *the Lord*
[a]Acts 14:23 [b]Acts 14:3; 20:24
[c]Acts 9:31 [d]Acts 26:18; Eph. 1:14; 5:5; Col. 1:12; 3:24; Heb. 9:15; 1 Pet. 1:4

33 [a]1 Cor. 9:4-18; 2 Cor. 11:7-12; 12:14-18; 1 Thess. 2:5f.

34 [a]Acts 18:3 [b]Acts 19:22

36 [a]Acts 9:40; 21:5; Luke 22:41

37 [1]Lit., *a considerable weeping of all occurred*
[2]Lit., *fell on Paul's neck*
[a]Luke 15:20

38 [1]Lit., *suffering pain*
[a]Acts 20:25 [b]Acts 15:3

1 [a]["we"] Acts 21:1-18; 16:10 [b]Acts 16:11

2 ᵃActs 11:19; 21:3

3 ᵃActs 4:36; 21:16 ᵇMatt.
4:24 ᶜActs 12:20; 21:7 ᵈActs
21:2

4 ¹I.e., because of
impressions made by the
Spirit
ᵃActs 21:16; 11:26 ᵇActs
21:11; 20:23

5 ¹Lit., *we had completed
the days*
ᵃActs 15:3 ᵇActs 9:40; 20:36;
Luke 22:41

6 ᵃJohn 19:27

7 ᵃActs 12:20; 21:3 ᵇActs
1:15; 21:17

8 ᵃActs 8:40; 21:16 ᵇActs
6:5 ᶜEph. 4:11; 2 Tim. 4:5

9 ᵃActs 13:1; Luke 2:36;
1 Cor. 11:5

10 ᵃActs 11:28

11 ᵃ1 Kin. 22:11; Is. 20:2;
Jer. 13:1-11; 19:1, 11; John
18 ᵇActs 8:29 ᶜActs 9:16;
21:33 ᵈMatt. 20:19

12 ᵃActs 21:15

13 ᵃActs 20:24 ᵇActs 5:41;
9:16

14 ᵃLuke 22:42

15 ᵃActs 21:12

16 ᵃActs 21:4 ᵇActs 8:40
ᶜActs 4:36; 21:3

2 and having found a ship crossing over to ᵃPhoenicia, we went aboard and set sail.

3 And when we had come in sight of ᵃCyprus, leaving it on the left, we kept sailing to ᵇSyria and landed at ᶜTyre; for ᵈthere the ship was to unload its cargo.

4 And after looking up ᵃthe disciples, we stayed there seven days; and they kept telling Paul ¹ᵇthrough the Spirit not to set foot in Jerusalem.

5 And when it came about that ¹our days there were ended, we departed and started on our journey, while they all, with wives and children, ᵃescorted us until *we were* out of the city. And after ᵇkneeling down on the beach and praying, we said farewell to one another.

6 Then we went on board the ship, and they returned ᵃhome again.

7 And when we had finished the voyage from ᵃTyre, we arrived at Ptolemais; and after greeting ᵇthe brethren, we stayed with them for a day.

8 And on the next day we departed and came to ᵃCaesarea; and entering the house of ᵇPhilip the ᶜevangelist, who was ᵇone of the seven, we stayed with him.

9 Now this man had four virgin daughters who were ᵃprophetesses.

10 And as we were staying there for some days, a certain prophet named ᵃAgabus came down from Judea.

11 And coming to us, he ᵃtook Paul's belt and bound his own feet and hands, and said, "This ᵇis what the Holy Spirit says: 'In this way the Jews at Jerusalem will ᶜbind the man who owns this belt and ᵈdeliver him into the hands of the Gentiles.' "

12 And when we had heard this, we as well as the local residents *began* begging him ᵃnot to go up to Jerusalem.

13 Then Paul answered, "What are you doing, weeping and breaking my heart? For ᵃI am ready not only to be bound, but even to die at Jerusalem for ᵇthe name of the Lord Jesus."

14 And since he would not be persuaded, we fell silent, remarking, "ᵃThe will of the Lord be done!"

15 And after these days we got ready and ᵃstarted on our way up to Jerusalem.

16 And *some* of ᵃthe disciples from ᵇCaesarea also came with us, taking us to Mnason of ᶜCyprus,

a ddisciple of long standing with whom we were to lodge.

17 And when we had come to Jerusalem, athe brethren received us gladly.

18 And now the following day Paul went in with us to 1aJames, and all bthe elders were present.

19 And after he had greeted them, he abegan to relate one by one the things which God had done among the Gentiles through his bministry.

20 And when they heard it they began aglorifying God; and they said to him, "You see, brother, how many 1thousands there are among the Jews of those who have believed, and they are all bzealous for the Law;

21 and they have been told about you, that you are ateaching all the Jews who are among the Gentiles to forsake Moses, telling them bnot to circumcise their children nor to walk according to cthe customs.

22 "What, then, is to be done? They will certainly hear that you have come.

23 "Therefore do this that we tell you: We have four men who 1aare under a vow;

24 take them and apurify yourself along with them, and 1pay their expenses in order that they may bshave their 2heads; and all will know that there is nothing to the things which they have been told about you, but that you yourself also walk orderly, keeping the Law.

25 "But concerning the Gentiles who have believed, we wrote, ahaving decided that they should abstain from 1meat sacrificed to idols and from blood and from what is strangled and from fornication."

26 Then Paul 1took the men, and the next day apurifying himself along with them bwent into the temple, giving notice of the completion of the days of purification, until the sacrifice was offered for each one of them.

27 And when athe seven days were almost over, bthe Jews from 1cAsia, upon seeing him in the temple, began to stir up all the multitude and laid hands on him,

28 crying out, "Men of Israel, come to our aid! aThis is the man who preaches to all men everywhere against our people, and the Law, and this place; and besides he has even brought Greeks into the temple and has bdefiled this aholy place."

16 dActs 15:7 marg.

17 aActs 1:15; 21:7

18 1Or, Jacob
aActs 12:17 bActs 11:30

19 aActs 14:27 bActs 1:17

20 1Lit., ten thousands
aMatt. 9:8 bActs 15:1; 22:3;
Rom. 10:2; Gal. 1:14

21 aActs 21:28 bActs
15:19ff.; 1 Cor. 7:18f. cActs
6:14

23 1Lit., have a vow on
them
aActs 18:18

24 1Lit., spend on them
2Lit., head
aActs 21:26; 24:18; John
11:55 bActs 18:18

25 1Lit., the thing
aActs 15:19f., 29

26 1Or, took the men the
next day, and purifying
himself
aActs 21:24; 24:18; John
11:55 bNum. 6:13; Acts 24:18

27 1I.e., west coast province
of Asia Minor
aNum. 6:9, 13-20 bActs
24:18; 20:19 cActs 16:6

28 aActs 6:13 bActs 24:6;
Matt. 24:15; Acts 6:13f.

29 ªActs 20:4 ᵇActs 18:19

30 ¹Lit., *a running together
of the people occurred*
ªActs 26:21; 2 Kin. 11:15;
Acts 16:19

31 ¹Lit., *chiliarch*, in
command of one thousand
troops ²Or, *Battalion*
ªActs 10:1

32 ¹Vs. 31 note
ªActs 23:27

33 ¹Vs. 31 note
ªActs 20:23; 21:11; 22:29;
26:29; 28:20; 2 Tim. 1:16;
2:9; Eph. 6:20 ᵇActs 12:6

34 ¹Lit., *certainty*
ªActs 19:32 ᵇActs 21:37;
22:24; 23:10, 16, 32

35 ¹Or, *multitude*
ªActs 21:40

36 ªActs 22:22; Luke 23:18;
John 19:15

37 ¹Vs. 31 note
ªActs 21:34; 22:24; 23:10, 16,
32

38 ¹Lit., *days*
ªActs 5:36 ᵇMatt. 24:26

39 ªActs 22:3; 9:11 ᵇActs 6:9

40 ¹Lit., *occurred* ²I.e.,
Jewish Aramaic
ªActs 21:35 ᵇActs 12:17 ᶜActs
22:2; 26:14; 1:19; John 5:2

1 ªActs 7:2

29 For they had previously seen ªTrophimus the ᵇEphesian in the city with him, and they supposed that Paul had brought him into the temple.

30 And all the city was aroused, and ¹the people rushed together; and taking hold of Paul, they ªdragged him out of the temple; and immediately the doors were shut.

31 And while they were seeking to kill him, a report came up to the ¹commander of the ªRoman ²Cohort that all Jerusalem was in confusion.

32 And at once he ªtook along *some* soldiers and centurions, and ran down to them; and then they saw the ¹commander and the soldiers, they stopped beating Paul.

33 Then the ¹commander came up and took hold of him, and ordered him to be ªbound with ᵇtwo chains; and he *began* asking who he was and what he had done.

34 But among the crowd ªsome were shouting one thing *and* some another, and when he could not find out the ¹facts on account of the uproar, he ordered him to be brought into ᵇthe barracks.

35 And when he got to ªthe stairs, it so happened that he was carried by the soldiers because of the violence of the ¹mob;

36 for the multitude of the people kept following behind, crying out, "ªAway with him!"

37 And as Paul was about to be brought into ªthe barracks, he said to the ¹commander, "May I say something to you?" And he *said, "Do you know Greek?

38 "Then you are not ªthe Egyptian who some ¹time ago stirred up a revolt and led the four thousand men of the Assassins out ᵇinto the wilderness?"

39 But Paul said, "ªI am a Jew of Tarsus in ᵇCilicia, a citizen of no insignificant city; and I beg you, allow me to speak to the people."

40 And when he had given him permission, Paul, standing on ªthe stairs, ᵇmotioned to the people with his hand; and when there ¹was a great hush, he spoke to them in the ²ᶜHebrew dialect, saying,

CHAPTER 22

"ªBRETHREN and fathers, hear my defense which I now *offer* to you."

2 And when they heard that he was addressing them in the [1a]Hebrew dialect, they became even more quiet; and he *said,

3 "[a]I am [b]a Jew, born in [c]Tarsus of [d]Cilicia, but brought up in this city, [e]educated [1]under [f]Gamaliel, [2g]strictly according to the law of our fathers, being zealous for God, just as [h]you all are today.

4 "And [a]I persecuted this [b]Way to the death, binding and putting both men and women into prisons,

5 as also [a]the high priest and all [b]the Council of the elders [1]can testify. From them I also [c]received letters to [d]the brethren, and started off for [e]Damascus in order to bring even those who were there to Jerusalem [2]as prisoners to be punished.

6 "[a]And it came about that as I was on my way, approaching Damascus about noontime, a very bright light suddenly flashed from heaven all around me,

7 and I fell to the ground and heard a voice saying to me, 'Saul, Saul, why are you persecuting Me?'

8 "And I answered, 'Who art Thou, Lord?' And He said to me, 'I am [a]Jesus the Nazarene, whom you are persecuting.'

9 "And those who were with me [a]beheld the light, to be sure, but [b]did not [1]understand the voice of the One who was speaking to me.

10 "And I said, '[a]What shall I do, Lord?' And the Lord said to me, 'Arise and go on into Damascus; and there you will be told of all that has been appointed for you to do.'

11 "But since I [a]could not see because of the [1]brightness of that light, I was led by the hand by those who were with me, and came into Damascus.

12 "And a certain [a]Ananias, a man who was devout by the standard of the Law, *and* [b]well spoken of by all the Jews who lived there,

13 came to me, and standing near said to me, '[a]Brother Saul, receive your sight!' And [1b]at that very time I looked up at him.

14 "And he said, '[a]The God of our fathers has [b]appointed you to know His will, and to [c]see the [d]Righteous One, and to hear an [1]utterance from His mouth.

15 'For you will be [a]a witness for Him to all men of [b]what you have seen and heard.

16 'And now why do you delay? [a]Arise, and be

2 [1]I.e., Jewish Aramaic
[a]Acts 21:40

3 [1]Lit., *at the feet of* [2]Lit., *according to the strictness of the ancestral law*
[a]Acts 22:3-16; 9:1-22; 26:9-18
[b]Acts 21:39 [c]Acts 9:11 [d]Acts 6:9 [e]Deut. 33:3; 2 Kin. 4:38; Luke 10:39 [f]Acts 5:34 [g]Acts 26:5; Phil. 3:6; Acts 23:6
[h]Acts 21:20

4 [a]Acts 8:3; 22:19f. [b]Acts 9:2

5 [1]Lit., *testifies for me* [2]Lit., *having been bound*
[a]Acts 9:1 [b]Luke 22:66 [Gr.]; 1 Tim 4:14 [Gr.], Acts 5:21 [Gr.] [c]Acts 9:2 [d]Acts 2:29; 3:17; 13:26; 23:1; 28:17, 21; Rom 9:3 [e]Acts 9:2

6 [a]Acts 22:6-11: Acts 9:3-8; 26:12-18

8 [a]Acts 26:9

9 [1]Or, *hear* (with comprehension)
[a]Acts 26:13 [b]Acts 9:7

10 [a]Acts 16:30

11 [1]Or, *glory*
[a]Acts 9:8

12 [a]Acts 9:10 [b]Acts 6:3; 10:22

13 [1]Or, *instantly*; lit., *at that very hour*
[a]Acts 9:17 [b]Acts 9:18

14 [1]Or, *message*; lit., *voice*
[a]Acts 3:13 [b]Acts 9:15; 26:16 [c]Acts 9:17; 26:16; 1 Cor. 9:1; 15:8 [d]Acts 7:52

15 [a]Acts 23:11; 26:16 [b]Acts 22:14

16 [a]Acts 9:18

16 [b]1 Cor. 6:11; Heb. 10:22; Acts 2:38; Eph. 5:26 [c]Acts 7:59

17 [a]Acts 9:26; 26:20 [b]Acts 10:10

18 [a]Acts 9:29

19 [a]Acts 8:3; 22:4 [b]Acts 26:11; Matt. 10:17

20 [a]Acts 7:58f.; 8:1; 26:10

21 [a]Acts 9:15

22 [a]Acts 21:36; 1 Thess. 2:16 [b]Acts 25:24

23 [a]Acts 7:58 [b]2 Sam. 16:13

24 [1]Lit., *chiliarch*, in command of one thousand troops [a]Acts 21:34 [b]Acts 22:29

25 [1]Lit., *for the thongs* [a]Acts 16:37

26 [1]Vs. 24 note

27 [1]Vs. 24 note

28 [1]Vs. 24 note

29 [1]Or, *withdrew from* [2]Vs. 24 note [3]Lit., *bound him* [a]Acts 22:24 [b]Acts 16:38 [c]Acts 22:24f.

30 [a]Acts 23:28 [b]Acts 21:33

baptized, and [b]wash away your sins, [c]calling on His name.'

17 "And it came about that when I [a]returned to Jerusalem and was praying in the temple, I [b]fell into a trance,

18 and I saw Him saying to me, '[a]Make haste, and get out of Jerusalem quickly, because they will not accept your testimony about Me.'

19 "And I said, 'Lord, they themselves understand that in one synagogue after another [a]I used to imprison and [b]beat those who believed in Thee.

20 'And [a]when the blood of Thy witness Stephen was being shed, I also was standing by approving, and watching out for the cloaks of those who were slaying him.'

21 "And He said to me, 'Go! For I will send you far away [a]to the Gentiles.'"

22 And they listened to him up to this statement, and *then* they raised their voices and said, "[a]Away with such a fellow from the earth, for [b]he should not be allowed to live!"

23 And as they were crying out and [a]throwing off their cloaks and [b]tossing dust into the air,

24 the [1]commander ordered him to be brought into [a]the barracks, stating that he should be [b]examined by scourging so that he might find out the reason why they were shouting against him that way.

25 And when they stretched him out [1]with thongs, Paul said to the centurion who was standing by, "Is it lawful for you to scourge [a]a man who is a Roman and uncondemned?"

26 And when the centurion heard *this*, he went to the [1]commander and told him, saying, "What are you about to do? For this man is a Roman."

27 And the [1]commander came and said to him, "Tell me, are you a Roman?" And he said, "Yes."

28 And the [1]commander answered, "I acquired this citizenship with a large sum of money." And Paul said, "But I was actually born *a citizen*."

29 Therefore those who were about to [a]examine him immediately [1]let go of him; and the [2]commander also [b]was afraid when he found out that he was a Roman, and because he had [3c]put him in chains.

30 But on the next day, [a]wishing to know for certain why he had been accused by the Jews, he [b]released him and ordered the chief priests and all

ᶜthe ¹Council to assemble, and brought Paul down and set him before them.

CHAPTER 23

AND Paul, looking intently at ᵃthe ¹Council, said, "ᵇBrethren, ᶜI have ²lived my life with a perfectly good conscience before God up to this day."

2 And the high priest ᵃAnanias commanded those standing beside him ᵇto strike him on the mouth.

3 Then Paul said to him, "God is going to strike you, ᵃyou white-washed wall! And do you ᵇsit to try me according to the Law, and in violation of the Law order me to be struck?"

4 But the bystanders said, "Do you revile God's high priest?"

5 And Paul said, "I was not aware, brethren, that he was high priest; for it is written, 'ᵃYOU SHALL NOT SPEAK EVIL OF A RULER OF YOUR PEOPLE.' "

6 But perceiving that one party were ᵃSadducees and the other Pharisees, Paul *began* crying out in ᵇthe ¹Council, "ᶜBrethren, ᵈI am a Pharisee, a son of Pharisees; I am on trial for ᵉthe hope and resurrection of the dead!"

7 And as he said this, there arose a dissension between the Pharisees and Sadducees; and the assembly was divided.

8 For ᵃthe Sadducees say that there is no resurrection, nor an angel, nor a spirit; but the Pharisees acknowledge them ¹all.

9 And there arose a great uproar; and some of ᵃthe scribes of the Pharisaic party stood up and *began* to argue heatedly, saying, "ᵇWe find nothing wrong with this man; ᶜsuppose a spirit or an angel has spoken to him?"

10 And as a great dissension was developing, the ¹commander was afraid Paul would be torn to pieces by them and ordered the troops to go down and take him away from them by force, and bring him into ᵃthe barracks.

11 But on ᵃthe night *immediately* following, the Lord stood at his side and said, "ᵇTake courage; for ᶜas you have ᵈsolemnly witnessed to My cause at Jerusalem, so you must witness at Rome also."

12 And when it was day, ᵃthe Jews formed a ¹conspiracy and ᵇbound themselves under an oath,

---

30 ¹Or, *Sanhedrin*
ᶜMatt. 5:22

1 ¹Or, *Sanhedrin* ²Or, *conducted myself as a citizen*
ᵃActs 22:30; 23:6, 15, 20, 28
ᵇActs 22:5 ᶜActs 24:16;
2 Cor. 1:12; 2 Tim. 1:3

2 ᵃActs 24:1 ᵇJohn 18:22

3 ᵃMatt. 23:27 ᵇLev. 19:15;
Deut. 25:2; John 7:51

5 ᵃEx. 22:28

6 ¹Or, *Sanhedrin*
ᵃMatt. 22:23; 3:7 ᵇActs
22:30; 23:1, 15, 20, 28 ᶜActs
22:5 ᵈActs 26:5; Phil. 3:5
ᵉActs 24:15, 21; 26:8

8 ¹Lit., *both*
ᵃMatt. 22:23; Acts 3:7

9 ᵃMark 2:16; Luke 5:30
ᵇActs 23:29 ᶜActs 22:6ff.;
John 12:29

10 ¹Lit., *chiliarch*, in command of one thousand troops
ᵃActs 21:34; 23:16, 32

11 ᵃActs 18:9 ᵇMatt. 9:2
ᶜActs 19:21 ᵈActs 28:23;
Luke 16:28

12 ¹Or, *mob*
ᵃActs 23:30; Acts 9:23;
1 Thess. 2:16 ᵇActs 23:14, 21

303

14 ªActs 23:12, 21

15 ¹Lit., *with* ²Or,
Sanhedrin ³Vs. 10 note
ªActs 22:30; 23:1, 6, 20, 28

16 ¹Or, *having been
present* with them, *and he
entered*
ªActs 21:34; 23:10, 32

17 ¹Vs. 10 note

18 ¹Vs. 10 note
ªEph. 3:1

19 ¹Vs. 10 note

20 ¹Or, *Sanhedrin*
ªActs 23:14f. ᵇActs 22:30;
23:1, 6, 15, 28

21 ¹Lit., *be persuaded by
them*
ªLuke 11:54 ᵇActs 23:12, 14

22 ¹Vs. 10 note

23 ¹I.e., 9 p.m. ²Lit., *and*
³Or, *slingers or bowmen*
ªActs 8:40; 23:33

24 ªActs 23:26, 33; 24:1, 3,
10; 25:14

saying that they would neither eat nor drink until they had killed Paul.

13 And there were more than forty who formed this plot.

14 And they came to the chief priests and the elders, and said, "We have ªbound ourselves under a solemn oath to taste nothing until we have killed Paul.

15 "Now, therefore, you ¹and ªthe ²Council notify the ³commander to bring him down to you, as though you were going to determine his case by a more thorough investigation; and we for our part are ready to slay him before he comes near *the place.*"

16 But the son of Paul's sister heard of their ambush, ¹and he came and entered ªthe barracks and told Paul.

17 And Paul called one of the centurions to him and said, "Lead this young man to the ¹commander, for he has something to report to him."

18 So he took him and led him to the ¹commander and *said, "Paul ªthe prisoner called me to him and asked me to lead this young man to you since he has something to tell you."

19 And the ¹commander took him by the hand and stepping aside, *began* to inquire of him privately, "What is it that you have to report to me?"

20 And he said, "ªThe Jews have agreed to ask you to bring Paul down tomorrow to ᵇthe ¹Council, as though you were going to inquire somewhat more thoroughly about him.

21 "So do not ¹listen to them, for more than forty of them are ªlying in wait for him who have ᵇbound themselves under a curse not to eat or drink until they slay him; and now they are ready and waiting for the promise from you."

22 Therefore the ¹commander let the young man go, instructing him, "Tell no one that you have notified me of these things."

23 And he called to him two of the centurions, and said, "Get two hundred soldiers ready by ¹the third hour of the night to proceed to ªCaesarea, ²with seventy horsemen and two hundred ³spearmen."

24 *They were* also to provide mounts to put Paul on and bring him safely to ªFelix the governor.

25 And he wrote a letter having this form:

26 "Claudius Lysias, to the ªmost excellent governor Felix, ᵇgreetings,

27 "When this man was arrested by the Jews and ªwas about to be slain by them, ªI came upon them with the troops and rescued him, ᵇhaving learned that he was a Roman.

28 "And ªwanting to ascertain the charge for which they were accusing him, I ᵇbrought him down to their ¹ᶜCouncil;

29 and I found him to be accused over ªquestions about their Law, but ¹under ᵇno accusation deserving death or ²imprisonment.

30 "And when I was ªinformed that there would be ᵇa plot against the man, I sent him to you at once, also instructing ᶜhis accusers to ¹bring charges against him before you.²"

31 So the soldiers, in accordance with their orders, took Paul and brought him by night to Antipatris.

32 But the next day, leaving ªthe horsemen to go on with him, they returned to ᵇthe barracks.

33 And when these had come to ªCaesarea and delivered the letter to ᵇthe governor, they also presented Paul to him.

34 And when he had read it, he asked from what ªprovince he was; and when he learned that ᵇhe was from Cilicia,

35 he said, "I will give you a hearing after your ªaccusers arrive also," giving orders for him to be ᵇkept in Herod's ¹Praetorium.

CHAPTER 24

Aⁿᴅ after ªfive days the high priest ᵇAnanias came down with some elders, ¹with a certain ²attorney *named* Tertullus; and they ³brought charges to ᶜthe governor against Paul.

2 And after *Paul* had been summoned, Tertullus began to accuse him, saying *to the governor,*

"Since we have through you attained much peace, and since by your providence reforms are being carried out for this nation,

3 we acknowledge *this* in every way and everywhere, ªmost excellent Felix, with all thankfulness.

26 ªActs 24:3; 26:25; Luke 1:3 ᵇActs 15:23

27 ªActs 21:32f. ᵇActs 22:25-29

28 ¹Or, *Sanhedrin* ªActs 22:30 ᵇActs 23:10 ᶜActs 23:1

29 ¹Lit., *having* ²Lit., *bonds* ªActs 18:15; Acts 25:19 ᵇActs 25:25; 26:31; 28:18; 23:9

30 ¹Lit., *speak against him* ²Some mss. add, *Farewell* ªActs 23:20f. ᵇActs 23:12; 9:24 ᶜActs 23:35; 24:19; 25:16

32 ªActs 23:23 ᵇActs 23:10

33 ªActs 8:40; 23:23 ᵇActs 23:24, 26; 24:1, 3, 10; 25:14

34 ªActs 25:1 ᵇActs 21:39; 6:9

35 ¹Or, *governor's official residence* ªActs 23:30; 24:19; 25:16 ᵇActs 24:27

1 ¹Lit., *and* ²Lit., *orator* ³Or, *presented their evidence,* or *case* ªActs 24:11 ᵇActs 23:2 ᶜActs 23:24

3 ªActs 23:26; 26:25

4 [1]Lit., *to hear. . . . briefly*

5 [1]Lit., *the inhabited earth*
[a]Acts 15:5; 24:14

6 [1]Lit., *also* [2]Some later mss. add, *[And we wanted to judge him according to our own Law.* 7 *"But Lysias the commander came along, and with much violence took him out of our hands,* 8 *ordering his accusers to come before you.]*
[a]Acts 21:28

9 [a]1 Thess. 2:16

10 [a]Acts 23:24

11 [a]Acts 21:18, 27; 24:1

12 [1]Lit., *an attack of a mob*
[a]Acts 25:8 [b]Acts 24:18

13 [a]Acts 25:7

14 [1]Lit., *the ancestral god*
[a]Acts 24:22; 9:2 [b]Acts 15:5; 24:5 [c]Acts 3:13 [d]Acts 25:8; 26:4ff., 22f.; 28:23

15 [a]Dan. 12:2; John 5:28f.; 11:24; Acts 23:6

16 [1]Lit., *practice myself*
[a]Acts 23:1

17 [1]Or, *gifts to charity*
[a]Acts 20:31 [b]Rom. 15:25-28; 1 Cor. 16:1-4; 2 Cor. 8:1-4; 9:1, 2, 12; Acts 11:29f.; Gal. 2:10

18 [1]I.e., west coast province of Asia Minor
[a]Acts 21:26 [b]Acts 24:12 [c]Acts 21:27

19 [a]Acts 23:30

4 "But, that I may not weary you any further, I beg you [1]to grant us, by your kindness, a brief hearing.

5 "For we have found this man a real pest and a fellow who stirs up dissension among all the Jews throughout [1]the world, and a ringleader of the [a]sect of the Nazarenes.

6 "And he even tried to [a]desecrate the temple; and [1]then we arrested him.[2]

7 (See marginal note[2], vs. 6.)

8 "And by examining him yourself concerning all these matters, you will be able to ascertain the things of which we accuse him."

9 And [a]the Jews also joined in the attack, asserting that these things were so.

10 And when [a]the governor had nodded for him to speak, Paul responded:

"**K**nowing that for many years you have been a judge to this nation, I cheerfully make my defense,

11 since you can take note of the fact that no more than [a]twelve days ago I went up to Jerusalem to worship.

12 "And [a]neither in the temple, nor in the synagogues, nor in the city *itself* did they find me carrying on a discussion with anyone or [b]causing [1]a riot.

13 "[a]Nor can they prove to you the charges of which they now accuse me.

14 "But this I admit to you, that according to [a]the Way which they call a [b]sect I do serve [1c]the God of our fathers, [d]believing everything that is in accordance with the Law, and that is written in the Prophets;

15 having a hope in God, which [a]these men cherish themselves, that there shall certainly be a resurrection of both the righteous and the wicked.

16 "In view of this, [a]I also [1]do my best to maintain always a blameless conscience *both* before God and before men.

17 "Now [a]after several years I [b]came to bring [1]alms to my nation and to present offerings;

18 in which they found me *occupied* in the temple, having been [a]purified, without *any* [b]crowd or uproar. But *there were* certain [c]Jews from [1]Asia—

19 who ought to have been present before you, and to [a]make accusation, if they should have anything against me.

20 "Or else let these men themselves tell what misdeed they found when I stood before ᵃthe ¹Council,

21 other than for this one statement which ᵃI shouted out while standing among them, 'For the resurrection of the dead I am on trial before you today.' "

22 But Felix, having a more exact knowledge about ᵃthe Way, put them off, saying, "When Lysias the ¹commander comes down, I will decide your case."

23 And he gave orders to the centurion for him to be ᵃkept in custody and *yet* ᵇhave *some* freedom, and not to prevent any of ᶜhis friends from ministering to him.

24 But some days later, Felix arrived with Drusilla, his ¹wife who was a Jewess, and sent for Paul, and heard him *speak* about ᵃfaith in Christ Jesus.

25 And as he was discussing ᵃrighteousness, ᵇself-control and ᶜthe judgment to come, Felix became frightened and said, "Go away for the present, and when I find time, I will summon you."

26 At the same time too, he was hoping that ᵃmoney would be given him by Paul; therefore he also used to send for him quite often and converse with him.

27 But after two years had passed, Felix ¹was succeeded by Porcius ᵃFestus; and ᵇwishing to do the Jews a favor, Felix left Paul ᶜimprisoned.

CHAPTER 25

F ESTUS therefore, having arrived in ᵃthe province, three days later went up to Jerusalem from ᵇCaesarea.

2 And the chief priests and the leading men of the Jews ᵃbrought charges against Paul; and they were urging him,

3 requesting a ¹concession against ²Paul, that he might ³have him brought to Jerusalem, (*at the same time*, ᵃsetting an ambush to kill him on the way).

4 Festus then ᵃanswered that Paul ᵇwas being kept in custody at ᶜCaesarea and that he himself was about to leave shortly.

5 "Therefore," he ⃰said, "let the influential men among you ¹go there with me, and if there is anything wrong ²about the man, let them ³prosecute him."

20 ¹Or, *Sanhedrin*
ᵃMatt. 5:22

21 ᵃActs 23:6; 24:15

22 ¹Lit., *chiliarch*, in command of one thousand troops
ᵃActs 24:14

23 ᵃActs 23:35 ᵇActs 28:16
ᶜActs 23:16; 27:3

24 ¹Lit., *own wife*
ᵃActs 20:21

25 ᵃTitus 2:12 ᵇGal. 5:23;
2 Pet. 1:6; Titus 1:8 ᶜActs 10:42

26 ᵃActs 24:17

27 ¹Lit., *received a successor, Porcius Festus*
ᵃActs 25:1, 4, 9, 12; 26:24f.,
32 ᵇActs 25:9; 12:3 ᶜActs 23:35; 25:14

1 ᵃActs 23:34 ᵇActs 8:40;
25:4, 6, 13

2 ᵃActs 24:1; 25:15

3 ¹Or, *favor* ²Lit., *him*
³Lit., *send for him to Jerusalem*
ᵃActs 9:24

4 ᵃActs 25:16 ᵇActs 24:23
ᶜActs 8:40; 25:1, 6, 13

5 ¹Lit., *go down* ²Lit., *in*
³Or, *accuse*

6 ªActs 8:40; 25:1, 4, 13
ᵇMatt. 27:19; Acts 25:10,
17

7 ªActs 24:5f. ᵇActs 24:13

8 ªActs 24:12; 28:17; 6:13

9 ¹Lit., *be judged*
ªActs 24:27; 12:3 ᵇActs 25:20

10 ªMatt. 27:19; Acts 25:10,
17

11 ªActs 25:21, 25; 26:32;
28:19

12 ªA different body from
that mentioned Acts 4:15
and subsequently [e.g. Acts
24:20]

13 ¹Lit., *greeting Festus*
ªActs 8:40; 25:1, 4, 6

14 ªActs 24:27

15 ªActs 24:1; 25:2

16 ªActs 25:4f. ᵇActs 23:30

17 ªMatt. 27:19; Acts 25:6,
10

6 And after he had spent not more than eight or ten days among them, he went down to ªCaesarea; and on the next day he took his seat on ᵇthe tribunal and ordered Paul to be brought.

7 And after he had arrived, the Jews who had come down from Jerusalem stood around him, bringing ªmany and serious charges against him ᵇwhich they could not prove;

8 while Paul said in his own defense, "ªI have committed no offense either against the Law of the Jews or against the temple or against Caesar."

9 But Festus, ªwishing to do the Jews a favor, answered Paul and said, "ᵇAre you willing to go up to Jerusalem and ¹stand trial before me on these charges?"

10 But Paul said, "I am standing before Caesar's ªtribunal, where I ought to be tried. I have done no wrong to *the* Jews, as you also very well know.

11 "If then I am a wrongdoer, and have committed anything worthy of death, I do not refuse to die; but if none of those things is *true* of which these men accuse me, no one can hand me over to them. I ªappeal to Caesar."

12 Then when Festus had conferred with ªhis council, he answered, "You have appealed to Caesar, to Caesar you shall go."

13 Now when several days had elapsed, King Agrippa and Bernice arrived at ªCaesarea, ¹and paid their respects to Festus.

14 And while they were spending many days there, Festus laid Paul's case before the king, saying, "There is a certain man ªleft a prisoner by Felix;

15 and when I was at Jerusalem, the chief priests and the elders of the Jews ªbrought charges against him, asking for a sentence of condemnation upon him.

16 "And I ªanswered them that it is not the custom of the Romans to hand over any man before ᵇthe accused meets his accusers face to face, and has an opportunity to make his defense against the charges.

17 "And so after they had assembled here, I made no delay, but on the next day took my seat on ªthe tribunal, and ordered the man to be brought.

18 "And when the accusers stood up, they *be-*

gan bringing charges against him not of such crimes as I was expecting;

19 but they *simply* had some ªpoints of disagreement with him about their own [1b]religion and about a certain dead man, Jesus, whom Paul asserted to be alive.

20 "And ªbeing at a loss how to investigate [1]such matters, I asked whether he was willing to go to Jerusalem and there stand trial on these matters.

21 "But when Paul ªappealed to be held in custody for [1]the Emperor's decision, I ordered him to be kept in custody until I send him to Caesar."

22 And ªAgrippa *said* to Festus, "I also would like to hear the man myself." "Tomorrow," he *said, "you shall hear him."

23 And so, on the next day when ªAgrippa had come [1]together with ªBernice, amid great pomp, and had entered the auditorium [2]accompanied by the [3]commanders and the prominent men of the city, at the command of Festus, Paul was brought in.

24 And Festus *said, "King Agrippa, and all you gentlemen here present with us, you behold this man about whom ªall the people of the Jews appealed to me, both at Jerusalem and here, loudly declaring that [b]he ought not to live any longer.

25 "But I found that he had committed ªnothing worthy of death; and since he himself [b]appealed to [1]the Emperor, I decided to send him.

26 "[1]Yet I have nothing definite about him to write to my lord. Therefore I have brought him before you *all* and especially before you, King Agrippa, so that after the investigation has taken place, I may have something to write.

27 "For it seems absurd to me in sending a prisoner, not to indicate also the charges against him."

CHAPTER 26

AND ªAgrippa said to Paul, "You are permitted to speak for yourself." Then Paul stretched out his hand and *proceeded* to make his defense:

2 "In regard to all the things of which I am accused by the Jews, I consider myself fortunate, King Agrippa, that I am about to make my defense before you today;

3 [1]especially because you are an expert in all ªcustoms and [2]questions among *the* Jews; therefore I beg you to listen to me patiently.

4 "So then, all Jews know ªmy manner of life

19 [1]Or, *superstition*
ªActs 18:15; 23:29 [b]Acts 17:22

20 [1]Lit., *these*
ªActs 25:9

21 [1]Lit., *the Augustus* (in this case Nero)
ªActs 25:11f.

22 ªActs 9:15

23 [1]Lit., *and Bernice* [2]Lit., *and with* [3]Lit., *chiliarchs,* in command of one thousand troops
ªActs 25:13; 26:30

24 ªActs 25:2, 7 [b]Acts 22:22

25 [1]Note vs. 21
ªActs 23:29 [b]Acts 25:11f.

26 [1]Lit., *About whom I have nothing definite*

1 ªActs 9:15

3 [1]Or, *because you are especially expert* [2]Or, *controversial issues*
ªActs 6:14; 25:19; 26:7

4 ªGal. 1:13f.; Phil. 3:5

5 ªActs 23:6 ᵇActs 22:3
ᶜActs 15:5

6 ¹Lit., *being tried*
ªActs 28:20; 24:15 ᵇActs
13:32

7 ªJames 1:1 ᵇActs 28:20;
24:15 ᶜActs 26:2

8 ªActs 23:6

9 ª1 Tim. 1:13; John 16:2
ᵇJohn 15:21

10 ¹Lit., *also* ²I.e., true
believers; lit., *holy ones*
ªActs 8:3; 9:13 ᵇActs 9:1f.
ᶜActs 22:20

11 ¹Or, *outlying*
ªActs 22:19; Matt. 10:17
ᵇActs 9:1 ᶜActs 22:5

12 ¹Lit., *In which things*
ªActs 26:12-18; 9:3-8; 22:6-11

13 ¹Lit., *above the
brightness of*

14 ¹I.e., Jewish Aramaic
ªActs 9:7 ᵇActs 21:40

16 ¹Some early mss. read,
seen Me
ªEzek. 2:1; Dan. 10:11 ᵇActs
22:14 ᶜLuke 1:2 ᵈActs 22:15

17 ªJer. 1:8, 19 ᵇ1 Chr.
16:35; Acts 9:15

18 ªIs. 35:5; 42:7, 16; Eph.
5:8; Col. 1:13; 1 Pet. 2:9
ᵇJohn 1:5; Eph. 5:8; Col.
1:12f.; 1 Thess. 5:5; 1 Pet. 2:9

from my youth up, which from the beginning was spent among my *own* nation and at Jerusalem;

5 since they have known about me for a long time previously, if they are willing to testify, that I lived *as* a ªPharisee ᵇaccording to the strictest ᶜsect of our religion.

6 "And now I am ¹standing trial ªfor the hope of ᵇthe promise made by God to our fathers;

7 *the promise* ªto which our twelve tribes hope to attain, as they earnestly serve *God* night and day. And for this ᵇhope, O King, I am being ᶜaccused by Jews.

8 "Why is it considered incredible among you *people* ªif God does raise the dead?

9 "So then, ªI thought to myself that I had to do many things hostile to ᵇthe name of Jesus of Nazareth.

10 "And this is ¹just what I ªdid in Jerusalem; not only did I lock up many of the ²saints in prisons, having ᵇreceived authority from the chief priests, but also when they were being put to death I ᶜcast my vote against them.

11 "And ªas I punished them often in all the synagogues, I tried to force them to blaspheme; and being ᵇfuriously enraged at them, I kept pursuing them ᶜeven to ¹foreign cities.

12 "¹While thus engaged ªas I was journeying to Damascus with the authority and commission of the chief priests,

13 at midday, O King, I saw on the way a light from heaven, ¹brighter than the sun, shining all around me and those who were journeying with me.

14 "And when we had ªall fallen to the ground, I heard a voice saying to me in the ¹ᵇHebrew dialect, 'Saul, Saul, why are you persecuting me? It is hard for you to kick against the goads.'

15 "And I said, 'Who art Thou, Lord?' And the Lord said, 'I am Jesus whom you are persecuting.

16 'But arise, and ªstand on your feet; for this purpose I have appeared to you, to ᵇappoint you a ᶜminister and ᵈa witness not only to the things which you have ¹seen, but also to the things in which I will appear to you;

17 ªdelivering you ᵇfrom the *Jewish* people and from the Gentiles, to whom I am sending you,

18 to ªopen their eyes so that they may turn from ᵇdarkness to light and from the dominion of

ᶜSatan to God, in order that they may receive ᵈfor-giveness of sins and an ᵉinheritance among those who have been sanctified by ᶠfaith in Me.'

19 "Consequently, King Agrippa, I did not prove disobedient to the heavenly vision,

20 but *kept* declaring both ᵃto those of Damascus first, and *also* ᵇat Jerusalem and *then* throughout all the region of Judea, and *even* ᶜto the Gentiles, that they should ᵈrepent and turn to God, performing deeds ᵉappropriate to repentance.

21 "For this reason *some* Jews ᵃseized me in the temple and tried ᵇto put me to death.

22 "And so, having obtained help from God, I stand to this day ᵃtestifying both to small and great, stating nothing but what ᵇthe Prophets and Moses said was going to take place;

23 ¹ᵃthat ²the Christ was ³to suffer, *and* ¹that ᵇby reason of *His* resurrection from the dead He should be the first to proclaim ᶜlight both to the *Jewish* people and to the Gentiles."

24 And while *Paul* was saying this in his defense, Festus *said in a loud voice, "Paul, you are out of your mind! ¹*Your* great ᵃlearning is ²driving you mad."

25 But Paul *said, "I am not out of my mind, ᵃmost excellent Festus, but I utter words ¹of sober truth.

26 "For the king ¹ᵃknows about these matters, and I speak to him also with confidence, ²since I am persuaded that none of these things escape his notice; for this has not been done in a corner.

27 "King Agrippa, do you believe the Prophets? I know that you do."

28 And Agrippa *replied* to Paul, "¹In a short time you ²will persuade me to ³become a ᵃChristian."

29 And Paul *said, "¹I would to God, that whether ²in a short or long time, not only you, but also all who hear me this day, might become such as I am, except for these ᵃchains."

30 And ᵃthe king arose and the governor and Bernice, and those who were sitting with them,

31 and when they had drawn aside, they *began* talking to one another, saying, "ᵃThis man is not doing anything worthy of death or ¹imprisonment."

32 And Agrippa said to Festus, "This man

18 ᶜMatt. 4:10 ᵈLuke 24:47; Acts 2:38 ᵉActs 20:32 ᶠActs 20:21

20 ᵃActs 9:19ff. ᵇActs 9:26-29; 22:17-20 ᶜActs 13:46; 9:15 ᵈActs 3:19 ᵉMatt. 3:8; Luke 3:8

21 ᵃActs 21:27, 30 ᵇActs 21:31

22 ᵃLuke 16:28 ᵇActs 10:43; 24:14

23 ¹Lit., *whether* ²I.e., the Messiah ³Lit., *subject to suffering* ᵃMatt. 26:24; Acts 3:18 ᵇ1 Cor. 15:20, 23; Col. 1:18; Rev. 1:5 ᶜLuke 2:32; 2 Cor. 4:4

24 ¹Lit., *The many letters* ²Lit., *turning you to madness* ᵃJohn 7:15; 2 Tim. 3:15

25 ¹Lit., *of truth and rationality* ᵃActs 23:26; 24:3

26 ¹Or, *understands* ²Or, *for* ᵃActs 26:3

28 ¹Or, *with a little* ²Or, *try to convince* ³Lit., *make* ᵃActs 11:26

29 ¹Lit., *I would pray to* ²Or, *with a little or with much* ᵃActs 21:33

30 ᵃActs 25:23

31 ¹Lit., *bonds* ᵃActs 23:29

32 ªActs 28:18 ᵇActs 25:11

1 ¹Or, *Battalion*
ª[we] Acts 27:1-28; 16:10
ᵇActs 25:12, 25 ᶜActs 18:2;
27:6 ᵈActs 10:1

2 ¹I.e., west coast province
of Asia Minor
ªActs 2:9 ᵇActs 19:29 ᶜActs
16:9 ᵈActs 17:1

3 ªMatt. 11:21 ᵇActs 27:43
ᶜActs 24:23

4 ªActs 4:36 ᵇActs 27:7

5 ªActs 6:9 ᵇActs 13:13

6 ªActs 28:11 ᵇActs 18:2;
27:1

7 ªActs 27:4 ᵇActs 27:12f.,
21, Titus 1:5; Acts 2:11;
Titus 1:12

8 ªActs 27:13 [Gr.]

9 ¹I.e., the Day of
Atonement in October
ªLev. 16:29-31; 23:27-29;
Num. 29:7

10 ªActs 27:21

11 ¹Or, *owner*
ªRev. 18:17

12 ¹Or possibly, *southwest
and northwest*
ªActs 27:13, 21; Titus 1:5;
Acts 2:11; Titus 1:12

13 ¹Lit., *a south wind
having gently blown*

312

might have been ªset free if he had not ᵇappealed to Caesar."

CHAPTER 27

AND when it was decided that ªwe ᵇshould sail for ᶜItaly, they proceeded to deliver Paul and some other prisoners to a centurion of the Augustan ¹ᵈCohort named Julius.

2　And embarking in an Adramyttian ship, which was about to sail to the regions along the coast of ¹ªAsia, we put out to sea, accompanied by ᵇAristarchus, a ᶜMacedonian of ᵈThessalonica.

3　And the next day we put in at ªSidon; and Julius ᵇtreated Paul with consideration and ᶜallowed him to go to his friends and receive care.

4　And from there we put out to sea and sailed under the shelter of ªCyprus because ᵇthe winds were contrary.

5　And when we had sailed through the sea along the coast of ªCilicia and ᵇPamphylia, we landed at Myra in Lycia.

6　And there the centurion found an ªAlexandrian ship sailing for ᵇItaly, and he put us aboard it.

7　And when we had sailed slowly for a good many days, and with difficulty had arrived off Cnidus, ªsince the wind did not permit us *to go* farther, we sailed under the shelter of ᵇCrete, off Salmone;

8　and with difficulty ªsailing past it we came to a certain place called Fair Havens, near which was the city of Lasea.

9　And when considerable time had passed and the voyage was now dangerous, since even ªthe ¹Fast was already over, Paul *began* to admonish them,

10　and said to them, "Men, I perceive that the voyage will certainly be *attended* with ªdamage and great loss, not only of the cargo and the ship, but also of our lives."

11　But the centurion was more persuaded by the ªpilot and the ¹captain of the ship, than by what was being said by Paul.

12　And because the harbor was not suitable for wintering, the majority reached a decision to put out to sea from there, if somehow they could reach Phoenix, a harbor of ªCrete, facing ¹northeast and southeast, and spend the winter *there*.

13　And ¹when a moderate south wind came

up, supposing that they had gained their purpose, they weighed anchor and *began* ᵃsailing along ᵇCrete, close *inshore.*

14   But before very long there ᵃrushed down from ¹the land a violent wind, called ²Euraquilo;

15   and when the ship was caught *in it,* and could not face the wind, we gave way *to it,* and let ourselves be driven along.

16   And running under the shelter of a small island called ¹Clauda, we were scarcely able to get the *ship's* boat under control.

17   And after they had hoisted it up, they used ¹supporting cables in undergirding the ship; and fearing that they might ᵃrun aground on *the shallows* of Syrtis, they let down the ²sea anchor, and so let themselves be driven along.

18   The next day as we were being violently storm-tossed, ¹they began to ᵃjettison the cargo;

19   and on the third day they threw the ship's tackle overboard with their own hands.

20   And since neither sun nor stars appeared for many days, and no small storm was assailing *us,* from then on all hope of our being saved was gradually abandoned.

21   And ¹when they had gone a long time without food, then Paul stood up in their midst and said, "ᵃMen, you ought to have ²followed my advice and not to have set sail from ᵇCrete, and ³incurred this ᵃdamage and loss.

22   "And *yet* now I urge you to ᵃkeep up your courage, for there shall be no loss of life among you, but *only* of the ship.

23   "For this very night ᵃan angel of the God to whom I belong and ᵇwhom I serve ᶜstood before me,

24   saying, 'Do not be afraid, Paul; ᵃyou must stand before Caesar; and behold, God has granted you ᵇall those who are sailing with you.'

25   "Therefore, ᵃkeep up your courage, men, for I believe God, that ¹it will turn out exactly as I have been told.

26   "But we must ᵃrun aground on a certain ᵇisland."

27   But when the fourteenth night had come, as we were being driven about in the Adriatic Sea, about midnight the sailors *began* to surmise that ¹they were approaching some land.

28   And they took soundings, and found *it to*

13 ᵃActs 27:8 [Gr.] ᵇActs 27:12f., 21; Titus 1:5; Acts 2:11; Titus 1:12

14 ¹Lit., *it* ²I.e., a northeaster ᵃMark 4:37

16 ¹Some ancient mss. read, *Cauda*

17 ¹Lit., *helps* ²Or possibly, *sail* ᵃActs 27:26, 29

18 ¹Lit., *they were doing a throwing out* ᵃActs 27:38; Jonah 1:5

21 ¹Lit., *there being much abstinence from food* ²Lit., *obeyed me* ³Lit., *gained* ᵃActs 27:10 ᵇActs 27:7

22 ᵃActs 27:25, 36

23 ᵃActs 5:19 ᵇRom. 1:9 ᶜActs 23:11; 18:9; 2 Tim. 4:17

24 ᵃActs 23:11 ᵇActs 27:44; Acts 27:31, 42

25 ¹Lit., *it will be* ᵃActs 27:22, 36

26 ᵃActs 27:17, 29 ᵇActs 28:1

27 ¹Lit., *some land was approaching them*

be twenty fathoms; and a little farther on they took another sounding and found *it to be* fifteen fathoms.

29 And fearing that we might ᵃrun aground somewhere on the ¹rocks, they cast four anchors from the stern and ²wished for daybreak.

30 And as the sailors were trying to escape from the ship, and had let down ᵃthe *ship's* boat into the sea, on the pretense of intending to lay out anchors from the bow,

31 Paul said to the centurion and to the soldiers, "Unless these men remain in the ship, you yourselves cannot be saved."

32 Then the soldiers cut away the ᵃropes of the *ship's* boat, and let it fall away.

33 And until the day was about to dawn, Paul was encouraging them all to take some food, saying, "Today is the fourteenth day that you have been constantly watching and going without eating, having taken nothing.

34 "Therefore I encourage you to take some food, for this is for your preservation; for ᵃnot a hair from the head of any of you shall perish."

35 And having said this, he took bread and ᵃgave thanks to God in the presence of all; and he broke it and began to eat.

36 And all ᵃof them ¹were encouraged, and they themselves also took food.

37 And all of us in the ship were two hundred and seventy-six ¹ᵃpersons.

38 And when they had eaten enough, they *began* to lighten the ship by ᵃthrowing out the wheat into the sea.

39 And when day came, ᵃthey ¹could not recognize the land; but they ²did observe a certain bay with a beach, and they ³resolved to ⁴drive the ship onto it if they could.

40 And casting off ᵃthe anchors, they ¹left them in the sea while at the same time they were loosening the ropes of the rudders, and hoisting the foresail to the wind, they were heading for the beach.

41 But striking a ¹reef where two seas met, they ran the vessel aground; and the prow stuck fast and remained immovable, but the stern *began* to be broken up by the force *of the waves.*

42 And the soldiers' plan was to ᵃkill the prison-

ers, that none *of them* should swim away and escape;

43 but the centurion, [a]wanting to bring Paul safely through, kept them from their intention, and commanded that those who could swim should [1]jump overboard first and get to land,

44 and the rest *should follow,* some on planks, and others on various things from the ship. And thus it happened that [a]they all were brought safely to land.

43 [1]Lit., *cast themselves*
[a]Acts 27:3

44 [a]Acts 27:22, 31

CHAPTER 28

AND when [a]they had been brought safely through, [b]then we found out that [c]the island was called [1]Malta.

2 And [a]the [1]natives showed us extraordinary kindness; for because of the rain that had set in and because of the cold, they kindled a fire and [b]received us all.

3 But when Paul had gathered a bundle of sticks and laid them on the fire, a viper came out [1]because of the heat, and fastened on his hand.

4 And when [a]the [1]natives saw the creature hanging from his hand, they *began* saying to one another, "[b]Undoubtedly this man is a murderer, and though he has been saved from the sea, [2]Justice has not allowed him to live."

5 However [a]he shook the creature off into the fire and suffered no harm.

6 But they were expecting that he was about to swell up or suddenly fall down dead. But after they had waited a long time and had seen nothing unusual happen to him, they changed their minds and [a]*began* to say that he was a god.

7 Now in the neighborhood of that place were lands belonging to the leading man of the island, named Publius, who welcomed us and entertained us courteously three days.

8 And it came about that the father of Publius was lying *in bed* afflicted with *recurrent* fever and dysentery; and Paul went in *to see* him and after he had [a]prayed, he [b]laid his hands on him and healed him.

9 And after this had happened, the rest of the people on the island who had diseases were coming to him and getting cured.

10 And they also honored us with many [1]marks

1 [1]Or, *Melita.* Some mss. read, *Melitene*
[a]"we": Acts 27:1 [16:10]
[b]Acts 27:39 [c]Acts 27:26

2 [1]Lit., *barbarians*
[a]Rom 1:14; 1 Cor. 14:11, Col. 3:11; Acts 28:4 [b]Rom. 14:1

3 [1]Or, *from the heat*

4 [1]Lit., *barbarians* [2]I.e., personification of a goddess
[a]Acts 28:2 [b]Luke 13:2, 4

5 [a]Mark 16:18

6 [a]Acts 14:11

8 [a]Acts 9:40; James 5:14f. [b]Mark 5:23

10 [1]Lit., *honors*

Acts 28

The Voyage Resumed.   Arrival at Rome.
Paul Addresses the Jews.

10 [2]Or, *put on board* [3]Lit., the things pertaining to the needs

11 [1]Gr., *the Dioscuri*, i.e., the twin sons of Zeus, Castor and Pollux
[a]Acts 27:6

13 [1]Some early mss. read, *weighed anchor*

14 [1]Lit., *where*
[a]Acts 1:15

15 [1]Lat., Appii Forum, a station about 43 miles from Rome [2]Lat., Tres Tabernae, a station about 33 miles from Rome
[a]Acts 1:15

16 [a]Acts 24:23

17 [1]Or, *forefathers*
[a]Acts 13:50; 25:2 [b]Acts 22:5
[c]Acts 25:8 [d]Acts 6:14

18 [1]Lit., *of death in me*
[a]Acts 26:32 [b]Acts 23:29

19 [1]Lit., *spoke against it*
[a]Acts 25:11

20 [1]Or, *invited you to see me and speak with me*
[a]Acts 21:33 [b]Acts 26:6f.

21 [a]Acts 22:5

22 [1]Lit., *you think*
[a]Acts 24:14 [b]1 Pet. 2:12; 3:16; 4:14, 16

23 [a]Philem. 22 [b]Luke 16:28; Acts 1:3; 23:11

of respect; and when we were setting sail, they [2]supplied *us* with [3]all we needed.

11   And at the end of three months we set sail on [a]an Alexandrian ship which had wintered at the island, and which had [1]the Twin Brothers for its figurehead.

12   And after we put in at Syracuse, we stayed there for three days.

13   And from there we [1]sailed around and arrived at Rhegium, and a day later a south wind sprang up, and on the second day we came to Puteoli.

14   [1]There we found *some* [a]brethren, and were invited to stay with them for seven days; and thus we came to Rome.

15   And the [a]brethren, when they heard about us, came from there as far as the [1]Market of Appius and [2]Three Inns to meet us; and when Paul saw them, he thanked God and took courage.

16   And when we entered Rome, Paul was [a]allowed to stay by himself, with the soldier who was guarding him.

17   And it happened that after three days he called together those who were [a]the leading men of the Jews, and when they had come together, he *began* saying to them, "[b]Brethren, [c]though I had done nothing against our people, or [d]the customs of our [1]fathers, yet I was delivered prisoner from Jerusalem into the hands of the Romans.

18   "And when they had examined me, they [a]were willing to release me because there was [b]no ground [1]for putting me to death.

19   "But when the Jews [1]objected, I was forced to [a]appeal to Caesar; not that I had any accusation against my nation.

20   "For this reason therefore, I [1]requested to see you and to speak with you, for I am wearing [a]this chain for [b]the sake of the hope of Israel."

21   And they said to him, "We have neither received letters from Judea concerning you, nor have any of [a]the brethren come here and reported or spoken anything bad about you.

22   "But we desire to hear from you what [1]your views are; for concerning this [a]sect, it is known to us that [b]it is spoken against everywhere."

23   And when they had set a day for him, they came to him at [a]his lodging in large numbers; and he was explaining to them by solemnly [b]testifying

about the kingdom of God, and trying to persuade them concerning Jesus, cfrom both the Law of Moses and from the Prophets, from morning until evening.

24 And ᵃsome were being persuaded by the things spoken, but others would not believe.

25 And when they did not agree with one another, they *began* leaving after Paul had spoken one parting word, "The Holy Spirit rightly spoke through Isaiah the prophet to your fathers,

26   saying,

'ᵃGo to this people and say,
"¹ᵇYou will keep on hearing, ²but will
    not understand;
And ³you will keep on seeing, but will
    not perceive;

27   ᵃFor the heart of this people has be-
        come dull,
    And with their ears they scarcely
        hear,
    And they have closed their eyes;
    Lest they should see with their eyes,
    And hear with their ears,
    And understand with their heart and
        turn again,
    And I should heal them."'

28 "Let it be known to you therefore, that ᵃthis salvation of God has been sent ᵇto the Gentiles; they will also listen."

29 (See marginal note.¹)

30 And he stayed two full years ¹in his own rented quarters, and was welcoming all who came to him,

31   ¹ᵃpreaching the kingdom of God, and teaching concerning the Lord Jesus Christ ᵇwith all openness, unhindered.

23 ᶜActs 8:35

24 ᵃActs 14:4

26 ¹Lit., *with a hearing*
²Lit., *and* ³Lit., *seeing you will see*
ᵃIs. 6:9 ᵇActs 28:26, 27; Matt. 13:14f.

27 ᵃIs. 6:10

28 ᵃActs 13:26; Ps. 98:3; Luke 2:30 ᵇActs 13:46; 9:15

29 ¹Some mss. add vs. 29, *And when he had spoken these words, the Jews departed, having a great dispute among themselves.*

30 ¹Or, *at his own expense*

31 ¹Or, *proclaiming*
ᵃMatt. 4:23; Acts 20:25; 28:23 ᵇ2 Tim. 2:9

THE EPISTLE OF PAUL TO THE
ROMANS

Salutation. Personal Explanations.

1 ¹Lit., *a called apostle*
ᵃ1 Cor. 1:1; 9:1; 2 Cor. 1:1
ᵇActs 9:15; 13:2; Gal. 1:15
ᶜMark 1:14; Rom. 15:16;
2 Cor. 11:7; 1 Thess. 2:2, 8, 9;
1 Pet. 4:17; 2 Cor. 2:12

2 ᵃTitus 1:2; ᵇLuke 1:70;
Rom. 3:21; 16:26

3 ᵃMatt. 1:1 ᵇRom. 4:1;
9:3, 5; 1 Cor. 10:18; John
1:14

4 ¹Or, *in an act of power*
²Or, *as a result of* ³Or, *spirit*
ᵃMatt. 4:3

5 ¹Lit., *for obedience*
ᵃActs 1:25; Gal. 1:16 ᵇRom.
16:26; Acts 6:7 ᶜActs 9:15

6 ᵃJude 1; Rev. 17:14

7 ¹I.e., *true believers; lit.,
holy ones*
ᵃ1 Thess. 1:4; Rom. 5:5ff.;
8:39 ᵇ1 Cor. 1:2, 24; Rom.
8:28ff.; Acts 9:13 ᶜ1 Cor. 1:3;
2 Cor. 1:2; Gal. 1:3; Eph. 1:2;
Phil. 1:2; Col. 1:2; 1 Thess.
1:1; 2 Thess. 1:2; 1 Tim. 1:2;
2 Tim. 1:2; Titus 1:4;
Philem. 3; 2 John 3; 2 Pet.
1:2; Num. 6:25f.

8 ᵃ1 Cor. 1.4, Eph. 1:15f.;
Phil. 1:3f.; Col. 1:3f.;
1 Thess. 1:2; 2:13; 2 Thess.
1:3; 2:13; 2 Tim. 1:3; Philem.
4 ᵇRom. 16:19; Acts 28:22

9 ᵃRom. 9:1; 2 Cor. 1:23;
11:31; Phil. 1:8; 1 Thess. 2:5,
10 ᵇActs 24:14; 2 Tim. 1:3
ᶜEph. 1:16; Phil. 1:3f.;
1 Thess. 1:2f.; 2 Tim. 1:3;
Philem. 4

10 ᵃRom. 15:32; Acts 18:21

11 ᵃRom. 15:23; Acts 19:21

13 ᵃRom. 11:25; 1 Cor.
10:1; 12:1; 2 Cor. 1:8;
1 Thess. 4:13 ᵇRom. 7:1;
1 Cor. 1:10; 14:20, 26; Gal.
3:15; Acts 1:15 ᶜRom.
15:22f.; Acts 19:21 ᵈJohn
4:36; 15:16; Phil. 1:22; Col.
1:6

14 ¹Lit., *debtor*
ᵃ1 Cor. 9:16 ᵇActs 28:2

318

P AUL, a bond-servant of Christ Jesus, ¹ᵃcalled *as* an apostle, ᵇset apart for ᶜthe gospel of God,

2   which He ᵃpromised beforehand through His ᵇprophets in the holy Scriptures,

3   concerning His Son, who was born ᵃof the seed of David ᵇaccording to the flesh,

4   who was declared ¹with power *to be* ᵃthe Son of God ²by the resurrection from the dead, according to the ³Spirit of holiness, Jesus Christ our Lord,

5   through whom we have received grace and ᵃapostleship ¹to bring about *the* ᵇobedience of faith among ᶜall the Gentiles, for His name's sake,

6   among whom you also are the ᵃcalled of Jesus Christ;

7   to all who are ᵃbeloved of God in Rome, called *as* ¹ᵇsaints: ᶜGrace to you and peace from God our Father and the Lord Jesus Christ.

8   First, ᵃI thank my God through Jesus Christ for you all, because ᵇyour faith is being proclaimed throughout the whole world.

9   For ᵃGod, whom I ᵇserve in my spirit in the *preaching of the* gospel of His Son, is my witness *as to* how unceasingly ᶜI make mention of you,

10   always in my prayers making request, if perhaps now at last by ᵃthe will of God I may succeed in coming to you.

11   For ᵃI long to see you in order that I may impart some spiritual gift to you, that you may be established;

12   that is, that I may be encouraged together with you *while* among you, each of us by the other's faith, both yours and mine.

13   And ᵃI do not want you to be unaware, ᵇbrethren, that often I ᶜhave planned to come to you (and have been prevented thus far) in order that I might obtain some ᵈfruit among you also, even as among the rest of the Gentiles.

14   ᵃI am ¹under obligation both to Greeks and to ᵇbarbarians, both to the wise and to the foolish.

15 Thus, [a]for my part, I am eager to [b]preach the gospel to you also who are in Rome.

16 For I am not [a]ashamed of the gospel, for [b]it is the power of God for salvation to every one who believes, to the [c]Jew first and also to [d]the Greek.

17 For in it [a]*the* righteousness of God is revealed [1]from faith to faith; as it is written, "[2b]BUT THE RIGHTEOUS *man* SHALL LIVE BY FAITH."

18 For [a]the wrath of God is revealed from heaven against all ungodliness and unrighteousness of men, who [b]suppress the truth [1]in unrighteousness,

19 because [a]that which is known about God is evident [1]within them; for God made it evident to them.

20 For [a]since the creation of the world His invisible attributes, His eternal power and divine nature, have been clearly seen, [b]being understood through what has been made, so that they are without excuse.

21 For even though they knew God, they did not [1]honor Him as God, or give thanks; but they became [a]futile in their speculations, and their foolish heart was darkened.

22 [a]Professing to be wise, they became fools,

23 and [a]exchanged the glory of the incorruptible God for an image in the form of corruptible man and of birds and four-footed animals and [1]crawling creatures.

24 Therefore [a]God gave them over in the lusts of their hearts to impurity, that their bodies might be [b]dishonored among them.

25 For they exchanged the truth of God for [1a]a [a]lie, and worshiped and served the creature rather than the Creator, [b]who is blessed [2]forever. Amen.

26 For this reason [a]God gave them over to [b]degrading passions; for their women exchanged the natural function for that which is [1]unnatural,

27 and in the same way also the men abandoned the natural function of the woman and burned in their desire towards one another, [a]men with men committing [1]indecent acts and receiving in [2]their own persons the due penalty of their error.

28 And just as they did not see fit [1]to acknowledge God any longer, [a]God gave them over to a depraved mind, to do those things which are not proper,

29 being filled with all unrighteousness, wick-

---

15 [a]Rom. 12:18 [b]Rom. 15:20

16 [a]2 Tim. 1:8, 12, 16 [b]1 Cor. 1:18, 24 [c]Acts 3:26; Rom. 2:9 [d]John 7:35

17 [1]Or, *by* [2]Or, *"But he who is righteous by faith shall live."* [a]Rom. 3:21; Phil. 3:9; Rom. 9:30 [b]Hab. 2:4; Gal. 3:11; Heb. 10:38

18 [1]Or, *by* [a]Eph. 5:6; Col. 3:6; Rom. 5:9 [b]2 Thess. 2:6f. [Gr.]

19 [1]Or, *among* [a]Acts 14:17; 17:24ff.

20 [a]Mark 10:6 [b]Ps. 19:1-6; Job 12:7-9; Jer. 5:21f.

21 [1]Lit., *glorify* [a]2 Kin. 17:15; Jer. 2:5; Eph. 4:17f.

22 [a]Jer. 10:14; 1 Cor. 1:20

23 [1]Or possibly, *reptiles* [a]Ps. 106:20; Jer. 2:11; Acts 17:29

24 [a]Rom. 1:26, 28; Eph. 4:19 [b]Eph. 2:3

25 [1]Lit., *the lie* [2]Lit., *unto the ages* [a]Is. 44:20; Jer. 10:14; 13:25; 16:19 [b]Rom. 9:5; 2 Cor. 11:31

26 [1]Lit., *against nature* [a]Rom. 1:24 [b]1 Thess. 4:5

27 [1]Lit., *the shameless deed* [2]Lit., *themselves* [a]Lev. 18:22; 20:13; 1 Cor. 6:9

28 [1]Lit., *to have God in knowledge* [a]Rom. 1:24

319

29 a2 Cor. 12:20

30 1Or, *hateful to God*
aPs. 5:5 b2 Tim. 3:2

31 a2 Tim. 3:3

32 aRom. 6:21 bLuke 11:48;
Acts 8:1; 22:20

1 aRom. 1:20 bRom. 2:3;
9:20; Luke 12:14 c2 Sam.
12:5-7; Matt. 7:1; Rom.
14:22

2 1Lit., *is according to
truth against . . .*

3 1Lit., *who pass
judgment*
aRom. 2:1; 9:20; Luke 12:14

4 aRom. 9:23; 11:33;
2 Cor. 8:2; Eph. 1:7, 18; 2:7;
Phil. 4:19; Col. 1:27; 2:2;
Titus 3:6 bRom. 11:22
cRom. 3:25 dRom. 9:22;
1 Tim. 1:16; 1 Pet. 3:20;
2 Pet. 3:15; Ex. 34:6 e2 Pet.
3:9

5 1Or, *in accordance with*
aDeut. 32:34f.; Prov. 1:18
bPs. 110:5; Jude 6; 2 Cor.
5:10; 2 Thess. 1:5

6 aPs. 62:12; Matt. 16:27

7 aLuke 8:15; Heb. 10:36
bRom. 2:10; Heb. 2:7; 1 Pet.
1:7 c1 Cor. 15:42, 50, 53f.;
Eph. 6:24 marg.; 2 Tim. 1:10
marg. dMatt. 25:46

8 aPhil. 1:17 marg.; 2 Cor.
12:20; Gal. 5:20; Phil. 2:3;
James 3:14, 16 b2 Thess. 2:12

9 1Lit., *upon*
aRom. 8:35 b1 Pet. 4:17; Acts
3:26; Rom. 1:16

10 aRom. 2:7; Heb. 2:7;
1 Pet. 1:7 bRom. 2:9

11 aActs 10:34

12 1Or, *without law*
a1 Cor. 9:21; Acts 2:23

edness, greed, malice; full of envy, murder, strife, deceit, malice; *they are* agossips,

30　slanderers, 1ahaters of God, insolent, arrogant, boastful, inventors of evil, bdisobedient to parents,

31　without understanding, untrustworthy, aunloving, unmerciful;

32　and, although they know the ordinance of God, that those who practice such things are worthy of adeath, they not only do the same, but also bgive hearty approval to those who practice them.

CHAPTER 2

Therefore you are awithout excuse, bevery man *of you* who passes judgment, for in that cyou judge another, you condemn yourself; for you who judge practice the same things.

2　And we know that the judgment of God 1rightly falls upon those who practice such things.

3　And do you suppose this, aO man, 1when you pass judgment upon those who practice such things and do the same *yourself*, that you will escape the judgment of God?

4　Or do you think lightly of athe riches of His bkindness and cforbearance and dpatience, not knowing that ethe kindness of God leads you to repentance?

5　But 1because of your stubbornness and unrepentant heart ayou are storing up wrath for yourself bin the day of wrath and revelation of the righteous judgment of God;

6　awho WILL RENDER TO EVERY MAN ACCORDING TO HIS DEEDS:

7　to those who by aperseverance in doing good seek for bglory and honor and cimmortality, deternal life;

8　but to those who are aselfishly ambitious and bdo not obey the truth, but obey unrighteousness, wrath and indignation.

9　*There will be* atribulation and distress 1for every soul of man who does evil, of the Jew bfirst and also of the Greek,

10　but aglory and honor and peace to every man who does good, to the Jew bfirst and also to the Greek.

11　For athere is no partiality with God.

12　For all who have sinned 1awithout the Law

will also perish [1]without the Law; and all who have sinned [2]under the Law will be judged [3]by the Law;

13   for [a]not the hearers [1]of the Law are [2]just before God, but the doers [1]of the Law will be justified.

14   For when Gentiles who do not have [1]the Law do [2a]instinctively the things of the Law, these, not having [1]the Law, are a law to themselves,

15   in that they show [a]the work of the Law written in their hearts, their conscience bearing witness, and their thoughts alternately accusing or else defending themselves,

16   on the day when, [a]according to my gospel, [b]God will judge the secrets of men through Christ Jesus.

17   But if you bear the name 'Jew,' and [a]rely [1]upon the Law, and boast in God,

18   and know *His* will, and [1a]approve the things that are essential, being instructed out of the Law,

19   and are confident that you yourself are a guide to the blind, a light to those who are in darkness,

20   a [1]corrector of the foolish, a teacher of [2]the immature, having in the Law [a]the embodiment of knowledge and of the truth;

21   you therefore [a]who teach another, do you not teach yourself? You who [1]preach that one should not steal, do you steal?

22   You who say that one should not commit adultery, do you commit adultery? You who abhor idols, do you [a]rob temples?

23   You who [a]boast [1]in the Law, through your breaking the Law, do you dishonor God?

24   For "[a]THE NAME OF GOD IS BLASPHEMED AMONG THE GENTILES [b]BECAUSE OF YOU," just as it is written.

25   For indeed circumcision is of value, if you [a]practice [1]the Law; but if you are a transgressor [2]of the Law, [b]your circumcision has become uncircumcision.

26   [a]If therefore [b]the [1]uncircumcised man [c]keep the requirements of the Law, will not his uncircumcision be regarded as circumcision?

27   And will not [a]he who is physically uncircumcised, if he keeps the Law, will he not [b]judge you who [1]though having the letter *of the Law* and circumcision are a transgressor [2]of the Law?

28   For [a]he is not a Jew who is one outwardly;

12 [1]Or, *without law* [2]Or, *under law* [3]Or, *by law*

13 [1]Or, *of law* [2]Or, *righteous*
[a]James 1:22f., 25; Matt. 7:21, 24ff.; John 13:17

14 [1]Or, *law* [2]Lit., *by nature*
[a]Rom. 2:15; Rom. 1:19; Acts 10:35

15 [a]Rom. 2:14, 27

16 [a]Rom. 16:25; 2 Tim. 2:8; 1 Cor. 15:1; Gal. 1:11; 1 Tim. 1:11 [b]Acts 10:42; 17:31; Rom. 3:6; 14:10

17 [1]Or, *upon law*
[a]Rom. 2:23; 9:4; Mic. 3:11; John 5:45

18 [1]Or, *distinguish between the things which differ*
[a]Phil. 1:10

20 [1]Or, *instructor* [2]Lit., *infants*
[a]2 Tim. 1:13; Rom. 3:31

21 [1]Or, *proclaim*
[a]Matt. 23:3ff.

22 [a]Acts 19:37

23 [1]Or, *in law*
[a]Rom. 2:17; 9:4; Mic. 3:11; John 5:45

24 [a]Is. 52:5 [b]Ezek. 36:20ff.; 2 Pet. 2:2

25 [1]Or, *law* [2]Or, *of law*
[a]Rom. 2:13f., 27 [b]Jer. 4:4; 9:25f.

26 [1]Lit., *uncircumcision*
[a]1 Cor. 7:19 [b]Eph. 2:11; Rom. 3:30 [c]Rom. 8:4; 2:25, 27

27 [1]Lit., *through the letter* [2]Or, *of law*
[a]Eph. 2:11; Rom. 3:30 [b]Matt. 12:41

28 [a]Rom. 9:6; John 8:39; Gal. 6:15; Rom. 2:17

29 ªPhil. 3:3; Col. 2:11
ᵇRom. 7:6; 2 Cor. 3:6; Rom.
2:27 ᶜ1 Cor. 4:5; 2 Cor.
10:18; John 5:44, 12:43

1 ¹Lit., *is the advantage of
the Jew*

2 ªDeut. 4:8; Ps. 147:19;
Rom. 9:4 ᵇActs 7:38

3 ¹Or, *were unfaithful*
²Or, *unfaithfulness*
ªRom. 10:16; Heb. 4:2

4 ¹Or, *dost enter into
judgment*
ªLuke 20:16; Rom. 3:6, 31
ᵇRom. 3:7; Ps. 116:11 ᶜPs.
51:4

5 ¹Or, *commends*
ªRom. 5:8; 2 Cor. 6:4; 7:11
[Gr.]; Gal. 2:18 [Gr.] ᵇRom.
7:7; 8:31; 9:14, 30; 4:1 ᶜRom.
6:19; 1 Cor. 9:8; Gal. 3:15;
1 Cor. 15:32

6 ªLuke 20:16; Rom. 3:4,
31 ᵇRom. 2:16

7 ªRom. 3:4 ᵇRom. 9:19

8 ¹Lit., *Whose*
ªRom. 6:1

9 ¹Or possibly, *Are we
worse*
ªRom. 3:1 ᵇRom. 2:1-29
ᶜRom. 1:18-32 ᵈRom. 3:19,
23; 11:32; Gal. 3:22

10 ªPs. 14:1-3; 53:1-4

13 ªPs. 5:9; Ps. 140:3

neither is circumcision that which is outward in the flesh;

29 but ªhe is a Jew who is one inwardly; and circumcision is that which is of the heart, by the ᵇSpirit, not by the letter; ᶜand his praise is not from men, but from God.

CHAPTER 3

THEN what ¹advantage has the Jew? Or what is the benefit of circumcision?

2 Great in every respect. First of all, that ªthey were entrusted with the ᵇoracles of God.

3 What then? If ªsome ¹did not believe, their ²unbelief will not nullify the faithfulness of God, will it?

4 ªMay it never be! Rather, let God be found true, though every man *be found* ᵇa liar, as it is written,

"ᶜThat Thou mightest be justified in Thy
words,
And mightest prevail when Thou ¹art
judged."

5 But if our unrighteousness ¹ªdemonstrates the righteousness of God, ᵇwhat shall we say? The God who inflicts wrath is not unrighteous, is He? (ᶜI am speaking in human terms.)

6 ªMay it never be! For otherwise how will ᵇGod judge the world?

7 But if through my lie ªthe truth of God abounded to His glory, ᵇwhy am I also still being judged as a sinner?

8 And why not *say* (as we are slanderously reported and as some affirm that we say), "ªLet us do evil that good may come"? ¹Their condemnation is just.

9 What then? ¹ªAre we better than they? Not at all; for we have already charged that both ᵇJews and ᶜGreeks are ᵈall under sin;

10 as it is written,
"ªThere is none righteous, not even
one;
11 There is none who understands,
There is none who seeks for God;
12 All have turned aside, together they
have become useless;
There is none who does good,
There is not even one."
13 "ªTheir throat is an open grave,

WITH THEIR TONGUES THEY KEEP DECEIVING,"

"THE POISON OF ASPS IS UNDER THEIR LIPS;"

14 "^aWHOSE MOUTH IS FULL OF CURSING AND BITTERNESS;"

15 "^aTHEIR FEET ARE SWIFT TO SHED BLOOD,

16 DESTRUCTION AND MISERY ARE IN THEIR PATHS,

17 AND THE PATH OF PEACE HAVE THEY NOT KNOWN."

18 "^aTHERE IS NO FEAR OF GOD BEFORE THEIR EYES."

19 Now we know that whatever the ^aLaw says, it speaks to ^bthose who are ¹under the Law, that every mouth may be closed, and ^call the world may become accountable to God;

20 because ^aby the works ¹of the Law no flesh will be justified in His sight; for ^{2b}through the Law *comes* the knowledge of sin.

21 But now apart ¹from the Law ^a*the* righteousness of God has been manifested, being ^bwitnessed by the Law and the Prophets;

22 even *the* ^arighteousness of God through ^bfaith ^cin Jesus Christ for ^dall those who believe; for ^ethere is no distinction;

23 for ¹all ^ahave sinned and fall short of the glory of God,

24 being justified as a gift ^aby His grace through ^bthe redemption which is in Christ Jesus;

25 whom God displayed publicly as ^aa ¹propitiation ^{2b}in His blood through faith. *This was* to demonstrate His righteousness, ³because in the ^cforbearance of God He ^dpassed over the sins previously committed;

26 for the demonstration, *I say*, of His righteousness at the present time, that He might be just and the justifier of the one who ¹has faith in Jesus.

27 Where then is ^aboasting? It is excluded. By ^bwhat kind of law? Of works? No, but by a law of faith.

28 ¹For ^awe maintain that a man is justified by faith apart from works ²of the Law.

29 Or ^ais God *the God* of Jews only? Is He not *the God* of Gentiles also? Yes, of Gentiles also—

30 if indeed ^aGod is one—and ^bHe will justify the ¹circumcised ²by faith and the ³uncircumcised through faith.

14 ^aPs. 10:7

15 ^aIs. 59:7f.

18 ^aPs. 36:1

19 ¹Lit., *in*
^aJohn 10:34 ^bRom. 2:12
^cRom. 3:9

20 ¹Or, *of law* ²Or, *through law*
^aActs 13:39; Gal. 2:16; Ps. 143:2 ^bRom. 7:7; 4:15; 5:13, 20

21 ¹Or, *from law*
^aRom. 1:17; 9:30 ^bRom. 1:2; Acts 10:43

22 ^aRom. 1:17; 9:30 ^bRom. 4:5 ^cActs 3:16; Gal. 2:16, 20; 3:22; Eph. 3:12 ^dRom. 4:11, 16; 10:4 ^eRom. 10:12; Gal. 3:28; Col. 3:11

23 ¹Or, *all sinned*
^aRom. 3:9

24 ^aRom. 4:4f. 16; Eph. 2:8 ^bEph. 1:7; Col. 1:14; Heb. 9:15; 1 Cor. 1:30

25 ¹Or, *a propitiatory sacrifice* ²Or, *by* ³Lit., *because of the passing over of the sins previously committed in the forbearance of God*
^a1 John 2:2; 4:10 ^b1 Cor. 5:7; Heb. 9:14, 26; 1 Pet. 1:19; Rev. 1:5 ^cRom. 2:4 ^dActs 17:30; 14:16

26 ¹Lit., *is of the faith of Jesus.*

27 ^aRom. 2:17, 23; 4:2; 1 Cor. 1:29 ff. ^bRom. 9:31

28 ¹Some ancient mss. read, *Therefore* ²Or, *of law*
^aRom. 3:20, 21; Acts 13:39; Eph. 2:9; James 2:20, 24, 26

29 ^aRom. 9:24; 10:12; 15:9; Gal. 3:28; Acts 10:34f.

30 ¹Lit., *circumcision* ²Lit., *out of* ³Lit., *uncircumcision*
^aRom. 10:12 ^bRom. 4:11f. 16; Gal. 3:8; Rom. 3:22

323

31 [1]Or, *law*
[a]Luke 20:16; Rom. 3:4
[b]Rom. 4:3; 8:4; Matt. 5:17

1 [1]Or, *our forefather, has found according to the flesh*
[a]Rom. 1:3

2 [1]Lit., *toward*
[a]1 Cor. 1:31

3 [a]Gen. 15:6; Rom. 4:9, 22; Gal. 3:6; James 2:23

4 [a]Rom. 11:6

5 [a]Rom. 3:22; John 6:29

7 [a]Ps. 32:1

8 [1]Or, *reckon*
[a]Ps. 32:2 [b]2 Cor. 5:19

9 [1]Lit., *circumcision* [2]Lit., *uncircumcision*
[a]Rom. 3:30 [b]Rom. 4:3 [c]Gen. 15:6

10 [1]Lit., *in circumcision* [2]Lit., *in uncircumcision*

11 [a]Gen. 17:10f. [b]John 3:33 [c]Rom. 4:16f.; Luke 19:9 [d]Rom. 3:22; 4:16

13 [1]Lit., *seed* [2]Or, *through law*
[a]Rom. 9:8; Gal. 3:16 [b]Gen. 17:4-6; 22:17f.

31 Do we then nullify [1]the Law through faith? [a]May it never be! On the contrary, we [b]establish the Law.

CHAPTER 4

W HAT then shall we say that Abraham, [1]our forefather [a]according to the flesh, has found?

2 For if Abraham was justified by works, he has something to boast about; but [a]not [1]before God.

3 For what does the Scripture say? "[a]AND ABRAHAM BELIEVED GOD, AND IT WAS RECKONED TO HIM AS RIGHTEOUSNESS."

4 Now to the one who [a]works, his wage is not reckoned as a favor but as what is due.

5 But to the one who does not work, but [a]believes in Him who justifies the ungodly, his faith is reckoned as righteousness.

6 Just as David also speaks of the blessing upon the man to whom God reckons righteousness apart from works:

7 "[a]BLESSED ARE THOSE WHOSE LAWLESS DEEDS
  HAVE BEEN FORGIVEN,
AND WHOSE SINS HAVE BEEN COVERED.

8 "[a]BLESSED IS THE MAN WHOSE SIN THE LORD
  WILL NOT [1b]TAKE INTO ACCOUNT."

9 Is this blessing then upon [1a]the circumcised, or upon the [2]uncircumcised also? For [b]we say, "[c]FAITH WAS RECKONED TO ABRAHAM AS RIGHTEOUSNESS."

10 How then was it reckoned? While he was [1]circumcised, or [2]uncircumcised? Not while [1]circumcised, but while [2]uncircumcised;

11 and he [a]received the sign of circumcision, [b]a seal of the righteousness of the faith which he had while uncircumcised, that he might be [c]the father of [d]all who believe without being circumcised, that righteousness might be reckoned to them,

12 and the father of circumcision to those who not only are of the circumcision, but who also follow in the steps of the faith of our father Abraham which he had while uncircumcised.

13 For [a]the promise to Abraham or to his [1]descendants [b]that he would be heir of the world was not [2]through the Law, but through the righteousness of faith.

14 For [a]if those who are [1]of the Law are heirs, faith is made void and the promise is nullified;

15 for [a]the Law brings about wrath, but [b]where there is no law, neither is there violation.

16 For this reason *it is* [1]by faith, that *it might be* in accordance with [a]grace, in order that the promise may be certain to [b]all the [2]descendants, not only to [3]those who are of the Law, but also to [3]those who are of the faith of Abraham, who is [c]the father of us all,

17 (as it is written, "[a]A FATHER OF MANY NATIONS HAVE I MADE YOU") in the sight of Him whom he believed, *even* God, [b]who gives life to the dead and [1c]calls into being [d]that which does not exist.

18 In hope against hope he believed, in order that he might become [a]a father of many nations, according to that which had been spoken, "[b]SO SHALL YOUR [1]DESCENDANTS BE."

19 And without becoming weak in faith he contemplated his own body, now [a]as good as dead since [b]he was about a hundred years old, and [c]the deadness of Sarah's womb;

20 yet, with respect to the promise of God, he did not waver in unbelief, but grew strong in faith, [a]giving glory to God,

21 and [a]being fully assured that [b]what He had promised, He was able also to perform.

22 Therefore also [a]IT WAS RECKONED TO HIM AS RIGHTEOUSNESS.

23 Now [a]not for his sake only was it written, that "IT WAS RECKONED TO HIM,"

24 but for our sake also, to whom it will be reckoned, as those [a]who believe in Him who [b]raised Jesus our Lord from the dead,

25 *Him* who was [a]delivered up because of our transgressions, and was [b]raised because of our justification.

CHAPTER 5

T HEREFORE having been justified by faith, [1b]we have peace with God through our Lord Jesus Christ,

2 through whom also we have [a]obtained our introduction by faith into this grace [b]in which we stand; and [1]we exult in hope of the glory of God.

3 [a]And not only this, but [1]we also [b]exult in

14 [1]Or, *of law*
[a]Gal. 3:18

15 [a]Rom. 7:7, 10-25; 1 Cor. 15:56; Gal. 3:10 [b]Rom. 3:20

16 [1]Or, *of* [2]Lit., *seed* [3]Lit., *that which is*
[a]Rom. 3:24 [b]Rom. 4:11; 9:8; 15:8 [c]Rom. 4:11; Luke 19:9

17 [1]Lit., *calls the things which do not exist as existing*
[a]Gen. 17:5 [b]John 5:21 [c]Is. 48:13; 51:2 [d]1 Cor. 1:28

18 [1]Lit., *seed*
[a]Rom. 4:17 [b]Gen. 15:5

19 [a]Heb. 11:12 [b]Gen. 17:17 [c]Gen. 18:11

20 [a]Matt. 9:8

21 [a]Rom. 14:5 [b]Gen. 18:14; Heb. 11:19

22 [a]Rom. 4:3

23 [a]Rom. 15:4; 1 Cor. 9:9f.; 10:11; 2 Tim. 3:16f.

24 [a]Rom. 10:9; 1 Pet. 1:21 [b]Acts 2:24

25 [a]Rom. 5:6, 8; 8:32; Gal. 2:20; Eph. 5:2 [b]1 Cor. 15:17; 2 Cor. 5:15; Rom. 5:18

1 [1]Some ancient mss. read, *let us have*
[a]Rom. 3:28 [b]Rom. 5:11

2 [1]Or, *let us exult*
[a]Eph. 2:18; 3:12; Heb. 10:19f.; 1 Pet. 3:18 [b]1 Cor. 15:1

3 [1]Or, *let us also exult*
[a]Rom. 5:11; 8:23; 9:10; 2 Cor. 8:19 [b]Matt. 5:12; James 1:2f.

325

Romans 5

**Christ's Death for Sinners.
Adam and Christ Contrasted.**

3 cLuke 21:19

4 aLuke 21:19 bPhil. 2:22;
James 1:12

5 aPs. 119:116; Rom. 9:33;
Heb. 6:18f. bActs 2:33; 10:45;
Titus 3:6; Gal. 4:6

6 aRom. 5:8, 10 bGal. 4:4
cRom. 4:25; 5:8; 8:32; Gal.
2:20; Eph. 5:2

8 aRom. 3:5 bRom. 8:39;
John 3:16; 15:13 cRom. 4:25;
5:6; 8:32; Gal. 2:20; Eph. 5:2

9 1Or, in
aRom. 3:25 b1 Thess 1:10;
Rom. 1:18

10 1Or, in
aRom. 11:28; Eph. 2:3; Col.
1:21f.; 2 Cor. 5:18f. bRom.
8:34; Heb. 7:25; 1 John 2:1

11 1Lit., but also exulting
aRom. 5:3; 8:23; 9:10; 2 Cor.
8:19 bRom. 5:10; 11:15;
2 Cor. 5:18f.

12 aGen. 2:17; 3:6, 19;
1 Cor. 15:21f.; Rom. 5:15,
16, 17 bRom. 6:23; 1 Cor.
15:56; James 1:15 cRom.
5:14, 19, 21; 1 Cor. 15:22

13 1Or, until law
aRom. 4:15

14 1Or, foreshadowing
aHos. 6:7 b1 Cor. 15:45

15 1Lit., not as the trespass,
so also is the free gift
aRom. 5:12, 18 bRom. 5:19;
Rom. 5:18 cActs 15:11

16 1Lit., to condemnation
2Lit., to an act of
righteousness
a1 Cor. 11:32 [Gr.]

17 aGen. 2:17; 3:6, 19;
1 Cor. 15:21f.; Rom. 5:12,
15, 16

our tribulations; knowing that tribulation brings about cperseverance;

4 and aperseverance, bproven character; and proven character, hope;

5 and hope adoes not disappoint; because the love of God has been bpoured out within our hearts through the Holy Spirit who was given to us.

6 For while we were still ahelpless, bat the right time cChrist died for the ungodly.

7 For one will hardly die for a righteous man; though perhaps for the good man someone would dare even to die.

8 But God ademonstrates bHis own love toward us, in that while we were yet sinners, cChrist died for us.

9 Much more then, having now been justified 1aby His blood, we shall be saved bfrom the wrath of God through Him.

10 For if while we were aenemies, we were reconciled to God through the death of His Son, much more, having been reconciled, we shall be saved 1bby His life.

11 aAnd not only this, 1but we also exult in God through our Lord Jesus Christ, through whom we have now received bthe reconciliation.

12 Therefore, just as through aone man sin entered into the world, and bdeath through sin, and cso death spread to all men, because all sinned—

13 for 1until the Law sin was in the world; but asin is not imputed when there is no law.

14 Nevertheless death reigned from Adam until Moses, even over those who had not sinned ain the likeness of Adam's offense, who is a 1btype of Him who was to come.

15 But 1the free gift is not like the transgression. For if by the transgression of athe one bthe many died, much more did the grace of God and the gift by cthe grace of the one Man, Jesus Christ, abound to bthe many.

16 And the gift is not like that which came through the one who sinned; for on the one hand athe judgment arose from one transgression 1resulting in condemnation, but on the other hand the free gift arose from many transgressions 2resulting in justification.

17 For if by the transgression of the one, death reigned athrough the one, much more those who receive the abundance of grace and of the gift of

righteousness will [b]reign in life through the One, Jesus Christ.

18 So then as through [a]one transgression [1]there resulted condemnation to all men; even so through one [b]act of righteousness [2]there resulted [c]justification of life to all men.

19 For as through the one man's disobedience [a]the many [b]were made sinners, even so through [c]the obedience of the One [a]the many will be made righteous.

20 And [1a]the Law came in that the transgression might increase; but where sin increased, [b]grace abounded all the more,

21 that, as [a]sin reigned in death, even so [b]grace might reign through righteousness to eternal life through Jesus Christ our Lord.

a   Chapter 6

WHAT shall we say then? Are we to [b]continue in sin that grace might increase?

2 [a]May it never be! How shall we who [b]died to sin still live in it?

3 Or do you not know that all of us who have been [a]baptized into [b]Christ Jesus have been baptized into His death?

4 Therefore we have been [a]buried with Him through baptism into death, in order that as Christ was [b]raised from the dead through the [c]glory of the Father, so we too might walk in [d]newness of life.

5 For [a]if we have become [1]united with *Him* in the likeness of His death, certainly we shall be also [2]in the likeness of His resurrection,

6 knowing this, that our [a]old [1]self was [b]crucified with *Him*, that our [c]body of sin might be [2]done away with, that we should no longer be slaves to sin;

7 for [a]he who died is [1]freed from sin.

8 Now [a]if we have died with Christ, we believe that we shall also live with Him,

9 knowing that Christ, having been [a]raised from the dead, is never to die again; [b]death no longer is master over Him.

10 For the death that He died, He died to sin, once for all; but the life that He lives, He lives to God.

11 Even so consider yourselves to be [a]dead to sin, but alive to God in Christ Jesus.

17 [b]2 Tim. 2:12; Rev. 22:5

18 [1]Lit., *to condemnation* [2]Lit., *to justification* [a]Rom. 5:12, 15 [b]Rom. 3:25 [c]Rom. 4:25

19 [a]Rom. 5:15, 18 [b]Rom. 5:12; 11:32 [c]Phil. 2:8

20 [1]Or, *law* [a]Gal. 3:19; Rom. 3:20; 7:7f. [b]Rom. 6:1; 1 Tim. 1:14

21 [a]Rom. 5:12, 14 [b]John 1:17; Rom. 6:23

[a]Rom. 3:5 [b]Rom. 6:15; 3:8

2 [a]Luke 20:16; Rom. 6:15 [b]Rom. 6:11; 7:4, 6; Gal. 2:19; Col. 2:20; 3:3; 1 Pet. 2:24

3 [a]Matt. 28:19 [b]Acts 2:38; 8:16; 19:5; Gal. 3:27

4 [a]Col. 2:12 [b]Acts 2:24; Rom. 6:9 [c]John 11:40; 2 Cor. 13:4 [d]Rom. 7:6; 2 Cor. 5:17; Gal. 6:15; Eph. 4:23f.; Col. 3:10

5 [1]Or, *united with the likeness* [2]Or, *with* [a]2 Cor. 4:10; Phil. 3:10f.; Col. 2:12; 3:1

6 [1]Lit., *man* [2]Or, *made powerless* [a]Eph. 4:22; Col. 3:9 [b]Gal. 2:20; 5:24; 6:14 [c]Rom. 7:24

7 [1]Or, *acquitted* [a]1 Pet. 4:1

8 [a]2 Tim. 2:11; 2 Cor. 4:10; Rom. 6:4

9 [a]Acts 2:24; Rom. 6:4 [b]Rev. 1:18

11 [a]Rom. 6:2; 7:4, 6; Gal. 2:19; Col. 2:20; 3:3; 1 Pet. 2:24

12 ªRom. 6:14

13 ¹Lit., *your members to sin* ²Or, *weapons* ªRom. 7:5; Col. 3:5; Rom. 6:16, 19 ᵇRom. 12:1; 2 Cor. 5:14f.; 1 Pet. 2:24

14 ªRom. 8:2, 12 ᵇRom. 6:12 ᶜRom. 7:4, 6; Gal. 4:21; Rom. 5:18 ᵈRom. 5:17, 21

15 ªRom. 6:1 ᵇLuke 20:16; Rom. 6:2

16 ¹Lit., *to death* ²Lit., *to righteousness* ªRom. 11:2; 1 Cor. 3:16; 5:6; 6:2, 3, 9, 15, 16, 19; 9:13, 24 ᵇJohn 8:34; 2 Pet. 2:19 ᶜRom. 6:21, 23

17 ¹Lit., *you were slaves . . . but you became* ªRom. 1:8; 2 Cor. 2:14 ᵇ2 Tim. 1:13

18 ªRom. 8:2; John 8:32; Rom. 6:22

19 ¹Lit., *to lawlessness* ²Lit., *to sanctification* ªRom. 3:5 ᵇRom. 6:13

20 ªRom. 6:16; Matt. 6:24

21 ¹Lit., *fruit* ²Lit., *having* ³Lit., *in* ªRom. 7:5; Jer. 12:13; Ezek. 16:63 ᵇRom. 6:16, 23; 1:32; 8:6, 13; Gal. 6:8; Rom. 5:12

22 ¹Lit., *have* ²Lit., *fruit* ³Lit., *to sanctification* ªRom. 8:2; John 8:32; Rom. 6:18 ᵇ1 Cor. 7:22; 1 Pet. 2:16 ᶜRom. 7:4 ᵈ1 Pet. 1:9

23 ªRom. 6:16, 21; 1:32; 8:6, 13; Gal. 6:8; Rom. 5:12 ᵇRom. 5:21; 8:39; Matt. 25:46

1 ªRom. 1:13

2 ª1 Cor. 7:39

12 Therefore do not let sin ªreign in your mortal body that you should obey its lusts,

13 and do not go on ªpresenting ¹the members of your body to sin *as* ²instruments of unrighteousness; but ᵇpresent yourselves to God as those alive from the dead, and your members *as* ²instruments of righteousness to God.

14 For ªsin shall not ᵇbe master over you, for ᶜyou are not under law, but ᵈunder grace.

15 What then? ªShall we sin because we are not under law but under grace? ᵇMay it never be!

16 Do you not ªknow that when you present yourselves to someone *as* ᵇslaves for obedience, you are slaves of the one whom you obey, either of ᶜsin ¹resulting in death, or of obedience ²resulting in righteousness?

17 But ªthanks be to God that ¹though you were slaves of sin, you became obedient from the heart to that ᵇform of teaching to which you were committed,

18 and having been ªfreed from sin, you became slaves of righteousness.

19 ªI am speaking in human terms because of the weakness of your flesh. For just ᵇas you presented your members *as* slaves to impurity and to lawlessness, ¹resulting in *further* lawlessness, so now present your members *as* slaves to righteousness, ²resulting in sanctification.

20 For ªwhen you were slaves of sin, you were free in regard to righteousness.

21 Therefore what ¹ªbenefit were you then ²deriving ³from the things of which you are now ashamed? For the outcome of those things is ᵇdeath.

22 But now having been ªfreed from sin and ᵇenslaved to God, you ¹derive your ²ᶜbenefit, ³resulting in sanctification, and ᵈthe outcome, eternal life.

23 For the wages of ªsin is death, but the free gift of God is ᵇeternal life in Christ Jesus our Lord.

CHAPTER 7

 OR do you not know, ªbrethren (for I am speaking to those who know the law), that the law has jurisdiction over a person as long as he lives?

2 For ªthe married woman is bound by law to her husband while he is living; but if her husband

dies, she is released from the law concerning the husband.

3 So then if, while her husband is living, she is joined to another man, she shall be called an adulteress; but if her husband dies, she is free from the law, so that she is not an adulteress, though she is joined to another man.

4 Therefore, my brethren, you also were [a]made to die [b]to the Law [c]through the body of Christ, that you might be joined to another, to Him who was raised from the dead, that we might bear fruit for God.

5 For while we were [a]in the flesh, the sinful passions, which were [b]*aroused* by the Law, were at work [c]in [1]the members of our body to bear fruit for death.

6 But now we have been [a]released from the Law, having [b]died to that by which we were bound, so that we serve in [c]newness of [d]the [1]Spirit and not in oldness of the letter.

7 [a]What shall we say then? Is the Law sin? [b]May it never be! On the contrary, [c]I would not have come to know sin except [1]through the Law; for I would not have known about [2]coveting if the Law had not said, "[d]You shall not [3]covet."

8 But sin, [a]taking opportunity [b]through the commandment, produced in me [1]coveting of every kind; for [c]apart [2]from the Law sin *is* dead.

9 And I was once alive apart [1]from the Law; but when the commandment came, sin became alive, and I died;

10 and this commandment, which was [1a]to result in life, proved [2]to result in death for me;

11 for sin, [a]taking opportunity [b]through the commandment, [c]deceived me, and through it killed me.

12 [a]So then, the Law is holy, and the commandment is holy and righteous and good.

13 Therefore did that which is good become *a cause of* death for me? [a]May it never be! Rather it was sin, in order that it might be shown to be sin by effecting my death through that which is good, that through the commandment sin might become utterly sinful.

14 For we know that the Law is [a]spiritual; but I am [a]of flesh, [b]sold [1c]into bondage to sin.

15 For that which I am doing, [a]I do not

4 [a]Rom. 7:6; 6:2 [b]Gal. 2:19; 5:18; Rom. 8:2 [c]Col. 1:22

5 [1]Lit., *our members to bear* [a]Rom. 8:8f.; 2 Cor. 10:3 [b]Rom. 7:7f. [c]Rom. 6:13, 21, 23

6 [1]Or, *spirit* [a]Rom. 7:2 [b]Rom. 6:2 [c]Rom. 6:4 [d]Rom. 2:29

7 [1]Or, *through law* [2]Or, *lust* [3]Or, *LUST* [a]Rom. 3:5 [b]Luke 20:16 [c]Rom. 3:20; 4:15; 5:20 [d]Ex. 20:17; Deut. 5:21

8 [1]Or, *lust* [2]Or, *from law* [a]Rom. 7:11 [b]Rom. 3:20; 7:11 [c]1 Cor. 15:56

9 [1]Or, *from law*

10 [1]Lit., *to life* [2]Lit., *to death* [a]Lev. 18:5; Rom. 10:5; Gal. 3:12; Luke 10:28

11 [a]Rom. 7:8 [b]Rom. 3:20; 7:8 [c]Gen. 3:13

12 [a]Rom. 7:16; 1 Tim. 1:8

13 [a]Luke 20:16

14 [1]Lit., *under sin* [a]1 Cor. 3:1 [b]1 Kin. 21:20, 25; 2 Kin. 17:17; Rom. 6:6; Gal. 4:3 [c]Rom. 3:9

15 [a]John 15:15

15 [b]Gal. 5:17; Rom. 7:19

16 [a]Rom. 7:12; 1 Tim. 1:8

17 [a]Rom. 7:20

18 [a]Rom. 7:25; 8:3; John 3:6

19 [a]Rom. 7:15

20 [a]Rom. 7:17

21 [1]Lit., *law*
[a]Rom. 7:23, 25; 8:2

22 [1]Or, *concerning*
[a]2 Cor. 4:16; Eph. 3:16;
1 Pet. 3:4

23 [1]Lit., *my members* [2]Lit.,
in
[a]Gal. 5:17; James 4:1; 1 Pet.
2:11; Rom. 6:19 [b]Rom. 7:25
[c]Rom. 7:21, 25; 8:2

24 [1]Or, *this body of death*
[a]Rom. 6:6; Col. 2:11 [b]Rom.
8:2

25 [a]1 Cor. 15:57 [b]Rom.
7:21, 23; 8:2

1 [a]Rom. 8:34; 5:16 [b]Rom.
8:9f. [c]Rom. 8:2, 11, 39; 16:3

2 [1]Or, *has set you free in
Christ Jesus* [2]Some ancient
mss. read, *me*
[a]1 Cor. 15:45 [b]Rom. 8:1, 11,
39; 16:3 [c]Rom 6:14, 18; 7:4;
John 8:32, 36

3 [1]Lit., *wherein it was
weak* [2]Lit., *flesh of sin*
[a]Heb. 10:1ff.; Acts 13:39
[b]Heb. 7:18; Rom. 7:18f.
[c]Phil. 2:7; Heb. 2:14, 17; 4:15

4 [a]Luke 1:6; Rom. 2:26
[b]Gal. 5:16, 25

5 [a]Gal. 5:19-21 [b]Gal. 5:22-
25

understand; for I am not practicing [b]what I *would* like to *do*, but I am doing the very thing I hate.

16 But if I do the very thing I do not wish *to do*, I agree with [a]the Law, *confessing* that it is good.

17 So now, [a]no longer am I the one doing it, but sin which indwells me.

18 For I know that nothing good dwells in me, that is, in my [a]flesh; for the wishing is present in me, but the doing of the good *is* not.

19 For [a]the good that I wish, I do not do; but I practice the very evil that I do not wish.

20 But if I am doing the very thing I do not wish, [a]I am no longer the one doing it, but sin which dwells in me.

21 I find then [a]the [1]principle that evil is present in me, the one who wishes to do good.

22 For I joyfully concur with the law of God [1]in [a]the inner man,

23 but I see [a]a different law in [1]the members of my body, waging war against the [b]law of my mind, and making me a prisoner [2]of [c]the law of sin which is in my members.

24 Wretched man that I am! Who will set me free from [1a]the body of this [b]death?

25 [a]Thanks be to God through Jesus Christ our Lord! So then, on the one hand I myself with my mind am serving the law of God, but on the other, with my flesh [b]the law of sin.

CHAPTER 8

THERE is therefore now no [a]condemnation for those who are [b]in [c]Christ Jesus.

2 For [a]the law of the Spirit of life [1]in [b]Christ Jesus [c]has set [2]you free from the law of sin and of death.

3 For [a]what the Law could not do, [1b]weak as it was through the flesh, God *did*: sending His own Son in [c]the likeness of [2]sinful flesh and *as an offering* for sin, He condemned sin in the flesh,

4 in order that the [a]requirement of the Law might be fulfilled in us, who [b]do not walk according to the flesh, but according to the Spirit.

5 For those who are according to the flesh set their minds on [a]the things of the flesh, but those who are according to the Spirit, [b]the things of the Spirit.

6   ªFor the mind set on the flesh is ᵇdeath, but the mind set on the Spirit is life and peace;

7   because the mind set on the flesh is ªhostile toward God; for it does not subject itself to the Law of God, for it is not even able *to do so;*

8   and those who are ªin the flesh cannot please God.

9   However you are not ªin the flesh but in the Spirit, if indeed the Spirit of God ᵇdwells in you. But ᶜif anyone does not have the Spirit of Christ, he does not belong to Him.

10   And ªif Christ is in you, though the body is dead because of sin, yet the spirit is ¹alive because of righteousness.

11   But if the Spirit of Him who ªraised Jesus from the dead dwells in you, ᵇHe who raised ᶜChrist Jesus from the dead will also give life to your mortal bodies ¹through His Spirit who indwells you.

12   So then, brethren, we are under obligation, not to the flesh, to live according to the flesh—

13   for ªif you are living according to the flesh, you ¹must die; but if by the Spirit you are ᵇputting to death the deeds of the body, you will live.

14   For all who are ªbeing led by the Spirit of God, these are ᵇsons of God.

15   For you ªhave not received a spirit of slavery ¹leading to fear again, but you ᵇhave received ²a spirit of adoption as sons by which we cry out, "ᶜAbba! Father!"

16   The Spirit Himself ªbears witness with our spirit that we are ᵇchildren of God,

17   and if children, ªheirs also, heirs of God and fellow-heirs with Christ, ᵇif indeed we suffer with *Him* in order that we may also be glorified with *Him.*

18   For I consider that the sufferings of this present time ªare not worthy to be compared with the ᵇglory that is to be revealed to us.

19   For the ªanxious longing of the creation waits eagerly for ᵇthe revealing of the ᶜsons of God.

20   For the creation ªwas subjected to ᵇfutility, not of its own will, but ᶜbecause of Him who subjected it, ¹in hope

21   that ªthe creation itself also will be set free from its slavery to corruption into the freedom of the glory of the children of God.

22   For we know that the whole creation ªgroans

6 ªGal. 6:8 ᵇRom. 6:21; 8:13

7 ªJames 4:4

8 ªRom. 7:5

9 ªRom. 7:5 ᵇRom. 8:11; 1 Cor. 3:16; 6:19; 2 Cor. 6:16; 2 Tim. 1:14; John 14:23 ᶜJohn 14:17; Gal. 4:6; Phil. 1:19; 1 John 4:13

10 ¹Lit., *life* ªGal. 2:20; Eph. 3:17; Col. 1:27; John 17:23

11 ¹Some ancient mss. read, *because of* ªActs 2:24; Rom. 6:4 ᵇJohn 5:21 ᶜRom. 8:1, 2, 39; 16:3

13 ¹Or, *are about to* ªRom. 8:6 ᵇCol. 3:5

14 ªGal. 5:18 ᵇHos. 1:10; [Rom. 9:26]; Matt. 5:9; John 1:12; 2 Cor. 6:18; Gal. 3:26; 1 John 3:1; Rev. 21:7; Rom. 8:16, 19; 9:8

15 ¹Lit., *for fear again* ²Or, *the Spirit* ª2 Tim. 1:7; Heb. 2:15 ᵇGal. 4:5f.; Rom. 8:23 ᶜMark 14:36; Gal. 4:6

16 ªActs 5:32 ᵇHos. 1:10; [Rom. 9:26]; Matt. 5:9; John 1:12; 2 Cor. 6:18; Gal. 3:26; 1 John 3:1; Rev. 21:7; Rom. 8:14, 19; 9:8

17 ªGal. 4:7; Acts. 20:32; Gal. 3:29; Eph. 3:6; Titus 3:7; Heb. 1:14; Rev. 21:7 ᵇ2 Cor. 1:5, 7; Phil. 3:10; 2 Tim. 2:12; 1 Pet. 4:13; Col. 1:24

18 ª2 Cor. 4:17; 1 Pet. 4:13 ᵇCol. 3:4; Titus 2:13; 1 Pet. 5:1; 1:5

19 ªPhil. 1:20 ᵇ1 Cor. 1:7f.; Col. 3:4; 1 Pet. 1:7, 13; 1 John 3:2; Rom. 8:18 ᶜHos. 1:10; [Rom. 9:26]; Matt. 5:9; John 1:12; 2 Cor. 6:18; Gal. 3:26; 1 John 3:1; Rev. 21:7; Rom. 8:14, 16; 9:8

20 ¹Some ancient mss. read, *in hope; because the creation . . .* ªGen. 3:17-19 ᵇPs. 39:5f.; Eccl. 1:2 ᶜGen. 3:17; 5:29

21 ªActs 3:21; 2 Pet. 3:13; Rev. 21:1

22 ªJer. 12:4, 11

23 ªRom. 5:3 ᵇ2 Cor. 1:22;
Rom. 8:16 ᶜ2 Cor. 5:2, 4
ᵈRom. 8:19, 25; 8:15; Gal.
5:5 ᵉRom. 7:24

24 ¹Some ancient mss.
read, *who hopes for what he
sees?*
ªRom. 8:20; 1 Thess. 5:8;
Titus 3:7 ᵇ2 Cor. 5:7 [cf.
Rom. 4:18]; Heb. 11:1

25 ª1 Thess. 1:3

26 ªMatt. 20:22; 2 Cor. 12:8
ᵇJohn 14:16; Eph. 6:18;
Rom. 8:15f.

27 ¹I.e., *true believers;* lit.,
holy ones
ªPs. 139:1f.; Luke 16:15; Rev.
2:23; Acts 1:24 ᵇRom. 8:6
ᶜRom. 8:34

28 ¹Some ancient mss.
read, *all things work
together for good*
ªRom. 8:32 ᵇRom. 8:30;
9:24; 1 Cor. 1:9; Gal. 1:6, 15;
5:8; Eph. 1:11; 3:11; 2 Thess.
2:14; Heb. 9:15; 1 Pet. 2:9;
3:9; Rom. 11:29

29 ªRom. 11:2; 1 Pet. 1:2,
20; 2 Tim. 1:9; 1 Cor. 8:3
ᵇ1 Cor. 2:7; Eph. 1:5, 11;
Rom. 9:23 ᶜ1 Cor. 15:49;
Phil. 3:21; Col. 3:10; 1 John
3:2 ᵈCol. 1:18; Heb. 1:6

30 ª1 Cor. 2:7; Eph. 1:5, 11;
Rom. 9:23 ᵇRom. 8:28; 9:24;
1 Cor. 1:9; Gal. 1:6, 15; 5:8;
Eph. 1:11; 3:11; 2 Thess.
2:14; Heb. 9:15; 1 Pet. 2:9;
3:9; Rom. 11:29 ᶜ1 Cor. 6:11
ᵈJohn 17:22; 1 Cor. 2:7;
Rom. 8:21; 9:23

31 ªRom. 3:5; 4:1 ᵇPs.
118:6; Matt. 1:23

32 ªJohn 3:16; Rom. 5:8
ᵇRom. 4:25

33 ªLuke 18:7 ᵇIs. 50:8f.

34 ¹Some ancient mss.
read, *raised from the dead*
ªRom. 8:1 ᵇRom. 5:6f. ᶜActs
2:24 ᵈMark 16:19 ᵉHeb. 7:25;
Rom. 8:27; Heb. 9:24;
1 John 2:1

35 ¹Some ancient mss.
read, *God*
ªRom. 8:37f. ᵇRom. 2:9;
2 Cor. 4:8 ᶜ1 Cor. 4:11;
2 Cor. 11:26f.

36 ªPs. 44:22; 1 Cor. 4:9;
15:30f.; 2 Cor. 1:9; 4:10f.;
6:9; 11:23; Acts 20:24

and suffers the pains of childbirth together until now.

23 ªAnd not only this, but also we ourselves, having ᵇthe first fruits of the Spirit, even we ourselves ᶜgroan within ourselves, ᵈwaiting eagerly for *our* adoption as sons, ᵉthe redemption of our body.

24 For ªin hope we have been saved, but ᵇhope that is seen is not hope; for ¹why does one also hope for what he sees?

25 But ªif we hope for what we do not see, with perseverance we wait eagerly for it.

26 And in the same way the Spirit also helps our weakness; for ªwe do not know how to pray as we should, but ᵇthe Spirit Himself intercedes for *us* with groanings too deep for words;

27 and ªHe who searches the hearts knows what ᵇthe mind of the Spirit is, because He ᶜintercedes for the ¹saints according to *the will of* God.

28 And we know that ¹God causes ªall things to work together for good to those who love God, to those who are ᵇcalled according to *His* purpose.

29 For whom He ªforeknew, He also ᵇpredestined *to become* ᶜconformed to the image of His Son, that He might be the ᵈfirst-born among many brethren;

30 and whom He ªpredestined, these He also ᵇcalled; and whom He called, these He also ᶜjustified; and whom He justified, these He also ᵈglorified.

31 ªWhat then shall we say to these things? ᵇIf God *is* for us, who *is* against us?

32 He who ªdid not spare His own Son, but ᵇdelivered Him up for us all, how will He not also with Him freely give us all things?

33 Who will bring a charge against ªGod's elect? ᵇGod is the one who justifies;

34 who is the one who ªcondemns? Christ Jesus is He who ᵇdied, yes, rather who was ¹ᶜraised, who is ᵈat the right hand of God, who also ᵉintercedes for us.

35 Who shall separate us from ªthe love of ¹Christ? Shall ᵇtribulation, or distress, or ᶜpersecution, or ᶜfamine, or ᶜnakedness, or ᶜperil, or sword?

36 Just as it is written,
    "ªFor Thy sake we are being put to
        death all day long;
    We were considered as sheep to be
        slaughtered."

37 But in all these things we overwhelmingly [a]conquer through [b]Him who loved us.

38 For I am convinced that neither [a]death, nor life, nor [b]angels, nor principalities, nor [c]things present, nor things to come, nor powers,

39 nor height, nor depth, nor any other created thing, shall be able to separate us from [a]the love of God, which is [b]in Christ Jesus our Lord.

a   CHAPTER 9

I AM telling the truth in Christ, I am not lying, my conscience bearing me witness in the Holy Spirit,

2 that I have great sorrow and unceasing grief in my heart.

3 For [a]I could [1]wish that I myself were [b]accursed, *separated* from Christ for the sake of my brethren, my kinsmen [c]according to the flesh,

4 who are [a]Israelites, to whom belongs [b]the adoption as sons and [c]the glory and [d]the covenants and [e]the giving of the Law and [f]the *temple* service and [g]the promises,

5 whose are [a]the fathers, and [b]from whom is [1]the Christ according to the flesh, [c]who is over all, [d]God [e]blessed [2]forever. Amen.

6 But *it is* not as though [a]the word of God has failed. [b]For they are not all Israel who are *descended* from Israel;

7 neither are they all children [a]because they are Abraham's [1]descendants, but: "[b]THROUGH ISAAC YOUR [1]DESCENDANTS WILL BE NAMED."

8 That is, it is not the children of the flesh who are [a]children of God, but the [b]children of the promise are regarded as [1]descendants.

9 For this is a word of promise: "[a]AT THIS TIME I WILL COME, AND SARAH SHALL HAVE A SON."

10 [a]And not only this, but there was [b]Rebekah also, when she had conceived *twins* by one man, our father Isaac;

11 for though *the twins* were not yet born, and had not done anything good or bad, in order that [a]God's purpose according to *His* choice might stand, not because of works, but because of Him who calls,

12 it was said to her, "[a]THE OLDER WILL SERVE THE YOUNGER."

13 Just as it is written, "[a]JACOB I LOVED, BUT ESAU I HATED."

37 [a]1 Cor. 15:57; John 16:33 [b]Gal. 2:20; Eph. 5:2; Rev. 1:5

38 [a]1 Cor. 3:22 [b]1 Cor. 15:24; Eph. 1:21; 1 Pet. 3:22 [c]1 Cor. 3:22

39 [a]Rom. 5:8 [b]Rom. 8:1

1 [a]2 Cor. 11:10; Gal. 1:20; 1 Tim. 2:7; Rom. 1:9

3 [1]Lit., *pray* [a]Ex. 32:32 [b]1 Cor. 12:3; 16:22; Gal. 1:8f. [c]Rom. 11:14; Eph. 6:5; Rom. 1:3

4 [a]Rom. 9:6 [b]Ex. 4:22; Rom. 8:15 [c]Ex. 40:34; 1 Kin. 8:11; Ezek. 1:28; Heb. 9:5 [d]Gen. 17:2; Deut. 29:14; Eph. 2:12; Luke 1:72; Acts 3:25 [e]Deut. 4:13f.; Ps. 147:19 [f]Heb. 9:1, 6; Deut. 7:6; 14:1f. [g]Acts 2:39; 13:32; Eph. 2:12

5 [1]I.e., the Messiah [2]Lit., *unto the ages* [a]Rom. 11:28; Acts 3:13 [b]Matt. 1:1-16; Rom. 1:3 [c]Col. 1:16-19 [d]John 1:1; Col. 2:9 [e]Rom. 1:25

6 [a]Num. 23:19 [b]Rom. 2:28f.; Gal. 6:16; John 1:47

7 [1]Lit., *seed* [a]Gal. 4:23; John 8:33, 39 [b]Gen. 21:12; Heb. 11:18

8 [1]Lit., *seed* [a]Rom. 8:14 [b]Rom. 4:13, 16; Gal. 3:29; 4:28; Heb. 11:11

9 [a]Gen. 18:10

10 [a]Rom. 5:3 [b]Gen. 25:21

11 [a]Rom. 8:28; 4:17

12 [a]Gen. 25:23

13 [a]Mal. 1:2f.

14 ªRom. 3:5 ᵇ2 Chr. 19:7;
Rom. 2:11 ᶜLuke 20:16

15 ªEx. 33:19

16 ªGal. 2:2 ᵇEph. 2:8

17 ¹Lit., *in*
ªEx. 9:16

18 ªEx. 4:21; 7:3; 9:12;
10:20, 27; 11:10; 14:4, 17;
Deut. 2:30; Josh. 11:20; John
12:40; Rom. 11:7, 25

19 ªRom. 11:19; 1 Cor.
15:35; James 2:18 ᵇRom. 3:7
ᶜ2 Chr. 20:6; Job 9:12; Dan.
4:35

20 ªRom. 2:1 ᵇJob. 33:13
ᶜIs. 29:16; 45:9; 64:8; Jer.
18:6; 2 Tim. 2:20; Rom
9:22f.

21 ¹Lit., *for honor* ²Lit., *for
dishonor*

22 ªRom. 2:4 ᵇProv. 16:4;
1 Pet. 2:8

23 ªRom. 2:4; Eph. 3:16
ᵇActs 9:15 ᶜRom. 8:29f.

24 ªRom. 8:28 ᵇRom. 3:29

25 ªHos. 2:23; 1 Pet. 2:10

26 ªHos. 1:10 ᵇMatt. 16:16

27 ªIs. 10:22 ᵇGen. 22:17;
Hos. 1:10 ᶜRom. 11:5

14   ªWhat shall we say then? ᵇThere is no injustice with God, is there? ᶜMay it never be!

15   For He says to Moses, "ªI WILL HAVE MERCY ON WHOM I HAVE MERCY, AND I WILL HAVE COMPASSION ON WHOM I HAVE COMPASSION."

16   So then it *does* not *depend* on the man who wills or the man who ªruns, but on ᵇGod who has mercy.

17   For the Scripture says to Pharaoh, "ªFOR THIS VERY PURPOSE I RAISED YOU UP, TO DEMONSTRATE MY POWER IN YOU, AND THAT MY NAME MIGHT BE PROCLAIMED ¹THROUGHOUT THE WHOLE EARTH."

18   So then He has mercy on whom He desires, and He ªhardens whom He desires.

19   ªYou will say to me then, "ᵇWhy does He still find fault? For ᶜwho resists His will?"

20   On the contrary, who are you, ªO man, who ᵇanswers back to God? ᶜThe thing molded will not say to the molder, "Why did you make me like this," will it?

21   Or does not the potter have a right over the clay, to make from the same lump one vessel ¹for honorable use, and another ²for common use?

22   What if God, although willing to demonstrate His wrath and to make His power known, endured with much ªpatience vessels of wrath ᵇprepared for destruction?

23   And *He did so* in order that He might make known ªthe riches of His glory upon ᵇvessels of mercy, which He ᶜprepared beforehand for glory,

24   *even* us, whom He also ªcalled, ᵇnot from among Jews only, but also from among Gentiles.

25   As He says also in Hosea,

"ªI WILL CALL THOSE WHO WERE NOT MY
    PEOPLE, 'MY PEOPLE.'
AND HER WHO WAS NOT BELOVED,
    'BELOVED.'"

26   "ªAND IT SHALL BE THAT IN THE PLACE
    WHERE IT WAS SAID TO THEM, 'YOU ARE
    NOT MY PEOPLE.'
THERE THEY SHALL BE CALLED SONS OF
    ᵇTHE LIVING GOD."

27   And Isaiah cries out concerning Israel, "ªTHOUGH THE NUMBER OF THE SONS OF ISRAEL BE ᵇAS THE SAND OF THE SEA, IT IS ᶜTHE REMNANT THAT WILL BE SAVED;

28   ᵃFOR THE LORD WILL EXECUTE HIS WORD
UPON THE EARTH, ¹THOROUGHLY AND ²QUICKLY."

29   And just as Isaiah foretold,
"ᵃEXCEPT ᵇTHE LORD OF ¹SABAOTH HAD
  LEFT TO US A ²POSTERITY,
ᶜWE WOULD HAVE BECOME AS SODOM, AND
  WOULD HAVE ³RESEMBLED GOMORRAH."

30   ᵃWhat shall we say then? That Gentiles,
who did not pursue righteousness, attained righteousness, even ᵇthe righteousness which is ¹by
faith;

31   but Israel, ᵃpursuing a law of righteousness,
did not ᵇarrive at *that* law.

32   Why? Because *they did* not *pursue it* ¹by
faith, but as though *it were* ¹by works. They
stumbled over ᵃTHE STUMBLING-STONE,

33   just as it is written,
"ᵃBEHOLD, I LAY IN ZION A STONE OF STUM-
  BLING AND A ROCK OF OFFENSE,
ᵇAND HE WHO BELIEVES IN HIM ᶜWILL NOT
  BE ¹DISAPPOINTED."

CHAPTER 10

BRETHREN, my heart's desire and my prayer to
God for them is for *their* salvation.

2   For I bear them witness that they have ᵃa
zeal for God, but not in accordance with
knowledge.

3   For not knowing about ᵃGod's righteousness, and ᵇseeking to establish their own, they did
not subject themselves to the righteousness of
God.

4   For ᵃChrist is the ¹end of the law for righteousness to ᵇeveryone who believes.

5   For Moses writes that the man who practices the righteousness which is ¹based on law ᵃshall
live ²by that righteousness.

6   But ᵃthe righteousness ¹based on faith
speaks thus, "ᵇDO NOT SAY IN YOUR HEART, 'WHO
WILL ASCEND INTO HEAVEN?' (that is, to bring Christ
down),

7   or 'WHO WILL DESCEND INTO THE ᵃABYSS?'
(that is, to ᵇbring Christ up from the dead)."

8   But what does it say? "ᵃTHE WORD IS NEAR
YOU, IN YOUR MOUTH AND IN YOUR HEART"—that is,
the word of faith which we are preaching,

---

28 ¹Lit., *finishing it* ²Lit.,
cutting it short
ᵃIs. 10:23

29 ¹I.e., Hosts ²Lit., *seed*
³Lit., *been made like*
ᵃIs. 1:9 ᵇJames 5:4 ᶜDeut.
29:23; Is. 13:19; Jer. 49:18;
50:40; Amos 4:11

30 ¹Lit., *out of*
ᵃRom. 9:14 ᵇRom. 10:6; Gal.
2:16; 3:24; Phil. 3:9; Heb.
11:7; Rom. 1:17; 3:21f.

31 ᵃIs. 51:1; Rom. 10:2f.;
11:7; 9:30; 10:20 ᵇGal. 5:4

32 ¹Lit., *out of*
ᵃIs. 8:14; 1 Pet. 2:6, 8

33 ¹Lit., *put to shame*
ᵃIs. 28:16 ᵇRom. 10:11
ᶜRom. 5:5

2 ᵃActs 21:20

3 ᵃRom. 1:17 ᵇIs. 51:1;
Rom. 10:2f.; 11:7; 8:30; 10:20

4 ¹Or, *goal*
ᵃGal. 3:24; 4:5; Rom. 7:1-4
ᵇRom. 3:22

5 ¹Lit., *out of, from* ²Lit.,
by it
ᵃLev. 18:5; Neh. 9:29; Ezek.
20:11, 13, 21; Rom. 7:10

6 ¹Lit., *out of, from*
ᵃRom. 9:30 ᵇDeut. 30:12f.

7 ᵃLuke 8:31 ᵇHeb. 13:20

8 ᵃDeut. 30:14

335

9 ¹Or, *because*
ᵃMatt. 10:32; Luke 12:8;
Rom. 14:9; 1 Cor. 12:3; Phil.
2:11 ᵇRom. 4:24; Acts 16:31
ᶜActs 2:24

10 ¹Lit., *to righteousness*
²Lit., *to salvation*

11 ¹Lit., *put to shame*
ᵃIs. 28:16; Rom. 9:33

12 ᵃRom. 3:22, 29 ᵇActs
10:36 ᶜRom. 3:29

13 ᵃJoel 2:32; Acts 2:21

14 ᵃEph. 2:17; 4:21 ᵇActs
8:31; Titus 1:3

15 ¹Or, *preach the gospel*
ᵃIs. 52:7 ᵇRom. 1:15; 15:20

16 ¹Lit., *gospel*
ᵃRom. 3:3 ᵇIs. 53:1; John
12:38

17 ¹Or, *concerning Christ*
ᵃGal. 3:2, 5 ᵇCol. 3:16

18 ¹Or, *inhabited earth*
ᵃPs. 19:4; Col. 1:6, 23;
1 Thess. 1:8; Rom. 1:8

19 ᵃDeut. 32:21 ᵇRom.
11:11, 14

20 ᵃIs. 65:1; Rom. 9:30

21 ᵃIs. 65:2

9 ¹that ᵃif you confess with your mouth Jesus *as* Lord, and ᵇbelieve in your heart that ᶜGod raised Him from the dead, you shall be saved;

10 for with the heart man believes, ¹resulting in righteousness, and with the mouth he confesses, ²resulting in salvation.

11 For the Scripture says, "ᵃWHOEVER BELIEVES IN HIM WILL NOT BE ¹DISAPPOINTED."

12 For ᵃthere is no distinction between Jew and Greek; for the same *Lord* is ᵇLord of ᶜall, abounding in riches for all who call upon Him;

13 for "ᵃWHOEVER WILL CALL UPON THE NAME OF THE LORD WILL BE SAVED."

14 How then shall they call upon Him in whom they have not believed? And how shall they believe in Him ᵃwhom they have not heard? And how shall they hear without ᵇa preacher?

15 And how shall they preach unless they are sent? Just as it is written, "ᵃHOW BEAUTIFUL ARE THE FEET OF THOSE WHO ¹ᵇBRING GLAD TIDINGS OF GOOD THINGS!"

16 However, they ᵃdid not all heed the ¹glad tidings; for Isaiah says, "ᵇLORD, WHO HAS BELIEVED OUR REPORT?"

17 So faith *comes* from ᵃhearing, and hearing by ᵇthe word ¹of Christ.

18 But I say, surely they have never heard, have they? Indeed they have:

"ᵃTHEIR VOICE HAS GONE OUT INTO ALL THE EARTH,

AND THEIR WORDS TO THE ENDS OF THE ¹WORLD."

19 But I say, surely Israel did not know, did they? At the first Moses says,

"ᵃI WILL ᵇMAKE YOU JEALOUS BY THAT WHICH IS NOT A NATION,

BY A NATION WITHOUT UNDERSTANDING WILL I ANGER YOU."

20 And Isaiah is very bold and says,

"ᵃI WAS FOUND BY THOSE WHO SOUGHT ME NOT,

I BECAME MANIFEST TO THOSE WHO DID NOT ASK FOR ME."

21 But as for Israel he says, "ᵃALL THE DAY LONG I HAVE STRETCHED OUT MY HANDS TO A DISOBEDIENT AND OBSTINATE PEOPLE."

CHAPTER 11

I SAY then, God has not [a]rejected His people, has He? [b]May it never be! For [c]I too am an Israelite, [1]a descendant of Abraham, of the tribe of Benjamin.

2   God [a]has not rejected His people whom He [b]foreknew. [c]Or do you not know what the Scripture says in *the passage about* Elijah, how he pleads with God against Israel?

3   "Lord, [a]THEY HAVE KILLED THY PROPHETS, THEY HAVE TORN DOWN THINE ALTARS, AND I ALONE AM LEFT, AND THEY ARE SEEKING MY [1]LIFE."

4   But what [1]is the divine response to him? "[a]I HAVE KEPT for Myself SEVEN THOUSAND MEN WHO HAVE NOT BOWED THE KNEE TO BAAL."

5   In the same way then, there has also come to be at the present time [a]a remnant according to *God's* [1]gracious choice.

6   But [a]if it is by grace, it is no longer on the basis of works, otherwise grace is no longer grace.

7   What then? That which [a]Israel is seeking for, it has not obtained, but [1]those who were chosen obtained it, and the rest were [b]hardened;

8   just as it is written,

"[a]GOD GAVE THEM A SPIRIT OF STUPOR,
EYES TO SEE NOT AND EARS TO HEAR NOT,
DOWN TO THIS VERY DAY."

9   And David says,

"[a]LET THEIR TABLE BECOME A SNARE and a trap,
AND A STUMBLING-BLOCK AND A RETRIBUTION TO THEM.

10   [a]LET THEIR EYES BE DARKENED TO SEE NOT,
AND BEND THEIR BACKS FOREVER."

11   [a]I say then, they did not stumble so as to fall, did they? [b]May it never be! But by their transgression [c]salvation *has come* to the Gentiles, to [d]make them jealous.

12   Now if their transgression be riches for the world and their failure be riches for the Gentiles, how much more will their [1a]fulfillment be!

13   But I am speaking to you who are Gentiles. Inasmuch then as [a]I am an apostle of Gentiles, I magnify my ministry,

14   if somehow I might [a]move to jealousy [b]my [1]fellow-countrymen and [c]save some of them.

15   For if their rejection be the [a]reconciliation

---

1 [1]Lit., *of the seed of Abraham*
[a]1 Sam. 12:22; Jer. 31:37; 33:24-26 [b]Luke 20:16 [c]2 Cor. 11:22; Phil. 3:5

2 [a]Ps. 94:14 [b]Rom. 8:29 [c]Rom. 6:16

3 [1]Gr., *soul-life*
[a]1 Kin. 19:10

4 [1]Lit., *says*
[a]1 Kin. 19:18

5 [1]Lit., *choice of grace*
[a]Rom. 9:27; 2 Kin. 19:4

6 [a]Rom. 4:4

7 [1]Lit., *the election*
[a]Rom. 9:31 [b]Mark 6:52; 2 Cor. 3:14; Rom. 11:25; 9:18

8 [a]Is. 29:10; Deut. 29:4; Matt. 13:13f.

9 [a]Ps. 69:22f.

10 [a]Ps. 69:23

11 [a]Rom. 11:1 [b]Luke 20:16 [c]Acts 28:28 [d]Rom. 11:14

12 [1]Or, *fulness*
[a]Rom. 11:25

13 [a]Acts 9:15

14 [1]Lit., *flesh*
[a]Rom. 11:11 [b] Rom. 9:3; Gen. 29:14; 2 Sam. 19:12f. [c]1 Cor. 7:16; 9:22; 1 Tim. 1:15; 2:4; 2 Tim. 1:9; Titus 3:5; 1 Cor. 1:21

15 [a]Rom. 5:11

337

15 bLuke 15:24, 32

16 aNum. 15:18ff.; Neh.
10:37; Ezek. 44:30

17 1Lit., *root of the fatness*
aJer. 11:16; John 15:2 bEph.
2:11ff.

18 aJohn 4:22

19 aRom. 9:19

20 a2 Cor. 1:24; 1 Cor.
10:17; Rom. 5:2 bRom.
12:16, 1 Tim. 6:17; 1 Pet.
1:17

22 aRom. 2:4 b1 Cor. 15:2;
Heb. 3:6, 14 cJohn 15:2

23 a2 Cor. 3:16

25 aRom. 1:13 bRom.
16:25; 1 Cor. 2:7-10; Eph.
3:3-5, 9; Matt. 13:11 cRom.
12:16 dRom. 11:7 eRom.
11:12; Luke 21:24; John
10:16

26 aIs. 59:20, 21

27 1Lit., *the covenant from
Me*
aIs. 27:9; Heb. 8:10, 12

28 1Lit., *according to the
gospel* 2Lit., *according to
the election*
aRom. 5:10 bRom. 9:5; Deut.
7:8; 10:15

29 a1 Cor. 1:26; Eph. 1:18;
4:1, 4; Phil. 3:14; 2 Thess.
1:11; 2 Tim. 1:9; Heb. 3:1;
2 Pet. 1:10; Rom. 8:28 bHeb.
7:21

of the world, what will *their* acceptance be but blife from the dead?

16   And if the afirst piece *of dough* be holy, the lump is also; and if the root be holy, the branches are too.

17   But if some of the abranches were broken off, and byou, being a wild olive, were grafted in among them and became partaker with them of the 1rich root of the olive tree,

18   do not be arrogant toward the branches; but if you are arrogant, *remember that* ait is not you who supports the root, but the root *supports* you.

19   aYou will say then, "Branches were broken off so that I might be grafted in."

20   Quite right, they were broken off for their unbelief, and you astand *only* by your faith. bDo not be conceited, but fear;

21   for if God did not spare the natural branches, neither will He spare you.

22   Behold then the kindness and severity of God; to those who fell, severity, but to you, God's akindness, bif you continue in His kindness; otherwise you also cwill be cut off.

23   And they also, aif they do not continue in their unbelief, will be grafted in; for God is able to graft them in again.

24   For if you were cut off from what is by nature a wild olive tree, and were grafted contrary to nature into a cultivated olive tree, how much more shall these who are the natural *branches* be grafted into their own olive tree?

25   For aI do not want you, brethren, to be uninformed of this bmystery, lest you be cwise in your own estimation, that a partial dhardening has happened to Israel until the efulness of the Gentiles has come in;

26   and thus all Israel will be saved; just as it is written,

"aThe Deliverer will come from Zion,
   He will remove ungodliness from Jacob."

27   "aAnd this is 1My covenant with them,
   When I take away their sins."

28   1From the standpoint of the gospel they are aenemies for your sake, but 2from the standpoint of God's choice they are beloved for bthe sake of the fathers;

29   for the gifts and the acalling of God bare irrevocable.

30 For just as you once were disobedient to God but now have been shown mercy because of their disobedience,

31 so these also now have been disobedient, in order that because of the mercy shown to you they also may now be shown mercy.

32 For ªGod has shut up all in disobedience that He might show mercy to all.

33 Oh the depth of ªthe riches ¹both of the ᵇwisdom and knowledge of God! ᶜHow unsearchable are His judgments and unfathomable His ways!

34 FOR ªWHO HAS KNOWN THE MIND OF THE LORD, OR WHO BECAME HIS COUNSELOR?

35 OR ªWHO HAS FIRST GIVEN TO HIM ¹THAT IT MIGHT BE PAID BACK TO HIM AGAIN?

36 For ªfrom Him and through Him and to Him are all things. ᵇTo Him *be* the glory ¹forever. Amen.

a   CHAPTER 12

I URGE you therefore, brethren, by the mercies of God, to ᵇpresent your bodies a living and holy sacrifice, ¹acceptable to God, *which is* your ²spiritual service of worship.

2 And do not ªbe conformed to ᵇthis ¹world, but be transformed by the ᶜrenewing of your mind, that you may ᵈprove what the will of God is, that which is good and ²acceptable and perfect.

3 For through ªthe grace given to me I say to every man among you ᵇnot to think more highly of himself than he ought to think; but to think so as to have sound judgment, as God has allotted to ᶜeach a measure of faith.

4 For ªjust as we have many members in one body and all the members do not have the same function,

5 so we, ªwho are many, are ᵇone body in Christ, and individually members one of another.

6 And since we have gifts that ªdiffer according to the grace given to us, *let each exercise them accordingly:* if ᵇprophecy, according to the proportion of his faith;

7 if ¹ªservice, in his serving; or he who ᵇteaches, in his teaching;

8 or he who ªexhorts, in his exhortation; he

32 ªGal. 3:22f.; Rom. 3:9

33 ¹Or, *and the wisdom* ªEph. 3:8; Rom. 2:4 ᵇCol. 2:3; Eph. 3:10 ᶜJob 5:9; 11:7; 15:8

34 ªIs. 40:13f.; 1 Cor. 2:16

35 ¹Lit., *and it will be paid back* ªJob 35:7; 41:11

36 ¹Lit., *to the ages* ª1 Cor. 8:6; 11:12; Col. 1:16; Heb. 2:10 ᵇRom. 16:27; Eph. 3:21; Phil. 4:20; 1 Tim. 1:17; 2 Tim. 4:18; 1 Pet. 4:11; 5:11; 2 Pet. 3:18; Jude 25; Rev. 1:6; 5:13; 7:12

1 ¹Or, *well-pleasing* ²Or, *rational* ª1 Cor. 1:10; 2 Cor. 10:2; Eph. 4:1; 1 Pet. 2:11 ᵇRom. 6:13, 16, 19; 1 Cor. 6:20; Heb. 13:15; 1 Pet. 2:5

2 ¹Or, *age* ²Or, *well-pleasing* ª1 Pet. 1:14 ᵇMatt. 13:22; Gal. 1:4; 1 John 2:15 ᶜTitus 3:5; Eph. 4:23 ᵈEph. 5:10, 17; Col. 1:9

3 ªRom. 15:15; 1 Cor. 3:10; 15:10; Gal. 2:9; Eph. 3:7f.; Rom. 1:5 ᵇRom. 11:20; 12:16; ᶜ1 Cor. 7:17; 2 Cor. 10:13; Eph. 4:7; 1 Pet. 4:11

4 ª1 Cor. 12:12-14; Eph. 4:4, 16

5 ª1 Cor. 10:17, 33 ᵇ1 Cor. 12:20, 27; Eph. 4:12, 25

6 ª1 Cor. 7:7; 12:4; 1 Pet. 4:10f.; Rom. 12:3 ᵇ1 Cor. 12:10; Acts 13:1

7 ¹Or, *office of service* ª1 Cor. 12:5, 28; Acts 6:1 ᵇ1 Cor. 12:28; 14:26; Acts 13:1

8 ªActs 4:36; 11:23; 13:15

339

8 ¹Or, *simplicity* ²Or, *gives aid*
ᵇ2 Cor. 8:2; 9:11, 13 ᶜ1 Tim. 5:17; 1 Cor. 12:28 ᵈ2 Cor. 9:7

9 ᵃ2 Cor. 6:6; 1 Tim. 1:5
ᵇ1 Thess. 5:21f.

10 ¹Or, *outdo one another in showing honor*
ᵃ1 Thess. 4:9; Heb. 13:1; 2 Pet. 1:7; John 13:34 ᵇPhil. 2:3; Rom. 13:7; 1 Pet. 2:17

11 ᵃActs 18:25 ᵇActs 20:19

12 ᵃRom. 5:2 ᵇHeb. 10:32, 36 ᶜActs 1:14

13 ¹I.e., *true believers; lit., holy ones* ²Lit., *pursuing*
ᵃRom. 15:25; 1 Cor. 16:15; 2 Cor. 9:1; Heb. 6:10
ᵇ1 Tim. 3:2; Matt. 25:35

14 ¹Some ancient mss. omit, *you*
ᵃMatt. 5:44; Luke 6:28; 1 Cor. 4:12

15 ᵃJob 30:25; Heb. 13:3

16 ¹Or, *accommodate yourself to lowly things*
ᵃRom. 15:5; 2 Cor. 13:11; Phil. 2:2; 4:2; 1 Pet. 3:8
ᵇRom. 12:3; Rom. 11:20
ᶜRom. 11:25; Prov. 3:7

17 ¹Lit., *take thought for*
ᵃProv. 20:22; 24:29; Rom. 12:19 ᵇ2 Cor. 8:21

18 ᵃRom. 1:15 ᵇMark 9:50; Rom. 14:19

19 ¹Lit., *give a place*
ᵃProv. 20:22; 24:29; Rom. 12:17 ᵇDeut. 32:35; Heb. 10:30; 1 Thess. 4:6; Ps. 94:1

20 ᵃProv. 25:21f.; Matt. 5:44; Luke 6:27 ᵇ2 Kin. 6:22

1 ¹Lit., *soul* ²Lit., *by*
ᵃActs 2:41 ᵇTitus 3:1; 1 Pet. 2:13f. ᶜJohn 19:11; Dan. 2:21; 4:17

3 ¹Lit., *the good work*
ᵃ1 Pet. 2:14

who gives, with ¹ᵇliberality; ᶜhe who ²leads, with diligence; he who shows mercy, with ᵈcheerfulness.

9 Let ᵃlove be without hypocrisy. ᵇAbhor what is evil; cleave to what is good.

10 Be ᵃdevoted to one another in brotherly love; ¹give preference to one another ᵇin honor;

11 not lagging behind in diligence, ᵃfervent in spirit, ᵇserving the Lord;

12 ᵃrejoicing in hope, ᵇpersevering in tribulation, ᶜdevoted to prayer,

13 ᵃcontributing to the needs of the ¹saints, ²ᵇpracticing hospitality.

14 ᵃBless those who persecute ¹you; bless and curse not.

15 ᵃRejoice with those who rejoice, and weep with those who weep.

16 ᵃBe of the same mind toward one another; do not be haughty in mind, ᵇbut ¹associate with the lowly. ᶜDo not be wise in your own estimation.

17 ᵃNever pay back evil for evil to anyone. ¹ᵇRespect what is right in the sight of all men.

18 If possible, ᵃso far as it depends on you, ᵇbe at peace with all men.

19 ᵃNever take your own revenge, beloved, but ¹leave room for the wrath *of God*, for it is written, "ᵇVᴇɴɢᴇᴀɴᴄᴇ ɪs Mɪɴᴇ, I ᴡɪʟʟ ʀᴇᴘᴀʏ, sᴀʏs ᴛʜᴇ Lᴏʀᴅ."

20 "ᵃBᴜᴛ ɪғ ʏᴏᴜʀ ᴇɴᴇᴍʏ ɪs ʜᴜɴɢʀʏ, ғᴇᴇᴅ ʜɪᴍ, ᴀɴᴅ ɪғ ʜᴇ ɪs ᴛʜɪʀsᴛʏ, ɢɪᴠᴇ ʜɪᴍ ᴀ ᴅʀɪɴᴋ; ғᴏʀ ᵇɪɴ sᴏ ᴅᴏɪɴɢ ʏᴏᴜ ᴡɪʟʟ ʜᴇᴀᴘ ʙᴜʀɴɪɴɢ ᴄᴏᴀʟs ᴜᴘᴏɴ ʜɪs ʜᴇᴀᴅ."

21 Do not be overcome by evil, but overcome evil with good.

Cʜᴀᴘᴛᴇʀ 13

Lᴇᴛ every ¹ᵃperson be in ᵇsubjection to the governing authorities. For ᶜthere is no authority except ²from God, and those which exist are established by God.

2 Therefore he who resists authority has opposed the ordinance of God; and they who have opposed will receive condemnation upon themselves.

3 For ᵃrulers are not a cause of fear for ¹good behavior, but for evil. Do you want to have no fear of authority? Do what is good, and you will have praise from the same;

4 for it is a minister of God to you for good. But if you do what is evil, be afraid; for it does not bear the sword for nothing; for it is a minister of God, an ªavenger who brings wrath upon the one who practices evil.

5 Wherefore it is necessary to be in subjection, not only because of wrath, but also ªfor conscience' sake.

6 For because of this you also pay taxes, for *rulers* are servants of God, devoting themselves to this very thing.

7 ªRender to all what is due them: ᵇtax to whom tax *is due;* ᶜcustom to whom custom; fear to whom fear; honor to whom honor.

8 Owe nothing to anyone except to love one another; for ªhe who loves ¹his neighbor has fulfilled *the* law.

9 For this, "ªYOU SHALL NOT COMMIT ADULTERY, YOU SHALL NOT MURDER, YOU SHALL NOT STEAL, YOU SHALL NOT COVET," and if there is any other commandment, it is summed up in this saying, "ᵇYOU SHALL LOVE YOUR NEIGHBOR AS YOURSELF."

10 Love ¹does no wrong to a neighbor; ªlove therefore is the fulfillment of *the* law.

11 And this *do,* knowing the time, that it is ªalready the hour for you to ᵇawaken from sleep; for now ¹salvation is nearer to us than when we believed.

12 ªThe night is almost gone, and ᵇthe day is at hand. Let us therefore lay aside ᶜthe deeds of darkness and put on ᵈthe armor of light.

13 Let us ¹ªbehave properly as in the day, ᵇnot in carousing and drunkenness, not in sexual promiscuity and sensuality, not in strife and jealousy.

14 But ªput on the Lord Jesus Christ, and make no provision for the flesh ᵇin regard to *its* lusts.

CHAPTER 14

NOW ªaccept the one who is ᵇweak in faith, *but* not for *the purpose of* passing judgment on his opinions.

2 ªOne man has faith that he may eat all things, but he who is ᵇweak eats vegetables *only.*

3 Let not him who eats ªregard with contempt him who does not eat, and let not him who

---

4 ª1 Thess. 4:6

5 ª1 Pet. 2:19; 1 Pet. 2:13; Eccl. 8

7 ªMatt. 22:21 ᵇLuke 20:22; 23:2 ᶜMatt. 17:25

8 ¹Lit., *the other* ªMatt. 22:39f.; Gal. 5:14; Rom. 13:10; Matt. 7:12; John 13:34; James 2:8

9 ªEx. 20:13ff.; Deut. 5:17ff. ᵇLev. 19:18; Matt. 19:19

10 ¹Lit., *works no evil* ªMatt. 22:39f.; Gal. 5:14; Rom. 13:8; Matt. 7:12; John 13.34; James 2:8

11 ¹Or, *our salvation is nearer than when . . .* ª1 Cor. 7:29f.; 10:11; James 5:8; 1 Pet. 4:7; 2 Pet. 3:9, 11; 1 John 2:18; Rev. 1:3; 22:10 ᵇ1 Cor. 15:34; Eph. 5:14; 1 Thess. 5:6; Mark 13:37

12 ª1 Cor. 7:29f.; 10:11; James 5:8; 1 Pet. 4:7; 2 Pet. 3:9, 11; 1 John 2:18; Rev. 1:3; 22:10 ᵇHeb. 10:25; 1 John 2:8; Rev. 1:3; 22:10 ᶜEph. 5:11 ᵈ2 Cor. 6:7; 10:4; Eph. 6:11, 13; 1 Thess. 5:8

13 ¹Lit., *walk* ª1 Thess. 4:12 ᵇLuke 21:34; Gal. 5:21; Eph. 5:18; 1 Pet. 4:3

14 ªGal. 3:27; Job 29:14; Eph. 4:24; Col. 3:10, 12 ᵇGal. 5:16; 1 Pet. 2:11

1 ªRom. 14:3; 15:7; Acts 28:2; Rom. 11:15 ᵇRom. 14:2; Rom. 15:1; 1 Cor. 8:9ff.; 9:22

2 ªRom. 14:14 ᵇRom. 14:1; 15:1; 1 Cor. 8:9ff.; 9:22

3 ªRom. 14:10; Luke 18:9

3 bCol. 2:16; Rom. 14:10,
13 cRom. 14:1; 15:7; Acts
28:2; Rom. 11:15

4 1Or, *house-servant* 2Lit.,
lord
aJames 4:12; Rom. 9:20

5 1Lit., *judges*
aGal. 4:10 bRom. 4:21; Luke
1:1; Rom. 14:23

6 1Lit., *eats*
a1 Cor. 10:30; 1 Tim. 4:3f.;
Matt. 14:19

7 a2 Cor. 5:15; Gal. 2:20;
Phil. 1:20f.; Rom. 8:38

8 aPhil. 1:20; 1 Thess.
5:10; Rev. 14:13; Luke 20:38

9 aRev. 1:18; 2:8 bPhil.
2:11; Matt. 28:18; John
12:24; 1 Thess. 5:10

10 aRom. 14:3; Luke 18:9
bRom. 2:16; 2 Cor. 5:10

11 1Or, *confess*
aIs. 45:23 bPhil. 2:10f.

12 aMatt. 12:36; 1 Pet. 4:5;
Matt. 16:27

13 aRom. 14:3; Matt. 7:1
b1 Cor. 8:13

14 aRom. 14:2, 20; Acts
10:15 b1 Cor. 8:7

15 aEph. 5:2 b1 Cor. 8:11;
Rom. 14:20

16 1Lit., *blasphemed*
a1 Cor. 10:30; Titus 2:5

17 a1 Cor. 8:8 bGal. 5:22;
Rom. 15:13

does not eat [b]judge him who eats, for God has [c]accepted him.

4   [a]Who are you to judge the [1]servant of another? To his own [2]master he stands or falls; and stand he will, for the Lord is able to make him stand.

5   [a]One man [1]regards one day above another, another regards every day *alike*. Let each man be [b]fully convinced in his own mind.

6   He who observes the day, observes it for the Lord, and he who eats, [1]does so for the Lord, for he [a]gives thanks to God; and he who eats not, for the Lord he does not eat, and gives thanks to God.

7   For not one of us [a]lives for himself, and not one dies for himself;

8   for if we live, we live for the Lord, or if we die, we die for the Lord; therefore [a]whether we live or die, we are the Lord's.

9   For to this end [a]Christ died and lived *again*, that He might be [b]Lord both of the dead and of the living.

10   But you, why do you judge your brother? Or you again, why do you [a]regard your brother with contempt? For [b]we shall all stand before the judgment-seat of God.

11   For it is written,

"[a]As I live, says the Lord, [b]every knee
    shall bow to Me,
And every tongue shall [1]give praise to
    God."

12   So then [a]each one of us shall give account of himself to God.

13   Therefore let us not [a]judge one another any more, but rather determine this — [b]not to put an obstacle or a stumbling block in a brother's way.

14   I know and am convinced in the Lord Jesus that [a]nothing is unclean in itself; but to him who [b]thinks anything to be unclean, to him it is unclean.

15   For if because of food your brother is hurt, you are no longer [a]walking according to love. [b]Do not destroy with your food him for whom Christ died.

16   Therefore [a]do not let what is for you a good thing be [1]spoken of as evil;

17   for the kingdom of God [a]is not eating and drinking, but righteousness and [b]peace and [b]joy in the Holy Spirit.

18   For he who in this *way* [a]serves Christ is [b]acceptable to God and approved by men.

19   So then [1]let us [a]pursue the things which make for peace and the [b]building up of one another.

20   [a]Do not tear down the work of God for the sake of food. [b]All things indeed are clean, but [c]they are evil for the man who eats [1]and gives offense.

21   [a]It is good not to eat meat or to drink wine, or *to do anything* by which your brother stumbles.

22   The faith which you have, have [1]as your own conviction before God. Happy is he who [a]does not condemn himself in what he approves.

23   But [a]he who doubts is condemned if he eats, because *his eating is* not from faith; and whatever is not from faith is sin.

CHAPTER 15

N OW we who are strong ought to bear the weaknesses of [a]those without strength and not *just* please ourselves.

2   Let each of us [a]please his neighbor [1]for his good, to his [b]edification.

3   For even [a]Christ did not please Himself; but as it is written, "[b]THE REPROACHES OF THOSE WHO REPROACHED THEE FELL UPON ME."

4   For [a]whatever was written in earlier times was written for our instruction, that through perseverance and the encouragement of the Scriptures we might have hope.

5   Now may the [a]God [1]who gives perseverance and encouragement grant you [b]to be of the same mind with one another according to Christ Jesus;

6   that with one accord you may with one [1]voice glorify [a]the God and Father of our Lord Jesus Christ.

7   Wherefore, [a]accept one another, just as Christ also accepted [1]us to the glory of God.

8   For I say that Christ has become a servant to [a]the circumcision on behalf of the truth of God to confirm [b]the promises *given* to the fathers,

9   and for [a]the Gentiles to [b]glorify God for His mercy; as it is written,

"[c]THEREFORE I WILL [1]GIVE PRAISE TO THEE
        AMONG THE GENTILES,
   AND I WILL SING TO THY NAME."

10   And again he says,

"[a]REJOICE, O GENTILES, WITH HIS PEOPLE."

18 [a]Rom. 16:18 [b]2 Cor. 8:21; Phil. 4:8; 1 Pet. 2:12

19 [1]Many ancient mss. read, *we pursue* [a]Ps. 34:14; 1 Cor. 7:15; 2 Tim. 2:22; Heb. 12:14; Rom. 12:18 [b]Rom. 15:2; 1 Cor. 10:23; 14:3f., 26; 2 Cor. 12:19; Eph. 4:12, 29

20 [1]Lit., *with offense* [a]Rom. 14:15 [b]Rom. 14:2, 14; Acts 10:15 [c]1 Cor. 8:9-12

21 [a]1 Cor. 8:13

22 [1]Lit., *according to yourself* [a]1 John 3:21

23 [a]Rom. 14:5

1 [a]Rom. 14:1; Gal. 6:2; 1 Thess. 5:14

2 [1]Lit., *for what is good to edification* [a]1 Cor. 10:33; 9:22; 10:24; 2 Cor. 13:9 [b]Rom. 14:19; 1 Cor. 10:23; 14:3f., 26; 2 Cor. 12:19; Eph. 4:12, 29

3 [a]2 Cor. 8:9 [b]Ps. 69:9

4 [a]Rom. 4:23f.; 2 Tim. 3:16

5 [1]Lit., *of perseverance* [a]2 Cor. 1:3 [b]Rom. 12:16

6 [1]Lit., *mouth* [a]Rev. 1:6

7 [1]Some mss. read, *you* [a]Rom. 14:1

8 [a]Matt. 15:24; Acts 3:26 [b]Rom. 4:16; 2 Cor. 1:20

9 [1]Or, *confess* [a]Rom. 3:29; 11:30 [b]Matt. 9:8 [c]Ps. 18:49 [or 2 Sam. 22:50]

10 [a]Deut. 32:43

11 aPs. 117:1

12 aIs. 11:10 bRev. 5:5; 22:16 cMatt. 12:21

13 aRom. 14:17 bRom. 15:19; 1 Cor. 2:4; 1 Thess. 1:5

14 aEph. 5:9; 2 Thess. 1:11 b1 Cor. 1:5; 13:2; 1 Cor. 8:1, 7, 10; 12:8

15 1Some mss. read, by God aRom. 12:3

16 aRom. 11:13; Acts 9:15 bRom. 15:19, 20; 1:1 cEph. 5:2; Phil. 2:17; Rom. 12:1

17 aPhil. 3:3 bHeb. 2:17; 5:1

18 1Or, which Christ has not accomplished 2Lit., to the obedience aActs 15:12; 21:19; Rom. 1:5; 2 Cor. 3:5

19 1Or, attesting miracles 2Lit., fulfilled aJohn 4:48 bRom. 15:13; 1 Cor. 2:4; 1 Thess. 1:5 cActs 22:17-21 dActs 20:1f.

20 aRom. 1:15; 10:15; 15:16 b2 Cor. 10:15f.; 1 Cor. 3:10

21 aIs. 52:15

22 aRom. 1:13; 1 Thess. 2:18

23 aActs 19:21; Rom. 1:10f.; 15:29, 32

24 aRom. 15:28 bActs 15:3

11 And again,
"aPRAISE THE LORD ALL YOU GENTILES,
AND LET ALL THE PEOPLES PRAISE HIM."
12 And again Isaiah says,
"aTHERE SHALL COME bTHE ROOT OF JESSE,
AND HE WHO ARISES TO RULE OVER THE GENTILES;
cIN HIM SHALL THE GENTILES HOPE."
13 Now may the God of hope fill you with all ajoy and peace in believing, that you may abound in hope bby the power of the Holy Spirit.
14 And concerning you, my brethren, I myself also am convinced that you yourselves are full of agoodness, filled with ball knowledge, and able also to admonish one another,
15 But I have written very boldly to you on some points, so as to remind you again, because of athe grace that was given me 1from God,
16 to be aa minister of Christ Jesus to the Gentiles, ministering as a priest the bgospel of God, that my coffering of the Gentiles might become acceptable, sanctified by the Holy Spirit.
17 Therefore in Christ Jesus I have found areason for boasting in bthings pertaining to God.
18 For I will not presume to speak of anything 1except what aChrist has accomplished through me, 2resulting in the obedience of the Gentiles by word and deed,
19 in the power of 1asigns and awonders, bin the power of the Spirit; so that cfrom Jerusalem and round about as dfar as Illyricum I have 2fully preached the gospel of Christ.
20 And thus I aspired to apreach the gospel, not where Christ was already named, bthat I might not build upon another man's foundation;
21 but as it is written,
"aTHEY WHO HAD NO NEWS OF HIM SHALL SEE,
AND THEY WHO HAVE NOT HEARD SHALL UNDERSTAND."
22 For this reason aI have often been hindered from coming to you;
23 but now, with no further place for me in these regions, and since I ahave had for many years a longing to come to you
24 whenever I ago to Spain — for I hope to see you in passing, and to be bhelped on my way there

by you, when I have first ^cenjoyed your company ¹for awhile —

25 but now, ^aI am going to Jerusalem ^bserving the ¹saints.

26 For ^aMacedonia and ^bAchaia have been pleased to make a contribution for the poor among the ¹saints in Jerusalem.

27 Yes, they were pleased *to do so*, and they are indebted to them. For ^aif the Gentiles have shared in their spiritual things, they are indebted to minister to them also in material things.

28 Therefore, when I have finished this, and ^ahave ¹put my seal on this fruit of theirs, I will ^bgo on by way of you to Spain.

29 And I know that when ^aI come to you, I will come in the fulness of the blessing of Christ.

30 Now I urge you, brethren, by our Lord Jesus Christ and by ^athe love of the Spirit to ^bstrive together with me in your prayers to God for me,

31 that I may be ^adelivered from those who are disobedient in Judea, and *that* my ^bservice for Jerusalem may prove acceptable to the ^{1c}saints;

32 so that ^aI may come to you in joy by ^bthe will of God and find *refreshing* rest in your company.

33 Now ^athe God of peace be with you all. Amen.

<h3 style="text-align:center">Chapter 16</h3>

I ^aCOMMEND to you our sister Phoebe, who is a ¹servant of the church which is at ^bCenchrea;

2 that you ^areceive her in the Lord in a manner worthy of the ^{1b}saints, and that you help her in whatever matter she may have need of you; for she herself has also been a helper of many, ²and of myself as well.

3 Greet ^aPrisca and ^aAquila my fellow-workers ^bin ^cChrist Jesus,

4 who for my life risked their own necks, to whom not only do I give thanks, but also all the churches of the Gentiles;

5 also *greet* ^athe church that is in their house. Greet Epaenetus my beloved, who is the ^bfirst convert to Christ from ^{1c}Asia.

6 Greet Mary, who has worked hard for you.

7 Greet Andronicus and ¹Junias, my ^akinsmen, and my ^bfellow-prisoners, who are outstanding

24 ¹Lit., *in part*
^cRom. 1:12

25 ¹I.e., true believers; lit., *holy ones*
^aActs 19:21 ^bActs 24:17

26 ¹Note vs. 25
^a1 Cor. 16:5; 2 Cor. 1:16; 2:13; 7:5; 8:1; 9:2, 4; 11:9; Phil. 4:15; 1 Thess. 1:7f.; 4:10; 1 Tim. 1:3; Acts 16:9
^bActs 18:12; 19:21

27 ^a1 Cor. 9:11

28 ¹Lit., *sealed to them this fruit*
^aJohn 3:33
^bRom. 15:24

29 ^aActs 19:21; Rom. 1:10f.; Rom. 15:23, 32

30 ^aGal. 5:22; Col. 1:8 ^bCol. 4:12; 2 Cor. 1:11

31 ¹Note vs. 25
^a2 Cor. 1:10; 2 Thess. 3:2; 2 Tim. 3:11; 4:17
^bRom. 15:25f.; 2 Cor. 8:4; 9:1 ^cActs 9:13, 15

32 ^aRom. 15:23 ^bRom. 1:10; Acts 18:21

33 ^aRom. 16:20; 2 Cor. 13:11; Phil. 4:9; 1 Thess. 5:23; Heb. 13:20; 2 Thess. 3:16

1 ¹Or, *deaconess*
^a2 Cor. 3:1 ^bActs 18:18

2 ¹I.e., true believers; lit., *holy ones* ²Lit., *and of me, myself*
^aPhil. 2:29 ^bActs 9:13, 15

3 ^aActs 18:2 ^b2 Cor. 5:17; 12:2; Gal. 1:22; Rom. 16:7, 9, 10; 8:11ff. ^cRom. 8:1

5 ¹I.e., west coast province of Asia Minor
^a1 Cor. 16:19; Col. 4:15; Philem. 2 ^b1 Cor. 16:15
^cActs 16:6

7 ¹Or, *Junia* (fem.)
^aRom. 16:11, 21; 9:3 ^bCol. 4:10; Philem. 23

7 c2 Cor. 5:17; 12:2; Gal. 1:22; Rom. 16:3, 9, 10; 8:11ff.

9 a2 Cor. 5:17; 12:2; Gal. 1:22; Rom. 16:3, 7, 10; 8:11ff.

10 a2 Cor. 5:17; 12:2; Gal. 1:22; Rom. 16:3, 7, 9; 8:11ff. b1 Cor. 1:11

11 aRom. 16:7, 21; 9:3 b1 Cor. 1:11

13 aMark 15:21

15 1Note 1, vs. 2 aRom. 16:2, 14

16 a1 Cor. 16:20; 2 Cor. 13:12; 1 Thess. 5:26; 1 Pet. 5:14

17 1Lit., *occasions of stumbling* a1 Tim. 1:3; 6:3 bGal. 1:8f.; 2 Thess. 3:6, 14; Titus 3:10; 2 John 10; Matt. 7:15

18 1Lit., *belly* aRom. 14:18 bPhil. 3:19 cCol. 2:4; 2 Pet. 2:3

19 aRom. 1:8 b1 Cor. 14:20; Matt. 10:16; Jer. 4:22

20 aRom. 15:33 bMatt. 4:10 c1 Cor. 16:23; 2 Cor. 13:14; Gal. 6:18; Phil. 4:23; 1 Thess. 5:28; 2 Thess. 3:18; Rev. 22:21

21 aActs 16:1 bActs 13:1 [?] cActs 17:5 [?] dActs 20:4 [?] eRom. 16:7, 11; 9:3

22 a1 Cor. 16:21; Gal. 6:11; Col. 4:18; 2 Thess. 3:17; Philem. 19

23 a1 Cor. 1:14; Acts 20:4 [?] bActs 19:22

24 1Some ancient mss. add vs. 24, *The grace of our Lord Jesus Christ be with you all. Amen.*

25 aEph. 3:20; Jude 24 bRom. 2:16

among the apostles, who also were cin Christ before me.

8 Greet Ampliatus my beloved in the Lord.

9 Greet Urbanus our fellow-worker ain Christ, and Stachys my beloved.

10 Greet Apelles the approved ain Christ. Greet bthose who are of the *household* of Aristobulus.

11 Greet Herodion my akinsman. bGreet those of the *household* of Narcissus, who are in the Lord.

12 Greet Tryphaena and Tryphosa, workers in the Lord. Greet Persis the beloved, who has worked hard in the Lord.

13 Greet aRufus, a choice man in the Lord, also his mother and mine.

14 Greet Asyncritus, Phlegon, Hermes, Patrobas, Hermas and the brethren with them.

15 Greet Philologus and Julia, Nereus and his sister, and Olympas, and all athe 1saints who are with them.

16 aGreet one another with a holy kiss. All the churches of Christ greet you.

17 Now I urge you, brethren, keep your eye on those who cause dissensions and 1hindrances acontrary to the teaching which you learned, and bturn away from them.

18 For such men are aslaves not of our Lord Christ but of btheir own 1appetites; and by their csmooth and flattering speech they deceive the hearts of the unsuspecting.

19 For the report of your obedience ahas reached to all; therefore I am rejoicing over you, but bI want you to be wise in what is good, and innocent in what is evil.

20 And athe God of peace will soon crush bSatan under your feet.

cThe grace of our Lord Jesus be with you.

21 aTimothy my fellow-worker greets you; and so do bLucius and cJason and dSosipater, my ekinsmen.

22 I Tertius, who awrite this letter, greet you in the Lord.

23 aGaius, host to me and to the whole church, greets you. bErastus, the city treasurer greets you, and Quartus, the brother.

24 (See marginal note.1)

25 aNow to Him who is able to establish you baccording to my gospel and the preaching of Jesus

Christ, according to the revelation of ᶜthe mystery which has been kept secret for ᵈlong ages past,

26 but now is manifested, and by ᵃthe Scriptures of the prophets, according to the commandment of the eternal God, has been made known to all the nations, *leading* to ᵇobedience of faith;

27 to the only wise God, through Jesus Christ, ᵃto whom be the glory forever. Amen.

THE FIRST EPISTLE OF PAUL TO THE
CORINTHIANS

Salutation.   Thanksgiving.

PAUL, ᵃcalled *as* an apostle of Jesus Christ ¹by ᵇthe will of God, and ᶜSosthenes our ᵈbrother,

2 to ᵃthe church of God which is at ᵇCorinth, to those who have been sanctified in Christ Jesus, ¹saints ᶜby calling, with all who in every place ᵈcall upon the name of our Lord Jesus Christ, their *Lord* and ours:

3 ᵃGrace to you and peace from God our Father and the Lord Jesus Christ.

4 ᵃI thank ¹my God always concerning you, for the grace of God which was given you in Christ Jesus,

5 that in everything you were ᵃenriched in Him, in all ᵇspeech and ᵇall knowledge,

6 even as ᵃthe testimony concerning Christ was confirmed ¹in you,

7 so that you are not lacking in any gift, ᵃawaiting eagerly the revelation of our Lord Jesus Christ,

8 ᵃwho shall also confirm you to the end, blameless in ᵇthe day of our Lord Jesus Christ.

9 ᵃGod is faithful, through whom you were ᵇcalled into ᶜfellowship with His Son, Jesus Christ our Lord.

10 Now ᵃI exhort you, ᵇbrethren, by the name of our Lord Jesus Christ, that you all ¹agree, and there be no ²ᶜdivisions among you, but you be ³made complete in ᵈthe same mind and in the same judgment.

11 For I have been informed concerning you, my brethren, by ᵃChloe's *people*, that there are quarrels among you.

25 ᶜ1 Cor. 2:1, 7; 4:1; Eph. 1:9; 3:3, 9; 6:19; Col. 1:26f.; 2:2; 4:3; 1 Tim. 3:16; Rom. 11:25; Matt. 13:35 ᵈ2 Tim. 1:9; Titus 1:2

26 ᵃRom. 1:2 ᵇRom. 1:5

27 ᵃRom. 11:36

1 ¹Lit., *through*
ᵃRom. 1:1 ᵇRom. 15:32; 2 Cor. 1:1; Eph. 1:1; Col. 1:1; 2 Tim. 1:1; Rom. 1:10; 2 Cor. 8:5 ᶜActs 18:17 ᵈActs 1:15

2 ¹I.e., true believers; lit., *holy ones*
ᵃ1 Cor. 10:32 ᵇActs 18:1 ᶜRom. 1:7; 8:28 ᵈActs 7:59

3 ᵃRom. 1:7

4 ¹Some ancient mss. omit *my*
ᵃRom. 1:8

5 ᵃ2 Cor. 9:11 ᵇ2 Cor. 8:7; Rom. 15:14

6 ¹Or, *among*
ᵃ2 Tim. 1:8; 2 Thess. 1:10; 1 Tim. 2:6; Rev. 1:2

7 ᵃRom. 8:19, 23; Phil. 3:20; Luke 17:30; 2 Pet. 3:12

8 ᵃPhil. 1:6; Col. 2:7; 1 Thess. 3:13; 5:23; Rom. 8:19 ᵇ1 Cor. 5:5; 2 Cor. 1:14; Phil. 1:6, 10; 2:16; 1 Thess. 5:2; 2 Thess. 2:2; Luke 17:24, 30

9 ᵃDeut. 7:9; Is. 49:7; 1 Cor. 10:13; 2 Cor. 1:18; 1 Thess. 5:24; 2 Thess. 3:3 ᵇMatt. 8:28 ᶜ1 John 1:3

10 ¹Lit., *speak the same thing* ²Lit., *schisms* ³Or, *united*
ᵃRom. 12:1 ᵇRom. 1:13 ᶜ1 Cor. 11:18 ᵈRom. 12:16; Phil. 1:27

11 ᵃRom. 16:10f.

347

12 ᵃ1 Cor. 3:4; Matt. 23:8-10 ᵇActs 18:24; 1 Cor. 3:22 ᶜJohn 1:42; 1 Cor. 3:22; 9:5; 15:5

13 ¹Or, *Christ has been divided!* or, *Christ is divided!* ²Lit., *into* ᵃMatt. 28:19; Acts 2:38

14 ¹Some ancient mss. read, *I give thanks that* ᵃActs 18:8 ᵇRom. 16:23

15 ¹Lit., *into*

16 ᵃ1 Cor. 16:15 [17]

17 ¹Lit., *wisdom* ᵃJohn 4:2; Acts 10:48 ᵇ1 Cor. 2:1, 4, 13; 2 Cor. 10:10; 11:6

18 ¹Or, *perish* ²Or, *are saved* ᵃ2 Cor. 2:15; 4:3; 2 Thess. 2:10; Acts 2:47 ᵇ1 Cor. 1:21, 23, 25; 2:14; 4:10 ᶜ1 Cor. 1:24; Rom. 1:16

19 ᵃIs. 29:14

20 ᵃJob 12:17; Is. 19:11f.; 33:18 marg. ᵇMatt. 13:22; 1 Cor. 2:6, 8; 3:18, 19 ᶜRom. 1:20ff. ᵈ1 Cor. 1:27f.; 6:2; 11:32; John 12:31; James 4:4

21 ¹Lit., *preaching* ᵃ1 Cor. 1:27f.; 6:2; 11:32; John 12:31; James 4:4; ᵇGal. 1:15; Col. 1:19; Luke 12:32 ᶜ1 Cor. 1:18, 23, 25; 2:14; 4:10 ᵈ1 Tim. 4:16; 2 Tim. 2:10; 3:15; 4:18; Heb. 7:25; James 5:20; Rom. 11:14

22 ¹Or, *attesting miracles* ᵃMatt. 12:38

23 ¹I.e., *Messiah* ᵃ1 Cor. 2:2; Gal. 3:1; 5:11 ᵇLuke 2:34; 1 Pet. 2:8 ᶜ1 Cor. 1:18, 21, 25; 2:14; 4:10

24 ᵃRom. 8:28 ᵇ1 Cor. 1:18; Rom. 1:16 ᶜLuke 11:49; 1 Cor. 1:30

25 ᵃ1 Cor. 1:18, 21, 23; 2:14; 1 Cor. 4:10 ᵇ2 Cor. 13:4

26 ¹Lit., *see* ²Or, *human standards* ᵃRom. 11:29 ᵇ1 Cor. 2:8; 1:20; Matt. 11:25

27 ᵃJames 2:5 ᵇ1 Cor. 1:20

28 ᵃ1 Cor. 1:20

12 Now I mean this, that ᵃeach one of you is saying, "I am of Paul," and "I of ᵇApollos," and "I of ᶜCephas," and "I of Christ."

13 ¹Has Christ been divided? Paul was not crucified for you, was he? Or were you ᵃbaptized ²in the name of Paul?

14 ¹I thank God that I ᵃbaptized ¹none of you, except ᵃCrispus and ᵇGaius,

15 that no man should say you were baptized ¹in my name.

16 Now I did baptize also the ᵃhousehold of Stephanas; beyond that, I do not know whether I baptized any other.

17 ᵃFor Christ did not send me to baptize, but to preach the gospel, ᵇnot in ¹cleverness of speech, that the cross of Christ should not be made void.

18 For the word of the cross is to ᵃthose who ¹are perishing ᵇfoolishness, but to us who ²are being saved it is ᶜthe power of God.

19 For it is written,

"ᵃI WILL DESTROY THE WISDOM OF THE WISE,
AND THE CLEVERNESS OF THE CLEVER I
WILL SET ASIDE."

20 ᵃWhere is the wise man? Where is the scribe? Where is the debater of ᵇthis age? Has not God ᶜmade foolish the wisdom of ᵈthe world?

21 For since in the wisdom of God ᵃthe world through its wisdom did not *come to* know God, ᵇGod was well pleased through the ᶜfoolishness of the ¹message preached to ᵈsave those who believe.

22 For indeed ᵃJews ask for ¹signs, and Greeks search for wisdom;

23 but we preach ¹ᵃChrist crucified, ᵇto Jews a stumbling-block, and to Gentiles ᶜfoolishness,

24 but to those who are ᵃthe called, both Jews and Greeks, Christ ᵇthe power of God and ᶜthe wisdom of God.

25 Because the ᵃfoolishness of God is wiser than men, and ᵇthe weakness of God is stronger than men.

26 For ¹consider your ᵃcall, brethren, that there were ᵇnot many wise according to ²the flesh, not many mighty, not many noble;

27 but ᵃGod has chosen the foolish things of ᵇthe world to shame the wise, and God has chosen the weak things of ᵇthe world to shame the things which are strong,

28 and the base things of ᵃthe world and the

despised, God has chosen, [b]the things that are not, that He might [c]nullify the things that are,

29 that [a]no [1]man should boast before God.

30 But [1]by His doing you are in [a]Christ Jesus, who became to us [b]wisdom from God, [2]and [c]righteousness and [d]sanctification, and [e]redemption,

31 that, just as it is written, "[a]LET HIM WHO BOASTS, BOAST IN THE LORD."

CHAPTER 2

AND when I came to you, brethren, I [a]did not come with superiority of speech or of wisdom, proclaiming to you [b]the [1]testimony of God.

2 For I determined to know nothing among you except [a]Jesus Christ, and Him crucified.

3 And I [a]was with you in [b]weakness and in [c]fear and in much trembling.

4 And my [1]message and my preaching were [a]not in persuasive words of wisdom, but in demonstration of [b]the Spirit and of power,

5 that your faith should not [1]rest on the wisdom of men, but on [a]the power of God.

6 Yet we do speak wisdom among those who are [a]mature; a wisdom, however, not of [b]this age, nor of the rulers of [b]this age, who are [c]passing away;

7 but we speak God's wisdom in a [a]mystery, the hidden *wisdom*, which God [b]predestined before the [c]ages to our glory;

8 *the wisdom* [a]which none of the rulers of [b]this age has understood; for if they had understood it, they would not have crucified [c]the Lord of glory;

9 but just as it is written,

"[a]THINGS WHICH EYE HAS NOT SEEN AND EAR HAS NOT HEARD,

AND *which* HAVE NOT ENTERED THE HEART OF MAN,

ALL THAT GOD HAS PREPARED FOR THOSE WHO LOVE HIM."

10 [1][a]For to us God revealed *them* [b]through the Spirit; for the Spirit searches all things, even the [c]depths of God.

11 For who among men knows the *thoughts* of a man except the [a]spirit of the man, which is in him? Even so the *thoughts* of God no one knows except the Spirit of God.

12 Now we [a]have received, not the spirit of

28 [b]Rom. 4:17 [c]1 Cor. 2:6; Job 34:19; 2 Thess. 2:8; Heb. 2:14

29 [1]Lit., *flesh*
[a]Eph. 2:9

30 [1]Lit., *of Him* [2]Or, *both*
[a]1 Cor. 4:15; Rom. 8:1
[b]1 Cor. 1:24 [c]2 Cor. 5:21; Phil. 3:9; Jer. 23:5f.; 33:16
[d]1 Cor. 1:2; 6:11; 1 Thess. 5:23 [e]Eph. 1:7, 14; Col. 1:4; Rom. 3:24

31 [a]Jer. 9:23f.; 2 Cor. 10:17

1 [1]Some ancient mss. read, *mystery*
[a]1 Cor. 2:4, 13; 1:17 [b]1 Cor. 2:7

2 [a]Gal. 6:14; 1 Cor. 1:23

3 [a]Acts 18:1, 6, 12 [b]1 Cor. 4:10; 2 Cor. 11:30; 12:5, 9f.; 13:9 [c]Is. 19:16; Eph. 6:5; 2 Cor. 7:15

4 [1]Lit., *word*
[a]1 Cor. 2:1, 13; 1:17 [b]Rom. 15:19; 1 Cor. 4:20

5 [1]Lit., *be*
[a]2 Cor. 4:7; 6:7; 2 Cor. 12:9

6 [a]Eph. 4:13; Phil. 3:15 marg.; Heb. 5:14; 6:1 [b]1 Cor. 1:20; Matt. 13:22 [c]1 Cor. 1:28

7 [a]1 Cor. 2:1; Rom. 11:25; 16:25f. [b]Rom. 8:29f. [c]Heb. 1:2; 11:3

8 [a]1 Cor. 2:6; 1:26 [b]1 Cor. 1:20; Matt. 13:22 [c]Acts 7:2; James 2:1

9 [a]Is. 64:4; 65:17

10 [1]Some ancient mss. use, *But*
[a]Matt. 11:25; 13:11; 16:17; Gal. 1:12; Eph. 3:3, 5 [b]John 14:26 [c]Rom. 11:33ff.

11 [a]Prov. 20:27

12 [a]Rom. 8:15

12 [b]1 Cor. 1:27

13 [1]Or, *interpreting spiritual things to spiritual men*
[a]1 Cor. 1:17; 1 Cor. 2:1, 4

14 [1]Or, *unspiritual* [2]Or, *examined*
[a]1 Cor. 15:44, 46; James 3:15 marg.; Jude 19 marg. [b]John 14:17 [c]1 Cor. 1:18

15 [a]1 Cor. 3:1; 14:37; Gal. 6:1

16 [a]Is. 40:13; Rom. 11:34 [b]John 15:15

1 [a]1 Cor. 2:15; 14:37; Gal. 6:1 [b]Rom. 7:14; 1 Cor. 2:14 [c]Heb. 5:13; 1 Cor. 2:6; Eph. 1.11

2 [a]Heb. 5:12f.; 1 Pet. 2:2 [b]John 16:12

3 [1]Lit., *according to man* [a]Rom. 13:13; 1 Cor. 1:10f.; 11:18 [b]1 Cor. 3:4

4 [a]1 Cor. 1:12 [b]1 Cor. 3:3

5 [a]2 Cor. 6:4; Eph. 3:7; Col. 1:25; Rom. 15:16; 2 Cor. 3:3, 6; 4:1; 5:18; 1 Tim. 1:12 [b]Rom. 12:6; 1 Cor. 3:10

6 [a]Acts 18:4-11, 18; 1 Cor. 4:15; 9:1; 15:1; 2 Cor. 10:14f. [b]Acts 18:27; 1 Cor. 1:12 [c]1 Cor. 15:10

8 [1]Or, *wages* [a]1 Cor. 3:14; 1 Cor. 4:5; 9:17; Gal. 6:4

9 [1]Or, *cultivated land* [a]Mark 16:20; 2 Cor. 6:1 [b]Is. 61:3; Matt. 15:13 [c]Eph. 2:20-22; Col. 2:7; 1 Pet. 2:5; 1 Cor. 3:16

10 [a]Rom. 12:3; 1 Cor. 15:10 [b]Rom. 15:20; 1 Cor. 3:11f. [c]1 Thess. 3:2

[b]the world, but the Spirit who is from God, that we might know the things freely given to us by God,

13 which things we also speak, [a]not in words taught by human wisdom, but in those taught by the Spirit, [1]combining spiritual *thoughts* with spiritual *words.*

14 But a [1a]natural man [b]does not accept the things of the Spirit of God; for they are [c]foolishness to him, and he cannot understand them, because they are spiritually [2]appraised.

15 But he who is [a]spiritual appraises all things, yet he himself is appraised by no man.

16 For [a]WHO HAS KNOWN THE MIND OF THE LORD, THAT HE SHOULD INSTRUCT HIM? But [b]we have the mind of Christ.

CHAPTER 3

AND I, brethren, could not speak to you as to [a]spiritual men, but as to [b]men of flesh, as to [c]babes in Christ.

2 I gave you [a]milk to drink, not solid food; for you [b]were not yet able *to receive it.* Indeed, even now you are not yet able,

3 for you are still fleshly. For since there is [a]jealousy and strife among you, are you not fleshly, and are you not walking [1b]like mere men?

4 For when [a]one says, "I am of Paul," and another, "I am of Apollos," are you not *mere* [b]men?

5 What then is Apollos? And what is Paul? [a]Servants through whom you believed, even [b]as the Lord gave *opportunity* to each one.

6 [a]I planted, [b]Apollos watered, but [c]God was causing the growth.

7 So then neither the one who plants nor the one who waters is anything, but God who causes the growth.

8 Now he who plants and he who waters are one; but each will [a]receive his own [1]reward according to his own labor.

9 For we are God's [a]fellow-workers; you are God's [1b]field, God's [c]building.

10 According to [a]the grace of God which was given to me, as a wise masterbuilder [b]I laid a foundation, and [c]another is building upon it. But let each man be careful how he builds upon it.

11   For no man can lay a [a]foundation other than the one which is laid, which is Jesus Christ.

12   Now if any man builds upon the foundation with gold, silver, [1]precious stones, wood, hay, straw,

13   [a]each man's work will become evident; for [b]the day will show it, because it is *to be* revealed with fire; and the fire itself will test [1]the quality of each man's work.

14   If any man's work which he has built upon it remains, he shall [a]receive a reward.

15   If any man's work is burned up, he shall suffer loss; but he himself shall be saved, yet [a]so as through fire.

16   [a]Do you not know that [b]you are a [1]temple of God, and *that* the Spirit of God dwells in you?

17   If any man destroys the [1]temple of God, God will destroy him, for the [1]temple of God is holy, and [2]that is what you are.

18   [a]Let no man deceive himself. [b]If any man among you thinks that he is wise in [c]this age, let him become foolish that he may become wise.

19   For [a]the wisdom of this world is foolishness before God. For it is written, "*He is* [b]THE ONE WHO CATCHES THE WISE IN THEIR CRAFTINESS";

20   and again, "[a]THE LORD KNOWS THE REASONINGS of the wise, THAT THEY ARE USELESS."

21   So then [a]let no one boast in men. For [b]all things belong to you,

22   [a]whether Paul or Apollos or Cephas or the world or [b]life or death or things present or things to come; all things belong to you,

23   and [a]you belong to Christ; and [b]Christ belongs to God.

CHAPTER 4

LET a man regard us in this manner, as [a]servants of Christ, and [b]stewards of [c]the mysteries of God.

2   In this case, moreover, it is required [1]of stewards that one be found trustworthy.

3   But to me it is a very small thing that I should be examined by you, or by *any* human [1]court; in fact, I do not even examine myself.

4   I [a]am conscious of nothing against myself, yet I am not by this [b]acquitted; but the one who examines me is the Lord.

5   Therefore [a]do not go on [1]passing judgment

11 [a]Is. 28:16; 1 Pet. 2:4ff.; Eph. 2:20

12 [1]Or, *costly*

13 [1]Lit., *of what sort each man's work is* [a]1 Cor. 4:5 [b]2 Thess. 1:7-10; 2 Tim. 1:12, 18; 4:8; 1 Cor. 1:8; Matt. 10:15; 1 Cor. 4:3 marg.

14 [a]1 Cor. 3:8; 4:5; 9:17; Gal. 6:4

15 [a]Job 23:10; Ps. 66:10, 12; Jude 23

16 [1]Or, *sanctuary* [a]Rom. 6:16 [b]1 Cor. 6:19; 2 Cor. 6:16; Eph. 2:21f.; Rom. 8:9

17 [1]Or, *sanctuary* [2]Lit., *which you are*

18 [a]Is. 5:21 [b]1 Cor. 8:2; Gal. 6:3 [c]1 Cor. 1:20

19 [a]1 Cor. 1:20 [b]Job 5:13

20 [a]Ps. 94:11

21 [a]1 Cor. 4:6 [b]Rom. 8:32

22 [a]1 Cor. 1:12; 3:5, 6 [b]Rom. 8:38

23 [a]1 Cor. 15:23; 2 Cor. 10:7; Gal. 3:29 [b]1 Cor. 11:3; 15:28

1 [a]Luke 1:2 [b]1 Cor. 9:17; Titus 1:7; 1 Pet. 4:10 [c]Rom. 11:25; 16:25

2 [1]Lit., *in*

3 [1]Lit., *day*

4 [a]2 Cor. 1:12; Acts 23:1 [b]Ps. 143:2; Rom. 2:13

5 [1]Lit., *judging anything* [a]Matt. 7:1; Rom. 2:1

5 [2] I.e., the appointed time
of judgment
[b] Rom. 2:16; John 21:22
[c] 1 Cor. 3:13 [d] 2 Cor. 10:18;
Rom. 2:29; 1 Cor. 3:8

6 [1] Lit., *puffed up*
[a] 1 Cor. 1:19, 31; 3:19f.
[b] 1 Cor. 4:18f.; 1 Cor. 8:1;
13:4 [c] 1 Cor. 1:12; 3:4

7 [a] John 3:27; Rom. 12:3, 6;
1 Pet. 4:10

8 [a] Rev. 3:17f.

9 [1] Or, *and to angels and
to men*
[a] 1 Cor. 15:31; 2 Cor. 11:23;
Rom. 8:36 [b] Heb. 10:33

10 [a] 1 Cor. 1:18; Acts 17:18;
26:24 [b] 2 Cor. 11:19; 1 Cor.
1:19f.; 3:18 [c] 2 Cor. 13:9;
1 Cor. 2:3

11 [a] Rom. 8:35; 2 Cor.
11:23-27

12 [a] Acts 18:3 [b] 1 Pet. 3:9
[c] John 15:20; Rom. 8:35

13 [1] Or, *console*
[a] Lam. 3:45

14 [a] 1 Cor. 6:5; 15:34
[b] 2 Cor. 6:13; 12:14; 1 Thess.
2:11; 1 John 2:1; 3 John 4

15 [a] Gal. 3:24f. [b] 1 Cor. 1:30;
[c] Philem. 10; Gal. 4:19;
1 Cor. 3:8; Num. 11:12
[d] 1 Cor. 9:12, 14, 18, 23; 15:1

16 [a] 1 Cor. 11:1; Phil. 3:17;
4:9; 1 Thess. 1:6; 2 Thess. 3:9

17 [a] 1 Cor. 16:10 [b] Acts 16:1
[c] 1 Tim. 1:2, 18; 2 Tim. 1:2;
1 Cor. 4:14 [d] 1 Cor. 7:17;
11:34; 14:33; 16:1; Titus 1:5

18 [1] Lit., *puffed up*
[a] 1 Cor. 4:6 [b] 1 Cor. 4:21

352

before [2] the time, *but wait* [b] until the Lord comes who will both [c] bring to light the things hidden in the darkness and disclose the motives of *men's* hearts; and then each man's [d] praise will come to him from God.

6 Now these things, brethren, I have figuratively applied to myself and Apollos for your sakes, that in us you might learn not to exceed [a] what is written, in order that no one of you might [b] become [1] arrogant [c] in behalf of one against the other.

7 For who regards you as superior? And [a] what do you have that you did not receive? But if you did receive it, why do you boast as if you had not received it?

8 You are [a] already filled, you have already become rich, you have become kings without us; and would indeed that you had become kings so that we also might reign with you.

9 For, I think, God has exhibited us apostles last of all, as men [a] condemned to death; because we [b] have become a spectacle to the world, [1] both to angels and to men.

10 We are [a] fools for Christ's sake, but [b] you are prudent in Christ; [c] we are weak, but you are strong; you are distinguished, but we are without honor.

11 To this present hour we are both [a] hungry and thirsty, and are poorly clothed, and are roughly treated, and are homeless;

12 and we toil, [a] working with our own hands; when we are [b] reviled, we bless; when we are [c] persecuted, we endure;

13 when we are slandered, we try to [1] conciliate; we have [a] become as the scum of the world, the dregs of all things, *even* until now.

14 I do not write these things to [a] shame you, but to admonish you as my beloved [b] children.

15 For if you were to have countless [a] tutors in Christ, yet *you would* not *have* many fathers; for in [b] Christ Jesus I [c] became your father through the [d] gospel.

16 I exhort you therefore, be [a] imitators of me.

17 For this reason I [a] have sent to you [b] Timothy, who is my [c] beloved and faithful child in the Lord, and he will remind you of my ways which are in Christ, [d] just as I teach everywhere in every church.

18 Now some have become [1] [a] arrogant, as though I were not [b] coming to you.

19 But I [a]will come to you soon, [b]if the Lord wills, and I shall find out, not the [1]words of those who are [c]arrogant, but their power.

20 For the kingdom of God does [a]not consist in [1]words, but in power.

21 What do you desire? [a]Shall I come to you with a rod or with love and a spirit of gentleness?

Chapter 5

IT is actually reported that there is immorality among you, and immorality of such a kind as does not exist even among the Gentiles, that someone has [a]his father's wife.

2 And [1]you [a]have become [2]arrogant, and [3]have not [b]mourned instead, in order that the one who had done this deed might be [c]removed from your midst.

3 For I, on my part, though [a]absent in body but present in spirit, have already judged him who has so committed this, as though I were present.

4 [a]In the name of our Lord Jesus, when you are assembled, and [1]I with you in spirit, [b]with the power of our Lord Jesus,

5 *I have decided* to [a]deliver such a one to [b]Satan for the destruction of his flesh, that his spirit may be saved in [c]the day of the Lord [1]Jesus.

6 [a]Your boasting is not good. [b]Do you not know that [c]a little leaven leavens the whole lump *of dough?*

7 Clean out the old leaven, that you may be a new lump, just as you are *in fact* unleavened. For Christ our [a]Passover also has been sacrificed.

8 Let us therefore celebrate the feast, [a]not with old leaven, nor with the leaven of malice and wickedness, but with the unleavened bread of sincerity and truth.

9 I wrote you in my letter [a]not to associate with immoral people;

10 I *did* not at all *mean* with the immoral people of this world, or with the covetous and swindlers, or with [a]idolaters; for then you would have to go out of the world.

11 But [1]actually, I wrote to you not to associate [2]with any so-called [a]brother if he should be an immoral person, or covetous, or [b]an idolater, or a reviler, or a drunkard, or a swindler—not even to eat with such a one.

---

19 [1]Lit., *word*
[a]1 Cor. 11:34; 16:5f.; 1 Cor. 16:8; 2 Cor. 1:15f.; Acts 19:21; 20:2 [b]Acts 18:21
[c]1 Cor. 4:6

20 [1]Lit., *word*
[a]1 Cor. 2:4

21 [a]2 Cor. 1:23; 2:1, 3; 12:20; 13:2, 10

1 [a]Lev. 18:8; Deut. 22:30; 27:20

2 [1]Or, *have you . . . ?* [2]Lit., *puffed up* [3]Or, *have you . . . ?*
[a]1 Cor. 4:6 [b]2 Cor. 7:7-10
[c]1 Cor. 5:13

3 [a]Col. 2:5; 1 Thess. 2:17

4 [1]Lit., *my spirit, with the power*
[a]2 Thess. 3:6 [b]John 20:23; 2 Cor. 2:6, 10; 13:3, 10; 1 Tim. 5:20

5 [1]Some ancient mss. omit, *Jesus*
[a]Luke 22:31; 1 Tim. 1:20; Prov. 23:14 [b]Matt. 4:10
[c]1 Cor. 1:8

6 [a]James 4:16; 1 Cor. 5:2 [b]Rom. 6:16 [c]Gal. 5:9; Matt. 16:6, 12; Hos. 7:4

7 [a]Mark 14:12; 1 Pet. 1:19

8 [a]Ex. 12:19; 13:7; Deut. 16:3

9 [a]2 Cor. 6:14; Eph. 5:11; 2 Thess. 3:6

10 [a]1 Cor. 10:27

11 [1]Or, *now I write* [2]Lit., *together if any man called a brother should be*
[a]2 Thess. 3:6; Acts 1:15
[b]1 Cor. 10:7, 14, 20f.

12 ªMark 4:11 ᵇ Cor. 5:3-5; 6:1-4

13 ¹Or. *will judge*
ªl Cor. 5:2; Deut. 13:5; 17:7, 12; 21:21; 22:21

1 ¹Lit., *matter* ²I.e., true believers; lit., *holy ones*
ªMatt. 18:17

2 ¹Note 2, vs. 1 ²Or, try *the trivial cases?*
ªRom. 6:16 ᵇMatt. 19:28; Dan. 7:18, 22, 27 ᶜl Cor. 1:20

3 ªRom. 6:16

4 ¹Or, *appoint them . . . . church.*

5 ªl Cor. 15:34; 4:14 ᵇActs 1:15; 1 Cor. 6:1 and Acts 9:13

6 ª2 Cor. 6:14f.; 1 Tim. 5:8

7 ªMatt. 5:39f.

8 ªl Thess. 4:6

9 ¹I.e., effeminate, by perversion
ªRom. 6:16 ᵇl Cor. 15:50; Gal. 5:21; Eph. 5:5; Acts 20:32 ᶜl Cor. 15:33, Gal. 6.7, James 1 16; Luke 21;8; 1 John 3:7 ᵈRom. 13:13; 1 Cor. 5:11; Gal. 5:19-21; Eph. 5:5; 1 Tim. 1:10; Rev. 21:8; 22:15

10 ªl Cor. 15:50; Gal. 5:21; Eph. 5:5; Acts 20:32

11 ªl Cor. 12:2; Eph. 2:2f.; Col. 3:5-7; Titus 3:3-7 ᵇActs 22:16; Eph. 5:26 ᶜl Cor. 1:2, 30 ᵈRom. 8:30

12 ªl Cor. 10:23

13 ¹Lit., *belly* ²Lit., *it and them*
ªMatt. 15:17 ᵇCol. 2:22 ᶜl Cor. 6:15, 19 ᵈGal. 5:24; Eph. 5:23

12 For what have I to do with judging ªoutsiders? ᵇDo you not judge those who are within *the church?*

13 But those who are outside God ¹judges. ªRemove the wicked man from among yourselves.

Chapter 6

DOES any one of you, when he has a ¹case against his neighbor, dare to go to law before the unrighteous, and ªnot before the ²saints?

2 Or ªdo you not know that ᵇthe ¹saints will judge ᶜthe world? And if the world is judged by you, are you not competent to ²*constitute* the smallest law courts?

3 ªDo you not know that we shall judge angels? How much more, matters of this life?

4 If then you have law courts dealing with matters of this life, ¹do you appoint them as judges who are of no account in the church?

5 ªI say *this* to your shame. *Is it* so, *that* there is not among you one wise man who will be able to decide between his ᵇbrethren,

6 but brother goes to law with brother, and that before ªunbelievers?

7 Actually, then, it is already a defeat for you, that you have lawsuits with one another. ªWhy not rather be wronged? Why not rather be defrauded?

8 On the contrary, you yourselves wrong and defraud, and that *your* ªbrethren.

9 Or ªdo you not know that the unrighteous shall not ᵇinherit the kingdom of God? ᶜDo not be deceived; ᵈneither fornicators, nor idolaters, nor adulterers, nor ¹effeminate, nor homosexuals,

10 nor thieves, nor covetous, nor drunkards, nor revilers, nor swindlers, shall ªinherit the kingdom of God.

11 And ªsuch were some of you; but you were ᵇwashed, but you were ᶜsanctified, but you were ᵈjustified in the name of the Lord Jesus Christ, and in the Spirit of our God.

12 ªAll things are lawful for me, but not all things are profitable. All things are lawful for me, but I will not be mastered by anything.

13 ªFood is for the ¹stomach, and the ¹stomach is for food; but God will ᵇdo away with both ²of them. Yet the body is not for immorality, but ᶜfor the Lord; and ᵈthe Lord is for the body.

14   Now God has not only [a]raised the Lord, but [b]will also raise us up through His power.

15   [a]Do you not know that [b]your bodies are members of Christ? Shall I then take away the members of Christ and make them members of a harlot? [c]May it never be!

16   Or [a]do you not know that the one who joins himself to a harlot is one body *with her?* For He says, "[b]THE TWO WILL BECOME ONE FLESH."

17   But the one who joins himself to the Lord is [a]one spirit *with Him.*

18   [a]Flee immorality. Every *other* sin that a man commits is outside the body, but the [1]immoral man sins against his own body.

19   Or [a]do you not know that [b]your body is a [1]temple of the Holy Spirit who is in you, whom you have from [2]God, and that [c]you are not your own?

20   For [a]you have been bought with a price: therefore glorify God in [b]your body.

CHAPTER 7

Now concerning the things about which you wrote, it is [a]good for a man not to touch a woman.

2   But because of immoralities, let each man have his own wife, and let each woman have her own husband.

3   Let the husband [1]fulfill his duty to his wife, and likewise also the wife to her husband.

4   The wife does not have authority over her own body, but the husband *does;* and likewise also the husband does not have authority over his own body, but the wife *does.*

5   · [a]Stop depriving one another, except by agreement for a time that you may devote yourselves to prayer, and [1]come together again lest [b]Satan tempt you because of your lack of self-control.

6   But this I say by way of concession, [a]not of command.

7   [1]Yet I wish that all men were [a]even as I myself am. However, [b]each man has his own gift from God, one in this manner, and another in that.

8   But I say to the unmarried and to widows that it is [a]good for them if they remain [b]even as I.

9   But if they do not have self-control, [a]let them marry; for it is better to marry than to [1]burn.

10   But to the married I give instructions, [a]not

14 [a]Acts 2:24 [b]1 Cor. 15:23; John 6:39f.

15 [a]1 Cor. 6:3 [b]1 Cor. 6:13; Rom. 12:5; 12:27; Eph. 5:30 [c]Luke 20:16

16 [a]1 Cor. 6:3 [b]Gen. 2:24; Matt. 19:5; Mark 10:8; Eph. 5:31

17 [a]John 17:21-23; Rom. 8:9-11; Gal. 2:20; 1 Cor. 6:15

18 [1]Or, *one who practices immorality* [a]2 Cor. 12:21; Eph. 5:3; Col. 3:5; Heb. 13:4; 1 Cor. 6:9

19 [1]Or, *sanctuary* [2]Or, *God? And you . . . own* [a]1 Cor. 6:3 [b]John 2:21 [c]Rom. 14:7f.

20 [a]1 Cor. 7:23; Acts 20:28; 1 Pet. 1:18f.; 2 Pet. 2:1; Rev. 5:9 [b]Rom. 12:1; Phil. 1:20

1 [a]1 Cor. 7:8, 26

3 [1]Lit., *render*

5 [1]Lit., *be* [a]Ex. 19:15; 1 Sam. 21:5 [b]Matt. 4:10

6 [a]2 Cor. 8:8

7 [1]Some ancient mss. read, *For* [a]1 Cor. 7:8; 9:5 [b]1 Cor. 12:4, 11, Rom. 12:6, Matt. 19:11f.

8 [a]1 Cor. 7:1, 26 [b]1 Cor. 7:7; 9:5

9 [1]I.e., burn with passion [a]1 Tim. 5:14

10 [a]1 Cor. 7:6; Mal. 2:16; Matt. 5:32; 19:3-9; Mark 10:2-12; Luke 16:18

355

10 [1]Lit., *depart from*

11 [1]Or, *leave his wife*

12 [1]Or, *leave her*
[a]1 Cor. 7:6; 2 Cor. 11:17

13 [1]Or, *leave her husband*

14 [1]Lit., *the brother*
[a]Ezra 9:2; Mal. 2:15

15 [1]Some ancient mss. read, *you* [2]Lit., *in*
[a]Rom. 14:19

16 [a]1 Pet. 3:1; Rom. 11:14

17 [a]Rom. 12:3 [b]1 Cor. 4:17
[c]1 Cor. 14:33; 11:16; 2 Cor. 8:18; 11:28; Gal. 1:22;
1 Thess. 2:14; 2 Thess. 1:4

18 [a]Acts 15:1ff.

19 [a]Gal. 5:6; 6:15; Col. 3:11; Rom. 2:27, 29; Gal. 3:28
[b]Rom. 2:25

20 [1]Lit., *calling*
[a]1 Cor. 7:24

21 [1]Lit., *Let it not be a care to you* [2]Lit., *use*

22 [a]John 8:32, 36; Philem. 16 [b]Eph. 6:6; Col. 3:24;
1 Pet. 2:16

23 [a]1 Cor. 6:20

24 [a]1 Cor. 7:20

25 [1]Lit., *has had mercy shown on him by the Lord to be trustworthy*
[a]1 Cor. 7:6 [b]2 Cor. 4:1;
1 Tim. 1:13, 16

I, but the Lord, that the wife should not [1]leave her husband

11 (but if she does leave, let her remain unmarried, or else be reconciled to her husband), and that the husband should not [1]send his wife away.

12 But to the rest [a]I say, not the Lord, that if any brother has a wife who is an unbeliever, and she consents to live with him, let him not [1]send her away.

13 And a woman who has an unbelieving husband, and he consents to live with her, let her not [1]send her husband away.

14 For the unbelieving husband is sanctified through his wife, and the unbelieving wife is sanctified through [1]her believing husband; for otherwise your children are unclean, but now they are [a]holy.

15 Yet if the unbelieving one leaves, let him leave; the brother or the sister is not under bondage in such *cases*, but God has called [1]us [2a]to peace.

16 For how do you know, O wife, whether you will [a]save your husband? Or how do you know, O husband, whether you will save your wife?

17 Only, [a]as the Lord has assigned to each one, as God has called each, in this manner let him walk. And [b]thus I direct in [c]all the churches.

18 Was any man called *already* circumcised? Let him not become uncircumcised. Has anyone been called in uncircumcision? [a]Let him not be circumcised.

19 [a]Circumcision is nothing, and uncircumcision is nothing, but *what matters is* [b]the keeping of the commandments of God.

20 [a]Let each man remain in that [1]condition in which he was called.

21 Were you called while a slave? [1]Do not worry about it; but if you are able also to become free, rather [2]do that.

22 For he who was called in the Lord while a slave, is [a]the Lord's freedman; likewise he who was called while free, is [b]Christ's slave.

23 [a]You were bought with a price; do not become slaves of men.

24 Brethren, [a]let each man remain with God in that *condition* in which he was called.

25 Now concerning virgins I have [a]no command of the Lord, but I give an opinion as one who [1b]by the mercy of the Lord is trustworthy.

26 I think then that this is good in view of the

[1]present [a]distress, that [b]it is good for a man [2]to remain as he is.

27 Are you bound to a wife? Do not seek to be released. Are you released from a wife? Do not seek a wife.

28 But if you should marry, you have not sinned; and if a virgin should marry, she has not sinned. Yet such will have [1]trouble in this life, and I am trying to spare you.

29 But this I say, brethren, [a]the time has been shortened, so that from now on both those who have wives should be as though they had none;

30 and those who weep, as though they did not weep; and those who rejoice, as though they did not rejoice; and those who buy, as though they did not possess;

31 and those who use the world, as though they did not [a]make full use of it; for [b]the form of this world is passing away.

32 But I want you to be free from concern. One who is [a]unmarried is concerned about the things of the Lord, how he may please the Lord;

33 but one who is married is concerned about the things of the world, how he may please his [1]wife,

34 and *his interests* are divided. And the woman who is unmarried, and the virgin, is concerned about the things of the Lord, that she may be holy both in body and spirit; but one who is married is concerned about the things of the world, how she may please her husband.

35 And this I say for your own benefit; not to put a restraint upon you, but [1]to promote what is seemly, and *to secure* undistracted devotion to the Lord.

36 But if any man thinks that he is acting unbecomingly toward his virgin *daughter*, if she should be of full age, and if it must be so, let him do what he wishes, he does not sin; let [1]her marry.

37 But he who stands firm in his heart, [1]being under no constraint, but has authority [2]over his own will, and has decided this in his own heart, to keep his own [3]virgin *daughter*, he will do well.

38 So then both he who gives his own virgin *daughter* in marriage does well, and he who does not give her in marriage will do better.

39 [a]A wife is bound as long as her husband

---

26 [1]Or, *impending* [2]Lit., *so to be*
[a]Luke 21:23; 2 Thess. 2:2
[b]1 Cor. 7:1, 8

28 [1]Lit., *tribulation in the flesh*

29 [a]Rom. 13:11f.; 1 Cor. 7:31

31 [a]1 Cor. 9:18 [b]1 Cor. 7:29; 1 John 2:17

32 [a]1 Tim. 5:5

33 [1]Some mss. read, *wife. And there is a difference also between the wife and the virgin. One who is unmarried is concerned . . . .*

35 [1]Lit., *for what is seemly*

36 [1]Lit., *them*

37 [1]Lit., *having no necessity* [2]Lit., *pertaining to* [3]Or, *virgin*

39 [a]Rom. 7:2

39 [1]Lit., *has fallen asleep*
[b]2 Cor. 6:14

40 [a]1 Cor. 7:6, 25

1 [1]Lit., *puffs up*
[a]1 Cor. 8:4, 7, 10; Acts 15:20
[b]1 Cor. 8:7, 10; 10:15; Rom.
15:14 [c]1 Cor. 4:6 [d]Rom.
14:19

2 [a]1 Cor. 3:18 [b]1 Cor.
13:8, 9, 12; 1 Tim. 6:4

3 [a]Gal. 4:9; Rom. 8:29;
11:2; Ps. 1:6; Jer. 1:5; Amos
3:2

4 [1]I.e., has no real
existence
[a]1 Cor. 8:1, 7, 10; Acts 15:20
[b]1 Cor. 10:19; Acts 14:15;
Gal. 4:8 [c]1 Cor. 8:6; Deut.
4:35, 39; 6:4

5 [a]2 Thess. 2:4

6 [a]1 Cor. 8:4; Deut. 4:35,
39; 6:4 [b]Mal. 2:10; Eph. 4:6
[c]Rom. 11:36 [d]1 Cor. 1:2;
Eph. 4:5; John 13:13; 1 Tim.
2:5 [e]John 1:3; Col. 1:16

7 [a]1 Cor. 8:4ff. [b]Rom.
14:14, 22f.

8 [1]Or, *present* 2I it,
lacking [3]Lit., *abounding*
[a]Rom. 14:17

9 [1]Lit., *right*
[a]Rom. 14:13, 21; 1 Cor.
10:28; Gal. 5:13 [b]1 Cor.
8:10f.; Rom. 14:1

10 [a]1 Cor. 8:4ff. [b]1 Cor. 8:1,
4, 7; Acts 15:20

11 [a]1 Cor. 8:4ff. [b]Rom.
14:15, 20

12 [a]Matt. 18:6; Rom. 14:20
[b]Matt. 25:45

13 [a]Rom. 14:21; 1 Cor.
10:32; 2 Cor. 6:3; 11:29

lives; but if her husband [1]is dead, she is free to be married to whom she wishes, only [b]in the Lord.

40 But [a]in my opinion she is happier if she remains as she is; and I think that I also have the Spirit of God.

CHAPTER 8

NOW concerning [a]things sacrificed to idols, we know that we all have [b]knowledge. Knowledge [1c]makes arrogant, but love [d]edifies.

2 [a]If any one supposes that he knows anything, he has not yet [b]known as he ought to know;

3 but if any one loves God, he [a]is known by Him.

4 Therefore concerning the eating of [a]things sacrificed to idols, we know that [1]there is [b]no such thing as an idol in the world, and that [c]there is no God but one.

5 For even if [a]there are so-called gods whether in heaven or on earth, as indeed there are many gods and many lords,

6 yet for us [a]there is *but* one God, [b]the Father, [c]from whom are all things, and we *exist* for Him; and [d]one Lord, Jesus Christ, [e]through whom are all things, and we *exist* through Him.

7 However not all men [a]have this knowledge; but [b]some, being accustomed to the idol until now, eat food as if it were sacrificed to an idol; and their conscience being weak is defiled.

8 But [a]food will not [1]commend us to God; we are neither [2]the worse if we do not eat, nor [3]the better if we do eat.

9 But [a]take care lest this [1]liberty of yours somehow become a stumbling-block to the [b]weak.

10 For if someone sees you who have [a]knowledge dining in an idol's temple, will not his conscience, if he is weak, be strengthened to eat [b]things sacrificed to idols?

11 For through [a]your knowledge he who is weak [b]is ruined, the brother for whose sake Christ died.

12 [a]And thus, by sinning against the brethren and wounding their conscience when it is weak, you sin [b]against Christ.

13 Therefore, [a]if food causes my brother to stumble, I will never eat meat again, that I might not cause my brother to stumble.

CHAPTER 9

AM I not [a]free? Am I not an [b]apostle? Have I not [c]seen Jesus our Lord? Are you not [d]my work in the Lord?

2 If to others I am not an apostle, at least I am to you; for you are the [a]seal of my [b]apostleship in the Lord.

3 My defense to those who examine me is this:

4 [1][a]Do we not have a right to eat and drink?

5 [1][a]Do we not have a right to take along a [2]believing wife, even as the rest of the apostles, and the [b]brothers of the Lord, and [c]Cephas?

6 Or do only [1][a]Barnabas and I not have a right to refrain from working?

7 Who at any time serves [a]as a soldier at his own expense? Who [b]plants a vineyard, and does not eat the fruit of it? Or who tends a flock and does not [1]use the milk of the flock?

8 I am not speaking these things [a]according to [1]human judgment, am I? Or does not the Law also say these things?

9 For it is written in the Law of Moses, "[a]YOU SHALL NOT MUZZLE THE OX WHILE HE IS THRESHING." God is not concerned about [b]oxen, is He?

10 Or is He speaking altogether for our sake? Yes, [a]for our sake it was written, because [b]the plowman ought to plow in hope, and the thresher *to thresh* in hope of sharing *the crops.*

11 [a]If we sowed spiritual things in you, is it too much if we should reap material things from you?

12 If others share the right over you, do we not more? Nevertheless, we [a]did not use this right, but we endure all things, [b]that we may cause no hindrance to the [c]gospel of Christ.

13 [a]Do you not know that those who [b]perform sacred services eat the *food* of the temple, *and* those who attend regularly to the altar have their share with the altar?

14 So also [a]the Lord directed those who proclaim the [b]gospel to [c]get their living from the gospel.

15 But I have [a]used none of these things. And I am not writing these things that it may be done so in my case; for it would be better for me to die than have any man make [b]my boast an empty one.

16 For if I preach the gospel, I have nothing to

1 [a]1 Cor. 9:19; 10:29 [b]Acts 14:14; 2 Cor. 12:12; 1 Thess. 2:6; 1 Tim. 2:7; 2 Tim. 1:11; Rom. 1:1 [c]Acts 9:3, 17; 18:9; 22:14, 18; 23:11; 1 Cor. 15:8 [d]1 Cor. 3:6; 4:15

2 [a]John 3:33; 2 Cor. 3:2f. [b]Acts 1:25

4 [1]Lit., *It is not that we have no right to eat and drink, is it?* [a]1 Cor. 9:14; 1 Thess. 2:6, 9; 2 Thess. 3:8f.

5 [1]Lit., *It is not that we have no right to take along . . . Cephas, is it?* [2]Lit., *sister, as wife* [a]1 Cor. 7:7f. [b]Matt. 12:46 [c]Matt. 8:14; John 1:42

6 [1]Lit., *I and Barnabas* [a]Acts 4:36

7 [1]Lit., *eat of* [a]2 Cor. 10:4; 1 Tim. 1:18; 2 Tim. 2:3f. [b]1 Cor. 3:6, 8; Deut. 20:6; Prov. 27:18

8 [1]Lit., *man* [a]Rom. 3:5

9 [a]Deut. 25:4; 1 Tim. 5:18 [b][Deut. 22:1-4; Prov. 12:10]

10 [a]Rom. 4:23f. [b]2 Tim. 2:6

11 [a]Rom. 15:27; 1 Cor. 9:14

12 [a]1 Cor. 9:15, 18; Acts 18:3; Acts 20:33 [b]2 Cor. 6:3; 11:12 [c]1 Cor. 4:15; 9:14; 16, 18, 23; 2 Cor. 2:12

13 [a]Rom. 6:16 [b]Lev. 6:16, 26; 7:6, 31ff.; Num. 5:9f.; 18:8-20, 31; Deut. 18:1

14 [a]Matt. 10:10; Luke 10:7; 1 Tim. 5:18 [b]1 Cor. 4:15; 9:12, 16, 18, 23; 2 Cor. 2:12 [c]1 Cor. 9:4; Luke 10:8

15 [a]1 Cor. 9:12, 18; Acts 18:3; Acts 20:33 [b]2 Cor. 11:10

16 ªRom. 1:14; Acts 9:15
ᵇl Cor. 4:15; 9:12, 14, 18, 23;
2 Cor. 2:12

17 ªl Cor. 9:18; John 4:36
[Gr.]; 1 Cor. 3:8 ᵇl Cor. 4:1;
Gal. 2:7; Eph. 3:2 marg.;
Phil. 1:16; Col. 1:25 marg.

18 ªl Cor. 9:17; John 4:36
[Gr.]; 1 Cor. 3:8 ᵇ2 Cor.
11:7; 12:13; Acts 18:3 ᶜl Cor.
7:31; 9:12

19 ªl Cor. 9:1 ᵇ2 Cor. 4:5
marg.; Gal. 5:13 ᶜMatt.
18:15; 1 Pet. 3:1

20 ¹Or, *law*
ªActs 16:3; 21:23-26; Rom.
11:14 ᵇGal. 2:19

21 ªRom. 2:12, 14 ᵇGal. 2:3;
3:2 ᶜGal. 6:2; 1 Cor. 7:22

22 ª2 Cor. 11:29; Rom.
14:1; 15:1 ᵇl Cor. 10:33
ᶜRom. 11:14

24 ªl Cor. 9:13 ᵇPhil. 3:14;
Col. 2:18 ᶜHeb. 12:1; 2 Tim.
4:7; Gal. 2:2

25 ªl Tim 6:12; 2 Tim. 2:5;
4:7; Eph. 6:12 ᵇ2 Tim. 4:8;
James 1:12; 1 Pet. 5:4; Rev.
2:10; 3:11

26 ªHeb. 12:1; 2 Tim. 4:7;
Gal. 2:2 ᵇl Cor. 14:9

27 ¹Lit., *bruise*
ªRom. 8:13

1 ªRom. 1:13 ᵇEx. 13:21;
Ps. 105:39 ᶜEx. 14:22, 29; Ps.
66:6

2 ¹Some ancient mss.
read, *received baptism*
ªRom. 6:3; Gal. 3:27; 1 Cor.
1:13

3 ªEx. 16:4, 35; Deut. 8:3;
Neh. 9:15, 20; Ps. 78:24f.;
John 6:31

boast of, for ªI am under compulsion; for woe is me if I do not preach ᵇthe gospel.

17 For if I do this voluntarily, I have a ªreward; but if against my will, I have a ᵇstewardship entrusted to me.

18 What then is my ªreward? That, when I preach the gospel, I may offer the gospel ᵇwithout charge, so as ᶜnot to make full use of my right in the gospel.

19 For though I am ªfree from all *men*, I have made myself ᵇa slave to all, that I might ᶜwin the more.

20 And ªto the Jews I became as a Jew, that I might win Jews; to those who are under ¹the Law, as under ¹the Law, though ᵇnot being myself under ¹the Law, that I might win those who are under ¹the Law;

21 to those who are ªwithout law, ᵇas without law, though not being without the law of God but ᶜunder the law of Christ, that I might win those who are without law.

22 To the ªweak I became weak, that I might win the weak; I have become ᵇall things to all men, ᶜthat I may by all means save some.

23 And I do all things for the sake of the gospel, that I may become a fellow-partaker of it.

24 ªDo you not know that those who run in a race all run, but *only* one receives ᵇthe prize? ᶜRun in such a way that you may win.

25 And everyone who ªcompetes in the games exercises self-control in all things. They then *do it* to receive a perishable ᵇwreath, but we an imperishable.

26 Therefore I ªrun in such a way, as not without aim; I box in such a way, as not ᵇbeating the air;

27 but I ¹buffet ªmy body and make it my slave, lest possibly, after I have preached to others, I myself should be disqualified.

CHAPTER 10

FOR ªI do not want you to be unaware, brethren, that our fathers were all ᵇunder the cloud, and all ᶜpassed through the sea;

2 and all ¹were ªbaptized into Moses in the cloud and in the sea;

3 and all ªate the same spiritual food;

4   and all [a]drank the same spiritual drink, for they were drinking from a spiritual rock which followed them; and the rock was [1]Christ.

5   Nevertheless, with most of them God was not well pleased; for [a]they were laid low in the wilderness.

6   Now these things happened as [a]examples for us, that we should not crave evil things, as [b]they also craved.

7   And do not be [a]idolaters, as some of them were; as it is written, "[b]THE PEOPLE SAT DOWN TO EAT AND DRINK, AND STOOD UP TO [c]PLAY."

8   Nor let us act immorally, as [a]some of them [1]did, and [b]twenty-three thousand fell in one day.

9   Nor let us try the Lord, as [a]some of them [1]did, and were destroyed by the serpents.

10   Nor grumble, [a]as some of them [1]did, and [b]were [2]destroyed by the [c]destroyer.

11   Now these things happened to them as an [a]example, and [b]they were written for our instruction, upon whom [c]the ends of the ages have come.

12   Therefore let him who [a]thinks he stands take heed lest he fall.

13   No temptation has overtaken you but such as is common to man; and [a]God is faithful, who will not allow you to be [b]tempted beyond what you are able; but with the temptation will provide the way of escape also, that you may be able to endure it.

14   Therefore, my [a]beloved, flee from [b]idolatry.

15   I speak as to wise men; you judge what I say.

16   Is not the [a]cup of blessing which we bless a sharing in the blood of Christ? Is not the [1b]bread which we break a sharing in the body of Christ?

17   Since there is one [1]bread, we [a]who are many are one body; for we all partake of the one [1]bread.

18   Look at [1]the nation [a]Israel; are not those who [b]eat the sacrifices sharers in the altar?

19   What do I mean then? That a thing sacrificed to idols is anything, or [a]that an idol is anything?

20   No; but *I say* that the things which the Gentiles sacrifice, they [a]sacrifice to demons, and not to God; and I do not want you to become sharers in demons.

21   [a]You cannot drink the cup of the Lord, and

4 [1]I.e., the Messiah
[a]Ex. 17:6; Num. 20:11; Ps. 78:15

5 [a]Num. 14:29ff., 37; 26:65; Heb. 3:17; Jude 5

6 [a]1 Cor. 10:11 [b]Num. 11:4, 34; Ps. 106:14

7 [a]Ex. 32:4; 1 Cor. 10:14; 5:11 [b]Ex. 32:6 [c]Ex. 32:19

8 [1]Lit., *acted immorally*
[a]Num. 25:1ff. [b]Num. 25:9

9 [1]Lit., *made trial*
[a]Num. 21:5f.

10 [1]Lit., *grumbled* [2]Lit., *being destroyed*
[a]Num. 16:41; 17:5, 10 [b]Num. 16:49 [c]Ex. 12:23; 2 Sam. 24:16; 1 Chr. 21:15; Heb. 11:28

11 [a]1 Cor. 10:6 [b]Rom. 4:23 [c]Rom. 13:11

12 [a]Rom. 11:20; 2 Pet. 3:17

13 [a]1 Cor. 1:9 [b]2 Pet. 2:9

14 [a]Heb. 6:9 [b]1 Cor. 10:7; 1 Cor. 10:19f.; 1 John 5:21

16 [1]Lit., *loaf*
[a]Matt. 26:27f.; 1 Cor. 11:25 [b]Matt. 26:26; 1 Cor. 11:32f.; Acts 2:42

17 [1]Lit., *loaf*
[a]Rom. 12:5; 1 Cor. 12:12f., 27; Eph. 4:4, 16; Col. 3:15

18 [1]Lit., *Israel according to the flesh*
[a]Rom. 1:3 [b]Lev. 7:6, 14f.; Deut. 12:17f.

19 [a]1 Cor. 8:4

20 [a]Deut. 32:17; Ps. 106:37; Rev. 9:20; Gal. 4:8

21 [a]2 Cor. 6:16

1 Corinthians 10, 11

**The Use of Christian Liberty.
Covering the Head.**

21 ᵇIs. 65:11

22 ᵃDeut. 32:21 ᵇEccl. 6:10;
Is. 45:9

23 ᵃ1 Cor. 6:12 ᵇRom.
14:19

24 ¹Or, *the other*
ᵃ1 Cor. 10:33; 13:5; Phil.
2:21; 2 Cor. 12:14; Rom. 15:2

25 ᵃActs 10:15; 1 Cor. 8:7

26 ᵃPs. 24:1; Ps. 50:12;
1 Tim. 4:4

27 ᵃ1 Cor. 5:10 ᵇLuke 10:8

28 ᵃ1 Cor. 8.7, 10-12

29 ᵃ1 Cor. 9:19; Rom. 14:16

30 ᵃ1 Cor. 9:1 ᵇRom. 14:6

31 ᵃCol. 3:17; 1 Pet. 4:11

32 ᵃ1 Cor. 8:13; Acts 24:16
ᵇActs 20:28 marg.; 1 Cor.
1:2; 11:22; 15:9; 2 Cor. 1:1;
Gal. 1:13; 1 Tim. 3:5, 15;
1 Cor. 7:17; Phil. 3:6

33 ᵃ1 Cor. 9:22; Rom. 15.2,
Gal. 1:10 ᵇ1 Cor. 13:5; Phil.
2:21; 2 Cor. 12:14; Rom. 15:2
ᶜ1 Thess. 2:16; Rom. 11:14

1 ᵃ1 Cor. 4:16

2 ᵃ1 Cor. 11:17, 22 ᵇ1 Cor.
4:17; 15:2; 1 Thess. 1:6; 3:6
ᶜ2 Thess. 2:15; 3:6

3 ¹I.e., the Messiah
ᵃEph. 1:22; 4:15; 5:23; Col.
1:18; 2:19 ᵇEph. 5:23; Gen.
3:16 ᶜ1 Cor. 3:23

4 ᵃActs 13:1; 1 Thess. 5:20

5 ¹Lit., *who is shaved*
ᵃLuke 2:36; Acts 21:9; 1 Cor.
14:34 ᵇDeut. 21:12

the cup of demons; you cannot partake of the table of the Lord, and ᵇthe table of demons.

22 Or do we ᵃprovoke the Lord to jealousy? We are not ᵇstronger than He, are we?

23 ᵃAll things are lawful, but not all things are profitable. All things are lawful, but not all things ᵇedify.

24 Let no one ᵃseek his own *good*, but that of his ¹neighbor.

25 ᵃEat anything that is sold in the meat market, without asking questions for conscience' sake;

26 ᵃFOR THE EARTH IS THE LORD'S, AND EVERYTHING THAT IS IN IT.

27 If ᵃone of the unbelievers invites you, and you wish to go, ᵇeat anything that is set before you, without asking questions for conscience' sake.

28 But ᵃif anyone should say to you, "This is meat sacrificed to idols," do not eat it, for the sake of the one who informed *you*, and for conscience' sake;

29 I mean not your own conscience, but the other *man's*; for ᵃwhy is my freedom judged by another's conscience?

30 If I partake with thankfulness, ᵃwhy am I slandered concerning that for which I ᵇgive thanks?

31 Whether, then, you eat or drink or ᵃwhatever you do, do all to the glory of God.

32 ᵃGive no offense either to Jews or to Greeks or to ᵇthe church of God;

33 just as I also ᵃplease all men in all things, ᵇnot seeking my own profit, but the *profit* of the many, ᶜthat they may be saved.

ᵃ CHAPTER 11

BE imitators of me, just as I also am of Christ.

2 Now ᵃI praise you because you ᵇremember me in everything, and ᶜhold firmly to the traditions, just as I delivered them to you.

3 But I want you to understand that ¹Christ is the ᵃhead of every man, and ᵇthe man is the head of a woman, and God is the ᶜhead of ¹Christ.

4 Every man who has *something* on his head while praying or ᵃprophesying, disgraces his head.

5 But every ᵃwoman who has her head uncovered while praying or prophesying, disgraces her head; for she is one and the same with her ¹whose head is ᵇshaved.

6   For if a woman does not cover [1]her head, let her also [2]have her hair cut off; but if it is disgraceful for a woman to [2]have her hair cut off or [1]her head shaved, let her cover [1]her head.

7   For a man ought not to have his head covered, since he is the [a]image and glory of God; but the woman is the glory of man.

8   For [a]man [1]does not originate from woman, but woman from man;

9   for indeed man was not created for the woman's sake, but [a]woman for the man's sake.

10   Therefore the woman ought to have *a symbol of* authority on her head, because of the angels.

11   However, in the Lord, neither is woman [1]independent of man, nor is man [1]independent of woman.

12   For as the woman [1]originates from the man, so also the man has his birth through the woman; and [a]all things [2]originate [b]from God.

13   [a]Judge [1]for yourselves: is it proper for a woman to pray to God *with head* uncovered?

14   Does not even nature itself teach you that if a man has long hair, it is a dishonor to him,

15   but if a woman has long hair, it is a glory to her? For her hair is given to her for a covering.

16   But if one is inclined to be contentious, [a]we have no [1]other practice, nor have [b]the churches of God.

17   But in giving this instruction, [a]I do not praise you, because you come together not for the better but for the worse.

18   For, in the first place, when you come together [1]as a church, I hear that [2a]divisions exist among you; and in part, I believe it.

19   For there [a]must also be factions among you, [b]in order that those who are approved may have become [1]evident among you.

20   Therefore when you meet together, it is not to eat the Lord's Supper,

21   for in your eating each one takes his own supper first; and one is hungry and [a]another is drunk.

22   What! Do you not have houses in which to eat and drink? Or do you despise the [a]church of God, and [b]shame those who have nothing? What shall I say to you? Shall [c]I praise you? In this I will not praise you.

23   For [a]I received from the Lord that which I

6 [1]Lit., *herself* [2]Lit., *shear herself*

7 [a]James 3:9; Gen. 1:26; 5:1; 9:6

8 [1]Lit., *is not from*
[a]Gen. 2:21-23; 1 Tim. 2:13

9 [a]Gen. 2:18

11 [1]Lit., *without*

12 [1]Lit., *is* [2]Lit., *are*
[a]2 Cor. 5:18 [b]Rom. 11:36

13 [1]Lit., *in*
[a]Luke 12:57

16 [1]Lit., *such*
[a]1 Cor. 9:1-3, 6; 4:5 [b]1 Cor. 7:17

17 [a]1 Cor. 11:2, 22

18 [1]Lit., *in church* [2]Lit., *schisms*
[a]1 Cor. 1:10; 3:3

19 [1]Or, *manifest*
[a]Matt. 18:7; Luke 17:1; 1 Tim. 4:1; 2 Pet. 2:1 [b]1 John 2:19; Deut. 13:3

21 [a]Jude 12

22 [a]1 Cor. 10:32 [b]James 2:6 [c]1 Cor. 11:2, 17

23 [a]1 Cor. 15:3; Gal. 1:12; Col. 3:24

23 b1 Cor. 11:23-25: *Matt. 26:26-28; Mark 14:22-24; Luke 22:17-20; 1 Cor. 10:16*

24 ¹*Some ancient mss. read, is broken*

25 a1 Cor. 10:16 b2 Cor. 3:6; Luke 22:20

26 a1 Cor. 4:5; John 21:22

27 aHeb. 10:29

28 a2 Cor. 13:5; Gal. 6:4; Matt. 26.22

30 aActs 7:60

32 a2 Sam. 7:14; Ps. 94:12; Heb. 12:7-10; Rev. 3:19 b1 Cor. 1:20

34 a1 Cor. 11:21 b1 Cor. 11:22 c1 Cor. 7:17; 16:1; 1:17 d1 Cor. 4:19

1 a1 Cor. 14:1; 12:4 bRom. 1:13

2 aEph. 2:11f.; 1 Pet. 4:3; 1 Cor. 6:11 b1 Thess. 1:9 cHab. 2:18f.; Ps. 115:5; Is. 46:7; Jer. 10:5

3 ¹Or, *in* ²Gr. *anathema* a1 John 4:2f.; Matt. 22:43; Rev. 1:10, bRom. 9:3 cJohn 13:13; Rom. 10:9

4 aRom. 12:6f.; 1 Cor. 12:11; Eph. 4:4ff., 11; Heb. 2:4

also delivered to you, that ᵇthe Lord Jesus in the night in which He was betrayed took bread;

24   and when He had given thanks, He broke it, and said, "This is My body, which ¹is for you; do this in remembrance of Me."

25   In the same way ᵃthe cup also, after supper, saying, "This cup is the ᵇnew covenant in My blood; do this, as often as you drink *it*, in remembrance of Me."

26   For as often as you eat this bread and drink the cup, you proclaim the Lord's death ᵃuntil He comes.

27   Therefore whoever eats the bread or drinks the cup of the Lord in an unworthy manner, shall be ᵃguilty of the body and the blood of the Lord.

28   But let a man ᵃexamine himself, and so let him eat of the bread and drink of the cup.

29   For he who eats and drinks, eats and drinks judgment to himself, if he does not judge the body rightly.

30   For this reason many among you are weak and sick, and a number ᵃsleep.

31   But if we judged ourselves rightly, we should not be judged.

32   But when we are judged, we are ᵃdisciplined by the Lord in order that we may not be condemned along with ᵇthe world.

33   So then, my brethren, when you come together to eat, wait for one another.

34   If anyone is ᵃhungry, let him eat ᵇat home, so that you may not come together for judgment. And the remaining matters I shall ᶜarrange ᵈwhen I come.

CHAPTER 12

Now concerning ᵃspiritual *gifts*, brethren, ᵇI do not want you to be unaware.

2   ᵃYou know that when you were pagans, *you were* ᵇled astray to the ᶜdumb idols, however you were led.

3   Therefore I make known to you, that no one speaking ¹ᵃby the Spirit of God says, "Jesus is ²ᵇaccursed"; and no one can say, "Jesus is ᶜLord," except ¹ᵃby the Holy Spirit.

4   Now there are ᵃvarieties of gifts, but the same Spirit.

5   And there are varieties of ministries, and the same Lord.

6   And there are varieties of effects, but the same [a]God who works all things in all *persons.*

7   But to each one is given the manifestation of the Spirit [a]for the common good.

8   For to one is given the word of [a]wisdom through the Spirit, and to another the word of [b]knowledge according to the same Spirit;

9   to another [a]faith [1]by the same Spirit, and to another [b]gifts of [2]healing [1]by the one Spirit,

10   and to another the [1]effecting of [2a]miracles, and to another [b]prophecy, and to another the [3c]distinguishing of spirits, to another *various* [d]kinds of tongues, and to another the [e]interpretation of tongues.

11   But one and the same Spirit works all these things, [a]distributing to each one individually just as He wills.

12   For even [a]as the body is one and *yet* has many members, and all the members of the body, though they are many, are one body, [b]so also is Christ.

13   For [1a]by one Spirit we were all baptized into one body, whether [b]Jews or Greeks, whether slaves or free, and we were all made to [c]drink of one Spirit.

14   For [a]the body is not one member, but many.

15   If the foot should say, "Because I am not a hand, I am not *a part* of the body," it is not for this reason [1]any the less *a part* of the body.

16   And if the ear should say, "Because I am not an eye, I am not *a part* of the body," it is not for this reason [1]any the less *a part* of the body.

17   If the whole body were an eye, where would the hearing be? If the whole were hearing, where would the sense of smell be?

18   But now God has [a]placed the members, each one of them, in the body, [b]just as He desired.

19   And if they were all one member, where would the body be?

20   But now [a]there are many members, but one body.

21   And the eye cannot say to the hand, "I have no need of you"; or again the head to the feet, "I have no need of you."

22   On the contrary, [1]it is much truer that the

6 [a]1 Cor. 15:28; Eph. 1:23; 4:6

7 [a]Eph. 4:12; 1 Cor. 12:12-30; 14:26

8 [a]1 Cor. 2:6; 2 Cor. 1:12 [b]Rom. 15:14; 1 Cor. 2:11, 16; 2 Cor. 2:14; 4:6; 8:7; 11:6

9 [1]Or, *in* [2]Lit., *healings* [a]1 Cor. 13:2; 2 Cor. 4:13 [b]1 Cor. 12:28, 30

10 [1]Lit., *effects* [2]Or, *works of power* [3]Lit., *distinguishings* [a]1 Cor. 12:28f.; Gal. 3:5 [b]1 Cor. 11:4; 13:2, 8 [c]1 Cor. 14:29; 1 John 4:1 [d]1 Cor. 12:28, 30; 13:1; 14:2ff.; Mark 16:17 [e]1 Cor. 12:30; 14:26

11 [a]1 Cor. 12:4 and ref.

12 [a]Rom. 12:4; 1 Cor. 10:17 [b]1 Cor. 12:27

13 [1]Or, *in* [a]Eph. 2:18 [b]Gal. 3:28; Col. 3:11; Eph. 2:13-18; Rom. 3:22 [c]John 7:37-39

14 [a]1 Cor. 12:20

15 [1]Lit., *not a part*

16 [1]Lit., *not a part*

18 [a]1 Cor. 12:28 [b]1 Cor. 12:11; Rom. 12:6

20 [a]1 Cor. 12:14; 12:12

22 [1]Lit., *to a much greater degree the members*

23 [1]Or, *think to be* [2]Or, *these we clothe with*

25 [1]Lit., *schism*

26 [1]Lit., *glorified*

27 [a]1 Cor. 12:12; 1:2; Eph. 1:23; 4:12; Col. 1:18, 24; 2:19 [b]Eph. 5:30; Rom. 12:5

28 [1]Lit., *set some in* [2]Or, *works of power* [a]1 Cor. 12:18 [b]1 Cor. 10:32 [c]Eph. 4:11 [d]Eph. 2:20; 3:5; Acts 13:1 [e]Acts 13:1 [f]1 Cor. 12:10, 29 [g]1 Cor. 12:9, 30 [h]Rom. 12:8 [i]1 Cor. 12:10

29 [1]Or, *works of power*

30 [a]1 Cor. 12:10

31 [a]1 Cor. 14:1, 39

1 [a]1 Cor. 12:10 [b]2 Cor. 12:4; Rev. 14:2 [c]Ps. 150:5 Sept.

2 [a]Acts 13:1; 1 Cor. 11:4; 13:8; 14:1, 39; Matt. 7:22 [b]1 Cor. 14:2; 15:51 [c]Rom. 15:14 [d]1 Cor. 12:9 [e]Matt. 17:20; 21:21

3 [1]Some ancient mss. read, *that I may boast* [a]Matt. 6:2 [b]Dan. 3:28

4 [a]Prov. 10:12; 17:9; 1 Thess. 5:14; 1 Pet. 4:8 [b]Acts 7:9 [c]1 Cor. 4:6

5 [a]1 Cor. 10:24; Phil. 2:21

members of the body which seem to be weaker are necessary;

23   and those *members* of the body, which we [1]deem less honorable, [2]on these we bestow more abundant honor, and our unseemly *members come to* have more abundant seemliness,

24   whereas our seemly *members* have no need *of it.* But God has *so* composed the body, giving more abundant honor to that *member* which lacked,

25   that there should be no [1]division in the body, but *that* the members should have the same care for one another.

26   And if one member suffers, all the members suffer with it; if *one* member is [1]honored, all the members rejoice with it.

27   Now you are [a]Christ's body, and [b]individually members of it.

28   And God has [1a]appointed in [b]the church, first [c]apostles, second [d]prophets, third [e]teachers, then [2f]miracles, then [g]gifts of healings, helps, [h]administrations, *various* [i]kinds of tongues.

29   All are not apostles, are they? All are not prophets, are they? All are not teachers, are they? All are not *workers of* [1]miracles, are they?

30   All do not have gifts of healings, do they? All do not speak with tongues, do they? All do not [a]interpret, do they?

31   But [a]earnestly desire the greater gifts.

And I show you a still more excellent way.

CHAPTER 13

IF I speak with the [a]tongues of men and of [b]angels, but do not have love, I have become a noisy gong or a [c]clanging cymbal.

2   And if I have *the gift of* [a]prophecy, and know all [b]mysteries and all [c]knowledge; and if I have [d]all faith, so as to [e]remove mountains, but do not have love, I am nothing.

3   And if I [a]give all my possessions to feed *the poor,* and if I [b]deliver my body [1]to be burned, but do not have love, it profits me nothing.

4   Love [a]is patient, love is kind, *and* [b]is not jealous; love does not brag *and* is not [c]arrogant,

5   does not act unbecomingly; it [a]does not

seek its own, is not provoked, [b]does not take into account a wrong *suffered,*

6 [a]does not rejoice in unrighteousness, but [b]rejoices with the truth;

7 [1][a]bears all things, believes all things, hopes all things, endures all things.

8 Love never fails; but if *there are gifts of* [1][a]prophecy, they will be done away; if *there are* [b]tongues, they will cease; if *there is* knowledge, it will be done away.

9 For we [a]know in part, and we prophesy in part;

10 but when the perfect comes, the partial will be done away.

11 When I was a child, I used to speak as a child, think as a child, reason as a child; when I became a man, I did away with childish things.

12 For now we [a]see in a mirror [1]dimly, but then [b]face to face; now I know in part, but then I shall know fully just as I also [c]have been fully known.

13 But now abide faith, hope, love, these three; but the [1]greatest of these is [a]love.

5 [b]2 Cor. 5:19

6 [a]2 Thess. 2:12 [b]2 John 4; 3 John 3f.

7 [1]Or, *covers*
[a]1 Cor. 9:12

8 [1]Lit., *prophecies*
[a]1 Cor. 13:2 [b]1 Cor. 13:1

9 [a]1 Cor. 13:12; 8:2

12 [1]Lit., *in a riddle*
[a]2 Cor. 5:7; Phil. 3:12; James 1:23 [b]Gen. 32:30; Num. 12:8; 1 John 3:2 [c]1 Cor. 8:3

13 [1]Lit., *greater*
[a]Gal. 5:6

1 [a]1 Cor. 16:14 [b]1 Cor. 12:31; 14:39 [c]1 Cor. 12:1 [d]1 Cor. 13:2

CHAPTER 14

a

PURSUE love, yet [b]desire earnestly [c]spiritual *gifts,* but especially that you may [d]prophesy.

2 For one who [a]speaks in a tongue does not speak to men, but to God; for no one [1]understands, but [2]in *his* spirit he speaks [b]mysteries.

3 But one who prophesies speaks to men for [a]edification and [b]exhortation and consolation.

4 One who [a]speaks in a tongue [b]edifies himself; but one who [c]prophesies [b]edifies the church.

5 Now I wish that you all [a]spoke in tongues, but [b]*even* more that you would prophesy; and greater is one who prophesies than one who [a]speaks in tongues, unless he interprets, so that the church may receive [c]edifying.

6 But now, brethren, if I come to you speaking in tongues, what shall I profit you, unless I speak to you either by way of [a]revelation or of [b]knowledge or of [c]prophecy or of [d]teaching?

7 Yet *even* lifeless things, either flute or harp, in producing a sound, if they do not produce a

2 [1]Lit., *hears* [2]Or, *by the Spirit*
[a]1 Cor. 12:10, 28, 30; 13:1; 14:18ff.; Mark 16:17 [b]1 Cor. 13:2

3 [a]1 Cor. 14:5, 12, 17, 26; Rom. 14:19 [b]Acts 4:36

4 [a]1 Cor. 12:10, 28, 30; 13:1; 14:18ff., 26f.; Mark 16:17 [b]1 Cor. 14:5, 12, 17, 26; Rom. 14:19 [c]1 Cor. 13:2

5 [a]1 Cor. 12:10, 28, 30; 13:1; 14:18ff., 26f.; Mark 16:17 [b]Num. 11:29 [c]1 Cor. 14:4, 12, 17, 26; Rom. 14:19

6 [a]1 Cor. 14:26; Eph. 1:17 [b]1 Cor. 12:8 [c]1 Cor. 13:2 [d]1 Cor. 14:26; Acts 2:42; Rom. 6:17

8 [1]Lit., *trumpet*
[a]Num. 10:9; Jer. 4:19; Ezek. 33:3-6; Joel 2:1

9 [a]1 Cor. 9:26

10 [1]Lit., *voices*

11 [1]Or, *foreigner* [2]Or, *in my estimation*
[a]Acts 28:2

12 [1]Lit., *spirits*
[a]1 Cor. 14:4, 5, 17, 26; Rom. 14:19

15 [a]1 Cor. 14:26; Acts 21:22
[b]Eph. 5:19; Col. 3:16

16 [1]Or, *with the* [2]I.e., unversed in spiritual gifts
[a]Deut. 27:15-26; 1 Chr. 16:36 [Ps. 106:48]; Neh. 5:13; 8:6; Jer. 11:5; 28:6; Rev. 5:14; 7:12 [b]Matt. 15:36

17 [a]1 Cor. 14:4, 5, 12, 26; Rom. 14:19

20 [a]Rom. 1:13 [b]Eph. 4:14; Heb. 5:12f. [c]Ps. 131:2; Rom. 16:19; 1 Pet. 2:2; Matt. 18:3

21 [a]John 10:34; 1 Cor. 14:34 [b]Is. 28:11f.

22 [a]1 Cor. 14:1

distinction in the tones, how will it be known what is played on the flute or on the harp?

8 For if [a]the [1]bugle produces an indistinct sound, who will prepare himself for battle?

9 So also you, unless you utter by the tongue speech that is clear, how will it be known what is spoken? For you will be [a]speaking into the air.

10 There are, perhaps, a great many kinds of [1]languages in the world, and no *kind* is without meaning.

11 If then I do not know the meaning of the language, I shall be to the one who speaks a [1]abarbarian, and the one who speaks will be a [1]barbarian [2]to me.

12 So also you, since you are zealous of [1]spiritual *gifts*, seek to abound for the [a]edification of the church.

13 Therefore let one who speaks in a tongue pray that he may interpret.

14 For if I pray in a tongue, my spirit prays, but my mind is unfruitful.

15 [a]What is *the outcome* then? I shall pray with the spirit and I shall pray with the mind also; I shall [b]sing with the spirit and I shall sing with the mind also.

16 Otherwise if you bless [1]in the spirit *only*, how will the one who fills the place of the [2]ungifted say [a]the "Amen" at your [b]giving of thanks, since he does not know what you are saying?

17 For you are giving thanks well enough, but the other man is not [a]edified.

18 I thank God, I speak in tongues more than you all;

19 however, in the church I desire to speak five words with my mind, that I may instruct others also, rather than ten thousand words in a tongue.

20 [a]Brethren, [b]do not be children in your thinking; yet in evil [c]be babes, but in your thinking be mature.

21 In [a]the Law it is written, "[b]BY MEN OF STRANGE TONGUES AND BY THE LIPS OF STRANGERS I WILL SPEAK TO THIS PEOPLE, AND EVEN SO THEY WILL NOT LISTEN TO ME," says the Lord.

22 So then tongues are for a sign, not to those who believe, but to unbelievers; but [a]prophecy *is for a sign*, not to unbelievers, but to those who believe.

23 If therefore the whole church should

assemble together and all speak in tongues, and [1]ungifted men or unbelievers enter, will they not say that [a]you are mad?

24 But if all [a]prophesy, and an unbeliever or an [1]ungifted man enters, he is [b]convicted by all, he is called to account by all;

25 [a]the secrets of his heart are disclosed; and so he will [b]fall on his face and worship God, [c]declaring that God is certainly among you.

26 [a]What is *the outcome* then, [b]brethren? When you assemble, [c]each one has a [d]psalm, has a [e]teaching, has a [e]revelation, has a [f]tongue, has an [g]interpretation. Let [h]all things be done for edification.

27 If any one speaks in a [a]tongue, *it should be* by two or at the most three, and *each* in turn, and let one [b]interpret;

28 but if there is no interpreter, let him keep silent in the church; and let him speak to himself and to God.

29 And let two or three [a]prophets speak, and let the others [b]pass judgment.

30 But if a revelation is made to another who is seated, let the first keep silent.

31 For you can all prophesy one by one, so that all may learn and all may be exhorted;

32 and the spirits of prophets are subject to prophets;

33 for God is not *a God* of [a]confusion but of [1]peace, as in [b]all the churches of the [c]saints.

34 Let the women [a]keep silent in the churches; for they are not permitted to speak, but [b]let them subject themselves, just as [c]the Law also says.

35 And if they desire to learn anything, let them ask their own husbands at home; for it is [1]improper for a woman to speak in church.

36 [1]Was it from you that the word of God *first* went forth? Or has it come to you only?

37 [a]If any one thinks he is a prophet or [b]spiritual, let him recognize that the things which I write to you [c]are the Lord's commandment.

38 But if any one [1]does not recognize *this*, he is not recognized.

39 Therefore, my brethren, [a]desire earnestly to [b]prophesy, and do not forbid to speak in tongues.

40 But [a]let all things be done properly and in an orderly manner.

23 [1]Note 2, vs. 16
[a]Acts 2:13

24 [1]Note 2, vs. 16
[a]1 Cor. 14:1 [b]John 16:8

25 [a]John 4:19 [b]Luke 17:16 [c]Is. 45:14; Zech. 8:23; Dan. 2:47; Acts 4:13

26 [a]1 Cor. 14:15 [b]Rom. 1:13 [c]1 Cor. 12:8-10 [d]Eph. 5:19 [e]1 Cor. 14:6 [f]1 Cor. 14:2 [g]1 Cor. 14:5, 13, 27f.; 12:10 [h]Rom. 14:19

27 [a]1 Cor. 14:2 [b]1 Cor. 14:5, 13, 26ff.; 12:10

29 [a]1 Cor. 14:32, 37; 13:2 [b]1 Cor. 12:10

33 [1]Or, *peace. As in all . . . saints, let . . .* [a]1 Cor. 14:40 [b]1 Cor. 4:17; 7:17 [c]Acts 9:13

34 [a]1 Cor. 11:5, 13 [b]1 Tim. 2:11f.; 1 Pet. 3:1 [c]1 Cor. 14:21

35 [1]Or, *disgraceful*

36 [1]Lit., *Or was*

37 [a]2 Cor. 10:7 [b]1 Cor. 2:15 [c]1 Cor. 7:40; 1 John 4:6

38 [1]Some ancient mss. read, *is ignorant, let him be ignorant*

39 [a]1 Cor. 12:31 [b]1 Cor. 14:1; 13:2

40 [a]1 Cor. 14:33

**The Resurrection of Christ.
The Resurrection of the Dead.**

1 Corinthians 15

1 ªGal. 1:11; Rom. 2:16
ᵇ1 Cor. 3:6; 4:15; Rom. 2:16
ᶜRom. 5:2; 11:20; 2 Cor. 1:24

2 ¹Lit., *to what word I*
ªRom. 11:22 ᵇGal. 3:4

3 ¹Lit., *among the first*
ª1 Cor. 11:23 ᵇJohn 1:29;
Gal. 1:4; Heb. 5:1, 3; 1 Pet.
2:24 ᶜIs. 53:5-12; Matt. 26:24;
Luke 24:25-27; Acts 8:32f.;
17:2f.; 26:22

4 ªMatt. 16:21; John
2:21f.; Acts 2:24 ᵇPs. 16:8ff.;
Acts 2:31; 26:22f.

5 ªLuke 24:34 ᵇ1 Cor. 1:12
ᶜMark 16:14

6 ªActs 7:60; 1 Cor. 15:18,
20

7 ¹Lit., *Jacob* ªActs 12:17
ᵇLuke 24:33, 36f.; Acts 1:3f.

8 ¹Lit., *to an untimely
birth*
ª1 Cor. 9:1; Acts 9:3-8; 22:6-
11; 26:12-18

9 ªEph. 3:8; 2 Cor. 12:11;
1 Tim. 1:15 ᵇActs 8:3

10 ªRom. 12:3 ᵇ2 Cor.
11:23; Col. 1:29; 1 Tim. 4:10
ᶜ1 Cor. 3:6; 2 Cor. 3:5; Phil.
2:13

12 ªActs 17:32; 23:8; 2 Tim.
2:18

14 ª1 Thess. 4:14

15 ¹Or, *concerning* ²I.e.,
the Messiah
ªActs 2:24

17 ªRom. 4:25

NOW ªI make known to you, brethren, the ᵇgospel which I preached to you, which also you received, ᶜin which also you stand,

2 by which also you are saved, ªif you hold fast ¹the word which I preached to you, ᵇunless you believed in vain.

3 For ªI delivered to you ¹as of first importance what I also received, that Christ died ᵇfor our sins ᶜaccording to the Scriptures,

4 and that He was buried, and that He was ªraised on the third day ᵇaccording to the Scriptures,

5 and that ªHe appeared to ᵇCephas, then ᶜto the twelve.

6 After that He appeared to more than five hundred brethren at one time, most of whom remain until now, but some ªhave fallen asleep;

7 then He appeared to ¹ªJames, then to ᵇall the apostles;

8 and last of all, as it were ¹to one untimely born, ªHe appeared to me also.

9 For I am ªthe least of the apostles, who am not fit to be called an apostle, because I ᵇpersecuted the church of God.

10 But by ªthe grace of God I am what I am, and His grace toward me did not prove vain; but I ᵇlabored even more than all of them, yet ᶜnot I, but the grace of God with me.

11 Whether then *it was* I or they, so we preach and so you believed.

12 Now if Christ is preached, that He has been raised from the dead, how do some among you say that there ªis no resurrection of the dead?

13 But if there is no resurrection of the dead, not even Christ has been raised;

14 and ªif Christ has not been raised, then our preaching is vain, your faith also is vain.

15 Moreover we are even found *to be* false witnesses of God, because we witnessed ¹against God that He ªraised ²Christ, whom He did not raise, if in fact the dead are not raised.

16 For if the dead are not raised, not even Christ has been raised;

17 and if Christ has not been raised, your faith is worthless; ªyou are still in your sins.

18 Then those also who [a]have fallen asleep in Christ have perished.

19 If we have only hoped in Christ in this life, we are [a]of all men most to be pitied.

20 But now Christ [a]has been raised from the dead, the [b]first fruits of those who [c]are asleep.

21 For since [a]by a man *came* death, by a man also *came* the resurrection of the dead.

22 For [a]as in Adam all die, so also in [1]Christ all shall be made alive.

23 But each in his own order: Christ [a]the first fruits, after that [b]those who are Christ's at [c]His coming,

24 then *comes* the end, when He delivers up [a]the kingdom to the [b]God and Father, when He has abolished [c]all rule and all authority and power.

25 For He must reign [a]until He has put all His enemies under His feet.

26 The last enemy that will be [a]abolished is death.

27 For [a]HE HAS PUT ALL THINGS IN SUBJECTION UNDER HIS FEET. But when He says, "[b]All things are put in subjection," it is evident that He is excepted who put all things in subjection to Him.

28 And when [a]all things are subjected to Him, then the Son Himself also will be subjected to the one who subjected all things to Him, that God may be all in all.

29 Otherwise, what will those do who are baptized for the dead? If the dead are not raised at all, why then are they baptized for them?

30 Why are we also [a]in danger every hour?

31 I protest, brethren, by the boasting in you, which I have in Christ Jesus our Lord, [a]I die daily.

32 If [1]from human motives I [a]fought with wild beasts at [b]Ephesus, what does it profit me? If the dead are not raised, [c]LET US EAT AND DRINK, FOR TOMORROW WE DIE.

33 [a]Do not be deceived: "Bad company corrupts good morals."

34 [a]Become sober-minded [1]as you ought, and stop sinning; for some have [b]no knowledge of God. [c]I speak *this* to your shame.

35 But [a]some one will say, "How are [b]the dead raised? And with what kind of body do they come?"

36 [a]You fool! That which you [b]sow does not come to life unless it dies;

18 [a]1 Thess. 4:16; Rev. 14:13; 1 Cor. 15:6

19 [a]1 Cor. 4:9; 2 Tim. 3:12

20 [a]1 Pet. 1:3; Acts 2:24 [b]1 Cor. 15:23; Acts 26:23; Rev. 1:5 [c]1 Thess. 4:16; Rev. 14:13; 1 Cor. 15:6

21 [a]Rom. 5:12

22 [1]I.e., the Messiah [a]Rom. 5:14-18

23 [a]1 Cor. 15:20; Acts 26:23; Rev. 1:5 [b]1 Cor. 15:52; 6:14; 1 Thess. 4:16 [c]1 Thess. 2:19

24 [a]Dan. 2:44; 7:14, 27; 2 Pet. 1:11 [b]Eph. 5:20 [c]Rom. 8:38

25 [a]Ps. 110:1; Matt. 22:44

26 [a]2 Tim. 1:10; Rev. 20:14; 21:4

27 [a]Ps. 8:7 [b]Eph. 1:22; Heb. 2:8; Matt. 11:27; 28:18

28 [a]Phil. 3:21 [b]1 Cor. 12:6; 3:23

30 [a]2 Cor. 11:26

31 [a]Rom. 8:36

32 [1]Lit., *according to man* [a]2 Cor. 1:8 [b]1 Cor. 16:8f.; Acts 18:19 [c]Is. 22:13; 56:12; Luke 12:19

33 [a]1 Cor. 6.9

34 [1]Lit., *righteously* [a]Rom. 13:11 [b]Matt. 22:29; Acts 26:8 [c]1 Cor. 6:5

35 [a]Rom. 9:19 [b]Ezek. 37:3

36 [a]Luke 11:40 [b]John 12:24

37 and that which you sow, you do not sow the body which is to be, but a bare grain, perhaps of wheat or of [1]something else.

38 But God gives it a body just as He wished, and [a]to each of the seeds a body of its own.

39 All flesh is not the same flesh, but there is *one flesh* of men, and another flesh of beasts, and another flesh of birds, and another of fish.

40 There are also heavenly bodies and earthly bodies, but the glory of the heavenly is one, and the *glory* of the earthly is another.

41 There is one glory of the sun, and another glory of the moon, and another glory of the stars; for star differs from star in glory.

42 [a]So also is the resurrection of the dead. It is sown [1b]a perishable *body*, it is raised [2c]an imperishable *body;*

43 it is sown in dishonor, it is raised in [a]glory; it is sown in weakness, it is raised in power;

44 it is sown a [a]natural body, it is raised a [b]spiritual body. If there is a natural body, there is also a spiritual *body.*

45 So also it is written, "The first [a]MAN, Adam, BECAME A LIVING SOUL." The [b]last Adam *became* a [c]life-giving spirit.

46 However, the spiritual is not first, but the natural; then the spiritual.

47 The first man is [a]from the earth, [1b]earthy; the second man is from heaven.

48 As is the earthy, so also are those who are earthy; and as is the heavenly, [a]so also are those who are heavenly.

49 And just as we have [a]borne the image of the earthy, [1]we [b]shall also bear the image of the heavenly.

50 Now I say this, brethren, that [a]flesh and blood cannot [b]inherit the kingdom of God; nor does [1]the perishable inherit [2c]the imperishable.

51 Behold, I tell you a [a]mystery; we shall not all sleep, but we shall all be [b]changed,

52 in a moment, in the twinkling of an eye, at the last trumpet; for [a]the trumpet will sound, and [b]the dead will be raised [1]imperishable, and [c]we shall be changed.

53 For this [1]perishable must put on [2a]the imperishable, and this [b]mortal must put on immortality.

54 But when this [1]perishable will have put on [1]the imperishable, and this mortal will have put on

---

37 [1]Lit., *some of the rest*

38 [a]Gen. 1:11

42 [1]Lit., *in corruption* [2]Lit., *in incorruption*
[a]Dan. 12:3; Matt. 13:43
[b]1 Cor. 15:50; Rom. 8:21; Gal. 6:8 [c]Rom. 2:7

43 [a]Phil. 3:21; Col. 3:4

44 [a]1 Cor. 2:14 [b]1 Cor. 15:50

45 [a]Gen. 2:7 [b]Rom. 5:14 [c]John 5:21, 6:57f., Rom. 8:2

47 [1]Lit., *made of dust* [a]John 3:31 [b]Gen. 2:7; 3:19

48 [a]Phil. 3:20f.

49 [1]Some ancient mss. read, *let us also* [a]Gen. 5:3 [b]Rom. 8:29

50 [1]Lit., *corruption* [2]Lit., *incorruption* [a]Matt. 16:17; John 3:5f. [b]1 Cor. 6:9 [c]Rom. 2:7

51 [a]1 Cor. 13:2 [b]2 Cor. 5:2, 4

52 [1]Lit., *incorruptible* [a]Matt. 24:31 [b]John 5:28 [c]1 Thess. 4:15, 17

53 [1]Lit., *corruptible* [2]Lit., *incorruption* [a]Rom. 2:7 [b]2 Cor. 5:4

54 [1]Note vs. 53

immortality, then will come about the saying that is written, "ᵃDEATH IS SWALLOWED UP IN VICTORY.

55 "ᵃO DEATH, WHERE IS YOUR VICTORY? O DEATH, WHERE IS YOUR STING?"

56 The sting of ᵃdeath is sin, and ᵇthe power of sin is the law;

57 but ᵃthanks be to God, who gives us the ᵇvictory through our Lord Jesus Christ.

58 ᵃTherefore, my beloved brethren, be steadfast, immovable, always abounding in ᵇthe work of the Lord, knowing that your toil is not *in* vain in the Lord.

CHAPTER 16

NOW concerning ᵃthe collection for ᵇthe saints, as ᶜI directed the churches of ᵈGalatia, so do you also.

2 On ᵃthe first day of every week let each one of you ¹put aside and save, as he may prosper, that ᵇno collections be made when I come.

3 And when I arrive, ᵃwhomever you may approve, I shall send them with letters to carry your gift to Jerusalem;

4 and if it is fitting for me to go also, they will go with me.

5 But I ᵃshall come to you after I go through ᵇMacedonia, for I ᶜam going through Macedonia;

6 and perhaps I shall stay with you, or even spend the winter, that you may ᵃsend me on my way wherever I may go.

7 For I do not wish to see you now ᵃ*just* in passing; for I hope to remain with you for some time, ᵇif the Lord permits.

8 But I shall remain in ᵃEphesus until ᵇPentecost;

9 for a ᵃwide door ¹for effective *service* has opened to me, and ᵇthere are many adversaries.

10 Now if ᵃTimothy comes, see that he is with you without ¹cause to be afraid; for he is doing ᵇthe Lord's work, as I also am.

11 ᵃLet no one therefore despise him. But ᵇsend him on his way ᶜin peace, so that he may come to me; for I expect him with the brethren.

12 But concerning ᵃApollos our brother, I encouraged him greatly to come to you with the brethren; and it was not at all *his* desire to come now, but he will come when he has opportunity.

---

54 ᵃIs. 25:8

55 ᵃHos. 13:14

56 ᵃRom. 5:12 ᵇRom. 3:20; 4:15; 7:8

57 ᵃ2 Cor. 2:14; Rom. 7:25 marg. ᵇRom. 8:37; Heb. 2:14f.; 1 John 5:4; Rev. 21:4

58 ᵃ2 Pet. 3:14 ᵇ1 Cor. 16:10

1 ᵃActs 24:17 ᵇActs 9:13 ᶜ1 Cor. 4:17 ᵈActs 16:6

2 ¹Lit., *put by himself* ᵃActs 20:7 ᵇ2 Cor. 9:4f.

3 ᵃ2 Cor. 8:18f.; 3:1

5 ᵃ1 Cor. 4:19 ᵇRom. 15:26 ᶜActs 19:21

6 ᵃ1 Cor. 16:11; Acts 15:3

7 ᵃ2 Cor. 1:15f. ᵇActs 18:21

8 ᵃActs 18:19 ᵇActs 2:1

9 ¹Lit., *and* ᵃActs 14:27 ᵇActs 19:9

10 ¹Lit., *fear; for* ᵃActs 16:1; 1 Cor. 4:17; 2 Cor. 1:1 ᵇ1 Cor. 15:58

11 ᵃ1 Tim. 4:12; Titus 2:15 ᵇ1 Cor. 16:6; Acts 15:3 ᶜActs 15:33

12 ᵃActs 18:24 [1 Cor. 1:12; 3:5f.]

13 ᵃMatt. 24:42 ᵇGal. 5:1; Phil. 1:27; 4:1; 1 Thess. 3:8; 2 Thess. 2:15; 1 Cor. 15:1 ᶜ1 Sam. 4:9; 2 Sam. 10:12; Is. 46:8 ᵈPs. 31:24; Eph. 6:10; 3:16; Col. 1:11

14 ᵃ1 Cor. 14:1

15 ¹Lit., *it was* ᵃ1 Cor. 1:16 ᵇRom. 16:5 ᶜActs 18:12 ᵈRom. 15:31 ᵉ1 Cor. 16:1

16 ᵃ1 Thess. 5:12; Heb. 13:17

17 ¹Or, *presence* ²Or, *made up for your absence* ᵃ2 Cor. 7:6f. ᵇPhil. 2:30; 2 Cor. 11:9

18 ᵃ2 Cor. 7:13; Philem. 7, 20 ᵇPhil. 2:29; 1 Thess. 5:12

19 ᵃActs 16:6 ᵇActs 18:2 ᶜRom. 16:5

20 ᵃRom. 16:16

21 ¹Lit., *Paul's* ᵃCol. 4:18; 2 Thess. 3:17; Rom. 16:22; Gal. 6:11; Philem. 19

22 ¹Gr., anathema ²I.e., O [our] Lord come! ᵃRom. 9:3 ᵇRev. 22:20; Phil. 4:5

23 ᵃRom. 16:20

13 ᵃBe on the alert, ᵇstand firm in the faith, ᶜact like men, ᵈbe strong.

14 Let all that you do be done ᵃin love.

15 Now I urge you, brethren (you know the ᵃhousehold of Stephanas, that ¹they were the ᵇfirst fruits of ᶜAchaia, and that they have devoted themselves for ᵈministry to ᵉthe saints),

16 that ᵃyou also be in subjection to such men and to everyone who helps in the work and labors.

17 And I rejoice over the ¹ᵃcoming of Stephanas and Fortunatus and Achaicus; because they have ²supplied ᵇwhat was lacking on your part.

18 For they ᵃhave refreshed my spirit and yours. Therefore ᵇacknowledge such men.

19 The churches of ᵃAsia greet you. ᵇAquila and Prisca greet you heartily in the Lord, with ᶜthe church that is in their house.

20 All the brethren greet you. ᵃGreet one another with a holy kiss.

21 The greeting is in ᵃmy own hand—¹Paul.

22 If any one does not love the Lord, let him be ¹ᵃaccursed. ²ᵇMaranatha.

23 ᵃThe grace of the Lord Jesus be with you.

24 My love be with you all in Christ Jesus. Amen.

THE SECOND EPISTLE OF PAUL TO THE
CORINTHIANS

Salutation.   The Divine Comfort.

1 ¹I.e., true believers; lit., *holy ones* ᵃEph. 1:1; Col. 1:1; 2 Tim. 1:1; Titus 1:1; Rom. 1:1; Gal. 1:1 ᵇGal. 3:26 ᶜ1 Cor. 1:1 ᵈ2 Cor. 1:19; 1 Cor. 16:10; Acts 16:1 ᵉ1 Cor. 10:32 ᶠActs 18:1 ᵍActs 18:12

2 ᵃRom. 1:7

3 ᵃEph. 1:3; 1 Pet. 1:3 ᵇRom. 15:5

4 ᵃ2 Cor. 7:6, 7, 13; Is. 51:12; 66:13

5 ¹Lit., *to us* ᵃ2 Cor. 4:10; Phil. 3:10; Col. 1:24

PAUL, ᵃan apostle of ᵇChrist Jesus ᶜby the will of God, and ᵈTimothy *our* brother, to ᵉthe church of God which is at ᶠCorinth with all the ¹saints who are throughout ᵍAchaia:

2 ᵃGrace to you and peace from God our Father and the Lord Jesus Christ.

3 ᵃBlessed *be* the God and Father of our Lord Jesus Christ, the Father of mercies and ᵇGod of all comfort;

4 who ᵃcomforts us in all our affliction so that we may be able to comfort those who are in any affliction with the comfort with which we ourselves are comforted by God.

5 For just ᵃas the sufferings of Christ are ¹ours

in abundance, so also our comfort is abundant through Christ.

6 But if we are afflicted, it is [a]for your comfort and salvation; or if we are comforted, it is for your comfort, which is effective in the patient enduring of the same sufferings which we also suffer;

7 and our hope for you is firmly grounded, knowing that [a]as you are sharers of our sufferings, so also you are *sharers* of our comfort.

8 For [a]we do not want you to be unaware, brethren, of our [b]affliction which came *to us* in [1][c]Asia, that we were burdened excessively, beyond our strength, so that we despaired even of life;

9 [1]indeed, we had the sentence of death within ourselves in order that we should not trust in ourselves, but in God who raises the dead;

10 who [a]delivered us from so great a *peril of* death, and will deliver *us*, [1]He [b]on whom we have set our hope. And He will yet deliver us,

11 you also joining in [a]helping us through your prayers, that thanks may be given by [b]many persons on our behalf for the favor bestowed upon us through *the prayers of* many.

12 For our [1]proud confidence is this, the testimony of [a]our conscience that in holiness and [b]godly sincerity, [c]not in fleshly wisdom but in the grace of God, we have conducted ourselves in the world, and especially toward you.

13 For we write nothing else to you than what you read and understand, and I hope you will understand [a]until the end;

14 just as you also partially did understand us, that we are your reason to be proud as you also are ours, in [a]the day of our Lord Jesus.

15 And in this confidence I intended at first to [a]come to you, that you might [1]twice receive a [2][b]blessing;

16 [1]that is, to [a]pass [2]your way into [b]Macedonia, and again from Macedonia to come to you, and by you to be [c]helped on my journey [d]to Judea.

17 Therefore, I was not vacillating when I intended to do this, was I? Or that which I purpose, do I purpose [a]according to the flesh, that with me there should be yes, yes and no, no *at the same time?*

18 But as [a]God is faithful, [b]our word to you is not yes and no.

19 For [a]the Son of God, Christ Jesus, who was

6 [a]2 Tim. 2:10; 2 Cor. 4:15; 12:15; Eph. 3:1, 13

7 [a]Rom. 8:17

8 [1]I.e., west coast province of Asia Minor [a]Rom. 1:13 [b]Acts 19:23; 1 Cor. 15:32 [c]Acts 16:6

9 [1]Lit., *but we ourselves*

10 [1]Or, *on whom we have set our hope that He will also . . .* [a]Rom. 15:31 [b]1 Tim. 4:10

11 [a]Rom. 15:30; Phil. 1:19; Philem. 22 [b]2 Cor. 4:15; 9:11f.

12 [1]Lit., *boasting* [a]Acts 23:1; 1 Thess. 2:10; Heb. 13:18 [b]2 Cor. 2:17 [c]1 Cor. 1:17; James 3:15

13 [a]1 Cor. 1:8

14 [a]1 Cor. 1:8

15 [1]Lit., *have a second grace* [2]Some ancient mss. read, *joy* [a]1 Cor. 4:19 [b]Rom. 1:11; 15:29

16 [1]Lit., *and* [2]Lit., *through you into* [a]Acts 19:21; 1 Cor. 16:5-7 [b]Rom. 15:26 [c]Acts 15:3; 1 Cor. 16:6, 11 [d]Acts 19:21

17 [a]2 Cor. 10:2f.; 11:18

18 [a]1 Cor. 1:9 [b]2 Cor. 2:17

19 [a]Matt. 16:16; 26:63, 4:3

19 [b]1 Thess. 1:1; 2 Thess.
1:1; 1 Pet. 5:12; Acts 15:22
[c]2 Cor. 1:1 [d]Heb. 13:8

20 [a]Rom. 15:8 [b]Heb. 13:8
[c]1 Cor. 14:16; Rev. 3:14

21 [a]1 Cor. 1:8 [b]1 John 2:20,
27

22 [1]Or, *down payment*
[a]John 3:33 [b]2 Cor. 5:5; Eph.
1:14; Rom. 8:16

23 [1]Lit., *upon*
[a]Rom. 1:9; Gal. 1:20 [b]1 Cor.
4:21; 2 Cor. 2:1, 3 [c]2 Cor. 1:1

24 [a]1 Pet. 5:3; 2 Cor. 4:5;
11:20 [b]Rom 11:20; 1 Cor.
15:1

1 [1]Or, *as far as I am
concerned*
[a]1 Cor. 4:21; 2 Cor. 12:21

2 [a]2 Cor. 7:8

3 [a]2 Cor. 2:9; 7:8, 12
[b]1 Cor. 4:21; 2 Cor. 12:21
[c]Gal. 5:10; 2 Thess. 3:4;
Philem. 21

4 [a]2 Cor. 2:9; 7:8, 12

5 [1]Lit., *that I be not
burdensome*
[a]1 Cor. 5:1f.

6 [a]1 Cor. 5:4f.; 2 Cor. 7:11

7 [a]Gal. 6:1; Eph. 4:32

9 [1]Lit., *know the proof of
you*
[a]2 Cor. 2:3f. [b]Phil. 2:22;
2 Cor. 8:2 [c]2 Cor. 7:15; 10:6

10 [a]1 Cor. 5:4; 2 Cor. 4:6

preached among you by us,—by me and [b]Silvanus and [c]Timothy—was not yes and no, but is yes [d]in Him.

20 For [a]as many as may be the promises of God, [b]in Him they are yes; wherefore also by Him is [c]our Amen to the glory of God through us.

21 Now He who [a]establishes us with you in Christ and [b]anointed us is God,

22 who also [a]sealed us and [b]gave *us* the Spirit in our hearts as a [1]pledge.

23 But [a]I call God as witness [1]to my soul, that [b]to spare you I came no more to [c]Corinth.

24 Not that we [a]lord it over your faith, but are workers with you for your joy; for in your faith you are [b]standing firm.

CHAPTER 2

BUT I determined this [1]for my own sake, that I [a]would not come to you in sorrow again.

2 For if I [a]cause you sorrow, who then makes me glad but the one whom I made sorrowful?

3 And this is the very thing I [a]wrote you, lest, [b]when I came, I should have sorrow from those who ought to make me rejoice; having [c]confidence in you all, that my joy would be *the joy* of you all.

4 For out of much affliction and anguish of heart I [a]wrote to you with many tears; not that you should be made sorrowful, but that you might know the love which I have especially for you.

5 But [a]if any has caused sorrow, he has caused sorrow not to me, but in some degree—[1]in order not to say too much—to all of you.

6 Sufficient for such a one is [a]this punishment which was *inflicted by* the majority,

7 so that on the contrary you should rather [a]forgive and comfort *him*, lest somehow such a one be overwhelmed by excessive sorrow.

8 Wherefore I urge you to reaffirm *your* love for him.

9 For to this end also [a]I wrote that I might [1][b]put you to the test, whether you are [c]obedient in all things.

10 But whom you forgive anything, I *forgive* also; for indeed what I have forgiven, if I have forgiven anything, *I did it* for your sakes [a]in the presence of Christ,

11 in order that no advantage be taken of us by ᵃSatan; for ᵇwe are not ignorant of his schemes.

12 Now when I came to ᵃTroas for the ᵇgospel of Christ and when a ᶜdoor was opened for me in the Lord,

13 I ᵃhad no rest for my spirit, not finding ᵇTitus my brother; but ᶜtaking my leave of them, I went on to ᵈMacedonia.

14 ᵃBut thanks be to God, who always ᵇleads us in His triumph in Christ, and manifests through us the ᶜsweet aroma of the ᵈknowledge of Him in every place.

15 For we are a ᵃfragrance of Christ to God among ᵇthose who are being saved and among those who are perishing;

16 ᵃto the one an aroma from death to death, to the other an aroma from life to life. And who is ᵇadequate for these things?

17 For we are not like many, ¹ᵃpeddling the word of God, but ᵇas from sincerity, but as from God, we speak in Christ ᶜin the sight of God.

CHAPTER 3

Aʀᴇ we beginning to ᵃcommend ourselves again? Or do we need, as some, ᵇletters of commendation to you or from you?

2 ᵃYou are our letter, written in our hearts, known and read by all men;

3 being manifested that you are a letter of Christ, ¹ᵃcared for by us, written not with ink, but with the Spirit of ᵇthe living God, not on ᶜtablets of stone, but on ᵈtablets of ²ᶜhuman hearts.

4 And such ᵃconfidence we have through Christ toward God.

5 Not that we are adequate in ourselves to consider anything as *coming* from ourselves, but ᵃour adequacy is from God,

6 who also made us adequate *as* ᵃservants of a ᵇnew covenant, not of ᶜthe letter, but of the Spirit; for the letter kills, but ᵈthe Spirit gives life.

7 But if the ᵃministry of death, ᵇin letters engraved on stones, came ¹with glory, ᶜso that the sons of Israel could not look intently at the face of Moses because of the glory of his face, fading *as* it was,

8 how shall the ministry of the Spirit fail to be even more with glory?

11 ᵃMatt. 4:10 ᵇLuke 22:31; 2 Cor. 4:4; 1 Pet. 5:8

12 ᵃActs 16:8 ᵇ2 Cor. 4:3, 4; 8:18; 9:13; 10:14; 11:4, 7; 1 Thess. 3:2; Rom. 1:1 ᶜActs 14:27

13 ᵃ2 Cor. 7:5 ᵇ2 Cor. 7:6, 13f.; 8:6, 16, 23; 12:18; Gal. 2:1, 3; 2 Tim. 4:10; Titus 1:4 ᶜMark 6:46 ᵈRom. 15:26

14 ᵃRom. 1:8; 6:17; 1 Cor. 15:57; 2 Cor. 8:16; 9:15 ᵇCol. 2:15 [Gr.] ᶜEph. 5:2; Phil. 4:18; Song of Sol. 1:3; Ezek. 20:41 ᵈ1 Cor. 12:8

15 ᵃEph. 5:2; Phil. 4:18; Song of Sol. 1:3; Ezek. 20:41 ᵇ1 Cor. 1:18

16 ᵃLuke 2:34; John 9:39; 1 Pet. 2:7f. ᵇ2 Cor. 3:5f.

17 ¹Or, *corrupting* ᵃ2 Cor. 4:2; Gal. 1:6-9 ᵇ2 Cor. 1:12; 1 Cor. 5:8; 1 Thess. 2:4; 1 Pet. 4:11 ᶜ2 Cor. 12:19

1 ᵃ2 Cor. 5:12; 10:12, 18; 12:11 ᵇActs 18:27; Rom. 16:1; 1 Cor. 16:3

2 ᵃ1 Cor. 9:2

3 ¹Lit., *served* ²Lit., *hearts of flesh* ᵃ2 Cor. 3:6 ᵇMatt. 16:16 ᶜ2 Cor. 3:7; Ex. 24:12; 31:18; 32:15f. ᵈProv. 3:3; 7:3; Jer. 17:1 ᵉJer. 31:33; Ezek. 11:19

4 ᵃEph. 3:12

5 ᵃ1 Cor. 15:10

6 ᵃ1 Cor. 3:5 ᵇLuke 22:20 ᶜRom. 2:29 ᵈJohn 6:63; Rom. 7:6

7 ¹Or, *in glory* ᵃ2 Cor. 3:9; Rom. 7:5f.; Gal. 3:10, 21f.; Rom. 4:15; 5:20 ᵇ2 Cor. 3:3; Ex. 24:12; 31:18; 32:15f. ᶜ2 Cor. 3:13; Ex. 34:29-35

9 a2 Cor. 3:7; Deut. 27:26; Heb. 12:18-21 bRom. 1:17; 3:21f.

11 1Lit., through

12 a2 Cor. 7:4 b2 Cor. 7:4; Eph. 6:19; Acts 4:13, 29; 1 Thess. 2:2

13 a2 Cor. 3:7

14 1Or, remains, it not being revealed that it is done away in Christ. aRom. 11:7; 2 Cor. 4:4 bActs 13:15 c2 Cor. 3:6

16 aEx. 34:34; Rom. 11:27

17 aGal. 4:6; Is. 61:1f. bJohn 8:32; Gal. 5:1, 13

18 a1 Cor. 13:12 b2 Cor. 4:4, 6; John 17:22, 24 cRom. 8:29 d2 Cor. 3:17

1 a1 Cor. 3:5 b1 Cor. 7:25 c2 Cor. 4:16; Luke 18:1; Gal. 6:9; Eph. 3:13; 2 Thess. 3:13

2 aRom. 6:21; 1 Cor. 4:5 b2 Cor. 2:17 c2 Cor. 5:11f.

3 1Lit., in a2 Cor. 2:12 b2 Cor. 3:14; 1 Cor. 2:6ff. c1 Cor. 1:18; 2 Cor. 2:15

4 1Lit., age 2Or, that the light . . . image of God, should not dawn upon them aJohn 12:31 bMatt. 13:22 c2 Cor. 3:14 d2 Cor. 4:6; Acts 26:18 e2 Cor. 3:18; 4:6 fCol. 1:15; Phil. 2:6; Heb. 1:3; John 1:18

5 1Or, through Jesus a1 Thess. 2:6f. [1 Cor. 4:15f.]

6 aGen. 1:3 b2 Pet. 1:19

9 For if ªthe ministry of condemnation has glory, much more does the ᵇministry of righteousness abound in glory.

10 For indeed what had glory, in this case has no glory on account of the glory that surpasses *it*.

11 For if that which fades away *was* ¹with glory, much more that which remains *is* in glory.

12 ªHaving therefore such a hope, ᵇwe use great boldness in *our* speech,

13 and *are* not as Moses, ªwho used to put a veil over his face that the sons of Israel might not look intently at the end of what was fading away.

14 But their minds were ªhardened; for until this very day at the ᵇreading of ᶜthe old covenant the same veil ¹remains unlifted, because it is removed in Christ.

15 But to this day whenever Moses is read, a veil lies over their heart;

16 ªBUT WHENEVER A MAN TURNS TO THE LORD, THE VEIL IS TAKEN AWAY.

17 Now the Lord is the Spirit; and where ªthe Spirit of the Lord is, ᵇthere is liberty.

18 But we all, with unveiled face ªbeholding as in a mirror the ᵇglory of the Lord, are being ᶜtransformed into the same image from glory to glory, just as from ᵈthe Lord, the Spirit.

CHAPTER 4

THEREFORE since we have this ªministry, as we ᵇreceived mercy, we ᶜdo not lose heart,

2 but we have renounced the ªthings hidden because of shame, not walking in craftiness or ᵇadulterating the word of God, but by the manifestation of truth ᶜcommending ourselves to every man's conscience in the sight of God.

3 And even if our ªgospel is ᵇveiled, it is veiled ¹to ᶜthose who are perishing,

4 in whose case ªthe god of ᵇthis ¹world has ᶜblinded the minds of the unbelieving, ²that they might not see the ᵈlight of the gospel of the ᵉglory of Christ, who is the ᶠimage of God.

5 For we ªdo not preach ourselves but Christ Jesus as Lord, and ourselves as your bond-servants ¹for Jesus' sake.

6 For God, who said, "ªLight shall shine out of darkness," is the One who has ᵇshone in our

hearts to give the ᶜlight of the knowledge of the glory of God in the face of Christ.

7 But we have this treasure in ᵃearthen vessels, that the surpassing greatness of ᵇthe power may be of God and not from ourselves;

8 *we are* ᵃafflicted in every way, but not ᵇcrushed; ᶜperplexed, but not despairing;

9 ᵃpersecuted, but not ᵇforsaken; ᶜstruck down, but not destroyed;

10 ᵃalways carrying about in the body the dying of Jesus, that ᵇthe life of Jesus also may be manifested in our body.

11 For we who live are constantly being delivered over to death for Jesus' sake, that the life of Jesus also may be manifested in our mortal flesh.

12 So death works in us, but life in you.

13 But having the same ᵃspirit of faith, according to what is written, "ᵇI BELIEVED, THEREFORE I SPOKE," we also believe, therefore also we speak;

14 knowing that He who ᵃraised the Lord Jesus ᵇwill raise us also with Jesus and will ᶜpresent us with you.

15 For all things *are* ᵃfor your sakes, that the grace which is ¹ᵇspreading to more and more people may cause the giving of thanks to abound to the glory of God.

16 Therefore we ᵃdo not lose heart, but though our outer man is decaying, yet our ᵇinner man is ᶜbeing renewed day by day.

17 For momentary, ᵃlight affliction is producing for us an eternal weight of glory far beyond all comparison,

18 while we ᵃlook not at the things which are seen, but at the things which are not seen; for the things which are seen are temporal, but the things which are not seen are eternal.

CHAPTER 5

FOR we know that if ¹the ᵃearthly ᵇtent which is our house is torn down, we have a building from God, a house ᶜnot made with hands, eternal in the heavens.

2 For indeed in this *house* we ᵃgroan, longing to be ᵇclothed with our dwelling from heaven;

3 inasmuch as we, having put it on, shall not be found naked.

4 For indeed while we are in this tent, we

---

6 ᶜ2 Cor. 4:4; Acts 26:18

7 ᵃ2 Cor. 5:1; 2 Tim. 2:20; Job 4:19; 10:9; 33:6; Lam. 4:2 ᵇ1 Cor. 2:5; Judg. 7:2

8 ᵃ2 Cor. 7:5; 1:8 ᵇ2 Cor. 6:12 ᶜGal. 4:20

9 ᵃJohn 15:20; Rom. 8:35f. ᵇHeb. 13:5; Ps. 129:2 ᶜPs. 37:24; Prov. 24:16; Mic. 7:8

10 ᵃRom. 6:5; 8:36; Gal. 6:17 ᵇRom. 6:8

13 ᵃ1 Cor. 12:9 ᵇPs. 116:10

14 ᵃActs 2:24 ᵇ1 Thess. 4:14 ᶜEph. 5:27; Col. 1:22; Jude 24; Luke 21:36

15 ¹Lit., *being multiplied through the many* ᵃ2 Cor. 1:6; Rom. 8:28 ᵇ2 Cor. 1:11; 1 Cor. 9:19

16 ᵃ2 Cor. 4:1 ᵇRom. 7:22 ᶜCol. 3:10; Is. 40:29, 31

17 ᵃRom. 8:18

18 ᵃ2 Cor. 5:7; Rom. 8:24; Heb. 11:1, 13

1 ¹Lit., *our earthly house of the tent* ᵃ1 Cor. 15:47; 2 Cor. 4:7; Job 4:19 ᵇ2 Pet. 1:13f. ᶜMark 14:58; Acts 7:48; Heb. 9:11, 24

2 ᵃRom. 8:23; 2 Cor. 5:4 ᵇ1 Cor. 15:53f.; 2 Cor. 5:4

379

2 Corinthians 5

**At Home with the Lord.
The New Creature.**

4 ª2 Cor. 5:2 b1 Cor.
15:53f.; 2 Cor. 5:2 c1 Cor.
15:54

5 ¹Or, *down payment*
ª2 Cor. 1:22; Rom. 8:23

6 ªHeb. 11:13f.

7 ¹Or, *appearance*
ª2 Cor. 4:18; 1 Cor. 13:12

8 ªPhil. 1:23 bJohn 12:26;
Phil. 1:23

9 ªRom. 14:18; Col. 1:10;
1 Thess. 4:1

10 ¹Lit., *the things through
the body*
ªMatt. 16:27; Acts 10:42;
Rom. 2:16; 14:10, 12, Eph.
6:8

11 ªHeb. 10:31; 12:29; Jude
23 b2 Cor. 4:2

12 ª2 Cor. 3:1 b2 Cor. 1:14;
Phil. 1:26

13 ¹Lit., *were*
ª2 Cor. 11:1, 16ff.; 12:11;
Mark 3:21

14 ªActs 18:5 bRom. 5:15;
6:6f.; Gal. 2:20; Col. 3:3

15 ªRom. 14:7-9

16 ¹I.e., by what he is in the
flesh ª2 Cor. 11:18; Phil. 3:4;
John 8:15

17 ¹Or, *there is* a new
creation
ªRom. 16:7 bGal. 6:15; John
3:3; Rom. 6:4 cIs. 43:18f.;
65:17; Eph. 4:24; Rev. 21:4f.

18 ª1 Cor. 11:12 bCol. 1:20;
Rom. 5:10 c1 Cor. 3:5

19 ¹Lit., *having committed*
²Lit., *placed in us*
ªCol. 2:9 bRom. 4:8; 1 Cor.
13:5

380

ªgroan, being burdened, because we do not want to be unclothed, but to be bclothed, in order that what is cmortal may be swallowed up by life.

5 Now He who prepared us for this very purpose is God, who ªgave to us the Spirit as a ¹pledge.

6 Therefore, being always of good courage, and knowing that ªwhile we are at home in the body we are absent from the Lord—

7 for ªwe walk by faith, not by ¹sight—

8 we are of good courage, I say, and ªprefer rather to be absent from the body and bto be at home with the Lord.

9 Therefore also we have as our ambition, whether at home or absent, to be ªpleasing to Him.

10 For we must all appear before ªthe judgment-seat of Christ, that each one may be recompensed for ¹his deeds in the body, according to what he has done, whether good or bad.

11 Therefore knowing the ªfear of the Lord, we persuade men, but we are made manifest to God; and I hope that we are bmade manifest also in your consciences.

12 We are not ªagain commending ourselves to you but *are* giving you an boccasion to be proud of us, that you may have *an answer* for those who take pride in appearance, and not in heart.

13 For if we ¹are ªbeside ourselves, it is for God; if we are of sound mind, it is for you.

14 For the love of Christ ªcontrols us, having concluded this, that bone died for all, therefore all died;

15 and He died for all, that they who live should no longer ªlive for themselves, but for Him who died and rose again on their behalf.

16 Therefore from now on we recognize no man ¹ªaccording to the flesh; even though we have known Christ ¹according to the flesh, yet now we know *Him thus* no longer.

17 Therefore if any man is ªin Christ, ¹*he is* ba new creature; cthe old things passed away; behold, new things have come.

18 Now ªall *these* things are from God, bwho reconciled us to Himself through Christ, and gave us the cministry of reconciliation,

19 namely, that ªGod was in Christ reconciling the world to Himself, bnot counting their trespasses against them, and ¹He has ²committed to us the word of reconciliation.

20 Therefore, we are [a]ambassadors for Christ, [b]as though God were entreating through us; we beg you on behalf of Christ, be [c]reconciled to God.

21 He made Him who [a]knew no sin *to be* [b]sin on our behalf, that we might become the [c]righteousness of God in Him.

CHAPTER 6

A ND [a]working together *with Him*, [b]we also urge you not to receive [c]the grace of God in vain;—

2 for He says,

"[a]AT THE ACCEPTABLE TIME I LISTENED TO YOU,

AND ON THE DAY OF SALVATION I HELPED YOU";

behold, now is "THE ACCEPTABLE TIME," behold, now is "THE DAY OF SALVATION";—

3 [a]giving no cause for offense in anything, in order that the ministry be not discredited,

4 but in everything [a]commending ourselves as [1][b]servants of God, [c]in much endurance, in afflictions, in hardships, in distresses,

5 in [a]stripes, in [a]imprisonments, in [b]tumults, in labors, in watchings, in [c]fastings,

6 in purity, in [a]knowledge, in [b]patience, in kindness, in the [c]Holy Spirit, in [d]genuine love,

7 in [a]the word of truth, in [b]the power of God; by [c]the weapons of righteousness for the right hand and the left,

8 by glory and [a]dishonor, by [b]evil report and good report; *regarded* as [c]deceivers and yet [d]true;

9 as unknown yet well-known, as [a]dying yet behold, [b]we live; as [1]punished yet not put to death,

10 as [a]sorrowful yet always [a]rejoicing, as [b]poor yet making many rich, as [c]having nothing yet possessing [d]all things.

11 [a]Our mouth [1]has spoken freely to you, O Corinthians, our [b]heart is opened wide.

12 You are not restrained [1]by us, but [a]you are restrained in your own [2]affections.

13 Now in a like [a]exchange—I speak as to [b]children,—open wide *to us* also.

14 [a]Do not be [1]bound together with [b]unbelievers; for what [c]partnership have righteousness and lawlessness, or what fellowship has light with darkness?

15 Or what [a]harmony has Christ with [1]Belial,

20 [a]Eph. 6:20; Mal. 2:7
[b]2 Cor. 6:1 [c]Col. 1:20; Rom. 5:10

21 [a]Heb. 4:15; 7:26; 1 Pet. 2:22; 1 John 3:5; Acts 3:14, [b]Rom. 8:3; Gal. 3:13; Rom. 3:25; 4:25 [c]Rom. 1:17; 3:21f.; 1 Cor. 1:30

1 [a]1 Cor. 3:9 [b]2 Cor. 5:20 [c]Acts 11:23

2 [a]Is. 49:8

3 [a]1 Cor. 8:9, 13; 9:12

4 [1]Or, *ministers* [a]Rom. 3:5 [b]1 Cor. 3:5; 2 Tim. 2:24f. [c]2 Cor. 6:4ff.; 4:8-11; 11:23-27; 12:10; Acts 9:16

5 [a]Acts 16:23 [b]Acts 19:23ff. [c]1 Cor. 4:11

6 [a]2 Cor. 11:6; 1 Cor. 12:8 [b]2 Cor. 1:23; 2:10; 13:10 [c]1 Thess. 1:5; 1 Cor. 2:4 [d]Rom. 12:9

7 [a]2 Cor. 2:17; 4:2 [b]1 Cor. 2:5 [c]2 Cor. 10:4; Rom. 13:12; Eph. 6:11ff.

8 [a]1 Cor. 4:10 [b]1 Cor. 4:13; Rom. 3:8; 2 Cor. 12:16 [c]Matt. 27:63 [d]2 Cor. 1:18; 4:2; 1 Thess. 2:3f.

9 [1]Or, *disciplined* [a]Rom. 8:36 [b]2 Cor. 1:8, 10; 4:11

10 [a]2 Cor. 7:4; 1 Thess. 1:6; Phil. 2:17; 4:4; Col. 1:24; John 16:22 [b]2 Cor. 8:9; 1 Cor. 1:5 [c]Acts 3:6 [d]Rom. 8:32; 1 Cor. 3:21

11 [1]Lit., *is open to you* [a]Ezek. 33:22; Eph. 6:19 [b]2 Cor. 7:3; Is. 60:5

12 [1]Or, *in us* [2]Lit., *inward parts* [a]2 Cor. 7:2

13 [a]Gal. 4:12 [b]1 Cor. 4:14

14 [1]Lit., *unequally yoked* [a]Deut. 22:10; 1 Cor. 5:9f. [b]1 Cor. 6:6 [c]Eph. 5:7, 11; 1 John 1:6

15 [1]Gr., *Beliar* [a]1 Cor. 10:21

15 [2]Lit., *what part has a believer with an unbeliever*
[b]Acts 5:14; 1 Pet. 1:21
[c]1 Cor. 6:6

16 [a]1 Cor. 10:21 [b]1 Cor. 3:16 [c]Matt. 16:16 [d]Lev. 26:12; Ex. 29:45; Ezek. 37:27; Jer. 31:1 [e]Ex. 25:8; John 14:23 [f]Rev. 2:1

17 [a]Is. 52:11 [b]Rev. 18:4

18 [a]Hos. 1:10; Is. 43:6 [b]Rom. 8:14

1 [a]Heb. 6:9 [b]1 Pet. 1:15f.

2 [a]2 Cor. 6:12f.; 12:15

3 [a]2 Cor. 6:11f. [b]Phil. 1:7

4 [1]Lit., *to* [a]2 Cor. 3:12 [b]2 Cor. 7:14; 8:24; 9:2f.; 10:8; 2 Thess. 1:4; Phil. 1:26 [c]2 Cor. 1:4 [d]2 Cor. 6:10

5 [a]2 Cor. 2:13; Rom. 15:26 [b]2 Cor. 4:8 [c]Deut. 32:25

6 [1]Or, *humble* [a]2 Cor. 1:3f. [b]2 Cor. 7:13 [c]2 Cor. 2:13; 7:13f.

8 [a]2 Cor. 2:2

or [2]what has a [b]believer in common with an [c]unbeliever?

16 Or [a]what agreement has the temple of God with idols? For we are [b]the temple of [c]the living God; just as God said,

"[d]I WILL [e]DWELL IN THEM AND [f]WALK AMONG
　　THEM;
AND I WILL BE THEIR GOD, AND THEY SHALL
　　BE MY PEOPLE.

17 "[a]Therefore, [b]COME OUT FROM THEIR MIDST
　　AND BE SEPARATE, says the Lord.
AND DO NOT TOUCH WHAT IS UNCLEAN;
AND I WILL WELCOME YOU.

18　　[a]AND I WILL BE A FATHER TO YOU.
AND YOU SHALL BE [b]SONS and daughters TO
　　ME,
SAYS THE LORD ALMIGHTY."

CHAPTER 7

THEREFORE, having these promises, [a]beloved, [b]let us cleanse ourselves from all defilement of flesh and spirit, perfecting holiness in the fear of God.

2 [a]Make room for us *in your hearts*; we wronged no one, we corrupted no one, we took advantage of no one.

3 I do not speak to condemn you; for I have said [a]before that you are [b]in our hearts to die together and to live together.

4 Great is my [a]confidence [1]in you, great is my [b]boasting on your behalf; I am filled with [c]comfort. I am overflowing with [d]joy in all our affliction.

5 For even when we came into [a]Macedonia our flesh had no rest, but we were [b]afflicted on every side: [c]conflicts without, fears within.

6 But [a]God, who comforts the [1]depressed, [b]comforted us by the coming of [c]Titus;

7 and not only by his coming, but also by the comfort with which he was comforted in you, as he reported to us your longing, your mourning, your zeal for me; so that I rejoiced even more.

8 For though I [a]caused you sorrow by my letter, I do not regret it; though I did regret it,—*for* I see that that letter caused you sorrow, though only for a while—

9 I now rejoice, not that you were made sorrowful, but that you were made sorrowful to *the*

point of repentance; for you were made sorrowful according to *the will of* God, in order that you might not suffer loss in anything through us.

10 For the sorrow that is according to *the will of* God produces a [a]repentance [1]without regret, *leading* to salvation; but the sorrow of the world produces death.

11 For behold what earnestness this very thing, this [1]godly sorrow, has produced in you, what vindication of yourselves, what indignation, what fear, what [a]longing, what zeal, what [b]avenging of wrong! In everything you [c]demonstrated yourselves to be innocent in the matter.

12 So although [a]I wrote to you *it was* not for the sake of [b]the offender, nor for the sake of the one offended, but that your earnestness on our behalf might be made known to you in the sight of God.

13 For this reason we have been [a]comforted.

And besides our comfort, we rejoiced even much more for the joy of [b]Titus, because his [c]spirit has been refreshed by you all.

14 For if in anything I have [a]boasted to him about you, I was not put to shame; but as we spoke all things to you in truth, so also our boasting before [b]Titus proved to be *the* truth.

15 And his [1]affection abounds all the more toward you, as he remembers the [a]obedience of you all, how you received him with [b]fear and trembling.

16 I rejoice that in everything [a]I have confidence in you.

CHAPTER 8

NOW, brethren, we *wish to* make known to you the grace of God which has been [a]given in the churches of [b]Macedonia,

2 that in a great ordeal of affliction their abundance of joy and their deep poverty overflowed in the [a]wealth of their liberality.

3 For I testify that [a]according to their ability, and beyond their ability *they gave* of their own accord,

4 begging us with much entreaty for the [a]favor of participation in the [1b]support of the [2]saints,

5 and *this*, not as we had [1]expected, but they first [a]gave themselves to the Lord and to us by [b]the will of God.

10 [1]Or, *leading to a salvation without regret*
[a]Acts 11:18

11 [1]Lit., *sorrow according to God*
[a]2 Cor. 7:7 [b]2 Cor. 2:6
[c]Rom. 3:5

12 [a]2 Cor. 7:8; 2:3, 9 [b]1 Cor. 5:1f.

13 [a]2 Cor. 7:6 [b]2 Cor. 2:13; 7:6, 14 [c]1 Cor. 16:18

14 [a]2 Cor. 7:4; 8:24; 9:2f.; 10:8; 2 Thess. 1:4; Phil. 1:26 [b]2 Cor. 2:13; 7:6, 13

15 [1]Lit., *inward parts* [a]2 Cor. 2:9 [b]Phil. 2:12; 1 Cor. 2:3

16 [a]2 Cor. 2:3

1 [a]2 Cor. 8:5 [b]Acts 16:9

2 [a]Rom. 2:4

3 [a]2 Cor. 8:11; 1 Cor. 16:2

4 [1]Lit., *service to the saints* [2]I.e., true believers; lit., *holy ones* [a]Rom. 15:25f.; Acts 24:17 [b]2 Cor. 8:19f.; 9:1, 12f.; Rom. 15:31

5 [1]Lit., *hoped* [a]2 Cor. 8:1 [b]1 Cor. 1:1

6 ᵃ2 Cor. 8:17; 12:18
ᵇ2 Cor. 8:16, 23; 2:13 ᶜ2 Cor.
8:10 ᵈRom. 15:25f.; Acts
24:17

7 ¹Lit., *love from us in
you*; some ancient mss. read,
your love for us
ᵃ2 Cor. 9:8 ᵇ1 Cor. 1:5; 12:8;
Rom. 15:14

8 ᵃ1 Cor. 7:6

9 ᵃ2 Cor. 13:14 ᵇPhil. 2:6f.;
Matt. 20:28; 2 Cor. 6:10

10 ᵃ1 Cor. 7:25, 40 ᵇ2 Cor.
9:2; 1 Cor. 16:2f.

11 ¹Lit., *the doing*
ᵃ2 Cor. 8:12, 19; 9:2

12 ᵃMark 12:43f.; Luke
21:3; 2 Cor. 9:7

14 ᵃ2 Cor. 9:12; Acts 4:34

15 ᵃEx. 16:18

16 ᵃ2 Cor. 2:14 ᵇRev. 17:17
ᶜ2 Cor. 8:6, 23; 2:13

17 ᵃ2 Cor. 8:6; 12:18

18 ᵃ2 Cor. 12:18; 1 Cor.
16:3 ᵇ2 Cor. 2:12 ᶜ1 Cor.
7:17; 4:17

19 ᵃRom. 5:3 ᵇ1 Cor. 16:3f.;
Acts 14:23 ᶜ2 Cor. 8:4, 6
ᵈ2 Cor. 8:11, 12; 9:2

20 ¹Lit., *avoiding this*

6   Consequently we ᵃurged ᵇTitus that as he had previously ᶜmade a beginning, so he would also complete in you ᵈthis gracious work as well.

7   But just as you ᵃabound ᵇin everything, in faith and utterance and knowledge and in all earnestness and in the ¹love we inspired in you, *see* that you ᵃabound in this gracious work also.

8   I ᵃam not speaking *this* as a command, but as proving through the earnestness of others the sincerity of your love also.

9   For you know ᵃthe grace of our Lord Jesus Christ, that ᵇthough He was rich, yet for your sake He became poor, that you through His poverty might become rich.

10   And I ᵃgive *my* opinion in this matter, for this is to your advantage, who were the first to begin ᵇa year ago not only to do *this*, but also to desire *to do it*.

11   But now finish ¹doing it also; that just as *there was* the ᵃreadiness to desire it, so *there may be* also the completion of it by your ability.

12   For if the readiness is present, it is acceptable ᵃaccording to what *a man* has, not according to what he does not have.

13   For *this* is not for the case of others *and* for your affliction, but by way of equality—

14   at this present time your abundance *being a supply* for ᵃtheir want, that their abundance also may become *a supply* for ᵃyour want, that there may be equality;

15   as it is written, "ᵃHE WHO *gathered* MUCH DID NOT HAVE TOO MUCH, AND HE WHO *gathered* LITTLE HAD NO LACK."

16   But ᵃthanks be to God, who ᵇputs the same earnestness on your behalf in the heart of ᶜTitus.

17   For he not only accepted our ᵃappeal, but being himself very earnest, he has gone to you of his own accord.

18   And we have sent along with him ᵃthe brother whose fame in *the things of* the ᵇgospel *has spread* through ᶜall the churches;

19   ᵃand not only *this*, but he has also been ᵇappointed by the churches to travel with us in ᶜthis gracious work, which is being administered by us for the glory of the Lord Himself, and *to show* our ᵈreadiness,

20   ¹taking precaution that no one should discredit us in our administration of this generous gift;

21 for we [a]have regard for what is honorable, not only in [b]the sight of the Lord, but also in the sight of men.

22 And we have sent with them our brother, whom we have often tested and found diligent in many things, but now even more diligent, because of *his* great confidence in you.

23 As for [a]Titus, *he is* my [b]partner and fellow-worker [1]among you; as for our [c]brethren, *they are* [2][d]messengers of the churches, [e]a glory to Christ.

24 Therefore [1]openly before the churches [2]show them the proof of your love and of our [a]reason for boasting about you.

CHAPTER 9

FOR [a]it is superfluous for me to write to you about this [b]ministry to the [1]saints;

2 for I know your readiness, of which I [a]boast about you to the [b]Macedonians, *namely*, that [c]Achaia has been prepared since [d]last year, and your zeal has stirred up most of them.

3 But I have sent the brethren, that our [a]boasting about you may not be made empty in this case, that, [b]as I was saying, you may be prepared;

4 lest if any [a]Macedonians come with me and find you unprepared, we (not to speak of you) should be put to shame by this confidence.

5 So I thought it necessary to urge the [a]brethren that they would go on ahead to you and arrange beforehand your previously promised [1][b]bountiful gift, that the same might be ready as a [1c]bountiful gift, and not [2d]affected by covetousness.

6 Now this *I say*, [a]he who sows sparingly shall also reap sparingly; and he who sows [1]bountifully shall also reap [1]bountifully.

7 Let each one *do* just as he has purposed in his heart; not [a]grudgingly or under compulsion; for [b]God loves a cheerful giver.

8 And [a]God is able to make all grace abound to you, that always having all sufficiency in everything, you may have an abundance for every good deed;

9 as it is written,

"[a]HE SCATTERED ABROAD, HE GAVE TO THE POOR,
HIS RIGHTEOUSNESS ABIDES FOREVER."

21 [a]Rom. 12:17 [b]Rom. 14:18

23 [1]Lit., *for you* [2]Lit., *apostles* [a]2 Cor. 8:6 [b]Philem. 17 [c]2 Cor. 8:18, 22 [d]Phil. 2:25; John 13:16 [e]1 Cor. 11:7

24 [1]Lit., *in the face of the churches* [2]Or, *show the proof . . . for boasting to them about you* [a]2 Cor. 7:4

1 [1]I.e., true believers; lit., *holy ones* [a]1 Thess. 4:9 [b]2 Cor. 8:4

2 [a]2 Cor. 7:4 [b]Rom. 15:26 [c]Acts 18:12 [d]2 Cor. 8:10

3 [a]2 Cor. 7:4 [b]1 Cor. 16:2

4 [a]Rom. 15:26

5 [1]Gr., *blessing* [2]Lit., *as covetousness* [a]2 Cor. 9:3 [b]Gen. 33:11; Judg. 1:15; 2 Cor. 9:6 [c]Phil. 4:17 [d]2 Cor. 12:17f.

6 [1]Lit., *with blessings* [a]Prov. 11:24f.; 22:9; Gal. 6:7, 9

7 [a]Deut. 15:10; 1 Chr. 29:17; Rom. 12:8; 2 Cor. 8:12 [b]Prov. 22:8 [Sept.]; Ex. 25:2; 2 Cor. 8:12

8 [a]Eph. 3:20

9 [a]Ps. 112:9

10 ªIs. 55:10 ᵇHos. 10:12

11 ª1 Cor. 1:5 ᵇ2 Cor. 1:11

12 ¹I.e., true believers; lit.,
holy ones
ª2 Cor. 8:14 ᵇ2 Cor. 1:11

13 ¹Or, *sharing with them*
ª2 Cor. 8:4; Rom. 15:31
ᵇRom. 9:8 ᶜ1 Tim. 6:12f.;
Heb. 3:1; 4:14; 10:23 ᵈ2 Cor.
2:12

15 ª2 Cor. 2:14 ᵇRom.
5:15f.

1 ¹Lit., *lowly*
ªGal. 5:2; Eph. 3:1; Col. 1:23
ᵇRom. 12:1 ᶜMatt. 11:29;
1 Cor. 4:21; Phil. 4:5 ᵈ2 Cor.
10:10; 1 Cor. 2:3f.

2 ª2 Cor. 13:2, 10; 1 Cor.
4:21 ᵇ1 Cor. 4:18f. ᶜ2 Cor.
1:17; Rom. 8:4

3 ª2 Cor. 1:17; Rom. 8:4

4 ¹Or, *mighty before God*
ª2 Cor. 6:7; 1 Cor. 9:7;
1 Tim. 1:18 ᵇActs 7:20 marg.
ᶜJer. 1:10; 2 Cor. 10:8; 13:10

5 ªIs. 2:11f. ᵇ2 Cor. 9:13

6 ª2 Cor. 2:9

7 ¹Or, *Look at . . . ,* or, *Do
you look at . . . ?* ²Lit., *what
is before your face*
ªJohn 7:24; 2 Cor. 5:12
ᵇ1 Cor. 1:12; 14:37 ᶜ2 Cor.
11:23; 1 Cor. 9:1; Gal. 1:12

8 ¹Or, *more abundantly*
ª2 Cor. 7:4 ᵇ2 Cor. 13:10

386

10   Now He who supplies ªseed to the sower and bread for food, will supply and multiply your seed for sowing and ᵇincrease the harvest of your righteousness;

11   you will be ªenriched in everything for all liberality, which through us is producing ᵇthanksgiving to God.

12   For the ministry of this service is not only fully supplying ªthe needs of the ¹saints, but is also overflowing ᵇthrough many thanksgivings to God.

13   Because of the proof given by this ªministry they will ᵇglorify God for *your* obedience to your ᶜconfession of the ᵈgospel of Christ, and for the liberality of your ¹contribution to them and to all,

14   while they also, by prayer on your behalf, yearn for you because of the surpassing grace of God in you.

15   ªThanks be to God for His indescribable ᵇgift!

CHAPTER 10

Now ªI Paul myself ᵇurge you by the ᶜmeekness and gentleness of Christ,—I who ᵈam ¹meek when face to face with you, but bold toward you when absent!—

2   I ask that ªwhen I am present I may not be bold with the confidence with which I propose to be courageous against ᵇsome, who regard us as if we walked ᶜaccording to the flesh.

3   For though we walk in the flesh, we do not war ªaccording to the flesh,

4   for the ªweapons of our warfare are not of the flesh, but ¹ᵇdivinely powerful ᶜfor the destruction of fortresses.

5   We *are* destroying speculations and every ªlofty thing raised up against the knowledge of God, and *we are* taking every thought captive to the ᵇobedience of Christ,

6   and we are ready to punish all disobedience, whenever ªyour obedience is complete.

7   ¹ªYou are looking at ²things as they are outwardly. ᵇIf any one is confident in himself that he is Christ's, let him consider this again within himself, that just as he is Christ's, ᶜso also are we.

8   For even if ªI should boast somewhat ¹further about our ᵇauthority, which the Lord gave for

building you up and not for destroying you, I shall not be put to shame,

9 ¹for I do not wish to seem as if I would terrify you by my letters.

10 For they say, "His letters are weighty and strong, but his ¹personal presence is ᵃunimpressive, and ᵇhis speech contemptible."

11 Let such a person consider this, that what we are in word by letters when absent, such persons *we are* also in deed when present.

12 For we are not bold to class or compare ourselves with ¹some of those who ᵃcommend themselves; but when they measure themselves by themselves, and compare themselves with themselves, they are without understanding.

13 But we will not boast ᵃbeyond *our* measure, but ¹ᵇwithin the measure of the sphere which God apportioned to us as a measure, to reach even as far as you.

14 For we are not overextending ourselves, as if we did not reach to you, for ᵃwe were the first to come even as far as you in the ᵇgospel of Christ;

15 not boasting ᵃbeyond *our* measure, *that is*, in ᵇother men's labors, but with the hope that as ᶜyour faith grows, we shall be, ¹within our sphere, ᵈenlarged even more by you,

16 so as to ᵃpreach the gospel even to ᵇthe regions beyond you, *and* not to boast ¹ᶜin what has been accomplished in the sphere of another.

17 But ᵃHE WHO BOASTS, LET HIM BOAST IN THE LORD.

18 For not he who ᵃcommends himself is approved, but ᵇwhom the Lord commends.

CHAPTER 11

I WISH that you would ᵃbear with me in a little ᵇfoolishness; but ¹indeed you are bearing with me.

2 For I am jealous for you with a godly jealousy; for I ᵃbetrothed you to one husband, that to Christ I might ᵇpresent you *as* a pure virgin.

3 But I am afraid, lest as the ᵃserpent deceived Eve by his craftiness, your minds should be led astray from the simplicity and purity *of devotion* to Christ.

4 For if one comes and preaches ᵃanother Jesus whom we have not preached, or you receive a ᵇdifferent spirit which you have not received, or a

---

9 ¹Lit., *that I may not seem* . . .

10 ¹Lit., *bodily presence is weak*
ᵃ1 Cor. 2:3; 2 Cor. 12:7; Gal. 4:13f. ᵇ1 Cor. 1:17; 2 Cor. 11:6

12 ¹Or, *any*
ᵃ2 Cor. 10:18; 3:1

13 ¹Lit., *according to the measure*
ᵃ2 Cor. 10:15 ᵇRom. 12:3; 2 Cor. 10:15f.

14 ᵃ1 Cor. 3:6 ᵇ2 Cor. 2:12

15 ¹Lit., *according to our sphere*
ᵃ2 Cor. 10:13 ᵇRom. 15:20 ᶜ2 Thess. 1:3 ᵈActs 5:13

16 ¹Lit., *to the things prepared in the* . . .
ᵃ2 Cor. 11:7 ᵇActs 19:21 ᶜRom. 15:20

17 ᵃJer. 9:24; 1 Cor. 1:31

18 ᵃ2 Cor. 10:12 ᵇRom. 2:29; 1 Cor. 4:5

1 ¹Or, *do indeed bear with me*
ᵃ2 Cor. 11:4, 19f.; Matt. 17:17; 2 Cor. 11:16 ᵇ2 Cor. 11:17, 21; 5:13

2 ᵃHos. 2:19f.; Eph. 5:26f. ᵇ2 Cor. 4:14

3 ᵃGen. 3:4, 13; 1 Tim. 2:14; Rev. 12:9, 15; John 8:44; 1 Thess. 3:5

4 ᵃ1 Cor. 3:11 ᵇRom. 8:15

4 cGal. 1:6 d2 Cor. 11:1
eMark 7:9

5 1Or, *super-apostles*
a2 Cor. 12:11; Gal. 2:6

6 a1 Cor. 1:17 b1 Cor.
12:8; Eph. 3:4 c2 Cor. 4:2

7 a2 Cor. 12:13 bRom. 1:1;
2 Cor. 2:12 c1 Cor. 9:18; Acts
18:3

8 aPhil. 4:15, 18; 1 Cor.
4:12; 9:6

9 1Lit., *and I will keep*
a2 Cor. 12:13f., 16 bActs 18:5
cRom. 15:26

10 aRom. 9:1; 1:9; 2 Cor.
1:23; Gal. 2:20 b1 Cor. 9:15
cActs 18:12

11 a2 Cor. 12:15 b2 Cor.
11:31; 2 Cor. 12:2f.; Rom.
1:9; 2 Cor. 2:17

12 1Lit., *found*
a1 Cor. 9:12

13 aRev. 2:2; Acts 20:30;
Gal. 1:7; 2:4; Phil. 1:15; Titus
1:10f.; 2 Pet. 2:1 bPhil. 3:2

14 aMatt. 4:10; Eph. 6:12;
Col. 1:13 bCol. 1:12

15 aRom. 2:6; 3:8

16 a2 Cor. 11:1

17 1Lit., *in accordance
with the Lord*
a1 Cor. 7:12, 25 b2 Cor.
11:21

18 aPhil. 3:3f. b2 Cor. 5:16

19 a1 Cor. 4:10

20 aGal. 2:4; 2 Cor. 1:24;
Gal. 4:3, 9; 5:1 bMark 12:40
cLuke 5:5; 2 Cor. 11:3; 12:16
d2 Cor. 10:5 e1 Cor. 4:11

21 a2 Cor. 6:8

cdifferent gospel which you have not accepted, you
dbear *this* ebeautifully.

5 For I consider myself anot in the least inferior to the 1most eminent apostles.

6 But even if I am aunskilled in speech, yet I
am not *so* in bknowledge; in fact, in every way we
have cmade *this* evident to you in all things.

7 Or adid I commit a sin in humbling myself
that you might be exalted, because I preached the
bgospel of God to you cwithout charge?

8 I robbed other churches, ataking wages *from
them* to serve you;

9 and when I was present with you and was in
need, I was anot a burden to anyone; for when bthe
brethren came from cMacedonia, they fully
supplied my need, and in everything I kept myself
from abeing a burden to you, 1and will continue to
do so.

10 aAs the truth of Christ is in me, bthis boasting of mine will not be stopped in the regions of
cAchaia.

11 Why? aBecause I do not love you? bGod
knows *I do!*

12 But what I am doing, I will continue to do,
athat I may cut off opportunity from those who
desire an opportunity to be 1regarded just as we are
in the matter about which they are boasting.

13 For such men are afalse apostles, bdeceitful
workers, disguising themselves as apostles of Christ.

14 And no wonder, for even aSatan disguises
himself as an bangel of light.

15 Therefore it is not surprising if his servants
also disguise themselves as servants of righteousness; awhose end shall be according to their deeds.

16 aAgain I say, let no one think me foolish;
but if *you do,* receive me even as foolish, that I also
may boast a little.

17 That which I am speaking, I am not speaking 1aas the Lord would, but as bin foolishness, in
this confidence of boasting.

18 Since amany boast baccording to the flesh, I
will boast also.

19 For you, abeing *so* wise, bear with the foolish gladly.

20 For you bear with anyone if he aenslaves
you, if he bdevours you, if he ctakes advantage of
you, if he dexalts himself, if he ehits you in the face.

21 To *my* ashame I *must* say that we have been

ᵇweak *by comparison.* But in whatever respect anyone *else* ᶜis bold (I ᵈspeak in foolishness), I am just as bold myself.

22 Are they ᵃHebrews? ᵇSo am I. Are they ᶜIsraelites? ᶜSo am I. Are they ¹ᵈdescendants of Abraham? ᵉSo am I.

23 Are they ᵃservants of Christ? (I speak as if insane) I more so; in ¹ᵇfar more labors, in ¹ᶜfar more imprisonments, ²ᵈbeaten times without number, often in ᵉdanger of death.

24 Five times I received from the Jews ᵃthirty-nine *lashes.*

25 Three times I was ᵃbeaten with rods, once I was ᵇstoned, three times I was shipwrecked, a night and a day I have spent in the deep.

26 *I have been* on frequent journeys, in dangers from rivers, dangers from robbers, dangers from *my* ᵃcountrymen, dangers from the ᵇGentiles, dangers in the ᶜcity, dangers in the wilderness, dangers on the sea, dangers among ᵈfalse brethren;

27 *I have been* in ᵃlabor and hardship, ¹through many sleepless nights, in ᵇhunger and thirst, often ᶜwithout food, in cold and ²ᵈexposure.

28 Apart from *such* ¹external things, there is the daily pressure upon me *of* concern for ᵃall the churches.

29 Who is ᵃweak without my being weak? Who is ¹led into sin ²without my intense concern?

30 If I have to boast, I will boast of what pertains to my ᵃweakness.

31 The God and Father of the Lord Jesus, ᵃHe who is blessed forever, ᵇknows that I am not lying.

32 In ᵃDamascus the ethnarch under Aretas the king was ᵇguarding the city of the Damascenes in order to seize me,

33 and I was let down in a basket ᵃthrough a window ¹in the wall, and *so* escaped his hands.

ᵃ   Cʜᴀᴘᴛᴇʀ 12

Bᴏᴀsᴛɪɴɢ is necessary, though it is not profitable; but I will go on to visions and ᵇrevelations ¹of the Lord.

2 I know a man ᵃin Christ who fourteen years ago—whether in the body I do not know, or out of the body I do not know, ᵇGod knows—such a man was ᶜcaught up to the ᵈthird heaven.

3 And I know how such a man—whether in

21 ᵇ2 Cor. 10:10 ᶜ2 Cor. 10:2 ᵈ2 Cor. 11:17

22 ¹Lit., *seed*
ᵃActs 6:1 ᵇPhil. 3:5 ᶜRom. 9:4 ᵈGal. 3:16 ᵉRom. 11:1

23 ¹Lit., *more abundantly* ²Lit., *exceedingly in stripes* ᵃ2 Cor. 3:6; 1 Cor. 3:5; 2 Cor. 10:7 ᵇ1 Cor. 15:10 ᶜ2 Cor 6:5 ᵈActs 16:23; 2 Cor. 6:5 ᵉRom. 8:36

24 ᵃDeut. 25:3

25 ᵃActs 16:22 ᵇActs 14:19

26 ᵃActs 9:23; 13:45, 50; 14:5; 17:5, 13; 18:12; 20:3, 19; 21:27; 23:10, 12; 25:3; 1 Thess. 2:15 ᵇActs 14:5, 19; 19:23ff.; 27:42 ᶜActs 21:31 ᵈGal. 2:4

27 ¹Lit., *often in wakefulness* ²Lit., *nakedness,* lack of clothing ᵃ1 Thess. 2:9; 2 Thess. 3:8 ᵇ1 Cor. 4:11; Phil. 4:12 ᶜ2 Cor. 6:5 ᵈ1 Cor. 4:11

28 ¹Or, *the things unmentioned* ᵃ1 Cor. 7:17

29 ¹Lit., *made to stumble* ²Lit., *and I do not burn* ᵃ1 Cor. 9:22; 1 Cor. 8:9, 13

30 ᵃ1 Cor. 2:3

31 ᵃRom. 1:25 ᵇ2 Cor. 11:11

32 ᵃActs 9:2 ᵇActs 9:24

33 ¹Lit., *through* ᵃActs 9:25

1 ¹Or possibly, *from* ᵃ2 Cor. 11:30; 11:16, 18; 12:5, 9 ᵇ2 Cor. 12:7; Gal. 1:12; 2:2; Eph. 3:3; 1 Cor. 14:6

2 ᵃRom. 16:7 ᵇ2 Cor. 11:11 ᶜ2 Cor. 12:4; 1 Thess. 4:17; Rev. 12:5; Acts 8:39; Ezek. 8:3 ᵈDeut. 10:14; Ps. 148:4; Eph. 4:10; Heb. 4:14

3 a2 Cor. 11:11

4 a2 Cor. 12:2; 1 Thess.
4:17; Rev. 12:5; Acts 8:39;
Ezek. 8:3 bLuke 23:43

5 a2 Cor. 12:1 b1 Cor. 2:3;
2 Cor. 12:9f.

6 a2 Cor. 11:16f.; 2 Cor.
12:11; 2 Cor. 5:13 b2 Cor.
7:14

7 a2 Cor. 12:1 bNum.
33:55; Ezek. 28:24; Hos. 2:6
cJob 2:6; 1 Cor. 5:5; Matt.
4:10

8 aMatt. 26:44

9 1Later mss. read, My
power
aPhil. 4:13; 1 Cor. 2:5; Eph.
3:16 b1 Cor. 2:3; 2 Cor. 12:5

10 1Or, mistreatment
aRom. 5:3; 8:35 b2 Cor. 6:4
c2 Thess. 1:4; 2 Tim. 3:11
d2 Cor. 5:15, 20 e2 Cor. 13:4

11 1Or, super-apostles
a2 Cor. 11:16f.; 12:6; 5:13
b2 Cor. 11:5; 1 Cor. 15:10
c1 Cor. 3:7; 13:2; 15:9

12 1Or, attesting miracles
2Lit., of the apostle 3Or,
works of power
a1 Cor. 9:1; Rom. 15:19; esp.
John 4:48

13 a1 Cor. 9:12, 18; 2 Cor.
11:9; 12:14 b2 Cor. 11:7

14 a2 Cor. 13:1; 1:15; 13:2
b1 Cor. 9:12, 18; 2 Cor. 11:9;
12:13 c1 Cor. 10:24, 33
d1 Cor. 9:19 e1 Cor. 4:14f.;
Gal. 4:19 fProv. 19:14; Ezek.
34:2

15 a2 Cor. 1:6; Rom. 9:3;
Phil. 2:17; Col. 1:24; 1 Thess.
2:8; 2 Tim. 2:10 b2 Cor.
11:11

the body or apart from the body I do not know, [a]God knows—

4　was [a]caught up into [b]Paradise, and heard inexpressible words, which a man is not permitted to speak.

5　[a]On behalf of such a man will I boast; but on my own behalf I will not boast, except in regard to *my* [b]weaknesses.

6　For if I do wish to boast I shall not be [a]foolish, [b]for I shall be speaking the truth; but I refrain *from this,* so that no one may credit me with more than he sees *in* me or hears from me.

7　And because of the surpassing greatness of the [a]revelations, for this reason, to keep me from exalting myself, there was given me a [b]thorn in the flesh, a [c]messenger of Satan to buffet me—to keep me from exalting myself!

8　Concerning this I entreated the Lord [a]three times that it might depart from me.

9　And He has said to me, "My grace is sufficient for you, for [1a]power is perfected in weakness." Most gladly, therefore, I will rather [b]boast about my weaknesses, that the power of Christ may dwell in me.

10　Therefore [a]I am well content with weaknesses, with [1]insults, with [b]distresses, with [c]persecutions, with [b]difficulties, [d]for Christ's sake; for [e]when I am weak, then I am strong,

11　I have become [a]foolish; you yourselves compelled me. Actually I should have been commended by you, for [b]in no respect was I inferior to the [1]most eminent apostles, even though [c]I am a nobody.

12　The [1a]signs [2]of a true apostle were performed among you with all perseverance, by [1]signs and wonders and [3]miracles.

13　For in what respect were you treated as inferior to the rest of the churches, except that [a]I myself did not become a burden to you? Forgive me [b]this wrong!

14　Here [a]for this third time I am ready to come to you, and I [b]will not be a burden to you; for I [c]do not seek what is yours, but [d]you; for [e]children are not responsible to save up for *their* parents, but [f]parents for *their* children.

15　And I will [a]most gladly spend and be expended for your souls. If [b]I love you the more, am I to be loved the less?

16 But be that as it may, I [a]did not burden you myself; nevertheless, crafty fellow that I am, I [b]took you in by deceit.

17 [a]Certainly I have not taken advantage of you through any of those whom I have sent to you, have I?

18 I [a]urged [b]Titus *to go,* and sent [c]the brother with him. Titus did not take any advantage of you, did he? Did we not [1]conduct ourselves [2]in the same [d]spirit *and walk* [e]in the same steps?

19 All this time [1]you have been thinking that we are defending ourselves to you. *Actually,* [a]it is in the sight of God that we have been speaking in Christ; and [b]all for your upbuilding, [c]beloved.

20 For I am afraid that perhaps [a]when I come I may find you to be not what I wish and may be found by you to be not what you wish; that perhaps *there may be* [b]strife, jealousy, [c]angry tempers, [d]disputes, [e]slanders, [f]gossip, [g]arrogance, [h]disturbances;

21 I am afraid that when I come again my God may humiliate me before you, and I may mourn over many of those who have [a]sinned in the past and not repented of the [b]impurity, [1]immorality and sensuality which they have practiced.

a   CHAPTER 13

THIS is the third time I am coming to you. [b]Every [1]fact [2]is to be confirmed by the [3]testimony of two or three witnesses.

2 I have previously said when present the second time, and though now absent I say in advance to those who have [a]sinned in the past and to all the rest as well, that [b]if I come again, I will not [c]spare *anyone,—*

3 since you are [a]seeking for proof of the [b]Christ who speaks in me, and who is not weak toward you, but [c]mighty in you.

4 For indeed He was [a]crucified because of weakness, yet He lives [b]because of the power of God. For we also are [c]weak [1]in Him, yet [d]we shall live with Him because of the power of God *directed* toward you.

5 [a]Test yourselves *to see* if you are in the faith; [b]examine yourselves! Or do you not recognize this about yourselves, that Jesus Christ is in you—unless indeed you [1c]fail the test?

6 [1]Lit., *are not unapproved*

7 [1]Lit., *be as*

9 [1]Lit., *your completion*
[a]2 Cor. 13:4; 12:10 [b]1 Cor. 1:10; 2 Cor. 13:11; Eph. 4:12; 1 Thess. 3:10

10 [a]2 Cor. 2:3 [b]Titus 1:13 [c]2 Cor. 10:8; 1 Cor. 5:4

11 [1]Or possibly, *farewell* [2]Or, *put yourselves in order* [a]1 Thess. 4:1; 2 Thess. 3:1, [b]1 Cor. 1:10; 2 Cor. 13:9; Eph. 4:12; 1 Thess. 3:10 [c]Rom. 12:16 [d]Mark 9:50 [e]Rom. 15:33; Eph. 6:23

12 [a]Rom. 16:16

13 [1]I.e., true believers; lit., *holy ones* [a]Phil. 4:22

14 [a]Rom. 16:20; 2 Cor. 8:9 [b]Rom. 5:5; Jude 21 [c]Phil. 2:1

6 But I trust that you will realize that we ourselves [1]do not fail the test.

7 Now we pray to God that you do no wrong; not that we ourselves may appear approved, but that you may do what is right, even though we should [1]appear unapproved.

8 For we can do nothing against the truth, but *only* for the truth.

9 For we rejoice when we ourselves are [a]weak but you are strong; this we also pray for, [1]that you be [b]made complete.

10 For this reason I am writing these things while absent, in order that when present [a]I may not use [b]severity in accordance with the [c]authority which the Lord gave me for building up and not for tearing down.

11 [a]Finally, brethren, [1]rejoice, [2][b]be made complete, be comforted, [c]be like-minded, [d]live in peace; and [e]the God of love and peace shall be with you.

12 [a]Greet one another with a holy kiss.

13 [a]All the [1]saints greet you.

14 [a]The grace of the Lord Jesus Christ, and the [b]love of God, and the [c]fellowship of the Holy Spirit, be with you all.

THE EPISTLE OF PAUL TO THE
GALATIANS

Salutation. The Galatians' Falling Away.
The Gospel I Preach Came from Christ.

1 [a]2 Cor. 1:1 [b]Gal. 1:11f. [c]Acts 20:24; 9:15; Gal. 1:15f. [d]Acts 2:24

2 [a]Phil. 4:21 [b]1 Cor. 16:1; Acts 16:6

3 [1]Some early mss. read, *God the Father, and our Lord Jesus Christ* [a]Rom. 1:7

4 [1]Or, *world* [a]Matt. 20:28; Rom. 4:25; 1 Cor. 15:3; Gal. 2:20 [b]Matt. 13:22; Rom. 12:2; 2 Cor. 4:4 [c]Phil. 4:20; 1 Thess. 1:3; 3:11, 13

5 [a]Rom. 11:36

P AUL, [a]an apostle ([b]not *sent* from men, nor through the agency of man, but [c]through Jesus Christ, and God the Father, who [d]raised Him from the dead),

2 and all [a]the brethren who are with me, to [b]the churches of Galatia:

3 [a]Grace to you and peace from [1]God our Father, and the Lord Jesus Christ,

4 who [a]gave Himself for our sins, that He might deliver us out of [b]this present evil [1]age, according to the will of [c]our God and Father,

5 [a]to whom *be* the glory forevermore. Amen.

6 I am amazed that you are [a]so quickly deserting [b]Him who called you [1]by the grace of Christ, for a [c]different gospel;

7 which is *really* not another; only there are some who are [a]disturbing you, and want to distort the gospel of Christ.

8 But even though we, or [a]an angel from heaven, should preach to you a gospel [1]contrary to that which we have preached to you, let him be [2b]accursed.

9 As we [a]have said before, so I say again now, [b]if any man is preaching to you a gospel [1]contrary to that which you received, let him be [2c]accursed.

10 For am I now [a]seeking the favor of men, or of God? Or am I striving to please men? If I were still trying to please men, I would not be a [b]bond-servant of Christ.

11 For [a]I would have you know, brethren, that the gospel which was preached by me is [b]not according to man.

12 For [a]I neither received it from man, nor was I taught it, but *I received it* through a [b]revelation of Jesus Christ.

13 For you have heard of [a]my former manner of life in Judaism, how I [b]used to persecute [c]the church of God beyond measure, and [d]tried to destroy it;

14 and I [a]was advancing in Judaism beyond many of my contemporaries among my [1]countrymen, being more extremely zealous for my [b]ancestral traditions.

15 But when He who had set me apart, *even* from my mother's womb, and [a]called me through His grace, was [b]pleased

16 to reveal His Son in me, that I might [a]preach Him among the Gentiles, [b]I did not immediately consult with [1c]flesh and blood,

17 [a]nor did I go up to Jerusalem to those who were apostles before me; but I went away to Arabia, and returned once more to [b]Damascus.

18 Then [a]three years later I went up [b]to Jerusalem to [1]become acquainted with [c]Cephas, and stayed with him fifteen days.

19 But I did not see any other of the apostles except [1a]James the Lord's brother.

20 (Now in what I am writing to you, [1]I assure you [a]before God *that* I am not lying.)

6 [1]Lit., *in*
[a]Acts 16:6; 18:23; Gal. 4:13
[b]Gal. 5:8; 1:15; Rom. 8:28
[c]2 Cor. 11:4; 1 Tim. 1:3; Gal. 1:7, 11; 2:2, 7; Gal. 5:14

7 [a]Acts 15:24; Gal. 5:10

8 [1]Or, *other than, more than* [2]Gr., *anathema*
[a]2 Cor. 11:14 [b]Rom. 9:3

9 [1]Or, *other than, more than* [2]Gr., *anathema*
[a]Acts 18:23 [b]Rom. 16:17
[c]Rom. 9:3

10 [a]1 Thess. 2:4; 1 Cor. 10:33 [b]Rom. 1:1; Phil. 1:1

11 [a]1 Cor. 15:1; Rom. 2:16
[b]1 Cor. 9:8; 3:4

12 [a]Gal. 1:1; 1 Cor. 11:23
[b]Gal. 1:16; 1 Cor. 2:10;
2 Cor. 12:1; Gal. 2:2

13 [a]Acts 26:4f. [b]Acts 8:3
[c]1 Cor. 10:32 [d]Acts 9:21

14 [1]Lit., *race*
[a]Acts 22:3 [b]Matt. 15:2; Mark 7:3; Col. 2:8; Jer. 9:14

15 [a]Gal. 1:6 [b]Acts 9:15;
Rom. 1:1; Is. 49:1, 5; Jer. 1:5

16 [1]I.e., human beings
[a]Gal. 2:9; Acts 9:15 [b]Acts 9:20 [c]Matt. 16:17

17 [a]Acts 9:19-22 [b]Acts 9:2

18 [1]Or, *visit Cephas*
[a]Acts 9:22f. [b]Acts 9:26f.
[c]John 1:42; Gal 2:9, 11, 14

19 [1]Or, *Jacob*
[a]Matt. 12:46; Acts 12:17

20 [1]Lit., *behold before God*
[a]Rom. 9:1; 2 Cor. 1:23; 11:31

21 ªActs 9:30 ᵇActs 15:23, 41 ᶜActs 6:9

22 ¹Lit., *face*
ªl Thess. 2:14; 1 Cor. 7:17
ᵇRom. 16:7

23 ªActs 6:7; Gal. 6:10 ᵇActs 9:21

24 ¹Lit., *in me*
ªMatt. 9:8

1 ªActs 15:2 ᵇActs 4:36; Gal. 2:9, 13 ᶜ2 Cor. 2:13; Gal. 2:3

2 ¹Lit., *according to revelation I went up*
ªActs 15:2; Gal. 1:12 ᵇGal. 1:6 ᶜGal. 5:7; Phil. 2:16; Rom. 9:16; 1 Cor. 9:24ff.; Heb. 12:1; 2 Tim. 4:7

3 ª2 Cor. 2:13; Gal. 2:1
ᵇActs 16:3; 1 Cor. 9:21

4 ªGal. 1:7; Acts 15:1, 24; 2 Cor. 11:13, 26 ᵇ2 Pet. 2:1; Jude 4 ᶜGal. 5:1, 13; James 1:25 ᵈ2 Cor. 11:20; Rom. 8:15

5 ªGal. 2:14; Col. 1:5; Gal. 1:6

6 ¹Lit., *seemed to be something* ²Lit., *does not receive a face.*
ªGal. 2:9; Gal. 6:3; 2 Cor. 11:5; 12:11 ᵇActs 10:34

7 ¹Lit., *of the uncircumcision* ²Lit., *of the circumcision*
ªl Thess. 2:4; 1 Tim. 1:11; 1 Cor. 9:17 ᵇGal. 1:16; Acts 9:15 ᶜGal. 2:9, 11, 14; Gal. 1:18

8 ¹Lit., *of the circumcision*
ªActs 1:25

9 ¹Or, *Jacob* ²Lit., *hands*
ªRom. 12:3 ᵇActs 12:17; Gal. 2:12 ᶜGal. 2:7, 11, 14; 1:18; Luke 22:8 ᵈGal. 2:2, 6; 6:3; 2 Cor. 11:5; 12:11 ᵉRev. 3:12; 1 Tim. 3:15 ᶠActs 4:36; Gal. 2:1, 13 ᵍ2 Kin. 10:15; Ezra 10:19 ʰGal. 1:16

10 ªActs 24:17

11 ªGal. 2:6, 9, 14; Gal. 1:18 ᵇActs 11:19; Acts 15:1

21 Then ªI went into the regions of ᵇSyria and ᶜCilicia.

22 And I was *still* unknown by ¹sight to ªthe churches of Judea which were ᵇin Christ;

23 but only, they kept hearing, "He who once persecuted us is now preaching ªthe faith which he once ᵇ*tried to* destroy."

24 And they ªwere glorifying God ¹because of me.

CHAPTER 2

THEN after an interval of fourteen years I ªwent up again to Jerusalem with ᵇBarnabas, taking ᶜTitus along also.

2 And ¹it was because of a ªrevelation that I went up; and I submitted to them the ᵇgospel which I preach among the Gentiles, but I did so in private to those who were of reputation, for fear that I might be ᶜrunning, or had run, in vain.

3 But not even ªTitus who was with me, though he was a Greek, was ᵇcompelled to be circumcised.

4 But *it was* because of the ªfalse brethren who ᵇhad sneaked in to spy out our ᶜliberty which we have in Christ Jesus, in order to ᵈbring us into bondage.

5 But we did not yield in subjection to them for even an hour, so that ªthe truth of the gospel might remain with you.

6 But from those who ¹were of high ªreputation (what they were makes no difference to me; ᵇGod ²shows no partiality)—well, those who were of reputation contributed nothing to me.

7 But on the contrary, seeing that I had been ªentrusted with the ᵇgospel ¹to the uncircumcised, just as ᶜPeter with *the gospel* ²to the circumcised

8 (for He who effectually worked for Peter in *his* ªapostleship ¹to the circumcised effectually worked for me also to the Gentiles),

9 and recognizing ªthe grace that had been given to me, ¹ᵇJames and ᶜCephas and John, who were ᵈreputed to be ᵉpillars, gave to me and ᶠBarnabas the ᵍright ²hand of fellowship, that we might ʰgo to the Gentiles, and they to the circumcised.

10 *They* only *asked* us to remember the poor—ªthe very thing I also was eager to do.

11 But when ªCephas came to ᵇAntioch, I op-

posed him to his face, because he [1]stood condemned.

12 For prior to the coming of certain men from [1a]James, he used to [b]eat with the Gentiles; but when they came, he *began* to withdraw and hold himself aloof, [c]fearing the [2]party of the circumcision.

13 And the rest of the Jews joined him in hypocrisy, with the result that even [a]Barnabas was carried away by their hypocrisy.

14 But when I saw that they [a]were not [1]straightforward about [b]the truth of the gospel, I said to [c]Cephas in the presence of all, "If you, being a Jew, [d]live like the Gentiles and not like the Jews, how *is it that* you compel the Gentiles to live like Jews?[2]

15 "We *are* [a]Jews by nature, and not [b]sinners from among the Gentiles;

16 nevertheless knowing that [a]a man is not justified by the works of [1]the Law but through faith in Christ Jesus, even we have believed in Christ Jesus, that we may be justified by [b]faith in Christ, and not by the works of [1]the Law; since [c]by the works of [1]the Law shall no [2]flesh be justified.

17 "But if, while seeking to be justified in Christ, we ourselves have also been found [a]sinners, is Christ then a minister of sin? [b]May it never be!

18 "For if I rebuild what I have *once* destroyed, I [a]prove myself to be a transgressor.

19 "For through [1]the Law I [a]died to [1]the Law, that I might live to God.

20 "I have been [a]crucified with Christ; and it is no longer I who live, but [b]Christ lives in me; and [1]the *life* which I now live in the flesh I live by faith in [c]the Son of God, who [d]loved me, and [e]delivered Himself up for me.

21 "I do not nullify the grace of God; for [a]if righteousness *comes* through [1]the Law, then Christ died needlessly."

[1]   CHAPTER 3

YOU foolish [a]Galatians, who has bewitched you, before whose eyes Jesus Christ [b]was publicly portrayed *as* crucified?

2 This is the only thing I want to find out from you: Did you receive the Spirit by the works of [1]the Law, or by [2a]hearing with faith?

11 [1]Or, *was to be condemned*; lit., *was one who was condemned*, or, was self condemned

12 [1]Or, *Jacob* [2]Or, *converts from the circumcised*; lit., *those from the circumcision* [a]Acts 12:17; Gal. 2:9 [b]Acts 11:3 [c]Acts 11:2

13 [a]Acts 4:36; Gal. 2:1, 9

14 [1]Or, *progressing toward*; lit., *walking straightly* [2]Some close the direct quotation here, others extend it through vs. 21. [a]Heb. 12:13 [b]Gal. 2:5; Col. 1:5; Gal. 1.6 [c]Gal. 2.7, 9, 11; 1:18 [d]Gal. 2:12; Acts 10:28

15 [a]Phil. 3:4f. [b]1 Sam. 15:18; Luke 24:7; 1 Cor. 6:1

16 [1]Or, *law* [2]Or, *mortal man* [a]Gal. 3:11; Acts 13:39 [b]Rom. 9:30 [c]Rom. 3:20; Ps. 143:2

17 [a]Gal. 2:15 [b]Gal. 3:21; Luke 20:16

18 [a]Rom. 3:5 [Gr.]

19 [1]Or, *law* [a]Rom. 7:4; 6:2; 1 Cor. 9:20

20 [1]Or, *insofar as I* [a]Rom. 6:6; Gal. 5:24; 6:14 [b]Rom. 8:10 [c]Matt. 4:3 [d]Rom. 8:37 [e]Gal. 1:4

21 [1]Or, *law* [a]Gal. 3:21

1 [1]Lit., *O* [a]Gal. 1:2 [b]1 Cor. 1:23; Gal. 5:11

2 [1]Or, *law* [2]Lit., *the hearing of faith* [a]Rom. 10:17

395

Galatians 3

**The Blessing of Faith.
The Preparatory Character of the Law.**

3 [1]Or, *with* [2]Or, *ending with*

4 [a]1 Cor. 15:2

5 [1]Or, *works of power* [2]Or, *law* [3]Lit., *the hearing of faith*
[a]Phil. 1:19; 2 Cor. 9:10
[b]1 Cor. 12:10 [c]Rom. 10:17

6 [1]Lit., *Just as*
[a]Rom. 4:3 [b]Gen. 15:6

7 [1]Lit., *know*
[a]Gal. 3:9 [b]Luke 19:9; Gal. 6:16

8 [1]Lit., *justifies* [2]Lit., *nations*
[a]Gen. 12:3

9 [1]Lit., *the believing Abraham*
[a]Gal. 3:7

10 [1]Or, *law*
[a]Deut. 27:26

11 [1]Or, *in* [2]Or, *law* [3]Or, *"But he who is righteous by faith shall live."*
[a]Gal. 2:16 [b]Hab. 2:4; Rom. 1:17; Heb. 10:38

12 [1]Or, *and* [2]Or, *based on* [3]Or, *in*
[a]Lev. 18:5; Rom. 10:5

13 [1]Or, *cross;* lit., *wood*
[a]Gal. 4:5 [b]Deut. 21:23 [c]Acts 5:30

14 [1]Or, *occur*
[a]Rom. 4:9, 16; Gal. 3:28
[b]Gal. 3:2 [c]Acts 2:33; Eph. 1:13

15 [1]Lit., *according to man* [2]Or, *will,* or, *testament* [3]Or, *a codicil*
[a]Gal. 6:18; Rom. 1:13; Acts 1:15 [b]Rom. 3:5 [c]Heb. 6:16

16 [a]Luke 1:55; Rom. 4:13, 16; 9:4 [b]Gen. 13:15 [c]Gen. 17:8; Acts 3:25

17 [a]Ex. 12:40; Gen. 15:13f.; Acts 7:6

3 Are you so foolish? Having begun [1]by the Spirit, are you now [2]being perfected by the flesh?
4 Did you suffer so many things in vain—[a]if indeed it was in vain?
5 Does He then who [a]provides you with the Spirit and [b]works [1]miracles among you, do it by the works of [2]the Law, or by [3]hearing with faith?
6 [1]Even so [a]Abraham [b]BELIEVED GOD, AND IT WAS RECKONED TO HIM AS RIGHTEOUSNESS.
7 Therefore, [1]be sure that [a]it is those who are of faith that are [b]sons of Abraham.
8 And the Scripture, foreseeing that God [1]would justify the [2]Gentiles by faith, preached the gospel beforehand to Abraham, *saying,* "[a]ALL THE NATIONS SHALL BE BLESSED IN YOU."
9 So then [a]those who are of faith are blessed with [1]Abraham, the believer.
10 For as many as are of the works of [1]the Law are under a curse; for it is written, "[a]CURSED IS EVERY ONE WHO DOES NOT ABIDE BY ALL THINGS WRITTEN IN THE BOOK OF THE LAW, TO PERFORM THEM."
11 Now that [a]no one is justified [1]by [2]the Law before God is evident; for, "[3b]THE RIGHTEOUS MAN SHALL LIVE BY FAITH."
12 [1]However, the Law is not [2]of faith; on the contrary, "[a]HE WHO PRACTICES THEM SHALL LIVE [3]BY THEM."
13 Christ [a]redeemed us from the curse of the Law, having become a curse for us—for it is written, "[b]CURSED IS EVERY ONE WHO HANGS ON [c]A [1]TREE"—
14 in order that [a]in Christ Jesus the blessing of Abraham might [1]come to the Gentiles, so that we [b]might receive [c]the promise of the Spirit through faith.
15 [a]Brethren, [b]I speak [1]in terms of human relations: [c]even though it is *only* a man's [2]covenant, yet when it has been ratified, no one sets it aside or adds [3]conditions to it.
16 Now the promises were spoken [a]to Abraham and to his seed. He does not say, "[b]AND TO SEEDS," as *referring* to many, but *rather* to one, "[c]AND TO YOUR SEED," that is, Christ.
17 What I am saying is this: the Law, which came [a]four hundred and thirty years later, does not invalidate a covenant previously ratified by God, so as to nullify the promise.

18 For ^aif the inheritance is ¹based on law, it is no longer ¹based on a promise; but ^bGod has granted it to Abraham by means of a promise.

19 ^aWhy the Law then? It was added ¹because of transgressions, having been ^bordained through angels ^cby the ²agency of a mediator, until ^dthe seed should come to whom the promise had been made.

20 Now ^aa mediator is not ¹for one *party only;* whereas God is *only* one.

21 Is the Law then contrary to the promises of God? ^aMay it never be! For ^bif a law had been given which was able to impart life, then righteousness ¹would indeed have been ²based on law.

22 But the Scripture has ^ashut up all ^{1b}men under sin, that the promise by faith in Jesus Christ might be given to those who believe.

23 But before faith came, we were kept in custody under the law, ^abeing shut up to the faith which was later to be revealed.

24 Therefore the Law has become our ^{1a}tutor *to lead us* to Christ, that ^bwe may be justified by faith.

25 But now that faith has come, we are no longer under a ^{1a}tutor.

26 For you are all ^asons of God through faith in ^bChrist Jesus.

27 For all of you who were ^abaptized into Christ have ^bclothed yourselves with Christ.

28 ^aThere is neither Jew nor Greek, there is neither slave nor free man, there is ¹neither male nor female; for ^byou are all one in ^cChrist Jesus.

29 And if ^ayou ¹belong to Christ, then you are Abraham's ²offspring, heirs according to ^bpromise.

CHAPTER 4

Now I say, as long as the heir is a ¹child, he does not differ at all from a slave although he is ²owner of everything,

2 but he is under guardians and ¹managers until the date set by the father.

3 So also we, while we were children, were held ^ain bondage under the ^{1b}elemental things of the world.

4 But when ^athe fulness of the time came, God sent forth His Son, ^bborn of a woman, born ^cunder ¹the Law,

18 ¹Lit., *out of, from*
^aRom. 4:14 ^bHeb. 6:14

19 ¹Or, *for the sake of defining* ²Lit., *hand*
^aRom. 5:20 ^bActs 7:53 ^cEx. 20:19; Deut. 5:5 ^dGal. 3:16

20 ¹Lit., *of one*
^a1 Tim. 2:5; Heb. 8:6; 9:15; 12:24

21 ¹Or, *would indeed be* ²Lit., *out of, from*
^aLuke 20:16; Gal. 2:17 ^bGal. 2:21

22 ¹Lit., *things*
^aRom. 11:32 ^b1 Cor. 1:27

23 ^aRom. 11:32

24 ¹Lit., *a child-conductor*
^a1 Cor. 4:15 ^bGal. 2:16

25 ¹Lit., *a child-conductor*
^a1 Cor. 4:15

26 ^aGal. 4:5 Rom. 8:14
^bGal. 3:28; 4:14; 5:6, 24; Rom. 8:1; Eph. 1:1; Col. 1:4; Phil. 1:1; 1 Tim. 1:12; 2 Tim. 1:1; Titus 1:4

27 ^aMatt. 28:19; Rom. 6:3; 1 Cor. 10:2 ^bRom. 13:14

28 ¹Lit., *not male and female*
^a1 Cor. 12:13; Col. 3:11; Rom. 3:22 ^bJohn 17:11; Eph. 2:15 ^cGal. 3:26; 4:14; 5:6, 24; Rom. 8:1; Eph. 1:1; Col. 1:4; Phil. 1:1; 1 Tim. 1:12; 2 Tim. 1:1; Titus 1:4

29 ¹Lit., *are Christ's* ²Lit., *seed*
^a1 Cor. 3:23 ^bGal. 3:18; 4:28; Rom. 9:8

1 ¹Or, *minor* ²Lit., *lord*

2 ¹Or, *stewards*

3 ¹Or, *rudimentary teachings,* or, *principles*
^aGal. 4:8f.; 4:24f.; 2:4 ^bCol. 2:8, 20; Heb. 5:12; Gal. 4:9

4 ¹Or, *law*
^aMark 1:15 ^bJohn 1:14; Rom. 1:3; 8:3; Phil. 2:7 ^cLuke 2:21f., 27

5 [1]Or, *law*
[a]Gal. 3:26; Rom. 8:14

6 [a]Rom. 5:5; 8:9, 16;
2 Cor. 3:17; Acts 16:7 [b]Mark
14:36; Rom. 8:15

7 [1]I.e., through the
gracious act of
[a]Rom. 8:17

8 [a]1 Cor. 1:21; 1 Thess.
4:5; 2 Thess. 1:8; Eph. 2:12
[b]Gal. 4:3 [c]2 Chr. 13:9; Is.
37:19; Jer. 2:11; 1 Cor. 8:4f.;
1 Cor. 10:20

9 [1]Or, *rudimentary
teachings*, or *principles*
[a]1 Cor. 8:3 [b]Col. 2:20 [c]Gal.
4:3 and marg.

10 [a]Rom. 14:5; Col. 2:16

11 [1]Or, *for*

12 [a]Gal. 6:18 [b]2 Cor. 6:11,
13

13 [1]Lit., *weakness of the
flesh* [2]Or, *former*

14 [1]Or, *temptation* [2]Lit.,
flesh [3]Lit., *spit out at*
[a]Matt. 10:40; 1 Thess. 2:13
[b]Gal. 3:26

15 [1]Lit., *the
congratulation of yourselves*

16 [1]Or, *dealing truthfully
with you*
[a]Amos 5:10

18 [a]Gal. 4:13f.

19 [a]1 John 2:1 [b]1 Cor. 4:15
[c]Eph. 4:13

20 [a]2 Cor. 4:8

398

5   in order that He might redeem those who were under [1]the Law, that we might receive the adoption as [a]sons.

6   And because you are sons, [a]God has sent forth the Spirit of His Son into our hearts, crying, "[b]Abba! Father!"

7   Therefore you are no longer a slave, but a son; and [a]if a son, then an heir [1]through God.

8   However at that time, [a]when you did not know God, you were [b]slaves to [c]those which by nature are no gods.

9   But now that you have come to know God, or rather to be [a]known by God, [b]how is it that you turn back again to the weak and worthless [1]elemental things, to which you desire to be enslaved all over again?

10   You [a]observe days and months and seasons and years.

11   I fear for you, that perhaps I have labored [1]over you in vain.

12   I beg of you, [a]brethren, [b]become as *I am*, for I also *have become* as you *are*. You have done me no wrong;

13   but you know that it was because of a [1]bodily illness that I preached the gospel to you the [2]first time;

14   and that which was a [1]trial to you in my [2]bodily condition you did not despise or [3]loathe, but [a]you received me as an angel of God, as [b]Christ Jesus *Himself*.

15   Where then is [1]that sense of blessing you had? For I bear you witness, that if possible, you would have plucked out your eyes and given them to me.

16   Have I therefore become your enemy [a]by [1]telling you the truth?

17   They eagerly seek you, not commendably, but they wish to shut you out, in order that you may seek them.

18   But it is good always to be eagerly sought in a commendable manner, and [a]not only when I am present with you.

19   [a]My children, with whom [b]I am again in labor until [c]Christ is formed in you —

20   but I could wish to be present with you now and to change my tone, for [a]I am perplexed about you.

21 Tell me, you who want to be under law, do you not ªlisten to the law?

22 For it is written that Abraham had two sons, one by the bondwoman and one by the free woman.

23 But ªthe son by the bondwoman was born according to the flesh, and ᵇthe son by the free woman through the promise.

24 ¹ªThis contains an allegory: for these *women* are two covenants, one *proceeding* from ᵇMount Sinai bearing children ²who are to be ᶜslaves; ³she is Hagar.

25 Now this Hagar is Mount Sinai in Arabia, and corresponds to the present Jerusalem, for she is in slavery with her children.

26 But ªthe Jerusalem above is free; ¹she is our mother,

27 For it is written,

> "ªREJOICE, BARREN WOMAN WHO DOES NOT
>   BEAR;
> BREAK FORTH AND SHOUT, YOU WHO ARE
>   NOT IN LABOR;
> FOR MORE ARE THE CHILDREN OF THE
>   DESOLATE
> THAN OF THE ONE WHO HAS A HUSBAND."

28 And you brethren, ªlike Isaac, are ᵇchildren of promise.

29 But as at that time ªhe who was born according to the flesh ᵇpersecuted him *who was born* according to the Spirit, ᶜso it is now also.

30 But what does the Scripture say?

> "ªCAST OUT THE BONDWOMAN AND HER SON,
> FOR ᵇTHE SON OF THE BONDWOMAN SHALL
>   NOT BE AN HEIR WITH THE SON OF THE
>   FREE WOMAN."

31 So then, brethren, we are not children of a bondwoman, ¹but of the free woman.

_{1a}   CHAPTER 5

IT was for freedom that Christ set us free; therefore ᵇkeep standing firm and do not be subject again to a ᶜyoke of slavery.

2 Behold I, ªPaul, say to you that if you receive ᵇcircumcision, Christ will be of no benefit to you.

3 And I ªtestify again to every man who re-

21 ªLuke 16:29

23 ªGal. 4:29; Rom. 9:7
ᵇGal. 4:28; Gen. 17:16ff.;
18:10ff.; 21:1; Heb. 11:11

24 ¹Lit., *which things are
allegorical utterances* ²Lit.,
into slavery ³Lit., *which*
ª1 Cor. 10:11 ᵇDeut. 33:2
ᶜGal. 4:3

26 ¹Lit., *which*
ªHeb. 12:22; Rev. 3:12; 21:2,
10

27 ªIs. 54:1

28 ªGal. 4:23 ᵇGal. 3:29;
Rom. 9:7ff.

29 ªGal. 4:23 ᵇGen. 21:9
ᶜGal. 5:11

30 ªGen. 21:10, 12 ᵇJohn
8:35

31 ¹Note next vs., 5:1

1 ¹Some authorities prefer
to join with 4:31 and render,
*but with the freedom of the
free woman Christ set us
free*
ªGal. 2:4; 5:13; John 8:32, 36;
Rom. 8:15; 2 Cor. 3:17
ᵇ1 Cor. 16:13 ᶜActs 15:10,
Gal. 2:4

2 ª2 Cor. 10:1 ᵇActs 15:1;
Gal. 5:3, 6, 11

3 ªLuke 16:28

399

3 [b]Acts 15:1; Gal. 5:2, 6, 11
[c]Rom. 2:25

4 [1]Or, *would be*
[a]2 Pet. 3:17; Heb. 12:15
marg.

5 [a]Rom. 8:23; 1 Cor. 1:7

6 [a]Gal. 3:26 [b]1 Cor. 7:19;
Gal. 6:15 [c]Col. 1:4f.;
1 Thess. 1:3; James 2:18, 20,
22

7 [a]Gal. 2:2

8 [a]Rom. 8:28; Gal. 1:6

9 [a]1 Cor. 5:6

10 [1]Lit., *toward*
[a]2 Cor. 2:3 [b]Phil. 3:15; Gal.
5:7 [c]Gal. 1:7; 5:12

11 [a]Gal. 4:29; 6:12 [b]1 Cor.
1:23; Rom. 9:33

12 [1]Or, *cut themselves off*
[a]Gal. 5:10; 2:4 [b]Deut. 23:1

13 [a]Gal. 5:1 [b]1 Cor. 8:9;
1 Pet. 2:16 [c]1 Cor. 9:19; Eph.
5:21

14 [a]Matt. 7:12; 22:40; Rom.
13:8, 10; Gal. 6:2 [b]Lev. 19:18;
Matt. 19:19; John 13:34

15 [a]Phil. 3:2; Gal. 5:20

16 [a]Rom. 8:4; 13:14; Gal.
5:24f. [b]Eph. 2:3; Rom. 13:14

17 [1]Lit., *lusts against* [2]Lit.,
wish
[a]Rom. 7:18, 23; 8:5ff. [b]Rom.
7:15ff.

18 [a]Rom. 8:14 [b]Rom. 6:14;
7:4; 1 Tim. 1:9

19 [1]I.e., *sexual immorality*
[a]1 Cor. 6:9, 18; 2 Cor. 12:21

20 [1]Or, *heresies*
[a]Rev. 21:8 [b]2 Cor. 12:20
[c]Rom. 2:8; James 3:14ff.
[d]1 Cor. 11:19

21 [a]Rom. 13:13

400

ceives [b]circumcision, that he is under obligation to [c]keep the whole Law.

4 You have been severed from Christ, you who [1]are seeking to be justified by law; you have [a]fallen from grace.

5 For we through the Spirit, by faith, are [a]waiting for the hope of righteousness.

6 For in [a]Christ Jesus [b]neither circumcision nor uncircumcision means anything, but [c]faith working through love.

7 You were [a]running well; who hindered you from obeying the truth?

8 This persuasion *did* not *come* from [a]Him who calls you.

9 [a]A little leaven leavens the whole lump *of dough.*

10 [a]I have confidence [1]in you in the Lord, that you [b]will adopt no other view; but the one who is [c]disturbing you shall bear his judgment, whoever he is.

11 But I, brethren, if I still preach circumcision, why am I still [a]persecuted? Then [b]the stumbling-block of the cross has been abolished.

12 Would that [a]those who are troubling you would even [1b]mutilate themselves.

13 For you were called to [a]freedom, brethren; [b]only *do* not *turn* your freedom into an opportunity for the flesh, but through love [c]serve one another.

14 For [a]the whole Law is fulfilled in one word, in the *statement,* "[b]YOU SHALL LOVE YOUR NEIGHBOR AS YOURSELF."

15 But if you [a]bite and devour one another, take care lest you be consumed by one another.

16 But I say, [a]walk by the Spirit, and you will not carry out [b]the desire of the flesh.

17 For [a]the flesh [1]sets its desire against the Spirit, and the Spirit against the flesh; for these are in opposition to one another, [b]so that you may not do the things that you [2]please.

18 But if you are [a]led by the Spirit, [b]you are not under the Law.

19 Now the deeds of the flesh are evident, which are: [1a]immorality, impurity, sensuality,

20 idolatry, [a]sorcery, enmities, [b]strife, jealousy, outbursts of anger, [c]disputes, dissensions, [1d]factions,

21 envyings, [a]drunkenness, carousings, and

things like these, of which I forewarn you just as I have forewarned you that those who practice such things shall not ^binherit the kingdom of God.

22 But ^athe fruit of the Spirit is ^blove, joy, peace, patience, kindness, goodness, faithfulness,

23 gentleness, ^aself-control; against such things ^bthere is no law.

24 Now those who ¹belong to ^aChrist Jesus have ^bcrucified the flesh with its passions and ^cdesires.

25 If we live by the Spirit, let us also ¹walk ^aby the Spirit.

26 Let us not become ^aboastful, challenging one another, envying one another.

^a

CHAPTER 6

BRETHREN, even if a man is caught in any trespass, you who are ^bspiritual, ^crestore such a one ^din a spirit of gentleness; looking to yourself, lest you too be tempted.

2 ^aBear one another's burdens, and thus fulfil ^bthe law of Christ.

3 For ^aif anyone thinks he is something when he is nothing, he deceives himself.

4 But let each one ^aexamine his own work, and then he will have *reason for* ^bboasting in regard to himself alone, and not in regard to another.

5 For ^aeach one shall bear his own load.

6 And ^alet the one who is taught ^bthe word share all good things with him who teaches.

7 ^aDo not be deceived, ^bGod is not mocked; for ^cwhatever a man sows, this he will also reap.

8 ^aFor the one who sows to his own flesh shall from the flesh reap ^bcorruption, but ^cthe one who sows to the Spirit shall from the Spirit reap eternal life.

9 And ^alet us not lose heart in doing good, for in due time we shall reap if we ^bdo not grow weary.

10 So then, ^{1a}while we have opportunity, let us do good to all men, and especially to those who are of the ^bhousehold of ^cthe faith.

11 See with what large letters I ¹am writing to you ^awith my own hand.

12 Those who desire ^ato make a good showing in the flesh try to ^bcompel you to be circumcised, simply that they ^cmay not be persecuted ¹for the cross of Christ.

21 ^b1 Cor. 6:9

22 ^aMatt. 7:16ff.; Rom. 6:21; Eph. 5:9 ^b1 Cor. 13:4; Rom. 5:1-5; Col. 3:12-15

23 ^aActs 24:25 ^bGal. 5:18

24 ¹Lit., *are of Christ Jesus* ^aGal. 3:26 ^bRom. 6:6; Gal. 2:20; 6:14 ^cGal. 5:16f.

25 ¹Or, *follow the Spirit* ^aGal. 5:16

26 ^aPhil. 2:3

1 ^aGal. 6:18; 1 Thess. 4:1 ^b1 Cor. 2:15 ^c2 Cor. 2:7; 2 Thess. 3:15; Heb. 12:13; James 5:19f. ^d1 Cor. 4:21

2 ^aRom. 15:1 ^b1 Cor. 9:21; James 1:25; 2:12; Rom. 8:2; 2 Pet. 3:2

3 ^a1 Cor. 3:18; 2 Cor. 12:11; Acts 5:36

4 ^a1 Cor. 11:28 ^bPhil. 1:26

5 ^aProv. 9:12; Rom. 14:12; 1 Cor. 3:8

6 ^a1 Cor. 9:11, 14 ^b2 Tim. 4:2

7 ^a1 Cor. 6:9 ^bJob 13:9 ^c2 Cor. 9:6

8 ^aJob 4:8; Hos. 8:7; Rom. 6:21 ^b1 Cor. 15:42 ^cJames 3:18; Rom. 8:11

9 ^a2 Cor. 4:1; 1 Cor. 15:58 ^bHeb. 12:3, 5; James 5:7f.; Matt. 10:22

10 ¹Or, *as* ^aProv. 3:27; John 12:35 ^bEph. 2:19; Heb. 3:6; 1 Pet. 2:5; 4:17 ^cActs 6:7; Gal. 1:23

11 ¹Or, *have written* ^a1 Cor. 16:21

12 ¹Or, *because of* ^aMatt. 23:27f. ^bActs 15:1 ^cGal. 5:11

401

13 [1]Some ancient mss. read, *have been* [2]Or, *law* [a]Rom. 2:25 [b]Phil. 3:3

14 [1]Or, *whom* [a]Gal. 2:17; 3:21; Luke 20:16 [in the Gr.] [b]1 Cor. 2:2 [c]Gal. 2:20; Col. 2:20 [d]Rom. 6:2, 6; Gal. 2:19f.; 5:24

15 [1]Or, *creature* [a]Gal. 5:6; 1 Cor. 7:19; Rom. 2:26, 28 [b]2 Cor. 5:17; Eph. 2:10, 15; 4:24; Col. 3:10

16 [1]Or, *follow this rule* [a]Rom. 9:6; Gal. 3:7, 29; Phil. 3:3

17 [a]Is. 44:5 marg.; Ezek. 9:4; Rev. 13:16; 2 Cor. 4:10; 11:23

18 [a]Rom. 16:20 [b]2 Tim. 4:22 [c]Gal. 3:15; 4:12, 28, 31; Rom. 1:13; Acts 1:15

1 [1]Lit., *through* [2]I.e., true believers; lit., *holy ones* [3]Some ancient mss. omit, *at Ephesus* [a]2 Cor. 1:1 [b]Eph. 2:6, 7, 10, 13, 20; 3:1, 6, 11, 21; Col. 1:4; 2:6; 4:12; Rom. 8:1; Gal. 3:26 [c]1 Cor. 1:1 [d]Acts 9:13; Phil. 1:1; Col. 1:1 [e]Acts 18:19 [f]Col. 1:2

2 [a]Rom. 1:7

3 [a]2 Cor. 1:3 [b]Eph. 1:20; 2:6; 3:10; 6:12; Phil. 3:20

4 [1]Or, *Him, in love* [a]2 Thess. 2:13f.; Eph. 2:10 [b]Matt. 25:34 [c]Eph. 5:27; Col. 1:22; 2 Tim. 1:9 [d]Eph. 4:2, 15, 16; 5:2

5 [1]Lit., *having predestined* [2]Lit., *good pleasure* [a]Eph. 1:11; Rom. 8:29f.; Acts 13:48 [b]Rom. 8:14ff.; Gal. 4:5 [c]Luke 12:32; 1 Cor. 1:21; Gal. 1:15; Phil. 2:13; Col. 1:19

6 [a]Eph. 1:12, 14 [b]Matt. 3:17

7 [1]Lit., *whom* [a]Col. 1:14 [b]Eph. 1:14; 1 Cor. 1:30; Rom. 3:24 [c]Acts 20:28; Rom. 3:25 [d]Acts 2:38 [e]Rom. 2:4; Eph. 1:18; 2:7; 3:8, 16; Col. 1:27

8 [1]Lit., *made abundant toward* [2]Or, *us, in all wisdom and insight*

13 For those who [1]are circumcised do not even [a]keep [2]the Law themselves, but they desire to have you circumcised, that they may [b]boast in your flesh.

14 But [a]may it never be that I should boast, [b]except in the cross of our Lord Jesus Christ, [c]through [1]which the world has been crucified to me, and [d]I to the world.

15 For [a]neither is circumcision anything, nor uncircumcision, but a [b]new [1]creation.

16 And those who will [1]walk by this rule, peace and mercy *be* upon them, and upon the [a]Israel of God.

17 From now on let no one cause trouble for me, for I bear on my body the [a]brand-marks of Jesus.

18 [a]The grace of our Lord Jesus Christ be [b]with your spirit, [c]brethren. Amen.

THE EPISTLE OF PAUL TO THE

EPHESIANS

Salutation. The Blessings of Redemption.

PAUL, [a]an apostle of [b]Christ Jesus [1c]by the will of God, to the [2d]saints who are [3]at [e]Ephesus, and [f]*who are* faithful in [h]Christ Jesus:

2 [a]Grace to you and peace from God our Father and the Lord Jesus Christ.

3 [a]Blessed *be* the God and Father of our Lord Jesus Christ, who has blessed us with every spiritual blessing in [b]the heavenly *places* in Christ,

4 just as [a]He chose us in Him before [b]the foundation of the world, that we should be [c]holy and blameless before [1]Him. [d]In love

5 [1]He [a]predestined us to [b]adoption as sons through Jesus Christ to Himself, [c]according to the [2]kind intention of His will,

6 [a]to the praise of the glory of His grace, which He freely bestowed on us in [b]the Beloved.

7 [a]In [1]Him we have [b]redemption [c]through His blood, the [d]forgiveness of our trespasses, according to [e]the riches of His grace,

8 which He [1]lavished upon [2]us. In all wisdom and insight

9 He [1a]made known to us the mystery of His will, [b]according to His [2]kind intention which He [c]purposed in Him

10 with a view to an administration [1]suitable to [a]the fulness of the times, *that is,* [b]the summing up of all things in Christ, things [2]in the heavens and things upon the earth. In Him

11 [1]also we [2a]have obtained an inheritance, having been [b]predestined [c]according to His purpose who works all things [d]after the counsel of His will,

12 to the end that we who were the first to hope in [1]Christ should be [a]to the praise of His glory.

13 In [1]Him, you also, after listening to [a]the message of truth, the gospel of your salvation—having also [2]believed, you were [b]sealed in [1]Him with [c]the Holy Spirit of promise,

14 who is [1a]given as a pledge of [b]our inheritance, with a view to the [c]redemption of [d]*God's own* possession, [e]to the praise of His glory.

15 For this reason I too, [a]having heard of the faith in the Lord Jesus which *exists* among you, and [1]your love for [b]all the [2]saints,

16 [a]do not cease giving thanks for you, [b]while making mention *of you* in my prayers;

17 that the [a]God of our Lord Jesus Christ, [b]the Father of glory, may give to you a spirit of [c]wisdom and of [d]revelation in the [1]knowledge of Him.

18 *I pray that* [a]the eyes of your heart [1]may be enlightened, so that you may know what is the [b]hope of His [c]calling, what are [d]the riches of the glory of [e]His inheritance in [f]the [2]saints,

19 and what is the surpassing greatness of His power toward us who believe. [a]*These are* in accordance with the working of the [b]strength of His might

20 which He brought about in Christ, when He [a]raised Him from the dead, and [b]seated Him at His right hand in [c]the heavenly *places,*

21 far above [a]all rule and authority and power and dominion, and every [b]name that is named, not only in [c]this age, but also in the one to come.

22 And He [a]put all things in subjection under His feet, and gave Him as [b]head over all things to the church,

23 which is His [a]body, the [b]fulness of Him who [c]fills [d]all in all.

9 [1]Lit., *making known*
[2]Lit., *good pleasure*
[a]Rom. 11:25; 16:25; Eph. 3:3
[b]Luke 12:32; 1 Cor. 1:21;
Gal. 1:15; Phil. 2:13; Col.
1:19 [c]Eph. 1:11; Rom. 8:28

10 [1]Lit., *of* [2]Lit., *upon*
[a]Mark 1:15 [b]Col. 1:16, 20;
Eph. 3:15; Phil. 2:9f.

11 [1]Lit., *in whom also* [2]Or,
were made a heritage
[a]Eph. 1:14, 18; Titus 2:14;
Deut. 4:20; 9:26, 29; 32:9
[b]Eph. 1:5 [c]Eph. 3:11; Rom.
8:28f. [d]Rom. 9:11; Heb. 6:17

12 [1]I.e., the Messiah
[a]Eph. 1:6, 14

13 [1]Lit., *whom* [2]Or,
*believed in Him, you were
sealed*
[a]Col. 1:5; Acts 13:26; Eph.
4:21 [b]Eph. 4:30; John 3:33
[c]Acts 1:4f.; 2:33

14 [1]Or, *down payment*
[a]2 Cor. 1:22 [b]Acts 20:32
[c]Eph. 1:7 [d]Eph. 1:11 [e]Eph.
1:6, 12

15 [1]Many ancient mss.
omit, *your love* [2]Note 2, vs. 1
[a]Col. 1:4; Philem. 5; Rom.
1:8 [b]Eph. 3:18; Eph. 1:1

16 [a]Col. 1:9; Rom. 1:8f.
[b]Rom. 1:9

17 [1]Or, *true knowledge*
[a]John 20:17; Rom. 15:6
[b]Acts 7:2; 1 Cor. 2:8 [c]Col. 1:9
[d]1 Cor. 14:6

18 [1]Lit., *being* [2]I.e., true
believers; lit., *holy ones*
[a]Acts 26:18; 2 Cor. 4:6; Heb.
6:4 [b]Eph. 4:4 [c]Rom. 11:29
[d]Eph. 1:7 [e]Eph. 1:11 [f]Col.
1:12; Acts 9:13

19 [a]Eph. 3:7; Phil. 3:21;
Col. 1:29 [b]Eph. 6:10

20 [a]Acts 2:24 [b]Mark 16:19
[c]Eph. 1:3

21 [a]Col. 1:16; Eph. 3:10;
Rom. 8:38; Matt. 28:18
[b]Phil. 2:9; Heb. 1:4; Rev.
19:12; John 17:11 [c]Eph. 2:2;
Matt. 12:32

22 [a]1 Cor. 15:27 [fr. Ps. 8:6]
[b]Eph. 4:15; 5:23; Col. 1:18;
2:19; 1 Cor. 11:3

23 [a]Eph. 4:12; 5:30; Col.
1:18, 24; 2:19; 1 Cor. 12:27
[b]John 1:16; Eph. 3:19 [c]Eph.
4:10 [d]Col. 3:11

CHAPTER 2

1 [1]Lit., *being* [2]Or, *by reason of*
[a]Eph. 2:5; Col. 2:13; Luke 15:24, 32

2 [1]Lit., *age*
[a]Eph. 2:3, 11, 13; 5:8; Col. 3:7; Rom. 13:13; 1 Cor. 6:11; 1 Pet. 4:3 [b]Eph. 1:21 [c]Eph. 6:12; John 12:31 [d]Eph. 5:6

3 [1]Lit., *doing* [2]Lit., *thoughts*
[a]Eph. 2:2 [b]Gal. 5:16f. [c]Rom. 2:14; Gal. 2:15 [d]Rom. 5:10; Col. 1:21; 2 Pet. 2:14 [e]Rom. 5:12, 19; 1 Thess. 4:13; 5:6

4 [a]Eph. 1:7 [b]John 3:16

5 [1]Or, *by reason of* [2]Some ancient mss. read, *in Christ*
[a]Eph. 2:1 [b]Eph. 2:8; Acts 15:11

6 [a]Col. 2:12 [b]Eph. 1:20 [c]Eph. 1:3 [d]Eph. 1:1; 2:10, 13

7 [a]Rom. 2:4; Eph. 1:7 [b]Titus 3:4

8 [1]I.e., that salvation
[a]Eph. 2:5; Acts 15:11 [b]1 Pet. 1:5 [c]John 4:10; Heb. 6:4

9 [a]2 Tim. 1:9; Titus 3:5; Rom. 3:28 [b]1 Cor. 1:29

10 [a]Eph. 2:15; 4:24; Col. 3:10 [b]Eph. 1:1; 2:6, 13 [c]Titus 2:14 [d]Eph. 1:4 [e]Eph. 4:1

11 [a]Eph. 2:2, 3, 13; 5:8; Col. 3:7; Rom. 13:13; 1 Cor. 6:11; 1 Pet. 4:3 [b]1 Cor. 12:2; Eph. 5:8 [c]Col. 2:11, 13; Rom. 2.28f.

12 [1]Or, *alienated*
[a]Rom. 9:4; Col. 1:21 [b]Gal. 3:17; Heb. 8:6 [c]1 Thess. 4:13 [d]Gal. 4:8; 1 Thess. 4:5; Eph. 4:18

13 [1]Lit., *became*, or, *were made* [2]Or, *in*
[a]Eph. 1:1; 2:6, 10 [b]Eph. 2:2, 3, 11; 5:8; Col. 3:7; Rom. 13:13; 1 Cor. 6:11; 1 Pet. 4:3 [c]Eph. 2:17; Acts 2:39; Is. 57:19 [d]Col. 1:20; Rom. 3:25

14 [1]Lit., *the dividing wall of the barrier*
[a]Eph. 2:15; Col. 3:15; Gal. 3:28; Col. 3:11; Is. 9:6 [b]1 Cor. 12:13

15 [1]Or, *the enmity, by abolishing in His flesh the Law* [2]Lit., *create*
[a]Eph. 2:16; Col. 1:21f. [b]Col. 2:14; 2:20 [c]Eph. 2:10; 4:24; Col. 3:10 [d]Gal. 3:28; Col. 3:10f. [e]Eph. 2:14; Col. 3:15; Gal. 3:28; Col. 3:11; Is. 9:6

A ND you [1]were [a]dead [2]in your trespasses and sins,

2 in which you [a]formerly walked according to the [1]course of [b]this world, according to [c]the prince of the power of the air, of the spirit that is now working in [d]the sons of disobedience.

3 Among them we too all [a]formerly lived in [b]the lusts of our flesh, [1]indulging the desires of the flesh and of the [2]mind, and were [c]by nature [d]children of wrath, [e]even as the rest.

4 But God, being [a]rich in mercy, because of [b]His great love with which He loved us,

5 even when we were [a]dead [1]in our transgressions, [a]made us alive together [2]with Christ ([b]by grace you have been saved),

6 and [a]raised us up with Him, and [b]seated us with Him in [c]the heavenly *places*, in [d]Christ Jesus,

7 in order that in the ages to come He might show the surpassing [a]riches of His grace in [b]kindness toward us in Christ Jesus.

8 For [a]by grace you have been saved [b]through faith; and [1]that not of yourselves, *it is* [c]the gift of God;

9 [a]not as a result of works, that [b]no one should boast.

10 For we are His workmanship, [a]created in [b]Christ Jesus for [c]good works, which God [d]prepared beforehand, that we should [e]walk in them.

11 Therefore remember, that [a]formerly [b]you, the Gentiles in the flesh, who are called ["Uncircumcision"] by the so-called ["Circumcision,"] *which is* performed in the flesh by human hands—

12 *remember* that you were at that time separate from Christ, [1a]excluded from the commonwealth of Israel, and strangers to [b]the covenants of promise, having [c]no hope and [d]without God in the world.

13 But now in [a]Christ Jesus you who [b]formerly were [c]far off [1]have [c]been brought near [2d]by the blood of Christ.

14 For He Himself is [a]our peace, [b]who made both *groups into* one, and broke down the [1]barrier of the dividing wall,

15 [1]by [a]abolishing in His flesh the enmity, *which is* [b]the Law of commandments *contained* in ordinances, that in Himself He might [2c]make the two into [d]one new man, *thus* establishing [e]peace,

16 and might ᵃreconcile them both in ᵇone body to God through the cross, ¹by it having ᶜput to death the enmity.

17 AND ᵃHE CAME AND PREACHED ᵇPEACE TO YOU WHO WERE ᶜFAR AWAY, AND PEACE TO THOSE WHO WERE ᶜNEAR;

18 for through Him we both have ᵃour access in ᵇone Spirit to ᶜthe Father.

19 So then you are no longer ᵃstrangers and aliens, but you are ᵇfellow-citizens with the ¹saints, and are of ᶜGod's household,

20 having been ᵃbuilt upon ᵇthe foundation of ᶜthe apostles and prophets, ᵈChrist Jesus Himself being the ᵉcornerstone,

21 ᵃin whom the whole building, being fitted together is growing into ᵇa holy ¹temple in the Lord;

22 in whom you also are being ᵃbuilt together into a ᵇdwelling of God in the Spirit.

CHAPTER 3

FOR this reason I Paul, ᵃthe prisoner of ᵇChrist Jesus ᶜfor the sake of you ᵈGentiles—

2 if indeed you have heard of the ᵃstewardship of God's grace which was given to me for you;

3 ᵃthat ᵇby revelation there was ᶜmade known to me ᵈthe mystery, ᵉas I wrote before in brief.

4 ¹And by referring to this, when you read you can understand ᵃmy insight ²into the ᵇmystery of Christ,

5 which in other generations was not made known to the sons of men, as it has now been revealed to His holy ᵃapostles and prophets ¹in the Spirit;

6 *to be specific*, that the Gentiles are ᵃfellow-heirs and ᵇfellow-members of the body, and ᶜfellow-partakers of the promise in ᵈChrist Jesus through the gospel,

7 ᵃof which I was made a ᵇminister, according to the gift of ᶜGod's grace which was given to me ᵈaccording to the working of His power.

8 To me, ᵃthe very least of all ¹saints, this grace was given, to ᵇpreach to the Gentiles the unfathomable ᶜriches of Christ,

9 and to bring to light what is the administration of the ᵃmystery which for ages has been ᵇhidden in God, ᶜwho created all things;

16 ¹Or, *in Himself*
ᵃCol. 1:20, 22; 2 Cor. 5:18
ᵇEph. 4:4; 1 Cor. 10:17 ᶜEph. 2:15

17 ᵃIs. 57:19; Rom. 10:14;
Eph. 4:21 ᵇActs 10:36; Eph. 2:14 ᶜEph. 2:13; Acts 2:39; Is. 57:19

18 ᵃEph. 3:12; Rom. 5:2
ᵇEph. 4:4; 1 Cor. 12:13 ᶜCol. 1:12

19 ¹I.e., true believers; lit., *holy ones*
ᵃEph. 2:12; Heb. 11:13;
1 Pet. 2:11 ᵇPhil. 3:20; Heb. 12:22f. ᶜGal. 6:10

20 ᵃ1 Cor. 3:9 ᵇMatt. 16:18;
Rev. 21:14; 1 Cor. 3:10
ᶜ1 Cor. 12:28; Eph. 3:5
ᵈ1 Cor. 3:11 ᵉLuke 20:17 [Ps. 118:22]; 1 Pet. 2:6 [Is. 28:16]

21 ¹Or, *sanctuary*
ᵃEph. 4:15f.; Col. 2:19
ᵇ1 Cor. 3:16f.

22 ᵃ1 Cor. 3:9, 16; 2 Cor. 6:16 ᵇEph. 3:17

1 ᵃActs 23:18; Eph. 4:1;
2 Tim. 1:8; Philem. 1, 9; 23
ᵇGal. 5:24 ᶜEph. 3:13; 2 Cor. 1:6 ᵈEph. 3:8

2 ᵃCol. 1:25; 1 Tim. 1:4;
Eph. 1:10; 3:9

3 ᵃActs 22:17, 21; 26:16ff.
ᵇGal. 1:12 ᶜEph. 1:9; 3:4, 9
ᵈEph. 3:4, 9; 6:19; Col. 1:26f.; 4:3; Rom. 11:25; 16:25
ᵉEph. 1:9f. [Heb. 13:22;
1 Pet. 5:12]

4 ¹Lit., *to which, when you read* ²Lit., *in*
ᵃ2 Cor. 11:6 ᵇEph. 3:3, 9;
6:19; Col. 1:26f.; 4:3; Rom. 11:25; 16:25

5 ¹Or, *by*
ᵃ1 Cor. 12:28; Eph. 2:20

6 ᵃGal. 3:29 ᵇEph. 2:16
ᶜEph. 5:7 ᵈGal. 5:24

7 ᵃCol. 1:23, 25 ᵇ1 Cor. 3:5
ᶜEph. 3:2; Rom. 12:3; Acts 9:15 ᵈEph. 1:19; 3:20

8 ¹I.e., true believers; lit., *holy ones*
ᵃ1 Cor. 15:9 ᵇEph. 3:1f.; Acts 9:15 ᶜEph. 3:16; 1:7; Rom. 2:4

9 ᵃEph. 3:3, 4; 6:19; Col. 1:26f.; 4:3; Rom. 11:25; 16:25
ᵇCol. 3:3 ᶜRev. 4:11

10 ªRom. 11:33; 1 Cor. 2:7
ᵇ1 Pet. 1:12; Eph. 1:23 ᶜEph.
1:21; 6:12; Col. 2:10, 15
ᵈEph. 1:3

11 ¹Lit., *purpose of the ages*
²Or, *formed*
ªEph. 1:11 ᵇGal. 5:24; Eph.
3:1

12 ¹Lit., *access in
confidence* ²Lit., *of Him*
ªHeb. 4:16; 10:19, 35; 1 John
2:28; 3:21 ᵇ2 Cor. 3:4 ᶜEph.
2:18

13 ¹Or, *that I may not lose*
²Lit., *which are*
ª2 Cor. 4:1 ᵇEph. 3:1

14 ªPhil. 2:10

15 ¹Or, *the whole*

16 ªEph. 3:8; 1:18 ᵇPhil.
4:13; Col. 1:11; 1 Cor. 16:13
ᶜRom. 7:22

17 ªJohn 14:23; Rom. 8:9f.;
2 Cor. 13:5; Eph. 2:22 ᵇCol.
2:7; 1 Cor. 3:6 ᶜCol. 1:23

18 ¹Note vs. 8
ªEph. 1:15 ᵇJob 11:8f.

19 ªRom. 8:39; 8:35 ᵇPhil.
4:7 ᶜCol. 2:10 ᵈEph. 1:23

20 ªRom. 16:25 ᵇ2 Cor. 9:8
ᶜEph. 3:7

21 ¹Lit., *of the age of the
ages*
ªRom. 11:36

1 ªEph. 3:1 ᵇRom. 12:1
ᶜCol. 1:10; 1 Thess. 2:12;
Eph. 2:10; Col. 2:6 ᵈRom.
11:29 ᵉRom. 8:28f.

2 ªCol. 3:12f. ᵇEph. 1:4

3 ªCol. 3:14f.

4 ªEph. 2:16, 18; 1 Cor.
12:4ff. ᵇEph. 1:18

5 ª1 Cor. 8:6

10 in order that the manifold ªwisdom of God might now be ᵇmade known through the church to the ᶜrulers and the authorities in ᵈthe heavenly *places.*

11 *This was* in ªaccordance with the ¹eternal purpose which He ²carried out in ᵇChrist Jesus our Lord,

12 in whom we have ªboldness and ¹ᵇconfident ᶜaccess through faith ²in Him.

13 Therefore I ask ¹you not ªto lose heart at my tribulations ᵇon your behalf, ²for they are your glory.

14 For this reason, I ªbow my knees before the Father,

15 from whom ¹every family in heaven and on earth derives its name,

16 that He would grant you, according to ªthe riches of His glory, to be ᵇstrengthened with power through His Spirit in ᶜthe inner man;

17 so that ªChrist may dwell in your hearts through faith; *and* that you, being ᵇrooted and ᶜgrounded in love,

18 may be able to comprehend with ªall the ¹saints what is ᵇthe breadth and length and height and depth,

19 and to know ªthe love of Christ which ᵇsurpasses knowledge, that you may be ᶜfilled up to all the ᵈfulness of God.

20 ªNow to Him who is ᵇable to do exceeding abundantly beyond all that we ask or think, ᶜaccording to the power that works within us,

21 ªto Him *be* the glory in the church and in Christ Jesus to all generations ¹forever and ever. Amen.

CHAPTER 4

I, THEREFORE, ªthe prisoner of the Lord, ᵇentreat you to ᶜwalk in a manner worthy of the ᵈcalling with which you have been ᵉcalled,

2 with all ªhumility and gentleness, with patience, showing forbearance to one another ᵇin love,

3 being diligent to preserve the unity of the Spirit in the ªbond of peace.

4 *There is* ªone body and one Spirit, just as also you were called in one ᵇhope of your calling;

5 ªone Lord, one faith, one baptism,

6   one God and Father of all [a]who is over all and through all and in all.

7   But [a]to each one of us [b]grace was given [c]according to the measure of Christ's gift.

8   Therefore [1]it says,

"[a]WHEN HE ASCENDED ON HIGH,
HE [b]LED CAPTIVE A HOST OF CAPTIVES,
AND HE GAVE GIFTS TO MEN."

9   (Now this *expression*, "He [a]ascended," what [1]does it mean except that He also [2]had descended into [b]the lower parts of the earth?

10   He who descended is Himself also He who ascended [a]far above all the heavens, that He might [b]fill all things.)

11   And He [a]gave [b]some *as* apostles, and some *as* prophets, and some *as* [c]evangelists, and some *as* pastors and [d]teachers,

12   [a]for the equipping of the [1]saints for the work of service, to the building up of [b]the body of Christ;

13   until we all attain to [a]the unity of the faith, and of the [1b]knowledge of the Son of God, to a [c]mature man, to the measure of the stature [2]which belongs to the [d]fulness of Christ.

14   [1]As a result, we are [a]no longer to be children, [b]tossed here and there by waves, and carried about by every wind of doctrine, by the trickery of men, by [c]craftiness [2]in [d]deceitful scheming;

15   but [1]speaking the truth [a]in love, we [2]are to [b]grow up in all *aspects* into Him, who is the [c]head, *even* Christ,

16   from whom [a]the whole body, being fitted and held together [1]by that which every joint supplies, according to the [2]proper working of each individual part, causes the growth of the body for the building up of itself [b]in love.

17   [a]This I say therefore, and [b]affirm together with the Lord, [c]that you walk no longer just as the Gentiles also walk, in the [d]futility of their mind,

18   being [a]darkened in their understanding, [1]excluded from [b]the life of God, because of the [c]ignorance that is in them, because of the [d]hardness of their heart;

19   and they, having [a]become callous, [b]have given themselves over to [c]sensuality, [1]for the practice of every kind of impurity with greediness.

20   But you did not [a]learn [1]Christ in this way,

---

6 [a]Rom. 11:36; Col. 1:16

7 [a]1 Cor. 12:7, 11 [b]Eph. 3:2 [c]Rom. 12:3

8 [1]Or, *He*
[a]Ps. 68:18 [b]Judg. 5:12; Col. 2:15

9 [1]Lit., *is it except* [2]Some ancient mss. read, *had first descended*
[a]John 3:13 [b]Is. 44:23; Ps. 63:9

10 [a]Heb. 4:14; 7:26; 9:24; Eph. 1:20f. [b]Eph. 1:23

11 [a]Eph. 4:8 [b]1 Cor. 12:28; Acts 13:1 [c]Acts 21:8 [d]Acts 13:1

12 [1]I.e., true believers; lit., *holy ones*
[a]2 Cor. 13:9 [b]Eph. 1:23; 1 Cor. 12:27

13 [1]Or, *true knowledge* [2]Lit., *of the fulness*
[a]Eph. 4:3, 5 [b]Eph. 1:17; Phil. 3:10; John 6:69 [c]Heb. 5:14; 1 Cor. 14:20; Col. 1:28 [d]John 1:16; Gal. 4:19; Eph. 1:23

14 [1]Lit., *that we may no longer be* [2]Lit., *with regard to the scheming of deceit*
[a]1 Cor. 14:20 [b]James 1:6; Jude 12 [c]1 Cor. 3:19; 2 Cor. 4:2; 11:3 [d]Eph. 6:11

15 [1]Or, *holding to, or, walking in* [2]Lit., *may grow up*
[a]Eph. 4:4 [b]Eph. 2:21 [c]Eph. 1:22

16 [1]Lit., *through every joint of the supply* [2]Lit., *working in measure*
[a]Col. 2:19; Rom. 12:4f.; 1 Cor. 10:17 [b]Eph. 1:4

17 [a]Col. 2:4 [b]Luke 16:28 [c]Eph. 2:2; 4:22 [d]Rom. 1:21; Col. 2:18; 1 Pet. 1:18; 2 Pet. 2:18

18 [1]Or, *alienated*
[a]Rom. 1:21 [b]Eph. 2:1, 12 [c]Acts 17:30; Heb. 5:2; 9:7; 1 Pet. 1:14; Acts 3:17; 1 Cor. 2:8 [d]Mark 3:5; Rom. 11:7, 25; 2 Cor. 3:14

19 [1]Or, *greedy for the practice of every kind of impurity*
[a]1 Tim. 4:2 [b]Rom. 1:24 [c]Col. 3:5

20 [1]I.e., the Messiah
[a]Matt. 11:29

The Christian's Walk in Love and Light.

21 ᵃRom. 10:14; Eph. 1:13; 2:17; Col. 1:5 ᵇCol. 2:7

22 ¹Lit., *man* ᵃEph. 4:25, 31; Col. 3:8; Heb. 12:1 [Gr.]; James 1:21; 1 Pet. 2:1 ᵇRom. 6:6 ᶜ2 Cor. 11:3; Heb. 3:13

23 ᵃRom. 12:2

24 ¹Lit., *man* ²Lit., *according to God* ᵃRom. 13:14 ᵇCol. 3:10; Rom. 6:4; 7:6; 12:2; 2 Cor. 5:17 ᶜEph. 2:10

25 ᵃEph. 4:22, 31; Col. 3:8; Heb. 12:1 [Gr.]; James 1:21; 1 Pet. 2:1 ᵇZech. 8:16; Col. 3:9; Eph. 4:15 ᶜRom. 12:5

26 ᵃPs. 4:4 ᵇDeut. 24:15

27 ¹Lit., *place* ᵃJames 4:7; Rom. 12:19

28 ᵃActs 20:35; 1 Cor. 4:12; Gal. 6:10 ᵇ1 Thess. 4:11; 2 Thess. 3:8, 11f.; Titus 3:8, 14 ᶜLuke 3:11; 1 Thess. 4:12

29 ¹Lit., *rotten* ²Lit., *of the need* ᵃEph. 5:4; Col. 3:8; Matt. 12:34 ᵇRom. 14:19; Col. 4:6; Eccl. 10:12

30 ¹Lit., *in* ᵃIs. 63:10; 1 Thess. 5:19 ᵇEph. 1:13; John 3:33

31 ᵃCol. 3:8, 19; Rom. 3:14 ᵇEph. 4:22 ᶜ1 Pet. 2:1

32 ¹Some ancient mss. read, *us* ᵃCol. 3:12f.; 1 Cor. 13:4, 1 Pet. 3:8 ᵇMatt. 6:14f.; 2 Cor. 2:10

1 ᵃEph. 4:32; Luke 6:36; Matt. 5:48

2 ¹Some ancient mss. read, *us* ²Lit., *for an odor of fragrance* ᵃRom. 14:15; Col. 3:14 ᵇJohn 13:34; Rom. 8:37 ᶜEph. 5:25; Gal. 2:20; Rom. 4:25; John 6:51 ᵈHeb. 7:27; 9:14; 10:10, 12 ᵉ2 Cor. 2:14; Ex. 29:18, 25

3 ¹Lit., *and all* ²I.e., true believers; lit., *holy ones* ᵃCol. 3:5

4 ᵃEph. 4:29; Col. 3:8; Matt. 12:34 ᵇRom. 1:28 ᶜEph. 5:20

5 ᵃ1 Cor. 6:9; Col. 3:5

21 if indeed you ᵃhave heard Him and have ᵇbeen taught in Him, just as truth is in Jesus,

22 that, in reference to your former manner of life, you ᵃlay aside the ᵇold ¹self, which is being corrupted in accordance with the ᶜlusts of deceit,

23 and that you be ᵃrenewed in the spirit of your mind,

24 and ᵃput on the ᵇnew ¹self, which ²ᶜin *the likeness of* God has been created in righteousness and holiness of the truth.

25 Therefore, ᵃlaying aside falsehood, ᵇSPEAK TRUTH, EACH ONE *of you,* WITH HIS NEIGHBOR, for we are ᶜmembers of one another.

26 ᵃBE ANGRY, AND *yet* DO NOT SIN; do not let ᵇthe sun go down on your anger,

27 and do not ᵃgive the devil an ¹opportunity.

28 Let him who steals steal no longer; but rather ᵃlet him labor, ᵇperforming with his own hands what is good, ᶜin order that he may have *something* to share with him who has need.

29 Let no ¹ᵃunwholesome word proceed from your mouth, but only such *a word* as is good for ᵇedification ²according to the need *of the moment,* that it may give grace to those who hear.

30 And ᵃdo not grieve the Holy Spirit of God, ¹by whom you were ᵇsealed for the day of redemption.

31 ᵃLet all bitterness and wrath and anger and clamor and slander be ᵇput away from you, along with all ᶜmalice.

32 And ᵃbe kind to one another, tender-hearted, forgiving each other, ᵇjust as God in Christ also has forgiven ¹you.

CHAPTER 5

THEREFORE be imitators of God, as beloved children;

2 and ᵃwalk in love, just as Christ also ᵇloved ¹you, and ᶜgave Himself up for us, an ᵈoffering and a sacrifice to God ²as a ᵉfragrant aroma.

3 But do not let ᵃimmorality ¹or any impurity or greed even be named among you, as is proper among ²saints;

4 and *there must be no* ᵃfilthiness and silly talk, or coarse jesting, which ᵇare not fitting, but rather ᶜgiving of thanks.

5 For this you know with certainty, that ᵃno

[1]immoral or impure person or covetous man, who is an idolater, has an inheritance in the kingdom [b]of Christ and God.

6   [a]Let no one deceive you with empty words, for because of these things [b]the wrath of God comes upon [c]the sons of disobedience.

7   Therefore do not be [a]partakers with them;

8   for [a]you were formerly [b]darkness, but now you are light in the Lord; walk as [c]children of light

9   (for [a]the fruit of the light *consists* in all [b]goodness and righteousness and truth),

10   [1a]trying to learn what is pleasing to the Lord.

11   And [a]do not participate in the unfruitful [b]deeds of [c]darkness, but instead even [1d]expose them;

12   for it is disgraceful even to speak of the things which are done by them in secret.

13   But all things become visible [a]when they are [1]exposed by the light, for everything that becomes visible is light.

14   For this reason [1a]it says,
"[b]Awake, sleeper,
And arise from [c]the dead,
And Christ [d]will shine on you."

15   Therefore [1]be careful how you [a]walk, not [b]as unwise men, but as wise,

16   [1a]making the most of your time, because [b]the days are evil.

17   So then do not be foolish, but [a]understand what the will of the Lord is.

18   And [a]do not get drunk with wine, [1]for that is [b]dissipation, but be [c]filled with the Spirit,

19   [a]speaking to [1]one another in [b]psalms and [c]hymns and spiritual [d]songs, [e]singing and making melody with your heart to the Lord;

20   [a]always giving thanks for all things in the name of our Lord Jesus Christ to [1b]God, even the Father;

21   [1a]and be subject to one another in the [2b]fear of Christ.

22   [a]Wives, [b]*be subject* to your own husbands, [c]as to the Lord.

23   For [a]the husband is the head of the wife, as Christ also is the [b]head of the church, He Himself [c]*being* the Savior of the body.

24   But as the church is subject to Christ, so

5 [1]I.e., one who commits sexual immorality
[b]Col. 1:13

6 [a]Col. 2:8 [b]Rom. 1:18; Col. 3:6 [c]Eph. 2:2; Col. 3:6

7 [a]Eph. 3:6

8 [a]Eph. 2:2 [b]Acts 26:18; Col. 1:12f. [c]Luke 16:8; John 12:36; Rom. 13:12

9 [a]Gal. 5:22 [b]Rom. 15:14

10 [1]Lit., *proving what*
[a]Rom. 12:2

11 [1]Or, *reprove*
[a]1 Cor. 5:9; 2 Cor. 6:14 [b]Rom. 13:12 [c]Acts 26:18; Col. 1:12f. [d]1 Tim. 5:20

13 [1]Or, *reproved*
[a]John 3:20f.

14 [1]Or, *He*
[a]Is. 26:19; Is. 51:17; 52:1; 60:1 [b]Rom. 13:11 [c]Eph. 2:1 [d]Luke 1:78f.

15 [1]Lit., *look carefully*
[a]Eph. 5:2 [b]Col. 4:5

16 [1]Lit., *redeeming the time*
[a]Col. 4:5 [b]Eph. 6:13; Gal. 1:4

17 [a]Rom. 12:2; Col. 1:9; 1 Thess. 4:3

18 [1]Lit., *in which is*
[a]Prov. 20:1; 23:31f.; Rom. 13:13; 1 Cor. 5:11; 1 Thess. 5:7 [b]Titus 1:6; 1 Pet. 4:4 [c]Luke 1:15

19 [1]Or, *yourselves*
[a]Col. 3:16; James 5:13 [b]1 Cor. 14:26 [c]Acts 16:25 [d]Rev. 5:9 [e]1 Cor. 14:15

20 [1]Lit., *the God and Father*
[a]Eph. 5:4; Col. 3:17; Rom. 1:8 [b]1 Cor. 15:24

21 [1]Lit., *being subject* [2]Or, *reverence*
[a]Gal. 5:13; 1 Pet. 5:5; Phil. 2:3 [b]2 Cor. 5:11

22 [a]Eph. 5:22 to Eph. 6:9; *Col. 3:18 to 4:1* [b]1 Cor. 14:34f.; Titus 2:5; 1 Pet. 3:1 [c]Eph. 6:5

23 [a]1 Cor. 11:3 [b]Eph. 1:22 [c]1 Cor. 6:13

25 aEph. 5:28, 33; 1 Pet. 3:7
bEph. 5:2

26 aHeb. 10:10, 14, 29;
13:12; Titus 2:14 b2 Pet. 1:9
cTitus 3:5; Acts 22:16; 1 Cor.
6:11 dJohn 15:3; 17:17; Eph.
6:17; Rom. 10:8f.

27 1Lit., glorious
a2 Cor. 11:2; Col. 1:22;
2 Cor. 4:14 bEph. 1:4

28 aEph. 5:25, 33; 1 Pet. 3:7

30 a1 Cor. 6:15; 12:27 bEph.
1:23

31 aGen. 2:24; Matt. 19:5;
Mark 10:7f.

33 1Lit., fear
aEph. 5:25, 28; 1 Pet. 3:7
b1 Pet. 3:2, 5f.

1 aCol. 3:20; Prov. 6:20;
23:22

2 aEx. 20:12; Deut. 5:16

3 aEx. 20:12; Deut. 5:16

4 aCol. 3:21 bGen. 18:19;
Deut. 6:7; 11:19; Ps. 78:4;
Prov. 22:6; 2 Tim. 3:15

5 1I.e., earthly masters,
with fear
aCol. 3:22; 1 Tim. 6:1; Titus
2:9 b1 Cor. 2:3 cEph. 5:22

6 1Lit., according to 2Lit.,
soul
aCol. 3:22 bGal. 1:10 c1 Cor.
7:22

7 1Lit., rendering
aCol. 3:23

8 aCol. 3:24 bMatt. 16:27;
2 Cor. 5:10; Col. 3:24f.

also the wives *ought to be* to their husbands in everything.

25 aHusbands, love your wives, just as Christ also loved the church and bgave Himself up for her;

26 athat He might sanctify her, having bcleansed her by the cwashing of water with dthe word,

27 that He might apresent to Himself the church 1in all her glory, having no spot or wrinkle or any such thing; but that she should be bholy and blameless.

28 So husbands ought also to alove their own wives as their own bodies. He who loves his own wife loves himself;

29 for no one ever hated his own flesh, but nourishes and cherishes it, just as Christ also *does* the church,

30 because we are amembers of His bbody.

31 aFOR THIS CAUSE A MAN SHALL LEAVE HIS FATHER AND MOTHER, AND SHALL CLEAVE TO HIS WIFE; AND THE TWO SHALL BECOME ONE FLESH.

32 This mystery is great; but I am speaking with reference to Christ and the church.

33 Nevertheless let each individual among you also alove his own wife even as himself; and *let* the wife *see to it* that she 1brespect her husband.

a   CHAPTER 6

CHILDREN, obey your parents in the Lord, for this is right.

2 aHONOR YOUR FATHER AND MOTHER (which is the first commandment with a promise),

3 aTHAT IT MAY BE WELL WITH YOU, AND THAT YOU MAY LIVE LONG ON THE EARTH.

4 And, afathers, do not provoke your children to anger; but bbring them up in the discipline and instruction of the Lord.

5 aSlaves, be obedient to those who are your 1masters according to the flesh, with bfear and trembling, in the sincerity of your heart, cas to Christ;

6 anot 1by way of eyeservice, as bmen-pleasers, but as cslaves of Christ, doing the will of God from the 2heart.

7 With good will 1render service; aas to the Lord, and not to men,

8 aknowing that bwhatever good thing each

one does, this he will receive back from the Lord, ^cwhether slave or free.

9 And, masters, do the same things to them, and ^agive up threatening, knowing that ^bboth their Master and yours is in heaven, and there is ^cno partiality with Him.

10 Finally, ^abe strong in the Lord, and in ^bthe strength of His might.

11 ^aPut on the full armor of God, that you may be able to stand firm against the ^bschemes of the devil.

12 For our ^astruggle is not against ^1b flesh and blood, but ^cagainst the rulers, against the powers, against the ^dworld-forces of this ^edarkness, against the ^fspiritual *forces* of wickedness in ^gthe heavenly *places*.

13 Therefore take up ^athe full armor of God, that you may be able to ^bresist in ^cthe evil day, and having done everything, to stand firm.

14 Stand firm therefore, ^aHAVING GIRDED YOUR LOINS WITH TRUTH, AND HAVING ^bPUT ON THE ^cBREASTPLATE OF RIGHTEOUSNESS,

15 and having ^ashod YOUR FEET WITH THE PREPARATION OF THE GOSPEL OF PEACE;

16 ^1in addition to all, taking up the ^ashield of faith with which you will be able to extinguish all the ^bflaming missiles of ^cthe evil *one*.

17 And take the ^ahelmet of salvation, and the ^bsword of the Spirit, which is ^cthe word of God.

18 With all ^aprayer and petition ^1b pray at all times ^cin the Spirit, and with this in view, ^2d be on the alert with all ^eperseverance and ^fpetition for all the saints,

19 and ^apray on my behalf, that utterance may be given to me ^bin the opening of my mouth, to make known with ^cboldness ^dthe mystery of the gospel,

20 for which I am an ^aambassador ^bin ^1chains; that ^2in *proclaiming* it I may speak ^cboldly, ^das I ought to speak.

21 ^aBut that you also may know about my circumstances, how I am doing, ^bTychicus, ^cthe beloved brother and faithful minister in the Lord, will make everything known to you.

22 ^1And ^aI have sent him to you for this very purpose, so that you may know ^2about us, and that he may ^bcomfort your hearts.

23 ^aPeace be to the brethren, and ^blove with

8 ^cl Cor. 12:13; Col. 3:11

9 ^aLev. 25:43 ^bJob 31:13ff.; John 13:13 ^cActs 10:34; Col. 3:25

10 ^al Cor. 16:13; 2 Tim. 2:1 ^bEph. 1:19

11 ^aEph. 6:13; Rom. 13:12 ^bEph. 4:14

12 ^1Lit., *blood and flesh* ^al Cor. 9:25 ^bMatt. 16:17 ^cEph. 1:21; 2:2; 3:10 ^dJohn 12:31 ^eActs 26:18; Col. 1:13 ^fEph. 3:10 ^gEph. 1:3

13 ^aEph. 6:11 ^bJames 4:7 ^cEph. 5:16

14 ^aIs. 11:5; Luke 12:35; 1 Pet. 1:13 ^bEph. 6:13; Rom. 13:12 ^cIs. 59:17; 1 Thess. 5:8

15 ^aIs. 52:7; Rom. 10:15

16 ^1Lit., *in all* ^al Thess. 5:8 ^bPs. 7:13; 120:4 ^cMatt. 5:37

17 ^aIs. 59:17 ^bHeb. 4:12; Is. 49:2; Hos. 6:5 ^cHeb. 6:5; Eph. 5:26

18 ^1Lit., *praying* ^2Lit., *being* ^aPhil. 4:6 ^bLuke 18:1; Col. 1:3; 4:2; 1 Thess. 5:17 ^cRom. 8:26f. ^dMark 13:33 ^eActs 1:14 [Gr.] ^fl Tim. 2:1

19 ^aCol. 4:3; 1 Thess. 5:25 ^b2 Cor. 6:11 ^c2 Cor. 3:12 ^dEph. 3:3

20 ^1Lit., *a chain* ^2Some ancient mss. read, *I may speak it boldly* ^a2 Cor. 5:20; Philem. 9 marg. ^bActs 21:33; 28:20; Col. 4:3; Eph. 3:1; Phil. 1:7 ^c2 Cor. 3:12 ^dCol 4:4

21 ^aEph. 6:21, 22: Col. 4:7-9 ^bActs 20:4 ^cCol. 4:7

22 ^1Lit., *whom I have sent to you* ^2Lit., *the things about us* ^aCol. 4:8 ^bCol. 2:2; 4:8

23 ^aGal. 6:16; 2 Thess. 3:16; 1 Pet. 5:14; Rom. 15:33 ^bGal. 5:6; 1 Thess. 5:8

24 [1]Lit., *in incorruption*

faith, from God the Father and the Lord Jesus Christ.

24   Grace be with all those who love our Lord Jesus Christ [1]with *a love* incorruptible.

THE EPISTLE OF PAUL TO THE
PHILIPPIANS

Salutation.   Thanksgiving and Supplication.

1 [1]I.e., true believers; lit., *holy ones*
[a]2 Cor. 1:1; Col. 1:1; Philem. 1; 1 Thess. 1:1; 2 Thess. 1:1 [b]Acts 16:1 [c]Rom. 1:1; Gal. 1:10 [d]Phil. 1:8; 2:5; 3:3, 8, 12, 14; 4:7, 19, 21; Gal. 3:26 [e]2 Cor. 1:1; Col. 1:2 [f]Acts 9:13 [g]Acts 16:12 [h]Acts 20:28; 1 Tim. 3:1f.; Titus 1:7 [i]1 Tim. 3.8ff.

2 [a]Rom. 1:7

3 [a]Rom. 1:8

4 [a]Rom. 1:9

5 [1]Or, *sharing in the preaching of the gospel* [a]Acts 2:42; Phil. 4:15 [b]Phil. 1:7, 12, 16, 27; 2:22; 4:3, 15 [c]Phil. 2:12; 4:15; Acts 16:12-40

6 [a]1 Cor. 1:8; Phil. 1:10; 2:16

7 [1]Lit., *Just as it is right* [2]Lit, *bonds* [a]2 Pet. 1:13 [b]2 Cor. 7:3 [c]Phil. 1:13f., 17; Acts 21:33; Eph. 6:20 [d]Phil. 1:16 [e]Phil. 1:5, 12, 16, 27; 2:22; 4:3, 15

8 [1]Lit., *inward parts* [a]Rom. 1:9 [b]Phil. 1:1; 2:5; 3:3, 8, 12, 14; 4:7, 19, 21; Gal. 3:26

9 [a]1 Thess. 3:12 [b]Col. 1:9

10 [1]Or, *distinguish between the things which differ* [2]Lit., *for* [a]Rom. 2:18 [b]1 Cor. 1:8; Phil. 1:6; 2:16

11 [a]James 3:18

12 [a]Luke 21:13 [b]Phil. 1:5, 7, 16, 27; 2:22; 4:3, 15

13 [1]Lit., *bonds* [a]Phil. 1:7; 2 Tim. 2:9

[a]Paul and [b]Timothy, [c]bond-servants of [d]Christ Jesus, to [e]all the [1f]saints in Christ Jesus who are in [g]Philippi, including the [h]overseers and [i]deacons:

2   [a]Grace to you and peace from God our Father and the Lord Jesus Christ.

3   [a]I thank my God in all my remembrance of you,

4   always offering prayer with joy in [a]my every prayer for you all,

5   in view of your [1a]participation in the [b]gospel [c]from the first day until now.

6   *For I am* confident of this very thing, that He who began a good work in you will perfect it until [a]the day of Christ Jesus.

7   [1]For [a]it is only right for me to feel this way about you all, because I [b]have you in my heart, since both in my [2c]imprisonment and in the [d]defense and confirmation of the [e]gospel, you all are partakers of grace with me.

8   For [a]God is my witness, how I long for you all with the [1]affection of [b]Christ Jesus.

9   And this I pray, that [a]your love may abound still more and more in [b]real knowledge and all discernment,

10   so that you may [1a]approve the things that are excellent, in order to be sincere and blameless [2]until [b]the day of Christ;

11   having been filled with the [a]fruit of righteousness which *comes* through Jesus Christ, to the glory and praise of God.

12   Now I want you to know, brethren, that my circumstances [a]have turned out for the greater progress of the [b]gospel,

13   so that my [1a]imprisonment in *the cause of*

Christ has become well-known throughout the whole [2]praetorian guard and to [b]everyone else,

14 and that most of the [1]brethren, trusting in the Lord because of my [2a]imprisonment, have [b]far more courage to speak the word of God without fear.

15 [a]Some, to be sure, are preaching Christ even from envy and strife, but some also from good will;

16 [1]the latter *do it* out of love, knowing that I am [a]appointed for the defense of the [b]gospel;

17 the former proclaim Christ [a]out of selfish ambition, [1]rather than from pure motives, thinking to cause me distress in my [2b]imprisonment.

18 What then? Only that in every way, whether in pretense or in truth, Christ is proclaimed; and in this I rejoice, yes, and I will rejoice.

19 For I know that this shall turn out for my [1]deliverance [a]through your [2]prayers and the provision of [b]the Spirit of Jesus Christ,

20 according to my [a]earnest expectation and [b]hope, that I shall not be [b]put to shame in anything, but *that* with [c]all boldness, Christ shall even now, as always, be [d]exalted in my body, [e]whether by life or by death.

21 For to me, [a]to live is Christ, and to die is gain.

22 [1]But if *I am* to live *on* in the flesh, this *will mean* [a]fruitful labor for me; and I do not know [2]which to choose.

23 But I am hard pressed from both *directions*, having the [a]desire to depart and [b]be with Christ, for *that* is very much better;

24 yet to remain on in the flesh is more necessary for your sake.

25 And [a]convinced of this, I know that I shall remain and continue with you all for your progress and joy in the faith,

26 so that your [a]proud confidence in me may abound in Christ Jesus through my coming to you again.

27 Only conduct yourselves in a manner [a]worthy of the [b]gospel of Christ; so that whether I come and see you or remain absent, I may hear of you that you are [c]standing firm in [d]one spirit, with one [1]mind [e]striving together for the faith of the gospel;

28 in no way alarmed by *your* opponents— which is a [a]sign of destruction for them, but of salvation for you, and that *too*, from God.

13 [2]Or, *governor's palace*
[b]Acts 28:30

14 [1]Or, *brethren in the Lord, trusting because of my bonds* [2]Lit., *bonds*
[a]Phil. 1:7; 2 Tim. 2:9 [b]Phil. 1:20; 2 Cor. 3:12; 7:4; Acts 4:31

15 [a]2 Cor. 11:13

16 [1]Some later mss. reverse the order of vss. 16 and 17
[a]1 Cor. 9:17 [b]Phil. 1:5, 7, 12, 27; 2:22; 4:3, 15

17 [1]Lit., *not sincerely* [2]Lit., *bonds*
[a]Phil. 2:3; Rom. 2:8 [b]Phil. 1:7; 2 Tim. 2:9

19 [1]Or, *salvation* [2]Lit., *supplication*
[a]2 Cor. 1:11 [b]Acts 16:7

20 [a]Rom. 8:19 [b]Rom. 5:5; 1 Pet. 4:16 [c]Phil. 1:14; 2 Cor. 3:12; 7:4; Acts 4:31 [d]1 Cor. 6:20 [e]Rom. 14:8

21 [a]Gal. 2:20

22 [1]Or, *But if to live in the flesh, this will be fruitful labor for me, then I . . .* [2]Lit., *what I shall choose*
[a]Rom. 1:13

23 [a]2 Cor. 5:8; 2 Tim. 4:6 [b]John 12:26

25 [a]Phil. 2:24

26 [a]2 Cor. 5:12; 7:4; Phil. 2:16

27 [1]Lit., *soul*
[a]Eph. 4:1 [b]Phil. 1:5 [c]Phil. 4:1; 1 Cor. 16:13 [d]Acts 4:32 [e]Jude 3

28 [a]2 Thess. 1:5

Philippians 1, 2

**The Lowly Mind of Christ.
Exhortations to Obedience.**

29 a Matt. 5:12 b Acts 14:22

30 a 1 Thess. 2:2; Heb. 10:32; also Col. 1:29; 2:1; 1 Tim. 6:12; 2 Tim. 4:7; Heb. 12:1, [Gr.] b Acts 16:19-40; Phil. 1:13

1 ¹Lit., *inward parts* a 2 Cor. 13:14 [Gr.] b Col. 3:12

2 ¹Lit., *that you be* a John 3:29 b Rom. 12:16; Phil. 4:2

3 ¹Or, *contentiousness* a Phil. 1:17 marg.; Rom. 2:8 b Gal. 5:26 c Rom. 12:10; Eph. 5:21

4 a Rom. 15:1f.

5 ¹Or, *among* a Matt. 11:29; Rom. 15:3 b Phil. 1:1

6 a John 1:1 b 2 Cor. 4:4 c John 5:18; 10:33; 14:28

7 ¹I.e., laid aside His privileges a 2 Cor. 8:9 b Matt. 20:28 c John 1:14; Rom. 8:3; Gal. 4:4; Heb. 2:17

8 ¹Lit., *of* a 2 Cor. 8:9 b Heb. 5:8; Matt. 26:39; John 10:18; Rom. 5:19 c Heb. 12:2

9 a Heb. 1:9 b Matt. 28:18; Acts 2:33; Heb. 2:9 c Eph. 1:21

10 a Rom. 14:11 b Eph. 1:10

11 a John 13:13; Rom. 10:9; 14:9

12 a Phil. 1:5, 6; 4:15 b Heb. 5:9 c 2 Cor. 7:15

13 a 1 Cor. 12:6; 15:10; Rom. 12:3; Heb. 13:21 b Eph. 1:5

414

29 For to you ᵃit has been granted for Christ's sake, not only to believe in Him, but also to ᵇsuffer for His sake,

30 experiencing the same ᵃconflict which ᵇyou saw in me, and now hear *to be* in me.

CHAPTER 2

IF therefore there is any encouragement in Christ, if there is any consolation of love, if there is any ᵃfellowship of the Spirit, if any ¹ᵇaffection and compassion,

2 ᵃmake my joy complete ¹by ᵇbeing of the same mind, maintaining the same love, united in spirit, intent on one purpose.

3 Do nothing from ¹ᵃselfishness or ᵇempty conceit, but with humility of mind let ᶜeach of you regard one another as more important than himself;

4 ᵃdo not *merely* look out for your own personal interests, but also for the interests of others.

5 ᵃHave this attitude ¹in yourselves which was also in ᵇChrist Jesus,

6 who, although He ᵃexisted in the ᵇform of God, ᶜdid not regard equality with God a thing to be grasped,

7 but ¹ᵃemptied Himself, taking the form of a ᵇbond-servant, *and* ᶜbeing made in the likeness of men.

8 And being found in appearance as a man, ᵃHe humbled Himself by becoming ᵇobedient to the point of death, even ᶜdeath ¹on a cross.

9 ᵃTherefore also God ᵇhighly exalted Him, and bestowed on Him ᶜthe name which is above every name,

10 that at the name of Jesus ᵃevery knee should bow, of ᵇthose who are in heaven, and on earth, and under the earth,

11 and that every tongue should confess that Jesus Christ is ᵃLord, to the glory of God the Father.

12 So then, my beloved, ᵃjust as you have always obeyed, not as in my presence only, but now much more in my absence, work out your ᵇsalvation with ᶜfear and trembling;

13 for it is ᵃGod who is at work in you, both to will and to work ᵇfor *His* good pleasure.

14 Do all things without [a]grumbling or disputing;

15 that you may [1]prove yourselves to be [a]blameless and innocent, [b]children of God above reproach in the midst of a [c]crooked and perverse generation, among whom you [2d]appear as [3e]lights in the world,

16 holding [1]fast the word of life, so that in [a]the day of Christ I may have cause to glory because I did not [b]run in vain nor [c]toil in vain.

17 But even if I am being [a]poured out as a drink offering upon [b]the sacrifice and service of your faith, I rejoice and share my joy with you all.

18 And you too, *I urge you*, rejoice in the same way and share your joy with me.

19 But I hope [1]in the Lord Jesus to [a]send [b]Timothy to you shortly, so that I also may be encouraged when I learn of your condition.

20 For I have no one *else* [a]of kindred spirit who will genuinely be concerned for your welfare.

21 For they all [a]seek after their own interests, not those of Christ Jesus.

22 But you know [a]of his proven worth that [b]he served with me in the furtherance of the gospel [c]like a child *serving* his father.

23 [a]Therefore I hope to send him immediately, as soon as I see how things *go* with me;

24 and [a]I trust in the Lord that I myself also shall be coming shortly.

25 But I thought it necessary to send to you [a]Epaphroditus, my brother and [b]fellow-worker and [c]fellow-soldier, who is also your [1d]messenger and [e]minister to my need;

26 because he was longing [1]for you all and was distressed because you had heard that he was sick.

27 For indeed he was sick to the point of death, but God had mercy on him, and not on him only but also on me, lest I should have sorrow upon sorrow.

28 Therefore I have sent him all the more eagerly in order that when you see him again you may rejoice and I may be less concerned *about you*.

29 Therefore [a]receive him in the Lord with all joy, and [b]hold men like him in high regard;

30 because he came close to death [a]for the work of Christ, risking his life to [b]complete [1]what was deficient in your service to me.

14 [a]1 Cor. 10:10; 1 Pet. 4:9

15 [1]Or, *become* [2]Or, *shine* [3]Or, *luminaries, stars* [a]Luke 1:6; Phil. 3:6 [b]Matt. 5:45; Eph. 5:1 [c]Acts 2:40 [d]Matt. 24:27 [e]Gen. 1:16

16 [1]Or, *forth* [a]Phil. 1:6 [b]Gal. 2:2 [c]Gal. 4:11; 1 Thess. 3:5; Is. 49:4

17 [a]2 Tim. 4:6; 2 Cor. 12:15 [b]Rom. 15:16; Num. 28:6, 7

19 [1]Or, *trusting in* [a]Phil. 2:23 [b]Phil. 1:1

20 [a]1 Cor. 16:10; 2 Tim. 3:10

21 [a]1 Cor. 10:24; 13:5; Phil. 2:4

22 [a]Rom. 5:4 [Gr.] [b]1 Cor. 16:10; 2 Tim. 3:10 [c]1 Cor. 4:17

23 [a]Phil. 2:19

24 [a]Phil. 1:25

25 [1]Lit., *apostle* [a]Phil. 4:18 [b]Rom. 16:3, 9, 21; Phil. 4:3; Philem. 1, 24 [c]Philem. 2 [d]2 Cor. 8:23; John 13:16 [e]Phil. 4:18

26 [1]Some ancient mss. read, *to see you all*

29 [a]Rom. 16:2 [b]1 Cor. 16:18

30 [1]Lit., *your deficiency of service* [a]Acts 20:24 [b]1 Cor. 16:17; Phil. 4:10

1 ªPhil. 4:4; Phil. 2:18

2 ¹Lit., *mutilation* (Gr., katatomé)
ªPs. 22:16, 20; Rev. 22:15; Gal. 5:15 ᵇ2 Cor. 11:13

3 ¹Gr., peritomé
ªRom. 2:29; 9:6; Gal. 6:15
ᵇGal. 5:25 ᶜRom. 15:17; Gal. 6:14 ᵈPhil. 3:12; Phil. 1:1; Rom. 8:39

4 ª2 Cor. 11:18; 5:16

5 ªLuke 1:59 ᵇ2 Cor. 11:22; Rom. 11:1 ᶜRom. 11:1 ᵈActs 22:3; 23:6; 26:5

6 ªActs 8:3 ᵇPhil. 3:9 ᶜPhil. 2:15

7 ªLuke 14:33

8 ¹Lit., *the knowledge of*
ªJohn 17:3; Eph. 4:13; 2 Pet. 1:3; Phil. 3:10; Jer. 9:23f.
ᵇPhil. 3:12; 1:1; Rom. 8:39

9 ªRom. 10:5; Phil. 3:6
ᵇRom. 9:30; 1 Cor. 1:30

10 ¹Or, *participation in*
ªJohn 17:3; Eph. 4:13; 2 Pet. 1:13; Phil. 3:8; Jer. 9:23f.
ᵇRom. 6:5 ᶜRom. 8:17
ᵈRom. 6:5; 8:36; Gal. 6:17

11 ¹Lit., *if somehow*
ª1 Cor. 15:23; Rev. 20:5f.; Acts 26:7

12 ¹Lit., *if I may even* ²Or, *because also*
ª1 Cor. 9:24f.; 1 Tim. 6:12, 19 ᵇ1 Cor. 13:10 ᶜ1 Tim. 6:12, 19 ᵈActs 9:5f. ᵉPhil. 3:3, 8, Phil. 1:1; Rom. 8:39

13 ªLuke 9:62

14 ª1 Cor. 9:24; Heb. 6:1
ᵇRom. 11:29; 8:28; 2 Tim. 1:9 ᶜPhil. 3:3

15 ¹Or, *mature*
ª1 Cor. 2:6 Matt. 5:48

416

CHAPTER 3

FINALLY, my brethren, ªrejoice in the Lord. To write the same things *again* is no trouble to me, and it is a safeguard for you.

2 Beware of the ªdogs, beware of the ᵇevil workers, beware of the ¹false circumcision;

3 for ªwe are the *true* ¹circumcision, who ᵇworship in the Spirit of God and ᶜglory in ᵈChrist Jesus and put no confidence in the flesh,

4 although ªI myself might have confidence even in the flesh. If anyone else has a mind to put confidence in the flesh, I far more:

5 ªcircumcised the eighth day, of the ᵇnation of Israel, of the ᶜtribe of Benjamin, a ᵇHebrew of Hebrews, as to the Law, ᵈa Pharisee;

6 as to zeal, ªa persecutor of the church, as to the ᵇrighteousness which is in the Law, found ᶜblameless.

7 But ªwhatever things were gain to me, those things I have counted as loss for the sake of Christ.

8 More than that, I count all things to be loss in view of the surpassing value of ¹ªknowing ᵇChrist Jesus my Lord, for whom I have suffered the loss of all things, and count them but rubbish in order that I may gain Christ,

9 and may be found in Him, not having ªa righteousness of my own derived from *the* Law, but that which is through faith in Christ, ᵇthe righteousness which *comes* from God on the basis of faith,

10 that I may ªknow Him, and ᵇthe power of His resurrection and ¹ᶜthe fellowship of His sufferings, being ᵈconformed to His death;

11 ¹in order that I may ªattain to the resurrection from among the dead.

12 Not that I have already ªobtained *it*, or have already ᵇbecome perfect, but I press on ¹in order that I may ᶜlay hold of that ²for which also I ᵈwas laid hold of by ᵉChrist Jesus.

13 Brethren, I do not regard myself as having laid hold of *it* yet; but one thing I *do*: ªforgetting what *lies* behind and reaching forward to what *lies* ahead,

14 I ªpress on toward the goal for the prize of the ᵇupward call of God in ᶜChrist Jesus.

15 Let us therefore, as many as are ¹ªperfect, have this attitude; and if in anything you have a

^bdifferent attitude, ^cGod will reveal that also to you;

16 however, let us keep ^{1a}living by that same *standard* to which we have attained.

17 Brethren, ^ajoin in following my example, and observe those who walk according to the ^bpattern you have in us.

18 For ^amany walk, of whom I often told you, and now tell you even ^bweeping, *that they are* enemies of ^cthe cross of Christ,

19 whose end is destruction, whose god is *their* ^{1a}appetite, and *whose* ^bglory is in their shame, who ^cset their minds on earthly things.

20 For ^aour ¹citizenship is in heaven, from which also we eagerly ^bwait for a Savior, the Lord Jesus Christ;

21 who will ^atransform ¹the body of our humble state into ^bconformity with ²the ^cbody of His glory, ^dby the exertion of the power that He has even to ^esubject all things to Himself.

CHAPTER 4

THEREFORE, my beloved brethren ¹whom I ^along *to see*, my joy and crown, so ^bstand firm in the Lord, my beloved.

2 I urge Euodia and I urge Syntyche to ^{1a}live in harmony in the Lord.

3 Indeed, true comrade, I ask you also to help these women who have shared my struggle in *the cause of* the gospel, together with Clement also, and the rest of my ^afellow-workers, whose ^bnames are in the book of life.

4 ^aRejoice in the Lord always; again I will say, rejoice!

5 Let your forbearing *spirit* be known to all men. ^aThe Lord is ¹near.

6 ^aBe anxious for nothing, but in everthing by ^bprayer and supplication with thanksgiving let your requests be made known to God.

7 And ^athe peace of God, which ^bsurpasses all ¹comprehension, shall ^cguard your hearts and your ^dminds in ^eChrist Jesus.

8 Finally, brethren, ^awhatever is true, whatever is honorable, whatever is right, whatever is pure, whatever is lovely, whatever is ¹of good repute, if there is any excellence and if anything worthy of praise, ²let your mind dwell on these things.

15 ^bGal. 5:10 ^cEph. 1:17;
1 Thess. 4:9; John 6:45

16 ¹Lit., *following in line*
^aGal. 6:16

17 ^a1 Cor. 4:16; Phil. 4:9
^b1 Pet. 5:3

18 ^a2 Cor. 11:13 ^bActs 20:31
^cGal. 6:14

19 ¹Lit., *belly*
^aRom. 16:18; Titus 1:12
marg. ^bRom. 6:21; Jude 13
^cRom. 8:5f.; Col. 3:2

20 ¹Lit., *commonwealth*
^aEph. 2:19; Phil. 1:27 marg.;
Col. 3:1; Heb. 12:22 ^b1 Cor.
1:7

21 ¹Or, *our lowly body* ²Or,
His glorious body
^a1 Cor. 15:43-53 ^bRom. 8:29;
Col. 3:4 ^c1 Cor. 15:43, 49
^dEph. 1:19 ^e1 Cor. 15:28

1 ¹Lit., *and longed for*
^aPhil. 1:8 ^b1 Cor. 16:13; Phil.
1:27

2 ¹Or, *be of the same
mind*
^aPhil. 2:2

3 ^aPhil. 2:25 ^bLuke 10:20

4 ^aPhil. 3:1

5 ¹Or, *at hand*
^a1 Cor. 16:22 marg.; Heb.
10:37; James 5:8f.

6 ^aMatt. 6:25 ^bEph. 6:18;
1 Tim. 2:1; 5:5

7 ¹Lit., *mind*
^aIs. 26:3; Phil. 4:9; John
14:27; Col. 3:15 ^bPhil. 3:19
^c1 Pet. 1:5 ^d2 Cor. 10:5 ^ePhil.
1:1; 4:19, 21

8 ¹Or, *attractive* ²Lit.,
ponder these things
^aRom. 14:18; 1 Pet. 2:12

417

Philippians 4

Learn to be Content. "I Can do All Things."
"God Shall Supply All Your Needs." Farewell.

9 ^aPhil. 3:17 ^bRom. 15:33

10 ^a2 Cor. 11:9; Phil. 2:30

11 ¹Lit., *according to* ²Or, *self-sufficient* ^a1 Tim. 6:6, 8; 2 Cor. 9:8; Heb. 13:5

12 ^a1 Cor. 4:11 ^b2 Cor. 11:9

13 ¹Lit., *in* ^a2 Cor. 12:9; Eph. 3:16; Col. 1:11

14 ^aHeb. 10:33; Rev. 1:9, [in Gr.]

15 ¹Lit., *beginning of* ^aPhil. 1:5 ^bRom. 15:26 ^c2 Cor. 11:9

16 ^aActs 17:1; 1 Thess. 2:9

17 ¹Lit., *fruit* ^a2 Cor. 9:5; 1 Cor. 9:11f.

18 ¹Lit., *made full* ²Lit , *the things from you* ³Lit., *an odor of fragrance* ^aPhil. 2:25 ^b2 Cor. 2:14; Eph 5:2

19 ¹Or, *every need of yours* ^a2 Cor. 9:8 ^bRom. 2:4

20 ¹Lit., *to the ages of the ages* ^aGal. 1:4 ^bRom. 11:36

21 ¹I.e., true believer; lit., *holy one* ^aGal. 1:2

22 ¹Note vs. 21 ^a2 Cor. 13:13 ^bActs 9:13

23 ^aRom. 16:20 ^b2 Tim. 4:22

9   The things you have learned and received and heard and seen ^ain me, practice these things; and ^bthe God of peace shall be with you.

10   But I rejoiced in the Lord greatly, that now at last ^ayou have revived your concern for me; indeed, you were concerned *before*, but you lacked opportunity.

11   Not that I speak ¹from want; for I have learned to be ^{2a}content in whatever circumstances I am.

12   I know how to get along with humble means, and I also know how to live in prosperity; in any and every circumstance I have learned the secret of being filled and going ^ahungry, both of having abundance and ^bsuffering need.

13   I can do all things ¹through Him who ^astrengthens me.

14   Nevertheless, you have done well to ^ashare *with me* in my affliction.

15   And you yourselves also know, Philippians, that at the ^{1a}first preaching of the gospel, after I departed from ^bMacedonia, no church ^cshared with me in the matter of giving and receiving but you alone;

16   for even in ^aThessalonica you sent *a gift* more than once for my needs.

17   ^aNot that I seek the gift itself, but I seek for the ¹profit which increases to your account.

18   But I have received everything in full, and have an abundance; I am ¹amply supplied, having received from ^aEpaphroditus ²what you have sent, ^{3b}a fragrant aroma, an acceptable sacrifice, well pleasing to God.

19   And ^amy God shall supply ¹all your needs according to His ^briches in glory in Christ Jesus.

20   Now to ^aour God and Father ^b*be* the glory ¹forever and ever. Amen.

21   Greet every ¹saint in Christ Jesus. ^aThe brethren who are with me greet you.

22   ^aAll the ^{1b}saints greet you, especially those of Caesar's household.

23   ^aThe grace of the Lord Jesus Christ ^bbe with your spirit.

THE EPISTLE OF PAUL TO THE
COLOSSIANS

Salutation. Thanksgiving for their Attainments.

^a

P AUL, ^ban apostle of Jesus Christ ^{1c}by the will of God, and ^dTimothy ²our brother,

2   to the ^{1a}saints and faithful brethren in Christ *who are* at Colossae: ^bGrace to you and peace from God our Father.

3   ^aWe give thanks to God, ^bthe Father of our Lord Jesus Christ, praying always for you,

4   ^asince we heard of your faith in Christ Jesus and the ^blove which you have ¹for ^call the ²saints;

5   because of the ^ahope ^blaid up for you in ¹heaven, of which you previously ^cheard in the word of truth, ²the gospel,

6   which has come to you, just as ^{1a}in all the world also it is constantly bearing ^bfruit and ²increasing, even as *it has been doing* in you also since the day you ^cheard *of it* and ³understood the grace of God in truth;

7   just as you learned *it* from ^aEpaphras, our ^bbeloved fellow bond-servant, who is a faithful servant of Christ on ¹our behalf,

8   and he also informed us of your ^alove in the Spirit.

9   For this reason also, ^asince the day we heard *of it,* ^bwe have not ceased to pray for you and to ask that you may be filled with the ^{1c}knowledge of His will in all spiritual ^dwisdom and understanding,

10   so that you may ^awalk in a manner worthy of the Lord, ^{1b}to please *Him* in all respects, ^cbearing fruit in every good work and ²increasing in the ³knowledge of God;

11   ^astrengthened with all power, according to ¹His glorious might, ²for the attaining of all steadfastness and ³patience, ^bjoyously

12   giving thanks to ^athe Father, who has qualified us ¹to share in ^bthe inheritance of the ²saints in ^clight.

13   For He delivered us from the ^{1a}domain of darkness, and transferred us to the kingdom of ^{2b}His beloved Son,

14   ^ain whom we have redemption, the forgiveness of sins.

1 ¹Lit., *through* ²Lit., *the*
^aPhil. 1:1 ^b2 Cor. 1:1 ^c1 Cor. 1:1 ^d2 Cor. 1:1; 1 Thess. 3:2; Philem. 1; Heb. 13:23

2 ¹I.e., true believers; lit., *holy ones*
^aActs 9:13; Eph. 1:1; Phil. 1:1 ^bRom. 1:7; Col. 4:18

3 ^aRom. ' 8 ^bRom. 15:6; 2 Cor. 1:3

4 ¹Or, *toward* ²I.e., true believers; lit., *holy ones*
^aEph. 1:15 ^bGal. 5:6 ^cEph. 6:18

5 ¹Lit., *the heavens* ²Or, *of the gospel*
^aCol. 1:23; Rom. 5:2; 1 Thess. 5:8; Titus 1:2; Acts 23:6 ^b2 Tim. 4:8; 1 Pet. 1:4 ^cEph. 1:13; Col. 1:6, 23

6 ¹Or, *it is in the world* ²Or, *spreading abroad* ³Or, *came really to know*
^aRom. 10:18; 1 Tim. 3:16; Col. 1:23 ^bRom. 1:13 ^cEph. 4:21; Col. 1:5

7 ¹Some later mss. read, *your*
^aCol. 4:12; Philem. 23 ^bCol. 4:7

8 ^aRom. 15:30

9 ¹Or, *real knowledge*
^aCol. 1:4 ^bEph. 1:16 ^cEph. 5:17; Phil. 1:9 ^dEph. 1:17

10 ¹Lit., *unto all pleasing* ²Or, *growing by the knowledge* ³Or, *real knowledge*
^aEph. 4:1; Col. 2:6 ^b2 Cor. 5:9; Eph. 5:10 ^cRom. 1:13

11 ¹Lit., *the might of His glory* ²Lit., *unto all* ³Or, *patience with joy*
^aEph. 3:16; 1 Cor. 16:13 ^bEph. 4:2

12 ¹Lit., *unto the portion of* ²I.e., true believers; lit., *holy ones*
^aEph. 2:18 ^bActs 20:32 ^cActs 26:18; Eph. 6:12

13 ¹Lit., *authority* ²Lit., *the Son of His love*
^aActs 26:18; Eph. 6:12 ^bMatt. 3:17; Eph. 1:6

14 ^aEph. 1:7; Rom. 3:24

419

15 ª2 Cor. 4:4 ᵇ1 Tim. 1:17; Heb. 11:27; John 1:18 ᶜCol. 1:17f.; Rom. 8:29

16 ªEph. 1:10 ᵇEph. 1:20f.; Col. 2:15 ᶜJohn 1:3; Rom. 11:36; 1 Cor. 8:6

17 ¹Or, has existed prior to ²Or, endure ªJohn 1:1; 8:58

18 ªEph. 1:22 ᵇEph. 1:23; Col. 1:24; Col. 2:19 ᶜRev. 3:14 ᵈActs 26:23

19 ¹Or, all the fulness was pleased to dwell ²I.e., fulness of diety ªEph. 1:5 ᵇJohn 1:16

20 ¹Lit., the heavens ²2 Cor. 5:18; Eph. 2:16 ᵇRom. 5:1; Eph. 2:14 ᶜEph. 2:13 ᵈCol. 1:16

21 ªRom. 5:10; Eph. 2:3; 2:12

22 ª2 Cor. 5:18; Eph. 2:16 ᵇRom. 7:4 ᶜEph. 5:27; Col. 1:28 ᵈEph. 1:4

23 ¹Or omit, the ²Lit., became ³Or, servant ªEph. 3:17; Col. 2:7 ᵇCol. 1:5 ᶜCol. 1:6; Mark 16:15; Acts 2:5 ᵈCol. 1:25; Eph. 3:7 ᵉ1 Cor. 3:5

24 ¹Or, represen-tatively . . . fill up ²Lit., of ªPhil. 2:17; Rom. 8:17; 2 Cor. 1:5; 12:15 ᵇ2 Tim. 1:8; 2:10 ᶜCol. 1:18

25 ¹Lit., became ²Lit., make full the word of God ªCol. 1:23 ᵇEph. 3:2

26 ¹I.e., true believers; lit., holy ones ªEph. 3:3f.; Rom. 16:25f.; Col. 2:2; 4:3

27 ªMatt. 13:11 ᵇEph. 1:18; 3:16; Eph. 1:7 ᶜRom. 8:10 ᵈ1 Tim. 1:1

28 ¹Lit., in ªActs 20:31; Col. 3:16 ᵇ1 Cor. 2:6f.; Col. 2:3

15   And He is the ªimage of the ᵇinvisible God, the ᶜfirstborn of all creation.

16   For ªin Him all things were created, ª*both* in the heavens and on earth, visible and invisible, whether ᵇthrones or dominions or rulers or authori-ties—ᶜall things have been created through Him and for Him.

17   And He ¹ªis before all things, and in Him all things ²hold together.

18   He is also ªhead of ᵇthe body, the church; and He is ᶜthe beginning, ᵈthe first-born from the dead; so that He Himself might come to have first place in everything.

19   For ¹it was ªthe *Father's* good pleasure for all ᵇthe ²fulness to dwell in Him,

20   and through Him to ªreconcile all things to Himself, having made ᵇpeace through ᶜthe blood of His cross; through Him, *I say,* ᵈwhether things on earth or things in ¹heaven.

21   And although you were ªformerly alienated and hostile in mind, *engaged* in evil deeds,

22   yet He has now ªreconciled you in His flesh-ly ᵇbody through death, in order to ᶜpresent you before Him ᵈholy and blameless and beyond re-proach—

23   if indeed you continue in ¹the faith firmly ªestablished and steadfast, and not moved away from the ᵇhope of the gospel that you have heard, which was proclaimed ᶜin all creation under heav-en, ᵈand of which I Paul ²was made a ³ᵉminister.

24   ªNow I rejoice in my sufferings for your sake, and in my flesh ᵇI ¹do my share on behalf of ᶜHis body (which is the church) in filling up that which is lacking ²in Christ's afflictions.

25   ªOf *this church* I ¹was made a minister ac-cording to the ᵇstewardship from God bestowed on me for your benefit, that I might ²fully carry out the *preaching of* the word of God,

26   *that is,* ªthe mystery which has been hidden from the *past* ages and generations; but has now been manifested to His ¹saints,

27   to whom ªGod willed to make known what is ᵇthe riches of the glory of this mystery among the Gentiles, which is ᶜChrist in you, the ᵈhope of glory.

28   And we proclaim Him, ªadmonishing every man and teaching every man ¹with all ᵇwisdom,

that we may ^cpresent every man ^{2d}complete in Christ.

29 And for this purpose also I ^alabor, ^bstriving ^caccording to His ¹power, which ²mightily works within me.

CHAPTER 2

FOR I want you to know how great a ^astruggle I have on your behalf, and for those who are at ^bLaodicea, and for all those who have not ¹personally seen my face,

2 that their ^ahearts may be encouraged, having been ^bknit together in love, and *attaining* to all ^cthe wealth ¹that comes from the ^dfull assurance of understanding, *resulting* in a ^etrue knowledge of ^fGod's mystery, *that is,* Christ *Himself,*

3 in whom are hidden all ^athe treasures of wisdom and knowledge.

4 ^aI say this in order that no one may delude you with ^bpersuasive argument.

5 For even though I am ^aabsent in body, nevertheless I am with you in spirit, rejoicing ¹to see ²your ^bgood discipline and the ^cstability of your faith in Christ.

6 As you therefore have received ^aChrist Jesus the Lord, *so* ^{1b}walk in Him,

7 having been firmly ^arooted *and now* being ^bbuilt up in Him and ^cestablished ¹in your faith, just as you ^dwere instructed, *and* overflowing ²with gratitude.

8 ^aSee to it that no one takes you captive through ^bphilosophy and empty deception, according to the tradition of men, according to the ^celementary principles of the world, ¹rather than according to Christ.

9 For in Him all the ^afulness of Deity dwells in bodily form,

10 and in Him you have been ^amade ¹complete, and ^bHe is the head ²over all ^crule and authority;

11 and in Him ^ayou were also circumcised with a circumcision made without hands, in the removal of ^bthe body of the flesh by the circumcision of Christ;

12 having been ^aburied with Him in baptism, in which you were also ^braised up with Him

28 ²Or, *perfect*
^cCol. 1:22 ^dMatt. 5:48; Eph. 4:13

29 ¹Lit., *working* ²Lit., *in power*
^a1 Cor. 15:10 ^bCol. 4:12; 2:1 ^cEph. 1:19; Col. 2:12

1 ¹Lit., *in the flesh*
^aCol. 4:12; 1:29 ^bCol. 4:13, 15f.; Rev. 1:11

2 ¹Lit., *of the full assurance*
^aEph. 6:22; Col. 4:8; 1 Cor. 14:31 ^bCol. 2:19 ^cEph. 1:18; 3:16; 1:7 ^dLuke 1:1 [Gr.] ^eMatt. 13:11 ^fEph. 3:3f.; Rom. 16:25f.; Col. 1:26; 4:3

3 ^aIs. 11:2; Rom. 11:33

4 ^aEph. 4:17 ^bRom. 16:18

5 ¹Lit., *and seeing* ²Or, *your ordered array*
^a1 Cor. 5:3 ^b1 Cor. 14:40 ^c1 Pet. 5:9

6 ¹Or, *lead your life*
^aGal. 3:26 ^bCol. 1:10

7 ¹Or, *by* ²Some mss. read, *in it with*
^aEph. 3:17 ^bEph. 2:20; 1 Cor. 3:9 ^c1 Cor. 1:8 ^dEph. 4:21

8 ¹Lit., *and not*
^a1 Cor. 8:9; 10:12; Gal. 5:15; Heb. 3:12 ^bCol. 2:23; 1 Tim. 6:20; Eph. 5:6 ^cCol. 2:20; Gal. 4:3

9 ^aCol. 1:19; 2 Cor. 5:19

10 ¹Or, *full* ²Lit., *of*
^aEph. 3:19 ^bEph. 1:21f. ^cCol. 2:15; Eph. 3:10; 1 Cor. 15:24

11 ^aRom. 2:29; Eph. 2:11 ^bRom. 6:6; 7:24; Gal. 5:24; Col. 3:5

12 ^aRom. 6:4f. ^bRom. 6:5; Eph. 2:6; Col. 2:13; 3:1

421

12 cActs 2:24

13 [1]Or, *by reason of*
aEph. 2:1 bEph. 2:1, 5; Col. 2:12

14 aEph. 2:15; Col. 2:20
bl Pet. 2:24

15 [1]Or, *divested Himself of*
[2]Or, *it*; i.e., the cross.
aEph. 4:8 bCol. 2:10; Eph. 3:10; 1 Cor. 15:24 cIs. 53:12; Matt. 12:29; Luke 10:18; John 12:31; Eph. 4:8 d2 Cor. 2:14 [Gr.]

16 [1]Lit., *judge you* [2]Or, *days*
aRom. 14:3 bMark 7:19; Rom. 14:17, Heb. 9.10 nLev. 23:2; Rom. 14:5 d1 Chr. 23:31; 2 Chr. 31:3; Neh. 10:33; cMark 2:27f.; Gal. 4:10f.

17 [1]Lit., *body* [2]Lit., *of Christ*
aHeb. 8:5; 10:1

18 [1]Or, *giving judgment against you* [2]Or, *humility*
al Cor. 9:24; Phil. 3:14 bCol. 2:23 cl Cor. 4:6 dRom. 8:7

19 [1]Lit., *bonds* [2]Lit., *of God*
aEph. 1:22 bEph. 1:23; 4:16

20 [1]Lit., *from*
aRom. 6:2 bCol. 2:8 cGal. 4:9 dCol. 2:14, 16

22 [1]Or, *by being consumed*
al Cor. 6:13 bIs. 29:13; Matt. 15:9; Titus 1:14

23 [1]Or, *delight in religiousness*
aCol. 2:18 bl Tim. 4:3 cRom. 13:14; 1 Tim. 4:8

1 aCol. 2:12 bMark 16:19

2 [1]Or, *Be intent on*
aPhil. 3:19, 20; Matt. 16:23

through faith in the working of God, who craised Him from the dead.

13 And when you were adead [1]in your transgressions and the uncircumcision of your flesh, He bmade you alive together with Him, having forgiven us all our transgressions,

14 having cancelled out athe certificate of debt consisting of decrees against us *and* which was hostile to us; and bHe has taken it out of the way, having nailed it to the cross.

15 When He had [1]adisarmed the brulers and authorities, He cmade a public display of them, having dtriumphed over them through [2]Him.

16 Therefore let no one [1]aact as your judge in regard to bfood or bdrink or in respect to a cfestival or a dnew moon or a eSabbath [2]day—

17 things which are aa *mere* shadow of what is to come; but the [1]substance [2]belongs to Christ.

18 Let no one keep [1]adefrauding you of your prize by bdelighting in [2]self-abasement and the worship of the angels, taking his stand on *visions* he has seen, cinflated without cause by his dfleshly mind,

19 and not holding fast to athe Head, from whom bthe entire body, being supplied and held together by the joints and [1]ligaments, grows with a growth [2]which is from God.

20 aIf you have died with Christ [1]to the belementary principles of the world, cwhy, as if you were living in the world, do you submit yourself to ddecrees, such as,

21 "Do not handle, do not taste, do not touch!"

22 (which all *refer* ato things destined to perish [1]with the using)—in accordance with the bcommandments and teachings of men?

23 These are matters which have, to be sure, the appearance of wisdom in [1]aself-made religion and self-abasement and bsevere treatment of the body, *but are* of no value against cfleshly indulgence.

CHAPTER 3

IF then you have been araised up with Christ, keep seeking the things above, where Christ is, bseated at the right hand of God.

2 [1]aSet your mind on the things above, not on the things that are on earth.

**What to Put Away and What to
Put on.   Family Matters.**

Colossians 3

3 For you have [a]died and your life is hidden with Christ in God.

4 When Christ, [a]who is our life, is revealed, [b]then you also will be revealed with Him in glory.

5 [a]Therefore [1]consider [b]the members of your earthly body as dead to [2c]immorality, impurity, passion, evil desire, and greed, which [3]amounts to idolatry.

6 For it is on account of these things that [a]the wrath of God will come[1],

7 and [a]in them you also once walked, when you were living in them.

8 But now you also, [a]put them all aside: [b]anger, wrath, malice, slander, *and* [c]abusive speech from your mouth.

9 [1a]Do not lie to one another, since you [b]laid aside the old [2]self with its *evil* practices,

10 and have [a]put on the new [1]self who is being [2b]renewed to a true knowledge [c]according to the image of the One who [d]created him,

11 —a *renewal* in which [a]there is no *distinction between* Greek and Jew, [b]circumcised and uncircumcised, [c]barbarian, Scythian, [d]slave and freeman, but [e]Christ is all, and in all.

12 And so, as those who have been [a]chosen of God, holy and beloved, [b]put on a [c]heart of compassion, kindness, [d]humility, gentleness and [1e]patience;

13 [a]bearing with one another, and [b]forgiving each other, whoever has a complaint against any one; [b]just as the Lord forgave you, so also should you.

14 And beyond all these things *put on* love, which is [1a]the perfect bond of [b]unity.

15 And let [a]the peace of Christ [1]rule in your hearts, to which [2]indeed you were called [b]one body; and [3]be thankful.

16 Let [a]the word of [1]Christ richly dwell within you; [2]with all wisdom [b]teaching and admonishing one another [c]with psalms *and* hymns *and* spiritual songs, [d]singing [3]with thankfulness in your hearts to God.

17 And [a]whatever you do in word or deed, *do* all in the name of the Lord Jesus, [b]giving thanks through Him to God the Father.

18 [a]Wives, [b]be subject to your husbands, as is fitting in the Lord.

19 [a]Husbands, love your wives, and do not be embittered against them.

3 [a]Rom. 6:2; 2 Cor. 5:14; Col. 2:20

4 [a]Gal. 2:20; John 11:25 [b]1 Cor. 1:7; 1 Pet. 1:13; 1 John 2:28; 3:2; Phil. 3:21

5 [1]Lit., *put to death the members which are upon the earth* [2]Lit., *fornication* [3]Lit., *is* [a]Rom. 8:13 [b]Col. 2:11 [c]Mark 7:21f.; Gal. 5:19; 1 Cor. 6:9f., 18; 2 Cor. 12:21; Eph. 4:19; 5:3, 5

6 [1]Some early mss. add, *upon the sons of disobedience* [a]Rom. 1:18; Eph. 5:6

7 [a]Eph. 2:2

8 [a]Eph. 4:22 [b]Eph. 4:31 [c]Eph. 4:29

9 [1]Or, *Stop lying* [2]Lit., *man* [a]Eph. 4:25 [b]Eph. 4:22

10 [1]Lit., *man* [2]Lit., *renovated* [a]Eph. 4:24 [b]Rom. 12:2; 2 Cor. 4:16; Eph. 4:23 [c]Rom. 8:29 [d]Eph. 2:10

11 [a]Rom. 10:12; 1 Cor. 12:13; Gal. 3:28 [b]1 Cor. 7:19; Gal. 5:6 [c]Acts 28:2 [d]Eph. 6:8 [e]Eph. 1:23

12 [1]I.e., forbearance toward others [a]Luke 18:7 [b]Eph. 4:24 [c]Gal. 5:22f.; Phil. 2:1; Luke 1:78 marg. [d]Eph. 4:2; Phil. 2:3 [e]2 Cor. 6:6; 1 Cor. 13:4

13 [a]Eph. 4:2 [b]Eph. 4:32; Rom. 15:7

14 [1]Lit., *the uniting bond of perfectness* [a]Eph. 4:3 [b]Heb. 6:1; John 17:23

15 [1]Or, *act as arbiter* [2]Lit., *also* [3]Or, *show yourselves thankful* [a]John 14:27 [b]Eph. 2:16

16 [1]Some mss. read, *the Lord*; others read, *God* [2]Or, *in* [3]Or, *by*; lit., *in His grace* [a]Rom. 10:17; Eph. 5:26; 1 Thess. 1:8 [b]Eph. 5:19; Col. 1:28 [c]Eph. 5:19 [d]1 Cor. 14:15

17 [a]1 Cor. 10:31 [b]Eph. 5:20; Col. 3:15

18 [a]Col. 3:18 to 4:1: *Eph. 5:22 to 6:9* [b]Eph. 5:22

19 [a]Eph. 5:25

20 ¹Lit., *in*
ᵃEph. 6:1

21 ¹Some early mss. read,
provoke to anger
ᵃEph. 6:4

22 ¹Lit., *according to the
flesh* ²Lit., *eye-service*
ᵃEph. 6:5 ᵇEph. 6:6

23 ¹Lit., *from the soul* ²Lit.,
and not
ᵃEph. 6:7

24 ¹I.e., consisting of
ᵃEph. 6:8 ᵇActs 20:32; 1 Pet.
1:4 ᶜ1 Cor. 7:22

25 ¹Lit., *there is no
partiality*
ᵃEph. 6:8 ᵇActs 10:34; Eph.
6:9

2 ᵃActs 1:14; Eph. 6:18

3 ᵃEph. 6:19 ᵇActs 14:27
ᶜ2 Tim. 4:2 ᵈEph. 3:3, 4; 6:19
ᵉEph. 6:20

4 ᵃEph. 6:20

5 ¹Lit., *Walk* ²Lit.,
redeeming the time
ᵃEph. 5:15 ᵇMark 4:11 ᶜEph.
5:16

6 ¹Or, *gracious* ᵃEph. 4:29
ᵇMark 9:50 ᶜ1 Pet. 3:15

7 ᵃCol. 4:7-9; *Eph.* 6:21, 22
ᵇActs 20:4 ᶜEph. 6:21; Col.
1:7

8 ᵃEph. 6:22 ᵇCol. 2:2

9 ¹Lit., *along with
Onesimus*
ᵃPhilem. 10 ᵇCol. 1:7 ᶜCol.
4:12

10 ᵃActs 19:29 ᵇRom. 16:7
ᶜActs 12:12; 15:37, 39; 4:36

424

20   ᵃChildren, be obedient to your parents in all things, for this is well pleasing ¹to the Lord.

21   ᵃFathers, do not ¹exasperate your children, that they may not lose heart.

22   ᵃSlaves, in all things obey those who are your masters ¹on earth, ᵇnot with ²external service, as those who *merely* please men, but with sincerity of heart, fearing the Lord.

23   Whatever you do, do your work ¹heartily, ᵃas for the Lord ²rather than for men;

24   ᵃknowing that from the Lord you will receive the reward ¹of ᵇthe inheritance. It is the Lord Christ whom you ᶜserve.

25   For ᵃhe who does wrong will receive the consequences of the wrong which he has done, and ¹ᵇthat without partiality.

CHAPTER 4

MASTERS, grant to your slaves justice and fairness, knowing that you too have a Master in heaven.

2   ᵃDevote yourselves to prayer, keeping alert in it with *an attitude of* thanksgiving;

3   praying at the same time ᵃfor us as well, that God may open up to us a ᵇdoor for ᶜthe word, so that we may speak forth ᵈthe mystery of Christ, for which I have also ᵉbeen imprisoned;

4   in order that I may make it clear ᵃin the way I ought to speak.

5   ¹ᵃConduct yourselves with wisdom toward ᵇoutsiders, ²ᶜmaking the most of the opportunity.

6   ᵃLet your speech always be ¹with grace, seasoned, *as it were*, with ᵇsalt, so that you may know how you should ᶜrespond to each person.

7   ᵃAs to all my affairs, ᵇTychicus, *our* ᶜbeloved brother and faithful servant and fellow-bondslave in the Lord, will bring you information.

8   ᵃFor I have sent him to you for this very purpose, that you may know *about* our circumstances and that he may ᵇencourage your hearts;

9   ¹and with him ᵃOnesimus, *our* faithful and ᵇbeloved brother, ᶜwho is one of your *number*. They will inform you about the whole situation here.

10   ᵃAristarchus, my ᵇfellow prisoner, sends you his greetings; and *also* ᶜBarnabas' cousin Mark

Conclusion and Benediction.

(about whom you received ¹instructions: ᵈif he comes to you, welcome him);

11 and *also* Jesus who is called Justus; these are the only ᵃfellow-workers for the kingdom of God ᵇwho are from the circumcision; and they have proved to be an encouragement to me.

12 ᵃEpaphras, ᵇwho is one of your number, a bondslave of Jesus Christ, sends you his greetings, always ᶜlaboring earnestly for you in his prayers, that you may ¹stand ²ᵈperfect and ³ᵉfully assured in all the will of God.

13 For I bear him witness that he has ¹a deep concern for you and for those who are in ᵃLaodicea and Hierapolis.

14 ᵃLuke, the beloved physician, sends you his greetings, and *also* ᵇDemas.

15 Greet the brethren who are in ᵃLaodicea and also ¹Nympha and ᵇthe church that is in ²her house.

16 And ᵃwhen ¹this letter is read among you, have it also read in the church of the Laodiceans; and you, for your part ᵃread ¹my letter *that is coming* from ᵇLaodicea.

17 And say to ᵃArchippus, "Take heed to the ᵇministry which you have received in the Lord, that you may ¹fulfill it."

18 ¹I, Paul, ᵃwrite this greeting with my own hand. ᵇRemember my ²ᶜimprisonment. ᵈGrace be with you.

THE FIRST EPISTLE OF PAUL TO THE
THESSALONIANS

Salutation. Thanksgiving for their Reception of the Gospel.

ᵃ

PAUL and ᵇSilvanus and ᶜTimothy to the ᵈchurch of the Thessalonians in God the Father and the Lord Jesus Christ: ᵉGrace to you and peace.

2 ᵃWe give thanks to God always for all of you, ᵇmaking mention *of you* in our prayers;

3 constantly bearing in mind your ᵃwork of faith and labor of ᵇlove and ¹ᶜsteadfastness of hope

3 ²Lit., *of*
ᵈGal. 1:4

4 ª2 Thess. 2:13; Rom. 1:7
ᵇ2 Pet. 1:10; Rom. 9:11

5 ¹Lit., *became*
ª2 Cor. 2:12; 1 Cor. 9:14;
1 Thess. 2:2, 4, 8f.; 3:2;
2 Thess. 2:14 ᵇRom. 15:19;
1 Cor. 2:4; 2 Cor. 6:6 ᶜCol.
2:2; Luke 1:1 [Gr.] ᵈ1 Thess.
2:10

6 ¹Lit., *inspired by*
ª1 Cor. 4:16; 11:1f. ᵇActs
17:5-10 ᶜ2 Tim. 4:2 ᵈActs
13:52; 2 Cor. 6:10; Gal. 5:22

7 ªRom. 15:26 ᵇActs 18:12

8 ª2 Thess. 3:1; Col. 3:16
ᵇRom. 10:18 ᶜRom. 15:26
ᵈActs 18:12 ᵉRom. 1:8;
2 Cor. 2:14; Rom. 16:19

9 ¹Lit., *entrance* ²Lit., *to*
³Or, *the idols* ⁴Or, *the*
ª1 Thess. 2:1 ᵇActs 14:15
ᶜ1 Cor. 12:2 ᵈMatt. 16:16

10 ¹Lit., *the heavens*
ªMatt. 16:27f.; 1 Cor. 1:7
ᵇActs 2:24 ᶜRom. 5:9 ᵈMatt.
3:7; 1 Thess. 2:16; 5:9

1 ¹Lit., *entrance*
ª1 Thess. 1:9 ᵇ2 Thess. 1:10

2 ¹Or, *struggle, conflict*
ªPhil. 1:30; Acts 14:5 ᵇActs
16:22-24 ᶜActs 17:1-9 ᵈRom.
1:1 ᵉPhil. 1:30

3 ¹Lit., *in deceit*
ªActs 13:15 ᵇ2 Thess. 2:11
ᶜ1 Thess. 4:7 ᵈ2 Cor. 4:2

4 ¹Or, *approves*
ª2 Cor. 2:17 ᵇGal. 2:7 ᶜGal.
1:10 ᵈRom. 8:27

5 ¹Lit., *in a word of
flattery*
ªActs 20:33; 2 Pet. 2:3
ᵇ1 Thess. 2:10; Rom. 1:9

6 ¹Or, *been burdensome*
ªJohn 5:41, 44; 2 Cor. 4:5
ᵇ1 Cor. 9:1f.

²in our Lord Jesus Christ in the presence of ᵈour God and Father;

4 knowing, ªbrethren beloved by God, ᵇ*His* choice of you,

5 for our ªgospel did not come to you in word only, but also ᵇin power and in the Holy Spirit and with ᶜfull conviction; just as you know ᵈwhat kind of men we ¹proved to be among you for your sake.

6 You also became ªimitators of us and of the Lord, ᵇhaving received ᶜthe word in much tribulation with the ᵈjoy ¹of the Holy Spirit,

7 so that you became an example to all the believers in ªMacedonia and in ᵇAchaia.

8 For ªthe word of the Lord has ᵇsounded forth from you, not only in ᶜMacedonia and ᵈAchaia, but also ᵉin every place your faith toward God has gone forth, so that we have no need to say anything.

9 For they themselves report about us what kind of a ¹ªreception we had ²with you, and how you ᵇturned to God ᶜfrom ³idols to serve ⁴ᵈa living and true God,

10 and to ªwait for His Son from ¹heaven, whom He ᵇraised from the dead, *that is* Jesus, who ᶜdelivers us from ᵈthe wrath to come.

CHAPTER 2

FOR you yourselves know, brethren, that our ¹ªcoming to you ᵇwas not in vain,

2 but after we had already suffered and been ªmistreated in ᵇPhilippi, as you know, we had the boldness in our God ᶜto speak to you the ᵈgospel of God amid much ¹ᵉopposition.

3 For our ªexhortation does not *come* from ᵇerror or ᶜimpurity or ¹by way of ᵈdeceit;

4 ªbut just as we have been approved by God to be ᵇentrusted with the gospel, so we speak, ᶜnot as pleasing men but God, who ¹ᵈexamines our hearts.

5 For we never came ¹with flattering speech, as you know, nor with ªa pretext for greed—ᵇGod is witness —

6 nor did we ªseek glory from men, either from you or from others, even though as ᵇapostles of Christ we might have ¹asserted our authority.

7 But we [1]proved to be [2a]gentle [3]among you, [b]as a nursing *mother* [4]tenderly cares for her own children.

8 Having thus a fond affection for you, were well pleased to [a]impart to you not only the [b]gospel but also our own [1]lives, because you had become [2]very dear to us.

9 For you recall, brethren, our [a]labor and hardship, *how* [b]working night and day so as not to be a [c]burden to any of you, we proclaimed to you the [d]gospel of God.

10 You are witnesses, and *so is* [a]God, [b]how devoutly and uprightly and blamelessly we [1]behaved toward you [2]believers;

11 just as you know how we *were* [a]exhorting and encouraging and [1b]imploring each one of you as [c]a father *would* his own children,

12 so that you may [a]walk in a manner worthy of the God who [b]calls you into His own kingdom and [c]glory.

13 And for this reason we also constantly [a]thank God that when you received from us the [b]word of God's message, you accepted *it* [c]not *as* the word of men, but *for* what it really is, the word of God, [d]which also performs its work in you who believe.

14 For you, brethren, became [a]imitators of [b]the churches of God in Christ Jesus that are [c]in Judea, for [d]you also endured the same sufferings at the hands of your own countrymen, [e]even as they *did* from the Jews,

15 [a]who both killed the Lord Jesus and [b]the prophets, and [1]drove us out; [2]they are not pleasing to God, [3]but hostile to all men,

16 [a]hindering us from speaking to the Gentiles [b]that they might be saved; with the result that they always [c]fill up the measure of their sins. But [d]wrath has come upon them [1]to the utmost.

17 But we, brethren, having been bereft of you for a [1]short while—[a]in [2]person, not in [3]spirit—were all the more eager with great desire [b]to see your face.

18 [1]For [a]we wanted to come to you—I, Paul, [2b]more than once—and *yet* [c]Satan [d]thwarted us.

19 For who is our hope or [a]joy or crown of exultation? Is it not even you, in the presence of our Lord Jesus at His [1b]coming?

20 For you are [a]our glory and joy.

7 [1]Lit., *became gentle*
[2]Some ancient mss. read,
babes [3]Lit., *in the midst of
you* [4]Or, *cherishes*
[a]2 Tim. 2:24 [b]1 Thess. 2:11;
Gal. 4:19

8 [1]Or, *selves*, lit., *souls*
[2]Lit., *beloved*
[a]2 Cor. 12:5; 1 John 3:16
[b]Rom. 1:1

9 [a]2 Thess. 3:8; Phil. 4:16
[b]Acts 18:3 [c]2 Cor. 11:9;
1 Cor. 9:4f. [d]Rom. 1:1

10 [1]Lit., *became* [2]Or, *who
believe*
[a]1 Thess. 2:5 [b]1 Thess. 1:5;
2 Cor. 1:12

11 [1]Or, *testifying*
[a]1 Thess. 5:14 [b]Luke 16:28;
1 Thess. 4:6 [c]1 Cor. 4:14;
1 Thess. 2:7

12 [a]Eph. 4:1 [b]1 Thess. 5:24;
2 Thess. 2:14; Rom. 8:28
[c]1 Pet. 5:10; 2 Cor. 4:6

13 [a]Rom. 1:8; 1 Thess. 1:2
[b]Heb. 4:2; Rom. 10:17 [c]Gal.
4:14; Matt. 10:20 [d]Heb. 4:12

14 [a]1 Thess. 1:6 [b]1 Cor.
7:17; 10:32 [c]Gal. 1:22 [d]Acts
17:5; 1 Thess. 3:4; 2 Thess.
1:4f. [e]Heb. 10:33f.

15 [1]Or, *persecuted us* [2]Lit.,
and [3]Lit., *and*
[a]Luke 24:20; Acts 2:23 [b]Acts
7:52; Matt. 5:12

16 [1]Or, *forever; or,
altogether*
[a]Acts 9:23; 13:45, 50; 14:2, 5,
19; 17:5, 13; 18:12; 21:21f.,
27; 25:2, 7 [b]1 Cor. 10:33
[c]Gen. 15:16; Dan. 8:23;
Matt. 23:32 [d]1 Thess. 1:10

17 [1]Lit., *occasion of an
hour* [2]Lit., *face* [3]Lit., *heart*
[a]1 Cor. 5:3 [b]1 Thess. 3:10

18 [1]Or, *because* [2]Lit., *both
once and twice*
[a]Rom. 15:22 [b]Phil. 4:16
[c]Matt. 4:10 [d]Rom. 15:22;
1:13

19 [1]Or, *presence*
[a]Phil. 4:1 [b]1 Thess. 3:13;
4:15; 5:23; Matt. 16:27; Mark
8:38; John 21:22

20 [a]2 Cor. 1:14

427

CHAPTER 3

1 [a]1 Thess. 3:5; Phil. 2:19 [b]Acts 17:15f.

2 [a]2 Cor. 1:1; Col. 1:1

3 [1]Or, *deceived* [a]Acts 9:16; 14:22

4 [1]Lit., *just as* [2]Lit., *and* [a]1 Thess. 2:14

5 [1]Or, *to know, to ascertain* [a]1 Thess. 3:1; Phil. 2:19 [b]1 Thess. 3:2 [c]Matt. 4:3 [d]Phil. 2:16; 2 Cor. 6:1

6 [a]Acts 18:5 [b]1 Thess. 1:3 [c]1 Cor. 11:2

8 [a]1 Cor. 6:13

9 [a]1 Thess. 1:2

10 [a]2 Tim. 1:3 [b]1 Thess. 2:17 [c]2 Cor. 13:9

11 [a]2 Thess. 2:16 [b]Gal. 1:4; 1 Thess. 3:13 [c]1 Thess. 4:16; 5:23; 2 Thess. 2:16; 3:16; Rev. 21:3 [d]2 Thess. 3:5

12 [a]Phil. 1:9; 1 Thess. 4:1, 10; 2 Thess. 1:3

13 [1]Or, *presence* [2]I.e., true believers; lit., *holy ones* [a]1 Cor. 1:8; 1 Thess. 3:2 [b]Luke 1:6 [c]Gal. 1:4; 1 Thess. 3:11 [d]1 Thess. 2:19 [e]Matt. 25:31; Mark 8:38; 2 Thess. 1:7; 1 Thess. 4:17

1 [1]Or, *conduct yourselves* [a]2 Thess. 3:1; 2 Cor. 13:11 [b]1 Thess. 5:12; 2 Thess. 1:3; 2:1; 3:1, 13; Gal. 6:1 [c]Eph. 4:1

THEREFORE [a]when we could endure *it* no longer, we thought it best to be left behind at [b]Athens alone;

2 and we sent [a]Timothy, our brother and God's fellow-worker in the gospel of Christ, to strengthen and encourage you as to your faith;

3 so that no man may be [1]disturbed by these afflictions; for you yourselves know that [a]we have been destined for this.

4 For indeed when we were with you, we *kept* telling you in advance that we were going to suffer affliction; [1a]and so it came to pass, [2]as you know.

5 For this reason, [a]when I could endure *it* no longer, I also [b]sent to [1]find out about your faith, for fear that [c]the tempter might have tempted you, and [d]our labor should be in vain.

6 But now that [a]Timothy has come to us from you, and has brought us good news of [b]your faith and love, and that you always [c]think kindly of us, longing to see us just as we also long to see you,

7 for this reason, brethren, in all our distress and affliction we were comforted about you through your faith;

8 for now we *really* live, if you [a]stand firm in the Lord.

9 For [a]what thanks can we render to God for you in return for all the joy with which we rejoice before our God on your account,

10 as we [a]night and day keep praying most earnestly that we may [b]see your face, and may [c]complete what is lacking in your faith?

11 [a]Now may [b]our God and Father [c]Himself and Jesus our Lord [d]direct our way to you;

12 and may the Lord cause you to increase and [a]abound in love for one another, and for all men, just as we also *do* for you;

13 so that He may [a]establish your hearts [b]unblamable in holiness before [c]our God and Father at the [1d]coming of our Lord Jesus [e]with all His [2]saints.

a

CHAPTER 4

FINALLY then, [b]brethren, we request and exhort you in the Lord Jesus that, as you received from us *instruction* as to how you ought to [1c]walk and

Exhortation to Sanctification.
Brotherly Love.

ᵈplease God (just as you actually do ¹walk), that you may ᵉexcel still more.

2 For you know what commandments we gave you ¹by *the authority of* the Lord Jesus.

3 For this is the will of God, your sanctification; *that is,* that you ᵃabstain from ¹sexual immorality;

4 that ᵃeach of you know how to ¹possess his own ²ᵇvessel in sanctification and ᶜhonor,

5 not in ¹ᵃlustful passion, like the Gentiles who ᵇdo not know God;

6 *and* that no man transgress and ᵃdefraud his brother ᵇin the matter because ᶜthe Lord is *the* avenger in all these things, just as we also ᵈtold you before and solemnly warned *you.*

7 For ᵃGod has not called us for ᵇthe purpose of impurity, but ¹in sanctification.

8 Consequently, he who rejects *this* is not rejecting man but the God who ᵃgives His Holy Spirit to you.

9 Now as to the ᵃlove of the brethren, you ᵇhave no need for *any one* to write to you, for you yourselves are ᶜtaught by God to love one another;

10 for indeed ᵃyou do practice it toward all the brethren who are in all Macedonia. But we urge you, brethren, to ᵇexcel still more,

11 and to make it your ambition ᵃto lead a quiet life and ᵇattend to your own business and ᶜwork with your hands, just as we commanded you;

12 so that you may ¹ᵃbehave properly toward ᵇoutsiders and ²ᶜnot be in any need.

13 But ᵃwe do not want you to be uninformed, brethren, about those who ᵇare asleep, that you may not grieve, as do ᶜthe rest who have ᵈno hope.

14 For if we believe that Jesus died and rose again, ᵃeven so God will bring with Him ᵇthose who have fallen asleep ¹in Jesus.

15 For this we say to you ᵃby the word of the Lord, that ᵇwe who are alive, ¹and remain until ᶜthe coming of the Lord, shall not precede ᵈthose who have fallen asleep.

16 For the Lord ᵃHimself ᵇwill descend from heaven with a ¹ᶜshout, with the voice of ᵈ*the* archangel, and with the ᵉtrumpet of God; and ᶠthe dead in Christ shall rise first.

17 Then ᵃwe who are alive ¹and remain shall be ᵇcaught up together with them ᶜin the clouds to

---

1 ¹Or, *conduct yourselves*
ᵈ2 Cor. 5:9 ᵉPhil. 1:9;
1 Thess. 3:12; 4:10; 2 Thess. 1:3

2 ¹Lit., *through the Lord*

3 ¹Or, *fornication*
ᵃ1 Cor. 6:18

4 ¹Or, *acquire* ²I.e., body, or possibly, *wife*
ᵃ1 Cor. 7:2, 9 ᵇ1 Pet. 3:7;
2 Cor. 4:7 ᶜRom. 1:24

5 ¹Lit., *passion of lust*
ᵃRom. 1:26 ᵇGal. 4:8

6 ᵃ1 Cor. 6:8 ᵇ2 Cor. 7:11
ᶜHeb. 13:4; Rom. 12:19; 13:4
ᵈLuke 16:28; 1 Thess. 2:11;
Heb. 2:6

7 ¹I.e., in the state or sphere of
ᵃ1 Pet. 1:15 ᵇ1 Thess. 2:3

8 ᵃRom. 5:5; 2 Cor. 1:22;
Gal. 4:6; 1 John 3:24

9 ᵃJohn 13:34; Rom. 12:10
ᵇ1 Thess. 5:1; 2 Cor. 9:1
ᶜJohn 6:45; 1 John 2:27; Jer. 31:33f.

10 ᵃ1 Thess. 1:7 ᵇ1 Thess. 3:12

11 ᵃ2 Thess. 3:12 ᵇ1 Pet. 4:15 ᶜEph. 4:28; 2 Thess. 3:10-12; Acts 18:3

12 ¹Lit., *walk* ²Lit., *have need of nothing*
ᵃRom. 13:13; Col 4:5 ᵇMark 4:11 ᶜEph. 4:28

13 ᵃRom. 1:13 ᵇActs 7:60
ᶜ1 Thess. 5:6; Eph. 2:3 ᵈEph. 2:12

14 ¹Lit., *through*
ᵃRom. 14:9; 2 Cor. 4:14
ᵇ1 Cor. 15:18; 1 Thess. 4:13

15 ¹Lit., *who*
ᵃ1 Kin. 13:17f.; 20:35; Gal. 1:12; 2 Cor. 12:1 ᵇ1 Cor. 15:52; 1 Thess. 5:10
ᶜ1 Thess. 2:19 ᵈ1 Cor. 15:18; 1 Thess. 4:13

16 ¹Or, *cry of command*
ᵃ1 Thess. 3:11 ᵇ2 Thess. 1:7;
1 Thess. 1:10 ᶜJoel 2:11
ᵈJude 9 ᵉMatt. 24:31 ᶠ1 Cor. 15:23; 2 Thess. 2:1; Rev. 14:13

17 ¹Lit., *who*
ᵃ1 Cor. 15:52; 1 Thess. 5:10
ᵇ2 Cor. 12:2 ᶜDan. 7:13; Acts 1:9; Rev. 11:12

17 ᵈJohn 12:26

1 ᵃActs 1:7 ᵇ1 Thess. 4:9

2 ¹Lit., *is coming*
ᵃ1 Cor. 1:8 ᵇLuke 21:34;
1 Thess. 5:4; 2 Pet. 3:10;
Rev. 3:3; 16:15

3 ¹Or, *sudden destruction*
²Lit., *is at hand*
ᵃJer. 6:14; 8:11; Ezek. 13:10
ᵇ2 Thess. 1:9 ᶜJohn 16:21

4 ¹Some early mss. read,
like thieves
ᵃ1 John 2:8; Acts 26:18
ᵇLuke 21:34; 1 Thess. 5:2;
2 Pet. 3:10; Rev. 3:3; 16:15

5 ᵃLuke 16:8 ᵇ1 John 2:8;
Acts 26:18

6 ¹Lit., *the remaining
ones* ²Or, *self-controlled*
ᵃRom. 13:11; 1 Thess. 5:10
ᵇEph. 2:3; 1 Thess. 4:13
ᶜ1 Pet. 1:13

7 ᵃActs 2:15; 2 Pet. 2:13

8 ¹Or, *self-controlled*
ᵃ1 Thess. 5:5 ᵇ1 Pet. 1:13
ᶜEph. 6:14 ᵈEph. 6:23 ᵉEph.
6:17 ᶠRom. 8:24

9 ᵃ1 Thess. 1:10 ᵇ2 Thess.
2:13f.

10 ᵃRom. 14:9

11 ¹Or, *comfort*
ᵃEph. 4:29

12 ¹Lit., *know* ²Or,
admonition
ᵃ1 Cor. 16:18; 1 Tim. 5:17;
Ps. 144:3 ᵇ1 Cor. 16:16;
Rom. 16:6, 12; 1 Cor. 15:10
ᶜHeb. 13:17

13 ᵃMark 9:50

14 ¹Or, *undisciplined*
ᵃ2 Thess. 3:6, 7, 11 ᵇIs. 35:4
[Sept.] ᶜRom. 14:1f.; 1 Cor.
8:7ff. [Rom. 15:1] ᵈ1 Cor.
13:4

15 ᵃRom. 12:17; 1 Pet. 3:9;
Matt. 5:44 ᵇRom. 12:9;
1 Thess. 5:21; Gal. 6:10

16 ᵃPhil. 4:4

430

meet the Lord in the air, and thus we shall always ᵈbe with the Lord.
18   Therefore comfort one another with these words.

CHAPTER 5

Now as to the ᵃtimes and the epochs, brethren, you ᵇhave no need of anything to be written to you.
2   For you yourselves know full well that ᵃthe day of the Lord ¹will come ᵇjust like a thief in the night.
3   While they are saying, "ᵃPeace and safety!" then ¹ᵇdestruction ²will come upon them suddenly like ᶜbirth pangs upon a woman with child; and they shall not escape.
4   But you, brethren, are not in ᵃdarkness, that the day should overtake you ¹ᵇlike a thief,
5   for you are all ᵃsons of light and sons of day. We are not of night nor of ᵇdarkness;
6   so then let us not ᵃsleep as ¹ᵇothers do, but let us be alert and ²ᶜsober.
7   For those who sleep do their sleeping at night, and those who get drunk get ᵃdrunk at night.
8   But since ᵃwe are of *the* day, let us ᵇbe ¹sober, having put on the ᶜbreastplate of ᵈfaith and love, and as a ᵉhelmet, the ᶠhope of salvation.
9   For God has not destined us for ᵃwrath, but for ᵇobtaining salvation through our Lord Jesus Christ,
10   ᵃwho died for us, that whether we are awake or asleep, we may live together with Him.
11   Therefore ¹encourage one another, and ᵃbuild up one another, just as you also are doing.
12   But we request of you, brethren, that you ¹ᵃappreciate those ᵇwho diligently labor among you, and ᶜhave charge over you in the Lord and give you ²instruction,
13   and that you esteem them very highly in love because of their work. ᵃLive in peace with one another.
14   And we urge you, brethren, admonish ᵃthe ¹unruly, encourage ᵇthe fainthearted, help ᶜthe weak, be ᵈpatient with all men.
15   See that ᵃno one repays another with evil for evil, but always ᵇseek after that which is good for one another and for all men.
16   ᵃRejoice always;

17 [a]pray without ceasing;

18 in everything [a]give thanks; for this is God's will for you in Christ Jesus.

19 [a]Do not quench the Spirit;

20 do not despise [a]prophetic [1]utterances.

21 But [a]examine everything *carefully*; [b]hold fast to that which is good;

22 abstain from every [1]form of evil.

23 Now [a]may the God of peace [b]Himself sanctify you entirely; and may your [c]spirit and soul and body be preserved complete, [d]without blame at [e]the coming of our Lord Jesus Christ.

24 [a]Faithful is He who [b]calls you, and He also will bring it to pass.

25 Brethren, [a]pray for us[1].

26 [a]Greet all the brethren with a holy kiss.

27 I adjure you by the Lord to [a]have this letter read to all the [b]brethren.

28 [a]The grace of our Lord Jesus Christ be with you.

17 [a]Eph. 6:18

18 [a]Eph. 5:20

19 [a]Eph. 4:30

20 [1]Or, *gifts*
[a]Acts 13:1; 1 Cor. 14:31

21 [a]1 Cor. 14:29; 1 John 4:1
[b]Rom. 12:9; 1 Thess. 5:15;
Gal. 6:10

22 [1]Or, *appearance*

23 [a]Rom. 15:33 [b]1 Thess.
3:11 [c]Luke 1:46f.; Heb. 4:12
[d]2 Pet. 3:14; James 1:4
[e]1 Thess. 2:19

24 [a]1 Cor. 1:9; 2 Thess. 3:3
[b]1 Thess. 2:12

25 [1]Some mss. add, *also*
[a]Eph. 6:19; 2 Thess. 3:1;
Heb. 13:18

26 [a]Rom. 16:16

27 [a]Col. 4:16 [b]Acts 1:15

28 [a]Rom. 16:20; 2 Thess.
3:18

THE SECOND EPISTLE OF PAUL TO THE
THESSALONIANS

**Salutation.   Thanksgiving for their Faith and
Perseverance.**

[a]
PAUL and [b]Silvanus and [c]Timothy to the [d]church of the Thessalonians in God our Father and the Lord Jesus Christ:

2 [a]Grace to you and peace from God the Father and the Lord Jesus Christ.

3 We ought always [a]to give thanks to God for you, [b]brethren, as is *only* fitting, because your faith is greatly enlarged, and the [c]love of each one of you all toward one another grows *ever* greater;

4 therefore, we ourselves [a]speak proudly of you among [b]the churches of God for your [1]perseverance and faith [b]in the midst of all your persecutions and afflictions which you endure.

5 *This is* a [a]plain indication of God's righteous judgment so that you may be [b]considered worthy of the kingdom of God, for which indeed you are suffering.

1 [a]1 Thess. 1:1 [b]2 Cor.
1:19 [c]Acts 16:1 [1 Thess. 1:1]
[d]1 Thess. 1:1; Acts 17:1

2 [a]Rom. 1:7

3 [a]1 Thess. 1:2; 2 Thess.
2:13; Rom. 1:8; Eph. 5:20
[b]1 Thess. 4:1; 2 Thess. 2:1
[c]1 Thess. 3:12

4 [1]Or, *steadfastness*
[a]2 Cor. 7:4; 1 Thess. 2:19
[b]1 Thess. 2:14; 1 Cor. 7:17

5 [a]Phil. 1:28 [b]Luke 20:35;
2 Thess. 1:11

431

6 ¹Lit., *If indeed* ²Or, *in the sight of*
ᵃEx. 23:22; Col. 3:25; Heb. 6:10

7 ¹Lit., *along with us* ²Lit., *at the revelation of the Lord Jesus* ³Lit., *the angels of His power*
ᵃLuke 17:30 ᵇ1 Thess. 4:16
ᶜJude 14 ᵈ1 Cor. 3:13; Heb. 10:27; 12:29; 2 Pet. 3:7; Jude 7; Rev. 14:10; Ex. 3:2; 19:18; Is. 66:15; Ezek. 1:13f.; Dan. 7:9; Matt. 25:41

8 ᵃGal. 4:8 ᵇRom 2:8

9 ᵃ1 Thess. 5:3; Phil. 3:19
ᵇIs. 2:10, 19, 21; 2 Thess. 2:8

10 ¹Or, *in the persons of* ²I.e., true believers; lit., *holy ones*
ᵃJohn 17:10; 1 Thess. 2:12; Is. 49:3 ᵇ1 Cor. 5:13; Is. 2:11ff. ᶜ1 Thess. 2:1; 1 Cor. 1:6

11 ¹Or, *make*
ᵃCol. 1:9 ᵇ2 Thess. 1:5
ᶜRom. 11:29 ᵈRom. 15:14
ᵉ1 Thess. 1:3

12 ¹Or omit, *the*
ᵃPhil. 2:9ff.; Is. 24:15; 66:5; Mal. 1:11

1 ¹Or, *presence*
ᵃ2 Thess. 1:3 ᵇ1 Thess. 2:19
ᶜMark 13:27; 1 Thess. 4:15-17

2 ¹Lit., *mind* ²Lit., *word*
ᵃ1 Cor. 14:32; 1 John 4:1
ᵇ2 Thess. 2:15; 1 Thess. 5:2
ᶜ2 Thess. 3:17 ᵈ1 Cor. 1:8
ᵉ1 Cor. 7:26

3 ¹Or, *falling away* from the faith ²Some early mss. read, *sin*
ᵃEph. 5:6 ᵇ1 Tim. 4:1
ᶜ2 Thess. 2:8; Dan. 7:25; 8:25; 11:36; Rev. 13:5ff.
ᵈJohn 17:12

4 ¹Or, *all that is called God*
ᵃ1 Cor. 8:5 ᵇIs. 14:14; Ezek. 28:2

5 ᵃ1 Thess. 3:4

6 ᵃ2 Thess. 2:7

7 ᵃRev. 17:5, 7 ᵇ2 Thess. 2:6

432

6 ¹For after all ᵃit is *only* just ²for God to repay with affliction those who afflict you,

7 and *to give* relief to you who are afflicted ¹and to us as well ²ᵃwhen the Lord Jesus shall be revealed ᵇfrom heaven ᶜwith ³His mighty angels ᵈin flaming fire,

8 dealing out retribution to those who ᵃdo not know God and to those who ᵇdo not obey the gospel of our Lord Jesus.

9 And these will pay the penalty of ᵃeternal destruction, ᵇaway from the presence of the Lord and from the glory of His power,

10 when He comes to be ᵃglorified ¹in His ²saints on that ᵇday, and to be marveled at among all who have believed—for our ᶜtestimony to you was believed.

11 To this end also we ᵃpray for you always that our God may ¹ᵇcount you worthy of your ᶜcalling, and fulfill every desire for ᵈgoodness and the ᵉwork of faith with power;

12 in order that the ᵃname of our Lord Jesus may be glorified in you, and you in Him, according to the grace of our God and ¹the Lord Jesus Christ.

CHAPTER 2

NOW we request you, ᵃbrethren, with regard to the ¹ᵇcoming of our Lord Jesus Christ, and our ᶜgathering together to Him,

2 that you may not be quickly shaken from your ¹composure or be disturbed either by a ᵃspirit or a ²ᵇmessage or a ᶜletter as if from us, to the effect that ᵈthe day of the Lord ᵉhas come.

3 ᵃLet no one in any way deceive you, for *it will not come* unless the ¹ᵇapostasy comes first, and the ᶜman of ²lawlessness is revealed, the ᵈson of destruction,

4 who opposes and exalts himself above ¹ᵃevery so-called god or object of worship, so that he takes his seat in the temple of God, ᵇdisplaying himself as being God.

5 Do you not remember that ᵃwhile I was still with you, I was telling you these things?

6 And you know ᵃwhat restrains him now, so that in his time he may be revealed.

7 For ᵃthe mystery of lawlessness is already at work; only ᵇhe who now restrains *will do so* until he is taken out of the way.

8 And then that lawless one [a]will be revealed whom the Lord will slay [b]with the breath of His mouth and bring to an end by the [c]appearance of His [1]coming;

9 *that is,* the one whose [1]coming is in accord with the activity of [a]Satan, with all power and [2b]signs and false wonders,

10 and with [1]all the deception of wickedness for [a]those who perish, because they did not receive the love of [b]the truth so as to be saved.

11 And for this reason [a]God [1]will send upon them [2]a [b]deluding influence so that they might believe [3]what is false,

12 in order that they all may be [1]judged who [a]did not believe the truth, but [2b]took pleasure in wickedness.

13 [a]But we should always give thanks to God for you, [b]brethren beloved by the Lord, because [c]God has chosen you [1]from the beginning [d]for salvation [2e]through sanctification [3]by the Spirit and faith in the truth.

14 And it was for this He [a]called you through [b]our gospel, [1]that you may gain the glory of our Lord Jesus Christ.

15 So then, brethren, [a]stand firm and [b]hold to the traditions which you were taught, whether [c]by word *of mouth* or [c]by letter [1]from us.

16 [a]Now may our Lord Jesus Christ [b]Himself and God our Father, who has [c]loved us and given us eternal comfort and [d]good hope by grace,

17 [a]comfort and [b]strengthen your hearts in every good work and word.

CHAPTER 3

[a] FINALLY, brethren, [b]pray for us that [c]the word of the Lord may [1]spread rapidly and be glorified, just as *it did* also with you;

2 and that we may be [a]delivered from [1]perverse and evil men; for not all have [2]faith.

3 But [a]the Lord is faithful, and [1]He will strengthen and protect you [2]from [b]the evil *one.*

4 And we have [a]confidence in the Lord concerning you, that you [b]are doing and will continue to do what we command.

5 And may the Lord [a]direct your hearts into the love of God and into the steadfastness of Christ.

8 [1]Or, *presence*
[a]2 Thess. 2:3; Dan. 7:25; 8:25; 11:36; Rev. 13:5ff. [b]Is. 11:4; Rev. 2:16; 19:15 [c]1 Tim. 6:14; 2 Tim. 1:10; 4:1, 8; Titus 2:13

9 [1]Or, *presence* [2]Or, *attesting miracles* [a]Matt. 4:10 [b]Matt. 24:24; John 4:48

10 [1]Or, *every deception* [a]1 Cor. 1:18 [b]2 Thess. 2:12; 2:13

11 [1]Lit., *sends* [2]Lit., *an activity of error* [3]Or, *the lie* [a]Rom. 1:28; 1 Kin. 22:22 [b]1 Thess. 2:3; 2 Tim. 4:4

12 [1]Or, *condemned* [2]Or, *approved* [a]Rom. 2:8 [b]Rom. 1:32; 1 Cor. 13:6

13 [1]Some ancient mss. read, *first fruits* [2]Lit., *in* [3]Lit., *of* [a]2 Thess. 1:3 [b]1 Thess. 1:4 [c]Eph. 1:4ff. [d]1 Thess. 5:9; 2:12; 1 Pet. 1:5; 1 Cor. 1:21 [e]1 Pet. 1:2; 1 Thess. 4:7

14 [1]Lit., *to the gaining of* [a]1 Thess. 2:12 [b]1 Thess. 1:5

15 [1]Lit., *of* [a]1 Cor. 16:13 [b]1 Cor. 11:2; 2 Thess. 3:6 [c]2 Thess. 2:2

16 [a]1 Thess. 3:11 [b]1 Thess. 3:11 [c]John 3:16 [d]Titus 3:7; 1 Pet. 1:3

17 [a]1 Thess. 3:2, 13 [b]2 Thess. 3:3

1 [1]Lit., *run* [a]1 Thess. 4:1 [b]1 Thess. 5:25 [c]1 Thess. 1:8

2 [1]Lit., *improper* [2]Or, *the faith* [a]Rom. 15:31

3 [1]Lit., *will* [2]Or, *from evil* [a]1 Cor. 1:9; 1 Thess. 5:24 [b]Matt. 5:37

4 [a]2 Cor. 2:3 [b]1 Thess. 4:10

5 [a]1 Thess. 3:11

433

Final Exhortations and Benediction.

6 ¹Or, *avoid* ²Lit., *walks disorderly* ³Or, *undisciplined* ⁴Many ancient mss. read, *they*
ᵃ1 Cor. 5:4 ᵇRom. 16:17; 1 Cor. 5:11; 2 Thess. 3:14
ᶜ1 Thess. 5:14; 2 Thess. 3:7, 11 ᵈ1 Cor. 11:2; 2 Thess. 2:15

7 ¹Lit., *imitate us*
ᵃ1 Thess. 1:6; 2 Thess. 3:9

8 ¹Lit., *from any one* ²Lit., *freely*
ᵃ1 Cor. 9:4 ᵇ1 Thess. 2:9
ᶜActs 18:3; Eph. 4:28

9 ¹Lit., *imitate us*
ᵃ1 Cor. 9:4ff. ᵇ2 Thess. 3:7

10 ᵃ1 Thess. 3:4 ᵇ1 Thess. 4:11

11 ᵃ2 Thess. 3:6 ᵇ1 Tim. 5:13; 1 Pet. 4:15

12 ᵃ1 Thess. 4:1 ᵇ1 Thess. 4:11

13 ᵃ1 Thess. 4:1 ᵇGal. 6:9; 2 Cor. 4:1

14 ¹Lit., *word* ²Lit., *through* ³Lit., *not to associate*
ᵃCol. 4:16 ᵇ2 Thess. 3:6
ᶜ1 Cor. 4:14

15 ¹Or, *keep admonishing*
ᵃGal. 6:1 ᵇ1 Thess. 5:14
ᶜ2 Thess. 3:6, 13

16 ¹Lit., *way*
ᵃRom. 15:33 ᵇ1 Thess. 3:11
ᶜRuth 2:4

17 ¹Lit., *the greeting by my hand of Paul*
ᵃ1 Cor. 16:21

18 ᵃRom. 16:20; 1 Thess. 5:28

6 Now we command you, brethren, ᵃin the name of our Lord Jesus Christ, that you ¹ᵇkeep aloof from every brother who ²leads an ³ᶜunruly life and not according to ᵈthe tradition which ⁴you received from us.

7 For you yourselves know how you ought to ¹ᵃfollow our example; because we did not act in an undisciplined manner among you,

8 nor did we ᵃeat ¹anyone's bread ²without paying for it, but with ᵇlabor and hardship we *kept* ᶜworking night and day so that we might not be a burden to any of you;

9 not because we do not have ᵃthe right *to this*, but in order to offer ourselves ᵇas a model for you, that you might ¹follow our example.

10 For even ᵃwhen we were with you, we used to give you this order: ᵇIf anyone will not work, neither let him eat.

11 For we hear that some among you are ᵃleading an undisciplined life, doing no work at all, but acting like ᵇbusybodies.

12 Now such persons we command and ᵃexhort in the Lord Jesus Christ to ᵇwork in quiet fashion and eat their own bread.

13 But as for you, ᵃbrethren, ᵇdo not grow weary of doing good.

14 And if anyone does not obey our ¹instruction ²ᵃin this letter, take special note of that man ³ᵇand do not associate with him, so that he may be ᶜput to shame.

15 And yet ᵃdo not regard him as an enemy, but ¹ᵇadmonish him as a ᶜbrother.

16 Now ᵃmay the Lord of peace ᵇHimself continually grant you peace in every ¹circumstance. ᶜThe Lord be with you all!

17 ¹I Paul write this greeting ᵃwith my own hand, and this is a distinguishing mark in every letter: this is the way I write.

18 ᵃThe grace of our Lord Jesus Christ be with you all.

THE FIRST EPISTLE OF PAUL TO
TIMOTHY

Salutation. Charge Respecting Misuse of the Law. Personal Thanksgiving.

PAUL, [a]an apostle of [b]Christ Jesus [c]according to the commandment of [d]God our Savior, and of [b]Christ Jesus, *who is* our [e]hope;

2 to [a]Timothy, [b]*my* true child in *the* faith: [c]Grace, mercy *and* peace from God the Father and [d]Christ Jesus our Lord.

3 As I urged you [1]upon my departure for [a]Macedonia, [2]remain on at [b]Ephesus, in order that you may instruct certain men not to [c]teach strange doctrines,

4 nor to [1]pay attention to [a]myths and endless [b]genealogies, which give rise to mere [c]speculation rather than [d]*furthering* [2]God's provision which is by faith.

5 But the goal of our [1a]instruction is love [b]from a pure heart and a [c]good conscience and a sincere [d]faith.

6 For some men, straying from these things, have turned aside to [a]fruitless discussion,

7 [a]wanting to be [b]teachers of the Law, even though they do not understand either what they are saying or the matters about which they make confident assertions.

8 But we know that [a]the Law is good, if one uses it lawfully,

9 realizing the fact that [a]law is not made for a righteous man, but for those who are lawless and [b]rebellious, for the [c]ungodly and sinners, for the unholy and [d]profane, for those who kill their fathers or mothers, for murderers

10 [1]and [2a]immoral men [1]and [b]homosexuals [1]and [c]kidnappers [1]and [d]liars [1]and [e]perjurers, and whatever else is contrary to [f]sound teaching,

11 according to [a]the glorious gospel of [b]the blessed God, with which I have been [c]entrusted.

12 I thank [a]Christ Jesus our Lord, who has [b]strengthened me, because He considered me faithful, [c]putting me into service;

13 even though I was formerly a blasphemer and a [a]persecutor and a violent aggressor. And yet I

1 [a]2 Cor. 1:1; 2 Tim. 1:1
[b]1 Tim. 1:12 [c]Titus 1:3
[d]Luke 1:47; Titus 1:3 [e]Col. 1:27

2 [a]Acts 16:1; 2 Tim. 1:2
[b]2 Tim. 1:2; Titus 1:4
[c]2 Tim. 1:2; Titus 1:4; Rom. 1:7 [d]1 Tim. 1:12

3 [1]Lit., *while departing*
[2]Lit., *to remain*
[a]Rom. 15:26 [b]Acts 18:19
[c]1 Tim. 6:3; Rom. 16:17;
2 Cor. 11:4; Gal. 1:6f.

4 [1]Or, *occupy themselves with* [2]Lit., *the administration of God which*
[a]1 Tim. 4:7; 2 Tim. 4:4;
Titus 1:14; 2 Pet. 1:16 [b]Titus 3:9 [c]1 Tim. 6:4; 2 Tim. 2:23;
Titus 3:9 [d]Eph. 3:2

5 [1]Lit., *commandment*
[a]1 Tim. 1:18 [b]2 Tim. 2:22
[c]1 Pet. 3:16, 21; 1 Tim. 1:19;
3:9; 2 Tim. 1:3 [d]2 Tim. 1:5

6 [a]Titus 1:10

7 [a]James 3:1 [b]Luke 2:46

8 [a]Rom. 7:12, 16

9 [a]Gal. 5:23 [b]Titus 1:6, 10
[c]1 Pet. 4:18; Jude 15 [d]1 Tim. 4:7; 6:20; 2 Tim. 2:16; Heb. 12:16

10 [1]Lit., *for* [2]Or, *fornicators*
[a]1 Cor. 6:9 [b]Lev. 18.22 [c]Ex. 21:16; Rev. 18:13 [d]Rev. 21:8, 27; 22:15 [e]Matt. 5:33; 23:16 [f]2 Tim. 4:3; Titus 1:9; 2:1;
1 Tim. 4:6; 6:3; 2 Tim. 1:13;
Titus 1:13; 2:2

11 [a]2 Cor. 4:4 [b]1 Tim. 6:15
[c]Gal. 2:7

12 [a]1 Tim. 1:1, 2, 15; 2:5;
6:13; Titus 1:4; Gal. 3:26
[b]Phil. 4:13; 2 Tim. 4:17; Acts 9:22 [c]Acts 9:15

13 [a]Acts 8:3; Phil. 3:6

13 bl Tim. 1:16; 1 Cor. 7:25
cActs 26:9

14 aRom. 5:20; 2 Cor. 4:15;
1 Cor. 3:10; 1:13-16 b2 Tim.
1:13; 1 Thess. 1:3; 1 Tim.
2:15; 4:12; 6:11; 2 Tim. 2:22;
Titus 2:2

15 al Tim. 3:1; 4:9; 2 Tim.
2:11; Titus 3:8 bMark 2:17;
Luke 15:2ff.; 19:10 cRom.
11:14 dl Cor. 15:9; Eph. 3:8

16 1Or, destined to
al Tim. 1:13; 1 Cor. 7:25
bEph. 2:7

17 1Lit., of the ages 2Lit.,
the ages of the ages
aRev. 15:3 [Gr.] bl Tim. 6:16
cCol. 1:15 dl Tim. 6:15; Jude
25; John 5:44 cRom. 11:36;
2:7, 10; Heb. 2:7

18 1Lit., child
al Tim. 1:5 bl Tim. 1:2
cl Tim. 4:14 d2 Cor. 10:4;
2 Tim. 2:3f.; 4:7; 1 Tim. 6:12

19 1Lit., the
al Tim. 1:5 bl Tim. 6:12, 21;
2 Tim. 2:18

20 1Lit., of
a2 Tim. 2:17 b2 Tim. 4:14
cl Cor. 5:5 dl Cor. 11:32;
Heb. 12:5ff.

1 aEph. 6:18

2 1Or, a high position 2Or,
seriousness
aEzra 6:10; Rom. 13:1

3 al Tim. 1:1, Luke 1:47;
1 Tim. 4:10

4 1Or, recognition
aEzek. 18:23, 32; 1 Tim.
4:10; Titus 2:11; 2 Pet. 3:9;
John 3:17 bRom. 11:14
c2 Tim. 2:25; 3:7; Titus 1:1;
Heb. 10:26

5 aRom. 3:30; 10:12;
1 Cor. 8:4 bGal. 3:20; 1 Cor.
8:6 cMatt. 1:1; Rom. 1:3

6 1Or, to be borne 2Lit., its
own times
aMatt. 20:28; Gal. 1:4
bl Cor. 1:6 cl Tim. 6:15;
Titus 1:3; Gal. 4:4; Mark
1:15

7 1Or, herald
a2 Tim. 1:11; 1 Tim. 1:11;
Eph. 3:8 bl Cor. 9:1 cRom.
9:1 dActs 9:15

436

was bshown mercy, because cI acted ignorantly in unbelief;

14 and the agrace of our Lord was more than abundant, with the bfaith and love which are *found* in Christ Jesus.

15 aIt is a trustworthy statement, deserving full acceptance, that bChrist Jesus came into the world to csave sinners, among whom dI am foremost *of all.*

16 And yet for this reason I afound mercy, in order that in me as the foremost Jesus Christ might bdemonstrate His perfect patience, as an example for those 1who would believe in Him for eternal life.

17 Now to the aKing 1eternal, bimmortal, cinvisible, the donly God, cbe honor and glory 2forever and ever. Amen.

18 This acommand I entrust to you, Timothy, bmy 1son, in accordance with the cprophecies previously made concerning you, that by them you may dfight the good fight,

19 keeping afaith and a good conscience, which some have rejected and suffered shipwreck in regard to 1btheir faith.

20 1Among these are aHymenaeus and bAlexander, whom I have cdelivered over to Satan, so that they may be dtaught not to blaspheme.

CHAPTER 2

FIRST of all, then, I urge that aentreaties *and* prayers, petitions *and* thanksgivings, be made on behalf of all men,

2 afor kings and all who are in 1authority, in order that we may lead a tranquil and quiet life in all godliness and 2dignity.

3 This is good and acceptable in the sight of aGod our Savior,

4 awho desires all men to be bsaved and to ccome to the 1knowledge of the truth.

5 For there is aone God, *and* bone mediator also between God and men, *the* cman Christ Jesus,

6 who agave Himself as a ransom for all, the btestimony 1*borne* at 2cthe proper time.

7 aAnd for this I was appointed a 1preacher and ban apostle (cI am telling the truth, I am not lying) as a teacher of dthe Gentiles in faith and truth.

8 Therefore [a]I want the men [b]in every place to pray, [c]lifting up [d]holy hands, without wrath and dissension.

9 Likewise, *I want* [a]women to adorn themselves with proper clothing, [1]modestly and discreetly, not with braided hair and gold or pearls or costly garments;

10 but rather by means of good works, as befits women making a claim to godliness.

11 [a]Let a woman quietly receive instruction with entire submissiveness.

12 [a]But I do not allow a woman to teach or exercise authority over a man, but to remain quiet.

13 [a]For it was Adam who was first [1]created, *and* then Eve.

14 And *it was* not Adam *who* was deceived, but [a]the woman being quite deceived, fell into transgression.

15 But she shall be [1]preserved through the bearing of children if *the women* continue in [a]faith and love and sanctity with [2]self restraint.

[a]

CHAPTER 3

IT is a trustworthy statement; if any man aspires to the [b]office of [1]overseer, it is a fine work he desires *to do*.

2 [1a]An overseer, then, must be above reproach, [b]the husband of one wife, [c]temperate, prudent, respectable, [d]hospitable, [e]able to teach,

3 [a]not addicted to wine [1]or pugnacious, but gentle, uncontentious, [b]free from the love of money.

4 *He must be* one who [a]manages his own household well, keeping his children under control with all dignity

5 (but if a man does not know how to manage his own household, how will he take care of [a]the church of God?);

6 *and* not a new convert, lest he become [a]conceited and fall into the [b]condemnation [1]incurred by the devil.

7 And he must [a]have a good reputation with [b]those outside *the church*, so that he may not fall into reproach and [c]the snare of the devil.

8 [a]Deacons likewise *must be* men of dignity, not [1]doubletongued, [2b]or addicted to much wine [2c]or fond of sordid gain,

8 [a]1 Tim. 5:14; Phil. 1:12; Titus 3:8, [in Gr.] [b]John 4:21; 1 Cor. 1:2; 2 Cor. 2:14; 1 Thess. 1:8 [c]Ps. 63:4; Luke 24:50 [d]Ps. 24:4; James 4:8

9 [1]Lit., *with modesty* [a]1 Pet. 3:3

11 [a]1 Cor. 14:34; Titus 2:5

12 [a]1 Cor. 14:34; Titus 2:5

13 [1]Or, *formed* [a]Gen. 2:7, 22; 3:16; 1 Cor. 11:8ff.

14 [a]Gen. 3:6, 13; 2 Cor. 11:3

15 [1]Lit., *saved* [2]Or, *discretion* [a]1 Tim. 1:14

1 [1]Or, *bishop* [a]1 Tim. 1:15 [b]Acts 20:28; Phil. 1:1

2 [1]Lit., *the* [a]1 Tim. 3:2-4; Titus 1:6-8 [b]Titus 1:6; Luke 2:36f.; 1 Tim. 5:9 [c]1 Tim. 3:11; Titus 2:2; 1 Tim. 3:8 [d]Titus 1:8; Rom. 12:13; Heb. 13:2; 1 Pet. 4:9 [e]2 Tim. 2:24

3 [1]Lit., *not* [a]Titus 1:7 [b]Heb. 13:5; 1 Tim. 6:10; Titus 1:7; 1 Tim. 3:8

4 [a]1 Tim. 3:12

5 [a]1 Cor. 10:32; 1 Tim. 3:15

6 [1]Lit., *of the devil* [a]1 Tim. 6:4; 2 Tim. 3:4 [b]1 Tim. 3:7

7 [a]2 Cor. 8:21 [b]Mark 4:11 [c]2 Tim. 2:26; 1 Tim. 6:9

8 [1]Or, *given to double-talk* [2]Lit., *not* [a]Phil. 1:1; 1 Tim. 3:12 [b]Titus 2:3; 1 Tim. 5:23 [c]Titus 1:7; 1 Tim. 3:3; 1 Pet. 5:2

F34

9 ᵃ1 Tim. 1:19; 1 Tim. 1:5

10 ᵃ1 Tim. 5:22

11 ¹I.e., either deacons'
wives or deaconesses
ᵃ2 Tim. 3:3; Titus 2:3
ᵇ1 Tim. 3:2

12 ¹Lit., *managing well*
ᵃPhil. 1:1; 1 Tim. 3:8 ᵇ1 Tim.
3:2 ᶜ1 Tim. 3:4

13 ¹Lit., *good*
ᵃMatt. 25:21

15 ¹Lit., *if I delay* ²Or, *you
ought to conduct yourself*
ᵃEph. 2:21f.; 1 Cor. 3:16;
2 Cor. 6:16; 1 Pet. 2:5; 4:17
ᵇ1 Tim. 3:5 ᶜMatt. 16:16;
1 Tim. 4:10 ᵈGal. 2:9; 2 Tim.
2:19

16 ¹Some later mss. read,
God ²Or, *justified* ³Or, *by*
ᵃRom. 16:25 ᵇJohn 1:14;
1 Pet. 1:20; 1 John 3:5, 8
ᶜRom. 3:4 ᵈLuke 2:13; 24:4;
1 Pet. 1:12 ᵉRom. 16:26;
2 Cor. 1:19; Col. 1:23
ᶠ2 Thess. 1:10 ᵍMark 16:19;
Acts 1:9

1 ᵃJohn 16:13; Acts 20:23;
21:11; 1 Cor. 2:10f. ᵇ2 Thess.
2:3ff.; 2 Tim. 3:1; 2 Pet. 3:3;
Jude 18 ᶜ1 John 4:6 ᵈJames
3:15

2 ᵃEph. 4:19

3 ᵃHeb. 13:4 ᵇCol. 2:16;
2:23 ᶜGen. 1:29; 9:3 ᵈ1 Tim.
4:4; Rom. 14:6; 1 Cor.
10:30f.

4 ᵃ1 Cor. 10:26 ᵇ1 Tim.
4:3; Rom. 14:6; 1 Cor.
10:30f.

5 ᵃGen. 1:25, 31; Heb. 11:3

6 ᵃActs 1:15 ᵇ2 Cor. 11:23

9 ᵃ*but* holding to the mystery of the faith with a clear conscience.

10 And ᵃlet these also first be tested; then let them serve as deacons if they are beyond reproach.

11 ¹Women *must* likewise *be* dignified, ᵃnot malicious gossips, but ᵇtemperate, faithful in all things.

12 Let ᵃdeacons be ᵇhusbands of *only* one wife, *and* ¹ᶜgood managers of *their* children and their own households.

13 For those who have served well as deacons ᵃobtain for themselves a ¹high standing and great confidence in the faith that is in Christ Jesus.

14 I am writing these things to you, hoping to come to you before long;

15 but ¹in case I am delayed, *I write* so that you may know how ²one ought to conduct himself in ᵃthe household of God, which is the ᵇchurch of ᶜthe living God, the ᵈpillar and support of the truth.

16 And by common confession great is ᵃthe mystery of godliness:

¹He who was ᵇrevealed in the flesh,
Was ²ᶜvindicated ³in the Spirit,
ᵈBeheld by angels,
ᵉProclaimed among the nations,
ᶠBelieved on in the world,
ᵍTaken up in glory.

CHAPTER 4

BUT ᵃthe Spirit explicitly says that ᵇin later times some will fall away from the faith, paying attention to ᶜdeceitful spirits and ᵈdoctrines of demons,

2 by means of the hypocrisy of liars ᵃseared in their own conscience as with a branding iron,

3 *men* who ᵃforbid marriage *and advocate* ᵇabstaining from foods, which ᶜGod has created to be ᵈgratefully shared in by those who believe and know the truth.

4 For ᵃeverything created by God is good, and nothing is to be rejected, if it is ᵇreceived with gratitude:

5 for it is sanctified by means of ᵃthe word of God and prayer.

6 In pointing out these things to ᵃthe brethren, you will be a good ᵇservant of Christ Jesus, *constantly* nourished on the words of the faith and

of the [1c]sound doctrine which you [d]have been following.

7 But have nothing to do with [a]worldly [b]fables fit only for old women. On the other hand, discipline yourself for the purpose of [c]godliness;

8 for [a]bodily discipline is only little profit, but [b]godliness is profitable for all things, since it [c]holds promise for the [d]present life and *also* for the *life* to come.

9 [a]It is a trustworthy statement deserving full acceptance.

10 For it is for this we labor and strive, because we have fixed [a]our hope on [b]the living God, who is [c]the Savior of all men, especially of believers.

11 [1a]Prescribe and teach these things.

12 [a]Let no one look down on your youthfulness, but *rather* in speech, conduct, [b]love, faith *and* purity, show yourself [c]an example [1]of those who believe.

13 [a]Until I come, give attention to the *public* [b]reading of *Scripture*, to exhortation and teaching.

14 Do not neglect the spiritual gift within you, which was bestowed upon you through [a]prophetic utterance with [b]the laying on of hands by the [1c]presbytery.

15 Take pains with these things; be *absorbed* in them, so that your progress may be evident to all.

16 [a]Pay close attention to yourself and to your teaching; persevere in these things; for as you do this you will [1b]insure salvation both for yourself and for those who hear you.

[a]   CHAPTER 5

DO not sharply rebuke an [b]older man, *but rather* appeal to him as a father; [c]the younger men as brothers,

2 the older women as mothers, *and* the younger women as sisters, in all purity.

3 Honor widows who are [a]widows indeed;

4 but if any widow has children or grandchildren, [a]let them first learn to practice piety in regard to their own family, and to [1]make some return to their parents; for this is [b]acceptable in the sight of God.

5 Now she who is a [a]widow indeed and who has been left alone [b]has fixed her hope on God,

6 [1]Lit., *good*
[c]1 Tim. 1:10 [d]Luke 1:3 [Gr.]; 2 Tim. 3:10; Phil. 2:20, 22

7 [a]1 Tim. 1:9 [b]1 Tim. 1:4 [c]1 Tim. 4:8; 6:3, 5f.; 2 Tim. 3:5

8 [a]Col. 2:23 [b]1 Tim. 4:7; 6:3, 5f.; 2 Tim. 3:5 [c]Ps. 37:9, 11; Prov. 19:23; 22:4; Matt. 6:33 [d]Matt. 12:32; 6:33; Mark 10:30

9 [a]1 Tim. 1:15

10 [a]2 Cor. 1:10; 1 Tim. 6:17 [b]1 Tim. 3:15 [c]1 Tim. 2:4; John 4:42

11 [1]Or, *Keep commanding and teaching* [a]1 Tim. 5:7; 6:2

12 [1]Or, *to* [a]1 Cor. 16:11; Titus 2:15 [b]1 Tim. 1:14 [c]Titus 2:7; 1 Pet. 5:3

13 [a]1 Tim. 3:14 [b]2 Tim. 3:15ff.

14 [1]Or else, *board of elders* [a]1 Tim. 1:18 [b]1 Tim. 5:22; 2 Tim. 1:6; Acts 6:6 [c][in Gr.] Acts 11:30

16 [1]Lit., *save both yourself and those . . .* [a]Acts 20:28 [b]1 Cor. 1:21

1 [a]Lev. 19:32 [b]Titus 2:2 [c]Titus 2:6

3 [a]1 Tim. 5:5, 16; Acts 6:1; 9:39, 41

4 [1]Lit., *give back recompenses* [a]Eph. 6:2 [b]1 Tim. 2:3

5 [a]1 Tim. 5:3, 16; Acts 6:1; 9:39, 41 [b]1 Pet. 3:5; 1 Cor. 7:34

5 cLuke 2:37; 1 Tim. 2:1;
2 Tim. 1:3

6 aJames 5:5 bRev. 3:1;
Luke 15:24; 2 Tim. 3:6

7 1Or, *Keep commanding*
a1 Tim. 4:11

8 a2 Tim. 2:12; Titus 1:16;
2 Pet. 2:1; Jude 4

9 a1 Tim. 5:16 b1 Tim. 3:2

10 1I.e., true believers; lit.,
holy ones
aActs 9:36; 1 Tim. 6:18;
1 Pet. 2:12; Titus 2:7; 3:8
b1 Tim. 3:2 cLuke 7:44; John
13:14 d1 Tim. 5:16

11 aRev. 18:7

12 1Lit., *faith*

13 a3 John 10 [Gr.]
b2Thess. 3:11 cTitus 1:11

14 a1 Tim. 2:8 b1 Cor. 7:9;
1 Tim. 4:3 cTitus 2:5 d1 Tim.
6:1

15 a1 Tim. 1:20 bMatt. 4:10

16 a1 Tim. 5:4 b1 Tim. 5:10
c1 Tim. 5:3

17 1Lit., *in word*
aActs 11:30; 1 Tim. 5:19;
4:14 [Gr.] bRom. 12:8
c1 Thess. 5:12

18 aDeut. 25:4; 1 Cor. 9:9
bMatt. 10:10; Luke 10:7;
1 Cor. 9:14; Lev. 19:13;
Deut. 24:15

19 aActs 11:30; 1 Tim. 5:17;
4:14 [Gr.] bMatt. 18:16

20 aEph. 5:11; Gal. 2:14;
2 Tim. 4:2 b2 Cor. 7:11

21 a1 Tim. 6:13; 2 Tim. 4:1;
2:14; Luke 9:26

and continues in centreaties and prayers night and day.

6 But she who agives herself to wanton pleasure is bdead even while she lives.

7 1aPrescribe these things as well, so that they may be above reproach.

8 But if any one does not provide for his own, and especially for those of his household, he has adenied the faith, and is worse than an unbeliever.

9 Let a widow be aput on the list only if she is not less than sixty years old, *having been* bthe wife of one man,

10 having a reputation for agood works; *and if* she has brought up children, if she has bshown hospitality to strangers, if she chas washed the 1saints' feet, if she has dassisted those in distress, *and if* she has devoted herself to every good work.

11 But refuse *to put* younger widows on the *list*, for when they feel asensual desires in disregard of Christ, they want to get married,

12 *thus* incurring condemnation, because they have set aside their previous 1pledge.

13 And at the same time they also learn *to be* idle, as they go around from house to house; and not merely idle, but also agossips and bbusybodies, talking about cthings not proper *to mention.*

14 Therefore, aI want younger *widows* to get bmarried, bear children, ckeep house, *and* dgive the enemy no occasion for reproach;

15 for some ahave already turned aside to follow bSatan.

16 If any woman who is a believer ahas *dependent* widows, let her bassist them, and let not the church be burdened, so that it may assist those who are cwidows indeed.

17 Let athe elders who brule well be considered worthy of double honor, especially those who cwork hard 1at preaching and teaching.

18 For the Scripture says, "aYOU SHALL NOT MUZZLE THE OX WHILE HE IS THRESHING," and "bThe laborer is worthy of his wages."

19 Do not receive an accusation against an aelder except on the basis of btwo or three witnesses.

20 Those who continue in sin, arebuke in the presence of all, bso that the rest also may be fearful *of sinning.*

21 aI solemnly charge you in the presence of God and of Christ Jesus and of *His* chosen angels,

to maintain these *principles* without bias, doing nothing in a *spirit of* partiality.

22   ᵃDo not lay hands upon any one *too* hastily and ¹thus share ᵇ*responsibility for* the sins of others; keep yourself ²free from sin.

23   No longer drink water *exclusively*, but ᵃuse a little wine for the sake of your stomach and your frequent ailments.

24   The sins of some men are quite evident, going before them to judgment; for others, their *sins* ᵃfollow after.

25   Likewise also, deeds that are good are quite evident, and ᵃthose which are otherwise cannot be concealed.

Chapter 6

ᵃLET all who are under the yoke as slaves regard their own masters as worthy of all honor so ᵇthat the name of God and *our* doctrine may not be spoken against.

2   And let those who have believers as their masters not be disrespectful to them because they are ᵃbrethren, but let them serve them all the more, because those who ¹partake of the benefit are believers and beloved. ᵇTeach and ²preach these *principles*.

3   If any one ᵃadvocates a different doctrine, and does not ¹agree with ᵇsound words, those of our Lord Jesus Christ, and with the doctrine ᶜconforming to godliness,

4   he is ᵃconceited *and* understands nothing; but he ¹has a morbid interest in ᵇcontroversial questions and ᶜdisputes about words, out of which arise envy, strife, abusive language, evil suspicions,

5   and constant friction between ᵃmen of depraved mind and deprived of the truth, who ᵇsuppose that ¹godliness is a means of gain.

6   ᵃBut godliness *actually* is a means of ᵇgreat gain, when accompanied by ᶜcontentment.

7   For ᵃwe have brought nothing into the world, ¹so we cannot take anything out of it either.

8   And if we ᵃhave food and covering, with these we shall be content.

9   ᵃBut those who want to get rich fall into temptation and ᵇa snare and many foolish and harmful desires which plunge men into ruin and destruction.

22 ¹Lit., *do not share* ²Lit., *pure*
ᵃ1 Tim. 4:14; 3:10 ᵇEph. 5:11; 1 Tim. 3:2-7

23 ᵃ1 Tim. 3:8

24 ᵃRev. 14:13

25 ᵃProv. 10:9

1 ᵃTitus 2:9; 1 Pet. 2:18; Eph. 6:5 ᵇTitus 2:5

2 ¹Or, *benefit by their service* ²Lit., *exhort, urge* ᵃActs 1:15; Gal. 3:28; Philem. 16 ᵇ1 Tim. 4:11

3 ¹Lit., *come to*, or, *come with* ᵃ1 Tim. 1:3 ᵇ1 Tim. 1:10 ᶜTitus 1:1

4 ¹Lit., *is sick about* ᵃ1 Tim. 3:6 ᵇ1 Tim. 1:4 ᶜ2 Tim. 2:14; Acts 18:15

5 ¹Or, *religion* ᵃ2 Tim. 3:8; Titus 1:15 ᵇTitus 1:11; 2 Pet. 2:3

6 ᵃ1 Tim. 6:6-10; Luke 12:15-21 ᵇ1 Tim. 4:8 ᶜPhil. 4:11; Heb. 13:5

7 ¹Later mss. read, *it is clear that* ᵃJob 1:21; Eccl. 5:15

8 ᵃProv. 30:8

9 ᵃProv. 15:27; 23:4; 28:20; 1 Tim. 6:17; Luke 12:21 ᵇ1 Tim. 3:7

10 [1]Lit., *the evils*
[a]1 Tim. 6:9; 3:3; Col. 3:5
[b]Rom. 11:16ff. [c]James 5:19

11 [1]Or, *steadfastness*
[a]2 Tim. 2:22 [b]2 Tim. 3:17
[c]1 Tim. 1:14 [d]2 Tim. 3:10

12 [a]1 Cor. 9:25f.; Phil. 1:30;
1 Tim. 1:18 [b]1 Tim. 1:19
[c]Phil. 3:12; 1 Tim. 6:19 [d]Col.
3:15 [e]2 Cor. 9:13; 1 Tim.
6:13 [f]2 Tim. 2:2; 1 Tim. 4:14

13 [1]Or, *preserves alive*
[a]1 Tim. 5:21 [b]1 Tim. 1:12,
15; 2:5; Gal. 3:26 [c]2 Cor.
9:13; 1 Tim. 6:12 [d]John
18:37; Matt. 27:2

14 [a]2 Thess. 2:8

15 [1]Lit., *show* [2]Lit., *those
who reign as kings* [3]Lit.,
those who rule as lords
[a]1 Tim. 2:6 [b]1 Tim. 1:11
[c]1 Tim. 1:17 [d]Rev. 19:16;
17:14; Deut. 10:17 [e]Ps. 136:3

16 [a]1 Tim. 1:17 [b]Ps. 104:2;
1 John 1:5; James 1:17 [c]John
1:18 [d]1 Tim. 1:17

17 [a]2 Tim. 4:10; Titus 2:12;
Matt. 12:32 [b]Ps. 62:10; Luke
12:20; 1 Tim. 6:9; Rom.
11:20 [c]1 Tim. 4:10 [d]Acts
14:17

18 [1]Or, *deeds*
[a]1 Tim. 5:10 [b]Rom. 12:8;
Eph. 4:28

19 [a]Matt. 6:20 [b]1 Tim. 6:12

20 [a]1 Tim. 1:2 [b]2 Tim. 1:12,
14 [c]2 Tim. 2:16; 1 Tim. 1:9

21 [1]Lit., *concerning*
[a]2 Tim. 2:18 [b]1 Tim. 1:19
[c]Col. 4:18

10 For [a]the love of money is a [b]root of all [1]sorts of evil, and some by longing for it have [c]wandered away from the faith, and pierced themselves with many a pang.

11 But [a]flee from these things, you [b]man of God; and pursue after righteousness, godliness, [c]faith, [d]love, [1]perseverance *and* gentleness.

12 [a]Fight the good fight of [b]faith; [c]take hold of the eternal life [d]to which you were called, and you made the good [e]confession in the presence of [f]many witnesses.

13 [a]I charge you in the presence of God, who [1]gives life to all things, and of [b]Christ Jesus, who testified the [c]good confession [d]before Pontius Pilate;

14 that you keep the commandment without stain or reproach, until the [a]appearing of our Lord Jesus Christ,

15 which He will [1]bring about at [a]the proper time—He who is [b]the blessed and [c]only Sovereign, [d]the King of [2]kings and [e]Lord of [3]lords;

16 [a]who alone possesses immortality and [b]dwells in unapproachable light; [c]whom no man has seen or can see. [d]To Him *be* honor and eternal dominion! Amen.

17 Instruct those who are rich in [a]this present world [b]not to be conceited or to [c]fix their hope on the uncertainty of riches, but on God, [d]who richly supplies us with all things to enjoy.

18 *Instruct them* to do good, to be rich in [a]good [1]works, [b]to be generous and ready to share,

19 [a]storing up for themselves the treasure of a good foundation for the future, so that they may [b]take hold of that which is life indeed.

20 O [a]Timothy, guard [b]what has been entrusted to you, avoiding [c]worldly *and* empty chatter *and* the opposing arguments of what is falsely called 'knowledge'—

21 which some have professed and thus [a]gone astray [1]from [b]the faith.

[c]**G**race be with you.

THE SECOND EPISTLE OF PAUL TO
TIMOTHY

Salutation. Timothy Charged to Guard His Trust.

PAUL, ªan apostle of ᵇChrist Jesus ¹ᶜby the will of God, according to the promise of ᵈlife in Christ Jesus,

2 to ªTimothy, my beloved ¹ᵇson: ᶜGrace, mercy *and* peace from God the Father and Christ Jesus our Lord.

3 ªI thank God, whom I ᵇserve with a ᶜclear conscience ¹the way my forefathers did, ᵈas I constantly remember you in my ²prayers night and day,

4 ªlonging to see you, ᵇeven as I recall your tears, so that I may be filled with joy.

5 ¹For I am mindful of the ªsincere faith within you, which first dwelt in your grandmother Lois, and ᵇyour mother Eunice, and I am sure that *it is* in you as well.

6 And for this reason I remind you to kindle afresh ªthe gift of God which is in you through ªthe laying on of my hands.

7 For God has not given us a ªspirit of timidity, but of power and love and ¹discipline.

8 Therefore ªdo not be ashamed of the ᵇtestimony of our Lord, or of me ᶜHis prisoner; but join with *me* in ᵈsuffering for the ᵉgospel according to the power of God;

9 who has ªsaved us, and ᵇcalled us with a holy ᶜcalling, ᵈnot according to our works, but according to His own ᵇpurpose and grace which was granted us in ᵉChrist Jesus from ᶠall eternity,

10 but ªnow has been revealed by the ᵇappearing of our Savior ᶜChrist Jesus, who ᵈabolished death, and brought life and immortality to light through the gospel,

11 ªfor which I was appointed a preacher and an apostle and a teacher.

12 For this reason I also suffer these things, but ªI am not ashamed; for I know ᵇwhom I have believed and I am convinced that He is able to ᶜguard what I have entrusted to Him ¹until ᵈthat day.

13 ¹ªRetain the ᵇstandard of ᶜsound words

1 ¹Lit., *through*
ª2 Cor. 1:1 ᵇ2 Tim. 1:2, 9, 13; 2:1, 3, 10; 3:12, 15; 1 Tim. 1:12; Gal. 3:26 ᶜ1 Cor. 1:1 ᵈ1 Tim. 6:19

2 ¹Lit., *child*
ªActs 16:1; 1 Tim. 1:2 ᵇ1 Tim. 1:2; 2 Tim. 2:1; Titus 1:4 ᶜ1 Tim. 1:2

3 ¹Lit., *from my forefathers* ²Or, *petitions*
ªRom. 1:8 ᵇActs 24:14 ᶜActs 23:1; 24:16; 1 Tim. 1:5 ᵈRom. 1:9

4 ª2 Tim. 4:9, 21 ᵇActs 20:37

5 ¹Lit., *Receiving remembrance of*
ª1 Tim. 1:5 ᵇActs 16:1; 2 Tim. 3:15

6 ª1 Tim. 4:14

7 ¹Or, *sound judgment*
ªRom. 8:15; John 14:27

8 ª2 Tim. 1:12, 16; Mark 8:38; Rom. 1:16 ᵇ1 Cor. 1:6 ᶜEph. 3:1; 2 Tim. 1:16 ᵈ2 Tim. 2:3, 9; 4:5 ᵉ2 Tim. 1:10; 2:8

9 ªRom. 11:14 ᵇRom. 8:28f. ᶜRom. 11:29 ᵈEph. 2:9 ᵉ2 Tim. 1:1 ᶠTitus 1:2; Rom. 16:25; Eph. 1:4

10 ªRom. 16:26 ᵇTitus 2:11; 2 Thess. 2:8; 2 Tim. 4:1, 8 ᶜ2 Tim. 1:1 ᵈ1 Cor. 15:26; Heb. 2:14f.

11 ª1 Tim. 2:7

12 ¹Or, *for*
ª2 Tim. 1:8; 1:16 ᵇTitus 3:8 ᶜ2 Tim. 1:14; 1 Tim. 6:20 ᵈ2 Tim. 1:18; 4:8; 1 Cor. 3:13; 1:8

13 ¹Or, *Hold the example*
ª2 Tim. 3:14; Titus 1:9 ᵇRom. 2:20; 6:17 ᶜ1 Tim. 1:10

13 ^d2 Tim. 2:2 ^e1 Tim. 1:14
^f2 Tim. 1:1

14 ¹Lit., *good deposit*
^aRom. 8:9 ^b2 Tim. 1:12;
1 Tim. 6:20

15 ¹I.e., the province of
Asia
^aActs 2:9 ^b2 Tim. 4:10, 11, 16

16 ¹Lit., *chain*
^a2 Tim. 4:19 ^b2 Tim. 1:8
^cEph. 6:20

18 ^a2 Tim. 1:12; 4:8; 1 Cor.
3:13; 1:8 ^bActs 18:19; 1 Tim.
1:3

1 ¹Lit., *child*
^a2 Tim. 1:2 ^bEph. 6:10
^c2 Tim. 1:1

2 ^a2 Tim. 1:13 ^b1 Tim.
6:12 ^c1 Tim. 1:18 ^d1 Tim.
1:12 ^e[in Gr.] 2 Cor. 2:16; 3:5

3 ^a2 Tim. 1:8 ^b1 Cor. 9:7;
1 Tim. 1:18 ^c2 Tim. 1:1

4 ^a2 Pet. 2:20

5 ¹Lit., *not crowned*
^a1 Cor. 9:25

6 ^a1 Cor. 9:10

8 ^aActs 2:24 ^bMatt. 1:1
^cRom. 2:16

9 ¹Lit., *in which*
^a2 Tim. 1:8; 2:3 ^bPhil. 1:7
^cLuke 23:32 ^d1 Thess. 1:8
^eActs 28:31; 2 Tim. 4:17

10 ^aCol. 1:24 ^bLuke 18:7;
Titus 1:1 ^c2 Cor. 1:6;
1 Thess. 5:9 ^d1 Cor. 1:21
^e2 Tim. 2:1, 3; 2 Tim. 1:1
^f2 Cor. 4:17; 1 Pet. 5:10

11 ^a1 Tim. 1:15

^dwhich you have heard from me, in the ^efaith and love which are in ^fChrist Jesus.

14 Guard through the Holy Spirit who ^adwells in us, the ^{1b}treasure which has been entrusted to *you.*

15 You are aware of the fact that all who are in ^{1a}Asia ^bturned away from me, among whom are Phygelus and Hermogenes.

16 The Lord grant mercy to ^athe house of Onesiphorus for he often refreshed me, and ^bwas not ashamed of my ^{1c}chains;

17 but when he was in Rome, he eagerly searched for me, and found me—

18 the Lord grant to him to find mercy from the Lord on ^athat day—and you know very well what services he rendered at ^bEphesus.

Chapter 2

Y OU therefore, my ^{1a}son, ^bbe strong in the grace that is in ^cChrist Jesus.

2 And the things ^awhich you have heard from me in the presence of ^bmany witnesses, these ^centrust to ^dfaithful men, who will be ^eable to teach others also.

3 ^aSuffer hardship with *me,* as a good ^bsoldier of ^cChrist Jesus.

4 No soldier in active service ^aentangles himself in the affairs of everyday life, so that he may please the one who enlisted him as a soldier.

5 And also if any one ^acompetes as an athlete, he ¹does not win the prize unless he competes according to the rules.

6 ^aThe hard-working farmer ought to be the first to receive his share of the crops.

7 Consider what I say, for the Lord will give you understanding in everything.

8 Remember Jesus Christ, ^aarisen from the dead, ^bdescendant of David, ^caccording to my gospel;

9 ¹for which I ^asuffer hardship even to ^bimprisonment as a ^ccriminal, but ^dthe word of God ^eis not imprisoned.

10 For this reason ^aI endure all things for ^bthe sake of those who are chosen, ^cthat they also may obtain the ^dsalvation which is in ^eChrist Jesus *and* with *it* ^feternal glory.

11 ^aIt is a trustworthy statement:

For [b]if we died with Him, we shall also live with Him;

12 If we endure, [a]we shall also reign with Him;
If we [1][b]deny Him, He also will deny us;

13 If we are faithless, [a]He remains faithful; for [b]He cannot deny Himself.

14 Remind *them* of these things, and solemnly [a]charge *them* in the presence of God not to [b]wrangle about words, which is useless, *and leads* to the ruin of the hearers.

15 Be diligent to [a]present yourself approved to God as a workman who does not need to be ashamed, handling accurately [b]the word of truth.

16 But [a]avoid [b]worldly *and* empty chatter, for [1]it will lead to further ungodliness,

17 and their [1]talk will spread like [2]gangrene. Among them are [a]Hymenaeus and Philetus,

18 *men* who have gone astray from the truth saying that [a]the resurrection has already taken place, and thus they upset [b]the faith of some.

19 Nevertheless, the [a]firm foundation of God stands, having this [b]seal, "[c]The Lord knows those who are His," and, "[d]Let every one who names the name of the Lord abstain from wickedness."

20 Now in a large house there are not only gold and silver vessels, but also vessels of wood and of earthenware, and [a]some to honor and some to dishonor.

21 Therefore, if a man cleanses himself from [a]these *things*, he will be a vessel for honor, sanctified, useful to the Master, [b]prepared for every good work.

22 Now [a]flee from youthful lusts, and [a]pursue after righteousness, [b]faith, love *and* peace, with those who [c]call on the Lord [d]from a pure heart.

23 But refuse foolish and ignorant [a]speculations, knowing that they [b]produce [1]quarrels.

24 And [a]the Lord's bond-servant must not be quarrelsome, but be kind to all, [b]able to teach, patient when wronged,

25 [a]with gentleness correcting those who are in opposition; [b]if perhaps God may grant them repentance leading to [c]the knowledge of the truth,

26 and they may come to their senses *and* escape from [a]the snare of the devil, having been [b]held captive [1]by him to do his will.

11 [b]Rom. 6:8; 1 Thess. 5:10

12 [1]Lit., *shall deny*
[a]Luke 22:29; Matt. 19:28;
Rom. 5:17; 8:17 [b]Matt. 10:33; 1 Tim. 5:8

13 [a]1 Cor. 1:9; Rom. 3:3
[b]Num. 23:19; Titus 1:2

14 [a]1 Tim. 5:21; 2 Tim. 4:1
[b]1 Tim. 6:4; 2 Tim. 2:23;
Titus 3:9

15 [a]Rom. 6:13; James 1:12
[b]Eph. 1:13; James 1:18

16 [1]Lit., *they will make further progress in ungodliness*
[a]Titus 3:9 [b]1 Tim. 6:20; 1:9

17 [1]Lit., *word* [2]Or, *cancer*
[a]1 Tim. 1:20

18 [a]1 Cor. 15:12 [b]1 Tim. 1:19; Titus 1:11

19 [a]1 Tim. 3:15; Is. 28:16f.
[b]John 3:33 [c]John 10:14;
1 Cor. 8:3 [d]Luke 13:27;
1 Cor. 1:2

20 [a]Rom. 9:21

21 [a]2 Tim. 2:16-18; 1 Tim. 6:11 [b]2 Tim. 3:17; 2 Cor. 9:8;
Eph. 2:10

22 [a]1 Tim. 6:11 [b]1 Tim. 1:14 [c]Acts 7:59 [d]1 Tim. 1:5

23 [1]Lit., *fightings*
[a]1 Tim. 6:4; Titus 3:9,
2 Tim. 2:14 [b]Titus 3:9;
James 4:1

24 [a]1 Tim. 3:3; Titus 1:7
[b]1 Tim. 3:2

25 [a]Titus 3:2; Gal. 6:1;
1 Pet. 3:15 [b]Acts 8:22
[c]1 Tim. 2:4

26 [1]Or possibly, *by him, to do His will*
[a]1 Tim. 3:7 [b]Luke 5:10

CHAPTER 3

1 a1 Tim. 4:1

2 aPhil. 2:21 bLuke 16:14;
1 Tim. 3:3; 6:10 cRom. 1:30
d2 Pet. 2:10-12 eLuke 6:35
f1 Tim. 1:9

3 1Lit., *not loving good*
aRom. 1:31 b1 Tim. 3:11
cTitus 1:8

4 aActs 7:52 [Gr.] bActs
19:36 [Gr.] c1 Tim. 3:6 dPhil.
3:19

5 1Or, *religion*
aRom. 2:20 b1 Tim. 4:7
c1 Tim. 5:8 d2 Thess. 3:6;
Matt. 7:15

6 1Or, *creep into*
aJude 4 b1 Tim. 5:6; Titus
1:3 cTitus 2:3

7 1Or, *recognition*
a2 Tim. 2:25

8 aEx. 7:11 bActs 13:8
c1 Tim. 6:5

9 aLuke 6:11 [Gr.] bEx.
7:12; 8:18; 9:11

10 1Or, *steadfastness*
a1 Tim. 4:6; Luke 1:3 [Gr.];
Phil. 2:20, 22 b1 Tim 6:11

11 a2 Cor. 12:10 b2 Cor.
1:5, 7 cActs 13:14, 45, 50
dActs 14:5 eActs 14:19
f2 Cor. 11:23-27 gRom. 15:31

12 aJohn 15:20; Acts 14:22;
2 Cor. 4:9f.

13 a2 Tim. 2:16 bTitus 3:3

14 a Tim. 1:13; Titus 1:9

15 a2 Tim. 1:5 bJohn 5:47;
Rom. 2:27 cPs. 119:98f.
d1 Cor. 1:21 e2 Tim. 1:1

16 1Or, possibly, *Every
Scripture inspired by God is
also* . . . 2Lit., *God-breathed*
3Lit., *training which is in*
aRom. 4:23f.; 15:4; 2 Pet.
1:20f.

17 a1 Tim. 6:11 b2 Tim.
2:21; Heb. 13:21

BUT realize this, that ain the last days difficult times will come.

2 For men will be alovers of self, blovers of money, cboastful, carrogant, drevilers, cdisobedient to parents, eungrateful, funholy,

3 aunloving, irreconcilable, bmalicious gossips, without self-control, brutal, 1chaters of good,

4 atreacherous, breckless, cconceited, dlovers of pleasure rather than lovers of God;

5 holding to a aform of 1bgodliness, although they have cdenied its power; and davoid such men as these.

6 For among them are those who 1aenter into households and captivate bweak women weighed down with sins, led on by cvarious impulses,

7 always learning and never able to acome to the 1knowledge of the truth.

8 And just as aJannes and Jambres bopposed Moses, so these *men* also oppose the truth, cmen of depraved mind, rejected as regards the faith.

9 But they will not make further progress; for their afolly will be obvious to all, bas also that of those *two* came to be.

10 But you afollowed my teaching, conduct, purpose, faith, patience, blove, 1perseverance,

11 apersecutions, bsufferings, such as happened to me at cAntioch, at dIconium *and* at eLystra; what fpersecutions I endured, and out of them all gthe Lord delivered me!

12 And indeed, all who desire to live godly in Christ Jesus awill be persecuted.

13 But evil men and impostors awill proceed *from bad* to worse, bdeceiving and being deceived.

14 You, however, acontinue in the things you have learned and become convinced of, knowing from whom you have learned *them;*

15 and that afrom childhood you have known bthe sacred writings which are able to cgive you the wisdom that leads to dsalvation through faith which is in eChrist Jesus.

16 1aAll Scripture is 2inspired by God and profitable for teaching, for reproof, for correction, for 3training in righteousness;

17 that athe man of God may be adequate, bequipped for every good work.

a   CHAPTER 4

I SOLEMNLY charge *you* in the presence of God and of Christ Jesus, who is to ᵇjudge the living and the dead, and by His ᶜappearing and His kingdom:

2 preach ᵃthe word; be ready in season *and* out of season; ᵇreprove, rebuke, exhort, with ¹great ᶜpatience and instruction.

3 For ᵃthe time will come when they will not endure ᵇsound doctrine; but *wanting* to have their ears tickled, they will accumulate for themselves teachers in accordance to their own desires;

4 and ᵃwill turn away their ears from the truth, and ᵇwill turn aside to myths.

5 But you, ᵃbe sober in all things, ᵇendure hardship, do the work of an ᶜevangelist, ᵈfulfill your ᵉministry.

6 For I am already being ᵃpoured out as a drink-offering, and the time of ᵇmy departure has come.

7 ᵃI have fought the good fight, I have finished ᵇthe course, I have kept ᶜthe faith;

8 in the future there ᵃis laid up for me ᵇthe crown of righteousness, which the Lord, the righteous Judge, will award to me on ᶜthat day; and not only to me, but also to ᵈall who have loved His ᵉappearing.

9 ᵃMake every effort to come to me soon;

10 for ᵃDemas, having loved ᵇthis present ¹world, has deserted me and gone to ᶜThessalonica; Crescens *has gone* to ²ᵈGalatia, ᵉTitus to Dalmatia.

11 ᵃOnly ᵇLuke is with me. Pick up ᶜMark and bring him with you, ᵈfor he is useful to me for service.

12 But ᵃTychicus I have sent to ᵇEphesus.

13 When you come bring the cloak which I left at ᵃTroas with Carpus, and the books, especially the parchments.

14 ᵃAlexander the coppersmith did me much harm; ᵇthe Lord will repay him according to his deeds.

15 Be on guard against him yourself, for he vigorously opposed our ¹teaching.

16 At my first defense no one supported me, but all deserted me; ᵃmay it not be counted against them.

17 But the Lord stood with me, and ᵃstrengthened me, in order that through me ᵇthe procla-

1 ᵃ2 Tim. 2:14; 1 Tim. 5:21 ᵇActs 10:42 ᶜ2 Thess. 2:8; 2 Tim. 4:8; 1:10

2 ¹Lit., *all* ᵃGal. 6:6; Col. 4:3; 1 Thess. 1:6 ᵇ1 Tim. 5:20; Titus 1:13; 2:15 ᶜ2 Tim. 3:10

3 ᵃ2 Tim. 3:1 ᵇ1 Tim. 1:10; 2 Tim. 1:13

4 ᵃ2 Thess. 2:11; Titus 1:14 ᵇ1 Tim. 1:4

5 ᵃ1 Pet. 1:13 ᵇ2 Tim. 1:8 ᶜActs 21:8 ᵈLuke 1:1 ᵉCol. 4:17; Eph. 4:12

6 ᵃPhil. 2:17 ᵇPhil. 1:23; 2 Pet. 1:14

7 ᵃ1 Tim. 6:12; 1 Cor. 9:25f.; Phil. 1:30; 1 Tim. 1:18 ᵇ1 Cor. 9:24; Acts 20:24 ᶜ2 Tim. 3:10

8 ᵃCol. 1:5; 1 Pet. 1:4 ᵇ1 Cor. 9:25; 2 Tim. 2:5 ᶜ2 Tim. 1:12 ᵈPhil. 3:11 ᵉ2 Tim. 4:1

9 ᵃ2 Tim. 1:4; 4:21; Titus 3:12

10 ¹Or, *age* ²Some ancient mss. read, *Gaul* ᵃCol. 4:14 ᵇ1 Tim. 6:17 ᶜActs 17:1 ᵈActs 16:6 ᵉ2 Cor. 2:13

11 ᵃ2 Tim. 1:15 ᵇCol. 4:14 ᶜActs 12:12 ᵈCol. 4:10; 2 Tim. 2:21

12 ᵃActs 20:4 ᵇActs 18:19

13 ᵃActs 16:8

14 ᵃ1 Tim. 1:20; Acts 19:33 ᵇRom. 12:19; 2:6

15 ¹Lit., *words*

16 ᵃActs 7:60; 1 Cor. 13:5

17 ᵃ2 Tim. 2:1; 1 Tim. 1:12 ᵇTitus 1:3

447

17 [1]Or, *be fulfilled*
[c]2 Tim. 4:5 [d]Acts 9:15; Phil.
1:12ff. [e]2 Tim. 3:11; Rom.
15:31 [f]Ps. 22:21; 1 Sam.
17:37

18 [1]Or, *save me for* [2]Lit.,
whom
[a]1 Cor. 1:21 [b]2 Tim. 4:1;
1 Cor. 15:50; Heb. 11:16;
12:22 [c]Rom. 11:36; 2 Pet.
3:18

19 [a]Acts 18:2 [b]2 Tim. 1:16

20 [a]Acts 19:22 [b]Acts 18:1
[c]Acts 20:15

21 [a]2 Tim. 4:9 [b]Titus 3:12

22 [a]Gal. 6:18; Phil. 4:23;
Philem. 25 [b]Col. 4:18

1 [1]Or, *according to*
[a]James 1:1; Rev. 1:1; Rom.
1:1 [b]2 Cor. 1:1 [c]Luke 18:7
[d]1 Tim. 2:4 [e]1 Tim. 6:3

2 [1]Lit., *before times
eternal*
[a]Titus 3:7; 2 Tim. 1:1
[b]2 Tim. 2:13 [c]Rom. 1:2
[d]2 Tim. 1:9

3 [a]1 Tim. 2:6 [b]2 Tim. 4:17;
Rom. 16:25 [c]1 Tim. 1:11
[d]1 Tim. 1:1 [e]1 Tim. 1:1;
Titus 2:10; 3:4; Luke 1:47

4 [1]Lit., *according to*
[a]2 Cor. 2:13 [b]2 Tim. 1:2
[c]2 Pet. 1:1 [d]Rom. 1:7
[e]1 Tim. 1:12; 2 Tim. 1:1

5 [a]Acts 27:7; Titus 1:12
[b]Acts 14:23 [c]Acts 11:30

6 [a]Titus 1:6-8; 1 Tim. 3:2-4
[b]1 Tim. 3:2 [c]Eph. 5:18
[d]Titus 1:10

7 [1]Or, *bishop*
[a]1 Tim. 3:2 [b]1 Cor. 4:1
[c]2 Pet. 2:10

448

mation might [1]be [c]fully accomplished, and that all [d]the Gentiles might hear; and I was [e]delivered out of [f]the lion's mouth.

18 The Lord will deliver me from every evil deed, and will [1a]bring me safely to His [b]heavenly kingdom; [c]to [2]Him *be* the glory forever and ever. Amen.

19 Greet Prisca and [a]Aquila, and [b]the household of Onesiphorus.

20 [a]Erastus remained at [b]Corinth; but Trophimus I left sick at [c]Miletus.

21 [a]Make every effort to come before [b]winter. Eubulus greets you, also Pudens and Linus and Claudia and all the brethren.

22 [a]The Lord be with your spirit. [b]Grace be with you.

THE EPISTLE OF PAUL TO

TITUS

Salutation.   Qualifications of an Elder.

P AUL, [a]a bondservant of God, and an [b]apostle of Jesus Christ, [1]for the faith of those [c]chosen of God and [d]the knowledge of the truth which is [e]according to godliness,

2 in [a]the hope of eternal life, which God, [b]who cannot lie, [c]promised [1d]long ages ago,

3 but [a]at the proper time manifested, *even* His word, in [b]the proclamation [c]with which I was entrusted [d]according to the commandment of [e]God our Savior;

4 to [a]Titus, [b]my true child [1]in a [c]common faith: [d]Grace and peace from God the Father and [e]Christ Jesus our Savior.

5 For this reason I left you in [a]Crete, that you might set in order what remains, and [b]appoint [c]elders in every city as I directed you,

6 namely, [a]if any man be above reproach, the [b]husband of one wife, having children who believe, not accused of [c]dissipation or [d]rebellion.

7 For the [1a]overseer must be above reproach as [b]God's steward, not [c]self-willed, not quick-tem-

pered, not ^daddicted to wine, not pugnacious, ^enot fond of sordid gain,

8   but ^ahospitable, ^bloving what is good, sensible, just, devout, self-controlled,

9   ^aholding fast the faithful word which is in accordance with the teaching, that he may be able both to exhort in ^bsound doctrine and to refute those who contradict.

10   ^aFor there are many ^brebellious men, ^cempty talkers and deceivers, especially ^dthose of the circumcision,

11   who must be silenced because they are upsetting ^awhole families, teaching ^bthings they should not *teach,* ^cfor the sake of sordid gain.

12   ^aOne of themselves, a prophet of their own, said, "^bCretans are always liars, evil beasts, lazy gluttons."

13   This testimony is true. For this cause ^areprove them ^bseverely that they may be ^csound in the faith,

14   not paying attention to Jewish ^amyths and ^bcommandments of men who ^cturn away from the truth.

15   ^aTo the pure, all things are pure; but ^bto those who are defiled and unbelieving, nothing is pure, but both their ^cmind and their conscience are defiled.

16   ^aThey profess to know God, but by *their* deeds they ^bdeny *Him,* being ^cdetestable and ^ddisobedient, and ^eworthless ^ffor any good deed.

CHAPTER 2

B<small>UT</small> as for you, speak the things which are fitting for ^asound doctrine.

2   ^aOlder men are to be ^btemperate, dignified, ^bsensible, ^csound ^din faith, in love, in ¹perseverance.

3   Older women likewise are to be reverent in their behavior, ^anot malicious gossips, nor ^benslaved to much wine, teaching what is good,

4   that they may ¹encourage the young women to love their husbands, to love their children,

5   *to be* sensible, pure, ^aworkers at home, kind, being ^bsubject to their own husbands, ^cthat the word of God may not be dishonored.

6   Likewise urge ^athe young men to be ^{1b}sensible;

7   in all things show yourself to be ^aan

7 ^d1 Tim. 3:3 ^e1 Tim. 3:3, 8

8 ^a1 Tim. 3:2 ^b2 Tim. 3:3

9 ^a1 Tim. 1:19; 2 Tim. 1:13; 2 Thess. 2:15 ^b1 Tim. 1:10; Titus 2:1

10 ^a2 Cor. 11:13 ^bTitus 1:6 ^c1 Tim. 1:6 ^dActs 11:2

11 ^a1 Tim. 5:4 [in Gr.]; 2 Tim. 3:6 ^b1 Tim. 5:13 ^c1 Tim. 6:5

12 ^aActs 17:28. The Gr. hexameter is said to be taken from a work by the Cretan poet Epimenides ^bActs 2:11; 27:7

13 ^a1 Tim. 5:20; 2 Tim. 4:2; Titus 2:15 ^b2 Cor. 13:10 ^cTitus 2:2

14 ^a1 Tim. 1:4 ^bCol. 2:22 ^c2 Tim. 4:4

15 ^aLuke 11:41; Rom. 14:20 ^bRom. 14:14, 23 ^c1 Tim. 6:5

16 ^a1 John 2:4 ^b1 Tim. 5:8 ^cRev. 21:8 ^dTitus 3:3 ^e2 Tim. 3:8 ^f2 Tim. 3:17; Titus 3:1

1 ^aTitus 1:9

2 ¹Or, *steadfastness* ^aPhilem. 9 ^b1 Tim. 3:2 ^cTitus 1:13 ^d1 Tim. 1:2, 14

3 ^a1 Tim. 3:11 ^b1 Tim. 3:8

4 ¹Or, *train*

5 ^a1 Tim. 5:14 ^bEph. 5:22 ^c1 Tim. 6:1

6 ¹Or, *sensible in all things; show . . .* ^a1 Tim. 5:1 ^b1 Tim. 3:2

7 ^a1 Tim. 4:12

449

7 [1]Or, *soundness*, lit., *uncorruptness*

8 [a]1 Pet. 2:12; 2 Thess. 3:14

9 [1]Lit., *contradicting* [a]Eph. 6:5; 1 Tim. 6:1

10 [a]Titus 1:3

11 [1]Or, *to all men, bringing* [a]2 Tim. 1:10; Titus 3:4 [b]1 Tim. 2:4

12 [1]Or, *disciplining* [a]1 Tim. 6:9; Titus 3:3 [b]2 Tim. 3:12 [c]1 Tim. 6:17

13 [1]Or, *the great God and our Savior* [a]2 Thess. 2:8 [b]2 Pet. 1:1, 1 Tim. 1:1; 2 Tim. 1:2; Titus 1:4

14 [a]1 Tim. 2:6 [b]Ps. 130:8; 1 Pet. 1:18f. [c]Heb. 1:3; 9:14; 1 John 1:7 [d]Ex. 19:5; Deut. 14:2; 1 Pet. 2:9; Eph. 1:11 [e]Eph. 2:10; Titus 3:8; 1 Pet. 3:13

15 [1]Lit., *command* [a]1 Tim. 4:13; 5:20; 2 Tim. 4:2 [b]1 Tim. 4:12

1 [a]2 Tim. 2:14 [b]Rom. 13:1 [c]2 Tim. 2:21

2 [a]1 Tim. 3:3; 1 Pet. 2.18 [b]2 Tim. 2:25

3 [a]Rom. 11:30; 1 Cor. 6:11; Col. 3:7 [b]Titus 1:16 [c]2 Tim. 3:13 [d]Rom. 6:6, 12 [e]2 Tim. 3:6; Titus 2:12 [f]Rom. 1:29

4 [a]Eph. 2:7; Rom. 2:4; 1 Pet. 2:3 [b]Titus 2:10 [c]Titus 2:11

5 [a]2 Tim. 1:9; Rom. 11:14 [b]Eph. 2:9 [c]1 Pet. 1:3; Eph. 2:4 [d]Eph. 5:26; John 3:5; 1 Pet. 3:21 [e]Rom. 12:2

6 [a]Rom. 5:5 [b]Rom. 2:4; 1 Tim. 6:17

7 [1]Or, *of eternal life according to hope* [a]Rom. 8:17, 24; Titus 1:2; Matt. 25:34; Mark 10:17

example of good deeds, *with* [1]purity in doctrine, dignified,

8 sound *in* speech which is beyond reproach, in order [a]that the opponent may be put to shame, having nothing bad to say about us.

9 Urge [a]bond-slaves to be subject to their own masters in everything, to be well pleasing, not [1]argumentative,

10 not pilfering, but showing all good faith that they may adorn the doctrine of [a]God our Savior in every respect.

11 For the grace of God has [a]appeared, [1b]bringing salvation to all men,

12 [1]instructing us to deny ungodliness and [a]worldly desires and [b]to live sensibly, righteously and godly [c]in the present age,

13 looking for the blessed hope and the [a]appearing of the glory of [1b]our great God and Savior, Christ Jesus;

14 who [a]gave Himself for us, [b]that HE MIGHT REDEEM US FROM EVERY LAWLESS DEED AND [c]PURIFY FOR HIMSELF A [d]PEOPLE FOR HIS OWN POSSESSION, [e]zealous for good deeds.

15 These things speak and [a]exhort and [a]reprove with all [1]authority. [b]Let no one disregard you.

[a]   CHAPTER 3

REMIND them [b]to be subject to rulers, to authorities, to be obedient, to be [c]ready for every good deed,

2 to malign no one, [a]to be uncontentious, [a]gentle, [b]showing every consideration for all men.

3 [a]For we also once were foolish ourselves, [b]disobedient, [c]deceived, [d]enslaved to [e]various lusts and pleasures, spending our life in [f]malice and [f]envy, hateful, hating one another.

4 But when the [a]kindness of [b]God our Savior and *His* love for mankind [c]appeared,

5 [a]He saved us, [b]not on the basis of deeds which we have done in righteousness, but [c]according to His mercy, by the [d]washing of regeneration and [e]renewing by the Holy Spirit,

6 [a]whom He poured out upon us [b]richly through Jesus Christ our Savior,

7 that being justified by His grace we might be made [a]heirs [1]according to *the* hope of eternal life.

8 ᵃThis is a trustworthy statement, and concerning these things I ᵇwant you to speak confidently, so that those who have ᶜbelieved God may be careful to ᵈengage in good deeds. These things are good and profitable for men.

9 But ᵃshun ᵇfoolish controversies and ᶜgenealogies and strife and ᵈdisputes about the Law; for they are ᵉunprofitable and worthless.

10 ᵃReject a ᵇfactious man ᶜafter a first and second warning,

11 knowing that such a man is ᵃperverted and is sinning, being self-condemned.

12 When I send Artemas or ᵃTychicus to you, ᵇmake every effort to come to me at ᶜNicopolis, for I have decided to ᵈspend the winter there.

13 ᵃDiligently help Zenas the ᵇlawyer and ᶜApollos on their way so that nothing is lacking for them.

14 And let ᵃour *people* also learn to ᵇengage in good ¹deeds to meet ᶜpressing needs, that they may not be ᵈunfruitful.

15 ᵃAll who are with me greet you. Greet those who love us ᵇin *the* faith.
ᶜ**G**race be with you all.

8 ᵃ1 Tim. 1:15 ᵇ1 Tim. 2:8
ᶜ2 Tim. 1:12 ᵈTitus 3:14; 2:7,
14

9 ᵃ2 Tim. 2:16 ᵇ2 Tim.
2:23; 1 Tim. 1:4 ᶜ1 Tim. 1:4
ᵈJames 4:1 ᵉ2 Tim. 2:14

10 ᵃ2 John 10 ᵇRom. 16:17
ᶜMatt. 18:15f.

11 ᵃTitus 1:14

12 ᵃActs 20:4; 2 Tim. 4:12
ᵇ2 Tim. 4:9 ᶜ2 Tim. 4:10
ᵈ2 Tim. 4:21

13 ᵃActs 15:3 ᵇMatt. 22:35
ᶜActs 18:24

14 ¹Or, *occupations*
ᵃTitus 2:8 ᵇTitus 3:8 ᶜRom.
12:13; Phil. 4:16 ᵈMatt. 7:19;
Phil. 1:11; Col. 1:10

15 ᵃActs 20:34 ᵇ1 Tim. 1:2
ᶜCol. 4:18

THE EPISTLE OF PAUL TO

PHILEMON

Salutation. Thanksgiving for Philemon's Love and Fellowship.

ᵃ

PAUL, ᵇa prisoner of ᶜChrist Jesus, and ᵈTimothy ¹our brother, to Philemon our beloved *brother* and ᵉfellow-worker,

2 and to Apphia ¹ᵃour sister, and to ᵇArchippus our ᶜfellow-soldier, and to ᵈthe church in your house:

3 ᵃGrace to you and peace from God our Father and the Lord Jesus Christ.

4 ᵃI thank my God always, ᵇmaking mention of you in my prayers,

5 because I ᵃhear of your love, and of the faith which you have toward the Lord Jesus, and toward all the ¹saints;

6 *and I pray* that the fellowship of your faith

1 ¹Lit., *the*
ᵃPhil. 1:1 ᵇPhilem. 9, 23;
Eph. 3:1 ᶜPhilem. 9, 23; Gal.
3:26; 1 Tim. 1:12 ᵈ2 Cor. 1:1;
Col. 1:1 ᵉPhilem. 24; Phil.
2:25

2 ¹Lit., *the*
ᵃRom. 16:1 ᵇCol. 4:17 ᶜPhil.
2:25; 2 Tim. 2:3 ᵈRom. 16:5

3 ᵃRom. 1:7

4 ᵃRom. 1:8 ᵇRom. 1:9

5 ¹I.e., true believers; lit.,
holy ones
ᵃEph. 1:15; Col. 1:4; 1 Thess.
3:6

6 [1]Or, *in* [2]Some ancient mss. read, *us* [3]Lit., *toward Christ*
[a]Phil. 1:9; Col. 1:9; 3:10

7 [1]Lit., *inward parts* [2]I.e., true believers; lit., *holy ones*
[a]2 Cor. 7:4, 13 [b]Philem. 20; 1 Cor. 16:18; 2 Cor. 7:13

8 [1]Lit., *much*
[a]2 Cor. 3:12; 1 Thess. 2:6 [b]Eph. 5:4

9 [1]Or, *an ambassador*
[a]Rom. 12:1 [b]Titus 2:2 [c]Philem. 1 [d]Philem. 9, 23; Gal. 3:26; 1 Tim. 1:12

10 [1]Lit., *bonds* [2]I.e., Useful
[a]Rom. 12:1 [b]1 Cor. 4:14f. [c]Col. 4:9

13 [1]Lit., *bonds*
[a]Philem. 10; Phil. 1:7

14 [a]1 Pet. 5:2; 2 Cor. 9:7

15 [a]Gen. 45:5, 8

16 [a]1 Cor. 7:22 [b]Matt. 23:8; 1 Tim. 6:2 [c]Eph. 6:5; Col. 3:22

17 [a]2 Cor. 8:23; Philem. 6

19 [1]Lit., *say*
[a]1 Cor. 16:21; 2 Cor. 10:1; Gal. 5:2 [b]2 Cor. 9:4

20 [a]Philem. 7

21 [a]2 Cor. 2:3

22 [a]Acts 28:23 [b]Phil. 1:25; 2:24 [c]2 Cor. 1:11 [d]Acts 27:24; Heb. 13:19

23 [a]Col. 1:7 [b]Rom. 16:7; Philem. 1 [c]Philem. 1

24 [a]Acts 12:12 [b]Acts 19:29; Col. 4:10 [c]Col. 4:14; 2 Tim. 4:10f. [d]Philem. 1

may become effective [1]through the [a]knowledge of every good thing which is in [2]you [3]for Christ's sake.

7 For I have come to have much [a]joy and comfort in your love, because the [1]hearts of the [2]saints have been [2b]refreshed through you, brother.

8 Therefore, [a]though I have [1]enough confidence in Christ to order you *to do* that which is [b]proper,

9 yet for love's sake I rather [a]appeal *to you*— since I am such a person as Paul [1]the [b]aged, and now also [c]a prisoner of [d]Christ Jesus—

10 I [a]appeal to you for my [b]child, whom I have begotten in my [1]imprisonment, [2c]Onesimus,

11 who formerly was useless to you, but now is useful both to you and to me.

12 And I have sent him back to you in person, that is, *sending* my very heart;

13 whom I wished to keep with me, that in your behalf he might minister to me in my [1a]imprisonment for the gospel;

14 but without your consent I did not want to do anything, that your goodness should [a]not be as it were by compulsion, but of your own free will.

15 For perhaps [a]he was for this reason parted *from you* for a while, that you should have him back forever.

16 [a]no longer as a slave, but more than a slave, [b]a beloved brother, especially to me, but how much more to you, both [c]in the flesh and in the Lord.

17 If then you regard me a [a]partner, accept him as *you would* me.

18 But if he has wronged you in any way, or owes you anything, charge that to my account;

19 [a]I, Paul, am writing this with my own hand, I will repay it ([b]lest I should [1]mention to you that you owe to me even your own self as well).

20 Yes, brother, let me benefit from you in the Lord; [a]refresh my heart in Christ.

21 [a]Having confidence in your obedience, I write to you, since I know that you will do even more than what I say.

22 And at the same time also prepare me a [a]lodging; for [b]I hope that through [c]your prayers [d]I shall be given to you.

23 [a]Epaphras, my [b]fellow-prisoner in [c]Christ Jesus, greets you;

24 *as do* [a]Mark, [b]Aristarchus, [c]Demas, [c]Luke, my [d]fellow-workers.

25 [a]The grace of the Lord Jesus Christ be [b]with your spirit.[1]

THE EPISTLE TO THE
HEBREWS

God's Final Word spoken through His Son, Who is Superior to the Angels.

GOD, after He [a]spoke long ago to the fathers in [b]the prophets in many portions and [c]in many ways,

2 [1][a]in these last days [b]has spoken to us in [c]*His* Son, whom He appointed [d]heir of all things, [e]through whom also He made the [2f]world.

3 [1]And He is the radiance of His glory and the exact [a]representation of His nature, and [2b]upholds all things by the word of His power. When He had made [c]purification of sins, He [d]sat down at the right hand of the [e]Majesty on high;

4 having become as much better than the angels, as He has inherited a more excellent [a]name than they.

5 For to which of the angels did He ever say,
"[a]THOU ART MY SON,
TODAY I HAVE BEGOTTEN THEE"?
And again,
"[b]I WILL BE A FATHER TO HIM,
AND HE SHALL BE A SON TO ME"?

6 And [1]when He again [a]brings the first-born into [2b]the world, He says,
"[c]AND LET ALL THE ANGELS OF GOD WORSHIP HIM."

7 And of the angels He says,
"[a]WHO MAKES HIS ANGELS WINDS,
AND HIS MINISTERS A FLAME OF FIRE."

8 But of the Son *He says,*
"[a]THY [b]THRONE, O GOD, IS FOREVER AND EVER,
AND THE RIGHTEOUS SCEPTER IS THE SCEPTER OF [1]HIS KINGDOM.

9 "[a]THOU HAST LOVED RIGHTEOUSNESS AND HATED LAWLESSNESS;
[b]THEREFORE GOD, THY GOD, HATH [c]ANOINTED THEE
WITH THE OIL OF GLADNESS ABOVE THY COMPANIONS."

25 [1]Some ancient mss. add, *Amen*
[a]Gal. 6:18 [b]2 Tim. 4:22

1 [a]Heb. 2:2f.; 3:5; 4:8; 5:5; 11:18; 12:25; John 9:29; 16:13 [b]Acts 2:30; 3:21 [c]Num. 12:6, 8; Joel 2:28

2 [1]Or, *at the end of these days* [2]Lit., *ages*
[a]Heb. 9:26; 1 Pet. 1:20; Matt. 13:39 [b]Heb. 2:2f.; 3:5; 4:8; 5:5; 11:18; 12:25; John 9:29; John 16:13 [c]Heb. 3:6; 5:8; 7:28; John 5:26, 27 [d]Ps. 2:8; Matt. 28:18; Mark 12:7; Rom. 8:17; Heb. 2:8 [e]John 1:3; Col. 1:16; 1 Cor. 8:6 [f]Heb. 11:3; 1 Cor. 2:7

3 [1]Lit., *who being* [2]Lit., *upholding*
[a]2 Cor. 4:4 [b]Col. 1:17 [c]Titus 2:14; Heb. 9:14 [d]Heb. 8:1; 10:12; 12:2; Mark 16:19 [e]2 Pet. 1:17

4 [a]Eph. 1:21; Phil. 2:9

5 [a]Ps. 2:7; Acts 13:13; Heb. 5:5 [b]2 Sam. 7:14

6 [1]Or, *again when He brings* [2]Lit., *the inhabited earth*
[a]Heb. 10:5 [b]Matt. 24:14 [c]Deut. 32:43 Sept.; Ps. 97:7

7 [a]Ps. 104:4

8 [1]Some mss. read, *Thy*
[a]Ps. 45:6 [b]Deut. 33:27; Ps. 71:3; 90:1; 91:2, 9

9 [a]Ps. 45:7 [b]Phil. 2:9; John 10:17; Heb. 2:9 [c]Is. 61:1, 3

453

10 ªPs. 102:25

11 ªPs. 102:26 ᵇIs. 51:6; Heb. 8:13

12 ªPs. 102:26, 27 ᵇHeb. 13:8

13 ªPs. 110:1; Matt. 22:44; Heb. 1:3 ᵇHeb. 10:13; Josh. 10:24

14 ªDan. 7:10; Ps. 103:20f. ᵇMatt. 25:34; Mark 10:17; Titus 3:7; Heb. 6:12 ᶜHeb. 2:3; 5:9; 9:28; Rom. 11:14; 1 Cor. 1:21

1 ¹Lit., *the things that have been heard* ªProv. 3:21 [Sept.]

2 ¹Or, *steadfast* ªHeb. 1:1 ᵇActs 7:53 ᶜHeb. 10:28 ᵈHeb. 10:35; 11:26

3 ¹Lit. *which was* ªHeb. 10:29; 12:25 ᵇHeb. 1:14; 5:9; 9:28; Rom. 11:14; 1 Cor. 1:21 ᶜHeb. 1:1 ᵈMark 16:20, Luke 1:2, 1 John 1:1

4 ¹Or, *works of power* ²Lit., *distributions* ªJohn 4:48 ᵇMark 6:14 ᶜ1 Cor. 12:4, 11; Eph. 4:7 ᵈEph. 1:5

5 ¹Lit., *the inhabited earth* ªHeb. 6:5; Matt. 24:14; Heb. 1:6

6 ª1 Thess. 4:6 ᵇHeb. 4:4 ᶜPs. 8:4

7 ¹Or, *a little lower* ªPs. 8:5, 6

10　And,
　"ªThou, Lord, in the beginning didst lay the foundation of the earth,
　And the heavens are the works of Thy hands;

11　ªThey will perish, but Thou remainest;
　ᵇAnd they all will become old as a garment,

12　ªAnd as a mantle Thou wilt roll them up;
　As a garment they will also be changed.
　But Thou art ᵇthe same,
　And Thy years will not come to an end."

13　But to which of the angels has He ever said,
　"ªSit at My right hand,
　ᵇUntil I make Thine enemies
　A footstool for Thy feet"?

14　Are they not all ªministering spirits, sent out to render service for the sake of those who will ᵇinherit ᶜsalvation?

CHAPTER 2

FOR this reason we must pay much closer attention to ¹what we have heard, lest ªwe drift away *from it.*

2　For if the word ªspoken through ᵇangels proved ¹unalterable, and ᶜevery transgression and disobedience received a just ᵈrecompense,

3　ªhow shall we escape if we neglect so great a ᵇsalvation? ¹After it was at the first ᶜspoken through the Lord, it was ᵈconfirmed to us by those who heard,

4　God also bearing witness with them, both by ªsigns and ªwonders and by ᵇvarious ¹miracles and by ²ᶜgifts of the Holy Spirit ᵈaccording to His own will.

5　For He did not subject to angels ¹ªthe world to come, concerning which we are speaking.

6　But one has ªtestified ᵇsomewhere, saying,
　"ᶜWhat is man, that Thou rememberest him?
　Or the son of man, that Thou art concerned about him?

7　"ªThou hast made him ¹for a little while lower than the Angels;

Thou hast crowned him with glory
and honor,
[2]And hast appointed him over the
works of Thy hands;

8   [a]Thou hast put all things in subjection under his feet."

For in subjecting all things to him, He left nothing
that is not subject to him. But now [b]we do not yet
see all things subjected to him.

9   But we do see Him who has been [a]made
[1]for a little while lower than the angels, *namely*,
Jesus, [b]because of the suffering of death [c]crowned
with glory and honor, that [d]by the grace of God He
might [e]taste death [f]for every one.

10   For [a]it was fitting for Him, [b]for whom are
all things, and [b]through whom are all things, in
bringing many sons to glory, to [c]perfect the [1d]author
of their salvation through sufferings.

11   For both He who [a]sanctifies and those who
[b]are [1]sanctified are all [c]from one *Father*; for which
reason He is not ashamed to call them [d]brethren,

12   saying,
"[a]I will proclaim Thy name to My
brethren,
In the midst of the [1]congregation I
will sing Thy praise."

13   And again,
"[a]I will put My trust in Him."
And again,
"[b]Behold, I and the children whom God
has given me."

14   Since then the children share in [1a]flesh and
blood, [b]He Himself likewise also partook of the
same, that [c]through death He might render powerless [d]him who had the power of death, that is, the
devil;

15   and might deliver those who through [a]fear
of death were subject to slavery all their lives.

16   For assuredly He does not [1]give help to angels, but He gives help to the [2]seed of Abraham.

17   Therefore, He [1]had [a]to be made like His
brethren in all things, that He might [b]become a
merciful and faithful [c]high priest in [d]things pertaining to God, to [e]make propitiation for the sins of
the people.

18   For since He Himself was [a]tempted in that
which He has suffered, He is able to come to the
aid of those who are tempted.

7 [2]Some ancient mss.
omit, *And . . . . hands*

8 [a]Ps. 8:6; 1 Cor. 15:27
[b]1 Cor. 15:25

9 [1]Or, *a little lower*
[a]Heb. 2:7 [b]Phil. 2:9; Heb. 1:9
[c]Acts 2:33; 3:13; 1 Pet. 1:21
[d]John 3:16 [e]Matt. 16:28;
John 8:52 [f]Heb. 6:20; 7:25

10 [1]Or, *leader*
[a]Luke 24:26 [b]Rom. 11:36
[c]Heb. 5:9; 7:28; Luke 13:32
[d]Acts 3:15; 5:31

11 [1]Or, *being sanctified*
[a]Heb. 13:12 [b]Heb. 10:10
[c]Acts 17:28 [d]Matt. 25:40;
Mark 3:34f.; John 20:17

12 [1]Lit., *church*
[a]Ps. 22:22

13 [a]Is. 8:17 [b]Is. 8:18

14 [1]Lit., *blood and flesh*
[a]Matt. 16:17 [b]John 1:14;
Heb. 7:13 marg. [c]1 Cor.
15:54-57; 2 Tim. 1:10
[d]1 John 3:8; John 12:31

15 [a]Rom. 8:15

16 [1]Lit., *take hold of
angels, but He takes hold of*
[2]I.e., offspring

17 [1]Lit., *was obligated to
be*
[a]Heb. 2:14; Phil. 2:7 [b]Heb.
4:15f.; 5:2 [c]Heb. 3:1; 4:14f;
5:5, 10; 6:20; 7:26, 28; 8:1, 3;
9:11; Heb. 10:21 [d]Heb. 5:1;
Rom. 15:17 [e]1 John 2:2;
4:10; Dan. 9:24

18 [a]Heb. 4:15

455

1 ªHeb. 2:11; 3:12; 10:19; 13:22; Acts 1:15 ᵇPhil. 3:14 ᶜJohn 17:3 ᵈHeb. 2:17; 4:14f.; 5:5, 10; 6:20; 7:26, 28; 8:1, 3; 9:11; Heb. 10:21 ᵉHeb. 4:14; 10:23; 2 Cor. 9:13

2 ¹Lit., *being faithful* ²Or, *made* ªHeb. 3:5; Num. 12:7; Ex. 40:16

3 ª2 Cor. 3:7-11

5 ªHeb. 3:2; Num. 12:7; Ex. 40:16 ᵇEx. 14:31; Num. 12:7 ᶜDeut. 18:18f. ᵈHeb. 1:1

6 ªHeb. 1:2 ᵇ1 Tim. 3:15; 1 Cor. 3:16 ᶜRom. 11:22; Heb. 3:14; 4:14 ᵈHeb. 4:16; 10:19, 35; Eph. 3:12 ᵉRom. 5:2 marg. ᶠHeb. 6:11; 7:19; 10:23; Heb. 11:1; 1 Pet. 1:3

7 ªHeb. 9:8; 10:15; Acts 28:25 ᵇPs. 95:7; Heb. 3:15; 4:7

8 ¹Lit., *in the provocation* ªPs. 95:8

9 ªPs. 95:9, 10 ᵇActs 7:36

10 ªPs. 95:10

11 ªPs. 95:11; Heb. 4:3, 5

12 ªHeb. 12:25; Col. 2:8 ᵇHeb. 9:14; 10:31; 12:22; Matt. 16:16

13 ªHeb. 10:24f. ᵇEph. 4:22

14 ªHeb. 3:6 ᵇHeb. 11:1 [Gr.]

15 ¹Lit., *in the provocation* ªPs. 95:7f.

16 ªJer. 32:29; 44:3, 8

456

CHAPTER 3

THEREFORE, ªholy brethren, partakers of a ᵇheavenly calling, consider Jesus, ᶜthe Apostle and ᵈHigh Priest of our ᵉconfession.

2 ¹He was faithful to Him who ²appointed Him, as ªMoses also was in all His house.

3 ªFor He has been counted worthy of more glory than Moses, by just so much as the builder of the house has more honor than the house.

4 For every house is built by someone, but the builder of all things is God.

5 Now ªMoses was faithful in all His house as ᵇa servant, ᶜfor a testimony of those things ᵈwhich were to be spoken later;

6 but Christ *was faithful* as ªa Son over His house ᵇwhose house we are, ᶜif we hold fast our ᵈconfidence and the ᵉboast of our ᶠhope firm until the end.

7 Therefore just as ªthe Holy Spirit says,
"ᵇTODAY IF YOU HEAR HIS VOICE,

8 ªDO NOT HARDEN YOUR HEARTS AS ¹WHEN THEY PROVOKED ME,
AS IN THE DAY OF TRIAL IN THE WILDERNESS,

9 ªWHERE YOUR FATHERS TRIED *Me* BY TESTING *Me*,
AND SAW MY WORKS FOR ᵇFORTY YEARS.

10 "ªTHEREFORE I WAS ANGRY WITH THIS GENERATION,
AND SAID, 'THEY ALWAYS GO ASTRAY IN THEIR HEART,
AND THEY DID NOT KNOW MY WAYS';

11 ªAS I SWORE IN MY WRATH,
'THEY SHALL NOT ENTER MY REST.' "

12 ªTake care, brethren, lest there should be in any one of you an evil, unbelieving heart, in falling away from ᵇthe living God.

13 But ªencourage one another day after day, as long as it is *still* called "Today," lest any one of you be hardened by the ᵇdeceitfulness of sin.

14 For we have become partakers of Christ, ªif we hold fast the beginning of our ᵇassurance firm until the end;

15 while it is said,
"ªTODAY IF YOU HEAR HIS VOICE,
DO NOT HARDEN YOUR HEARTS, AS ¹WHEN THEY PROVOKED ME."

16 For who ªprovoked *Him* when they had

heard? Indeed, [b]did not all those who came out of Egypt *led* by Moses?

17 And with whom was He angry for forty years? Was it not with those who sinned, [a]whose bodies fell in the wilderness?

18 And to whom did He swear [a]that they should not enter His rest, but to those who were [b]disobedient?

19 And *so* we see that they were not able to enter because of [a]unbelief.

CHAPTER 4

THEREFORE, let us fear lest, while a promise remains of entering His rest, any one of you should seem to have [a]come short of it.

2 For indeed we have had good news preached to us, just as they also; but [a]the word [1]they heard did not profit them, because [2]it was not united by faith in those who heard.

3 [1]For we who have believed enter that rest; just as He has said,

"[a]AS I SWORE IN MY WRATH,
THEY SHALL NOT ENTER MY REST,"
although His works were finished [b]from the foundation of the world.

4 For He has thus said [a]somewhere concerning the seventh *day*, "[b]AND GOD [c]RESTED ON THE SEVENTH DAY FROM ALL HIS WORKS";

5 and again in this *passage*, "[a]THEY SHALL NOT ENTER MY REST."

6 Since therefore it remains for some to enter it, and those who formerly had good news preached to them failed to enter because of [a]disobedience,

7 He again fixes a certain day, "Today," saying [1a]through David after so long a time just [b]as has been said before.

"[c]TODAY IF YOU HEAR HIS VOICE,
DO NOT HARDEN YOUR HEARTS."

8 For [a]if Joshua had given them rest, He would not have [b]spoken of another day after that.

9 There remains therefore a Sabbath rest for the people of God.

10 For the one who has entered His rest has himself also [a]rested from his works, as [b]God did from His.

11 Let us therefore be diligent to enter that

16 [b]Num. 14:2, 11; Deut. 1:35; Num. 14:30; Deut. 1:36, 38

17 [a]Num. 14:29; 1 Cor. 10:5

18 [a]Num. 14:23; Deut. 1:34f.; Heb. 4:2 [b]Heb. 4:6, 11; Rom. 11:30-32

19 [a]John 3:36

1 [a]Heb. 12:15

2 [1]Lit., *of hearing* [2]Or, *they were. . .faith with those who heard* [a]1 Thess. 2:13

3 [1]Some ancient mss. read, *Therefore* [a]Ps. 95:11; Heb. 3:11 [b]Matt. 25:34

4 [a]Heb. 2:6 [b]Gen. 2:2 [c]Ex. 20:11; 31:17

5 [a]Ps. 95:11; Heb. 3:11

6 [a]Heb. 3:18; 4:11

7 [1]Or, *in* [a]Ps. 95 title in Sept. [b]Heb. 3:7f. [c]Ps. 95:7f.

8 [a]Josh. 22:4 [b]Heb. 1:1

10 [a]Rev. 14:13 [b]Heb. 4:4

Hebrews 4, 5

The Power of the Word of God. The Sympathetic High Priest. The Son as a High Priest.

11 [a]2 Pet. 2:6 [b]Heb. 3:18; 4:6

12 [a]1 Pet. 1:23; Jer. 23:29; Heb. 6:5; Eph. 5:26 [b]Acts 7:38 [c]1 Thess. 2:13 [d]Eph. 6:17 [e]1 Thess. 5:23 [f]John 12:48; 1 Cor. 14:24f.

13 [a]2 Chr. 16:9; Ps. 33:13-15 [b]Job 26:6

14 [a]Heb. 2:17 [b]Eph. 4:10; Heb. 6:20; 8:1; 9:24 [c]Heb. 6:6; 7:3; 10:29; Matt. 4:3; Heb. 1:2 [d]Heb. 3:1

15 [a]Heb. 2:17 [b]Heb. 2:18 [c]2 Cor. 5:21; Heb. 7:26

16 [a]Heb. 7:19 [b]Heb. 3:6

1 [a]Ex. 28:1 [b]Heb. 2:17 [c]Heb. 8:3f.; 9:9; 7:27; 10:11 [d]Heb. 7:27; 10:12; 1 Cor. 15:3

2 [1]Lit., *being able to* [2]Or, *subject to weakness* [a]Heb. 2:18; 4:15 [b]Heb. 9:7 marg.; Eph. 4:18 [c]James 5:19; 1 Pet. 2:25 [d]Heb. 7:28

3 [a]Heb. 7:27; 10:12; 1 Cor. 15:3 [b]Heb. 7:27; 9:7; Lev. 9:7; 16:6

4 [a]Num. 16:40; 18:7; 2 Chr. 26:18 [b]Ex. 28:1; 1 Chr. 23:13

5 [a]John 8:54 [b]Heb. 2:17; 5:10 [c]Heb. 1:1, 5 [d]Ps. 2:7

6 [a]Ps. 110:4; Heb. 7:17 [b]Heb. 5:10; 6:20; 7:11, 17

7 [1]Or, *out of* [a]Matt. 26:39, 42, 44; Mark 14:36, 39; Luke 22:41, 44 [b]Matt. 27:46, 50; Mark 15:34, 37; Luke 23:46 [c]Mark 14:36 [d]Heb. 12:28 marg.; Heb. 11:7

rest, lest anyone fall through *following* the same [a]example of [b]disobedience.

12 For [a]the word of God is [b]living and [c]active and sharper than any two-edged [d]sword, and piercing as far as the division of [e]soul and [e]spirit, of both joints and marrow, and [f]able to judge the thoughts and intentions of the heart.

13 And [a]there is no creature hidden from His sight, but all things are [b]open and laid bare to the eyes of Him with whom we have to do.

14 Since then we have a great [a]high priest who has [b]passed through the heavens, Jesus [c]the Son of God, let us hold fast our [d]confession.

15 For we do not have [a]a high priest who cannot sympathize with our weaknesses, but one who has been [b]tempted in all things as *we are*, yet [c]without sin.

16 Let us therefore [a]draw near with [b]confidence to the throne of grace, that we may receive mercy and may find grace to help in time of need.

CHAPTER 5

FOR every high priest [a]taken from among men is appointed on behalf of men in [b]things pertaining to God in order to [c]offer both gifts and sacrifices [d]for sins;

2 [1]he can deal gently with the [b]ignorant and [c]misguided, since he himself also is [2][d]beset with weakness;

3 and because of it he is obligated to offer *sacrifices* [a]for sins, [b]as for the people, so also for himself.

4 And [a]no one takes the honor to himself, but *receives it* when he is called by God, even [b]as Aaron was.

5 So also Christ [a]did not glorify Himself so as to become a [b]high priest, but He who [c]said to Him,

"[a]THOU ART MY SON,
TODAY I HAVE BEGOTTEN THEE";

6 just as He says also in another *passage*,

"[a]THOU ART A PRIEST FOREVER
ACCORDING TO [b]THE ORDER OF MELCHIZEDEK."

7 In the days of His flesh, [a]when He offered up both prayers and supplications with [b]loud crying and tears to Him who was [c]able to save Him [1]from death, and who was heard because of His [d]piety,

8 although He was ªa Son, He learned ᵇobedience from the things which He suffered;

9 and having been made ªperfect, He became to all those who obey Him the source of eternal salvation;

10 being designated by God as ªa high priest according to ᵇthe order of Melchizedek.

11 Concerning ¹him we have much to say, and *it is* hard to explain, since you have become dull of hearing.

12 For though ¹by this time you ought to be teachers, you have need again for some one to teach you ªthe ²ᵇelementary principles of the ᶜoracles of God, and you have come to need ᵈmilk and not solid food.

13 For every one who partakes *only* of milk is not accustomed to the word of righteousness, for he is a ªbabe.

14 But solid food is for ªthe mature, who because of practice have their senses ᵇtrained to ᶜdiscern good and evil.

CHAPTER 6

THEREFORE ªleaving ᵇthe ¹elementary teaching about the ²Christ, let us press on to ³ᶜmaturity, not laying again a foundation of repentance from ᵈdead works and of faith toward God,

2 of ªinstruction about washings, and ᵇlaying on of hands, and the ᶜresurrection of the dead, and ᶜeternal judgment.

3 And this we shall do, ªif God permits.

4 For in the case of those who have once been ªenlightened and have tasted of ᵇthe heavenly gift and have been made ᶜpartakers of the Holy Spirit,

5 and ªhave tasted the good ᵇword of God and the powers of ᶜthe age to come,

6 and *then* have fallen away, it is ªimpossible to renew them again to repentance, ¹ᵇsince they again crucify to themselves the Son of God, and put Him to open shame.

7 For ground that drinks the rain which often ¹falls upon it and brings forth vegetation useful to those ªfor whose sake it is also tilled, receives a blessing from God;

8 but if it yields thorns and thistles, it is worthless and ªclose ¹to being cursed, and ²it ends up being burned.

8 ªHeb. 1:2 ᵇPhil. 2:8

9 ªHeb. 2:10

10 ªHeb. 2:17; 5:5 ᵇHeb. 5:6

11 ¹Or, *Him*; or, *this*

12 ¹Lit., *because of the time* ²Lit., *elements of the beginning* ªGal. 4:3 ᵇHeb. 6:1 ᶜActs 7:38 ᵈ1 Cor. 3:2; 1 Pet. 2:2

13 ª1 Cor. 3:1; 1 Cor. 14:20; 1 Pet. 2:2

14 ª1 Cor. 2:6; Eph. 4:13; Heb. 6:1 marg ᵇ1 Tim. 4:7 ᶜRom. 14:1

1 ¹Lit., *word of the beginning* ²I.e., Messiah ³Or, *perfection* ªPhil. 3:13f. ᵇHeb. 5:12 ᶜHeb. 5:14 and marg. ᵈHeb. 9:14; John 8:21

2 ªActs 19:3f.; John 3:25 ᵇActs 6:6 ᶜActs 17:31f.

3 ªActs 18:21

4 ªHeb. 10:32; 2 Cor. 4:4, 6 ᵇEph. 2:8; John 4:10 ᶜHeb. 2:4; Gal. 3:2

5 ª1 Pet. 2:3 ᵇEph. 6:17 ᶜHeb. 2:5

6 ¹Or, *while* ªHeb. 10:26f.; 1 John 5:16; 2 Pet. 2:21; Matt. 19:26 ᵇHeb. 10:29

7 ¹Lit., *comes* ª2 Tim. 2:6

8 ¹Lit., *to a curse* ²Lit., *its end is for burning* ªDeut. 29:22ff.

459

9 [1]Or, *belong to*
[a]1 Cor. 10:14; 2 Cor. 7:1;
12:19; 1 Pet. 2:11; 2 Pet. 3:1;
1 John 2:7; Jude 3

10 [1]I.e., true believers; lit.,
holy ones
[a]Prov. 19:17; Matt. 10:42;
25:40; Acts 10:4 [b]1 Thess. 1:3
[c]Heb. 10:32-34; Rom. 15:25

11 [1]Lit., *to the full*
[a]Heb. 10:22; Luke 1:1 [b]Heb.
3:6

12 [a]Heb. 13:7 [b]2 Thess. 1:4;
James 1:3; Rev. 13:10 [c]Heb.
1:14

13 [a]Gal. 3:15, 18 [b]Gen.
22:16; Luke 1:73

14 [a]Gen. 22:16f.

15 [a]Gen. 12:4; 21:5

16 [a]Gal. 3:15 [b]Ex. 22:11

17 [1]Or, *Therefore God* [2]Or,
guaranteed
[a]Heb. 11:9 [b]Ps. 110:4; Prov.
19:21; Heb. 6:18

18 [a]Titus 1:2; Num. 23:19
[b]Heb. 3:6; 7:19

19 [1]Lit., *which we have*
[2]Or, *inside*
[a]Lev. 16:2; Heb. 9:2f.

20 [a]Heb. 4:14; John 14:2
[b]Heb. 5:6; 2:17

1 [a]Gen. 14:18-20; Heb. 7:6
[b]Mark 5:7

9 But, [a]beloved, we are convinced of better things concerning you, and things that [1]accompany salvation, though we are speaking in this way.

10 For [a]God is not unjust so as to forget [b]your work and the love which you have shown toward His name, in having [c]ministered and in still ministering to the [1]saints.

11 And we desire that each one of you show the same diligence [1]so as to realize the [a]full assurance of [b]hope until the end,

12 that you may not be sluggish, but [a]imitators of those who through [b]faith and patience [c]inherit the promises.

13 For [a]when God made the promise to Abraham, since He could swear by no one greater, He [b]swore by Himself,

14 saying, "[a]I WILL SURELY BLESS YOU, AND I WILL SURELY MULTIPLY YOU."

15 And thus, [a]having patiently waited, he obtained the promise.

16 [a]For men swear by one greater *than themselves*, and with them [b]an oath *given* as confirmation is an end of every dispute.

17 [1]In the same way God, desiring even more to show to [a]the heirs of the promise [b]the unchangeableness of His purpose, [2]interposed with an oath,

18 in order that by two unchangeable things, in which [a]it is impossible for God to lie, we may have strong encouragement, we who have fled for refuge in laying hold of [b]the hope set before us.

19 [1]This hope we have as an anchor of the soul, a *hope* both sure and steadfast and one which [a]enters [2]within the veil,

20 [a]where Jesus has entered as a forerunner for us, having become a [b]high priest forever according to the order of Melchizedek.

CHAPTER 7

FOR this [a]Melchizedek, king of Salem, priest of the [b]Most High God, who met Abraham as he was returning from the slaughter of the kings and blessed him,

2 to whom also Abraham apportioned a tenth part of all *the spoils*, was first of all, by the translation *of his name*, king of righteousness, and then also king of Salem, which is king of peace.

3 Without father, without mother, ^awithout genealogy, having neither beginning of days nor end of life, but made like ^bthe Son of God, he abides a priest perpetually.

4 Now observe how great this man was to whom Abraham, the ^apatriarch, gave a tenth of the choicest spoils.

5 And those indeed of ^athe sons of Levi who receive the priest's office have commandment ¹in the Law to collect ²a tenth from the people, that is, from their brethren, although these ³are descended from Abraham.

6 But the one ^awhose genealogy is not traced from them ^bcollected ¹a tenth from Abraham, and ^bblessed the one who ^chad the promises.

7 But without any dispute the lesser is blessed by the greater.

8 And in this case mortal men receive tithes, but in that case one *receives them,* ^aof whom it is witnessed that he lives on.

9 And, so to speak, through Abraham even Levi, who received tithes, paid tithes,

10 for he was still in the loins of his father when Melchizedek met him.

11 ^aNow if perfection was through the Levitical priesthood (for on the basis of it ^bthe people received the Law), what further need *was there* for another priest to arise ^caccording to the order of Melchizedek, and not be designated according to the order of Aaron?

12 For when the priesthood is changed, of necessity there takes place a change of law also.

13 For ^athe one concerning whom ^bthese things are spoken belongs to another tribe, from which no one has officiated at the altar.

14 For it is evident that our Lord ¹was ^adescended from Judah, a tribe with reference to which Moses spoke nothing concerning priests.

15 And this is clearer still, if another priest arises according to the likeness of Melchizedek,

16 who has become *such* not on the basis of a law of ^aphysical requirement, but according to the power of ^ban indestructible life.

17 For it is witnessed *of Him,*
"^aThou art a priest forever
According to the order of Melchizedek."

18 For, on the one hand, there is a setting aside

3 ^aHeb. 7:6 ^bHeb. 7:28; 7:1; Matt. 4:3

4 ^aActs 2:29

5 ¹Lit., *according to* ²Or, *tithes* ³Lit., *have come out of the loins of* ^aNum. 18:21, 26; 2 Chr. 31:4f.

6 ¹Or, *tithes* ^aHeb. 7:3 ^bHeb. 7:1f. ^cRom. 4:13

8 ^aHeb. 5:6; 6:20

11 ^aHeb. 7:18f.; 8:7 ^bHeb. 9:6; 10:1 ^cHeb. 7:17; 5:6

13 ^aHeb. 7:14 ^bHeb. 7:11

14 ¹Lit., *rose from* ^aRev. 5:5; Matt. 2:6 [Mic. 5:2]; Is. 11:1; Num. 24:17

16 ^aHeb. 9:10 ^bHeb. 9:14

17 ^aPs. 110:4; Heb. 7:21; 5:6

of a former commandment [a]because of its weakness and uselessness

19   (for [a]the Law made nothing perfect), and on the other hand there is a bringing in of a better [b]hope, through which we [c]draw near to God.

20   And inasmuch as *it was* not without an oath

21   (for they indeed became priests without an oath, but He with an oath through the One who said to Him,

"[a]THE LORD HAS SWORN

AND [b]WILL NOT CHANGE HIS MIND,

'THOU ART A PRIEST [c]FOREVER' ");

22   so much the more also Jesus has become the [a]guarantee of [b]a better covenant.

23   And the *former* priests, on the one hand, existed in greater numbers, because they were prevented by death from continuing,

24   but He, on the other hand, because He abides [a]forever, holds His priesthood permanently.

25   Hence also He is able to [a]save [1]forever those who [b]draw near to God through Him, since He always lives to [c]make intercession for them.

26   For it was fitting that we should have such a [a]high priest, [b]holy, [c]innocent, undefiled, separated from sinners and [d]exalted above the heavens;

27   who does not need daily, like those high priests, to [a]offer up sacrifices, [b]first for His own sins, and then for the *sins* of the people, because this He did [c]once for all when He [d]offered up Himself.

28   For the Law appoints men as high priests [a]who are weak, but the word of the oath, which came after the Law, *appoints* [b]a Son, [c]made perfect forever.

CHAPTER 8

NOW the main point in what has been said *is this*: we have such a [a]high priest, who has taken His seat at [b]the right hand of the throne of the [b]Majesty in the heavens,

2   a [a]minister [1]in the sanctuary, and [1]in the [b]true [2]tabernacle, which the Lord [c]pitched, not man.

3   For every [a]high priest is appointed [b]to offer both gifts and sacrifices; hence it is necessary that this *high priest* also have something to offer.

4   Now if He were on earth, He would not be a priest at all, since there are those who [a]offer the gifts according to the Law;

---

18 [a]Heb. 7:11; Rom. 8:3; Gal. 3:21

19 [a]Heb. 9:9; 10:1; Acts 13:39; Rom. 3:20; 7:7f.; Gal. 2:16; 3:21 [b]Heb. 3:6 [c]Heb. 7:25; 4:16; 10:1, 22; Lam. 3:57; James 4:8

21 [a]Ps. 110:4; Heb. 7:17; Heb. 5:6 [b]Num. 23:19; 1 Sam. 15:29; Rom. 11:29 [c]Heb. 7:23f., 28

22 [a]Ps. 119:122; Is. 38:14 [b]Heb. 8:6

24 [a]Heb. 7:23f.

25 [1]Or, *completely* [a]1 Cor. 1:21 [b]Heb. 7:19 [c]Rom. 8:34; Heb. 9:24

26 [a]Heb. 2:17 [b]2 Cor. 5:21; Heb. 4:15 [c]1 Pet. 2:22 [d]Heb. 4:14

27 [a]Heb. 5:1 [b]Heb. 5:3 [c]Heb. 9:12; 10:10; 9:28 [d]Eph. 5:2; Heb. 9:14, 28; 10:10, 12

28 [a]Heb. 5:2 [b]Heb. 1:2 [c]Heb. 2:10

1 [a]Heb. 2:17 [b]Heb. 1:3

2 [1]Or, *of* [2]Or, *sacred tent* [a]Heb. 10:11 [b]Heb. 9:11, 24 [c]Ex. 33:7

3 [a]Heb. 2:17 [b]Heb. 5:1; 8:4

4 [a]Heb. 5:1; 8:3

5 who serve ᵃa copy and ᵇshadow of the heavenly things, just as Moses is ᶜwarned *by God* when he was about to erect the ¹tabernacle; for, "ᵈSᴇᴇ," He says, "ᴛʜᴀᴛ ʏᴏᴜ ᴍᴀᴋᴇ ᴀʟʟ ᴛʜɪɴɢs ᴀᴄᴄᴏʀᴅɪɴɢ ᴛᴏ ᴛʜᴇ ᴘᴀᴛᴛᴇʀɴ ᴡʜɪᴄʜ ᴡᴀs sʜᴏᴡɴ ʏᴏᴜ ᴏɴ ᴛʜᴇ ᴍᴏᴜɴᴛᴀɪɴ."

6 But now He has obtained a more excellent ministry, by as much as He is also the ᵃmediator of ᵇa better covenant, which has been enacted on better promises.

7 For ᵃif that first *covenant* had been faultless, there would have been no occasion sought for a second.

8 For finding fault with them, He says,

"ᵃBᴇʜᴏʟᴅ, ᴅᴀʏs ᴀʀᴇ ᴄᴏᴍɪɴɢ, sᴀʏs ᴛʜᴇ Lᴏʀᴅ,
¹Wʜᴇɴ I ᴡɪʟʟ ᴇꜰꜰᴇᴄᴛ ᵇᴀ ɴᴇᴡ ᴄᴏᴠᴇɴᴀɴᴛ
Wɪᴛʜ ᴛʜᴇ ʜᴏᴜsᴇ ᴏꜰ Isʀᴀᴇʟ ᴀɴᴅ ᴡɪᴛʜ ᴛʜᴇ ʜᴏᴜsᴇ ᴏꜰ Jᴜᴅᴀʜ;
9 ᵃNᴏᴛ ʟɪᴋᴇ ᴛʜᴇ ᴄᴏᴠᴇɴᴀɴᴛ ᴡʜɪᴄʜ I ᴍᴀᴅᴇ ᴡɪᴛʜ ᴛʜᴇɪʀ ꜰᴀᴛʜᴇʀs
Oɴ ᴛʜᴇ ᴅᴀʏ ᴡʜᴇɴ I ᵇᴛᴏᴏᴋ ᴛʜᴇᴍ ʙʏ ᴛʜᴇ ʜᴀɴᴅ
Tᴏ ʟᴇᴀᴅ ᴛʜᴇᴍ ᴏᴜᴛ ᴏꜰ ᴛʜᴇ ʟᴀɴᴅ ᴏꜰ Eɢʏᴘᴛ;
Fᴏʀ ᴛʜᴇʏ ᴅɪᴅ ɴᴏᴛ ᴄᴏɴᴛɪɴᴜᴇ ɪɴ Mʏ ᴄᴏᴠᴇɴᴀɴᴛ,
Aɴᴅ I ᴅɪᴅ ɴᴏᴛ ᴄᴀʀᴇ ꜰᴏʀ ᴛʜᴇᴍ, sᴀʏs ᴛʜᴇ Lᴏʀᴅ.
10 "ᵃFᴏʀ ᵇᴛʜɪs ɪs ᴛʜᴇ ᴄᴏᴠᴇɴᴀɴᴛ ᴛʜᴀᴛ I ᴡɪʟʟ ᴍᴀᴋᴇ ᴡɪᴛʜ ᴛʜᴇ ʜᴏᴜsᴇ ᴏꜰ Isʀᴀᴇʟ
Aꜰᴛᴇʀ ᴛʜᴏsᴇ ᴅᴀʏs, sᴀʏs ᴛʜᴇ Lᴏʀᴅ:
I ᴡɪʟʟ ᴘᴜᴛ Mʏ ʟᴀᴡs ɪɴᴛᴏ ᴛʜᴇɪʀ ᴍɪɴᴅs,
Aɴᴅ I ᴡɪʟʟ ᴡʀɪᴛᴇ ᴛʜᴇᴍ ᶜᴜᴘᴏɴ ᴛʜᴇɪʀ ʜᴇᴀʀᴛs.
Aɴᴅ I ᴡɪʟʟ ʙᴇ ᴛʜᴇɪʀ Gᴏᴅ,
Aɴᴅ ᴛʜᴇʏ sʜᴀʟʟ ʙᴇ Mʏ ᴘᴇᴏᴘʟᴇ.
11 "ᵃAɴᴅ ᴛʜᴇʏ sʜᴀʟʟ ɴᴏᴛ ᴛᴇᴀᴄʜ ᴇᴠᴇʀʏ ᴏɴᴇ ʜɪs ꜰᴇʟʟᴏᴡ-ᴄɪᴛɪᴢᴇɴ,
Aɴᴅ ᴇᴠᴇʀʏ ᴏɴᴇ ʜɪs ʙʀᴏᴛʜᴇʀ, sᴀʏɪɴɢ, 'Kɴᴏᴡ ᴛʜᴇ Lᴏʀᴅ,'
Fᴏʀ ᵇᴀʟʟ sʜᴀʟʟ ᴋɴᴏᴡ Mᴇ,
Fʀᴏᴍ ᴛʜᴇ ʟᴇᴀsᴛ ᴛᴏ ᴛʜᴇ ɢʀᴇᴀᴛᴇsᴛ ᴏꜰ ᴛʜᴇᴍ.
12 "ᵃFᴏʀ I ᴡɪʟʟ ʙᴇ ᴍᴇʀᴄɪꜰᴜʟ ᴛᴏ ᴛʜᴇɪʀ ɪɴɪϙᴜɪᴛɪᴇs,
ᵇAɴᴅ I ᴡɪʟʟ ʀᴇᴍᴇᴍʙᴇʀ ᴛʜᴇɪʀ sɪɴs ɴᴏ ᴍᴏʀᴇ."

13 ¹When He said, "ᵃA new *covenant*," He

---

5 ¹Or, *sacred tent*
ᵃHeb. 9:23 ᵇCol. 2:17; Heb. 10:1 ᶜHeb. 11:7; 12:25; Matt. 2:12; ᵈEx. 25:40

6 ᵃ1 Tim. 2:5 ᵇHeb. 7:22; 8:8; 9:15; 12:24; Luke 22:20

7 ᵃHeb. 7:11

8 ¹Lit., *and*
ᵃJer. 31:31 ᵇHeb. 8:13; 9:15; 12:24; 2 Cor. 3:6; Luke 22:20; Heb. 7:22; 8:6

9 ᵃJer. 31:32 ᵇHeb. 2:16 marg.; Ex. 19:5f.

10 ᵃJer. 31:33 ᵇHeb. 10:16; Rom. 11:27 ᶜ2 Cor. 3:3

11 ᵃJer. 31:34 ᵇIs. 54:13; John 6:45; 1 John 2:27

12 ᵃJer. 31:34 ᵇHeb. 10:17

13 ¹Or, *In His saying*
ᵃHeb. 8:8; 9:15; 12:24; 2 Cor. 3:6; Luke 22:20; Heb. 7:22; 8:6

Hebrews 8, 9

**The Earthly Sanctuary.
The Blood of the New Covenant.**

13 [2]Or, *near*
[b]Heb. 1:11; 2 Cor. 5:17

1 [a]Heb. 9:10 [b]Ex. 25:8;
Heb. 9:11, 24; 8:2

2 [1]Or, *sacred tent* [2]Lit.,
first [3]Lit., *loaves of
presentation*
[a]Ex. 25:8, 9 [b]Ex. 25:31-39
[c]Ex. 25:23-29 [d]Ex. 25:30;
Lev. 24:5ff.[Matt. 12:4]

3 [1]Or, *sacred tent*
[a]Ex. 26:31-33 [b]Ex. 26:33

4 [1]Or, *censer*
[a]Ex. 30:1-5; 37:25f. [b]Ex.
25:10ff.; 37:1ff. [c]Ex. 16:32f.
[d]Num. 17:10 [e]Ex. 31:18;
32:15; Deut. 9:9, 11, 15

5 [a]Ex. 25:18ff. [b]Ex. 25:17,
20

6 [1]Lit., *first* [2]Or, *sacred
tent*
[a]Num. 28:3 [b]Ex. 25:8, 9

7 [1]Lit., *ignorance of the
people*
[a]Heb. 9:3 [b]Lev. 16:12ff. [c]Ex.
30:10, Lev. 16:34; Heb. 10:3
[d]Lev. 16:11, 14 [e]Heb. 5:3
[f]Num. 15:25; Heb. 5:2

8 [1]Lit., *first*
[a]Heb. 3:7 [b]Heb. 10:20; John
14:6

9 [a]Heb. 11:19; 10:1 [b]Heb.
5:1 [c]Heb. 7:19

10 [1]Lit., *flesh*
[a]Lev. 11:2ff.; Col. 2:16
[b]Num. 6:3 [c]Lev. 11:25;
Num. 19:13; Mark 7:4 [d]Heb.
7:16 [e]Heb. 7:12

11 [1]Some ancient mss.
read, *that have come* [2]Or,
sacred tent
[a]Heb. 2:17 [b]Heb. 10:1 [c]Heb.
9:24; 8:2 [d]Mark 14:58; 2 Cor.
5:1 [e]2 Cor. 4:18; Heb. 12:27;
13:14

12 [1]Or, *obtaining*
[a]Lev. 4:3; 16:6, 15; Heb. 9:19
[b]Heb. 9:14; 13:12 [c]Heb. 9:24
[d]Heb. 7:27 [e]Heb. 9:15; 5:9

464

has made the first obsolete. [b]But whatever is becoming obsolete and growing old is [2]ready to disappear.

CHAPTER 9

NOW even the first *covenant* had [a]regulations of divine worship and [b]the earthly sanctuary.

2   For there was [a]a [1]tabernacle prepared, the [2]outer one, in which *were* [b]the lampstand and [c]the table and [d]the [3]sacred bread; this is called the holy place.

3   And behind [a]the second veil, there was a [1]tabernacle which is called the [b]Holy of Holies,

4   having a golden [1a]altar of incense and [b]the ark of the covenant covered on all sides with gold, in which *was* [c]a golden jar holding the manna, and [d]Aaron's rod which budded, and [e]the tables of the covenant.

5   And above it *were* the [a]cherubim of glory [b]overshadowing the mercy seat; but of these things we cannot now speak in detail.

6   Now when these things have been thus prepared, the priests [a]are continually entering [b]the [1]outer [2]tabernacle, performing the divine worship,

7   but into [a]the second only [b]the high priest *enters*, [c]once a year, [d]not without *taking* blood, which he [e]offers for himself and for the [1f]sins of the people committed in ignorance.

8   [a]The Holy Spirit *is* signifying this, [b]that the way into the holy place has not yet been disclosed, while the [1]outer tabernacle is still standing;

9   which *is* [a]a symbol for the time *then* present, according to which both gifts and sacrifices are [b]offered which cannot [c]make the worshiper perfect in conscience,

10   since they *relate* only to [a]food and [b]drink and various [c]washings, [d]regulations for the [1]body imposed until [e]a time of reformation.

11   But when Christ appeared *as* a [a]high priest of the [b]good things [1]to come, *He entered* through [c]the greater and more perfect [2]tabernacle, [d]not made with hands, that is to say, [e]not of this creation;

12   and not through [a]the blood of goats and calves, but [b]through His own blood, He [c]entered the holy place [d]once for all, [1]having obtained [e]eternal redemption.

13 For if ᵃthe blood of goats and bulls and ᵇthe ashes of a heifer sprinkling those who have been defiled, sanctify for the ¹cleansing of the flesh,

14 how much more will ᵃthe blood of Christ, who through ¹ᵇthe eternal Spirit ᶜoffered Himself without blemish to God, ᵈcleanse ²your conscience from ᵉdead works to serve ᶠthe living God?

15 And for this reason ᵃHe is the ᵇmediator of a ᶜnew covenant, in order that since a death has taken place for the redemption of the transgressions that were *committed* under the first covenant, those who have been ᵈcalled may ᵉreceive the promise of ᶠthe eternal inheritance.

16 For where a ¹covenant is, there must of necessity ²be the death of the one who made it.

17 For a ¹covenant is valid *only* when ²men are dead, ³for it is never in force while the one who made it lives.

18 Therefore even the first *covenant* was not inaugurated without blood.

19 For when every commandment had been ᵃspoken by Moses to all the people according to the Law, ᵇhe took the ᶜblood of the calves and the goats, with ᵈwater and scarlet wool and hyssop, and sprinkled both ᵉthe book itself and all the people,

20 saying, "ᵃTHIS IS THE BLOOD OF THE COVENANT WHICH GOD COMMANDED YOU."

21 And in the same way he sprinkled both the ¹ᵃtabernacle and all the vessels of the ministry with the blood.

22 And according to the ¹Law, *one may* ᵃalmost *say*, all things are cleansed with blood, and ᵇwithout shedding of blood there is no forgiveness.

23 Therefore it was necessary for the ᵃcopies of the things in the heavens to be cleansed with these, but ᵃthe heavenly things themselves with better sacrifices than these.

24 For Christ ᵃdid not enter a holy place made with hands, a *mere* copy of ᵇthe true one, but into ᶜheaven itself, now ᵈto appear in the presence of God for us;

25 nor was it that He should offer Himself often, as ᵃthe high priest enters ᵇthe holy place ᵃyear by year with blood not his own.

26 Otherwise, He would have needed to suffer often since ᵃthe foundation of the world; but now ᵇonce at ᶜthe consummation He has been ᵈmanifested to put away sin ¹ᵉby the sacrifice of Himself.

13 ¹Lit., *purity*
ᵃHeb. 9:19; 10:4 ᵇNum. 19:9, 17f.

14 ¹Or, His *eternal spirit*
²Some ancient mss. read, *our*
ᵃHeb. 9:12; 13:12 ᵇ1 Cor. 15:45; 1 Pet. 3:18 ᶜEph. 5:2; Heb. 7:27; 10:10, 12 ᵈActs 15:9; Titus 2:14; Heb. 10:2, 22; 1:3 ᵉHeb. 3:1; ᶠMatt. 16:16; Heb. 3:12

15 ᵃRom. 3:24 ᵇ1 Tim. 2:5; Heb. 8:6; 12:24 ᶜHeb. 8:8 ᵈRom. 8:28f.; Heb. 3:1; Matt. 22:3ff. ᵉHeb. 6:15; 10:36; Heb. 11:39 ᶠActs 20:32

16 ¹Or, *testament* ²Lit., *be brought*

17 ¹Note vs. 16 ²Lit., *over the dead* ³Some ancient mss. read, *for is it then . . . lives?*

19 ᵃHeb. 1:1 ᵇEx. 24:6ff. ᶜHeb. 9:12 ᵈLev. 14:4, 7; Num. 19:6, 18 ᵉEx. 24:7

20 ᵃEx. 24:8; Matt. 26:28

21 ¹Or, *sacred tent*
ᵃEx. 40:9; 24:6; Lev. 8:15, 19; 16:14-16

22 ¹Or, *Law, almost all things*
ᵃLev. 5:11f. ᵇLev. 17:11

23 ᵃHeb. 8:5

24 ᵃHeb. 9:12; 4:14 ᵇHeb. 8:2 ᶜHeb. 9:12 ᵈHeb. 7:25; Matt. 18:10

25 ᵃHeb. 9:7 ᵇHeb. 9:2; 10:19

26 ¹Or, *by His sacrifice*
ᵃMatt. 25:34; Heb. 4:3 ᵇHeb. 9:12; 7:27 ᶜMatt. 13:39; Heb. 1:2 ᵈ1 John 3:5, 8 ᵉHeb. 9:12, 14

27 [1]Lit., *laid up*
[a]Gen. 3:19 [b]2 Cor. 5:10;
1 John 4:17

28 [1]Lit., *without sin*
[a]Heb. 7:27 [b]1 Pet. 2:24 [c]Acts
1:11 [d]Heb. 4:15 [e]1 Cor. 1:7;
Titus 2:13 [f]Heb. 5:9

1 [1]Lit., *image* [2]Some
ancient mss. read, *they can*
[a]Heb. 8:5 [b]Heb. 9:11 [c]Heb.
10:4, 11; 9:9; Rom. 8:3 [d]Heb.
7:19

2 [a]1 Pet. 2:19 marg.

3 [1]Lit., *them there is*
[a]Heb. 9:7

4 [a]Heb. 10:1, 11 [b]Heb.
9:12f.

5 [a]Heb. 1:6 [b]Ps. 40:6
[c]1 Pet. 2:24; Heb. 2:14; 5:7

6 [a]Ps. 40:6

7 [a]Ps. 40:7, 8 [b]Jer. 36:2;
Ezek. 2:9; 3:1f.; Ezra 6:2
[Sept.]

8 [a]Ps. 40:6; Heb. 10:5f.
[b]Mark 12:33 [c]Rom. 8:3
marg.

9 [a]Ps. 40:7, 8; Heb. 10:7

10 [1]Lit., *which*
[a]Eph. 5:26; Heb. 10:14, 29;
2:11; 13:12; John 17:19
[b]Heb. 7:27; 9:14, 28; 10:12;
Eph. 5:2; John 6:51 [c]1 Pet.
2:24; Heb. 2:14; 5:7 [d]Heb.
7:27

11 [a]Heb. 5:1 [b]Heb. 10:1, 4;
Mic. 6:6-8

12 [a]Heb. 5:1

27 And inasmuch as [a]it is [1]appointed for men to die once, and after this [b]*comes* judgment;

28 so Christ also, having been [a]offered once to [b]bear the sins of many, shall appear [c]a second time, [1d]not to bear sin, to those who [e]eagerly await Him, for [f]salvation.

CHAPTER 10

FOR the Law, since it has *only* [a]a shadow of [b]the good things to come *and* not the very [1]form of things, [2]can [c]never by the same sacrifices year by year, which they offer continually, [d]make perfect those who draw near.

2 Otherwise, would they not have ceased to be offered, because the worshipers, having once been cleansed, would no longer have had [a]consciousness of sins?

3 But [a]in [1]those *sacrifices* there is a reminder of sins year by year.

4 For it is [a]impossible for the [b]blood of bulls and goats to take away sins.

5 Therefore, [a]when He comes into the world, He says,

"[b]SACRIFICE AND OFFERING THOU HAST NOT DESIRED,
BUT [c]A BODY THOU HAST PREPARED FOR ME;
6 [a]IN WHOLE BURNT OFFERINGS AND *sacrifices*
FOR SIN THOU HAST TAKEN NO PLEASURE.
7 "[a]THEN I SAID, 'BEHOLD, I HAVE COME
(IN [b]THE ROLL OF THE BOOK IT IS WRITTEN OF
ME)
TO DO THY WILL, O GOD.'"

8 After saying above, "[a]SACRIFICES AND OFFERINGS AND [b]WHOLE BURNT OFFERINGS AND *sacrifices* [c]FOR SIN THOU HAST NOT DESIRED, NOR HAST THOU TAKEN PLEASURE *in them*" (which are offered according to the Law),

9 then He said, "[a]BEHOLD, I HAVE COME TO DO THY WILL." He takes away the first in order to establish the second.

10 By [1]this will we have been [a]sanctified through [b]the offering of [c]the body of Jesus Christ [d]once for all.

11 And every priest stands daily ministering and [a]offering time after time the same sacrifices, which [b]can never take away sins;

12 but He, having offered one sacrifice [a]for

[1]sins [b]for all time, [c]sat down at the right hand of God,

13   waiting from that time onward [a]UNTIL HIS ENEMIES BE MADE A FOOTSTOOL FOR HIS FEET.

14   For by one offering He has [a]perfected [b]for all time those who are [1]sanctified.

15   And [a]the Holy Spirit also bears witness to us; for after saying,

16   "[a]THIS IS THE COVENANT THAT I WILL MAKE
     WITH THEM
AFTER THOSE DAYS, SAYS THE LORD:
I WILL PUT MY LAWS UPON THEIR HEART,
AND UPON THEIR MIND I WILL WRITE THEM,"
He then says,

17   "[a]AND THEIR SINS AND THEIR LAWLESS DEEDS
     I WILL REMEMBER NO MORE."

18   Now where there is forgiveness of these things, there is no longer *any* offering for sin.

19   Since therefore, brethren, we [a]have confidence to [b]enter the holy place by the blood of Jesus,

20   by [a]a new and living way which He inaugurated for us through [b]the veil, that is, His flesh,

21   and since *we have* [a]a great priest [b]over the house of God,

22   let us [a]draw near with a [1]sincere heart in [b]full assurance of faith, having our hearts [c]sprinkled *clean* from an evil conscience and our body [d]washed with pure water.

23   Let us hold fast the [a]confession of our [b]hope without wavering, for [c]He who promised is faithful;

24   and let us consider how [a]to stimulate one another to love and [b]good deeds,

25   not forsaking our own [a]assembling together, as is the habit of some but [b]encouraging *one another*; and all the more, as you see [c]the day drawing near.

26   For if we go on [a]sinning willfully after receiving [b]the knowledge of the truth, there no longer remains a sacrifice for sins,

27   but a certain terrifying expectation of [a]judgment, and THE [b]FURY OF A FIRE WHICH WILL CONSUME THE ADVERSARIES.

28   [a]Anyone who has set aside the Law of Moses dies without mercy on *the testimony of* two or three witnesses.

29   [a]How much severer punishment do you

---

12 [1]Or, *sins, forever sat down*
[b]Heb. 10:14 [c]Heb. 1:3

13 [a]Ps. 110:1; Heb. 1:13

14 [1]Or, *being sanctified*
[a]Heb. 10:1 [b]Heb. 10:12

15 [a]Heb. 3:7

16 [a]Jer. 31:33; Heb. 8:10

17 [a]Jer. 31:34; Heb. 8:12

19 [a]Heb. 10:35; 3:6 [b]Heb. 9:25

20 [a]Heb. 9:8 [b]Heb. 6:19; 9:3

21 [a]Heb. 2:17 [b]Heb. 3:6; 1 Tim. 3:15

22 [1]Lit., *true*
[a]Heb. 10:1; 7:19 [b]Heb. 6:11 [c]Heb. 12:24; 1 Pet. 1:2; Heb. 9:19; Ezek. 36:25 [d]Acts 22:16; 1 Cor. 6:11; Eph. 5:26; Titus 3:5; 1 Pet. 3:21

23 [a]Heb. 3:1 [b]Heb. 3:6 [c]Heb. 11:11; 1 Cor. 1:9; 10:13

24 [a]Heb. 13:1 [b]Titus 3:8

25 [a]Acts 2:42 [b]Heb. 3:13 [c]1 Cor. 3:13

26 [a]Heb. 5:2; 6:4-8; 2 Pet. 2:20f.; Num. 15:30 [b]1 Tim. 2:4

27 [a]John 5:29; Heb. 9:27 [b]Is. 26:11; 2 Thess. 1:7

28 [a]Deut. 17:2-6; Matt. 18:16; Heb. 2:2

29 [a]Heb. 2:3

Hebrews 10, 11

**The Need for Endurance.
Faith Defined and its Triumphs Set Forth.**

29 bHeb. 6:6 cHeb. 13:20;
Matt. 26:28, dEph. 5:26;
Rev. 1:5; Heb. 9:13f. eHeb.
6:4; Eph. 4:30; 1 Cor. 6:11

30 aDeut. 32:35; Rom.
12:19 bDeut. 32:36

31 a2 Cor. 5:11 bMatt.
16:16; Heb. 3:12

32 1Lit., in which
aHeb. 5:12 bHeb. 6:4 cPhil.
1:30

33 a1 Cor. 4:9; Heb. 12:4
bPhil. 4:14 [Gr.]; 1 Thess.
2:14

34 aHeb. 13:3 bMatt. 5:12
cHeb. 9:15; 11:16; 13:14;
1 Pet. 1.1f.

35 aHeb. 10:19 bHeb. 2:2

36 1Lit., the promise
aHeb. 12:1; Luke 21:19
bHeb. 9:15

37 aHab. 2:3; Heb. 10:25;
Rev. 22:20 bMatt. 11:3

38 aHab. 2:4 Rom. 1:17;
Gal. 3:11

39 1Lit., we are not of
shrinking back . . . but of
faith 2Or. possessing

1 1Or, substance 2Or,
evidence
aHeb. 3:14 [Gr.] bHeb. 3:6
cRom. 8:24; 2 Cor. 4:18; 5:7;
Heb. 11:7, 27

2 1Lit., obtained a
testimony
aHeb. 1:1 bHeb. 11:4, 39

3 1Lit., ages
aHeb. 1:2 bGen. 1; Heb. 1:2
cHeb. 6:5; 2 Pet. 3:5 dRom.
4:17

4 1I.e., by receiving his
gifts 2Lit., it
aGen. 4:4; Matt. 23:35;
1 John 3:12 bHeb. 11:2
cHeb. 5:1 dGen. 4:8-10; Heb.
12:24

468

think he will deserve bwho has trampled under foot the Son of God, and has regarded as unclean cthe blood of the covenant dby which he was sanctified, and has einsulted the Spirit of grace?

30 For we know Him who said, "aVENGEANCE IS MINE, I WILL REPAY." And again, "bTHE LORD WILL JUDGE HIS PEOPLE."

31 It is a aterrifying thing to fall into the hands of the bliving God.

32 But remember athe former days, 1when, after being benlightened, you endured a great cconflict of sufferings,

33 partly, by being amade a public spectacle through reproaches and tribulations, and partly by becoming bsharers with those who were so treated.

34 For you ashowed sympathy to the prisoners, and accepted bjoyfully the seizure of your property, knowing that you have for yourselves ca better possession and an abiding one.

35 Therefore, do not throw away your aconfidence, which has a great breward.

36 For you have need of aendurance, so that when you have done the will of God, you may breceive 1what was promised.

37 aFOR YET IN A VERY LITTLE WHILE,
bHE WHO IS COMING WILL COME, AND WILL NOT DELAY.

38 aBUT MY RIGHTEOUS ONE SHALL LIVE BY FAITH;
AND IF HE SHRINKS BACK, MY SOUL HAS NO PLEASURE IN HIM.

39 But 1we are not of those who shrink back to destruction, but of those who have faith to the 2preserving of the soul.

CHAPTER 11

Now faith is the 1aassurance of *things* bhoped for, the 2conviction of cthings not seen.

2 For by it the amen of old 1bgained approval.

3 By faith we understand that the 1aworlds were prepared bby the cword of God, so that what is seen dwas not made out of things which are visible.

4 By faith aAbel offered to God a better sacrifice than Cain, through which he bobtained the testimony that he was righteous, God testifying 1about his cgifts, and through 2faith, though dhe is dead, he still speaks.

5 By faith [a]Enoch was taken up so that he should not [b]see death; and he was not found because God took him up; for he obtained the witness that before his being taken up he was pleasing to God.

6 And without faith it is impossible to please *Him*, for he who [a]comes to God must believe that He is, and *that* He is a rewarder of those who seek Him.

7 By faith [a]Noah, being [b]warned *by God* about [c]things not yet seen, [1][d]in reverence [e]prepared an ark for the salvation of his household, by which he condemned the world, and became an heir of [f]the righteousness which is according to faith.

8 By faith [a]Abraham, when he was called, obeyed by going out to a place which he was to [b]receive for an inheritance; and he went out, not knowing where he was going.

9 By faith he lived as an alien in [a]the land of promise, as in a foreign *land*, [b]dwelling in tents with Isaac and Jacob, [c]fellow-heirs of the same promise;

10 for he was looking for [a]the city which has [b]foundations, [c]whose architect and builder is God.

11 By faith even [a]Sarah herself received [1]ability to conceive, even beyond the proper time of life, since she considered Him [b]faithful who had promised;

12 therefore also there was born of one man, and [a]him as good as dead [1]at that, *as many descendants* [b]AS THE STARS OF HEAVEN IN NUMBER, AND INNUMERABLE AS THE SAND WHICH IS BY THE SEASHORE.

13 [a]All these died in faith, [b]without receiving the promises, but [c]having seen them and having welcomed them from a distance, and [d]having confessed that they were strangers and exiles on the earth.

14 For those who say such things make it clear that they are seeking a country of their own.

15 And indeed if they had been [1]thinking of that *country* from which they went out, [a]they would have had opportunity to return.

16 But as it is, they desire a better *country*, that is a [a]heavenly one. Therefore [b]God is not [1]ashamed to be [c]called their God; for [d]He has prepared a city for them.

17 By faith [a]Abraham, when he was tested,

5 [a]Gen. 5:21-24 [b]Luke 2:26; John 8:51; Heb. 2:9

6 [a]Heb. 7:19

7 [1]Lit., *having become reverent* [a]Gen. 6:13-22 [b]Heb. 8:5 [c]Heb. 11:1 [d]Heb. 5:7 [e]1 Pet. 3:20 [f]Gen. 6:9; Ezek. 14:14, 20; Rom. 4:13; 9:30

8 [a]Gen. 12:1-4; Acts 7:2-4 [b]Gen. 12:7

9 [a]Acts 7:5 [b]Gen. 12:8; 13:3, 18; 18:1, 9 [c]Heb. 6:17

10 [a]Heb. 12:22; 13:14 [b]Rev. 21:14ff. [c]Heb. 11:16

11 [1]Lit., *power for the laying down of seed* [a]Gen. 17:19; 18:11-14; 21:2 [b]Heb. 10:23

12 [1]Lit., *in these things* [a]Rom. 4:19 [b]Gen. 15:5; 22:17; 32:12

13 [a]Matt. 13:17 [b]Heb. 11:39 [c]John 8:56; Heb. 11:27 [d]Gen. 23:4; 47:9; Ps. 39:12; Eph. 2:19; 1 Pet. 1:1; 2:11

15 [1]Or, *remembering* [a]Gen. 24:6-8

16 [1]Lit., *ashamed of them, to be* [a]2 Tim. 4:18 [b]Mark 8:38; Heb. 2:11 [c]Gen. 26:24; 28:13; Ex. 3:6, 15; 4:5 [d]Heb. 11:10; Rev. 21:2

17 [a]Gen. 22:1-10; James 2:21

17 [b]Heb. 11:13

18 [a]Gen. 21:12; Rom. 9:7

19 [1]Lit., *Considering* [2]Or, *figuratively speaking*; lit., *in a parable* [a]Rom. 4:21 [b]Heb. 9:9

20 [a]Gen. 27:27-29, 39f.

21 [a]Gen. 48:1, 5, 16, 20 [b]Gen. 47:31 [Sept.]; 1 Kin. 1:47

22 [a]Gen. 50:24f.; Ex. 13:19

23 [a]Ex. 2:2 [Sept.] [b]Ex. 1.16, 22

24 [a]Ex. 2:10, 11ff.

25 [a]Heb. 11:37

26 [1]I.e., the Messiah [a]Luke 14:33; Phil. 3:7f. [b]Heb. 2:2

27 [a]Ex. 12;50f.; 13:17f.; Ex. 2:15 [b]Ex. 10:28f.; Ex. 2:14 [c]Heb. 11:1, 13; Col. 1:15

28 [a]Ex. 12;21ff. [b]Ex. 12:23, 29f.; 1 Cor. 10:10

29 [1]Lit., *swallowed up* [a]Ex. 14:22-29

30 [a]Josh. 6:20 [b]Josh. 6:15f.

31 [1]Lit., *with* [a]Josh. 2:9ff.; 6:23; James 2:25

32 [a]Judg. 6-8 [b]Judg. 4-5 [c]Judg. 13-16 [d]Judg. 11-12 [e]1 Sam. 16:1, 13 [f]1 Sam. 1:20

33 [a]Judg. 4, 7, 11, 14; 2 Sam. 5:17; 8:2; 10:12 [b]1 Sam. 12:4; 2 Sam. 8:15 [c]2 Sam. 7:11f. [d]Dan. 6:22; Judg. 14:6; 1 Sam.17:34

offered up Isaac; and he who had [b]received the promises was offering up his only begotten *son;*

18   *it was he* to whom it was said, "[a]IN ISAAC YOUR SEED SHALL BE CALLED."

19   [1]He considered that [a]God is able to raise *men* even from the dead; from which he also received him back [2]as a [b]type.

20   By faith [a]Isaac blessed Jacob and Esau, even regarding things to come.

21   By faith [a]Jacob, as he was dying, blessed each of the sons of Joseph, and [b]worshiped, *leaning* on the top of his staff.

22   By faith [a]Joseph, when he was dying, made mention of the exodus of the sons of Israel, and gave orders concerning his bones.

23   By faith [a]Moses, when he was born, was hidden for three months by his parents, because they saw he was a beautiful child; and they were not afraid of the [b]king's edict.

24   By faith Moses, [a]when he had grown up, refused to be called the son of Pharaoh's daughter;

25   choosing rather to [a]endure ill-treatment with the people of God, than to enjoy the passing pleasures of sin;

26   [a]considering the reproach of [1]Christ greater riches than the treasures of Egypt; for he was looking to the [b]reward.

27   By faith he [a]left Egypt, not [b]fearing the wrath of the king; for he endured, as [c]seeing Him who is unseen.

28   By faith he [a]kept the Passover and the sprinkling of the blood, so that [b]he who destroyed the first-born might not touch them.

29   By faith they [a]passed through the Red Sea as though *they were passing* through dry land; and the Egyptians, when they attempted it, were [1]drowned.

30   By faith [a]the walls of Jericho fell down, [b]after they had been encircled for seven days.

31   By faith [a]Rahab the harlot did not perish along with those who were disobedient, after she had welcomed the spies [1]in peace.

32   And what more shall I say? For time will fail me if I tell of [a]Gideon, [b]Barak, [c]Samson, [d]Jephthah; of [e]David and [f]Samuel and the prophets;

33   who by faith [a]conquered kingdoms, [b]performed *acts of* righteousness, [c]obtained promises, [d]shut the mouths of lions,

34 [a]quenched the power of fire, [b]escaped the edge of the sword, from weakness were made strong, [c]became mighty in war, [c]put foreign armies to flight.

35 [a]Women received *back* their dead by resurrection; and others were tortured, not accepting their [1]release, in order that they might obtain a better resurrection;

36 and others [1]experienced mockings and scourgings, yes, also [a]chains and imprisonment.

37 They were [a]stoned, they were [b]sawn in two, [1]they were tempted, they were [c]put to death with the sword; they went about [d]in sheepskins, in goatskins; being destitute, afflicted, [e]ill-treated

38 (*men* of whom the world was not worthy), [a]wandering in deserts and mountains and caves and holes [1]in the ground.

39 And all these, having [1a]gained approval through their faith, [b]did not receive [2]what was promised,

40 because God had [1]provided [a]something better for us, so that [b]apart from us they should not be made perfect.

CHAPTER 12

THEREFORE, since we have so great a cloud of witnesses surrounding us, let [a]us also [b]lay aside every encumbrance, and the sin which so easily entangles us, and let us [c]run with [d]endurance the race that is set before us,

2 [1]fixing our eyes on Jesus the [2a]author and perfecter of faith, who for the joy set before Him [b]endured the cross, [c]despising the shame, and has [d]sat down at the right hand of the throne of God.

3 For [a]consider Him who has endured such hostility by sinners against Himself, so that you may not grow weary [1b]and lose heart.

4 [a]You have not yet resisted [1b]to the point of shedding blood, in your striving against sin;

5 and you have forgotten the exhortation which is addressed to you as sons,

"[a]MY SON, DO NOT REGARD LIGHTLY THE DISCIPLINE OF THE LORD,

NOR [b]FAINT WHEN YOU ARE REPROVED BY HIM;

6 [a]FOR THOSE [b]WHOM THE LORD LOVES HE DISCIPLINES,

---

34 [a]Dan. 3:23ff. [b]Ex. 18:4; 1 Sam. 18:11; 19:10; Ps. 144:10; 1 Kin. 19; 2 Kin. 6 [c]Judg. 7:21; 15:8, 15f.; 1 Sam. 17:51f.; 2 Sam. 8:1-6; 10:15ff.

35 [1]Lit., *redemption* [a]1 Kin. 17:23; 2 Kin. 4:36f.

36 [1]Lit., *received the trial of* [a]Gen. 39:20; Jer. 20:2; 37:15

37 [1]Some mss. omit, *they were tempted* [a]2 Chr. 24:21; 1 Kin. 21:13 [b]2 Sam. 12:31; 1 Chr. 20:3 [c]1 Kin. 19:10; Jer. 26:23 [d]1 Kin. 19:13, 19; 2 Kin. 2:8, 13f.; Zech. 13:4 [e]Heb. 11:25; 13:3

38 [1]Lit., *of* [a]1 Kin. 18:4, 13; 19:9

39 [1]Lit., *obtained a testimony* [2]Lit., *the promise* [a]Heb. 11:2 [b]Heb. 11:13; 10:36

40 [1]Or, *foreseen* [a]Heb. 11:16 [b]Rev. 6:11

1 [a]Heb. 10:39 [b]Eph. 4:22 [Gr.]; Rom. 13:12 [c]1 Cor. 9:24; Gal. 2:2 [d]Heb. 10:36

2 [1]Lit., *looking to* [2]Or, *leader* [a]Heb. 2:10 [b]Heb. 2:9; Phil. 2:8f. [c]1 Cor. 1:18, 23; Heb. 13:13 [d]Heb. 1:3

3 [1]Lit., *fainting in your souls* [a]Matt. 10:24; Rev. 2:3 [b]Gal. 6:9; Heb. 12:5

4 [1]Lit., *as far as blood* [a]Heb. 10:32ff.; 13:13 [b]Phil. 2:8

5 [a]Prov. 3:11 [b]Heb. 12:3

6 [a]Prov. 3:12 [b]Ps. 119:75; Rev. 3:19

471

7 ᵃDeut. 8:5; 2 Sam. 7:14; Prov. 13:24; 19:18; 23:13f.

8 ᵃ1 Pet. 5:9

9 ¹Lit., *fathers of our flesh* ²Or, *our spirits* ᵃLuke 18:2 ᵇNum. 16:22; 27:16; Rev. 22:6 ᶜIs. 38:16

10 ¹Lit., *were disciplining* ᵃ2 Pet. 1:4

11 ᵃ1 Pet. 1:6 ᵇJames 3:17f.; Is. 32:17; 2 Tim. 4:8

12 ¹Lit., *make straight* ᵃIs. 35:3

13 ᵃProv. 4:26; Gal. 2:14 ᵇJames 5:16; Gal. 6:1

14 ᵃRom. 14:19 ᵇRom. 6:22; Heb. 12:10 ᶜMatt. 5:8; Heb. 9:28

15 ᵃHeb. 4:1; 2 Cor. 6:1; Gal. 5:4 ᵇDeut. 29:18 ᶜTitus 1:15

16 ᵃHeb. 13:4 ᵇ1 Tim. 1:9 ᶜGen. 25:33f.

17 ᵃGen. 27:30-40

18 ᵃHeb. 12:18ff.; 2 Cor. 3:7-13 ᵇEx. 19:12, 16ff.; 20:18; Deut. 4:11; 5:22

19 ᵃEx. 19:16, 19; 20:18; Matt. 24:31 ᵇDeut. 4:12; Ex. 19:19 ᶜEx. 20:19; Deut. 5:25; 18:16

20 ᵃEx. 19:12f.

AND HE SCOURGES EVERY SON WHOM HE RECEIVES."

7 It is for discipline that you endure; ᵃGod deals with you as with sons; for what son is there whom *his* father does not discipline?

8 But if you are without discipline, ᵃof which all have become partakers, then you are illegitimate children and not sons.

9 Furthermore, we had ¹earthly fathers to discipline us, and we ᵃrespected them; shall we not much rather be subject to ᵇthe Father of ²spirits, and ᶜlive?

10 For they ¹disciplined us for a short time as seemed best to them, but He disciplines us for *our* good, ᵃthat we may share His holiness.

11 All discipline ᵃfor the moment seems not to be joyful, but sorrowful; yet to those who have been trained by it, afterwards it yields the ᵇpeaceful fruit of righteousness.

12 Therefore, ¹ᵃstrengthen the hands that are weak and the knees that are feeble,

13 and ᵃmake straight paths for your feet, so that *the limb* which is lame may not be put out of joint, but rather ᵇbe healed.

14 ᵃPursue after peace with all men, and after the ᵇsanctification without which no one will ᶜsee the Lord.

15 See to it that no one ᵃcomes short of the grace of God; that no ᵇroot of bitterness springing up cause trouble, and by it many be ᶜdefiled;

16 that *there be* no ᵃimmoral or ᵇgodless person like Esau, ᶜwho sold his own birthright for a single meal.

17 For you know that even afterwards, ᵃwhen he desired to inherit the blessing, he was rejected, for he found no place for repentance, though he sought for it with tears.

18 ᵃFor you have not come to ᵇ*a mountain* that may be touched and to a blazing fire, and to darkness and gloom and whirlwind,

19 and to the ᵃblast of a trumpet and the ᵇsound of words which *sound was such that* those who heard ᶜbegged that no further word should be spoken to them.

20 For they could not bear the command, "ᵃIF EVEN A BEAST TOUCHES THE MOUNTAIN, IT WILL BE STONED."

21 And so terrible was the sight, *that* Moses said, "ᵃI AM FULL OF FEAR AND TREMBLING."

22 But ᵃyou have come to Mount Zion and to ᵇthe city of ᶜthe living God, ᵈthe heavenly Jerusalem, and to ᵉmyriads of ¹angels,

23 to the general assembly and ᵃchurch of the first-born who ᵇare enrolled in heaven, and to God ᶜthe Judge of all, and to the ᵈspirits of righteous men made perfect,

24 and to Jesus the ᵃmediator of a new covenant and to the ᵇsprinkled blood, which speaks better than ᶜ*the blood* of Abel.

25 ᵃSee to it that you do not refuse him who is ᵇspeaking. For ᶜif those ¹did not escape when they ᵈrefused him who ᵉwarned *them* on earth, much ²less *shall* we *escape* who turn away from Him who ᵉ*warns* from heaven.

26 And ᵃHis voice shook the earth then, but now He has promised, saying, "ᵇYET ONCE MORE I WILL SHAKE NOT ONLY THE EARTH, BUT ALSO THE HEAVEN."

27 And this *expression*, "Yet once more," denotes ᵃthe removing of those things which can be shaken, as of created things, in order that those things which cannot be shaken may remain.

28 Therefore, since we receive a ᵃkingdom which cannot be shaken, let us ¹show gratitude, by which we may ᵇoffer to God an acceptable service with reverence and awe;

29 for ᵃour God is a consuming fire.

CHAPTER 13

LET ᵃlove of the brethren continue.

2 Do not neglect to ᵃshow hospitality to strangers, for by this some have ᵇentertained angels without knowing it.

3 ᵃRemember ᵇthe prisoners, as though in prison with them; and those who are ill-treated, since you yourselves also are in the body.

4 ᵃ*Let* marriage *be held* in honor among all, and let the *marriage* bed *be* undefiled; ᵇfor fornicators and adulterers God will judge.

5 Let your way of life be ᵃfree from the love of money, ᵇbeing content with what you have; for He Himself has said, "ᶜI WILL NEVER DESERT YOU, NOR WILL I EVER FORSAKE YOU,"

6 so that we confidently say,

21 ᵃDeut. 9:19

22 ¹Or, *angels in festal assembly, and to the church . . .*
ᵃRev. 14:1 ᵇHeb. 11:10; Eph. 2:19; Phil. 3:20; Rev. 21:2 ᶜHeb. 3:12 ᵈGal. 4:26; Heb. 11:16 ᵉRev. 5:11

23 ᵃHeb. 2:12 marg.; Ex. 4:22 ᵇLuke 10:20 ᶜGen. 18:25; Ps. 50:6; 94:2 ᵈRev. 6:9, 11; Heb. 11:40

24 ᵃ1 Tim. 2:5; Heb. 8:6; 9:15 ᵇHeb. 9:19; 10:22; 1 Pet. 1:2 ᶜHeb. 11:4

25 ¹Lit., *were not escaping* ²Lit., *more*
ᵃHeb. 3:12 ᵇHeb. 1:1 ᶜHeb. 2:2f.; 10:28f. ᵈHeb. 12:19 [Gr.] ᵉHeb. 8:5; 11:7

26 ᵃEx. 19:18; Judg. 5:4f. ᵇHag. 2:6

27 ᵃ1 Cor. 7:31; Rom. 8:19, 21; Heb. 1:10ff.; Is. 34:4; 54:10; 65:17

28 ¹Lit., *have* ᵃDan. 2:44 ᵇHeb. 13:15, 21

29 ᵃDeut. 4:24; 9:3; Is. 33:14; 2 Thess. 1:7; Heb. 10:27, 31

1 ᵃRom. 12:10; 1 Thess. 4:9; 1 Pet. 1:22

2 ᵃMatt. 25:35; Rom. 12:13; 1 Pet. 4:9 ᵇGen. 18:3; 19:2

3 ᵃCol. 4:18 ᵇHeb. 10:34; Matt. 25:36

4 ᵃ1 Cor. 7:38; 1 Tim. 4:3 ᵇ1 Cor. 6:9; Gal. 5:19, 21; 1 Thess. 4:6

5 ᵃ1 Tim. 3:3; Eph. 5:3; Col 3:5 ᵇPhil. 4:11 ᶜDeut. 31:6; Josh. 1:5

6 ªPs. 118:6

7 ¹Or, *end of their life*
ªHeb. 13:17, 24 ᵇLuke 5:1;
ᶜHeb. 6:12

8 ª2 Cor. 1:19; Heb. 1:12

9 ¹Lit., *walked*
ªEph. 4:14; Jude 12 ᵇ2 Cor.
1:21; Col. 2:7 ᶜCol. 2:16
ᵈHeb. 9:10

10 ¹Or, *sacred tent*
ª1 Cor. 10:18 ᵇHeb. 8:5

11 ªEx. 29:14; Lev. 4:12, 21;
9:11; 16:27; Num. 19:3, 7

12 ªEph. 5:26; Heb. 2:11
ᵇHeb. 9:12 ᶜJohn 19:17

13 ªHeb. 11:26; 12:2; Luke
9:23

14 ªHeb. 10:34; 12:27 ᵇHeb.
11:10, 16; 12:22; 2:5; Eph.
2:19

15 ¹Lit., *confess*
ª1 Pet. 2:5 ᵇLev. 7:12 ᶜIs.
57:19; Hos. 14.2 marg.

16 ªRom. 12:13 ᵇPhil. 4:18

17 ¹Lit., *in order that they
may do this* ²Lit., *groaning*
ªHeb. 13:7, 24; 1 Cor. 16:16
ᵇIs. 62:6; Ezek. 3:17; Acts
20:28

18 ª1 Thess. 5:25 ᵇActs
24:16; 1 Tim. 1:5

19 ªPhilem. 22

20 ¹Or, *in*
ªRom. 15:33 ᵇActs 2:24;
Rom. 10:7 ᶜIs. 63:11 marg.;
John 10:11; 1 Pet. 2:25
ᵈZech. 9:11; Heb. 10:29 ᵉIs.
55:3; Jer. 32:40; Ezek. 37:26

21 ª1 Pet. 5:10 ᵇPhil. 2:13
ᶜ1 John 3:22; Heb. 12:28
ᵈRom. 11:36

"ªTHE LORD IS MY HELPER, I WILL NOT BE AFRAID.

WHAT SHALL MAN DO TO ME?"

7   Remember ªthose who led you, who spoke ᵇthe word of God to you; and considering the ¹outcome of their way of life, ᶜimitate their faith.

8   ªJesus Christ *is* the same yesterday and today, *yes* and forever.

9   ªDo not be carried away by varied and strange teachings; for it is good for the heart to ᵇbe strengthened by grace, not by ᶜfoods, ᵈthrough which those who ¹were thus occupied were not benefited.

10   We have an altar, ªfrom which those ᵇwho serve the ¹tabernacle have no right to eat.

11   For ªthe bodies of those animals whose blood is brought into the holy place by the high priest *as an offering* for sin, are burned outside the camp.

12   Therefore Jesus also, ªthat He might sanctify the people ᵇthrough His own blood, suffered ᶜoutside the gate.

13   Hence, let us go out to Him outside the camp, ªbearing His reproach.

14   For here ªwe do not have a lasting city, but we are seeking ᵇ*the city* which is to come.

15   ªThrough Him then let us continually offer up a ᵇsacrifice of praise to God, that is, ᶜthe fruit of lips that ¹give thanks to His name.

16   And do not neglect doing good and ªsharing; for ᵇwith such sacrifices God is pleased.

17   ªObey your leaders, and submit *to them*; for ᵇthey keep watch over your souls, as those who will give an account. ¹Let them do this with joy and not ²with grief, for this would be unprofitable for you.

18   ªPray for us, for we are sure that we have a ᵇgood conscience, desiring to conduct ourselves honorably in all things.

19   And I urge *you* all the more to do this, ªthat I may be restored to you the sooner.

20   Now ªthe God of peace, who ᵇbrought up from the dead the ᶜgreat Shepherd of the sheep ¹through ᵈthe blood of the ᵉeternal covenant, *even* Jesus our Lord,

21   ªequip you in every good thing to do His will, ᵇworking in us that ᶜwhich is pleasing in His sight, through Jesus Christ; ᵈto whom *be* the glory forever and ever. Amen.

22 But [a]I urge you, [b]brethren, [1]bear with [2]this [b]word of exhortation, for [c]I have written to you briefly.

23 Take notice that [a]our brother Timothy has been released; with whom, if he comes soon, I shall see you.

24 Greet [a]all of your leaders and all the [1b]saints. Those from [c]Italy greet you.

25 [a]Grace be with you all.

22 [1]Or, *listen to* [2]Lit., *the*
[a]Heb. 13:19; 3:13; 10:25;
12:5; Acts 13:15 [b]Heb. 3:1
[c]1 Pet. 5:12

23 [a]Acts 16:1; Col. 1:1

24 [1]I.e., *true believers; lit.,
holy ones*
[a]Heb. 13:7, 17; 1 Cor. 16:16
[b]Acts 9:13 [c]Acts 18:2

25 [a]Col. 4:18

THE EPISTLE OF

JAMES

Address and Greeting. Pray in Faith.
Rejoice in Lowliness.

[1a]

JAMES, a [b]bond-servant of God and [c]of the Lord Jesus Christ, to [d]the twelve tribes who are [2e]dispersed abroad, [f]greetings.

2 [a]Consider it all joy, my brethren, when you encounter [b]various [1]trials;

3 knowing that [a]the testing of your [b]faith produces [1c]endurance.

4 And let [1a]endurance have *its* perfect [2]result, that you may be [3b]perfect and complete, lacking in nothing.

5 But if any of you [a]lacks wisdom, let him ask of God, who gives to all men generously and [1]without reproach, and [b]it will be given to him.

6 But let him [a]ask in faith [b]without any doubting, for the one who doubts is like the surf of the sea [c]driven and tossed by the wind.

7 For let not that man expect that he will receive anything from the Lord,

8 *being* a [1a]double-minded man, [b]unstable in all his ways.

9 [a]But let the [1]brother of humble circumstances glory in his high position;

10 and *let* the rich man *glory* in his humiliation, because [a]like [1]flowering grass he will pass away.

11 For the sun rises with [1a]a scorching wind, and [b]withers the grass; and its flower falls off, and the beauty of its appearance is destroyed; so too

1 [1]Or, *Jacob* [2]Lit., *in the
Dispersion*
[a]Acts 12:17, 2 [b]Titus 1:1
[c]Rom. 1:1; 2 Pet. 1:1; Jude 1
[d]Luke 22:30; Acts 26:7
[e]1 Pet. 1:1; Phil. 3:20; Heb.
13:14; John 7:35 [f]Acts 15:23

2 [1]Or, *temptations*
[a]Matt. 5:12; James 1:12; 5:11
[b]1 Pet. 1:6

3 [1]Or, *steadfastness*
[a]1 Pet. 1:7 [b]Heb. 6:12 [c]Luke
21:19

4 [1]Note vs. 3 [2]Lit., *work*
[3]Or, *mature*
[a]Luke 21:19 [b]James 3:2;
Matt. 5:48; Col. 4:12;
1 Thess. 5:23

5 [1]Lit., *does not reproach*
[a]1 Kin. 3:9ff.; Prov. 2:3-6;
James 3:17 [b]Matt. 7:7

6 [a]Matt. 21:21 [b]Mark
11:23; Acts 10:20 [c]Eph. 4:14
[Matt. 14:28-31]

8 [1]Or, *doubting,
hesitating*
[a]James 4:8 [b]2 Pet. 2:14

9 [1]I.e., church member
[a]Luke 14:11

10 [1]Lit., *the flower of the
grass*
[a]1 Pet. 1:24; 1 Cor. 7:31

11 [1]Lit., *the*
[a]Matt. 20:12 [b]Is. 40:7f.; Ps.
102:4, 11

12 [1]Or, *passed the test*
[a]James 5:11; Luke 6:22;
1 Pet. 3:14; 4:14 [b]1 Cor. 9:25
[c]James 2:5; Ex. 20:6 [d]1 Cor.
2:9; 8:3

13 [1]Lit., *from* [2]Lit., *of evil
things*
[a]Gen. 22:1

15 [a]Job 15:35; Ps. 7:14; Is.
59:4 [b]Rom. 5:12; 6:23

16 [a]1 Cor. 6:9 [b]James 1:2,
19; 2:1, 5, 14; 3:1, 10; 4:11;
5:12, 19; Acts 1:15

17 [1]Lit., *shadow of turning*
[a]James 3:15, 17; John 3:3 [b]Ps.
136:7; 1 John 1:5 [c]Mal. 3:6

18 [1]Lit., *a certain first
fruits* [2]Lit., *of*
[a]John 1:13 [b]James 1:15;
1 Pet. 1:3, 23 [c]2 Cor. 6:7;
Eph. 1:13; 2 Tim. 2:15 [d]Jer.
2:3; Rev. 14:4

19 [1]Or, *Know this*
[a]John 2:21 [b]James 1:2, 16;
2:1, 5, 14; 3:1, 10; 4:11; 5:12,
19; Acts 1:15 [c]Prov. 10:19;
17:27 [d]Prov. 16:32; Eccles.
7:9

20 [a]Matt. 5:22, Eph. 4:26

21 [1]Lit., *abundance of
malice* [2]Or, *gentleness*
[a]Eph. 4:22; 1 Pet. 2:1 [b]1 Pet.
1:22f.; Eph. 1:13

22 [a]James 1:22-25; Matt.
7:24-27 [Luke 6:46-49];
Rom. 2:13; James 2:14-20

23 [1]Lit., *the face of his
birth;* or, *nature*
[a]1 Cor. 13:12

24 [1]Lit., *and he*

25 [1]Lit., *a doer of a work*
[2]Lit., *his doing*
[a]James 2:12; Gal. 2:4; John
8:32; Rom. 8:2; Gal. 6:2;
1 Pet. 2:16 [b]John 13:17

26 [a]James 3:2-12; Ps. 39:1;
141:3

476

the rich man in the midst of his pursuits will fade away.

12 [a]Blessed is a man who perseveres under trial; for once he has [1]been approved, he will receive [b]the crown of life, which *the Lord* [c]has promised to those who [d]love Him.

13 Let no one say when he is tempted, "[a]I am being tempted [1]by God"; for God cannot be tempted [2]by evil, and He Himself does not tempt any one.

14 But each one is tempted when he is carried away and enticed by his own lust.

15 Then [a]when lust has conceived, it gives birth to sin; and when [b]sin is accomplished, it brings forth death.

16 [a]Do not be deceived, [b]my beloved brethren.

17 Every good thing bestowed and every perfect gift is [a]from above, coming down from [b]the Father of lights, [c]with whom there is no variation, or [1]shifting shadow.

18 In the exercise of [a]His will He [b]brought us forth by [c]the word of truth, so that we might be [1]as it were the [d]first fruits [2]among His creatures.

19 [1]*This* [a]you know, [b]my beloved brethren. But let every one be quick to hear, [c]slow to speak *and* [d]slow to anger;

20 for [a]the anger of man does not achieve the righteousness of God.

21 Therefore [a]putting aside all filthiness and *all* [1]that remains of wickedness, in [2]humility receive [b]the word implanted, which is able to save your souls.

22 [a]But prove yourselves doers of the word, and not merely hearers who delude themselves.

23 For if any one is a hearer of the word and not a doer, he is like a man who looks at his [1]natural face [a]in a mirror;

24 for *once* he has looked at himself and gone away, [1]he has immediately forgotten what kind of person he was.

25 But one who looks intently at the perfect law, [a]the *law* of liberty and abides by it, not having become a forgetful hearer but [1]an effectual doer, this man shall be [b]blessed in [2]what he does.

26 If any one thinks himself to be religious, and yet does not [a]bridle his tongue but deceives his *own* heart, this man's religion is worthless.

27　This is pure and undefiled religion [a]in the sight of *our* God and Father, to [b]visit [c]orphans and widows in their distress, *and* to keep oneself unstained [1]by [d]the world.

27 [1]Lit., *from*
[a]Rom. 2:13; Gal 3:11 [b]Matt. 25:36 [c]Deut. 14:29; Job 31:16, 17, 21; Ps. 146:9; Is. 1:17, 23 [d]James 4:4; Titus 2:12; 2 Pet. 1:4; 2:20; Eph. 2:2; Matt. 12:32; 1 John 2:15-17

a

CHAPTER 2

My brethren, [b]do not hold your faith in our [c]glorious Lord Jesus Christ with *an attitude of* [d]personal favoritism.

1 [a]James 1:16 [b]Heb. 12:2 [c]1 Cor. 2:8; Acts 7:2 [d]James 2:9; Acts 10:34

2　For if a man comes into your [1]assembly with a gold ring and dressed in [2a]fine clothes, and there also comes in a poor man in [b]dirty clothes,

2 [1]Or, *synagogue* [2]Or, *bright*
[a]Luke 23:11; James 2:3 [b]Zech. 3:3f.

3　and you [1]pay special attention to the one who is wearing the [a]fine clothes, and say, "You sit here in a good place," and you say to the poor man, "You stand over there, or sit down by my footstool";

3 [1]Lit., *look upon*
[a]Luke 23:11; James 2:3

4　have you not made distinctions among yourselves, and become judges [a]with evil [1]motives?

4 [1]Lit., *reasonings*
[a]Luke 18:6 marg.; John 7:24

5　Listen, [a]my beloved brethren: did not [b]God choose the poor [1]of this world *to be* [c]rich in faith and [d]heirs of the kingdom which He [e]promised to those who love Him?

5 [1]Lit., *to the*
[a]James 1:16 [b]1 Cor. 1:27f.; Job 34:19 [c]Luke 12:21; Rev. 2:9 [d]Matt. 5:3; 25:34 [e]James 1:12

6　But you have dishonored the poor man. Is it not the rich who oppress you and [1]personally [a]drag you into [2]court?

6 [1]Lit., *they themselves* [2]Lit., *courts*
[a]Acts 8:3; 16:19

7　[a]Do they not blaspheme the fair name [1]by which you have been called?

7 [1]Lit., *which has been called upon you*
[a]1 Pet. 4:16; Acts 11:26

8　If, however, you [a]are fulfilling the [1]royal law, according to the Scripture, "[b]YOU SHALL LOVE YOUR NEIGHBOR AS YOURSELF," you are doing well.

8 [1]Or, *of our King*
[a]Matt. 7:12 [b]Lev. 19:18

9　But if you [a]show partiality, you are committing sin *and* are [b]convicted by the [1]law as transgressors.

9 [1]Or, *Law*
[a]James 2:1; Acts 10:34 [b]Deut. 1:17

10　For whoever keeps the whole [1]law and yet [a]stumbles in one *point*, he has become [b]guilty of all.

10 [1]Or, *Law*
[a]James 3:2; 2 Pet. 1:10; Jude 24 [b]Gal. 5:3; Matt. 5:19

11　For He who said, "[a]DO NOT COMMIT ADULTERY," also said, "[b]DO NOT COMMIT MURDER." NOW if you do not commit adultery, but do commit murder, you have become a transgressor of the [1]law.

11 [1]Or, *Law*
[a]Ex. 20:14; Deut. 5:18 [b]Ex. 20:13; Deut. 5:17

12　So speak and so act, as those who are to be judged by [a]*the* law of liberty.

12 [a]James 1:25

13　For [a]judgment *will be* merciless to one who

13 [a]Matt. 5:7; 18:32-35; Luke 6:37f.; Prov. 21:13

13 ¹Lit., *boasts against*

14 ¹Lit., *the*
ªJames 1:22ff. ᵇJames 1:16

15 ªMatt. 25:35f.; Luke 3:11

16 ª1 John 3:17f.

17 ªGal. 5:6; James 2:20, 26

18 ¹Lit., *will*
ªRom. 9:19 ᵇRom. 3:28; 4:6; Heb. 11:33 ᶜJames 3:13 ᵈMatt. 7:16f.; Gal. 5:6

19 ¹Or, *there is one God*
ªDeut. 6:4; Mark 12:29 ᵇJames 2:8 ᶜMatt. 8:29; Mark 1:24; 5:7; Luke 4:34; Acts 19:15

20 ªRom. 9:20; 1 Cor. 15:36 ᵇGal. 4:6; James 2:17, 26

21 ªGen. 22:9, 10, 12, 16-18

22 ¹Or, *by the deeds* ²Or, *completed*
ªHeb. 11:17; John 6:29 ᵇ1 Thess. 1:3

23 ªGen. 15:6; Rom. 4:3 ᵇIs. 41:8; 2 Chr. 20:7

25 ªHeb. 11:31 ᵇJosh. 2:4, 6, 15

26 ªGal. 5:6; James 2:17, 20

1 ¹Or, *greater condemnation*
ªMatt. 23:8; Rom. 2:20f.; 1 Tim. 1:7 ᵇJames 1:16; 3:10

2 ¹Lit., *word*
ªJames 2:10 ᵇJames 3:2-12; Matt. 12:34-37

has shown no mercy; mercy ¹triumphs over judgment.

14 ªWhat use is it, ᵇmy brethren, if a man says he has faith, but he has no works? Can ¹that faith save him?

15 ªIf a brother or sister is without clothing and in need of daily food,

16 and one of you says to them, "ªGo in peace, be warmed and be filled"; and yet you do not give them what is necessary for *their* body; what use is that?

17 Even so ªfaith, if it has no works, is dead, *being* by itself.

18 ªBut someone ¹may *well* say, "You have faith, and I have works; show me your ᵇfaith without the works, and I will ᶜshow you my faith ᵈby my works."

19 You believe that ¹ªGod is one. ᵇYou do well; ᶜthe demons also believe, and shudder.

20 But are you willing to recognize, ªyou foolish fellow, that ᵇfaith without works is useless?

21 ªWas not Abraham our father justified by works, when he offered up Isaac his son on the altar?

22 You see that ªfaith was working with his works, and ¹as a result of the ᵇworks faith was ²perfected;

23 and the Scripture was fulfilled which says, "ªAND ABRAHAM BELIEVED GOD, AND IT WAS RECKONED TO HIM AS RIGHTEOUSNESS," and he was called ᵇthe friend of God.

24 You see that a man is justified by works, and not by faith alone.

25 And in the same way was not ªRahab the harlot also justified by works, ᵇwhen she received the messengers and sent them out by another way?

26 For just as the body without *the* spirit is dead, so also ªfaith without works is dead.

ª

CHAPTER 3

LET not many *of you* become teachers, ᵇmy brethren, knowing that as such we shall incur a ¹stricter judgment.

2 For we all ªstumble in many *ways*. ᵇIf any one does not stumble in ¹what he says, he is a

^cperfect man, able to ^dbridle the whole body as well.

3 Now ^aif we put the bits into the horses' mouths so that they may obey us, we direct their entire body as well.

4 Behold, the ships also, though they are so great and are driven by strong winds, are still directed by a very small rudder, wherever the inclination of the pilot desires.

5 So also the tongue is a small part of the body, and *yet* it ^aboasts of great things. ^bBehold, how great a forest is set aflame by such a small fire!

6 And ^athe tongue is a fire, the *very* world of iniquity; the tongue is set among our members as that which ^bdefiles the entire body, and sets on fire the course of *our* ¹life, and is set on fire by ^{2c}hell.

7 For every ¹species of beasts and birds, of reptiles and creatures of the sea, is tamed, and has been tamed by the human ¹race.

8 But no one can tame the tongue; *it is* a restless evil *and* full of ^adeadly poison.

9 With it we bless ^a*our* Lord and Father; and with it we curse men, ^bwho have been made in the likeness of God;

10 from the same mouth come *both* blessing and cursing. My brethren, these things ought not to be this way.

11 Does a fountain send out from the same opening *both* ¹fresh and bitter *water*?

12 ^aCan a fig tree, my brethren, produce olives, or a vine produce figs? Neither *can* salt water produce ¹fresh.

13 Who among you is wise and understanding? ^aLet him show by his ^bgood behavior his deeds in the gentleness of wisdom.

14 But if you have bitter ^ajealousy and ¹selfish ambition in your heart, do not be arrogant and *so* lie against ^bthe truth.

15 This wisdom is not that which comes down ^afrom above, but is ^bearthly, ^{1c}natural, ^ddemonic.

16 For where ^ajealousy and ¹selfish ambition exist, there is disorder and every evil thing.

17 But the wisdom ^afrom above is first ^bpure, then ^cpeaceable, ^dgentle, ¹reasonable, ^efull of mercy and good fruits, ^funwavering, without ^ghypocrisy.

18 And the ^{1a}seed whose fruit is righteousness is sown in peace ²by those who make peace.

2 ^cJames 1:4 ^dJames 1:26

3 ^aPs. 32:9

5 ^aPs. 12:3f.; 73:8f. ^bProv. 26:20f.

6 ¹Or, *existence, origin* ²Gr., *Gehenna* ^aPs. 120:3, 4; Prov. 16:27 ^bMatt. 15:11, 18f.; 12:36f. ^cMatt. 5:22

7 ¹Lit., *nature*; Gr., genos

8 ^aPs. 140:3; Rom. 3:13; Eccles. 10:11 marg.

9 ^aJames 1:27 ^b1 Cor. 11:7

11 ¹Lit., *sweet*

12 ¹Note vs. 11 ^aMatt. 7:16

13 ^aJames 2:18 ^b1 Pet. 2:12

14 ¹Or, *strife* ^aJames 3:16; Rom. 2:8; 2 Cor. 12:20 ^bJames 5:19; 1:18; 1 Tim. 2:4

15 ¹Or, *unspiritual* ^aJames 1:17 ^b1 Cor. 2:6; 3:19 ^c2 Cor. 1:12; Jude 19 ^d2 Thess. 2:9f.; 1 Tim. 4:1; Rev. 2:24

16 ¹Note vs. 14 ^aJames 3:14; Rom 2:8; 2 Cor. 12:20

17 ¹Or, *willing to yield* ^aJames 1:17 ^bJames 4:8; 2 Cor. 7:11 ^cMatt. 5:9; Heb. 12:11 ^dTitus 3:2; Phil. 4:5 marg. ^eLuke 6:36; James 2:13 ^fJames 2:4 [Gr.] ^gRom. 12:9; 2 Cor. 6:6

18 ¹Lit., *fruit of righteousness* ²Or, *for* ^aProv. 11:18; Is. 32:17; Hos. 10:12; Amos 6:12; Phil. 1:11; Gal. 6:8

James 4

**Quarrels and Conflicts. "Draw Near to God."
Uncertainty of Life.**

Cross references (left column):

1 ¹Lit., *Whence wars and whence fightings* ²Lit., Are they *not* hence, from your . . .
ᵃTitus 3:9 ᵇRom. 7:23

2 ᵃ1 John 3:15; James 5:6

3 ¹Lit., *wickedly* ²Lit., *in*
ᵃ1 John 3:22; 5:14

4 ᵃIs. 54:5; Jer. 2:2; Ezek. 16:32; Matt. 12:39 ᵇJames 1:27 ᶜRom. 8:7; 1 John 2:15 ᵈJohn 15:19; Matt. 6:24

5 ¹Or, *The Spirit which He has made to dwell in us jealously desires us* ²Lit., *desires to jealousy*
ᵃNum. 23:19 ᵇ1 Cor. 6:19; 2 Cor. 6:16

6 ᵃIs. 54:7f.; Matt. 13:12 ᵇProv. 3:34; 1 Pet. 5:5; Ps. 138:6; Matt. 23:12

7 ᵃ1 Pet. 5:6 ᵇ1 Pet. 5:8f.; Eph. 4:27; 6:11f.

8 ᵃ2 Chr. 15:2; Zech. 1:3; Mal. 3:7; Heb. 7:19 ᵇIs. 1:16; Job 17:9; 1 Tim. 2:8 ᶜJer. 4:14; 1 Pet. 1:22; 1 John 3:3; James 3:17 ᵈJames 1:8

9 ᵃLuke 6:25; Prov. 14:13; Neh. 8:9

10 ᵃJames 4:6; Job 5:11; Ezek. 21:26; Luke 1:52

11 ᵃ2 Cor. 12:20; 1 Pet. 2:1; James 5:9 ᵇJames 5:7, 9, 10; 1:16 ᶜMatt. 7:1; Rom. 14:4 ᵈJames 2:8 ᵉJames 1:22

12 ᵃIs. 33:22; James 5:9 ᵇMatt. 10:28 ᶜRom. 14:4

13 ᵃJames 5:1 ᵇProv. 27:1; Luke 12:18-20

14 ¹Lit., *who do not . . .* ²Some mss. read, *the morrow; for what kind of life is yours*
ᵃPs. 102:3; Job 7:7; Ps. 39:5; 144:4

CHAPTER 4

1 WHAT is the source of quarrels and ᵃconflicts among you? ²Is not the source your pleasures that wage ᵇwar in your members?

2 You lust and do not have; *so* you ᵃcommit murder. And you are envious and cannot obtain; *so* you fight and quarrel. You do not have because you do not ask.

3 You ask and ᵃdo not receive, because you ask ¹with wrong motives, so that you may spend *it* ²on your pleasures.

4 You ᵃadulteresses, do you not know that friendship with ᵇthe world is ᶜhostility toward God? ᵈTherefore whoever wishes to be a friend of the world makes himself an enemy of God.

5 Or do you think that the Scripture ᵃspeaks to no purpose: "¹He ²jealously desires ᵇthe spirit which He has made to dwell in us"?

6 But ᵃHe gives a greater grace. Therefore *it* says, "ᵇGOD IS OPPOSED TO THE PROUD, BUT GIVES GRACE TO THE HUMBLE."

7 ᵃSubmit therefore to God. ᵇResist the devil and he will flee from you.

8 ᵃDraw near to God and He will draw near to you. ᵇCleanse your hands, you sinners; and ᶜpurify your hearts, you ᵈdouble-minded.

9 ᵃBe miserable and mourn and weep; let your laughter be turned into mourning, and your joy to gloom.

10 ᵃHumble yourselves in the presence of the Lord, and He will exalt you.

11 ᵃDo not speak against one another, ᵇbrethren. He who speaks against a brother, or ᶜjudges his brother, speaks against ᵈthe law, and judges the law; but if you judge the law, you are not ᵉa doer of the law, but a judge *of it.*

12 There is *only* one ᵃLawgiver and Judge, the One who is ᵇable to save and to destroy; but ᶜwho are you who judges your neighbor?

13 ᵃCome now, you who say, "ᵇToday or tomorrow, we shall go to such and such a city, and spend a year there and engage in business and make a profit."

14 ¹Yet you do not know ²what your life will be like tomorrow. ᵃYou are *just* a vapor that appears for a little while and then vanishes away.

15 ¹Instead, *you ought* to say, "ᵃIf the Lord wills, we shall live and also do this or that."

16 But as it is, you boast in your ¹arrogance; ᵃall such boasting is evil.

17 Therefore, ᵃto one who knows *the* ¹right thing to do, and does not do it, to him it is sin.

ᵃ   CHAPTER 5

COME now, ᵇyou rich, ᶜweep and howl for your miseries which are coming upon you.

2 ᵃYour riches have rotted and your garments have become moth-eaten.

3 Your gold and your silver have rusted; and their rust will be a witness against you and will consume your flesh like fire. It is ᵃin the Last Days that you have stored up your treasure!

4 Behold, ᵃthe pay of the laborers who mowed your fields, *and* which has been withheld by you, cries out *against you*; and ᵇthe outcry of those who did the harvesting has reached the ears of ᶜthe Lord of ¹Sabaoth.

5 You have ᵃlived luxuriously on the earth and led a life of wanton pleasure; you have ¹fattened your hearts in ᵇa day of slaughter.

6 You have condemned and ¹ᵃput to death ᵇthe righteous *man;* he does not resist you.

7 Be patient, therefore, ᵃbrethren, ᵇuntil the coming of the Lord. ᶜBehold, the farmer waits for the precious produce of the soil, being patient about it, until ¹it gets ᵈthe early and late rains.

8 ᵃYou too be patient; ᵇstrengthen your hearts, for ᶜthe coming of the Lord is ᵈat hand.

9 ᵃDo not ¹complain, ᵇbrethren, against one another, that you yourselves may not be judged; behold, ᶜthe Judge is standing ²ᵈright at the ³door.

10 As an example, ᵃbrethren, of suffering and patience, take ᵇthe prophets who spoke in the name of the Lord.

11 Behold, we count those ᵃblessed who endured. You have heard of ᵇthe ¹endurance of Job and have seen ᶜthe ²outcome of the Lord's dealings, that ᵈthe Lord is full of compassion and *is* merciful.

12 But above all, ᵃmy brethren, ᵇdo not swear, either by heaven or by earth or with any other oath; but ¹let your yes be yes, and your no, no; so that you may not fall under judgment.

15 ¹Lit., *instead of your saying*
ᵃActs 18:21

16 ¹Or, *pretensions*
ᵃ1 Cor. 5:6

17 ¹Or, *good*
ᵃLuke 12:47; 2 Pet. 2:21; John 9:41

1 ᵃJames 4:13 ᵇLuke 6:24; 1 Tim. 6:9 ᶜIs. 13:6; 15:3; Ezek. 30:2

2 ᵃJob 13:28; Is. 50:9; Matt. 6:19f.

3 ᵃJames 5:7, 8

4 ¹I.e., Hosts
ᵃLev. 19:13; Job 24:10f.; Jer. 22:13; Mal. 3:5 ᵇDeut. 24:15; Job 31:38f.; Ex. 2:23 ᶜRom. 9:29

5 ¹Lit., *nourished*
ᵃLuke 16:19; 2 Pet. 2:13; Ezek. 16:49; 1 Tim. 5:6 ᵇJer. 12:3; 25:34

6 ¹Or, *murdered*
ᵃJames 4:2 ᵇHeb. 10:38; 1 Pet. 4:18

7 ¹Or, *he*
ᵃJames 4:11; 5:9, 10 ᵇJohn 21:22; 1 Thess. 2:19 ᶜGal. 6:9 ᵈDeut. 11:14; Jer. 5:24; Joel 2:23

8 ᵃLuke 21:19 ᵇ1 Thess. 3:13 ᶜJohn 21:22; 1 Thess. 2:19 ᵈRom. 13:11, 12; 1 Pet. 4:7

9 ¹Lit., *groan* ²Lit., *before* ³Lit., *doors*
ᵃJames 4:11 ᵇJames 4:11; 5:7, 10 ᶜJames 4:12; 1 Cor. 4:5; Heb. 10:25; 1 Pet. 4:5 ᵈMatt. 24:33; Mark 13:29

10 ᵃJames 4:11; 5:7, 9 ᵇMatt. 5:12

11 ¹Or, *steadfastness* ²Lit., *end of the Lord*
ᵃMatt. 5:10; 1 Pet. 3:14 ᵇJob 1:21f.; 2:10 ᶜJob 42:10, 12 ᵈEx. 34:6; Ps. 103:8

12 ¹Lit., *let yours be the yes, yes, and the no, no*
ᵃJames 1:16 ᵇMatt. 5:34-37

13 aJames 5:10 bPs. 50:15
cCol. 3:16; 1 Cor. 14:15

14 1Lit., *having anointed*
aActs 11:30 bMark 6:13;
16:18

15 1Lit., *of* 2Or, *save* 3Lit., *it*
aJames 1:6 b1 Cor. 1:21;
James 5:20 cJohn 6:39;
2 Cor. 4:14

16 1Lit., *supplication*
aMatt. 3:6; Mark 1:5; Acts
19:18 bHeb. 12:13; 1 Pet.
2:24 cGen. 18:23-32, John
9:31

17 1Lit., *with prayer*
aActs 14:15 b1 Kin. 17:1; 18:1
cLuke 4:25

18 1Lit., *heaven* 2Lit., *gave*
a1 Kin. 18:42 b1 Kin. 18:45

19 aMatt. 18:15; Gal. 6:1
bJames 3:14

20 aRom. 11:14; 1 Cor.
1:21; James 1:21 b1 Pet. 4:8

13 Is anyone among you [a]suffering? [b]Let him pray. Is anyone cheerful? Let him [c]sing praises.

14 Is anyone among you sick? Let him call for [a]the elders of the church, and let them pray over him, [1][b]anointing him with oil in the name of the Lord;

15 and the [a]prayer [1]offered in faith will [2][b]restore the one who is sick, and the Lord will [c]raise him up, and if he has committed sins, [3]they will be forgiven him.

16 Therefore, [a]confess your sins to one another, and pray for one another, so that you may be [b]healed. [c]The effective [1]prayer of a righteous man can accomplish much.

17 Elijah was [a]a man with a nature like ours, and [b]he prayed [1]earnestly that it might not rain; and it did not rain on the earth for [c]three years and six months.

18 And he [a]prayed again, and [b]the [1]sky [2]poured rain, and the earth produced its fruit.

19 My brethren, [a]if any among you strays from [b]the truth, and one turns him back;

20 let him know that he who turns a sinner from the error of his way will [a]save his soul from death, and will [b]cover a multitude of sins.

THE FIRST EPISTLE OF

PETER

Salutation.   Our Living Hope through Christ's Resurrection.

1 a2 Pet. 1:1 b1 Pet. 2:11
cJames 1:1 dActs 2:9 cActs
16:6 fActs 16:7 gMatt. 24:22;
Luke 18:7

2 1Lit., *unto obedience
and sprinkling* 2Lit., *be
multiplied for you*
aRom. 8:29; 1 Pet. 1:20
b2 Thess. 2:13 c1 Pet. 1:14,
22; Rom. 1:5; 6:16; 16:19
dHeb. 10:22; 12:24 e2 Pet.
1:2

3 a2 Cor. 1:3 bTitus 3:5;
Gal. 6:16 c1 Pet. 1:23; James
1:18 d1 Pet. 1:13, 21; 3:5, 15;
Heb. 3:6; 2 Thess. 2:16;
1 John 3:3

[a]
P ETER, an apostle of Jesus Christ, to those who reside as [b]aliens, [c]scattered throughout [d]Pontus, [e]Galatia, [d]Cappadocia, [d]Asia, and [f]Bithynia, [g]who are chosen

2 according to the [a]foreknowledge of God the Father, [b]by the sanctifying work of the Spirit, [1]that you may [c]obey Jesus Christ and be [d]sprinkled with His blood: [e]May grace and peace [2]be yours in fullest measure.

3 [a]Blessed be the God and Father of our Lord Jesus Christ, who [b]according to His great mercy [c]has caused us to be born again to [d]a living hope

through the ᵉresurrection of Jesus Christ from the dead,

4 to *obtain* an ᵃinheritance *which is* imperishable and undefiled and ᵇwill not fade away, ᶜreserved in heaven for you,

5 who are ᵃprotected by the power of God ᵇthrough faith for ᶜa salvation ready ᵈto be revealed in the last time.

6 ᵃIn this you greatly rejoice, even though now ᵇfor a little while, ᶜif necessary, you have been distressed by ᵈvarious ¹trials,

7 that the ¹ᵃproof of your faith, *being* more precious than gold which ²is perishable, ᵇeven though tested by fire, ᶜmay be found to result in praise and glory and honor at ᵈthe revelation of Jesus Christ;

8 and ᵃthough you have not seen Him, you ᵇlove Him, and though you do not see Him now, but believe in Him, you greatly rejoice with joy inexpressible and ¹full of glory,

9 obtaining as ᵃthe outcome of your faith the salvation of ¹your souls.

10 ᵃAs to this salvation, the prophets who ᵇprophesied of the ᶜgrace that *would come* to you made careful search and inquiry,

11 ¹seeking to know what person or time ᵃthe Spirit of Christ within them was indicating as He ᵇpredicted the sufferings of Christ and the glories ²to follow.

12 It was revealed to them that they were not serving themselves but you in these things which now have been announced to you through those who ᵃpreached the gospel to you by ᵇthe Holy Spirit sent from heaven,—things into which ᶜangels long to ¹look.

13 Therefore, ᵃgird ¹your minds for action, ²ᵇkeep sober *in spirit*, fix your ᶜhope completely on the ᵈgrace ³to be brought to you at ᵉthe revelation of Jesus Christ.

14 As ¹ᵃobedient children, do not ²ᵇbe conformed to the former lusts *which were yours* in your ᶜignorance,

15 but ¹ᵃlike the Holy One who called you, ²ᵇbe holy yourselves also ᶜin all *your* behavior;

16 because it is written, "ᵃYOU SHALL BE HOLY, FOR I AM HOLY."

17 And if you ᵃaddress as Father the One who ᵇimpartially ᶜjudges according to each man's work,

3 ᶜl Pet. 3:21; 1 Cor. 15:20

4 ᵃActs 20:32; Rom. 8:17; Col. 3:24 ᵇl Tim. 5:4 ᶜ2 Tim. 4:8; Heb. 11:16

5 ᵃPhil. 4:7; John 10:28 ᵇEph. 2:8 ᶜl Cor. 1:21; 2 Thess. 2:13 ᵈl Pet. 4:13; 5:1; Rom. 8:18

6 ¹Or, *temptations* ᵃRom. 5:2 ᵇl Pet. 5:10 ᶜl Pet. 3:17 ᵈJames 1:2; 1 Pet. 4:12

7 ¹Or, *genuineness* ²Lit., *perishes* ᵃJames 1:3 ᵇJob 23:10; Ps. 66:10; Prov. 17:3; Is. 48:10; Zech. 13:9; Mal. 3:3; 1 Cor. 3:13 ᶜRom. 2:7, 10; 2 Cor. 4:17; Heb. 12:11 ᵈl Pet. 1:13; 4:13; Luke 17:30

8 ¹Lit., *glorified* ᵃJohn 20:29 ᵇEph. 3:19

9 ¹Some ancient mss. omit *your* ᵃRom. 6:22

10 ᵃl Pet. 1:10-12; Matt. 13:17; Luke 10:24 ᵇMatt. 26:24; Luke 24:27, 44 ᶜl Pet. 1:13; Col. 3:4

11 ¹Lit., *inquiring* ²Lit., *after these* ᵃRom. 8:9; 2 Pet. 1:21 ᵇMatt. 26:24; Luke 24:27, 44

12 ¹Or, *gain a clear glimpse* ᵃl Pet. 1:25; 4:6 ᵇActs 2:2-4 ᶜLuke 2:13; Eph. 3:10; 1 Tim. 3:16

13 ¹Lit., *the loins of your mind* ²Lit., *be sober* ³Or, *which is announced* ᵃEph. 6:14 ᵇl Pet. 4:7; 5:8; 1 Thess. 5:6, 8; 2 Tim. 4:5; Rom. 12:3; Titus 2:6 ᶜl Pet. 1:3 ᵈl Pet. 1:10; Col. 3:4 ᵉl Pet. 1:7; 4:13; Luke 17:30

14 ¹Lit., *children of obedience* ²Or, *conform yourselves* ᵃl Pet. 1:2 ᵇRom. 12:2; 1 Pet. 4:2f. ᶜEph. 4:18

15 ¹Lit., *according to* ²Or, *become* ᵃl Thess. 4:7; 1 John 3:3 ᵇ2 Cor. 7:1 ᶜJames 3:13

16 ᵃLev. 11:44f.; 19:2; 20:7

17 ᵃPs. 89:26; Jer. 3:19; Mal. 1:6; Matt. 6:9 ᵇActs 10:34 ᶜMatt. 16:27

483

17 d1 Pet. 3:15; 2 Cor. 7:1;
Heb. 12:28 e1 Pet. 2:11; Eph.
2:19

18 1Or, *ransomed*
a Is. 52:3; 1 Cor. 6:20; Titus
2:14; Heb. 9:12; 2 Pet. 2:1;
Matt. 20:28 bEph. 4:17

19 aActs 20:28; 1 Pet. 1:2
bJohn 1:29; Heb. 9:14

20 1Lit., *at the end of the
times*
aActs 2:23; 1 Pet. 1:2; Eph.
1:4; Rev. 13:8 bMatt. 25:34
cHeb. 9:26 dHeb. 2:14

21 aRom. 4:24; 10:9 bHeb.
2:9; 1 Tim. 3:16; John 17:5,
24 c1 Pet. 1:3

22 1Lit., *unhypocritical*
2Some mss. read, *a clean
heart*
a1 Pet. 1:2 bJames 4:8 cJohn
13:34; Rom. 12:10 Heb.
13:1; 1 Pet. 2:17; 3:8

23 a1 Pet. 1:3; John 3:3
bJohn 1:13 cHeb. 4:12

24 aIs. 40:6ff.; James 1:10f.

25 1Lit., *preached as good
news to you*
aIs. 40:8 bHeb. 6:5

1 1Or, *wickedness* 2plural
nouns
aEph. 4:22, 25, 31; James
1:21 bJames 4:11

2 1Or, *unadulterated* 2Or,
spiritual (Gr., logikos) *milk*
3Or, *up to salvation*
aMatt. 18:3; 19:14; Mark
10:15; Luke 18:17; 1 Cor.
14:20 b1 Cor. 3:2 cEph.
4:15f.

3 1Lit., *that the Lord is
kind*
aHeb. 6:5 bPs. 34:8; Titus 3:4

4 1Lit., *chosen;* or, *elect*
a1 Pet. 2:7

5 1Or, *allow yourselves to
be built up;* or, *build
yourselves up*
a1 Cor. 3:9 b1 Tim. 3:15;
Gal. 6:10 c1 Pet. 2:9; Is. 61:6;
66:21; Rev. 1:6 dHeb. 13:15;
Rom. 15:16

6 1Or, *a scripture*
2Or, *it* 3Or, *put to shame*
aIs. 28:16; 1 Pet. 2:6, 8; Rom.
9:32, 33; 10:11 bEph. 2:20

484

conduct yourselves din fear during the time of your
estay *upon earth;*

18 knowing that you were not 1aredeemed with
perishable things like silver or gold from your bfu-
tile way of life inherited from your forefathers,

19 but with precious ablood, as of a blamb un-
blemished and spotless, *the blood* of Christ.

20 For He was aforeknown before bthe foundation of the world, but has cappeared 1in these last
times dfor the sake of you

21 who through Him are abelievers in God,
who raised Him from the dead and bgave Him
glory, so that your faith and chope are in God.

22 Since you have ain obedience to the truth
bpurified your souls for a 1csincere love of the brethren, fervently love one another from 2the heart,

23 for you have been aborn again bnot of seed
which is perishable but imperishable, *that is,*
through the living and abiding cword of God.

24 For,

"aALL FLESH IS LIKE GRASS,
AND ALL ITS GLORY LIKE THE FLOWER OF
    GRASS.
THE GRASS WITHERS,
AND THE FLOWER FALLS OFF,

25 aBUT THE WORD OF THE LORD ABIDES
    FOREVER."
And this is bthe word which was 1preached to you.

CHAPTER 2

THEREFORE, aputting aside all 1malice and all
guile and 2hypocrisy and 2envy and all 2bslander,

2 alike newborn babes, long for the 1bpure
milk 2of the word, that by it you may cgrow 3in
respect to salvation,

3 if you have atasted 1bthe kindness of the
Lord.

4 And coming to Him as to a living stone,
arejected by men, but 1choice and precious in the
sight of God,

5 ayou also, as living stones, 1are being built
up as a bspiritual house for a holy cpriesthood, to
doffer up spiritual sacrifices acceptable to God
through Jesus Christ.

6 For *this* is contained in 1Scripture:

"aBEHOLD I LAY IN ZION A CHOICE STONE, A
bPRECIOUS CORNER *STONE,*
AND HE WHO BELIEVES IN 2HIM SHALL NOT
BE 3DISAPPOINTED."

**The Example of Christ's Sufferings.
Human Institutions.**

1 Peter 2

7 ªThis precious value, then, is for you who believe, but for those who disbelieve,

"ᵇTHE STONE WHICH THE BUILDERS ᶜREJECTED, THIS BECAME THE VERY CORNER STONE,

8 and,

"ªA STONE OF STUMBLING AND A ROCK OF OFFENSE";

ᵇfor they stumble because they are disobedient to the word, ᶜand to this *doom* they were also appointed.

9 But you are ªA CHOSEN RACE, A ROYAL ᵇPRIESTHOOD, A ᶜHOLY NATION, ᵈA PEOPLE FOR God's OWN POSSESSION, that you may proclaim the excellencies of Him who has called you ᵉout of darkness into His marvelous light;

10 ªfor you once wcrc NOT A PEOPLE, but now you are THE PEOPLE OF GOD; you had NOT RECEIVED MERCY, but now you have RECEIVED MERCY.

11 ªBeloved, ᵇI urge you as ᶜaliens and strangers to abstain from ᵈfleshly lusts, which wage ᵉwar against the soul.

12 ªKeep your behavior excellent among the Gentiles, so that in the thing in which they ᵇslander you as evildoers, they may ¹on account of your good deeds, as they observe *them*, ᶜglorify God ᵈin the day of ²visitation.

13 ªSubmit yourselves for the Lord's sake to every human institution: whether to a king as the one in authority;

14 or to governors as sent ¹by him ªfor the punishment of evildoers and the ᵇpraise of those who do right.

15 For ªsuch is the will of God that by doing right you may ᵇsilence the ignorance of foolish men.

16 *Act* as ªfree men, and do not use your freedom as a covering for evil, but *use it* as ᵇbondslaves of God.

17 ªHonor all men; ᵇlove the brotherhood, ᶜfear God, ᵈhonor the ¹king.

18 ªServants, be submissive to your masters with all respect, not only to those who arc good and ᵇgentle, but also to those who are ¹unreasonable.

19 For this *finds* ¹favor, if for the sake of ªconscience toward God a man bears up under sorrows when suffering unjustly.

7 ª1 Pet. 2:7, 8; 2 Cor. 2:16 ᵇPs. 118:22; Matt. 21:42; Luke 2:34 ᶜ1 Pet. 2:4

8 ªIs. 8:14 ᵇ1 Cor. 1:23; Gal. 5:11 ᶜRom. 9:22

9 ªDeut. 10:15; Is. 43:20f. ᵇ1 Pet. 2:5; Is. 61:6; 66:21; Rev. 1:6 ᶜEx. 19:6; Deut. 7:6 ᵈTitus 2:14 ᵉActs 26:18; Is. 42:16; 2 Cor. 4:6

10 ªHos. 1:10; 2:23; Rom. 9:25; Rom. 10:19

11 ªHeb. 6:9; 1 Pet. 4.12 ᵇRom. 12:1 ᶜLev. 25:23; Ps. 39:12; 1 Pet. 1:17; Heb. 11:13; Eph. 2:19 ᵈRom. 13:14; Gal. 5:16, 24 ᵉJames 4:1

12 ¹Or, *as a result of* ²I.e., Christ's coming again in judgment ª1 Pet. 2:15; 3:16; 2 Cor. 8:21; Phil. 2:15; Titus 2:8 ᵇActs 28:22 ᶜ1 Pet. 4:11, 16; Matt. 5:16; Matt. 9:8; John 13:31 ᵈIs. 10:3; Luke 19:44

13 ªRom. 13:1

14 ¹Lit., *through* ªRom. 13:4 ᵇRom. 13:3

15 ª1 Pet. 3:17 ᵇ1 Pet. 2:12

16 ªJohn 8:32; James 1:25 ᵇ1 Cor. 7:22; Rom. 6:22

17 ¹Or, *emperor* ªRom. 12:10; 13:7 ᵇ1 Pet. 1:22 ᶜProv. 24:21 ᵈProv. 24:21; Matt. 22:21; 1 Pet. 2:13

18 ¹Or, *perverse* ªEph. 6:5 ᵇJames 3:17

19 ¹Or, *grace* ª1 Pet. 3:14, 17; Rom. 13:5

20 [1]Note vs. 19
[a]1 Pet. 3:17

21 [a]1 Pet. 3:9; Acts 14:22
[b]1 Pet. 3:18; 4:1, 13 [c]Matt.
11:29; 16:24

22 [a]Is. 53:9; 2 Cor. 5:21

23 [1]Lit., who [2]Lit., was not
reviling
[a]1 Pet. 3:9; Is. 53:7; Heb.
12:3

24 [1]Or, carried . . . up to
the cross [2]Lit., wood [3]Lit.,
sins [4]Lit., wound, or welt
[a]Is. 33.4, 11; 1 Cor. 15:3;
Heb. 9:28 [b]Acts 5:30 [c]Rom.
6:2, 13 [d]Is. 53:5 [e]Heb.
12:13; James 5:16

25 [1]Or, Bishop, Overseer
[a]Is. 53:6 [b]John 10:11; 1 Pet.
5:4

1 [a]1 Pet. 2:18; 3:7 [b]Eph.
5:22 [c]1 Cor. 9:19

2 [1]Lit., with fear

3 [a]1 Tim. 2:9; Is. 3:18ff.

4 [a]Rom. 7:22

5 [a]1 Tim. 5:5; 1 Pet. 1:3

6 [1]Lit., and are not
[a]Gen. 18:12 [b]1 Pet. 3:14

7 [a]Eph. 5:25; Col. 3:19
[b]1 Thess. 4:4

486

20   For what credit is there if, when you sin and are harshly treated, you endure it with patience? But if [a]when you do what is right and suffer *for it* you patiently endure it, this *finds* [1]favor with God.

21   For [a]you have been called for this purpose, [b]since Christ also suffered for you, leaving you [c]an example for you to follow in His steps,

22   WHO [a]COMMITTED NO SIN, NOR WAS ANY DE- CEIT FOUND IN HIS MOUTH;

23   [1]and while being [a]reviled, He [2]did not revile in return; while suffering, He uttered no threats, but kept entrusting *Himself* to Him who judges righteously;

24   and He Himself [1a]bore our sins in His body on the [2b]cross, that we [c]might die to [3]sin and live to righteousness; for [d]by His [4]wounds you were [e]healed.

26   For you were [a]continually straying like sheep, but now you have returned to the [b]Shepherd and [1]Guardian of your souls.

[a]   CHAPTER 3

IN the same way, you wives, [b]be submissive to your own husbands so that even if any *of them* are disobedient to the word they may be [c]won without a word by the behavior of their wives,

2   as they observe your chaste and [1]respectful behavior.

3   [a]And let not your adornment be external *only*—braiding the hair, and wearing gold jewelry, and putting on dresses;

4   but *let it be* [a]the hidden person of the heart, with the imperishable quality of a gentle and quiet spirit, which is precious in the sight of God.

5   For in this way in former times the holy women also, [a]who hoped in God, used to adorn themselves, being submissive to their own hus- bands.

6   Thus Sarah obeyed Abraham, [a]calling him lord, and you have become her children if you do what is right [1b]without being frightened by any fear.

7   [a]You husbands likewise, live with your wives in an understanding way, as with a weaker [b]vessel, since she is a woman; and grant her honor as a fellow-heir of the grace of life, so that your prayers may not be hindered.

8 [1]To sum up, [a]let all be harmonious, sympathetic, [b]brotherly, [c]kind-hearted, and [d]humble in spirit;

9 [a]not returning evil for evil, or [b]insult for insult, but [1]giving a [c]blessing instead; for [d]you were called for the very purpose that you might [e]inherit a blessing.

10 For
"[a]LET HIM WHO MEANS TO LOVE LIFE AND
    SEE GOOD DAYS
REFRAIN HIS TONGUE FROM EVIL AND HIS
    LIPS FROM SPEAKING GUILE.

11 "[a]AND LET HIM TURN AWAY FROM EVIL AND
    DO GOOD;
LET HIM SEEK PEACE AND PURSUE IT.

12 "[a]FOR THE EYES OF THE LORD ARE UPON THE
    RIGHTEOUS,
AND HIS EARS ATTEND TO THEIR PRAYER,
BUT THE FACE OF THE LORD IS AGAINST
    THOSE WHO DO EVIL."

13 And [a]who is there to harm you if you prove zealous for what is good?

14 But even if you should [a]suffer for the sake of righteousness, [b]*you are* blessed. [c]AND DO NOT FEAR THEIR [1]INTIMIDATION, AND DO NOT BE TROUBLED,

15 but [1]SANCTIFY [a]Christ as Lord in your hearts, always *being* ready [b]to make a defense to every one who asks you to give an account for the [c]hope that is in you, yet [d]with gentleness and [2]reverence;

16 [1]and keep a [a]good conscience so that in the thing in which [b]you are slandered, those who revile your good behavior in Christ may be put to shame.

17 For [a]it is better, [b]if [1]God should will it so, that you suffer for doing what is right rather than for doing what is wrong.

18 For [a]Christ also died for sins [b]once for all, *the* just for *the* unjust, in order that He might [c]bring us to God, having been put to death [d]in the flesh, but made alive [e]in the [1]spirit;

19 in [1]whom also He went and [a]made proclamation to the spirits *now* in prison,

20 who once were disobedient, when the [a]patience of God [b]kept waiting in the days of Noah, during the construction of [c]the ark, in which a few, that is, [d]eight [e]persons, were brought safely through *the* water.

21 [a]And corresponding to that, baptism now

8 [1]Or, *Finally*
[a]Rom. 12:16 [b]1 Pet. 1:22
[c]Eph. 4:32 [d]Eph. 4:2; Phil. 2:3; 1 Pet. 5:5

9 [1]Lit., *blessing instead*
[a]Rom. 12:17; 1 Thess. 5:15
[b]1 Pet. 2:23; 1 Cor. 4:12
[c]Luke 6:28; Rom. 12:14;
1 Cor. 4:12 [d]1 Pet. 2:21 [e]Gal. 3:14; Heb. 6:14; 12:17

10 [a]Ps. 34:12, 13

11 [a]Ps. 34:14

12 [a]Ps. 34:15, 16

13 [a]Prov. 16:7

14 [1]Lit., *fear*
[a]1 Pet. 2:19ff.; 4:15f. [b]James 5:11 [c]Is. 8:12f.; 1 Pet. 3:6

15 [1]I.e., set apart [2]Or, *fear*
[a]1 Pet. 1:3 [b]Col. 4:6 [c]1 Pet. 1:3 [d]2 Tim. 2:25 [e]1 Pet. 1:17

16 [1]Lit., *having a good . . .*
[a]1 Pet. 3:21; 1 Tim. 1:5;
Heb. 13:18 [b]1 Pet. 2:12, 15

17 [1]Lit., *the will of God*
[a]1 Pet. 2:20; 4:15f. [b]1 Pet. 1:6; 2:15; 4:19; Acts 18:21

18 [1]Or, *Spirit*
[a]1 Pet. 2:21 [b]Heb. 9:26, 28;
10:10 [c]Rom. 5:2; Eph. 3:12
[d]1 Pet. 4:1; Col. 1:22 [e]1 Pet. 4:6

19 [1]Or, *which*
[a]1 Pet. 4:6

20 [a]Rom. 2:4 [b]Gen. 6:3, 5, 13f.; Heb. 11:7 [c]2 Pet. 2:5;
Gen. 8:18 [e]Acts 2:41; 1 Pet. 1:9, 22; 2:25; 4:19

21 [a]Titus 3:5; Acts 16:33

487

21 ᵇHeb. 9:14; 10:22 ᶜ1 Pet.
3:16; 1 Tim. 1:5; Heb. 13:18
ᵈ1 Pet. 1:3

22 ᵃMark 16:19 ᵇHeb. 4:14;
6:20 ᶜRom. 8:38f.; Heb. 1:6

1 ¹I.e., suffered death
ᵃ1 Pet. 2:21 ᵇEph. 6:13
ᶜRom. 6:7

2 ᵃRom. 6:2; Col. 3:3
ᵇ1 Pet. 1:14

3 ¹Lit., lawless
ᵃ1 Cor. 12:2 ᵇRom. 13:13;
Eph. 2:2; 4:17ff.

4 ᵃEph. 5:18 ᵇ1 Pet. 3:16

5 ᵃActs 10.42; 2 Tim. 4:1;
Rom. 14:9

6 ᵃ1 Pet. 1:12; 3:19

7 ¹Lit., has come near
²Lit., prayers
ᵃRom. 13:11; James 5:8;
Heb. 9:26; 1 John 2:18
ᵇ1 Pet. 1:13

8 ᵃ1 Pet. 1:22 ᵇProv. 10:12;
James 5:20; 1 Cor. 13:4ff.

9 ᵃ1 Tim. 3:2; Heb. 13:2
ᵇPhil. 2:14

10 ᵃRom. 12:6f. ᵇ1 Cor. 4:1

11 ¹Lit., from
ᵃ1 Thess. 2:4; Titus 2:1, 15;
Heb. 13:7 ᵇActs 7:38 ᶜEph.
6:10; 1:19 ᵈ1 Cor. 10:31;
1 Pet. 2:12 ᵉRev. 1:6; 5:13;
1 Pet. 5:11; Rom. 11:36

12 ᵃ1 Pet. 2:11 ᵇ1 Pet. 1:6f.

saves you—ᵇnot the removal of dirt from the flesh, but an appeal to God for a ᶜgood conscience—through ᵈthe resurrection of Jesus Christ,

22 ᵃwho is at the right hand of God, ᵇhaving gone into heaven, ᶜafter angels and authorities and powers had been subjected to Him.

CHAPTER 4

THEREFORE, since ᵃChrist has ¹suffered in the flesh, ᵇarm yourselves also with the same purpose, because ᶜhe who has ¹suffered in the flesh has ceased from sin,

2 ᵃso as to live ᵇthe rest of the time in the flesh no longer for the lusts of men, but for the will of God.

3 For ᵃthe time already past is sufficient *for you to have carried out the desire of the Gentiles,* ᵇhaving pursued a course of sensuality, lusts, drunkenness, carousals, drinking parties and ¹abominable idolatries.

4 And in *all* this, they are surprised that you do not run with *them* into the same excess of ᵃdissipation, and they ᵇmalign *you;*

5 but they shall give account to Him who is ready to judge ᵃthe living and the dead.

6 For ᵃthe gospel has for this purpose been preached even to those who are dead, that though they are judged in the flesh as men, they may live in the spirit according to *the will of* God.

7 ᵃThe end of all things ¹is at hand; therefore, ᵇbe of sound judgment and sober *spirit* for the purpose of ²prayer.

8 Above all, ᵃkeep fervent in your love for one another, because ᵇlove covers a multitude of sins.

9 ᵃBe hospitable to one another without ᵇcomplaint.

10 ᵃAs each one has received a *special* gift, employ it in serving one another, as good ᵇstewards of the manifold grace of God.

11 ᵃWhoever speaks, *let him speak,* as it were, the ᵇutterances of God; whoever serves, *let him do so* as ¹ᶜby the strength which God supplies; so that ᵈin all things God may be glorified through Jesus Christ, ᵉto whom belongs the glory and dominion forever and ever. Amen.

12 ᵃBeloved, do not be surprised at the ᵇfiery ordeal among you, which comes upon you for your

testing, as though some strange thing were happening to you;

13 but to the degree that you [a]share the sufferings of Christ, keep on rejoicing; so that also at the [b]revelation of His glory, [c]you may rejoice with exultation.

14 If you are reviled [1][a]for the name of Christ, [b]you are blessed, [c]because the Spirit of glory and of God rests upon you.

15 By no means [a]let any of you suffer as a murderer, or thief, or evil-doer, or a [1][b]troublesome meddler;

16 but if *anyone suffers* as a [a]Christian, let him not feel ashamed, but in that name let him [b]glorify God.

17 For *it is* time for judgment [a]to begin [1]with [b]the household of God; and if *it* [c]*begins* with us first, what *will be* the outcome for those [d]who do not obey the [e]gospel of God?

18 [a]AND IF IT IS WITH DIFFICULTY THAT THE RIGHTEOUS IS SAVED, [1]WHAT WILL BECOME OF THE [b]GODLESS MAN AND THE SINNER?

19 Therefore, let those also who suffer according to [a]the will of God entrust their souls to a faithful Creator in doing what is right.

[a] CHAPTER 5

THEREFORE, I exhort the elders among you, as *your* [b]fellow-elder and [c]witness of the sufferings of Christ, and a [d]partaker also of the glory that is to be revealed,

2 shepherd [a]the flock of God among you, [b]not under compulsion, but voluntarily, according to *the will of* God; and [c]not for sordid gain, but with eagerness;

3 nor yet as [a]lording it over [1]those allotted to your charge, but [2]proving to be [b]examples to the flock.

4 And when the Chief [a]Shepherd appears, you will receive the [b]unfading [1][c]crown of glory.

5 [a]You younger men, likewise, [b]be subject to your elders; and all of you, clothe yourselves with [c]humility toward one another, for [d]GOD IS OPPOSED TO THE PROUD, BUT GIVES GRACE TO THE HUMBLE.

6 [a]Humble yourselves, therefore, under the mighty hand of God, that He may exalt you at the proper time,

13 [a]Phil. 3:10; 2 Cor. 1:5; 4:10; Rom. 8:17 [b]1 Pet. 1:7; 5:1 [c]2 Tim. 2:12

14 [1]Lit., *in* [a]John 15:21; 1 Pet. 4:16; Heb. 11:26 [b]Matt. 5:11; Luke 6:22; Acts 5:41 [c]2 Cor. 4:10f., 16

15 [1]Lit., *one who oversees others' affairs* [a]1 Pet. 2:19f.; 3:17 [b]1 Thess. 4:11; 2 Thess. 3:11; 1 Tim. 5:13

16 [a]Acts 5:41; 28:22; James 2:7 [b]1 Pet. 4:11

17 [1]Lit., *from* [a]Jer. 25:29; Ezek. 9:6; Amos 3:2 [b]1 Tim. 3:15; Heb. 3:6; 1 Pet. 2:5 [c]Rom. 2:9 [d]2 Thess. 1:8 [e]Rom. 1:1

18 [1]Lit., *where will appear* [a]Prov. 11:31; Luke 23:31 [b]1 Tim. 1:9

19 [a]1 Pet. 3:17

1 [a]Acts 11:30 [b]2 John 1; 3 John 1 [c]Luke 24:48; Heb. 12:1 [d]1 Pet. 1:5, 7; 4:13; Rev. 1:9

2 [a]John 21:16; Acts 20:28 [Gr.] [b]Philem. 14 [c]1 Tim. 3:8

3 [1]Lit., *the allotments* [2]Or, *becoming* [a]Ezek. 34:4; Matt. 20:25f. [b]Phil. 3:17; 1 Thess. 1:7; 2 Thess. 3:9; 1 Tim. 4:12; Titus 2:7; John 13:15

4 [1]Lit., *wreath* [a]1 Pet. 2:25 [b]1 Pet. 1:4 [c]1 Cor. 9:25

5 [a]Luke 22:26; 1 Tim. 5:1 [b]Eph. 5:21 [c]1 Pet. 3:8 [d]Prov. 3:34; James 4:6

6 [a]James 4:10

7 ªMatt. 6:25

8 ª1 Pet. 1:13 ᵇMatt. 24:42
ᶜJames 4:7 ᵈ2 Tim. 4:17

9 ¹Lit., *whom resist* ²Lit.,
brotherhood
ªJames 4:7 ᵇCol. 2:5 ᶜActs
14:22; Heb. 12:8

10 ¹Omitted by some
ancient mss.
ª1 Pet. 1:6 ᵇ1 Pet. 4:10
ᶜ1 Cor. 1:9; 1 Thess. 2:12
ᵈ2 Cor. 4:17; 2 Tim. 2:10
ᵉ1 Cor. 1:10; Heb. 13:21
ᶠRom. 16:25; 2 Thess. 2:17;
3:3

11 ªRom. 11:36; 1 Pet. 4:11

12 ¹Lit., *(as I consider)*
ª2 Cor. 1:19 ᵇHeb. 13:22
ᶜ1 Pet. 1:13; 4:10; Acts 11:23
ᵈ1 Cor. 15:1

13 ¹Some mss. read, *The
church which*
ªActs 12:12

14 ªRom. 16:16 ᵇEph. 6:23

7 casting all your ªanxiety upon Him, because He cares for you.

8 ªBe of sober *spirit*, ᵇbe on the alert. Your adversary, ᶜthe devil, prowls about like a roaring ᵈlion, seeking someone to devour.

9 ¹ªBut resist him, ᵇfirm in *your* faith, knowing that ᶜthe same experiences of suffering are being accomplished by your ²brethren who are in the world.

10 And after you have suffered ªfor a little, the ᵇGod of all grace, who ᶜcalled you to His ᵈeternal glory in Christ, will Himself ᵉperfect, ᶠconfirm, strengthen *and* ¹establish you.

11 ªTo Him *be* dominion forever and ever. Amen.

12 Through ªSilvanus, our faithful brother (¹for so I regard *him*), ᵇI have written to you briefly, exhorting and testifying that this is ᶜthe true grace of God. ᵈStand firm in it!

13 ¹She who is in Babylon, chosen together with you, sends you greetings, and *so does* my son, ªMark.

14 ªGreet one another with a kiss of love. ᵇPeace be to you all who are in Christ.

THE SECOND EPISTLE OF
PETER

Salutation. Growth in Christian Virtue.

1 ¹Most early mss. read,
Simeon ²Or, *value* ³Or, *in*
ªRom. 1:1; Phil. 1:1; Jude 1;
James 1:1 ᵇ1 Pet. 1:1 ᶜRom.
1:12; 2 Cor. 4:13; Titus 1:4
ᵈRom. 3:21-26 ᵉTitus 2:13

2 ª1 Pet. 1:2; Rom. 1:7
ᵇ2 Pet. 1:3, 8; 2:20; 3:18;
John 17:3; Phil. 3:8

3 ¹Or possibly, *to* ²Or,
virtue
ª1 Pet. 1:5 ᵇ2 Pet. 1:2, 8;
2:20; 3:18; John 17:3; Phil.
3:8 ᶜ1 Thess. 2:12; 2 Thess.
2:14; 1 Pet. 5:10

4 ¹Lit., *through which*
(things)
ª2 Pet. 3:9, 13 ᵇEph. 4:13, 24;
Heb. 12:10; 1 John 3:2
ᶜ2 Pet. 2:18, 20 ᵈ2 Pet. 2:19
ᵉJames 1:27

1

SIMON PETER, a ªbond-servant and ᵇapostle of Jesus Christ, to those who have received ᶜa faith of the same ²kind as ours, ³by ᵈthe righteousness of ᵉour God and Savior, Jesus Christ:

2 ªGrace and peace be multiplied to you in ᵇthe knowledge of God and of Jesus our Lord;

3 seeing that His ªdivine power has granted to us everything pertaining to life and godliness, through the true ᵇknowledge of Him who ᶜcalled us ¹by His own glory and ²excellence.

4 ¹For by these He has granted to us His precious and magnificent ªpromises, in order that by them you might become ᵇpartakers of *the* divine nature, having ᶜescaped the ᵈcorruption that is in ᵉthe world by lust.

5 Now for this very reason also, applying all diligence, in your faith ᵃsupply ᵇmoral ¹excellence, and in *your* moral excellence, ᶜknowledge;

6 and in *your* knowledge, ᵃself-control, and in *your* self-control, ᵇperseverance, and in *your* perseverance, ᶜgodliness;

7 and in *your* godliness, ᵃbrotherly kindness, and in *your* brotherly kindness, *Christian* love.

8 For if these *qualities* are yours and are increasing, they render you neither useless nor ᵃunfruitful in the true ᵇknowledge of our Lord Jesus Christ.

9 For he who lacks these *qualities* is ᵃblind *or* short-sighted, having forgotten *his* ᵇpurification from his former sins.

10 Therefore, brethren, be all the more diligent to make certain about His ᵃcalling and ᵇchoosing you; for as long as you practice these things, you will never ᶜstumble;

11 for in this way the entrance into ᵃthe eternal kingdom of our ᵇLord and Savior Jesus Christ will be ᶜabundantly ᵈsupplied to you.

12 Therefore, ᵃI shall always be ready to remind you of these things, even though you *already* know *them*, and have been established in ᵇthe truth which is present with *you*.

13 And I consider it ᵃright, as long as I am in ᵇthis *earthly* dwelling, to ᶜstir you up by way of reminder,

14 knowing that ᵃthe laying aside of my *earthly* dwelling is imminent, ᵇas also our Lord Jesus Christ has made clear to me.

15 And I will also be diligent that at any time after my ᵃdeparture you may be able to call these things to mind.

16 For we did not follow cleverly devised ᵃtales when we made known to you the ᵇpower and coming of our Lord Jesus Christ, but we were ᶜeyewitnesses of His majesty.

17 For when He received honor and glory from God the Father, such an ¹ᵃutterance as this was ²made to Him by the ᵇMajestic Glory, "This is My beloved Son with whom I am well pleased," —

18 and we ourselves heard this ¹utterance made from heaven when we were with Him on the ᵃholy mountain.

19 ¹And *so* we have ᵃthe prophetic word *made* more ᵇsure, to which you do well to pay attention

5 ¹Or, *virtue*
ᵃ2 Pet. 1:11 ᵇ2 Pet. 1:3 ᶜCol. 2:3; 2 Pet. 1:2

6 ᵃActs 24:25 ᵇLuke 21:19 ᶜ2 Pet. 1:3

7 ᵃRom. 12:10; 1 Pet. 1:22

8 ᵃCol. 1:10 ᵇ2 Pet. 1:2, 3; 2:20; 3:18; John 17:3; Phil. 3:8

9 ᵃ1 John 2:11 ᵇEph. 5:26; Titus 2:14

10 ᵃRom. 11:29; 2 Pet. 1:3; Matt. 22:14 ᵇ1 Thess. 1:4 ᶜJude 24; 2 Pet. 3:17; James 2:10

11 ᵃ2 Tim. 4:18 ᵇ2 Pet. 2:20; 3:18 ᶜRom. 2:4; 1 Tim. 6:17 ᵈ2 Pet. 1:5

12 ᵃJude 5; Phil. 3:1; 1 John 2:21 ᵇCol. 1:5f.; 2 John 2

13 ᵃPhil. 1:7 ᵇ2 Cor. 5:1, 4; 2 Pet. 1:14 ᶜ2 Pet. 3:1

14 ᵃ2 Tim. 4:6; 2 Cor. 5:1 ᵇJohn 13:36; 21:19

15 ᵃLuke 9:31

16 ᵃ1 Tim. 1:4; 2 Pet. 2:3 ᵇMark 13:26; 14:62; 1 Thess. 2:19 ᶜMatt. 17:1ff.; Mark 9:2ff.; Luke 9:28ff.

17 ¹Lit., *voice* ²Lit., *borne* ᵃMatt. 17:5; Mark 9:7; Luke 9:35 ᵇHeb. 1:3

18 ¹Lit., *voice borne* ᵃEx. 3:5; Josh. 5:15

19 ¹Or, *And we have the even surer prophetic word* ᵃ1 Pet. 1:10f. ᵇHeb. 2:2

491

19 cPs. 119:105 dLuke 1:78
eRev. 22:16 f2 Cor. 4:6

20 a2 Pet. 3:3 bRom. 12:6

21 aJer. 23:26; 2 Tim. 3:16
b1 Pet. 1:11; 2 Sam. 23:2;
Luke 1:70; Acts 1:16; 3:18

1 aDeut. 13:1ff.; Jer. 6:13,
b2 Cor. 11:13 c1 Tim. 4:1;
Matt. 7:15 dGal. 2:4; Jude 4
e1 Cor. 11:19; Gal. 5:20
fJude 4 gRev. 6:10 h1 Cor.
6:20

2 aGen. 19:5ff.; Jude 4;
2 Pet. 2:7, 18 bActs 16.17;
22:4; 24:14 c[Gr.] Rom. 2:24;
1 Tim. 6:1

3 a2 Pet. 2:14; 1 Tim. 6:5;
Jude 16 b2 Cor. 2:17 marg.;
1 Thess. 2:5 cRom. 16:18;
2 Pet. 1:16 dDeut. 32:35

4 aGen. 6; Jude 6 bRev.
20:1f.

5 1Or, herald
a2 Pet. 3:6; Ezek. 26:20
b1 Pet. 3:20 c2 Pet. 3:6

6 aGen. 19:24; Jude 7
bJude 7; Matt. 10:15; 11:23;
Rom. 9:29 [Is. 1:9] cJude 15

7 aGen. 19:16, 29 bGen.
19:5ff.; Jude 4; 2 Pet. 2:2, 18
c2 Pet. 3:17

8 aHeb. 11:4

9 1Or, trial
a1 Cor. 10:13; Rev. 3:10
bMatt. 10:15; Jude 6

10 1Lit., go after 2Lit.,
glories
a2 Pet. 3:3; Jude 16, 18 bJude
8; Ex. 22:28 cTitus 1:7

as to ca lamp shining in a dark place, until the dday dawns and the emorning star arises fin your hearts. 20 But aknow this first of all, that bno prophecy of Scripture is *a matter* of one's own interpretation, 21 for ano prophecy was ever made by an act of human will, but men bmoved by the Holy Spirit spoke from God.

CHAPTER 2

BUT afalse prophets also arose among the people, just as there will also be bfalse teachers camong you, who will dsecretly introduce edestructive heresies, even fdenying the gMaster who hbought them, bringing swift destruction upon themselves. 2 And many will follow their asensuality, and because of them bthe way of the truth will be cmaligned; 3 and in *their* agreed they will bexploit you with cfalse words; dtheir judgment from long ago is not idle, and their destruction is not asleep. 4 For aif God did not spare angels when they sinned, but cast them into hell and bcommitted them to pits of darkness, reserved for judgment; 5 and did not spare athe ancient world, but preserved bNoah, a 1preacher of righteousness, with seven others, when He brought a cflood upon the world of the ungodly; 6 and if He acondemned the cities of Sodom and Gomorrah to destruction by reducing *them* to ashes, having made them an bexample to those who would clive ungodly thereafter; 7 and if He arescued righteous Lot, oppressed by the bsensual conduct of cunprincipled men 8 (for by what he saw and heard *that* arighteous man, while living among them, felt *his* righteous soul tormented day after day with *their* lawless deeds), 9 athen the Lord knows how to rescue the godly from 1temptation, and to keep the unrighteous under punishment for the bday of judgment, 10 and especially those who 1aindulge the flesh in *its* corrupt desires and bdespise authority. Daring, cself-willed, they do not tremble when they brevile 2angelic majesties,

11 ªwhereas angels who are greater in might and power do not bring a reviling judgment against them before the Lord.

12 But ªthese, like unreasoning animals, ᵇborn as creatures of instinct to be captured and killed, reviling where they have no knowledge, will in ¹the destruction of those creatures also be destroyed,

13 suffering wrong as ªthe wages of doing wrong. They count it a pleasure to ᵇrevel in the ᶜdaytime. They are stains and blemishes, ᵇrevelling in their ¹deceptions, as they ᵈcarouse with you;

14 having eyes full of adultery and that never cease from sin; ªenticing ᵇunstable souls, having a heart trained in ᶜgreed, ᵈaccursed children;

15 forsaking ªthe right way they have gone astray, having followed ᵇthe way of Balaam, the son of Beor, who loved ᶜthe wages of unrighteousness,

16 but he received a rebuke for his own transgression; ªfor a dumb donkey, speaking with a voice of a man, restrained the madness of the prophet.

17 These are ªsprings without water, and mists driven by a storm, ᵇfor whom the ¹black darkness has been reserved.

18 For speaking out ªarrogant *words* of ᵇvanity they ᶜentice by fleshly desires, by ᵈsensuality, those who barely ᵉescape from the ones who live in error,

19 promising them freedom while they themselves are slaves of corruption; for ªby what a man is overcome, by this he is enslaved.

20 For if after they have ªescaped the defilements of the world by ᵇthe knowledge of the ᶜLord and Savior Jesus Christ, they are again ᵈentangled in them and are overcome, ᵉthe last state has become worse for them than the first.

21 ªFor it would be better for them not to have known the way of righteousness, than having known it, to turn away from ᵇthe holy commandment ᶜdelivered to them.

22 It has happened to them according to the true proverb, "ªA DOG RETURNS TO ITS OWN VOMIT," and, "A sow, after washing, *returns* to wallowing in the mire."

CHAPTER 3

THIS is now, ªbeloved, the second letter I am writing to you in which I am ᵇstirring up your sincere mind by way of reminder,

---

11 ªJude 9

12 ¹Lit., *their destruction also*
ªJude 10 ᵇJer. 12:3; Col. 2:22

13 ¹Some ancient mss. read, *love-feasts*, cf. Jude 12
ª2 Pet. 2:15 ᵇRom. 13:13
ᶜ1 Thess. 5:7 ᵈJude 12; 1 Cor. 11:21

14 ª2 Pet. 2:18 ᵇJames 1:8; 2 Pet. 3:16 ᶜ2 Pet. 2:3 ᵈEph. 2:3

15 ªActs 13:10 ᵇNum. 22:5, 7; Deut. 23:4; Neh. 13:2; Jude 11; Rev. 2:14 ᶜ2 Pet. 2:13

16 ªNum. 22:21, 23, 28, 30f.

17 ¹Lit., *blackness of darkness*
ªJude 12 ᵇJude 13

18 ªJude 16 ᵇEph. 4:17 ᶜ2 Pet. 2:14 ᵈ2 Pet. 2:2 ᵉ2 Pet. 2:20; 1:4

19 ªRom. 6:16; John 8:34

20 ª2 Pet. 2:18 ᵇ2 Pet. 1:2 ᶜ2 Pet. 1:11; 3:18 ᵈ2 Tim. 2:4 ᵉMatt. 12:45; Luke 11:26

21 ªEzek. 18:24; Heb. 6:4ff.; 10:26f.; James 4:17 ᵇ2 Pet. 3:2; Gal. 6:2; 1 Tim. 6:14 ᶜJude 3

22 ªProv. 26:11

1 ª2 Pet. 3:8, 14, 17; 1 Pet. 2:11 ᵇ2 Pet. 1:13

493

2 ªJude 17 ᵇLuke 1:70;
Acts 3:21; Eph. 3:5 ᶜ2 Pet.
2:21; Gal. 6:2; 1 Tim. 6:14

3 ª2 Pet. 1:20 ᵇ1 Tim. 4:1;
Heb. 1:2 ᶜJude 18 ᵈ2 Pet.
2:10

4 ªIs. 5:19; Jer. 17:15;
Ezek. 11:3; 12:22, 27; Mal.
2:17; Matt. 24:48 ᵇ2 Pet.
3:12; 1 Thess. 2:19 ᶜActs 7:60
ᵈMark 10:6

5 ¹Or, they are willfully
ignorant of this fact, that
ªGen. 1:6, 9; Heb. 11:3 ᵇCol.
1:17 [Gr.]; Ps. 24:2; 136:6

6 ª2 Pet. 2:5 ᵇGen. 7:21f.

7 ª2 Pet. 3:10, 12 ᵇIs.
66:15; Dan. 7:9f.; 2 Thess.
1:7; Heb. 12:29 ᶜMatt. 10:15;
1 Cor. 3:13; Jude 7

8 ª2 Pet. 3:1 ᵇPs. 90:4

9 ªHab. 2:3; Heb. 10:37;
Rom. 13:11 ᵇRom. 2:4; Rev.
2:21 ᶜ1 Tim. 2:4; Rev. 2:21

10 ¹Lit., the works in it
²Some ancient mss. read,
discovered
ª1 Cor. 1:8 ᵇ1 Thess. 5:2;
Matt. 24:43; Rev. 3:3; 16:15
ᶜ2 Pet. 3:7, 12 ᵈMatt. 24:35;
Rev. 21:1 ᵉIs. 34:4; 24:19;
Mic. 1:4; Gal. 4:3 marg.
ᶠ2 Pet. 3:7

12 ª1 Cor. 1:7 ᵇ2 Pet. 3:7,
10 ᶜIs. 34:4; 24:19; Mic. 1:4;
Gal. 4:3 marg.

13 ªIs. 65:17; 66:22 ᵇRev.
21:1; Rom. 8:21 ᶜIs. 60:21;
65:25; Rev. 21:27

14 ª2 Pet. 1:10; 1 Cor. 15:58
ᵇ2 Pet. 3:1 ᶜ1 Pet. 1:7 ᵈPhil.
2:15; 1 Tim. 6:14; James
1:27; 1 Thess. 5:23

15 ª2 Pet. 3:9

494

2   that you should ªremember the words spoken beforehand by ᵇthe holy prophets and ᶜthe commandment of the Lord and Savior *spoken* by your apostles.

3   ªKnow this first of all, that ᵇin the last days ᶜmockers will come with *their* mocking, ᵈfollowing after their own lusts,

4   and saying, "ªWhere is the promise of His ᵇcoming?" For *ever* since the fathers ᶜfell asleep, all continues just as it was ᵈfrom the beginning of creation.

5   For ¹when they maintain this, it escapes their notice that ªby the word of God *the* heavens existed long ago and *the* earth was ᵇformed out of water and by water,

6   through which ªthe world at that time was ᵇdestroyed, being flooded with water.

7   But ªthe present heavens and earth by His word are being reserved for ᵇfire, kept for ᶜthe day of judgment and destruction of ungodly men.

8   But do not let this one *fact* escape your notice, ªbeloved, that with the Lord one day is as a thousand years, and ᵇa thousand years as one day.

9   ªThe Lord is not slow about His promise, as some count slowness, but ᵇis patient toward you, ᶜnot wishing for any to perish but for all to come to repentance.

10   But ªthe day of the Lord ᵇwill come like a thief, in which ᶜthe heavens ᵈwill pass away with a roar and the ᵉelements will be destroyed with intense heat, and ᶠthe earth and ¹its works will be ²burned up.

11   Since all these things are to be destroyed in this way, what sort of people ought you to be in holy conduct and godliness,

12   ªlooking for and hastening the coming of the day of God, on account of which ᵇthe heavens will be destroyed by burning, and the ᶜelements will melt with intense heat.

13   But according to His ªpromise we are looking for ᵇnew heavens and a new earth, ᶜin which righteousness dwells.

14   ªTherefore, ᵇbeloved, since you look for these things, be diligent to be ᶜfound by Him in peace, ᵈspotless and blameless,

15   and regard the ªpatience of our Lord *to be*

salvation; just as also [b]our beloved brother Paul, [c]according to the wisdom given him, wrote to you,

16 as also in all *his* letters, speaking in them of [a]these things, [b]in which are some things hard to understand, which the untaught and [c]unstable distort, as *they do* also [d]the rest of the Scriptures, to their own destruction.

17 You therefore, [a]beloved, knowing this beforehand, [b]be on your guard lest, being carried away by [c]the error of [d]unprincipled men, you [e]fall from your own steadfastness,

18 but grow in the grace and [a]knowledge of our [b]Lord and Savior Jesus Christ. [c]To Him *be* the glory, both now and to the day of eternity. Amen.

15 [b]Acts 9:17; 15:25; 2 Pet. 3:2 [c]1 Cor. 3:10; Eph. 3:3

16 [a]2 Pet. 3:14 [b]Heb. 5:11 [c]2 Pet. 2:14 [d]Is. 28:13; 2 Pet. 3:2

17 [a]2 Pet. 3:1 [b]1 Cor. 10:12 [c]2 Pet. 2:18 [d]2 Pet. 2:7 [e]Rev. 2:5

18 [a]2 Pet. 1:2 [b]2 Pet. 1:11; 2:20 [c]Rom. 11:36; 2 Tim. 4:18; Rev. 1:6

THE FIRST EPISTLE OF
JOHN

Introduction. "Walk in the light... Even as He Walked." The Contrasted Darkness.

W HAT was [a]from the beginning, what we have [b]heard, what we have [c]seen with our eyes, what we [d]beheld and our hands [e]handled, concerning the [f]Word of life—

2 and [a]the life was manifested, and we have [b]seen and [c]bear witness and proclaim to you [d]the eternal life, which was [e]with the Father and was [a]manifested to us—

3 what we have [a]seen and [b]heard we proclaim to you also, that you also may have fellowship with us; and indeed our [c]fellowship is with the Father, and with His Son Jesus Christ.

4 And [a]these things we write, so that our [b]joy may be made complete.

5 And [a]this is the message we have heard from Him and announce to you, that [b]God is light, and in Him there is no darkness at all.

6 [a]If we say that we have fellowship with Him and *yet* walk in the darkness, we [b]lie and [c]do not practice the truth;

7 but if we [a]walk in the light as [b]He Himself is in the light, we have fellowship with one another,

1 [a]John 1:1f.; 1 John 2:13, 14 [b]1 John 1:3; Acts 4:20 [c]1 John 1:2; John 19:35; 2 Pet. 1:16 [d]John 1:14; 1 John 4:14 [e]Luke 24:39; John 20:27 [f]John 1:1, 4

2 [a]John 1:4; Rom. 16:26; 1 Tim. 3:16; 1 Pet. 1:20; 1 John 3:5, 8; 5:20 [b]1 John 1:1; John 19:35 [c]1 John 4:14; John 15:27 [d]1 John 2:25; 5:11, 13, 20; John 10:28; 17:3 [e]John 1:1

3 [a]1 John 1:1; John 19:35; 2 Pet. 1:16 [b]1 John 1:1; Acts 4:20 [c]John 17:3, 21; 1 Cor. 1:9

4 [a]1 John 2:1 [b]John 3:29

5 [a]1 John 3:11; John 1:19 [b]1 Tim. 6:16; James 1:17

6 [a]John 8:12; 2 Cor. 6:14; Eph. 5:8; 1 John 2:11 [b]John 8:55; 1 John 2:4; 4:20 [c]John 3:21

7 [a]Is. 2:5 [b]1 Tim. 6:16

7 ᶜHeb. 9:14; Rev. 7:14; Titus 2:14

8 ᵃJob 15:14; Prov. 20:9; Rom. 3:10ff.; James 3:2 ᵇ1 John 2:4; John 8:44

9 ᵃPs. 32:5; Prov. 28:13 ᵇHeb. 9:14; Rev. 7:14; Titus 2:14

10 ᵃJob 15:14; Prov. 20:9; Rom. 3:10ff.; James 3:2 ᵇ1 John 5:10; John 3:33 ᶜ1 John 2:14

1 ¹Gr., *Paracletos,* one called alongside to help ᵃ1 John 2:12, 28; 3:7, 18; 4:4; 5:21; John 13:33; Gal. 4:19 ᵇ1 John 1:4 ᶜRom. 8:34; 1 Tim. 2:5; Heb. 7:25; 9:24 ᵈJohn 14:16

2 ¹Or, *satisfaction* ᵃ1 John 4:10; Rom. 3:25; Heb. 2:17 ᵇ1 John 4:11; John 4:42; 11:51f.

3 ᵃ1 John 2:5; 3:24; 4:13; 5:2 ᵇ1 John 2:4; 3:6; 4:7f. ᶜ1 John 3:22, 24; 5:3; John 14:15; 15:10; Rev. 12:17; 14:12

4 ᵃTitus 1:10 ᵇ1 John 3:6; 4:7f ᶜ1 John 1:6 ᵈ1 John 1:8

5 ᵃJohn 14:23 ᵇ1 John 4:12 ᶜ1 John 2:3; 3:24; 4:13; 5:2

6 ᵃJohn 15:4 ᵇJohn 13:15; 15:10; 1 Pet. 2:21

7 ¹Lit., *were having* ᵃ1 John 3:2, 21; 4:1, 7, 11; Heb. 6:9 ᵇ1 John 3:11, 23; 4:21; 2 John 5 ᶜ1 John 2:24; 3:11; 2 John 5, 6

8 ¹Lit., *Again* ᵃJohn 13:34 ᵇEph. 5:8; 1 Thess. 5:4f.; Rom. 13:12 ᶜJohn 1:9

9 ᵃ1 John 2:11; 3:15; 4:20 ᵇ1 John 3:10, 16; 4:20f.; Acts 1:15

10 ᵃ1 John 2:10, 11; John 11:9 and ref.

11 ᵃ1 John 2:9; 3:15; 4:20 ᵇJohn 12:35; 1 John 1:6 ᶜ2 Cor. 4:4; 2 Pet. 1:9

12 ᵃ1 John 2:1 ᵇ1 Cor. 6:11; Acts 13:38

and ᶜthe blood of Jesus His Son cleanses us from all sin.

8 ᵃIf we say that we have no sin, we are deceiving ourselves, and the ᵇtruth is not in us.

9 ᵃIf we confess our sins, He is faithful and righteous to forgive us our sins and ᵇto cleanse us from all unrighteousness.

10 ᵃIf we say that we have not sinned, we ᵇmake Him a liar, and ᶜHis word is not in us.

ᵃ CHAPTER 2

MY little children, I am writing ᵇthese things to you that you may not sin. And if anyone sins, ᶜwe have an ¹ᵈAdvocate with the Father, Jesus Christ the righteous;

2 and He Himself is ᵃthe ¹propitiation for our sins; and not for ours only, but also ᵇfor *those of* the whole world.

3 And ᵃby this we know that we have come to ᵇknow Him, if we ᶜkeep His commandments.

4 The one who says, "ᵃI have come to ᵇknow Him," and does not keep His commandments, is a ᶜliar, and ᵈthe truth is not in him;

5 but whoever ᵃkeeps His word, in him the ᵇlove of God has truly been perfected. ᶜBy this we know that we are in Him:

6 the one who says he ᵃabides in Him ᵇought himself to walk in the same manner as He walked.

7 ᵃBeloved, I am ᵇnot writing a new commandment to you, but an old commandment which you ¹have had ᶜfrom the beginning; the old commandment is the word which you have heard.

8 ¹On the other hand, I am writing ᵃa new commandment to you, which is true in Him and in you, because ᵇthe darkness is passing away, and ᶜthe true light is already shining.

9 The one who says he is in the light and *yet* ᵃhates his ᵇbrother is in the darkness until now.

10 ᵃThe one who loves his brother abides in the light and there is no cause for stumbling in him.

11 But the one who ᵃhates his brother is in the darkness and ᵇwalks in the darkness, and does not know where he is going because the darkness has ᶜblinded his eyes.

12 I am writing to you, ᵃlittle children, because ᵇyour sins are forgiven you for His name's sake.

13 I am writing to you, fathers, because you

know Him ^awho has been from the beginning. I am writing to you, young men, because ^byou have overcome ^cthe evil one. I have written to you, children, because ^dyou know the Father.

14 I have written to you, fathers, because you know Him ^awho has been from the beginning. I have written to you, young men, because you are ^bstrong, and the ^cword of God abides in you, and ^dyou have overcome the evil one.

15 Do not love ^athe world, nor the things in the world. ^bIf any one loves the world, the love of the Father is not in him.

16 For all that is in the world, ^athe lust of the flesh and ^bthe lust of the eyes and ^cthe boastful pride of life, is not from the Father, but is from the world.

17 And ^athe world is passing away, and *also* its lusts; but the one who does the will of God abides forever.

18 Children, ^ait is the last hour; and just as you heard that ^bantichrist is coming, ^ceven now many antichrists have arisen; from this we know that it is the last hour.

19 ^aThey went out from us, but they were not *really* of us; for if they had been of us, they would have remained with us; but *they went out,* ^bin order that ¹it might be shown that they all are not of us.

20 ¹But you have an ^aanointing from ^bthe Holy One, and ^{2c}you all know.

21 I have not written to you because you do not know the truth, but ^abecause you do know it, and ¹because no lie is ^bof the truth.

22 Who is the liar but ^athe one who denies that Jesus is the ¹Christ? This is ^bthe antichrist, the one who denies the Father and the Son.

23 ^aWhoever denies the Son does not have the Father; the one who confesses the Son has the Father also.

24 As for you, let that abide in you which you heard ^afrom the beginning. If what you heard from the beginning abides in you, you also ^bwill abide in the Son and in the Father.

25 And ^athis is the promise which He Himself ¹made to us, the eternal life.

26 These things I have written to you concerning those who are trying to ^adeceive you.

27 And as for you, the ^aanointing which you

13 ^a1 John 1:1 ^b1 John 2:14; 1 John 4:4; 5:4f.; Rev. 2:7; John 16:33 ^cMatt. 5:37; 1 John 2:14; 3:12; 5:18f. ^d1 John 2:3; John 14:7

14 ^a1 John 1:1 ^bEph. 6:10 ^c1 John 1:10; John 5:38; 8:37 ^d1 John 2:13

15 ^aJames 1:27; Rom. 12:2 ^bJames 4:4

16 ^aRom. 13:14; Eph. 2:3; 1 Pet. 2:11 ^bProv. 27:20 ^cJames 4:16

17 ^a1 Cor. 7:31

18 ^aRom. 13:11; 1 Tim. 1:1, 1 Pet. 4:7 ^b1 John 2:22; 4:3; 2 John 7; Matt. 24:5, 24 ^c1 John 4:1, 3; Mark 13:22

19 ¹Lit., *they might be made manifest* ^aActs 20:30 ^b1 Cor. 11:19

20 ¹Lit., *And* ²Some ancient mss. read, *you know all things* ^a1 John 2:27; 2 Cor. 1:21 ^bMark 1:24; Acts 10:38 ^c1 John 2:27; Prov. 28:5; Matt. 13:11; John 14:26; 1 Cor. 2:15f.

21 ¹Or, know *that* ^aJames 1:19; 2 Pet. 1:12; Jude 5 ^b1 John 3:19; John 8:44; 18:37

22 ¹I.e., Messiah ^a1 John 4:3; 2 John 7 ^b1 John 2:18; 4:3; 2 John 7; Matt. 24:5, 24

23 ^a1 John 4:15, 5:1; 2 John 9; John 8:19; 16:3; 17:3

24 ^a1 John 2:7 ^b1 John 1:3; John 14:23; 2 John 9

25 ¹Lit., *promised us* ^aJohn 3:15; 6:40; 1 John 1:2

26 ^a1 John 3:7; 2 John 7

27 ^a1 John 2:20; John 14:16

1 John 2, 3

God's Children Show Righteousness and Brotherly Love. Practicing Sin.

27 ¹Or, *abide in Him*
ᵇJohn 14:26; 1 Cor. 2:12;
1 Thess. 4:9 ᶜJohn 14:17

28 ¹Lit., *be put to shame from Him* ²Or, *in His presence*
ᵃ1 John 2:1 ᵇ1 John 3:2; Col.
3:4; Luke 17:30 ᶜ1 John 3:21;
4:17; 5:14; Eph. 3:12 ᵈMark
8:38 ᵉ1 Thess. 2:19

29 ¹Or, *begotten*
ᵃ1 John 3:7; John 7:18
ᵇ1 John 3:9; 4:7; 5:1, 4, 18
[3 John 11]; John 1:13; 3:3

1 ¹Lit., *what kind of love*
ᵃ1 John 4:10; John 3:16
ᵇ1 John 3:2, 10; John 1:12;
11:52; Rom. 8:16 ᶜJohn
15:21; 16:3; 15:18

2 ᵃ1 John 2:7 ᵇ1 John 3:1,
10; John 1:12; 11:52; Rom.
8:16 ᶜRom. 8:19, 23f.
ᵈ1 John 2:29; Col. 3:4; Luke
17:30 ᵉRom. 8:29; 2 Pet. 1:4
ᶠJohn 17:24; 2 Cor. 3:18

3 ᵃRom. 15:12; 1 Pet. 1:3
ᵇ2 Cor. 7:1; 2 Pet. 3:13f.;
1 John 2:6; John 17:19

4 ᵃ1 John 5:17; Rom. 4:15

5 ᵃ1 John 1:2; 3:8 ᵇJohn
1:29; 1 Pet. 1:18-20; 1 John
2:2 ᶜ2 Cor. 5:21; 1 John 2:29

6 ¹Or, *has known*
ᵃ1 John 3:9 ᵇ1 John 2:3;
3 John 11

7 ᵃ1 John 2:1 ᵇ1 John 2:26
ᶜ1 John 2:29

8 ¹Lit., *sins*
ᵃ1 John 3:10; Matt. 13:38;
John 8:44 ᵇMatt. 4:3 ᶜ1 John
3:5 ᵈJohn 16:11; John 12:31

9 ¹Or, *begotten*
ᵃ1 John 2:29; 4:7; 5:1, 4, 18
[3 John 11]; John 1:13; 3:3
ᵇ1 John 3:6; 5:18; James 1:18;
1 Pet. 1:23

10 ᵃ1 John 3:1, 2; John 1:12;
11:52; Rom. 8:16 ᵇ1 John
3:8; Matt. 13:38; John 8:44
ᶜ1 John 4:8; Rom. 13:8ff.;
Col. 3:14; 1 Tim. 1:5 ᵈ1 John
2:9

11 ᵃ1 John 1:5 ᵇ1 John 2:7
ᶜJohn 13:34f.; 15:12; 1 John
4:7, 11f., 21; 2 John 5

498

received from Him abides in you, and you have no need for any one to teach you; but as His anointing ᵇteaches you about all things, and is ᶜtrue and is not a lie, and just as it has taught you, ¹you abide in Him.

28 And now, ᵃlittle children, abide in Him, so that if He ᵇshould appear, we may have ᶜconfidence and ᵈnot ¹shrink away from Him in shame ²at His ᵉcoming.

29 If you know that ᵃHe is righteous, you know that every one also who practices righteousness ᵇis ¹born of Him.

CHAPTER 3

SEE ¹ᵃhow great a love the Father has bestowed upon us, that we should be called ᵇchildren of God; and *such* we are. For this reason the world does not know us, because ᵉit did not know Him.

2 ᵃBeloved, now we are ᵇchildren of God, and ᶜit has not appeared as yet what we shall be. We know that, if He ᵈshould appear, we shall be ᵉlike Him, because we shall ᶠsee Him just as He is.

3 And every one who has this ᵃhope *fixed* on Him ᵇpurifies himself, just as He is pure.

4 Every one who practices sin also practices lawlessness; and ᵃsin is lawlessness.

5 And you know that He ᵃappeared in order to ᵇtake away sins; and ᶜin Him there is no sin.

6 No one who abides in Him ᵃsins; no one who sins has seen Him or ¹ᵇknows Him.

7 ᵃLittle children, let no one ᵇdeceive you; ᶜthe one who practices righteousness is righteous, just as He is righteous;

8 the one who practices sin is ᵃof the devil; for the devil ¹has sinned from the beginning. ᵇThe Son of God ᶜappeared for this purpose, ᵈthat He might destroy the works of the devil.

9 No one who is ¹ᵃborn of God ᵇpractices sin, because His seed abides in him; and he cannot sin, because he is ¹born of God.

10 By this the ᵃchildren of God and the ᵇchildren of the devil are obvious; any one who does not practice righteousness is not of God, nor the one who ᶜdoes not love his ᵈbrother.

11 ᵃFor this is the message ᵇwhich you have heard from the beginning, ᶜthat we should love one another;

12 not as [a]Cain *who* was of [b]the evil one, and slew his brother. And for what reason did he slay him? Because [c]his deeds were evil, and his brother's were righteous.

13 Do not marvel, brethren, if [a]the world hates you.

14 We know that we have [a]passed out of death into life, [b]because we love the brethren. He who does not love abides in death.

15 Every one who [a]hates his brother is a murderer; and you know that [b]no murderer has eternal life abiding in him.

16 We know love by this, that [a]He laid down His life for us; and [b]we ought to lay down our lives for the [c]brethren.

17 But [a]whoever has the world's goods, and beholds his brother in need and [b]closes his [1]heart [2]against him, [c]how does the love of God abide in him?

18 [a]Little children, let us not love with word or with tongue, but in deed and [b]truth.

19 We shall know by this that we are [a]of the truth, and shall [1]assure our heart [2]before Him,

20 in whatever our heart condemns us; for God is greater than our heart, and knows all things.

21 [a]Beloved, if our heart does not condemn us, we have [b]confidence [1]before God;

22 and [a]whatever we ask we receive from Him, because we [b]keep His commandments and do [c]the things that are pleasing in His sight.

23 And this is His commandment, that we [1a]believe in [b]the name of His Son Jesus Christ, and love one another, just as [c]He [2]commanded us.

24 And the one who [a]keeps His commandments [b]abides in Him, and He in him. And [c]we know by this that [d]He abides in us, by the Spirit which He has given us.

CHAPTER 4

[a]BELOVED, do not believe every [b]spirit, but test the spirits to see whether they are from God; because [c]many false prophets have gone out into the world.

2 By this you know the Spirit of God: [a]every spirit that [b]confesses that [c]Jesus Christ has come in the flesh is from God;

3 and every spirit that [a]does not confess Jesus

12 [a]Gen. 4:8 [b]1 John 2:13f.; Matt. 5:37 [c]Ps. 38:20; Prov. 29:10; John 8:40, 41

13 [a]John 15:18; 17:14

14 [a]John 5:24 [b]1 John 2:10; John 13:35

15 [a]Matt. 5:21f.; John 8:44 [b]Gal. 5:20f.; Rev. 21:8

16 [a]John 15:13; John 10:11 [b]Phil. 2:17; 1 Thess. 2:8 [c]1 John 2:9

17 [1]Lit., *inward parts* [2]Lit., *from* [a]James 2:15f. [b]Deut. 15:7 [c]1 John 4:20

18 [a]1 John 3:7; 1 John 2:1 [b]2 John 1; 3 John 1

19 [1]Or, *persuade* [2]Or, *before Him; because if our heart . . .* [a]1 John 2:21

21 [1]Lit., *toward* [a]1 John 2:7 [b]1 John 5:14; 2:28

22 [a]Job 22:26f.; Matt. 21:22; 7:7; John 9:31 [b]1 John 2:3 [c]John 8:29; Heb. 13:21

23 [1]Or, *believe the name* [2]Or, *gave us a commandment* [a]John 6:29 [b]John 1:12; 2:23; 3:18 [c]John 13:34; 15:12; 1 John 2:8

24 [a]1 John 2:3 [b]John 2:6, 24; 4:15; John 6:56; 10:38 [c]1 John 4:13; John 14:17; Rom. 8:9, 14, 16; 1 Thess. 4:8 [d]1 John 2:5

1 [a]1 John 2:7 [b]Jer. 29:8; 1 Cor. 12:10; 2 Thess. 2:2; 1 Thess. 5:20f. [c]1 John 2:18; Jer. 14:14; 2 Pet. 2:1

2 [a]1 Cor. 12:3 [b]1 John 2:23 [c]1 John 1:2; John 1:14

3 [a]2 John 7; 1 John 2:22

3 ᵇ1 John 2:22; 2:18
ᶜ1 John 2:18; 2 Thess. 2:3-7

4 ᵃ1 John 2:1 ᵇ1 John 2:13
ᶜ1 John 3:20; 2 Kin. 2:16;
Rom. 8:31 ᵈJohn 12:31

5 ᵃJohn 15:19; 17:14, 16

6 ᵃ1 John 4:4; John 8:23
ᵇJohn 8:47; 10:3ff.; 18:37
ᶜ1 Cor. 14:37 ᵈJohn 14:17
ᵉ1 Tim. 4:1

7 ¹Or, *begotten*
ᵃ1 John 2:7 ᵇ1 John 3:11
ᶜ1 John 5:1 ᵈ1 John 2:29
ᵉ1 John 2:3; 1 Cor. 8:3

8 ᵃ1 John 4:16; 1 John 4:7

9 ¹Or, *in our case* ²Or,
unique, only one of His kind
ᵃ1 John 4:16; John 9:3 ᵇJohn
3:16f.; 1 John 4:10; 5:11

10 ¹Some mss. read, *had
loved*
ᵃRom. 5:8, 10; 1 John 4:19
ᵇJohn 3:16f.; 1 John 4:9; 5:11
ᶜ1 John 2:2

11 ᵃ1 John 2:7 ᵇ1 John 4:7

12 ᵃJohn 1:18; 1 Tim. 6:16;
1 John 4:20 ᵇ1 John 2:5;
4:17f.

13 ᵃ1 John 3:24; Rom. 8:9

14 ᵃ1 John 1:2; John 15:27
ᵇJohn 3:17; 4:42; 1 John 2:2

15 ᵃ1 John 2:23 ᵇ1 John 5:5;
3:23; 4:2; 5:1; Rom. 10:9
ᶜ1 John 2:24; 3:24

16 ¹Lit., *in*
ᵃJohn 6:69 ᵇ1 John 4:9; John
9:3 ᶜ1 John 4:8; 4:7 ᵈ1 John
4:12f.

17 ᵃ1 John 2:5; 4:12 ᵇ1 John
2:28 ᶜMatt. 10:15 ᵈ1 John
2:6; 3:1, 7, 16; John 17:22

18 ¹Lit., *has*
ᵃRom. 8:15; Gal. 4:30f.
ᵇ1 John 4:12

19 ᵃ1 John 4:10

is not from God; and this is the *spirit* of the ᵇantichrist, of which you have heard that it is coming, and ᶜnow it is already in the world.

4 You are from God, ᵃlittle children, and ᵇhave overcome them; because ᶜgreater is He who is in you than ᵈhe who is in the world.

5 ᵃThey are from the world; therefore they speak *as* from the world, and the world listens to them.

6 ᵃWe are from God; ᵇhe who knows God listens to us; ᶜhe who is not from God does not listen to us. By this we know ᵈthe spirit of truth and ᵉthe spirit of error.

7 ᵃBeloved, let us ᵇlove one another, for love is from God; and ᶜevery one who loves is ¹ᵈborn of God and ᵉknows God.

8 The one who does not love does not know God, for ᵃGod is love.

9 By this the love of God was manifested ¹ᵃin us, that ᵇGod has sent His ²only begotten Son into the world so that we might live through Him.

10 In this is love, ᵃnot that we ¹loved God, but that ᵇHe loved us and sent His Son *to be* ᶜthe propitiation for our sins.

11 ᵃBeloved, if God so loved us, ᵇwe also ought to love one another.

12 ᵃNo one has beheld God at any time; if we love one another, God abides in us, and His ᵇlove is perfected in us.

13 ᵃBy this we know that we abide in Him and He in us, because He has given us of His Spirit.

14 And we have beheld and ᵃbear witness that the Father has ᵇsent the Son *to be* the Savior of the world.

15 ᵃWhoever confesses that ᵇJesus is the Son of God, God ᶜabides in him, and he in God.

16 And ᵃwe have come to know and have believed the love which God has ¹ᵇfor us. ᶜGod is love, and the one who ᵈabides in love abides in God, and God abides in him.

17 By this, ᵃlove is perfected with us, that we may have ᵇconfidence in ᶜthe day of judgment; because ᵈas He is, so also are we in this world.

18 There is no fear in love; but ᵃperfect love casts out fear, because fear ¹involves punishment, and the one who fears is not ᵇperfected in love.

19 ᵃWe love, because He first loved us.

20 [a]If some one says, "I love God," and [b]hates his brother, he is a [c]liar; for [d]the one who does not love his brother whom he has seen, [1e]cannot love God whom he has not seen.

21 And [a]this commandment we have from Him, that the one who loves God [b]should love his brother also.

CHAPTER 5

W[a]HOEVER believes that Jesus is the [1]Christ is [2b]born of God; and whoever loves the [3]Father [c]loves the *child* [2]born of Him.

2 [a]By this we know that [b]we love the children of God, when we love God and [1]observe His commandments.

3 For [a]this is the love of God, that we [b]keep His commandments; and [c]His commandments are not burdensome.

4 For whatever is [1a]born of God [b]overcomes the world; and this is the victory that has overcome the world—our faith.

5 And who is the one who overcomes the world, but he who [a]believes that Jesus is the Son of God?

6 This is the one who came [a]by water and blood, Jesus Christ; not [1]with the water only, but [1]with the water and [1]with the blood.

7 And it is [a]the Spirit who bears witness, because the Spirit is[1]the truth.

8 For there are [a]three that bear witness, [1]the Spirit and the water and the blood; and the three are [2]in agreement.

9 [a]If we receive the witness of men, the witness of God is greater; for this is the witness of God, that [b]He has borne witness concerning His Son.

10 The one who believes in the Son of God has the witness in himself; the one who does not believe God has made Him a liar, because he has not believed in the witness that God has borne concerning His Son.

11 And the witness is this, that [a]God has given us [b]eternal life, and this life is in His Son.

12 [a]He who has the Son has the life; he who does not have the Son of God does not have the life.

13 [a]These things I have written to you who believe in the name of the Son of God, in order that you may know that you have eternal life.

20 [1]Some mss. read, *how can he love God . . . seen?*
[a]1 John 1:6, 8, 10; 2:4
[b]1 John 2:9, 11 [c]1 John 1:6
[d]1 John 3:17 [e]1 John 4:12;
1 Pet. 1:8

21 [a]Matt. 5:43f.; 22:37ff.;
John 13:34; Lev. 19:18
[b]1 John 3:11

1 [1]I.e., Messiah [2]Or,
begotten [3]Lit., *one who
begets*
[a]1 John 4:2; 4:15; 2:22f.
[b]1 John 5:4, 18; 2:29; John
1:13; 3:3 marg. [c]John 8:42

2 [1]Lit., *do*
[a]1 John 2:5 [b]1 John 3:14

3 [a]John 14:15; 2 John 6
[b]1 John 2:3 [c]Matt. 11:30;
23:4

4 [1]Or, *begotten*
[a]1 John 5:1, 18; 2:29; John
1:13; 3:3 marg. [b]1 John 2:13;
4:4

5 [a]1 John 4:15; 1 John 5:1

6 [1]Lit., *in*
[a]John 19:34

7 [a]John 15:26; 16:13-15
[Matt. 3:16f.]

8 [1]A few late mss. read *in
heaven, the Father, the
Word, and the Holy Spirit,
and these three are one. And
there are three that bear
witness on earth, the
Spirit. . . .* [2]Lit., *for the one
thing*
[a]Matt. 18:16

9 [a]John 5:34, 37; 8:18
[b]Matt. 3:17; John 5:32, 37

Rev. .
John 3:16, 1 Gal. 4:6;
. . .

11 [a]1 John 5:13, 20; .
2:25; 4:9 [b]John 1:4

12 [a]John 3:15f., 36

13 [a]John 20:31

13 [b]1 John 3:23 [c]1 John 5:11, 20; 1:2; 2:25; 4:9

14 [1]Lit., *toward* [a]1 John 3:21f.; 2:28 [b]1 John 3:22; Matt. 7:7; John 14:13

15 [a]1 John 5:18, 19, 20

16 [1]Lit., *sinning* [a]James 5:15 [b]Heb. 6:4-6; 10:26; Num. 15:30 [c]Jer. 7:16; 14:11

17 [a]1 John 3:4 [b]1 John 2:1f.; 5:16

18 [1]Or, *begotten* [a]1 John 5:15, 19, 20 [b]1 John 3:9 [c]James 1:27; Jude 21 [d]1 John 2:13 [e]John 14:30

19 [a]1 John 5:15, 18, 20 [b]1 John 4:6 [c]John 12:31; 17:15; Gal. 1:4

20 [a]1 John 5:15, 18, 19 [b]1 John 5:5; John 8:42 [c]Luke 24:45 [d]John 17:3; Rev. 3:7 [e]John 1:18; 14:9; 1 John 2:23; Rev. 3:7 [f]1 John 1:2 [g]1 John 5:11

21 [a]1 John 2:1 [b]1 Cor. 10:7, 14; 1 Thess. 1:9

[b]believe in the name of the Son of God, in orde[r] that you may know that you have [c]eternal life.

14 And this is [a]the confidence which we have [1]before Him, that, [b]if we ask anything according to His will, He hears us.

15 And if we know that He hears us *in* whatever we ask, [a]we know that we have the requests which we have asked from Him.

16 If any one sees his brother [1]committing a sin not *leading* to death, [a]he shall ask and *God* will for him give life to those who commit sin not *leading* to death. [b]There is a sin *leading* to death; [c]I do not say that he should make request for this.

17 [a]All unrighteousness is sin, and [b]there is a sin not *leading* to death.

18 [a]We know that [b]no one who is [1]born of God sins; but He who was [1]born of God [c]keeps him and [d]the evil one does not [e]touch him.

19 [a]We know that [b]we are of God, and [c]the whole world lies in *the power of* the evil one.

20 And [a]we know that [b]the Son of God has come, and has [c]given us understanding, in order that we might know [d]Him who is true, and we [e]are in Him who is true, in His Son Jesus Christ. [f]This is the true God and [g]eternal life.

21 [a]Little children, guard yourselves from [b]idols.

OF

THE SECON[D]

[... partial torn text ...]

"Abide in the Teachings of Christ."
Farewell.

4 ªI was very glad to find *some* of your children walking in truth, just as we have received commandment *to do* from the Father.

5 And now I ask you, lady, ªnot as writing to you a new commandment, but the one which we have had ªfrom the beginning, that we ᵇlove one another.

6 And ªthis is love, that we walk according to His commandments. This is the commandment, ᵇjust as you have heard ᶜfrom the beginning, that you should walk in it.

7 For ªmany deceivers have ᵇgone out into the world, those who ᶜdo not acknowledge Jesus Christ *as* coming in the flesh. This is ªthe deceiver and the ᵈantichrist.

8 ªWatch yourselves, ᵇthat you might not lose what ¹we have accomplished, but that you may receive a full reward.

9 Any one who ¹goes too far and ªdoes not abide in the teaching of Christ, does not have God; the one who abides in the teaching, he has both the Father and the Son.

10 If any one comes to you and does not bring this teaching, ªdo not receive him into *your* house, and do not give him a greeting;

11 for the one who gives him a greeting ªparticipates in his evil deeds.

12 ªHaving many things to write to you, I do not want to *do so* with paper and ink; but I hope to come to you and speak face to face, that ¹your ᵇjoy may be made full.

13 The children of your ªchosen sister greet you.

4 ª3 John 3f.

5 ª1 John 2:7 ᵇ1 John 3:11

6 ª1 John 5:3; 2:5 ᵇ1 John 2:24 ᶜ1 John 2:7

7 ª1 John 2:26 ᵇ1 John 4:1; 2:19 ᶜ1 John 4:2f. ᵈ1 John 2:18

8 ¹Some ancient mss. read, *you* ªMark 13:9 ᵇHeb. 10:35; 1 Cor. 3:8

9 ¹Lit., *goes on ahead* ªJohn 8:31; 7:16; 1 John 2:23

10 ªRom. 16:17; 1 Kin. 13:16f.

11 ª1 Tim. 5:22; Jude 23

12 ¹Some ancient mss. read, *our* ª3 John 13, 14 ᵇ1 John 1:4; John 3:29

13 ª2 John 1

THE THIRD EPISTLE OF
JOHN

Address to Gaius.   Prayer for His Prosperity. "The One Who Does Good is of God."

1 ᵃ2 John 1 ᵇ1 John 3:18;
2 John 1

3 ¹Or, *am very glad when
brethren come and bear
witness*
ᵃ2 John 4 ᵇ3 John 5, 10; Acts
1:15; Gal. 6:10

4 ¹Lit., *these things that I
hear*
ᵃ1 John 2:1; 1 Cor. 4:14f.;
2 Cor. 6:13; Gal. 4:19;
1 Thess. 2:11; 1 Tim. 1:2;
2 Tim. 1:2; Philem. 10
ᵇ2 John 3

5 ᵃ3 John 3, 10; Acts 1:15;
Gal. 6:10 ᵇRom. 12:13, Heb.
13:2

6 ᵃActs 15:3; Titus 3:13
ᵇ1 Thess. 2:12; Col. 1:10

7 ᵃActs 5:41; John 15:21;
Phil. 2:9 ᵇActs 20:33, 35

8 ¹Or, *receive such men as
guests* ²Or, *for*

9 ¹Lit., *us*
ᵃ2 John 9 marg.

10 ᵃ2 John 12 ᵇ3 John 5;
2 John 10 ᶜ3 John 3, 5; Acts
1:15; Gal. 6:10 ᵈJohn 9:34

11 ᵃPs. 34:14; 37:27;
ᵇ1 John 2:29; 3:10 ᶜ1 John
3:6

12 ᵃActs 6:3; 1 Tim. 3:7
ᵇJohn 21:24; John 19:35

13 ᵃ2 John 12

ᵃ

T‌HE elder to the beloved Gaius, whom I ᵇlove in truth.

2   Beloved, I pray that in all respects you may prosper and be in good health, just as your soul prospers.

3   For I ¹ᵃwas very glad when ᵇbrethren came and bore witness to your truth, *that is,* how you ᵃare walking in truth.

4   I have no greater joy than ¹this, to hear of ᵃmy children ᵇwalking in the truth.

5   Beloved, you are acting faithfully in whatever you accomplish for the ᵃbrethren, and especially *when they are* ᵇstrangers;

6   and they bear witness to your love before the church; and you will do well to ᵃsend them on their way in a manner ᵇworthy of God.

7   For they went out for the sake of ᵃthe Name, ᵇaccepting nothing from the Gentiles.

8   Therefore we ought to ¹support such men, that we may be fellow-workers ²with the truth.

9   I wrote something to the church; but Diotrephes, who loves to ᵃbe first among them, does not accept ¹what we say.

10   For this reason, ᵃif I come, I will call attention to his deeds which he does, unjustly accusing us with wicked words; and not satisfied with this, neither does he himself ᵇreceive the ᶜbrethren, and he forbids those who desire *to do so,* and ᵈputs *them* out of the church.

11   Beloved, ᵃdo not imitate what is evil, but what is good. ᵇThe one who does good is of God; ᶜthe one who does evil has not seen God.

12   Demetrius ᵃhas received a good testimony from every one, and from the truth itself; and we also bear witness, and ᵇyou know that our witness is true.

13   ᵃI had many things to write to you, but I am not willing to write *them* to you with pen and ink;

14   but I hope to see you shortly, and we shall

speak face to face. ᵃPeace *be* to you. The friends greet you. Greet the friends ᵇby name.

14 ᵃ1 Pet. 5:14; Eph. 6:23; John 20:19, 21, 26 ᵇJohn 10:3

THE EPISTLE OF
JUDE

General Salutation. "Contend Earnestly for the Faith."

1a

JUDE, a ᵇbond-servant of Jesus Christ, and brother of ²James, to ᶜthose who are the called, beloved in God the Father, and ᵈkept for Jesus Christ:

2 ᵃMay mercy and peace and love ᵇbe multiplied to you.

3 ᵃBeloved, while I was making every effort to write you about our ᵇcommon salvation, I felt the necessity to write to you appealing that you ᶜcontend earnestly for ᵈthe faith which was once for all ᵉdelivered to ᶠthe ¹saints.

4 For certain persons have ᵃcrept in unnoticed, those who were long beforehand ¹ᵇmarked out for this condemnation, ungodly persons who turn ᶜthe grace of our God into ᵈlicentiousness and ᵉdeny our only Master and Lord, Jesus Christ.

5 Now I desire to ᵃremind you, though ᵇyou know all things once for all, that ¹the Lord, ᶜafter saving a people out of the land of Egypt, ²subsequently destroyed those who did not believe.

6 And ᵃangels who did not keep their own domain, but abandoned their proper abode, He has ᵇkept in eternal bonds under darkness for the judgment of the great day.

7 Just as ᵃSodom and Gomorrah and the ᵇcities around them, since they in the same way as these indulged in gross immorality and ᶜwent after strange flesh, are exhibited as an ¹ᵈexample, in undergoing the ᵉpunishment of eternal fire.

8 Yet in the same manner these men also by dreaming ᵃdefile the flesh, and ᵃreject authority, and ᵃrevile ¹angelic majesties.

9 But ᵃMichael ᵇthe archangel, when he disputed with the devil and argued about ᶜthe body of Moses did not dare pronounce against him a railing judgment, but said, "ᵈTHE LORD REBUKE YOU."

1 ¹Gr. *Judas* ²Lit., *Jacob* ᵃMatt. 13:55; Mark 6:3; [Luke 6:16; John 14:22; Acts 1:13?] ᵇRom. 1:1 ᶜRom. 1:6f. ᵈJohn 17:11f.; Jude 21; 1 Pet. 1:5

2 ᵃGal. 6:16; 1 Tim. 1:2 ᵇ1 Pet. 1:2; 2 Pet. 1:2

3 ¹I.e., true believers; lit., *holy ones* ᵃHeb. 6:9; Jude 1, 17, 20 ᵇTitus 1:4 ᶜ1 Tim. 6:12 ᵈJude 20; Acts 6:7 ᵉ2 Pet. 2:21 ᶠActs 9:13

4 ¹Or, *written about* ᵃ2 Tim. 3:6; Gal. 2:4 ᵇ1 Pet. 2:8 ᶜActs 11:23 ᵈ2 Pet. 2:7 ᵉ2 Pet. 2:1; 2 Tim. 2:12; Titus 1:16; 1 John 2:22

5 ¹Some ancient mss. read, *Jesus* ²Lit., *the second time* ᵃ2 Pet. 1:12f.; 3:1f. ᵇ1 John 2:20 ᶜ1 Cor. 10:5-10; Heb. 3:16f.

6 ᵃ2 Pet. 2:4 ᵇ2 Pet. 2:9

7 ¹Or, *example of eternal fire, in undergoing punishment* ᵃ2 Pet. 2:6 ᵇDeut. 29:23; Hos. 11:8 ᶜ2 Pet. 2:6 ᵈ2 Pet. 2:6 ᵉMatt. 25:41; 2 Thess. 1:8f.; 2 Pet. 3:7

8 ¹Lit., *glories* ᵃ2 Pet. 2:10

9 ᵃDan. 10:13, 21; 12:1; Rev. 12:7 ᵇ1 Thess. 4:16; 2 Pet. 2:11 ᶜDeut. 34:6 ᵈZech. 3:2

505

Jude 1

**The Warnings of History to the Ungodly.
Warnings of the Apostles.**

10 ¹Lit., *corrupted*
ᵃ2 Pet. 2;12 ᵇPhil. 3:19

11 ¹Lit., *they have poured
themselves out*
ᵃGen. 4:3-8; Heb. 11:4;
1 John 3:12 ᵇ2 Pet. 2:15;
Num. 31:16; Rev. 2:14
ᶜNum. 16:1-3, 31-35

12 ¹Or, *stains* ²Lit., *twice*
ᵃ2 Pet. 2:13 and marg.;
1 Cor. 11:20ff. ᵇEzek. 34:2,
8, 10 ᶜProv. 25:14; 2 Pet. 2:17
ᵈEph. 4:14 ᵉMatt. 15:13

13 ¹Or, *shameless deeds*
²Lit., *blackness of darkness;
or, nether gloom*
ᵃIs. 57:20 ᵇPhil. 3:19 ᶜ2 Pet.
2:17; Jude 6

14 ¹Lit., *His holy ten
thousands*
ᵃGen. 5:18, 21ff. ᵇDeut. 33:2;
Matt. 16:27; Dan. 7:10; Heb.
12:22

15 ᵃ2 Pet. 2:6ff. ᵇ1 Tim. 1:9

16 ¹Lit., *their mouth speaks*
ᵃNum. 16:11, 41; 1 Cor.
10:10 ᵇ2 Pet. 2:10; Jude 18
ᶜ2 Pet. 2:18 ᵈ2 Pet. 2:3

17 ᵃJude 3 ᵇ2 Pet. 3:2 ᶜHeb.
2:3

18 ᵃ2 Pet. 3:3; Acts 20:29;
1 Tim. 4:1; 2 Tim. 3:1f.; 4:3
ᵇJude 4, 16

19 ¹Or, *merely natural*
²Lit., *not having*
ᵃ1 Cor. 2:14f.; James 3:15

20 ᵃJude 3 ᵇCol. 2:7;
1 Thess. 5:11 ᶜEph. 6:18

21 ᵃTitus 2:13; Heb. 9:28;
2 Pet. 3:12

22 ¹Some ancient mss.
read, *convince*

23 ᵃAmos 4:11; Zech. 3:2;
1 Cor. 3:15 ᵇRev. 3:4; Zech.
3:3f.

10 But ᵃthese men revile the things which they do not understand; and ᵇthe things which they know by instinct, ᵃlike unreasoning animals, by these things they are ¹destroyed.

11 Woe to them! For they have gone ᵃthe way of Cain, and for pay ¹they have rushed headlong into ᵇthe error of Balaam, and ᶜperished in the rebellion of Korah.

12 These men are those who are ¹hidden reefs ᵃin your love-feasts when they feast with you ᵇwithout fear, caring for themselves; ᶜclouds without water, ᵈcarried along by winds; autumn trees without fruit, ²doubly dead, ᵉuprooted;

13 ᵃwild waves of the sea, casting up ᵇtheir own ¹shame like foam; wandering stars, ᶜfor whom the ²black darkness has been reserved forever.

14 And about these also ᵃEnoch, *in the seventh generation from Adam prophesied, saying, "ᵇBehold, the Lord came with ¹many thousands of His holy ones,*

15 ᵃto execute judgment upon all, and to convict all the ungodly of all their ungodly deeds which they have done in an ungodly way, and of all the harsh things which ᵇungodly sinners have spoken against Him."

16 These are ᵃgrumblers, finding fault, ᵇfollowing after their *own* lusts, ¹they speak ᶜarrogantly, flattering people ᵈfor the sake of *gaining an* advantage.

17 But you, ᵃbeloved, ᵇought to remember the words that were spoken beforehand by ᶜthe apostles of our Lord Jesus Christ;

18 that they were saying to you, "ᵃIn the last time there shall be mockers, ᵇfollowing after their own ungodly lusts."

19 These are the ones who cause divisions, ¹worldly-minded, ²devoid of the Spirit.

20 But you, ᵃbeloved, ᵇbuilding yourselves up on your most holy ᵃfaith; ᶜpraying in the Holy Spirit;

21 keep yourselves in the love of God, ᵃwaiting anxiously for the mercy of our Lord Jesus Christ to eternal life.

22 And ¹have mercy on some, who are doubting;

23 save others, ᵃsnatching them out of the fire; and on some have mercy with fear, ᵇhating even the garment polluted by the flesh.

24 [a]Now to Him who is able to keep you from stumbling, and to [b]make you stand in the presence of His glory blameless with [c]great joy,
25 to the [a]only [b]God our Savior, through Jesus Christ our Lord, [c]be glory, majesty, dominion and authority, [d]before all time and now and [1]forever. Amen.

24 [a]Rom. 16:25 [b]2 Cor. 4:14 [c]1 Pet. 4:13

25 [1]Lit., *to all the ages* [a]John 5:44; 1 Tim. 1:17 [b]Luke 1:47 [c]Rom. 11:36 [d]Heb. 13:8

THE REVELATION OF JOHN

The Revelation of Jesus Christ.
The Message to
the Seven Churches.

THE Revelation of Jesus Christ, which [a]God gave Him to [b]show to His bond-servants, [c]the things which must shortly take place; and He sent and [1]communicated *it* [d]by His angel to His bond-servant [e]John;

2 who bore witness to [a]the word of God and to [b]the testimony of Jesus Christ, *even* to all that he saw.

3 [a]Blessed is he who reads and those who hear the words of the prophecy, and [1]heed the things which are written in it; [b]for the time is near.

4 [a]John to [b]the seven churches that are in [c]Asia: [d]Grace to you and peace, from [e]Him who is and who was and who is to come; and from [f]the seven Spirits who are before His throne;

5 and from Jesus Christ, [a]the faithful witness, the [b]first-born of the dead, and the [c]ruler of the kings of the earth. To Him who [d]loves us, and released us from our sins [1]by His blood,

6 and He has made us *to be* a [a]kingdom, [a]priests to [1b]His God and Father; [c]to Him *be* the glory and the dominion forever and ever. Amen.

7 [a]BEHOLD, HE IS COMING WITH THE CLOUDS, and [b]every eye will see Him, even those who pierced Him; AND ALL THE TRIBES OF THE EARTH WILL [c]MOURN OVER HIM. Even so. Amen.

1 [1]Or, *signified* [a]Rev. 5:7; John 17:8 [b]Rev. 22:6 [c]Rev. 1:19; Dan. 2:28f. [d]Rev. 17:1; 19:9f.; 21:9; 22:16 [e]Rev. 1:4, 9; 22:8

2 [a]Rev. 1:9; 6:9; 20:4; 12:17; 1 Cor. 1:6 [b]Rev. 12:17

3 [1]Or, *keep* [a]Rev. 22:7; Luke 11:28 [b]Rev. 22:10; 3:11; 22:7, 12; Rom. 13:11

4 [a]Rev. 1:1, 9; 22:8 [b]Rev. 1:20; 1:11 [c]Acts 2:9 [d]Rom. 1:7 [e]Rev. 1:8; 4:8; Ex. 3:14; Rev. 16:5; 1:17; Heb. 13:8; Is. 41:4 [f]Rev. 3:1; 4:5; 5:6; Is. 11:2; Rev. 8:2

5 [1]Or, *in* [a]Rev. 3:14; John 8:14; 18:37; 1 Tim. 6:13; Rev. 19:11 [b]1 Cor. 15:20; Col. 1:18 [c]Rev. 17:14; 19:16; 1 Tim. 6:15; Dan. 2:47 [d]Rom. 8:37

6 [1]Or, *God and His Father* [a]Rev. 20:6; 1 Pet. 2:5, 9; Ex. 19:6; Is. 61:6 [b]Rom. 15:6 [c]Rom. 11:36

7 [a]Matt. 16:27f.; 24:30; Dan. 7:13 [b]Zech. 12:10; John 19:37 [c]Luke 23:28

8 ªRev. 21:6; 22:13; Is. 41:4
ᵇRev. 4:8; 11:17; 15:3; 16:7;
21:22; 19:6 ᶜRev. 1:4

9 ¹Or, *steadfastness*
ªRev. 1:1 ᵇActs 1:15 ᶜ2 Cor.
1:7; Phil. 4:14; Matt. 20:23;
Acts 14:22 ᵈRev. 1:6; 2 Tim.
2:12 ᵉRev. 3:10; 2 Thess. 3:5
ᶠRev. 1:2

10 ¹Or, *in spirit*
ªRev. 4:2; 17:3; 21:10; Matt.
22:43 ᵇActs 20:7 ᶜRev. 4:1

11 ¹Or, *scroll*
ªRev. 1:19; 1:2 ᵇRev. 1:4, 20
ᶜRev. 2:1 ᵈRev. 2:8 ᵉRev.
2:12 ᶠRev. 2:18, 24; Acts
16:14 ᵍRev. 3:1, 4 ʰRev. 3:7
ⁱRev. 3:14; Col. 2:1

12 ªRev. 1:20; 2:1; Ex.
25:37; 37:23; Zech. 4:2

13 ¹Or, *the Son of Man*
ªRev. 2:1 ᵇRev. 14:14; Ezek.
1:26; Dan. 7:13; 10:16 ᶜDan.
10:5 ᵈRev. 15:6

14 ªDan. 7:9 ᵇRev. 2:18;
19:12; Dan. 7:9; 10:6

15 ªRev. 2:18; Ezek. 1:7;
Dan. 10:6 ᵇRev. 14:2; 19:6;
Ezek. 43:2

16 ¹Lit., *shines*
ªRev. 1.20; 2:1; 3:1 ᵇRev.
2:12, 16; 19:15; Is. 49:2; Heb.
4:12 ᶜMatt. 17:2; Rev. 10:1
ᵈJudg. 5:31

17 ªDan. 8:17; 10:9, 10, 15
ᵇDan. 8:18; 10:10, 12 ᶜMatt.
14:27; 17:7 ᵈRev. 2:8; 22:13;
Is. 41:4; 44:6; 48:12

18 ¹Lit., *became*
ªLuke 24:5; Rev. 4:9f. ᵇRev.
2:8; Rom. 6:9; Rev. 10:6; 15:7
ᶜRev. 9:1; 20:1; Job 38:17;
Matt. 16:19; 11:23

19 ªRev. 1:11 ᵇRev. 1:12-16
ᶜRev. 4:1

20 ªRom. 11:25 ᵇRev. 1:16;
2:1; 3:1 ᶜRev. 1:12; 2:1; Ex.
25:37; 37:23; Zech. 4:2 ᵈRev.
1:4, 11 ᵉMatt. 5:14f.

8 "I am ªthe Alpha and the Omega," says the ᵇLord God, "ᶜwho is and who was and who is to come, the Almighty."

9 ªI, John, your ᵇbrother and ᶜfellow-partaker in the tribulation and ᵈkingdom and ¹ᵉperseverance *which are* in Jesus, was on the island called Patmos, ᶠbecause of the word of God and the testimony of Jesus.

10 I was ¹ªin the Spirit on ᵇthe Lord's day, and I heard behind me a loud voice ᶜlike *the sound* of a trumpet,

11 saying, "ªWrite in a ¹book what you see, and send *it* to the ᵇseven churches: to ᶜEphesus and to ᵈSmyrna and to ᵉPergamum and to ᶠThyatira and to ᵍSardis and to ʰPhiladelphia and to ⁱLaodicea."

12 And I turned to see the voice that was speaking with me. And having turned I saw ªseven golden lampstands;

13 and ªin the middle of the lampstands one ᵇlike ¹a son of man, ᶜclothed in a robe reaching to the feet, and ᵈgirded across His breasts with a golden girdle.

14 And His head and His ªhair were white like white wool, like snow; and ᵇHis eyes were like a flame of fire;

15 and His ªfeet *were* like burnished bronze, when it has been caused to glow in a furnace, and His ᵇvoice *was* like the sound of many waters.

16 And in His right hand He held ªseven stars; and out of His mouth came a ᵇsharp two-edged sword; and His ᶜface was like ᵈthe sun ¹shining in its strength.

17 And when I saw Him, I ªfell at His feet as a dead man. And He ᵇlaid His right hand upon me, saying, "ᶜDo not be afraid; ᵈI am the first and the last,

18 and the ªliving One; and I ¹ᵇwas dead, and behold, I am alive forevermore, and I have ᶜthe keys of death and of Hades.

19 "ªWrite therefore ᵇthe things which you have seen, and the things which are, and the things which shall take place ᶜafter these things.

20 "As for the ªmystery of the ᵇseven stars which you saw in My right hand, and the ᶜseven golden lampstands, the ᵇseven stars are the angels of ᵈthe seven churches, and the seven ᵉlampstands are the seven churches.

CHAPTER 2

"TO the angel of the church in ᵃEphesus write: 'The One who holds ᵇthe seven stars in His right hand, the One who walks ¹ᶜamong the seven golden lampstands, says this:

2 'ᵃI know your deeds and your toil and ¹perseverance, and that you cannot endure evil men, and you ᵇput to the test those who call themselves ᶜapostles, and they are not, and you found them *to be* false;

3 and you have ¹perseverance and have endured ᵃfor My name's sake, and have not grown weary.

4 'But I have *this* against you, that you have ᵃleft your first love.

5 'Remember therefore from where you have fallen, and ᵃrepent and ᵇdo the ¹deeds you did at first; or else I am coming to you, and will remove your ᶜlampstand out of its place — unless you repent.

6 'Yet this you do have, that you hate the deeds of the ᵃNicolaitans, which I also hate.

7 'ᵃHe who has an ear, let him hear what the Spirit says to the churches. ᵇTo him who overcomes, I will grant to eat of ᶜthe tree of life, which is in the ᵈParadise of God.'

8 "And to the angel of the church in ᵃSmyrna write:

'ᵇThe first and the last, who ¹ᶜwas dead, and has come to life, says this:

9 'I know your ᵃtribulation and your ᵇpoverty (but you are ᵇrich), and the blasphemy by those who ᶜsay they are Jews and are not, but are a synagogue of ᵈSatan.

10 'Do not fear what you are about to suffer. Behold, the devil is about to cast some of you into prison, that you may be ᵃtested, and you will have tribulation ᵇten days. Be ᶜfaithful until death, and I will give you ᵈthe crown of life.

11 'ᵃHe who has an ear, let him hear what the Spirit says to the churches. ᵇHe who overcomes shall not be hurt by the ᶜsecond death.'

12 "And to the angel of the church in ᵃPergamum write:

'The One who has ᵇthe sharp two-edged sword says this:

13 'I know where you dwell, where ᵃSatan's

1 ¹Lit., *in the middle of*
ᵃRev. 1:11 ᵇRev. 1:16 ᶜRev. 1:12f.

2 ¹Or, *steadfastness*
ᵃRev. 2:19; 3:1, 8, 15 ᵇ1 John 4:1; John 6:6 ᶜ2 Cor. 11:13

3 ¹Note vs. 2
ᵃJohn 15:21

4 ᵃMatt. 24:12; Jer. 2:2

5 ¹Lit., *first deeds*
ᵃRev. 2:16, 22; 3:3, 19 ᵇRev. 2:2; Heb. 10:32 ᶜRev. 1:20; Matt. 5:14ff.; Phil. 2:15

6 ᵃRev. 2:15

7 ᵃRev. 2:17; 3:6, 13, 22; 13:9; Matt. 11:15 ᵇRev. 2:11, 17, 26; 3:5, 12, 21; 21:7 ᶜRev. 22:2, 14; Gen. 2:9 [3:22]; Prov. 3:18; 11:30; 13:12; 15:4 ᵈEzek. 31:8 [Sept.]; Luke 23:43

8 ¹Lit., *became*
ᵃRev. 1:11 ᵇRev. 1:17 ᶜRev. 1:18

9 ᵃRev. 1:9 ᵇ2 Cor. 6:10; 8:9; James 2:5 ᶜRev. 3:9 ᵈRev. 2:13, 24; Matt. 4:10

10 ᵃRev. 3:10; 13:14ff. ᵇDan. 1:12, 14 ᶜRev. 2:13; 17:14; 12:11 ᵈ1 Cor. 9:25; Rev. 3:11

11 ᵃRev. 2:7, 17, 29; 3:6, 13, 22; 13:9; Matt. 11:15 ᵇRev. 2:7, 17, 26; 3:5, 12, 21; 21:7 ᶜRev. 20:6, 14; 21:8

12 ᵃRev. 1:11 ᵇRev. 2:16; 1:16

13 ᵃRev. 2:13, 24; Matt. 4:10

13 ᵇRev. 14:12; 1 Tim. 5:8
ᶜRev. 1:5; 11:3; 17:6 marg.;
Acts 22:20 ᵈRev. 2:10; 17:14;
12:11 ᵉRev. 2:9

14 ᵃRev. 2:20 ᵇ2 Pet. 2:15
ᶜRev. 2:20; Acts 15:29; 1 Cor.
10:20

15 ᵃRev. 2:6

16 ᵃRev. 2:5 ᵇRev. 22:7, 20
ᶜRev. 1:16; 2 Thess. 2:8

17 ᵃRev. 2:7 ᵇJohn 6:49f.
ᶜIs. 56:5; 62:2; 65:15 ᵈRev.
19:12; Rev. 14:3

18 ¹Lit., *His eyes*
ᵃRev. 2:24; 1:11 ᵇMatt. 4:3
ᶜRev. 1:14f.

19 ¹Or, *steadfastness* ²Lit.,
last deeds ³Lit., *the first*
ᵃRev. 2:2

20 ᵃRev. 2:14 ᵇ1 Kin. 16.31,
21:25; 2 Kin. 9:7 ᶜRev. 2:14;
Acts 15:29; 1 Cor. 10:20

21 ᵃRom. 2:4; 2 Pet. 3:9
ᵇRev. 9:20f.; 16:9, 11; Rom.
2:5

22 ¹Lit., *I cast* ²Lit., *into*
³Some mss. read, *their*
ᵃRev. 17:2; 18:9

23 ¹Or, *death* ²Lit.,
kidneys, figurative for inner
man
ᵃPs. 7:9; 26:2; 139:1; Jer.
11:20; 17:10; Luke 16:15;
Acts 1:24; Rom. 8:27; Matt.
16:27

24 ᵃRev. 2:18 ᵇ1 Cor. 2:10
ᶜActs 15:28

throne is; and you hold fast My name, and did not deny ᵇMy faith, even in the days of Antipas My ᶜwitness, My ᵈfaithful one, who was killed among you, ᵉwhere Satan dwells.

14 'But ᵃI have a few things against you, because you have there some who hold the ᵇteaching of Balaam, who kept teaching Balak to put a stumbling block before the sons of Israel, ᶜto eat things sacrificed to idols, and to commit *acts of immorality.*

15 'Thus you also have some who in the same way hold the teaching of the ᵃNicolaitans.

16 'ᵃRepent therefore; or else ᵇI am coming to you quickly, and I will make war against them with ᶜthe sword of My mouth.

17 'ᵃHe who has an ear, let him hear what the Spirit says to the churches. ᵃTo him who overcomes, to him I will give *some* of the hidden ᵇmanna, and I will give him a white stone, and a ᶜnew name written on the stone ᵈwhich no one knows but he who receives it.'

18 "And to the church in ᵃThyatira write:

'ᵇThe Son of God, ᶜwho has ¹eyes like a flame of fire, and His feet are like burnished bronze, says this:

19 'ᵃI know your deeds, and your love and faith and service and ¹perseverance, and that your ²deeds of late are greater than ³at first.

20 'But ᵃI have *this* against you, that you tolerate the woman ᵇJezebel, who calls herself a prophetess, and she teaches and leads my bond-servants astray, so that they ᶜcommit *acts of* immorality and eat things sacrificed to idols.

21 'And ᵃI gave her time to repent; and she ᵇdoes not want to repent of her immorality.

22 'Behold, ¹I will cast her ²upon a bed *of sickness,* and those who ᵃcommit adultery with her into great tribulation, unless they repent of ³her deeds.

23 'And I will kill her children with ¹pestilence; and all the churches will know that I am He who ᵃsearches the ²minds and hearts; and I will give to each one of you according to your deeds.

24 'But I say to you, the rest who are in ᵃThyatira, who do not hold this teaching, who have not known the ᵇdeep things of Satan, as they call them — I ᶜplace no other burden on you.

25 'Nevertheless ᵃwhat you have, hold fast ᵇuntil I come.

26 'And ᵃhe who overcomes, and he who keeps My deeds ᵇuntil the end, ᶜTO HIM I WILL GIVE AUTHORITY OVER THE ¹NATIONS;

27 AND HE SHALL ¹ᵃRULE THEM WITH A ROD OF IRON, ᵇAS THE VESSELS OF THE POTTER ARE BROKEN TO PIECES, as I also have received *authority* from My Father;

28 and I will give him ᵃthe morning star.

29 'ᵃHe who has an ear, let him hear what the Spirit says to the churches.'

CHAPTER 3

"AND to the angel of the church in ᵃSardis write: 'He who has ᵇthe seven Spirits of God, and ᶜthe seven stars, says this: ᵈI know your deeds, that you have a name that you are alive, and you are ᵉdead.

2 'Wake up, and strengthen the things that remain, which were about to die; for I have not found your deeds completed in the sight of My God.

3 'ᵃRemember therefore ¹what you have received and heard; and keep *it*, and ᵃrepent. If therefore you will not wake up, ᵇI will come ᶜlike a thief, and you will not know at ᵈwhat hour I will come upon you.

4 'But you have a few ¹ᵃpeople in ᵇSardis who have not ᶜsoiled their garments; and they will walk with Me ᵈin white; for they are worthy.

5 'ᵃHe who overcomes shall thus be clothed in ᵇwhite garments; and I will not ᶜerase his name from the book of life, and ᵈI will confess his name before My Father, and before His angels.

6 'ᵃHe who has an ear, let him hear what the Spirit says to the churches.'

7 "And to the angel of the church in ᵃPhiladelphia write:

'ᵇHe who is holy, ᶜwho is true, who has ᵈthe key of David, who opens and no one will shut, and who shuts and no one opens, says this:

8 'ᵃI know your ¹deeds. Behold, I have put before you ᵇan open door which no one can shut, because you have a little power, and have kept My word, and ᶜhave not denied My name.

25 ᵃRev. 3:11 ᵇJohn 21:22

26 ¹Or, *Gentiles*
ᵃRev. 2:7 ᵇMatt. 10:22; Heb. 3:6 ᶜPs. 2:8; Rev. 3:21; 20:4

27 ¹Or, *shepherd*
ᵃRev. 12:5; 19:15 ᵇIs. 30:14; Jer. 19:11

28 ᵃRev. 22:16; 1 John 3:2

29 ᵃRev. 2:7

1 ᵃRev. 1:11 ᵇRev. 1:4 ᶜRev. 1:16 ᵈRev. 3:8, 15; 2:2 ᵉ1 Tim. 5:6

3 ¹Lit., *how*
ᵃRev. 2:5 ᵇRev. 2:5 ᶜRev. 16:15; 1 Thess. 5:2; 2 Pet. 3:10 ᵈMatt. 24:43

4 ¹Lit., *names*
ᵃRev. 11:13 marg.; Acts 1:15 marg. ᵇRev. 1:11 ᶜJude 23 ᵈRev. 3:5, 18; 4:4; 6:11; 7:9, 13f.; 19:14; 19:8; Eccles. 9:8

5 ᵃRev. 2:7 ᵇRev. 3:4 ᶜRev. 13:8; 17:8; 20:12, 15; 21:27; Luke 10:20 ᵈMatt. 10:32; Luke 12:8

6 ᵃRev. 2:7

7 ᵃRev. 1:11 ᵇRev. 6:10 ᶜRev. 3:14; 19:11; 1 John 5:20 ᵈIs. 22:22; Matt. 16:19; Rev. 1:18; Job 12:14

8 ¹Or, *deeds (behold . . . shut), that you* ᵃRev. 3:1 ᵇActs 14:27 ᶜRev. 2:13

9 ¹Lit., *give* ²Lit., *before*
ªRev. 2:9 ᵇIs. 45:14; 49:23;
60:14 ᶜIs. 43:4; John 17:23

10 ¹Or, *steadfastness* ²Or,
temptation ³Lit., *inhabited
earth* ⁴Or, *tempt*
ªRev. 3:8; John 17:6 ᵇRev.
1:9 ᶜ2 Pet. 2:9; 2 Tim. 2:12
ᵈRev. 2:10 ᶜRev. 16:14;
Matt. 24:14 ᶠRev. 6:10; 8:13;
11:10; 13:8, 14; 17:8

11 ªRev. 22:7, 12, 20; 1:3
ᵇRev. 2:25 ᶜRev. 2:10

12 ªRev. 3:5 ᵇ1 Kin. 7:21;
Jer. 1:18; Gal. 2:9 ᶜRev. 14:1;
22:4 ᵈRev. 21:2; Ezek. 48:35
ᶜRev. 21:2, 10; Gal. 4:26;
Heb. 13:14 ᶠRev. 2:17

13 ªRev. 3:6

14 ¹I.e., origin or source
ªRev. 1:11 ᵇIs. 65:16 marg.;
2 Cor. 1:20 ᶜRev. 1:5; 3:7
ᵈJohn 1:3; Col. 1:18; Rev.
21:6; 22:13; Gen. 49:3; Deut.
21:17; Prov. 8:22 marg.

15 ªRev. 3:1 ᵇRom. 12:11

16 ¹Lit., *vomit*

17 ªHos. 12:8; Zech. 11:5;
1 Cor. 1:8; Matt. 5:3

18 ªIs. 55:1; Matt. 13:44
ᵇ1 Pet. 1:7 ᶜRev. 3:4 ᵈRev.
16:15

19 ªHeb. 12:6; 1 Cor. 11:32
ᵇRev. 2:5

20 ªMatt. 24:33; James 5:9
ᵇLuke 12:36; John 10:3 ᶜJohn
14:23

21 ªRev. 2:7 ᵇRev. 20:4;
2:26; Matt. 19:28; 2 Tim.
2:12 ᶜRev. 5:5; 6:2; 17:14;
John 16:33

22 ªRev. 2:7

512

9 'Behold, I ¹will cause *those* of ªthe synagogue of Satan, who say that they are Jews, and are not, but lie — behold, I will make them to ᵇcome and bow down ²at your feet, and to know that ᶜI have loved you.

10 'Because you have ªkept the word of ᵇMy ¹perseverance, ᶜI also will keep you from the hour of ²ᵈtesting, that *hour* which is about to come upon the whole ³ᵉworld, to ⁴test ᶠthose who dwell upon the earth.

11 'ªI am coming quickly; ᵇhold fast what you have, in order that no one take your ᶜcrown.

12 'ªHe who overcomes, I will make him a ᵇpillar in the temple of My God, and he will not go out from it any more; and I will write upon him the ᶜname of My God, and ᵈthe name of the city of My God, ᵉthe new Jerusalem, which comes down out of heaven from My God, and My ᶠnew name.

13 'ªHe who has an ear, let him hear what the Spirit says to the churches.'

14 "And to the angel of the church in ªLaodicea write:

'ᵇThe Amen, ᶜthe faithful and true Witness, ᵈthe ¹Beginning of the creation of God, says this:

15 'ªI know your deeds, that you are neither cold nor hot; ᵇI would that you were cold or hot.

16 'So because you are lukewarm, and neither hot nor cold, I will ¹spit you out of My mouth.

17 'Because you say, "ªI am rich, and have become wealthy, and have need of nothing," and you do not know that you are wretched and miserable and poor and blind and naked.

18 'I advise you to ªbuy from Me ᵇgold refined by fire, that you may become rich, and ᶜwhite garments, that you may clothe yourself, and *that* ᵈthe shame of your nakedness may not be revealed, and eyesalve to anoint your eyes, that you may see.

19 'ªThose whom I love, I reprove and discipline; be zealous therefore, and ᵇrepent.

20 'Behold, I stand ªat the door and ᵇknock; if any one hears My voice and opens the door, ᶜI will come in to him, and will dine with him, and he with Me.

21 'ªHe who overcomes, I will grant to him ᵇto sit down with Me on My throne, as ᶜI also overcame, and sat down with My Father on His throne.

22 'ªHe who has an ear, let him hear what the Spirit says to the churches.' "

CHAPTER 4

AFTER ᵃthese things I looked, and behold, ᵇa door *standing* open in heaven, and the first voice which I had heard, ᶜlike *the sound* of a trumpet speaking with me, ¹said, "ᵈCome up here, and I will ᵉshow you what must take place after these things."

2 Immediately I was ¹ᵃin the spirit; and behold, ᵇa throne was standing in heaven, and ᶜOne sitting on the throne.

3 And He who was sitting *was* like a ᵃjasper stone and a ᵇsardius in appearance; and *there was* a ¹ᶜrainbow around the throne, like an ᵈemerald in appearance.

4 And ᵃaround the throne *were* ᵇtwenty-four thrones; and upon the thrones *I saw* ᶜtwenty-four elders ᵈsitting, clothed in ᵉwhite garments, and ᶠgolden crowns on their heads.

5 And from the throne proceed ᵃflashes of lightning and sounds and peals of thunder. And *there were* ᵇseven lamps of fire burning before the throne, which are ᶜthe seven Spirits of God;

6 and before the throne *there was*, as it were, a ᵃsea of glass like crystal; and in the ¹center and ᵇaround the throne, ᶜfour living creatures ᵈfull of eyes in front and behind.

7 ᵃAnd the first creature *was* like a lion, and the second creature like a calf, and the third creature had a face like that of a man, and the fourth creature *was* like a flying eagle.

8 And the ᵃfour living creatures, each one of them having ᵇsix wings, are ᶜfull of eyes around and within; and ᵈday and night ¹they do not cease to say,

"ᵉHOLY, HOLY, HOLY, *is* THE ᶠLORD GOD, THE ALMIGHTY, ᵍwho was and who is and who is to come."

9 And when the living creatures give glory and honor and thanks to Him who ᵃsits on the throne, to ᵇHim who lives forever and ever,

10 the ᵃtwenty-four elders will ᵇfall down before Him who ᶜsits on the throne, and will worship ᵈHim who lives forever and ever, and will cast their ᵉcrowns before the throne, saying,

11 "ᵃWorthy art Thou, our Lord and our God, to receive glory and honor and power; for Thou ᵇdidst create all things, and because

1 ¹Lit., *saying*
ᵃRev. 1:12ff., 19 ᵇRev. 19:11;
Ezek. 1:1 ᶜRev. 1:10 ᵈRev.
11:12 ᵉRev. 1:19; 22:6

2 ¹Or, *in spirit*
ᵃRev. 1:10 ᵇRev. 4:9f.; 1 Kin.
22:19; Is. 6:1; Ezek. 1:26;
Dan. 7:9 ᶜRev. 4:9

3 ¹Or, *halo*
ᵃRev. 21:11 ᵇRev. 21:20
ᶜEzek. 1:28; Rev. 10:1 ᵈRev.
21:19

4 ᵃRev. 4:6; 5:11; 7:11
ᵇRev. 11:16 ᶜRev. 4:10; 5:6, 8,
14; 19:4 ᵈRev. 20:4; 2:26;
Matt. 19:28; 2 Tim. 2:12
ᶜRev. 3:18 ᶠRev. 4:10

5 ᵃRev. 8:5; 11:19; 16:18;
Ex. 19:16 ᵇRev. 4:2; Ex.
25:37 ᶜRev. 1:4

6 ¹Lit., *middle of the
throne and around . . .*
ᵃRev. 15:2; 21:18, 21; Ezek.
1:22 ᵇRev. 4:4 ᶜEzek. 1:5;
Rev. 4:8f.; 5:6; 6:1, 6; 7:11;
14:3; 15:7; 19:4 ᵈEzek. 1:18;
10:12

7 ᵃEzek. 1:10; 10:14

8 ¹Lit., *they have no rest,
saying,*
ᵃEzek. 1:5; Rev. 4:6, 9; 5:6;
6:1, 6; 7:11; 14:3; 15:7; 19:4
ᵇIs. 6:2 ᶜEzek. 1:18; 10:12
ᵈRev. 14:11 ᶜIs. 6:3 ᶠRev. 1:8
ᵍRev. 1:4

9 ᵃRev. 4:2, Is. 6:1; Ps. 47:8
ᵇRev. 10:6; 15:7; Deut. 32:40;
Dan. 4:34; 12:7

10 ᵃRev. 4:4 ᵇRev. 5:8, 14;
7:11; 11:16; 19:4 ᶜRev. 4:2; Is.
6:1; Ps. 47:8 ᵈRev. 10:6; 15:7;
Deut. 32:40; Dan. 4:34; 12:7
ᶜRev. 4:4

11 ᵃRev. 5:12; 1:6 ᵇRev.
10:6; 14:7; Acts 14:15

11 ¹Lit., *were*

1 ¹Lit., *upon* ²Or, *scroll*
ªRev. 5:7, 13; 4:9 ᵇEzek. 2:9,
10 ᶜIs. 29:11; Dan. 12:4

2 ¹Or, *scroll*
ªRev. 10:1; 18:21

3 ¹Or, *scroll*
ªRev. 5:13; Phil. 2:10

4 ¹Or, *scroll*

5 ¹Or, *scroll*
ªGen. 49:9 ᵇHeb. 7:14 ᶜRev.
22:16; Is. 11:1, 10; Rom.
15:12

6 ¹Lit., *in the middle of
the throne and of the four
living creatures, and in the
middle of the elders*
ªRev. 5:8, 14; 4:4 ᵇRev. 5:8,
12f.; 13:8; John 1:29 ᶜRev.
5:9, 12; 13:8 ᵈDan. 8:3f.
ᵉZech. 3:9; 4:10 ᶠRev. 1:4

7 ªRev. 5:1

8 ¹Or, *scroll* ²I.e., *true
believers; lit., holy ones*
ªRev. 5:6, 11, 14; 4:6 ᵇRev.
5:6, 14, 4.1 ᶜRev. 4:10 ᵈRev
5:6, 12f.; 1 Cor. 6:20 ᵉRev. 7:9;
ᶜRev. 14:2; 15:2 ᶠRev. 15:7
ᵍRev. 8:3f.; Ps. 141:2

9 ¹Or, *scroll*
ªRev. 14:3; 15:3; Ps. 40:3;
98:1; 149:1; Is. 42:10 ᵇRev.
4:11 ᶜRev. 5:6, 12; 13:8 ᵈRev.
14:3f.; 1 Cor. 6:20 ᵉRev. 7:9;
11:9; 13:7; 14:6; 10:11; 17:15;
Dan. 3:4; 5:19

10 ªRev. 1:6 ᵇRev. 20:4;
3:21

11 ªRev. 4:4 ᵇRev. 5:6, 8, 14;
4:6 ᶜRev. 5:6, 14; 4:4 ᵈDan.
7:10; Rev. 9:16; Heb. 12:22;
Jude 14

514

of Thy will they ¹existed, and were created."

CHAPTER 5

AND I saw ¹in the right hand of Him who ªsat on the throne a ²ᵇbook written inside and on the back, ᶜsealed up with seven seals.

2 And I saw a ªstrong angel proclaiming with a loud voice, "Who is worthy to open the ¹book and to break its seals?"

3 And no one ªin heaven, or on the earth, or under the earth, was able to open the ¹book, or to look into it.

4 And I *began* to weep greatly, because no one was found worthy to open the ¹book, or to look into it;

5 and one of the elders *said to me, "Stop weeping; behold, the ªLion that is ᵇfrom the tribe of Judah, the ᶜRoot of David, has overcome so as to open the ¹book and its seven seals."

6 And I saw ¹between the throne (with the four living creatures) and ªthe elders a ᵇLamb standing, as if ᶜslain, having seven ᵈhorns and ᵉseven eyes, which are ᶠthe seven Spirits of God, sent out into all the earth.

7 And He came, and He took ªit out of the right hand of Him who ªsat on the throne.

8 And when He had taken the ¹book, the ªfour living creatures and the ᵇtwenty-four elders ᶜfell down before the ᵈLamb, having each one a ᵉharp, and ᶠgolden bowls full of incense, which are the ᵍprayers of ²saints.

9 And they *sang a ªnew song, saying,

"ᵇWorthy art Thou to take the ¹book, and
to break its seals; for Thou wast ᶜslain,
and didst ᵈpurchase for God with Thy
blood *men* from ᵉevery tribe and tongue
and people and nation.

10 "And Thou hast made them *to be* a ªkingdom and ªpriests to our God; and they will ᵇreign upon the earth."

11 And I looked, and I heard the voice of many angels ªaround the throne and the ᵇliving creatures and the ᶜelders; and the number of them was ᵈmyriads of myriads, and thousands of thousands;

12 saying with a loud voice,

"ªWorthy is the ᵇLamb that was ᵇslain to receive power and riches and wisdom and might and honor and glory and blessing."

13 And ªevery created thing which is in heaven and on the earth and under the earth and on the sea, and all things in them, I heard saying, "To Him who ᵇsits on the throne, and to the ᶜLamb, ᵈbe blessing and honor and glory and dominion forever and ever."

14 And the ªfour living creatures kept saying, "ᵇAmen." And the ᶜelders ᵈfell down and worshiped.

CHAPTER 6

AND I saw when the ªLamb broke one of the ᵇseven seals, and I heard one of the ᶜfour living creatures saying as with a ᵈvoice of thunder, "Come.¹"

2 And I looked, and behold, a ªwhite horse, and he who sat on it had a bow; and ᵇa crown was given to him; and he went out ᶜconquering, and to conquer.

3 And when He broke the second seal, I heard the ªsecond living creature saying, "Come.¹"

4 And another, ªa red horse, went out; and to him who sat on it, it was granted to ᵇtake peace from the earth, and that *men* should slay one another; and a great sword was given to him.

5 And when He broke the third seal, I heard the ªthird living creature saying, "Come.¹" And I looked, and behold, a ᵇblack horse; and he who sat on it had a ᶜpair of scales in his hand.

6 And I heard as it were a voice in the center of the ªfour living creatures saying, "A ¹quart of wheat for a ²denarius, and three ¹quarts of barley for a ²denarius; and ᵇdo not harm the oil and the wine."

7 And when He broke the fourth seal, I heard the voice of the ªfourth living creature saying, "Come.¹"

8 And I looked, and behold, an ¹ªashen horse; and he who sat on it had the name "ᵇDeath"; and ᵇHades was following with him. And authority was given to them over a fourth of the earth, ᶜTO KILL WITH SWORD AND WITH FAMINE AND WITH ²PESTILENCE AND BY THE WILD BEASTS OF THE EARTH.

12 ªRev. 1:6; 4:11; 5:9 ᵇRev. 5:6, 13; 13:8; John 1:29

13 ªPhil. 2:10; Rev. 5:3 ᵇRev. 5:1 ᶜRev. 5:6, 12f. 13:8; John 1:29 ᵈRom. 11:36; Rev. 1:6

14 ªRev. 5:6, 8, 11; 4:6 ᵇ1 Cor. 14:16; Rev. 7:12; 19:4 ᶜRev. 5:6, 8; 4:4 ᵈRev. 4:10

1 ¹Some mss. add, *and see* ªRev. 5:6, 12f.; 13:8; John 1:29 ᵇRev. 5:1 ᶜRev. 5:6, 8, 11, 14; 4:6 ᵈRev. 14:2; 19:6

2 ªRev. 19:11; Zech. 1:8; 6:3f. ᵇRev. 14:14; 9:7; 19:12; Zech. 6:11 ᶜRev. 3:21

3 ¹Some mss. add, *and see* ªRev. 4:7

4 ªZech. 1:8; 6:2 ᵇMatt. 10:34

5 ¹Some mss. add, *and see* ªRev. 4:7 ᵇZech. 6:2 ᶜEzek. 4:16

6 ¹Lit., *choenix*; a dry measure almost equal to a quart ²A denarius was worth about 18 cents in silver, equal to a day's wage ªRev. 4:6f. ᵇRev. 7:3; 9:4

7 ¹Some mss. add, *and see* ªRev. 4:7

8 ¹Or, *sickly pale* ²Or, *death* ªZech. 6:3 ᵇRev. 1:18; 20:13f.; Prov. 5:5; Hos. 13:14; Matt. 11:23 ᶜJer. 15:2f.; 24:10; 29:17f. Ezek. 5:12, 17; 14:21

9 aEx. 29:12; Lev. 4:7;
John 16:2 bRev. 14:18; 16:7
cRev. 20:4 dRev. 1:2, 9 eRev.
12:17

10 1Or, *Master* 2Lit., *dost
Thou not judge and avenge*
aZech. 1:12 b2 Pet. 2:1; Luke
2:29 cRev. 3:7 dRev. 19:2;
Deut. 32:43; Ps. 79:10; Luke
18:7 eRev. 3:10

11 aRev. 3:5; 7:9; 3:4 bRev.
14:13; 2 Thess. 1:7; Heb.
4:10 cHeb. 11:40 dActs 20:24;
2 Tim. 4:7

12 aRev. 8:5; 11:13; 16:18;
Matt. 24:7 bMatt. 24:29 cIs.
50:3; Matt. 11:21

13 aRev. 8:10; 9:1; Matt.
24:29 bIs. 34:4

14 aIs. 34:4; Rev. 20:11;
21:1; 2 Pet. 3:10 bRev. 16:20;
Is. 54:10; Jer. 4:24; Ezek.
38:20; Nah. 1:5

15 1Lit., *chiliarch,* in
command of one thousand
troops
aIs. 2:10f., 19, 21; 24:21; Rev.
19:18

16 1Lit., *face*
aLuke 23:30; Rev. 9:6 bRev.
4:9; 5:1 cMark 3:5

17 aIs. 63:4; Jer. 30:7; Joel
1:15; 2:1f., 11, 31; Zeph.
1:14f.; Rev. 16:14 bPs. 76:7;
Nah. 1:6; Mal. 3:2; Luke
21:36

1 aRev. 9:14 bRev. 20:8; Is.
11:12; Ezek. 7:2 cJer. 49:36;
Zech. 6:5; Matt. 24:31; dRev.
7:3; 8:7; 9:4

2 aRev. 16:12; Is. 41:2
bRev. 9:4; 7:3 cMatt. 16:16
dRev. 9:14

9 And when He broke the fifth seal, I saw aunderneath the baltar the csouls of those who had been slain dbecause of the word of God, and because of the ctestimony which they had maintained;

10 and they cried out with a loud voice, saying, "aHow long, O 1bLord, choly and true, 2wilt Thou refrain from djudging and avenging our blood on ethose who dwell on the earth?"

11 And athere was given to each of them a white robe; and they were told that they should brest for a little while longer, cuntil *the number of* their fellow-servants and their brethren who were to be killed even as they had been, should be dcompleted also.

12 And I looked when He broke the sixth seal, and there was a great aearthquake; and the bsun became black as csackcloth *made* of hair, and the whole moon became like blood;

13 and athe stars of the sky fell to the earth, bas a fig tree casts its unripe figs when shaken by a great wind.

14 And athe sky was split apart like a scroll when it is rolled up; and bevery mountain and island were moved out of their places.

15 And athe kings of the earth and the great men and the 1commanders and the rich and the strong and every slave and free man, hid themselves in the caves and among the rocks of the mountains;

16 and they *said to the mountains and to the rocks, "Fall on us and hide us from the 1presence of Him bwho sits on the throne, and from the cwrath of the Lamb;

17 for athe great day of their wrath has come; and bwho is able to stand?"

CHAPTER 7

After this I saw afour angels standing at the bfour corners of the earth, holding back cthe four winds of the earth, dso that no wind should blow on the earth or on the sea or on any tree.

2 And I saw another angel ascending afrom the rising of the sun, having the bseal of cthe living God; and he cried out with a loud voice to the dfour angels to whom it was granted to harm the earth and the sea,

3   saying, "ᵃDo not harm the earth or the sea or the trees, until we have ᵇsealed the bond-servants of our God on their ᶜforeheads."

4   And I heard the ᵃnumber of those who were sealed, ᵇone hundred and forty-four thousand sealed from every tribe of the sons of Israel:

5   from the tribe of Judah, twelve thousand *were* sealed, from the tribe of Reuben twelve thousand, from the tribe of Gad twelve thousand,

6   from the tribe of Asher twelve thousand, from the tribe of Naphtali twelve thousand, from the tribe of Manasseh twelve thousand,

7   from the tribe of Simeon twelve thousand, from the tribe of Levi twelve thousand, from the tribe of Issachar twelve thousand,

8   from the tribe of Zebulun twelve thousand, from the tribe of Joseph twelve thousand, from the tribe of Benjamin, twelve thousand *were* sealed.

9   After these things I looked, and behold, a great multitude, which no one could count, from ᵃevery nation and *all* tribes and peoples and tongues, standing ᵇbefore the throne and ᶜbefore the Lamb, clothed in ᵈwhite robes, and ᵉpalm branches *were* in their hands;

10   and they cry out with a loud voice, saying, "ᵃSalvation to our God ᵇwho sits on the throne, and to the Lamb."

11   And all the angels were standing ᵃaround the throne and *around* ᵃthe elders and the ᵇfour living creatures; and they ᶜfell on their faces before the throne and worshiped God,

12   saying,
"ᵃAmen, ᵇblessing and glory and wisdom and thanksgiving and honor and power and might, *be* to our God forever and ever. ᵃAmen."

13   And one of the elders ᵃanswered, saying to me, "These who are clothed in the ᵇwhite robes, who are they, and from where have they come?"

14   And I ¹said to him, "My lord, you know." And he said to me, "These are the ones who come out of the ᵃgreat tribulation, and they have ᵇwashed their robes and made them ᶜwhite in the ᵈblood of the Lamb.

15   "For this reason, they are ᵃbefore the throne of God; and they ᵇserve Him day and night in His ¹ᶜtemple; and ᵈHe who sits on the throne shall spread His ᵉtabernacle over them.

3 ᵃRev. 6:6 ᵇRev. 7:3-8; John 3:33 ᶜRev. 14:1; 22:4; Ezek. 9:4, 6; Rev. 13:16; 14:9; 20:4

4 ᵃRev. 9:16 ᵇRev. 14:1, 3

9 ᵃRev. 5:9 ᵇRev. 7:15 ᶜRev. 22:3 ᵈRev. 6:11; 7:14 ᵉLev. 23:40

10 ᵃRev. 12:10; 19:1; Ps. 3:8 ᵇRev. 22:3

11 ᵃRev. 4:4 ᵇRev. 4:6 ᶜRev. 4:10

12 ᵃRev. 5:14 ᵇRev. 5:12

13 ᵃActs 3:12 ᵇRev. 7:9

14 ¹Lit., *have said* ᵃMatt. 24:21 ᵇRev. 22:14; Zech. 3:3-5 ᶜRev. 6:11; 7:9 ᵈHeb. 9:14; 1 John 1:7

15 ¹Or, *sanctuary* ᵃRev. 7:9 ᵇRev. 22:3; 4:8 ᶜRev. 11:19; 21:22 ᵈRev. 4:9 ᵉRev. 21:3; Lev. 26:11; Ezek. 37:27; John 1:14

517

Revelation 7, 8

Opening of the Seventh Seal.   The Sounding of the First Three Trumpets.

16 [1]Lit., *fall*
[a]Is. 49:10; Ps. 121:5f.

17 [1]Lit., *waters*
[a]Ps. 23:1f.; Matt. 2:6; John 10:11 [b]Rev. 21:6; 22:1; John 4:14 [c]Rev. 21:4; Is. 25:8; Matt. 5:4

1 [a]Rev. 5:1; 6:1, 3, 5, 7, 9, 12 [b]Rev. 5:9

2 [a]Rev. 8:6-13; 9:1, 13; 11:15; 1:4; Matt. 18:10 [b]1 Cor. 15:52; 1 Thess. 4:16

3 [1]Lit., *give* [2]I.e., true believers; lit., *holy ones* [a]Rev. 7:2 [b]Rev. 6:9; Amos 9:1 [c]Heb. 9:4 [d]Rev. 5:8 [e]Ex. 30:1, 3; Num. 4:11; Rev. 8:5; 9:13

4 [1]Or, *for* [2]Note 2, v. 3 [a]Ps. 141:2

5 [a]Lev. 16:12 [b]Ezek. 10:2 [c]Rev. 4:5 [d]Rev. 6:12

6 [a]Rev. 8:2

7 [a]Ezek. 38:22; Is. 28:2; Joel 2:30 [b]Rev. 8:7-12; 9:15, 18; 12:4; Zech. 13:8, 9 [c]Rev. 9:4

8 [a]Jer. 51:25 [b]Rev. 8:7-12; 9:15, 18; 12:4, Zech. 13:8, 9 [c]Rev. 16:3; 11:6; Ex. 7:17ff.

9 [1]Lit., *those which had* [a]Rev. 8:7-12; 9:15, 18; 12:4; Zech. 13:8, 9 [b]Is. 2:16

10 [a]Rev. 9:1; 6:13; Is. 14:12 [b]Rev. 8:7-12; 9:15, 18; 12:4; Zech. 13:8, 9 [c]Rev. 14:7; 16:4

11 [a]Rev. 8:7-12; 9:15, 18; 12:4; Zech. 13:8, 9 [b]Jer. 9:15; 23:15

16 "[a]They shall hunger no more, neither thirst any more; neither shall the sun [1]beat down on them, nor any heat;

17 for the Lamb in the center of the throne shall be their [a]shepherd, and shall guide them to springs of the [1b]water of life; and [c]God shall wipe every tear from their eyes."

CHAPTER 8

AND when He broke the [a]seventh seal, there was [b]silence in heaven for about half an hour.

2 And I saw [a]the seven angels who stand before God; and seven [b]trumpets were given to them.

3 And [a]another angel came and stood at the [b]altar, holding a [c]golden censer; and much [d]incense was given to him, that he might [1]add it to the [d]prayers of all the [2]saints upon the [e]golden altar which was before the throne.

4 And [a]the smoke of the incense, [1]with the prayers of the [2]saints, went up before God out of the angel's hand.

5 And the angel took the censer; and he [a]filled it with the fire of the altar and [b]threw it to the earth; and there followed [c]peals of thunder and sounds and flashes of lightning and an [d]earthquake.

6 [a]And the seven angels who had the seven trumpets prepared themselves to sound them.

7 And the first sounded, and there came [a]hail and fire, mixed with blood, and they were thrown to the earth; and [b]a third of the earth was burnt up, and [b]a third of the [c]trees were burnt up, and all the green [c]grass was burnt up.

8 And the second angel sounded, and *something* like a great [a]mountain burning with fire was thrown into the sea; and [b]a third of the [c]sea became blood;

9 and [a]a third of the creatures, which were in the sea [1]and had life, died; and a third of the [b]ships were destroyed.

10 And the third angel sounded, and a great star [a]fell from heaven, burning like a torch, and it fell on a [b]third of the rivers and on the [c]springs of waters;

11 and the name of the star is called Wormwood; and a [a]third of the waters became [b]worm-

wood; and many men died from the waters, because they were made bitter.

12 And the fourth angel sounded, and a ᵃthird of the ᵇsun and a third of the ᵇmoon and a ᵃthird of the ᵇstars were smitten, so that a ᵃthird of them might be darkened and the day might not shine for a ᵃthird of it, and the night in the same way.

13 And I looked, and I heard ¹an eagle flying in ᵃmid-heaven, saying with a loud voice, "ᵇWoe, woe, woe, to ᶜthose who dwell on the earth; because of the remaining blasts of the trumpet of the ᵈthree angels who are about to sound!"

CHAPTER 9

AND the ᵃfifth angel sounded, and I saw a ᵇstar from heaven which had fallen to the earth; and the ᶜkey of the ¹ᵈbottomless pit was given to him.

2 And he opened the ¹bottomless pit; and ᵃsmoke went up out of the pit, like the smoke of a great furnace; and ᵇthe sun and the air were darkened by the smoke of the pit.

3 And out of the smoke came forth ᵃlocusts ¹upon the earth; and power was given them, as the ᵇscorpions of the earth have power.

4 And they were told that they should not ᵃhurt the ᵇgrass of the earth, nor any green thing, nor any tree, but only the men who do not have the ᶜseal of God on their foreheads.

5 And ¹they were not permitted to kill ²anyone, but to torment for ᵃfive months; and their torment was like the torment of a ᵇscorpion when it ³stings a man.

6 And in those days ᵃmen will seek death and will not find it; and they will long to die and death flees from them.

7 And the ¹ᵃappearance of the locusts was like horses prepared for battle; and on their heads, as it were, crowns like gold, and their faces were like the faces of men.

8 And they had hair like the hair of women, and their ᵃteeth were like *the teeth* of lions.

9 And they had breastplates like breastplates of iron; and the ᵃsound of their wings was like the sound of chariots, of many horses rushing to battle.

10 And they have tails like ᵃscorpions, and stings; and in their ᵇtails is their power to hurt men for ᶜfive months.

12 ᵃRev. 8:7-12; 9:15, 18; 12:4; Zech. 13:8, 9 ᵇRev. 6:12f.; Ex. 10:21ff.

13 ¹Lit., *one eagle* ᵃRev. 14:6; 19:17 ᵇRev. 9:12; 11:14; 12:12 ᶜRev. 3:10 ᵈRev. 8:2

1 ¹Lit., *shaft of the abyss* ᵃRev. 8:2 ᵇRev. 8:10 ᶜRev. 1:18 ᵈLuke 8:31; Rev. 9:2, 11

2 ¹Note v. 1 ᵃGen. 19:28; Ex. 19:18 ᵇJoel 2:2, 10

3 ¹Lit., *into* ᵃRev. 9:7; Ex. 10:12-15 ᵇRev. 9:5, 10; 2 Chr. 10:11, 14; Ezek. 2:6

4 ᵃRev. 6:6 ᵇRev. 8:7 ᶜRev. 7:2, 3

5 ¹Lit., *it was given to them* ²Lit., *them* ³Lit., *strikes* ᵃRev. 9:10 ᵇRev. 9:3, 10; 2 Chr. 10:11, 14; Ezek. 2:6

6 ᵃJob 3:21; 7:15; Jer. 8:3; Rev. 6:16

7 ¹Lit., *appearances* ᵃJoel 2:4

8 ᵃJoel 1:6

9 ᵃJoel 2:5; Jer. 47:3

10 ᵃRev. 8:3, 5; 2 Chr. 10:11, 14; Ezek. 2:6 ᵇRev. 9:19 ᶜRev. 9:5

11 [1]Or, *Destruction* [2]Or, *Destroyer*
[a]Luke 8:31; Rev. 9:1, 2 [b]Rev. 16:16; John 5:2 [c]Job 26:6; 28:22 marg.; 31:12 marg.; Ps. 88:11 marg.; Prov. 15:11

12 [a]Rev. 8:13; 11:14

13 [1]Lit., *one voice* [2]Some ancient mss. omit, *four*
[a]Ex. 30:2f., 10 [b]Rev. 8:3

14 [a]Rev. 7:1 [b]Gen. 15:18; Deut. 1:7; Josh. 1:4; Rev. 16:12

15 [1]Lit., *men*
[a]Rev. 20:7 [b]Rev. 9:18; 8:7

16 [a]Rev. 5:11 [b]Rev. 7:4

17 [1]Lit., *thus I saw* [2]Or, *sulphur*
[a]Dan. 8:2; 9:21 [b]Rev. 9:18; 14:10; 19:20; 20:10; 21:8 [c]Rev. 11:5

18 [1]Lit., *men* [2]Or, *sulphur*
[a]Rev. 9:15; 8:7 [b]Rev. 9:17

20 [1]Lit., *men*
[a]Rev. 2:21 [b]Deut. 4:28; Jer. 1:16; Mic. 5:13; Acts 7:41 [c]1 Cor. 10:20 [d]Ps. 115:4-7; 135:15-17; Dan. 5:23

21 [a]Rev. 9:20 [b]Is. 47:9, 12; Rev. 18:23 [c]Rev. 17:2, 5

1 [a]Rev. 5:2 [b]Rev. 18:1; 20:1 [c]Rev. 4:3 [d]Rev. 1:16; Matt. 17:2 [e]Rev. 1:15

2 [a]Rev. 10:8-10; Rev. 5:1

11   They have as king over them, the angel of the [a]abyss; his name in [b]Hebrew is [1c]Abaddon, and in the Greek he has the name [2]Apollyon.

12   [a]The first Woe is past; behold, two Woes are still coming after these things.

13   And the sixth angel sounded, and I heard [1]a voice from the [2]four [a]horns of the [b]golden altar which is before God,

14   one saying to the sixth angel who had the trumpet, "Release the [a]four angels who are bound at the [b]great river Euphrates."

15   And the four angels, who had been prepared for the hour and day and month and year, were [a]released, so that they might kill a [b]third of [1]mankind.

16   And the number of the armies of the horsemen was [a]two hundred million; [b]I heard the number of them.

17   And [1]this is how I saw [a]in the vision the horses and those who sat on them: *the riders* had breastplates *the color* of fire and of hyacinth and of [2b]brimstone; and the heads of the horses are like the heads of lions; and [c]out of their mouths proceed fire and smoke and [2b]brimstone.

18   A [a]third of [1]mankind was killed by these three plagues, by the [b]fire and the smoke and the [2]brimstone, which proceeded out of their mouths.

19   For the power of the horses is in their mouth and in their tails; for their tails are like serpents and have heads; and with them they do harm.

20   And the rest of [1]mankind, who were not killed by these plagues, [a]did not repent of [b]THE WORKS OF THEIR HANDS, so as not to [c]worship DE-MONS, AND [d]THE IDOLS OF GOLD AND OF SILVER AND OF BRASS AND OF STONE AND OF WOOD, WHICH CAN NEITHER SEE NOR HEAR NOR WALK;

21   and they [a]did not repent of their murders nor of their [b]sorceries nor of their [c]immorality nor of their thefts.

CHAPTER 10

AND I saw another [a]strong angel [b]coming down out of heaven, clothed with a cloud; and the [c]rainbow was upon his head, and [d]his face was like the sun, and his [e]feet like pillars of fire;

2   and he had in his hand a [a]little book which

was open. And he placed [b]his right foot on the sea and his left on the land;

3   and he cried out with a loud voice, [a]as when a lion roars; and when he had cried out, the [b]seven peals of thunder [1]uttered their voices.

4   And when the seven peals of thunder had spoken, [a]I was about to write; and I [b]heard a voice from heaven saying, "[c]Seal up the things which the seven peals of thunder have spoken, and do not write them."

5   And the angel whom I saw standing on the sea and on the land [a]LIFTED UP HIS RIGHT HAND TO HEAVEN,

6   AND SWORE BY [a]HIM WHO LIVES FOREVER AND EVER, WHO [b]CREATED HEAVEN AND THE THINGS IN IT, AND THE EARTH AND THE THINGS IN IT, AND THE SEA AND THE THINGS IN IT, that [c]there shall be delay no longer,

7   but in the days of the voice of the [a]seventh angel, when he is about to sound, then [b]the mystery of God is finished, as He [1]preached to His servants the prophets.

8   And [a]the voice which I heard from heaven, *I heard* again speaking with me, and saying, "Go, take [b]the [1]book which is open in the hand of the angel who [b]stands on the sea and on the land."

9   And I went to the angel, telling him to give me the little book. And he *said to me, "[a]Take it, and eat it; and it will make your stomach bitter, but in your mouth it will be sweet as honey."

10   And I took the little book out of the angel's hand and ate it, and it was in my mouth sweet as honey; and when I had eaten it, my stomach was made bitter.

11   And [a]they *said to me, "You must [b]prophesy again concerning [c]many peoples and nations and tongues and [d]kings."

CHAPTER 11

AND there was given me a [1a]measuring rod like a staff; [2]and [b]someone said, "Rise and measure the [3]temple of God, and the altar, and those who worship in it.

2   "And [1]leave out the [a]court which is outside the [2]temple, and do not measure it, for [b]it has been given to the nations; and they will [b]tread under foot [c]the holy city for [d]forty-two months.

2 [b]Rev. 10:5, 8

3 [1]Or, *spoke*
[a]Is. 31:4; Hos. 11:10 [b]Rev. 4:5; Ps. 29:3-9

4 [a]Rev. 1:11, 19 [b]Rev. 10:8 [c]Dan. 8:26; 12:4, 9; Rev. 22:10

5 [a]Gen. 14:22; Ex. 6:8; Num. 14:30; Deut. 32:40; Ezek. 20:5; Dan 12:7

6 [a]Rev. 4:9 [b]Rev. 4:11 [c]Rev. 6:11; 12:12; 16:17; 21:6

7 [1]Lit., *preached the gospel* [a]Rev. 11:15 [b]Amos 3:7; Rom. 16:25

8 [1]Or, *scroll* [a]Rev. 10:4 [b]Rev. 10:2

9 [a]Ezek. 2:8; 3:1-3; Jer. 15:16

11 [a]Rev. 11:1 [b]Ezek. 37:4, 9 [c]Rev. 5:9 [d]Rev. 17:10, 12

1 [1]Lit., *reed* [2]Lit., *saying* [3]Or, *sanctuary* [a]Rev. 21:15f.; Ezek. 40:3-42:20; Zech. 2:1 [b]Rev. 10:11

2 [1]Lit., *throw out* [2]Or, *sanctuary* [a]Ezek. 40:17, 20 [b]Luke 21:24 [c]Is. 52:1; Matt. 27:53; 4:5; Rev. 21:2, 10; 22:19 [d]Rev. 12:6; 13:5; Dan. 7:25; 12:7

9 ¹Lit., *inhabited earth*
ªRev. 12:3 ᵇRev. 12:15; 20:2;
Gen. 3:1; 2 Cor. 11:3 ᶜMatt.
4:10; 25:41 ᵈRev. 20:3, 8, 10;
13:14 ᵉLuke 10:18; John
12:31

10 ªRev. 11:15 ᵇRev. 7:10
ᶜJob 1:11; 2:5; Zech. 3:1;
Luke 22:31; 1 Pet. 5:8

11 ªRev. 15:2; John 16:33;
1 John 2:13 ᵇRev. 7:14 ᶜRev.
6:9 ᵈRev. 2:10; Luke 14:26

12 ¹Or, *tabernacle*
ªRev. 18:20; Ps. 96:11; Is.
11.23 ᵇNav. 17:6 ᶜR ov. 8:13
ᵈRev. 12:9 ᵉRev. 10:6

13 ªRev. 12:3 ᵇRev. 12:5

14 ¹Lit., *face*
ªEx. 19:4; Deut. 32:11; Is.
40:31 ᵇRev. 12:6 ᶜDan. 7:25,
12:7

15 ¹Lit., *threw*
ªRev. 12:9; 20:2; Gen. 3:1;
2 Cor. 11:3 ᵇHos. 5:10; Is.
59:19

16 ¹Lit., *threw*

17 ªRev. 11:7; 13:7 ᵇGen.
3:15 ᶜRev. 14:12; 1 John 2:3
ᵈRev. 1:2; 6:9; [14:12]; 19:10

1 ¹Some mss. read, *I stood*
²Lit., *sea*
ªRev. 13:14, 15; 15:2; 16:13;
Rev. 11:7; 17:8; Dan. 7:3
ᵇRev. 12:3 ᶜRev. 12:3; 17:12
ᵈRev. 17:3; Dan. 7:8; 11:36

524

8   and they were not strong enough, and there was no longer a place found for them in heaven.

9   And the great ªdragon was thrown down, the ᵇserpent of old who is called the Devil and ᶜSatan, who ᵈdeceives the whole ¹world; he was ᵉthrown down to the earth, and his angels were thrown down with him.

10   And I heard ªa loud voice in heaven, saying, "**N**ow the ᵇsalvation, and the power, and the ªkingdom of our God and the authority of His Christ have come, for the ᶜaccuser of our brethren has been thrown down, who accuses them before our God day and night.

11   "And they ªovercame him because of ᵇthe blood of the Lamb and because of ᶜthe word of their testimony, and they ᵈdid not love their life even to death.

12   "For this reason, ªrejoice, O heavens and ᵇyou who ¹dwell in them. ᶜWoe to the earth and the sea; because ᵈthe devil has come down to you, having great wrath, knowing that he has *only* ᵉa short time."

13   And when the ªdragon saw that he was thrown down to the earth, he persecuted ᵇthe woman who gave birth to the male *child*.

14   And the ªtwo wings of the great eagle were given to the woman, in order that she might fly ᵇinto the wilderness to her place, where she *was nourished for ᶜa time and times and half a time, from the ¹presence of the serpent.

15   And the ªserpent ¹poured water ᵇlike a river out of his mouth after the woman, so that he might cause her to be swept away with the flood.

16   And the earth helped the woman, and the earth opened its mouth and drank up the river which the dragon ¹poured out of his mouth.

17   And the dragon was enraged with the woman, and went off to ªmake war with the rest of her ᵇoffspring, who ᶜkeep the commandments of God and ᵈhold to the testimony of Jesus.

CHAPTER 13

AND ¹he stood on the sand of the ²seashore.

And I saw a ªbeast coming up out of the sea, having ᵇten horns and ᵇseven heads, and on his horns *were* ᶜten diadems, and on his heads *were* ᵈblasphemous names.

2   And the beast which I saw was ᵃlike a leopard, and his feet were *like those* of ᵇa bear, and his mouth like the mouth of ᶜa lion. And the ᵈdragon gave him his power and his ᵉthrone and great authority.

3   And *I saw* one of his heads as if it had been ¹slain, and his ᵃfatal wound was healed. And the whole earth ᵇwas amazed *and followed* after the beast;

4   and they worshiped the ᵃdragon, because he ᵃgave his authority to the beast; and they worshiped the beast, saying, "ᵇWho is like the beast, and who is able to wage war with him?"

5   And there was given to him a mouth ᵃspeaking ¹arrogant words and blasphemies; and authority to ²act for ᵇforty-two months was given to him.

6   And he opened his mouth in blasphemies against God, to blaspheme His name and His tabernacle, *that is,* ᵃthose who ¹dwell in heaven.

7   And it was given to him to ᵃmake war with the ¹saints and to overcome them; and authority over ᵇevery tribe and people and tongue and nation was given to him.

8   And all who ᵃdwell on the earth will worship him, *every one* ᵇwhose name has not been ¹written ᶜfrom the foundation of the world in the book of life of ᵈthe Lamb who has been slain.

9   ᵃIf any one has an ear, let him hear.

10   ᵃIf any one ¹*is destined* for captivity, to captivity he goes; ᵇif any one kills with the sword, with the sword he must be killed. Here is ᶜthe ²perseverance and the faith of the ³saints.

11   And ᵃI saw another beast coming up out of the earth; and he ¹had ᵇtwo horns like a lamb, and he ²spoke as a ᶜdragon.

12   And he ᵃexercises all the authority of the first beast ¹ᵇin his presence. And he makes ᶜthe earth and those who dwell in it to ᵈworship the first beast, whose ᵉfatal wound was healed.

13   And he ᵃperforms great signs, so that he even makes ᵇfire come down out of heaven to the earth in the presence of men.

14   And he ᵃdeceives ᵇthose who dwell on the earth because of ᶜthe signs which it was given him to perform ¹ᵈin the presence of the beast, telling those who dwell on the earth to make an image to the beast who *had the ᵉwound of the sword and has come to life.

2 ᵃDan 7:6; Hos. 13:7f.
ᵇDan. 7:5 ᶜDan. 7:4 ᵈRev.
13:4, 12; 12:3 ᵉRev. 2:13;
16:10

3 ¹Lit., *smitten to death*
ᵃRev. 13:21; Rev. 13:14
ᵇRev. 17:8

4 ᵃRev. 13:2, 12; 12:3
ᵇRev. 18:18; Ex. 15:11; Is.
46:5

5 ¹Lit., *great things* ²Lit.,
do
ᵃDan. 7:8, 11, 20, 25; 11:36;
2 Thess. 2:3f. ᵇRev. 11:2

6 ¹Or, *tabernacle*
ᵃRev. 12:12; 7:15

7 ¹I.e., true believers; lit.,
holy ones
ᵃRev. 11:7 ᵇRev. 5:9

8 ¹Or, *written in the
book . . . slain from the
foundation of the world*
ᵃRev. 13:12, 14; 3:10 ᵇRev.
3:5 ᶜRev. 17:8; Matt. 25:34
ᵈRev. 5:6

9 ᵃRev. 2:7

10 ¹Or, *leads into captivity*
²Or, *steadfastness* ³I.e., true
believers; lit., *holy ones*
ᵃIs. 33:1; Jer. 15:2; 43:11
ᵇGen. 9:6; Matt. 26:52; Rev.
11:18 ᶜHeb. 6:12; Rev. 14:12

11 ¹Lit., *was having* ²Lit.,
was speaking
ᵃRev. 13:1, 14; 16:13 ᵇDan.
8:3 ᶜRev. 13:4

12 ¹Or, *by his authority*
ᵃRev. 13:4 ᵇRev. 13:14; 19:20
ᶜRev. 13:8 ᵈRev. 13:15; 14:9,
11; 16:2; 19:20; 20:4 ᵉRev.
13:3

13 ᵃRev. 19:20; 16:14; Matt.
24:24 ᵇRev. 20:9; 1 Kin.
18:38; Luke 9:54; Rev. 11:5

14 ¹Lit., *by the authority of*
ᵃRev. 12:9 ᵇRev. 13:8
ᶜ2 Thess. 2:9f. ᵈRev. 13:12;
19:20 ᶜRev. 13:3

15 ¹Some ancient mss.
read, *speak, and he will
cause*
ᵃDan. 3:3ff. ᵇRev. 13:12;
14:9, 11; 16:2; 19:20; 20:4

16 ¹Lit., *that they give to
them a mark*
ᵃRev. 11:18; 19:5, 18 ᵇRev.
14:9; 20:4; Gal. 6:17; Rev. 7:3

17 ᵃRev. 14:9; 20:4; Gal.
6:17; Rev. 7:3 ᵇRev. 14:11
ᶜRev. 15:2

18 ¹Some mss. read, 616
ᵃRev. 17:9 ᵇRev. 21:17

1 ᵃRev. 5:6 ᵇPs. 2:6; Heb.
12:22 ᶜRev. 14:3; 7:4 ᵈRev.
3:12 ᵉRev. 7:3

2 ᵃRev. 1:15 ᵇRev. 6:1
ᶜRev. 5:8

3 ¹Some ancient mss.
read, *sing, as it were, a new
song*
ᵃRev. 5:9 ᵇRev. 4:6 ᶜRev. 4:4
ᵈRev. 2:17 ᵉRev. 14:1; 7:4

4 ¹Or, *chaste men, lit.,
virgins*
ᵃMatt. 19:12 Rev. 3:4; 2 Cor.
11:2; Eph. 5:27 ᵇRev. 7:17;
Rev. 3:4; 17:14 ᶜRev. 5:9
ᵈJames 1:18; Heb. 12:23

5 ᵃZeph. 3:13; Ps. 32:2;
Mal. 2:6; John 1:47; 1 Pet.
2:22 ᵇJude 24; Heb. 9:14;
1 Pet. 1:19

6 ¹Lit., *sit*
ᵃRev. 8:13 ᵇRev. 10:7; 1 Pet.
1:25 ᶜRev. 3:10 ᵈRev. 5:9

7 ᵃRev. 15:4 ᵇRev. 11:13
ᶜRev. 4:11 ᵈRev. 8:10

15 And there was given to him to give breath to the image of the beast, that the image of the beast might even ¹speak and cause ᵃas many as do not ᵇworship the image of the beast to be killed.

16 And he causes all, ᵃthe small and the great, and the rich and the poor, and the free men and the slaves, ¹to be given a ᵇmark on their right hand, or on their forehead,

17 and *he provides* that no one should be able to buy or to sell, except the one who has the ᵃmark, *either* ᵇthe name of the beast or ᶜthe number of his name.

18 ᵃHere is wisdom. Let him who has understanding calculate the number of the beast, for the number is that ᵇof a man; and his number is ¹six hundred and sixty-six.

CHAPTER 14

AND I looked, and behold, ᵃthe Lamb *was* standing on ᵇMount Zion, and with Him ᶜone hundred and forty-four thousand, having ᵈHis name and the ᵈname of His Father written ᵉon their foreheads.

2 And I heard a voice from heaven, like ᵃthe sound of many waters and like the ᵇsound of loud thunder, and the voice which I heard *was* like *the sound* of ᶜharpists playing on their harps.

3 And they ¹*sang ᵃa new song before the throne and before the ᵇfour living creatures and the ᶜelders; and ᵈno one could learn the song except the ᵉone hundred and forty-four thousand who had been ᵃpurchased from the earth.

4 ᵃThese are the ones who have not been defiled with women, for they are ¹celibates. These *are* the ones who ᵇfollow the Lamb wherever He goes. These have been ᶜpurchased from among men ᵈas first fruits to God and to the Lamb.

5 And no lie was found ᵃin their mouth; they are ᵇblameless.

6 And I saw another angel flying in ᵃmidheaven, having ᵇan eternal gospel to preach to ᶜthose who ¹live on the earth, and to ᵈevery nation and tribe and tongue and people;

7 and He said with a loud voice, "ᵃFear God, and ᵇgive Him glory, because the hour of His judgment has come; and worship Him who ᶜmade the heaven and the earth and sea and ᵈsprings of waters."

8 And another angel, a second one, followed, saying, "ªFallen, fallen is ᵇBabylon the great, she who has ᶜmade all the nations drink of the ᵈwine of the ¹passion of her immorality."

9 And another angel, a third one, followed them, saying with a loud voice, "If any one ªworships the beast and his ᵇimage, and receives a ᶜmark on his forehead or upon his hand,

10 he also will drink of the ªwine of the wrath of God, which is mixed ¹in full strength ᵇin the cup of His anger; and he will be tormented with ᶜfire and brimstone in the presence of the ᵈholy angels and in the presence of the Lamb.

11 "And the ªsmoke of their torment goes up forever and ever; and ᵇthey have no rest day and night, those who ᶜworship the beast and his ᶜimage, and whoever receives the ᵈmark of his name."

12 Here is ªthe ¹perseverance of the ²saints who ᵇkeep the commandments of God and ³ᶜtheir faith in Jesus.

13 And I heard a voice from heaven, saying, "Write, 'ªBlessed are the dead who ᵇdie in the Lord ᶜfrom now on!' " "Yes," ᵈsays the Spirit, "that they may ᵉrest from their labors, for their ᶠdeeds follow with them."

14 And I looked, and behold, a ªwhite cloud, and sitting on the cloud *was* one ᵇlike ¹a son of man, having a golden ᶜcrown on His head, and a sharp sickle in His hand.

15 And another angel ªcame out of the ¹temple, crying out with a loud voice to Him who sat on the cloud, "²ᵇPut in your sickle and reap, because the hour to reap has come, because the ᶜharvest of the earth ³is ripe."

16 And He who sat on the cloud ¹swung His sickle over the earth; and the earth was reaped.

17 And another angel ªcame out of the ¹temple which is in heaven, ²and he also had a sharp sickle.

18 And another angel, ªthe one who has power over fire, came out from ᵇthe altar; and he called with a loud voice to him who had the sharp sickle, saying, "¹ᶜPut in your sharp sickle, and gather the clusters ²from the vine of the earth, ᵈbecause her grapes are ripe."

19 And the angel ¹swung his sickle to the earth, and gathered *the clusters from* the vine of the

8 ¹Or, *wrath*
ªRev. 18:2; Is. 21:9; Jer. 51:8
ᵇRev. 16:19; 17:5; 18:10;
Dan. 4:30 ᶜJer. 51:7 ᵈRev. 18:3; 17:2, 4

9 ªRev. 14:11; Rev. 13:12
ᵇRev. 14:11; 13:14f. ᶜRev. 13:16

10 ¹Lit., *unmixed*
ªRev. 16:19; 19:15; Is. 51:17; Jer. 25:15f., 27 ᵇRev. 18:6; Ps. 75:8 ᶜRev. 19:20; 20:10, 14f.; 21:8; Ezek. 38:22; 2 Thess. 1:7 ᵈMark 8:38

11 ªRev. 18:9, 18; 19:3; Is. 34:8-10 ᵇRev. 4:8 ᶜRev. 14:9; 13:12 ᵈRev. 13:17

12 ¹Or, *steadfastness* ²I.e., true believers; lit., *holy ones* ³Lit., *the faith of* ªRev. 13:10 ᵇRev. 12:17 ᶜRev. 2:13

13 ªRev. 20:6 ᵇ1 Cor. 15:18; 1 Thess. 4:16 ᶜRev. 11:18 ᵈRev. 2:7; 22:17 ᵉRev. 6:11; Heb. 4:9f. ᶠ1 Tim. 5:25

14 ¹Or, *the Son of Man* ªMatt. 17:5 ᵇRev. 1:13 ᶜRev. 6:2; Ps. 21:3

15 ¹Or, *sanctuary* ²Lit., *Send forth* ³Lit., *has become dry* ªRev. 14:17; 15:6; 16:17; 11:19 ᵇRev. 14:18; Mark 4:29; Joel 3:13 ᶜMatt. 13:39-41; Jer. 51:33

16 ¹Lit., *cast*

17 ¹Or, *sanctuary* ²Lit., *having himself also* ªRev. 14:15; 15:6; 16:17; 11:19

18 ¹Lit., *Send forth* ²Lit., *of* ªRev. 16:8 ᵇRev. 6:9; 8:3 ᶜRev. 14:15; Mark 4:29; Joel 3:13 ᵈJoel 3:13

19 ¹Lit., *cast*

527

19 ªRev. 19:15; Is. 63:2f.

20 ¹Lit., *from two hundred miles* ²Lit., *sixteen hundred stadia.* A stadion was about six hundred feet. ªHeb. 13:12; Rev. 11:8 ᵇGen. 49:11; Deut. 32:14

1 ªRev. 12:1, 3 ᵇRev. 15:6-8; 16:1; 17:1; 21:9 ᶜLev. 26:21, ᵈRev. 9:20

2 ªRev. 4:6 ᵇRev. 12:11 ᶜRev. 13:1 ᵈRev. 13:14f. ᵉRev. 13:17 ᶠRev. 5:8

3 ¹Some ancient mss. read, *ages* ªEx. 15:1ff. ᵇJosh. 22:5; Heb. 3:5 ᶜRev. 5:9f., 12f. ᵈDeut. 32:3f.; Ps. 111:2; 139:14; Hos. 14:9 ᵉRev. 1:8 ᶠ1 Tim. 1:17 marg.

4 ¹Or, *judgments* ªRev. 14:7; Jer. 10:7 ᵇPs. 86:9; Is. 66:23 ᶜRev. 19:8

5 ¹Or, *sanctuary* ªRev. 11:19 ᵇEx. 38:21; Num. 1:50; Heb. 8:5; Rev. 13:6

6 ¹Or, *sanctuary* ²Some mss. read, *stone* ªRev. 15:1 ᵇRev. 14:15 ᶜEzek. 28:13 ᵈRev. 1:13

7 ªRev. 4:6 ᵇRev. 15:1 ᶜRev. 5:8 ᵈRev. 15:1; 14:10 ᵉRev. 4:9

8 ¹Or, *sanctuary* ªEx. 19:18; Is. 6:4; Ex. 40:34f.; Lev. 16:2; 1 Kin. 8:10f.; 2 Chr. 5:13f.

528

earth, and threw them into ªthe great wine press of the wrath of God.

20 And the wine press was trodden ªoutside the city, and ᵇblood came out from the wine press, up to the horses' bridles, ¹for a distance of ²two hundred miles.

CHAPTER 15

AND I saw ªanother sign in heaven, great and marvelous, ᵇseven angels who had ᶜseven plagues, *which are* ᵈthe last, because in them the wrath of God is finished.

2 And I saw, as it were, a ªsea of glass mixed with fire, and those who had ᵇcome off victorious from the ᶜbeast and from ᵈhis image and from the ᵉnumber of his name, standing on the ªsea of glass, holding ᶠharps of God.

3 And they *sang the ªsong of Moses ᵇthe bond-servant of God and the ᶜsong of the Lamb, saying,

"ᵈGREAT AND MARVELOUS ARE THY WORKS,
ᵉO LORD GOD, THE ALMIGHTY;
RIGHTEOUS AND TRUE ARE THY WAYS,
THOU ᶠKING OF THE ¹NATIONS.

4 "ªWHO WILL NOT FEAR, O LORD, AND GLORIFY
THY NAME?
FOR THOU ALONE ART HOLY;
FOR ᵇALL THE NATIONS WILL COME AND WOR-
SHIP BEFORE THEE,
For Thy ¹ᶜrighteous acts have been revealed."

5 After these things I looked, and ªthe ¹temple of the ᵇtabernacle of testimony in heaven was opened,

6 and the ªseven angels who had the seven plagues ᵇcame out of the ¹temple, clothed ᶜin ²linen, clean *and* bright, and ᵈgirded around their breasts with golden girdles.

7 And one of the ªfour living creatures gave to the ᵇseven angels seven ᶜgolden bowls full of the ᵈwrath of God, who ᵉlives forever and ever.

8 And the ¹temple was filled with ªsmoke from the glory of God and from His power; and no one was able to enter the ¹temple until the seven plagues of the seven angels were finished.

CHAPTER 16

AND I heard a loud voice from [a]the [1]temple, saying to the [b]seven angels, "Go and [c]pour out the [d]seven bowls of the wrath of God into the earth."

2 And the first *angel* went and poured out his bowl [a]into the earth; and it became a loathsome and malignant [b]sore upon the men [c]who had the mark of the beast and who worshiped his image.

3 And the second *angel* poured out his bowl [a]into the sea, and it became blood like *that* of a dead man; and every living [1]thing in the sea died.

4 And the third *angel* poured out his bowl into the [a]rivers and the springs of waters; and [1]they [b]became blood.

5 And I heard the angel of the waters saying, "[a]Righteous art Thou, [b]who art and who wast, O [c]Holy One, because Thou didst [d]judge these things;

6 for they poured out [a]the blood of saints and prophets, and Thou hast given them [b]blood to drink. They [1]deserve it."

7 And I heard [a]the altar saying, "Yes, O [b]Lord God, the Almighty, [c]true and righteous are Thy judgments."

8 And the fourth *angel* poured out his bowl upon [a]the sun; [b]and it was given to it to scorch men with fire.

9 And men were scorched with [1]fierce heat; and they [a]blasphemed the name of God who has the power over these plagues; and they [b]did not repent, so as to [c]give Him glory.

10 And the fifth *angel* poured out his bowl upon the [a]throne of the beast; and his kingdom became [b]darkened; and they gnawed their tongues because of pain,

11 and they [a]blasphemed the [b]God of heaven because of their pains and their [c]sores; and they [d]did not repent of their deeds.

12 And the sixth *angel* poured out his bowl upon the [a]great river, the Euphrates; and [b]its water was dried up, that [c]the way might be prepared for the kings [d]from the [1]east.

13 And I saw *coming* out of the mouth of the [a]dragon and out of the mouth of the [b]beast and out of the mouth of the [c]false prophet, three [d]unclean spirits like [e]frogs;

14 for they are [a]spirits of demons, [b]performing

1 [1]Or, *sanctuary* [a]Rev. 11:19 [b]Rev. 15:1 [c]Rev. 16:2ff.; Ps. 79:6; Jer. 10:25; Ezek. 22:31; Zeph. 3:8 [d]Rev. 5:8

2 [a]Rev. 8:7 [b]Rev. 16:11; Ex. 9:9-11; Deut. 28:35 [c]Rev. 13:15-17; 14:9

3 [1]Lit., *soul.* Some ancient mss. read, *thing, the things in the sea.* [a]Rev. 8:8f.; Ex. 7:17-21; Rev. 11:6

4 [1]Some ancient mss. read, *it became* [a]Rev. 8:10 [b]Ex. 7:17-20; Rev. 11:6

5 [a]John 17:25 [b]Rev. 11:17 [c]Rev. 15:4 [d]Rev. 6:10

6 [1]Lit., *are worthy* [a]Rev. 18:24; Rev. 17:6 [b]Is. 49:26; Luke 11:49-51

7 [a]Rev. 6:9; 14:18 [b]Rev. 1:8 [c]Rev. 19:2; 15:3

8 [a]Rev. 6:12 [b]Rev. 14:18

9 [1]Lit., *great* [a]Rev. 16:11, 21 [b]Rev. 2:21 [c]Rev. 11:13

10 [a]Rev. 13:2 [b]Rev. 8:12; 9:2; Ex. 10:21f.; Is. 8:22

11 [a]Rev. 16:9, 21 [b]Rev. 11:13 [c]Rev. 16:2 [d]Rev. 2:21

12 [1]Lit., *rising of the sun* [a]Rev. 9:14 [b]Is. 11:15f.; 44:27; Jer. 51:32, 36 [c]Is. 41:2, 25; 46:11 [d]Rev. 7:2

13 [a]Rev. 12:3 [b]Rev. 13:1 [c]Rev. 19:20; 20:10; Rev. 13:11, 14 [d]Rev. 18:2 [e]Ex. 8:6

14 [a]1 Tim. 4:1 [b]Rev. 13:13

529

14 ¹Lit., *inhabited earth*
ᶜRev. 3:10 ᵈRev. 20:8;
17:14; 19:19; 1 Kin. 22:21-23
ᵉRev. 6:17

15 ¹Lit., *they*
ᵃRev. 3:3, 11 ᵇLuke 12:37
ᶜRev. 3:18

16 ¹Some authorities read,
Armageddon
ᵃRev. 19:19 ᵇRev. 9:11 ᶜJudg.
5:19; 2 Kin. 23:29f.; 2 Chr.
35:22; Zech. 12:11

17 ¹Or, *sanctuary*
ᵃEph. 2:2 ᵇRev. 11:15 ᶜRev.
14:15 ᵈRev. 21:6; Rev. 10:6

18 ᵃRev. 4:5 ᵇRev. 6:12
ᶜDan. 12:1; Matt. 24:21

19 ¹Or, *Gentiles*
ᵃRev. 17:18; 18:10, 18f., 21;
11:8 ᵇRev. 14:8 ᶜRev. 18:5
ᵈRev. 14:10

20 ᵃRev. 6:14; 20:11

21 ¹Lit., *hail* ²Lit., *the
weight of a talent* ³Lit.,
great
ᵃRev. 11:19; 8:7 ᵇRev. 16:9,
11 ᶜEx. 9:18-25

1 ᵃRev. 21:9; 1:1 ᵇRev.
15:1 ᶜRev. 15:7 ᵈRev. 16:19
ᶜRev. 17:5, 15f.; 19:2; Nah.
3:4; Is. 1:21; Jer. 2:20 ᶠRev.
17:15; Jer. 51:13

2 ᵃRev. 18:3, 9; 2:22 ᵇRev.
17:8; 3:10 ᶜRev. 14:8

3 ¹Or, *in spirit*
ᵃRev. 21:10 ᵇRev. 1:10 ᶜRev.
12:6, 14; 21:10 ᵈRev. 18:12,
16; Matt. 27:28 ᶜRev. 13:1
ᶠRev. 17:7, 9, 12, 16; 12:3

4 ¹Lit., *gilded* ²Lit., *stone*
ᵃRev. 18:16; 18:12; Ezek.
28:13 ᵇJer. 51:7; Rev. 18:6

530

signs, which go out to the kings of the ᶜwhole ¹world, to ᵈgather them together for the war of the ᵉgreat day of God, the Almighty.

15 (Behold, ᵃI am coming like a thief. ᵇBlessed is the one who stays awake and keeps his garments, ᶜlest he walk about naked and ¹men see his shame.)

16 And they ᵃgathered them together to the place which ᵇin Hebrew is called ¹Har-ᶜMagedon.

17 And the seventh *angel* poured out his bowl upon ᵃthe air; and a ᵇloud voice came out of the ¹ᶜtemple from the throne, saying, "ᵈIt is done."

18 And there were flashes of ᵃlightning and sounds and peals of thunder; and there was ᵇa great earthquake, ᶜsuch as there had not been since man came to be upon the earth, so great an earthquake *was it, and* so mighty.

19 And ᵃthe great city was split into three parts, and the cities of the ¹nations fell. And ᵇBabylon the great was ᶜremembered before God, to give her ᵈthe cup of the wine of His fierce wrath.

20 And ᵃevery island fled away, and the mountains were not found.

21 And ᵃhuge ¹hailstones, about ²one hundred pounds each, *came down from heaven upon men; and men ᵇblasphemed God because of the ᶜplague of the hail, because its plague *was extremely ³severe.

ᵃ   CHAPTER 17

AND one of the ᵇseven angels who had the ᶜseven bowls came and spoke with me, saying, "Come here, I shall show you ᵈthe judgment of the ᵉgreat harlot who ᶠsits on many waters,

2 with whom ᵃthe kings of the earth committed *acts of* immorality, and ᵇthose who dwell on the earth were ᶜmade drunk with the wine of her immorality."

3 And ᵃhe carried me away ¹ᵇin the Spirit ᶜinto a wilderness; and I saw a woman sitting on a ᵈscarlet beast, full of ᵉblasphemous names, having ᶠseven heads and ten horns.

4 And the woman ᵃwas clothed in purple and scarlet, and ¹adorned with gold and precious ²stones and pearls, having in her hand ᵇa gold cup full of abominations and of the unclean things of her immorality,

5 and upon her forehead a name *was* written,

a ªmystery, "ᵇBABYLON THE GREAT, THE MOTHER OF HARLOTS AND OF ᶜTHE ABOMINATIONS OF THE EARTH."

6 And I saw the woman drunk with the ªblood of the ¹saints, and with the blood of the witnesses of Jesus. And when I saw her, I wondered ²greatly.

7 And the angel said to me, "Why ¹do you wonder? I shall tell you the ªmystery of the woman and of the beast that carries her, which has the ᵇseven heads and the ten horns.

8 "The beast that you saw ªwas and is not, and is about to ᵇcome up out of the ᶜabyss and ¹to ᵈgo to destruction. And ᵉthose who dwell on the earth will ᶠwonder, ᵍwhose name has not been written in the book of life ʰfrom the foundation of the world, when they see the beast, that ªhe was and is not and will come.

9 "ªHere is the mind which has wisdom. The ᵇseven heads are seven mountains on which the woman sits,

10 and they are seven ªkings; five have fallen, one is, the other has not yet come; and when he comes, he must remain a little while.

11 "And the beast which ªwas and is not, is himself also an eighth, and is *one* of the seven, and he ᵇgoes to destruction.

12 "And the ªten horns which you saw are ten kings, who have not yet received a kingdom, but they receive authority as kings with the beast ᵇfor one hour.

13 "These have ªone ¹purpose and they give their power and authority to the beast.

14 "These will wage ªwar against the Lamb, and the Lamb will ᵇovercome them, because He is ᶜLord of lords and ᶜKing of kings, and ᵈthose who are with Him *are the* ᵉcalled and chosen and faithful."

15 And he *said to me, "The ªwaters which you saw where the harlot sits, are ᵇpeoples and multitudes and nations and tongues.

16 "And the ªten horns which you saw, and the beast, these will hate the harlot and will make her ᵇdesolate and ᶜnaked, and will ᵈeat her flesh and will ᵉburn her up with fire.

17 "For ªGod has put it in their hearts to execute His ¹purpose ²by ᵇhaving a common purpose, and by giving their kingdom to the beast, until the ᶜwords of God should be fulfilled.

5 ªRev. 17:7; 2 Thess. 2:7; Rev. 1:20 ᵇRev. 14:8; 16:19 ᶜRev. 17:2

6 ¹I.e., true believers; lit., holy ones ²Lit., with great wonder ªRev. 16:6

7 ¹Lit., *have you wondered* ªRev. 17:5; 2 Thess. 2:7; Rev. 1:20 ᵇRev. 17:3

8 ¹Some ancient mss. read, *he goes* ªRev. 17:11; 13:3, 12, 14 ᵇRev. 11:7; 13:1 ᶜRev. 9:1; 13:1 ᵈRev. 17:11; 13:10 ᵉRev. 3:10 ᶠRev. 13:3 ᵍRev. 3:5 ʰRev. 13:8; Matt. 25:34

9ªRev. 13:18 ᵇRev. 17:3

10 ªRev. 10:11

11 ªRev. 17:8; 13:3, 12, 14 ᵇRev. 17:8; 13:10

12 ªRev. 17:16; 12:3; 13:1 ᵇRev. 18:10, 17, 19

13 ¹Or, *mind* ªRev. 17:17

14 ªRev. 16:14 ᵇRev. 3:21 ᶜRev. 19:16; 1 Tim. 6:15 ᵈRev. 2:10f. ᵉMatt. 22:14

15 ªRev. 17:1; Is. 8:7; Jer. 47:2 ᵇRev. 5:9

16 ªRev. 17:12 ᵇRev. 18:17, 19 ᶜEzek. 16:37, 39 ᵈRev. 19:18 ᵉRev. 18:8

17 ¹Or, *mind* ²Lit., *even to do one mind and to give* ª2 Cor. 8:16 ᵇRev. 17:13 ᶜRev. 10:7

18 ¹Lit., *has a kingdom*
ªRev. 16:19; 11:8

1 ªRev. 17:1, 7 ᵇRev. 10:1
ᶜEzek. 43:2

2 ¹Or, *haunt*
ªRev. 14:8 ᵇIs. 13:21f.; 34:11,
13-15; Jer. 50:39; 51:37;
Zeph. 2:14f. ᶜRev. 16:13

3 ¹Many ancient mss.
read, *have fallen by* ²Lit.,
wrath ³Lit., *power* ⁴Or,
luxury
ªRev. 14:8 ᵇRev. 18:9; 17:2
ᶜRev. 18:11, 15; 18:19, 23;
Ezek. 27:9-25 ᵈRev. 18:7, 9;
1 Tim. 5:11

4 ªIs. 52:11; Jer 50:8; 51:6,
9, 45; 2 Cor. 6:17

5 ¹Lit., *joined together*
ªJer. 51:9 ᵇRev. 16:19

6 ¹Lit., *double to her*
ªPs. 137:8; Jer. 50:15, 29
ᵇRev. 17:4

7 ¹Or, *luxuriously*
ªEzek. 28:2-8 ᵇRev. 18:3, 9;
1 Tim. 5:11 ᶜIs. 47:7f.; Zeph.
2:15

8 ¹Or, *death*
ªIs. 47:9; Jer. 50:31f.; Rev.
18:10 ᵇRev. 17:16 ᶜJer. 50:34;
Rev. 11:17f.

9 ¹Or, *luxuriously*
ªRev. 18:3; 17:2 ᵇRev. 18:3,
7; 1 Tim. 5:11 ᶜEzek. 26:16f.;
27:35 ᵈRev. 18:18; 14:11;
19:3

10 ªRev. 18:15, 17 ᵇRev.
18:16, 19 ᶜRev. 18:16, 18, 19,
21; 11:8; 16:19 ᵈRev. 18:17,
19; 17:12; 18:8

11 ªRev. 18:3, 15; 18:19, 23;
Ezek. 27:9-25 ᵇEzek. 27:27-
34

532

18 "And the woman whom you saw is ªthe great city, which ¹reigns over the kings of the earth."

CHAPTER 18

AFTER these things I saw ªanother angel ᵇcoming down from heaven, having great authority, and the earth was ᶜillumined with his glory.

2 And he cried out with a mighty voice, saying, "ªFallen, fallen is Babylon the great! And she ᵇhas become a dwelling place of demons and a ¹prison of every ᶜunclean spirit, and a ¹prison of every unclean and hateful bird.

3 "For all the nations ¹have drunk of the ªwine of the ²passion of her immorality, and ᵇthe kings of the earth have committed *acts of* immorality with her, and the ᶜmerchants of the earth have become rich by the ³wealth of her ⁴ᵈsensuality."

4 And I heard another voice from heaven, saying, "ªCome out of her, my people, that you may not participate in her sins and that you may not receive of her plagues;

5 for her sins have ¹ªpiled up as high as heaven, and God has ᵇremembered her iniquities.

6 "ªPay her back even as she has paid, and ¹give back *to her* double according to her deeds; in the ᵇcup which she has mixed, mix twice as much for her.

7 "ªTo the degree that she glorified herself and ᵇlived ¹sensuously, to the same degree give her torment and mourning; for she says in her heart, 'ᶜI sit *as* a queen and I am not a widow, and will never see mourning.'

8 "For this reason ªin one day her plagues will come, ¹pestilence and mourning and famine, and she will be ᵇburned up with fire; for the Lord God who judges her ᶜis strong.

9 "And ªthe kings of the earth, who committed *acts of* immorality and ᵇlived ¹sensuously with her, will ᶜweep and lament over her when they ᵈsee the smoke of her burning,

10 ªstanding at a distance because of the fear of her torment, saying, 'ᵇWoe, woe, ᶜthe great city, Babylon, the strong city! For in ᵈone hour your judgment has come.'

11 "And the ªmerchants of the earth ᵇweep and mourn over her, because no one buys their cargoes any more;

12   cargoes of [a]gold and silver and precious [1]stones and pearls and fine linen and purple and silk and scarlet, and every *kind of* citron wood and every article of ivory and every article *made* from very costly wood and [2]bronze and iron and marble, 13   and cinnamon and [1]spice and incense and perfume and frankincense and wine and olive oil and fine flour and wheat and cattle and sheep, and *cargoes* of horses and chariots and [2]slaves, and [3a]human lives.

14   "And the fruit [1]you long for has gone from you, and all things that were luxurious and splendid have passed away from you and *men* will no longer find them.

15   "The [a]merchants of [b]these things, who became rich from her, will [c]stand at a distance because of the fear of her torment, weeping and mourning,

16   saying, '[a]Woe, woe, [b]the great city, she who [c]was clothed in fine linen and purple and scarlet, and [1]adorned with gold and precious [2]stones and pearls;

17   for in [a]one hour such great wealth has been laid [b]waste.' And [c]every shipmaster and every [1]passenger and sailor, and as many as make their living by the sea, [a]stood at a distance,

18   and were [a]crying out as they [b]saw the smoke of her burning, saying, '[c]What *city* is like [d]the great city?'

19   "And they threw [a]dust on their heads and were crying out, weeping and mourning, saying, '[b]Woe, woe, the great city, in which all who had ships at sea [c]became rich by her [1]wealth, for in [b]one hour she has been laid [d]waste.'

20   "[a]Rejoice over her, O heaven, and you [1]saints and [b]apostles and prophets, because [c]God has [2]pronounced judgment for you against her."

21   And [1a]a [a]strong angel [b]took up a stone like a great millstone and threw it into the sea, saying, "Thus will Babylon, [c]the great city, be thrown down with violence, and will not be found any longer.

22   "And [a]the sound of harpists and musicians and flute-players and trumpeters will not be heard in you any longer; and no craftsman of any craft will be found in you any longer; and the [b]sound of a mill will not be heard in you any longer;

23   and the light of a lamp will not shine in you

12 [1]Lit., *stone* [2]Or, *brass*
[a]Rev. 17:4; Ezek. 27:12-22

13 [1]Lit., *amomum* [2]Lit., *bodies* [3]Lit., *souls of men*
[a]Ezek. 27:13; 1 Chr. 5:21 marg.; 1 Tim. 1:10

14 [1]Lit., *of your soul's desire*

15 [a]Rev. 18:3 [b]Rev. 18:12, 13 [c]Rev. 18:10

16 [1]Lit., *gilded* [2]Lit., *stone and pearl*
[a]Rev. 18:10, 19 [b]Rev. 18:10, 18, 19, 21 [c]Rev. 17:4

17 [1]Lit., *one who sails anywhere*
[a]Rev. 18:10 [b]Rev. 18:19; 17:16 [c]Ezek. 27:28f.

18 [a]Ezek. 27:30 [b]Rev. 18:9 [c]Ezek. 27:32; Rev. 13:4 [d]Rev. 18:10

19 [1]Lit., *costliness*
[a]Josh. 7:6; Job 2:12; Lam. 2:10 [b]Rev. 18:10 [c]Rev. 18:3, 15 [d]Rev. 18:17; 17:16

20 [1]I.e., true believers; lit., holy ones [2]Lit., *judged your judgment of her*
[a]Jer. 51:48; Rev. 12:12 [b]Luke 11:49f. [c]Rev. 19:2, 18.6ff.; 6:10

21 [1]Lit., *one*
[a]Rev. 5:2; 10:1 [b]Jer. 51:63f. [c]Rev. 18:10

22 [a]Is. 24:8; Ezek. 26:13; Matt. 9:23 [b]Eccles. 12:4; Jer. 25:10

Revelation 18, 19

**The Fourfold Hallelujah.
The Marriage Supper of the Lamb.**

23 ªJer. 7:34; 16:9 ᵇIs. 23:8;
Rev. 18:3; 6:15 ᶜNah. 3:4;
Rev. 9:21

24 ¹I.e., true believers, lit.,
holy ones
ªRev. 16:6; 17:6 ᵇMatt. 23:35

1 ªRev. 19:6; 11:15; Jer.
51:48 ᵇRev. 19:3, 4, 6; Ps.
104:35 marg. ᶜRev. 7:10
ᵈRev. 4:11

2 ¹Lit., *from her hand*
ªPs. 19:9 ᵇRev. 6:10 ᶜRev.
16:7 ᵈRev. 17:1 ᶜDeut. 32:43;
Rev. 18:20; 16:6; 2 Kin. 9:7

3 ªIs. 34:10; Rev. 19:1, 4, 6;
Ps. 104:35 ᵇRev. 14:11

4 ªRev. 4:4, 10 ᵇRev. 4:6
ᶜRev. 4:10 ᵈRev. 5:14; Ps.
106:48 and marg. ᶜRev. 19:3,
6; Ps. 104:35

5 ªPs. 115:13; 134:1; 135:1
ᵇRev. 11:18

6 ªRev. 19:1, 11.15; Jer.
51.48 ᵇRev. 1.15 ᶜRev. 6:1
ᵈRev. 1:8

7 ¹Lit., *wife*
ªRev. 11:13 ᵇRev. 19:9;
Matt. 22:2; 25:10; Luke
12:36; John 3:29; Eph. 5:23,
32 ᶜRev. 21:2; Matt. 1:20;
Rev. 21:9

8 ¹I.e., true believers; lit.,
holy ones
ªRev. 19:14; Rev. 15:6 marg.
ᵇRev. 15:4

9 ªRev. 19:10; 17:1 ᵇRev.
1:19 ᶜLuke 14:15; 22:16
ᵈRev. 21:5; 22:6; 17:17

10 ªRev. 22:8 ᵇRev. 22:9;
Acts 10:26 ᶜRev. 1:1f.

534

any longer; and the ªvoice of the bridegroom and bride will not be heard in you any longer; for your ᵇmerchants were the great men of the earth, because all the nations were deceived ᶜby your sorcery.

24 "And in her was found the ªblood of prophets and of ¹saints and of ᵇall who have been slain on the earth."

CHAPTER 19

AFTER these things I heard, as it were, a ªloud voice of a great multitude in heaven, saying,

"ᵇHallelujah! ᶜSalvation and ᵈglory and power belong to our God;

2 ªBECAUSE HIS ᵇJUDGMENTS ARE ᶜTRUE AND RIGHTEOUS; for He has judged the ᵈgreat harlot who was corrupting the earth with her immorality, and HE HAS ᶜAVENGED THE BLOOD OF HIS BOND-SERVANTS ¹ON HER."

3 And a second time they said, "ªHALLELUJAH! HER ᵇSMOKE RISES UP FOREVER AND EVER."

4 And the ªtwenty-four elders and the ᵇfour living creatures ᶜfell down and worshiped God who sits on the throne saying, "ᵈAmen. ᶜHallelujah!"

5 And a voice came from the throne, saying, "ªGIVE PRAISE TO OUR GOD, ALL YOU HIS BOND-SERVANTS, ᵇYOU WHO FEAR HIM, THE SMALL AND THE GREAT."

6 And I heard, as it were, ªthe voice of a great multitude and as ᵇthe sound of many waters and as the ᶜsound of mighty peals of thunder, saying,

"ªHallelujah! For the ᵈLord our God, the Almighty, reigns.

7 "Let us rejoice and be glad and ªgive the glory to Him, for ᵇthe marriage of the Lamb has come and His ¹ᶜbride has made herself ready."

8 And it was given to her to clothe herself in ªfine linen, bright *and* clean; for the fine linen is the ᵇrighteous acts of the ¹saints.

9 And ªhe *said to me, "ᵇWrite, 'ᶜBlessed are those who are invited to the marriage supper of the Lamb.' " And he *said to me, "ᵈThese are true words of God."

10 And ªI fell at his feet to worship him. ᵇAnd he *said to me, "Do not do that; I am a ᶜfellow-

servant of yours and your brethren who ᵈhold the testimony of Jesus; worship God. For the testimony of Jesus is the spirit of prophecy."

11 And I saw ᵃheaven opened; and behold, a ᵇwhite horse, and He who sat upon it *is* called ᶜFaithful and True; and in ᵈrighteousness He judges and wages war.

12 And His ᵃeyes *are* a flame of fire, and upon His head *are* many ᵇdiadems; and He has a ᶜname written *upon Him* which no one knows except Himself.

13 And *He is* clothed with a ᵃrobe dipped in blood; and His name is called ᵇThe Word of God.

14 And the armies which are in heaven, clothed in ᵃfine linen, ᵇwhite *and* clean, were following Him on white horses.

15 And ᵃfrom His mouth comes a sharp sword, so that ᵇwith it He may smite the nations; and He will ¹ᶜrule them with a rod of iron; and ᵈHe treads the ²wine press of the fierce wrath of God, the Almighty.

16 And on His robe and on His thigh He has ᵃa name written, "ᵇKING OF KINGS, AND LORD OF LORDS."

17 And I saw ¹an angel standing in the sun; and he cried out with a loud voice, saying to ᵃall the birds which fly in ᵇmidheaven, "ᶜCome, assemble for the ᵈgreat supper of God;

18 in order that you may ᵃeat the flesh of kings and the flesh of ¹commanders and the flesh of mighty men and the flesh of horses and of those who sit on them and the flesh of all men, ᵇboth free men and slaves, and ᶜsmall and great."

19 And I saw ᵃthe beast and ᵇthe kings of the earth and their armies, assembled to make war against Him who ᶜsat upon the horse, and against His army.

20 And the beast was seized, and with him the ᵃfalse prophet who ᵇperformed the signs ¹ᶜin his presence, by which he ᵈdeceived those who had received the ᶜmark of the beast and those who ᶠworshiped his image; these two were thrown alive into the ᵍlake of ʰfire which burns with brimstone.

21 And the rest were killed with the sword which ᵃcame from the mouth of him who ᵇsat upon the horse, and ᶜall the birds were filled with their flesh.

10 ᵈRev. 12:17

11 ᵃRev. 4:1; John 1:51
ᵇRev. 19:19, 21; 6:2 ᶜRev.
3:14 ᵈIs. 11:4

12 ᵃRev. 1:14 ᵇRev. 6:2;
12:3 ᶜRev. 19:16; 2:17

13 ᵃIs. 63:3 ᵇJohn 1:1

14 ᵃRev. 19:8 ᵇRev. 3:4;
19:8

15 ¹Or, *shepherd* ²Lit.,
*wine press of the wine of His
fierce wrath*
ᵃRev. 1:16; 19:21 ᵇIs. 11:4;
2 Thess. 2:8 ᶜRev. 2:27 ᵈRev.
14:19, 20

16 ᵃRev. 19:12; 2:17 ᵇRev.
17:14

17 ¹Lit., *one*
ᵃRev. 19:21 ᵇRev. 8:13 ᶜJer.
12:9; Ezek. 39:17; 1 Sam.
17:44 ᵈIs. 34:6; Jer. 46:10

18 ¹Lit., *chiliarchs, in
command of one thousand
troops*
ᵃEzek. 39:18-20 ᵇRev. 6:15
ᶜRev. 11:18; 13:16; 19:5

19 ᵃRev. 11:7; 13:1 ᵇRev.
16:14, 16 ᶜRev. 19:11, 21

20 ¹Or, *by his authority*
ᵃRev. 16:13 ᵇRev. 13:13
ᶜRev. 13:12 ᵈRev. 13:14
ᶜRev. 13:16f. ᶠRev. 13:15 [12]
ᵍRev. 20:10, 14f.; 21:8 ʰRev.
14:10; Is. 30:33; Dan. 7:11

21 ᵃRev. 19:15 ᵇRev. 19:11,
19 ᶜRev. 19:17

Revelation 20

Satan Bound. The Millennial Reign. Satan Loosed. The Great White Throne Judgment.

CHAPTER 20

1 ¹Lit., *upon*
ªRev. 10:1 ᵇRev. 1:18; 9:1

2 ªRev. 12:9 ᵇIs. 24:22;
2 Pet. 2:4; Jude 6

3 ªRev. 20:1 ᵇDan. 6:17;
Matt 27:66 ᶜRev. 20:8, 10;
12:9

4 ªDan. 7:9 ᵇRev. 3:21;
Matt. 19:28 ᶜDan. 7:22;
1 Cor. 6:2 ᵈRev. 6:9 ᵉRev. 1:9
ᶠRev. 13:15 [12] ᵍRev. 13:16f.
ʰJohn 14:19; Is. 26:14 ⁱRev.
20:6; 22:5; 3:21; 5:10

5 ªLuke 14:14; Phil. 3:11;
1 Thess. 4:16

6 ªRev. 14:13 ᵇRev. 20:14;
2:11 ᶜRev. 1:6 ᵈRev. 20:4;
22:5; 3:21; 5:10

7 ªRev. 20:2

8 ¹Lit., *sea*
ªRev. 20:3, 10; 12:9 ᵇRev. 7:1
ᶜEzek. 38.2, 39.1, 6 ᵈRev.
16:14 ᵉHeb. 11:12

9 ¹Lit., *breadth of the
earth* ²I.e., true believers;
lit., *holy ones*
ªEzek. 38:9, 16; Hab. 1:6
ᵇDeut. 23:14 ᶜPs. 87:2 ᵈEzek.
38:22; 39:6; Rev. 13:13

10 ªRev. 20:2f. ᵇRev. 20:14,
15; 19:20 ᶜRev. 16:13 ᵈRev.
14:10f.

11 ¹Lit., *face*
ªRev. 4:2 ᵇRev. 6:14; 21:1

536

AND I saw ªan angel coming down from heaven, having the ᵇkey of the abyss and a great chain ¹in his hand.

2 And he laid hold of the ªdragon, the serpent of old, who is the Devil and Satan, and ᵇbound him for a thousand years,

3 and threw him into the ªabyss, and shut *it* and ᵇsealed *it* over him, so that he should ᶜnot deceive the nations any longer, until the thousand years were completed; after these things he must be released for a short time.

4 And I saw ªthrones, and ᵇthey sat upon them, and ᶜjudgment was given to them. And I *saw* ᵈthe souls of those who had been ᵈbeheaded because of the ᵉtestimony of Jesus and because of the word of God, and those who had not ᶠworshiped the beast or his image, and had not received the ᵍmark upon their forehead and upon their hand; and they ʰcame to life and ⁱreigned with Christ for a thousand years.

5 The rest of the dead did not come to life until the thousand years were completed. ªThis is the first resurrection.

6 ªBlessed and holy is the one who has a part in the first resurrection; over these the ᵇsecond death has no power, but they will be ᶜpriests of God and of Christ and will ᵈreign with Him for a thousand years.

7 And when the thousand years are completed, Satan will be ªreleased from his prison,

8 and will come out to ªdeceive the nations which are in the ᵇfour corners of the earth, ᶜGog and Magog, to ᵈgather them together for the war; the number of them is like the ᵉsand of the ¹seashore.

9 And they ªcame up on the ¹broad plain of the earth and surrounded the ᵇcamp of the ²saints and the ᶜbeloved city, and ᵈfire came down from heaven and devoured them.

10 And ªthe devil who ªdeceived them was thrown into the ᵇlake of fire and brimstone, where the ᶜbeast and the ᶜfalse prophet are also; and they will be ᵈtormented day and night forever and ever.

11 And I saw a great white ªthrone and Him who sat upon it, from whose ¹presence ᵇearth and

heaven fled away, and ^cno place was found for them.

12   And I saw the dead, the ^agreat and the small, standing before the throne, and ^{1b}books were opened; and another ²book was opened, which is ^c*the book* of life; and the dead ^dwere judged from the things which were written in the ¹books, ^eaccording to their deeds.

13   And the sea gave up the dead which were in it, and ^adeath and Hades ^bgave up the dead which were in them; and they were judged, every one *of them* ^caccording to their deeds.

14   And ^adeath and Hades were thrown into ^bthe lake of fire. This is the ^csecond death, the lake of fire.

15   And if ¹anyone's name was not found written in ^athe book of life, he was thrown into the lake of fire.

CHAPTER 21

AND I saw ^aa new heaven and a new earth; for ^bthe first heaven and the first earth passed away, and there is no longer *any* sea.

2   And I saw ^athe holy city, ^bnew Jerusalem, ^ccoming down out of heaven from God, ^dmade ready as a bride adorned for her husband.

3   And I heard a loud voice from the throne, saying, "Behold, ^athe tabernacle of God is among men, and He shall ^{1b}dwell among them, and they shall be His peoples, and God Himself shall be among them,²

4   and He shall ^awipe away every tear from their eyes; and ^bthere shall no longer be *any* death; ^cthere shall no longer be *any* mourning, or crying, or pain: ^dthe first things have passed away."

5   And ^aHe who sits on the throne said, "Behold, I am ^bmaking all things new." And He *said, "Write, for ^cthese words are faithful and true."

6   And He said to me, "^{1a}It is done. I am the ^bAlpha and the Omega, the beginning and the end. ^cI will give to the one who thirsts from the spring of the ^dwater of life without cost.

7   "^aHe who overcomes shall inherit these things, and ^bI will be his God and he will be My son.

8   "^aBut for the cowardly and ¹unbelieving and abominable and murderers and immoral persons

11 ^cDan. 2:35; Rev. 12:8

12 ¹Or, *scrolls* ²Or, *scroll* ^aRev. 11:18 ^bDan. 7:10; Jer. 17:1, 10 ^cRev. 20:15; 3:5 ^dRev. 11:18 ^eRev. 20:13; 2:23; Matt. 16:27

13 ^aRev. 6:8; Rev. 1:18; 21:4; 1 Cor. 15:26 ^bIs. 26:19 ^cRev. 20:12; 2:23; Matt. 16:27

14 ^aRev. 6:8; 1:18; 21:4; 1 Cor. 15:26 ^bRev. 20:10, 15; 19:20 ^cRev. 20:6

15 ¹Lit., *anyone was* ^aRev. 20:12; 3:5

1 ^aIs. 65:17; 66:22; 2 Pet. 3:13 ^bRev. 20:11; 2 Pet. 3:10

2 ^aRev. 21:10; 22:19; 11:2 ^bRev. 3:12; 21:10 ^cRev. 21:10; Heb. 11:10, 16 ^dRev. 21:9; 22:17; 19:7; Is. 61:10

3 ¹Or, *tabernacle* ²Some ancient mss. add, and be *their God* ^aLev. 26:11f.; Ezek. 37:27; 48:35; Rev. 7:15; Heb. 8:2 ^bJohn 14:23; 2 Cor. 6:16

4 ^aRev. 7:17 ^bRev. 20:14; 1 Cor. 15:26 ^cIs. 25:8; 35:10; 51:11; 65:19 ^d2 Cor. 5:17; Heb. 12:27

5 ^aRev. 20:11; 4:9 ^b2 Cor. 5:17; Heb. 12:27 ^cRev. 22:6; 19:9

6 ¹Lit., *They are* ^aRev. 16:17; 10:6 ^bRev. 1:8; 22:13 ^cRev. 22:17; Is. 55:1; John 4:10; Rev. 7:17 ^dRev. 7:17

7 ^aRev. 2:7 ^bRev. 21:3; 2 Sam. 7:14; 2 Cor. 6:16, 18

8 ¹Or, *untrustworthy* ^aRev. 21:27; 22:15; 1 Cor. 6:9; Gal. 5:19-21; Rev. 9:21

8 bRev. 19:20 cRev. 2:11

9 1Lit., *who were full*
aRev. 17:1 bRev. 15:7 cRev.
15:1 dRev. 17:1 eRev. 21:2;
19:7

10 1Or, *in spirit*
aRev. 17:3; Ezek. 40:2 bRev.
1:10 cRev. 21:2

11 1Lit. *luminary*
aRev. 15:8; 21:23; Is. 60:1f.;
Ezek. 43:2; Rev. 22:5 bRev.
21:18, 19; 4:3 cRev. 4:6

12 1Lit., *having*
aEzek. 48:31-34 bRev. 21:15,
21, 25; 22:14

14 aEph. 2:20; Heb. 11:10
bActs 1:26

15 1Lit., *measure, a gold
reed*
aRev. 11:1 bRev. 21:21, 25;
21:12

16 1Lit., *reed* 2Lit., *twelve
thousand stadia,* a stadion
was about 600 ft.

17 1Lit., *one hundred forty-
four cubits* 2Lit., *measure*
aDeut. 3:11; Rev. 13:18
bRev. 21:9

18 1Lit., *pure*
aRev. 21:11 bRev. 21:21
cRev. 4:6

19 aIs. 54:11f.; Rev. 21:19,
20; Ex. 28:17-20; Ezek. 28:13
bRev. 21:11 cRev. 4:3

20 aRev. 4:3

21 aRev. 21:15, 25; 21:12
bRev. 17:4; Is. 54:12

538

and sorcerers and idolaters and all liars, their part *will be* in bthe lake that burns with fire and brimstone, which is the csecond death."

9 aAnd one of the seven angels who had the bseven bowls 1full of the cseven last plagues, came and spoke with me, saying, "dCome here, I shall show you the ebride, the wife of the Lamb."

10 And ahe carried me away 1bin the Spirit to a great and high mountain, and showed me cthe holy city, Jerusalem, coming down out of heaven from God,

11 having athe glory of God. Her 1brilliance was like a very costly stone, as a bstone of ccrystal-clear jasper.

12 1It had a great and high wall, 1awith twelve bgates, and at the gates twelve angels; and names *were* written on them, which are *those* of the twelve tribes of the sons of Israel.

13 *There were* three gates on the east and three gates on the north and three gates on the south and three gates on the west.

14 And the wall of the city had atwelve foundation stones, and on them *were* the twelve names of the btwelve apostles of the Lamb.

15 And the one who spoke with me had a 1gold measuring arod to measure the city, and its bgates and its wall.

16 And the city is laid out as a square, and its length is as great as the width; and he measured the city with the 1rod, 2fifteen hundred miles; its length and width and height are equal.

17 And he measured its wall, 1seventy-two yards, *according to* ahuman 2measurements, which are *also* bangelic *measurements*.

18 And the material of the wall was ajasper; and the city was bpure gold, like 1clear cglass.

19 aThe foundation stones of the city wall were adorned with every kind of precious stone. The first foundation stone was bjasper; the second, sapphire; the third, chalcedony; the fourth, cemerald;

20 the fifth, sardonyx; the sixth, asardius; the seventh, chrysolite; the eighth, beryl; the ninth, topaz; the tenth, chrysoprase; the eleventh, jacinth; the twelfth, amethyst.

21 And the twelve agates were twelve bpearls; each one of the gates was a single pearl. And the

street of the city was ᶜpure gold, like transparent ᵈglass.

22 And I saw ᵃno ¹temple in it, for the ᵇLord God, the Almighty, and the ᶜLamb, are its ¹temple.

23 And the city ᵃhas no need of the sun or of the moon to shine upon it, for ᵇthe glory of God has illumined it, and its lamp *is* the ᶜLamb.

24 And ᵃthe nations shall walk by its light, and the ᵇkings of the earth ¹shall bring their glory into it.

25 And in the daytime (for ᵃthere shall be no night there) ᵇits gates ᶜshall never be closed;

26 and ᵃthey shall bring the glory and the honor of the nations into it;

27 and nothing unclean and no one who practices abomination and lying, ᵃshall ever come into it, but only those ¹whose names are ᵇwritten in the Lamb's book of life.

CHAPTER 22

Aᴺᴰ ᵃhe showed me a ᵇriver of the ᶜwater of life, ¹clear ᵈas crystal, coming from the throne of God and of ²the Lamb,

2 in the middle of ᵃits street. And ᵇon either side of the river was ᶜthe tree of life, bearing twelve ¹kinds of fruit, yielding its fruit every month; and the ᵇleaves of the tree were for the healing of the nations.

3 And ᵃthere shall no longer be any curse; and ᵇthe throne of God and of the Lamb shall be in it, and His bond-servants shall ᶜserve Him;

4 and they shall ᵃsee His face, and His ᵇname *shall be* on their ᶜforeheads.

5 And ᵃthere shall no longer be *any* night; and they ¹shall not have need ᵇof the light of a lamp nor the light of the sun, because the Lord God shall illumine them; and they shall ᶜreign forever and ever.

6 And ᵃhe said to me, "ᵇThese words are faithful and true"; and the Lord, the ᶜGod of the spirits of the prophets, ᵈsent His angel to show to His bond-servants the things which must shortly take place.

7 "And behold, ᵃI am coming quickly. ᵇBlessed is he who ¹heeds ᶜthe words of the prophecy of this book."

8 And ᵃI, John, am the one who heard and saw

---

21 ᶜRev. 21:18 ᵈRev. 4:6

22 ¹Or, *sanctuary*
ᵃJohn 4:21; Matt. 24:2 ᵇRev. 1:8 ᶜRev. 5:6; 7:17; 14:4

23 ᵃIs. 60:19, 20; 24:23; Rev. 21:25; 22:5 ᵇRev. 21:11 ᶜRev. 5:6; 7:17; 14:4

24 ¹Lit., *bring*
ᵃIs. 60:3, 5; Rev. 22:2 ᵇPs. 72:10f.; Is. 49:23; 60:16; Rev. 21:26

25 ᵃRev. 22:5; 21:23; Zech. 14:7 ᵇRev. 21:15; 21:12 ᶜIs. 60:11

26 ᵃPs. 72:10f.; Is. 49:23; 60:16

27 ¹Lit., *who are*
ᵃRev. 22:14f.; Is. 52:1; Ezek. 44:9; Zech. 14:21 ᵇRev. 3:5

1 ¹Lit., *bright* ²Or, *the Lamb. In the middle of its street, and on either side of the river, was*
ᵃRev. 21:9; 22:6; 1:1 ᵇPs. 46:4; Ezek. 47:1 ᶜRev. 22:17; 7:17 ᵈRev. 4:6

2 ¹Or, *crops of fruit*
ᵃRev. 21:21 ᵇEzek. 47:12 ᶜRev. 22:14, 19; 2:7

3 ᵃZech. 14:11 ᵇRev. 21:3, 23 ᶜRev. 7:15

4 ᵃMatt. 5:8; Ps. 17:15; 42:2 ᵇRev. 14:1 ᶜRev. 7:3

5 ¹Lit., *do not have*
ᵃRev. 21:25; Zech. 14:7 ᵇRev. 21:23 ᶜDan. 7:18, 27; Rev. 20:4; Matt. 19:28; Rom. 5:17

6 ᵃRev. 21:9; 1:1 ᵇRev. 21:5; 19:9 ᶜ1 Cor. 14:32; Heb. 12:9 ᵈRev. 22:16; 1:1

7 ¹Or, *keeps*
ᵃRev. 22:12, 20; 3:11; 1:3; 3:3; 16:15 ᵇRev. 1:3; 16:15 ᶜRev. 22:10, 18f.; 22:9; 1:11

8 ᵃRev. 1:1

8 bRev. 19:10

9 1Or, *keep*
aRev. 19:10 bRev. 1:1 cRev.
22:10, 18f.; Rev. 1:11

10 aRev. 10:4; Dan. 8:26
bRev. 22:18f.; 22:9; 1:11
cRev. 1:3

11 aEzek. 3:27; Dan. 12:10

12 1Lit., *as his work is*
aRev. 22:7 bIs. 40:10; 62:11
cRev. 2:23; Jer. 17:10; Matt.
16:27

13 aRev. 1:8 bRev. 1:17
cRev. 21:6

14 aRev. 7:14 bRev. 22:2
cRev. 21:27 dRev. 21:12

15 aRev. 21:8; 1 Cor. 6:9f.;
Gal. 5:19ff.; Matt. 8:12
bDeut. 23:18; Matt. 7:6; Phil.
3:2

16 1Or, *concerning*
aRev. 1:1 bRev. 22:6; 1:1
cRev. 1:4, 11; 3:22 dRev. 5:5
eMatt. 1:1 fRev. 2:28; Matt.
2:2

17 aRev. 2:7; 14:13 bRev.
21:9; 21:2 cRev. 21:6 dRev.
7:17; 22:1

18 aRev. 22:7 bDeut. 4:2;
12:32; Prov. 30:6 cRev. 15:6-
16, 21 dRev. 22:7

19 1Lit., *out of*
aDeut. 4:2; 12:32; Prov. 30:6
bRev. 22:7 cRev. 22:2 dRev.
21:10-22:5

20 aRev. 1:2 bRev. 22:7
c1 Cor. 16:22 marg.

21 1Some ancient mss.
read, *the saints*
aRom. 16:20

540

these things. And when I heard and saw, bI fell down to worship at the feet of the angel who showed me these things.

9 And ahe *said to me, "Do not do that; I am a bfellow-servant of yours and of your brethren the prophets and of those who 1heed the words of cthis book: worship God."

10 And he *said to me, "aDo not seal up bthe words of the prophecy of this book, cfor the time is near.

11 "aLet the one who does wrong, still do wrong; and let the one who is filthy, still be filthy; and let the one who is righteous, still practice righteousness; and let the one who is holy, still keep himself holy.

12 "Behold, aI am coming quickly, and My bre-ward is with Me, cto render to every man 1accord-ing to what he has done.

13 "I am the aAlpha and the Omega, bthe first and the last, cthe beginning and the end."

14 Blessed are those who awash their robes, that they may have the right to bthe tree of life, and may center by the dgates into the city.

15 aOutside are the bdogs and the sorcerers and the immoral persons and the murderers and the idolaters, and everyone who loves and practices lying.

16 "aI, Jesus, have sent bMy angel to testify to you these things 1cfor the churches. I am dthe root and the eoffspring of David, the bright fmorning star."

17 And the dSpirit and the bbride say, "Come." And let the one who hears say, "Come." And clet the one who is thirsty come; let the one who wishes take the dwater of life without cost.

18 I testify to everyone who hears athe words of the prophecy of this book: if anyone badds to them, God shall add to him cthe plagues which are written in dthis book;

19 and if anyone atakes away from the bwords of the book of this prophecy, God shall take away his part from cthe tree of life and 1from the holy city, dwhich are written in this book.

20 He who atestifies to these things says, "Yes, bI am coming quickly." Amen. cCome, Lord Jesus.

21 aThe grace of the Lord Jesus be with 1all. Amen.

3

Dear Dick and Karen

On this your wedding day, may God give you His blessing as you begin life together.

We pray that God's Word will be your light along life's way.

Sincerely in Christ,

Pastor Wayne & Clara Stark
First Covenant Church
San Jose, California

Philippians 4:13